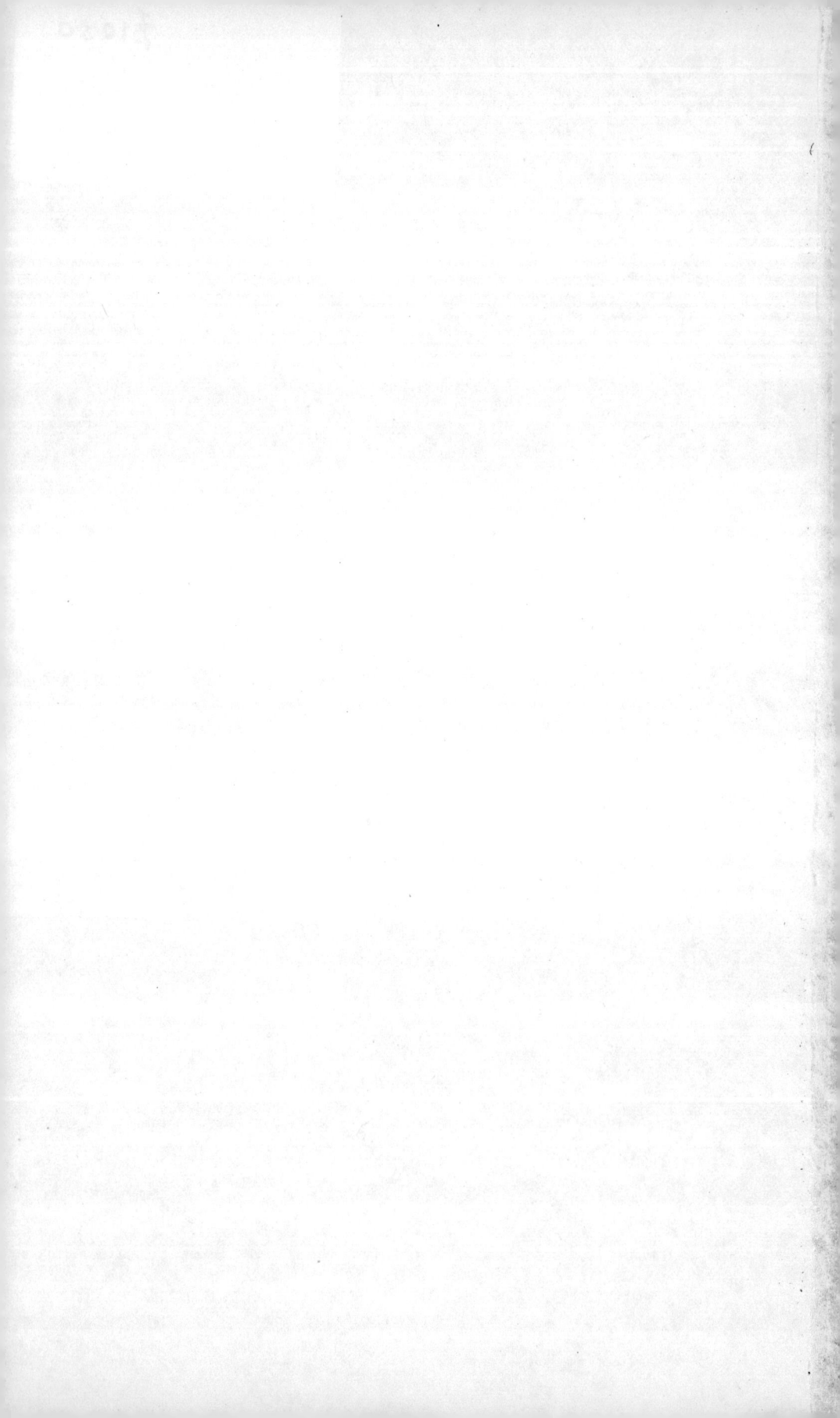

THE NEW
EXTINCT PEERAGE 1884-1971

By the same author

The Stuarts of Traquair
The House of Wavell
The Middle Sea
The Story of Heraldry
Trace Your Ancestors
The Golden Book of the Coronation
They Came with the Conqueror
The Story of the Peerage
Tales of the British Aristocracy
The House of Constantine
Teach Yourself Heraldry and Genealogy
The Twilight of Monarchy
A Guide to Titles
Princes of Wales
American Origins
Your Family Tree
Ramshackledom, A Critical Appraisal
  of the Establishment
Heirs of the Conqueror
Heraldry, Ancestry and Titles, Questions and
  Answers
The Story of Surnames
After Their Blood
Tradition and Custom in Modern Britain
The Genealogist's Encyclopedia
The Story of Titles
International Heraldry
Acteon: A History of Hunting
Highland Clans
Sons of the Conqueror

PLATE 1

BARON ABERCROMBY.

EN DIEV EST TOVT

BARON ALINGTON.

BARON ARDILAUN.

BARON ARMITSTEAD.

BARON ARUNDELL OF WARDOUR.

EARL OF ASHBURNHAM.

The New
Extinct Peerage
1884-1971

Containing Extinct, Abeyant
Dormant & Suspended Peerages
with Genealogies and Arms

L. G. Pine

B.A. LOND., F.S.A. Scot.,
F.J.I., F.A.M.S., F.R.G.S.
Barrister-at-Law, Inner Temple

Heraldry Today
10, Beauchamp Place, London, S.W.3
1972

Published 1972
by Heraldry Today
10, Beauchamp Place
London, S.W.3

© L. G. Pine

I.S.B.N. 0 90045523 3

Printed in England by
Hollen Street Press, Ltd.
Slough, Bucks.

Contents

Preface

THIS book deals with the peerages which have become extinct between 1 January 1884 and 31 December 1971. Also included are peerages which became dormant or abeyant in the same period, and the three peerages—Albany, Cumberland and Taaffe—which were suspended under the Titles Deprivation Act of 1917. In addition it was necessary to include some peerages which became extinct before 1884, and which were not included in Sir Bernard Burke's edition of the *Extinct Peerage* in 1883. These articles are marked with two asterisks in the present work. All articles are entered alphabetically under the highest title held: in the index the surnames give the title under which they will be found. Subsidiary titles are also given in the Index. Hyphenated surnames are entered under the first name. Surnames of peers are given in the narrative in each generation, in accordance with the principle of the *Complete Peerage*. The practice of leaving off a peer's surname, e.g. from his tombstone, can be most confusing.

I wish to thank the following. The University Library of Cambridge for allowing me to use the Library. I cannot speak too highly of the efficiency of the service provided. Miss Dorothy M. White, Chief Librarian of Ipswich has been very helpful. Mr. Patrick Montague-Smith, Editor of Debrett's Peerage was kind enough to supply a list of peerages extinct in 1970 and 1971. *The Times* gave a copy of the entry of the item on the barony intended for Sir J. Forrest, and the Clerk of the Journals at the House of Lords supplied exact dates of creation for seven peerages. Major D. M. Maitland-Titterton, Ormond Pursuivant of Lyon Court, furnished information in connection with the entry for Muir Mackenzie. Miss Williams of the Bristol Archives Office for ready assistance with the Colston pedigree, under Roundway. Lastly I record my appreciation of sound constructive criticism throughout by my British publisher, Mrs. Rosemary Pinches.

The writing of the book has been of the greatest interest, since the peerage creations and extinctions of the last 90 years do illustrate the enormous changes political, social and economic which have occurred during that time. Here will be found in the lives of noted men and women, many indications of the change from Empire to Commonwealth; from the Liberal to the Labour Party; the advent of the trade union peer to sit beside the industrialist and the old landed aristocracy; and the decay of the latter. Many articles touch upon points of peerage law. In this century there has been more legislation on the House of Lords than at any other time. There is a great difference between the facts of peerage as seen by historians and the established law on the subject. I have therefore written and included a treatment of Peerage in History and in Law.

L. G. PINE

Peerage in History
and in Law

THAT there is a very considerable divergence in the conception of peerage held respectively by lawyers and by historians will be apparent to anyone who uses the *Complete Peerage* or the works of J. H. Round. This difference is manifested most in the treatment of peerages other than those created by letters patent, i.e. by writ of summons. It is the contention of the writer that a second example of divergence of view point arises in the peerage legislation of the present century, which is more extensive than in any other previous age.

Here is a quotation taken at random from a volume of the *Complete Peerage* the italics being those of the writer. "Among the representatives of Eleanor and Joan any hereditary barony *which may be supposed to have been created by the writ of 1309* is in abeyance". The 14 volumes of the *Complete Peerage* abound in sentences and notes of this nature, which may be fairly summed up as expressing the learned editors' views that certain legal doctrines concerning the nature of peerage will not endure the criticism of historical inquiry. A few examples will serve to illustrate the differences between the ideas of peerage which can be taken to be settled law and those of learned scholars who have devoted many years to the study of medieval dignities. In Vol. 13 Part I p.321 of the *Complete Peerage* the view is set forth that the rolls of attendance at the Great Council and those of attendance in Parliament were sometimes mixed: thus when in 1916 the barony of Strabolgi was revived in favour of the Rev. Matthias Kenworthy, in reality an entirely new barony was created, for the earlier Lords Strabolgi attended the Council and not the Parliament. If this were indeed the case, then it would follow that a peerage was created as it were by mistake, and the Strabolgi barony would date from 1916. Again in Vol. 4 of the work just cited there is an appendix which deals with the subject of "Earldoms and Baronies in History and Law, and the Doctrines of Abeyance". At p.723 of this volume occurs the following passage: "It is time that a strong protest be entered against the continuance of the practice of calling out of abeyance so-called baronies in fee, most of which never had any existence. The co-heirship possessed by the petitioners usually represents only a small fraction of the alleged barony, and in nearly every case the lands have been alienated for centuries. Their right to an estate of honour which is the most endurable that can be bestowed has no basis in fact: yet most of these parvenus are given precedence in the House of Lords over the heads of peers of like degree whose right to their dignities is unquestioned."

Lest the above be thought the prejudiced opinion of a layman, the considered judgment of a Queen's Counsel may be quoted. "The doctrine of abeyance is a legal fiction which has not found favour with historians . . .

The historical absurdity of the doctrine was underlined . . . when the non-existent barony of Strabolgi was held to have been in abeyance for no less than 496 years". (G. D. Squibb, Q.C. in Foreword to *Earldoms in Fee* by the late Sir Geoffrey Ellis 1963).

To examine this charge adequately it is necessary to understand the nature of peerage creation. Today all peerages are created by letters patent. (A very rare exception to this rule occurred in 1951 when the present (3rd) Earl of Ancaster was summoned to the House of Lords by writ as Lord Willoughby de Eresby, his father being unable owing to ill-health to discharge the duties of Lord Great Chamberlain though such a writ does not create a new peerage but merely constitutes a summons in the father's barony.)It was not always so and some of the oldest peerages have been created by writ of summons to the Lords. A relic of this mode of creation is found in the writs issued to peers to attend Parliament. There have been other methods of creation, e.g. by charter, which may be taken to be a form of letters patent, and at one time by tenure. Of this last method the only remainder consists in the sometimes quoted myth that a peerage by the tenure exists in the case of Arundel Castle, so that whoever owned this property would become Earl of Arundel. (On the alleged Arundel tenure it is enough to say that in the Berkeley Case 8 H.L.C. 21, in 1861 the notion that there are peerages by tenure was finally and effectively disposed of, see Sir Francis Palmer, *Peerage Law*, 1907, pp.183-186.)

The House of Lords and the peerage evolved like other English institutions over a long period, and in a typically English and pragmatic manner. To find the beginnings of the peerage we have to go back to the Witan of the Old English kings, well over one thousand years ago. The full title, Witenagemot, the gathering of the wise men of the land, meant an assembly of the great ones, ecclesiastical and lay, under the king who summoned them. In the earlier pre-Conquest period the magnates were referred to as aldermen (ealdormen), or old or senior men. This term gave place after the Danish invasions in the ninth-eleventh centuries to the English earl based on the Norse jarl, or chief, referring to the magnates who were nearest to the raiders' kings. The ealdorman was an official holding high place under the king; as such he was entitled to a third of the revenues in the area which he administered. The latter perquisite was the origin of the later so called third penny to which the feudal earls were entitled. Along with the term ealdorman went the much more familiar lord and lady. The former came from O.E. hlaford—bread keeper. With the establishment of the Danish monarchy in England, 1017-42, the number of ealdormen was reduced and those who discharged their functions were called earls and had much wider areas of administration. By the generation preceding the Conquest there were three or four great earldoms in England: Northumbria, Wessex and Mercia, the last being loosely equivalent to the Midlands. These earldoms were functional; a man might hold one for some years, then lose it or receive another in place of it. A tendency to inheritance of an earldom did naturally show itself. The Leofricsons of Mercia could show a succession for four generations. "Leofwine, Earl of Mercia, was succeeded at some date between 1024 and 1032 by his son Leofric, who in turn in 1057 was succeeded by his son Alfgar; about 1062 the fourth generation came into possession of the earldom in the person of Alfgar's elder son, Edwin, who held it until after the Conquest" (Enoch Powell & Keith Wallis, *The House of Lords in the Middle Ages*, 1968, p.7).

The other great house of the old England, that of the Godwinsons, who for ten months had tenure of the throne, possessed more than one earldom during Edward the Confessor's reign (1042-1066) and it is highly probable that they would have retained the position if not the actual area. In fact Harold II who was killed at Hastings in 1066, succeeded his father Godwin as Earl of Wessex.

After the Norman Conquest, the old aristocracy were soon replaced by foreigners. The great majority of the former landowners gave way to those to whom William I allotted their estates. In the Domesday Book (1086) the Crown owned about one seventh of the total area, or rather retained this amount under its own control, for in feudal theory all land in England belonged to the king who let it out to his vassals. Some two sevenths of the country was held by the Church. The remaining four sevenths was held by the king's tenants in chief, numbering about 180. They were termed the king's barons, a word whose etymology seems curious, for in classical Latin it meant 'dunce', in low Latin a slave or servant, and eventually the king's man. These tenants *in capite* were the magnates who formed the Great Council and from the nucleus of whom the modern peerage and the House of Lords was derived.

Parliament, in the sense of Commons as well as Lords, developed from the 13th century onwards. Not until the 14th century are the Lords as a separate House beginning to be distinguished from the Commons; at the end of that century appear the terms Lords Spiritual and Temporal. It was not until 1387 that a peerage was created which was not connected with the holding of land, and which purported to be given for services rendered to the king. On 10 October, 1387, Richard II issued letters patent creating John Beaumont of Holt, Lord Beauchamp and Baron of Kidderminster, thus establishing the precedent for the now invariable mode of procedure. The same monarch created the first Marquessate in England, when on 1 December, 1385, he issued letters patent to his favourite, Robert de Vere, Earl of Oxford, creating him Marquess of Dublin. It should be specially noted that this creation was for life. The term Marquess (in France Marquis) came from a word 'march' or frontier, and on the Continent it had denoted the ruler of a march, similar to the Lords Marchers who kept the border with Wales. It had no such connotation in England. The rank of Viscount, from vice comes or deputy of the count (earl), came into the peerage in December 1440 when Henry VI made John Beaumont, who was a Baron, Viscount Beaumont. The first dukedom created in England occurred when Edward the Black Prince was made

Duke of Cornwall by Edward III in 1337. This was a special case, not only because the recipient was heir to the throne but because the lands of the duchy were annexed to the dukedom for ever and because the title is held by the reigning sovereign's eldest son, reverting to the Crown when there is no such person.

It should be added that post Conquest earldoms were never as powerful as those of the old kingdom except those of the palatinates, Chester, Pembroke and Durham, the last named being held by the bishop of the see. The title *Comes Palatinus* was of continental origin denoting a great official of the Palace. In England it meant the ruler of a jurisdiction able to exercise the full powers of the king and it will be observed that the English Palatinates were on the borders of Scotland and Wales or in the latter.

Thus it came about, slowly and over a long period of time, that a peerage system was evolved. It was perhaps unfortunate that in the process the word baron should have been used both in the old feudal sense and in a more modern meaning. Mr. I. J. Sanders in his work, *English Baronies, a Study of Their Origin and Descent*, 1086-1327, has made it abundantly clear that the older baronies had no necessary relationship with our modern conception of peerage. The author states that neither the king nor the tenants in chief knew clearly what was the origin of tenure *per baroniam* or why a tenant in chief was considered a baron. He adds that the most searching test as to baronial status was the payment of baronial relief. The mere use of such language takes us at once into a feudal world in which the modern idea of peerage (modern here is taken to mean the legal conception over the past 400 years) is out of place. The feudal baron was not what we or the Tudor lawyers would call a lord; he was the holder of Crown land of which he was the tenant in chief. This feudal conception has gone out of England. It still exists in Scotland where a considerable distinction is made between a minor baron, who is a laird and holder of a medieval barony, and a 'Lord of Parliament'. The late Lord Lyon, Sir Thomas Innes of Learney, in writing on this subject left little doubt as to which of the dignities—feudal baron or modern Lord of Parliament—he considered superior.

It may be added that the law of Scotland recognises and regulates heraldry, which is another survival from the feudal ages, in a most distinct and certain manner, for the Lord Lyon, besides being the head of the Scottish heraldic system, is also a judge from whom appeal lies to the Court of Session and to the House of Lords. Disregard of his decisions implies contempt of court and his judgments can seldom be reversed even on appeal to the House of Lords. A recent study of the Scottish heraldic system, *The Nature of Arms* by Colonel Gayre of Gayre and Nigg, makes clear how much Scottish law (and this applies to peerages also) has adhered to the medieval conceptions.

In other words, the English peerage evolved over centuries out of a feudal baronage. One popular phrase will illustrate this point yet further. We are accustomed to refer to the great Earl of Warwick, the King-

Maker, as the Last of the Barons. The barons of the middle ages were a generic class, whereas the baron created by letters patent is a peer, the holder of the lowest rank in the peerage. The oldest terms of nobility in this land are baron and earl. Yet the doctrine grew up that peerages were created by writ and that a person who had received such a writ was considered to have received the equivalent of a peerage by letters patent, which would carry with it the right to inheritance on the part of his son. Peerages thus held to be created by writ of summons differed, however, from peerages by letters patent in that a barony by writ passes into abeyance between several co-heirs. It exists, but no one enjoys it, and it can be called out of abeyance at the will of the Crown.

This doctrine with reference to peerages by writ of summons cannot be substantiated by historical research, but rather the reverse. A degree of fluidity is essential to all schemes of evolution, and in the process of the development of the peerage a fixed doctrine such as the above is quite out of place. The propositions relating to peerages created by writ and those which are in abeyance have been reached over the past 300-400 years, being themselves an example of the evolution of the peerage and of thinking about it. There would be nothing wrong with this but for the maxim that the law relating to peerage is held to have been always the law, to the limit of legal memory, i.e. the reign of Richard I. The theory of abeyance owes a great deal to the authority of Sir Edward Coke. It is a bold challenge to say that the greatest common lawyer of English history is wrong, but it is true that historical research into medieval dignities has given all peerage scholars a knowledge of the subject not possessed by this immensely learned man.

However moderately the view contrary to Coke's may be expressed, there is none the less at best an uncertainty that anything resembling modern peerage law could have existed in medieval times. Few persons would care to have contested a view expressed by the great Professor F. W. Maitland, yet in his *Constitutional History of England* (1908, p.168) this is what he says: "It is held that a mere writ of summons directed to A.B., if obeyed by him, confers on him a right descendible to his heirs. Whether the kings of the 13th and 14th centuries meant that this should be so may well be doubted, but on the whole the practice of summoning the heir was regularly observed, and in the 16th century the rule that summons and sitting gives a descendible right was regarded as fixed". The clear meaning here is that the conception of peerage has developed over centuries. To which may be added the following quotation "No Baron had any inherent right to a Writ of Summons to Parliament, as we find that Barons summoned to one Parliament were not summoned to another Parliament, and their heirs were sometimes summoned and sometimes not; which would appear to be inconsistent with a later theory, now acknowledged to be a legal fiction, that a single summons to Parliament followed by a sitting in Parliament gave a peerage inheritable by heirs general in perpetuity." (C. F. L. St. George—The Composition of the House of Lords, in *The Future of the House of Lords*, a symposium, 1954.)

Furthermore, with process of time, baronies in abeyance were called out of abeyance long after the time from which they were said to have fallen into the same. In 1764 the Botetourt barony was summoned out of abeyance after a period of 358 years. It was this practice which led eventually to the meeting of a Select Committee on Peerages in Abeyance, which was set up in 1926. This committee in its report pointed out that with reference to the 14th and 15th centuries there was grave reason to doubt whether, during those two centuries either sovereign or subject had ever any idea that by summons to a Parliament a hereditary right either was being or had been created. The committee said that the law as settled could not, however, be upset; but it recommended that no abeyance should be terminated the first commencement of which occurred more than one hundred years before the presentation of the petition. This last recommendation has at least prevented some petitions dealing with peerages of extreme antiquity. (*Report from the Select Committee on Peerages in Abeyance* 1927.)

In reference to the creation of a Viscount by Henry VI, the authors of the most detailed account of the medieval peerage write: "From that moment onward a new conundrum posed itself. There would henceforth be two sorts of lordship of parliament, of peerage. About the origin and descent of the one, there was no doubt at all: they were created by patent in tail male. But how and when were the others 'created', and why had they in historical fact normally, though not invariably, descended through the female—to heirs general? Given the question thus posed, there could be only one answer, and that a preposterous one: they were created by the first recorded writ which summoned an ancestor to parliament, though why the dignity thus created was heritable through the female— was it, or was a 'new' barony created in such cases by a new writ, but with the precedence of the old barony?—admitted of no satisfactory explanation". (Enoch Powell & Keith Wallis, op. cit. p.xix, a work which all writers on the peerage henceforth will have to consult.)

It can thus be seen clearly that the law on peerage is still at variance with the historical facts. Nor is it only in the sphere of abeyance that the law has made decisions which are not supported by historical research. Peerages created for life are far from unknown in English peerage history. They became an anachronism, however, to the extent that in 1856 in the *Wensleydale (Peerage) Case* (5.H.L.Cas. 958) the Committee of Privileges was led to declare that the letters patent of a life peer could not entitle him to sit in the Lords, not even when the writ of summons was annexed to the letters patent. Yet no less than 29 instances can be collected of the grant of a life peerage, including several made in Parliament with the assent of Lords and Commons. Both Coke and Selden recognise nobility for life only; as do William Cruise (*On Dignities*) and the Redesdale Committee in its Report on Peerage Dignity (1820-25).

Despite the fact that life peerages, like other honours, can proceed without let or hindrance from the Fountain of Honour, it has been found necessary to pass Acts of Parliament from 1876 to 1958 to permit the creation of life peerages, which such great authorities as those cited above agree are well within the power of the Crown.

A similar position exists with regard to the subject of the surrender of peerages. Here again until 1678 this right to surrender a peerage did exist, subject to formalities. Cases exist which demonstrate this completely. In Scottish peerage law there are many instances of the surrender of peerages, and there are well-authenticated cases in England. Reference to Scots law does not of course imply that at the present day a Scottish peerage case could be decided on lines fundamentally different from those of English law, because in the last resort the Scottish case would come before the Committee of Privileges of the House of Lords. Yet in two respects Scottish nobiliary law (this term is purposely used in the present context instead of peerage law) does differ from its counterpart in England. The Court of the Lord Lyon does decide cases relating to the lesser nobility, cases which rarely come to the House of Lords; and in a Scottish peerage case there will usually be a much less rigorous interpretation than in the corresponding English case, even in the House of Lords. Proof of this came some years ago in the *Dundee* case. The Proceedings before the Committee of Privileges, Dudhope Peerage, 1952 and Earldom of Dundee, 1953, both titles adjudged to the same person, show conclusively that rules of interpretation, e.g. as to acceptance of secondary evidence, were accepted by the committee, as would hardly have been the rule in an English case. This was due to the peculiar circumstances of Scottish life in past ages. Also the *Dundee* case was easily outside the limits of time laid down by the committee and as noted above. Nearly three centuries had passed since the Earldom of Dundee and other peerages of the Scrymgeour family had been in use. (*Proceedings before the Committee of Privileges & Judgment Dudhope Peerage 1952 & Earldom of Dundee 1953.*)

The above considerations have received the greater force owing to the case *In re Bristol South East Parliamentary Election* (1961) 3 (All E.R. 354) heard in Queen's Bench Division (Gorman and McNair, JJ.). This case is likely to take its place in the law of the peerage after the celebrated *Viscountess Rhondda's Claim* (128 L.T.Rep. 155; (1922) 2 A.C. 339) and to become with that case essential reading for all who wish to study the peerage and its law. The election case deserves detailed study not only because it illustrates the inability of a peer in the present century before 1963 to surrender his peerage but also because the case led to the 1963 Peerage Act.

The facts in the case can soon be given. In 1942 William Wedgwood Benn was created a peer of the United Kingdom with the title of Viscount Stansgate of Stansgate, in the county of Essex, with succession in the peerage to the heirs male of his body lawfully begotten, i.e. the normal limitation given in letters patent which create a peerage. The eldest son of the first Lord Stansgate died in 1944 of injuries received on active service. The second son, Anthony Neil Wedgwood Benn, was elected member of Parliament for Bristol South East in 1950. He was returned as member for the same constituency at the general election of 1959. Lord Stansgate died on 17 November 1960. On 13 April, 1961, the House of Commons, confirming the report of its committee of privileges, resolved that Mr. Anthony Wedgwood Benn had ceased to be a member of that House on succeeding to the Viscounty of Stansgate on 17th November 1960. The House of Commons further resolved that a writ should be issued for the election of a new member for Bristol South East. At the by-election held at Bristol South East on 4th May, 1961, the result was that Mr. Benn received a majority over his only opponent (himself the heir presumptive to a Scottish peerage)—a majority which, it should be observed, was more than double that which he obtained against the same opponent at the general election in 1959. It may also be remarked at this stage that while, under election law, it is clearly known that a peer is among those disqualified from sitting in the House of Commons, this fact does not prevent a peer from being put forward for nomination as a candidate at a parliamentary election. It is also laid down with equal clarity that at a nomination, while certain objections may be made to a candidate, these objections must relate to particulars of the candidate or the persons subscribing the paper as not being those required by law, or the objection must be that the paper is not subscribed as required by law. It is expressly stated that the grounds for objection do not include objections to the qualifications of a candidate; these are matters which can only be questioned on petition. Lest there should be any query regarding this latter item, reference may be made to so easily accessible a work as the *Parliamentary Election Manual*, issued by the Conservative and Unionist Central Office, mainly for the guidance of candidates and agents at elections. It is suggested that, while this item with regard to election law is not relevant to the main subject of this article, it does help to explain the anomalies and curious positions which result from ignoring the differences that undoubtedly do exist between the legal and the historical expositions of peerage.

To resume with that which for general convenience may be referred to as the Stansgate case: On 5th May, 1961, Mr. Benn (hereafter called 'the respondent') was returned as the duly elected member of Parliament for Bristol South East. He went to the entrance of the Chamber of the House of Commons and was refused admittance. Prior to the date of the by-election Mr. Malcolm St. Clair, the defeated candidate, had sent out notices to all persons entitled to vote stating that the respondent was a peer of the United Kingdom, and had been so found by the House of Commons; he did in fact take every possible step before the by-election and during the election to advise voters in the constituency that votes cast for the respondent would be thrown away. On the result of the election, the petitioner, Mr. Malcolm St. Clair, with one John Malcolm

Harris, presented a petition on 8th May, 1961, asking that it be determined that Anthony Neil Wedgwood Benn, the respondent, was not duly elected or returned as member of Parliament for Bristol South East, and that the first named petitioner, namely Malcolm St. Clair, was duly elected. There is no need to go into the court's reasons for its findings, in so far as they relate to the law of elections. Suffice to say that it was held that "on the evidence before the court, the facts which in law created the respondent's incapacity to be elected a member of Parliament were known to the electors before they cast their votes and the court was therefore bound to declare that the votes cast for the respondent had been thrown away and that the petitioner was duly elected as the member of Parliament for the constituency".

Turning to the peerage law expressed in this case, the court said that the respondent had not contended that the instrument of renunciation which he had signed in this case amounted to a renunciation of the peerage. (This referred to an attempt by the respondent before the by-election took place to surrender his letters patent to the Queen and to execute a deed of renunciation of his peerage.) Their lordships quoted the respondent as having said: "It is really not for me to say whether I think a peerage can be surrendered. All that I can say is that in this case I am placing no reliance whatsoever on the instrument of renunciation which I have executed. It is not for me to say whether or not a peerage can be surrendered." None the less, the court did give consideration to the question whether in law a peer has the right to renounce or surrender a peerage. The court considered the *Norfolk (Earldom) Peerage Claim* (95 L.T.Rep. 682: (1907) A.C.10). This in itself dealt with three earlier decisions—the *Oxford (Earldom) Petitions* (1625 Collins's Baronies by writ 173) the *Grey de Ruthyn Case* (1640, ibid.195,256) and *Purbeck's Case* (1678, ibid,293). The *Norfolk* case is of great importance because the earldom itself was surrendered to King Edward I in 1302 by Roger le Bygod. It was held that this surrender was invalid; that the charter of 1312 by which Edward II granted the surrendered earldom to Thomas de Brotherton was invalid; that the sitting in Parliament under the king's writ could not create an earldom; and that Lord Mowbray (the claimant who was the proven descendant of Thomas de Brotherton) had not made out his claim. The plain meaning of this is that in 1302 the law was wrongly stated. The law has always been what it is today, that a peerage cannot be surrendered. Therefore in 1302 not only was Bygod wrong, but King Edward I was wrong, and so was the king's chancellor. They did not know the law, and it may be said at once that this is not surprising, for no one could know of a law which was not declared until some hundreds of years after his death.

From the *Norfolk* case the court passed to the famous case of *Viscountess Rhondda*, which has already been mentioned. In that case Lord Wrenbury said that a peerage was an inalienable, incorporeal hereditament.

Such then was held to be the law as to the surrender of peerages before 1963. Peerage history and peerage law were again in conflict, nor can the solution of the impasse be regarded as historically satisfactory.

It can be shown without shadow of doubt that peerages have been surrendered, and as accessible an authority as Sir Francis B. Palmer's *Peerage Law in England* cites no less than eight cases between 1378 and 1639. None of these is among those quoted already, where the surrender has been held of no effect. The outstanding case is that of Roger Stafford 1639. Here a very ancient barony by writ was surrendered by the heir, namely one Roger Stafford. The sovereign (Charles I) had wanted the barony for his courtier, Sir William Howard, who was married to Mary, the heir general of the Stafford family. Roger Stafford surrendered the barony by means of a fine which was levied in the Common Pleas, with the Crown as plaintiff and Roger Stafford as deforceant. It is true that this case was challenged the next year, in the *Grey de Ruthyn* case, but the results of Roger Stafford's surrender still stand. After the surrender Sir William Howard was created, with his wife, Baron and Baroness Stafford, and this barony still remains in the descendants. But, if the decision in the *Norfolk* case is correct, then should not the grant of the barony of Stafford to Sir William Howard also be invalid? If the surrender of the barony in 1639 was wrong in law, how could that barony be validly granted anew to another person? So far as is known there has not been any attempt to assert this view, but it is surely valid on the premises given, and presents once more an example of the difficulties which beset peerage law at every turn.

Peerage legislation in this century starts from the Parliamentary crisis of 1909-11, when Conservative peers had imposed a veto on legislative forwarded to the Upper House by the Liberal Government. The Parliament Act of 1911 withdrew Money Bills passed by the Commons from any veto by the Lords. The Lords' veto was reduced to two years in the case of any other Bill; after two years within the life of the Government which forwarded the Bill, it would on re-presentation become law.

In the preamble of the 1911 Act it was stated that it was "intended to substitute for the House of Lords as it at present exists a Second Chamber constituted on a popular instead of hereditary basis, but such substitution cannot be immediately brought into operation".

Inter-party conferences have been unable, in 1917-18 and in 1948, to reach agreement on House of Lords' reform mainly on the subject of the delaying powers of the Lords. In 1949 the Parliament Act, passed by the then Labour Government, further reduced the Lords' veto to less than one year on other than Money Bills.

No reform of the Lords as envisaged in 1911 has taken place but the 1963 Peerage Act is the nearest approach to such a reform. It affords once more an interesting contrast between legal and historical views. Why was it necessary for the main part of the Act, that relating to the surrender of Peerages to be passed by Parliament? Could not the Prime Minister have advised the Sovereign, who is the Fountain of Honour, to exercise the powers which past sovereigns had undoubtedly possessed of receiving the surrender of peerages?

The Peerage Act, 1963, was described in the popular press as Mr. Wedgwood Benn's Enabling Act, and even in periodicals which are accustomed to a more thoughtful analysis there was a strong tendency to overlook those sections of the Act which are not necessarily connected with any question of surrender of peerages. Even in textbooks this statute may receive a popular title, as in the case of the Libel Acts of 1845 which are so frequently mentioned even when lawyers are writing for lawyers and law students as Lord Campbell's Libel Acts or even simply as Lord Campbell's Acts. It is certainly true that the name of Mr. Wedgwood Benn will for ever be associated with the Peerage Act of 1963. Without his pertinacity over two years the Act would be unlikely to have reached the Statute book. None the less, the Act included within its provisions several heterogeneous features. It is as though some distinct lines of reform of the House of Lords had been brought together and their full force focussed by Mr. Wedgwood Benn's campaign to surrender his peerage.

The full title of the Act makes the position quite clear: that some things much more varied than the right of a peer to disclaim his peerage are involved. "An Act to authorise the disclaimer for life of certain hereditary peerages; to include among the peers qualified to sit in the House of Lords all peers in the peerage of Scotland and peeresses in their own right in the peerages of England, Scotland, Great Britain and the United Kingdom; to remove certain disqualifications of peers in the peerage of Ireland in relation to the House of Commons and elections thereto; and for purposes connected with the matters aforesaid."

It may be noted that the first clause only in the full title is concerned with the problem made familiar by Mr. Benn, how to remain a member of the House of Commons despite succession to the Lords. It is true that out of seven sections of the Act, three, and those the largest, deal with disclaimer, but that is because there are various categories of persons who may wish to disclaim a peerage and the Act must set out the procedure to be adopted in each case.

It is next well to note that the term used to cover the resignation of a peer from the peerage is always "disclaimer", and that the term 'surrender' is not used. This is the more interesting because in the Report of the Joint Committee on House of Lords Reform, 1962, which is the foundation of the Act, the term to "surrender" a peerage is regularly used. The Act speaks of a "disclaimer" for life of certain hereditary peerages. Perhaps it is felt that 'surrender' has an association with the more ancient history of the peerage, before the later 17th century when the surrender of a peerage was undoubtedly legal. It should be realized that the present Act completely ignores the contradiction between the conception of peerage in law and peerage in history to which several distinguished scholars have drawn attention.

To proceed with the analysis of the Act, C.1.s (1) provides that any person who henceforth succeeds to a peerage in the peerage of England, Scotland, Great Britain or the United Kingdom, may disclaim that peerage for his life by an Act of disclaimer delivered to the Lord Chancellor. Irish peerages are not mentioned in this section, as they come under C.5. and do not debar their holders from sitting in the Commons. C.1.ss (2)—(5) deal with the procedure to be adopted by a peer who wished to disclaim. The prescribed period in which a disclaimer may be made is 12 months from the day of succession; in the case of a minor, the period begins to run from the day he attains his majority. As to those who have succeeded to a peerage before the beginning of the Act, they have 12 months from the commencement of the Act in which to decide. Consideration is given to the fact of illness or other incapacity and time does not begin to run during the period of infirmity. Schedule 1 of the Act gives the form of the instrument of disclaimer. Coming to C.2, there is the case of succession to a peerage of a member of the House of Commons and of a parliamentary candidate. The former is allowed one month from the date of his succession to the peerage. With the latter, he may continue with his candidature and if elected to the Commons, he then has a month in which to consider his position. Candidature in this section does not of course cover the position of a prospective candidate, who comes under C.1.s(2), but deals only with a candidate nominated at an actual election.

C.3.s.(1) outlines the effects of disclaimer. Disclaimer is irrevocable, once he has made a disclaimer, the former peer is divested of all titles, rights, offices, privileges and precedence attaching to the peerage. This applies to his wife also, an important provision in view of the social conditions of today, when divorced women who have remarried continue to use titles derived from their first husbands. The disclaimer "shall not accelerate the succession to that peerage, nor effect its devolution on his death". This sub-section again resolutely bars the way to the old Scottish system whereby a renunciation of peerage could be followed by succession of the next heir.

Under C.3.s.(2) no hereditary peerages shall be conferred upon the person who has disclaimed a peerage. Subsection (3) preserves the right of succession to any property which may devolve with the peerage.

The machinery of disclaimer having been dealt with, the Act comes to C.4 which concerns Scottish peerages. This is short and succinct: "The holder of a peerage in the peerage of Scotland shall have the same right to receive writs of summons to attend the House of Lords, and to sit and vote in that House as the holder of a peerage in the peerage of the United Kingdom; and the enactments relating to the election of Scottish representative peers shall cease to have effect". Behind this lies a very long history. Schedule 2 lists 10 statutes relating to Scottish peers. Of these Acts, three are entirely repealed; while sections of the other seven are also repealed. When the Treaty of Union between England and Scotland was negotiated and became law in 1707, only 16 of the Scottish peers were allowed to sit in the House of Lords. The whole body of the Scottish peers numbered between 154 and 170 (the different numbers come from equally good authorities) and under the Treaty of Union they were to choose 16 of their number to represent them at Westminster, for the life of each Parliament. This was a gross injustice and dictated solely by the English peers, fearing that they would be swamped by the arrival of so many Scottish peers. In the intervening period, the number of the Scottish peers has greatly declined. Today there are only 31 peers of Scotland who could elect 16 of their number to sit in the Lords. There are other peers of Scotland but they hold in addition to their Scottish peerages, peerages of the United Kingdom, and as such could not vote in the election of peers. In addition, Scottish peers, unlike Irish peers, have not been allowed to sit in the House of Commons or to vote in the elections to the same. This very considerable injustice to the Scottish peers, was removed by this section of the Act. Scottish peerages henceforth, like those of England, of Great Britain and of the United Kingdom, carry with them the right to a seat in the Lords. The Joint Committee had recommended that for the avoidance of doubt, it should be enacted that no further peerages of Scotland should be created. This recommendation was not embodied in the Act, but perhaps the fact that for over 250 years no Scottish peerages have been created was held sufficient as proof that none would be created. The next section C.5. is devoted to the Irish peerage, of which presently. C.6. is concerned with peeresses in their own right. Ever since the passing of the Sex Disqualification (Removal) Act of 1919, there have been persistent advocates of the entry of women into the Lords. The Rhondda Peerage case in 1922, in which the Committee of Privilege of the House of Lords decided against the admission of peeresses was notable for the judgment of the then Lord Chancellor, the 1st Earl of Birkenhead. This judgment is necessary reading for the student of the peerage and of constitutional history, but its main contention has always seemed to be an example of the worst feature of legal reasoning. However, the judgment stood as the last on the subject, despite several efforts, until the Life Peerage Act of 1958. This measure allowed the creation of women as peeresses for life and hence as able to sit in the Lords. It then became patently illogical to admit a woman as a member of the Lords in her capacity as a life peeress, while refusing her admission as an hereditary peeress, which was exactly the position of Lady Ravensdale who possessed a hereditary and a life barony. The cause of feminism triumphed and peeresses in their own right have the right to receive writs of Summons to the Lords. These ladies have the same privilege of disclaimer of peerage as their male counterparts.

Coming now to C.5 which deals with the peerage of Ireland, two slight changes were made. C.5 (a) allows that an Irish peer can be elected as a member of the House of Commons for any constituency in the United Kingdom. Up to the passing of the present Act, an Irish peer who was not a representative peer was able to be elected a member for any constituency other than those in Northern Ireland. Now this latter restriction is removed. Then under C.5. (b) an Irish peer may not vote at elections for the House of Commons whether or not he is a member of that House. Previously Irish peers could vote at parliamentary elections only if they were sitting members of the House of Commons.

With the general position of Irish peers, the Act does not, however deal, and in this it follows the judgment of the Joint Committee which was "that the Committee were not in favour of the revival of any form of representation for the peerage of Ireland in the House of Lords nor of any scheme for the surrender by Irish peers of their peerages". Under the Act of Union of 1800 between Great Britain and Ireland, provision was made for the election by the Irish peers of 28 of their number to represent them in the Lords. Peers thus elected held their places for life, those not elected could offer themselves as candidates for the Commons. Earl Winterton, an Irish peer, did indeed sit for 47 years as an M.P. The machinery for the election of Irish representative peers was that the writs should be issued by the Lord Chancellor of Ireland. No election has taken place since 1919, and after the establishment of the Irish Free State in 1921, the office of Lord Chancellor was abolished. The last Irish representative peer, the late Earl of Kilmorey died in 1961. Despite several memoranda to the Joint Committee with regard to the Irish peers, nothing is to be done to cover the case of the peers who hold peerages exclusively of Ireland. It follows that these peers will have no official check upon their successions. It likewise follows that should an impostor or a person whose claim is unproven choose to take up one of these peerages there will be no means of dealing officially with his claim.

Very few peers have in fact disclaimed their peerages; not a dozen out of a total of more than 1,100. Other piecemeal changes have occurred. The Criminal Justice Act, 1948 abolished the right of a peer to be tried by his peers. Payment of expenses for peers attending sessions was introduced from 1951; peers who do not desire to attend the House can now formally apply for leave of absence. The Life Peerage Act of 1958 has greatly increased the number of life peers. Since 1964 no hereditary peerages have been created. Since most life peerages go to the over 60s, the voice of youth is unlikely to be heard in the Lords except when a young hereditary peer takes his seat.

NOTE: The following articles in the present volume illustrate points of peerage law. Berkeley (alleged creation of peerage by writ of summons); Carnwath (attainder and subsequent restoration and reference to abolition of attainder etc.); Cobham, Conyers, Fauconberge, Ferrers of Chartley, Fitzwalter, Grey de Ruthyn (cases of abeyance); Rhondda (claim of peeresses in own right to sit in Lords); Turnour (Irish earl created and sat as U.K. baron)—: Hamilton (creation of life dukedom and other peerages).

List of Abbreviations

A.A.	.. ..	Athletic Association (now A.A.A.)
A.A.G. ..	..	Assistant Adjutant General
A.C.A. ..	..	Associate of Institute of Chartered Accountants
A/Cdre ..	..	Air Commodore
A.D.C. ..	..	Aide-de-Camp
Adm. ..	..	Admiral; admitted
A.M.I.C.E.	..	Associated Member of the Institute of Civil Engineers
A.O.C. (in C.) ..		Air Officer Commanding (in chief)
A.R.I.B.A.	..	Associate of the Royal Institute of British Architects
A.R.A. ..	..	Associate of the Royal Academy
A.R.P. ..	..	Air Raid Precautions
A.R.R.C.	..	Associate of the Royal Red Cross
A.S.C. ..	..	Army Service Corps
A.T.S. ..	..	Auxiliary Territorial Service
A/V/M. ..	..	Air Vice Marshal
B.	.. ..	Baron
B.A.	.. ..	Bachelor of Arts
B.B.C. ..	..	British Broadcasting Corporation
B.C.	.. ..	Bachelor of Surgery (Chirugery)
B.C.L. ..	..	Bachelor of Civil Law
B.Chir ..	..	Bachelor of Surgery
B.C.S. ..	..	Bengal Civil Service
B.D.	.. ..	Bachelor of Divinity
B.E.M. ..	..	British Empire Medal
B.L.G. ..	..	Burke's Landed Gentry
B.Litt. ..	..	Bachelor of Letters
B.M.	.. ..	Bachelor of Medicine
B.M.A. ..	..	British Medical Association
Bn.	.. ..	Battalion
B.R.C. ..	..	British Red Cross
Brev.	.. ..	Brevet
B.S.	.. ..	Bachelor of Surgery
B.Sc.	.. ..	Bachelor of Science
Bt.	.. ..	Baronet
C.A.	.. ..	Chartered Accountant; county alderman
C.B.	.. ..	Companion of the Order of the Bath
C.C.	.. ..	County Council; County Counsellor; Corpus Christi
C.D.	.. ..	Civil Defence
C.E.	.. ..	Civil Engineer
C.F.	.. ..	Chaplain to the Forces
C.H.	.. ..	Companion of Honour
Chm.	.. ..	Chairman
Ch.Ch. ..	..	Christ Church
C.I.	.. ..	Lady of the Imperial Order of Crown of India
C.I.E.	.. ..	Companion of the Order of the Indian Empire
C.in-C. ..	..	Commander in Chief
Cmdr. ..	..	Commander
C.P.	.. ..	Complete Peerage
C.S.	.. ..	Civil Service
C.S.I.	.. ..	Companion of the Order of the Star of India
C.St.J. ..	..	Commander of the Order of St. John of Jerusalem

Cttee	..	.. Committee
C.V.O. ..	..	Commander of the Royal Victorian Order
D.	..	.. Duke
D.A.A.G.	..	Deputy Assistant Adjutant General
D.A.Q.M.G.	..	Deputy Assistant Quarter Master General
D.B.E. ..	..	Dame Commander of the Order of the British Empire
D.C.L. ..	..	Doctor of Civil Law
D.C.L.I.	..	Duke of Cornwall's Light Infantry
D.C.V.O.	..	Dame Commander of Royal Victorian Order
D.D.	..	.. Doctor of Divinity
D.F.C. ..	..	Distinguished Flying Cross
D.G.St.J.	..	Dame of Grace of the Order of St. John of Jerusalem
D.J.St.J.	..	Dame of Justice of Order of St. John of Jerusalem
D.J.A.(G.)	..	Deputy Judge Advocate (General)
D.L.	..	.. Deputy Lieutenant
D.M.R. ..	..	Diploma in Medical Radiology
D.N.B. ..	..	Dictionary of National Biography
D.P.H. ..	..	Diploma in Public Health
D.Sc.	..	.. Doctor of Science
D.S.C. ..	..	Distinguished Service Cross
D.S.M. ..	..	Distinguished Service Medal
D.S.O. ..	..	Companion of the Distinguished Service Order
d.s.p.	..	.. decessit sine prole (died without issue)
d.s.p.l. ..	..	decessit sine prole legitima (died without legitimate issue)
d.s.p.m. (s)	..	decessit sine prole mascula superstite (died without (surviving) male issue)
d.s.p.s. ..	..	decessit sine prole superstite (died without surviving issue)
d.s.p.v.p.	..	decessit sine prole vita patris (died without issue in the lifetime of the father)
d.v.p.	..	.. decessit vita patris (died in the father's lifetime)
E.	..	.. Earl
F.A.I. ..	..	Fellow of Chartered Auctioneers and Estate Agents Institute
F.A.G.S.	..	Fellow of American Geographical Society
F.A.N.Y.	..	First Aid Nursing Yeomanry
F.B.A. ..	..	Fellow of the British Academy
F.B.O.A.	..	Fellow of the British Optical Association
F.B.S. ..	..	Fellow of the Building Societies Institute
F.E.I.S. ..	..	Fellow of the Educational Institute of Scotland
F.F.	..	.. Frontier Force
F.I.L.	..	.. Fellow of the Institute of Linguists

Fin. Sec.	..	Financial Secretary
F.I.J. ..	..	Fellow of the Institute of Journalists
F.L.S. ..	..	Fellow of the Linnean Society
F/Lt. ..	..	Flight Lieutenant
F.R.A.S.	..	Fellow of the Royal Asiatic Society; of the Royal Astronomical Society
F.R.C.P.	..	Fellow of the Royal College of Physicians
F.R.C.S.	..	Fellow of the Royal College of Surgeons
F.R.E.S.	..	Fellow of the Royal Entomological Society
F.R.Ecom.S.	..	Fellow of the Royal Economic Society
F.R.G.S.	..	Fellow of the Royal Geographical Society
F.R.Hist.S.	..	Fellow of the Royal Historical Society
F.R.Hort.S.	..	Fellow of the Royal Horticultural Society
F.R.I.B.A.	..	Fellow of the Royal Institute of British Architects
F.R.I.C...	..	Fellow of the Royal Institute of Chemistry
F.R.Met.S.	..	Fellow of the Royal Meteorological Society
F.R.S. ..	..	Fellow of the Royal Society
F.R.S.E.	..	Fellow of the Royal Society of Edinburgh
F.R.S.L.	..	Fellow of the Royal Society of Literature
F.S.A. ..	..	Fellow of the Society of Antiquaries
F.S.A.Scot.	..	Fellow of the Society of Antiquaries of Scotland
F.S.A.S.M.	..	Fellow of the South Australian School of Mines
F.S.G. ..	..	Fellow of the Society of Genealogists
F.Z.S. ..	..	Fellow of the Zoological Society
G.B.E. ..	..	Knight or Dame Grand Cross of the Order of the British Empire
G.C.B. ..	..	Knight Grand Cross of the Order of the Bath
G.C.H.	..	Knight Grand Cross of Order of Hanover
G.C.I.E...	..	Knight Grand Commander of the Order of the Indian Empire
G.C.M.G.	..	Knight or Dame Grand Cross of the Order of St. Michael & St. George
G.C.S.I.	..	Knight Grand Commander of the Order of the Star of India
G.C.V.O.	..	Knight or Dame Grand Cross of the Royal Victorian Order
G.M. ..	..	Grand Master
G.O.C. ..	..	General Officer Commanding
Grm.	..	Grammar
G.S.O. ..	..	General Staff Officer
H.E.I.C.S.	..	Honourable East India Company's Service
H.I.H. ..	..	His or Her Imperial Highness
I.A. ..	..	Indian Army
I.C.S. ..	..	Indian Civil Service
I.L.P. ..	..	Independent Labour Party
I.M.S. ..	..	Indian Medical Service
I.P.M. ..	..	Inquisitio post mortem
I.S.O. ..	..	Imperial Service Order
J.A.G. ..	..	Judge Advocate General
J.P. ..	..	Justice of the Peace
K.B. ..	..	Knight of the Bath
K.B.E. ..	..	Knight Commander of the Order of the British Empire
K.C. ..	..	King's Counsel
K.C.B. ..	..	Knight Commander of the Bath
K.C.H.	..	Knight Commander of Order of Hanover
K.C.M.G.	..	Knight Commander of Order of St. Michael & St. George
K.C.S. ..	..	Knight of Charles III of Spain
K.C.S.I.	..	Knight Commander of the Order of the Star of India
K.C.V.O.	..	Knight Commander of the Royal Victorian Order
K.F. ..	..	Knight of San Fernando
K.G. ..	..	Knight of the Garter
K.H. ..	..	Knight of the Order of Hanover
K.G.St.J.	..	Knight of Grace of Order of St. John of Jerusalem
K.J.St.J...	..	Knight of Justice of Order of St. John of Jerusalem
K.O.S.B.	..	King's Own Scottish Borderers
K.P. ..	..	Knight of St. Patrick
K.R.R.C.	..	King's Royal Rifle Corps
K.St.J. ..	..	Knight of the Order of St. John of Jerusalem
K.T. ..	..	Knight of the Thistle
Kt.Bach	..	Knight Bachelor
L.A. ..	..	Legislative Assembly
L.C.C. ..	..	London County Council
L.D.S. ..	..	Licentiate in Dental Surgery
L.G.St.J.	..	Lady of Grace of Order of St. John of Jerusalem
L.I. ..	..	Light Infantry
L.J.St.J.	..	Lady of Justice of St. John of Jerusalem
LL.B. ..	..	Bachelor of Laws
LL.D. ..	..	Doctor of Laws
L.N.E.R.	..	London North Eastern Railway
L.N.W.R.	..	London North Western Railway
L.R.C.P.	..	Licentiate of Royal College of Physicians
L.R.C.S.	..	Licentiate of Royal College of Surgeons
Lt. Cmdr.	..	Lieutenant Commander
M.	..	Marquess
M.A. ..	..	Master of Arts
M.B. ..	..	Bachelor of Medicine
M.B.E. ..	..	Member of the Order of the British Empire
M.C. ..	..	Military Cross
M.D. ..	..	Doctor of Medicine
M.I. ..	..	Monumental inscription
M.I.C.E.	..	Member of Institute of Civil Engineers
M.I.N.A.	..	Member of Institution of Naval Architects
M.I.M.E.	..	Member of Institution of Mechanical Engineers
M.L.A. ..	..	Member of Legislative Assembly
M.L.C. ..	..	Member of Legislative Council
M.R.C.P.	..	Member of Royal College of Physicians
M.R.C.S.	..	Member of Royal College of Surgeons
M.V.O. ..	..	Member of Royal Victorian Order
N.U.R. ..	..	National Union of Railwaymen
N.Z. ..	..	New Zealand
O.B.E. ..	..	Officer of Order of British Empire
O.M. ..	..	Order of Merit
O.St.J. ..	..	Officer of Order of St. John of Jerusalem
P.C. ..	..	Privy Counsellor
P.C.C. ..	..	Prerogative Court of Canterbury
Ph.D. ..	..	Doctor of Philosophy

Ppr	.. ..	proper
P.U.S.	.. ..	Permanent Under Secretary
Q.C.	.. ..	Queen's Counsel
Q.S.	.. ..	Queen's Scholar
R.A.	.. ..	Royal Artillery; Royal Academy
R.A.A.F.	..	Royal Australian Air Force
R.A.F.V.R.	..	Royal Air Force Volunteer Reserve
R.A.M.C.	..	Royal Army Medical Corps
R.A.N.	..	Royal Australian Navy
R.A.S.C.	..	Royal Army Service Corps
R.C.S.	..	Royal College of Surgeons
R.E.	..	Royal Engineers
R.F.A.	..	Royal Field Artillery
R.G.A.	..	Royal Garrison Artillery
R.G.S.	..	Royal Geographical Society
R.H.A.	..	Royal Horse Artillery
R.M.	..	Royal Marines
R.M.A.	..	Royal Military College (Sandhurst)
R.M.C.	..	Royal Military Academy (Woolwich)
R.N.A.S.	..	Royal Naval Air Service
R.N.I.	..	Royal National Institute
R.N.R.	..	Royal Naval Reserve
R.N.V.R.	..	Royal Naval Volunteer Reserve

s...	.. ..	succeeded; succeeding; surviving
sch.	.. ..	school; scholar
Sjt.	.. ..	Serjeant
S/Ldr.	..	Squadron Leader
S.R.	..	Special Reserve
S.S. St.J.	..	Serving Sister of Order of St. John of Jerusalem
T.A.	..	Territorial Army
T.D.	..	Territorial Decoration
Terr.	..	Territorial
U.D.C.	..	Urban District Council
V.	..	Viscount
V.D.	..	Victorian Decoration
V.P.	..	Vita patris, in lifetime of father
V.C.	..	Victoria Cross
W.A.A.F.	..	Women's Auxiliary Air Force
W/Cmdr.	..	Wing Commander
W.R.	..	West Riding
W.R.N.S.	..	Women's Royal Naval Service
W.S.	..	Writer to the Signet
W.V.S.	..	Women's Voluntary Service
ygr. yr.	..	younger
ygst. yst.	..	youngest
Yeo.	..	Yeomanry

List of Illustrations

Publisher's Note: The illustrations are in the main taken from the spirited work of Fr. Anselm and Forbes Nixon. It will be noticed that tilting helmets are sometimes used instead of helmets of degree and coronets are not always included.

ABERCROMBY

PEERAGE—U.K. Baron Abercromby of Aboukir and Tullibody, co. Clackmannan.
SURNAME—Abercromby.
CR.—28 May 1801. **EXT.** 7 Oct. 1924.
HISTORY—Sir Alexander Abercromby, 1st Bt. of Birkenbog (see that title in extant peerages) had a second son, Alexander Abercromby, Advocate and M.P. Clackmannanshire 1703-07, inherited the estate of Tullibody in that county from his cousin, George Abercromby of Skelth. He m. Mary, dau. of Alexander Duff, and had (with a second son, Alexander, of Alloa, who m. 1732, Rebecca, dau. of Alexander Colquhoun) an elder son, George Abercromby of Tullibody, Advocate, m. Mary, dau. of Ralph Dundas of Manour, co. Peebles, and d. 8 June 1800, leaving issue,

1. Ralph, Sir, (see below).
2. Burnet, of Brucefield, Capt. H.E.I.C.S., M.P. for Clackmannan, who d.s.p. 24 March 1792.
3. Robert, Sir, G.C.B., of Brucefield, Gen., C. in C. in India, 1793, Gov. of Edinburgh Castle, M.P. Clackmannan 1798-1802; b. 21 Oct. 1740, d. 3 Nov. 1827.
4. Alexander, as Lord Abercromby, a Lord of Session, b. 15 Oct. 1745 d. unm. 17 Nov. 1795.
1. Helen, m. 6 June 1754, Robert Bruce, Lord Kennet, a lord of justiciary and d. 1786 (Balfour B.).
2. Mary, m. Major Alexander Joass, Gov. of Stirling Castle and had issue.

The eldest son, Sir Ralph Abercromby, K.B. (1795) P.C. (Ireland) 1798, b. 25 Oct. 1734; educ. Rugby; cornet 2nd Dragoon Guards 1756; Capt. 1762; Col. 103rd Foot, 1781-83, Major Gen. 1787; Col. 7th Dragoon Guards 1795-96, Col. 2nd Dragoons, 1796-1801; M.P. co. Clackmannan 1774-80 and 1796-98, Gov. of Inverness 1798-1801; Lt. Gen. 1797. He was C. in C. the West Indies 1795, had chief command of forces in Ireland 1798; had chief military command in Scotland. In 1801 he commanded the British forces in Egypt, landed his troops at Aboukir and fought the famous battle of Alexandria, in which he was mortally wounded on 21 March and d. 28 March 1801 on board *H.M.S. Foudroyant* in Aboukir Bay. (There is a detailed account of the campaign in Sir John Fortescue's *History of the British Army*. vol. IV chs. XXVIII and XXIX.) His body was buried in the Commandery of the Grand Master of Malta. By order of the House of Commons a monument was erected in St. Paul's Cathedral. He had married 17 Nov. 1767, Mary Anne, second dau. and coheir of John Menzies of Ferntower, in Crieff, co. Perth. She was cr. **Baroness Abercromby** of Aboukir and Tullibody co. Clackmannan, 28 May 1801, in reward for her late husband's gallant service, with remainder to the heirs male of her body by Sir Ralph. She was also granted a pension of £2,000 per year, this being settled on the three successors in the title. Sir Ralph and Baroness Abercromby had issue,

1. George, **2nd Baron** (see below).
2. John, Sir, G.C.B. Gen. and Col. 53rd Regt. who captured Mauritius 1809, b. 2 April 1772; d. unm. 14 Feb. 1817.
3. James, 1st Baron Dunfermline (1883 Extinct Peerage, Addenda).

4. Alexander, C.B. Lt. Col. 28th Regt.; served in the Peninsular War, and at Waterloo, M.P. Clackmannanshire, 1817; b. 4 March 1784 d. 27 Aug. 1853.
1. Anne, m. 1795, Donald Cameron, of Lochiel and d. 17 Sept. 1844.
2. Mary, d. 1825.
3. Catherine, m. Dec. 1871, Thomas Buchanan, and d. 7 May 1841.

Baroness Abercromby d. 11 Feb. 1821, being s. by her eldest son, George Abercromby, **2nd Baron Abercromby**, b. 14 Oct. 1770; Advocate, M.P. (Whig) Edinburgh 1805-06, and co. Clackmannan, 1806-07, and 1812-15, Lord Lieut. co. Stirling, 1837 43, m. 25 Jan. 1799, Montague, 3rd dau. of Henry Dundas, 1st Viscount Melville and by her (who d. March 1837) had issue,

1. George Ralph, **3rd Baron** (see below).
1. Montague, b. 25 May 1807; m. 4 Aug. 1831, F. M. Ramsay, 11th Earl of Dalhousie and d.s.p. 11 Nov. 1853.
2. Mary Anne, b. 7 Dec. 1811; m. 13 July 1857, Col. N. R. Brown, and d. 24 Sept. 1898.

The 2nd Baron d. 14 Feb. 1843 being s. by his son, George Ralph Abercromby, **3rd Baron Abercromby**, Major 3rd Dragoons 1826 and Col., M.P. (Whig) co. Clackmannan 1824-26 and 1830-31, co. Stirling 1838-41, cos. Clackmannan and Kinross, 1841-42, Lord Lt. co. Clackmannan 1840-52; b. 30 May 1800; m. 3 April 1832, Louisa Penuel, dau. of John Hay Forbes, Lord Medwyn as a Judge of Session (Forbes of Pitsligo Bt.) and by her (who d. 20 April 1882) had issue

1. George Ralph Campbell, **4th Baron** (see below).
2. John, **5th Baron** (see below).
3. Ralph, Lt. 60th Rifles, b. 11 Feb. 1842; d. unm. 21 June 1897.
1. Montague. b. 11 Aug. 1835; m. 29 April 1856, 6th Earl of Glasgow and had issue.

The 3rd Baron d. 25 June 1852, being s. by his eldest son, George Ralph Campbell Abercromby, **4th Baron Abercromby**. b. 23 Sept. 1838, J.P. cos. Stirling and Clackmannan, D.L. co. Stirling, 1860; m. 1858 Julia Janet Georgina, only dau. of Adam Duncan, 2nd Earl of Camperdown, one of the Ladies of the Bedchamber to Queen Victoria, 1874-85. She d.s.p. 8 Dec. 1915. He d.s.p. being s. by his brother, John Abercromby, **5th Baron Abercromby**. Lt. Rifle Brig.; LL.D (Hon) Edinburgh, Pres. of Soc. of Antiquaries of Scotland, b. 15 Jan. 1841; m. 26 Aug. 1876, his cousin, Adele Wilhelmina Marika, dau. of Chevalier Charles von Heidenstern, Swedish Min. at the Court of Greece, and d. 7 Oct. 1924 having had issue, Edla Louisa Montague, b. 23 Aug. 1877, m. 10 Oct. 1906, Georges N. Nasos, Dir. of the Conservatoire of Music at Athens.

The 5th Baron's marriage was dissolved in 1879 on his suit by the Court of Session.
ARMS—Argent a fesse embattled gules therefrom issuant in chief a dexter arm embowed in armour ppr., garnished or, encircled by a wreath of laurel, the hand supporting the French standard in bend sinister also ppr.; in base (for Abercromby) a chevron indented gules between three boars' heads erased azure.
CREST—A bee volant ppr.
SUPPORTERS—Two greyhounds per fesse argent and or each plain collared with line

reflexed over the back gules and charged on the shoulder with a thistle ppr.

MOTTO—Vive ut vivas.

The seats of the Lords Abercromby were Tullibody Castle, co. Clackmannan and Fern Tower, Crieff, co. Perth. Their London house was 41 Brompton Square.

ABERTAY

PEERAGE—U.K. Baron Abertay of Tullybelton.

SURNAME—Barrie.

CR.—18 June 1940. **EXT.** 6 Dec. 1940.

HISTORY—Charles Barrie of Coldside, Dundee, had issue, Sir Charles Barrie of Airlie Park, Broughty Ferry, J.P., D.L., Dundee, 1902-15, cr. Kt. Bach. 1919, b. 1840; m. 25 Dec. 1872, the dau. of Alexander Cathro of Arbroath and had issue, an eldest son, Sir Charles Coupar Barrie, **Baron Abertay**, b. 1875: educ. Blairlodge Sch., Polmont; M.P. Elgin Burghs 1918; Banffshire 1918-24, Southampton 1931-40; partner in Charles Barrie and Sons, Dundee, shipowners and merchants; a director of many cos, cr. Baron Abertay of Tullybelton, co. Perth 18 June 1940 He m. 1 June 1926, Ethel, only dau. of Sir James Thomson Broom M.L.C. Ceylon, and d. 6 Dec. 1940, leaving issue, three daus.,

1. June Jane Coupar, b. 1928; m. 1952, Lt. Col. A. N. Breitmeyer, and had issue.
2. Rosemary Ethel Coupar, b. 1931; m. 1952, J. S. Maitland, and had issue.
3. Caroline Barbara Coupar, b. 1933; m. 1955, Capt. J. N. Buchanan Baillie-Hamilton and had issue, (Haddington E.).

ADAMS

PEERAGE—U.K. Baron Adams of Ennerdale, co. Cumberland.

SURNAME—Adams.

CR.—16 Feb. 1949. **EXT.** 23 Aug. 1960.

HISTORY—One of the numerous creations of the Labour Government 1945-51. John Jackson Adams was born 12 Oct. 1890, the 7th son of Thomas and Mary (née Bowness) Adams of Arlecdon, a parish near Whitehaven in Cumberland. His life was associated with his native county. He went to the Council School at Arlecdon and entered local politics early, being Chairman of the Arlecdon and Frizington U.D.C., 1919-23, and by 1934, J.P. and County Alderman, also from 1919 a member of the Health Cttee. of the Cumberland C.C., and Chairman of the Cttee. 1942-47. He was Chm. of Governors of Whitehaven School, Deputy Regional Controller of the Board of Trade for Cumberland Westmorland Sub-region 1944-48, was awarded the O.B.E. 1944, and held several other appointments in connection with Cumberland. Durham Univ. conferred an Hon. M.A. in 1948. Cr. **Baron Adams** of Ennerdale, co. Cumberland 16 Feb. 1949. He m. 1914, Agnes Jane, the only dau. of Thomas Birney. Their only child, Thomas was b. 22 and d. 27 Dec. 1923. The family home was at Wybrow Terrace, Workington, Cumberland. Lord Adams d. 23 Aug. 1960.

ARMS—Vert a torch erect, between in chief two cog wheels and issuant from the base a sun rising or thereon an open book proper bound and clasped gules.

CREST—On the head of a well a fieldfare rising proper.

SUPPORTERS—Dexter, A miner holding in the interior hand a lamp and supporting in the exterior a pickaxe; Sinister, An agricultural labourer resting the exterior hand on a fork.

MOTTO—Labore omnia vincit.

ALBANY

PEERAGE—U.K. Baron Arklow, co. Wicklow. Earl of Clarence. Duke of Albany.

SURNAME—None.

CR.—24 May 1881. In suspense since 28 March 1919.

HISTORY—H.R.H. Leopold George Duncan Albert, Prince of Great Britain and Ireland, also Duke of Saxony, the 4th and yst. son of Queen Victoria, b. 7 April 1853; matric. at Ch.Ch. Oxford 1872; made P.C. 1874, K.G. 1869, K.T. 1871; G.C.S.I. 1877, G.C.M.G. 1880; cr. **Baron Arklow**, co. Wicklow, **Earl of Clarence** in England, **Duke of Albany** in Scotland (the practice of the Royal family since the time of George III being to take a peerage title from each one of the three kingdoms). Col. in the Army and Hon. Col. 3rd Seaforth Highlanders. He m. 27 April 1882, Helene Friederike Auguste, 5th dau. of George Victor reigning Prince of Waldeck and Pyrmont, and d. suddenly at Cannes, 28 March 1884, having had issue, H.R.H. Leopold Charles Edward George Albert, Prince of Great Britain and Ireland, **2nd Duke of Albany, Earl of Clarence** and 2nd **Baron Arklow**, also Duke of Saxony, and by s. to his uncle Prince Alfred, Duke of Saxe Coburg and Gotha, 30 July 1900; b. posthumously 19 July 1884; G.C.V.O. 1901; K.G. 1902; m. 11 Oct. 1905, Victoria Adelheid Helena Louise Marie Frederike, dau. of Frederick Ferdinand George Christian Carl Wilhelm, Duke of Schleswig-Holstein-Sonderburg-Glücksburg. He was struck off the roll of the Order of the Garter, 13 May 1915. His titles in the peerage of the U.K. were removed from the roll of the peers following an Order of the King in Council 28 March 1919. He had issue three sons and two daus. The eldest son is H.H. Johann Leopold Wilhelm Albert Ferdinand Viktor, "in whom is vested the right to petition for restoration to the Roll of Peers on the death of his father" (*Suspended Peerages*, an article by the late Philip Thomas in B.P. 1953 in which the subject of the Albany, Cumberland and Taaffe peerages is discussed).

ARMS—(of 1st Duke). The royal arms differenced by a label of three points argent, the centre point charged with St. George's Cross, and each of the other points with a heart gules; in the centre of the said royal arms an escutcheon of the august House of Saxony, viz., barry of ten or and sable, a crown of rue in bend vert.

CREST—On a coronet composed of crosses pattée and fleur-de-lis, a lion statant guardant or, crowned with the like coronet and differenced with a label of three points charged as in the arms.

SUPPORTERS—The royal supporters differenced with the like coronet and label.

ALCESTER

PEERAGE—U.K. Baron Alcester, of Alcester, co. Warwick.
SURNAME—Seymour.
CR.—24 Nov. 1882. **EXT.**—30 Mar. 1895.
HISTORY—Lord Alcester was the only surv. son of Sir Horace Beauchamp Seymour, K.C.H., and Col. in the Army, by his wife, Elizabeth Malet, dau. of Sir Lawrence Palk, 2nd Bt., (see Haldon, B. in present work), and grandson of Adm. Lord Hugh Seymour, 5th son of the 1st Marquess of Hertford, (by Lady Anne Horatia, his wife, 3rd dau. of 2nd Earl Waldegrave). (see extant peerage works). Sir Frederick Beauchamp Paget Seymour, **Baron Alcester**, b. 12 April 1821; educ. Eton; entered R.N. 1834; Cmdr. 1847; Capt. 1854; Rear Adm. 1870; Vice Adm. 1876; and Adm. 1882. He took the Meteor floating battery to the Crimea and back to Portsmouth, 1855-56; cmd. naval brigade in New Zealand, during the Maori War, 1860-61; became Lord of the Admiralty, 1872-74; and 1883-85; cmd. Channel Fleet, 1874-77; C. in C. Mediterranean Fleet, 1880-83, and cmd. at bombardment of Alexandria, 1882, and in consideration of his services then was raised to the peerage as Baron Alcester, of Alcester, co. Warwick, 24 Nov. 1882. He was also cr. C.B. 1861, K.C.B. 1877, and G.C.B. 1881. He was A.D.C. to Queen Victoria, 1866. He d. unm. 30 Mar. 1895.
ARMS—Quarterly 1 and 4, Or on a pile gules between six fleur-de-lis azure, three lions passant guardant, in pale, or; 2 and 3, Gules two wings conjoined in lure or.
CREST—Out of a ducal coronet or, a phoenix in flames ppr.
SUPPORTERS—Dexter, A sailor; Sinister, A private of the Royal Marines, both habited, each holding in the exterior hand a musket, and each standing on an Armstrong gun, all ppr.
MOTTO—Foy pour devoir.
Lord Alcester's town residence was 22 Ryder Street, London, S.W. His clubs were United Service; Marlborough; Travellers; Garrick, Pratt's; Naval and Military.

ALEXANDER OF HILLSBOROUGH

PEERAGE—U.K. Earl Alexander of Hillsborough. Viscount Alexander of Hillsborough. Baron Weston-super-Mare.
SURNAME—Alexander.
CR.—Viscounty, 27 Jan. 1950. Barony and Earldom 30 Jan. 1963. **EXT.**—11 Jan. 1965.
HISTORY—Albert Alexander of Weston-super-Mare, Somerset, was father of Albert Victor Alexander, **Earl Alexander** of Hillsborough, **Viscount Alexander** of Hillsborough and Baron Weston-super-Mare, b. 1 May 1885; educ. Barton Hill elementary sch. Bristol; worked for Somerset C.C. Educ. Cttee., 1903; served in World War I, 1914-18 as Capt.; M.P. for Hillsborough Div. of Sheffield, 1922-31, and 1935-50, held several ministerial posts, inc.

Chancellor of Duchy of Lancaster, 1950-51; made P.C. 1929, cr. C.H. 1941, and Viscount Alexander of Hillsborough, City of Sheffield 27 Jan. 1950, and an Earl and Baron as above 1963. He m. 6 June 1908, Esther Ellen (d. 18 Oct. 1969) dau. of George Chapple, of Tiverton, Devon and d. 11 Jan. 1965 having had issue a dau., Beatrix Dora, who m. W. B. Evison and had issue.
Earl Alexander's residences were Wellhouse Farm, West Mersea, Essex and 31, Bellingham Mansions, London W.8. He was a member of the Savage Club.

ALINGTON

PEERAGE—U.K. Baron Alington of Crichel, Dorset.
SURNAME—Sturt.
CR.—15 Jan. 1876. **EXT.**—17 Sept. 1940.
HISTORY—Henry Gerard Sturt, **1st Baron Alington**, was the eldest son of Henry Charles Sturt of Crichel, Dorset and the great-great-grandson of Diana Napier who m. 1717/18 Humphrey Sturt of Horton, Dorset. She was the dau. of the Hon. Catherine Alington, sister and coheiress of Giles Alington, 2nd Baron Alington of Wymondley, co. Hertford (cr. 5 Dec. 1682 in the English peerage) and 4th Baron Alington of Killard, co. Cork, in the peerage of Ireland, 28 July 1642. Giles d.s.p. 18 Sept. 1691 when the English peerage expired and the Irish peerage reverted to his uncle, Hildebrand, 5th Baron Alington of the Irish creation who d.s.p. Feb. 1772/3 (see Burke's Extinct Peerage. 1883).
Henry Gerard Sturt, **1st Baron Alington**, of Crichel, Dorset, so created 15 Jan. 1876, was b. 16 May 1825; M.A. Oxford, M.P. for Dorchester, 1847-56, and for Dorset 1856-76; m. (1) 10 Sept 1853 Lady Augusta Bingham, dau. of the 3rd Earl of Lucan, and by her (d. 3 July 1880) had issue with four daus.,
Humphrey Napier, **2nd Baron Alington** (see below). He m. (2) 10 Feb. 1892, Evelyn Henrietta, dau. of H. B. Leigh and d. 17 Feb. 1904 when he was s. by his only son,
Humphrey Napier Sturt, **2nd Baron**, K.C.V.O., M.P. for East Dorset, 1891-1904, b. 20 Aug. 1839; m. 29 June 1883 Lady Feodorowna Yorke, dau. of the 5th Earl of Hardwicke, and had with a third son d. young and three daus.,
1. Gerard Philip Montagu Napier, Capt. Coldstream Guards, b. 9 April 1893; d. 11 Nov. 1918, of wounds received in action.
2. Napier George Henry, **3rd Baron** (see below).
The 2nd Baron d. 30 July 1919 being s. by his elder surviving son, Napier George Henry Sturt, **3rd Baron Alington**, served in World War I (Capt. R.A.F.) b. 4 Nov. 1896; m. 27 Nov. 1928, Lady Mary Sibell Ashley-Cooper, dau. of the 9th Earl of Shaftesbury, and d. 17 Sept. 1940, having had issue, a dau. Mary Anna Sibell Elizabeth.
ARMS—Vert on a fesse or, between three colts courant argent, as many roses gules.
CREST—A demi-lion holding a banner gules charged with a rose argent, the staff and fringe or.

SUPPORTERS—On either side, a talbot argent, billety sable, holding in the mouth a rose gules, slipped and leaved ppr.
MOTTO—En Dieu est tout.
The family seat was at Crichel, Wimborne, Dorset.

ALLEN OF HURTWOOD

PEERAGE—U.K. Baron Allen of Hurtwood, co. Surrey.
SURNAME—Allen.
CR.—18 Jan. 1932. EXT.—3 Mar. 1939.
HISTORY—Walter Allen, b. 1855; m. 7 Mar. 1885, Frances Augusta Baker (d. 1903) and d. 19 July 1913 having had with a ygr. son and two daus., an elder son, Reginald Clifford Allen, **Baron Allen** of Hurtwood, co. Surrey, so cr. 18 Jan. 1932, b. 9 May 1889; B.A. Peterhouse, Camb., during World War I, Chm. No Conscription Fellowship, and 1916-17 three times imprisoned for conscientious objection; Sec. and Gen. Man. of the *Daily Citizen* 1911-15, Chm. *New Leader* 1922-26, Treasurer and Chm. Independent Labour Party 1922-26, and Dir. *Daily Herald*, 1925-30; m. 17 Dec. 1921, Marjory, dau. of George Gill and d. 3 Mar. 1939 having had issue a dau. Joan Collette Clifford.
Lord Allen's residence was Hurtwood House, Albury, Guildford, Surrey.

ALNESS

PEERAGE—U.K. Baron Alness, of Alness in co. of Ross and Cromarty.
SURNAME—Munro.
CR.—27 June 1934. EXT.—6 Oct. 1955.
HISTORY—Robert Munro, **Baron Alness,** was one of the children of the Rev. Alexander Rose Munro, of Alness (1835-1903), by his wife, Margaret, dau. of the Rev. John Sinclair, Minister of Bruan, Caithness, and grandson of Robert Munro, of Bonar Bridge, Sutherland. He was b. 28 May 1868, and had a distinguished legal and political career, being an Advocate of the Scots Bar, 1893, K.C., 1910, Counsel to Board of Inland Revenue, an Advocate Depute, Lord Advocate of Scotland 1913-16, Lord Justice Clerk and Lord Pres. of 2nd Div. of Court of Session, 1922-23, Hon. Bencher, Lincoln's Inn 1924. He was M.P. for Wick Burghs, 1910-18, and for Roxburgh and Selkirk, 1918-22. He held several directorships and was Lord in Waiting to King George VI, 1945. He became Sec. of State for Scotland, 1916-22, was made P.C. 1913, and G.B.E. 1947, was D.L. Edinburgh, and M.A. LL.D. Edinburgh, LL.D. Aberdeen & St. Andrews. He m. twice (1) 1898, Edith Gwladys, who d. in 1920, dau. of the Rev. John L. Evans of the Parsonage, Peebles, and (2) 1921, Olga Marie, dau. of Jean Georges Grumler of Dinard, France. Lord Alness d. 6 Oct. 1955.

ALVERSTONE

PEERAGE—U.K. Baron Alverstone of Alverstone in the Isle of Wight, co. Southampton and Viscount Alverstone.

SURNAME—Webster.
CR.—Barony 18 June 1900. Viscounty 1913. (Also a baronetcy cr. 29 Jan. 1900). EXT.—15 Dec. 1915.
HISTORY—William Webster of Tong St. James near Leeds, by Jane his wife had issue, Thomas Webster, b. circa 1744; m. 14 June 1774, Susanna, dau. of John Scott, of Bratoft, co. Lincoln, and d. 20 Sept. 1779, leaving issue,
1. Thomas, b. 30 April, d. 12 Aug. 1775.
2. Thomas, Rev. (see below).
1. Susanna, b. 1 Mar. 1777.
2. Elizabeth, b. 28 Oct. 1778.
The second son, The Rev. Thomas Webster, M.A., vicar of Oakington and rector of St. Botolph's Cambridge, had by Mary Anne, his wife, a son,
Thomas Webster of Beachfield, Sandown, Isle of Wight, M.A., Trin. Coll. Camb., F.R.S., Q.C., Bencher, Lincoln's Inn, b. 16 Oct. 1810; m. (1) 16 Oct. 1839, Elizabeth Anne, dau. of Richard Calthrop of Swineshead Abbey, co. Lincoln. By her who d. 3 Dec. 1847 he had issue,
1. Thomas Calthrop, Rev. M.A., Trin. Coll. Camb. rector of Rettendon, Essex, b. 23 Sept. 1840; m. Elizabeth Neill (d. 1 April 1913) dau. of William Waugh, of Hornsey and d. 7 May 1906 having had issue.
2. Richard Everard, **Baron and Viscount Alverstone** (see below).
3. Henry George, b. 5 Mar. 1843; m. Annie Marie Christine (d. 27 April 1909) dau. of Col. Roche, of Canterbury and d. 24 Aug. 1890 having had issue,
(1) Redmond Charles Calthrop. d. an infant 18 Aug. 1873.
(2) Cyril Gray, b. 3 Nov. 1874.
(3) Everard Francis, b. 26 April 1877.
1. Mary Emily, d. unm. July 1885.
2. Laura Alice, b. 6 Sept. 1847.
Thomas Webster m. (2) 8 Sept. 1853, Mary Frances, elder dau. of Joseph Collier Cookworthy, M.D. of Plymouth and d. 3 June 1875 having by her (who d. 26 Jan. 1911) had further issue,
4. Francis Joseph, Taxing Master of the Supreme Court, b. 6 Sept. 1860 m. 3 Jan. 1903, Helen Beatrice dau. of A. S. Hay of Sacombe Park, Herts, and d.s.p. 31 Aug. 1904.
3. Helen Avice, b. 30 Oct. 1863.
The second son, Sir Richard Everard Webster, Bt., **Baron Alverstone** and **Viscount Alverstone,** b. 22 Dec. 1842; educ. King's Coll. Sch., the Charterhouse and Trin. Coll. Camb., B.A. 1865, M.A. 1868; Barrister-at-law 1868, Q.C. 1878, M.P. Launceston 1885 and Isle of Wight 1885-1900, Attorney Gen. 1885, 1886-92, and 1895-1900; Master of the Rolls 1900, and Lord Chief Justice of England 1900-13. cr. Kt. Bach. 1885, G.C.M.G. 1893, a baronet 29 Jan. 1900 a peer as Baron Alverstone of Alverstone in the Isle of Wight, co. Southampton, 18 June 1900, and Viscount Alverstone 1913. He was made P.C. 1900, was F.R.S. and K.G. St. J. He m. 20 Aug. 1872, Mary Louisa, only dau. of William Charles Calthrop of Withern, co. Lincoln and by her who d. 22 Mar. 1877 had issue,
Arthur Harold, Lt. 14th Middlesex Vols., M.A. Camb., b. 16 June 1874; m. 10 May 1898, Gwladys Marie de Grasse, dau. of Sir Francis Henry Evans Bt., and d.s.p. 8 Aug.

1902. She m. (2) 1905 Iain Ramsey and had issue, Dora Marion, b. 18 May 1873; m. 19 April 1902, A. S. Mallor and had issue.

Viscount Alverstone d.s.p.m.s. 15 Dec. 1915.

ARMS—Azure two pallets or five swans in cross argent between four annulets gold.

CREST—A swan's head erased argent encircled by an annulet azure and holding in the beak a like annulet.

SUPPORTERS—On either side a seal ppr. gorged with a chain of annulets interlaced or, suspended therefrom an escutcheon azure charged with a swan argent.

MOTTO—Veritas puritas.

Viscount Alverstone's residences were Winterfold, Cranleigh, co. Surrey and Horntren Lodge, Pitt Street, Kensington.

AMMON

PEERAGE—U.K. Baron Ammon of Camberwell, co. Surrey.

SURNAME—Ammon.

CR.—31 Jan. 1944. EXT.—2 April 1960.

HISTORY—Charles George Ammon, **Baron Ammon,** was b. 22 April 1873, the son of Charles George and Mary (née Kempley) Ammon of London and was educated at state elementary schools and by private study. Worked in the Post Office and became Organizing Sec. of the Post Office Workers, was member of the L.C.C. 1919-25, and 1934-46 being Chm. 1941-42, Alderman of Camberwell Borough Council from 1935, Mayor of Camberwell 1950 and Freeman, 1951. Entered national politics 1922, M.P. North Camberwell 1922-31 and 1935-44 when cr. a peer 1944 and P.C. 1945. He held many appointments, the most important being a member of several commissions to the West Indies, West Africa, Newfoundland and China, and of Cttee. dealing with national expenditure 1939-44; Chm. Nat. Dock Labour Corpn. 1944-46, and at Nat. Dock Labour Board 1946-48; Capt. the Hon. Corps of Gentlemen-at-Arms, 1945-49. He m. 1898, Ada Ellen, dau. of David May of Walworth, S.E. She d. 1958. They had, with one son, Charles Kempley (1907-09), two daus. Ada Mary, Mayoress of Camberwell, 1950, and May Joyce, a teacher. Lord Ammon d. 2 April 1960. Lord Ammon's home was at 70 Ferndene Road, Herne Hill, London, S.E.24.

ANNESLEY

PEERAGE—U.K. Baron Annesley of Bletchington, co. Oxford.

SURNAME—Annesley.

CR.—7 May 1917. EXT.—6 Oct. 1949.

HISTORY—Arthur Annesley, 11th Viscount Valentia, (see that title in extant peerages), was cr. **Baron Annesley,** of Bletchington, co. Oxford, in the peerage of the U.K. on 7 May 1917. He d. 20 Jan. 1927 and was succeeded by his only sur. son, Caryl Arthur James Annesley, 12th Viscount Valentia, and **2nd Baron Annesley,** who d. unm. 6 Oct. 1949, when the U.K. Barony became extinct and when he was s. by his kinsman, the Rev. William Monckton Annesley, styled 13th Viscount Valentia, who

never proved his claim to the Viscounty and who d.s. p. 26 Feb. 1951, when he was s. by his cousin, who established his succession, as 14th Viscount (see extant peerages).

ANSLOW

PEERAGE—U.K. Baron Anslow of Iver, co. Buckingham.

SURNAME—Mosley.

CR.—28 June 1916. EXT.—20 Aug. 1933.

HISTORY—Sir Tonman Mosley, 3rd Bt. (see Extant Peerage & Baronetage, Mosley Bt.) had a second son, Tonman Mosley, **Baron Anslow** b. 16 Jan. 1850; B.A. Corpus Christi Coll. Oxford 1872, Barrister-at-Law, Inner Temple, 1874; Chm. Quarter Sessions, co. Derby, 1897-1902, Chm. Bucks C.C. 1904-21, Chm. North Staffordshire Railway Co., 1904-23, was created C.B. 19 June 1911, and Baron Anslow of Iver, co. Buckingham, 28 June 1916. He m. 22 Feb. 1881, Lady Hilda Rose Montgomerie (d. 18 June 1928), dau. of the 13th Earl of Eglinton and d.s.p. m.s. 20 Aug. 1933, having had issue two sons and two daus.

ARMS—Sable a chevron between three pickaxes argent.

CREST—An eagle displayed ermine.

SUPPORTERS—Dexter, A stork ppr., charged with a Stafford knot or. Sinister, A swan wings inverted also ppr. gorged with an antique crown gold.

MOTTO—Mos legem regit.

ARDILAUN

PEERAGE—U.K. Baron Ardilaun, of Ashford, co. Galway.

SURNAME—Guinness.

CR.—1 May 1880. EXT.—20 Jan. 1915.

HISTORY—Sir Benjamin Lee Guinness, 1st Bt. (see extant peerages) had an eldest son, Sir Arthur Edward Guinness, 2nd Bt. **Baron Ardilaun** of Ashford, co. Galway, so cr. 1 May 1880; was b. 1 Nov. 1840; educ. Eton and Trin. Coll. Dublin, B.A. 1863, M.A. 1866; M.P. for City of Dublin, 1868-69; and 1874-80; s. his father as 2nd Bt., 19 March 1868; m. 16 Feb. 1871; Olivia Charlotte, dau. of William Henry Hare Hedges-White, 3rd Earl of Bantry and d. 20 Jan. 1915, when the Barony became extinct and the baronetcy developed upon his nephew, Sir Algernon Guinness, 3rd Bt. (see extant peerages).

ARMS—Quarterly 1 and 4, Per saltire gules and azure, a lion rampant or, on a chief ermine, a dexter hand, couped at the wrist of the first; a crescent for difference, (Guinness); 2 and 3; Argent on a fesse between three crescents sable, a trefoil slipped or (Lee).

CRESTS—1, A boar passant, quarterly or and gules; a crescent for difference (Guinness); 2, On a pillar argent, encircled by a ducal coronet or, an eagle preying on a bird's leg erased ppr. (Lee).

SUPPORTERS—On either side a stag gules, attired and gorged with a collar gemmel, pendant therefrom by a chain gold an escutcheon, the dexter charged with the arms of Guinness, and the sinister with those of Lee.

MOTTO—Spes mea in Deo.

ARLINGTON

PEERAGE—England. Baron Arlington of Arlington, co. Middlesex (this being usually spelt Harlington, near Hounslow), with special remainder failing issue male to the heirs of his body, 28 Sept. 1663. England. Baron Arlington of Arlington, Middlesex. Viscount Thetford, co. Norfolk and Earl of Arlington, 22 April 1672, with a similar special remainder and in default of heirs of his body, with a further remainder to his brother, Sir John Bennet, K.B. (cr. 1682 Baron Ossulston, see Tankerville, E.).
SURNAME—Bennet, later Fitzroy.
CR.—Dates as above. **ABEYANCE**—4 Aug. 1936.
HISTORY—The history of the Bennet family is given in extant peerages under Tankerville, E. Sir Henry Bennet for whom the peerages mentioned above were cr., was one of the members of the famous or infamous Cabal ministry in the reign of Charles II. Of him Lord Macaulay wrote: "Henry Bennet, Lord Arlington, then Sec. of State, had since he came to manhood, resided principally on the Continent and had learned that cosmopolitan indifference to constitutions and religions which is so often observable in persons whose life has been passed in vagrant diplomacy". (*History of England*, vol i ch. 2, p.159. Everyman edition). Arlington was also mentioned under the symbolic name of Eliab in John Dryden's poem *Absalom and Achitophel*, Part II lines 985-995.

"His age with only one mild heiress blest
In all the bloom of smiling nature drest
And blest again to see his flower allied
To David's stock and made young
    Othniel's bride"

In the above David is of course Charles II and Othniel his bastard son by the Duchess of Cleveland, Henry Fitzroy 1st Duke of Grafton. Cleveland did not want his son to marry Arlington's daughter though the girl was a considerable heiress. The C.P. considered that the generous remainder arrangement of the 1672 creation arose from King Charles having in mind a match between the little heiress and his son, Grafton. The extensive remainder of the creation of 1665 is not thus explained. Henry, **Earl of Arlington** Viscount Thetford and Baron Arlington was b. circa 1620; m. soon after March 1664/65, Isabella dau. of Louis de Nassau, Baron of Leck and Beverwaet, in Holland, by Elizabeth, dau. of Jean, Count of Hornes, Seigneur de Kessel, and d.s.p.m. 28 July 1685 leaving issue an only dau.,

Isabella Bennet, who inherited all her father's titles. She was m. 1 Aug. 1672 to Henry Fitzroy, 1st Duke of Grafton (he being aged 9 and she about 4), and m. him again 6 Nov. 1679. The Duke d. 9 Oct. 1690, after being wounded at the storming of Cork where he fought for William III. The Duchess m. 2ndly (lic. 14 Oct.) 1698, Sir Thomas Hanmer, 3rd Bt. and d. 7 Feb. 1722/23. By the Duke of Grafton she had a son,

Charles Fitzroy, 2nd Duke of Grafton, and **3rd Earl of Arlington** etc. In the C.P. the Earldom and the two Baronies of Arlington with the Viscounty of Thetford are described as then merged with the Dukedom of Grafton, and so they remained until the death of the 9th

Duke of Grafton on 4 Aug. 1936 when the four titles fell into abeyance between his sisters, Lady Jane Nelson and Lady Mary Rose Williams.
ARMS (of Bennet, Earl of Arlington)—Gules a besant between three demi-lions rampant couped argent which were granted by Camden to Sir Thomas Bennet, Lord Mayor of London, 1603, a collateral ancestor of Arlington.
CREST—Out of a mural crown or, a lion's head couped gules charged with a bezant. (This is the same as that of Bennet, Earl of Tankerville.)

ARMAGHDALE

PEERAGE—U.K. Baron Armaghdale of Armagh, co. Armagh.
SURNAME—Lonsdale.
CR.—17 Jan. 1918. **EXT.**—11 June 1924.
HISTORY—Thomas Lonsdale of Loughgall, co. Armagh. d. 1854 aged 76, having had issue. The yst. son, James Lonsdale of the Pavillion co. Armagh, J.P. and D.L., High Sheriff 1891, b. 10 Feb. 1826; m. (1) 7 Jan. 1846, Jane (who d. April 1855), dau. of William Brownlee, of Armagh, m. (2) 1856, Harriet, dau. of John Rolston and d. 26 Aug. 1913, having had issue by his first wife,

1. John Brownlee, Sir, **Baron Armaghdale,** (see below).
2. Thomas, of Hawthornden, Hooton, Cheshire, b. 5 Dec. 1854, m. 22 July 1891, Mary Alice, dau. of Lt. Col. G. A. J. McClintock, of Fellows Hall, Tynan, co. Armagh (Rathdonnell, B.) and had issue,
   (1) James Raymond McClintock, Lt. 4th Hussars, b. 16 March 1894; d. of wounds received in action Nov. 1914.
   (2) Thomas Leopold McClintock, b. 8 Aug. 1899.
   (1) Esme Georgina, b. 25 April 1895.
   (2) Vera Isabella, b. 9 May 1897.
1. Mary, b. 1851; m. J. W. Berry of Hopwood, Lancashire.
2. Jane, b. 1853; m. the Rev. F. E. Waldie, Vicar of Broadhempston, Totnes, Devon.

By his second wife James Lonsdale had a dau.

3. Sara, m. 1887, J. A. Reid, K.C. Scots Bar, and had issue.

The elder son, Sir John Brownlee Lonsdale, Bt., and **Baron Armaghdale,** b. 23 March 1850, educ. privately; entered business at 17 and became partner in J. and J. Lonsdale & Co.; J.P. and D.L., High Sheriff co. Armagh, 1895; M.P. (Cons.) for Mid-Armagh 1899-1918; was for 15 years Hon. Sec. and whip of the Irish Unionist Party in the House of Commons, and for 2 years leader of that party, a strong opponent of Home Rule; cr. a baronet 7 July 1911, and a peer as Baron Armaghdale of Armagh, co. Armagh, 17 Jan. 1918; m. 15 Sept. 1887, Florence, dau. of William Rumney, Stubbins House, Ramsbottom, Lancashire and d.s.p. 8 June 1924. Lady Armaghdale d. 2 Feb. 1937. They were buried in Putney Vale Cemetry.
ARMS—Azure on a pale between two bugle-horns or three hurts.
CREST—A demi stag azure charged with three bezants in pale, the forefeet resting on a harp and attired or.
MOTTO—Salus in fide.

ARMITSTEAD

PEERAGE—U.K. Baron Armitstead of Castle-hill in the City of Dundee.
SURNAME—Armitstead.
CR.—19 July 1906. EXT.—7 Dec. 1915.
HISTORY—John Armitstead of Austwick, Clapham, co. Yorks, had issue an only son, The Rev. John Armitstead, Vicar of Easingwold, co. Yorks, m. Mary, dau. of—Rocliffe and had issue a second son, George Armitstead of Riga, Russia, merchant, m. Emma Jacobs and had a second son, George Armitstead, **Baron Armitstead** b. 28 Feb. 1824, educ. Wiesbaden and Heidelberg; m. 1848, Jane Elizabeth, eldest dau. of Edward Baxter, of Kincaldrum, co. Forfar, entered firm of George Armitstead & Co., became senior partner of Armitstead & Co., London and of G. Armitstead & Co. of Dundee. M.P. Dundee 1868-73 and 1880-85; J.P. and D.L., co. Forfar, J.P. co. Perth, D.L. Dundee; F.R.G.S.; cr. Baron Armitstead, of Castlehill, in the City of Dundee 19 July 1906, and d. 7 Dec. 1915.
ARMS—Or a chevron embattled sable between three pheons gules, a bordure sable.
CREST—A sinister and a dexter arm embowed in armour, each hand grasping a spear erect ppr.
SUPPORTERS—Dexter, A mechanic holding in the exterior hand a cogged wheel; Sinister, A ship's carpenter holding in the exterior hand a saw all ppr.
MOTTO—Ever ready.
Lord Armitstead's seat was Butterstone House, Dunkeld. His London house was 4 Cleveland Square, London S.W.
In 1952 B.L.G. under Armitstead formerly of Cranage Hall, is a pedigree and arms, viz.—or a chevron embattled counterembattled sable between three pheons azure two flaunches gules each charged with a tilting spear erect of the field headed argent. Crest—A dexter and sinister arm embowed in armour each hand grasping a spear erect ppr. Motto—Pro Rege et Patria.

ARMSTRONG

PEERAGE—U.K. Baron Armstrong, of Cragside, co. Northumberland.
SURNAME—Armstrong.
CR.—6 July 1887. EXT.—27 Dec. 1900.
HISTORY—William Armstrong, b. 1778; was Mayor of Newcastle-on-Tyne, 1850; a corn merchant; was prominent in local affairs, much interested in mathematics, and an active member of local literary societies (D.N.B.). He had issue,
William George, Baron Armstrong.
Anne, who m. 17 Aug. 1826, as his first wife, Sir William Henry Watson, a Baron of the Exchequer. She d. 1 June, 1828, leaving issue, a son,
John William, who d. 30 Jan. 1909, having had with other issue, a son, William Henry Armstrong FitzPatrick, who by royal licence 1889, assumed the additional name and arms of Armstrong, and was cr. Baron Armstrong, of Bamburgh and Cragside, 4 Aug. 1903, the second creation of the name. (see extant peerage works).
The only son,

Sir William George Armstrong, **Baron Armstrong**, was b. 26 Nov. 1810; educ. Gr. Sch. Bishop Auckland, and studied law in London, becoming partner in legal firm of Donkin, Stable, and Armstrong, at Newcastle, 1833; subsequently had a great career as an inventor; he constructed water pressure wheel, 1839, and hydro-electric machine, 1844; became sec. and chm. of Whittle Dean, late Newcastle and Gateshead Water Co.; patented hydraulic crane, 1846; made F.R.S., 1846; was first manager of Elswick-on-Tyne engineering works, 1847; invented hydraulic pressure accumulator, 1850; in the Crimean War designed submarine mines; invented the rifled bore breech loading gun with cylinder constructed on scientific principles; patented his inventions and presented the patents to the nation; the Elswick Ordnance Co. was set up under his supervision, 1859, for purpose of making Armstrong guns, and he was appointed engineer of the rifled ordnance at Woolwich, cr. Kt. Bach. and C.B. 1859; but he resigned the appt. at Woolwich in 1863 when the Gov. returned to making of muzzle loaders. In 1880 the Gov. adopted once more the breech loading gun and Armstrong then finished a 6-inch breech loading gun. He established in 1882 a shipyard at Elswick for building of warships; he incorporated with his own business the works of Sir Joseph Whitworth, at Openshaw, near Manchester for making of Whitworth guns, 1897. He received many honours, and was cr. a peer as Baron Armstrong, of Cragside, (his residence) co. Northumberland. He was Telford Medallist of the Inst. of Civil Engineers, and received Albert Medal from Royal Soc. of Arts, 1878. Pres. of Inst. of Civil Engineers, 1882, and was Bessemer Medallist, 1891. He was a liberal donor to Newcastle; he wrote several works on engineering subjects. He m. 1 May 1835, Margaret, only dau. of William Ramshaw, of Bishop Auckland. She d. 2 Sept. 1893. He d.s.p. 27 Dec. 1900. Lord Armstrong held knighthoods of several foreign countries, including those of the Grand Officer of SS. Maurice and Lazarus of Italy, and the Knight Commandership of the Dannebrog of Denmark. He was High Sheriff of co. Northumberland, 1873., LL.D. Cambridge and D.C.L. Oxford.
ARMS—Gules a tilting spear in fess or, headed argent, between two dexter arms embowed in armour, fessewise ppr., hands of the last.
CREST—A dexter arm embowed in armour, holding a sledge hammer, encircled at the elbow by a wreath of oak, all ppr.
SUPPORTERS—On either side a smith, shirt sleeves rolled up, leather apron, and dark blue breeches, dark grey stockings, holding over the shoulder in the exterior hand, a sledge hammer, all ppr.
MOTTO—Fortis in armis.
Lord Armstrong's seat was Cragside, Rothbury, Northumberland; Jesmond Dene, Newcastle-on-Tyne, and he had a London house at 8 Great George Street, S.W. His club was the Athenaeum.

ARNOLD

PEERAGE—U.K. Baron Arnold of Hale, co. Chester.
SURNAME—Arnold.

CR.—12 Feb. 1924. **EXT.**—3 Aug. 1945.

HISTORY—William Ashness Arnold, a stock-broker, of Manchester, m. Sarah Ann, dau. of Charles Linney, and had issue, Sydney Arnold, **Baron Arnold,** of Hale, co. Chester, so cr. 12 Feb. 1924. He was b. at Altrincham, 13 Jan. 1878; educ. Manchester Gram. Sch. and privately; he entered the firm of W. A. Arnold & Sons in 1900, was mem. of Manchester Stock Exchange 1904-22, and retired 1921. He stood for Parliament in 1910 as a Liberal (Holderness Div. of East Riding Yorks.) and was Liberal M.P. for Holmfirth Div. of W.R. Yorks, 1912-18, and for Penistone Div. 1918-21, but resigned owing to ill health. Parl. Priv. Sec. to Pres. of Board of Education and Financial Sec. to Treasury 1914, but joined Labour Party 1922. Parl. Under-Sec. of State for Colonies, 1924, in first Labour Gov. and Paymaster Gen. 1929-31 in second Labour Gov. Resigned from Gov. in March 1931, in order to advance causes of Free Trade and of Temperance. He resigned from Labour Party in 1938. He d. 3 Aug. 1945.

ARMS—Per chevron azure and or, in chief two garbs and in base a pheon counter-changed.

CREST—In front of an eagle's head erased per chevron gules and or, two pheons fessewise sable.

SUPPORTERS—Dexter, A lion ppr. Sinister, A wolf also ppr., each charged on the shoulder with a pheon or.

MOTTO—Laborare est orare.

Lord Arnold's residence was Marley Corner nr. Haslemere, Surrey. His club was, The Reform.

ARUNDELL OF WARDOUR

PEERAGE—England. Baron Arundell of Wardour, co. Wiltshire.

SURNAME—Arundell.

CR.—4 May 1605. **EXT.**—25 Sept. 1944.

HISTORY—The earliest portion of the genealogy of Arundell is based on the account of the family given in *Genealogical Collections illustrating the history of Roman Catholic Families of England,* edited by J. Jackson Howard, LL.D., F.S.A., Maltravers Herald Extraordinary and J. Seymour Hughes. There is a pedigree derived from the Lawson Ms., which begins with a Roger de Arundel possessed of 28 lordships tempore Gulielmi Conquistoris etc. etc.; the pedigree based on documents and given in the above quoted work starts with, Sir Renfred de Arundel, who by his wife Margaret had,

1. Sir Ralf or Ralph, circa 1260.
2. Lawrence.
3. Odo.

The eldest son,

Sir Ralph de Arundel, Lord of Trelory and St. Colomb, Sheriff of Cornwall, 1260, m. Eva, eldest dau. and coheiress of Richard de Rupe, Lord of Tremodrud. She was living 1283. He was d. before Oct. 1275. They had issue,

Renfred de Arundel, m. Alice dau. of John de Lanhern and d. before 14 Dec. 1280, leaving issue,

John de Arundel, held Trelory 23 July 1279, m. Joan, dau. and coheiress of John le Sor, and had with other issue a son and heir,

Sir John Arundell, Lord of Lanherne, living 1334-35, m. Isabella, dau. and heiress of John de la Bere, of Talvern and had a son,

Sir John Arundell, living 1331, m. (1) 1334/35, Elizabeth dau. and co-heiress of Sir Oliver Carminow, and (2) Isabella, dau. of Sir Thomas Multon. By his first marriage he had,

Sir John Arundell of Lanherne, m. Joan, dau. of Sir William Luscote and d. 5 Nov. 1376 v.p. (said to have been drowned off the coast of Ireland in fleet going to Brittany) having had with other issue,

Sir John Arundell, K.B. (4th Oct. 1399 at coronation of Henry IV) of Lanherne, b. 1367; by an agreement dated 12 Feb. 1418 with Thomas Beaufort Duke of Exeter he took to France in 1418, 364 men-at-arms and 770 archers. He m. Eleanor, dau. and heiress of his stepfather, Sir William Lamborne of Lamborne by Joan his 2nd wife, the heiress of Ralph Le Sor, of Talvern, and had issue,

1. John who s. his father (see below).
2. Thomas, Sir, of Lanhadron, m. (1) Margery, dau. of Sir Warine Archeacon (scilicit Ercedekne or Archidicken) who d.s.p. 1420; (2) (marr. settlement 17 Dec. 1426), Elizabeth, dau. of Sir Thomas Paulet of Hinton St. John, and widow of William Bykbury and d. 24 June 1443, leaving by his 2nd wife (who m. 3rdly Robert Burton and d. 1477) a son,

    Sir John Arundell, of Tolvern, whose descentant was, Sir John Arundell, of Tolvern m. Ann, dau. of Thomas Godolphin and had issue,

    Sir Thomas Arundell, knighted by James I and who sold Tolvern. He m. Bridget, dau. and coheiress of Sir William Mohun, of Hall, parish of Lanteglos-juxta-Fowey and d. 1630 leaving a son and heir,

    Col. John Arundell, of Treethall parish of Tythney, Cornwall, in the royal army, deputy gov. of Pendennis castle, m. Mary dau. of John Coke of Tregassow and d. 1671, leaving a son, John Arundell, of Treethall who was grandfather of Robert Arundell, last of the Arundells of Tolvern.

3. Renfrey, Sir, m. (settlement 9 Sept. 1421) Joan, sister and heiress of Sir John Colshull and by her (who m. 2ndly John Nanfan and 3rdly Sir William Houghton, and d. 1497) had issue,

    (1) Humphrey (Renfrey), Sir, Sheriff of Cornwall 1462, m. Anne, dau. of Sir Andrew Ogard and had by her, (who m. 2ndly Robert Crane of Chelton, Suffolk) had a son, Sir Edmund Arundell, who m. Jean Walgrave and d.s.p. 27 Nov. 1503.

    (2) John, Bishop of Lichfield and Coventry 1496-1502 and of Exeter 1502-05. d. 1505.

Sir John Arundell, d. 7 Jan. 1434/35 and was s. by his eldest son,

John Arundell, Esq., m. (1) Elizabeth Rochford, d.s.p.; (2) Margaret dau. of Sir John Burgersh and widow of Sir John Grenville of Bideford, and by her had,

Sir John Arundell, served in France *temp.* Henry VI, m. (1) Elizabeth dau. of Thomas Morley, 5th Baron Morley (see Extinct Peerage 1883) and had issue,

1. Anne, m. (settlement 23 March 1469) Sir James Tyrrell of Gipping, Suffolk, the supposed instrumental murderer of the Princes in the Tower, Master of the Horse to Richard III, was given posts in Wales by Henry VII and general pardon; lieut. of Castle of Guisnes 1486 was concerned in the flight of Edmund de la Pole (titular) 3rd Duke of Suffolk 1501, and beheaded on Tower Hill, 6 May 1502 having confessed to the murder of the Princes. Anne had issue two sons.

Sir John, m. (2) (marr. settlement 5 March 1451), Katherine, dau. of co-heir of Sir John Chideocke (see 1883 Extinct Peerage, FitzPayne B.) and widow of Sir William Stafford of Frome, and by her had further issue,

1. Thomas his successor (see below).
2. Catherine, m. (1) Sir William Courtenay and (2) John Mayle of Eastwell, co. Kent.
3. Elizabeth, m. Giles Daubeney, 6th Baron Daubeney and had issue, a son, Henry, 1st Earl of Bridgewater (see 1883 Extinct Peerage).
4. Thomasine, m. as his 1st wife, Sir Henry Marney, 1st Baron Marney. (1883 Extinct Peerage).
5. Margaret, m. Sir William Capel and had issue.
6. Ellen, m. Ralph Coplestone.
7. Dorothy, m. Sir Henry Strangways.
8. Jane.

The only son, Sir Thomas Arundell, K.B. (at Coronation of Richard III), m. Catherine, dau. of Sir John Dynham, and had issue five sons and three daus., of whom,

1. John, Sir, his successor (see below).
2. Humphrey, of Yewton, Devon, m. Philippa, dau. of Sir Thomas Grenville of Stowe and widow of Francis Harris of Hayne, and d.s.p.
3. Roger, of Stelland, Devon, m. Joan, dau. and heir of Humphrey Calwoodley and d. 12 June 1536, leaving with other issue, a son, Humphrey of Stelland, leader of the Cornish Rebellion in 1549. The yr. Humphrey was executed at Holborn and his widow, Elizabeth, dau. of Sir John Fulford, m. Thomas Cary.
1. Alice, m. John Speke, who d.v.p. leaving issue.
2. Elizabeth, m. Sir Edward Stradling, ancestor of Stradling Bts of St. Donats.
3. Eleanor, m. (1) Thomas Sydenham and (2) Nicholas St. Loe.

The eldest son, Sir John Arundell, of Lanherne, K.B., and a knight banneret, m. (1) Lady Elizabeth, dau. of Thomas Grey, 1st Marquess of Dorset, and had issue,

1. John, Sir, of Lanherne from whom descended the Arundells of Lanherne, and of Chideoke, Dorset.
2. Thomas, Sir (see below).
1. Elizabeth, m. 1516, Sir Richard Edgcombe, as his 1st wife.

Sir John, m. (2) (settlement 10 May 1507) Jane, dau. of Sir Thomas Granville and had further issue,

2. Mary, m. (1) (as his 3rd wife) Robert Ratcliffe, 1st Earl of Sussex, K.G.; he d. 1542. By him she had issue, a son John (Sir) d.s.p. She m. (2) (as his 2nd wife) Henry FitzAlan 21st Earl of Arundel, K.G.

The second son, Sir Thomas Arundell, K.B.

(at Coronation of Anne Boleyn), had by gift from his father, some manors in Somerset and Dorset, and in 1547 he bought from Sir Fulke Greville the castle and manor of Wardour, Wilts. In the reign of Edward VI he was convicted with Edward Seymour, Duke of Somerset of conspiring to murder John Dudley, Duke of Northumberland and was beheaded 26 Feb. 1552. He m. Margaret, dau. and coheir of Lord Edmund Howard, 3rd son of Thomas Howard, 2nd Duke of Norfolk and had issue,

1. Matthew (Sir) his successor (see below).
2. Charles (Sir) d. 9 Dec. 1587.
1. Dorothy, m. Sir Henry Weston.
2. Jane, m. Sir William Beville.

The elder son, Sir Matthew Arundell of Wardour, m. Margaret, dau. of Sir Henry Willoughby of Wollaton, co. Notts, and d. 1598 leaving with another son, William, of London, who d. unm. 16 Feb. 1592, an elder son, Sir Thomas Arundell, **1st Baron Arundell of Wardour,** b. ca. 1560 and imprisoned in 1580 for his zeal as a Roman Catholic, but in 1588 subscribed £100 toward defeating the Spanish Armada. At an early age he went as a volunteer to the Imperial Army and served very valiantly against the Turks capturing a standard from them at Gran in Hungary. The Emperor, Rudolph II, thereupon created him a Count of the Holy Roman Empire. The Latin text of the imperial decree, 14 Dec. 1595 is given in John Seldon's *Titles of Honour* 1672 ed ., p. 347; from this it is clear in J. H. Round's words that the honour is 'descendible to all and each of the grantee's children, heir, posterity, and descendants of either sex, born or to be born, for ever' (*The Ancestor*, vol. ix, p.234). The Emperor's edict commended Arundel to Queen Elizabeth I, but she took a very different view of the matter on his return to England. In my Preface to the 102nd edition of Burke's Peerage 1959 in commenting on the use of foreign titles by British subjects I wrote (after consultation with the Home Office); "The classical case on which the question was formally raised and decided is that of Thomas, 1st Lord Arundell of Wardour who had gone with the Queen's consent and with letters of recommendation from her to serve the Emperor against the Turks. For the conspicuous bravery that he had shown in action he was made a Count of the Holy Roman Empire. When he came back with his new dignity he found the Queen furiously angry with him and public opinion on her side. The Peers made a formal representation against any recognition of his title, saying 'that it belongeth only to the Prince and not to any other to confer dignities on his own subjects!' He was committed to the Fleet Prison for two months and banished from court. The Queen settled the question of the recognition of foreign titles by a famous pronouncement: 'As chaste women ought not to cast their eyes upon any other than their own husbands, so neither ought subjects to cast their eyes upon any other prince than him whom God hath set over them. I would not have my sheep branded with another man's mark; I would not have them follow the whistle of a strange shepherd' (William Camden, *History of Elizabeth*, p. 528)". In Dec. 1598 Sir Thomas Arundell was a knight and was cr. **Baron Arundell of Wardour,** co. Wiltshire, 4 May 1605. He m. (1) (Marr.

settlement 19 June 1585) Mary, dau. of Henry Wriothesley, 2nd Earl of Southampton and by her (who was bur. 27 June 1607) had issue,
1. Thomas, **2nd Baron** (see below).
2. William of Horningsham, co. Wilts, m. Hon. Mary, dau. of Anthony Browne, 2nd Viscount Montagu (1883 Extinct Peerage), and widow of William Paulett, Viscount St. John, eldest son of Marquess of Winchester and by her (d. 13 Nov. 1692) had issue,
   (1) Mark, of Horningsham d.s.p.
   (2) Charles, m. Lady Mary Talbot, dau. of 10th Earl of Shrewsbury and was k. at Worcester. His widow m. 2ndly Mervyn Touchet, 4th Earl of Castle-haven. By her Charles Arundell had a son, Charles, of Horningsham whose only dau. Mary, m. ante 1708, John Biddulph and had issue.
   (1) Mary, m. Sir Henry Tichborne, 3rd Bt. and d. 24 Dec. 1698.
   (2) Katherine, d. 4 March 1642.
   1. Elizabeth Mary, m. (settlement 14 June 1606) as his first wife, Sir John Philpot and had issue.
Lord Arundell m. (2) 1 July 1608, Anne, dau. of Miles Philipson, of Crook, co. Westmorland. By her, who d. 28 June 1637 he had further issue,
3. Matthew, b. 1609. d. 1620.
2. Catherine, m. 1 Nov. 1627 Ralph Eure, 2nd son of 4th Lord Eure and had issue (1883 Extinct Peerage).
3. Mary, m. Sir John Somerset, 2nd son of 5th Earl of Worcester and had issue.
4. Anne, m. Cecil Calvert, 2nd Lord Baltimore and d. 1649 (1883 Extinct Peerage).
5. Frances, m. as his 2nd wife, John Talbot, 10th Earl of Shrewsbury and had issue.
6. Margaret, b. 1620; m. as his 1st wife, Sir John Fortescue, 2nd Bt. and had issue.
7. Clara, twin with Margaret, m. (settlement 7 July 1638) Humphrey Weld, of Lul-worth and had issue.
Lord Arundell d. 7 Nov. 1639 and was s. by his eldest son,
Thomas Arundell, **2nd Baron Arundell of Wardour,** m. (settlement 11 May 1607 after marriage) Blanche, dau. of Edward Somerset, 4th Earl of Worcester. She defended Wardour for nine days against the Parliamentarians and surrendered on honourable terms, which were not observed, the castle was sacked and Lady Arundell taken prisoner to Dorchester. Lord Arundell d. of wounds received at the battle of Stratton 16 May 1643 aged about 57. His wife d. 27 Oct. 1649 having had issue with two daus., (1) Katherine, m. Francis, son of Sir Charles Cornwallis, (2) Anne m. Roger Vaughan, an only son,
Henry Arundell, **3rd Baron Arundell of Wardour,** Master of the Horse to Queen Henrietta Maria, a strong Royalist who retook Wardour Castle from the Roundheads and destroyed it to prevent them using it as a stronghold. Being involved as a second in a duel in which his brother-in-law, Col. Henry Compton was k. by Lord Chandos, he and Chandos were found guilty of manslaughter 17 May 1653 and sentenced to be burnt in the hand. Accused by Titus Oates in the Popish Plot he was committed to the Tower, 1678-83. In 1686 he was made P.C. and Lord Privy Seal.

On the departure of James II from England in 1688, Lord Arundell retired to Breamore in Wilts where he kept a pack of hounds which were the progenitors of the Quorn. Wardour Street, Soho, built about 1686 was named after him, and also Arundel Street, Panton Square, about 1673. He m. Cicely, dau. of the Hon. Sir Henry Compton, of Brambletye, co. Sussex (Northampton, M.) and widow of Sir John Fermor of Somerton, co. Oxford. She d. 24 March 1675/6. He d. 28 Dec. 1694 aged 88. They had issue,
1. Thomas, **4th Baron** (see below).
2. Henry, m. (settlement 10 Feb. 1675) Mary, dau. of Edmund Scrope of Danby, co. York and widow of Thomas Kempe of Slindon, co. Sussex and had three sons who d. young.
1. Cicely a nun at Rouen, d. 1717.
The elder son, Thomas Arundell, **4th Baron Arundell of Wardour,** b. 1633, went in the suite of the Earl of Castlemaine on the Embassy to Pope Innocent XI in 1686. He m. Margaret, dau. of Thomas Spencer of Ufton, co. Warwick and widow of Robert Lucy of Charlcote, co. Warwick. She d. 23 Dec. 1704. He d. 10 Feb. 1711/12, and was s. by his eldest son,
Henry Arundell, **5th Baron Arundell of Wardour,** m. between 5 and 9 Aug. 1691, Elizabeth, dau. of Col. Thomas Panton of St. Martin's-in-the-Fields, Middlesex (a large proprietor of that parish and known as the 'celebrated Gamester') and a sister and coheir of Lt. Gen. Thomas Panton (d. 20 July 1753). She d. 9 May 1700. He d. 20 April 1726. They had issue,
1. Henry **6th Baron** (see below).
2. Thomas, b. 1696; m. Anne, dau. of John Mitchell and d. 6 April 1752.
1. Elizabeth, m. 24 May 1722, James Touchet, 6th Earl of Castlehaven and d. 24 June 1743.
The elder son, Henry Arundell, **6th Baron Arundell of Wardour,** b. 4 Oct. 1694; m. (1) (contract 28 Sept. 1716), Elizabeth Eleanor, dau. and heir of Raymond Everard of Fethard, co. Tipperary, and of Liège, a Baron of the Holy Roman Empire. She was bapt. 1 Jan. 1696/7 at Reckheim, in Belgium and d. 22 May 1728. He m. (2) (contr. 18 Jan. 1728/9) Anne, dau. of William Herbert, 2nd Marquess of Powis. She d.s.p. 2 Oct. 1757. He d. 30 June 1746. By his 1st wife the 6th Baron had issue,
1. Henry, **7th Baron** (see below).
2. Raymond Thomas, m. 19 May 1760, Mary, dau. of John Porter of Alfarthing co. Surrey, and d.s.p. 11 May 1768.
3. James Everard, of Ashcombe, co. Wilts, m. at Salisbury, 24 June 1751 Anne, dau. and heir of John Wyndham of The Close, Salisbury, and of Norrington, co. Wilts, elder brother of Thomas Wyndham (Lord Chancellor of Ireland, 1727 and Baron Wyndham of Finglass, co. Dublin (see 1883 Extinct Peerage). She d. 10 April 1796. He d. 20 March 1803, having had issue,
   (1) James Everard, **9th Baron** (see below).
   (2) Thomas Raymond, of Ashcombe, co. Wilts, b. 9 March 1765; m. 21 Aug. 1792, Elizabeth Mary Anne, dau. of Sir Edward Smythe, Bt. of Acton Burnell, co. Salop. She d. 3 Feb. 1843. He d. 18 Jan. 1829, having had issue,

1a Thomas Raymond, d. an infant.
2a Henry Raymond, b. 27 June 1799; m. (1) 27 Sept. 1827 Mary Isabel, dau. of Sir Thomas H. C. Constable Bt. She d. 2 Oct. 1828. By her he had issue,
  1b Theodore, b. 17 June 1828; m. 24 Oct. 1854, his cousin, Louisa, dau. of John Hussey, of Nash Court, co. Dorset. She d. 3 April 1907. He d. 21 Aug. 1868 leaving issue,
    1c Raymond Robert, b. 11 Nov. 1856. d. 1886.
    2c Edgar Clifford, **14th Baron** (see below).
    3c Gerald Arthur, **15th Baron** (see below).
    1c Agnes Mary d. unm. 29 Feb. 1912.
    2c Blanche Mary, a nun at Taunton, d. 6 Nov. 1928.
    3c Maud Mary, m. 9 Aug. 1887, William Maund who d. 1896.
Henry Raymond Arundell, m. (2) April 1830, Eliza, sister of Robert Tolver Gerard, 1st Baron Gerard. She d. 5 June 1872. He d. 1886 having had by her further issue,
  2b Raymond Everard, d. young 17 May 1833.
  3b Rodolph Alexis, worked in Admiralty, b. 1837 d. 23 Jan. 1877.
  4b Reinfric Thomas, R.N., b. 16 May 1838; d. unm. 1860, k. in New Zealand in 2nd Maori War.
  5b Henry Alphonsus, Lt. R.N., b. 4 April 1841. d. unm. 19 July 1872 at sea on board *H.M.S. Bittern.*
  6b Raymond Ignatius, d. young 27 March 1852.
  1b Mary Julia, d. young, 1 July 1833.
  2b Amy Mary, d. young 20 Sept. 1839.
  3b Isabel, m. 22 Jan. 1861, Capt. Sir Richard Burton the famous traveller and author, whose biography she wrote. She d.s.p. 22 March 1896.
  4b Blanche, m. 13 Aug. 1857, John Hugh Smyth Pigott, of Brockley Hall, co. Somerset. He d. 19 Jan. 1892. She d. 21 Sept. 1891, leaving issue.
  5b Elizabeth Mary Regis, m. 23 April 1873, Edward Gerald FitzGerald (who d. 1891) yst. son of Henry FitzGerald of Maperton, co. Somerset. She d. 18 Jan. 1902.
  6b Emmeline Mary, m. 11 July 1877, Richard Van Zeller, Portuguese vice consul in London, who d. 3 Sept. 1892; she d. 1913, leaving issue,
3a Charles Francis, b. 1803. d. 6 Dec. 1876.
4a Reinfric Edwards, b. 1805. d. 21 Feb. 1877.
5a William Edward, in the Austrian service.
6a Matthew, d. young.

1a Mary Christina, m. 8 Feb. 1820, John Hussey of Nash Court, co. Dorset, and d. 21 Nov. 1872, leaving issue.
2a Blanche Appollonia, m. 16 July 1822, Edmund de Pentheny O'Kelly and d. 20 Dec. 1875, leaving issue (see B.L.G. of Ireland 1958).
3a Eleanora, m. 27 Dec. 18, Samuel B. de Lisle Hayes, and and d.s.p. 12 May 1878.
(1) Eleanor Anne, d. unm.
(2) Mary Wyndham, b. 1757; m. 9 March 1779, Hon. Bartholomew Bouverie, son of 1st Earl of Radnor and d. 22 Feb. 1832 leaving issue.
(3) Katherine Elizabeth, b. 1759; m. 3 Jan. 1792, Adm. George Frederick Rynes and d. 1803, leaving issue.
The 6th Baron was s. by his eldest son,
Henry Arundell, **7th Baron Arundell of Wardour**, b. 4 Oct. 1717; m. 27 Jan. 1738/9, Mary, dau. and eventually sole heir of Richard Bellings-Arundell of Lanherne, Cornwall. (the last named was son of Sir Richard Bellings by Frances the dau. and coheir of Sir John Arundell of Lanherne). By this marriage the two branches of the Arundell family which had been separated for more than two centuries were united. As Oswald Barron stated, the Lords Arundell of Wardour were able to bear the whole coat of the house, though originally they were cadets of the main Lanherne stock, their shield being sable with six swallows silver, the hirondelles playing upon the name of Arundell. Lady Arundell brought with her a dower of £70,000. She d. 1769. He d. 12 Sept. 1756, leaving issue an only surviving son,
Henry Arundell, **8th Baron Arundell of Wardour**, b. 21 March 1740; educ. at St. Omer, under the name of Bellings, rebuilt Wardour Castle; m. 31 May 1763, Mary Christina, only dau. and heiress of Benedict Conquest of Irnham Hall, co. Lincoln. She d. 20 June 1813. He had by her, surviving issue,
1. Mary Christina, m. her cousin, 9th Baron (see below).
2. Eleanor Mary, m. 29 Nov. 1786, Charles Clifford, 6th Lord Clifford, and d. 24 Nov. 1835 leaving issue.
The 8th Baron d.s.p. m. 4 Dec. 1808, being s. by his cousin. James Everard Arundell, **9th Baron Arundell of Wardour**, b. 4 March 1763 m. (1) 3 Feb. 1785, Mary Christina, his cousin (see above), and by her who d. 14 Feb. 1805, had issue,
1. James Everard, **10th Baron** (see below).
2. Henry Benedict, **11th Baron** (see below).
1. Anna Maria, d. 14 March 1829.
2. Mary Laura Charlotte, b. 1789; m. 18 April 1820, Lt. Col. G. Macdonell, and d. 1854.
3. Juliana Mary, b. 1791; m. 17 Oct. 1815, Adm. Hon. Sir John Talbot (Talbot of Malahide B.).
4. Katherine, m. 26 June 1827 Sir Edward Doughty, 9th Bt., and d. 12 Dec. 1872 (see Tichborne, Bt.).
He m. (2) 18 Sept. 1806, Mary (d. 18 Nov. 1853) dau. of Robert Burnet Jones and d. 14 July 1817, having had further issue,
3. Henry, b. 24 July 1811; m. 30 Oct. 1832,

Elizabeth, dau. of Joseph Esdaile and d. 1857 having had issue, Rudolphus James Everard, b. 1825. d. 1841.

4. Robert Arthur, 2nd Life Guards, b. 24 Aug. 1815; m. (1) 8 Aug. 1837, Elizabeth Louisa, dau. of the Rev. John Jones and had issue three daus.; m. (2) 17 Feb. 1870, Charlotte Stuart, dau. of Henry Parkin, R.N., Inspector of Hospitals and Fleets and d. 16 April 1886 having had issue a dau. Mabile Mary, m. R. A. Talbot (Talbot of Malahide, B.) and a fifth dau., Katherine Mary, b. 14 Dec. 1876.

5. Mary, m. 7 Aug. 1828, Sir Richard Neave, Bt., and d. 30 Aug. 1849.

The 9th Baron was s. by his eldest son, James Everard Arundell, **10th Baron of Wardour,** b. 3 Nov. 1785; m. 26 Feb. 1811 at Buckingham House, Pall Mall (by special licence) and again the next day at the house of the Dowager Lady Arundell of Wardour in Baker Street, Marylebone, Mary Anne, only dau. of George Nugent-Temple-Grenville, 1st Marquiss of Buckingham. She d. 1 June 1845. He d.s.p. 21 June 1834, being s. by his brother, Henry Benedict Arundell, **11th Baron Arundell of Wardour,** b. 12 Nov. 1804; m. (1) 8 Aug. 1826, Lucy, only child of High Philip Smythe, of Acton Burnell, co. Salop. She d.s.p. 22 Feb. 1827; m. (2) 22 Sept. 1829, Frances Catharine, dau. of Sir Henry Tichborne, 8th Bt., and by her (who d. 19 April 1836), he had issue,

1. John Francis, **12th Baron** (see below).
2. Everard Aloysius Gonzaga, **13th Baron** (see below).

He m. (3) 19 June 1838, Theresa, dau. of William Stourton, 17th Lord Stourton and by her (who d. 26 Oct. 1878) had further issue,

3. Thomas, b. 27 May 1839; d. 12 April 1840.
4. Edward Ignatius, Lt. 12th Lancers, b. 20 Dec. 1842; d. unm. 31 Jan. 1896.
1. Theresa Mary, m. (1) 17 April 1861, Sir Alfred Doughty Tichborne, 11th Bt., and (2) 24 Feb. 1873, Capt. Henry Lamplugh Wickham. She d. 17 Sept. 1895.
2. Cecily Mary, a nun, d. Sept. 1925.
3. Gertrude Mary, d. unm. 28 Feb. 1929.

The 11th Baron d. 19 Oct. 1962 and was s. by his eldest son,

John Francis Arundell. **12th Baron Arundell of Wardour,** b. 28 Dec. 1831; educ. Stoney-hurst; m. 13 Oct. 1862, Anne Lucy, dau. of John Errington of High Warden, co. Northumberland. She d. 24 Oct. 1934. He d.s.p. 26 Oct. 1906 and was s. by his brother,

The Rev. Everard Aloysius Gonzaga Arundell. **13th Baron Arundell of Wardour,** B.A. London Univ., Priest of the Church of Rome, ordained 1862, b. 6 Sept. 1834; d. unm. 11 July 1907, being s. by his cousin,

Edgar Clifford Arundell, **14th Baron Arundell of Wardour,** b. 20 Dec. 1859; m. 28 Nov. 1895, Ellen Elizabeth (d. 22 July 1935) dau. of John Thatcher and widow of J. Melbourne Evans and d.s.p. 8 Dec. 1921, being s. by his brother,

Gerald Arthur Arundell, **15th Baron Arundell of Wardour,** b. 11 Dec. 1861 m. 9 Jan. 1906, Ivy Florence Mary, dau. of Capt. W. F. Segrave, 71st Highlanders and had issue,

1. John Francis, **16th Baron** (see below).
1. Blanche Mary, b. 5 Dec. 1908; m. 11 Jan. 1935, M. J. F. Hanbury-Tracy, (Sudeley, B.).

2. Mary Isabella, b. 3 Feb. 1913; m. 31 Jan. 1935 A/Cdre T. P. F. Fagan and had issue.

The 15th Baron d. 30 March 1939 and was s. by his only son,

John Francis Arundell, **16th Baron Arundell of Wardour,** B.A. New Coll. Oxford, Lt. 4th Bn. Wilts Regt., b. 18 June 1907; k. in action 25 Sept. 1944.

ARMS—Sable six swallows three two and one argent.

CREST—A wolf passant argent.

SUPPORTERS—Dexter, A lion guardant erminois ducally crowned or; Sinister, An owl wings displayed and inverted ermine ducally crowned or.

MOTTO—Deo data.

The family seat was Wardour Castle, Tisbury, co. Wilts.

ASHBURNHAM

PEERAGE—England, Baron Ashburnham of Ashburnham, co. Sussex. Great Britain, Viscount St. Asaph of the Principality of Wales and Earl of Ashburnham.

SURNAME—Ashburnham.

CR.—Barony, 20 May 1689; Viscounty and Earldom, 14 May 1730. **EXT.**—12 May 1924.

HISTORY—Thomas Ashburnham, of Ashburnham, co. Sussex, described as one of those of prime quality in that country, made an oath on behalf of himself and his retainers to observe the laws then made, anno 12. Henry VI, (1434). He m. Sarah, dau. and heir of Henry Waunsey, lineally descended from Sir Nicholas de Wauncy, sheriff of the cos. of Surrey and Sussex, 1250, and had issue,

1. John, his heir (see below).
2. Richard of Bromham, co. Sussex from whom descend the baronets of Ashburnham (see extant peerages) where the earlier descent of the house from Sir Reginald Ashburnham, circa 1166, is shown generation by generation. The early history of the family was examined by J. H. Round in his essay, *Tales of the Conquest in Peerage and Pedigree.* (1970 reprint, p. 302). The completely mythical nature of the alleged pre-conquest ancestry has been proved, and the descent of the family now begins securely from the survey of 1166.
3. Thomas of Gesling, co. Sussex, who had by Elizabeth his wife, a son, Thomas, and two daus., Ellen and Anne.

The eldest son,

John Ashburnham of Ashburnham, m. Elizabeth Peckham and d. 1491 being buried in the Chapel of St. James at Ashburnham. He was s. by his only son,

William Ashburnham of Ashburnham, m. Anne, dau. of Henry Hawley of Ore, co. Sussex, and had with a dau. Jane (who m. 1. William Apsley and 2. Richard Covert, of Slaugham, Sussex) an only son,

John Ashburnham of Ashburnham, m. Lora, dau. and coheir of Thomas Berkeley, of Aram, co. Hants and had issue,

1. John (see below).
1. Anne, m. (1) John Bolney, of Bolney, co. Sussex and (2) Thomas Culpeper of Wakehurst.
2. Jane, m. Oliver Denham.

3. Alice, m. John Daniel.

The only son, John Ashburnham, M.P. for Sussex, 1547-48; m. Isabel dau. of John Sackville, of Buckhurst, co. Kent (1883 Extinct Peerage Dorset E.) and d. 1563, leaving issue.

1. John, his heir (see below).
2. Thomas. 3. William. d. unm.
1. Eleanor, d. unm.
2. Anne, m. Thomas Pemberton of Suffolk.
3. Margaret, m. Jones of Monmouth.

The eldest son, John Ashburnham, of Ashburnham, m. 1569, Mary, dau. of George Fane of Badsel, co. Kent (Westmorland, E.) and d. 1591, leaving issue,

1. John, Sir, (see below).
2. Thomas. 3. William. 4. George.
5. Walter, all d. unm.
1. Mary, m. George Wentworth of Bretton, co. York.
2. Katherine, m. George Adlewick, of co. York.

The eldest son, Sir John Ashburnham, of Ashburnham, knighted at the Tower, 1604, m. Elizabeth, dau. of Sir Thomas Beaumont of Stoughton, co. Leicester and had issue,

1. John, (see below).
2. William, M.P. in 1640, was with other loyal members expelled from the Commons for fidelity to the Crown; was Major Gen. in the royal army and in 1644 Col. Gen. co. Dorset; after the Restoration was appointed Cofferer to Charles II. He m. Jane, dau. of John Butler, 1st Lord Butler and widow of James Ley, 1st Earl of Marlborough (1883 Peerage), but d.s.p. 1679.
1. Elizabeth, m. Frederich Cornwallis 1st Lord Cornwallis 1661, and had issue,
2. Frances, m. Frederick Turville.
3. Anne, m. Sir Edward Dering, 1st Bt.
4. Katherine, d. unm.

Sir John's widow m. (2) Sir Thomas Richardson, Lord Chief Justice of the Common Pleas, and was cr. Baroness Cramond, in the peerage of Scotland for life in 1628, with remainder to the son by a former wife of her 2nd husband (see 1883 Peerage). Sir John Ashburnham d. 1620, his eldest son,

John Ashburnham of Ashburnham, Groom of the Bedchamber to Charles I and to Charles II, was M.P. Hastings 1640 and after 1660 for co. Sussex. In 1646 he was the only person who attended Charles I on the latter leaving Oxford and was with Charles I when the King left Hampton Court on 11 Nov. 1647. Clarendon considered that the general opinion (which he did not share) was that John Ashburnham had been outwitted if not corrupted by Cromwell at that time (1647, see C.P. sub nomine Ashburnham, p. 271). He was committed to the Tower by Cromwell and there remained until Cromwell's death (1658). Clarendon's view of the general opinion of Ashburnham's conduct was given by the former to explain Charles II's failure to confer a peerage on Ashburnham. John Ashburnham m. (1) Frances, dau. and heir of William Holland of Westburton, and had issue,

1. William, m. Hon. Elizabeth, dau. of John Poulett, 1st Lord Poulet of Hinton St. George co. Somerset and d.v.p. 1665 leaving issue,

John, heir to his grandfather and 1st Baron Ashburnham (see below).

His widow m. (2) Sir William Hartop, of Rotherly, co. Leicester.

1. Frances, m. Sir Denny Ashburnham 1st Bt.
2. Elizabeth, m. Sir Hugh Smyth, 1st Bt. of Long Ashton, Somerset.

John Ashburnham m. (2) Elizabeth, dau. and heiress of Christopher Kenn, of Kenn, co. Somerset and widow of John Poulett, 1st Lord Poulett. He d. 15 June 1671, being bur. in Ashburnham Church (M.I.) and was s. by his grandson. John Ashburnham of Ashburnham, 1st Baron Ashburnham of Ashburnham, co. Sussex, in the peerage of England, so cr. 20 May 1689, on which C.P. (vol. II, p. 271) remarks: "It seems remarkable that John Ashburnham, who had done so much for the House of Stuart, should not have been raised to the peerage immediately after the Restoration of that House, while his grandson (whose chief claim to distinction appears to have been that he was such grandson) should have been cr. a Baron by the very King who had driven the House of Stuart into banishment" (C.P. then cites Clarendon's explanation as given above). Lord Ashburnham was b. 15 Jan. 1655/56. He was M.P. Hastings 1679-81, 1685-87 and 1689. He m. 22 July 1677, in Westminster Abbey, Bridget only dau. and heiress of Walter Vaughan, of Porthammel House, co. Brecon (pedigree of Vaughan in Jones's Breconshire, vol. ii, p. 341) and d. 21 Jan. 1709/10 leaving issue,

1. William, 2nd Baron (see below).
2. John, 3rd Baron (see below).
3. Bertram d.s.p.
1. Elizabeth, m. (1) Robert Cholmondeley, of Halford, co. Chester and (2) Seymour Cholmondeley, and d. 26 Jan. 1732.
2. Anne d. young.
3. Jane, m. William Hayes and d. Aug. 1731.

The eldest son,

William Ashburnham, 2nd Baron Ashburnham, b. 21 May 1679; M.P. Hastings 1702-10; m. 16 Oct. 1705, Catharine, dau. and sole heir of Thomas Taylor of Clapham, Beds, (pedigree, Visit. of Beds. 1634) and d.s.p. 16 June 1710; she d. 11 July 1710, both of the smallpox. He was s. in the barony by his next brother,

John Ashburnham, 3rd Baron Ashburnham, 1st Viscount St. Asaph in the Principality of Wales and Earl of Ashburnham in the peerage of Great Britain, so cr. 14 May 1730. He was bapt. 13 March 1687; M.P. Hastings 1710; Col. 1st Troop of Horse Guards 1713-15; Lord of the Bedchamber to Frederick, Prince of Wales 1728-31, Capt. the Yeomen of the Guard 1731-36. In 1730 he sold to the Crown the long lease of Ashburnham House in Little Dean's Yard, Westminster (now part of Westminster School) which had been built for his ancestor by Inigo Jones and of which the staircase is reckoned one of his finest works. He m. (1) 21 Oct. 1710, Mary, dau. of James Butler 2nd Duke of Ormonde, and she d.s.p. 2 Jan. 1712/13 in childbed; he m. (2) 24 July 1714, Henrietta Maria, dau. and heir of William Stanley, 9th Earl of Derby, and widow of 4th Earl of Anglesey. She d. 26 June 1718 aged 31, leaving an only dau. Henrietta d. unm. The Earl m. (3) 14 Mar. 1723/24 Jemima (d. 7 July 1731, aged 32) dau. and coheir of Henry de Grey, 1st Duke of Kent, and d. 10 Mar. 1736 being s. by his only son (by his 3rd marriage),

John Ashburnham, **2nd Earl of Ashburnham,** b. 30 Oct. 1724 a Lord of the Bedchamber 1748-62, LL.D. Camb. 1749, Lord Lt. Sussex 1754-57, appt. Keeper of Hyde Park and of St. James's Park, 1753-62; made P.C. 1765, Master of the Great Wardrobe 1765-75; first Lord of the Bedchamber and Groom of the Stole 1775-82. He m. 28 June 1756, Elizabeth, dau. and heiress of John Crawley, Alderman of London. Through her grandmother, Theodosia, (née Gascoyne) who m. Sir Ambrose Crowley, the estate of Barking in Suffolk came to the 5th Earl of Ashburnham, on the death in 1782 of Theodosia Crowley who survived all her children. Elizabeth Crowley, Countess of Ashburnham brought with her a fortune of £200,000. By her who d. 15 Feb. 1787 the Earl had issue,

1. George b. 2 and d. 13 Feb. 1758.
2. George, **3rd Earl** (see below).
1. Henrietta Theodosia, b. 8 Nov. 1750, d. 30 March 1847.
2. Jemima Elizabeth, b. 1 Jan. 1762; m. 26 Feb. 1785, James Graham later 3rd Duke of Montrose, and d. 18 Sept. 1786 having an only son who d. in infancy.
3. Elizabeth Frances, b. 10 May 1763; d. 16 April 1854.
4. Theodosia Maria, b. 16 June 1765; m. 4 June 1788, Robert Vyne of Gautby, co. Lincoln and d. 1822.

The 2nd Earl d. 8 April 1812, and was s. by his 2nd and surv. son, George Ashburnham, **3rd Earl of Ashburnham,** K.G. 1829; G.C.H. 1827; F.S.A. 1827, M.A. Trin. Coll. Camb. 1780, Lord of the Bedchamber to the Prince of Wales 1784-95, a Trustee of the British Museum 1810-30; he edited 1830 2 vols. of *A Narrative by John Ashburnham* (his ancestor) *of his attendance on Charles I prefixed to which was a vindication of his character etc.* He was b. 25 Dec. 1760; m. (1) 28 Aug. 1784, Sophia, dau. of Thomas Thynne, 1st Marquess of Bath. By her who d. in childbed 9 April 1791 he had issue.

1. George, b. 9 Oct. 1785, M.A. Trin. Coll. Camb. 1805; M.P. New Romney 1807-12 and Weobley 1812-13 d.v.p. 7 June 1813.
2. John b. 3 June 1789; drowned 1810.
1. Elizabeth Sophia, b. 16 Sept. 1786; d. 13 March 1879.

He m. (2) 25 July 1795, Charlotte, dau. of Algernon Percy, 1st Earl of Beverley (Northumberland D.) and by her (who d. 26 Nov. 1862) had further issue.

3. Bertram, **4th Earl** (see below).
4. Percy, b. 22 Nov. 1799; m. 23 Aug. 1838, Esther, dau. of Lt. Col. By, R.E. and d. 25 Jan. 1881, having had issue 2 daus., Esther Hemet, b. 1844; d. 1845, Mary Catherine, b. 1847; d. 1851.
5. Charles, Sec. H.M. Legation, Constantinople, b. 23 March 1803; m. 1832, Sarah Joanna, dau. of William Murray of Jamaica, and d. 22 Dec. 1848. She m. 2ndly 1851, Sir Godfrey Webster, 6th Bt. who d.s.p. May 1853.
6. Thomas, C.B. Gen., Col. 82nd Foot, b. 1866; m. 8 Feb. 1860, Adelaide, dau. of Thomas Foley, 3rd Lord Foley, and d. 2 March 1872.
7. Reginald, b. 1819; d. 5 March 1830.
2. Charlotte Susan, b. 23 Feb. 1801; d. 26 April 1865.
3. Theodosia Julia, b. 27 March 1802; d. unm. 22 Aug. 1887.

4. Georgiana Jemima, b. 11 May 1805; m. (1) 28 Feb. 1828, Henry Reveley Mitford and (2) 1842 Hon. F. G. Molyneur (Sefton, E.). The 1st marriage was dissolved by Act of Parliament. She d. May 1882.
5. Jane Henrietta, b. 19 July 1809; m. 19 May 1836, Adm. Charles H. Swinburne, R.N. and had with other issue, Algernon, the poet. She d. Nov. 1896
6. Katherine Frances, b. 31 March 1812; m. 21 June 1838, Henry W. Beauclerk and d. 6 April 1839.
7. Eleanor Isabel Bridget, b. 28 July 1814; m. 26 Nov. 1844, Rev. Algernon Wodehouse. She d. March 1895.
8. Mary Agnes Blanche, b. 23 Jan. 1816; m. 29 Aug. 1839, Sir Henry Percy Gordon, Bt. She d. 1899.

The 3rd Earl d. 27 Oct. 1830 and was s. by his son, Bertram Ashburnham, **4th Earl of Ashburnham,** b. 23 Nov. 1797; educ. St. John's Coll. Camb.; m. 8 Jan. 1840, Katherine Charlotte, dau. of George Baillie of Jerviswood (Haddington E.) and had issue,

1. Bertram, **5th Earl** (see below).
2. John, 2nd Sec. H.M. Diplomatic Service, J.P. Sussex, b. 6 March 1845; m. 21 May 1907, Maud Mary, dau. of Charles Royal-Dawson of S.E. Wynand, Madras Presidency and d.s.p. 12 April 1912. She m. 2ndly G. V. Grose
3. William, M.A., Barrister-at-Law, b. 29 March 1847; d. 27 May 1897.
4. Richard, Rev., M.A., b. 27 July 1848. d. 8 Dec. 1882.
5. Thomas, **6th Earl** (see below).
6. Edward, b. 23 Dec. 1857; d. 30 Mar. 1859.
7. George, b. 21 Oct. 1863; d. unm. 1911.
1. Katherine, b. 23 Nov. 1841; m. 20 Jan. 1874, (as his 2nd wife) Sir Alexander Bannerman, 4th Bt. and d. 30 Sept. 1885.
2. Margaret, b. 4 April 1851; m. 3 Aug. 1882, John Bickersteth and d. 1933 leaving issue.
3. Anne, b. 21 March 1853, d. 1 Dec. 1857.
4. Mary, b. 21 Dec. 1859; m. 23 Jan. 1883, 2nd Viscount Knutsford and d. 3 May 1947.

The 4th Earl d. 22 June 1878 and was s. by his eldest son,
Bertram Ashburnham, **5th Earl of Ashburnham,** b. 28 Oct. 1840; educ. Westminster; m. 25 Feb. 1888, Emily (d. 12 Feb. 1900) dau. of Richard Chaplin, Gent., and d. 15 Jan. 1913 having had issue,
Bertram Richard, b. 2 and d. 4 March 1888.
Mary Catherine Charlotte, J.P. East Sussex. b. 3 Jan. 1890 d. unm. 5 Jan. 1953 (At her death the ancient custom was observed of placing a hatchment of her arms over the door of her house).
The 5th Earl was s. by his next surv. brother,
Thomas Ashburnham, **6th Earl of Ashburnham,** b. 8 April 1855; Capt. 7th Hussars, served in the Egyptian Campaign, 1882, had the Order of the Medjidieh, 5th class; from 1885-86, was A.D.C. to the Lord Lieutenant of Ireland; m. 10 June, 1903 Maria Elizabeth, O. St. J., dau. of W. H. Anderson, of Frederickton, New Brunswick, and d.s.p. 12 May, 1924.
ARMS—Gules a fesse between six mullets argent.

CREST—Out of a ducal coronet or an ash tree ppr.
SUPPORTERS—Two greyhounds sable their faces, breasts and feet argent, collared and lined or.
MOTTOES—Le roy et l'estat, and Will God I shall.
The seats of the family were Ashburnham Place, Battle, co. Sussex; Barking Hall, Needham, co. Suffolk; Pembrey, co. Carmarthen. Their town house, Ashburnham House, 30 Dover Street was demolished before 1910.

ASHFIELD

PEERAGE—U.K. Baron Ashfield of Southwell, co. Nottingham.
SURNAME—Stanley.
CR.—9 Jan. 1920. EXT.—4 Nov. 1948.
HISTORY—Henry Stanley, of Detroit, m. Elizabeth, dau. of George Twigg, of Derby. She d. 30 April, 1925; he d. 19 Feb. 1932, having had issue, Sir Albert Henry Stanley, **Baron Ashfield,** b. 8 Nov. 1874; educ. at an American Coll. and technical schools; for some years was Gen. Man. of American Electric Railways, and in 1907 was Gen. Man. of Metropolitan District Railway and Tube Railways in London, 1907. Held numerous executive appts. including Chm. of London Passenger Transport Board, Chm. North Metropolitan Electric Power Supply Co., Dir. of Midland Bank and Imperial Chemical Industries; served in World War I as Col. of Railway and Staff Corps, 1914-18; M.P. Ashton-under-Lyne, 1916-20, Pres. of Board of Trade, 1916-19. He m. 5 Dec. 1904, Grace Lowrey, dau. of Edward Lowrey Woodruff, of Detroit, U.S.A. He was cr. Kt. Bach. 1914; made P.C. 1916 and cr. a peer as Baron Ashfield of Southwell, co. Nottingham, 9 Jan. 1920. He d. 4 Nov. 1948. He had issue,
1. Marian Woodruff, m. (1) 1927 James H. Rutland (m. diss by div. 1934) m. (2) 1934, J. H. Royds, (m. diss by div. 1940) m. (3) 1940, (m. diss by div. 1954) R. A. Hubbard, and has issue, m. (4) 1964 E. J. Braford.
2. Grace Lowrey, m. (1) 1928, E. J. Barford, (m. diss by div. 1940) m. (2) 1940 Capt. H. J. Buckmaster.
ARMS—Azure a pegasus rampant and, in chief three estoiles or.
CREST—A demi stag ppr., gorged with a wreath of oak vert, resting the sinister foot upon a bugle horn or.
SUPPORTERS—Dexter, An electrical mechanic holding in the exterior hand a coil of wire; Sinister, An electrical mechanic holding in the exterior hand a pair of pliers, all ppr.
MOTTO—In alta tende.
Lord Ashfield's residence was The Crossways, Sunningdale.

ASHTON

PEERAGE—U.K. Baron Ashton of Ashton, co. Lancaster.
SURNAME—Williamson.
CR.—25 July 1895. EXT.—27 May 1930.

HISTORY—James Williamson, of Parkfield, in Scotforth, co. Lancaster J.P., sometime Mayor of Lancaster, m. Eleanor, dau. of Leonard Miller, of Lancaster, and d. 3 Jan. 1879, having had with other issue a second son, James Williamson, **Baron Ashton,** of Ashton, co. Lancaster, so cr. 25 July 1895. He was b. 31 Dec. 1842, educ. Lancaster Gram. Sch.; was manufacturer of linoleum at Ashton; J.P. and D.L. and High Sheriff, co. Lancaster (1885); Liberal M.P. for Lancaster Div. of N. Lancashire, 1886-95; m. (1) 23 Sept. 1869, Margaret, dau. of Joseph Gayet, of Keswick, Cumberland. She d.s.p.m. 10 April 1877, leaving issue, Eleanor who m. 1899, William Peel, 1st Earl Peel and had issue. Lord Ashton m. (2) 23 Nov. 1880 Jessy Henrietta, who d. 1904, dau. of James Stewart, of Clapham, W.R. Yorks; m. (3) 30 July, 1909, Florence Maude, dau. of Rev. R. Daniel, and widow of Col. J. Lawson. He d. 27 May 1930.
ARMS—Party per chevron or and argent, a chevron nebuly between in chief two trefoils slipped and in base a demi eagle couped and is displayed sable.
CREST—A demi-eagle displayed or gutteé-de-poix each wing charged with a fesse and holding in the beak two trefoils in saltire sable.
SUPPORTERS—on either side an eagle regardant with wings enclosed or, gutteé-de-poix, holding in the beak by a ribbon gules an escutcheon argent charged with a trefoil vert.
MOTTO—Murus aeneus conscientia sana.
Lord Ashton's seats were at Ryelands, co. Lancaster, and Ashton Hall near Lancaster with a town house at Alford House, Prince's Gate, London S.W.

ASKWITH

PEERAGE—U.K. Baron Askwith, of St. Ives, co. Hunts.
SURNAME—Askwith.
CR.—24 March 1919. EXT.—2 June 1942.
HISTORY—John Askwith, of Ripon, co Yorks, had a son,
William Askwith, of Ripon, b. 1680; m. 23 Mar. 1706, Rebecca, dau. of John Bradley, of Farnely, Yorks, and d. Nov. 1723 having with other issue,
William Askwith, of Ripon, Alderman, b. 30 Aug. 1712; m. (1) 4 Dec. 1735, Ann, dau. of Robert Atkinson, of Gwendale, Yorks. She d. Jan. 1751. He m. (2) Jane, dau. of James Smith, of Northallerton, Yorks and (3) Elizabeth—. He d. June, 1776, having had issue by his first marr.,
1. William, (see below).
2. Robert, of Ripon, an attorney, bapt. 16 Aug. 1745; d. 9 July, 1779.
1. Alice, bapt. 15 July, 1738; m. John Haddon, of Ripon, and d. 14 Oct. 1811.
The elder son,
William Askwith, of Ripon, Alderman and Mayor of that town, bapt. 22 Sept. 1740; m. 10 Feb. 1777, Jane, dau. of Peter Handley, of Bishopdale, co. York, and d. Jan. 1815, leaving with other issue by her who d. 24 Sept. 1841,
John Haddon Askwith, of Pickhill and of Old Sleningford Hall, Yorks. b. 11 Feb. 1782; m. 15 Oct. 1810. Catherine, dau. of William Harrison, M.D., F.R.S., of Ripon, and d.

28 May, 1824, leaving by her who d. 11 Jan. 1824, an eldest son,

Gen. William Harrison Askwith, R.A., b. 7 Sept. 1811; 2nd Lt. R.A. 18 Dec. 1829; Capt. 23 Nov. 1841; Col. 26 Oct. 1858; and Gen. 27 June, 1879; apptd. Col. Commandant R.A., 15 April 1877; Superintendent of the Royal Gunpowder Factory at Waltham, 1855-68; served in the Carlist War in Spain 1838-40 as Brit., Mil. Attaché, and was mentioned in despatches, and received crosses of the Orders of San Fernando and Charles III, and was made a Knight Commander of the Order of Isabella the Catholic. He m. 14 Sept. 1854 Elizabeth, dau. of George Ranken, and d. 25 Nov. 1897, leaving by her who d. 12 Feb. 1914, an eldest son,

Sir George Ranken Askwith, **Baron Askwith**, b. 17 Feb. 1861; educ. Marlborough, and Brasenose Coll. Oxford, Scholar, 1880, B.A. 1884; M.A. 1887; Barrister-at-Law, Inner and Middle Temples, 1886; K.C. 1908; Junior Counsel for Great Britain, in Anglo-Venezuelan Boundary Arbitration, 1899; High Steward of the Manor of the Savoy, 1899; apptd. Counsel to Commissioner of Works, and for the Treasury on Peerage claims; 1900; as British Plenipotentiary signed the Treaty on International Copyright at Berlin Conference 1908; was Chm. of many commissions, and an arbitrator in many trade disputes; Mayor of St. Ives, Hunts, 1913; cr. C.B. 1909; K.C.B. 1911; and a peer as Baron Askwith of St. Ives, co. Huntingdon, 24 March, 1919; m. 20 Feb. 1908. Ellen, dau. of Archibald Peel, of Westlea, Broxbourne, Herts and widow of Major Henry Graham, and d. 2 June 1942 having had issue, Betty Ellen 26 June 1909. Lady Askwith was cr. C.B.E. 1918 for war services and was author of *The Tower of Siloam*, and *Disinherited of the Earth*. Lord Askwith wrote several works on law.

ARMS—Sable a fesse between in chief two cross crosslets and in base a rose argent.

CREST—A cross crosslet fitcheé between two wings erect sable each charged with a rose as in the arms.

SUPPORTERS—On either side a dove holding in the beak an olive branch all ppr.

ASQUITH OF BISHOPSTONE

PEERAGE—U.K. Life, Baron Asquith of Bishopstone, co. Sussex.
SURNAME—Asquith.
CR.—April 1951. EXT.—24 Aug. 1954.
HISTORY—Sir Cyril Asquith, **Baron Asquith of Bishopstone**, fourth son of Herbert Henry Asquith, 1st Earl of Oxford and Asquith, (see current peerage) b. 5 Feb. 1890; educ. Winchester and Balliol Coll. Oxford; Barrister-at-Law, Inner Temple 1920, K.C. 1936, Bencher 1939, a Judge of the King's Bench Div. 1938-46, a Lord Justice of Appeal 1946-51, and a Lord of Appeal in Ordinary 1951-54; served in World War I, Capt. 16th Bn. London Regt.; was knighted 1938 and made P.C. 1946 and cr. a life peer as Baron Asquith of Bishopstone, co. Sussex. April 1951; m. 12 Feb. 1918, Anne Stephanie (d. 1964) dau. of Sir Adrian Pollock (Pollock of Hatton, Bt.) and d. 24 Aug. 1954 having had issue two sons, Luke and Paul and two daus., Jane and Frances Rose.

ARMS—Sable on a fesse between three crosses crosslet argent a portcullis of the field.
CREST—Issuant out of clouds ppr. a mascle gules.
MOTTO—Sine macula macla.

ASQUITH OF YARNBURY

PEERAGE—U.K. Life. Baroness Asquith of Yarnbury of Yarnbury, co. Wilts.
SURNAME—Bonham Carter.
CR.—21 Dec. 1964. EXT.—19 Feb. 1969.
HISTORY—Lady (Helen) Violet Bonham Carter, D.B.E., **Baroness Asquith of Yarnbury**, elder dau. of Herbert Henry Asquith, 1st Earl of Oxford and Asquith, b. 15 April 1887; Pres. women's liberal Fedn. 1923-25, and 1939-45, Pres. Liberal Party Org. 1947-65, a Gov. of B.B.C. 1941-46, a Gov. of the Old Vic 1945 and a Trustee of Glyndebourne Arts Trust 1955; cr. D.B.E. 1953 and a life peeress as Baroness Asquith of Yarnbury of Yarnbury co. Wilts 21 Dec. 1964; m. 30 Nov. 1915, Sir Maurice Bonham Carter (B.L.G. 1952 Lubbock, formerly Bonham Carter) and d. 19 Feb. 1969, leaving issue,

1. Mark Raymond, M.P. Torrington, 1958-59 m. and has issue.
2. Raymond Henry, m. and has issue.
1. Helen Laura Cressida, m. J. A. M. Ridley and has issue.
2. Laura Miranda, m. Rt. Hon. Joseph Grimond, P.C., Leader of Liberal Party 1956-57.

ATHLONE

PEERAGES—U.K. Viscount Trematon in county of Cambridge and Earl of Athlone.
SURNAME—Cambridge.
CR.—16 July 1917. EXT.16 Jan. 1957.
HISTORY—Alexander, Duke of Würtemberg (1804-85) m. morganatically (1835) Claudine, (née Countess de Rhédey) Countess of Hohenstein and had issue, an only son, H.H. Francis Paul Charles Louis Alexander, (1837-1900) who received the Würtemberg title of Prince of Teck (from some ruins near Owen in the circle of the Danube, Würtemberg) with the qualification of Durchlaucht, (Highness or Serene Highness) 1863. He m. 12 June 1866, Princess Mary Adelaide Wilhelmina Elizabeth, C.I., (b. in Hanover, 27 Nov. 1833) second dau. of H.R.H. Adolphus Frederick, 1st Duke of Cambridge, and seventh son of King George III and had issue,

1. Adolphus Charles Alexander Albert Edward George Philip Louis Ladislas, 2nd Duke of Teck and later Marquess of Cambridge.
2. Francis Joseph Leopold Frederick, G.C.V.O., D.S.O. d. unm. 22 Oct. 1910.
3. Alexander Augustus Frederick William Alfred George, created **Earl of Athlone** (see below).

The third son, H.S.H. Prince Alexander of Teck, in 1917, at the time when King George V assumed the surname of Windsor for the royal family, relinquished for himself and for any children of his the Germanic styles and titles which he had formerly borne. This was on

14 July 1917 when he also took the surname of Cambridge, and his peerage creations followed on 16 July 1917. **The Earl** was the recipient of many honours being K.G., P.C., G.C.B., G.C.M.G., G.C.V.O., and D.S.O., Royal Victorian Chain, and was Chancellor of the Order of St. Michael and St. George 1934-36 and Grand Master of the Order from 1936. He was educated at Eton and Sandhurst, and had a long and distinguished military career, commissioned 1894 and serving in the Matabele War, the South African War and World War I, becoming hon. Major Gen. 1923. He was nominated Gov. Gen. of Canada in 1914, but did not proceed; he was Gov. Gen. of, and High Commissioner, S. Africa 1923-31. He was b. 14 April 1874; m. 10 Feb. 1904, H.R.H. Princess Alice Mary Victoria Augusta Pauline, G.C.V.O., G.B.E., only dau. of H.R.H. Prince Leopold Charles Edward George Albert, 1st Duke of Albany and fourth son of Queen Victoria. They had issue,

1. Rupert Alexander George Augustus, Viscount Trematon, b. 24 Aug. 1907, d. unm. 15 April 1928.
2. Maurice Francis George, b. 29 Mar. and d. 14 Sept. 1910.
1. May Helen Emma, b. 23 Jan. 1906, m. 24 Oct. 1931, Henry Abel Smith, created K.C.V.O., 1950, D.S.O., 1945, Col. in the Army, and had issue, (see Burke's Landed Gentry, 1952 edition, Smith, formerly of Wilford House, Notts, where the lineage is derived from Abel Smith of Nottingham and East Stoke, Notts, described as a banker, living ca. 1700. In B.L.G. 1952 under Smith-Dorien-Smith of Tresco Abbey, the Smith ancestry is traced to Hugh Smith, tenant of the manor of Cressing Temple, Essex, who d. in 1485. In the enormous newspaper publicity which attended the marriage of Lady May Cambridge in 1931, the original Smith ancestor was described as a woolcomber. In the genealogy of Lord Carrington, a collateral of the Smiths of Wilford House, the ancestry begins with John Smith circa 1623).

The Earl of Athlone d. 16 Jan. 1957.

ARMS—Quarterly 1st and 4th grand quarters, the Royal Arms as borne by George III (i.e. having an inescutcheon for the arms of the King's Hanoverian Dominions) with a label of three points for difference, the centre point charged with the St. George's cross and each of the other points with two hearts in pale gules; 2nd and 3rd grand quarters, or, three stags' attires fessways in pale, the points of each attire to the sinister sable; impaling or three lions passant in pale sable langued gules, the dexter forepaws gules, over all an inescutcheon paly bendy sable and or. in the centre of the grand quarters a crescent sable for difference.

CREST—A dog's head and neck paly bendy sinister sable and or langued gules, a crescent argent for difference.

SUPPORTERS—Dexter, A lion sable, the dexter forepaw gules; Sinister, A stag proper, each charged with a crescent argent for difference.

MOTTO—Fearless and faithful.

ATHLUMNEY

PEERAGE—Ireland. Baron Athlumney of Somerville and Dollardstown co. Meath U.K. Baron Meredyth, of Dollardstown, co. Meath.
SURNAME—Somerville.
CR.—Baron Athlumney, 14 Dec. 1863. Baron Meredyth 3 May 1866. **EXT.**—8 Jan. 1929.
HISTORY—James Somerville of Tullykilter, co. Fermanagh, described in some sources as descended from the Somervilles of Cambusnethan, co. Ayr, m. Elizabeth (d. 1665/6) dau. of Thomas Hamilton, of Brimhill, and d. March 1642, having with other issue, a third son,

Thomas Somerville of Drumadown, co. Fermanagh, m. Joan, dau. of Thomas Warnock of Enniskillen and d. 1669, having had with others, a third son,

Thomas Somerville, Alderman of Dublin, m. Katherine (d. 3 Feb. 1725) dau. of James King of Corrard (King of Corrard, Bt.) and d. 23 July 1718 (will dated 20 July, proved 26 Aug. 1718) having with four daus., an only son,

Sir James Somerville, Kt., and 1st Bt., lord mayor of Dublin 1736, M.P. Dublin 1729, s. his uncle Janes King of Corrard in the latter's estates in Meath; cr. a Baronet of Ireland 14 June 1748; m. 2 Feb. 1713, Elizabeth, (d. 10 Nov. 1725) dau. of Alderman William Quaile of Dublin (of a Manx family) and d. 16 Aug. 1748 leaving with other issue (for which see account in extant baronetage), an eldest son,

Sir Quaile Somerville, 2nd Bt., of Brownstone, co. Meath, bapt. 14 March 1714, m. (1) 19 Feb. 1740, Mary (d. 28 Feb. 1748) only dau. and heiress of George Warburton, and (2) 11 April 1755, Sarah, eldest dau. of Thomas Towers, of Archerstown, Meath and Borrisopane, co. Tipperary, by whom he had a dau. Martha Mathilda, m. 5th Viscount Boyne. Sir Quaile d. 5 Dec. 1772 being s. by his eldest son (two others d.s.p. or unm.), by his first wife,

Sir James Quaile Somerville, 3rd Bt., of Somerville, co. Meath, m. 16 June 1770, Catherine, dau. of Sir Marcus Lowther Crofton, 1st Bt., of Moate, co. Roscommon. She d. 1775. He d. circa 1800. They had with other issue an eldest son,

Sir Marcus Somerville, 4th Bt., M.P. 1800-31, m. (1) 1 Oct. 1801, Mary Anne, only dau. and heiress of Sir Richard Gorges Meredyth, Bt., of St. Katherine's Grove, co. Dublin; m (2) 7 April 1825, Elizabeth, eldest dau. of Piers Geale of Dublin, and d. 11 July 1831, having had with other issue by his first marriage, an eldest son,

Sir William Meredyth Somerville, 5th Bt., **Baron Athlumney and Baron Meredyth**, b. 1802; matric. Ch.Ch. Oxford 1822; Liberal M.P. Drogehda 1837-52 and Canterbury 1854-65; Chief Sec. for Ireland 1847-52; made P.C. 1847; cr. Baron Athlumney of Somerville and Bollardstown, co. Meath in the peerage of Ireland, 14 Dec. 1863, and Baron Meredyth of Dollardstown, co. Meath in the peerage of the U.K. 3 May 1866. He m. (1) 22 Dec. 1832, Maria Harriet, (d. 3 Dec. 1843) yst. dau. of Henry Conyngham, 1st Marquess Conyngham and had issue,

1. William Henry Marcus, d. an infant, 11 Sept. 1837.

1. Elizabeth Jane, m. 18 Dec. 1856, 3rd Earl of Charlemont and d.s.p., 31 May 1882.

He m. (2) 16 Oct. 1860, Maria Georgiana Elizabeth, only dau. of Herbert George Jones, Serjeant at Law, and d. 7 Dec. 1873, having had issue with seven daus.,

2. James Herbert Gustavus Meredyth, **2nd Baron** (see below).
3. Marcus Edward Francis Meredyth d. 17 Sept. 1871 aged nearly 4.

The eldest surviving son, Sir James Herbert Gustavus Meredyth Somerville, **2nd Baron Athlumney and Meredyth,** b. 23 March 1865; educ. Harrow, Lt. 5th Bn. Royal Canadians 1882; Lt. Coldstream Guards, A.D.C. to Lord Lieut. of Ireland; served in the Dongola Expedition 1896 (despatches) and in the S. African War 1900; m. 30 July 1900, Margery (d. 10 July 1946) dau. of Henry Boan of Australia and d.s.p. 8 Jan. 1929. The two baronies became extinct, the baronetcy became dormant.

ARMS—Azure three mullets or two and one between seven cross crosslets fitchée argent, three, one, two and one.

CREST—A demi-lion rampant sable charged on the shoulder with a cross crosslet fitchée and two mullets argent.

SUPPORTERS—Dexter, A greyhound ppr. collared gules and charged on the shoulder with a mullet and two cross crosslets fitchée sable; Sinister, A lion rampant sable collared and chained or, charged on the shoulder with a cross crosslet fitchée and two mullets argent.

MOTTO—Crains Dieu tant que tu viveras.

Lord Athlumney's seat was Somerville House, near Navan, co. Meath.

ATHOLSTAN

PEERAGE—U.K. Baron Atholstan of Huntingdon in the Province of Quebec and of Edinburgh.

SURNAME—Graham.

CR.—5 May 1917. **EXT.**—28 Jan. 1938.

HISTORY—Robert Walker Graham of Huntingdon, Quebec, had a son, Sir Hugh Graham, Kt. Bach. **Baron Atholstan,** newspaper proprietor in Canada, Pres. Montreal Star Co., b. 18 July 1848, made Kt. Bach. by patent, 9 Nov. 1908, and created a peer 5 May 1917; m. 17 March 1892, Annie Beekman, dau. of Edward Hamilton, of Exeter, Devon, and d. 28 Jan. 1938 having had issue a dau. Alice Hamilton, m. B. M. Hallward.

ARMS—Argent on a pale sable, between two thistles leaved and slipped azure, an estoile between two maple leaves slipped or.

CREST—An escallop gules between two branches of maple ppr.

SUPPORTERS—Dexter, A moose; Sinister, A beaver both ppr., each charged on the shoulder with three escallops two and one, gules.

MOTTO—Onward.

ATKIN

PEERAGE—U.K. Life. Baron Atkin of Aberdovey, co. Merioneth.

SURNAME—Atkin.

CR.—6 Feb. 1928. **EXT.**—25 June 1944.

HISTORY—Robert Travers Atkin, of Fernhill, co. Cork, m. Mary Elizabeth, dau. of Lawrence Ruck, of Merioneth, and had issue an eldest son, Sir James Richard Atkin, **Baron Atkin,** b. 28 Nov. 1867 at Brisbane; educ. Christ Coll. Brecon, and Magdalen Coll. Oxford, Barrister-at-Law, Gray's Inn, 1891, K.C. 1906, Bencher, 1906, Treasurer, 1913; Judge of the High Court of Justice, 1913-19, Lord Justice of Appeal, 1919-28; Chm. of the Council of Legal Education, 1919-34; knighted 1913 and made P.C. 1919; Lord of Appeal in Ordinary, and cr. a life peer, 6 Feb. 1928, as Baron Atkin, of Aberdovey, co. Merioneth; F.B.A. 1938; m. 6 May 1893, Lucy Elizabeth, dau. of William Hemmant, of Bulimba, Sevenoaks, Kent. He d. 25 June 1944, having had issue,

1. William Robert, b. 12 July, 1901; m. (1) Constance Emilia Bourchier and by her (d. 4 April 1930), had issue, William Richard Bourchier, b. 31 March, 1930; m. (2) Mary McMurtrie.
1. Lucy Owen, m. (1) 1913, (m. diss. by div.) Col. Stuart Low and had issue. (2) 6 July, 1935 Capt. G. E. Shelley, (Shelley-Rolls, Bt.).
2. Norah Mary Grace, m. 1916, Major J. L. P. Macnair, and had issue.
3. Margaret Lucy, m. 1918, Lt. Cmdr. R. H. K. Hope, R.N. and had issue.
4. Nancy m. (1) 1924, (m. diss. by div.) J. D. T. Eve, and m. (2) H. T. B. Morison, son of Lord Morison, K.C.
5. Elizabeth, m. 17 Dec. 1932, J. K. C. Millar,
6. Rosaline, B.A. London, Barrister-at-Law, Gray's Inn, 1937; m. 9 Feb. 1929 G. B. Youard, and had issue.

ATKINSON

PEERAGE—U.K. Life Baron Atkinson of Glenwilliam, co. Limerick.

SURNAME—Atkinson.

CR.—19 Dec. 1905. **EXT.**—13 March 1932.

HISTORY—Edward Atkinson of Glenwilliam Castle, co. Limerick, and Skea House, Enniskillen, M.D., J.P., co. Limerick and High Sheriff, 1824, B.A. Trin. Coll. Dublin; b. 1801; m. (1) 1843, Rosetta (d. 1849), dau. of Capt. J. S. M'Cullock, and (2) Emma, dau. of Major Durbin, and d. 1876 having had issue by his first marriage, John Atkinson, **Baron Atkinson,** b. 13 Dec. 1844; Barrister, King's Inns, Dublin, 1865, Q.C. 1880, Bencher 1885; Barrister Inner Temple, 1890, Bencher 1906; M.P. for N. Londonderry, 1895-1905; Solicitor Gen. for Ireland, 1889-92, Attorney Gen. 1892, and 1895-1905. He was made P.C. (Ireland) 1892, and England 1905; created a Lord of Appeal in Ordinary and a life peer, as Baron Atkinson of Glenwilliam, co. Limerick 19 Dec. 1905; m. 1873, Rowena, dau. of R. Chute, M.D. of Tralee, co. Kerry and d. 13 March 1932 having had issue four sons.

ARMS—Per pale gules and argent, an eagle displayed with two heads counterchanged, on a chief engrailed ermine a rose ppr. between two martlets or.

CREST—A falcon rising ppr. belled and jessed or, holding in its beak a fleur-de-lis per pale gules and argent.

SUPPORTERS—(registered U.O. 15 Feb. 1906) Dexter, A figure of Justice ppr. vested argent, semée of fleur-de-lis gules. Sinister, An eagle ppr. gorged with a collar flory counter flory and pendent therefrom a portcullis or.

AUSTIN

PEERAGE—U.K. Baron Austin of Langridge in the City of Birmingham.
SURNAME—Austin.
CR.—16 July, 1936. EXT.—23 May 1941.
HISTORY—Giles Stevens Austin, of Little Missenden, Bucks, m. Clara Jane, dau. of Willoughby Simpson, and had issue, Sir Herbert Austin, **Baron Austin**, b. 8 Nov. 1866; educ. Rotherham Gram. Sch. and Brampton Coll.; M.I.M.E., served his apprenticeship to engineering at Langlands Foundry, Melbourne, Australia, and managed several small works at Melbourne, until coming to England 1890 to manage the manufacture of the Wolseley Sheep Shearing Machine; he founded the Austin Motor Co. at Birmingham 1905; was M.P. King's Norton Div. Birmingham, 1918-24; Chm. Austin Motor Car Co., Ltd., and Pres. of the Inst. of Automobile Engineers; was Hon. Col. The Worcestershire Regt. T.A.; m. 26 Dec. 1887 Helen, dau. of James Dron of Melbourne, Australia and had issue,
1. Irene b. 1891, m. 1918, Col. A. C. R. Waite, M.C.
2. Zitz Elaine b. 1902, m. C. P. Lambert and had issue 1928.
He was cr. K.B.E. 1917 and a peer as Baron Austin, of Longridge, in the City of Birmingham, 16 July, 1936, He d. 23 May 1941.
ARMS—Gules a cross between in the 1st and 4th quarters a garb and in the 2nd and 3rd a lozenge or.
CREST—A garb or charged with a steering wheel and column winged gules.
SUPPORTERS—On either side a bull sable gorged with a collar of lozenges conjoined or.
MOTTO—Forward.
Lord Austin's residence was Lickey, Bromsgrove.

AVONMORE

PEERAGE—Ireland. Lord Yelverton, Baron Avonmore, co. Cork, Viscount Avonmore of Derry Island, co. Tipperary.
SURNAME—Yelverton.
CR.—Barony, 15 June 1795. Viscounty 29 Dec. 1800. DORMANT—3 Sept. 1910.
HISTORY—Frank Yelverton of Blackwater, co. Cork, 1705; m. 16 Aug. 1733 Elizabeth (d. 1804) dau. of Jonas Barry of Kilbrin, co. Cork, and d. 27 March 1746, having had with others, an elder son, Barry Yelverton, Lord Yelverton, Baron Avonmore and **Viscount Avonmore**, b. 28 May 1736; educ. Trin. Coll. Dublin, Sch. 1755, B.A. 1757, LL.B. 1761, LL.D. 1774; admitted Middle Temple 1759; Barrister-at-Law, King's Inns, Dublin, 1764, K.C. and Bencher 1772; M.P. Donegal Borough 1774-76, and Carrickfergus 1776-83; Attorney Gen. for Ireland 1782-83; P.C. Ireland 1782; Lord Chief Baron of the Ex-

chequer, 1783-1805; cr. Lord Yelverton, Baron Avonmore, co. Cork, 15 June 1795, and Viscount Avonmore of Derry Island co. Tipperary, 29 Dec. 1800; m. July 1761, Mary, dau. and coheiress of William Nugent, of Clonlost, co. Westmeath, by Ursula dau. of Richard Aglionby of Carlisle. She d. 1802. They had issue,
1. William Charles, **2nd Viscount** (see below).
2. Walter Aglionby, b. 1772; m. 28 Nov. 1791, Cecilia (d. 1801) eldest dau. of George Yelverton of Belle Isle, Newfoundland, and d. 3 June 1824, leaving issue,
   (1) Bentinck Walter, b. 1792; m. 1829, Hon. Anna Maria Bingham, dau. of 1st Lord Clanmorris and d. 15 Dec. 1837. She d. 21 Jan. 1866.
   (2) Benjamin Chapman Frederick, Rev., of Ballea, King's Co., m. 1838, Hon. Louisa Catherine Bingham, 3rd dau. of 1st Lord Clanmorris and d. 1849, leaving issue two daus.
      1a Julia Anna Florence, m. 5 Aug. 1868, Barrie Corrie R.N.
      2a Pauline, m. (1) 1854, R.A.G. Davies of Trednick, Cornwall and (2) 1866, Hon. Barry John Bingham, son of 3rd Lord Clanmorris.
   (1) Maria Letitia, m. 1823, James Egan, and d. 5 April 1884.
   (2) Cecilia Anna, d. unm. 21 Aug. 1881.
3. Barry, d. unm. June 1824.
1. Maria, m. 1791, John Bingham, 1st Lord Clanmorris.
The 1st Viscount Avonmore d. 19 Aug. 1805 and was s. by his eldest son, William Charles Yelverton, **2nd Viscount Avonmore**, b. 5 April 1762; Prin. Registrar of the Court of Chancery, Ireland; m. 1 Sept. 1787, Mary, dau. of John Reade, of East Hants, and had issue,
1. Barry John, **3rd Viscount** (see below).
2. William Henry, M.A., of Whitland Abbey, co. Carmarthen, b. 5 March 1791; m. 2 June 1825, Elizabeth Lucy, dau. and heiress of John Morgan of Furness, co. Carmarthen, and d. 28 April 1884, leaving,
   (1) William Henry Morgan, of Whitland Abbey, b. 7 Feb. 1840.
   (1) Mary Elizabeth, m. 17 Nov. 1855, the Rev. W. P. Roberts and d. 14 May 1893.
   (2) Louisa Anne, m. 20 June 1859, Mons. Louis Gaston Salmon, Capt. in the French service, and d. 31 March 1886.
   (3) Henrietta Maria.
3. Augustus, b. 2 Aug. 1802; m. 1825, Sarah Whiteside in Dublin and d. 1864 having had issue,*
   (1) Augustus Barrymore, twin with his sister, Caroline Bingham, bapt. 18 Aug. 1829 (1832 according to another account, but certificate of baptism does not state year of birth) in parish of Rushen. I. of Man; m. 1859, Eliza Jane Ridge, at Wellington, N.Z. and d. 1909. She d. 1910. They had issue,
      1a Barry Squance, b. 7 Aug. 1865, d. unm. 10 Aug. 1938.
*NOTE: Most of the above information of the descendents of Augustus Yelverton 1802-64 was supplied to the writer by Barry Augustus Yelverton and M. G. Yelverton, (the latter having been in England 1949-50).

2a Foster Goring, b. 1 Sept. 1867; m. 1895 at Carterton, N.Z., Ann Caroline, dau. of Alfred Mason of Featherston, N.Z. she d. 1947. He d. 1952, their children were,
1b Barry Augustus, b. 1895, educ. New Zealand Univ. served in World War I 1916-19 with N.Z. Expeditionary Force; m. 1921 at Wellington N.Z., Margaret Ethel, dau. of John Thomas Green of Christchurch, N.Z. and had issue,
1c Barry Goring, b. 1923, served in World War II 1944-45 with N.Z. Forces; m. 1950, Frances Winifred, dau. of William Francis Battersby, of Glasgow Terrace, Feilding, N.Z. and had
1d Ian Foster, b. 1950,
2d Avon Barry, b. 1954.
2c Michael Curran, b. 1928; m. 1949 Marjory Ruth, dau. of Arthur William Hall, of Gisborne, N.Z. and had issue
1d Kevin Barry, b. 1949.
1d Sharon Anne, b. 1950.
2b Hermann Stratton, b. 1896; served in World War I with N.Z. Expeditionary Force; m. 1923 Janetta Ferguson, dau. of John McEwen, of Palmerston North, N.Z. and had issue
1c Stratton Barton, b. 1926.
1c June Avonmore, b. 1924, m. 1944, Charles Herbert Dudley Scantlebury, son of William Addison Scantlebury of Tauranga, N.Z. and had issue.
2c Matel, b. 1928, m. 1951 Raymond William Watson of Mairangi Bay, Auckland N.Z. and had issue,
3b Macy Goring, b. 1898; served in R.N.V.R.; m. 1922 (in England), Pauline, dau. of Jarrett Owen Allen of Nottingham and had issue,
Enid, b. 1929; m. 1952 Arthur Joseph Byrne of Lyndhurst, co. Hants, and had issue.
3a William Henry, b. 29 Aug. 1875 d. unm. 1888.
4a Longworth Ridge, b. 16 Sept. 1876; m. 1900, Beatrice, dau. of Thomas Lawry of Featherston, N.Z. and d. 12 April 1936, having had issue,
William Henry, b. 1903; m. (1) 18 July 1934, Doris Elizabeth Rose (d. 1953) dau. of James Miller, of Dannervirke, N.Z.; m. (2) 1954 (m. diss. by div. 1960) Gwendolen Hilda Carter, dau. of W. E. Jones of Southampton, and m. (3) 1960 Zoe May, dau. of Samuel Burnett, of Wairoa, N.Z.
Octavia Mervyn b. 1901; m. 1928, Robert Henry son of John Sinclair of Opunake N.Z.

1a Cecilia, b. 1860. d. 1862.
2a Cecilia Ann, b. 1863. d. 1908.
3a Ada Caroline, b. 1869; m. 1891, at Greytown, N.Z., Henry Benton, (d. 1939) son of Thomas Benton, of Featherston, N.Z. and had issue.
4a Catherine Amelia, b. 1871; m. 1892 at Featherston, N.Z. Charles, son of Thomas Benton and d. 1928.
(1) Caroline Bingham, twin with her brother, Augustus Barrymore, bapt. 18 Aug. 1829 (or 32, see above) in Parish of Rushen, I of Man; m. Francis Severne and d. at Nelson, N.Z.
1. Mary of Thane Cottage, Arnsworth, co. Pembroke, b. 7 Feb. 1859.
2. Louisa Sarah, m. 1825, Rev. Andrew Sayers, M.A., Rector of St. Mary de Crypt, co. Gloucester and d. 19 April 1866.
The 2nd Viscount d. 28 Nov. 1814, being s. by his eldest son, Barry John Yelverton, **3rd Viscount Avonmore**, b. 21 Feb. 1790; m. (1) 1811, Jane, second dau. of Thomas Booth, of Whitehaven, and by her (who d. Oct. 1821) had issue,
1. Barry Charles, b. 21 Nov. 1814; Lt. 79th Foot, 1833; d. unm. v.p. 11 Jan. 1853.
2. George Frederick William, 64th Regt., b. 7 March 1818; m. 12 Feb. 1857, Louisa Menox, dau. of Guy Lenox Prendergast and d.v.p. and s.p. 26 Feb. 1860.
1. Sydney Eloisa; m. 16 July 1839, Foster Goring (Goring Bt.) and d. at Wellington, N.Z. 13 March 1883.
2. Mary Augusta, d. 7 Oct. 1843.
3. Adelaide Matilda, m. 7 July 1860, Lt. Gen. Humphrey Lyons, Indian Army and d. 13 June 1884.
The 3rd Viscount m. (2) 1 Aug. 1822 his cousin, Cecilia, eldest dau. of Charles O'Keefe (by Letitia, his wife, ygst. dau. of George Yelverton of Belle Isle, see above) and by her (who d. 1 Feb. 1876) had further issue,
3. William Charles, **4th Viscount** (see below).
4. Walter Aglionby, b. 16 Feb. 1832; d. 16 Jan. 1844.
4. Letitia.
5. Louisa Elizabeth, m. 2 Sept. 1873, Herr Hermann Hultzsch, of Dresden.
6. Cecilia Priscilla, m. 13 April 1853, Col. George Harrington Hawes, 9th Regt. and 18 Sept. 1854.
7. Anna, m. 28 April 1859, James Walker of Dalry.
8. Maletta, m. 7 Oct. 1868, Capt. Crofton T. B. Vandeleur, 12th Lancers.
The 3rd Viscount d. 24 Oct. 1870 and was s. by his first surv. son of his 2nd marriage, William Charles Yelverton, **4th Viscount Avonmore**, b. 27 Sept. 1824, Major R.A., served in the Crimean War, Knight of the Turkish Order of the Medjidie, 5th Class; was suspended from all military duties owing to the scandal occasioned by the case of *Thelwall v. Yelverton* which raised the question of validity of his marriage to Maria Theresa Longworth. A full account of the matter is given in *C.P.* vol. I. p. 363 with the decision of the House of Lords as to the invalidity of the Longworth/Yelverton ceremony, "whereby the validity of this

PLATE 2

BARON ASHTON.

BARON ATHLUMNEY.

BARON BARRYMORE.

VISCOUNT AVONMORE.

BARON ATKINSON.

PLATE 3

BARON BATEMAN.

EARL OF BERKELEY.

BARON BATTERSEA.

BARON BERWICK.

BARON BLYTHSWOOD.

BARON BORTHWICK.

scoundrel's marriage in 1858 became established". The last reference is to W. C. Yelverton's marriage on 26 June 1858 to Emily Marianne, ygst. dau. of Major Gen. Sir Charles Ashworth K.C.B., and widow of Edward Forbes, F.R.S. and had issue,
1. Barry Nugent, **5th Viscount** (see below).
2. William Walter Aglionby, b. 7 May 1860; d. 3 May 1861.
3. Algernon William **6th Viscount** (see below).
1. Olive Ursula, d. 5 Jan. 1862.
The 4th Viscount d. 1 April 1883 being s. by his eldest son,
Barry Nugent Yelverton, **5th Viscount Avonmore**, b. 11 Feb. 1859; educ. R.M.C. Sandhurst, 2nd Lt. 27th Foot 1878, Lt. 1879, Instructor of Musketry 1882, Capt. 1884, served in the Sudan and d. unm. 13 Feb. 1885 of enteric fever at Kerbekan, being s. by his brother,
Algernon William Yelverton, **6th Viscount Avonmore**, b. 19 Nov. 1866; Capt. 4th Brig. South Irish Div. R.A.; m. 17 Dec. 1890, Mabel Sarah, second dau. of George Evans of Gortmerron, Dungannon, co. Tyrone, and d. 3 Sept. 1910, having had issue,
Evelyn Marianne Mabel, b. 1 Dec. 1893 and d. unm. 16 Jan. 1956.
The titles have been dormant since the death of the 6th Viscount.
ARMS—Argent three lions rampant gules on a chief gules a cresent argent.
CREST—A lion passant reguardant gules.
SUPPORTERS—Two lions reguardant gules.
MOTTO—Renascentur.
The seat of the Viscounts was Belle Isle, near Roscrea, co. Tipperary, also Hazle Rock, co. Mayo.
(The shield of arms above is the same with the exception of the silver crescent as that of the English Yelvertons of Norfolk, a family who held the titles of Viscounts Longueville, Earls of Sussex and Barons Grey of Ruthyn. The Viscounty and the earldom became extinct in 1799 on the death of Henry Yelverton, 3rd Earl of Sussex. (1883 Extinct Peerage).

BADELEY

PEERAGE—U.K. Baron Badeley of Badley, co. Suffolk.
SURNAME—Badeley.
CR.—21 June 1949. **EXT.**—27 Sept. 1951.
HISTORY—Capt. Henry Badeley of Grey Harlings, Chelmsford, had a son, Sir Henry John Fanshawe Badeley, **Baron Badeley**, b. 27 June 1874; educ. Radley and Trin. Coll. Oxford; entered Parliament Office, House of Lords 1897; Prin. Clerk and Taxing Officer Judicial Dept., House of Lords, 1919 Clerk Asst. of Parliament 1930 and Clerk of Parliament 1934-49; cr. C.B.E. (Civil) 1929, K.C.B. (Civil) 1935 and Baron Badeley of Badley, co. Suffolk 21 June 1949. He d. 27 Sept. 1951.
ARMS—Gules a chevron between three boars' heads couped at the neck argent each charged with a trefoil slipped of the field.
CREST—A boar's head couped at the neck argent charged with a trefoil slipped gules.
SUPPORTERS—On either side an eagle, wings elevated, sable charged with a portcullis chained or.
MOTTO—Principiis obsta.

BANNERMAN OF KILDONAN

PEERAGE—U.K. Life, Baron Bannerman of Kildonan, of Kildonan, co. Sutherland.
SURNAME—Bannerman.
CR.—5 Dec. 1967. **EXT.**—10 May 1969.
HISTORY—John Roderick Bannerman had a a son, John MacDonald Bannerman, Baron Bannerman of Kildonan, b. 1 Sept. 1901; educ. Shawlands Acad., Glasgow High Sch., Glasgow Univ. and Balliol Coll. Oxford, M.A., B.Sc., Pres. Scottish Liberal Party, 1965, cr. O.B.E. 1952, and a life peer as **Baron Bannerman** of Kildonan, of Kildonan, co. Sutherland, 5 Dec. 1967; m. 1931 Ray, dau of W. Mundell, of Swordale, Evanton, co. Ross and d. 10 May 1969. They had issue two sons, John Walter Macdonald and Calum Ruairi Mundell, and two daus. Janet Ray, m. Mayor I. Michie and Elizabeth Mary, m. D. S. Munro.
Lord Bannerman's residence was The Old Manse, Balmaba, co. Stirling.

BANTRY

PEERAGE—Ireland. Baron Bantry of Bantry, co. Cork 24 March 1797.
Ireland. Viscount Bantry of Bantry co. Cork 29 Dec. 1800.
Ireland. Viscount Berehaven and Earl of Bantry, co. Cork 22 Jan. 1816.
SURNAME—White (later Hedges-White).
CR.—as above. **EXT.**—30 Nov. 1891.
HISTORY—Richard White settled at Bantry and had a son,
Richard White of Bantry, m. 1734, Martha, dau. of the Very Rev. Rowland Davis, Dean of Cork and Ross, and had issue (with a dau. Margaret m. Viscount Longueville),
Simon White of Bantry, m. 1760, Frances Jane (d. 1816) dau. of Richard Hedges Eyre, of Mount Hedges and d.v.p. leaving issue,
1. Richard, **1st Earl of Bantry** (see below).
2. Simon, Col. m. 1801, Sarah, dau. of John Newenham of Maryborough, co. Cork and d. 1838, leaving issue, Robert Hedges Eyre, of Glengariffe, b. 1809, m. 1834 Charlotte Mary, dau. of Thomas Dorman and had issue. Fanny Rosa Maria, m. 1830 John Lavallin Prinley of Dunbog Castle, co. Cork.
3. Hamilton, m. Lucinda Heaphy and d. 1804 leaving issue.
1. Helen m. R. D. Newenham of Maryborough, co. Cork.
2. Martha, m. 1800 M. G. Adams of Jamesbrook.
3. Frances, m. 1801, Gen. E. Dunne of Brittas, Queen's County.
The eldest son, Richard White, **Earl of Bantry**, s. his grandfather in the Bantry estate, b. 6 Aug. 1767; assisted in defeating the French invasion in 1797 at Bantry Bay; was cr. 24 March 1797 Baron Bantry of Bantry, co. Cork, on 29 Dec. 1800 Viscount Bantry of Bantry, co. Cork and on 22 Jan. 1816 Viscount Berehaven and Earl of Bantry, all in the peerage of Ireland. He was presented with a gold medal by the City of Cork for his exertions against the French. He m. 3 Nov. 1799, Margaret Anne, dau. of William Hare, 1st Earl of Listowel. She d. 19 Jan. 1835. He d. 2 May 1851. They had issue,

1. Richard, **2nd Earl** (see below).
2. William Henry Hare, **3rd Earl** (see below).
3. Simon, an officer in the Army, b. 1807, d. unm. 1837.
4. Robert Hedges, b. 1810 had issue an only son, Richard d. 1886 aged 22.
1. Maria (1805-17).

The eldest son, Richard White, **2nd Earl of Bantry**, b. 16 Nov. 1800; High Sheriff co. Cork 1835, was a Representative Peer for Ireland from 1854; m. 11 Oct. 1836 Mary, dau. of William O'Brien, 2nd Marquess of Thomond. She d. 19 July 1853. He d.s.p. 16 July 1868 and was s. by his brother,

William Henry Hare Hedges-White, **3rd Earl of Bantry**, b. 10 Nov. 1801; educ. Downing Coll. Camb. M.A., 1823. By Royal Licence 7 Sept. 1840 he took the additional surname of Hedges, in gratitude and respect to the memory of his maternal uncle, Robert Hedges Eyre, of Macroom Castle from whom he inherited. The 3rd Earl was from 1869 a Representative Peer for Ireland. He m. 16 April 1845, Jane dau. of Charles John Herbert, of Muckross Abbey, co. Kerry. She d. 7 July 1898. He d. 15 Jan. 1884 having had issue,

1. William Henry Hare, **4th Earl** (see below).
1. Elizabeth Mary Gore, b. 1847; m. 1874, Egerton Leigh, of Jodrell Hall, and High co. Chester and d. 1880 having had issue.
2. Emily Anne, d. 1860.
3. Olivia Charlotte, b. 1850; m. 1871 Lord Ardilaun.
4. Ina Maude, b. 1852; m. 1885 the 10th Earl Ferrers.
5. Jane Frances Anna, b. 1857; m. 1876 E. M. Kenney Hubert and had issue.

The only son, William Henry Hare Hedges-White, **4th Earl of Bantry**, b. 2 July 1854; m. 18 Feb. 1886, Rosamund Catherine, dau. of Hon. E. G. Petre (Petre, B.) and d.s.p. 30 Nov. 1891. The Countess m. 2ndly 1897 the 2nd Baron Trevor of Brynninalt.

ARMS—Quarterly 1, Gules an annulet or, in the chief point a crescent argent all within a bordure sable charged with ten estoiles gold; on a canton ermine a lion rampant of the third (White); 2, Azure three swans' heads erased ppr. (Hedges); 3, Argent on a chevron sable three quatrefoils or (Eyre); 4 Gules ten bezants, four, three, two and one, a canton ermine (Zouche).
CRESTS—1. (centre) A stork argent beaked and membered or charged with a crescent gules (White); 2. (on dexter) A swan's head and neck erased ppr. (Hedges); 3. (on sinister) a leg booted, armed and spurred, couped at the thigh per pale gules and argent, spur gold (Eyre).
SUPPORTERS—Dexter, A Dragoon officer with a drawn cutlass in his right hand all ppr. Sinister, A female figure representing Ireland habited in a long blue vest, an ancient crown or on her head, in her left hand a spear and standing in front of a harp all ppr.; military trophies behind the supporters and shield.
MOTTO—The noblest motive is the public good.
The seats of the Earls were Bantry House, Macroom Castle, Glengariff Lodge, co. Cork and East Ferry, Cork Harbour.
In *Misc. Gen. and Her.* N.S. vol. 8. p. 60 (1847) are some details of the White family, as having come from England (possibly Kent) between 1695 and 1702. John White then bought some forfeited lands in cos. Limerick and Tipperary. He lived at Cappagh, called Cappagh White after him, in Tipperary where he d. 1718. He m. (1) Susanna, sister of Richard Newport of Longford, co. Limerick. She d. 7 Dec. 1700 and was bur. in the family vault at Toem, co. Tipperary. He m. (2) Catherine Mary a widow and sister of Lord Muckerry. John White had by his first wife,

1. Richard.
2. Newport, Rev. m. Fanny Forster and had,
  (1) John, m. Catherine Hunt.
  (2) Richard d. at Smyrna.
  (3) Newport m. Mary Ievers.

John White (d. 1718) had three half brothers who came to Ireland with him. They were, Benjamin, William and Hamilton. Benjamin was ancestor of the Whites of Whitehall, Kincora near Killaloe; William of the Whites of Greenhall New Ross and Manister; Hamilton of the Bantry family.

The writer of the above account, John Davis White of St. Dominick's, Cashel, co. Tipperary, adds on the arms of the family "when Richard White was cr. Baron Bantry, he of course applied for a grant of arms. The heralds gave him the arms of Sir Thomas White of Rickmansworth, who was Lord Mayor of London in 1555 and these arms are now adopted by every branch of the family. I think the arms should properly have been those of Sir William White who was Lord Mayor of London in 1489, in which there are three covered cups and three martlets upon a chevron, as I was told that there was some old family plate which had 'covered cups' as part of the arms. The following arms are on the seal used by John White attached to a lease made by him. A chevron between three roses; Crest, An arm embowed holding a sword. There was an old family of White in Clonmel and on a tombstone belonging to one of the family, date about 1550, the arms were the same as on the seal used on the lease".

BARROGILL

PEERAGE—U.K. Baron Barrogill.
SURNAME—Sinclair.
CR.—1 May 1866. EXT.—25 May 1889.
HISTORY—James Sinclair, 14th Earl of Caithness, b. 16 Dec. 1821; Lord Lt. and Vice Adm. of Caithness, F.R.S., and a Representative Peer for Scotland, 1858-66, when he was created a peer of the United Kingdom, as **Baron Barrogill**, 1 May, 1866; m. (1) 17 July 1847, Louisa Georgiana, dau. of Sir George Richard Philips, 2nd and last Bt., and by her (who d. 31 July 1870) had an only son,

George Philips Alexander, 15th Earl of Caithness and **2nd Baron Barrogill** (see below). He m. (2) 6 Mar. 1872, Duchesse de Pomar, dau. of Senor Don José de Mariategui, and widow of Gen. Condé de Medina Pomar. The Earl d. 28 Mar. 1881, and was s. by his son,

George Philips Alexander Sinclair, 15th Earl of Caithness, and **2nd Baron Barrogill**, b. 30 Nov. 1858; Lord Lt. of Caithness, d. unm. 25 May 1889, when the Barony of Barrogill became extinct and the earldom passed to his kinsman, James Augustus Sinclair, 16th Earl of Caithness, (extant peerages).

ARMS—Quarterly 1, Azure a ship at anchor, sails furled, oars erect in saltire or, within the royal tressure of Scotland of the last (Orkney); 2 and 3, Or a lion rampant gules (Spar); 4 Azure a galley under sail or (Caithness); over all a cross engrailed sable (Sinclair).
CREST—A cock ppr.
SUPPORTERS—Two griffins sable, armed or.
MOTTO—Commit thy work to God.

BARRYMORE

PEERAGE—U.K. Baron Barrymore, of Barrymore, co. Cork.
SURNAME—Barry.
CR.—18 July 1902. **EXT.**—22 Feb. 1925.
HISTORY—James Barry, 4th Earl of Barrymore (1883 Extinct Peerage) had a yst. son, John Smith Barry, b. 28 July 1725; m. 1746, Dorothy, dau. and co-heir of Hugh Smith, and had issue with a younger son and a dau., an elder son,

James Hugh Smith Barry, or Marbury, Cheshire, and Fota Island, co. Cork, b. 1748, had an illegitimate son,

John Smith Barry, who m. Eliza Mary, dau. of Robert Courtney, and d. 24 Feb. 1837, having had with other issue,

James Hugh Smith Barry, of Marbury, Cheshire, and of Fota Island, co. Cork, m. Eliza (d. 14 March, 1915) dau. of Capt. Shallcross Jacson, of Newton Bank, Cheshire, and d. 31 Dec. 1856, having with other issue,

Arthur Hugh Smith Barry, **Baron Barrymore**, of Barrymore, co. Cork, so cr. 18 July, 1902, b. 17 Jan. 1843 at Leamington; educ. Eton and Ch.Ch. Oxford; M.P. co. Cork, 1867-74; and South Hunts, 1886-1900; High Sheriff, co. Cork, 1886; made P.C. Ireland, 12 March 1896; m. (1) 17 Aug. 1868, Mary Frances, dau. of 3rd Earl of Dunraven and Mountearl. She d. 21 Sept. 1884. By her her had issue,

1. James Hugh Smith, b 22 Oct. 1870; d. 18 May 1871.
1. Geraldine, b. 9 June, 1869; m. (1) 18 July 1893, Henry Burleigh Lethem Overend, who d. 1904. She m. (2) 9 Nov. 1917, Major J. W. D. Thomson.

He m. (2) 28 Feb. 1889, Elizabeth, dau. of Gen. James Wadsworth, of Geneseo, U.S.A., and Mil. Gove. of Washington during the Civil War. By her (d. 9 May 1930) he had further issue,

2. Dorothy Elizabeth, m. 6 Jan. 1917, Major W. B. Bell, 12th Lancers.

Lord Barrymore, who was made a P.C. of Ireland 1896, had a beautiful seat at Fota Island, Queenstown; he d.s.p.m.s. 22 Feb. 1925.
ARMS—Quarterly 1 and 4, Argent three bars gemel gules; 2 and 3, counterquartered I and IV, Gules on a chevron or between three bezants as many crosses patée fitchée sable; II and III, Azure a fess argent between three porcupines or, the whole within a bordure compony ermine and of the second.
CREST—A castle argent issuing from the battlements thereof a wolf's head sable charged with a cross patée fitchée or.
SUPPORTERS—On either side a wolf sable gorged with a ducal coronet attached thereto a chain reflexed over the back and charged on the shoulder with a cross patée fitchée or.
MOTTO—Boutez en avant.

BATEMAN

PEERAGE—U.K. Baron Bateman of Shobdon, co. Hereford.
SURNAME—Bateman-Hanbury.
CR.—30 Jan. 1837. **EXT.**—4 Nov. 1931.
HISTORY—William Hanbury of Kelmarsh, Northants, a member of the family of Hanbury of Worcestershire (see B.L.G. 1952) and of the Barons Sudeley. He was related to the Viscounts Bateman through his grandmother Anne, dau. of Sir James Bateman (see Burke's Extinct Peerage, 1883, Viscount Bateman). William Hanbury, of Kelmarsh m. 1778, Charlotte, dau. of Charles James Packe, of Prestwold Hall, co. Leicester and d. 16 Nov. 1800 having had with other issue, an eldest son, William Hanbury Bateman, **1st Baron Bateman**, b. 24 June, 1780, s. to the Bateman estate on the death of the 2nd Viscount Bateman in 1802, and was created Baron Bateman of Shobdon, co. Hereford, 30 Jan. 1837. By Royal Licence 4 Feb. 1838 he assumed the additional surname and arms of Bateman. He m. 16 Aug. 1822, Elizabeth dau. of Lord Spencer Stanley Chichester, (Donegall, M.) and d. 19 Sept. 1882 having had issue, with three other sons and four daus.,

1. William Bateman, **2nd Baron** (see below).
2. Charles Spencer Bateman-Hambury-Kincaid-Lennox, who assumed the additional surnames and arms of Kincaid-Lennox, by Royal Licence, and d.s.p. 1862.

Lord Bateman d. 22 July 1845 being s. by his eldest son,

William Bateman Bateman-Hanbury, **2nd Baron Bateman**, b. 1826; M.A. Camb., Lord Lieut. co. Hereford, 1852-1901, m. 13 May 1854, Agnes Burrell (d. 1918), dau. of Gen. Sir Edward Kerrison, 1st Bt., of Brome Hall, Eye, co. Suffolk and d. 30 Nov. 1901, having had issue with four other sons who d.s.p. and six daus., an eldest son,

William Spencer Bateman-Hanbury **3rd Baron Bateman**, b. 30 Sept. 1856; m. 23 July 1904, Marian Alice, dau. of J. J. Graham of New York and widow of H. C. Knapp, and d.s.p. 4 Nov. 1931.
ARMS—Quarterly 1 and 4, Or a bend engrailed vert plain cottised sable (Hanbury); 2 and 3, Or on a fesse sable between three Muscovy ducks ppr. a rose or (Bateman).
CRESTS—1, Out of a mural crown sable, a demi-lion or, holding in the dexter paw a battle axe sable helved or (Hanbury) (shown here contournée). 2 A Muscovy duck's head couped between two wings expanded sable (Bateman).
SUPPORTERS—Two lions argent, gorged with plain collars, each charged with a rose between two fleur-de-lis or, and chains of the latter affixed to each collar and reflexed over the back.
Lord Bateman's seat was Shobdon Court, Hereford.

BATTERSEA

PEERAGE—U.K. Baron Battersea, of Battersea, co. London, and of Overstrand, Norfolk.
SURNAME—Flower.
CR.—5 Sept. 1892. **EXT.**—27 Nov. 1907.

HISTORY—Philip William Flower, of Furze Down, Surrey, son of John Flower, m. Mary, dau. of Jonathan Flower, and had issue,
1. Cyril, **Baron Battersea** (see below).
2. Arthur, of the Hyde, Luton, m. 3 Feb. 1873, Isabel Margaretta Cockayne, dau. of Sir Philip Duncombe Pauncefort Duncombe, 1st. Bt., and had issue, five sons and four daus.
3. Herbert, m. 5 Aug. 1876, Agnes Cecil Emmeline Duff, dau. of 5th Earl of Fife, and d. 30 Dec. 1881.
4. Horace.   5. Louis.
1. Clara, m. W. Brand.

Mr. P. W. Flower d. 22 Feb. 1872. His eldest son, Cyril Flower, **Baron Battersea**, of Aston Clinton, Bucks, b. 30 Aug. 1843; educ. Harrow and Trin. Coll. Camb., Barrister, Inner Temple, 1870; Liberal M.P. for Brecknock, 1880-85, and Luton, 1885-92; junior Lord of the Treasury, 1886; D.L. City of London sometime Lt. Bucks Yeo. Cavalry; cr. Baron Battersea, of Battersea, co. London, and of Overstrand, co. Norfolk, 5 Sept. 1892. He m. 22 Nov. 1877, Constance, dau. and coheir of Sir Anthony de Rothschild, 1st. Bt., and d.s.p. 27 Nov. 1907.
ARMS—Or two flaunches, in pale three escutcheons vert each charged with a fleur-de-lis of the field.
CREST—Issuant from clouds a cubit arm erect, in the hand a rose and lily each slipped, all ppr.
SUPPORTERS—Dexter, A mermaid ppr. semée of fleur-de-lis az. holding in the dexter hand 3 arrows or. Sinister, A sea horse ppr., collared or semée of roses gu.
MOTTO—Flores curat Deus.
Seats of the family were, Aston Clinton, Tring, co. Bucks; Pleasaunce, Overstrand, Cromer, co. Norfolk; and town house was at Surrey House, 7 Marble Arch, W.

BAYFORD

PEERAGE—U.K. Baron Bayford, of Stoke Trister, co. Somerset.
SURNAME—Sanders.
CR.—18 June, 1929. **EXT.**—24 Feb. 1940.
HISTORY—Samuel Sanders, of Fernhill, Isle of Wight, who d. 10 March 1859, had a son, Arthur Sanders, of Fernhill, b 1826; m. 1866, Isabella, 4th dau. of John Synge, of Glenmore Castle, co. Wicklow, (B.L.G. of Ireland, 1958, Synge of Mill Grange) and d. 15 April 1886, leaving issue,
1. Robert Arthur, Sir, Bt. and **Baron Bayford** (see below).
2. George Herbert, C.B. 1919, C.M.G. 1917, D.S.O. 1915, Col. R.F.A., hon. Brig. Gen. 1919, b. 14 Sept. 1868; m. 9 Sept. 1897, Vivien Charlotte Lifford, dau. of Hon. A. C. C. Plunket (Plunket, B.), and d. 23 Oct. 1935, leaving issue.
3. Alfred Harry, Capt. Roy. Fus., b. 4 June, 1871; d. 9 May, 1903.
1. Elizabeth Katharine, b. 7 May 1873; d. 27 May, 1930.

The eldest son, Sir Robert Arthur Sanders, Bt., and **Baron Bayford**, b. 20 June, 1867; educ. Harrow and Balliol Coll. Oxford, M.A., Barrister-at-Law, Inner Temple, 1891; M.P.

Bridgwater, 1910-23, and Wells Div. of Somerset, 1924-29; Lt. Col. Roy. North Devon Yeo., 1911; served in World War I, in Gallipoli, Egypt and Palestine, (despatches), J.P. Devon, J.P. and D.L. Somerset, Chm. Somerset County Council, Treasurer of H.M. Household, 1918-19; Junior Lord of the Treasury, 1919-21; Under Sec. of State for War and Vice Pres. of the Army Council, 1921-22; Min. of Agriculture and Fisheries, 1922-24; was cr. a baronet, 28 Jan. 1920, made a P.C. 1922, and cr. a peer as Baron Bayford, of Stoke Trister, co. Somerset, 18 June, 1929. He m. 3 Aug. 1893, Lucy Sophia, dau. of William Halliday Halliday, of Glemthorne, Lynton, Devon, and had issue,
1. Arthur Thomas, b. 21 Dec. 1900; educ. Harrow and R.M.C. Sandhurst, joined Grenadier Guards, 2nd. Lt. 1920, and d. 22 Nov. 1920.
1. Vera Elizabeth, b. 18 Dec. 1902; m. 6 Dec. 1933, Col. the Hon. T. P. P. Butler, (Dunboyne B.).
2. Dorothy, b. 27 Aug. 1907, m. 20 April, 1932, H. F. L. Hartman, and d. 1969 having had issue.

Lord Bayford who was Master of the Devon and Somerset Staghounds 1895-1907, d. 24 Feb. 1940.
ARMS—Per pale argent and sable, three elephants' heads counter changed, tusks and a bordure or.
CREST—An elephant's head erased sable, tusked and charged on the neck with an escarbuncle or.
SUPPORTERS—Dexter, A hind. Sinister, A stag, both ppr. each gorged with a collar pendent therefrom a portcullis or.
MOTTO—Suum cuique.
Lord Bayford's seat was Bayford Lodge, Wincanton, Somerset.

BENNETT

PEERAGE—U.K. Viscount Bennett, of Mickleham, co. Surrey.
SURNAME—Bennett.
CR.—16 July, 1941. **EXT.**—27 June 1947.
HISTORY—Henry J. Bennett, J.P. and Henrietta Stiles, had a son, Richard Bedford Bennett, **Viscount Bennett**, b. 3 July 1870; educ. Public and High Schs. New Brunswick and Dalhousie Univ. Halifax; Barrister New Brunswick 1893 and N.W. Territories and Alberta 1897, K.C. 1907, Bencher of Alberta and Upper Canada, Hon. Bencher, Lincoln's Inn, and Osgoode Hall, Toronto 1930; M.L.A. N.W. Territories 1898-1905 and Alberta 1909-11; mem. Canadian House of Commons 1911-17 and 1925-38; Min. of Justice and Attorney Gen. Canada 1921 and Min. of Finance 1926; Leader of Conservative Party, Canada 1927-38 and Prime Min. and Sec. of State for External Affairs 1930-35; represented Canada at Imperial Conf. 1930; Chm. Imperial Economic Conf. Ottawa 1932; led Canadian Delegation to World Economic Conf. London, 1933; was made P.C. of Canada and of U.K. 1930, a K.G. St J., J.P. Surrey and cr. Viscount Bennett of Mickelham, co. Surrey; d. 27 June 1947.
ARMS—Argent within two bendlets gules three maple leaves ppr. all between two demilions rampant couped gules.

CREST—A demi-lion gules grasping in the dexter paw a battle axe in bend sinister or and resting the sinister paw on an escallop also gules.

SUPPORTERS—Dexter, A buffalo; Sinister, A moose both ppr.

MOTTO—Premi non opprimi.

Viscount Bennett's residence was at Juniper Hall, Mickleham, co. Surrey. His clubs were Athenaeum and Calrton and Rideau in Ottawa.

BENNETT OF EDGBASTON

PEERAGE—U.K. Baron Bennett of Edgbaston of Sutton Coldfield in county of Warwick.

SURNAME—Bennett.

CR.—1 July 1953. EXT.—27 Sept. 1957.

HISTORY—Peter Frederick Blaker Bennett b. 16 April 1880, son of Frederick G. Bennett of Dartford and his wife Annie, dau. of Peter Blaker, m. 1905 Agnes, J.P., elder dau. of Joseph Palmer. He had a distinguished career in industry, being Chm. and Joint Man. Dir. of Joseph Lucas (Industries) Ltd., and one of the Prime Minister's Panel of Industrial Advisers 1938-39; held several war time appointments, including Chairman of the Automatic Gun Board, 1941-44. He was educated at King Edward's School, Birmingham and Birmingham Univ., was J.P. Sutton Coldfield; Alderman Warwickshire C.C., M.P. for Edgbaston 1940-53; was made O.B.E. 1918 and Kt. Bach. 1941, Hon. LL.D. Birmingham, 1950; cr. **Baron Bennett** of Edgbaston of Sutton Coldfield in county of Warwick 1 July 1953. He lived at Ardencote, Luttrell Road, Four Oaks, Warwickshire. Lord Bennett d. 27 Sept. 1957.

BERESFORD

PEERAGE—U.K. Baron Beresford, of Metemmeh and Curraghmore, co. Waterford.

SURNAME—Beresford.

CR.—22 Jan. 1916. EXT.—6 Sept. 1919.

HISTORY—Sir Charles William de la Poer Beresford, **Baron Beresford**, known in earlier life by the courtesy title of Lord Charles Beresford, was the second son of John de la Poer Beresford, 4th Marquess of Waterford. He was b. 10 Feb. 1846; educ. Bayford Sch., and Mr. Foster's Sch. Stubbington, Hants; was cadet H.M.S. *Britannia*, 1859; Sub. Lt. R.N. 1866; Lt. 1868; Cmdr. 1875; in command of Royal Yacht *Osborne* 1879-81; Capt. 1882; served in the Egyptian campaign, 1882; and commanded H.M.S. *Condor* at bombardment of Alexandria, later Gov. of that city (despatches); served on Lord Wolseley's staff in the Nile Expedition, 1884-85 for the relief of Gen. Gordon, and was in command of the Naval Brigade at the battles of Abu Klea, Abu Kru and Metemmeh; in command of the expedition for the relief of Sir Charles Wilson, (mentioned three times in despatches and awarded C.B. 1885); a Lord Commissioner of the Admiralty, 1886-88; Rear Admiral, 1897; Vice Admiral, 1902; awarded K.C.B. and K.C.V.O. 1903; C. in C. Mediterranean Fleet, 1905-07;

Admiral 1906. G.C.V.O. 1906; C. in C. Channel Fleet, 1907-09; G.C.B. 1911; cr. a peer as Baron Beresford of Metemmeh and Curraghmore, co. Waterford 22 Jan. 1916. He had numerous foreign orders and held three medals for saving life. He m. 25 June 1878, Mina, dau. of Richard Gardner, M.P., by Lucy, dau. of Count Augustus Mandelsloh. He d. 6 Sept. 1919, having had issue.
1. Kathleen Mary De la Poer. b. 6 May, 1879; m. 1913 Major Gen. E. R. Blacque and d. 1939 having had issue.
2. Eileen Theresa Lucy De la Poer d. unm. 1939.

ARMS—Quarterly 1 and 4, Argent crusilly fitchée three fleur-de-lis within a bordure engailed sable, (Beresford): 2 and 3, Argent a chief indented sable (La Poer).

CREST—A dragon's head erased azure transfixed by a broken spear, the lower part through the neck, the upper part through the jaw ppr.

MOTTO—Nil nisi cruce.

Lord Beresford's residence was 14 Wilton Crescent, London S.W.

BERKELEY

PEERAGE—England, Viscount Dursley and Earl of Berkeley.

SURNAME—Berkeley.

CR.—11 Sept. 1679. EXT. or DORMANT—15 Jan. 1942.

HISTORY—For several reasons the story of the Berkeleys is one of the most interesting in the English Peerage. First as to descent: three holders of the Castle of Berkeley with the appendant property called Berkeley are known between 1068 and 1152. They were Roger, styled the senior who had been made Provost of the Manor of Berkeley between 1068-71, by William FitzOsbern to whom the Conqueror had granted this property. (It had in 1051 been held by Earl Godwin.) The office was confirmed to Roger by the King about 1080 and in the Domesday Survey 1086, he was farming Berkeley from the Crown and was also tenant in chief of Dursley and other neighbouring lands. He entered a monastery 17 Jan. 1091 at St. Peter's Gloucester and d. 1093. It is considered in the *C.P.* vol. ii, p. 124 that Roger styled Junior and his brother Eustace of Nympesfield were probably his sons. Roger de Berkeley began the building of Berkeley Castle in 1117, and d. before Michaelmas 1131. His son and heir, Roger de Berkeley completed the building of the Castle and suffered greatly in the Anarchy under Stephen and Matilda, being deprived in 1152 of the manor of Berkeley and other lands mainly it seems because he refused to recognize the authority of either contender. He d. about 1170 leaving issue, who continued at Dursley, a part of the estate to which Roger had been restored. This foreign derived line of Berkeley remained in possession of Dursley for eight generations until the death s.p. in 1382 of Nicholas Berkeley. The property was alienated by the heir general, Robert Wykes in 1564, but by 1404 the male line of the Norman Berkeleys derived from Roger of 1068 died out with the decease of Sir Nicholas Berkeley of Coherley, co. Gloucester. The forfeiture of 1152 was followed in 1153 or 1154 by a grant of the Castle and heiress of Berkeley from Henry Duke of Anjou, soon to be Henry II, to Robert FitzHarding who thereby became feudal Lord of Berkeley. This Robert, son of Harding, is considered to have been of English stock. "The parentage of this Harding (living circa 1125) has been long and hotly disputed. The view now generally accepted is that he was the son of Eadnoth (killed 1068) 'staller' to King Harold and to Edward the Confessor. E. A. Freeman pronounces this descent 'in the highest degree probable.' Eyton (in his *Shropshire*) devoted much attention to the subject etc." (*C.P.* vol. 2 p. 124). A staller was the equivalent of a chamberlain; Eadnoth's death occurred while fighting for the Conqueror against the invasion of Somerset by King Harold's sons. His son, Harding, is described as a wealthy merchant of Bristol, even then an important city and port; his grandson was the Robert FitzHarding mentioned above. He was host to the Irish Dermot MacMurrough, King of Leinster in 1068 when he came as an exile to request aid from Henry II, and, from which visit was derived the invasion of Ireland by Strongbow Earl of Pembroke and the beginning of the English colonisation of Ireland. (The authority of Henry II's interference in Ireland had been granted by Pope Adrian IV, the only English Pope, who reigned from 1154-59 and who gave it in the Bull Laudabiliter, produced probably in 1155; it had been very strongly confirmed by the three letters of Pope Alexander III in 1172 after the conquest of Ireland. See the text of these documents, with explicit reference to the appalling state of the Irish in *Irish Historical Documents* 1172-1922, publ. 1943, reprinted 1968).

Robert FitzHarding, 1st feudal Lord of Berkeley, m. Eve, who is alleged to have been sister of Durand, dau. of Sir Estmond by Godiva, his wife, a pedigree which J. H. Round denounces as 'obviously absurd'. (*C.P.* vol. ii. p. 125) Robert founded in 1141, the Abbey of St. Augustine, at Bristol (now Bristol Cathedral), of which he later became a canon. He d. 5 Feb. 1170/1, aged about 75; his wife had founded a nunnery on St. Michael's Hill, Bristol, where she became prioress and d. 12 March 1170, being bur. with her husband. They had an eldest son and heir,

Maurice FitzRobert FitzHarding, or de Berkeley, to whom confirmation of the grant of property was made by Henry II, 1155, and by Henry's widow, Queen Eleanor, on 30 Oct. 1189, acting as Regent for Richard I. He enlarged the castle at Berkeley, which became the principal seat of the family and from which their surname was derived. He m. 1153-54, Alice, eldest dau. (but not coheiress, as seen above) of Roger de Berkeley, who had been dispossessed of Berkeley but remained Lord of Dursley. With Alice, Maurice received as her dower, the manor of Slimbridge. He d. 16 June 1190. By this marriage a native English line was allied with the previous Norman owners, adopting their surname and outlasting them by centuries. We have thus an example of one of the greatest medieval baronial houses being of English origin, as indeed research has shown to be the case with the Earls FitzWilliam.

The descent of the Lords Berkeley is given in the extant peerages. In 1295 the 9th of the feudal lords, Thomas de Berkeley received a writ of Summons to the so called Model Parliament of 1295 and thus by the theory of English peerage law became the first peer or Lord of Parliament. That this theory has been shown to be totally at variance with the facts of history is demonstrated by the learned editors of the *C.P.* and by the great medievalist, J. H. Round. ("But of what account is a mere historian? His criticism is nothing worth, for it rests only upon fact. The lawyer's ways are not as his, they dwell in realms apart", J. H. R. *The Muddle of the Law*, p. 283 in *Peerage and Pedigree*, 1910, reprinted 1970).

From this first alleged peer descended Thomas de Berkeley, 5th Lord Berkeley, great great grandson of the 1st Lord of Parliament. The behaviour of this 5th Baron was to cause almost perpetual trouble to his family. His career was one of unbroken success. He was not unreasonably styled the Magnificent. Inheriting very large properties he increased them by being a favourite of Henry IV. That king made Thomas guardian of the Welsh marches and Admiral of the King's Fleet. "westward and southward from the mouth of the Thames, as Admiral he was entitled to three quarters of the spoils of naval actions. In 1405 a force of French knights, men at arms, and crossbowmen under the Marshal Jean de Rieux landed on the Pembrokeshire coast to aid the Welsh Prince Owen Glendower in his struggle against the English. Thomas Berkeley at once put to sea, caught the French fleet off Milford Haven, sank or burned fifteen of their ships and captured the remaining fourteen" (Jonathan Blow, *Nibley Green* in *History Today* Sept. 1952, from which the other incidents of Thomas's career are taken.). This Thomas gathered money from every source and as he had no son, but an only daughter, he enveloped the succession to his estates in mystery. By so doing he was able to marry off his daughter to Richard Beauchamp, Earl of Warwick; while making his nephew, James Berkeley, appear to be his heir, so that an advantageous marriage could be made for the latter. Under his will the disposition of his land was left unmentioned; hence a long and bitter wrangle between James, Lord Berkeley and the Earl of Warwick. This James is reckoned as the **1st Baron Berkeley** by a writ of summons of 20 Oct. 1421. From him descended the 9th Baron Berkeley who in May 1661 petitioned for a higher precedence in Parliament as being a Baron by tenure. The hearing of the claim by the House of Lords was long drawn out and was never resolved. In 1679 on 11 Sept. he was cr. **Viscount Dursley and Earl of Berkeley** as a convenient way of getting rid of the matter. From the 1st Earl of Berkeley descended the **8th Earl**, Randal Mowbray Thomas Berkeley, who was b. 30 Jan. 1865; entered R.N. 1881; Lt. 1887; established his right to the peerage 31 July 1891 (his father the **7th Earl** having d. 27 Aug. 1888). The **8th Earl** was elected F.R.S. 1908; m. (1) 9 Aug. 1887, Kate, dau. of William Brand, and widow of Arthur Jackson. She d. 29 March 1898. He m. (2) 1924 Mary Emlen Lloyd, dau. of John Lowell, of Boston, U.S.A., and d.s.p. 15 Jan. 1942, when the Viscounty and the Earldom became extinct or dormant. The right to the Barony of Berkeley had devolved on the death of the 6th *de jure* Earl of Berkeley on his niece, Louisa Mary Berkeley, 15th holder of the

Barony. (see extant peerages for the present holder).

ARMS—Gules a chevron between ten crosses-patée, six in chief and four in base argent.

CREST—A mitre gules labelled and garnished or, charged with a chevron and crosses patée as in the arms.

SUPPORTERS—Two lions argent, the sinister ducally crowned gules, collared and chained gold.

MOTTO—Dieu avec nous.

NOTE. An instance in which Thomas the Magnificent failed to get any remuneration is instanced by Mr. Blow in the article quoted above. He was present at Agincourt but secured no worthwhile prisoners. On the evening after the battle he was riding over the ground and came upon Louis, Duke of Bourbon, who was prisoner to an English 'other rank'. Thomas in his overbearing fashion told the private that he would relieve him of the Duke whereupon the Englishman, disappointed of his rich prize, stabbed Bourbon. In the reign of Henry VI, not the strongest of sovereigns, there was open feudal warfare between James, 1st Lord Berkeley of the 1421 creation, and the daughter of the Earl of Warwick, Margaret. The result was the battle of Nibley Green in Gloucestershire, the last private battle fought in England. This occurred in 1469, with 1,000 men on the Berkeley side. Viscount Lisle, Margaret's grandson aged 19 was killed in the approved medieval manner when he raised his vizor, received an arrow in the cheek and was despatched as he lay on the ground.

BERTIE OF THAME

PEERAGE—U.K. Baron Bertie of Thame and Viscount Bertie of Thame (Pro. Tame).

SURNAME—Bertie (pronounced Barty)*

CR.—Barony 28 June 1915, Viscounty 2 Sept. 1918. **EXT.**—29 Aug. 1954.

HISTORY—This was a branch of the Berties, Earls of Abingdon and Barons Norreys, and since 1938, Earls of Lindsey (surname of Earl of Abingdon and Lindsey—Townley-Bertie). Francis Leveson Bertie **Viscount Bertie** and Baron Bertie, b. 1844 was the second son of the 6th Earl of Abingdon. He was educated at Eton, entered the diplomatic service and Foreign Office, 1863, and after holding several positions in England in the Foreign Office, became Ambassador at Rome, 1903-05 and at Paris 1905-18. His honours included: K.C.B. (1902), P.C. (1903), G.C.V.O. (1903), G.C.M.G. (1904), G.C.B. (1908). He was created a baron 28 June 1915 and a viscount 2 Sept. 1918. He m. 11 April 1874, Lady Feodorowna Cecilia Wellesley, dau. of the

*The pronounciation is the more interesting as J. H. Round showed that the name of the founder of the family was Bartewe. Thomas Bartune (son of Robert Bartune of Bersted, Kent) from whom the family descend was a stone mason, mentioned in a roll of 1532/3 as working on Winchester Cathedral. He became in time Capt. of Hurst Castle, and had a grant of arms 1550. His son was Richard Bertie, who became a Fellow of Corpus Christie Coll. Oxford. (Round, *Peerage and Pedigree* vol. 1. pp. 1-54).

1st Earl Cowley. He d. 26 Sept. 1919. She d. 30 March 1920. They had issue. Vere Frederick Bertie, **2nd Viscount,** b. 1878; educ. Eton, Ch.Ch. Oxford, Trin. Hall Camb. and Inner Temple, Barrister-at-Law, (1902); m. 1901 Nora, dau. of Frederick Webb and d. 29 Aug. 1954. He had resided at Shirburn Lodge, Watlington, Oxfordshire, and his widow at Applemore House, Dibden, Hants.

ARMS—Quarterly 1 and 4, Argent three battering rams proper headed and garnished azure (Bertie); 2 and 3, Sable a shattered castle triple towered argent (Willoughby).

CREST—A Saracen's head couped at the shoulders ppr. ducally crowned or, charged on the chest with a fret azure and crescent for difference.

SUPPORTERS—Dexter, A friar vested in russet grey with a crutch and rosary all ppr. Sinister, A savage also proper wreathed about the temple and waist with leaves vert, each supporter charged on the breast with a fret azure, a crescent for difference.

MOTTO—Virtus ariete fortior.

BERWICK

PEERAGE—G.B. Baron Berwick of Attingham, co. Salop.

SURNAME—Noel-Hill

CR.—19 May 1784. **EXT.**—27 Jan. 1953.

HISTORY—Sir Richard Hill, a P.C., statesman and diplomat, son of Rowland Hill of Hawkstone, Salop, in the reigns of William III, Anne and George I, d. unm., having devised much of his considerable estate to his nephews, Samuel Barber and Thomas Harwood, both of whom assumed the surname of Hill.

Thomas (Harwood) Hill of Tern Hill, near Market Drayton, Salop, m. as his 2nd wife, Susanna Maria, eldest dau. of co-heir of William Noel, one of the judges of the Common Pleas and had an eldest son,

Noel Hill, **1st Baron Berwick,** three times M.P. Salop, was created a peer in 1784. He m. 17 Nov. 1768, Anna dau. of Henry Vernon, of Hilton in Staffordshire, she d. 23 March 1797. He d. 6 Jan. 1789. They had three daus. and three sons, each of whom succeeded to the title. The eldest son,

Thomas Noel Hill, **2nd Baron Berwick,** b. 21 Oct. 1770, m. 8 Feb. 1872 Sophia dau. of John James Dubocket and d. 1832. Having no issue he was s. by his next brother,

William Noel-Hill, **3rd Baron Berwick** who took the surname of Noel in addition to his patronymic, M.P. for Shrewsbury and Ambassador at Sardinia and Naples, d. unm. 1842 being s. by his next brother,

The Rev. Richard Noel-Hill, **4th Baron Berwick,** Rector of Thornton, Cheshire and Berrington, Salop; b. 1774, m. 16 Jan. 1800, Frances Maria, dau. of William Mostyn Owen, M.P. for Montgomeryshire. He took the additional surname of Noel by royal sign manual, 1824. He d. 28 Sept. 1848. His wife d. 1840. They had with other children, four sons, viz.

1. Richard Noel, **5th Baron** (see below).
2. William, **6th Baron** (see below).
3. Thomas Henry, the Rev., Rector of Berrington, Salop, b. 1804, m. 1845 Harriet Rebecca, dau. of John Humffreys

of Llwyn, Montgomeryshire and d. 1870 having had issue,

(1) Richard Henry, **7th Baron** (see below).
(2) Thomas Noel, the Rev. twin with his brother, was granted the precedence of a baron's younger son; was Rector of Berrington, m. 1874 Frederica Sarah, dau. of the Rev. William David Morrice. She d. 1883. He d. 1888. Their children were,
Thomas Henry, **8th Baron** (see below). Mary Selina, b. 1875, granted the precedence of a baron's dau. she d. unm. 1950.

(1) Harriet Maria Selina, b. 21 Sept. 1848, d. 4 Feb. 1893.
(2) Anne, b. 23 June 1852, d. 25 Nov. 1905.
Both these daus. d. unm. granted precedence of a Baron's dau.

4. Charles Arthur Wentworth Harwood. b. 22 April 1811; m. 29 Aug. 1846, Catherine Mary (d. 1894) eldest dau. of Charles Marsh Adams, of The Abbey, Shrewsbury, and d. 1853. Their children were.
Charles, Rev., Rector of Stockton, Salop, M.A. Exeter Coll. Oxford, b. 18 Feb. 1848; m. 6 Oct. 1891, Edith Mary, eldest dau. of the Rev. R. G. Benson, a cadet of the Bensons of Lutwyche Hall, Salop (B.L.G. 1952) and d. 1911 having had issue with 2 daus., Charles Michael Wentworth, 9th Baron.
Kate Maria Louisa Ada, b. 1847, d. 1921.

The eldest son of the 4th Baron,
Richard Noel-Hill, **5th Baron**, b. 21 Nov. 1800 and d. unm. 1861 when he was s. by his younger brother,
William Noel-Hill **6th Baron Berwick**, Col. in the Army and d. unm. 1822 when his nephew s. as,
Richard Henry Noel Hill, **7th Baron Berwick**, b. 1847; m. 1869 Ellen, (d. 1934) eldest dau. of Bruckspatron Nystrom of Malmöe, Sweden and d.s.p. 1897 being s. by his nephew,
Thomas Henry Noel Hill, **8th Baron Berwick**, Capt. Shropshire Yeo., M.A. Trin. Coll. Oxford, b. 2 June 1877; m. 1919, Edith Teresa, dau. of William Hulton of Venice and d.s.p. 1947, being s. by his cousin,
Charles Wentworth Noel Hill, **9th Baron Berwick**, b. 4 March 1897, sometime Lt. King's Shropshire L.I. and A.D.C. Viceroy of India. d. unm. 27 Jan. 1953.

The seat of the family was Attingham Park where the widow of the 8th Baron lived (circa 1960).

ARMS—Quarterly, 1 and 4, Ermine on a fesse sable a castle with two towers argent on a canton gules a martlet or (Hill); 2, Or fretty gules a canton ermine (Noel); 3 Or a chevron between three stags' heads caboshed gules (Harwood).
CRESTS—1. A stag statant argent (Hill), 2. On the battlements of a tower proper a hind statant argent collared and chained or (Noel), 3. A stag's head caboshed sable in the mouth a sprig of oak ppr. (Harwood).
SUPPORTERS—Dexter, A Pegasus argent gorged with a plain collar sable thereon a martlet or. Sinister, A stag argent attired or gorged with a plain collar sable thereon a

leopard's face gold and a chain reflexed over the back also gold.
MOTTO—Qui uti scit ei bona.

BEVERIDGE

PEERAGE—U.K. Baron Beveridge of Tuggall, co. Northumberland.
SURNAME—Beveridge.
CR.—25 June 1956. **EXT.**—16 March 1963.
HISTORY—William Henry Beveridge, **Baron Beveridge,** civil servant and economist, one of the most widely known thinkers of the 20th century, whose works were not however read in anything approaching their entirety by the multitudes to whom the 'Beveridge Report' (result of his Chairmanship of the Committee on Social Insurance and Allied Services, 1941) became at once a household word and a slogan. He was b. 5 March 1879, his parents were Henry Beveridge, I.C.S., of Pitfold, Shottermill, Surrey, who d. 1929 and his wife Annette, the dau. of William Akroyd, of Stourbridge, co. Worcester. His mother d. 1929. W. H. Beveridge had one sister, Annette Jeanie (d. 1956) who m. Prof. Richard Henry Tawney who d. 1962. W. H. Beveridge was educated at Charterhouse and Balliol Coll. Oxford, where he graduated B.A. 1901, M.A., and B.C.L. 1902, Hon. Fell. 1909, D.Sc.(Econ.) London Univ. 1930 and Barrister-at-Law, Inner Temple, 1904. He became actively interested in social reform in 1903 when he was sub-warden of Toynbee Hall. He entered the Civil Service higher administrative grade in 1908 and worked closely with David Lloyd George in laying foundations of social service legislation before 1914. He remained in the Civil Service until 1919, being for seven years (1909-16) Director of the Employment Exchanges, then newly created. In 1919 he left the Civil Service and became Director of the London School of Economics where he remained until 1937, then becoming Master of University Coll. Oxford until 1944. In 1944 he became Liberal M.P. for Berwick upon Tweed but was defeated in the 1945 general election. Almost the whole of his recommendations regarding the social security system were accepted by the war time Coalition Gov., and later constituted the framework of the Welfare State legislation. Beveridge was the author of several books of which the most important was *Full Employment in a Free Society.* It is often overlooked that as an economist he had based his scheme of social insurance on a high level of employment. Beveridge received very many honorary doctorates, was made F.B.A. 1937, C.B. 1916, knighted as K.C.B. 1919, and created a peer 1956. He m. 15 Dec. 1942 Jessy (Janet), O.B.E., dau. of William Philip of Fife and widow of David B. Mair. She d. 1959. Lord Beveridge d. 16 March 1963.
His home had been at Staverton House, 104, Woodstock Road, Oxford. He was a member of the Reform Club.

BILSLAND

PEERAGE—U.K. Baron Bilsland, of Kinrara, co. Inverness. (Also a baronetcy cr. 25 Nov. 1907.)

SURNAME—Bilsland.
CR.—31 Jan. 1950. EXT.—10 Dec. 1970.
HISTORY—Alexander Bilsland, of Gartagyre, Kilmarnock, co. Stirling, was father of James Bilsland, of Ballat, co. Stirling, and m. Agnes, dau. of William Blair, of Spittal, of Killearn, co. Stirling. She d. 1891. He d. 1886. They had surv. issue,

1. William, Sir, 1st. Bt.,
2. James, m. 1879, Emily Fairie.
3. Alexander, m. 1883, Jane Colville, and d. 8 Feb. 1919, having had
   James Alexander, (1886-1932).
   Jessie Barr, b. 1885; m. 1 June, 1911, Sir John Anderson, 1st and only Bt., who d. 11 April 1963. She d. 25 June 1940.
4. John b. 1857.

The eldest son, Sir William Bilsland, 1st Bt., b. 17 Mar. 1847; Lord Provost of Glasgow, and Lord Lt. of the County and City of Glasgow, 1905-08; was cr. a Baronet 25 Nov. 1907; had the Order of St. Olaf of Norway, (Kt. Cmdr.) and of Sacred Treasure of Japan; m. 16 Sept. 1885, Agnes Anne, dau. of Alexander Steven, of Provanside, Glasgow, and d. 27 Aug. 1921. She d. 23 July 1935. They had children,

1. William Blair, b. 18 July 1888; d. unm. 9 June 1911.
2. Alexander Steven, Sir, 2nd Bt. and **Baron Bilsland** (see below).
1. Agnes Anne, C.I., C. St. J., and Kaiser-i-Hind Gold Medal, b. 5 June 1896; m. 6 Oct. 1915, 1st Baron Clydesmuir, and had issue.
2. Helen Isabel, b. 28 Aug. 1896; m. 2 Sept. 1937, B. C. Thompson.

The only surv. son, Sir Alexander Steven Bilsland, 2nd Bt., and **Baron Bilsland,** of Kinrara, co. Inverness, so. cr. 31 Jan. 1950; and cr. K.T. 1955; b. 13 Sept. 1892; educ. St. John's Coll. Camb; was Capt. 8th Bn. Scottish Rifles, and in World War II District Comm. for Civil Defence, Scotland (Western) District; mem. of the Royal Co. of Archers (the Sovereign's Bodyguard for Scotland).; Chm. of Scottish National Trust Ltd., and of the Second and Third Scottish National Trust; Chm. of Glasgow Stockholders Trust Ltd., and of other cos.; Pres. of Scottish Council, (Development and Industry); m. 16 Feb. 1922, Amy, dau. of David Colville, of Jerviston House, Motherwell, (Clydesmuir, B. in extant peerages).
ARMS—Argent, on a fess azure two bulls' heads erased sable horned gules in chief and a mascle gules in base, a salmon on its back holding in its mouth a signet ring ppr.
CREST—A bull's head erased sable, horned gules.
SUPPORTERS—Two bulls sable, horned and hooved gules.
MOTTO—Certum pete finem.
Lord Bilsland's seats were Kinrara, Aviemore, co. Inverness and Garden, Buchlyvie, co. Stirling.

BINGLEY

PEERAGE—U.K. Baron Bingley of Bramham, co. York.
SURNAME—Lane-Fox.
CR.—24 July 1933. EXT.—11 Dec. 1947.

HISTORY—James Fox-Lane, of Bramham Park, co. York, M.P. for Horsham, inherited the estates of his uncle, Baron Bingley, of Bingley, co. York (see 1883 Extinct Peerage) and m. 23 July 1789, Hon. Marcia Lucy Pitt, dau. of 1st Baron Rivers and d. 7 April 1821 having had with other issue, an eldest son,
George Lane-Fox, of Bramham Park, M.P., m. 1814, Georgiana Henrietta, only dau. of E. P. Buckley, of Minestead Lodge, co. Hants, and d. 1848, leaving with two daus., an only son,
George Lane-Fox, of Bramham Park, High Sheriff, W.R. Yorks 1873, and of Leitrim 1846, b. 1816; m. 1837 Katherine Mary, dau of John Stein and d. 2 Nov. 1896 leaving with other issue, a second son,
James Thomas Richard Lane-Fox, of Bramham Park, and of Hope Hall, co. York, b. 28 Feb. 1841; m. 15 Sept. 1868, Lucy Frances Jane, dau. of Humphrey St. John Mildmay and d. 26 Feb. 1906. She d. 19 March 1920. They had with another son and a dau., an elder son,
George Richard Lane-Fox, **Baron Bingley,** b. 15 Dec. 1870; B.A. New Coll. Oxford, Barrister-at-Law, Inner Temple, served in World War I, 1914-19 (wounded), M.P. for Barkston Ash Div. of Yorks 1906-31; Parl. Sec. for Mines 1922-24, and 1924-28, Pres. Nat. Union of Conservative & Unionist Asscns. 1937, made P.C. 1926, created Baron Bingley, of Bramham, co. Yorks. 24 July 1933. He m. 17 Sept. 1903, Hon. Mary Agnes Emily Wood, dau. of 2nd Viscount Halifax and d. 11 Dec. 1947, having had issue four daus.
ARMS—Quarterly 1 and 4, A chevron between three foxes' heads erased gules (Fox); 2 and 3, Argent a lion rampant gules within a bordure sable, on a canton azure a harp and crown or (Lane).
CRESTS—none recorded.
SUPPORTERS—On either side a bear argent.

BLACHFORD

PEERAGE—U.K. Baron Blachford of Wisdome, co. Devon. (Also a Baronetcy cr. 21 Feb. 1699. Ext. 9 Mar. 1895.)
SURNAME—Rogers.
CR.—4 Nov. 1871. EXT.—21 Nov. 1889.
HISTORY—John Rogers, of Plymouth, a merchant, described as great-grandson of the Rev. Vincent Rogers, of Stratford-le-Bow, Essex, was M.P. for Plymouth and was cr. a baronet, 21 Feb. 1699. He was High Sheriff of Devonshire, 1708. He m. Mary, dau. of William Spencer Vincent, alderman, of London, and d. 1710, being s. by his only son, Sir John Rogers, 2nd Bt., M.P. and Recorder of Plymouth, m. Mary, dau. of Sir Robert Henley, of The Grange, co. Southampton, and d. 1743, leaving issue,

1. John, 3rd Bt. (see below).
2. Frederick, 4th Bt. (see below).

The elder son,
Sir John Rogers, 3:d Bt., M.P. for Plymouth, m. Hannah, dau. of Thomas Trefusis, and d.s.p., being s. by his brother,
Sir Frederick Rogers, 4th Bt., Recorder of Plymouth, and commissioner of the dockyard, m. (1) Miss Cooper, of Norfolk, and by her had one son; m. (2) Catherine dau. of Thomas

Vincent, and widow of Vice Adm. Durrell. He d. 1777, being s. by his son,

Sir Frederick Leman Rogers, **5th Bt.**, M.P. and Recorder for Plymouth, m. Jane, dau. of John Lillicrap, R.N., and d. 1797 having had with two other daus. who d. young,

1. John Leman, **6th Bt.** (see below).
2. Frederick Leman, **7th Bt.** (see below).
3. Robert Henley, Rear Adm. R.N. b. Aug. 1783; d. 3 Jan. 1857.
4. William Cooper, Major Gen., m. 31 Mar. 1835, Caroline, dau. of W. Bridges, of Laverstock, and d.s.p. 6 Nov. 1857.
1. Mary, m. Lt. Col. Templer, and d. 1851.
2. Catherine, d. unm. 27 Aug. 1850.
3. Jane, d. unm. 22 April 1870.
4. Anne, d. unm. 1825.
5. Louisa, d. unm. 1838.
6. Harriet, m. (1) 1810, Rev. Richard Strode, of Newnham Park, and (2) 1830, Lt. Gen. Sir Charles Phillips of Lyndhurst and d. 6 April 1847.

The eldest son, Sir John Leman Rogers, **6th Bt.**, b. 18 April 1780; d. unm. 10 Dec. 1847 being then s. by his brother, Sir Frederick Leman Rogers, **7th Bt.**, b. 11 Feb. 1782; m. 12 April 1810, Sophia, dau. of Lt. Col. C. R. Deare, Bengal Army, and d. 13 Dec. 1851. Lady Rogers d. 16 Feb. 1872. Their children were,

1. Frederick, Sir, **8th Bt.**, and **Baron Blachford** (see below).
2. John Charles, **9th Bt.** (see below).
3. Edward, Rev., **10th Bt.** (see below).
4. Henry, Lt. Col. R.A., b. 2 Jan. 1821; d. 8 May 1871.
1. Katherine, b. 1812; d. unm. 11 Jan. 1892.
2. Emily, b. 1813; d. unm. 22 Sept. 1837.
3. Marian, b. 1814; m. 12 May 1842, the Rev: the Hon. H. Legge, 4th son of the 2nd Earl of Darmouth (extant peerages), and d. 10 July 1890.
4. Sophia, b. 1816; d. unm. 19 Mar. 1889.

The eldest son, Sir Frederick Rogers, **8th Bt.**, and **Baron Blachford**, b. 31 Jan. 1811; educ. Eton and Oriel Coll. Oxford, Craven Sch. 1829, B.A. and double first class, 1832; Fell. 1833; Vinerian Sch. 1834; M.A. 1835; Vinerian Fell. and B.C.L. 1838; Barrister-at-Law, Lincoln's Inn, 1837; Registrar of Joint Stock Cos., 1845; Emigration Commissioner, 1846-60; Commissioner for sale of West Indian estates, 1857; P.U.S. for the Colonies, 1860-71; cr. K.C.M.G. 1869; made P.C. 1871; cr. a peer as Baron Blachford of Wisdome, co. Devon. on 4 Nov. 1871. Cr. G.C.M.G. 1883. The Wisdome in the peerage title was the name of a farmhouse on the Blachford estate, and was also the designation of the title of the baronetcy of Rogers. Lord Blachford m. 29 Sept. 1847, Georgiana Mary, dau. of Andrew Colville, previously Wedderburn, of Ochiltree and Craigflower, by his 2nd wife, Mary, Louisa, dau. of William Eden, 1st Baron Auckland. He d.s.p. 21 Nov. 1889, she d. 13 July 1900. The peerage became extinct at Lord Blachford's death, but he was s. in the baronetcy by his brother,

Sir John Charles Rogers, **9th Bt.**, b. 10 April 1818, d. unm. 25 Mar. 1894, being s. by his surv. brother,

The Rev. Edward Rogers, **10th Bt.**, M.A. Rector of Odcombe, co. Somerset, b. 5 Sept. 1819; d. unm. 9 Mar. 1895, when the baronetcy also became extinct.

ARMS—Argent a chevron gules between three stags courant sable.
CREST—On a mount vert a stag courant ppr.
SUPPORTERS—Dexter, A stag sable, attired or, gorged with a laurel wreath ppr. Sinister, A griffin sable.
MOTTO—Nos nostraque Deo.
Lord Blachford's seat was Blachford Park, near Ivybridge, co. Devon. His club was the Athenaeum.

BLACKBURN

PEERAGE—U.K. Life Baron Blackburn of Killearn, co. Stirling.
SURNAME—Blackburn.
CR.—16 Oct. 1876. **EXT.**—8 Jan. 1896.
HISTORY—John Blackburn, of Killearn, co. Stirling, m. Rebecca Leslie, dau. of the Rev. Colin Gillies, (son of the Rev. Dr. Gillies, of Glasgow), and had issue, with an elder son, (Peter Blackburn, M.P. for co. Stirling and a lord of the Treasury) a ygr. son, Sir Colin Blackburn, **Baron Blackburn**, b. 18 May, 1813; educ. Eton and Trin. Coll. Camb., B.A. and 8th Wrangler 1835; M.A. 1838; Student, Lincoln's Inn, 1835; Barrister-at-Law, Inner Temple, 1838; appointed a Justice of the Queen's Bench, 1859; cr. Kt. Bach. 1860; apptd. a Lord of Appeal in Ordinary, on 16 Oct. 1876, this being the first appointment so made under the Appellate Jurisdiction Act of 1876, and cr. a life peer as Baron Blackburn of Killearn, co. Stirling, also made P.C. 1876. He resigned office Dec. 1886 and ceased for a few months to be a member of the House of Lords, but this privilege was granted by the Act of 1887 to him and the other Lords of Appeal for life. He d. unm. 8 Jan. 1896, at his residence of Doonholm, near Alloway, co. Ayr. Lord Blackburn was for 8 years a joint editor of the Reports in the Court of Queen's Bench, wrote a legal work on *Sales* and enjoyed a large commercial practice.
ARMS—Argent on a pale sable three stags' heads erased argent.
CREST—A stag's head erased as in the arms.
Lord Blackburn's club was The Athenaeum.

BLANESBURGH

PEERAGE—U.K. Life. Baron Blanesburgh, of Alloa, co. Clackmannan.
SURNAME—Younger.
CR.—12 Oct. 1923. **EXT.**—17 Aug. 1946.
HISTORY—Sir Robert Younger, **Baron Blanesburgh**, fifth son of James Younger, of Alloa, (Younger of Leckie, V.), b. 12 Sept. 1861; educ. Edinburgh Academy, and Balliol Coll. Oxford, B.A. 1883, M.A. 1909; Hon. Fell. 1916 and Visitor, 1934; Fell. of King's Coll. London, and Chm. of the Delegacy; Barrister-at-Law, Inner Temple, 1884; Q.C. 1900; Bencher, Lincoln's Inn, 1907; Treasurer, 1932; Judge of the Chancery Div. of the High Court, 1915-19, knighted, 1915; made G.B.E. 1917; Lord Justice of Appeal, 1919-23; made P.C. 1919; appointed Lord of Appeal in Ordinary, 12 Oct. 1923, and cr. a life peer as Baron Blanesburgh, of Alloa, co. Clackmannan. He d. unm. 17 Aug. 1946.

ARMS—Parted per saltire or and gules a rose counterchanged, in base a martlet sable, on a chief indented azure three covered cups or.
CREST—An armed leg couped at the thigh ppr. garnished and spurred or.
SUPPORTERS—Dexter, A figure representing St. Blane; Sinister, An ermine, both ppr.
MOTTO—Celer et audax.

BLYTHSWOOD

PEERAGE—U.K. Baron Blythswood of Blythswood, co. Renfrew.
SURNAME—Campbell.
CR.—24 Aug. 1892. EXT.—14 Sept. 1940.
HISTORY—Colin Campbell of Ardkinglas living 1448 (see Argyll, D.) had with other issue, a yr son, Donald, of Ardentinny, co. Argyll, from whom descended the Campbells of Blythswood. Colin Campbell, 1st of Blythswood, m. (1) Margaret Fleming and (2) Janet, dau. of James Muir and had issue,

1. Colin, of Blythswood, m. 1657 Margaret, dau. of Sir John Lauder, Bt., and had issue, Mary, heiress of Blythswood, m. her cousin, Colin (see below).
2. Robert of Woodside, m. (1) Catherine dau. and co-heiress of John Napier and (2) Jean, dau. of James Dunlop, and had issue two daus.
3. John (see below).

The third son, John Campbell, of Woodside, m. Mary dau. and coheir of John Douglas of Mains and had issue,

1. Colin, m. his cousin Mary and d. 1746 leaving issue,
   (1) Colin, of Blythswood, d.s.p. 1739.
   (2) James, of Blythswood, m. Mary Walkinshaw and d.s.p. 1767.
2. James, (see below).

The second son, James Campbell later Douglas the surname which he assumed on s. to Mains co. Lanark, m. (1) Isobel, dau. of Hugh Corbet, of Hardgrey, by whom he had issue, John (see below); he m. (2) Rebecca Wallace by whom he had two sons and four daus. He d. 1743 and his eldest son,

John Douglas of Mains, m. 1732 Agnes Jones of Clober and had, with other issue who inherited Blythswood, a fourth son,
Robert Douglas of Mains, m. Sarah dau. of J. Davis of Sunbury and d. 1804 leaving with other issue,
Colin Douglas of Mains, b. 1781; m. 1805 Sophia Armine, dau. of J. Boydell and d. 29 April 1820 leaving issue, with a yr son, Colin, Lt. R.N. who s. to Mains but d.s.p. 16 July 1847, an elder son,
Archibald Douglas later Campbell, 17th Laird of Mains, Lt. 68th Regt., s. to Blythswood, 1838 as 12th Laird on the death of his cousin, Archibald Campbell, great grandson of John Douglas, ca. 1732 (see above). He then assumed the surname of Campbell. He m. Caroline Agnes, dau. of M. Dick, of Pitkerro, Angus. She d. 1897. He d. 1868. They had issue with two daus., and a third son who d. young,

1. Archibald Campbell, 1st Baron Blythswood (see below).
2. Sholto Douglas, 2nd Baron (see below).
3. Robert, bore surname of Douglas-Campbell, b. 1842; m. 1869 Catherine

Ellen, dau. of Capt. T. H. L. Miller and d. 1 June 1896 leaving issue, with three daus.
Archibald James Hamilton, recorded arms 28 Jan. 1920 as heir male of Blythswood, with Douglas-Campbell, b. 1884; m. 22 April 1913, Hon. Anna Leonora Beatrice Massey, dau. of 5th Baron Clarina and d. having had issue, three daus.
4. Barrington Bulkley, 3rd Baron (see below).
5. Walter James (surname Douglas-Campbell) b. 1850; d. 9 March 1914.
6. Montagu (surname Douglas Campbell), b. 1852; d. unm. 1916.

The eldest son, Sir Archibald Campbell, Bt. and 1st Baron Blythswood, b. 22 Feb. 1835, served in the Crimean War (wounded at Sebastopol), Col. Scots Guards, Lord Lieut. and convener co. Renfrew, M.P. co. Renfrew 1873-74 and 1885-92, was created a baronet 4 May 1880, and Baron Blythswood, of Blythswood, co. Renfrew, 24 Aug. 1892, the peerage succession being limited in default of the heirs male of his body, with remainder to his brothers in the order specified in the entail of the estates (the third brother, Robert was placed in the entail after the yst brother). He m. 7 July 1864, Hon. Augusta Carrington, dau. of 2nd Baron Carrington and d.s.p. 8 July 1908 when the baronetcy became extinct, but the barony devolved upon his next brother, The Rev. Sholto Douglas, later Campbell, 2nd Baron Blythswood b. 28 June 1839; M.A. Trin. Coll. Camb., D.D. Glasgow, 1915, Vicar of Nonington, Kent, 1871-72, of All Saints,' Derby, 1872-79, Rector of All Souls' St. Marylebone, London, 1879-86, and incumbent of St. Giles, Glasgow, 1886-1900. He s. to Douglas-Support (property held by the junior line from James Douglas ca. 1705 see above). In 1869 he assumed the additional surname of Douglas but resumed that of Campbell in 1908 on s. his brother as Lord Blythswood. He m. 1889, Violet Mary, dau. of Gen. Lord Alfred Paget (Anglesey, M.) and d.s.p. 30 Sept. 1916 when he was s. by his brother, Sir Barrington Bulkeley Douglas later Campbell, 3rd Baron Blythswood, K.C.B., C.V.O., Major Gen. 1898, Lt. Gov. and C. in C. Guernsey 1903-08, received Royal Humane Society's medal for saving life, 1889; b. 18 Feb. 1845; s. to Douglas-Support in 1908 and assumed the additional name of Douglas but resumed that of Campbell on s. his brother as 3rd Baron Blythswood. He m. 7 July 1869, Mildred, dau. of Sir Joseph Hawley, 3rd Bt. and had issue,
1. Archibald, 4th Baron (see below).
2. Barrington Sholto, 5th Baron (see below).
3. Leopold Colin Henry Douglas (Rev.) 6th Baron (see below).

The 3rd Baron Blythswood d. 11 March 1918 and was s. by his brother, Sir Archibald Campbell, 4th Baron Blythswood, K.C.V.O., b. 25 April 1870, Major Scots Guards (S.R.), Major 4th Bn. Argyll & Sutherland Highlanders, and Brig. Major, Brig. of Guards, 1916-19; Grand Master Mason Grand Lodge of Scotland 1926-29, and 1st Hon. Mem. of Grand Lodge of Ireland; on s. to Douglas-Support 1916 he assumed additional surname of Douglas which he relinquished in 1918 on s. to Blythswood; m. 25 July 1895, Evelyn, dau.

of John Fletcher, of Saltoun and d. 14 Nov. 1929, leaving issue a dau. Olive Douglas, m. Hon. L. P. Methuen son of 3rd Baron Methuen. He was s. by his brother,

Barrington Sholto Douglas Campbell, **5th Baron Blythswood,** b. 15 July, 1877, and d. unm. 3 March 1937, being s. by his brother,

The Rev. Leopold Colin Henry Douglas Campbell, **6th Baron Blythswood,** b. 5 March 1881; M.A. Trin. Coll. Camb.; Rector of Didmarton, Gloucestershire 1912-17, C.F. 1917-19, Vicar of Padbury, Bucks. 1919-23; curate of St. Luke's Victoria Docks, 1923-26, vicar of North Cave, Yorks, 1926-27, of Ringmer, Sussex, 1927-31, and of Stockcross, near Newbury, Berks. 1931, s. to Douglas-Support, 1929, and relinquished additional surname of Douglas on becoming 6th Baron Blythswood; m. 22 July 1908, Mabel, dau. of E. C. Dumbleton, Crown Counsel, Colombo, Ceylon, and d. 8 Feb. 1940 having had issue,

Philip Archibald Douglas Campbell, **7th Baron Blythswood,** 2nd Lt. Gen. List. b. 19 Feb. 1919; d. 14 Sept. 1940.

ARMS—Quarterly 1 and 4 grand quarters, counter quartered i and iv, Gyronny of eight or and sable each charged with a trefoil slipped and countercharged; ii and iii, Argent a lymphad sable; 2 and 3, Argent a fesse chequy gules and argent between three mullets in chief azure, a human heart in base ppr.

CRESTS—(1) A lymphad as in the arms (Motto. over- Vincit labor) (2) an oak tree with a lock hanging upon one of the branches ppr. (Motto. over-Quae serata secura).

SUPPORTERS—Dexter, A savage wreathed about the temples and loins with laurel and holding in the dexter hand a club resting on the exterior shoulder ppr., around his neck a gold chain pendent therefrom an escutcheon argent charged with a human heart gules. Sinister, A lion gules gorged with a collar flory counter flory or and pendent therefrom an escutcheon argent charged as the dexter supporter.

The seats of the Lords Blythswood were Blythswood House, Renfrew, and Douglas Support, Coatbridge, co. Lanark.

BORTHWICK

PEERAGE—Scotland. Lord (Baron) Borthwick.

SURNAME—Borthwick.

CR.—12 June 1452, (see note below under 1st Baron). **EXT. or DORMANT**—8 Oct. 1910.

HISTORY—Sir William Borthwick was employed as ambassador to England between 1398 and 1415. The Regent Albany granted him a charter in 1410 of the lands of Borthwick in Selkirkshire, which had been known under that name from the time of William the Lion. Sir William was a hostage for the safe return from England of King James I in 1421, a commissioner to treat for the King's release in 1423, and one of the assize for the trial of Duke Murdoch in 1425. From King James I he had on 2 June 1430, under the Great Seal, permission to build a castle in the Mote of Lochorwart, co. Edinburgh, this being Borthwick Castle. According to some sources he m. a dau. of Sir Thomas Hay of Lochorwart, and had issue,

1. William, Sir, **1st Lord Borthwick,** (see below).
1. Jane, m. as his 2nd wife, Sir James Douglas, 1st Lord Dalkeith.
2. Margaret, m. Sir William Abernethy, of Saltoun, k. at Harlaw, 1411. In 1421 she had a dispensation to m. William Douglas, the ygr. of Dalkeith stepson of his sister.

The son and heir, Sir William Borthwick, **1st Baron Borthwick,** was knighted v.p. Oct. 1430. He was cr. a Lord of Parliament as Lord Borthwick, 12 June 1452, this date being given in the Auchinleck Chronicle. There is no document creating the dignity but it appears from much later evidence that the peerage did not exist in 1450 but was existent in 1455. The *C.P.* adds that the accounts of the first four Lords are very obscure nor can the *Scots Peerage* clear up the difficulty. "It is conceivable that the first two Lords may be in fact the same man, but in that case this man must have lived to a great age. A Lord Borthwick is said to have been slain at Flodden but this is unlikely; probably the 4th Lord fought and was wounded at that battle." (*C.P.*) Of this first Lord Borthwick it is stated that he was prominent in the exchequer accounts as one of the magnates who habitually plundered the Customs. He had two ygr. sons, James of Glengelt, and Thomas, of Colliielaw, and the former had issue. His eldest son,

William, Borthwick, **2nd Lord Borthwick,** mentioned as ambassador to England in 1471 and 1473. He m. 1458 Mariot Hoppringle, a widow, and d. between 6 Oct. 1483 and 7 Feb. 1483/4 leaving issue,

Sir William Borthwick, **3rd Lord Borthwick,** knighted v.p., a guarantor of a treaty with England, 20 Sept. 1484, and a conservator of other treaties, 1497 and 1499. He was Master of the Household to James III, 1485, and d. 20 May 1503, leaving issue,

1. William, **4th Lord** (see below).
2. Alexander, of Nenthorn, co. Roxburgh, by Margaret, his wife, had a son, William, of Soltray, who d. before May 1541, leaving by Janet, his wife, a son, William, of Soltray who m. Katharine Crichton, and d. before Jan. 1564, leaving issue,
   (1) William, of Soltray, and Johnstonburn, who forfeited his estate in 1603, and d. 1640 having by his wife, Barbara Lawson, had issue,
   1a William, of Soltray and Johnstonburn, d. before 1669, leaving a son, Major William, who d. before 1693, leaving one son, Col. William, k. at Ramilies s.p. 1706, and daus. Barbara, m. William Borthwick, of Falahill, and Katherine, m. William Stewart.
   2a Alexander, living 1668, m. Sibilla Cairnes, and was father of William, of Pilmuir and Mayshiell, who m. 1st Marion Borthwick (by whom he had Mary, m. to Sir Alexander Livingstone, and Margaret, m. to John Campbell of Knockreoch); and 2ndly, Marjory Stewart by whom he had a son, Capt. Henry k. at Ramilies, leaving by his wife Mary, dau. of Sir Robert Pringle, of Stichill, Bt., two sons, William who d. unm. before 1723 and

Henry, see below as **12th Lord Borthwick.**

(2) Alexander, of Reidhall and Sauchnell, father of Andrew of Sauchnell, who m. Margaret Turnbull, and had a son, Archibald, minister, of Polwarth. Archibald d. before Sept. 1799, leaving a son Patrick, who m. Marion Scott, and d. 1772, leaving a son Archibald, who claimed the peerage in 1808; he m. Margaret Scott, and d. 1815, leaving (beside a dau. Rachel who d. 1876) a son, Patrick, de jure **17th Lord Borthwick,** (see below).

The eldest son and heir, William Borthwick, **4th Lord Borthwick,** to whom after the defeat of Flodden in 1513, was entrusted the governorship of Stirling Castle with the person of the infant James V. He sealed the treaty with England, 7 Oct. 1517. "On 21 Aug. 1538 he settled his lands in strict tail male with an ultimate remainder to his heirs male whatsoever bearing the name and arms of Borthwick." (*C.P.*). He m. 1491, Margaret, dau. of John Hay of Yester and d. 1543, having had issue,

1. Thomas or Arthur, according to differing authorities, who was styled Master of Borthwick, m. Mariot, dau. of George Seton, 3rd Lord Seton, a marriage disallowed and annulled by the Pope on account of consanguinety before 1530, and he d.s.p. and v.p. before 21 Aug. 1538.
2. John, **5th Lord Borthwick** (see below).

The only surv. son and heir, John Borthwick, **5th Lord Borthwick,** present at the battle of Ancrum Moor, Mar. 1544/45, opposed the Reformation, being an adherent of the Catholic Church, was a mem. of Scots P.C., m. before 1544, Isobel, dau. of David Lindsay, Earl of Crawford, (she m. 2ndly, George Preston of Cameron and d. 15 Nov. 1577) and d. Mar. 1565/66, leaving a son and heir,

William Borthwick, **6th Lord Borthwick,** a partizan of Mary, Queen of Scots, m. before 1570, Grissel, dau. of Sir Walter Scott, of Branxholm, and Buccleuch; she on 24 Sept. 1581 lodged a complaint against him for desertion and cruelty. He d. Oct. 1582 (She m. 2ndly Water Cairncross, of Colmslie,). They had issue.

1. William, Master of Borthwick, d. unm. and v.p. 17 Mar. 1570/71.
2. James, **7th Lord Borthwick** (see below).

The surv. son and heir, James Borthwick, **7th Lord Borthwick,** mem. P.C. of Scotland, 1594; m. 1582, Margaret, dau. of William Hay of Yester, and d. 1599 aged 29, being s. by his only son and heir,

John Borthwick, **8th Lord Borthwick,** who was served heir in the barony of Borthwick, 4 July 1621; m. before 1616, Lilias, dau. of Mark Kerr, 1st Earl of Lothian, and d. Nov. 1623, leaving issue, with a dau. m. Robert Dundas, of Harviestown, a son and heir,

John Borthwick, **9th Lord Borthwick,** b. 9 Feb. 1616, held out his castle of Borthwick against Cromwell to whom he surrendered on honourable terms, 18 Nov. 1650. He m. 23 Aug. 1649, Elizabeth, 2nd dau. of William Kerr, Earl of Lothian, and d.s.p. between 13 Mar. 1673/74 and 27 Nov. 1675, aged about 58.

From the death of the 9th Lord Borthwick, the title remained dormant for 90 years, and

was not assumed by any member of the family, until it was adjudged in 1762. The succession to the barony should have gone through the following:

Major William Borthwick, de jure **10th Lord Borthwick,** see above, as son of William Borthwick, of Soltray etc., served in the Army, m. 28 April 1665 Marion Moorhead, and lived until 7 June 1687 when his ygst. child, Robert, was baptized and d. before 28 June 1690. His only surv. son and heir,

William Borthwick, **11th Lord Borthwick** de jure, was bapt. 8 Feb. 1666. He was a Capt. in the Cameronian Regt., 1689, and a Col. in the Army. He m. Jean, dau. of Robert Kerr, of Kersland, and d.s.p. being slain at Ramilies, 12/23 May 1706, where he was bur. The peerage should have passed to his cousin and male heir, see above,

Henry Borthwick, of Pilmuir, de jure **12th Lord Borthwick,** who m. Mary, dau. of Sir Robert Pringle, 1st Bt. of Stichill, and was mortally wounded at Ramilies, 1706 and d. 16/27 May 1706, leaving issue,

1. William, of Pilmuir, de jure, **13th Lord Borthwick,** who d.s.p. before 28 Nov. 1723.
2. Henry, **14th Lord Borthwick** (see below).

The ygr. son, Henry Borthwick, **14th Lord Borthwick,** was in 1727, served heir male general to the first Lord. He voted from 1734 to 1762 at elections of Scots peers, but was then ordered by the House of Lords to abstain from voting until he had established his right. This he did on 8 April, 1762, by a successful petition to the House, being found heir male of the body of the 1st Lord Borthwick. He m. 5 Mar. 1770, Margaret, dau. of George Drummond, of Broich, co. Stirling and d.s.p. 6 Sept. 1772. At his death the title again became dormant for 98 years until adjudged in 1870. The succession would have gone through, Patrick Borthwick, **15th Lord Borthwick,** de jure, (see above under Alexander, of Reidhall; he was a merchant in Leith, who m. Marion Scott, and d. 6 Oct. 1772, having issue, Archibald Borthwick, de jure **16th Lord Borthwick,** b. 13 May 1732, at Inveresk, and was a merchant in Norway, later in Edinburgh, and as he was in Norway he did not present his claim to the peerage until 1807, and the House considered it 1808-10, and again 1812-13. It is stated that in 1774 John Borthwick of Crookston had presented a claim on the ground that he was descended from a ygr. son of the 1st Lord, but no judgment was pronounced on his claim. When the claim of 1808 was presented, but opposed by the son of the 1774 claimant who now rested his case on a denial of the legitimacy of Alexander Borthwick of Nenthorn, a plea which struck at the right of Henry, 14th Lord Borthwick, adjudged the peer in 1762. As there was a discrepancy between the pedigree submitted in 1762 and that asserted by the claimant, Archibald, (which arose from the accidental omission of a generation in the former), the Committee of Privileges allowed the question to be opened up. The matter was not then decided. The de jure 16th Lord d. 13 July 1815, aged 83, and left issue,

Patrick Borthwick, de jure **17th Lord Borthwick,** b. 12 Sept. 1779, manager of the National Bank of Scotland, Edinburgh, who claimed the peerage 8 April, 1816. He m.

13 Nov. 1804, Ariana, dau. of Cunninghame Corbet, of Tolcross, and of Glasgow, merchant, and d. 12 April 1840, leaving issue,

Archibald Borthwick, **18th Lord Borthwick,** de jure, b. 31 Aug. 1811; m. 1 Aug. 1840, Mary Louisa, dau. of John Home Home, of Longformacus, and d.s.p.m.s. 3 July 1863, with two daus.,

1. Louisa Ramsay, m. 3 June 1873, Lt. Col. Henry Philip Miles Wylie, K.R.R.C.
2. Mary Catherine, m. 27 April 1870, William George Spens, and had issue.

The de jure 18th Lord Borthwick was s. by his brother, Cunninghame Borthwick, **19th Lord Borthwick,** b. 16 June 1813; educ. High School and Univ. of Edinburgh, mem. of London Stock Exchange, 1853-77; bought estate of Ravenstone, co. Wigtown, 1870, advanced claim to peerage which was allowed 5 May 1870, and was a representative peer from 1880 to his death. He m. 18 July 1865, Harriet Alice, dau. of Thomas Hermitage Day, of Frinsbury, Kent, and of Rochester, Banker, and d. 24 Dec. 1885, having had issue,

1. Archibald Patrick Thomas, **20th Lord Borthwick** (see below).
1. Gabrielle Margaret Ariana, b. 30 June 1866.
2. Alice Rachel Anne, b. 17 Dec. 1868; m. 5 July 1893, Alexander Stratton Campbell of Swaffam, Norfolk.
3. Violet Dagma Marion Aga, b. 3 June 1871; m. 22 Nov. 1900, Capt. Lewis G. Freeland and had issue.
4. Mary Frances Harriet, b. 11 Feb. 1876; m. 1 July 1897, Harold Chaloner Dowdall, B.C.L., Barrister-at-Law, Inner Temple, of Liverpool.

The only son and heir, Archibald Patrick Thomas Borthwick, **20th Lord Borthwick,** b. 3 Sept. 1867; educ. Glenalmond, and Ch. Ch. Oxford; partner in firm of Borthwick, Wark and Co. stockbrokers, a representative peer from 1906 to his death. He m. 18 July, 1901, Susanna Mary, dau. of Sir Mark John McTaggart-Stewart, 1st Bt., and d. 4 Oct. 1910, His widow m. 2ndly, the Earl of Euston, son of 7th Duke of Grafton. The 20th Lord left issue, an only child,

Isolde Frances, b. 2 Feb. 1903.

At his death the title became extinct or dormant.

ARMS—Argent three cinquefoils sable.

CREST—A moor's head couped ppr.

SUPPORTERS—Two angels, ppr. winged or.

MOTTO—Qui conducit.

NOTE. In vol. 2 of *B.L.G.* (1969) John Henry Stewart Borthwick of Borthwick, T.D., was described as Feudal Lord of Borthwick, Castle, and as claiming to be 24th Lord Borthwick, in the Peerage of Scotland, Baron of Heriotmuir, 17th of Crookston, Midlothian, and as officially recognized by Lyon Court, as Borthwick of Borthwick and in that surname, 26 July 1944. The descent is stated as from John Borthwick second son of the 1st Lord Borthwick. He is said to be mentioned in a instrument of 24 June 1458, (the authenticity of parts whereof had been questioned by the Cttee. of Privileges, in 1808, but which after modern scientific investigation was judicially sustained as genuine by the Lyon Court, 26 July 1944).

BOSSOM

PEERAGE—U.K. Life. Baron Bossom of Maidstone, co. Kent.

SURNAME—Bossom.

CR.—20 Jan. 1960. **EXT.**—4 Sept. 1965.

HISTORY—Sir Alfred Charles Bossom, 1st Bart, and **Baron Bossom,** was b. 6 Oct. 1881, the son of Alfred Henry Bossom (see current peerages, Bossom Bt.); educ. St. Thomas, Charterhouse and Royal Acad. of Arts; F.R.I.B.A., had a very distinguished career as an architect and was Chm. and member of very many organizations; M.P. Maidstone, 1931-59, cr. a Baronet, 4 July 1953 and a life peer as Baron Bossom of Maidstone, co. Kent, 30 Jan. 1960; had numerous foreign orders. He m. (1) 26 April 1910, Emily, dau. of S. G. Bayne, of New York and had issue,

1. Bruce Bayne, b. 25 March 1911.
2. Clive, Hon. Sir, 2nd Bt. (see Extant Baronetcy).
3. Doric, b. 3 May 1922, m. 1949, June dau. of Vernon Bertram Longworth of Clevedon Court, Port Elizabeth, S. Africa, and d. 14 Oct. 1959 having had issue,
    Doric Alfred Howard, b. posthumously 27 Feb. 1960.

Mrs. Emily Bossom was k. with her eldest son in an air crash 27 July 1932. Alfred Charles Bossom m. (2) 30 July 1934 (m. diss. by div.), Elinor, dau. of S. Dittenhofer, of Minnesota, U.S.A. Lord Bossom d. 4 Sept. 1965 when he was s. in the baronetcy by his only surv. son, the Hon. Sir Clive Bossom, 2nd Bt.

ARMS—Gules a representation of a steel building column and three floor girders with wind bracing projecting therefrom to the sinister or, on a chief or an antique lamp inflamed sable, between on the dexter a rose gules barbed and seeded ppr., and on the sinister a thistle leaved and slipped also ppr.

CREST—Upon a mount vert an oak tree fructed charged with an eye irradiated ppr.

SUPPORTERS—Dexter, A Knight of the Shire in the time of Charles I; Sinister, A Green Mountain Boy of the American Revolutionary Force at Ticonderoga, both ppr.

MOTTO—Esto quod es.

(Lord Bossom had in 1908 undertaken the restoration of Ticonderoga Fort.)

BOWEN

PEERAGE—U.K. Life Baron Bowen, of Colwood, co. Sussex.

SURNAME—Bowen.

CR.—23 Sept. 1893. **EXT.**—10 April 1894.

HISTORY—Robert Bowen, of Ballyadama, Queen's Co., was granted that property and other lands in Queen's Co., by patent dated 31 Aug. 1578; apptd. Provost Marshall of Province of Leinster, and of cos. of West and East Meath; 1595; m. Alice, dau. of Walter Hartpole, of Rochester, Kent, and d. 31 July, 1621. She d. 4 June 1634. They had issue,

1. John, Sir, of whom below.
2. Oliver, who during the rebellion of 1641, went to Haskard, co. Pembroke, where he d.s.p. at home of his kinsman, Philip Bowen.
3. Thomas, of Liskellen, m. Elizabeth, dau.

of Gilbert Edmund, and had issue, a son Edmund, and whose grandson, Oliver, k. in a fight at Castlebar, co. Mayo, left a son, William, see below, the eventual heir of the house.

1. Margaret, m. Alexander Barrington, of Cullenagh, Queen's Co.
2. Margery, m. Henry Brereton, of Loughteog, Queen's Co.
3. Elizabeth, m. James Freeman, of Gishiden, co. Mayo.
4. Alice, m. Pierce Butler, of Castle Comer, co. Kilkenny.
5. Susan, m. Robert Hovenden, of Ballytoile, Queen's Co.
6. Mabel, m. Robert Hetherington, of Boherard, Queen's Co.

The eldest son, Sir John Bowen, of Ballyadama, which was regranted to him with special remainder that succession to the property could pass to the heirs male of the body of his grandfather; (patent of 16 April 1636), knighted 13 Nov. 1629; m. Alice ,dau. of Most Rev. Meyler Magrath, Archbishop of Cashel, and d. 9 Feb. 1641, having had issue, with an eldest son, Robert who d.s.p. and other sons, Henry, Arthur, Thomas and George, a second son and successor. William Bowen, of Ballyadama, m. (1) Bridget, dau. of Sir Robert Tynte, of Funlavin, co. Wicklow, and had issue,

1. Helena, m. Edward Brereton, of Loughteog.
2. Katherine, m. Pierce Butler, of Kilvelough.

He m. (2) Margaret, dau. of Sir William Domvile, of Templeogue, Attorney Gen. for Ireland ancestor of the Domvile Bts., and had in addition,

1. John, of whom presently.
3. Bridget, m. Thomas Carr.
4. Mary, d. unm.
5. Lucy, m. William Southwell.

William Bowen d. 11 April 1686, and was s. by his only son, John Bowen, of Ballyadama, who d.s.p. and also intestate, so that administration was granted 19 Jan. 1691 to his mother. The ultimate heir to his estates was his sister Mrs. Southwell, but his kinsman, (see above) became the male representative of the family, William Bowen, of Hollymount, co. Mayo, who by his wife, Sarah Blake had two sons,

1. Christopher, of whom presently.
2. William, m. Ellen Burke, and d. 1786 having had a son, Christopher.

The elder son, Christopher Bowen, of Hollymount, m. Anne Allen, and d. 1812, having had by his wife, a dau., Ann who m. Anthony Elwood, and had a son, Anthony, who took the name of Bowen. Mr. Christopher Bowen was s. by his nephew, Christopher Bowen, of Hollymount, m. 1800, Eliza, dau. of Crossdale Miller of Milford. She d. 1815. He d. 1828. Their children were,

1. Christopher, Rev. of whom below.
2. Croasdale, of Milford, who assumed by Royal Licence, 1 Feb. 1812, the name and arms of Miller.
3. Charles, m. Georgina, dau. of Joseph Lambert, of Brookhill, co. Mayo, and d. 1871, having had issue, with a dau. Letitia, two sons, who went to New Zealand, where they m.,
   (1) Charles Croasdale, m. Georgina Markham.

(2) Croasdale, m. Annette Wyles.
4. Robert, m. Jane Courtenay, of Drumselk, co. Down, and d. 1882.
5. William. 6. Edward.
1. Anne. 2. Elizabeth.

The elder son, The Rev. Christopher Bowen, of Hollymount, Rector of St. Thomas, Winchester, m. 1833, Catherine Emily, dau. of Sir Richard Steele, 3rd Bt., and d. 1890, leaving issue,

1. Charles Synge Christopher, **Baron Bowen** (see below).
2. Edward Ernest, b. Mar. 1836. Fell. Trin, Coll. Camb.

The elder son, Sir Charles Synge Christopher Bowen, **Baron Bowen**, b. 29 Aug. 1831, at Woolaston near Chepstow; educ. Rugby and Balliol Coll. Oxford, Scholar 1854; 1st class mods. 1856; Fell. 1857; B.A. and 1st Class, Pres. of Oxford Union, 1858; Hertford Scholarship 1855, Ireland Scholarship and Latin Verse Prize, 1857, and Arnold Prize, 1859; M.A. 1872. Barrister-at-Law, Lincoln's Inn, 1861; Junior Standing Counsel to Treasury and Recorder of Penzance, 1872; apptd. Judge of the Queen's Bench Div. of High Court of Justice, 1879-82, and cr. Kt. Bach. 1879; a Lord Justice of Appeal, 1882-93; made P.C. 1882; F.R.S. 1885; D.C.L. 1883 Oxford; Hon. LL.D. Edinburgh, 1888; made a Lord of Appeal in Ordinary 23 Sept. 1893, and cr. a Baron for life as Baron Bowen of Colwood, Sussex. Trustee of British Museum, 1893. He m. 7 Jan. 1862, Emily Frances, dau. of James Meadows Rendel, of Plymouth (see Rendel, B. in present work), and d.s.p. 10 April 1894. Lady Bowen d. 24 Mar. 1897. Lord Bowen's reputation as a great judge is enshrined in many law reports of cases which are found in all text books of the English law. After his death he was described by the Master of the Rolls, Lord Esher, as the most distinguished judge who had sat in an English Court during the period of more than 50 years in which Lord Esher had been conversant with those Courts.

ARMS—(of Bowen of Ballyadama)—Argent on a mount vert a stag lodged gules attired and unguled or. in the mouth a trefoil slipped vert.
CREST—On a mount vert in front of an oak tree ppr. acorned or, a stag as in the arms.

BOWLES

PEERAGE—U.K. Life Baron Bowles of Nuneaton, co. Warwick.
SURNAME—Bowles.
CR.—12 Dec. 1964. **EXT.**—29 Dec. 1970.
HISTORY—Francis Dominic Bowles, Common Councilman, City of London, and Chm. Pearl Assurance Co. Ltd., 1916-26, b. 1 Mar. 1851; m. 1873, dau. of Frederick Marsh, of Leicester, and d. 28 June 1926. She d. 1934. They had issue, Horace Edgar Bowles, F.R.I.C., of Caryl, Freshwater, I. of W., b. 5 Sept. 1874 m. (1) July 1901, Louisa, dau. of Rev. G. H. Vance, B.D., and by her who d. 8 July 1958, had issue,

1. Francis George, **Baron Bowles** (see below).
2. Roger Vincent, b. 4 July 1903; educ. Highgate and Univ. Coll. Hosp. M.D., M.R.D.S., L.R.C.P., Pres. Agricultural

Soc. of Kenya; m. (1) Evelyn, dau. of E. I. Greaves, and had issue,

(1) John Robin, Rev., b. 7 Jan. 1930; educ. Eton and Magdalene Coll. Camb.; Barrister-at-Law, Inner Temple, 1954, took Holy Orders, 1963.

(1) Margaret, b. 4 July 1932.

(2) Anne Marie, b. 12 Feb. 1937.

He m. (2) 1938, Patricia, dau. of Dr. Percy Bowles, of St. George's Hill, Weybridge, co. Surrey, and had further issue,

(2) Benjamin Roger, b. 28 Jan. 1940; educ. Sedbergh and McGill Univ.

3. Cecil Vance, b. 23 Nov. 1905; educ. Univ. Coll. London, B.Sc. 1927; Dip. Civil and Municipal Engineering, 1937, A.M.I.C.E. 1937, Fell. Inst. of Work Study, 1953; m. (1) 1930, Miriam, dau. of W. E. Searle, and had issue,

(1) Francis Dudley, b. 1931; educ. Glasgow Sch. of Art.

(1) Carole Miriam, b. 1933.

(2) Jacqueline Mary, b. 1938; m. 1961, R. M. Basker, and had issue.

He m. (2) Monica Elizabeth, dau. of Ernest Barker, and had further issue,

(3) Judith Anne, b. 1944.

(4) Rebecca Louise, b. 1960.

4. Terence Michael, b. 1908; d. 1957.

5. Vivian Horace, b. 30 Mar. 1910; educ. Dunstable Sch., Guy's Hospital and St. George's Hospital, L.D.S., R.C.S., M.R.C.S., L.R.C.P. 1938, D.M.R. 1951; srved in R.A.M.C. as Major; m. Sept. 1950, Zoe, dau. of William Peacock, and had issue,

(1) Melanie Jane, b. 1951,

(2) Stephanie Ann, b. 1953.

Horace Edgar Bowles m. (2) 1959, Agnes Michel, dau. of Rev. G. H. Vance, B.D. and d. 5 Jan. 1965. The eldest son, Francis George Bowles, **Baron Bowles**, of Nuneaton, co. Warwick, b. 2 May 1902; educ. Highgate, Univ. Coll. London, LL.B. 1923, and London Sch. of Economics, B.Sc. 1926; Admitted a Solicitor, 1925; Solicitor with Pearl Assurance Co. 1925-47; M.P. for Nuneaton, 1942-64; Vice Chm. Parl. Labour Party 1946-48; Dep. Chm. of Ways and Means, 1948-50; Capt. the Queen's Bodyguard the Yeomen of The Guard, 1964-70; Freeman of City of London; Adm. of Port of Brixham Trawler Race Asscn.; was cr. a life peer as Baron Bowles, of Nuneaton, co. Warwick, 12 Dec. 1964; m. 25 May 1950, Kathleen Amy, dau. of E. H. Musgrove, of Aelybryn, Dowlais, Glam., and widow of A. Cdre. E. D. M. Hopkins. He d. 29 Dec. 1970.

ARMS—Per chevron gules and or, in chief two boars' heads erect in standing bowls and in base a harp all counterchanged.

CREST—A dexter hand couped at the wrist grasping a pomegranate slipped and leaved ppr.

MOTTO—Creidimh gan Cealg.

Lord Bowles's residences were Redwells, Brixham, co. Devon and 88 St. James's Street, S.W.1.

BOYD-ORR

PEERAGE—U.K. Baron Boyd-Orr, of Brechin Mearns, co. Angus.

SURNAME—Boyd-Orr.

CR.—9 Mar. 1949. EXT.—25 June, 1971.

HISTORY—Robert Orr, by his wife, Mary (dau. of Andrew Clark, of Cubnishaw, West Kilbride, co. Ayr) had a son, Robert Clark Orr, described as a bonnet laird, a small property owner and quarrymaster, b. 1842; m. 1870, Annie Morton, (described in *The Times* obituary notice as a woman of strong intellect and determination, qualities which were as pronounced in her son as the "Boyd" which he put into his title) dau. of James Boyd, of Ardeer, Setevenson, co. Ayr and d. April 1914. She d. 1931. Their children were,

1. John, **Baron Boyd-Orr** (see below).

2. Robert, who had issue, Robert Clark, of 12 Baliol Street, Charing Cross, Glasgow.

3. William who left issue, Robert Clark and Arthur.

4. James, Capt. k. in action.

5. Andrew, Rev., M.A. Min. Emeritus, Borthwick, Midlothian.

1. Mary, b. April 1870; d. unm. 20 Dec. 1941.

2. Annie Boyd, of Borthwick Bank, Saltcoats, co. Ayr.

The eldest son, Sir John Boyd-Orr, **Baron Boyd-Orr,** was b. 23 Sept. 1880; educ. West Kilbride Public Sch., and Glasgow Univ. M.A. 1901. He taught in school for 4 years, then returned to Glasgow Univ. to study medicine. He graduated, gained Barbour Scholarship, and with his M.D. thesis, 1914 the Bellahouston Gold Medal; he then became for one month a locum tenens but returned to the university to study metabolic disease, and became D.Sc. 1919; served in World War I, winning M.C. with bar, and the D.S.O. in R.A.M.C. as regimental medical officer with the Sherwood Foresters, later transferring to the R.N. and serving in the Q. ships. He became F.R.S. 1932. F.R.S.E.,' Dir. Rowett Research Inst. Aberdeen, and of Scottish Board of Guardians, Insce. Co., Pres. Northern Dairies Ltd., and Dir. Gen. of Food and Agric. Organization U.N. 1945-48; was M.P. for Scottish Univs. 1945-47; Rector of Glasgow Univ. 1945-47 and Chancellor from 1947; he received the Nobel Peace Prize. He m. 21 Feb. 1915, Elizabeth Pearson, dau. of J. B. Callum, of West Kilbride co. Ayr. They had issue,

1. Donald Noel Boyd, b. 19 May 1921; served in World War II in R.A.F., and was k. in action Dec. 1941, on a Coastal Command mission.

1. Elizabeth Boyd, a doctor, b. 8 June 1916; m. 22 Aug. 1943, Lt. Col. Kenneth A. J. Barton, and had issue.

2. Helen Anne Boyd, a sculptor, b. 12 May 1919; m. David Miles Lubbock, (Avebury, B.). and had issue.

He was cr. Kt. Bach. 1935, C.H. 1968, and a peer as Baron Boyd-Orr, of Brechin Mearn, co. Angus 9 Mar. 1949. He d. 25 June 1971.

ARMS—Argent three piles conjoined in point gules each charged with a wheat ear or; on a chief chequy gules, and argent, a pale azure charged with an estoile of six rays argent.

CREST—On a dexter hand, couped at the wrist, a dove rising, her wings elevated, holding in her beak an olive twig.

SUPPORTERS—Two wheat sheaves all ppr.

MOTTO—Panis et pax.

Lord Boyd-Orr's residence was Newton of

PLATE 4

MARQUESS OF BREADALBANE.

EARL BROWNLOW.

BARON BURGHCLERE.

VISCOUNT BURNHAM.

BARON BURTON.

EARL OF CAMPERDOWN.

PLATE 5

VISCOUNT CANTERBURY.

BARON CARMICHAEL.

EARL OF CARYSFORT.

BARON CASTLETOWN.

EARL OF CHESTERFIELD.

MARQUESS OF CLANRICARDE.

Stracathro, Brechin, Angus. His clubs were Athenaeum, Farmers', Royal Scottish Automobile, and Strathcona, (Aberdeen).

BRACKEN

PEERAGE—U.K. Viscount Bracken of Christchurch, co. Southampton.
SURNAME—Bracken.
CR.—8 Jan. 1952. **EXT.**—8 Aug. 1958.
HISTORY—Brendan Bracken, **Viscount Bracken**, a prominent politician and business man, was b. 1901, the son of J. K. A. Bracken of Ardvillen House, Kilmallock, co. Limerick, Ireland, his father d. 1906, his mother m. 2ndly Patrick Loffan.

Brendan Bracken was educated in Sydney and at Sedbergh; he was a member of the House of Commons for 22 years, being M.P. for North Paddington, 1929-45, for Bournemouth 1945-50, and for East Bournemouth and Christchurch, 1950-51.

In Sir John Wheeler Bennett's life of *King George VI* (1959), p. 356 there is a note in which Bracken is mentioned, 'After the resignation of Mr. Eden the dissident Tories were divided into two groups: the followers of Mr. Churchill, consisting of Mr. Brendan Bracken etc.' Bracken's Ministerial appointments were all under the Churchill Gov. of 1940-45. He was Parl. Priv. Sec. to the Prime Minister 1940-41, Minister of Information 1941-48 and First Lord of the Admiralty in the 'Caretaker' Administration in 1945. In the six volumes of Winston Churchill's memoirs of the Second World War he is frequently mentioned. Bracken's business directorships were: Director of Eyre and Spottiswoode Ltd., 1924-40; Chm. Financial News, 1928-40 and Man. Dir. *The Economist* 1940-41. He was made a P.C. 1940 and a Viscount 1952. He d. 8 Aug. 1858.

Lord Bracken lived at 8 North Street, London S.W.1. He was a member of White's and Bucks.

To the above somewhat meagre account may be added the following: From the *Irish Times*, of 9 Aug. 1958. "Viscount Bracken, the Limerick born mem. of S.W.C.'s wartime cabinet . . . son of a Templemore, co. Tipperary building contractor, the late J. Kevin Bracken who was one of the seven men who met in Thurles in 1884 to found the Gaelic A.A. and who became vice president of the Assoc. Viscount Bracken was related to Sir Winston Churchill through Mrs. Morton Frewen of Cork, an aunt of the British wartime leader. Spent his childhood at Ardvillen, co. Limerick and was educated at Belvedere Coll. Dublin and at Mungret Coll. Limerick. Most of his teens were spent with relatives in Australia. 1919, he returned from Australia and was appointed to teaching staff of Winchester Sch. before going to London. In 1945 he was appointed chm. of the Union Corporation, an immense financial and mining concern, which carried a salary reputed to have been between £15 and £20,000 p.a. His mother, Mrs. Hannah Bracken, was at one time Chm. of Templemore, co. Tipperary, U.D.C." (The Frewen family referred to above, are the Frewens of Northiam, B.L.G. 1952.) From *The Times*, 9 Aug. 1958. An observer said "he seemed to have conquered London, to have got to know everyone, to have been able to make the most important do his bidding before he was 30." ". . . son of the late J. K. A. Bracken of Ardvillen House, Kilmallock, co. Limerick, he was sent to Australia at an early age and had most of his schooling in Sydney; but in 1920 (having it is strongly believed, made his own choice among the public schools) he turned up at Sedbergh, a self assured young man with his own cheque book, who entered himself and paid his own fees. He remained at Sedbergh for less than a year, but even in that short time he impressed the staff by his adult mind, his interest in world affairs and his skill as a debater. Going to no university Bracken turned his attention to the newspaper world. Having both money and ability, this precocious young man was already in 1922 running *English Life* with Robert Lutyens. One of the important elements in his early business career was his connection with the Eyre family and the family publishing firm of Eyre and Spottiswoode. He formed this friendship early in life with the Eyres and from a young age he was a director of E. and S. and a trustee of the principal Eyre family trust. The Eyre family and publishing interests were in effect his partners in the formation of the publishing group which he constituted in the 1920s. The group included *The Financial News, Investors Chronicle, The Banker, The Practitioner*, a controlling interest in the *Liverpool Journal of Commerce*, and a half share in *The Economist*. These various interests were acquired during a short period and were organized under a general umbrella of a holding company called Financial Newspaper Proprietors of which he was managing director. He was keenly interested in architecture as an intelligent layman, and when the Liverpool R.C. Cathedral was mooted he passed word to the Archbishop, Dr. Downey, by Prof. Reilly that if Sir Edwin Lutyens was appointed architect he would subscribe munificently towards the funds. He was Chm. of the Board of Govs. of Sedbergh, and apptd. Trustee of the Nat. Gallery in 1955. Bracken was a tall man with a great mass of ginger hair. He was well read, quick and a remarkably fertile conversationalist, of whom it had been said that 'conversation was his hobby'. He shared Sir Winston Churchill's liking for a good cigar. He had a pretty wit, and many anecdotes have been collected about its exercise. One of these may bear relating. On his entry into Parliament he was asked what he thought of the new Prayer Book. 'My dear sir,' he answered 'we print it.' " Lord Bracken left a request that there should be no funeral and no memorial service. Tributes were paid to him in *The Times* from the son of the head of Sedbergh during his time there, by Lord Moran and Sir Geoffrey Crowther. These tributes spoke of his devotion to Sedbergh and to Sir Winston Churchill.

BRAINTREE

PEERAGE—U.K. Baron Braintree of Braintree, co. Essex.
SURNAME—Crittall.
CR.—9 Feb. 1948. **EXT.**—21 May 1961.
HISTORY—Valentine George Crittall, a great

industrialist and a Socialist was b. 28 June 1884. His grandparents were Francis Berrington Crittall, and Fanny Crittall (née Godfrey), his father was Francis Henry Crittall, J.P., of Manors, Silver End, Witham, co. Essex, b. 1860; m. 6 Sept. 1883 Ellen Laura, dau. of George Carter of Birmingham and d. 1935. She d. 1934. They had four children, three sons and a dau., the eldest being, Valentine George Crittall, **Baron Braintree**, educ. at Uppingham, Chm. of Crittall Manufacturing Co. Ltd., and of many associated companies in England and abroad. Past President of Institute of Works Managers, J.P. Essex, M.P. for Maldon Div. of Essex, 1923-24, Parl. Priv. Sec. for Air, 1924 in first Labour Gov., but lost seat in 1924 general election. He was made a Kt. Bach. 1930, became a Director of the Bank of England 1948-55, and made a peer 1948. Lord Braintree was married three times. (1) 28 June 1915 to Olive Lillian, dau. of Charles Landay MacDermott, of Comber, Ontario, Canada. She d. 1932. (2) 1933 to Lydia Mabel, dau. of J. J. Revy and widow of Frank C. R. Reed. She d. 1947. (3) 1955 to Phyllis Dorothy, dau. of Curtis Cloutman, of Bristol and widow of George Henry Nelson Parker. He d. in 1961. By his first marriage Lord Braintree had three daus.

1. Hon. Valentine Ellen MacDermott, b. 1918, m. 1939 Karl Stewart Richardson of Hungry Hall, Witham, Essex, and had issue.
2. Hon. Jane Olive, b. 1921, m. 1947, T. A. T. Hall of 6, Windsor Terrace, Clifton, Bristol, and had issue.
3. Hon. Mary Frances, b. 1922, m. 1950 Germano Luigi Facetti, of 51, Gloucester Avenue, London N.W.1. and had issue.

Lord Braintree lived at Queen's Meadow, Bocking, Braintree, Essex.
ARMS—Argent fretty sable on a chief gules two fleurs-de-lis argent.
CREST—Within a mascle sable a sun in splendour or.
SUPPORTERS—Dexter, A blacksmith holding in the exterior hand a hammer. Sinister, A glazier holding in the exterior hand a file all ppr.
MOTTO—Why not?

BRAMPTON

PEERAGE—U.K. Baron Brampton of Brampton, co. Huntingdon.
SURNAME—Hawkins.
CR.—27 Jan. 1899. **EXT.**—6 Oct. 1907.
HISTORY—John Hawkins, solicitor of Hitchin, co. Herts, m. Susanna, dau. of Theed Pearse, of Bedford and had issue, Sir Henry Hawkins, **Baron Brampton**, b. 14 Sept. 1817; educ. Bedford; Barrister-at-Law Middle Temple 1843, Q.C. 1858 and Bencher, 1859. apptd a Judge of the High Court of Justice 2 Nov. 1876, transferred to the Exchequer Div. by sign manual, 14 Nov. 1876 and retired from Bench 1 Jan. 1899; cr. Kt. Bach. 1876, made a P.C. and cr. Baron Brampton of Brampton, co. Huntingdon 27 Jan. 1899. He m. (1) — Casey (d. 10 Sept. 1886) and (2) 17 Aug. 1887, Jane Louisa (d. 17 Nov. 1907) dau. of Henry Francis Reynolds of Hulme, Lancashire, and d. 6 Oct. 1907.

ARMS—Ermine, on a saltire azure, between in chief a balance ppr. and in base on a mount vert, a hind lodged ppr., three fleur-de-lis or.
CREST—On a fasces lying fesswise blade upwards ppr. a fox passant or.
SUPPORTERS—On either side a hawk standing on a fasces ppr. and gorged with a collar flory counter flory azure.
MOTTO—Toujours prest.

BRAMWELL

PEERAGE—U.K. Baron Bramwell of Hever, co. Kent.
SURNAME—Bramwell.
CR.—3 Feb. 1882. **EXT.**—9 May 1892.
HISTORY—George Bramwell, of London, a banker, who d. 15 Sept. 1858, aged 85, had with other issue,

1. George William Wilshire, **Baron Bramwell** (see below).
2. (third son) Frederick Joseph, Sir, Bt., b. 7 Mar. 1818; an engineer, apprenticed to John Hague, London engineer, 1834; studied methods of steam propulsion, and as manager to Hague, constructed a locomotive for Stockton and Darlington Railway, 1843; began business for himself, 1853; developed legal and consultative side of the engineering profession, and became adviser to all London water cos. and built sewage disposal scheme for Portsmouth; mem. Inst. of Mechanical Engineers, 1854, and Pres. 1874, Pres. of British Asscn. at Bath, 1888, and of Royal Soc. of Arts, 1901 Chm. of City and Guilds Inst. 1878-1903; cr. Kt. Bach. 1881; F.R.S. 1873; cr. Baronet 25 Jan. 1889; predicted supercession of the steam engine by the internal combustion engine, 1881. He m. 29 Mar. 1847 his first cousin, Harriet Leonora, dau. of Joseph Frith, and d. 30 Nov. 1903, having had issue,
   (1) George Frederick, (1851-58).
   (1) Harriet Eliza, (1848-52).
   (2) Laura, m. 21 July 1882, Harald Ehrenborg, of Liverpool, Swedish Consul and d. 10 May 1883.
   (3) Eldred, m. 4 Oct. 1887, Sir Victor A. H. Horsley, F.R.S. and had issue.
   (4) Florence m. 6 Nov. 1900, Sir Henry W. Bliss, K.C.I.E.

The eldest son, Sir George William Wilshire Bramwell, **Baron Bramwell**, b. 12 June 1808; Barrister-at-Law, Inner Temple, and Lincoln's Inn, 1838; Q.C. 1851; Bencher, Inner Temple, 1851; a Baron of the Exchequer, 1856-76; cr. Kt. Bach. 1856; made P.C. 1876; a Lord Justice of Appeal, 1876-81; cr. a peer as Baron Bramwell, of Hever, Kent, 3 Feb. 1882; F.R.S. 1882. He m. (1) 1830, in New York, Mary Jane, dau. of Bruno Silva. She d.s.p.m. 13 April 1836. He m. (2) 1861, Martha Sinden. She d. 5 June, 1879. He d.s.p. 9 May 1892. Baron Bramwell is described as having one dau. by his first wife, (1886 Burke's Peerage).
ARMS—Per fess ermine and azure a pale counterchanged, three griffins sergreant one and two argent.
CREST—Two lions' gambs in saltire or supporting a sword in fess ppr.
MOTTO—Diligenter.

BRAND

PEERAGE—U.K. Baron Brand, of Eydon, co. Northampton.
SURNAME—Brand.
CR.—17 July 1946. EXT.—23 Aug. 1963.
HISTORY—Henry Robert Brand, 2nd Viscount Hampton and 24th Baron Dacre, had a fourth son, The Hon. Robert Henry Brand, **Baron Brand**, b. 30 Oct. 1878; educ. Marlborough and New Coll. Oxford, B.A. 1901, M.A., 1905, Hon. Fellow, Fellow of All Souls, D.C.L. (Hon.) Oxford 1937; was Sec. International Colonial Council S. Africa 1902-09, Vice Pres. International Financial Conf., Brussels, 1920, Head of the British Food Mission to U.S.A. 1941-44, and British Treasury representative there, 1944-46; held many directorships being Man. Dir. of Lazard Bros., chm. North British and Mercantile Insurance Co., Director of Lloyd's Bank etc. Mr. Brand was created a C.M.G. in 1910 and made a peer in 1946. He m. 9 June 1917, Phyllis (d. 1937) dau. of Chiswell Dabney Langhorne, of Mirador, Greenwood, Virginia, U.S.A. They had a son and two daus., namely,
1. Robert James, b. 1923, served in second World War as Lt. Coldstream Guards and was k. on active service in western Europe in 1945.
1. Hon. Virginia, Lady Ford, b. 1918, m. 1stly 1929 John M. Polk who d. 1948, and 2ndly 1949 Sir Edward W. S. Ford and had issue by both marriages.
2. Hon. Dinah, b. 1920, m. 1stly 1943 Lyttleton Fox (divorce) and 2ndly 1953, Christopher C. C. Bridge and had issue by both marriages.
Lord Brand d. 23 Aug. 1963. His residence was Eydon Hall, Eydon, near Rugby, co. Northampton. He was a member of Brook's and the Athenaeum.
ARMS—Azure two swords in saltire points upwards argent, pommels and hilts or, between three escallops, one in chief and two in fesse or.
CREST—Out of a crown vallery or, a leopard's head argent semée of escallops and gorged with a collar gemel gules.
SUPPORTERS—Dexter, A wolf argent. Sinister, A bull gules bezanty armed and unguled or each gorged with a collar or.
MOTTO—Pour bien desirer.

BRASSEY

PEERAGE—U.K. Baron Brassey of Bulkeley, co. Chester, Earl Brassey, and Viscount Hythe of Hythe, co. Kent.
SURNAME—Brassey.
CR.—Barony 16 Aug. 1886, Earldom and Viscounty 5 July 1911. EXT.—12 Nov. 1919.
HISTORY—The account of the family as given in peerage works is extremely muddled, with a Ralph Brassey aged 21 in the Visitation of Cheshire of 1613, put as the great grandfather of Richard Brassey, whose age is given in the Visitation of Cheshire for 1663 as 68. It can be taken that the family were located in Cheshire from an early period. In the *C.P.*, Richard Brassey of 1663 is described as being descended from a Brassey who had acquired lands at Bulkeley, by marriage with one of the

Bulkeley family, and a quotation is given from Ormerod's *History of Cheshire* (1st edit. 1819, vol. ii. p. 363) as follows: "The Brassies continued resident there in great respectability for two and a half centuries. The family have retained their property but have sunk to the rank of yeomanry". Commencing then with Richard Brassie, of Bulkeley aged 68 at the Heralds' Visitation of Cheshire 1663; he m. 12 Oct. 1634, Eleanor, dau. of Edward Dutton of Hatton, and d. (bur. 17 April 1668 at Malpas) leaving with other issue, a fifth son,
Thomas Brassie of Bulkeley and of Buerton, co. Chester, d. 18 Dec. 1696, Elizabeth, dau. of Thomas Dulkeley of Bulkeley, and d. (bur. 30 March 1721) leaving issue an eldest son,
Thomas Brassie of Bulkeley, and Buerton, b. circa 1702; m. 10 Feb. 1729, Mary, dau. of George Harrison of Aldford, co. Chester. She d. 14 May 1776. He d. 2 May 1776. They had with other issue, a 4th son,
George Brassey, of Buerton, bapt. 31 May 1744; m. 17 Feb. 1768, Elizabeth Jackson, of Waverton, and d. 13 Nov. 1803 having by her (who d. 2 Feb. 1834 aged 84) had with other issue, a second son,
John Brassey, of Buerton, b. 19 May and bapt. 20 July 1778; m. 19 May 1805, Elizabeth (d. 31 March 1840) dau. of Ralph Perceval, of Haslington Hall, Cheshire and had issue,
1. Thomas (see below).
2. Ralph Perceval, b. 26 June 1808, d. 11 July 1830.
3. John, b. 29 Sept. 1811; d. 8 April 1829.
4. George of Cuddington Hall, Malpas, b. 19 Feb. 1816; m. 25 May 1841 Jane (d. 19 Jan. 1873) dau. of John Cawley of Swandley, co. Chester and had issue.
5. Richard, b. 14 June 1818, d. 15 Jan. 1836.
6. Robert, of the Grange, Bulkeley, b. 10 June 1822; m. 15 March 1843 Mary, dau. of Richard Dutton, of Bickerton, co. Chester and had issue.
1. Elizabeth, m. the Rev. James Wright, Vicar of St. James, Latchford, and d. 30 Nov. 1865 having had issue.
John Brassey, d. 28 Jan. 1831. His eldest son, Thomas Brassey of Bulkeley and of 56 Lawndas Square, London, (one of the greatest of railway contractors), b. 7 Nov. 1805; m. 20 Dec. 1831, Mary Farrington (d. 3 Jan. 1877), dau. of Joseph Harrison of Liverpool, and d. 8 Dec. 1870, having had issue,
1. Thomas, **Earl Brassey** (see below).
2. John, b. and d. 16 June 1839.
3. Henry Arthur, of Preston Hall, Aylesford, co. Kent, M.A., J.P. Kent, and High Sheriff 1890, M.P. Sandwich 1868-85, b. 14 July 1840; m. 24 June 1866, Anna Harriet (d. 15 July 1898) dau. of G. R. Stevenson, of Hawkhurst, Kent, and d. 13 May 1891 leaving issue.
4. Albert, of Heythorn Hall, Chipping Norton, co. Oxford, 14th Hussars, J.P., M.P. North Oxfordshire 1895, b. 22 Feb. 1844; m. 12 Jan. 1871, Matilda M. H. Bingham, dau. of 4th Lord Clanmorris and had issue.
The eldest son, Sir Thomas Brassey, **Earl Brassey**, b. 11 Feb. 1836; educ. Rugby and Univ. Coll. Oxford, B.A. 1859, M.A. 1862; Barrister-at-Law, Lincoln's Inn 1864; Liberal M.P. Devonport 1865, and Hastings 1868-86, a Lord of the Admiralty 1880-84, and Sec. to the Admiralty 1884-85. He was cr. K.C.B.

1881, Baron Brassey of Bulkeley co. Chester 16 Aug. 1886, G.C.B. 1906 and Viscount Hythe of Hythe, Kent, and Earl Brassey, 5th July 1911; m. (1) 9 Oct. 1860, Anna, only child of John Allnutt, of Clapham, Surrey. She d. 14 Sept. 1887 on board the yacht *Sunbeam* (of the voyage of which she had written giving account of her travels all over the world) and was bur. at sea off Port Darwin. By his first wife Earl Brassey had,

1. Thomas Allnutt, **2nd Earl** (see below).
1. Mabel Annie, L(J) St. J., m. 17 April 1888, C. A. Egerton (Egerton B.).
2. Constance Alberta, d. 24 Jan. 1873.
3. Muriel Agnes, m. 4 Aug. 1891 (m. diss. by div. 1902) 8th Earl de la Warr and had issue.
4. Marie Adelaide, m. 20 July 1892, 1st Baron Willingdon (Willingdon M.) and had issue.

The 1st Earl m. (2) 18 Sept. 1890, Sybil de Vere Capell, dau. of Viscount Malden (Essex, E.) and had further issue,

5. Helen de Vere, b. 4 Sept. 1892; m. 14 Aug. 1916, Major John Murray, Scottish Horse.

Earl Brassey was Gov. of Victoria 1895-1901. He d. 23 Feb. 1918 and was s. by his only son,

Thomas Allnutt Brassey, **2nd Earl Brassey,** b. 7 March 1863; M.A. Balliol Coll. Oxford; A.M.I.C.E., M. Inst. N.A. (on the Council), J.P. Sussex, K.G. St. J., served in S. African War 1900, acting Civil Commissioner of Pretoria, Mayor of Bexhill, 1909, Lt. Coll West Kent Yeo., had T.D., Hon. Fell. Ballio. Coll. Oxford; m. 27 Feb. 1889, Idina Mary (L. G. St. G.) and d.s.p. 12 Nov. 1919.

ARMS—Quarterly per fess indented sable and argent in the 1st quarter a mallard argent, beaked and legged gules.

CREST—A mallard argent, beaked and legged gules.

SUPPORTERS—On either side, a mallard argent, beaked, legged and collared gules, suspended from the collar an escutcheon of the arms of Bulkeley, viz. sable a chevron between three bulls' heads caboshed argent.

MOTTO—Arduis saepe, metu nunquam.

**BREADALBANE

PEERAGE—(1) U.K. Baron Breadalbane of Taymouth Castle, co. Perth, cr. 13 Nov. 1806; and Earl of Ormelie and Marquess of Breadalbane. CR.—12 Sept. 1831. EXT.—8 Nov. 1862.
(2) U.K. Baron Breadalbane of Kenmore, co. Perth, cr. 25 March 1873; and Earl of Ormelie, co. Caithness and Marquess of Breadalbane. CR.—11 July 1885. EXT.—19 Oct. 1922.

SURNAME—Campbell.

CR. and EXT.—as above.

HISTORY—The genealogy of the Earls of Breadalbane is given in the extant Peerages since their earldom is in the peerage of Scotland, but the two sets of U.K. peerages given above became extinct because in each respective case, the holder of the U.K. honours d.s.p., while the Scottish earldom, together with a baronetcy passed to kinsmen. John Campbell, 4th Earl of Breadalbane, b. 30 March 1762; educ. Winchester, was Rep-

resentative Peer for Scotland 1784-1806; F.R.S. 1784; Lt. Gen. in the Army 1814; cr. Baron Bredalbane of Taymouth Castle, co. Perth, 13 Nov. 1806, and **Earl of Ormelie and Marquess of Breadalbane,** 12 Sept. 1831, as one of the creations at the Coronation of William IV; m. 3 Sept. 1793, Mary Turner (d. 25 Sept. 1845) dau. of David Gavin of Langton House, co. Berwick and d. 29 March 1834, having had issue, with two daus. (see extant Peerage, Breadalbane, E.) an only son,

John Campbell, 5th Earl of Breadalbane (Scottish Peerage) and **2nd Marquess of Breadalbane** in the U.K. Peerage, b. 26 Oct. 1796; educ. Eton; M.P. (Whig) Okehampton 1820-26 and Perthshire 1832-34; F.R.S. 1834; K.T. 1838; Lord Chamberlain of the House-hold 1848-52, and 1853-58; Envoy Extra-ordinary to Prussia for the investiture of King William (afterwards German Emperor) with the Order of the Garter, 6 March 1861; m. 23 Nov. 1821, Eliza (d. 28 Aug. 1861) dau. of George Baillie (Haddington E.) and d.s.p. 8 Nov. 1862, when his U.K. peerages became extinct, but the Scottish earldom and baronetcy devolved on his cousin,

John Alexander Gavin Campbell, 6th Earl of Breadalbane (Scottish), b. 30 March 1824; m. 20 April 1853, Mary Theresa (d. 27 Feb. 1870) dau. of John Edwards of Dublin and d. 20 March 1871 having had with other issue, an eldest son,

Gavin Campbell, 7th Earl of Breadalbane and cr. **Baron Breadalbane** of Kenmore co. Perth, 25 March 1873, and Earl of Ormelie, co. Caithness and Marquess of Breadalbane, 11 July 1885, all in the U.K. Peerage. He was b. 9 April 1851; m. 27 July 1872, Alma Imogen Leonora Charlotta Graham, ygst. dau. of 4th Duke of Montrose and d.s.p. 19 Oct. 1922 when the Marquessate and other U.K. honours became extinct and the Scottish peerages devolved upon his nephew (see extant Peerage).

ARMS—Quarterly 1 and 4, Gyronny of eight or and sable (Campbell); 2, Argent a galley sable, sails furled oars in action, flags and pennons flying (Lorn); 3, Or a fesse chequy azure and argent (Stewart).

CREST—A boar's head erased ppr.

SUPPORTERS—Two stags ppr. attired and unguled or.

MOTTO—Follow me.

BROOKE OF OAKLEY

PEERAGE—U.K. Baron Brooke of Oakley, of Oakley, co. Northampton.

SURNAME—De Capell Brooke.

CR.—Barony 4 July 1939. EXT.—17 Nov. 1944.

HISTORY—Sir Arthur Richard De Capell Brooke, 5th Bt., and **1st Baron Brooke** of Oakley, s. his father as 4th Bt., in 1892 (see extant baronetcies). He was b. 12 Oct. 1869; educ. Eton and Ch. Ch. Oxford, B.A. 1893; Capt. and Hon. Major Northamptonshire Regt.; served in S. African War 1902, J.P. and D.L. and Chm. C.C. Northamptonshire, High Sheriff, Rutland 1899; three times stood for Parliament (unsuccessfully) Northamptonshire E. Div.; cr. Baron Brooke of Oakley, of Oakley, co. Northampton 4 July 1939; m. —— 1897, Fanny Cecil Talbot dau. of Capt. Duncan

McNeill of Colonsay (Shrewsbury, E.) she d. 1 Nov. 1942. He d. 17 Nov. 1944.
ARMS—Or on a fess azure three escallops of the field.
CREST—A demi-seahorse argent, finned and maned or.
SUPPORTERS—On either side a stag argent, attired or, holding in the mouth an oak leaf vert, the dexter charged on the shoulder with a hurt thereon a lozengy buckle, the tongue fessewise gold, and the sinister with an anchor azure.

BROTHERTON

PEERAGE—U.K. Baron Brotherton of Wakefield, co. York.
SURNAME—Brotherton.
CR.—17 June 1929. **EXT.**—21 Oct. 1930.
HISTORY—Theophilus Brotherton, of Manchester had as his father, Sir Edward Allen Brotherton, Bt., and **Baron Brotherton**, b. 1 April 1856; educ. Owens Coll. Manchester; became a chemical manufacturer, and gave great service in the first World War in the making of high explosives; M.P. Wakefield, 1902-10; and 1918-22; Mayor of Wakefield 1902-03, and Lord Mayor of Leeds 1913-14; was Hon. Col. of the 15th Service Bn. The West Yorkshire Regt. which he raised at his own charge in 1914; was a generous donor to Leeds University, bestowing on it his great collection of books, and also £100,000 to build a new library; cr. a baronet 27 June 1918; and Baron Brotherton of Wakefield, co. York, 17 June 1929. He d. unm. 21 Oct. 1930.
ARMS—Ermines within two bendlets between as many lions passant or a rose argent, between two roses gules barbed and seeded ppr.
CREST—In front of a dexter cubit arm grasping a club in bend sinister two swords saltirewise points downward ppr. pommels and hilts gold.
MOTTO—Studeo esse utilis.
Lord Brotherton's seat was Roundhay Hall, Leeds.

**BROUGHTON

PEERAGE—U.K. Baron Broughton of Broughton-de-Gyfford, co. Wilts.
SURNAME—Hobhouse.
CR.—26 Feb. 1851. **EXT.**—3 June 1869.
**This peerage is mentioned twice in cross references in the Extinct Peerage of 1883. On page 278 where Hobhouse-Baron Broughton is entered as See Addenda. On page 610, however, the second reference reads: Hobhouse-Baron Broughton, created 1851. See Burke's Extant Peerage and Baronetage, Hobhouse, Bt.
HISTORY—Sir Benjamin Hobhouse, 1st Bt., so cr. 22 Dec. 1812, had by his first wife Charlotte, dau. and heiress of Samuel Cam, of Chantry House, in Bradford-on-Avon, co. Wilts, an eldest son, Sir John Cam Hobhouse, 2nd Bt., (he s. his father on 15 Aug. 1831), and **Baron Broughton** of Broughton-de-Gyfford, co. Wilts, as he was cr. on 26 Feb. 1851, was b. 27 June 1786, at Redland (then) near Bristol

but now part of the city, and bapt. at Westbury-on-Tryme, co. Gloucester. He was educ. Westminster where he was admitted in 1800 and Trin. Coll. Camb. (adm. pensr. 1803) matric. 1806, Hulsean Prize 1808; B.A. 1808; M.A. 1811; founded the Cambridge Whig Club. He became F.R.S. 19 May 1814. He was a partner in the firm of Whitbread and Co. Brewers, of London. He wrote a pamphlet under the title, *A Trifling Mistake* which was held by the House of Commons to be a breach of privilege, and for this he was committed in Dec. 1819 to Newgate on the Speaker's warrant, where he stayed until Parliament rose in Feb. 1820; this did not prevent him from becoming (at the second attempt) M.P. for Westminster, 1820-33; for Nottingham 1834-47, and for Harwich, 1848-51. He became P.C. 1832; Sec. for War, 1832-33; Ch. Sec. for Ireland Mar. to May, 1833; Chief Commissioner of Woods and Forests July to Nov. 1834; Pres. of Board of Control 1835-41 and again 1846-52. He was cr. a peer as above on 26 Feb. 1851. He was cr. G.C.B. 1852. He m. 28 July 1828, Julia Tomlinson, dau. of George Hay, 7th Marquess of Tweeddale, who d. 3 April 1835. He d. 3 June 1869, having had issue,
    1. Julia Hay, d. unm. 5 Sept. 1849.
    2. Charlotte, m. 27 July 1854, 4th Baron Dorchester and d. 11 June 1914.
    3. Sophia, m. 31 July 1851, 5th Earl of Roden, and d. 3 Dec. 1916.
Lord Broughton was s. in the baronetcy by his nephew, Sir Charles Parry Hobhouse, 3rd Bt. for whom (with his descendants) see extant peerages (Hobhouse, Bt.). Lord Broughton was an intimate friend of Lord Byron, who dedicated to him the 4th Canto of *Childe Harold*. He was Byron's executor and as such advised the destruction of the *Memoirs* 1824, and also drew up a reply to Lady Byron's *Remarks*, 1830. He wrote *Recollections of a Long Life* (1865) in 6 vols. edited by his daughter, Lady Dorchester, 1910-11; he went in 1809 to Albania with Byron, and wrote an account of this in *Journey through Albania*. He is described as "one of the six founders of the Geographical Society, 1830; is said to have invented the phrase, 'His Majesty's Opposition'; his common place book while at school, containing the themes set, extracts from books, and occasional translations, is preserved amongst the MSS. in the British Museum" (*The Record of Old Westminsters*, Vol. 1. 1928).
ARMS—Per pale azure and gules three crescents argent issuant therefrom as many estoiles irradiated or.
CREST—Out of a ducal coronet per pale azure and gules an estoile issuant irradiated as in the arms.
SUPPORTERS—Two horses sable, each charged on the shoulder with an estoile radiated or.
MOTTO—Spes vitae melioris.

BROWNLOW

PEERAGE—U.K. Viscounty of Alford and Earldom of Brownlow.
SURNAME—Cust.
CR.—27 Nov. 1815. **EXT.**—17 March 1921.
HISTORY—The history of the Cust family is

given in the extant peerages under the title of the Baron Brownlow, who is also a baronet. The first baronet, Sir Richard Cust was so cr. 29 Sept. 1677. His great grandson, Sir John Cust, 3rd Bt., was Speaker of the House of Commons from 1761 until within a few days of his death which occurred 24 Jan. 1770. On the death of Sir John's uncle, John Brownlow, Viscount Tyrconnel without male issue Sir John inherited the latter's estates (For Tyrconnel see 1883 Extinct Peerage). In consideration of the services rendered by his father, Sir John Cust's only son, Sir Brownlow Cust was cr. a peer as Baron Brownlow, of Belton, co. Lincoln, 20 May 1776. His eldest son, John Cust, 2nd Baron Brownlow, was cr. **Viscount Alford** of Alford co. Lincoln and **Earl Brownlow**, 17 Nov. 1815. He was b. 19 Aug. 1779. Educ. Eton and Trin. Coll. Camb., M.A. 1801; M.P. Clitheroe, 1802-07; F.R.S., Lord Lieut. of Lincolnshire, 1809-52; a Gov. of King's Coll. London and Pres. of the Royal Archaeological Inst. 1841-49; m. (1) 24 July 1810, Sophia, dau. of Sir Abraham Hume, 2nd Bt., (she d. 21 Feb. 1814); he m. (2) 22 Sept. 1818, Caroline, dau. of George Fludyer. She d. 4 July 1824. He m. (3) 17 July 1828, Emma Sophia, dau. of Richard Edgcumbe, 2nd Earl of Mountedgcumbe. He d. 15 Sept. 1853. His widow d. 28 Jan. 1872. With other issue by his first and second marriages, either female or d.s.p. (see extant peerages), the Earl had by his first marriage an elder son, John Hume Cust, afterwards Home-Cust, and subsequently Egerton, styled Viscount Alford. He was b. 15 Oct. 1812; educ. Eton and Ch. Ch. Oxford, and Magdalene Coll. Camb., M.A. Camb. 1833. On the death of his grandfather Sir Abraham Hume he took the name of Home-Cust, in accordance with the will of Mrs. Elizabeth Home, cousin to Sir Abraham Hume, 1st Bt., his great-grandfather. Later on 15 March 1849 he took by royal licence the name of Egerton only, on s. to the estates of the Egerton family on the death of the Dowager Countess of Bridgwater, widow of his great uncle, the 7th Earl. He m. 10 Feb. 1841, Marianne Margaret, dau. of Spencer Compton, 2nd Marquess of Northampton. He d.v.p. 3 Jan. 1851. He left issue,

1. John William Spencer Brownlow, **2nd Earl** (see below).
2. Adelbert Wellington Brownlow, **3rd Earl** (see below).

The 1st Earl was s. by his elder grandson, John William Spencer Brownlow, (Egerton afterwards Egerton-Cust), known in the lifetime of his father by name of Cust, **2nd Earl Brownlow**. He was b. 28 June 1842, educ. Eton and Ch. Ch. Oxford; by royal licence 5 Sept. 1853, he took the name of Egerton only and by another licence 6 July 1863, the name of Egerton-Cust. He d. unm. 20 Feb. 1867, and was s. by his brother, Adelbert Wellington Brownlow Cust, **3rd Earl Brownlow**, b. 19 Aug. 1844; educ. Eton; Lt. Foot Guards, 1863-66; M.P. North Salop 1866-67; Lord Lieut. Lincolnshire, 1867; Paymaster General, 1887-89; Under Sec. of State for War, 1889-92; m. 22 June 1868, Adelaide, dau. of Henry John Talbot, 18th Earl of Shrewsbury, and d.s.p. 17 March 1921, when the earldom and viscounty became extinct, and the barony and baronetcy devolved on his kinsman Adelaide Salusbury

Cockayne Cust, (see extant peerages).
ARMS—Ermine on a chevron sable three fountains.
CREST—A lion's head erased sable collared paly wavy of six argent and azure.
SUPPORTERS—Two lions reguardant argent gorged with collars paly wavy of six argent and azure.
MOTTO—Esse quam videri.

BRUCE OF MELBOURNE

PEERAGE—U.K. Viscount Bruce of Melbourne of Westminster Gardens in the city of Westminster.
SURNAME—Bruce.
CR.—18 March 1947. **EXT.**—25 Aug. 1967.
HISTORY—Stanley Melbourne Bruce, **Viscount Bruce** of Melbourne, Australian statesman was b. 15 April 1883, son of John Munroe Bruce of Melbourne. educ. at Melbourne Grammar School, Trin. Hall, Cambridge, B.A. 1904, LL.D. (Hon.) 1923 and Middle Temple, Barrister-at-Law, 1907. He practised at the Bar in England until 1914 when he served in first World War with Worcestershire Regt. and Royal Fusiliers (Capt.) until 1917, being wounded twice, mentioned in despatches and awarded M.C. and Croix de Guerre avec Palme. Afterwards he returned to Australia where he entered politics and was elected to the Commonwealth Parliament as a member of the National Party, M.P. for Flinders, 1918-29, and 1931-33. He became Prime Minister and Minister for External Affairs in a National Country Party coalition from 1923-29. He was Australian Minister for London, 1932-33, High Commissioner for Australia in London 1933-45, and represented his country at many important international conferences, also Chm. World Food Council, 1947-51, Chm. Finance Corp. for Industry, 1947-57 and first Chancellor of Australian National Univ. Canberra 1951-61. He was made a P.C. 1923, C.H. 1927, and a peer 1947. He m. 1913, Ethel Dunlop, dau. of Andrew George Anderson of Edinburgh and Melbourne. Viscount Bruce d. 25 Aug. 1967. His London residence was at Flat 16, Prince's Gate, S.W.7. He was a member of the Athenaeum, Melbourne.
ARMS—Or a saltire gules cantoned between four mullets sable on a chief gules a pale argent charged with a saltire sable.
CREST—A lion passant tail extended gules supporting with his dexter paw a saltire sable.
SUPPORTERS—Two lyre birds ppr.

BRYCE

PEERAGE—U.K. Viscount Bryce, of Dechmount, co. Lanark.
SURNAME—Bryce.
CR.—28 Jan. 1914. **EXT.**—22 Jan. 1922.
HISTORY—This family was living at Dechmount, Lanarkshire about 1659, and two members of it were fighting in the Covenanting Army at Bothwell Bridge in 1679. Some sixty years later, Alexander Bryce d. having had a son, John Bryce, the last of the family to live at Dechmount. He had a son, The Rev. James Bryce, who was b. circa 1767 and d.

1857 at Killaig, nr. Coleraine, Londonderry, leaving issue, a third son, James Bryce, LL.D., Glasgow, F.S.G., b. at Killaig, 19 Oct. 1806; m. 1836 Margaret, dau. of James Young, of Abbeyville, co. Antrim, and d. 23 July 1877. She d. 18 Aug. 1903, aged 90. They had issue,

1. James, **Viscount Bryce** (see below).
2. John Annan, b. 1844, M.P. Inverness, 1906, Chm. Rangoon Chamber of Commerce, M.A. Glasgow, B.A. Balliol Coll. Oxford; m. 2 Aug. 1888, Violet, dau. of Capt. Champagne L'Estrange, and had issue, a son, Roland L'Estrange, B.A. Oxford; and two daus., Margaret Vincentia, and Rosalind L'Estrange.
1. Mary. 2. Katharine.

The elder son, James Bryce, **Viscount Bryce**, was b. 10 May 1838 at Belfast; educ. Glasgow High School, Glasgow Univ., and Trin. Coll. Oxford, where he was a Scholar, and gained the Craven and Vinerian Law Scholarships, the Latin Essay, the Gaisford and Arnold Prizes and obtained first in Classical Moderations, and a first class in final schools in classics, in law and in history, B.A. 1861; Fell. of Oriel, 1862; B.C.L. 1865; D.C.L. 1870; Barrister-at-Law, Lincoln's Inn, 1867; he received hon. degrees at very many universities throughout the world, and was a member of numerous English and European societies. He m. 23 July 1889, Elizabeth Marion, dau. of Thomas Ashton, of Hyde, Cheshire, (Ashton of Hyde, B.). He had a most distinguished career as a professor, politician, diplomat, and author. He was Regius Prof. of Civil Law at Oxford, 1870-93, and Prof. of Jurisprudence, Owens Coll. Manchester, 1870-75.; M.P. Tower Hamlets, 1880-85, and Aberdeen, 1885-1907; Under Sec. of State for Foreign Affairs, 1886; Chancellor of the Duchy of Lancaster, 1892-94; Pres. Board of Trade, 1894-95; Chief Sec. to Lord Lieut. of Ireland, 1905-07; and Ambassador to the United States, 1907-12. He was made P.C. in Ireland 1895; appointed O.M. 1907; cr. G.C.V.O. 1918, and a peer as Viscount Bryce of Dechmount, co. Lanark, 28 Jan. 1914. His writings included *Transcausia and Ararat*, *The American Commonwealth, Modern Democracy, Studies in History and Jurisprudence*, and perhaps most notable of all, *The Holy Roman Empire*. He spoke the chief European languages, and was described in *The Times* obituary as one who seemed to have been everywhere, known everybody, and read everything. He was, among his other accomplishments, a keen mountaineer, and Pres. of the Alpine Club; a mem. of the Senate of London Univ., a Bencher of Lincoln's Inn, a F.R.S., and Pres. of the British Academy. He d.s.p. 22 Jan. 1922.

ARMS—Gules on a saltire between four mullets or, two swords in saltire points upwards ppr., on a chief argent an open book also ppr. between two trefoils slipped vert.

CREST—In front of a mountain with two peaks a dexter cubit arm holding in the hand a scimitar all ppr.

SUPPORTERS—On either side a chamois ppr.

MOTTO—Do well, doubt not.

Lord Bryce's residences were at Hindleap, Forest Row, Sussex and 3 Buckingham Gate, London, S.W.

BUCKINGHAM AND CHANDOS

PEERAGE—G.B. Earl (of) Temple 18 Oct. 1749.
Ireland. Earl Nugent 21 July 1776.
G.B. Marquess of Buckingham 4 Dec. 1784.
U.K. Marquess of Chandos, Duke of Buckingham and Chandos and Earl Temple of Stour 4 Feb. 1822.
SURNAME—Temple - Nugent - Brydges - Chandos-Grenville.
CR.—As above. **EXT.**—26 March 1889.
HISTORY—Richard Grenville, of Wooton under Barnwood, co. Buckingham, High Sheriff 1636 and 1642 and M.P. for that county 1654, 1656 and 1658. He m. (1) Anne, dau. of Sir William Borlase, of Marlow, co. Bucks and (2) Eleanor, dau. of Sir Timothy Tirrel, of Oakley and widow of Sir Peter Temple, and d. 1665, having had one surv. son by his first marriage, Richard Grenville, of Wooton, m. Eleanor, dau. of Sir Peter Temple and d. 1719 leaving an only son, Richard Grenville of Wooton, M.P. for Andover and later for town of Buckingham. He m. Hester, dau. of Sir Richard Temple, 3rd Bt., of Stowe, co. Buckingham. (This lady was sister of Sir Richard Temple, 4th Bt. of Stowe, co. Buckingham, who was cr. Baron Cobham of Cobham, co. Kent 19 Oct. 1714 and further a Viscount and Baron Cobham 23 May 1718 with special remainder to his sister. On his death s.p. in 1749 the barony of 1714 became extinct, but the second barony and the viscounty passed to his sister. Mrs. Grenville then became Baroness and Viscountess Cobham and on 18 Oct. 1749 was cr. **Countess of Temple**, with inheritance by heirs male. She d. 6 Oct. 1752. Mr. Richard Grenville d. 17 Feb. 1726/27. Their issue were,

1. Richard, **2nd** holder of the title of **Temple** etc.
2. George, M.P. for town of Buckingham, Treasurer of the Navy, P.C., Sec. of State, First Lord of the Admiralty. In 1763, first lord of the Treasury and Chan. of the Exchequer. He was b. 1712; m. 1749, Elizabeth, dau. of Sir William Wyndham Bt., and d. 1770 leaving,
   (1) George, **3rd Earl Temple** (see below).
   (2) Thomas, Rt. Hon., M.P. for town of Buckingham, Pres. of the India Board 1806 and first Lord of the Admiralty, b. 1755.
   (3) William Wyndham of Dropmore, co. Buckingham, b. 1759; educ. Eton and Ch. Ch. Oxford, B.A. 1780, student Lincoln's Inn 1780, M.P. for Buckingham 1782-84 and for co. Buckingham 1784-90. He was chief Sec. for Ireland 1782-83, P.C. 1783, speaker House of Commons 1789, cr. Baron Grenville 25 Nov. 1790; Home Sec. 1789-90, Foreign Sec. 1791-1801; head of the Ministry of all the Talents 1806-07. He m. 18 July 1792, Hon. Anne Pitt, dau. of 1st Lord Camelford and d.s.p. 12 Jan. 1834. Lady Grenville d. 13 June 1864.
   (1) Charlotte, m. 1771, Sir William Wynn, 4th Bt. and d. 1832.
   (2) Elizabeth, m. 1st Earl of Carysfort and d. 1842.
   (3) Hester, m. 1st Earl Fortescue.
   (4) Catherine, m. 2nd Lord Braybrooke.

3. James, P.C., b. 1715; m. 1740 Mary dau. of James Smyth of Annable, co. Herts, and d. 1783 leaving issue,
(1) James, P.C., a Lord of the Treasury, cr. Lord Glastonbury 20 Oct. 1797 and d. unm. 1825.
(2) Richard, in the Army. d. unm. 1823.
4. Henry, Gov. of Barbados 1746 and Ambassador to Turkey 1762; m. 1757 Margaret Eleanora, dau. of Joseph Banks, of Revelsby Abbey, co. Lincoln and d. 1784 having an only dau., Louisa, m. 3rd Earl Stanhope.
5. Thomas, Capt. R.N., b. 1719, k. in fight at sea, 3 May 1747.
1. Hester, m. Rt. Hon. William Pitt, 1st Earl of Chatham.

The eldest son, Richard Grenville (later Nugent-Temple-Grenville) **2nd Earl Temple,** K.G., P.C. 1757, m. Anna, dau. and coheiress of Thomas Chambers of Hanworth, co. Middlesex and d.s.p. 11 Sept. 1779, being s. by his nephew,

George Grenville, **3rd Earl Temple** and **1st Marquess of Buckingham,** b. 17 June 1753; m. 16 April 1775 Lady Mary Elizabeth Nugent, elder dau. and coheir (with her sister Lady Louisa Nugent who m. Adm. Sir Eliab Harvey) of Earl Nugent. The 3rd Earl Temple by Royal Licence 2 Dec. 1779 assumed the surnames of Nugent and Temple before that of Grenville. He was cr. 4 Dec. 1784, Marquess of Buckingham. On the death of his father-in-law, 13 Oct. 1788 in accordance with a special limitation in the patent of the Irish earldom he inherited the earldom of Nugent. He twice held the office of Viceroy of Ireland in 1782 and 1787. He d. 11 Feb. 1813, having had issue,

1. Richard, **4th Earl** and **2nd Marquess** (see below).
2. George, Sir, G.C.M.G., Lord Commissioner of the Ionian Islands 1832-35 M.P. for Aylesbury. Inherited on the death of his mother on 16 March 1813, the Irish Barony of Nugent which had been granted to her on 29 Dec. 1800 with remainder to her second son. Lord Nugent was b. 31 Dec. 1789; m. 6 Sept. 1813, Anne Ludy dau. of Major Gen. the Hon. Vere Poulett (Poulett, E.) and d.s.p. 27 Nov. 1850.
1. Mary, m. 1811 the 10th Lord Arundell of Wardour (see that title in present work).

The elder son, Richard Nugent-Temple-Grenville (later Temple-Nugent-Brydges-Chandos-Grenville), **2nd Marquess of Buckingham,** 1st Marquess of Chandos and **1st Duke of Buckingham and Chandos,** K.G., assumed by Royal Licence the additional surnames of Brydges-Chandos. He was cr. 4 Feb. 1822 Earl Temple of Stowe with special limitation on failure of male issue under terms of the previous patent (that of the Countess of Temple, 1749), to his granddau. Anne Eliza Mary, He was further cr. 4 Feb. 1822 Marquess of Chandos and Duke of Buckingham and Chandos. He was b. 29 May 1776; m. 16 April 1796, Lady Anna Eliza, de jure Baroness Kinloss, dau. and sole heiress of James Brydges, 3rd and last Duke of Chandos of the family of Brydges. The Duke of Buckingham and Chandos d. 17 Jan. 1839. His Duchess d. 15 May 1836. They had an only son,

Richard Plantagenet Temple-Nugent-Brydges-Chandos Grenville, **2nd Duke of Buckingham and Chandos,** inherited Barony of Kinloss from his mother, K.G., G.C.H., b. 11 Feb. 1797; m. 13 May 1819, Mary, dau. of 1st Marquess of Breadalbane. She d. 28 June 1862. He d. 29 July 1861. Their issue were,
Richard Plantagenet Campbell, **3rd Duke** (see below).
Anna Eliza Mary, m. 1846, W. H. P. Gore-Langton and d. 1819 leaving with other issue,
William Stephen 4th Earl Temple of Stowe (see extant peerages).

The only son, Richard Plantagenet Campbell Temple-Nugent-Brydges-Chandos-Grenville, **3rd Duke of Buckingham and Chandos,** P.C., G.C.S.I., C.I.E., b. 10 Sept. 1823, m. (1) 1 Oct. 1851, Caroline dau. of Robert Harvey of Langley Park, co. Buckingham. She d. 28 Feb. 1874. He m. (2) 17 Feb. 1885 Alice Ann [m. 2ndly 1894 the 2nd Baron and only Earl Egerton of Tatton, (see that title in present work)], dau. of Sir Graham Montgomery, 3rd Bt. By his first marriage the Duke had issue,
1. Mary, s. her father as Baroness Kinloss (see extant peerages).
2. Anne, m. 1882 Lt. Col. G. R. Hadaway and had issue (Kinloss B.).

The 3rd Duke d.s.p.m. 26 March 1889.
ARMS—Quarterly 1 and 6, Vert on a cross argent five torteaux (Grenville); 2, quarterly 1st and 4th Or an eagle displayed sable (Leofric); 2nd and 3rd Argent two bars sable each charged with three martlets or (Temple); 3, Ermine two bars gules (Nugent); 4, Argent on a cross sable a leopard's face or (Brydges); 5, Or a pile gules (Chandos).
CRESTS—1. A garb vert (Grenville). 2. On a ducal coronet a martlet or (Temple), 3. The bust of an old man in profile couped below the shoulders ppr. habited paly of six argent and gules semée of roundels counter changed wreathed round the temples of the second and azure (Brydges). 4. A Saracen's head couped at the shoulders and affrontée ppr. wreathed about the temples argent and sable (Chandos).
SUPPORTERS—Dexter, A lion per fess embattled or and gules. Sinister, A horse argent semée of eaglets sable.
MOTTO—Templa quam delecta.
The Duke's seats were: Stowe, co. Buckingham (now the well-known school), and Wotton, Aylesbury. He had a town residence in Chandos House, Cavendish Square, W. His clubs were Athenaeum and Carlton.

NOTE. With reference to the quartering of Leofric in the arms given above, this is of course an anachronism since heraldic devices are not found in Europe until nearly a century after Leofric's death. As to the alleged descent of the Temple family from Leofric, Earl of Mercia and husband of Lady Godiva, there is an interesting comment on p. 1 (Ch. 1) of the *Life of William Temple, Archbishop of Canterbury* by F. A. Iremonger (1948). The Archbishop wrote "Of course Father used a coat of arms taken from the Duke of Buckingham's coat—and similarly the crest—so I suppose he convinced the College of Heralds of his right to do it. And his signature was the facsimile of that of Sir William Temple who was a prominent statesman at the end of the 17th century"

BUCKLAND

PEERAGE—U.K. Baron Buckland, of Bwlch, co. Brecknock.
SURNAME—Berry.
CR.—16 July 1926. **EXT.**—23 May 1928.
HISTORY—Henry Seymour Berry, **Baron Buckland,** was the eldest of the three Berry brothers, the sons of John Mathias Berry, J.P., the two younger brothers being Viscount Camrose and Viscount Kemsley (see extant peerages). He was b. 17 Sept. 1877 at Merthyr Tydfil, co. Glamorgan and educ. privately; he was a large coalowner, Chm. and Director of many colliery and shipping concerns, Chm. of Guest, Keen and Nettlefolds, and of John Lysaght Ltd. He was High Sheriff of co. Brecknock, 1924, and Knight of Grace of the Order of St. John of Jerusalem. He m. 5 Sept. 1907, Gwladys Mary, dau. of Simon Sandbrook of Merthyr Tydfil, and had issue,
  1. Gwladys Eileen, m. 1930, A.D.C.T. Thistlethwayte, and had issue.
  2. Mary Lorraine, m. 1934, Gwyn Morgan-Jones, and had issue.
  3. Dorothy Margaret. 4. Joan Sybil.
  5. Cecily Eveline.
He was cr. Baron Buckland, of Bwlch, co. Brecknock, 16 July 1926, and d. 23 May 1928, having been killed while riding near Bwlch. His title was taken from Buckland the property in Brecknockshire which he had bought from the widow and daughter of James Price William Gwynne-Holford.
ARMS—Argent three bars gules over all a pile ermine, charged with three martlets sable, in base the attires of a stag ppr.
CREST—A griffin sejant reguardant sable, resting the dexter claw on the attires of a stag or.
BADGE—A daffodil ppr. between two roses gules, all leaved and slipped ppr. enfiled by the circlet of a baron's coronet or.
SUPPORTERS—On a mount vert: Dexter, A buck ppr. charged on the shoulder with a divining rod also ppr.; Sinister, A dragon gules.
MOTTO—Cogitatione et constantia.
His seat was Buckland, Bwlch, Breconshire.

BURDETT-COUTTS

PEERAGE—U.K. Baroness Burdett-Coutts of Highgate and Brookfield, co. Middlesex.
SURNAME—Burdett-Coutts.
CR.—9 June 1871. **EXT.**—30 Dec. 1906.
HISTORY—In the *Liber Veritatis,* (1930 edition) William Beckford of Fonthill, author of *Vathek* refers to "the beautified elect of the stewpot, to the truly excellent Mrs. Coutts, mother of the Ladies Bute, Guilford and Burdett" (p. 109, *op. cit.*) and again on p. 130, see below. The pedigree based on this work and on the *C.P.* is as follows: Thomas Coutts, of Westminster, Banker, m. as his first wife Susan, dau. of ——— Starkie, a Lancashire yeoman, and a servant to Thomas's brother (*C.P.* under Bute), and by her had issue,
  1. Susan, m. 28 Feb. 1796, George Augustus North, 3rd Earl of Guilford.
  2. Frances, m. 7 Sept. 1800, (as his 2nd wife) John Crichton Stuart, 4th Earl of Bute and 1st Marquess of Bute). Of this marriage Beckford tells the extraordinary

story that the Marquess's heir was enamoured of Frances but that his father proposed to her in his place. "The melting mother of this angelic girl did honour to a glowing profession; she was a cook, ay, every inch a cook, of accurate taste and the most experienced proficiency. In despight of antiquated prejudices the young man tendered his nuptial hand to the fascinating young lady. His father, first stunned and then distracted at the news, stamped and raved about like a maniac, and in an agony of apprehension, and determined upon a wondrous and a more than Roman sacrifice. He thought that by offering himself instead of his son, the eldest branch of his male flock would be uncontaminated. Still more wonderful, the lady accepted the veteran peer in lieu of her blooming lover." She became the mother of Lord Dudley Coutts Crichton Stuart, "so called out of tender respect to his grandfather's immaculate memory."*
  3. Sophia, m. 5 Aug. 1793, Sir Francis Burdett, 5th Bt. and had with other issue, a 5th daughter,
    Angela Georgina, **Baroness Burdett-Coutts** (see below).
Thomas Coutts m. (2) Harriet, dau. of Matthew Mellon, who m. 2ndly, the 9th Duke of St. Albans. Angela Georgina Burdett-Coutts, **Baroness Burdett-Coutts,** was b. 25 April 1814. Under the will of her maternal step grandmother the Dowager Duchess of St. Albans she s. to considerable property. The Duchess d. 6 Aug. 1837. On 14 Sept. 1837 Miss Angela Georgina Burdett took by Royal Licence the name of Coutts after that of Burdett. On 9 June 1871, she was cr. Baroness Burdett-Coutts, of Highgate and Brookfield, both co. Middlesex, with remainder to the heirs male of her body. In 1872 she received the freedom of the city of London. She was principal partner in the banking house of Coutts. When her only brother, Sir Robert Burdett 6th Bt., died unm. 7 June 1880, she with her two sisters, Mrs. Trevannion and Mrs. Money-Coutts, became a coheiress to the baronies of Scales, Latimer and Badlesmere. She m. 12 Feb. 1881 ("she 66 and he 27" *C.P.*) William Lehman Ash Bartlett, yr. son of Ellis Bartlett, of Plymouth, Massachusetts, U.S.A., by Sophia, dau. of John King Ashmead. On 1 Feb. the bridegroom had taken the name of Burdett-Coutts before his surname of Bartlett, and on the 25th July following took the final name of Coutts in accordance with the will of Harriet, Duchess of St. Albans. Thus the surname of the husband of the Baroness was Burdett-Coutts-Bartlett, and afterwards Burdett-Coutts-Bartlett-Coutts. He was M.A. Keble Coll. Oxford, and M.P. Conservative for Westminster 1885 and a P.C. Lady Burdett-Coutts d. 30 Dec. 1906. He d. 28 July 1921. They had no issue. The body of the Baroness lay in state and was bur. in Westminster Abbey 5 Jan. 1907.
ARMS—Quarterly 1 and 4, Argent a stag's head, erased gules, between the attires a pheon azure, the whole within a bordure, embattled azure, charged with four buckles or (Coutts); 2 and 3, Azure two bars or each charged with three martlets gules. (Burdett).
SUPPORTERS—Dexter, A stag ppr. gorged

with a riband argent, pendent therefrom an escutcheon of the arms of Coutts; Sinister, A lion ppr. pendent from a like riband, an escutcheon of the arms of Burdett.

Baroness Burdett Coutts's seat was Holly Lodge, Highgate, N.W. and the town residence was 1, Stratton Street, Piccadilly.

*With regard to the validity of this story from Beckford, it is to be observed that while the various facts set out are confirmed from peerage histories, the central item, i.e. of the sacrifice made by the 4th Earl and 1st Marquess of Bute, scarcely agrees with dates of marriage. The 1st Marquess married for the second time, in 1800, but his eldest son, John Crichton Stuart, known as Lord Mount Stuart, who was father of the 2nd Marquess, and who died in the lifetime of his father (i.e. the 1st Marquess), married in 1792, Lady Elizabeth Penelope MacDowall-Crichton, dau. of the 6th Earl of Dumfries, and d. 1794. If therefore he was enamoured of Frances Coutts, the affair must have taken place 8 or more years before the father's "sacrifice." Beckford's *Liber Veritatis* was written between 1829 and 1844, and was described by him as being true in every syllable. It certainly contains some sneers at the alleged low origins of some of his contemporaries who were peers, a position to which he aspired without success. In his main attack on the aristocracy Beckford probably had right on his side, but the item about Bute and Coutts may not be correct.

BURGHCLERE

PEERAGE—U.K. Baron Burghclere of Walden, co. Essex.
SURNAME—Gardner.
CR.—3 Aug. 1895. **EXT.**—6 May 1921.
HISTORY—Alan Legge Gardner, 3rd Baron Gardner, m. twice. His first wife d.s.p. 1847. He m. 2ndly 1848 Julia Sarah Hayfield, dau. of Edward E. T. Fortescue by whom he had two daus., (see Gardner B.) and (before marriage) a son, Herbert Coulstoun Gardner, **Baron Burghclere**, of Walden, co. Essex, so cr. 3 Aug. 1895. He was b. 9 June 1846; educ. Harrow and Trin. Coll. Cambridge, M.A. 1872; was Liberal M.P. for Northern Div. of Essex, 1885-95; Pres. of the Board of Agric. 1892-95; an Ecclesiastical Comm. 1903 and Chm. of the Ancient Monuments Comm. He m. 4 March 1890, Winifred Anne Henrietta Christiana, dau. of Henry Howard Molyneux Herbert, 4th Earl of Carnarvon and widow of Capt. the Hon. Alfred G. Byng, and by her had issue,
1. Juliet Mary Evelyn Stanhope, b. 14 June 1892.
2. Alethea Margaret Gwendolin Valentine, b. 19 Aug. 1893; m. 30 June 1915, G. Fry, (see Fry Bt.).
3. Mary Sidney Katharine Almina, b. 27 Aug. 1896; m. 12 Dec. 1914, G. H. Morley, (see Hollenden B.) and had issue.
4. Evelyn Florence Margaret Winifred, b. 27 Sept. 1903.

Lord Burghclere d. 6 May 1921.
ARMS—Or on a chevron gules, between three griffins' heads erased, azure, an anchor with line reflexed between two lions passant,

contourne or, all within a bordure wavy sable (the arms of Gardner, with a sign—a bordure—used by English heralds within the last 150 years or so, to denote bastardy).
CREST—A demi-griffin azure, gorged with a collar, chain reflexed over the back, charged on the shoulder with a saltire wavy, and holding in the claws an anchor with line reflexed all or.
SUPPORTERS—On either side a wyvern reguardant vert wings elevated and addorsed, gorged with a collar flory counterflory and charged on the breast with an anchor with line reflexed or.
MOTTO—Valet anchora virtus.
Lord Burghclere's principal residence was at Debden House, near Saffron Walden, Essex, where in 1883, the estates were noted as being under 2000 acres. His town residence was 48 Charles Street, Berkeley Square, London, W.

BURNHAM

PEERAGE—Viscount Burnham.
SURNAME—Lawson.
CR.—16 May 1919. **EXT.**—20 July 1933.
HISTORY—The early history of this family is given in extant peerages under Burnham (Baron), beginning with Edward Levy, the son of Joseph Moses Levy, who assumed by royal licence the additional surname of Lawson, 11 Dec. 1875. He was cr. a baronet 15 Oct. 1892 and Baron Burnham, of Hall Barn, Beaconsfield, co. Bucks. 31 July 1903. He d. 9 Jan. 1916, having had issue,
1. Harry Lawson Webster, 2nd Baron and **Viscount Burnham.**
2. William Arnold Webster, 3rd Baron Burnham.

The elder son, Harry Lawson Webster Levy-Lawson, 2nd Baron Burnham and **Viscount Burnham**, b. 18 Dec. 1862; educ. Cheam, Eton and Balliol Coll. Oxford, M.A. 1888; Barrister-at-Law, Inner Temple, 1889; President of the Institute of Journalists, 1910, as had been his father in 1891-92, managing proprietor of *The Daily Telegraph* of which his grandfather Joseph Moses Levy had been the founder; M.P. West St. Pancras, 1885-92, Cirencester Div. of Gloucester, 1893-95; and for Tower Hamlets, 1905-06 and 1910-16; Mayor of Stepney 1907-09; served in the first World War, as Lt. Col. cmdg. Royal Bucks Yeo. 2nd Reserve Regt. (despatches). He was Chm. and member of many committees, President of many conferences and institutions; he was cr. C.H. 1917, G.C.M.G. 1927; and advanced to a Viscounty as Viscount Burnham, 16 May 1919. He m. 2 Jan. 1884, at St. Margaret's Westminster, Olive, dau. of Gen. Sir Henry de Bathe, Bt. and d. 20 July 1933, having had issue, a dau.,
Dorothy Olive, b. 26 Jan. 1885, m. 15 Jan. 1907, Major the Hon. John Spencer Coke, (see Leicester, E.).

The Viscounty became extinct at his death, while the barony and baronetcy devolved upon his brother, William Arnold Webster Levy Lawson (see extant peerages).
ARMS—Quarterly 1 and 4, Azure three bars gemel argent; over all a winged morion or; 2 and 3, Gules a saltire double parted and fretted or, between two rams' heads couped in fess argent.

CRESTS—1, In front of a terrestrial globe ppr. a winged morion or; 2, A ram argent holding in the mouth a trefoil slipped vert and resting the dexter foreleg on a quatrefoil or.
SUPPORTERS—Dexter, The figure of Clio, the Muse of History, Sinister, The figure of Hermes, vested argent, mantled azure, on the head a winged morion, on his heels wings, and in his exterior hand a caduceus or.
MOTTO—Of old I hold.

BURTON

PEERAGE—U.K. Baron Burton of Rangemore and Burton on Trent, co. Stafford.
SURNAME—Bass.
CR.—13 Aug. 1886. EXT.—1 Feb. 1909.
HISTORY—William Bass, b. 1717, bought the house and land at Burton, co. Stafford, where he built a brewery and founded the well known brewing business. He m. Mary Gibbons (d. 1786) and d. 2 March, 1787, being bur. in the family vault at Burton-on-Trent. He had issue,
Michael Thomas Bass, of Burton, b. 23 July 1760; m. 14 June, 1793 Sarah, dau. of Abram Hoskyns, of Newton Solney, co. Derby, and d. 9 March 1827, having had issue,
1. Michael Thomas (see below).
2. William of Dukinfield, co. Chester, b. 20 July 1801; d. 23 Sept. 1880.
3. Abraham, of Moat Bank, Burton, b. 23 Feb. 1804; m. 10 May 1852, Margaret Jane, dau. of Rev. George Wood Lloyd, D.D., Vicar of Gresley, co. Derby (she d. 1878) and d. 15 Jan. 1882, having had issue, Roger, of West Hallam Hall, near Derby, b. 15 April 1855; m. 27 April 1882, Thomasina Sarah Sophia, dau. of the Rev. Edward Dyer Green, M.A., Rector of Bromborough, co. Chester, and had issue,
(1) Roger Arthur, b. 1884;
(2) Alfred Edward, b. 1887.
(3) Victor Abram, b. 31 May 1888.
4. Roger, Rev., Vicar of Anstrey, co. Warwick, b. 15 April 1805; m. 1835, Anne, dau. of William Worthington, of Burton, and d.s.p. 8 April 1844. She d. 7 Feb. 1857.
1. Mary, m. 1843 Walter Joseph Gisborne, of Lingen, Presteign, co. Radnor, and d.s.p. 20 Dec. 1879.
2. Sarah, b. 15 Nov. 1796. d. unm. 1858.
3. Frances, m. 1838 Archibald Fox, of Blackheath, co. Kent, and d. 17 July 1881 aged 83 leaving issue.
The eldest son, Michael Thomas Bass, of Rangemore Hall, Tattenhill, co. Stafford, M.P. Derby, 1848-83, J.P. and D.L., b. 6 July, 1799; m. 8 Dec. 1835, Eliza Jane, dau. of Major Samuel Arden, of Longcroft, co. Stafford, (B.L.G. 1952, Arden, formerly of Longcroft). She d. 7 Aug. 1897. He d. 29 April 1884. They had issue,
1. Michael Arthur, Sir, Bt., and Baron Burton (see below).
2. Hamar Alfred, of Byrkley Lodge, Burton-on-Trent, M.P. Tamworth, 1878-85, and West Staffordshire, 1885-98, b. 30 July 1842; m. 22 Feb. 1879, Louisa Bagot, dau. of 3rd Lord Bagot. She m. 2ndly 28 Nov. 1901, Rev. B. D. D. Shaw, (Shaw, Bt.) and d. as result of an accident, 18 May

1942. He d. 8 April, 1898 having had issue,
(1) William Arthur Hamar, 2nd Bt. b. 24 Dec. 1879.
(2) Alexander Michael, b. 10 Feb. 1885; d. 9 March 1891.
(1) Sibell Lucia, b. 28 1881; m. 2 June 1900, Major J. T. Berkeley Levett.
1. Emily Frances Anne, m. 30 Sept. 1862, Sir William Chichele Plowden, and d. 29 Nov. 1915, having had issue.
2. Alice Jane, m. 21 Oct. 1868, Sir George Chetwode, 8th Bt. and d. 27 Nov. 1919 leaving issue.
The eldest son, Sir Michael Arthur Bass, 1st Bt., and 1st Baron Burton, b. 12 Nov. 1837; educ. Harrow and Trin. Coll. Cambridge, B.A., 1859; M.A. 1863; M.P. Stafford, 1865-68 and East Staffordshire, 1868-85, and for Burton Div., co. Stafford, 1885-86; m. 28 Oct. 1869, Harriet Georgiana, dau. of Edward Thornwill, of Dove Cliff, co. Stafford. He was cr. a Baronet, 17 May 1882, and a peer 13 Aug. 1886, as Baron Burton of Burton-on-Trent, and of Rangemore both co. Stafford, but having no male issue, he was cr. 29 Nov. 1897, Baron Burton, of Burton-on-Trent, and of Rangemore, with a special remainder failing heirs male of his body to his only dau. (The baronetcy had a special remainder to his brother, Hamar, and the heirs male of the latter). He was cr. K.C.V.O. 1904. He d. 1 Feb. 1909, after an operation on the kidneys. His only child was, Nellie Lisa, b. 27 Dec. 1873, m. 1894 Col. J. E. V. Baillie. She s. to the Barony of the second creation, while that of the first became extinct. For second Barony of Burton, see extant peerages. The Baronetcy inherited by Hamar Bass's son, Sir William Bass became extinct in 1952.
ARMS—Gules on a chevron cottised argent between three plates, each charged with a fleur-de-lis azure, a demi-lion rampant couped gules.
CREST—A demi-lion rampant, gules resting the dexter paw on a plate charged as in the arms, on the shoulder three annulets, two and one argent.
SUPPORTERS—On either side a lion rampant reguardant sable, each resting the inner leg on a stag's head ppr. and charged on the shoulder with a plate and fleur-de-lis as in the arms.
MOTTO—Basis virtutum constantia.
Lord Burton's seats were—Rangemore, Burton-on-Trent, co. Stafford. Glen Quioch, Inverness and for town residence, Chesterfield House, Mayfair.

BUTLER

PEERAGE—England. Baron Butler, of Moore Park, co. Hertford.
SURNAME—Butler.
CR.—17 Sept. 1666. ABEYANT—18 July 1905.
HISTORY—James Butler, 1st Duke of Ormonde, had a second son, Thomas Butler, styled, Earl of Ossory and commonly called, the gallant Ossory, who was summoned by writ to the Parliament of England on 17 Sept. 1666 as Baron Butler, of Moore Park in Hertford. Baron Butler m. 17 Nov. 1659, Lady Amelia de Nassau, eldest dau. of Henry de

Nassau, Lord of Auverquerque, and had issue,
1. James, who became 2nd Duke of Ormonde (extant peerages, Ormonde, M.) (see below).
2. Charles, de jure 3rd Duke and 14th Earl.
1. Henrietta, m. 12 Jan. 1697, Henry D'Auverquerque, Earl of Grantham, and d. 11 Oct. 1724, leaving issue, (see Lucas, B.).

Lord Butler d.v.p. 30 July 1680 being s. in the Barony by his son and heir James Butler, **2nd Baron Butler**, of Moore Park. The latter s. his grandfather as 2nd Duke of Ormonde, and was attained as a Jacobite supporter, 20 August. 1715, by which measure the Barony of Butler became forfeited. Eventually in 1871 Francis Thomas de Grey Cowper, Earl Cowper, the heir general to this Barony became Lord Butler, of Moore Park, also Lord Dingwall, by the reversal, under an Act of Parliament, of 31 July 1871, of the attainder which affected both these peerages. For further details, see under Cowper, Earl, in present work, and also under Ormonde, M. in extant peerage works.

BUXTON

PEERAGE—U.K. Viscount Buxton, of Newtimber, co. Sussex, and Earl Buxton, of Newtimber, co. Sussex.
SURNAME—Buxton.
CR.—11 May 1914, Barony; 8 Nov. 1920 Earldom. **EXT.**—15 Oct. 1934.
HISTORY—Sir Sydney Charles Buxton, **Viscount Buxton**, and **Earl Buxton**, b. 25 Oct. 1853, the yr. son of Charles Buxton, of Foxwarren, Cobham, and grandson of Sir Thomas Fowell Buxton, 1st Bt. (see that family in extant baronetage), educ. Clifton Coll., Bristol, and Trin. Coll. Camb. B.A. 1874; member of London Sch. Board, 1876-82; M.P. Liberal for Peterborough 1883-85 (he contested unsuccessfully as a Liberal, Boston in 1880, Peterborough in 1885, and Croydon in 1886); also sat as M.P. for the Tower Hamlets 1886-1914; member of various commissions and committees; Under Sec. of State for the Colonies, 1892-95; Postmaster Gen. with a seat in the Cabinet, 1905-1910, in which capacity he introduced penny postage to the U.S.A., the Canadian magazine post, cheap postage for the blind, and other reforms; made P.C. 1905; Pres. of the Board of Trade, 1910-14, and was cr. G.C.M.G. 1914; was cr. a peer as Viscount Buxton, of Newtimber, Sussex 11 May 1914; was Gov. Gen. of the Union of S. Africa, and High Commissioner for S. Africa, 1914-20, held several directorships, and was cr. Earl Buxton on 8 Nov. 1920. He m. (1) 5 Feb. 1882 Constance Mary (d. 3 Nov. 1892) dau. of 1st Baron Avebury. By her he had issue,
1. Charles Sydney, b. 26 May 1884; educ. Eton and Balliol Coll. Oxford, M.A. 1906; Vice Prin. of Ruskin Coll. Oxford, 1907-08; Priv. Sec. to Pres. of Board of Trade; d. unm. 31 Aug. 1911.
2. Kenneth Sydney, b. 4 Sept. 1886; d.v.p. 27 Aug. 1894.
1. Phyllis Sydney, O.B.E. (1918), b. 17 April 1888; m. 23 Sept. 1918, the Rev. Canon M. G. J. Ponsonby, M.C., (De Mauley, B.) and had issue.

Lord Buxton m. (2) 7 July 1896, Mildred Anne,

dau. of Hugh Colin Smith, of Mount Clare, Roehampton, Surrey. He had further issue by her,
3. Denis Bertram Sydney, 2nd Lt. Coldstream Guards, 1916; b. 29 Nov. 1897; educ. Eton; was k. in action v.p., and unm. 9 Oct. 1917 at Passchendale.
2. Doreen, twin with her brother, m. 24 Jan. 1918, Major C. A. E. Fitzroy, later 10th Duke of Grafton and d. 28 July 1923 leaving issue.
3. Alethea Constance Dorothy Sydney, b. 2 Aug. 1910; m. 13 July 1934, P.C. Eliot, (St. Germans, E.).

Earl Buxton was the author of several works, including *A Handbook to Political Questions*, 1880, of which 12 editions were published, a *Life of Gen. Botha*, (1924), with whom he had worked in S. Africa, and *Fishing and Shooting*, (1902). He d.s.p.m.s. 15 Oct. 1934.
ARMS—Argent a lion rampant tail elevated and turned over the head between two mullets sable.
CREST—A buck's head couped gules attired and gorged with a collar or therefrom pendent an escutcheon argent charged with an African's head sable.
SUPPORTERS—Dexter, A negro wreathed about the temples and waist with oak, holding in the dexter hand a leaf of a poplar tree all ppr. pendent from a gold cord round the neck an escutcheon argent charged with a carrier pigeon volant also ppr. Sinister, A buck gules attired and unguled or, pendant from the neck by a gold cord a shield argent charged with a ship in full sail on the sea, ppr.
MOTTO—Do it with thy might.
Earl Buxton's seat was Newtimber Place, Hassocks, Sussex.

BYNG OF VIMY

PEERAGE—U.K. Baron Byng of Vimy, of Thorpe-le-Soken, co. Essex, and Viscount Byng of Vimy.
SURNAME—Byng.
CR.—Barony 7 Oct. 1919. Viscounty 12 Jan. 1928. **EXT.**—6 June 1935.
HISTORY—Sir Julian Hedworth George Byng, **Baron Byng** and **Viscount Byng**, was b. 11 Sept. 1862, the seventh son of the 2nd Earl of Strafford, by his 2nd wife, Harriet Elizabeth, dau. of Charles Cavendish, 1st Baron Chesham. He was educ. Eton, and joined the 10th Royal Hussars, 1883; he served in the Sudan Expedition, 1884, Capt. 1889; served in the South African War 1899-1902, Brev. Lt. Col. 1902, mentioned in despatches, and awarded M.V.O. 1902; commanded 10th Royal Hussars, 1902-04; C.B., 1906; Major Gen. 1909; Gen. Officer cmdg. East Anglian Div. 1910-12; G.O.C. British Troops in Egypt, 1912-14; served in World War I as Cmdr. of 3rd Cavalry Div. 1914-15; cr. K.C.M.G. 1915; Lt. Gen. 1915; cmd. 9th Army Corps in the Dardanelles, 1915-16; K.C.B. 1916; cmd. 17th Army Corps 1916, and the Canadian Expeditionary Force 1916-17; Gen. 1917; Cmdr. 3rd Army 1917-19; G.C.B. 1919. At end of war, he received the thanks of Parliament with a grant of £30,000 and was cr. Baron Byng of Vimy, of Thorpe-le-Soken,

co. Essex, 7 Oct. 1919, and Viscount Byng of Vimy, 12 Jan. 1928. He was Gov. Gen. of Canada, 1921-26, G.C.M.G. 1921, Chief Commissioner of Metropolitan Police 1928-31; Field Marshal 1932, K.G. St. J. He m. 30 April 1902, Marie Evelyn, only child of the Hon. Sir Richard Charles Moreton, K.C.V.O., of Crookham House, Hants, (Ducie, E.) and d.s.p. 6 June 1935.

ARMS—Quarterly sable and argent in the first quarter a lion rampant argent, over all in bend sinister a representation of the colours of the 31st Regt.

CRESTS—1, Out of a mural crown an arm embowed grasping the colours of the 31st Regt. and pendent from the wrist by a ribbon the gold cross presented by command for Lord Strafford's gallant achievements all ppr., and on an escroll the word "Mouguerre". 2, An heraldic antelope statant ermine attired or.

SUPPORTERS—Dexter, An heraldic antelope ermine, attired or; Sinister, A lion or each charged on the shoulder with a rose gules.

MOTTO—Tuebor.

Lord Byng's seat was Thorpe Hall, Thorpe-le-Soken, Essex.

CABLE

PEERAGE—U.K. Baron Cable of Ideford, co. Devon.

SURNAME—Cable.

CR.—17 Jan. 1921. EXT.—28 March 1927.

HISTORY—William Cable of London, b. 1756. d. July 1841 leaving, with other issue,

George Cable of London, b. 1797; m. 11 Nov. 1819, Anne Elizabeth Dignam (d. 1848) and d. 15 Nov. 1836, having, with other issue, an eldest son,

George Herbert Cable of Calcutta, b. 19 Aug. 1823; m. 26 Mar. 1858 Emily Maria, dau. and eventual coheir of Richard Pickersgill, of St. Pancras, co. Middlesex and d. 10 Nov. 1876 leaving an only son,

Sir Ernest Cable, **Baron Cable,** b. 1 Dec. 1859, educ. Calcutta Univ.; Pres. of Bengal Chamber of Commerce; additional member of Council of Viceroy of India, sheriff of Calcutta, 1905, High Sheriff co. Devon 1916, cr. Kt. Bach and Baron Cable of Ideford, co. Devon 17 Jan. 1921; m. 10 Oct. 1888, Lilian Sarah, dau. of Weston Joseph Sparkes of Dawlish co. Devon and d. 28 Mar. 1927 having had issue,

1. George Pickersgill, b. 5 Dec 1891, Lt. 5th Bn. Rifle Brigade, attached 2nd Bn., served in World War I and was k. in action 9 May 1915.
1. Noorouz Weston, 15 Dec. 1908, Sir Lionel C. W. Alexander, 6th Bt. and had issue.
2. Ruth McCarthy, m. 11 May 1918, Capt. E. C. Benthall of Calcutta and had issue.

ARMS—Per pale vert and or fretty a fess dovetailed also per pale thereon a fret between two padlocks all counterchanged.

CREST—In front of a fret sable an escutcheon or charged with a padlock sable.

SUPPORTERS—On either side a gavial (i.e. crocodile) of the Ganges ppr. gorged with a mural crown or.

MOTTO—Probitate et labore.

CAMBRIDGE

PEERAGE—U.K. Baron of Culloden in North Britain, Earl of Tipperary in Ireland, and Duke of Cambridge.

SURNAME—None (before 1917).

CR.—27 Nov. 1801. EXT.—17 March 1904.

HISTORY—H.R.H. Adolphus Frederick, Prince of Great Britain, was the seventh and ygst. son of King George III. He was b. 24 Feb. 1774; educ. Kew and Univ. of Gottingen; Col. in the Hanoverian Army, 1793; becoming Lt. Gen. 1798, Gen. 1808, and Field Marshal 1813; cr. K.G. 1786, and **Baron of Culloden, Earl of Tipperary,** and **Duke of Cambridge,** 27 Nov. 1801. He m. 7 May 1818, at Cassel, and again on 1 June 1818, at Queen's Palace, London, (i.e. Buckingham House), Augusta Wilhelmia Louisa, dau. of Friedrich, Landgrave of Hesse Cassel Rumpenheim and d. 17 July 1850 at Kew. He had issue, with two daus. (see royal lineage in the extant peerages) a son, H.R.H. George William Frederick Charles, **2nd Duke of Cambridge,** b. 26 March 1819 at Hanover; Col. in the Army 1837, Major Gen. 1845, Field Marshal cmdg. in chief 1862-87; C. in C. by patent 1887-95; G.C.H. 1825; K.G. 1835; G.C.M.G. 1845, K.P. 1851; G.C.B. 1855; K.T. 1881; G.C.I.E. 1887; G.C.V.O. 1897; was for 39 years C. in C., and as such opposed every move towards army reform, being mentioned many times in Fortescue's *History of the British Army.* He m. in contravention of the Royal Marriage Act of 1772, on 8 Jan. 1847, at St. John's Clerkenwell (being described in the marriage register as George Frederick Cambridge, Gent. of St. Paul's, Deptford, Kent) Sarah, commonly called Louisa, dau. of Robert Fairbrother, an actress who d. 12 Jan. 1890. She was known after her marriage as Mrs. FitzGeorge. The Duke d. 17 March 1904, s.p.l. They had issue,

1. George William Adolphus FitzGeorge, b. 27 Aug. 1843, Col. 20th Hussars, m. 25 Nov. 1885 Rosa Fredericka, dau. of William Baring, of Norman Court, Hants (Northbrook, B.) and divorced wife of F. W. Arkwright, of Sanderstead Court, Surrey (B.L.G. 1952) and d. 2 Sept. 1907 having had issue.
2. Adolphus Augustus Frederick Fitz-George, b. 1846; Rear Adm. R.N. 1896, K.C.V.O. 1904, m. 1875, Sophia, Jane, dau. of Thomas Holden of Winestead Hall, Hull and had issue,
   Olga Mary Adelaide, b. 11 June 1877; m. (1) 18 Dec. 1897 (m. diss. by div. 1902) Sir Charles Edward Archibald Hamilton, 5th and 3rd Bt. (Hamilton of Trebinshun, Bt.). She m. (2) 5 Jan. 1905, R. C. Lane and had issue, a son, George Edward Archibald Augustus FitzGeorge, b. 1898; Lt. Gren. Guards, k. in action 18 May 1918, and a dau. b. and d. 5 May 1902.
3. Augustus Charles Frederick FitzGeorge b. 12 June 1847, Col. 11th Hussars, K.C.V.O. 1904; C.B. 1895.

ARMS—The royal arms of England as borne by King George III, differenced by a label of three points argent, the centre point charged with St. George's cross, and each of the other points with two hearts in pale gules.

Town House was Gloucester House, Piccadilly, where he died.

CAMPERDOWN

PEERAGE—U.K. Earl of Camperdown, of Lundie, co. Forfar and Gleneagles. co. Perth.

G.B. Baron Duncan of Lundie and Viscount Duncan of Camperdown.

SURNAME—Haldane-Duncan.

CR.—30 Oct. 1797 Viscounty & Barony. 12 Sept. 1831 Earldom. **EXT.**—5 Dec. 1933.

HISTORY—Alexander Duncan of Lundie, co. Angus (formerly Forfarshire) had issue by his wife Isabella, dau. of Sir Peter Murray Bt., (with a yr. son William, a physician, created a Baronet but d.s.p. 1774), an elder son, Alexander Duncan, of Lundie, Provost of Dundee, m. 1724 Helen, dau. of John Haldane, 14th of Gleneagles (see Chinnery-Haldane of Gleneagles, B.L.G. 1937 and 1952) she being his first cousin once removed, and d. May 1777 leaving with other issue, a third son, Adm. **Adam Duncan, 1st Baron Duncan** and **1st Viscount Duncan,** the famous naval commander, who gained the great victory off Camperdown (Kamperduin) Netherlands, over the Dutch fleet commanded by Adm. de Winter (but under French revolutionary direction) on 11 Oct. 1797. Previous to the engagement Duncan had been left with only two ships to resist invasion on the Downs because of the mutiny of the British fleet at the Nore, which was led by an ex-officer, Richard Parker, who styled himself President of the Floating Republic. This mutiny Duncan was largely instrumental in suppressing and on 30 June 1797 Parker was hanged from the yardarm of his ship. The Dutch fleet was overwhelmingly defeated and Adm. de Winter surrendered his sword to Duncan on the *Venerable.* Duncan was created Baron Duncan of Lundie and Viscount Duncan of Camperdown, 30 Oct. 1797, received the thanks of Parliament, and the freedom of the City of London, with a sword; George III went on board the Admiral's flagship to thank him and from the Crown Duncan was given a grant of £3000 per annum for the life of himself and his two next successors in the peerage. He was b. 1 July 1731; m. 6 June 1777, Henrietta, dau. of Robert Dundas of Arniston, Lord Pres. of the Court of Session, 1760-87. He inherited Gleneagles from his cousin George Cockburn afterwards Haldane, 18th of Gleneagles, and Lundie on the death of his brother, Alexander, who d.s.p. Viscount Duncan, 19th of Gleneagles d. 4 Aug. 1804 having had with other issue, an elder surviving son, Sir Robert Dundas Haldane-Duncan, **2nd Viscount Duncan** and **1st Earl of Camperdown,** of Lundie, and 20th of Gleneagles, was created K.T., and on 12 Sept. 1831 Earl of Camperdown, of Lundie and of Gleneagles. He assumed the additional surname of Haldane. He was b. 21 March 1785; m. 8 Jan. 1805, Jane (d. 1867) dau. of Sir Hew Hamilton Dalrymple, 3rd Bt., and d. 22 Dec. 1859, having had with other issue,

Adam Haldane-Duncan, **2nd Earl of Camperdown,** 21st of Gleneagles and of Lundie, M.P. successively for Southampton, Bath and Forfarshire, 1837-59, b. 25 March 1812; m. 23 March 1839, Juliana Cavendish (d. 1898), dau. of Sir George R. Philips, 2nd Bt., and d. 30 Jan. 1867, having had issue, with a dau. Julia, m. 4th Lord Abercromby,

1. Robert Adam Philips Haldane, **3rd Earl** (see below).
2. George Alexander Philips Haldane, **4th Earl** (see below).

The eldest son, Robert Adam Philips Haldane Haldane-Duncan, **3rd Earl of Camperdown,** 22nd of Gleneagles, and of Lundie, B.A. Balliol Coll. Oxford, civil Lord of the Admiralty, 1870-74, b. 28 May 1841; d. unm. 5 June 1918, being s. by his brother,

George Alexander Philips Haldane Haldane-Duncan, **4th Earl of Camperdown,** 23rd of Gleneagles, and of Lundie, b. 9 May 1845; m. 4 Feb. 1888, Laura, dau. of John Dove of Andover, Mass., U.S.A. and widow of J. A. Blanchard, of Boston, U.S.A. She d. 17 Aug. 1910. He d.s.p. 5 Dec. 1933. In 1918 he had resigned his right to Gleneagles in favour of the senior male representative of Lt. Col. James Haldane (see B.L.G. 1952).

ARMS—Quarterly 1 and 4 grand quarters, Gules in chief two cinquefoils and a bugle horn in base argent, stringed azure, in the centre, as an honourable augmentation, pendent by a ribbon of the second and third from a naval crown or a gold medal thereon two figures, the emblems of Victory and Britannia, Victory alighting on the prow of an antique vessel crowning Britannia with a wreath of laurel, below the medal the word 'Camperdown' (Duncan); 2 and 3 grand quarters, counter quartered i and iv, Argent a saltire engrailed sable (Haldane); ii, Argent a saltire between four roses gules (Lennox); iii, Or a bend chequy sable and argent (Menteith); in the centre a crescent azure for difference, all for Haldane of Gleneagles.

CRESTS—1. On waves of the sea a dismasted ship ppr. 2. An eagle's head ppr. (Haldane).

SUPPORTERS—Dexter, An angel crowned with a celestial crown, a scarf across her garments ppr., resting her exterior hand upon an anchor, the other holding a palm branch or. Sinister, A sailor holding in his exterior hand the union flag, with the tricoloured flag wrapped round the staff, all ppr.

MOTTOES—Above the 1st crest—Disce pati. Above the 2nd crest—Suffer. Under the shield —Secundis dubiisque rectus.

CAMPION

PEERAGE—U.K. Baron Campion, of Bowes, co. Surrey.

SURNAME—Campion.

CR.—6 July 1950. **EXT.**—6 April 1958.

HISTORY—Gilbert Francis Montriou Campion, **Baron Campion,** b. 11 May 1882, was the elder son of John Montriou Campion; he was educ. at Bedford School and Hertford Coll. Oxford, M.A. (1906) and Hon. Fell. 1946, D.C.L. (Hon.) Oxford 1950. He served as Capt. A.S.C., in the first World War, 1914-17. He was a Clerk Asst. in the House of Commons from 1921 and Clerk 1937-48, and was Editor of the 14th and 15th editions of *May's Parliamentary Practice.* He m. 1920, Hilda Mary, dau. of W. A. Spafford. He was cr. C.B. (1932), K.C.B. (1938), G.C.B. (1948) and a peer (1950). Lord Campion lived at Little Bowes, Abinger Hammer, Surrey, and was a member of the Athenaeum.

ARMS—Argent a chevron cottised between three talbots' heads erased sable.

CREST—Issuant from a crest coronet or, a talbot's head sable charged on the neck with a chevron cottised gold.
SUPPORTERS—Dexter, A lion azure charged on the shoulder with a portcullis chained or. Sinister, A lion gules charged on the shoulder with a lotus flower also or.

CANTERBURY

PEERAGE—U.K. Baron Bottesford, of Bottesford, co. Leicester and Viscount Canterbury of the city of Canterbury.
SURNAME—Manners-Sutton.
CR.—10 Mar. 1835. EXT.—26 Feb. 1941.
HISTORY—Lord George Manners (later Manners-Sutton), b. 1723, was the third son of the 3rd Duke of Rutland. On the death of his elder brother Lord Robert Manners-Sutton in 1762, he s. to the estates of his maternal grandfather, Robert Sutton, Baron Lexington (Extinct Peerage 1883) and assumed the additional surname of Sutton. He m. (1) 5 Dec. 1749, Diana, dau. of Thomas Chaplin (Chaplin V.) and by her (d. 13 May 1767) had with other issue a fourth son, Charles; (2) 5 Feb. 1768, Mary, dau. of Joshua Peart and by her had an only dau. Mary, m. Rev. R. Lockwood. He d. 7 Jan. 1883. His fourth son, The Most Rev. Charles Manners-Sutton D.D., b. 17 Feb. 1755; Bishop of Norwich 1792, Archbishop of Canterbury 1805. m. 3 April 1778, Mary dau. of Thomas Thoroton, of Screveton, co. Notts, and d. 21 July 1828. She d. 10 March 1832. They had with one other son and nine daus., an elder son,
Sir Charles Manners-Sutton, G.C.B., 1st Viscount Canterbury, Speaker of the House of Commons, 1817-34, created Baron Bottesford, of Bottesford, co. Leicester and Viscount Canterbury, 10 March 1835. b. 29 Jan. 1780; m. (1) 8 July 1811, Lucy (d. 7 Dec. 1815) dau. of John Denison, of Ossington, co. Notts, and had issue, with one dau.
1. Charles John, 2nd Viscount (see below).
2. John Henry Thomas, 3rd Viscount (see below).
He m. (2) 6 Dec. 1828, Ellen, dau. of Edmund Power, of Curragheen, co. Waterford, and widow of J. H. Purves by whom he had one dau., Frances, m. 18th Baron Hastings. Viscount Canterbury d. 21 July 1845 and was s. by his elder son, Charles John Manners-Sutton, 2nd Viscount Canterbury, b. 17 April 1812; d. unm. 13 Nov. 1869, being s. by his brother, Sir John Henry Thomas Manners-Sutton, 3rd Viscount Canterbury, G.C.M.G., K.C.B., Lt. Gov. New Brunswick, Gov. of Trinidad and Gov. of Victoria, b. 27 May 1814; m. 1838, Georgiana, dau. of Charles Tompson of Witchingham Hall, co. Norfolk, and d. 23 June 1877 having had issue with three sons d.s.p. and two daus.,
1. Henry Charles, 4th Viscount (see below).
2. Graham Edward Henry, b. 7 Feb. 1843; m. 1867 Charlotte Laura, dau. of Lt. Col. F. L'Estrange Astley (Hastings, B.) and d. 30 May 1888, having had with other issue, d. unm., a second son,
Charles Graham, 6th Viscount (see below).
The 3rd Viscount was s. by his eldest son,
Henry Charles Manners-Sutton, 4th Viscount Canterbury, b. 12 July 1839; m. 16 April

1872, Amye Rachel (d. 1935) dau. of Hon. F. Walpole (Orford, E.) and d. 19 Feb. 1914 being s. by his only son,
Henry Frederick Walpole Manners-Sutton 5th Viscount Canterbury, b. 8 April 1879; d. unm. 22 Oct. 1918, being s. by his cousin, Charles Graham Manners-Sutton. 6th Viscount Canterbury, b. 23 Jan. 1872, served in the S. African War, 1900-02, and in World War I, 1914-18, Capt. Submarine Miners, R.E.; m. 15 June 1903, Ethelwyn, dau. of Charles Hindle and d. 26 Feb. 1941, having had issue, Charlotte Ethelwyn, b. 22 April 1904 and d. 5 Feb. 1920.
ARMS—Quarterly 1 and 4, Argent a canton sable (Sutton); 2 and 3, Or two bars azure, a chief quarterly azure and gules, in the 1st and 4th quarters two fleurs-de-lys and in the 2nd and 3rd a lion passant guardant all or (Manners).
CREST—On a chapeau gules turned up ermine a peacock in pride, ppr.
SUPPORTERS—On either side a unicorn argent, armed, maned, tufted and unguled or; around the neck of the dexter a chain or therefrom pendent an escutcheon azure, charged with a mace erect gold; around the neck of the sinister a like chain therefrom pendent an escutcheon also azure charged with an archiepiscopal mitre.
MOTTO—Pour y parvenir.
The seats of the Lords Canterbury were Bergh-Apton, co. Norfolk and Lyndhurst, co. Hants.

CARDWELL

PEERAGE—U.K. Viscount Cardwell of Ellerbeck, co. Lancaster.
SURNAME—Cardwell.
CR.—6 Mar. 1874. EXT.—15 Feb. 1886.
HISTORY—Richard Cardwell of Blackburn, a ygr. son of Richard Cardwell of Stone Bridge was b. 22 April 1706; m. (1) Martha Holme, of Blackburn. She d.s.p. He m. (2) 1746, Elizabeth Stott (d. 31 May 1763) of Manchester and d. 10 March 1785 having an only son, Richard Cardwell of Blackburn, b. 28 May 1749; m. three times (1) Jane, dau. of John Hodson and by her had issue,
1. Richard, Rev. of Ellerbeck, b. 15 Dec. 1777, d. unm. 11 Dec. 1839.
2. James, b. 29 April 1779, d. unm. 31 May 1855.
3. John, see below.
4. Edward, Rev. D.D., b. 3 Aug. 1787, Camden Prof. of Ancient History, Oxford; m. 5 May 1829, Cecilia, dau. of Henry Feildien of Witton, co. Lancs, and d. 23 May 1861, leaving issue,
(1) Edward Henry, M.A. Univ. Coll, Oxford, b. 1833.
(2) Reginald, M.A. Ch. Ch. Oxford, b. 1834.
(3) Richard Arthur (1837-40).
(1) Cecilia Jane, m. 1857 Thomas Ellames Withington of Culcheth Hall, co. Lancs. and d. 1875.
(2) Frances Margaret.
(3) Isabella Eliza, d. 1848.
Richard Cardwell m. (2) Isabella, dau. of Richard Sclater of Bradford and (3) Anne, dau. of Thomas Thoresby and d. 4 June 1824. His third son,

John Cardwell, merchant of Liverpool, b. 31 July 1781, m. 15 Nov. 1831, leaving,

1. Edward, **Viscount Cardwell** (see below).
2. Charles, M.A. Oxford, b. 5 Dec. 1817.
1. Jane, m. 1843 Adm. Sir Edward Gennys Fanshawe, C.B. and had issue.
2. Elizabeth, m. 1856 Sir Henry Thring K.C.B., M.A., Barrister-at-Law 1845 and had issue.

The elder son, Edward Cardwell, **Viscount Cardwell**, was b. 24 July 1873; educ. Winchester and C.C. Oxford, Pres. of Oxford Union Soc. 1833-35, B.A. (double first) 1835 M.A. 1838. Fell. Balliol Coll. 1835, Barrister-at-Law, Inner Temple, 1838, was Conservative M.P. for Clitheroe 1842-47, as a Peelite for Liverpool 1847-52 and as a Liberal for Oxford City 1853-57 and 1857-74. He was Jt. Sec. to the Treasury 1845-46, Eccles Comm. 1852-82, Pres. of Board of Trade 1852-55, made P.C. 1852, Chief Sec. to Lord Lt. of Ireland 1859-61 and P.C. of Ireland, Chan. of the Duchy of Lancaster 1861-64, Sec. of State for the Colonies 1864-66, and Sec. of State for War 1868-74 when he made many far reaching reforms, including renaming regiments (the Cardwell system of stationing battalions in India etc.) F.R.S. 1873. He was cr. Viscount Cardwell of Ellerbeck, co. Lancaster 6 Mar. 1874. He m. 14 Aug. 1848, Annie, dau. of Charles Stuart Parker, of Fairlie, co. Ayr and d.s.p. 15 Feb. 1886. Viscountess Cardwell d. 20 Feb. 1887.

ARMS—Argent a chevron sable, in base a maiden's head erased ppr. ducally crowned or, on a chief of the second two maiden's heads erased also ppr. ducally crowned or.
CREST—A man in armour holding in the dexter hand a war mace all ppr. charged on the breast with a cross pattée gules.
SUPPORTERS—On either side a man in armour holding in the exterior hand a battle axe all ppr. charged on the breast with a cross pattée gules.
MOTTO—Vaillant et veillant.
Viscount Cardwell's seat was Ellerbeck Hall, Chorley, co. Lancaster.

CARISBROOKE

PEERAGE—U.K. Marquess of Carisbrooke, Earl of Berkhamsted and Viscount Launceston (the last in the county of Cornwall).
SURNAME—Mountbatten.
CR.—18 July 1917. **EXT.**—23 Feb. 1960.
HISTORY—Louis II, Grand Duke of Hesse and the Rhine (1777-1848) had with other issue, a third son, Prince Alexander of Hesse and the Rhine, G.C.B., b. 15 July 1823, m. morganatically 28 Oct. 1851 Julie Countess of Hauke who was cr. Countess of Battenberg in Hesse, 5 Nov. 1851, and Princess of Battenberg, 26 Dec. 1858, dau. of Count Maurice von Hauke. She d. 1895. He d. 1888. Their children were,

1. Louis Alexander, Prince of Battenberg, (later Mountbatten and Marquess of Milford Haven).
2. Alexander Joseph, Prince of Battenberg, from 1879-86, Alexander I, Prince of Bulgaria afterwards Count of Hartenau in Hesse, m. and left issue.

3. Henry Maurice, Prince of Battenberg. (see below).
4. Francis Joseph, Prince of Battenberg m. H.R.H. Princess Anne, dau. of King Nicholas I of Montenegro.
1. Marie Caroline, Princess of Battenberg, m. Gustave, Prince of Erbach-Schönberg and had issue.

The third son, H.R.H. Prince Henry Maurice of Battenberg, K.G., P.C., Capt. Gen. and Gov. of the Isle of Wight and Gov. of Carisbrooke Castle, was born 5 Oct. 1858; on the date and occasion of his marriage, 23 July 1885 to H.R.H. Princess Beatrice Mary Victoria Feodora, yst. dau. of Queen Victoria, was granted the style of Royal Highness by letters patent from the Queen. He was a Col. in the British Army and served in the Ashanti war of 1895. He d. at sea on 20 Jan. 1896 of fever as a result of military service. Princess Beatrice d. 1944. Their children were;

1. Alexander Albert, **Marquess of Carisbrooke** (see below).
2. Leopold Arthur Louis, G.C.V.O., b. 1889 and d. 1922. On 14 July 1917 at the request of King George V, H.H. Prince Leopold of Battenberg relinquished his Germanic styles and titles, and by Royal Licence assumed the surname of Mountbatten. On 11 Sept. 1917 he was granted by Royal Warrant, the title and precedence of the younger son of a marquess.
3. Maurice Victor Donald, K.C.V.O., b. 1891, served in first World War as Lt. K.R.R.C. and was k. in action 1914.
1. Victoria Eugenie Julia Eva, b. 1881, m. 1906 King Alfonso XIII of Spain and had issue.

The eldest son, Prince Alexander Albert of Battenberg, b. 23 Nov. 1886, educ. Wellington; m. 19 July 1917, Lady Irene Frances Adza Denison, only dau. of the 2nd Earl of Londesborough. He served in both the World Wars, and in each of the three services, having been in the R.N. 1902-08, then in the Grenadier Guards, 1911, serving from 1914 with his regiment and afterwards on the Staff (mentioned in despatches); retired from the Army 1919 as Capt.; was later F/Lt. R.A.F.V.R. and served in second World War. By Royal Warrant on 13 Dec. 1886 he was granted the style and title of Highness, but in common with other members of his family in Britain relinquished his Germanic styles and titles and assumed for himself and his issue the surname of Mountbatten by Royal Licence on 14 July 1917. On 18 July 1917 he was cr. a peer with the titles of Viscount Launceston in the county of Cornwall, Earl of Berkhamsted and **Marquess of Carisbrooke**. He d. 23 Feb. 1960 having had issue,

Iris Victoria Beatrice Grace, b. 1920, m. (1) 15 Feb. 1941 Major Hamilton Joseph Keyes O'Malley (m. diss. by div.). She resumed the surname of Mountbatten by deed poll, 1949, and m. (2) 1957 Michael N. Bryan.

The Marquess of Carisbrooke resided at Kensington Palace, W.8, and at King's Cottage, Kew Green, Richmond, Surrey. He belonged to the Naval and Military Club and Army and Navy Club.
ARMS—Quarterly, 1 and 4 grand quarters, the Royal Arms as borne by Queen Victoria, differenced by a label of three points argent, the centre point charged with a heart gules and

each of the other points with a rose gules, barbed and seeded ppr.; 2 and 3, grand quarters, quarterly I and IV azure a lion rampant, double queued barry of ten argent and gules, armed and langued compony of the 2nd and 3rd; II and III argent two pallets sable. CRESTS—1. Out of a coronet or two horns barry of ten argent and gules, issuing from each three linden leaves vert, and from the outer side of each four branches barwise having three like leaves pendant therefrom vert. 2. Out of a coronet or a plume of four ostrich feathers alternatively argent and sable. SUPPORTERS—On either side a lion guardant doubled queued or. MOTTO—In Te Domine Spero.

CARLINGFORD

PEERAGE—U.K. Baron Carlingford, of Carlingford, co. Louth.
SURNAME—Parkinson-Fortescue.
CR.—28 Feb. 1874. EXT.—30 Jan. 1898.
HISTORY—Sir John Fortescue, Lord Chief Justice of England, 1442, (see extant peerage works, under Fortescue, E.) had a son and heir, Martin Fortescue, who d.v.p. 12 Nov. 1472, having m. 10 Sept. 1454, Elizabeth, dau. and heiress of Richard Deynsell, of Filleigh and Wear Gifford, co. Devon. She m. 2ndly Sir Richard Pomeroy. Martin Fortescue had two sons, an elder, John, who was ancestor of the Fortescues, Earls and a ygr.,
William Fortescue, of Buckland Filleigh, co. Devon, m. Maud, dau. and heiress of John Atkyns, of Milton Abbot, and had an eldest son,
John Fortescue, of Buckland Filleigh, who by his wife, Christian, dau. of John Arscott, of Holdsworthy, co. Devon, had a son,
William Fortescue, of Buckland Filleigh, m. Ann, dau. of Sir Robert Giffard, and had with other children, an eldest son,
John Fortescue, of Buckland Filleigh, m. (1) Anne, dau. of Walter Porter, and widow of D. Thorne, and by her had a son, Roger, of Buckland Filleigh. Her m. (2) Susanna, dau. of Sir John Chichester (Chichester, Bt. in extant peerages), by whom he had further issue,
Sir Faithful Fortescue, went to Ireland in the beginning of James I's reign, and served under his mother's brother, Sir Arthur Chichester, Lord Chichester, Lord Deputy of Ireland. For his Irish services Sir Faithful was knighted, and rewarded with grants of extensive lands in Louth, Down and Antrim. He served under the royal banner in the great Civil War, and was at Worcester, later escaping to the Continent. On the Restoration, he was made a gentleman of the Privy Chamber to Charles II. He m. Hon. Anne Moore, second dau. of 1st Viscount Moore. She d. 5 Sept. 1634. He d. in 1666, and was bur. at Carisbrook, Isle of Wight. With other issue, they had a third son,
Sir Thomas Fortescue, of Dromisken, co. Louth, Lt. Col. in the Horse Guards, and Gov. of Carrickfergus Castle, was twice married, and by his first wife, Sydney, dau. of Col. Kingsmill, of Sidmonton, co. Hants, had issue,
1. Chichester, who s. his father.
2. William, of Newrath, co. Louth, whose son Thomas, was father of William Henry

Fortescue, who was cr. Baron Clermont 1770, Viscount Clermont, 1776, and Earl of Clermont, 1777 in the peerage of Ireland. The Earl d.s.p. in 1806, and was s. in the Barony and Viscounty by his nephew, William Charles, the son of his brother, James. The 2nd Viscount d. unm. 24 June 1829, and the honours became extinct. Of his three sisters, only Charlotte, who m. 1796, Sir Harry Goodricke, Bt., left issue, a son, Sir Henry James Goodricke, Bt., who d. unm. 1833. At this the estates of the Viscount Clermont passed to Thomas Fortescue, see below, Lord Clermont.
Sir Thomas Fortescue d. 1710, aged 90, and his elder son, Chichester Fortescue, of Dromisken, Col. in regt. of foot, served in the wars between William III and James II, in Londonderry; m. 1681, Frideswood, dau. of Francis Hall, of Mount Hall, co. Down, and had issue four daus. and an only son,
Thomas Fortescue, of Dromisken, m. 30 Aug. 1716, Anne dau. of John Garstin, of Bragganstown, co. Louth, and d. 19 May 1725, having had with a ygr. son John, and a dau., Anne, d. unm., an elder son,
Chichester Fortescue, of Dromisken, High Sheriff, of Down, 1744, M.P. for Trim, 1747-57; b. 5 June 1718; m. 9 April 1743, Hon. Elizabeth Wellesley, dau. of 1st Lord Mornington (Wellington, D.), She d. 10 Oct. 1752. He d. 16 July 1757. They had issue,
1. Thomas (see below).
2. Richard, (1749-74).
3. Chichester, Sir, Rear Adm., R.N., Ulster King of Arms, 31 Jan. 1788, b. 7 June 1750; m. 1791, Frances Anna, dau. of David Jones, of Bensfort in Meath. She d. 3 Jan. 1803. They had:
   (1) Richard (1791-1805).
   (2) Chichester, b. 28 Nov. 1794; d. 1876.
   (1) Sidney. (2) Elizabeth.
   (3) Frances Anne, m. (1) Rev. George Hamilton, and (2) Rev. G. H. Reade, and had issue.
   (4) Henrietta Catherine, m. H. Evanson, M.D.
4. Gerald, Ulster King of Arms, April 1787, b. 15 Nov. 1751; m. Elizabeth, dau. of John Tew, of Dublin, and d. 27 Oct. 1787, having had,
   Thomas, Civil Commissioner at Delhi, m. 19 Mar. 1850, Louisa Margaret, dau. of Major F. R. Eager, and d.s.p. 1872. Anne, m. Capt. W. R. Hopkins Northey, of Oving House, co. Buckingham.
1. Elizabeth, m. 9 June 1763, the 5th Marquess of Lothian,
The eldest son, Thomas Fortescue, of Dromisken, High Sheriff, co. Louth, 1770, and M.P. for Trim, was b. 1 May 1744; m. (1) Mar. 1770, Mary, dau. of Thomas Pakenham, 1st Baron Longford, by his wife, Elizabeth Cuff, who was cr. on 20 June 1785, Countess of Longford, Mary Fortescue d. 1775, leaving issue, with a son, Chichester, who d. young, two daus.,
1. Elizabeth, d. unm.
2. Anna Maria, m. 18 Jan. 1802, W. P. Buxton, Barrister, and M.P., of Redhouse, co. Louth.
He m. (2) Mary dau. of Edward Nicholson, and d. 1779, having had more issue,

1. Chichester, of whom below.
3. Harriet, m. 12 Nov. 1812, Rt. Hon. G. Knox, P.C., M.P., D.C.L., 5th son of Viscount Northland d. 21 Jan. 1816, leaving issue, (Ranfurly, E.).

The only surv. son, Chichester Fortescue, of Dromisken, High Sheriff, co. Louth. 1800, M.P. for Hillsborough, b. 12 Aug. 1777; m. 10 Aug. 1809 Martha Angel, dau. of Samuel Meade Hobson, of Muchridge House, co. Cork, Barrister-at-Law. He s. his 4th cousin once removed, Sir H. J. Goodricke, Bt., on 22 Aug. 1833, in the estates in co. Louth, as mentioned above. He d. 25 Nov. 1826, having had issue,

1. Thomas, b. 9 Mar. 1815; s. his distant cousin; educ. Exeter Coll. Oxford, B.A. 1833; was High Sheriff, co. Louth, 1839; sat as Liberal M.P. for co. Louth, 1840-41; was cr. Baron Clermont, of Dromisken, co. Louth, 11 Feb. 1852 in the Irish peerage, with a special remainder, failing the heirs male of his body, to his brother (see below). He m. 26 Sept. 1840, Louisa Grace, dau. of James Wandesforde Butler, 1st Marquess of Ormonde. He was further cr. 2 May 1866, Baron Clermont, of Clermont Park, co. Louth in the U.K. Peerage, but without special remainder. He d.s.p. 29 July 1887. Lady Clermont d. 8 Nov. 1896. The U.K. Barony became extinct, but in the Irish Barony, Lord Clermont was s. by his brother (see below).
2. Chichester Samuel, **Baron Carlingford,** and 2nd Baron Clermont (see below).
1. Martha Anne, m. 1828, Rev. E. M. Hamilton, and had issue.
2. Harriet, m. 5 Sept. 1854, David Urquhart, M.P. for Stafford, and had issue.

The second son, Sir Chichester Samuel Parkinson-Fortescue, 2nd Baron Clermont and only **Baron Carlingford,** b. 18 Jan. 1823; educ. Ch. Ch. Oxford, taking 1st class classics, B.A. 1845, Chancellor's prize for English Essay, 1846, and M.A. 1847; sat as Liberal M.P. for Louth. 1847-74; a Lord of the Treasury, 1854-55; Under Sec. of State for the Colonies, 1857-58; and 1859-65; he took the surname of Parkinson before that of Fortescue in 1863; made P.C. 1864 and P.C. (Ireland) 1866; Pres. of Board of Trade, 1871-74; Lord Lt. of Essex, 1873-92. Lord Privy Seal, 1881-85; Lord Pres. of the Council 1883-85; was cr. Baron Carlingford, of Carlingford, co. Louth, 28 Feb. 1874 and K.P. 1882. He m. 20 Jan. 1863, as her 4th husband, Frances Elizabeth Anne, dau. of John Braham, a tenor singer, (she had m. first John James Henry Waldegrave, illegitimate son of the 6th Earl Waldegrave, and secondly his legitimate brother, the 7th Earl Waldegrave, by these marriages obtaining all the Waldegrave estates, and for her third husband she m. George Granville Vernon-Harcourt, of Nuneham Park, co. Oxford). Lady Carlingford d. 5 July 1879. She left to her 4th husband, the Waldegrave estates, for life, with succession to Earl Waldegrave. Lord Carlingford and Clermont d.s.p. 30 Jan. 1898.

ARMS—Quarterly 1 and 4, Azure a bend engrailed argent, cotised or, (Fortescue). 2 and 3, Per chevron, gules and azure, on a chevron engrailed between three ostrich feathers, erect, argent, as many pellets, (Parkinson).

CRESTS—1. An heraldic tiger ppr., supporting with his forepaw a plain shield, argent (Fortescue), 2. A falcon, wings addorsed ppr., belled or, and charged on the breast with a pellet, in the beak an ostrich feather argent.
SUPPORTERS—Two moose deer ppr. attired or; each gorged with a collar of trefoils also ppr.
MOTTOES—Forte scutum salus ducum. (for Parkinson) Si celeres quatit pennas.

Lord Carlingford's seats were: Ravensdale Park, Newry; Chewton Priory, near Bath; Dudbrooke House, Brentwood, Essex; Red House, Ardree, co. Louth. His clubs were Reform; Brooks's; Travellers' and Athenaeum.

CARMICHAEL

PEERAGE—U.K. Baron Carmichael, of Skirling, co. Peebles.
SURNAME—Gibson-Carmichael.
CR.—7 Feb. 1912. EXT.—16 Jan. 1926.
HISTORY—Sir Thomas David Gibson-Carmichael, **Baron Carmichael,** was the eldest son of the Rev. Sir William Henry Gibson-Carmichael, 10th Bt., (see extant baronetage, Gibson-Craig-Carmichael), and was b. 18 Mar. 1859; educ. privately and St. John's Coll. Cambridge, B.A. 1881, M.A. 1884; Priv. Sec. to Sec. for Scotland, 1886; s. his father as 11th Bt. 1891; Chm. Scottish Liberal Association, 1892-1901, and of the Scottish Board of Lunacy, 1894-97; M.P. as Liberal for Midlothian, 1895-1900, having previously contested unsuccessfully, Peebles and Selkirk in 1892; Gov. of Victoria, 1908-11; of Madras, 1911-12; and of Bengal, 1912-17; he was a good judge of art and a keen entomologist, and was Trustee of the Nat. Gallery, the Nat. Portrait Gallery, of the Wallace Collection etc. He was cr. K.C.M.G. 1908, G.C.I.E. 1911, G.C.S.I. 1917, and Baron Carmichael of Skirling, co. Peebles, 7 Feb. 1912. He m. 1 July 1886, Mary Helen Elizabeth, L.G. St. J., dau. of Albert Llewellyn Nugent, Baron Nugent of the Austrian Empire and d.s.p. 16 Jan. 1926. The barony became extinct, but the baronetcy passed to his cousin Sir Henry Gibson-Craig.
ARMS—Quarterly. 1, Argent a fess wreathed azure and gules within a bordure of the last (Carmichael). 2 and 3, Gules, three keys fesswise in pale or (Gibson); 4. Ermine, on a fess sable three crescents argent (Craig).
CRESTS—1, A dexter arm embowed in armour, holding a broken lance in bend, all ppr. (Carmichael); 2. A pelican in her piety ppr. (Gibson).
SUPPORTERS—Two angels ppr.
MOTTOES—Toujours prest; and Caelestes pandite portae.
Seat was at Skirling, co. Peebles.

CARNWATH

PEERAGE—Scotland. Baron Dalzell, 18 Sept. 1628. Earl of Carnwath, and Baron Dalzell and Liberton. 21 April 1639. Also a baronetcy 11 April 1666.
SURNAME—Dalzell.
CR.—as above. EXT. or DORMANT— 9 March 1941.

HISTORY—The name of Thomas de Dalzelle occurs in the Ragman's Roll of Edward I, which was signed at Berwick-on-Tweed, 28 Aug. 1296. The name is derived from Dalziel, in N. Lanarkshire, pronounced Dee-eil. Sir Robert de Dalzell obtained from King David II grants of the serjeantship of Lanark on the resignation of Andrew Starheved, and of the lands of Croykstoune, co. Peebles; he had from the same king a charter—dilecto et fideli nostro Roberto de Dalzell militi, pro homagio et servicio suo, omnes terras nostras de Selkyrk, cum pertinenciis, exceptis annuis redditibus nostris et firmis nostris de burgo nostro de Selkyrk—to him and the legitimate heirs male of his body, 15 May 1365. He was one of the Scottish barons who were surety in 1379 to Haco, King of Norway, that Henry Sinclair, Earl of Orkney, should faithfully govern the islands of Orkney. He d. 1380. Sir William de Dalzell obtained from David II, 13 Aug. 1364, a grant of the fee of five pounds sterling per annum as serjeant of Lanark, either out of Sheriff Court, or the Justiceair held there. In 1388, Sir William lost an eye at the battle of Otterburn, and in 1390 accompanied Sir David Lindsay, of Glenesk (afterwards Earl of Crawford) to the famous tournament at London (on London Bridge) in which he defeated the English champion Sir Piers Courtenay. He recovered the estate of his ancestors and was styled—William de Dalzell, dominus ejusdem—and was witness to a charter of Johanna de Keith, Lady of Gallystoun, to her son Andrew de Hamyltoun, 11 Dec. 1406. Sir William's elder son, George de Dalzell, obtained, on the resignation of James Sandilands, the brother-in-law, of King Robert III, a charter of the barony of Dalzell, co. Lanark, to him and the heirs male of his body, failing which, to the heirs male of his father, Sir William de Dalzell, 5 July 1395. He d.s.p. before 1400, v.p., and the line is traced through his younger brother, Sir John de Dalzell, had a letter of safe conduct to pass into England, with four other knights and sixty horse in their train, to treat of national business, 24 July 1392; he had a charter of the lands of Kinmouth, Bouchtains, and half of Clune, co. Banff, from King Robert III, on the resignation of Alexander Keith. From the same King he had a grant of the St. Leonard's Hospital, near Lanark, with the whole lands and revenues thereto belonging, upon condition that he and his heirs should provide a priest to celebrate three masses once in every seven years for the salvation of the souls of the King, Annabella his Queen, and all their children for ever. This charter is dated 3 June 1400, with remainder to Walter, Adam, and Robert de Dalzell, his sons, and the heirs male of their bodies respectively, and was confirmed by King James II, 19 Feb. 1449-40, by which time Sir John was dead, he being termed, quondam in the confirmation. He had issue, as above, namely,

1. Walter, of Carlowrie, West Lothian, living, 4 June 1424, and 19 Jan. 1427, who left issue.
2. Adam, of Botheau and Elliotstown, living 5 Feb. 1423, and 10 Nov. 1426, who left issue.
3. Robert, see below.

The third son, Robert Dalzell, of Dalzell, s. to that estate before 27 June 1446, m. Agnes

Hamilton, and d. before 10 Nov. 1496, having had issue, with a ygr. son, John of Bracanrig and Brownside, who d. before 1490 leaving issue, an elder son,

William Dalzell of that ilk, s. also to the lands of Elliok, and was one of the Lords of Council, 14 Oct. 1495. He m. Gelis, or Elizabeth Hamilton, of Preston, and had issue,

1. Robert, living 1506, d.v.p. before 15 Dec. 1508, leaving a son, Robert, heir to his grandfather.
2. Thomas, living 14 July 1524, left issue.
3. Patrick.
4. George, M.A. Glasgow, living 29 April 1509.
5. John.
1. Marion, m. (1) 1500, John Montgomery, the ygr. of Skelmorlie and (2) before 1534, Michael Lindsay.

William Dazell, was slain in an affray at Dumfries, 1508, and was s. by his grandson, Robert Dalzell, of that ilk, m. Margaret Hamilton, and d. before 21 May 1550, having had issue,

1. Robert, of whom presently.
2. William, slain by John Douglas, 8 May 1555.
3. Paul, living 1512.
4. John, living 4 July 1524.
1. Christian m. (1) John Somervill, of Cambusneth, and (2) John Lindsay, of Covington, and (3) 1556, John Crichton, of Ryhill, by whom she had issue.
2. Margaret, m. Gavin Lockhart, of Kirkwood.

The eldest son, Robert Dalzell, of that ilk, had sasine of Dalzell, 26 May 1549, and by his first wife had issue,

1. Robert, his heir.
2. Andrew fought at Langside, 13 May 1568.
1. Christian, m. 1562 John Boswell, of Auchinleck.
2. Margaret, m. John Hamilton, of Bromhill. He m. (2)—contract made 29 Jan. 1551—Cristine, dau. of James Dundas, of Newliston, and by her, who m. 2ndly James Robertson, of Earnock, had further issue,

3. John, of Edinburgh, living 2 April 1574, said to have been ancestor of Dalzell, or Dalyell, of the Binns, Bt.,
4. James, of Edinburgh, living 1591.
3. Catherine, m. John Robertson, Sheriff Clerk of Lanark, and had issue,
4. Helen, m. (contract 16 Nov. 1590) John Stirling, of Baldoran.

He d. before 1563 and was s. by his eldest son, Robert Dalzell, of that ilk, fought for Queen Mary at Langside, 13 May 1568, M.P. for Wigtown, 1587, m. (contract 1 May 1558) Janet, dau. of Gavin Hamilton, commendator of Kilwinning, and d. before Feb. 1610, having had issue,

1. Robert, **1st Baron Dalzell** (see below).
2. Gavin, living 9 May 1580.
3. Archibald, m. 13 July 1599, Jean, dau. of Nicol Dalzell, of Dalzell, Mill. This marriage was annulled 25 Dec. 1601.
4. James, living 28 June 1592.
5. Claud, d. 1587.
6. Thomas, living 1597.
1. Christian, m. John Hamilton, of Orbiston, and had issue.
2. Janet, living 1586.
3. Margaret, m. (contract 5 Aug. 1601) Robert Nisbet.

4. Marion, living 1586.
5. Elizabeth, living 1586.

The eldest son, Robert Dalzell, **1st Lord Dalzell,** who had charters from his father of the lands of Ellioc, 1574, and of Dalzell, 1580, was cr. Lord Dalzell, 18 Sept. 1628, with remainder to his heirs male bearing the name and arms of Dalzell; m. (contract 28 March 1580) Margaret, dau. of Sir Robert Crichton, of Cluny, and by her had issue,

1. Robert, **2nd Lord Dalzell,** and **1st Earl of Carnwath** (see below).
2. John, Sir, of Glenae and Newton, who fought at the battle of Worcester, 3 Sept. 1651, and was taken prisoner, m. before 1625, Agnes, dau. of James Nesbit, of Restalrig, and d. before 23 Sept. 1669, having had issue,
   (1) Robert, Sir, 1st Bt., so cr. a baronet of Scotland, 11 April, 1666, M.P. for Dumfries, 1665-74, 1681-82, and 1685; m. (1) a dau. of Sandilands, and by her had issue,
   1a Mary, m. (contract 21 April 1652) Robert Lawrie, of Maxwelton.
   Sir Robert m. (2) (contract, 11 Oct. 1654, Margaret, dau. of James Johnstone, 1st Earl of Hartfell. She d.s.p. Oct. 1655. He m. (3) (contract 23 April 1657), Violet, dau. of Andrew Riddell, of Haining, and d. before April 1686, having by her had further issue,
   1a John, Sir, 2nd Bt., M.P. for Dumfries, 1686 and 1689; m. 16 June 1686, Henrietta, dau. of Sir William, Bt., of Stanhope, and d. March 1689, having had issue,
   1b Robert, Sir, 3rd Bt., later **5th Earl** (see below).
   2b John, Capt. in the Army, who resigned to join the Jacobite forces, and was captured at Preston, 14 Oct. 1715.
   1b Mary, m. (1) 1711, William, 6th Viscount Kenmure, who was beheaded 24 Feb. 1716, leaving issue. She m. (2) after 27 May, 1736, John Lumsden, cr. a baronet by the Pretender, 5 Jan. 1740. He d.s.p. 1751. She d. 16 Aug. 1776.
   2b Agnes, m. Sir John Johnstone, 1st Bt., of Westerhall, who d. 30 Sept. 1711.
   2a James, who joined the Jacobite forces, and was captured at Preston, 1715; m. the dau. of Graham and had issue, a son, John, of Barncrosh, Collector of Customs at Kirkcudbright; m. Henrietta, dau. of 6th Viscount Kenmure and had issue.
   3a Thomas, Col. Scots Guards, m. Nov. 1701, Isabel, only dau. of Robert Ferguson, of Craigdarroch, and d. Dec. 1743, having had issue,
   1b David of Glasgow, merchant d. 30 March 1772, having had issue.
   1b Jean, m. Thomas Gibson, and d. 1786, having had issue.
   2b Agnes.   3b. Henrietta.
   (1) Mary, m. (contract 8 July 1665),

Alexander, 5th Earl of Kellie, and had issue.

3. James, m. (contract 7 Aug. 1618) Marion, dau. of ——— Crauford, and widow of James Oswell, of Athellis.
4. Thomas, Burgess of Banff, 1640, living 1663.
5. William, living 1624.
1. Margaret, m. (contract 9 July, 1610), John Wilson, ygr. of Croglin.
2. A dau. m. before 1607, George Crawford, ygr. of Auchencross.
3. Mary m. Sir James Muirhead, of Lachop.

The first Lord Dalzell d. before July 1636, and was s. by his eldest son, Robert Dalzell, **2nd Baron Dalzell,** and **1st Earl of Carnwath.*** He had charters in 1634 and 1635 of the barony of Carnwath. He s. his father in the barony by July 1636, and on 21 April 1639 he was cr. Earl of Carnwath and Baron Dalzell and Liberton, with limitation to him and his heirs male bearing the name and arms of Dalzell. He was fined £10,000 Scots, having been accused by the Scottish Convention of having betrayed the designs of the Scots to King Charles I in June 1643. He became in even greater disfavour with them, for on 25 Feb. 1645 he was declared forfeit, and sentenced to death, the act providing that his son and heir should s. him as if he were dead. He fought at Naseby 14 June 1645 and was at Worcester 3 Sept. 1651, taken prisoner there, being confined in the Tower, but strangely enough being allowed out to enable him to go to Epsom to take the waters 25 June 1652. He m. (1) Christian, dau. of Sir William Douglas, of Hawick, who brought with her a tochter or portion of 20,000 marks. He m. (2) Katherine, dau. of John Abington, of Dowdeswell, co. Gloucester and d. (bur. 21 June) 1654. His widow (who m. 2ndly William Watkins, of Westminster, and thirdly, Samuel Collins, Dr. of Physic) d. (bur. 12 Aug.) 1712, being entered in the burial register as Dowager Countess of Carnwath. By his first wife, the 1st Earl had issue,

1. Gavin, **2nd Earl** (see below).
2. William, d. unm. 1647.
1. Anna, m. (contract 27 Sept. 1632) John Hamilton of Preston and d.s.p.

The elder son, Gavin Dalzell, **2nd Earl of Carnwath,** who was by 1646 referred to as Earl of Carnwath, but who was a royalist and fought at Worcester for Charles II, being captured and held prisoner for many years. He m. (1) (contract 21 July 1637) Margaret, eldest dau. and coheir of David Carnegy, son and heir of 1st Earl of Southesk, He m. (2) before 14 Dec. 1663, Mary, dau. of Alexander Erskine, son of 1st Earl of Kellie but by her had no issue. By his first wife, the Earl had issue,

1. James, **3rd Earl** (see below)
2. John, **4th Earl** (see below).
3. Robert.
1. Margaret.
2. Jane, m. Charles Muirhead, of Lachop.
3. Christian, d. 1650. 4. Mary, d. 1650.

The second Earl d. June 1674, and was s. by eldest son, James Dalzell, **3rd Earl of Carnwath,** was at Glasgow Univ. 1659. He sold the estate of Carnwath to Sir George Lockhart,

*See note 5 at end of article on the numbering of the earldom.

1682. He m. 10 Dec. 1676, Mary, dau. of George Seton, 3rd Earl of Wintoun, and d.s.p.m., 1683 (having had a dau., Elizabeth m. Lord John Hay, son of 2nd Marquess of Tweeddale) when he was s. by his brother,

John Dalzell, **4th Earl of Carnwath**, at Glasgow Univ. 1659; d. unm. 7 June 1702, being s. by his second cousin,

Sir Robert Dalzell, 3rd Bt., (see above) and **5th Earl of Carnwath**, b. circa 1687; educ. at Cambridge and was an English Episcopalian. He fought on the Jacobite side in the 1715 rising, and was captured at Preston. He was impeached 19 Jan. 1715/16, pleaded guilty, was sentenced to death as a traitor, and on being therefore attainted his estate and his peerages were forfeited. He was however pardoned as far as his life and estates were concerned, but the attainder stood as to his honours and titles. He m. (1) (contract 19 Jan. 1710) Grace, dau. of 9th Earl of Eglintoun. She d. Jan. 1713. By her he had issue,

1. Euphemia, b. 12 Feb. 1703, but d. young.
2. Margaret, d. unm. 18 April 1781.

He m. (2) 3 June 1720, Grizell, dau. of Alexander Urquhart, of Newhall. She was bur. 4 Sept. 1723, at Bath Abbey. By her he had,

1. Alexander, but for attainder, **6th Earl of Carnwath** (see below).

He m. (3) 15 Nov. 1728, Margaret, dau. of John Hamilton, of Bangour. By her who d. 13 Feb. 1730 he had issue,

3. Elizabeth, d. young, 12 Dec. 1737.

He m. (4) 19 June 1735, Margaret, dau. of Thomas Vincent, of Barnborough Grange, co. York, and by her (who d. 11 April 1758) had further issue,

2. Robert, m. 24 May 1761, Elizabeth, dau. of Richard Acklom, of Wiseton Hall, co. Nottingham. She d. 14 May 1817. He d. 29 July 1788, aged 50 leaving issue,
   (1) Robert Alexander, who was restored to the Earldom as **9th Earl of Carnwath.**
   (1) Elizabeth, d. unm. 24 Mar. 1819, aged 52.

The 5th Earl d. 4 Aug. 1737 aged about 50. His elder son, Alexander Dalzell, who but for the attainder would have been **6th Earl of Carnwath,** and who assumed the title, and so styled himself, was b. 2 Feb. 1721/2, and m. before 1753, Elizabeth Jackson, a spinster, by whom his issue was,

1. Richard, b. 23 July 1753; m. 1775, Elizabeth Johnson, and d. 5 July 1782, leaving an only dau., Elizabeth who m. Sir Alexander Gilbert Grierson, 6th Bt. of Lag, who d. 1840.
2. Robert (see below).
3. Alexander, b. 23 Aug. 1760, d. unm. 1788.
4. John, b. 19 Nov. 1765. Had issue a dau. Eliza Jane, who m. Jonas M. Leake, M.D.
1. Margaret, m. 1778, Sir Robert Grierson, 5th Bt. of Lag.
2. Elizabeth, d. unm. 23 Dec. 1830.

He d. 3 April 1787, aged 65, and his eldest surv. son, Robert Dalzell, but for the attainder **7th Earl of Carnwath,** but who never so styled himself, was b. 1755; mem. of Faculty of Advocates, Edinburgh, 1776; m. 18 Mar. 1783, Anne, dau. of David Armstrong, of Kirtleton, co. Dumfries, an advocate. She d. 21 Feb. 1797. He d. 13 Feb. 1808. They had issue,

1. John (see below).
1. Margaret, who s. to Glenae in 1814, b. 29 April 1784; m. 20 Aug. 1818, Major Douglas Stewart Dalzell. He d. 25 April 1847. She d. 29 April 1847, leaving issue,
2. Elizabeth, b. 20 Oct. 1790; m. 31 Aug, 1812, Henry Alexander Douglas, brother of the 5th Marquess of Queensberry. and had issue.

The only son, John Dalzell, of Glenae, but for the attainder **8th Earl of Carnwath**, an officer in the R.N., who fell in action off New Orleans, b. 18 Aug. 1795. He is said, in *C.P.*, to have been a Major in the Marines at the age of three. He d. unm. 10 Oct. 1814. We pass now to Lieut. Gen. Robert Alexander Dalzell, **6th Earl of Carnwath** but **9th Earl of Carnwath,** as he would have been but for the attainder, but who obtained a restoration to the dignity and title of Earl of Carnwath, on 26 May 1826. He was in the Gren. Guards, served in the Peninsula under Wellington, and was second in command in India, Major Gen. 1814, Lt. Gen. 1830. He was b. 13 Feb. 1768; m. (1) 23 Sept. 1789, Jane, dau. of Samuel Parkes, of Cork. She d. 30 Sept. 1791. By her he had issue, an only dau.,

1. Elizabeth, b. 12 Aug. 1790; d. 3 May 1801.

He m. (2) 26 April 1794, Andalusia, dau. of Lt. Col. Arthur Browne, of Knockduff, House, Kingsale. She d. March 1833. By her he had issue with others who d. young,

1. Thomas, **10th Earl** (see below).
2. Arthur Alexander, **9th Earl (12th)** (see below).
3. Harry Burrard, **10th Earl (13th)** (see below).
4. Robert Alexander George, C.B., Col. Gren. Guards, Knight of the Order of the Medjidie, b. 19 Aug. 1816; m. 27 Aug. 1846, Sarah Bushby, dau. of Capt. John Harris, R.N., of Eldon House, London, Canada, and d. 19 Oct. 1878 having by her (who d. 29 May 1916) had issue,
   (1) Robert Harris Carnwath, **11th Earl (14th)** (see below).
   (2) Arthur Edward, **13th Earl (16th)** (see below).
   (1) Amelia Andalusia, d. an infant, 15 Aug. 1850.
   (2) Mary Isabella, m. 30 July 1874, Major Thomas Leith, (Burgh, B.) and d. 5 Feb. 1836.
   (3) Charlotte Emma Maud, C.B.E. (1919), m. 25 Feb. 1882, Col. Sir Lancelot Rolleston, K.C.B., of Watnall Hall, co. Nottingham.
2. Emma, Maria, d. unm. 25 Dec. 1882.
3. Eleanor Jane Elizabeth, d. unm. 4 May 1835.
4. Charlotte Augusta, d. unm. 27 Dec. 1844.

The Earl m. (3) 11 Oct. 1838, Jane, dau. of John Cornell, of Corrednon and Hazel Hall, co. Kent, and widow of Major Alexander Morrison, of Gunnersbury Park, co. Middlesex. She d. 14 May 1863. The Earl d. 1 Jan. 1839, and was s. by his eldest son,

Thomas Henry Dalzell, **7th Earl of Carnwath (10th),** b. 2 Sept. 1797; m. (1) 9 Sept. 1834, Mary Anne, dau. of Rt. Hon. Henry Grattan, and widow of John Blachford, of Altadore, co. Wicklow; she d. 22 Sept. 1853. He m. (2) 2 May 1855, Isabella Eliza, dau. of Col. Yardley Wilmot, and widow of J. H. Lecky. She d. 16 Oct. 1902. The Earl d. 14 Dec. 1867, and was s. by his only son by his second marriage,

Henry Arthur Hew Dalzell, **8th Earl of Carnwath (11th)** b. at Heidelberg 12 April 1858, and d. unm. from the meazles, 13 Mar. 1873, being s. by his uncle,

Arthur Alexander Dalzell, **9th Earl of Carnwath (12th)**, Major Gen. 1858; Lt. Gen. 1865, and Gen. 1873, commanded the Dublin district, and from 1861-65, the Shorncliffe and South Eastern District. He was Asst. Sec. for Scotland, 1854-59. He was b. 15 Sept. 1799; d. unm. 28 April 1875, being s. by his brother,

Harry Burrard Dalzell, **10th Earl of Carnwath (13th)**, b. 11 Nov. 1804; Bengal Artillery, 1820; Col. 1835; Commissary of Ordnance at Agra, 1835-42; m. 16 Nov. 1827, Isabella, dau. of the Rev. Alexander Campbell. She d. 14 Oct. 1867. By her he had issue,

1. Arthur John, b. 8 April 1829; d. 9 April 1849.
2. Robert Augustus, Capt. Scots Fusilier Guards, b. 13 Oct. 1838; d. at Cannes, 20 April 1869.
1. Eleanor Carnwath, d. unm. 29 May 1867.
2. Edith Isabella, m. 31 July 1875, Adm. E. S. Adeane, C.M.G., and d. 7 May 1909, leaving issue.

The 10th Earl d. 1 Nov. 1887, and was s. by his nephew, Robert Harris Carnwath Dalzell, **11th Earl of Carnwath (14th)**, b. 1 July 1847; Major 79th Highlanders, 1882, and Lt. Col. 1st Bn. Queen's Own Cameron Highlanders, a Representative Peer for Scotland, 1892-1910; m. 19 Aug. 1873, Emily Sulivan, dau. of Henry Hippisley, of Lamborne Place, Berks, and Cote House, Oxon. She d. 7 May 1889, having had issue,

1. Robert Hippisley, b. 30 Sept. 1877; B.A. Trin. Coll. Camb; d. unm. v.p. 2 Aug. 1904.
2. Ronald Arthur, **12th Earl (15th)** (see below).
1. Ida Elizabeth, m. 8 June 1907, Frederick Ramon de Bertolano, 8th Marquis del Moral (for pedigree see Foreign Titles Section of Burke's Peerage in editions before that of 1949), and had issue.
2. Violet Charlotte, m. 19 Feb. 1901, Lt. Col. the Hon. H. G. Henderson, C.V.O., (Faringdon, B.) and had issue.

The Earl d. 8 March 1910, being s. by his only surv. son, Ronald Arthur Dalzell, **12th Earl of Carnwath (15th)**, Lt. Welsh Horse Yeo. b. 3 June 1883; m. 23 July 1910, Maude Maitland, dau. of John Eden Savile, of St. Martin's Stamford, and d.s.p. 11 July 1931, when he was s. by his uncle,

Sir Arthur Edward Dalzell, **13th Earl of Carnwath (16th)**, b. 25 Dec. 1851, a Representative Peer for Scotland, 1935; Col. 52nd Light Infantry, on Staff India, 1892-96, comm. No. 6 District, 1906-08; in World War I, raised and comm. 12th Service Bn. Cheshire Regt., comm. 207th Brigade, 1915-16, and was on special service in France, hon. Brig. Gen. 1917; he served in the Burmese War, 1891-92; in S. African War, (comm. a mobile column, and was present at several of the battles, and the occupation of Bloemfontein, mentioned in despatches, two medals and six clasps, and received C.B. 1900; was Comm. of Order of St. Nento' Avis, of Portugal; m. 4 Dec. 1902, Muriel Wyndham, dau. of Col. Norton Knatchbull (Brabourne, B.) and d. 9 March 1941, having had issue,

Arthur Robert Lancelot, b. 11 Mar. 1907; d. 28 Feb. 1909.

Muriel Marjorie, b. 22 Sept. 1903; m. 18 Jan. 1927, Major John Norton Taylor, I.A., and had issue. They assumed by Royal Licence, 18 Jan. 1927, the name and arms of Dalzell, in lieu of those of Taylor.

ARMS—Sable a naked man arms extended ppr.

CREST—A dagger erect azure, pommel and hilt or.

SUPPORTERS—Two armed men with targets in their exterior hands, all ppr.

MOTTO—I dar.

NOTE 1. The wife of the 11th Earl d. at Carnwath House, Fulham, where there is a road named Carnwath Road, in memory of the House and family. The 11th Earl, according to *C.P.* d. suddenly from syncope, dropping dead in St. Anne's Street, Westminster while walking to the House of Lords. He was bur. at Fulham.

NOTE 2. The very remarkable coat of arms of Dalzell, so simple and singular lends itself to illustration and it is shown in both John Woodward's *Treatise on Heraldry*, and in Sir Thomas Inne's *Scots Heraldry*.

NOTE 3. Dalyell of the Binns. The pedigree is given in the extant peerage works, with the name of Thomas Dalyell described as apparent heir of tailzie to the baronetcy and estate of the Binns. He is the grandson of the last Baronet and his mother married Col. Gordon Loch, who later assumed the name and arms of Dalyell of the Binns in lieu of those of Loch., 1938, Lyon Court.

NOTE 4. The numbering of the Earls of Carnwath in the above article follows the arrangement in the *C.P.*, and a note on the effect of attainder and of restoration may not be out of place. It appears to be settled peerage law that an attainder cannot be removed by the action of the Sovereign alone, but must be affected by Act of Parliament. This is certainly very extraordinary, in view of the well known position of the Sovereign as the Fountain of Honour. What the Crown gave, the Crown should apparently be able to restore. However, the view clearly expressed in Sir Francis Palmer's *Peerage Law* (ch. XVIII, edition 1907) is that an Act of Parliament is required to restore a peerage once passed under attainder. It might be thought that this arises from the circumstances of e.g. the rebellion of 1715, which could be viewed as having endangered the safety of the State as well as that of the Crown, or the new Hanoverian dynasty, and as therefore requiring an act of the State as well as the assent of the Sovereign. But in support of the view given in Palmer, Sir Edward Coke is cited as saying (Inst. III, chap. 106) "The reason wherefore the King may by his charter pardon the execution and restore the party or his heirs to the lands forfeited by the attainder and remaining in the Crown is for that no person hath thereby any prejudice; but to make restitution of his blood he cannot do it but by Act of Parliament, because it should be to the prejudice of others." The reason here is very difficult to follow; but it is interesting as an early example of the way in which great lawyers have sought to fetter the power of the Crown in matters of title, which seem peculiarly to be within the royal prerogative. The Life

Peerage Act of 1958 and the Peerage Act of 1963 are modern examples.

However, whatever the reasoning, the fact is clear that an attainder once passed, removes the title, and when the title is restored, as in the Carnwath case, to the descendant or collateral kinsman, the numbering must ignore those holders of the title who lived during the time of the attainder. Consequently the larger numbering is given above only in brackets, because the usual numbering in peerage works is clearly wrong.

It may be noted in passing that by sec. 1 of the Forfeiture Act, 1870, forfeiture of title is abolished. "No confession, verdict, inquest conviction, or judgment of or for any treason or felony or felo-de-se, shall cause any attainder or corruption of blood or any forfeiture or escheat."

NOTE 5 on the numbering of the first Earl of Carnwath.

There is a conflict between the numbering of the first Earl of Carnwath as given in Vol. 2 of the Scots Peerage (edited by Sir James Balfour Paul, Lord Lyon) and published in 1905, under Dalzell, Earl of Carnwath, page 408, and the C.P. likewise under Carnwath, Vol. 3, page 49. In view of the great value of both the Scots Peerage and the C.P., it is worthwhile, for the sake of those who will study both books, and the present account to give the reasons for preferring the numbering given in C.P. A note on page 49 of Vol. 3 of C.P. states that the proof of the numbering of Robert Dalzell, son and heir of Lord Dalzell (so. cr. 1628) as 1st Earl of Carnwath, was supplied to the Editor of C.P. by J. Maitland Thomson, LL.D., "The person who was *Master* of Dalzell, 11 July 1635, (Reg. Mag. Sig.) was Lord Dalzell at the date of his son's marriage contract, 21 July 1637 (Reg. of Deeds, 526, 69) and the first Lord Dalzell was dead July 1636 (Lanark Sas., Upper Ward, III, 342). 'It therefore follows as the night the day' that it was Robert the son who was cr. Earl of Carnwath 21 April 1639". In the above note the C.P. took definite notice of the account in the Scots Peerage. The first lord Dalzell is stated in the Scots Peerage to have died 1639, but in Vol. 4 of C.P. (published in 1916) his date of death is given as occurring between 11 July 1635 and July 1636, with the note "in all previous accounts he has been stated to have been cr. Earl of Carnwath, but see Vol. 3, page 49, note b. under that title", the gist of which is given above.

CARRON

PEERAGE—U.K. Life. Baron Carron of the city and co. of Kingston-upon-Hull.
SURNAME—Carron.
CR.—11 July 1967. EXT.—3 Dec. 1969.
HISTORY—Sir William John Carron, **Baron Carron**, was the son of John Carron of Carrowdean, co. Donegal and of Hull (1871-1917) by his wife, Frances Anne Richardson. William John Carron, b. 19 Nov. 1902; educ. St. Mary's R.C. Primary Sch. Hull, and Hull Tech. Coll., M.A. Oxford F.R.S.A., Pres. of A.E.U. 1956-67, mem. Gen. Council of T.U.C. 1954-68, Dir. Bank of England 1963 and of U.K. Atomic Energy Authority 1967. He was cr. Kt. Bach. 1963 and a Life Peer as Baron Carron of the city and county of Kingston-upon-Hull, 11 July 1967. A devout R.C. he was made a Kt. of the papal order of St. Gregory, 1959. He m. 5 Aug. 1931 Mary Emma, dau. of John McGuire, of Hull and d. 3 Dec. 1969 having had issue, two daus., Hilary Mary, m. J. S. Weidemann and had issue, and Patricia Anne.
ARMS—Azure a pile or (charged with a pile gules) thereon a passion cross argent, overall on a chief or a carronade ppr., the whole surmounted by a chain in orle argent.
CREST—An eagle rising ppr. gorged with an ancient crown or, the dexter claw resting on a cogwheel sable, in the beak a trefoil vert.
SUPPORTERS—Dexter, A beaver and sinister, A wolf both ppr. each gorged with an ancient crown or.
MOTTO—In veritate atque fortitudine.

CARSON

PEERAGE—U.K. Life. Baron Carson of Duncairn, co. Antrim.
SURNAME—Carson.
CR.—1 June 1921. EXT.—22 Oct. 1935.
HISTORY—Edward Henry Carson was father of a second son, Sir Edward Henry Carson, **Baron Carson**, b. 9 Feb. 1854; M.A. Trin. Coll. Dublin, Barrister-at-Law, King's Inns, 1877, Q.C. 1889, Bencher 1891; Solicitor Gen. for Ireland 1892-93; Barrister-at-Law Middle Temple, 1893, Q.C. 1894, Bencher 1900, Treasurer 1922, Solicitor Gen. for England 1900-05, Attorney Gen. 1915, First Lord of the Admiralty 1916-17 and mem. of the War Cabinet without portfolio 1917-18, M.P. for Trin. Coll. Dublin, 1892-1918, and for Duncairn Div. of Belfast 1918-21, a Lord of Appeal-in-Ordinary 1921-29; was made P.C. Ireland 25 April 1896, and of England 11 Dec. 1905, cr. Kt. Bach 1900 and a life peer as Baron Carson of Duncairn, co. Antrim 1 June 1921. He m. (1) 1879 Sarah Forster, dau. of H. P. Kirwan of Triston Lodge, co. Galway and by her (d. 6 April 1913) had issue two sons and two daus.; m. (2) 17 Sept. 1914 Ruby, dau. of Lt. Col. S. Frewen (B.L.G. 1952) and d. 22 Oct. 1935 having had by her a son, Edward. Lord Carson led the Ulster Unionists against Home Rule in Feb. 1910, and as Chm. of the Ulster Unionist Council was largely responsible for the creation of the Ulster Volunteer Force. He achieved part of his aim with the establishment of Northern Ireland in 1921. (*Chamber's Encyclopedia*).

CARYSFORT

PEERAGE—Ireland, Baron Carysfort, 23 Jan. 1752. Earl of Carysfort 18 Aug. 1789.
U.K. Baron Carysfort of Norman Cross, 21 Jan. 1801.
SURNAME—Proby.
CR.—see above. EXT.—4 Sept. 1909.
HISTORY—Randolph Proby of Chester, later of Brampton, co. Huntingdon, temp. Edward VI, m. Miss Bernard and had issue (with Ralph of Brampton d.s.p. 1605) Sir Peter Proby, of Brampton and of Elton, co. Huntingdon, also of Rans, co. Buckingham, Lord

Mayor of London 1652; m. Elizabeth, dau. of John Thorougood of Temple Cheston, co. Herts and Chiners, co. Essex and widow of Edward Henson of London and had issue,

1. Heneage, Sir, of Elton and Rans, m. Ellen, dau. of Edward Allen, of Finchley, co. Middlesex and d. 1652 leaving issue,
   (1) Thomas, Sir, cr. a baronet 7 Mar. 1662; m. Frances, dau. of Sir Thomas Cotton, Bt., of Conington and d. 1689 leaving an only surviving child, Alice who m. 1689, Hon. Thomas Watson Wentworth (Malton, E.).
   (2) John of Elton, Barrister-at-Law, m. Jane, dau. of Sir Richard Cust, Bt. and d. 1710 leaving an only child, Frances, d. unm. 1711.
   (3) Heneage, d. unm. 7 May 1699.
   (1) Elizabeth, Mrs. Sanders.
2. Henry, common serjeant of the city of London m. Ellen Bonham and d. 1660 leaving issue two sons, Henry and Edward, both d. unm. and 4 daus.
3. Edmund, Rev. D.D., Rector of Broughton Gifford, Wilts d.s.p. before 1684.
4. Emmanuel, see below.
1. Walsingham, m. William Downhall.
2. Frances.

The fourth son, Emmanuel Proby of St. Gregory, London, m. Mary dau. of John Bland of London, merchant and d. 1646 (will proved 28 April) leaving issue,

1. Peter, his heir (see below).
2. George, d.s.p.
3. Charles, mentioned in his brother Peter's will, m. sister of George Torriano of London, (who m. 2ndly, Thomas Lucas of Fort St. George, Madras) and had issue,
   (1) William, heir to his uncle.
   (2) Charles, Rev., D.D. Jesus Coll. Camb., rector of Tewin, Herts.
   (1) Elizabeth.
4. Samuel of London, merchant.
5. Nathaniel.
1. Susanna, m. George Torriano, merchant of London.
2. Mary.
3. Elizabeth, m. John Rogerson, alderman of Dublin.

The eldest son, Peter Proby of Putney, Surrey and of London, merchant, m. Grace, dau. of Sir Richard Ford, and d.s.p. (will proved 21 Nov. 1684). He was s. by his nephew, William Proby, of Rans, Bucks and Elton, co. Huntingdon, Gov. of Fort George, Madras, m. Henrietta, dau. of Robert Cornwall of Berrington and d. Jan. 1739, leaving with a dau., Editha, who m. Sir John Osborne, Bt., a son, John Proby of Elton, M.P. co. Huntingdon, m. 5 Jan. 1718-20, Jane, dau. of 1st Lord Gower. She d. 10 June 1726. He d. 1760. They had issue,

1. John, 1st Baron (see below).
2. William, d. unm.
3. Thomas, k. in attack on Ticonderoga, 1756.
4. Charles, Capt. R.N. commissioner of Chatham dockyard, m. 1758, Sarah, dau. of Philemon Pownall, of Plymouth and had issue.
5. Baptist, Very Rev. D.D., Dean of Lichfield, m. Mary, dau. of Rev. John Russell and d. 18 Jan. 1807, having had issue.
1. Caroline, d. unm.

The eldest son, Sir John Proby, K.B., **1st Baron Carysfort**, so cr. 23 Jan. 1757 in the peerage of Ireland, M.P. Hunts, a Lord of the Admiralty 1757; b. 25 Nov. 1720; m. 27 Aug. 1750, Elizabeth, dau. of 2nd Viscount Allen. She d. Mar. 1783. He d. 18 Oct. 1772. They had with a dau. Elizabeth who m. T. J. Storer, a son,

Sir John Joshua Proby, **2nd Baron Carysfort**, in Irish peerage; was cr. 18 Aug. 1789, **Earl of Carysfort** in the Irish peerage and 21 Jan. 1801, Baron Carysfort in the U.K. peerage. He was b. 12 Aug. 1751; m. (1) 18 Mar. 1774, Elizabeth, dau. of Sir William Osborne, Bt., of Newtown, co. Tipperary and by her (who d. Nov. 1783) had issue,

1. William Allen, Lord Proby, b. 19 June 1779, d.v.p. unm. 6 Aug. 1804.
2. John, 2nd Earl (see below).
3. Granville Leveson, 3rd Earl (see below).
1. Gertrude d. 1835.

The Earl m. (2) 12 May 1787, Elizabeth, dau. of Rt. Hon. George Grenville (Buckingham, D. in present work) had further issue,

2. Charlotte, d. unm. 23 Jan. 1860.
3. Frances, d. unm. 24 Mar. 1855.
4. Elizabeth, m. 2 Feb. 1816, Capt. W. Wells, R.N. and d. 17 Oct. 1869 leaving issue.

The 1st Earl d. 7 April 1828 being s. by his second son, John Proby, **2nd Earl of Carysfort**, Gen. in the Army, b. 1780. d. unm. 11 June 1855 and was s. by his brother,

Granville Leveson Proby, **3rd Earl of Carysfort**, Adm. R.N., was present at the battles of the Nile and Trafalgar, b. 1782; m. 5 April 1818, Isabella, dau. of Hon. Hugh Howard (Wicklow, E.). She d. 22 Jan. 1836. They had issue,

1. John Joshua, Lord Proby, b. 1823; d.v.p. 19 Nov. 1858.
2. Granville Leveson, 4th Earl (see below).
3. Hugh, d. 1852 in Austrlia.
4. William, 5th Earl (see below).
1. Frances, d. unm. 15 May 1863.
2. Emma Elizabeth, m. 7 Aug. 1844, Lord Claud Hamilton (Abercorn, D.).
3. Isabella d. 10 Jan. 1866.
4. Theodosia Gertrude m. 10 Sept. 1859, W. M. Baillie and had issue,

Adm. Lord Carysfort d. 3 Nov. 1868 and was s. by his second son, Sir Granville Leveson Proby, **4th Earl of Carysfort**, K.P., P.C., Capt. 74th Highlanders, comptroller of the Household, 1839-66, M.P. co. Wicklow, b. 14 Sept. 1824, m. 19 July 1853, Lady Augusta Hare, dau. of 2nd Earl of Listowel. She d. 24 Mar. 1887. He d.s.p. 18 May 1872, being s. by his brother,

Sir William Proby, K.P., **5th Earl of Carysfort**, Lieut. co. Wicklow, and High Sheriff 1865, J.P. and D.L. Hunts, J.P. Northants, M.A. Camb.; b. 18 Jan. 1836; m. 11 April 1860 Charlotte Mary, dau. of Rev. R. B. Heathcote (Ancaster, E.) and d. 4 Sept. 1909.

ARMS—Quarterly 1 and 4, Ermine on a fess gules, a lion passant or (Proby); 2 and 3, Argent two bars wavy and a plain chief azure on the latter an estoile between two escallops or. (Allen).

CREST—An ostrich's head erased at the neck argent, ducally gorged or; in the beak a key or.

SUPPORTERS—Dexter, An ostrich ppr. ducally gorged and in the beak a key or, Sinister, A talbot sable.

MOTTO—Manus haec inimica tyrannis.
The Earl's seats were Elton Hall, Peterborough and Glen Art Castle, Arklow co. Wicklow.

**CASTELMAINE

PEERAGE—Viscount Castlemaine, Ireland.
SURNAME—Handcock.
CR.—12 Jan. 1822. EXT.—7 Jan. 1839.
HISTORY—William Handcock, 1st Baron and only **Viscount Castlemaine,** was b. 28 Aug. 1761, the son and heir of the Very Rev. Richard Hancock, Dean of Achonry in Ireland, by his wife, Sarah, dau. and heiress of Richard Toler, of Ballintore, co. Kildare; he sat as M.P. for Athlone, from 1783 to 1803; was cr. in the Irish peerage Baron Castlemaine of Moydrum, co. Westmeath, on 21 Dec. 1812, with a special remainder, failing his heirs male, to his brother, Richard Handcock. He was further cr. on 12 Jan. 1822, Viscount Castlemaine, also in the Irish peerage but without special remainder. He m. 20 Mar. 1787, Florinda, dau. of William Power Keating Trench, 1st Earl of Clancarty, and d.s.p. 7 Jan. 1839. The Viscounty then became extinct, but the Barony was inherited by his brother, Richard Handcock, 2nd Baron Castlemaine, (for whom and his issue, see extant peerages).
ARMS—as under Castlemaine, B.
The Viscount's seat was at Moydrum Castle, co. Westmeath.

CASTLETOWN

PEERAGE—U.K. Baron Castletown of Upper Ossory, Queen's co.
SURNAME—FitzPatrick.
CR.—10 Dec. 1869. EXT.—29 May 1937.
HISTORY—John FitzPatrick, 2nd Earl of Upper Ossory, d. 1 Feb. 1818 without legitimate male issue and all his titles became extinct (see Extinct Peerage 1883). He had two sons John Wilson, (and Richard who d. unm. and a dau., Emma Mary who m. 1st Lord Lyveden). The elder son, John Wilson Fitz-Patrick, **1st Baron Castletown,** b. 23 Sept. 1811, s. to the Irish estates of the 2nd and last Earl of Upper Ossory; M.P. for Queen's co., Capt. in the Army; was made P.C. in Ireland 1848 and cr. Baron Castletown, of Upper Ossory, Queen's co. 10 Dec. 1869; m. 5 May 1830 Augusta, dau. of the Rev. Archibald Douglas, rector of Coote Hill, co. Monaghan and d. 22 Jan. 1883, having had issue, with six daus., an only son, Sir Bernard Edward Barnaby FitzPatrick, K.P., **2nd Baron Castletown,** b. 22 July 1849; B.A. Brasenose Coll. Oxford; served in Egypt 1882 and in the S. African War 1900-02, Lt. Col. 4th Bn. Leinster Regt., formerly 1st Life Guards; M.P. for Portarlington 1880-83, Chancellor of the Royal Univ. of Ireland 1906-09, m. 23 April 1874, Hon. Ursula St. Leger, dau. of 4th Viscount Doneraile. She d. 11 Mar. 1927. He d. 29 May 1937.
ARMS—Sable, a saltire argent, on a chief azure three fleur-de-lis, or, within a bordure wavy of the second.
CREST—A dragon on its back ppr. surmount-

ed by a lion passant sable, the whole debruised by a bendlet sinister wavy argent.
SUPPORTERS—Two lions sable, ducally crowned collared and chained or, each charged on the shoulder with three fleur-de-lis one and two or.
MOTTO—Ceart Laidir abu (Might and right for ever).
The seats of Lord Castletown were Granston Manor, Abbeyleix, Queen's Co. and Doneraile Court, co. Cork.

CAUTLEY

PEERAGE—U.K. Baron Cautley of Lindfield, co. Sussex.
SURNAME—Cautley.
CR.—14 July 1936. EXT.—21 Sept. 1946. Also a baronetcy, cr. 28 Jan. 1924.
HISTORY—The first three generations recorded were Clergymen of the Church of England; the Rev. John Cautley, rector of Donnington, Yorks had a son, Henry Cautley, F.R.C.S., of Hedon, Yorks who d. 1869 leaving issue, Henry Cautley, of Bramley and Burton Pidsea, Yorks, b. 1837; m. 1 Oct. 1860 Mary Ellen, dau. of Thomas Strother, of Killinghall, Yorks and Higham Park, Northants, and d. 30 Mar. 1897 having had with other issue, Sir Henry Strother Cautley, Bt., **Baron Cautley,** b. 9 Dec. 1863; B.A. Camb., Barrister-at-Law, Middle Temple, 1886, K.C., 1919, Bencher 1925. Recorder for Sunderland 1918-35, Mem. of the Bar Council 1926, M.P. for E. Leeds 1900-06 and for East Grinstead Div. of Sussex, 1910-36; cr. a baronet 28 Jan. 1924, and Baron Cautley of Lindfield, co. Sussex, 14 July 1936; m. 1 Oct. 1902, Alice Bohun, dau. of B.H.C. Fox, of Maplewell, Woodland Eaves, co. Leicester and d. 21 Sept. 1946.
ARMS—Gules, guttée de l'eau, a cross patonce or between three fountains.
CREST—In front of two swords in saltire points downwards ppr. a fountain.
SUPPORTERS—Dexter, A fox ppr., Sinister, An eagle wings addorsed and inverted or.
MOTTO—Ad alta.

CAVE

PEERAGE—U.K. Viscount Cave of Richmond, co. Surrey.
SURNAME—Cave.
CR.—14 Nov. 1918. EXT.—29 Mar. 1928.
HISTORY—Thomas Cave, of Queensberry House, Richmond, co, Surrey (described in some works as descended from Lyonnell Cave of Owlpen, co. Gloucester, 1649) Sheriff of London, 1863/64, J.P. Surrey, M.P. Barnstaple 1865-80, b. 16 Oct. 1825; m. 16 Mar. 1849, Elizabeth, dau. of Jasper Shallcross, of Banstead, Surrey, and d. 2 Nov. 1894, leaving issue,
  1. Thomas, of Carshalton Park House, Surrey, b. 12 Dec. 1854; m. 4 Mar. 1889, Ina, dau. of Gen. Sir George Bourchier, K.C.B. and d. 14 Feb. 1904, leaving issue,
    (1) Thomas Bourchier, m. 1913, Winifred Ellis, and was k. in action in France 11 Nov. 1916 leaving issue,
      Thomas Bourchier Ellis, b. 1916
      a dau. b. 1914.

(2) Estella Ina Mary, m. 1914 Ronald Griffith.
2. George, **Viscount Cave** (see below).
3. Edmund, b. 24 Nov. 1859; m. 3 Sept. 1888, Blanche Tankerville Chamberlaine and had issue,
    Edmund Shallcross Jasper, 2nd Lt. R.A.F., b. 23 Aug. 1892; k. in action in France, Aug. 1918.
    Blanche Harriet Shallcross, m. 1 Feb. 1910, Lt. Col. R. H. Lloyd, R.A.M.C. and had issue.
4. Basil Shillito, C.B. (1897) F.R.G.S., Consul Gen. at Zanzibar and later at Algiers, b. 14 Nov. 1865; m. 1892, Mary Creighton, dau. of Rev. J. B. McClellan, D.D., principal of the Roy. Agric. Coll., Cirencester and had issue,
    Kenneth McClellan, M.C., brevet Major, R.E., b. 16 Aug. 1893; m. 5 April 1916, Joyce Shore.
    Joy Mary.
5. Allan Mackinnon d. young.
1. Harriet Shallcross, m. 1873, Sir Max L. Waechter and d. 25 Nov. 1910.
2. Caroline d. young.
3. Caroline Elizabeth, m. 19 Nov. 1879, Francis Alexander Slache, C.S.I. and had issue.
4. Marion, m. 6 July 1892, Rev. John F. G. Glossop, Vicar of St. Mark's Battersea and had issue.
5. Edith Mary, m. 2 Jan. 1890. Rev. Nigel Freer and had issue.

The second son, Sir George Cave, **Viscount Cave**, b. 23 Feb. 1856; Barrister-at-Law, Inner Temple, 1880, K.C. 1904, Bencher 1912; recorder of Guildford 1904-13, M.P. Kingston Div. 1906-19, Attorney Gen. to the Prince of Wales 1913-15; standing counsel to Oxford Univ. 1913-18. Solicitor gen. 1915, Home Sec. 1916-19; Chm. Rhodesia Comm. 1919, cr. Kt. Bach. 1915, made P.C. 1915 and cr. Viscount Cave of Richmond, co. Surrey, 14 Nov. 1918. He was appt. a Lord of Appeal, Jan. 1919. He m. Anne Estella Sarah Penfold, dau. of William Withers Mathews of Wolston House, nr. Cadbury, co. Somerset and d. 29 Mar. 1928.
ARMS—Or fretty azure a cross moline within a bordure nebuly gules on a chief of the last two greyhounds' heads erased or.
CREST—A greyhound sejant or pelletée, resting the dexter leg on a cross moline gules.
MOTTO—Cave Deus videt.

CAVE OF RICHMOND

PEERAGE—U.K. Earl Cave of Richmond—Countess Cave of Richmond.
SURNAME—Cave.
CR.—8 May 1928. EXT.—7 Jan. 1938.
HISTORY—Viscount Cave, (see that title) d.s.p. 29 Mar. 1928. On that day it was announced that he was to be made an earl, but the letters patent had not passed the Great Seal. His widow was therefore granted by letters patent, 8 May 1928, the dignity of **Countess Cave of Richmond.** She was Anne Estella Sarah Penfold Cave, the dau. of W. W. Mathew, of Chard, co. Somerset, and the sister of Gen. Sir Lloyd William Mathew, K.C.M.G., of Zanzibar. She had the medal of

Queen Elizabeth of Belgium; she went to East Africa, South Africa, Canada, and America with her husband, and wrote of these journeys in an amusing book, being also the authoress of *Memories of Old Richmond* and *Odds and Ends* (the latter a volume of reminiscences). She wrote the introduction to Sir Charles Mallet's biography of Viscount Cave. Under the letters patent the grant of the title was that of Countess Cave of Richmond, and it was stated that at her decease the dignity of an earl of the U.K. was to pass to the heirs male of her body lawfully begotten by the name style and title of Earl Cave of Richmond. She d. 7 Jan. 1938 without issue. The wording of the patent implies that had it been physically possible for her to have had a son by a second husband, that son would have become Earl Cave of Richmond, a signally unimaginative wording.

CECIL OF CHELWOOD

PEERAGE—U.K. Viscount Cecil of Chelwood of Grinstead, co. Sussex.
SURNAME—Gascoyne-Cecil.
CR.—24 Dec. 1923. EXT.—24 Nov. 1958.
HISTORY—Edgar Algeinon Robert Gascoyne Cecil, **Viscount Cecil** of Chelwood, statesman, lawyer, and tireless worker in the cause of disarmament and peace. He was b. 14 Sept. 1864; 3rd son of 3rd Marquess of Salisbury, m. 22 Jan. 1889, Lady Eleanor Lambton, dau. of 2nd Earl of Durham. Lord Robert was M.A. and Hon. Fell. Univ. Coll. Oxford, Barrister-at-Law, Inner Temple, 1887, Q.C., 1899, a Member of the Gen. Council of the Bar, a Bencher of the Inner Temple, 1910, J.P. Herts, Chm. Quarter Sessions, Herts 1911-20; Chancellor of the Consistory Court of York and Vicar Gen. of the Archbishopric 1915. He sat in the House of Commons as a Conservative M.P. for East Marylebone 1906-10, and as an Independent for Hitchin Div.of Herts, 1911-23. He was made a P.C. 1915 and cr. a peer 1923. His political career included the holding of the following offices: Under Sec. of State for Foreign Affairs, 1915-18, Min. of Blockade, 1916-18, Lord Privy Seal, 1923-24, and Chancellor of the Duchy of Lancaster 1924-27. Lord Cecil had a large part in the drafting of the Covenant of the League of Nations and became President of the League of Nations Union with Prof. Gilbert Murray as its Chairman "Thus began the collaboration between Murray and Cecil in the great work of the age. Though born in different stations both belonged to the same élite, spoke the same language, felt the same feelings and took the same instinctive attitudes". (Salvador de Madariaga, a contribution—*Gilbert Murray and the League* in *Gilbert Murray An Unfinished Autobiography* (1960) p. 177). Viscount Cecil was awarded the Nobel Peace Prize in 1937. He was an Anglo Catholic in his religious allegiance. His residence was "Rock Platt", Chelwood Gate, Haywards Heath, Sussex. He d. 24 Nov. 1958.
ARMS—Quarterly 1 and 4 barry of ten argent and azure, over all six escutcheons sable three two and one, each charged with a lion rampant argent (Cecil). 2 and 3 argent on a pale sable a conger's head erased and erect and charged with an ermine spot (Gascoyne).

CRESTS—1. Six arrows in saltire or, barbed and flighted argent, girt together with a belt gules, buckled and garnished gold, over the arrows a morion cap ppr (Cecil). 2. A conger's head erased and erect or, charged with an ermine spot. Both arms and crest differenced by a mullet.
SUPPORTERS—On either side a lion ermine charged on the shoulder with a branch of olive fructed and slipped ppr.
MOTTO—Sero sed serio.

CHALMERS

PEERAGE—U.K. Baron Chalmers of Northiam, co. Sussex.
SURNAME—Chalmers.
CR.—24 April 1919. EXT.—17 Nov. 1938.
HISTORY—John Chalmers m. Julia, dau. of Robert Mackay and had an only son, Sir Robert Chalmers, **Baron Chalmers**, b. 18 Aug. 1858; educ. Oriel Coll. Oxford, B.A. 1881, M.A. 1908, Hon. Fell. 1918, entered Treasury 1882, Perm. Sec. to Treasury 1911-13, Gov. of Ceylon, 1913-16, Under Sec. to Lord Lieut. of Ireland 1916, Jt. Perm. Sec. to Treasury, 1916-19; Pres. Royal Asiatic Soc. 1922-25, Master of Peterhouse, Camb. 1924-31, a Trustee of Brit. Mus. 1924-31, F.B.A. 1927; cr. C.B. 1900, K.C.B. 1908, and G.C.B. 1916, made P.C. in Ireland 17 May 1916 and cr. Baron Chalmers of Northiam, co. Sussex 24 April 1919. He m. (1) 2 July 1888, Maud Mary (d. 2 July 1923) dau. of J. G. Pigott and by her had issue two sons, both k. in World War I and a dau. Mabel m. Sir Malcolm Stevenson. He m. (2) 1 June 1935, Iris Florence, dau. of Sir John Biles and widow of Prof. Robert Latta, and d. 17 Nov. 1938.
ARMS—Argent with two swords in pale ppr., pommelled gules, hilted or, each enfiled with a wreath of laurel vert, on a chief gules a crescent between two mullets or.
CREST—An elephant statant uprooting a tree eradicated all ppr.
SUPPORTERS—On either side an antelope reguardant argent collared and chain reflexed over the back or.
MOTTO—Felix merendo.

CHANNING OF WELLINGBOROUGH

PEERAGE—U.K. Baron Channing of Wellingborough, co. Northampton.
SURNAME—Channing.
CR.—9 July 1912. EXT.—20 Feb. 1926. Also a baronetcy, cr. 3 Dec. 1906.
HISTORY—John Channing, who is described as a member of a family which had resided for a long time near Maiden Newton, co. Dorset, emigrated to Boston, 17 June 1712, and settled in Newport, Rhode Island; he m. 1713, Mary Antram, and was father of, John Channing, of Newport, Rhode Island, m. Mary Chaloner by whom he had, Hon. William Channing, Attorney Gen. of Rhode Island, b. 11 June 1751; m. 1773, Lucy, dau. of Hon. William Ellery, (a signatory of the Declaration of Independence 1776) and d. 21 Sept. 1793, having had issue,
1. Francis Dana (see below).

2. William Ellery, Rev., D.D., writer and divine, b. 7 Apr. 1780; m. 1814, his cousin, Ruth Gibbs, granddau. of John Channing, of Newport, and had issue.
3. Walter, M.D., b. 15 Apr. 1786; m. 1815, Barbara Higginson Perkins, and left issue.
4. George, m. Mary Sigourney, and left issue.
1. Ann, m. 1809, Washington Allstom, A.R.A.
The eldest son, Francis Dana Channing, a lawyer, b. 16 Aug. 1775; m. 1806, Susan Cleveland Higginson, and d. 8 Nov. 1810, having had issue,
1. William Henry (see below).
1. Susan Cleveland, b. 1807; m. Francis J. Higginson, and had issue.
2. Lucy Ellery, b. 1809; d. unm. 1877.
The only son, The Rev. William Henry Channing, of Boston, and later of Kensington, B.A. Harvard; b. 25 May 1810; m. 9 Dec. 1836, Julia Maria, the only surv. dau. of William Allen, of Fishkill Point, and Hyde Park, New York, of a family settled in Pennsylvania, from Stirlingshire under James II. She d. 7 Dec. 1889. He d. 23 Dec. 1884, having had issue,
1. Francis, Allston, Sir, Bt., and Baron Channing of Wellingborough.
1. Frances Maria Adelaide, b. 21 Sept. 1837; m. 3 Aug. 1868, Sir Edwin Arnold, K.C.I.E., C.S.I. She d. 15 Mar. 1889, leaving issue.
2. Blanche Mary Susan Ethelind, d. unm. 9 Aug. 1902.
The only son, Sir Francis Allston Channing, Bt., **Baron Channing** of Wellingborough, b. 21 Mar. 1841; educ. Exeter Coll. Oxford, B.A. 1863, Chancellor's Prize English Essay, 1865, Arnold Essay, 1866, M.A., Fell. and Lecturer on Philisophy, Univ. Coll.; Barrister-at-Law, Lincoln's Inn; M.P. for East Div. of Northants 1885-1910; cr. Baronet 3 Dec. 1906 and Baron Channing of Wellingborough, Northants 9 July 1912; m. 21 July 1869, Elizabeth, dau. of Henry Bryant of Boston, U.S.A. He d. 20 Feb. 1926, having had issue with one son and one dau. both d. young, two other daus., Mary, m. C. H. Kennard, and had issue; and Julia Allen.
ARMS—Quarterly 1 and 4, Argent a fess nebuly gules between three blackamoors heads couped at the shoulders ppr. (Channing); 2 and 3, Per chevron in chief perpale gules and sable, two lions' heads erased or, and in base argent, three ermine spots one and two (Allen).
CREST—In front of a plate a blackamoor's head as in the arms.
SUPPORTERS—On either side a chestnut horse ppr. gorged with a coronet of fleur-de-lis argent, pendent therefrom a fountain.
MOTTO—Fortitudo mea Deus.
Lord Channing's residence was 40 Eaton Place, London, S.W. His clubs were Oxford and Cambridge; Reform; National Liberal and Royal Automobile.

CHARLEMONT

PEERAGE—Ireland Earl of Charlemont, co. Armagh, cr. 23 Dec. 1763.
U.K. Baron Charlemont of Charlemont, co. Armagh, cr. 13 Feb. 1837.
SURNAME—Caulfeild.
C.R.—as above EXT.—16 Jan. 1892.

HISTORY—James Caulfeild, 4th Viscount Charlemont and **Earl of Charlemont**, (see extant peerage works) was b. 18 Aug. 1728; spent a long time abroad, and returned to Ireland about 1749, when he took up the post of Gov. of co. Armagh; was cr. Earl of Charlemont, in peerage of U.K. 23 Dec. 1763. He was also cr. K.P. being one of the original 15 Knights of the Order, 18 Aug. 1783; Pres. of Royal Irish Academy from its establishment in 1785 until his death; F.R.S. and F.S.A., Hon. LL.D. Dublin; m. 2 July 1768, Mary dau. of Thomas Hickman, of Brickhill, co. Clare, and d. 4 Aug. 1799, having had with other issue,

1. Francis William, **2nd Earl** (see below).
2. Henry, of Hockley, co. Armagh, and M.P. Armagh, b. 20 July 1779; m. 30 Aug. 1819, Elizabeth Margaret, dau. of Dodwell Browne, of Rahins, co. Mayo, and d. 4 Mar. 1862. She d. 1878. Their issue were, with a dau. Margaret Zoe, m. Sir John Stronge, 4th Bt.,
   (1) James Molyneux, **4th Earl** (see below).
   (2) Henry William, 1822-67.

The elder son, Francis William Caulfeild, **2nd Earl of Charlemont**, and 5th Viscount, etc., b. 3 Jan. 1775; educ. Trin. Coll. Dublin, B.A., 1794; sat as M.P. for Armagh, 1797/99; was Representative Peer, 1806-63; cr. K.P. 1831, and Baron Charlemont, of Charlemont, co. Armagh, in the U.K. peerage, 13 Feb. 1837, with a special remainder allowing s. to his brother, Henry. He m. 9 Feb. 1802, Anne, dau. of William Bermingham, of Ross Hill, co. Galway, and d.s.p.s., having had two sons, who d. young, and two daus. who d. unm. He was s. in his peerage titles by his nephew,

James Molyneux Caulfeild, **3rd Earl of Charlemont**, and 6th Viscount Charlemont, b. 10 Oct. 1820; educ. Trin. Coll. Camb.; High Sheriff, co. Armagh and Liberal M.P. co. Armagh, 1847-57; Lord Lt. co. Armagh, 1849, and co. Tyrone, 1864; cr. K.P. 1865. He m. (1) 18 Dec. 1856, Elizabeth Jane, dau. of William Somerville, 1st Baron Athlumney. She d. 1882. He m. (2) 10 May 1883, Anna Lucy, dau. of the Rev. C. J. Lambert, Rector of Navan, co. Meath, and d.s.p. 12 Jan. 1892. The Earldom of Charlemont and the U.K. Barony of Charlemont, then became extinct, but the Viscounty, and the 1620 Irish Barony of Caulfeild of Charlemont passed to his cousin,

James Alfred Caulfeild, 7th Viscount Charlemont, and 11th Baron Caulfeild, of Charlemont, (for whom see extant peerage works).

ARMS—Barry of ten argent and gules, on a canton gules, a lion passant guardant or.
CREST—A dragon's head erased gules, gorged with a bar gemelle, argent.
SUPPORTERS—Two dragons gules wings endorsed sable, each gorged with a bar gemelle, argent.
MOTTO—Deo duce ferro comitante.
The principal seat of the Earls was Roxborough Castle, near Moy, co. Tyrone.

CHARNWOOD

PEERAGE—U.K. Baron Charnwood of Castle Donington, co. Leicester.
SURNAME—Benson.
CR.—29 June 1911. **EXT.**—1 Feb. 1955.

HISTORY—Thomas Benson of Stang End, co. Lancaster m. Elizabeth Sawrey and had issue,

George Benson of Stang End, b. 14 Aug. 1636; m. 12 July 1663, Margaret, the dau. and heiress of James Braithwaite of Croft Head, Hawkshead and d. 19 Oct. 1712 having had with other issue,

John Benson, of Stang End, b. 29 Dec. 1668; m. 11 Dec. 1691, Isabella dau. of Edward Forrest of Tockhow, and d. 15 July 1737 having had with other issue,

George Benson, of Stang End, b. Feb. 1699; m. 16 Sept. 1729, Abigail the dau. and heiress of William Braithwaite, of Elterwater, co. Westmorland and d. 13 Aug. 1761 having had with other children,

Robert Benson, b. 15 April 1749; m. 23 May 1781, Sarah, dau. of William Rathbone, of Liverpool, and d. 1 Nov. 1802, leaving with other issue,

Robert Benson of Liverpool, b. 1785; m. 4 Mar. 1872 Mary (d. 1824) dau. of David Dockray and d. 20 June 1846, having had with other issue,

William Benson, of Langtons, Alresford, co. Hants, J.P., M.A. Queen's Coll. Camb., Barrister, b. 3 Aug. 1876; m. 9 Dec. 1852, Elizabeth Soulsby, dau. of Thomas Smith of Colebrooke Park, Tonbridge and d. 31 Jan. 1887 having had with other issue, a younger son,

Godfrey Rathbone Benson, **1st Baron Charnwood**, being so created on 29 June 1911; J.P. and D.L. co. Stafford, Mayor of Lichfield 1902-11, M.P. Woodstock Div. of Oxfordshire, 1892-95, M.A. Oxford; b. 6 Nov. 1864; m. 11 May 1897, Dorothea Mary Roby, dau. of Roby Thorpe of Nottingham, the representative of the family of Roby of Donnington, and d. 3 Feb. 1945. Lady Charnwood d. 20 April 1942. They had with a son who d. young and two daus., an elder son who s. him,

John Roby Benson, **2nd Baron Charnwood**, a consulting optician, F.B.O.A., Liveryman of the Spectacle Makers' Co., educ. Eton and Balliol Coll. Oxford served in Second World War, Major 105 Field Brigade R.A. (T.A.), b. 31 Aug. 1901; m. 19 July 1933 Beryl Joan, elder dau. of Percy Cuthbert Quilter yst. son of Sir Cuthbert Quilter, Bart., and d.s.p. 1 Feb. 1955.
ARMS—Quarterly ermine and or a bend engrailed gules surmounted of another plain argent charged with three trefoils sable.
CREST—A bear's head erased argent muzzled, gorged with a collar and pendant therefrom an escutcheon azure charged with a trefoil or.
SUPPORTERS—On either side a roebuck supporting a staff all ppr. therefrom flying a banner charged with the arms of Thorpe, viz: sable an oak tree eradicated or, over all two bars dancetty argent.
MOTTO—Si Deus quis contra.

CHATTISHAM

PEERAGE—U.K. Baron Chattisham of Clitheroe.
SURNAME—Brass.
CR.—13 July 1945. **EXT.**—24 Aug. 1945.
HISTORY—William Brass had issue an only son, Sir William Brass, **Baron Chattisham,**

b. 11 Feb. 1886; educ. Eton and Trin. Coll. Camb.; served in World War I in France, Egypt and Italy, in R.F.C. and R.A.F.; M.P. Clitheroe Div. of Lancashire 1922-45; Chm. of the British Film Inst. and Director of Guardian Assurance Co. d. unm. 24 Aug. 1945.

CHERWELL

PEERAGE—U.K. Baron Cherwell of Oxford, co. Oxford and Viscount Cherwell.
SURNAME—Lindemann.
CR.—Barony 4 July 1941 and Viscounty 1956.
EXT.—3 July 1957.
HISTORY—Frederick Alexander Lindemann, **Baron Cherwell,** b. in 1886 was the son of Adolphus Frederick Lindemann of Sidholme, Sidmouth, a distinguished physical scientist, in the first World War he was an experimental pilot, and Director of the Physical Laboratory of the R.A.F. at Farnborough; in the second World War was Personal Asst. to the Prime Minister, 1940, Paymaster Gen. 1942-45 and 1951-53, Prof. of Experimental Philosophy, Oxford and Fell. Wadham Coll. Oxford. He was made a P.C. 1943 and a Companion of Honour 1953. Winston Churchill in his second vol. *of The Second World War* 1949, (ch. XIX, The Wizard War, p.p. 337-339) thus described Prof. Lindemann's services "There were no doubt greater scientists than Frederick Lindemann, though his credentials and genius command respect. But he had two qualifications of vital consequence to me. First . . . he was my trusted friend and confidant of twenty years . . . (Secondly) Lindemann could decipher the signals from the experts on the far horizons and explain to me in lucid, homely terms what the issues were." Lord Cherwell d. 3 July 1957.
ARMS—Gules an eagle rising or, on a chief gold a lime leaf vert between two mullets azure.
CREST—Between two mullets azure a demi-eagle displayed or charged on each wing with a lime leaf vert.
SUPPORTERS—On either side a savage wreathed about the loins with ivy and holding in his exterior hand a branch of lime all ppr.
MOTTO—In Stella Tutus.

CHESTERFIELD AND STANHOPE

PEERAGE—England. Baron Stanhope of Shelford, co. Nottingham 7 Nov. 1616. Earl of Chesterfield 4 Aug. 1628. Great Britain Earl Stanhope 1718.
SURNAME—Stanhope.
CR.—Dates as above. **EXT.**—15 Aug. 1967.
HISTORY—No fewer than 20 of the family are mentioned in the D.N.B. and have biographies. The Stanhopes take their name from Stanhope in co. Durham and had a seat at Shelford in Nottinghamshire, the latter being acquired by Sir John Stanhope of Rampton, Notts, who lived circa 1373 and m. twice (1) Elizabeth, the dau. and heiress of Stephen Manlovel of Rampton, and (2) Elizabeth dau. and heiress of Thomas Culley. Sir John's eldest son and successor was, Sir Richard Stanhope, of Rampton, K.B. (1399), M.P. for Nottinghamshire in several Parliaments under

the House of Lancaster. He inherited some property from his mother's family at Tuxford, Notts, and acquired further estates through his second marriage. He m., as his first wife, Elizabeth (or Joan) dau. of Ralph Staveley and, as his second, Maud, the sister and heiress of Ralph, Lord Cromwell. He had children by both marriages. His eldest son, Richard, d.v.p. 2 Mar. 1432 having m. Elizabeth (or Isabel) the dau. of Sir John Markham, Chief Justice of the King's Bench by whom he had issue a son, John. When Sir Richard Stanhope d. in 1436 he was therefore succeeded by his grandson,
John Stanhope of Rampton, M.P. for the county of Nottingham, 1450-72, and three times Sheriff of the counties of Nottingham and Derby. He m. circa 1427, Elizabeth dau. of Sir Thomas Talbot of Bashall, Yorks and left issue,
Thomas Stanhope of Rampton, served in France, 1474, m. Mary, dau. of John Jerningham, of Somerleyton, Suffolk, and had issue, with a yr. son John (from whom descended the family of Spencer Stanhope of Cannon Hall, Yorks, see B.L.G. 1952) an heir and successor,
Sir Edward Stanhope of Rampton, who served as a commander in the royal army at the battle of Stoke, 1487, and again at Blackheath, 1497, when he was knighted. He m. as his first wife, Avelina, dau. of Sir Gervase Clifton of Clifton, Notts, and by her had two sons, Richard and Michael (see below). His 2nd wife was Elizabeth dau. of Lord Fitzwarine by whom he had a daughter Anne, who m. the Protector, the Duke of Somerset, as his second wife. Sir Edward Stanhope, d. 6 June 1512 being s. by his elder son,
Richard Stanhope of Rampton, b. 1502; m. Anne, yst. dau. of John Strelly of Strelly, Notts, and d. 1583, leaving a dau. Sanchia, who inherited Rampton, and m. 1517 John Babington and left issue. The representation of the family passed to the younger son, (of Sir Edward Stanhope),
Sir Michael Stanhope, of Shelford, Notts and Elvaston, Derby, knighted by Henry VIII, 1545, and attained considerable position under Edward VI but was involved in the fall of his brother-in-law the Duke of Somerset and being charged with plotting the death of Dudley, Duke of Northumberland was beheaded on Tower Hill 25 Feb. 1552. His wife was Anne, the dau. of Nicholas Raw son of Aveley Bellhouse, Essex, and by her he had issue, (1) Thomas his heir and (2) John, who was made a peer, as Baron Stanhope of Harrington, Northants in 1605 (a title which became extinct in 1675, 1883 Extinct Peerage). The heir,
Sir Thomas Stanhope, of Shelford, M.P. for Notts under Queen Elizabeth I, m. Margaret, dau. and co-heiress of Sir John Port of Etwal, Derby and d. 1596 when he was s. by his eldest son,
Sir John Stanhope of Shelford, knighted 22 April 1603, m. 1stly Cordell, dau. and coheir of Richard Allington, by whom he had issue, an only son Philip. He m. 2ndly Catherine, dau. of Thomas Trentham of Rochester Priory, Staffs, and had further issue, including a son, John, of Elvaston. From this last descend the Earls of Harrington, who inherited in 1967 the barony of Stanhope of Elvaston and the viscounty of

Stanhope of Mahon (see below). Sir John d. 1611 and was s. by the son of his first marriage, Sir Philip Stanhope who was made a peer as **Baron Stanhope of Shelford** in the county of Notts on 7 Nov. 1616, and advanced to the **Earldom of Chesterfield,** 4 Aug. 1628. **The 1st Earl of Chesterfield** m. 1stly, 1605 Catherine, dau. of Francis, Lord Hastings. She d. 28 Aug. 1636. By her he had two daus. and eleven sons, of whom,

1. Henry, **Lord Stanhope,** K.B., m. 1628, Katherine, dau. and coheir of Thomas, 2nd Lord Wotton, and d.v.p. 1634. She was cr. **Countess of Chesterfield** for life, 29 May 1660. Lord Stanhope left issue with two daus. a son, Philip, **2nd Earl** (see below).

2. Arthur, ancestor of the 5th Earl, M.P. Nottingham from 1660. b. 1627, m. Anne dau. of Sir Henry Salisbury, 1st Bart. and had an only son, Charles, of Mansfield Woodhouse, Notts, b. 1655, m. 1674. Frances, only dau. of Sir Francis Topp, 1st Bart. and had issue,

 (1) Michael, Rev. D.D., Canon of Windsor, (1681-1737). He m. Penelope, dau. of Sir Salathiel Lovell, Baron of the Exchequer, and had with other issue,

  1a Arthur Charles of whom below as father of the **5th Earl** (see below).

  2a Ferdinand, ancestor of the **8th Earl** (see below).

 (2) Charles, ancestor of the **9th Earl** (see below).

The 1st Earl m. 2ndly Anne, dau. of Sir John Pakington and widow of Sir Humphrey Ferrers of Tamworth Castle and by her who d. 1667 had further issue, an only son,

3. Alexander, father of James 1st Earl Stanhope (see below).

When the 1st Earl d. in 1656 he was s. by his grandson, Philip Stanhope, **2nd Earl of Chesterfield,** P.C., who had no surviving issue by his first wife, Lady Anne Percy, eldest dau. of the 10th Earl of Northumberland and who d. 1654. By his second marriage to Lady Elizabeth Butler, dau. of James, 1st Duke of Ormonde, and who d. 1665, he had one surviving dau. Elizabeth, who m. the 4th Earl of Strathmore. The Earl of Chesterfield m. 3rdly Lady Elizabeth Dormer, eldest dau. and coheir of Charles, Earl of Caernarvon, and by her (who d. 1677) he had with other issue, a son, Philip. The 2nd Earl d. 28 Jan. 1713/14 and was s. by his son, Philip Stanhope, **3rd Earl of Chesterfield,** b. 3 Feb. 1672/3; m. 1691/2, Lady Elizabeth Savile, dau. of 1st Marquess of Halifax and d. 27 Jan. 1725/6 leaving with other issue, an eldest son, Philip Dormer Stanhope, **4th Earl of Chesterfield,** K.G., the author of the famous *Letters* written to his natural son, born to him by Mlle. du Bouchet, one of the most interesting figures in the 18th century—politician, wit, man of letters, scholar and polished gentleman—whose career in summary form fills a column in the *Concise D.N.B.* He was b. 1694, m. 1733 Melusina von der Schulenberg, Baroness of Aldborough, co. Suffolk and Countess of Walsingham, so cr. 1722, both being life peerages, and she being the natural dau. of King George I by his mistress Erengart Melusine Schulenberg, Princess of Eberstein, this rank being given to

her in 1719, she having also received seven other peerages for life only, including dukedoms, see 1883 Extinct Peerage. The Earl offended George II by this marriage but he threatened to sue the Crown to recover the legacy bequeathed to his mother-in-law by George I. In order to prevent any such action he was offered and accepted £20,000. The Earl held many important appointments including that of Ambassador to the Hague, 1728 and Lord Lieutenant of Ireland 1744-46 (where a monument to him stands in Phoenix Park, Dublin). The Countess d. 16 Sept. 1778. The Earl d.s.p.l. 24 Mar. 1773 when he was succeeded by his kinsman,

Philip Stanhope, **5th Earl of Chesterfield** only son of Arthur Charles Stanhope (1715-70) (see above), godson of the 4th Earl, by whom his education was directed, and was also a pupil of the Rev. Dr. William Dodd, author of *The Beauties of Shakespeare* and other works. Dodd who had been a royal chaplain, in 1777 forged a bond for £4,200 in the Earl's name, and on being detected was sentenced to be hanged for the forgery, which was duly carried out despite a great movement for mercy on his behalf. The Earl who was a P.C. a favourite with George III and held some public appointments, was b. 1755, m. 1stly, 1777, Anne (d. 1798) dau. of the Rev. Robert Thistlethwayte, and had a dau., Harriet, d. unm. 1803. He m. 2ndly 1799, Henrietta, 3rd dau. of 1st Marquess of Bath and d. 1815 having had with other issue,

George Stanhope, **6th Earl of Chesterfield,** P.C., b. 1805; m. 1830, Anne Elizabeth, eldest dau. of 1st Lord Forester, and d. 1866 when he was s. by his son,

George Cecil Arthur Stanhope, **7th Earl of Chesterfield,** b. 1831, d. unm. 1871, being s. by his cousin,

George Philip Stanhope, **8th Earl of Chesterfield,** the great grandson of Ferdinand Stanhope (see above). The latter d. 1790, leaving with other issue an eldest son, Rear Adm. John Stanhope, 1744-1800, who had with other issue, a son, Capt. Charles George Stanhope 29th Foot, 1789-1833, whose only son became the 8th Earl). The **8th Earl,** Lt., 29th Foot, b. 1822; m. 1stly, 1856 Marianne (d. 1875) dau. of William Roche; 2ndly, 1877, Catherine (d. 1880) only dau. of John Hildebrand Bond of Belfast and 3rdly 1882, Agnes, dau. of James Payne of Manchester. The only son of the first marriage, Philip Laurence John Stanhope, b. 1857; d. 1860. The 8th Earl d. 19 Oct. 1883 and was s. by his kinsman, Sir Henry Edwyn Chandos Scudamore Stanhope, 3rd Bart. who became **9th Earl** (see below). His ancestry was derived from Charles Stanhope (1700-59) a younger son of Charles Stanhope of Mansfield Woodhouse (see above). He m. Cecilia dau. of Dutton Stede, of Stede Hill, Kent and had an only son, Edwyn Francis Stanhope, (1729-1807), of Stanwell House, Middlesex. m. 9 Aug. 1753, Catherine, dau. and coheiress of John Brydges, Marquess of Carnarvon, son of the 1st Duke of Chandos (see 1883 Extinct Peerage) and widow of William Berkeley Lyon and had issue with a dau., a son, Sir Henry Edwyn Stanhope, 1st Bart., of Stanwell House, Middlesex, Rear Adm. of the Blue, served with distinction in the expedition against Copenhagen and was cr. a baronet, 13 Nov. 1807. He was b. 1754; m. 1783,

Margaret dau. of Francis Malbone, of Newport, Rhode Island, and d. 20 Dec. 1814, being s. by his only son, Sir Edwyn Francis Scudamore Stanhope, 2nd Bart., Capt. R.N., who assumed by Royal Licence, 17 Jan. 1827, the additional name and arms of Scudamore, b. 1793; m. 1820, Mary, dau. of Major Thomas Dowell, of Parker's Well, Devon, and d. 1874 having by her (d. 1859) had with other issue, an eldest son,

Sir Henry Edwyn Chandos Scudamore Stanhope, 3rd Bart., and **9th Earl of Chesterfield,** b. 1821; m. 1851, Dorothea (d. 1923) eldest dau. of Sir Adam Hay, 7th Bart., and d. 21 Jan. 1887, having had with other issue,

1. Edwyn Francis, **10th Earl** (see below).
2. Henry Athole, **11th Earl** (see below).
3. Evelyn Theodore, Chief Constable of Herefordshire 1895-1923. b. 1862; m. 1888, Julia Dasha, yst. dau. of John Gerald Potter, and d. 1925, leaving issue (with a dau., Enid Doreen Grace, m. Major Alexander Browne, and was granted predecence as dau. of an Earl 1938), a son, Edward Henry, **12th Earl** (see below).

The 10th Earl, Edwyn Francis Scudamore-Stanhope, **10th Earl of Chesterfield,** K.G., P.C., G.C.V.O., held several appointments at court, b. 1854; m. 1900, Enid Edith, 2nd dau. of 1st Baron Nunburnholme and d.s.p. 1933, when he was s. by his brother,

Henry Athole Scudamore-Stanhope **11th Earl of Chesterfield,** Capt. R.N., b. 1855, d. unm. 1935, being s. by his nephew,

Edward Henry Scudamore-Stanhope, **12th Earl of Chesterfield,** b. 1889; m. 1stly 1915 (m. diss. by div. 1925), Lorna, dau. of William Henry Lever, of Wellington, N.Z. and had issue a dau., Evelyn, who m. 1stly 1938 (m. diss. by div. 1947) Lt. Cmdr. Ian McDonald R.A.N. and 2ndly, 1947, John Harford Stanhope Lucas-Scudamore of Kentchurch Court, Herefordshire (see B.L.G. 1952). The 12th Earl m. 2ndly, 1931, Angela, dau. of Francis Hopkins, and d. 1952. The baronetcy cr. in 1807 then became extinct; the earldom of Chesterfield and the barony of Stanhope were inherited by the 7th Earl Stanhope (see below).

ARMS—(of Scudamore-Stanhope, Earls of Chesterfield). Quarterly, 1 and 4, Quarterly ermine and gules (Stanhope); 2 and 3, Gules, three stirrups with buckles and traps or (Scudamore), .

CRESTS—1. A tower azure thereon a demi lion rampant or ducally crowned gules, holding between the paws a grenade fired ppr. (Stanhope); 2. Out of a ducal coronet or, a bear's paw sable (Scudamore).

SUPPORTERS—Dexter, A wolf ducally crowned or; Sinister, A talbot ermine.

MOTTOES—A Deo et rege; In hoc signo vinces.

STANHOPE. Alexander Stanhope, a yr. son of the 1st Earl of Chesterfield (see above), b. 1638; and d. 1707 having by his wife Catheriné, dau. of Arnold Burghill, of Thinge-hill Parva, co. Hereford, with other issue an eldest son, James Stanhope, **1st Earl Stanhope,** had a very distinguished career in the army, in politics and diplomacy, and had considerable influence in bringing about the Hanoverian Succession in 1714, was two years a prisoner in France, having been captured at Briheuga in Spain. He captured Port Mahon in 1708. In 1717 he was cr. Baron Stanhope of Elvaston co. Derby and Viscount Stanhope of Mahon in the island of Minorca, with remainder in default of male issue, to the male issue of his cousin John Stanhope of Elvaston (ancestor of the Earls of Harrington, see above). Viscount Stanhope was further advanced in the peerage as Earl Stanhope, 14 April 1718. A full account of his career is given in D.N.B. LIV and a monument by Rysbrach was erected to him in Westminster Abbey. He was b. 1673; m. 24 Feb. 1713/4, Lucy (d. 1722/3) eldest dau. of Thomas Pitt, of Bosconnoc, Cornwall, and d. 5 Feb. 1720/21, having had with other issue,

Philip Stanhope, **2nd Earl Stanhope,** F.R.S., b. 1714; m. 1745, Grizel, dau. of Charles Hamilton, Lord Binning, son of the 6th Earl of Haddington and d. 1786 being s. by his surviving son,

Charles Stanhope, **3rd Earl Stanhope,** politician and scientist, F.R.S., author of many inventions, disinherited all his children; was b. 8 Aug. 1753; m. 1stly 19 Dec. 1774, Lady Hester Pitt, eldest dau. of 1st Earl of Chatham and by her (who d. 1780) had three daus., the eldest of whom was the famous Lady Hester Stanhope, the traveller and resident of remote places in the Near East. (A. W. Kinglake has a chapter on her in his *Eothen*). The Earl m. 2ndly, 19 Mar. 1781, Louisa (d. 1829) dau. and heiress of Hon. Henry Grenville, Gov. of Barbados and d. 15 Dec. 1816 having by her had with other issue, an eldest son,

Philip Henry Stanhope, **4th Earl Stanhope,** F.R.S., b. 4 Dec. 1781; m. 19 Nov. 1803, Catherine Lucy (d. 1843) 2nd dau. of 1st Baron Carrington, and d. 2 Mar. 1855 having had with other issue, an elder son,

Philip Henry Stanhope, **5th Earl Stanhope,** wrote many historical works including a History of England, and had a distinguished political career, b. 30 Jan. 1805; m. 10 July 1824, Emily Harriet (d. 1873) 2nd dau. of Sir Edward Jerrison, 1st Bart. and d. 24 Dec. 1875, having had with other issue (including a 4th son Philip James, cr. Baron Weardale of Stanhope co. Durham in 1906, peerage extinct 1923), an eldest son,

Arthur Philip Stanhope, **6th Earl Stanhope,** Lord Lieut. Kent, Capt. Grenadier Guards, M.P. Leominster 1868 and East Suffolk, 1870-75, b. 13 Sept. 1838; m. 1869 Evelyn Henrietta, only dau. of Richard Pennefather (see *Burke's Landed Gentry of Ireland*, 1958, Freese Pennefather of Rathsallagh) and d. 19 April 1905, having had with a yr. son, Richard Philip, k. in action 1916, s.p., an elder son,

James Richard Stanhope, **7th Earl Stanhope,** K.G., P.C., D.S.O., M.C., who became 13th Earl of Chesterfield on the death of his cousin, the 12th Earl on 2 Aug. 1952 (see above). He was b. 11 Nov. 1880; educ. Eton and Magdalen Coll. Oxford; joined the Grenadier Guards in 1901, served in the South African War, 1902, in first World War, 1914-18, being mentioned in despatches twice, awarded M.C. (1916), D.S.O. (1917) and Legion of Honour. He filled many political appointments; was made P.C. 1929 and K.G. (1934), F.R.S.A. 1953. He m. 16 April 1921, Lady Eileen Agatha Browne, (d. 1940) eldest dau. of the 6th

Marquess of Sligo and d. 15 Aug. 1967, when the two earldoms became extinct, also the barony of Stanhope of Shelford, while the barony of Stanhope of Mahon passed to the Earl of Harrington.

ARMS—Quarterly ermine and gules a crescent for difference.

CREST—As above under Chesterfield, also the *Supporters* but each of them marked on the shoulder with a crescent for difference. (The use of the crescent, traditionally the mark of cadency for a second son, as used here is one of the few instances of the retention of the cadency system in English heraldry.)

The seat of Earl Stanhope was at Chevening, near Sevenoaks, Kent.

NOTE. The 4th Earl of Chesterfield was the recipient of the famous letter, dated 7 Feb. 1755 written by Dr. Samuel Johnson, and reproduced in Boswell's *Life*, where it is also observed, such being Lord Chesterfield's command of himself that he was wont to point out the severest passages in the letter observing how well they were expressed. By contrast, Lord Chesterfield could exhibit a mordant wit, as in his celebrated description of sexual intercouse; "the posture ridiculous, the pleasure transient, and the price—damnable".

CHUTER EDE

PEERAGE—U.K. Life Baron Chuter-Ede.
SURNAME—Chuter-Ede.
CR.—1 Jan. 1964. EXT.—11 Nov. 1965.
HISTORY—James and Agnes Ede had issue, James Chuter Chuter-Ede, **Baron Chuter-Ede,** so cr. as a a life peer 1964, b. 1882; educ. Epsom Nat. Sch., Dorking High Sch., Battersea P.T. Centre and Christ's Coll. Camb.; m. 1917 Lilian Mary S. Williams, who d. 1948, was school teacher for some years, then entered local politics, mem. Epsom Urban Council 1908-27, and 1933-37, Charter Mayor of Epsom and Ewell 1937; mem. Surrey C.C. 1914-49; M.P. South Shields 1929-31 and 1935-64; Home Sec. 1945-51; mem. and Pres. of many asscns.; served in World War I 1914-18, Sgt. in East Surreys and R.Es.; made P.C. 1944, cr. C.H. 1953. He d. 11 Nov. 1965.

CILCENNIN

PEERAGE—U.K. Viscount Cilcennin of Hereford.
SURNAME—Thomas.
CR.—21 Dec. 1955. EXT.—13 July 1960.
HISTORY—James Llewellyn Lewes Thomas J.P. of Llangadock, Carmarthenshire, b. 1742; m. 1769, Letitia, dau. of George Miller of Queensferry, West Lothian, and d. 1797, having had issue (with a dau. Anne, who m. 1771, George Lyon, of Forfar, Angus and d. 1836) an only son,

James Miller Lewes Thomas of Caeglas, Llandilo, Carmarthenshire, b. 1778, m. 1810, Katherine, dau. of Charles Tregoning, and d. 1834 having had issue,

James Lewes Thomas, J.P., of Caeglas, Llandilo, b. 8 March 1818, m. 6 April 1857,

Elizabeth Anne, yst. dau. of John Weston Goss, I.C.S. and d. 5 Oct. 1875 leaving issue,

James Lewes Thomas, J.P., M.A., Pembroke Coll. Oxford, of Caeglas, Llandilo, Carmarthenshire, b. 20 March 1862, m. 28 Oct. 1898, Anne Louisa, dau. of Cmdr. George Purdon, R.N., of Tinerana, Killaloe, co. Clare (see entry in B.L.G. of Ireland, 1912 edition, Purdon of Tinerana, the senior line of which Purdon of Lisnabin is the junior, see Purdon of Lisnabin, in B.L.G. of Ireland 1958) and d. 13 Aug. 1910 having had issue (with a dau. Joan Philippa, b. 1 May, 1906),

James Purdon Lewes Thomas, **Viscount Cilcennin,** a professional politician, b. 13 Oct. 1903; educ. Rugby and Oriel Coll. Oxford, B.A. 1926, M.A. 1952; was Priv. Sec. to the Rt. Hon. Stanley Baldwin, 1929-31 (later Earl Baldwin); M.P. for Hereford Div. 1931-55; Parl. Priv. Sec. to Sec. of State for Dominions 1932-35; for Colonies, 1935-38, and for War 1940, Lord Commissioner of the Treasury, 1949-43, Fin. Sec. to the Admiralty 1943-45, Vice Chm. of the Conservative Party, 1945-51, First Lord of the Admiralty 1951-56, was made a P.C. 1951 and created a peer 1955. He d. 13 July 1960.

ARMS—Azure a dolphin naiant between three anchors or.

CREST—Upon a chapeau gules turned up ermine an eagle displayed azure in the beak a snake or.

SUPPORTERS—Dexter, A Hereford bull ppr. Sinister, A dragon gules, the wings semée of portcullises chained or.

MOTTO—Pro aris et focis.

Viscount Cilcennin's residence was The Bush Farm, Colwall, co. Hereford.

CLANBRASSILL

PEERAGE—U.K. Baron Clanbrassill, of Hyde Hall. co. Hertford.
SURNAME—Jocelyn.
CR.—17 July, 1821. EXT.—3 July, 1897.
HISTORY—Robert Jocelyn, **3rd Earl of Roden,** K.P., P.C. and a baronet, b. 27 Oct. 1788; m. (1) 9 Jan. 1813, Maria Frances Catherine, dau. of 16th Lord Le Despencer (see extant peerages, under Stapleton, Bt.). She d. 25 Feb. 1861. He m. (2) 16 Aug. 1862, Clementina Janet, dau. of Thomas Andrews, of Greenknowe, co. Dumfries, and widow of Capt. R. L. Reilly. She d. 9 July, 1903. The 3rd Earl was cr. a peer of the United Kingdom as **Baron Clanbrassill**, of Hyde Hall, co. Hertford, 17 July, 1821. He d. 20 Mar. 1870, having had with other issue by his first marriage (see extant peerages, Roden, E.),

1. Robert, b. 20 Feb. 1816; m. 9 April, 1841, Lady Frances Elizabeth Cowper, dau. of 5th Earl Cowper and d.v.p. 12 Aug. 1854, having had with a ygr. son who d. young and a dau., an elder son, Robert, **4th Earl of Roden** (see below),
2. John Strange, **5th Earl** (see below).

The 3rd Earl was s. by his grandson, Robert Jocely, **4th Earl of Roden,** and **2nd Baron Clanbrassill,** Lt. 1st Life Guards, b. 22 Nov. 1846; d. unm. 9 Jan. 1880, being s. by his uncle, John Strange Jocelyn, **5th Earl of Roden,** and **3rd Baron Clanbrassill,** Lt. Col. Scots Fus. Guards, b. 5 June 1823; served in the Crimean

War, and was present at the battles of the Alma, Balaclava and Inkerman, and was later cmdr. of the 2nd Jäger Corps of the British German Legion. He m. 31 July 1851, Hon. Sophia Hobhouse, dau. of 1st Baron Broughton (see that title in present work, and also under Hobhouse, Bt. in extant peerage works). The 5th Earl d.s.p. m. 3 July 1897, and the barony of Clanbrassill then became extinct.

ARMS—As under Roden, E., in extant peerages.

CLANRICARDE

PEERAGE—Ireland. Clanricarde, Marquess of, 26 Nov. 1825.
Ireland. Baron of Dunkellin and Earl of Clanricarde, 1 July 1543.
Ireland. Viscount Burke of Clanmories, co. Mayo, 20 April 1629.
U.K. Baron Somerhill, of Somerhill, co. Kent, 13 Dec. 1826.
SURNAME—De Burgh-Canning.
CR.—as above. EXT.—12 April 1916 (except Earldom of Clanricarde (Irish peerage) cr. 29 Dec. 1800, see end of history.

HISTORY—The name of this famous family is spelt variously as De Burgo, Burke, De Burgh or Bourke. William FitzAdelm and Hugh de Lacie were sent by Henry II to receive the submission of Roderick O'Connor, King of Connaught, and of O'Meleaghlin, King of Meath, and in the latter part of Ireland William FitzAdelm founded one of the most noble families among the Anglo-Norman nobles. William was made Governor of Wexford, and entrusted on Henry II's return to England with the management of his affairs in Ireland. In 1175 in a synod of the bishops and clergy at Waterford, he published the bull, and the privileges granted by Pope Alexander III, in confirmation of the bull of Pope Adrian IV, which constituted Henry II Lord of Ireland. In 1179 he obtained a grant of a large part of the province of Connaught. On his death in 1204 he was s. by his son, Richard de Burgh, surnamed the Great, Lord of Connaught, Lord Lieut. of Ireland in 1227; he built the castle of Galway in 1232, and that of Loughrea in 1236. On his way to meet the King of England at Bordeaux in Jan. 1243, he d. He m. Hodierrna, dau. of Robert de Gernon, and granddau. maternally of Cahill Crovderg, The Red Hand, King of Connaught. He had issue,

1. Walter, Lord of Connaught, m. Maud, dau. and heir of Hugh de Lacie, the ygr., and became jure uxoris Earl of Ulster, on the death of his father-in-law. He had an eldest son,
   Richard, 2nd Earl of Ulster, called The Red Earl, whose great-granddau. Lady Elizabeth de Burgh, the only child and heir of William, 3rd Earl of Ulster, m. Lionel, of Antwerp, Duke of Clarence, 3rd son of Edward III, who became in consequence, 4th Earl of Ulster, and Lord of Connaught, and had issue an only dau., Philippa, wife of Edward Mortimer, 3rd Earl of March and jure uxoris 5th Earl of Ulster, ancestor, through his granddau. the Lady Anne Mortimer, wife of Richard Plantagenet,

Earl of Cambridge, of Edward IV, King of England.

2. William, of whom below.

The 2nd son of Richard de Burgh, Lord of Connaught, William de Burgh, known by the surname of Athankip, from being put to death at that place by the King of Connaught. He had issue,

Sir William de Burgh, who d. 1324 leaving by his wife, a dau. of the family of Mac-Jordan,
1. Richard (see below).
2. Edmond, Sir, from whom came the extinct Viscounts Bourke of Mayo, the Bourkes of Partry, and the extant Earls of Mayo.
3. Walter, ancestor of the Burkes of Clogheroka and Tllyra, from whom descended the Burkes of Auberies, co. Essex, the family which produced the celebrated John Burke, founder of the Burke publications, his son Sir Bernard Burke, Ulster King of Arms, and the latter's sons, who carried on Sir Bernard's work. (See B.L.G. 1952 for an account of Burke of Auberies.)

The eldest son, Sir Richard de Burgh, of Clanricarde, m. Ismania and had issue with a ygr. son, Walter, whose son, Edmond, was hostage for his father in 1347, an elder son,

Ulick de Burgh, Lord of Clanricarde, m. a dau. of O'Flaherty, of Iar Connaught and had issue,
1. Richard (see below).
2. Redmond, ancestor of the Burkes of Castle Hackett, Ower Cloghan, and Athkip.
3. Edmond, ancestor of the Burkes of Pallice, Lisnard, and Derry.

The eldest son, Richard Burke, Lord of Clanricarde, also called MacWilliam Oughter, had two sons,
1. Ulick, his heir (see below).
2. William, whosd son, Rickard, was Tanist of Clanricarde, and d.s.p. 1439.

The Lord of Clanricarde d. 1424, and was s. by his elder son,

Ulick Burke, Lord of Clanricarde, called Ulick Roe, m. (1) Honora, dau. of Tiege O'Brien, son of Connor O'Brien, King of Thomond, and (2) More, dau. of O'Conor Faley, and had by his first wife,
1. Ulick, his successor.
2. Rickard, ancestor of the Burkes of Derrymacloghny.
3. Thomas. 4. Redmond. 5. Richard.

The Lord of Clanricarde d. 1467 and was s. by his eldest son, Ulick Burke, Lord of Clanricarde, called Ulick Fion, m. Slany O'Brien and had issue,
1. Ulick, his successor (see below).
2. Rickard, MacWilliam, Chief of Clanrickard, who m. April 1530 Margaret, dau. of Piers Butler, Earl of Ormond & Ossory and d. leaving,
   (1) Ulick, **1st Earl of Clanricarde,** (see below).
   (2) Rickard, whose son, William, m. his cousin, dau. of his uncle, Richard Oge Burke, and had two sons.
   (3) Theobald.
   (4) Rickard Oge, whose dau. m. her cousin, William Burke.
   (5) Redmond, of Tynae, who d.s.o. 20 Jan. 1580, when the Earl of Clanricarde was found to be his heir.

3. Thomas, k. 1517.

The Lord of Clanricarde, d. 1487 and was s. by his eldest son, Ulick Burke, Lord of Clanricarde, m. Slany, dau. of Suodha MacNamara, by whom (d. 1498) he had an only son,

Ulick, who s. his father as Lord of Clanricarde and d.s.p. 1520. The Lord of Clanricarde d. 1509 and was s. by his only son, at whose death in 1520 the feudal lordship passed to his cousin,

Ulick Burke, Lord of Clanricarde, and **1st Earl of Clanricarde**, s. to the headship of the clan as MacWilliam in 1541 on the deposition of his father's cousin Sir Ulick Burke. He was called by the Irish, Negan, or Beheader, from his practice of making a mound of the heads of the men slain in battle, which he then covered with earth. He surrendered his large estates into the hands of King Henry VIII and had a grant thereof with the monastery of De Via Nova, in the diocese of Clonfert. He was cr. Earl of Clanricarde and Baron of Dunkellin, on 1 July, 1543, with the designation of William Boruckalias Makwilliam. He m. (1) Grace or Grany, dau. of O'Carroll, Prince of Elyand and by her had issue an only legitimate son, Richard, **2nd Earl.** Grace was the widow of MacCoghlan. He was separated from her, but her marriage was upheld 1550. He m. (2) during the lifetime of his first wife, Honora, sister of Sir Ulick Burke (see above) and dau. of Rickard Oge MacWilliam, of Clanrickard. He is said to have m. (3) Mary Lynch, by whom he had a son, John, who claimed the earldom 4 Feb. 1568. In addition the first Earl had several concubines with whom he possibly went through some form of marriage. He d. 19 Oct. 1544, being s. by the only legitimate son,

Richard Bourke or de Burgh, **2nd Earl of Clanricarde,** was called the Saxon or Sassanagh, because his heirship of his father was according to English law, and also because he had assisted the English against the Irish rebels, between 1548 and 1553. On 22 June, 1559 he had a confirmation of his earldom and barony. He m. (1) 1548 Margaret, dau. of Murrough O'Brien, 1st Earl of Thomond, from whom he obtained a divorce on grounds that she had bewitched him, and m. (2) 24 Nov. 1553, Margaret, dau. of Donough O'Brien, 2nd Earl of Thomond She d. 1568. He m. (3) Gille, or Cecilia, dau. of Cormac Oge MacCarthy, of Muskerry, and widow of 1st Baron Dunboyne. The 2nd Earl d. 24 July, 1582, being s. by his only legitimate son, (by his first wife),

Ulick Bourke or de Burgh, **3rd Earl of Clanricarde,** who supported the English during Tyrone's rebellion 1598-1601 and was made commander of the forces in Connaught, 9 Jan. 1599/1600. He m. 25 Nov. 1564, Honora, dau. of John Burke, of Clogheroka and Tullyra, co. Galway, and d. 20 May, 1601, having had issue,

1. Richard, **4th Earl** (see below).
2. Thomas, Sir, m. Ursula, dau. of Sir Nicholas Malby, Chief Commissioner of Connaught and widow of Capt. Anthony Brabazon, of Ballynasloe, and d.s.p.
3. William, Sir, m. Joan, dau. of Dermot O'Shaughnessy, of Gort, and d. 2 Feb. 1625, having by her (who m. 2ndly Teige O'Brien),
   (1) Richard, **6th Earl** (see below),
   (2) William, **7th Earl** (see below).

4. John, of Dunsandle, cr. 20 April 1629, **Viscount Burke,** of Clanmories, co. Mayo, with remainder in default of his own male issue, to the issue male of his father. He m. Katherine, dau. of Capt. Anthony Brabazon, of Ballynasloe, and d. 16 Nov. 1633, having issue,
   Thomas, **2nd Viscount Burke,** of Clanmories, m. Margaret, dau. of Christopher, Lord Slane and d.s.p., but owing to the limitation mentioned, the peerage remained with the Earls of Clanricarde.
5. Edmond, of Kilcornan, co. Galway, m. Katherine, dau. of Thomas St. Lawrence of co. Tipperary, and d. 22 June 1639, leaving issue from whom descended the Burkes of Kilcornan, and the Burkes of Greenfield, co. Galway.

The eldest son, Richard Bourke, **4th Earl of Clanricarde,** was educ. at Ch. Ch. Oxford, 1584, M.A. 1598. He fought against the rebels, and was knighted on the field 24 Dec. 1601, at the battle of Kingsale, whence his sobriquet of Kingsale. He was Col. of Regt. of Foot, Gov. of Connaught, and Constable of Athlone Castle, Keeper of the King's House, 1603; Lord Pres. of Connaught, and Gov. of Galway, 1616. He was cr. 3 April 1624, Baron of Somerhill and Viscount Tunbridge, co. Kent, with the usual limitation to the heirs male of his body; he was further cr. on 23 Aug. 1628, Earl of St. Albans, co. Hertford, with usual remainder, and Baron of Imanney and Viscount Galway, Connaught, these last two peerages being limited, failing heirs male of his own body, to those of his father. He m. before 8 April 1603, Frances, dau. and heir of Sir Francis Walsingham, and widow of Sir Philip Sydney, and previously of Robert Devereux, Earl of Essex. She was bur. 17 Feb. 1631/2. He d. 12 Nov. 1635, will proved 15 Dec. 1635. He had issue,

1. Ulick, **5th Earl and Marquess of Clanricarde.**
   1. Mary, m. Hon. Edward Butler, (Ormonde M.) and had a son, d.s.p.
   2. Honora, m. (1) Garratt McCoghlan, of Clonecknose, son and heir of Sir John McCoghlan. He d. 17 April, 1629. She m. (2) about 1645, John Paulet, 5th Marquess of Winchester, and d. 10 March, 1661, leaving issue.

The only son, Ulick Bourke, **5th Earl of Clanricarde,** also 2nd Earl of St. Albans, Viscount Tunbridge and Baron Somerhill, etc., b. before 8 Dec. 1604, and s. his kinsman as Viscount Bourke of Clanmories (unless such succession was that of his successor). He was loyal to Gov. in the great rebellion of 1641-43, was Col. in his father's Regt. of Foot, Gov. of Galway, 1636, and knighted at Windsor, 20 May 1618. He was also Lieut. Gov. and C. in C. Connaught, 1644, and made a P.C. of Ireland, 1645. On 21 Feb. 1645/46 he was cr. Marquess of Clanricarde. He put up a strong resistance to Cromwell in Ireland in 1651 and by the latter's action he was excepted from pardon, though in 1652 he was able to leave Ireland for Kent. He m. Dec. 1622, Anne, dau. of William Compton, 1st Earl of Northampton, and by her had issue,
   Margaret, m. (1) after 2 Mar. 1659, Charles Maccarty, Viscount Muskerry, son and heir of Donough Maccarty, 1st Earl of Clancarty;

he d.v.p. being k. in a fight at sea against the Dutch, 3 June 1665. She m. (2) 1676 Robert Villiers, otherwise Danvers, styling himself Viscount Purbeck. He d. 1684. She m. (3) Robert Fielding, "Beau Fielding", who d. 1712. She d. Aug. 1698.

The 5th Earl and 1st Marquess of Clanricarde d. July 1657, when all his English honours became extinct and also the Marquessate of Clanricarde. The Irish honours went to his cousin and heir male,

Richard Bourke, **6th Earl of Clanricarde,** Viscount Burke of Clanmories, and Baron Dunkellin. He took his seat in the House of Lords, 1661, having in that year been in receipt of a Gov. pension of £1,500 until his estate (which had been sequestrated under Cromwell) should be restored to him. He m. Elizabeth, dau. of Walter Butler, 11th Earl of Ormonde, and had two daus. his coheirs, viz. Mary, wife of Sir John Burke, of Derrymacloghny, and Margaret, wife of Col. Garret Moore. He d.s.p.m. Aug. 1666, and was s. by his brother,

William Bourke, **7th Earl of Clanricarde,** Col. in Royal Army, 1640; Lieut. co. Galway, 1680; Gov. co. Galway, 1687; made P.C. of Ireland, 1681; m. (1) Lettice, dau. of Sir Henry Whirley Bt., by Dorothy, dau. of Robert Devereux, Earl of Essex. She was bur. 25 Sept. 1655. He m. (2) Helen, dau. of Donough Maccarty, 1st Earl of Clancarty, and widow of Sir John Fitzgerald, of Dromana, co. Waterford. The 7th Earl d. Oct. 1687, and his widow m. (3) before 1 Feb. 1699/1700, Thomas Bourke. By his first wife, the 7th Earl had,

1. Richard, **8th Earl** (see below).
2. John, **9th Earl** (see below).
3. Thomas, k. at Buda.

By his second wife the 7th Earl had further issue,

4. Ulick, cr. Baron Tyaquin and Viscount Galway, m. Hon. Frances Lane, dau. of George, 1st Viscount Lanesborough, and was k. at Aughrim, 12 July, 1691, s.p.
5. William, d.s.p.
1. Margaret, m. (1) Bryan, Viscount Magennis, of Iveagh; and (2) Col. Butler, of Kilcash.
2. Honor, m. (1) Patrick Sarsfield, Earl of Lucan; and (2) James FitzJames, Duke of Berwick.

The eldest son, Richard Bourke, **8th Earl of Clanricarde,** in command of a regt. of Foot for James II in his Irish Army in 1689, Gov. of Galway, surrendered that town to Gen. Ginkel, two weeks after Battle of Aughrim, and was outlawed 11 May 1691. He m. (1) 22 Jan. 1669/70, Elizabeth, ygst. dau. of — Bagnall, Page of the Backstairs to James I. and (2) Anne, dau. of Sir Thomas Cheke, of Pirgo, co. Essex, and widow of Robert Rich, Earl of Warwick, and of Richard Rogers, of Bryanston, Dorset. The 8th Earl d.s.p.m.s. (having had a son d. young, and a dau. Dorothy, m. Alexander Pendarves, of Roscrowe, co. Cornwall), and was s. by his brother,

John Bourke, **9th Earl of Clanricarde,** b. 1642; Col. of a regt. of foot for James II and cr. by the latter 2 April 1689, after his departure from the English throne, Baron Bourke of Bophin, co. Galway. He fought for James II, and was captured at Aughrim, 12 July 1691; was attainted, but having conformed to the

Established Church in 1699, he was by Act of 1 Anne, restored in blood and estate, having been acquitted of all treasons and attainders. He m. Oct. 1684, Mary, dau. of James Talbot, of Templeogue, co. Dublin, and Mount Talbot, co. Roscommon, and d. 16 Oct. 1722. She d. 27 June 1711. They had,

1. Michael, **10th Earl** (see below).
2. John, on whom his father settled Clondagoff, co. Galway, and who m. Mary, only dau. and heir of John Burke, of Clogheroka, and d.s.p.m. Aug. 1718.
3. Ulick, Col in the French army, d.sp. 4 Dec. 1762.
4. Thomas, of Lackan, co. Roscommon, m. Mary, dau. of Alexander, Eustace, and d.s.p.m. 1764.
5. Edward, Gen. in the Spanish army, d. unm. 7 Mar. 1743, of wounds received at the battle of Campo Santo.
6. William, in the French army, k. at Fontenoy, 11 May, 1745.
1. Letitia, m. Sir Festus Burke of Glinsk.
2. Bridget, m. Richard Dillon, Viscount Dillon.
3. Honora, m. John Kelly, of Clonlyon.
4. Mary, m. Garrett Moore.

The eldest son, Michael Bourke, **10th Earl of Clanricarde,** educ. Eton and Ch. Ch. Oxford; conformed to Established Church; sum. to House of Lords during father's lifetime as Baron Dunkellin, and took his seat 4 Oct. 1712. He m. 19 Sept. 1714, Anne, dau. of John Smith, of Beaufort Buildings, London, Commissioner of Excise, and widow of Hugh Parker, of Honington, co. Warwick. She d. 1 Jan. 1732/33 and was bur. in Westminster Abbey. He d. 29 Nov. 1726, having had with other issue,

1. John Smith, **11th Earl** (see below).
1. Anne, m. Denis Daly, of Raford, co. Galway, and had issue.
2. Mary. m. George Jennings, and had a dau.

The 1st 2nd but surv. son and heir, John Smith Bourke, **11th Earl of Clanricarde,** who resumed by sign manual 1752 the surname of De Burgh, in lieu of Bourke. He was b. 11 Nov. 1720, was F.R.S. 1753, F.S.A. 1753, and was made P.C. of Ireland 8 July 1761, but removed on 16 July 1761. He m. 1 July 1740, Hester Amelia, dau. of Sir Henry Vincent, 6th Bt. of Stoke Dabernon, co. Surrey, and d. 21 April, 1782, having had issue,

1. Henry, **12th Earl** (see below).
2. John Thomas, **13th Earl** (see below).
1. Hester Amelia, m. William Trenchard.
2. Margaret Augusta, m. Luke Dillon.

The elder son, Sir Henry de Burgh, **12th Earl of Clanricarde** and **Marquess of Clanricarde,** b. 8 Jan. 1742/43, M.P. co. Galway, 1768/69; Gov. co. Galway, 1782; cr. K.P. 1783, being one of the 15 original Knights of the Order; made P.C. of Ireland 1783, and cr. Marquess of Clanricarde, on 17 Aug. 1789. He m. 17 Mar. 1785, Urania Anne, dau. of George Paulet, 12th Marquess of Winchester, and d.s.p. 8 Dec. 1797, when the Marquessate became extinct. His widow m. (2) 28 Oct. 1799, Col. Peter Kington, who was k. in the attack on Buenos Aires 6 July 1807, and (3) Vice Adm. the Hon. Sir Joseph Sidney Yorke, K.C.B., who was accidentally drowned off his yacht in the Hamble river, 5 April 1831. She d. 27 Dec. 1843. The Earl was s. by his brother,

John Thomas de Burgh, **13th Earl of Clanricarde,** b. 22 Sept. 1744, Lt. Col. 68th Foot,

Major Gen. 1793, Lieut. Gen. 1798, Gen. 1803; cr. by letters patent 29 Dec. 1800 (the last date of creation of Irish peers before the Union with Great Britain) Earl of Clanricarde, with remainder failing his issue male to his first and every other dau. in priority of birth and to the heir male of the body of such dau., he having at that time no son. He was a representative peer 1801-08, being one of the original 28 so elected at the time of the Union. Gov. of Hull, 1801-08. He m. 17 Mar. 1799, Elizabeth, dau. of Sir Thomas Burke, 1st Bt., of Marble Hill, co. Galway and d. 27 July 1808, and his widow d. 26 Mar. 1854. They had issue,

1. Ulick John, **14th Earl of Clanricarde**, and **1st Marquess of Clanricarde.**
1. Hester Catherine, m. 4 Mar. 1816, Howe Peter Browne, 2nd Marquess of Sligo and d. 17 Feb. 1878. He d. 26 Jan. 1845, leaving with other issue, Henry Ulick Browne, 5th Marquess of Sligo, father of George Ulick Browne, 6th Marquess of Sligo, who s. in 1916 to the Earldom of Clanricarde which had been cr. 29 Dec. 1800.
2. Emily, m. 9 Jan. 1826, Thomas, 3rd Earl of Howth, and d. 5 Dec. 1842, leaving issue (Extinct Peerage 1883).

The 13th Earl's only son, Sir Ulick John de Burgh, **14th Earl of Clanricarde**, and **1st Marquess of Clanricarde**, b. 20 Dec. 1802; cr. Marquess of Clanricarde, 26 Nov. 1825 and Baron Somerhill, of Somerhill, Kent, 13 Dec. 1826; Under Sec. of State for Foreign Affairs, 1826-27; Capt. of the Yeomen of the Guard, 1830-34; made P.C. 1830; cr. K.P. 1831; Lord Lieut. of Galway, 1831-1874; Ambassador to St. Petersburg, 1838-41; Postmaster Gen. 1846-52; Lord Privy Seal, 1858 for about three weeks; m. 4 April 1825, Harriet, only dau. of Rt. Hon. George Canning, by Joan, suo jure, Viscountess Canning of Kilbrahan. She d. 13 April 1804. He d. 10 April 1874, having had issue,

1. Ulick Conding, Lord Dunkellin, b. 12 July 1827; educ. Eton; entered the Army, 1846; A.D.C. to Lord Lieut. of Ireland, 1846-52; State Steward to Lord Lieut. 1853-54; Lt. Col. Coldstream Guards, 1854-60; served in the Crimean War and was captured at Sebastopol; Mil. Sec. to Lord Canning, when the latter was Gov. Gen. of India, 1856; served as a volunteer on the staff during the Persian Expedition, 1856-57; M.P. for Galway, 1857-65, and for co. Galway. 1865-67. He d. unm. and v.p. 16 Aug. 1867.
2. Hubert George, **2nd Marquess** (see below).
1. Elizabeth Joanna, m. 17 July 1845, Viscount Lascelles, afterwards 4th Earl of Harewood, and d. 26 Feb. 1854, leaving issue.
2. Emily Chalotte, m. 20 July 1853; 9th Earl of Cork, and d. 10 Oct. 1912, leaving issue.
3. Catherine, m. 8 Aug. 1850, John Weyland, of Woodeaton, co. Oxford, and Woodriding, co. Norfolk and d. 9 April 1895 leaving issue.
4. Margaret Anne, m. 6 Mar. 1856, Wentworth Blackett Beaumont, afterwards Lord Allendale, and d. 31 Mar. 1888, leaving issue.

5. Harriet Augusta, m. 3 Mar. 1859, T. F. C. Vernon-Wentworth, and d. 18 Jan. 1901, leaving issue.

The only surv. son and heir, Hubert George de Burgh Canning, **15th Earl of Clanricarde,** and **2nd Marquess of Clanricarde**, b. 30 Nov. 1832; educ. Harrow; Attaché at Turin, 1852; Second Sec. there 1862; took the surname of Canning after that of De Burgh, in compliance with the will of his maternal uncle, Earl Canning, by royal licence 1862; M.P. for co. Galway, 1867-71. He d. unm. 12 April 1916, when all his honours became extinct except that for the Earldom of Clanricarde, cr. 29 Dec. 1800, which devolved in accordance with the special limitation to his kinsman the 6th Marquess of Sligo. His estates and property passed to his great nephew the 6th Earl of Harewood who m. Princess Royal (Princess Mary) dau. of George V.

ARMS—Quarterly 1 and 4, Argent three Moors' heads couped, in profile, ppr., wreathed round the temples argent and azure (Canning) 2 and 3, Or a cross gules, in the dexter canton a lion rampant sable (De Burgh).

CRESTS—1, A demi-lion rampant argent, charged with three trefoils vert, holding in the dexter paw an arrow, pheoned and flighted ppr., shaft or (Canning); and 2, A cat-a-mountain sejant guardant ppr., collared and chained or (De Burgh).

SUPPORTERS—Two cats-a-mountain guardant ppr., collared and chained or.

MOTTO—Ung roy, ung foy, ung loy.

The seat of the Earls and Marquesses was Portunna Castle, co. Galway.

CLARENCE AND AVONDALE

PEERAGE—U.K. Earl of Athlone, and Duke of Clarence and Avondale.

SURNAME—(sometimes given as Guelph, but no surname at that time).

CR.—24 May 1890. EXT.—14 Jan. 1892.

HISTORY—H.R.H. Prince Albert Victor Christian Edward, Prince of the United Kingdom of Great Britain and Ireland, Duke of Saxony, was b. 8 Jan. 1864, the eldest son of King Edward VII (born when the latter was Prince of Wales) by his Queen, the Princess Alexandra, eldest dau. of Christian IX, King of Denmark. The Prince entered the R.N. 1877; midshipman, 1880; Trin. Coll. Camb., 1883; Lt. 10th Hussars, 1886; Capt. 9th Lancers, Capt. 3rd K.R.R., and A.D.C. to Queen Victoria; 1887; Major 10th Hussars, 1889; was Hon. Col. 4th Regt. Bengal Infantry, 1st Punjab Cavalry, and 4th Bombay Cavalry. He was cr. K.G. 1883; K.P. 1887; was Hon. LL.D. Cambridge and Dublin; cr. **Earl of Athlone, and Duke of Clarence and Avondale**, 24 May 1890. (Avondale is in Lanarkshire). He d. unm. 14 Jan. 1892, of pneumonia at Sandringham. He had become betrothed only a few weeks previously to his cousin, the Princess Mary of Teck, who later m. his brother, the Duke of York, afterwards King George V.

ARMS—The royal arms differenced by a label of three points argent, the centre point charged with St. George's Cross; in the centre of the said royal arms an escutcheon of the august house of Saxony, viz., barry of ten or and sable, a crown of rue in bend vert.

CREST—On a coronet composed of crosses patteé and fleur-de-lis, a lion statant guardant or, crowned with a like coronet and differenced with a label of three points charged as in the arms.

SUPPORTERS—The royal supporters differenced with a like coronet and label.

CLARINA

PEERAGE—Ireland. Baron Clarina of Elm Park, co. Limerick.

SURNAME—Massey.

CR.—28 Dec. 1800. EXT.—4 Nov. 1952.

HISTORY—This family had an origin common with that of the present Baron Massey. Gen. Hugh Massey was a commander in the suppression of the Irish rebellion of 1641. For account of his son, Hugh, and his grandson, also Hugh, see the extant Peerage. The last named, Col. Hugh Massey, had with other issue, an eldest son, Hugh, 1st Baron Massy, and a sixth son,

Eyre Massey, **1st Baron Clarina**, Marshal of the British Army in Ireland, Col. 27th Foot, Gov. of Limerick, served at the battle of Culloden, 1746, and in North America. He was b. 24 May 1719; m. 27 Dec. 1767, Catherine, dau. of the Rt. Hon. Nathaniel Clements (see Leitrim E.); was cr. a peer of Ireland 28 Dec. 1800, as Baron Clarina, and d. 17 May 1804, having had with other children,

Nathaniel William Massey, **2nd Baron Clarina**, Major Gen., b. 23 May 1773; m. 29 May 1796 Penelope, dau. of Michael Roberts Westrop, and d. in Jan. 1810 leaving with other issue,

Eyre Massey, **3rd Baron Clarina**, a representative peer for Ireland, b. 6 May 1798; m. 9 Sept. 1828, Susan Elizabeth, yst. dau. of Hugh Barton, of Straffan, co. Kildare, and d. 18 Nov. 1872, having had with other issue,

1. Eyre Challoner Henry, **4th Baron** (see below).

2. Lionel Edward, **5th Baron** (see below).

The eldest son,

Eyre Challoner Henry Massey, **4th Baron Clarina**, Gen., C.B., commanded the Dublin District 1881-86, a representative peer, b. 29 April 1830; d. unm. 16 Dec. 1897 being s. by his brother,

Lionel Edward Massey, **5th Baron Clarina**, Lt. Col. Scots Fus. Guards, High Sheriff, co. Limerick, 1896, b. 20 April 1837; m. (1) 24 Nov. 1877, Elizabeth Ellen, dau. of Alexander Bannatyne, of Woodstown, co. Limerick. She d. 13 Jan. 1883, leaving with one dau., a son,

Eyre Nathaniel, **6th Baron** (see below).

The 5th Lord Clarina, m. (2) 23 Aug. 1889, Sophia Mary, dau. of James Butter of Castle Crine, co. Clare and had by her four more daus. She d. 1912. He d. 13 Oct. 1922 and was s. by his only son,

Eyre Nathaniel Massey, **6th Baron Clarina**, Capt. Scots Guards, served in the S. African War 1900-02 (wounded) and in the first World War, 1914-18, b. 8 Feb. 1880; m. 1 July 1906, Alice Erin, 4th dau. of Wilton Allhusen, of Pinhay, Lyme Regis, Dorset, and d. 4 Nov. 1952, having had issue, a dau.,

Erin Moira, b. 29 Nov. 1909; m. 2 Sept. 1939, Capt. Peter Roddam Holderness Rod-

dam, and has issue (see Burke's Landed Gentry, 1952. Roddam of Roddam).

Alice Erin, Baroness Clarina, who d. 12 May 1961 had a very distinguished record in the first World War. She served with the French Red Cross in France and Belgium, 1914-15, in a hospital and later opened a small canteen in a deserted house. She was mentioned in despatches by the officer, commanding the district. In 1916 she went to Greece and served on the Serbian-Bulgarian front with canteen units, being under fire and also bombed, and was wounded by an aircraft bullet. In 1917-18 served in Italy, then in Cologne. Not only wounded and twice mentioned in despatches, Lady Clarina was also awarded the M.M., and the Order of St. Sava of Serbia.

ARMS—Argent on a chevron between three fusils sable, a lion passant or.

CREST—Out of a ducal coronet or, a bull's head gules, armed sable.

SUPPORTERS—Two grenadier soldiers in the uniform of the 27th Foot ppr. each holding in his exterior hand a sword also ppr.

MOTTO—Pro liberate patriae.

NOTE. With regard to the presence of a ducal coronet in the crest, and having regard to the use of such a coronet in the crest of other families, the following note by an officer of the College of Arms is of interest. "Your question about the crest of Lord Clarina is not easy to answer. The Massy family seems to have established itself in Ireland in or about 1641. I have not found any pedigree showing its connection with any English family. There were several families of Massy in Lancashire and Cheshire and this particular family, for all I know with good reason, appears to have claimed descent from the Massys of Sale in Cheshire whose pedigree and arms were recorded at the Visitation of that county in 1663. At any rate it seems to have adopted the arms of that family with a small mark of difference and its crest with no difference at all. There does not appear to be any grant of arms to the Massys of Sale, and even if there was it is extremely improbable that it would give any reason for the ducal coronet. These crest coronets were fairly common and no particular significance seems to attach to them. They have not been granted for many years owing to the unfortunate and inevitable confusion that arose between them and a duke's coronet with which they have nothing to do". In Fox Davies's *Armorial Families* p. 1326, the registration of the arms of Lord Clarina is given as—Ireland 29 Dec. 1800.

CLAUSON

PEERAGE—U.K. Baron Clauson of Hawkeshead, co. Hertford.

SURNAME—Clauson.

CR.—20 Feb. 1942. EXT.—15 Mar. 1946.

HISTORY—Albert Charles Clauson, **Baron Clauson**, son of Charles Clauson, b. 14 Jan. 1870; educ. Merchant Taylors' School and St. John's Coll. Oxford, M.A. 1894, Hon. Fell. 1927, Barrister-at-Law, Lincoln's Inn, 1891, K.C. 1910, Bencher 1914, and Treasurer 1937; counsel Univ. of Oxford and standing counsel,

Roy. Coll. of Physicians 1923-26, a Judge of High Court, Chancery Div., 1926-38 and a Lord Justice of Appeal, 1938-42, mem. of Judicial Cttee of Privy Council 1942; cr. C.B.E. (civil) 1920, Kt. Bach. 1926, made P.C. 1938 and cr Baron Clauson of Hawkeshead, co. Hertford, 1942; m. 1902, Kate, dau. of J. T. Hopwood, of Lincoln's Inn, and widow of Lucas Thomasson and d. 15 Mar. 1946.

ARMS— Barry of four per pale sable and or countercharged three bendlets argent within two flaunches ermine.

CREST—A mullet of ten points encircled by an annulet or, between two wings sable, the dexter charged with three bendlets and the sinister with as many bendlets in sinister argent.

SUPPORTERS—On either side a hawk, wings elevated sable beaked and legged gules, belled or, the dexter charged on the wing with three bendlets and the sinister with as many bendlets sinister argent.

MOTTO—Spes et fides.

CLEVELAND

PEERAGE—Great Britain. Viscount Barnard of Barnards Castle, and Earl of Darlington, co. Durham, cr. 3 April 1754.

U.K. Marquess of Cleveland. 5 Oct. 1827.

U.K. Baron Raby, of Raby Castle, co. Durham, and Duke of Cleveland, 29 Jan. 1833.

SURNAME—Powlett, but previous to 1813, Vane.

CR.—As above. EXT.—21 Aug. 1891.

HISTORY—Henry Vane (or Fane), 3rd Baron Barnard, of the cr. of Baron Barnard of Barnard Castle, in the county of Palatine of Durham, of 1699 (see extant peerage works, under Barnard B.), who was b. about 1705; and s. his father as 3rd Baron Barnard, on 27 April 1753. He was cr. Viscount Barnard of Barnards Castle, and Earl of Darlington, co. Durham, on 3 April 1754. He m. 2 Sept. 1725, Lady Grace FitzRoy, dau. of the 1st Duke of Cleveland and Southampton, the son of Charles II by Barbara Villiers, Duchess of Cleveland. The 1st Earl of Darlington d. 6 Mar. 1758, and was s. by his eldest son, Henry Vane, 2nd Earl of Darlington, b. 1726; educ. Ch. Ch. Oxford, and M.A. Camb.; Capt. 1st Foot Guards, 1747; Lt. Col. Coldstream Guards, 1750; Col. 1779; Whig M.P. for Downton, 1749-53; and for co. Durham, 1753-58; was Lord Lt. of co. Durham, 1758-92; Gov. of Carlisle, 1763-92; m. 19 Mar. 1757, Margaret, dau. of Robert Lowther, (Lonsdale, E.), and d. 8 Sept. 1792, being s. by his son, William Harry Vane, 3rd Earl of Darlington, b. 27 July 1766; educ. Ch. Ch. Oxford; Whig M.P. for Totnes, 1788-90, and for Winchelsea 1790-92; Lord Lt. of Durham, 1793-1842; was cr. 5 Oct. 1827, Marquess of Cleveland, and on 29 Jan. 1833 Baron Raby, of Raby Castle, co. Durham, and Duke of Cleveland. The last title was taken from that of his ancestress, the infamous Barbara Villiers, Duchess of Cleveland. He was cr. K.G. 1839. He m. (1) 19 Sept. 1787, his cousin, Lady Katherine Powlett, dau. and coheiress of the 6th and last Duke of Bolton, by his 2nd wife, Katherine, dau. of Robert Lowther mentioned above. She d. 1807. He m. (2) 27 July 1813, Elizabeth dau. of

Robert Russell, a market gardener, of Newton House, in Burmiston, co. York. He d. 29 Jan. 1842. By his first wife he had with other issue.
1. Henry, 2nd Duke (see below).
2. William John Frederick, 3rd Duke (see below).
3. Harry George, 4th and last Duke (see below).

The eldest son, Henry Vane, 4th Earl of Darlington, and 2nd Duke of Cleveland b. 6 Aug. 1788; educ. Ch. Ch. Oxford; M.P. (Whig) for co. Durham, 1812-15; for Winchelsea, 1816-18; for Tregony, 1818-26, and for Totnes, 1826-30 (while in this constituency turning over to Toryism); afterwards Tory M.P. for Saltash, 1830-31; and South Salop 1832-42; served in the Army, from 1815, Lt. Col. 75th Foot, 1824; Major Gen. 1851; Lt. Gen. 1857; and Gen. 1863. He was cr. K.G. 1842. He m. 18 Nov. 1809, Lady Sophia, eldest dau. of the 4th Earl Poulett. She d. 1859. He d.s.p. 18 Jan. 1864 and was s. by his brother,

William John Frederick Vane (until 1813, when he took name of Powlett, but in 1864 resumed that of Vane), 5th Earl of Darlington and 3rd Duke of Cleveland, b. 3 April 1792; educ. Brasenose Coll. Oxford; M.A. 1812; He took the surname of Powlett in place of that of Vane, in compliance with the will of his maternal grandmother, the Duchess of Bolton, on 14 April 1813. He was M.P. for Winchilsea, 1812-15 as a Whig for co. Durham, 1815-31; then as a Tory for St. Ives, 1846-52, and Ludlow, 1852-57. He m. 3 July 1815, Lady Grace Caroline Lowther, dau. of 1st Earl of Lonsdale. Soon after his s. to the Dukedom in 1864, he by Royal Licence dated 4 Mar. that year resumed his surname of Vane. He d.s.p. 6 Sept. 1864 and was s. by his brother,

Harry George Vane, (later Powlett), 6th Earl of Darlington and 4th Duke of Cleveland, b. 19 April 1803; educ. Oriel Coll. Oxford, B.A. 1829; was Attaché in the Embassy at Paris, 1829, and Sec. of Legation at Stockholm, 1839-41; sat as Liberal M.P. for South Durham, 1841-59; and for Hastings, 1859-64. By Royal Licence, of 18 Nov. 1864, he took the surname of Powlett in lieu of that of Vane, in compliance with the will of his maternal grandmother, the Duchess of Bolton. He was cr. K.G. 1865. He m. 2 Aug. 1854, Lady Catherine Lucy Wilhelmina, dau. of 4th Earl Stanhope, and widow of Archibald Primrose, styled by courtesy, Lord Dalmeny, eldest son of 4th Earl of Rosebery. The Duchess was the author of the well known work, in 3 vols, The Battle Abbey Roll, publ. 1889. This book contains a great deal of sound genealogy, on various families, but its main foundation—of reliance on the anonymous work, The Norman People— completely vitiated its claim to vindicate the Roll. The 4th Duke d.s.p. 21 Aug. 1891. The Duchess d. 24 May 1901. They had no issue. The titles of the 4th Duke then all became extinct except for the Barony of Barnard cr. 1699, in which he was s. by his kinsman, Henry de Vere Vane who then became 9th Baron Barnard, (see that title in extant peerages).

ARMS—Quarterly 1 and 4, Azure, three sinister gauntlets, or (Vane). 2 and 3, Quarterly, I and IV. Quarterly France and England; II, Scotland; III, Ireland (being the arms of Charles II) charged on the centre point with a baton sinister ermine (for FitzRoy).

CRESTS—1, A dexter gauntlet ppr. bossed

and rimmed or, brandishing a sword also ppr. (Vane). 2, On a chapeau gules turned up ermine a lion passant guardant or, gorged with a collar componée ermine and azure, and crowned with a five leaved ducal coronet gold (FitzRoy).
SUPPORTERS—Dexter, A lion guardant or, crowned and gorged as in the crest (FitzRoy); Sinister, A greyhound argent, collared as the dexter.
MOTTO—Nec temere nec timide.
The Duke of Cleveland had estates in 11 English counties, amounting to some 55,000 acres in 1883. His principal seats were Raby Castle, co. Durham, now the seat of the Lords Barnard and Battle Abbey, Sussex. His total holding of land in the United Kingdom, in 1883 was over 100,000 acres. Battle Abbey, with 6,000 acres, was sold on 26 Nov. 1901, by auction for the sum of £200,000, to Sir Augustus Webster, 8th Bt., whose father, also Sir Augustus Webster, 7th Bt., had sold it to the 4th Duke in 1857. The house at Battle Abbey was used for some years as a school. The Webster baronetcy became extinct in 1923. The windows of the great hall at Battle were illuminated by the arms of the Vane family, with their various quarterings and heraldic alliances, probably arranged by the Duchess, wife of the 4th Duke.

CLONBROCK

PEERAGE—Ireland. Baron Clonbrock, of Clonbrock, co. Galway.
SURNAME—Dillon.
CR.—5 June 1790. **EXT.**—1 Nov. 1926.
HISTORY—This is a branch of the family of Dillon to which belonged also the Viscounts Dillon and the Earls of Roscommon. The family went to Ireland in the reign of Henry II, with Prince (later King) John, and received extensive grants of land in Longford and Westmeath, which were then named Dillon's County. The name was altered by statute 34th. Henry VIII to the Barony of Kilkenny West. The accounts of the earlier history of the family in Ireland as given in Extinct Peerage, 1883, and extant Peerages under Dillon cannot be reconciled, and therefore the present narrative begins with, Gerald Dillon, Lord of Dromrany, who m. Lady Emily Fitzgerald, dau. of the Earl of Desmond, and had issue,
1. Maurice, Sir, of Dromrany, ancestor of the Viscounts Dillon.
2. John.
3. Henry, Prior of St. John's, Newtown, near Trim.
4. James, Sir, of Proudstown.
The fourth son, Sir James Dillon, of Proudstown, m. Honor, dau. of Sir John D'Arcy, Lord Lieut. of Ireland and had issue,
Sir Robert Dillon, of Proudstown, m. a dau. of Sir James Bermingham, and had with other issue,
1. Richard, Sir, of Proudstown, distinguished at the battle of Verneuil, 1424, and was ancestor of the Earls of Roscommon.
2. Gerald, ancestor of Lord Clonbrock (see below).
The second son,
Gerald Dillon, m. Elizabeth, dau. of Lord Barry, and had with three other sons and three

daus., an eldest son, Richard Dillon, settled near Dublin, m. Mary, dau. of Lord Delvin, and had with a dau., Elinor who m. Robert Kent, of Danestown, co. Dublin, a son,
Thomas Dillon, a lawyer and second Justice of the Common Pleas in Ireland, who purchased the estate of Clonbrock, co. Galway, and m. a dau. of Alen, of Palmerstown, co. Dublin. He had issue,
Thomas Dillon, of Clonbrock, co. Galway, of Carraghboy, co. Roscommon, and of Ballineclogh, co. Sligo, Chamberlain of the Exchequer, and appointed by patent 6 Oct. 1603, Chief Justice of Connaught. He m. Ellen, sister of Sir James Shaen, and had, with other issue, a second son,
Robert Dillon of Clonbrock, aged 29 in 1606, m. Catherine dau. of Meyler Hussey, of Mulhussey, and d. 1628 (his will was proved 20 Feb. 1629) leaving an eldest son and heir,
Richard Dillon, of Clonbrock, aged 25 in 1628, m. (1) Frances, dau. of Edmund Malone, of Dublin, and (2) Gennett, dau. of Sir Dominick Browne, of Galway, and had by her with other issue, (his will was proved 8 Sept. 1676) a son,
Robert Dillon, of Clonbrock, who m. Mary, dau. of Geffery Browne, son of Sir Dominick Browne, and d. 1688, leaving,
Lucas Dillon, of Clonbrock, m. (1) Honora, dau. of Sir John Burke, of Glinsk, Bt., and (2) Ellis, widow of Sir Justin Aylmer, of Kildare, Bt. By his first wife he had five sons and four daus. of whom the eldest,
Robert Dillon, of Clonbrock, M.P. for Dungarvon, m. Feb. 1725, Margaret, dau. of Morgan Magan, of Togherstown, Westmeath, and widow of Sir Arthur Shaen, Bt., and d. 11 June 1746, leaving with two other sons Robert and Thomas,
Luke Dillon, of Clonbrock, m. Bridget, dau. of John Kelly, of Castle Kelly, co. Galway, and had with two daus.,
1. Robert, **1st Baron Clonbrock** (see below).
2. Luke, ancestor of Dillon-Trenchard, of Lytchett House, co. Dorset.
3. John, d. in 1790.
The eldest son, Robert Dillon, **1st Baron Clonbrock**, b. 27 Feb. 1754; M.P. for Lanesborough, 1776-90, cr. Baron Clonbrock, co. Galway, on 5 June 1790, and appointed P.C. June 1795, but never sworn. He m. 30 Jan. 1776, Letitia, only dau. and heir of John Greene, of Old Abbey, co. Limerick, by Catherine, sister of John, 1st Earl of Norbury and dau. of Daniel Toler, of Beechwood. He d. 22 July 1795. She m. 2ndly, May 1802, Clement Archer, State Surgeon in Ireland and d. 28 May 1841. The 1st Baron had issue,
1. Luke, **2nd Baron** (see below).
1. Catherine Bridget, m. 10 June 1797, Richard, Viscount Ennismore, and d. 13 Oct. 1828 (Listowel, E.).
2. Letitia Susannah, m. 21 Nov. 1845, Hon. Sir Robert le Poer Trench, and d. 25 Mar. 1865, (Clancarty, E.).
The only son and heir, Luke Dillon, **2nd Baron Clonbrock**, b. 24 April 1780, educ. Ch. Ch. Oxford, B.A. 1800; m. 6 Jan. 1803, Anastasia dau. and heir of Joseph Henry Blake, 1st Baron Wallscourt of Ardfry. She d. 5 June 1816. He d. 13 Dec. 1826. They had issue,
1. Robert, **3rd Baron** (see below).
1. Louisa Harriet, m. Nov. 1827, John Congreve, of Mount Congreve, co.

Waterford, and d. 4 Aug. 1881, leaving issue.

2. Letitia, d. unm. 19 Feb. 1837.

The only son and heir, Robert Dillon, **3rd Baron Clonbrock,** b. 29 Mar. 1807; educ. Eton and Ch. Ch. Oxford, B.A. 1827, M.A. 1830; was a representative peer 1838; Lord Lieut. of co. Galway, 1874-92. He m. 15 June 1830, Caroline Elizabeth, dau. of Francis Almeric Spencer, 1st Baron Churchill of Whichwood. She d. 17 Dec. 1864. He d. 4 Dec. 1893. They had issue,

1. Luke Almeric, b. 5 July 1832; d. Feb. 1833.
2. Luke Gerald, 4th Baron (see below).
3. Robert Villiers, Col. R.A., b. 10 Dec. 1838; m. 3 June 1873, Harriet Caroline Elizabeth, dau. of A. S. Gladstone. She d. 25 Feb. 1932. He served in the China War 1857 (medal and clasp) and d. 19 April 1923, having had issue,
   (1) Charles Henry, Lt. Rifle Brig., b. 31 Aug. 1877; d. of wounds in S. Africa, 8 June 1901.
   (1) Hilda May, b. 28 Oct. 1875; m. 12 Nov. 1901. R. E. Bucknall, O.B.E.
   (2) Stella Margaret, M.B.E., b. 26 Dec. 1889; m. 9 June 1926, Robert Skinner, of Bromham Hall, Bedford.
4. Francis William, b. 20 Dec. 1842; d. 9 April 1858.
1. Frances Letitia, d. unm. 26 Sept. 1911.
2. Caroline Anastasia, m. 30 Jan. 1877, William Dealtry, C.M.G., son of Archdeacon Dealtry, and d. 15 April 1907.
3. Helen Isabella, d. unm. 8 Nov. 1916.
4. Louisa Emilia, d. unm. 23 May 1927.
5. Georgiana Louisa, d. unm. 2 May 1892.
6. Alice Elizabeth, m. 26 July 1866, her cousin, Ambrose Congreve, of Mount Congreve, co. Waterford, and d. 18 Dec. 1878 having had issue.
7. Katherine Charlotte, d. unm. 14 Aug. 1927.
8. Elizabeth Octavia, m. 13 Jan. 1875, Sir Hugh J. Ellis-Nanney, Bt., of Gwynfryn, co. Carnarvon, and d. 12 Jan. 1928, leaving issue.

The 1st surv. son and heir, Sir Luke Gerald Dillon, **4th Baron Clonbrock,** b. 10 Mar. 1834; educ. Eton and Balliol Coll. Oxford, B.A.; second Sec. at Vienna, 1862; Sheriff of co. Galway, 1865; Priv. Sec. to the Viceroy of Ireland, 1866-68; and 1874-76, Lord Lieut. co. Galway, 1892; a representative peer 1895; was made P.C. of Ireland 1898, and K.P. 1900. He m. 18 July 1866, Augusta Caroline, O.B.E., only dau. of Edward Crofton, 2nd Baron Crofton, of Mote. She d. 5 Sept. 1928. He d. 12 May 1917. They had issue,

1. Robert Edward, **5th Baron** (see below).
1. Georgiana Caroline, b. 27 May 1867.
2. Edith Augusta, b. 9 Aug. 1878; m. 26 Jan. 1905, Sir William Henry Mahon, 5th Bt., and had issue.
3. Ethel Louisa, b. 16 Oct. 1880.

The only son and heir, Robert Edward Dillon, **5th Baron Clonbrock,** b. 21 May 1869; d. unm. 1 Nov. 1926.

ARMS—Argent a lion rampant, between three crescents each with an estoile between the horns, gules, over all a fess azure.

CREST—On a chapeau gules turned up ermine a falcon rising ppr. belled or.

SUPPORTERS—Dexter, A griffin wings elevated ppr.; Sinister, A falcon wings inverted ppr.

MOTTO—Auxilium ab alto.

The seat of the Lords Clonbrock was at Clonbrock, Ahascragh co. Galway.

CLONCURRY

PEERAGE—Ireland. Baron Cloncurry, co. Kildare.

U.K. Baron Cloncurry, co. Kildare.

SURNAME—Lawless.

CR.—I. Barony 22 Sept. 1789. U.K. Barony 14 Sept. 1831. Also a baronetcy, cr. 20 June 1776. **EXT.**—18 July 1929.

HISTORY—The family of Lawless came from Hoddesdon, co. Hertford, and had property at Shankill, co. Dublin in the 17th-18th century and at other places in Ireland. John Lawless, of Shankill, was father of Robert Lawless, of Abington, co. Limerick, who m. Mary, dau. of Dominick Hadsor of Dublin, and had issue, Sir Nicholas Lawless, Bt., and **1st Baron Cloncurry,** M.P. (Irish Parl.), cr. a Baronet 20 June 1776 and Baron Cloncurry 22 Sept. 1789. He was b. 1735, m. 1761, Margaret, dau. of Valentine Browne, of Dublin and d. 28 Aug. 1799 having had issue, with three daus., a son,

Sir Valentine Browne Lawless, Bt., and **2nd Baron Cloncurry,** cr. 14 Sept. 1831, Baron Cloncurry in the U.K. peerage. He was b. 19 Aug. 1773, and m. (1) 16 April 1803, Eliza, dau. of Major Gen. G. Morgan and by her had two daus. This marr. was dissolved by Act of Parliament, 7 April, 1871, and she m. the Rev. John Sandford. Lord Cloncurry m. (2) 1871, Emily, dau. of Archibald Douglas and widow of Hon. Joseph Leeson, and d. 28 Oct. 1853 having by her had issue, with a son Cecil John who d. 1853, and a dau. who d. young, an elder son,

Sir Edward Lawless, Bt., 2nd Baron Cloncurry (U.K.) and **3rd Baron** (I), b. 13 Sept. 1876; m. 17 Sept. 1839, Elizabeth, dau. of John Kirwan, of Castle Hackett, co. Galway, and d. 4 April 1869, having had issue, with two other sons, d. unm., and four daus.,

1. Valentine, **4th Baron** (see below).
2. Edward, of the Rifle Brigade and Hon. Col. 3rd Bn. Royal Dublin Fusiliers, b. 13 Sept. 1841; m. 16 June 1880, Mary, dau. of Rev. Benjamin Burton, of Burton Hall, co. Carlow, and d. 24 April 1921.
3. Frederick, **5th Baron** (I) (see below).

The eldest son, Sir Valentine Lawless, Bt., 3rd Baron Cloncurry (U.K.) and **4th Baron Cloncurry** (I), b. 2 Nov. 1840; m. 23 Jan. 1883, Hon. Laura Winn, dau. of 1st Lord St. Oswald and d. 12 Feb. 1928 having had issue two daus, Mary, d. 1922 and Kathleen Emily Marie. He was s. by his brother,

Sir Frederick Lawless, Bt., 4th Baron Cloncurry (U.K.) and **5th Baron Cloncurry** (I), b. 20 April 1847; educ. Eton, served on staff of two Lords Lieut. of Ireland, a Gov. of the National Gallery of Ireland, d. unm. 18 July 1929.

ARMS—Argent, On a chief indented sable three garbs or.

CREST—Out of a ducal coronet or, a demiman, in armour in profile, his visor closed, holding in his right hand a sword all ppr., the

helmet adorned with a plume of three feathers, the exterior two gules, the centre one argent.
SUPPORTERS—Dexter, A bull sable, armed and unguled argent; Sinister, A ram argent, armed and unguled or.
MOTTO—Virtute et numine.
The family seats were at Lyons, Hazelhatch, co. Kildare and Maretimo, Blackrock, near Dublin.

CLONMELL

PEERAGE—I. Baron Earlsfort of Lisson-Earl, co. Tipperary.
  I. Viscount Clonmell.
  I. Earl of Clonmell, co. Tipperary.
SURNAME—Scott.
CREATION—Barony, 10 May 1784. Viscounty, 18 Aug. 1789. Earldom, 20 Dec. 1793. **EXT.**—16 Jan. 1935.
HISTORY—Thomas Scott, of Urlings, co. Kilkenny, m. Rachel, dau. of Mark Prim of Johnswell, co. Kilkenny and had a son, John Scott, **Earl of Clonmell**, b. ca. 1740, entered Trin. Coll. Dublin 26 April 1756; Barrister-at-Law, King's Inn; Solicitor Gen., Attorney Gen. and Prime Sjt. of Ireland between 1774-1783; Chief Justice, Court of King's Bench 1784; cr. 10 May 1784, Baron Earlsfort of Lisson-Earl, co. Tipperary; 18 Aug. 1789, Viscount Clonmell, and 20 Dec. 1793, Earl of Clonmell. He m. (1) Catherine Anne Maria, dau. of Thomas Mathew (see Llandaff, E. Extinct Peerage 1883) and widow of P. Roe, by whom he had no s. issue. He m. (2) Margaret, dau. and heiress of Patrick Lawless, of Dublin (by his wife Mary, dau. of Robert Lawless of Abington, co. Limerick and only sister of 1st Lord Cloncurry). By this second marr. the Earl had Thomas his heir and a dau. Charlotte, m. 2nd Earl Beauchamp. The 1st Earl of Clonmell d. 23 May 1798 when he was s. by his only son,
Thomas Scott, **2nd Earl of Clonmell**, b. 15 Aug. 1783; m. 9 Feb. 1805, Henrietta Louisa Greville, dau. of 2nd Earl Brooke and Warwick, and had issue with seven daus.,
1. John Henry, **3rd Earl** (see below).
2. Charles Grantham, Col. b. 1 Mar. 1878, m. 9 Mar. 1843, Frances, dau. of R. W. Grey of Blackworth, Co. Northumberland and d. 5 Jan. 1885 leaving issue, with three daus.,
  (1) Beauchamp Henry, **6th Earl** (see below).
  (2) Louis Guy, b. 23 April 1850; m. 21 Feb. 1885, Inna, dau. of Col. the Hon. L. R. W. Milles (Sondes E.) and d. 23 April 1900 leaving issue a dau.
  (3) Dudley Alexander Charles, **8th Earl** (see below).
The 2nd Earl d. 18 Jan. 1838, being s. by his elder son,
John Henry Scott, **3rd Earl of Clonmell**, b. 4 Jan. 1817; m. 27 April 1838, Hon. Anne de Burgh, eldest dau. and co-heir of 2nd Lord Downes, and by her had issue with a third son d. young and four daus.
1. John Henry Reginald, **4th Earl** (see below)
2. Thomas Charles, **5th Earl** (see below).
The 3rd Earl d. 7 Feb. 1866 and was s. by his elder s. son, John Henry Reginald Scott, **4th**

Earl of Clonmell, b. 2 March 1839; and d. unm. 22 June 1891 being s. by his brother,
Thomas Charles Scott, **5th Earl of Clonmell**, Lt. Col. Rifle Brigade, sometime A.D.C. to Lord Lieutenant of Ireland, b. 18 Aug. 1830; m. 31 Mar. 1875, Agnes, dau. of R. G. Day and d.s.p. 18 June 1896, being s. by his cousin,
Beauchamp Henry John Scott, **6th Earl of Clonmell**, Capt. Scots Fusilier Guards, b. 28 Dec. 1847; m. 31 Mar. 1875, Lucy, dau. of Anthony Wilson, of Rauceby Hall, co. Lincoln and d. 2 Feb. 1898, being s. by his son,
Rupert Charles Scott, **7th Earl of Clonmell**, Capt. Warwickshire R.H.A., b. 10 Nov. 1877; m. 8 Aug. 1901, Rachel Estelle, dau. of Samuel Berridge of Rugby and d. 18 Nov. 1928, leaving issue two daus. He was s. by his uncle,
Dudley Alexander Charles Scott, **8th Earl of Clonmell**, b. 26 May 1853; m. 7 Aug. 1908, Rose Clare, dau. of G. Cutting of New York and d.s.p. 16 Jan. 1935.
ARMS—Or, on a bend azure an estoile between two crescents argent.
CREST—A buck trippant ppr.
SUPPORTERS—Dexter, A female figure representing Justice, holding in her right hand a sword, and with the left a balance, all ppr. Sinister, A female figure representing Mercy, her exterior hand resting on a sword, point downwards, all ppr.
MOTTO—Fear to transgress.
The seat of the Earls of Clonmell was Bishop's Court, Straffan, co. Kildare.

COBHAM

PEERAGE—England. Baron Cobham.
SURNAME(S)—Cobham, Brooke, Boothby, Thorp, Disney, Alexander.
CR.—By writ of summons 8 Jan. 1312-13.
  ABEYANCE—21 Feb. 1951.
HISTORY—The Cobham family derived its surname from the property of Cobham in Kent, where it is traced from 1211 in the reign of King John. The first of the family to be regarded—in the theory of English peerage lawyers—as a peer was Henry Cobham, born in 1260, who was summoned to Parliament from 8 Jan. 1312-13 to 22 Jan. 1335-36. He is therefore reckoned as **1st Baron Cobham.** He was s. by his son,
John Cobham, **2nd Baron Cobham**, summoned to Parliament from 25 Nov. 1350 to 2 Mar. 1353-54, and was s. by his son,
John Cobham, **3rd Baron Cobham**, summoned 20 Sept. 1355 to 21 Dec. 1405. He took a prominent part in public affairs, being in 1388 one of the Lords Appellant to impeach the King Richard II's favourites, and was himself impeached in 1397/8 and condemned to death, but was pardoned. He m. 1332/3 Margaret, dau. of Hugh Courtenay, Earl of Devon and d. 10 Jan. 1407/8 having had issue, an only child,
Joan, m. 1362, Sir John de la Pole, of Chrishall, Essex, and d.v.p. 1388, leaving an only child,
Joan de la Pole **(4th) Baroness Cobham**, was m. five times, her fourth husband, whom she m. before 1408, being the famous Lollard leader, Sir John Oldcastle, a soldier and friend of King Henry V, a fact which did not save him from being excommunicated

for heresy in 1413, declared a traitor to the King and put to death in 1417, hung over a slow fire which consumed him with the gallows. The Baroness was his third wife and in her right he was summoned to Parliament as Baron Cobham from 26 Oct. 1409 to 22 Mar. 1413/14. Baroness Cobham d. 13 Jan. 1433/4 and was s. by her only surviving child, by her second marriage,

Joan Braybrooke, **(5th holder) Baroness Cobham,** dau. of Sir Reginald Braybrooke, she m. 1409/10 Sir Thomas Brooke, of Brooke, Somerset. He d. 1439. She d. 1442 having had issue (with a ygr. son, Reginald, ancestor of the Brookes of Ufford) an elder son,

Edward Brooke, **6th Baron Cobham,** who fought on the Yorkist side in the Wars of the Roses, m. Elizabeth, dau. of James Tucket, Lord Audley, and d. 1464 being s. by his son,

John Brooke, **7th Baron Cobham,** a soldier, summoned to Parliament 19 Aug. 1472 to 28 Nov. 1511. On his death in 1511/12 he was s. by his son,

Thomas Brooke, **8th Baron Cobham,** summoned from 23 Nov. 1514 to 15 April 1523. He served in France at the siege of Tournay and the Battle of the Spurs 1513, was made knight banneret 1514. He m. 1stly, Dorothy, dau. of Sir Henry Heydon; 2ndly, Dorothy Southwell, a widow, and 3rdly, Elizabeth Hart. He had issue by his first and second marriages and was s. by his eldest surviving son,

George Brooke, **9th Baron Cobham,** K.G., in Parliament Nov. 1529 to Jan. 1557/8, a military commander in the north 1546-51, served as a peer on the trial of Anne Boleyn, and on that of the Protector Somerset. Accused of complicity in Sir Thomas Wyatt's rebellion under Mary I but was released. He had large grants of land on the dissolution of the monasteries. He m. Anne, eldest dau. of 1st Baron Braye and d. 29 Sept. 1558 having had issue ten sons and four daus.; the eldest son,

William Brooke, **10th Baron Cobham,** K.G., summoned to Parliament Nov. 1558-Feb. 1592/3, Lord Warden of the Cinque Ports, Constable of Dover, and Lord Chamberlain, 1596. He was b. 1 Nov. 1527; m. 1stly, Dorothy, dau. of George Nevill, Lord Abergavenny, and by her had issue a dau. Frances, m. 2ndly, 25 Feb. 1559/60 Frances, dau. of Sir John Newton and d. 6 Mar. 1596/7 having had with other issue by his second marriage,

1. Henry, **11th Baron** (see below).
2. George, Rev. Preb. of York, m. after 17 Jan. 1598/9, Elizabeth, dau. of 3rd Baron Burgh. He was involved in the Raleigh conspiracy with his brother and being found guilty of high treason, was executed in Dec. 1603, having had, with other issue,
   William (see below).
1. Margaret, m. Sir Thomas Sondes of Throwley, Kent and had issue from whom descended Sir Richard Temple, 4th Bart., created Viscount Cobham in 1718 with special limitation and the title is now held by the family of Lyttelton (see extant peerages, Viscount Cobham).

The s. to the 10th Baron, Henry Brooke, **11th Baron Cobham,** K.G., b 22 Nov. 1564, was

M.P. for Kent 1588-9 and for Hedon, E.R. Yorks., then summoned to Parliament as a peer Oct. 1597. With his brother George he was tried for participation in the so called Raleigh conspiracy, found guilty, attainted and condemned to death, also degraded from the Order of the Garter, but not executed though he was kept prisoner in the Tower until his death in 1618/19. He m. 1601, Frances, dau. of the 1st Earl of Nottingham but had no children. He would have been succeeded in the Barony but for the attainder by his nephew,

Sir William Brooke, K.B., of Sterborough, Surrey, and Cowling, Kent. He is styled in peerage accounts as **12th Baron Cobham** but for the attainder and this numbering is followed here. He was b. 1601 and was restored in blood by Act of Parliament 1609/10, but the title of Lord Cobham was not restored unless by the King's special favour. He m. 1stly, Pembroke, dau. of Henry, Lord Dacre (now represented by Viscount Hampden) and by her had a dau. Pembroke, who m. Sir Matthew Tomlinson, one of Cromwell's Other House, and whose issue became extinct in 1703. Sir William Booke m. 2ndly, Penelope, dau. of Sir Moyses Hill, and by her had issue three daus. and co-heiresses who despite the attainder, were granted the precedence of a baron's daughters 1665, this privilege not being granted to their half-sister, Pembroke. Sir William d. 20 Sept. 1643, leaving these three daus. by his 2nd marriage.

1. Hill, (see below).
2. Margaret, m. Sir John Denham and d.s.p. 6 Jan. 1666/7.
3. Frances, m. 1stly Sir Thomas Whitmore and 2ndly Matthew Harvey, and had issue, which became extinct in 1747.

The barony of Cobham then (1643) fell into abeyance between Sir William's four daus., but as by 1747 the issue of all but the second dau., Hill, had died out, the claim to succeed to the barony if removed from the attainder passed to the issue of, The Hon. Hill Brooke, m. 1657 (as his second wife), Sir William Boothby, *2nd Bart and d. 1704 leaving issue, of whom the eldest surviving son was,

Sir William Boothby, 4th Bart., who s. his nephew the 3rd Bart., bapt. 1 Jan. 1663/4; m. 1695, Frances, dau. of Sir Trevor Williams, 1st Bart., and d. 1731 having had issue,

> Gore, b. 1698; m. 1729, Elizabeth, dau. of John Bury, and d.v.p. 1730, having had issue an only child,
> > William (Sir), 5th Bart. (see below).
> Frances, b. 1696, sole heir through her issue of Henry Brooke, Lord Cobham (see Braye, B. and Burgh, B.).

Sir William Boothby, 4th Bart., was s. by his grandson, Sir William Boothby, 5th Bart., Major Gen., Col. 6th Foot and Master of the Horse to the Duke of York, 1761, bapt. 4 May, 1721. He would have been, but for the attainder, entitled to the barony of Cobham as **13th Baron,** owing to the failure of the issue of the other daus. and co-heirs of Sir William Brooke, K.B. in 1747. Sir William Boothby d. unm. 15 April, 1787. The baronetcy passed

*The number 1 is often given here and refers to the creation *de novo* of Sir William Boothby because his father's baronetcy had not passed the Great Seal. In peerage accounts he is usually given as 2nd Bart.

to his cousin, Sir Brooke Boothby, 6th Bart., but the right to the barony, subject to removal of the attainder, passed to his cousin and heir general,

Mary Thorp, but for the attainder **Baroness Cobham (14th holder).** Her descent from Sir William Boothby, 4th Bart. (see above), was from the latter's only dau. Frances, who m. (as his second wife), William Thorp of Nottingham, (bur. 29 Dec. 1746) and had issue, an only child, Mary Thorp. She was b. 25 Oct. 1716; m. 20 May 1736, Gervase Disney, of Nottingham and d. 14 Feb. 1789, leaving as her surviving issue, four daus. who were co-heiresses, and the attainted barony again fell into abeyance between her daus. They were,

1. Martha, m. 12 July 1763, the Rev. Robert Thorp, and had issue now represented by Burgh, B. (extant peerages).
2. Harriot (see below).
3. Henrietta, d. unm.
4. Lucy, m. 24 Feb. 1784, the Rev. Thomas Lund, and had issue (see present Strabolgi, B.).

The second dau., Harriot Disney, b. 4 Sept. 1744; m. 12 May 1768, Robert Alexander, of Halifax, Yorks. and d. May 1787, having had with other issue, a 3rd son, Gervase Alexander, of Halifax, b. 3 June, 1793; m. 26 Aug. 1800, Ellen, dau. of Robert Hudson, of Fordbridge, Lancashire, and d. 31 Dec. 1856 having had with other issue, a 3rd son,

William Alexander of Blackwall Lodge, Halifax, J.P. W.R. Yorks., F.R.C.P., b. 3 Sept. 1896; m. 4 Oct. 1837, Emily, dau. of Samuel Kirby, of Grove House, Sheffield, and d. 13 April 1888, leaving issue, a second son,

Reginald Gervase Alexander, of Blackwall Lodge, Halifax, M.A. Camb., M.D. Edin., F.L.S., b. 20 Feb. 1847; m. 29 May 1879, Alicia Mary, dau. of John Greenwood of Castle Hall, Mytholmroyd, Yorks., and d. 14 Feb. 1916. He had secured from the Committee of Privileges of the House of Lords a declaration, 22 July 1912, that he was one of the co-heirs of the barony of Burgh, and, saving the attainder, one of the co-heirs of the barony of Cobham; on 11 May 1914 he was likewise declared a co-heir of the barony of Strabolgi. As he died before the Crown could give effect to the resolutions of the Committee, his claim passed to his son, Gervase Disney Alexander, **15th Baron Cobham.** Dr. R. G. Alexander had issue,

1. Gervase Disney, **15th Baron** (see below)
2. Robert Disney, **16th Baron** (see below).
1. Mary Isabel, b. 11 June 1882; m. 1stly 27th April 1916, J. L. M. Shaw (d. 1923) and had issue; m. 2ndly, 21 May 1927, John Bazley-White (d. on active service 1940).
2. Muriel Helen, b. 15 Mar. 1887; m. 4 Mar. 1916 J. E. B. Thornely, and has issue.

Both daus. were granted the title and precedence, 9th May 1917, of a baron's daus. The elder son, Gervase Disney Alexander, **15th Baron Cobham,** B.A., B.C. Camb., M.R.C.S. Eng., L.R.C.P. Lond., b. 6 May 1880. The effects of the Act of Attainder of 1603 were removed by Act of Parliament, and the abeyance being terminated in his favour, he received a writ of summons to Parliament 8 Sept. 1916.

He d. unm. 10 June 1933 and was s. by his brother,

Robert Disney Leith Alexander, **16th Baron Cobham.** The barony had again fallen into abeyance but this was terminated in his favour by a writ of summons to the House of Lords, 5 Dec. 1933. He was b. 23 April 1885; m. 1stly, 1923, Christina Jean Honeybone, (marr. diss. by div. 1934); he m. 2ndly 10 Dec. 1934, Evelyn Sinclair (d. 1937), only dau. of John Turnure of New York, and widow of P. J. Britt; m. 3rdly, 1949, his first wife and d 21 Feb. 1951 when the barony again fell into abeyance.

ARMS—Paly wavy of six or and azure, a lion rampant erminois, on a chief gules three crosses flory ermine.

CREST—A demi lion or, gorged with a plain collar azure, charged with two bezants, and holding in the dexter claw a battleaxe ppr. and resting the sinister on a cross flory ermine.

MOTTO—Miseris succurrere disco.

COHEN OF BRIGHTON

PEERAGE—U.K. Life. Baron Cohen of Brighton, co. Sussex.

SURNAME—Cohen.

CR.—13 May 1965. **EXT.**—21 Oct. 1966.

HISTORY—Lewis Coleman Cohen, a general merchant of Edgbaston, co. Warwick, b. 1830; m. 30 Aug. 1854, Leah, dau. of Benjamin Lewis of Brighton and d. 1 Sept. 1874. She d. 8 Oct. 1880. They had issue, Hyam Cohen, a jeweller, of White Rock, Hastings. b. 13 July 1859; m. 16 Jan. 1895, Esther (d. 13 Sept. 1946), dau. of Moses Szapira of Brighton and d. 14 Feb. 1910 having had issue,

1. Lewis Coleman, **Baron Cohen of Brighton** (see below).
2. Maurice, b. 9 Jan. 1899; educ. Hastings and Brighton Gram. schs; m. 3 Mar. 1926, Valerie, dau. of Samuel Van den Burgh and had issue, Hyam Antony Van den Burgh, Solicitor 1955, b. 21 June 1928; educ. Whittingham Coll., Charterhouse and Emmanuel Coll., Camb., M.A., LL.B.; m. 4 July 1956, Judith, dau. of G. Tack and had issue, four sons.
3. Reginald Herbert Coleman, P.P.C.I.A., F.A.I., F.B.S., F.R.Econ.S., Dir. and Sec. of Alliance Bldg. Soc. (formerly Brighton and Sussex Bldg. Soc.); b. 23 Sept. 1902; educ. Brighton Gram. Sch. and Brighton Coll.; m. 12 July 1928, Joan Henrietta, dau. of J. M. Maurice.

The eldest son, Lewis Coleman Cohen, **Baron Cohen of Brighton,** b. 28 Mar. 1897; educ. Hastings and Brighton Gram. Schs., and École Moyenne de Saint-Giles, Brussels; Sec. Brighton and Sussex Bldg. Soc. 1929, Managing Dir. 1933, name being changed to Alliance Bldg. Soc. 1945 and Chm. and Managing Dir. 1959; mem. Brighton Town Council, 1930, Mayor of Brighton 1956-57, Alderman 1964, m. (1) 20 Sept. 1939, (m. diss. by div. 1952), Sonya, dau. of E. Lawson; (2) 5 Nov. 1961, Renie, dau. of Simon Frieze, and widow of L. Bodlender. He was cr. a life peer as Baron Cohen of Brighton, of Brighton, co. Sussex, 13 May 1965 and d. 21 Oct. 1966. By his first wife he had issue,

1. John Christopher Coleman, B.A. 1962, McGill Univ. Toronto, b. 13 July 1940; m. 20 Feb. 1965, Anne Marie, dau. of E. Kraus of Paris and had issue.
 1. Christine Joanna, m. 10 July 1965, David Maxwell Park and had issue.
 2. Madeleine Coleman.

ARMS—Per chevron flory at the top gules and or, in chief two bees volant and in base a lion rampant counter changed.

CREST—Issuant from a pavilion or lined and embellished sable with a forked pennant flying therefrom to the dexter gules, a lion passant supporting with the dexter forepaw a branch of coral gules.

SUPPORTERS—On either side a dolphin sable finned or, the dexter charged on the shoulder with a tower, the sinister likewise charged with a martlet or.

Lord Cohen's residence was 55, Dyke Road Avenue, Hove 4, Sussex.

COLCHESTER

PEERAGE—U.K. Baron Colchester of Colchester, co. Essex.
SURNAME—Abbot.
CR.—3 June 1817. EXT.—26 Feb. 1919.
HISTORY—The Rev. John Abbot, D.D., Rector of All Saints, Colchester, m. Sarah, dau. of Jonathan Farr, of Moorfields, Middlesex, citizen and draper of London, (she m. 2ndly Jeremy Bentham, father of the famous writer, and d. 27 Sept. 1809) and had issue, a second son, Charles Abbot, **1st Baron Colchester**, b. 14 Oct. 1757; educ. Westminster, Scholar, and Ch. Ch. Oxford, winning the Chancellor's prize for Latin verse in *Petrus Magnus* (for which he received a medal from the Empress Catherine) 1777; Vinerian Sch. 1781; B.C.L. 1783; Vinerian Fell. 1786-92; D.C.L. 1793; Barrister Middle Temple, 1783; Clerk of the Rules, Court of King's Bench, 1794; M.P. Helston, 1790, and 1795-1802, and Woodstock, 1802-06; Chm. in turn of the Finance Cttee., the Record, Cttee. and the Record Commission; Chief Sec. for Ireland 1801-02; Speaker of the House of Commons, 1802-1817, ret. and was cr. Baron Colchester of Colchester, co. Essex, 3 June, 1817, with a pension of £4,000 per annum for his own life, and £3,000 for his next successor. He was Bencher of the Middle Temple, and a trustee of the British Museum 1818 to 1829; he m. 29 Dec. 1796, Elizabeth, dau. of Sir Philip Gibbes, 1st Bt., and d. 8 May 1829. She d. 10 June 1847. They had issue,
 1. Charles, **2nd Baron** (see below).
 2. Philip Henry, b. 10 June 1802; Barrister-at-Law, Lincoln's Inn; m. 31 Dec. 1829, Frances Cecil (d. 7 Nov. 1855) dau. of the Very Rev. C. Talbot, Dean of Salisbury, and d. 8 Jan. 1835, leaving issue, Charles Henry Philip, Rev., M.A. Rector of Withington, near Hereford, b. 21 Mar. 1832; m. 3 Aug. 1865 Maria Lear, dau. of the Rev. John Comyns, of Wood, Bishopsteignton, S. Devon, and d.s.p. 28 Dec. 1878.
 1. Henrietta Elizabeth Agnes, d. unm. 17 Mar. 1851.
The elder son, Charles Abbot, **2nd Baron Colchester**, b. 12 Mar. 1798; educ. Westminster and the Royal Naval Coll., entered the Navy, 1811; Rear Adm. on reserve list 1854; Vice Adm. 1860; Adm. 1864; Pres. of Roy. Geog. Soc., 1845-47; made P.C. 1852; Vice Pres. of the Board of Trade and Paymaster Gen. 1852, and Postmaster Gen. 1850-59; m. 3 Feb. 1836, Elizabeth Susan, dau. of Edward Law, 1st Baron Ellenborough, and d. 18 Oct. 1867. She d. 31 Mar. 1883. They had an only child,
 Reginald Charles Edward Abbot, **3rd Baron Colchester**, b. 13 Feb. 1842; educ. Eton and Ch. Ch. Oxford, took 1st class in classics, in law and history, was Stanhope Prizeman and Pres. of the Union Soc.; B.A. 1864, M.A. 1864, Fell. of All Souls' Coll. 1864-69; Barrister-at-Law, Lincoln's Inn, 1867; Examiner in Law and History at Oxford, 1869-71; Priv. Sec. to Sir Stafford Northcote when he was Pres. of the Board of Trade, and to the Earl of Derby when the latter was First Lord of the Treasury; was a Charity Commissioner, 1880-83, and mem. of London Sc. Board, 1891-94; m. 28 Jan. 1869, Lady Isabella Grace Maude, eldest dau. of Cornwallis Maude, 1st and only Earl de Montalt (Hawarden, E.) and d. 26 Feb. 1919.

ARMS—Gules, on a chevron between three pears or, as many crosses raguly azure within a tressure flory of the second.

CREST—Out of a ducal coronet or a unicorn's head ermine, armed, crined and tufted or, between six ostrich feathers argent quilled gold.

SUPPORTERS—On either side a unicorn ermine, armed, crined and tufted or, gorged with a collar azure, within another gemelle flory counterflory gules, therefrom a chain reflexed over the back, gold and charged on the shoulder with a cross raguly of the second.

MOTTOES—Deo, patriae, amicis, and Perseverando.

Lord Colchester's residence was Forest Row, East Grinstead.

COLEBROOKE

PEERAGE—U.K. Baron Colebrooke of Stebunheath, co. Middlesex.
SURNAME—Colebrooke.
CR.—20 Feb. 1906. Also Baronetcy (G.B.) 12 Oct. 1759. EXT.—28 Feb. 1939.
HISTORY—James Colebrooke of Arundel, co. Sussex had a son, James Colebrooke, of Chilham Castle, co. Kent, b. 12 May 1680; m. 2 Jan. 1706, Mary Hudson, (d. 1753) and d. 18 Nov. 1752, having issue with 7 daus.,
 1. Robert, of Chilham Castle, M.P. Malden 1741-61, Ambassador to Turkey, 1765, b. 1718, m. twice but d.s.p. 1807.
 2. James, Sir, **1st Bt.** (see below).
 3. George, Sir, **2nd Bt.** (see below).
The second son, Sir James Colebrooke, **1st Bt.**, and Kt., M.P. for Gatton, 1851-61, b. 1722, cr. a baronet of G.B., 12 Oct. 1759 with remainder to his brother, George. He m. May 1747, Mary, eldest dau. and co-heir of Stephen Skynner, of Walthamstow, co. Essex, and had issue a son, d. 1754 and two daus. Sir James d. 10 May 1761 and was s. by his brother,
 Sir George Colebrooke, **2nd Bt.**, M.P. Arundel 1754-75, Chm. of court of directors of H.E.I.C. 1760 and 1771; b. 14 Jan. 1729; m. 23 July 1754, Mary, only dau. and heir of Peter Gaynor, of Antigua and had issue with three daus., and an eldest son who d.s.p., 1809,

1. James Edward, Sir, **3rd Bt.** (see below).
2. Henry Thomas, F.R.S., in Bengal C.S., mem. Bengal Council, a Sanskrit scholar, b. 15 June 1765; m. 1810, Elizabeth dau. of Johnson Wilkinson and d. 10 Mar. 1837 leaving with other sons who d. young, a second son, Thomas Edward, Sir, **4th Bt.** (see below).

Sir George d. 5 Aug. 1809, being s. by his elder s. son, Sir James Edward Colebrooke, **3rd Bt.**, b. 7 July 1761; m. 31 Jan. 1820 Louisa, widow of Capt. Stuart and d.s.p. 5 Nov. 1838, being s. by his nephew,

Sir Thomas Edward Colebrooke, **4th Bt.**, Lord Lieut. North Lanark, 1860-90, M.P. Taunton 1842-52, Lanarkshire 1857-68 and North Lanark 1868-85, b. 19 Aug. 1813; m. 15 Jan. 1857, Elizabeth Margaret (d. 1896) dau. of J. Richardson and d. 11 Jan. 1890, having had with two other sons who d. unm. and three daus., a second son,

Sir Edward Arthur Colebrooke, **5th Bt.**, **Baron Colebrooke**, G.C.V.O., b. 12 Oct. 1861, a lord in waiting to Edward VII, 1906-10, and to George V. 1910-11 and permanent lord-in-waiting 1924, Lord High Commissioner to the Church of Scotland 1906-07; made P.C. 1914, cr. K.C.V.O. 1922, G.C.V.O. 1927 and Baron Colebrooke of Stebunheath, co. Middlesex, 20 Feb. 1906. He m. 17 June 1889, Alexandras, dau. of Gen. Lord Alfred Paget (Anglesey, M.) and d. 28 Feb. 1939 having had issue one son who d. 1921 and two daus.

ARMS—Gules, a lion rampant ermine ducally crowned or, on a chief or three martlets sable.
CREST—A wyvern wings expanded or, resting the dexter foot upon an antique escutcheon gules.
SUPPORTERS—On either side a Cornish chough ppr. ducally gorged or, and charged on the breast with a bezant.
MOTTO—Sola bona quae honesta.
The family seat was Abington House, Abington, S. Lanarkshire.

COLLINS

PEERAGE—U.K. Life. Baron Collins of Kensington, co. London.
SURNAME—Collins.
CR.—6 Mar. 1907. **EXT.**—3 Jan. 1911.
HISTORY—John Collins was an officer in the Protestant Army of Charles I, which was disbanded in 1649. In satisfaction of arrears of pay he was granted lands in the co. and city of Limerick, under a patent of 22 Mar. 1666, made to the Earls of Roscommon and Orrery in trust for him and other officers. He was s. by, John Collins of Ballynere, co. Limerick and later of Rathcoole, co. Cork, which he obtained 1709. His will is dated 22 July 1708. He was s. by his son, Stephen Collins, of Rathcoole, m. Jane Purdin and d. before 1763, leaving a son and heir,

James Collins, of Rathcoole, m. 4 Feb. 1758, Diana, dau. and heiress of Abraham Coakley, by whom he acquired lands in co. Wexford which had been granted to her ancestor, Capt. Thomas Coakley, 28 June 1681. His will is dated 20 July 1770 and proved 1772. His son,

John Collins of Gurteenard, co. Cork, b.

1761; m. 1795, Mary, eldest dau. of William Allen of Greenfield, co. Cork, and d. 28 July 1808. She d. 1816. They had issue,

Stephen Collins, of Merrion Square, Dublin, Barrister-at-Law, Q.C., b. 10 June 1799; m. Jan. 1831, Francis, dau. of William Henn, Master in Chancery and d. 13 Sept. 1843. She d. 31 Jan. 1842. Their issue were,

1. John Stephen of Ardnalee, co. Cork, J.P., b. 14 Mar. 1834, Barrister-at-Law 1858; m. 16 April 1873, Henrietta Cecil, dau. of H. W. Wray, of Castle Wray, co. Donegal and had issue,
   (1) Lena Stephante, m. 27 Aug. 1891, Major J. C. O. Aldworth, of Sunny Hill, Marlow, co. Cork, and had issue.
   (2) Olive Susan, m. 28 April 1903, T. S. Reeves of Glandore House, co. Cork.
2. William Henry, Major R.E. m. Alice, dau. of E. B. Bradley and d. 1880 leaving issue, Alice Margaret.
3. Richard Henn, **Baron Collins.**
1. Susan Henn, m. 28 Feb. 1861, George Alexander, of Errndale, co. Carlow, and had issue.
2. Francis Ellinor d.s.p.

The third son, Sir Richard Henn Collins, **Baron Collins**, b. 1842, M.A. and Fell. Downing Coll. Camb. 1865; Barrister-at-Law, Middle Temple, 1867, Q.C. 1883; Bencher 1885; Treasurer 1905, Judge of the High Court, Queen's Bench Div. 1891-97, Lord Justice of the Court of Appeal, 1897-1901, Master of the Rolls 1901-07; cr. Kt. Bach. 1901; made P.C. 1897; cr. a Lord of Appeal in Ordinary and a peer for life as Baron Collins of Kensington, co. London, 6 Mar. 1907. He m. 1869, Jane Ogle, dau. of Very Rev. Ogle William Moore, Dean of Clogher and d. 3 Jan. 1911, having had issue,

1. Richard Henn, C.M.G., D.S.O., Capt. Royal Berks Regt., b. 2 April 1873; m. 1909 and had issue,
2. Stephen Ogle, C.B.E., K.C., m. 14 Dec. 1899, Agnes Julia, ygst. dau. of F. L. Lambert, of Garratt's Hall, Banstead (B.L.G. 1952) and had issue,
   (1) John Stephen, b. 21 May 1903.
   (1) Mary Pamela.
   (2) Agnes Patience.
1. Frances Helen, m. 1 Nov. 1905, Rev. Canon Henry Henn, Vicar of Bolton-le-Moors later Bishop of Burnley.
2. Hilda Jane, m. 30 Jan. 1906, Rev. J. A. Garton, Vicar of All Saints, Gordon Square, London W.C. and had issue.
3. Mary Brenda Nepenthe, m. 7 Dec. 1906, Capt. W. C. F. Vaudrey Barker-Mill, of Mottisfont Abbey, co. Hants and had issue.

ARMS—Argent two lions combatant ppr., on a chief azure a pelican argent, vulning herself gules.
CREST—A pelican as in the arms, gorged with a plain collar azure.
MOTTO—Dant vulnera vitam.

CONNAUGHT AND STRATHEARN

PEERAGE—U.K. Earl of Sussex, Duke of Connaught and Strathearn.
SURNAME—(after 1917) Windsor.
CR.—24 May 1874. **EXT.**—16 Jan. 1942.

HISTORY—H.R.H. Arthur William Patrick Albert (after 1917) Windsor, Prince of Great Britain and Ireland, also Duke of Saxony, third son of Queen Victoria, b. 1 May 1850; educ. Woolwich Academy, Lt. R.E. and R.A. 1868; m. 13 Mar. 1879, Luise Margarethe Alexandras Victoria Agnes, dau. of Prince Friedrich Karl Nikolaus, of Prussia, and had issue,

H.R.H. Arthur Frederick Patrick Albert, Prince of the United Kingdom, and Duke of Saxony, b. 13 Jan. 1883; cr. K.G. 1902, Major Gen., in the Army, Gov. Gen. of Union of South Africa 1920-24; m. 15 Oct. 1913, Princess Alexandra Victoria Alberta Edwina Louise, Duchess of Fife, elder dau. of 1st Duke of Fife, and d.v.p. 12 Sept. 1938, leaving issue,

H.R.H. Alastair Arthur, **2nd Duke,** (see below).

Prince Arthur was cr. K.G. 1867, K.P. 1869, K.T. 1869, G.C.M.G. 1870, P.C. 1871; G.C.I.E. 1887; K.C.B. 1890; G.C.V.O. 1896, G.C.B. 1898, and **Earl of Sussex, Duke of Connaught and Strathearn,** 24 May 1874. He was a Field Marshal, 1902 and Gov. Gen. of Canada, 1911. He d. 16 Jan. 1942, being s. by his grandson,

H.R.H. Alastair Arthur Windsor, **2nd Duke of Connaught and Strathearn,** Lt. the Royal Scots Greys, b. 9 Aug. 1914, d. unm. on active service at Ottawa, 26 April 1943.

ARMS—The royal arms differenced by a label of three points argent, the centre point charged with St. George's Cross, and each of the other points with a fleur-de-lis, azure; in the centre of the said royal arms an escutcheon of the august house of Saxony, viz., barry of or and sable, a crown of rue in bend vert.

CREST—On a coronet composed of crosses patée and fleur-de-lis, a lion statant guardant or, crowned with the like coronet, and differenced with a label of three points argent, charged as in the arms.

SUPPORTERS—The royal supporters differenced with the like coronet and label.

The Duke's residence was at Bagshot Park, Surrey.

CONNEMARA

PEERAGE—U.K. Baron Connemara, of Connemara, co. Galway.

SURNAME—Bourke.

CR.—12 May, 1887. **EXT.**—3 Sept. 1902.

HISTORY—Robert Bourke, third son of the 5th Earl of Mayo, (see extant peerages), b. 11 June, 1827; educ. Hall Place Sch., Bexley, Kent, and Trin. Coll. Dublin; Barrister-at-Law, Inner Temple, 1852; M.P. Lynn, 1868-86; Under Sec. for Foreign Affairs, 1874-80; and 1885-86; Gov. of Madras, 1886-90; was made P.C. 1880; cr. **Baron Connemara** of Connemara, co. Galway, 12 May 1887, and G.C.I.E. 21 June, 1887; m. (1) 21 Nov. 1863, (m. diss. by div. 1890), Susan Georgiana, eldest dau. and coheir of James Andrew Broun-Ramsay, 1st Marquess of Dalhousie. He m. (2), 22 Oct. 1894, Gertrude, (d. 23 Nov. 1898), widow of Edward Coleman, of Stoke Park, Bucks., and d.s.p. 3 Sept. 1902.

ARMS—Per fess or and ermine a cross gules, in the first quarter a lion rampant, and in the second a dexter hand couped at the wrist and erect both sable.

CREST—A cat-a-mountain sejant guardant ppr., collared and chained or.

SUPPORTERS—Those of the Earl of Mayo, with distinction of Third House.

MOTTO—A cruce salus.

CONSTANTINE

PEERAGE—U.K. Baron Life, Constantine of Maraval in Trinidad, and Tobago, and of Nelson in the co. Palatine of Lancaster.

SURNAME—Constantine.

CR.—24 Mar. 1969. **EXT.**—1 July, 1971.

HISTORY—In an interview on radio the late Lord Constantine once referred to his great-grandfather as having come from another country, possibly as a slave, to Trinidad. Lebrun Constantine, of Diego Martin, Trinidad, d. 1951. He had by his wife, Anna, who d. 1954, dau. of Ali Pascal, of Maraval, Trinidad, a son, Sir Learie Nicholas Constantine, **Baron Constantine,** who built a career notable for its achievement in various fields, on his original work as a professional cricketer. He was the first negro peer, and was also a solicitor's clerk who became a barrister and hon. Bencher of his Inn of Court. Lord Constantine was b. 21 Sept. 1901; educ. St. Ann's Roman Catholic Sch. Port of Spain, Trinidad; was employed in a solicitor's office, 1919-23; in the Civil Service in Trinidad, 1923-25; the Oil Co. Trinidad, 1925-29; was a professional and very great cricketer, 1929-41; he served in World War II as Equipment Offr. A.R.P. section Nelson Corp. 1939, Evacuation Officer, 1940-41; and Welfare Offr. Min. of Labour, 1941-46; Barrister-at-Law, Middle Temple, 1954; Hon. Bencher; Asst. Legal Adviser to Trinidad Leaseholds Ltd. 1955-56; mem. Legislative Council of Trinidad and Tobago, and Min. of Works and Transport, 1956-61; held various appts. in Trinidad and was High Commissioner in U.K. for Trinidad and Tobago, 1962; mem. B.B.C. Board of Govs. and Race Relations Bd., wrote five books on cricket and one on race relations. He m. July, 1927, Norma Agatha, dau. of Faustin Cox, of Port of Spain, and had issue,

Gloria Theresa, b. 2 April, 1928; m. 18 Dec. 1954, André Joseph Valere, son of Knolly Valere, of St. Joseph, Trinidad, and had issue, a son, Maurice André Constantine.

Lord Constantine was cr. M.B.E. 1945, Kt. Bach. 1961, and a life peer as Baron Constantine of Maraval in Trinidad and Tobago and of Nelson in the co. Palatine of Lancaster, 24 Mar. 1969. He d. 1 July, 1971, after a heart attack. His residence was 11 Kendal Court, Shoot-up Hill, N.W.2. His club was Marylebone Cricket.

The surname Constantine is a very old Norman name, and its use by the family of Lord Constantine is probably taken from the surname of the original slave owner.

CONWAY OF ALLINGTON

PEERAGE—U.K. Baron Conway of Allington, co. Kent.
SURNAME—Conway.
CR.—7 Dec. 1931. **EXT.**—19 April, 1937.
HISTORY—Thomas Conway, of Kennington, and Earlswood House, Reigate, b. 1762 and d. 10 July 1833, having had by his wife Ann Reeves, a son, The Rev. Willian Conway, Rector of St. Margaret's and Canon of Westminster, b. 16 April 1815, m. 20 Nov. 1850, Elizabeth, dau. of Dr. Adam Martin, of Rochester, and d. 22 Mar. 1876, having had. by her, who d. 1912, with other issue, Sir William Martin Conway, **Baron Conway** of Allington, a great traveller, and author of books on art and on mountaineering, b. 12 April 1856; educ. Trin. Coll. Camb.; M.A., Dir.Gen. of the Imperial War Museum and a Trustee of the National Portrait Gallery, Slade Prof. of Fine Arts, Camb. 1901-04, awarded gold medal of the R.G.S. 1905, M.P. English Universities 1918-31; cr. a Kt.Bach. 1895 and Baron Conway of Allington, co. Kent, 7 Dec. 1931. He m. (1) 10 June 1884, Katrina, dau. of Charles Lambard, of Maine, U.S.A., and by her (d. 22 Nov. 1933) had a dau. Agnes, m. G. W. Horsfield. He m. (2) 17 Nov. 1934, Iva, widow of Reginald Lawson and d. 19 April 1937.
ARMS—Argent, fourteen barrulets wavy azure, on a pale vert issuant from a mount in the base an ice axe or.
CREST—In front of a castle gate-house ppr. flying a banner argent charged with a cross gules, a shrapnel helmet also ppr.
SUPPORTERS—Dexter, An Astor Markor; Sinister, A Himalayan Ibex, each affrontée ppr.
The seat of Lord Conway was Allington Castle, Maidstone, co. Kent.

CONYERS

PEERAGE—England. Baron Conyers.
SURNAME(S)—Conyers, Darcy, Oxborne, Lane-Fox, Anderson-Pelham.
CR.—By writ or summons 17 Oct. 1509.
ABEYANT—7 Feb. 1948.
HISTORY—William Conyers, the **1st Baron Conyers**, was summoned by writ 17 Oct. 1509, by which he became Lord Conyers. His ancestry for several generations is given in extant peerages, under Yarborough, Earl, as also is the descent of the Conyers Barony through the families whose surnames are listed above. On 4 May 1859 when the 11th Baron Conyers died, (he was also 7th Duke of Leeds) he was succeeded in the baronies of Conyers and Darcy by his nephew, Sackville George Lane-Fox, **12th Baron Conyers**, and de jure 15th Baron Darcy de Knayth (according to *C.P.* he never used the latter title, being unaware that he had any right thereto). He was b. 14 Sept. 1827, m. 14 Aug. 1860, Mary, dau. of Capt. Reginald Curteis, of Windmill Hill, Sussex, and had issue, with a son, Sackville FitzRoy Henry Lane, who d. aged 18 in 1879, two daus.,
1. Marcia, Amelia Mary, **Baroness Conyers**, and Fauconberg (see below.)

2. Violet Ida Eveline, Baroness Darcy de Knayth (see that title in extant peerage).
The 12th Baron d. 24 Aug. 1888, when the Barony of Conyers fell into abeyance until terminated in favour of his elder dau., 8 June 1892. Marcia Amelia Mary, Lane-Fox, **13th** holder of the title, **Baroness Conyers**, b. 18 Oct. 1863; m. 5 Aug. 1886, Charles Alfred Worsley Anderson-Pelham, 4th Earl of Yarborough. On 29 Sept. 1903, the abeyance of the Barony of Fauconberg (see that title in present work), was terminated in her favour. By Royal Licence, 26 Oct. 1905, her husband assumed for himself and his issue the name and arms of Pelham only. (he had a female line descent from this medieval family). Baroness Conyers d. 17 Nov. 1926 and s. in the Barony by her second surviving son,
Sackville George Pelham, 5th Earl of Yarborough and **14th Baron Conyers** b. 17 Dec. 1888; m. 23 Sept. 1919, Nancye, dau. of Alfred Brocklehurst and niece of 1st and only Baron Ranksborough, and d. 7 Feb. 1948, having had issue,
1. Diana Mary, b. 5 July 1920; m. 15 Nov. 1952, Robert Miller, and had issue.
   (1) Marcia Anne, adopted by her aunt and uncle, Mr. and Mrs. M. H. L. Lycett, and renamed Anthea Theresa Lycett, b. 21 June 1954.
   (2) Beatrix Diana, b. 23 Aug. 1955.
2. June Wendy, b. 6 June 1924; m. 12 Oct. 1959, Michael Hildesley Lycett Lycett, Major Royal Scots Greys.
On the death of the 14th Baron Conyers, while his earldom of Yarborough passed to his brother, the baronies of Conyers and Faucomberg fell into abeyance between his two daus.
ARMS—(for 13th holder, Baroness Conyers)—Argent a chevron between three foxes' heads erased gules, (Fox).
SUPPORTERS—Two lions rampant azure.
The Baroness is said to have brought 153 quarterings into the Pelham family.

COOPER OF CULROSS

PEERAGE—U.K. Baron Cooper of Culross of Dunnet, co. Caithness.
SURNAME—Cooper.
CR.—31 July 1954. **EXT.**—15 July 1955.
HISTORY—Thomas Mackay Cooper, **Baron Cooper**, was the elder son of John Cooper, C.E., Burgh Engineer, of Edinburgh (b. 1843, d. 1901) by his wife Margaret, dau. of John Mackay of Dunnet, Caithness. T. M. Cooper was b. 24 September 1892; educ. George Watson's Coll. and Edin. Univ., M.A., LL.B., and was called to the Scottish Bar 1915. He was Junior Legal Assessor to the City of Edinburgh, 1922; Solicitor Gen. for Scotland, 1935, Lord Advocate for Scotland 1935-41, Lord Justice Clerk of Scotland, 1941-46, Lord Justice Gen. for Scotland and President of the Court of Session, 1947-54; Q.C. and Hon. Bencher of the Middle Temple, LL.D. (Hon.) Edinburgh and other univs; F.R.S.E., F.R.A.S., was cr. O.B.E., made P.C. (1935) and Baron Cooper of Culrose of Dunnet co. Caithness 21 July 1954. He d. 15 July 1955.

COPE

PEERAGE—U.K. Baron Cope of St. Mellons, co. Monmouth.
SURNAME—Cope.
CR.—14 July, 1945. **EXT.**—15 July, 1946.
HISTORY—William Cope, of 12, Bute Crescent, Cardiff, who d. 26 July, 1874, had a son, Matthew Cope, of Quarry Hill, St. Mellons, b. 2 Feb. 1843; m. 19 May, 1869, Margaret, dau. of John Harrison, of Beetham Hall, co. Westmorland, and d. 8 Nov. 1933. She d. 5 July, 1916. They had issue, Sir William Cope, Bt. and **Baron Cope**, b. 18 Aug. 1870; Barrister-at-Law, Inner Temple, 1894; K.C. 1933; M.A. Clare Coll. Camb.; High Sheriff, co. Glamorgan, 1932; Vice Chm. Quarter Sessions, 1932; M.P. Glamorgan (Llandaff and Barry Div.) 1918-29; a Junior Lord of the Treasury, 1923-24, and 1924-28; Comptroller to H.M. Household, 1928-29; Civil Commissioner for London and Home Counties in Gen. Strike, 1926; cr. a baronet 28 June, 1928, and a peer as Baron Cope of St. Mellons, co. Monmouth 14 July 1945; m. 5 Sept. 1900, Helen, dau. of Major Alexander Shuldham, of Flowerfield, co. Londonderry, and d. 15 July, 1946. Lady Cope d. 21 Jan. 1961. They had issue,

William Shuldham, b. 21 May, 1902, Educ. Eton.

Helen Margaret Letitia, m. 17 May, 1940, S. J. V. Simpson, and had issue.

ARMS—Per chevron argent and azure, in chief two roses gules barbed, seeded, slipped and leaved ppr., and in base a fleur-de-lis of the first.
CREST—In front of two roses, saltirewise gules barbed, seeded, slipped and leaved ppr., surmounted by a dragon's head also gules, a fleur-de-lis or.
SUPPORTERS—Dexter, A golden Labrador ppr., collared or. Sinister, A foxhound, also ppr.
Lord Cope's residence was Quarry Hill, St. Mellons, near Cardiff. His clubs were Carlton; and Oxford and Cambridge.

COURTAULD-THOMSON

PEERAGE—U.K. Baron Courtauld-Thomson of Dorneywood, co. Buckingham.
SURNAME—Courtauld-Thomson.
CR.—1 Feb. 1944. **EXT.**—1 Nov. 1954.
HISTORY—Robert William Thomson of Edinburgh and Stonehaven, Kincardineshire, m. Clara Hurst and had issue, Sir Courtauld Greenwood Courtauld-Thomson, **Baron Courtauld-Thomson**, who was born 16 Aug. 1865; educ. Eton and Magdalen Coll. Oxford, B.A. (1884), M.A. (1888); Chairman of many companies; served in World War I as B.R.C. Commissioner and was mentioned in despatches five times for work in France, Malta, Egypt, Macedonia, Italy and Near East; was Chm. or member of many commissions and committees. In 1942 he gave his home, Dorneywood, near Burnham, co. Bucks, to the National Trust for the use of the Prime Minister or at the latter's nomination for one of the Secretaries of State. He assumed by deed poll in 1944 the additional surname of Courtauld. He received many foreign decorations, was cr. Knight Bachelor 6 Mar. 1912, C.B. 1916, K.B.E. 1918, and a peer as Baron Courtauld-Thomson of Dorneywood, co. Bucks on 1 Feb. 1944. He d. 1 Nov. 1954.

ARMS—Quarterly 1 and 4, Or, a saltire flory between two lions rampant in pale and two towers in fess all gules (Thomson); 2 and 3, Argent, issuant from a mount in base a beech tree ppr. charged with a Maltese cross argent, on a chief gules two crosses voided argent (Courtauld).
CREST—On a tower argent, A lion sejant gules.
SUPPORTERS—On either side a pointer ppr.
MOTTO—Fortiter aut suaviter.

COURTHOPE

PEERAGE—U.K. Baron Courthope of Whiligh (near Etchingham), co. Sussex.
SURNAME—Courthope.
CR.—3 July 1945. **EXT.**—2 Sept. 1955.
HISTORY—As early as 1272 there is mention of Courthopes as land owners at Wadhurst, co. Sussex. The connected pedigree dates from the time of John Courthope, of Wadhurst and Hartfield, who m. Elizabeth, the dau. and heiress of William Saunders of Whiligh, co. Sussex, to whose property he s. in 1513. He had, with other children,

George Courthope, of Whiligh who m. Mary, dau. of Cyprian Warnett of Frantfold, co. Sussex and was bur. at Ticehurst, 1577, having had with other issue, an eldest son,

John Courthope, of Whiligh, m. 1583 Elizabeth, dau. and heiress of John Larkin, and was bur. at Ticehurst 1615 having had, with other issue,

Sir George Courthope, of Whiligh, knighted at Whitehall, 21 June 1641. He m. (1), Alice, dau. of Sir George Rivers, of Chafford, co. Kent, and had by her a son, George (see below) and a dau. Frances who m. Sir Charles Howard, (Effingham, E., in extant peerages). Sir George m. (2), Elizabeth, dau. of Thomas Symons, Alderman of London, and widow of Edward Hawes and had further issue, a dau.

The son and heir,

Sir George Courthope, of Whiligh and Ticehurst, Moseham in Wadhust, and Barnes in Brenchley, co. Kent, M.P. for East Grinstead, was knighted at Windsor, 1661. He m. (his step sister) Elizabeth, dau. and heiress of Edward Hawes, of London and was bur. in Ticehurst 1685, having had with a dau. Elizabeth who m. Sir Thomas Piers, Bt., and a ygr. son, Edward, an elder son,

George Courthope, of Whiligh, m. (1) 1674 Anne, dau. of John Fuller of Waldron, co. Sussex and (2), Albinia, only dau. of Sir William Eliot, of Godalming, co. Surrey, and d. 1714 aged 68, having had issue by his 2nd wife,

George Courthope, of Whiligh, bapt. 1686, m. Catherine, dau. of William Campion of Combwell, co. Kent, and d. 1741 having had with other issue, an elder son,

George Courthope, of Whiligh, b. 9 Nov. 1712; m. 11 Nov. 1735, Catherine, dau. of Henry Campion of Combwell by Barbara his wife, dau. and heiress of Peter Courthope of Danny Place, Hurstpierpoint, co. Sussex and

PLATE 6

BARON CLARINA.

BARON CLONBROCK

BARON CLONCURRY.

BARON COLCHESTER.

EARL OF CLONMELL.

BARON COLEBROOKE.

PLATE 7

BARON COLLINS.

LORD COURTNEY.

EARL OF DARTREY.

MARQUESS OF CREWE.

BARON de BLAQUIERE.

EARL OF DESART.

d. April 1793, having had, with other issue, an eldest son,

George Courthope of Whiligh and Uckfield, co. Sussex, b. 22 Nov. 1737; m. 1766, Frances Barbara, only dau. of William Campion of Danny Place, and d. 1828 having had with other issue,

George Courthope, of Whiligh, b. 1767; m. 1808, Amelia, dau. of William Campion of Lewes, co. Sussex and d. 1835, having had with other issue, an eldest son,

George Campion Courthope, of Whiligh, High Sheriff, Sussex, 1850. b. 1821; m. 1841 Anna, dau. of John Deacon of Mabledon, Tonbridge, co. Kent and d. 1895 having had with other issue, an eldest son,

Lt. Col. George John Courthope, of Whiligh, and of Sprivers, Horsmonden, co. Kent, b. 1848; educ. Eton and Ch. Ch. Oxford, M.A., Barrister-at-Law, Inner Temple. He m. 21 Sept. 1876, Elinor Sarah, dau. of Lt. Col. Edward Loyd of Lillesden, Hawkhurst, co. Kent, and d. 1910. She d. 1895. They had issue, with a surviving son, three other sons who d. young, and three daus. The eldest and surviving son,

Sir George Loyd Courthope, **Baron Courthope** of Whiligh, b. 1877; educ. Eton and Ch. Ch. Oxford, Barrister-at-Law, Inner Temple, Col. T.A. comm. 5th Batt. Royal Sussex Regt., and Kent and Sussex Terr. Inf. Brigade, served in World War I, mentioned in despatches, wounded and awarded M.C.; was M.P. for Rye Div. of Sussex, 1906-45, Master of the Company of Farmers, made P.C. 1937, cr. a Baronet, 1925 and a peer as Baron Courthope of Whiligh, co. Sussex, 3 July 1945. He m. (1), 14 June 1899, Hilda Gertrude only dau. of Major Gen. Henry Pelham Close, and by her, who d. 1940, had issue two daus., Hilda Beryl and Elinor Daphne. He m. (2) 5 Sept. 1944, Margaret, dau. of Frederick Barry of Westbury, Bristol and d. 2 Sept. 1955.

ARMS—Argent a fess azure between three estoiles of six points wavy sable.

CREST—A demi stag salient gules attired and charged with estoiles wavy or.

SUPPORTERS—Dexter, A forester holding in his exterior hand his hat; Sinister, A farmer holding in his exterior hand a pitchfork erect, all ppr.

MOTTO—Court hope.

COURTNEY OF PENWITH

PEERAGE—U.K. Baron Courtney of Penwith.

SURNAME—Courtney.

CR.—14 July, 1906. **EXT.**—11 May, 1918.

HISTORY—The arms of this family have as their main charge three bezants, having in their appearance in a black and white illustration, a resemblance to the three torteaux of the Courtenays, Earls of Devon. Consequently it is not surprising to find that in their entry in Burke's Peerage, (1917 edition, last issue before the extinction of this peerage) there is the following opening to the genealogy: "This family is descended from a branch of the Courtney family settled in Ilfracombe, from the time of Elizabeth till the beginning of the 19th century. John Courtney, m. at Ilfracombe, 20 November, 1580, Elizabeth Verchild. Their descendant",

John Courtney, of Ilfracombe, m. 4 Sept. 1726, Mary Williams, and had with other children, a son,

William Courtney, of Ilfracombe, b. 1739; m. 14 Sept. 1764, Thomasine, dau. of Richard Knill by his wife, Thomasine Chugg, and had issue,

James Courtney, of Ilfracombe, b. 28 Aug. 1778; m. 12 August 1802, Anne, dau. of Richard Cotton, of Trenance, St. Columb Minor, Cornwall. She d. 6 July, 1863. He d. 27 August 1860, having had with three daus.,

1. James Sampson (see below).
2. James Cotton, d.s.p.
3. Leonard, b. 23 May 1811, drowned 1838.
4. William Rice, bapt. 12 Mar. 1815; m. 7 Dec. 1836, Jane, dau. of James Brimacombe, and had issue.
5. James, b. 29 March, 1820; m. 18 August, 1846, Alice, dau. of Henry Vingoe, and had issue.

The eldest son, John Sampson Courtney, of Alverton House, Penzance, b. at Ilfracombe, 10 Oct. 1803; m. 20 Sept. 1831, Sarah, dau. of John Mortimer. She d. 19 Dec. 1859; he d. 10 Feb. 1881, having had issue,

1. Leonard Henry, **Baron Courtney** (see below).
2. John Mortimer, C.M.G., I.S.O., Dep. Min. of Finance, Canada, 1878-1906, b. 22 July, 1838; m. 5 Oct. 1870, Mary Elizabeth Sophia, dau. of Vennings Taylor, Clerk Asst. of the Senate of Canada, and had issue.
3. James, b. 25 August, 1840; d. unm. 28 Aug. 1886.
4. William Prideaux, d. an infant, 5 July, 1844.
5. William Prideaux, in the Ecclesiastical Commission, 1865-92 and author of *A Bibliography of Bibliographies*, and a *Parliamentary History of Cornwall*, b. 26 April, 1845; d. 14 Nov. 1913.
6. Richard Acutt, b. 11 June, 1847.
1. Margaret Ann, wrote *Cornish Feasts and Folklore*.
2. Mary Mortimer, m. 30 Mar. 1859, William Harvey Julyan, Alderman of Penzance, and had issue.
3. Louis d'Este, m. 19 Aug. 1885, Hon. Richard Oliver, of Dunedin, N.Z.

The eldest son, Leonard Henry Courtney, **Baron Courtney**, b. 6 July 1832; educ. privately and St. John's Coll. Camb., B.A. 1855, Fellow, 1856; M.A. 1858 and Hon. Fellow 1889; Barrister-at-Law, Lincoln's Inn, 1858, and Bencher, 1889; Hon. LL.D. Camb. and Manchester; Prof. of Political Economy at London Univ. 1872-75; M.P. Liskeard, 1876-85; and Bodmin Div. of Cornwall, 1885-1900; Under Sec. of State for Home Department 1880-81, for the Colonies, 1881-82, Financial Sec. to Treasury, 1882-84, Chm. of Cttee. of Ways and Means, and Deputy Speaker of House of Commons, 1886-92; made P.C. 1889, and cr. peer as Baron Courtney of Penwith, co. Cornwall, 14 July 1906; m. 15 Mar. 1883, Catharine, dau. of Richard Potter, of Standish House, co. Gloucester, and the Argoed, co. Monmouth. He d.s.p. 11 May, 1918. His *Life* was written by L. H. Gooch, and published in 1920.

ARMS—Gules, three bezants on a chief or as many Cornish choughs ppr.

CREST—A torteau charged with a dolphin or.

SUPPORTERS—On either side a doctor of civil law in the University of Cambridge, vested in his robes, the dexter holding in the right hand an open book, the sinister in the right hand a pen and in the left hand a scroll all ppr.

MOTTO—Ut liberati serviamus.

COWPER

PEERAGE—Great Britain, Cowper, Earl, and Fordwich, Viscount; England Cowper, Baron.

SURNAME—Cowper.

CR.—Barony of Cowper, of Wingham, co. Kent, 14 Dec. 1706. Viscount Fordwich, and Earl Cowper, 20 Mar. 1718. **EXT.**—18 July 1905.

HISTORY—John Cowper, of Strode, co. Sussex, temp. Edward IV, m. Joan, dau. of John Stanbridge, and widow of Stephen Brode. She m. (3) Robert Aucher, of Westwell, co. Kent. By her he had issue, John Cowper, of Strode, m. Mary Chaloner, and had issue, with two elder sons, (John d. unm., and Robert, ancestor of the Cowpers of Strode) a third son, William, of London, living temp. Henry VIII, m. Margaret, dau. of Thomas Spencer, of St. Peter's, Cornhill, and had issue,

John Cowper, of St. Michael's, Cornhill, Alderman of London, and Sheriff, 1551; m. Elizabeth, dau. of John Ironside, of co. Lincoln, and d. 3 June 1609, having had issue,
1. John d.s.p.
2. William, 1st Bt. (see below).
2. Edward, d.s.p. 4. Richard d.s.p.
5. Nicholas, m. Margaret, dau. of Robert Bourne, of Bobingworth, co. Essex.
1. Frances, d. unm.
2. Elizabeth, m. (1) Thomas Carryl, of Sussex, and (2) John Jacques, father of Sir John Jacques, Bt.
3. Katherine, m. John Tey, of Layer-de-la-Hay, co. Essex.
4. Judith, m. (1) Richard Bourne, of London, and (2) Thomas Hill, of Fulham, co. Middlesex.

The eldest surviving son, Sir William Cowper, 1st Bt., of Ratlin Court, co. Kent, cr. a Baronet 4 Mar. 1642. He was imprisoned for his loyalty to Charles I, but succeeded in overcoming his troubles, and later resided at Hertford Castle. He m. Martha, dau. of James Master, of East Langdon, co. Kent, and d. 10 Dec. 1664, leaving issue,
1. John, imprisoned like his father for loyalty to the King. He m. Martha, dau. of George Hewkley, of London, and d.v.p. in confinement, having had with a dau., Martha, who d. young, a son, William, Sir, 2nd Bt., (see below).
2. Edward, Sir, b. 5 Aug. 1614, d. unm. 10 Nov. 1685.
3. William, Sir, father of Sir John Cowper, who had issue.
4. Spencer, of Hertford Castle, d. unm. 6 Nov. 1676.
5. James, m. Mary, dau. of Sir Henry Wroth, of Durans, and d.s.p. She m. 2ndly the 4th Earl of Suffolk.
6. Henry, d. an infant.
1. Mary, d. unm.

2. Martha, m. John Hitson, of Cleasby, co. York, and d. 6 Nov. 1681.
3. Anne, m. John Richmond, of Hiddington, co. Norfolk.

Sir William's grandson, Sir William Cowper, 2nd Bt., M.P. Hertford, and a leading Whig, m. Sarah, dau. of Sir Samuel Holled, of London, and had issue,
1. William, Sir, 3rd Bt. and **1st Earl Cowper.**
2. Spencer, b. 1669; educ. Westminster and Christ's Coll. Camb., adm. to Middle Temple, 1687, Barrister-at-Law, 1693; was on the Home Circuit; "was tried with three others at the Hertford Assizes July 1699 for the murder of Sarah Stout, a Quakeress, and acquitted; there was practically no evidence of the crime against the accused, and the trial is a curious illustration of the crass stupidity of men's minds when blinded by religious and political fanaticism" (*The Record of Old Westminsters,* Vol. i. 1928, p. 224). He was adm. to Lincoln's Inn, 1713; Bencher, 1715; Treasurer, 1715; Bencher, Middle Temple, 1718; M.P. for Beeralston, 1705-10, and Truro, 1715-27; one of the managers of Dr. Sacheverell's impeachment, 1709-10; Attorney General to Prince of Wales, 1714-17; K.C. 1715; Chief Justice of Chester, 1717; Serjeant-at-Law, 1727; a Justice of the Common Pleas, 1724; m. (1) Pennington, dau. of John Goodeve, and (2) Theodora, widow of John Stepney. He d. 10 Dec. 1728, having had issue by his first wife,
(1) William, Clerk of the Parliaments, of St. Margaret's Westminster, who d. 1740, leaving issue,
 1a William, b. ca. 1722, educ. Westminster and Worcester Coll. Oxford, adm. Lincoln's Inn, 1740; s. his father as Clerk of Parliaments; M.P. Hertford, 1768; Major in Herts Militia, and is the Major Cowper, in the life of the poet. He m. his cousin Miss Madan and d. 27 Aug. 1769.
 2a Spencer, b. ca. 1726, educ. Westminster and Worcester Coll. Oxford, adm. Inner Temple, 1741; Ensign 1st Foot Guards, 1747; Lt. and Capt. 1760; Capt. Lt. 1761; Capt. and Lt. Col. 1761; Brevet Col. 1772; ret. from Guards, 1773; Major Gen. 1779; Lt. Gen. 1787, comm. a Brigade in American War, was the Gen. Cowper, of the poet's life. He d. 13 Mar. 1797. He was Gov. of Tynemouth, and was father of Henry Cowper, of Tewin Water, co. Herts, and Clerk of the House of Lords.
(2) John, Rev., educ. Westminster and Christ's Coll. Camb., but left and went to Merton Coll. Oxford, B.A. 1715, M.A. 1718; D.D. 1728; Rector of Great Berkhampstead, co. Herts., from 1722; m. Anne, only dau. of Roger Donne, of Ludham Hall, co. Norfolk, and d. 10 July 1756, leaving issue, two sons,
 1a William, the famous poet, b. 15 Nov. 1731; educ. Westminster; articled to a solicitor, 1750-52;

adm. to Middle Temple, 1748, Barrister-at-Law, 1754; d. 25 April, 1800.

2a John, Rev., b. 1737; d. unm. 10 May 1770.

(3) Ashley, Clerk of the Parliaments, and Barrister-at-Law, d. 1788, leaving issue three daus.,

 1b Harriet, the favourite correspondent of the poet, m. Sir Thomas Hesketh, Bt.

 2b Elizabeth Charlotta, m. 24 April 1759, Sir Archer Croft, Bt.,

 3b Theodora Jane, who was the object of her cousin the poet's affection and is the subject of some of his verse.

1. Judith, known as a poetess, m. Col. Martin Madan, M.P.

Sir William, 2nd Bt., was s. by his elder son, Sir William Cowper, 3rd Bt., and **1st Earl Cowper,** Lord Keeper of the Great Seal, 1705, cr. Baron Cowper, of Wingam, co. Kent, Dec. 1706, and one of the Commissioners to treat of the Union between England and Scotland. On 4 May 1707 he was appointed Lord High Chancellor. On the death of Queen Anne, he was one of the Lords Justices appointed until the arrival of George I; in 1716 he was Lord High Steward for the trials of the Jacobite lords; cr. Viscount Fordwich and Earl Cowper, with remainder to his brother Spencer Cowper and the heirs male of his body. He was Lord Lieut. of Herts. He m. (1) Judith, dau. and heir of Sir Robert Booth, of London, but had no sur. issue by her. He m. (2) Mary, dau. and heir of John Clavering, of Chopwell, co. Durham. She d. Feb. 1723. He d. 19 Oct. 1723, leaving issue,

1. William, **2nd Earl Cowper** (see below).

2. Spencer, Very Rev., educ. Westminster and Exeter Coll. Oxford, B.A. 1731, M.A. 1734; B.D. and D.D. 1746; Rector of Fordwich, co. Kent, 1742; Preb. of Canterbury, 1742; Dean of Durham 1746; m. 19 May 1743, Dorothy Townshend, dau. of 2nd Viscount Townshend and d.s.p. 25 Mar. 1774.

1. Sarah, d. unm. 1758.

2. Anne, m. 1731, James Edward Colleton, of Haynes Hill, co. Berks, and d. 26 Mar. 1750.

The elder son, William Cowper, later Clavering-Cowper (see below) **2nd Earl Cowper,** a lord of the Bedchamber to George II, Lord Lieut. of Herts; b. 13 Aug. 1709; assumed the surname of Clavering before that of Cowper, in accordance with the will of his maternal uncle. He m. (1) 27 June 1732, Henrietta, ygst. dau. and eventually sole heiress of Henry de Nassau d'Auverquerque, Earl of Grantham, son of the famous Marshal and the sole descendant of the legitimized children of Prince Maurice of Nassau. Her mother was Lady Henrietta Butler, dau. and eventually sole heiress of Thomas Butler, Lord Butler of Moore Park (see in present work), son of the 1st Duke of Ormonde by Lady Elizabeth, his wife, Baroness Dingwall (see below). Lord Cowper m. (2) 1 May 1750, Lady Georgiana Carteret, dau. of 1st Earl of Granville, and widow of Hon. John Spencer. He d. Dec. 1764, having had by his first wife, the following issue,

1. George Nassau, **3rd Earl Cowper** (see below).

1. Caroline, m. 24 July 1753; Henry Seymour (Somerset, D.) and d. 2 June 1773.

The only son, George Nassau Clavering-Cowper, **3rd Earl Cowper,** b. 26 Aug. 1738; m. at Florence, 2 June 1775, Anne, dau. of Charles Gore, of Horkstowe, co. Lincoln, and by her (d. 5 Sept. 1826), had issue,

1. George Augustus, **4th Earl Cowper** (see below).

2. Peter Leopold, **5th Earl Cowper** (see below).

3. Edward Spencer, of Digswell, co. Herts, M.P., b. 1779; m. 1808, Catharine, dau. of Thomas March Phillipps, of Garendon Park, co. Leicester d. 1823.

The 3rd Earl Cowper was cr. a Prince of the Holy Roman Empire by the Emperor Joseph II, as the sole remaining representative of the Princes and Counts of Nassau D'Auverquerque, and he was permitted to bear this title by George III, in a letter from Viscount Weymouth, Sec. of State. The Earl also became through his grandmother, heir general of the Dukes of Ormonde. He d. 1789 being s. by his eldest son,

George Augustus Clavering-Cowper, **4th Earl Cowper,** b. 9 Aug. 1776; d. unm. 12 Feb. 1799, and was s. by his brother,

Peter Leopold Louis Francis Nassau Clavering-Cowper, **5th Earl,** F.R.S., b. 6 May 1778; m. 20 July 1805, Amelia, (m. 2ndly last Viscount Palmerston, and d. 11 Sept. 1869) dau. of 1st Viscount Melbourne, and d. 27 June 1837, having had issue,

1. George Augustus Frederick, **6th Earl** (see below).

2. William Francis Cowper-Temple, P.C. cr. Lord Mount Temple 25 May 1880. b. 13 Dec. 1811; m. (1) 24 June 1843, Harriet Alicia, dau. of Daniel Gurney, of North Runcton, co. Norfolk. She d. Aug. 1844; he m. (2) 22 Nov. 1848, Georgiana, dau. of Adm. John R. D. Tollemache, (Tollemache, B.) and d.s.p. 17 Oct. 1888.

3. Charles Spencer, b. 9 June 1816; m. (1) 1 Sept. 1852, Lady Harriet Anne (Countess D'Orsay) ,dau. of the Earl of Blessington, and widow, of Alfred Count D'Orsay, and by her (who d. 17 Dec. 1869) had a dau. Mary Harriette, d. in infancy 1854. He m. (2) 11 April 1871, Jessie Mary, dau. of Col. Clinton McLean, and d. 30 Mar. 1879.

1. Emily Caroline Catherine Frances, m. 16 June 1830, the Earl of Shaftesbury.

2. Frances Elizabeth, m. 29 April 1841, Viscount Jocelyn and d. 26 Mar. 1880.

The sixth Earl, George Augustus Frederick Cowper, **6th Earl Cowper,** Lord Lieut. of Kent, b. 26 June 1806; m. 7 Oct. 1833, Anne Florence, Baroness Lucas, elder dau. of Thomas Philip Robinson, Earl de Grey, and had issue,

1. Francis Thomas de Grey, **7th Earl Cowper** (see below).

2. Henry Frederick, M.P. Herts 1865-85, b. 18 April 1836; d. 10 Nov. 1887.

1. Henrietta Emily Mary, d. unm. 28 June 1853.

2. Florence Amabell, m. 9 Aug. 1871, Hon. Auberon Herbert, (Carnarvon, E.) and had issue. She d. 26 April 1886.

3. Adine Eliza Anne, m. 29 Sept. 1866, Julian Fane, (Westmorland, E.) and d. 20 Oct. 1868.

4. Amabell, m. 1873, Lord Walter-Talbot Kerr. (Lothian, M.).

The 6th Earl Cowper d. 15 April 1856. His widow s. her father Earl de Grey in the Barony of Lucas on 14 Nov. 1859, and d. 25 July 1880. He was s. in the earldom by his elder son, Francis Thomas de Grey Cowper, **7th Earl Cowper,** Lord Lieut. of Bedfordshire, D.L. Kent and Notts, High Steward for Colchester, Capt. H.M.'s corps of Gentlemen-at-Arms, 1871-74; Lord Lieut. of Ireland, 1880-82; made P.C., and cr. K.G.; B.A. Oxford, 1861; b. 11 June 1834; m. 25 Oct. 1870, Katrine Cecilia, eldest dau. of 4th Marquess of Northampton. He s. to the Barony of Lucas on the death of his mother. He d.s.p. 18 July 1905, when the Earldom of Cowper, the Viscounty of Fordwich, and the Barony of Cowper became extinct, while the Barony of Butler fell into abeyance among his sisters and their heirs. The Baronies of Lucas and Dingwall devolved on his nephew and heir general Auberon Thomas Herbert who became 8th Baron Lucas and 11th Baron Dingwall. (see extant peerages under Lucas, B.).

ARMS—Quarterly I, Argent three martlets gules, on a chief engrailed of the last, as many annulets or. (Cowper); II, Quarterly 1, Azure billetté, a lion rampant or, (Nassau D'Auverquerque); 2, Or a lion rampant guardant gules ducally crowned azure; 3, Gules a fess argent; 4, Gules two lions passant guardant in pale or; over all an inescutcheon argent a lion rampant sable. III, Quarterly 1 and 4, Or a chief indented azure (Butler); 2 and 3, Gules three covered cups or. IV, Argent three unicorns' heads erased sable (Preston); V, Quarterly 1 and 4, Barry of six argent and azure (de Grey); 2 and 3, Vert a chevron between three stags at gaze trippant or (Robinson); VI, Argent on a saltire azure a bezant (Yorke); VII, Quarterly 1 and 4, Gyronny of eight or and sable; 2 Or a fess chequy argent and azure. 3, Argent a lymphad her sails furled and oars in action, all sable (Campbell); VIII, Barry of six argent and azure in chief three torteaux (Grey, Duke of Kent); IX, Argent a fess between six annulets gules (Lucas).

CREST—A lion's gamb, erect and erased or, holding a cherry branch vert fructed gules.

SUPPORTERS—On either side a light dun horse, with a large blaze down the face, mane close shorn, except a tuft upon the withers, a black list down the back, a bob tail, and three white feet, viz. the hind feet and near forefoot.

MOTTO—Tuum est.

CREWE

PEERAGE—U.K. Baron Crewe of Crewe, co. Chester, 25 Feb. 1806. Ext. 3 Jan. 1894. U.K. Earl of Crewe, co. Palatine of Chester, 17 July, 1895.
  U.K. Earl of Madeley, co. Stafford, and Marquess of Crewe, 22 June, 1911. Also Baron Houghton, of Great Houghton, W.R. Yorks. cr. 20 Aug. 1863.

SURNAME—Crewe-Milnes (originally Offley).

CR.—as above. EXT.—20 June, 1945, but see above for Barony cr. 1806.

HISTORY—John Crew, of Nantwich, co. Chester, m. Alice, dau. of Humphrey Main-

waring, of Nantwich, and d. 1598, aged 74, leaving issue,

1. Randolph, of whom below.
2. Thomas, Sir. serjeant-at-law, M.P. Northampton, and Speaker of the House of Commons, of Stene and Hinton, co. Northampton, from whom descended the Barons Crew of Stene (1883 Extinct Peerage), and also the baronets (in the female line, now extinct) of Crewe of Caulk Abbey, co. Derby.

The elder son, Sir Randolph Crewe, b. 1558, Speaker of the House of Commons, and Lord Chief Justice of the Court of King's Bench, 1624-26, who built Crewe Hall. He m. 1598, Julian, dau. and coheir of John Clippesby, Norfolk, and d. 1646, leaving issue, with others, an eldest son, Sir Clippesby Crewe, b. 1599; m. Joan, dau. and coheir of Sir John Pultney, of Pultney Misterton, co. Leicester, and d. 1648, leaving with other issue, an eldest son, John Crewe, of Crewe, b. 1626; m. Carew, dau. of Sir Arthur Gorges, of Chelsea, and d. 1684, when he was s. by his eldest dau. and eventual heir,

Ann Crewe, who m. John Offley, of Madeley Manor, co. Stafford. They had issue an elder son,

John Offley, later Crewe, of Crewe Hall, who s. to the estates of his maternal grandfather, and who assumed by Act of Parliament, 1708, the name of Crewe. He was M.P. for Cheshire. He m. Sarah, dau. of Morgan Price, of Nantgwared, co. Brecon, and d. 1749, leaving with other issue,

1. John, his heir (see below).
2. Randulph, Rev. LL.D., Rector of Bartholmey, m. Ann Read, and was ancestor of the family of Crewe-Read, of Llandinam.

The elder son, John Crewe, of Crewe Hall, M.P. for Cheshire, 1734-52, m. Anne, dau. of Richard Shuttleworth, of Gawthorp, co. Lancaster, and d. 18 Sept. 1752, leaving issue,

1. John, **1st Baron Crewe** (see below).
2. Richard, Major Gen., b. 27 Sept. 1749; m. Nilborough, dau. of Samuel Allpress and d. 17 June, 1814, leaving issue,
   (1) Richard, b. 1786; m. 1815 Frances, dau. of J. Hare, and left issue,
      1a Richard, Col. Madras Army, b. 1816; m. 2 Sept. 1862, Emma Louisa Frederica, widow of Capt. H. F. Siddons. She d. 16 Jan. 1878.
      2a Frederick, Capt. 17th Madras Native Inf., b. 1825; m. 1854 Elizabeth (she m. 2ndly 1862, the 7th Lord Calthorpe, and d. 26 August 1919), dau. of Capt. F. Chamier, R.N., and d. 1858, having had issue Charles Preston, Sir, K.C.M.G., C.B., V.D. Brig. Gen. S. African Defence Force, Colonial Sec., Cape of Good Hope, 1904-7, and Sec. for Agric. 1907-08, mem. Legis. Assembly, Cape of Good Hope, 1899-1910, mem. L.A. East London, Union of S. Africa Parl., 1910-19; served in Kaffir War, 1878-79; in Basutoland, 1880-81, in S. African War, 1900-02, and in World War I, in East Africa, as Brig. Gen.; was Dir. of War Recruiting, 1914-16, and chief owner of East London

Daily Despatch and Queenstown *Daily Representative*; was permitted to retain the title of Hon.; b. 11 Jan. 1858; m. 11 July, 1887, Helen Agnes Josephine, O.B.E. (1918), dau. of Joseph Orpen, Surveyor Gen. of Rhodesia, and d. 21 July, 1936, leaving issue, one son,

    Ranulphe Orpen, m. (1) Jan. 1927, Elaine Mary, (d. 4 Oct. 1929), dau. of T. Collier, and (2) 17 Dec. 1930, Dorothy Alice, dau. of W. Drummond Hamilton, of Dundrum, Dublin, and d. 23 Mar. 1937, having had a dau. Helen Joy, b. 2 and d. 11 Oct. 1931.

(2) John Frederick, Col. in the Army, b. 1788; m. 28 June, 1819, Hon. Harriet Smith, dau. of 1st Baron Carrington, (she d. 27 April, 1856) and d. 10 Nov. 1840, leaving an only son,

    Randolph Henry, of Loakes Hill, co. Bucks, Barrister-at-Law, b. 10 June, 1825; d. unm. 2 Jan. 1879.

(3) Willoughby, Rev., Rector of Mucklestone, co. Salop, b. 1792; m. 1816, Catherine, dau. of J. Harvey, and d. 9 April, 1850, having had two sons who d. unm.

(1) Emma, m. John Pusey Edwards.

1. Sarah, m. Obadiah Lane, and d. 1814.
2. Elizabeth, m. Dr. Hinchcliffe, Bishop of Peterborough.
3. Frances, m. Gen. Watson and had issue.
4. Emma, d. unm.

The elder son, John Crewe, **1st Baron Crewe,** of Crewe, co. Chester, so cr. 25 Feb. 1806; b. 27 Sept. 1742; educ. Ch. Ch. Oxford; High Sheriff, Cheshire 1764; M.P. for Stafford, 1765-68, for Cheshire, 1768-1802; m. 4 April, 1766, Frances, dau. of Fulke Greville, of Wilbury, co. Wilts. She d. 23 Dec. 1818, he d. 28 April, 1829. They had issue (with a dau. Emma, m. 21 April, 1809, Foster Cunliffe-Offley, son of Sir Foster Cunliffe, Bt., and d. 1850), an only son,

John Crewe, **2nd Baron Crewe,** bapt. 1772; served in the Army, Major Gen. 1808, Lt. Gen. 1813, Gen. 1830, ret. 1831; m. 5 May, 1807, Henrietta Maria Anne, dau. of George Walker-Jungerford, representative of the Hungerfords of Cadenham, co. Wilts., through her mother, Henrietta Maria, dau. of J. Hungerford. She d. 14 Jan. 1820. He d. 4 Dec. 1835. They had issue,

1. Hungerford, **3rd Baron** (see below).
1. Henrietta Mary, d. unm. 4 Feb. 1879.
2. Maria Hungerford, d. an infant, 1812.
3. Annabella Hungerford, m. 31 July 1851, Richard Monckton Milnes, 1st Lord Hougnton, and d. 24 Feb. 1874, leaving issue, Robert Offley Ashburton, cr. Marquess of Crewe (see below).

The only son, Hungerford Crewe, **3rd Baron Crewe,** b. 10 Aug. 1812; educ. Eton and Ch. Ch. Oxford; F.S.A. 1840; F.R.S. 1841. He d. unm. 3 Jan. 1894 being s. in his estates by his nephew, the 2nd Baron Houghton, and later Earl and Marquess of Crewe.

Lineage of Milnes. William Milnes, of Ashford, co. Derby, who lived in reign of Elizabeth I, had many children; from the eldest son,

Richard, descended the Milnes of Dunstone Hall, and Aldecar Park, co. Derby. His fourth son, James Milnes, of Tapton Hall, who d. 1651 had issue, Richard Milnes m. Elizabeth, dau. and heir of Richard Wilson, of Barton, co. Norfolk, and Eyam, co. Derby, and d. 1705, leaving issue with three other sons, Richard (eldest son), James and William, whose lines are extinct,

1. Robert, whose line we trace (see below).
2. John, ancestor of the Milnes Gaskells, of Thornes House, and Lupset Hall, near Wakefield.
1. Mary, m. 1698, John Wildbore, and had issue, a dau. and heir, Lilzabeth, m. Ichabod Wright, of Nottingham.

The second son, Robert Milnes, m. Hannah, dau. and coheir of Joseph Poole, of Drax Abbey, co. York, Capt. in the Parliamentary Army and d. 1737, having had issue (with a ygst. son John, of Wakefield, whose son, Sir Robert Shore Milnes, was cr. a Bt. 1801), an eldest son, Richard Milnes, b. 21 Mar. 1696; m. 1718, Bridget, dau. and heir of John Pemberton. She d. Jan. 1765. They had with others, an eldest son, Robert Milnes, m. (1) Feb. 1757, Joice (d. 1764), dau. of Adam Slater, M.D., of Chesterfield, and had issue. He m. (2) 1766, Esther, dau. of Samuel Shore, of Sheffield, who d.s.p. He d. April, 1771, leaving, with others by his first wife, an only surv. son,

Richard Slater Milnes, of Fryston Hall, co. York, M.P., City of York, b. 12 Dec. 1759; m. 30 May 1781, Rachael, dau. and (at the death of her sister Marianne, the wife of James Milnes) sole heir of Hans Busk, of Bull House, by Martha his wife, dau. and heir of Richard Rodes, of Great Houghton, co. York, and Martha his wife, sister and heir of Aymer Rich, of Penistone. By his wife Rachael, who d. 1835, Richard Slater Milnes had issue,

1. Robert Pemberton, his heir (see below).
2. Richard Rodes, b. 31 Oct. 1785; d. unm. 1835.
1. Martha.
2. Rachael, m. Marmaduke Wyvil, of Constable Burton, M.P. for York, and d. 1856.
3. Eliza, m. William Newton, of Elveden Hall, co. Suffolk, M.P. for Ipswich.
4. Mary Anne, m. Henry Spencer Waddington, M.P. co. Suffolk.
5. Louisa, b. 1791; d. 25 Nov. 1886.
6. Caroline, b. 1792; d. 4 April 1869.
7. Amelia Jane, b. 1801; d. 1 May 1885.

Richard Slater Milnes d. 2 June 1804 and was s. by his elder son, Robert Pemberton Milnes, of Fryston Hall and Bawtry Hall, co. York, M.P. for Pontefract, b. 20 May 1784; m. 22 Aug. 1808, Hon. Henrietta Maria Monckton, dau. of Robert Monckton Arundell, 4th Viscount Galway, d. Nov. 1858, having by her, who d. 1 May 1847, had issue (with a dau. Henrietta Maria, who m. 23 April 1838, 6th Viscount Galway, and d. 10 Sept. 1891), an only son,

Richard Monckton Milnes, **1st Baron Houghton,** b. 19 June 1809; m. 31 July 1851, Annabella Hungerford, dau. of 2nd Lord Crewe (see above), and by her (d. 24 Feb. 1874) had issue,

1. Robert Offley Ashburton, **2nd Baron Houghton** and **1st Marquess.**

1. Amicia Henrietta, m. 11 June 1881, Sir Gerald FitzGerald, K.C.M.G., who d. 11 Oct. 1912. She d. 4 July 1902, leaving issue.
2. Florence Ellen Hungerford, m. 20 June 1882, Major Gen. the Hon. Arthur Henry Henniker-Major, C.B., (Henniker, B.) and d.s.p. 4 April 1923.

Lord Houghton was a trustee of the British Museum, D.C.L., M.A., F.R.S., Hon. Fell. Trin. Coll. Camb., M.P. Pontefract 1837-63; author of many vols. of poems, monographs, and many pamphlets, also of *Life and Letters of John Keats*. He was cr. Baron Houghton, of Great Houghton, W.R. Yorks, 20 Aug. 1863 and d. 11 Aug. 1885 being s. by his only son,

Robert Offley Ashburton Milnes, afterwards Crewe-Milnes, **2nd Baron Houghton, Earl of Crewe, Earl of Madeley,** and **Marquess of Crewe,** b. 12 Jan. 1858; educ. Harrow and Trin. Coll. Camb., B.A. 1880, M.A. 1885; F.S.A. 1886; a Lord in Waiting 1886; made P.C. 1892; Viceroy of Ireland (as Lord Lt.) 1892-95. He inherited the estates of his maternal uncle, the 3rd Lord Crewe (see above) and by Royal Licence on 8 June 1894 he assumed the surname of Crewe before that of Milnes, and the arms of Crewe quarterly. He was Lord Pres. of the Council 1905-1908, Lord Privy Seal 1908-11, Colonial Sec. 1908-10; Sec. of State for India 1910-15; Lord Pres. of the Council 1915-16, Pres. of the Board of Education 1916 and Sec. of State for War and Pres. of the Army Council 1931, and Ambassador to France 1922-28. He was cr. Earl of Crewe, in the co. Palatine of Chester, 17 July 1895, K.G. 1908, Earl of Madeley, co. Stafford, and Marquess of Crewe 22 June 1911. He m. (1) 3 June 1880, Sibyl Marcia, dau. of Sir Frederick Graham, 3rd Bt., of Netherby, and by her (who d. 19 Sept. 1887) had issue,

1. Richard Charles Rodes, b. 30 July 1882; d. 20 Mar. 1890.
1. Annabel Hungerford, b. 31 Aug. 1881; m. (1) 21 Jan. 1902, Capt. the Hon. A. E. B. O'Neill, eldest son of 2nd Lord O'Neill, who was k. in action 5 Nov. 1914. She m. (2) 9 Feb. 1922, Major J. H. H. Dodds, and had issue.
2. Celia Hermione, b. 20 May 1884; m. 8 Oct. 1906, Sir Edward Clive Coates, 2nd Bt., and had issue.
3. Helen Cynthia, D.C.V.P., woman of the Bedchamber to Queen Mary, J.P. co. London, O.St.J., twin with Celia Hermione, m. 21 Jan. 1908 Hon. George Charles Colville, (Colville, V.) and had issue.

The Marquess m. (2) 20 April 1899, Lady Margaret Primrose, C.I., dau. of 5th Earl of Rosebery, and d. 20 June 1945, having had further issue,

2. Richard George Archibald John Lucian Hungerford, b. 7 Feb. 1911; d. 31 Mar. 1922.
4. Mary Evelyn Hungerford, b. 23 Mar. 1915; m. 24 Oct. 1935, 9th Duke of Roxburghe.

ARMS—Quarterly 1 and 4, Azure, a chevron between three windmill sails or, (Milnes); 2 and 3, Azure a lion rampant argent (Crewe).
CRESTS—1. A garb or charged with a fess dancettée azure, thereon three mullets argent

(Milnes); 2. Out of a ducal coronet or, a lion's gamb erect argent (Crewe).
SUPPORTERS—On either side, a pegasus argent, gorged with a collar dancetté azure, thereon three mullets argent, in the mouth a branch of laurel ppr.
MOTTO—Scio cui credidi.

The Marquess's seats were at West Horsley Place, co. Surrey and Madeley Manor, Newcastle, c. Stafford, with a town residence at Argyll House, 211, King's Road, Chelsea, London, S.W.3.

In some of the older peerge accounts the Crewes were said to be descended from the family of De Montalt, Barons, whose surname was Maude and whose arms the Crewes were said to bear undifferenced. It is much more probable that, as with many other coats of arms, before the rise and development of the College of Arms, the two families of Maude and Crewe had adopted simultaneously and without any connection the simple coat of azure a lion rampant argent.

ARMS (of Baron Crewe, extinct 1894). Quarterly 1 and 4, Azure a lion rampant argent (Crewe); 2 and 3, Argent a cross flory azure, charged with a lion passant or (Offley).
CRESTS—1, Out of a ducal coronet or, a lion's gamb erect argent (Crewe); 2, A demi lion rampant guardant or holding in the paws a slip of olive ppr. (Offley).
SUPPORTERS—Dexter, A lion argent collared azure, thereon three roses or. Sinister, A griffin sable, wings elevated argent, beaked and legged gules.
MOTTO—Sequor nec inferior.

The family seat of the Crewe family, Barons Crewe, was Crewe Hall, co. Cheshire, with a London house at 23 Hill Street, Berkeley Square. The last Baron's Clubs were Travellers' and White's.

CROOKSHANK

PEERAGE—U.K. Viscount Crookshank of Gainsborough, co. Lincoln.
SURNAME—Crookshank.
CR.—13 Jan. 1956. EXT.—17 Oct. 1961.
HISTORY—Crookshank, in its original form Cruickshank, is a Scottish name and is found in Aberdeenshire and other parts of Scotland in the middle ages. The genealogy of the present family is traced from its settlement in Dublin where William Crookshank b. in 1650 was son of Thomas and grandson of another Thomas Crookshank. William Crookshank d. 1719 having had with other issue, William Crookshank, Attorney, of Dublin and later of Drumhalry and Birrenagh, co. Longford, b. 8 Aug. 1699; m. 18 May 1725, Rebecca, dau. of George Tandy and d. 1780 having had with other issue, an eldest son, The Hon. Alexander Crookshank of Newtown Park, and Drumhalry and Birrenagh, M.P. for Belfast, 1777-83, Justice of the Court of Common Pleas, Dublin, 1784-1800, b. 30 June 1736; m. 12 July 1768, Esther, dau. of William Kennedy of Beechill, co. Down, and Alderman of Derry, and d. 10 Dec. 1873 having had eight sons of whom the second, George, inherited Drumhalry (see B.L.G. 1952, Crookshank of that place) while the ygst. son, Col. Chichester William Crookshank had a most distinguished career. He was

b. 24 May 1783 joined 58th Foot in 1799, and served in the West Indies, at the Cape of Good Hope 1806, at Monte Video in Uruguay where he was wounded and at the storming of Buenos Aires, Argentina, being captured, was in the battles of the Peninsular war and in the Walcheren Expedition; comm. 33rd Regt., cr. a K.H. (1835). In 1818 he m. Charlotte Elizabeth, dau. of the Rev. Charles Johnson of Southstake near Bath, Chaplain to the Prince Regent and d. 1 Sept. 1838 having had with other issue, an elder son,

Capt. Blackman Chichester Graham Crookshank, 21st and 51st Regts; b. 10 Jan. 1819; m. 4 Dec. 1849, Helen Elizabeth, dau. of George Bilton of Kimbolton Park, Hamilton, Tasmania and d. 24 April 1860 having had with other issue (B.L.G. 1952) a fifth son,

Harry Maule Crookshank, F.R.C.S. (Edin.) b. 13 Jan. 1849; educ. Cheltenham and Univ. Coll. Hospital, London, served in the Egyptian Admin., from 1883, being made Pasha and being awarded the Orders of Mejidieh (Grand Cordon) and Osmanieh (Cmdr.); m. 5 Aug. 1891, Emma, dau. of Major Samuel Comfort of New York and d. 25 Mar. 1914 having had issue with a dau., Helen who d. unm., a son,

Harry Frederick Comfort Crookshank, **Viscount Crookshank,** b. 27 May 1893; educ. Eton and Magdalen Coll. Oxford, M.A., served in World War I 1914-18, Capt. Hampshire Regt. and Grenadier Guards, wounded twice. Order of White Eagle of Serbia and Serbian Gold Medal for Valour; served in Diplomatic Service 1919; M.P. for Parts of Lindsey, Gainsborough, 1924-56; held several Government offices, being Postmaster Gen. 1943-45, Leader of the House of Commons and Minister of Health, 1951-52, and Lord Privy Seal, 1952-55. He was made P.C. 1939, appointed C.H. 1955 and cr. Viscount Crookshank of Gainsborough, co. Lincoln, 13 Jan. 1956, he d. 17 Oct. 1961.

ARMS—Or three bears' heads erased sable armed and langued azure, a bordure of the second.

CREST—A dexter cubit arm in armour, the hand naked holding a dagger in bend sinister ppr., hilt and pommel or.

MOTTO—Conferre gladio.

CUMBERLAND AND TEVIOTDALE

PEERAGE—Great Britain, Duke of Cumberland and Teviotdale.
Ireland. Earl of Armagh.
SURNAME—none (often given as Guelph).
CR.—24 April 1799. SUSPENDED—28 Mar. 1919.

HISTORY—H.R.H. Ernest Augustus, Prince of Great Britain and Ireland, also Duke of Brunswick-Luneburg, was the 5th son of King George III, by Charlotte Sophie, dau. of Karl Ludwig, Grand Duke of Mecklenburg-Strelitz, b. 5 June 1771; educ. Gottingen Univ.; entered 9th Hanoverian Hussars as Lt., 1790, Lt. Col. 1793, Major Gen. in Hanoverian Service, Feb. 1794; was wounded at Tournay, May 1794, and distinguished at Nimeguen, 10 Dec. 1794; received several promotions, becoming Field Marshal 1813, and Col. of the

15th Light Dragoons, 1801-27, and of the Royal Horse Guards, the Blues, 1827-30. On 24 April 1799 he was cr. **Earl of Armagh,** and **Duke of Cumberland and Teviotdale;** made a P.C. 1799. When his brother King William IV d. 20 June 1837, he s. to the kingdom of Hanover, owing to the operation of the Salic Law, to which his niece Queen Victoria could not succeed being a woman. He m. 29 Aug. 1815, Princess Friderike Louise Karoline Sophie Alexandrine, 3rd dau. of Karl Ludwig Friedrich, Grand Duke of Mecklenburg-Strelitz, who was the maternal uncle of the Duke of Cumberland. The bride was the former wife of Friedrich Wilhelm, Prince of Solms-Braunfels, who had divorced her and who d. 13 April 1814, and before that, wife of Prince Friedrich Ludwig Karl, of Prussia (who d. 28 Dec. 1796). The Duke of Cumberland, King of Hanover, d. 18 Nov. 1851. The Duchess, Queen of Hanover d. 29 June 1841. They had issue, one son,

H.R.H. George Frederick Alexander Charles Ernest Augustus, **2nd Duke of Cumberland and Teviotdale,** George V, King of Hanover, from 1851 to 1866, when he was deposed by the Prussians, after having been under their fire, until the final surrender of the Hanoverian army at Langensalza, 27 June 1866. He was also Duke of Brunswick-Luneburg. He was b. 27 May 1819; Col. in Chief, 4th Regt. of Dragoons in Hanoverian Army, and after his deposition, when he lived mostly in Paris, he became a Gen. in the British Army. He m. 18 Feb. 1843, Princess Marie Alexandrine Wilhelmine Katherine Charlotte Therese Henriette Louise Pauline Elisabeth Friedrike Georgine, 1st dau. of Joseph Georg Friedrich Ernst Karl, Duke of Saxe-Altenburg. He d. 12 June 1878, in Paris, and was bur. 25 June 1878, at Windsor. His Queen d. 9 Jan. 1907. They had issue with two daus. (see extant peerages, royal lineage), an only son,

H.R.H. Ernest Augustus William Adolphus George Frederick, **3rd Duke of Cumberland and Teviotdale,** and Duke of Brunswick-Luneburg, b. 21 Sept. 1845; Hanoverian Army, 1862, Col. of Infantry 42nd Regt. in Austrian Army, 1866; Major Gen. in British Army, 1886; Lt. Gen. 1892; Gen. 1898; appointed K.G. 1878. In 1884 on the death of his cousin, Wilhelm, Duke of Brunswick, he became the representative of that line, and announced, from Gmunden, in Austria, that he took possession of the Duchy of Brunswick, but no further action was taken. He m. 21 Dec. 1878, Thyra Amalie Karoline Charlotte Anna, ygst. dau. of Christian IX King of Denmark, and d. 14 Nov. 1923, having had issue, with two sons who d. unm., and three daus. (see royal lineage as supra), an eldest surv. son, Ernest Augustus Christian George, Duke of Brunswick-Luneburg. On 13 May 1915, the 3rd Duke of Cumberland was struck off the Roll of the Order of the Garter, and on 28 Mar. 1919, was deprived of his peerages and his title of a Prince of Great Britain by Order in Council. This is another instance of a suspended peerage, as noticed under Albany, Duke of.

ARMS—The royal arms of England as borne by King George III, differenced by a label of three points argent the centre point charged with a fleur-de-lis azure, and each of the other points with St. George's Cross.

CUNNINGHAM OF HYNDHOPE

PEERAGE—U.K. Baron Cunningham of Hyndhope, of Kirkhope, co. Selkirk and Viscount Cunningham of the same.
SURNAME—Cunningham.
CR.—Barony, 15 Sept. 1945; Viscounty 26 Jan. 1946 (also Baronetcy U.K. 7 July 1942). EXT.—12 June 1963.
HISTORY—This family is described as being descended from Alexander Cunningham, proprietor of Hyndhope which was owned by his family for a century, and who was a minister of the church at Ettrick (1641-62) until ejected as a nonconformist. The connected pedigree is as follows: John Cunningham, D.D., LL.D., Principal, St. Mary's Coll. St. Andrew's Univ., b. 1819; m. 1846 Susan Porteous, and d. 1893 having had issue, Daniel John Cunningham, D.C.L., LL.D., F.R.S., of Edinburgh and Dublin, b. 1850; m. 1878 Elizabeth, dau. of the Rev. Andrew Browne, of Beith, co. Ayr and d. 1909. She d. 1926. They had issue with two other sons, a second son, Sir Andrew Browne Cunningham, **Baron and Viscount Cunningham** of Hyndhope, one of the most distinguished naval commanders of World War II. He was b. 7 January 1883; educ. Edin. Acad., Stubbington House, Fareham, and H.M.S. *Britannia*. He entered the Royal Navy in 1896 and served in World War I, 1914-18 (despatches, D.S.O. two bars), A.D.C. to King George V 1932, Rear Adm. cmdg. Destroyer Flotillas Mediterranean, 1934-36, Vice Adm. cmdg. Battle Cruisers and 2nd in Command Mediterranean Fleet, 1937-38, Deputy Chief of Naval Staff 1938-39, C. in C. Mediterranean Fleet 1938-42, the most difficult period of the war in which he was responsible for the successful actions against the Italian Navy at Taranto and Matapan; received surrender, 1943 of Italian fleet, which while sailing under British safe conduct was severely bombed by its former allies, the Germans. He held several important positions, was First Sea Lord and Chief of Naval Staff, Oct. 1943-June 1946, Lord High Commissioner to the Church of Scotland 1950 and 1952. He received many honorary doctorates and other notable professional distinctions, with freedom of several cities. He was awarded many foreign decorations. Made D.S.O. 1915, with first bar 1919 and second 1920, C.B. 1934, K.C.B. 1939, G.C.B. 1941, K.T. 1945, O.M. 1946, and cr. a Baronet of Bishop's Waltham, co. Hants, 7 July 1942, Baron Cunningham of Hyndhope, of Kirkhope co. Selkirk 15 Sept. 1945 and Viscount Cunningham of Hyndhope, of Kirkhope, co. Selkirk 26 Jan. 1946. He m. 21 Dec. 1929, Nora Christine, dau. of Horace Byath, of Midhurst, co. Sussex, and d. 12 June 1963. His memoirs were published under the title of *A Sailor's Odyssey*.
ARMS—Argent a shake fork sable between a mullet in chief and two dolphins descending respectant vert, embouchée gules.
CREST—Issuant from a naval crown vert a unicorn's head argent armed, maned and tufted or, langued gules.
SUPPORTERS—Two albatrosses, their wings elevated ppr.
MOTTO—Over fork over.

CURRIE

PEERAGE—U.K. Baron Currie of Hawley.
SURNAME—Currie.
CR.—25 Jan. 1899. EXT.—12 May 1906.
HISTORY—The earliest recorded ancestor of the Currie family was William Currie, living in 1609, who was of a property called Currie Parks and whose predecessors had been of Dunse, co. Berwick. From him descended in a connected pedigree the baronets now entered in extant peerages, Currie. From the same stock also descended the family of Currie of Dingley Hall and Dunbeath Castle, formerly of Minley Manor, who are entered in *Burke's Landed Gentry*, 1952. Of the latter branch came Raikes Currie, M.P. for Northampton, b. 15 April 1801; m. 28 June 1825, Hon. Laura Sophia, eldest dau. of 2nd Baron Wodehouse, (Kimberley, E.), and d. 16 Oct. 1881, having had by her (who d. 17 Feb. 1869) with other issue (*B.L.G.* 1952 as cited), a fourth son, Sir Philip Henry Wodehouse Currie, **Baron Currie**, b. 13 Oct. 1834; educ. Eton; attached to Brit. Legation, St. Petersburg, 1856-57; Précis writer to the Foreign Sec. 1857-58; Sec. on several special missions, and Asst. Under-Sec. of State for Foreign Affairs 1882-89; Permanent Under Sec. of State for Foreign Affairs 1889-93; Ambassador to Constantinople 1893-98, and to Rome 1898-1903; cr. C.B. 1878; K.C.B. 1885, G.C.B. 1892, and Baron Currie of Hawley, 25 Jan. 1899. He m. 24 Jan. 1894, Mary Montgomerie, dau. of Charles James Saville Montgomerie Lamb, (Lamb, Bt.), and widow of Henry Sydenham Singleton of Mell, co. Louth, and Hazeley Heath, co. Hants. She d. 13 Oct. 1905. He d.s.p. 12 May 1906. Lady Currie was a writer under the pseudonym of Violet Fane, including some volumes of verse, and she was the Mrs. Sinclair of W. H. Mallock's *New Republic*.
ARMS—Gules, A saltire couped argent in the centre chief point a rose argent barbed and seeded ppr.
CREST—A cock ppr., resting its foot upon a rose argent barbed and seeded ppr.
SUPPORTERS—On either side a cock ppr. charged with a rose argent.

CURZON OF KEDLESTON

PEERAGE—Ireland. Baron Curzon of Kedleston, 11 Nov. 1898.
U.K. Earl Curzon of Kedleston, 2 Nov. 1911.
U.K. Marquess Curzon of Kedleston, 28 June 1912.
SURNAME—Curzon.
CR.—See above. EXT.—20 Mar. 1925.
HISTORY—George Nathaniel Curzon, **Marquess Curzon** of Kedleston, and holder of five other peerages plus two baronetcies, was b. 11 Jan. 1859, the eldest son of the Rev. Alfred Nathaniel Holden Curzon, 4th Baron Scarsdale (extant peerage, Scarsdale, V.). He was educ. Eton and Balliol Coll. Oxford, Pres. of Oxford Union Soc. 1880, Lothian Essay Prize, and Fell. of All Souls, 1883; was M.P. for Southport Div. of Lancashire 1886-89; Under Sec. of State for India 1891-92; Under Sec. of State for Foreign Affairs 1895-98; made P.C. 1895 and cr. Baron Curzon of Kedleston,

in the peerage of Ireland (the last creation in the Irish peerage) 11 Nov. 1898, having been appointed Viceroy and Gov. Gen. of India and cr. G.C.I.E. 1898. He took office in India in Jan. 1899 and continued until 1904, and 1904-05, Lord Warden of the Cinque Ports 1904-05; he was cr. Earl Curzon of Kedleston, co. Derby, 2 Nov. 1911, with rem. to the heirs male of his body, and also Viscount Scarsdale of Scarsdale, co. Derby, with rem. in default of male issue to his father, Baron Scarsdale, and the heirs male of his body, and also Baron Ravensdale, of Ravensdale, co. Derby, with rem. in default of male issue to his eldest dau. and the heirs male of her body, with like rem. to his second and every other dau. successively. He was Lord Privy Seal 1915-16. He s. his father in 1916 becoming 5th Baron Scarsdale, and s. to the two baronetcies, one of Scotland, the other of England; he was Pres. of the Air Board 1916, cr. K.G. 1916, Lord Pres. of the Council and mem. of the War Cabinet 1916-19, Leader of the House of Lords 1916-24; Lord Pres. of the Council and Leader of the Lords, 1924-1925. He m. (1) 22 April 1895, Mary Victoria, C.I., and Kaisar-i-Hind Gold Medal, dau. of Levi Zeighler Leiter, of Washington, U.S.A. She d. 18 July 1906, leaving issue,

1. Mary Irene, Baroness Ravensdale, (extant peerage). b. 20 Jan. 1896.
2. Cynthia Blanche, M.P. Stoke Div. Stoke-on-Trent, 1929-31; b. 23 Aug. 1898; m. 11 May 1920, Sir Oswald Mosley, 6th Bt., and d. 16 May 1933 leaving issue (extant baronetcies).
3. Alexandra Naldera, b. 20 Mar. 1904; m. 21 July 1925, (m. diss. by div. 1955) Major E. D. Metcalfe (see under Ravensdale in extant peerages), and had issue,

The Marquess Curzon d.s.p.m. 20 Mar. 1925 at 1 Carlton House Terrace, London, when the Marquessate, Earldom and Irish Barony became extinct. The Viscounty of Scarsdale and the Barony of Scarsdale, with two baronetcies went to his nephew and the Barony of Ravensdale was inherited by his eldest dau. The Marquess was a great traveller and writer. He had visited many countries in Asia and in 1895 had received the Gold Medal of the Royal Geographical Society. He was a profound scholar, and among other achievements he was the restorer of Bodiam Castle in Sussex, which he presented to the nation. The restoration of the building is one of the most successful of such efforts to have been made in England. The Marquess's monograph on Bodiam Castle represents every aspect of the architecture and history of this beautiful place. In India the Marquess was able to deal with many matters in connection with Indian archaeology and art, it being marvellous that he could do this in the midst of the arduous duties of his official position, but as a small instance may be cited the restoration of some plaques and paintings in the Red Fort at Delhi, together with some lights in the Taj Mahal.
ARMS—Argent, On a bend sable three popinjays or, collared gules.
CREST—A popinjay rising or collared gules.
SUPPORTERS—Dexter, The figure of Prudence, represented by a woman habited argent, mantled azure, holding in her sinister hand a javelin entwined with a remora (i.e. serpent) ppr. Sinister, The figure of Liberality, also represented by a woman habited argent, mantled purp. holding a cornucopia ppr.
MOTTOES—Let Curzon holde what Curzon helde; Recte et suaviter.
Lord Curzon's seats were at Kedleston (the home of the Curzon family for over 850 years, the Curzons being one of the very few families of male line Norman descent in the whole of the peerage) where there is a valuable museum of the Marquess's possessions; Hackwood, near Basing toke; and Montacute House, co. Somerset.

CUSHENDUN

PEERAGE—U.K. Baron Cushendun of Cushendun, co. Antrim.
SURNAME—McNeill.
CR.—7 Nov. 1927. **EXT.**—12 Oct. 1934.
HISTORY—Torquil MacNeill, chief of the Clan Neill, of Taynish and Gigha, b. circa 1380, Constable of Castle Sweyne in Knapdale, co. Argyll, had a second son,
Neill McNeill, whose eldest son,
Neill McNeill of Taynish, became in 1554 his heir-at-law to Gigha. He had an eldest son,
Torquil McNeill of Taynish and Gigha, who had two sons of whom the elder,
Neill McNeill, had with other issue a second son,
Neill Oge McNeill of Terfergus and Losset, co. Argyll, had by Mary McNeill of Colonsay his wife, with other issue, a third son,
Neill McNeill, settled in co. Antrim 1676, and by his wife, Rose Stuart of Garry, co. Antrim, had with other issue, an eldest son,
Lachlan McNeill of Cushendun, co. Antrim m. Jane McNaghten of Benvarden, co. Antrim and had, with other issue, an eldest son,
Neill McNeill of Cushendun, co. Antrim, m. Christian Hamilton of Londonderry and had, beside others, an eldest son,
Edmund McNeill of Cushendun, m. Elizabeth, dau. of John Hamilton of Londonderry and d. 1790 having had, with other issue, an eldest son,
Edmund Alexander McNeill of Cushendun, J.P., b. 1787. He was in 1850 in the Court of Session, Edinburgh served heir to the entailed estate of Ugudale in Kintyre but in an action to recover possession was defeated by the prescriptive title of the occupier. He m. 20 Oct. 1817, Rose, eldest dau. of Alexander McNeile, J.P. of Colliers Hall, Ballycastle, by his wife Mary, only dau. of John McNeile, J.P. of Culreskeskin and d. 29 May 1879 having by her (who d 25 Oct. 1868) had with other children,
Edmund McNeill of Craigdunn and Cushendun, co. Antrim, J.P. and D.L. High Sheriff 1879, b. 29 Nov. 1821; m. 11 June 1851, Mary (d. 10 Dec. 1909) eldest dau. of Alexander Miller of Ballycastle, co. Antrim by Jane his wife, second dau. of Alexander McNeile, of Colliers Hall, Ballycastle and d. 28 Sept. 1915 having had with other issue,
Ronald John McNeill, **Baron Cushendun**, b. 30 April 1861; M.A. Oxford, Barrister-at-Law, Lincoln's Inn 1888, M.P. St. Augustine's Div. Kent 1911-18 and Canterbury Div. 1918-27, Under Sec. of State for Foreign Affairs 1922-24 and 1924-25, Financial Sec. to the Treasury 1925-27; Chancellor of the

Duchy of Lancaster with a seat in the Cabinet 1927-29, made P.C. and cr. a peer as Baron Cushendun of Cushendun, co. Antrim, 7 Nov. 1927. He m. 9 Oct. 1884, Elizabeth Maud, dau. of William Bolitho of Polwithin, Penzance (*B.L.G.* 1952 Bolitho of Trengwainton) and had issue,

1. Esther Rose, m. 2 Mar. 1922, Major Geoffrey Cecil Gilbert Moss, of Ford Place, Ford, co. Sussex and had issue. He assumed by deed poll 9 May 1927, the surname of McNeill-Moss.
2. Mary Morvenna Bolitho, m. 5 June 1915, Major Philip Le Grand Gribble of Kingston Russell, co. Dorset and d. 14 Sept. 1924.
3. Loveday Violet.

Mrs. McNeil d. 20 June 1925. Lord Cushendun d. 12 Oct. 1934. His seat was Cushendun, co. Antrim. Town house was 18 Cadogan Place, London, S.W. His clubs were Carlton and Ulster (Belfast).

D'ABERNON

PEERAGE—U.K. Baron D'Abernon of Esher, co. Surrey, and Viscount D'Abernon of Esher and Stoke D'Abernon, co. Surrey.
SURNAME—Vincent.
CR.—Barony, 2 July 1914. Viscounty, 20 Feb. 1926. Also a Baronetcy 26 July 1620.
EXT.—1 Nov. 1941.
HISTORY—The Vincents possessed land in Swinford, co. Leicester, ca. 1307-27, but on marriage with the heiress of Sir John Bernach of Bernach, co. Northants, in the 15th century they removed to the county of Northampton and in the 16th century to Surrey. Sir Thomas Vincent of Bernach, m. Jane, dau. and heiress of Thomas Lyfield, of Stoke D'Abernon, co. Surrey and exchanged his property at Bernach with Thomas Cecil, Earl of Exeter for lands in Surrey. He was knighted by Elizabeth I at Stoke and d. 14 Dec. 1613 when he was s. by his eldest son, Sir Francis Vincent, **1st Bt.**, of Stoke D'Abernon, co. Surrey, knighted 23 July 1603 and cr. a baronet, 26 July 1620. He m. (1) Sarah, dau. of Sir Amyas Poulet and had with other issue, an only s. son. She d. 13 June 1608 and he m. (2) Mary, dau. of Sir Henry Archer, Kt., and (3) Eleanor, dau. and heiress of Robert Malet, but had no further issue. He d. 1640 (will proved 15 May 1640) and was s. by his son, Sir Anthony Vincent, **2nd Bt.**, knighted 11 Sept. 1617, High Sheriff, cos. Surrey and Sussex 1626-27, m. Elizabeth, dau. of Sir Arthur Acland, of Killerton, co. Devon, and d. 1642. His only son, Sir Francis Vincent, **3rd Bt.**, m. (1) 1645, Catherine, dau. of George Pitt and had issue. She d. 16 Feb. 1653/4 and he m. (2) Elizabeth, dau. of Sir Henry Vane, of Hadlow, co. Kent and had further issue. He d. 1670. His eldest son, Sir Anthony Vincent, **4th Bt.**, m. Anne, dau. of Sir James Austin, and had no male issue. He d. 1674 and was s. by his brother, Sir Francis Vincent, **5th Bt.**, M.P. co. Surrey, m. Rebecca, dau. of Jonathan Aske, of London and d. 10 Feb. 1735/6 having had with other issue, an eldest son, Sir Henry Vincent, **6th Bt.**, M.P. for Guildford 1728-34, m. Elizabeth, dau. of Bazaliel Sherman, of London and d. 10 Jan. 1757, having with other

issue, an eldest son, Sir Francis Vincent, **7th Bt.**, M.P. co. Surrey 1761-63, m. (1) 25 Aug. 1741 Elizabeth, dau. and heiress of David Kilmaine, of London, banker. She d.s.p. 22 Nov. 1744. He m. (2) 13 Mar. 1745, Mary, dau. of Lt. Gen. the Hon. Thomas Howard (Effingham, E.) and by her (who d. 16 Aug. 1757) had with other issue,

1. Francis, Sir, **8th Bt.** (see below).
2. Henry Dormer, b. 1751; m. 1794, Isabella, dau. of Hon. Felton Hervey (Bristol, M.) and d. 22 May 1833 having had with other issue, a yr. son,
   Frederick, Sir, **11th Bt.** (see below).

Sir Francis m. (3) Arabella, dau. and co-heiress of Sir John Astley, Bt. and widow of A. L. Swimmer. She d.s.p. 20 June 1795. Sir Francis d. 1775 and was s. by his son, Sir Francis Vincent, **8th Bt.**, Ambassador to Venice 1790, b. 1747, m. 12 July 1779, Mary, dau. of R. M. T. Chiswell, M.P. and d. 17 Aug. 1791, having had issue with a dau., an only son, Sir Francis Vincent, **9th Bt.**, b. 1780; m. 16 Jan. 1802, Jane, dau. of Hon. Edward Bouverie (Folkeston, V.) and d. 17 Jan. 1809, having had with a yr. son, Everard, who d. 1816, an elder son, Sir Francis Vincent, **10th Bt.**, b. 3 March 1803; m. 10 May, 1824, Augusta, dau. of Hon. Charles Herbert (Carnarvon, E.) and d. 6 July 1880, having had issue an only child, Blanche, m. J. R. C. Trevilian. He was s. in the baronetcy by his cousin, The Rev. Sir Frederick Vincent, **11th Bt.**, Rector of Slinfold, co. Sussex and Preb. of Chichester, b. 8 Jan. 1798; m. (1) 26 Oct. 1826, Louisa, dau. and co-heir of John Norris of Hughenden Manor, co. Bucks and by her (d. 23 May 1841) had with other issue,

1. William, Sir, **12th Bt.** (see below).

Sir Frederick m. (2) 4 Sept. 1844, Maria Copley (d. 1899), dau. of R. H. Young of Auchenskeoch, co. Dumfries, and had with other issue,

2. Frederick D'Abernon, Sir, **15th Bt.** (see below).
3. Edgar, Sir, **16th Bt.**, and **Baron and Viscount D'Abernon** (see below).

Sir Frederick d. 9 Jan. 1883 and was s. by his eldest son, The Rev. Sir William Vincent, **12th Bt.**, M.A. Ch. Ch. Oxford, Rector of Postwick, Chm. Surrey C.C., b. 20 Sept. 1834; m. (1) 24 April 1860, Lady Margaret Erskine (d. 22 Nov. 1872), dau. of 12th Earl of Buchan, and had issue,
Francis Erskine, Sir, **13th Bt.** (see below).
He m. (2) 10 May 1882, Hester Clara, dau. of Rev. E. B. Hawkshaw and had further issue. Sir William d. 16 Feb. 1914 being s. by his only s. son, Sir Francis Erskine Vincent, **13th Bt.**, b. 24 May 1869; m. 4 July 1893, Margaret, dau. of John Holmes of Brooke Hall, co. Norfolk, and d. 28 Aug. 1935 leaving an only s. son, Sir Anthony Francis Vincent, **14th Bt.**, C.E., served in Tank Corps (Lt.) b. 30 June 1894; m. 20 Feb. 1925, Dorothy Clare, dau. of Sir Charles Falk of Derryinch, co. Fermanagh and d. 24 Feb. 1936, having had issue, two daus. He was s. by his great uncle, Sir Frederick D'Abernon Vincent, **15th Bt.**, sometime Forest Dept., India, b. 12 Feb. 1852; m. 26 Dec. 1899, Emma Julia Bertha,

dau. of the Geheimrath Dr. Getz, of Frankfort-on-Main, and d. 2 Mar. 1936, having had issue a son d. an infant and a dau. Sybil, m. D. C. Fincham. He was s. by his brother,

Sir Edgar Vincent, **16th Bt., Baron and Viscount D'Abernon,** M.P. for Exeter 1899-1906, Ambassador at Berlin 1920-26, served on many boards and commissions; was made P.C. 13 Oct. 1920, cr. K.C.M.G. 1887, G.C.M.G. 1917, G.C.B. 1926, Baron D'Abernon of Esher, co. Surrey, 2 July 1914, and Viscount D'Abernon of Esher and Stoke D'Abernon, co. Surrey, 20 Feb. 1926. He was b. 19 Aug. 1857; m. 24 Sept. 1890, Lady Helen Venetia Duncombe, dau. of 1st Earl of Feversham and d. 1 Nov. 1941.

ARMS—Azure, three quatrefoils argent.
CREST—A figure representing the head of a Greek athlete couped at the shoulders and bound around the temples with a fillet of victory argent.
SUPPORTERS—On either side a bear sejant sable muzzled gules gorged with a collar gemel or pendent therefrom an escutcheon azure charged with a chevron or.
MOTTO—Quand même.

**DALLING AND BULWER OF DALLING

PEERAGE—U.K. Baron Dalling and Bulwer of Dalling, co. Norfolk.
SURNAME—Bulwer.
CR.—23 Mar. 1871. EXT.—23 May 1872.
HISTORY—Gen. William Earle Bulwer, of Wood Dalling and Heydon, co. Norfolk, m. in 1798, Elizabeth Barbara, dau. and heiress of Richard Warburton-Lytton, of Knebworth, co. Herts., and had three sons by her (who d. 19 Dec. 1843), namely,

1. William Earle Lytton Bulwer, of Wood Dalling and Heydon, from whom the Bulwers of Heydon in B.L.G. are descended.
2. William Henry Lytton Earle, Baron Dalling etc. see below.
3. Edward George Earle-Lytton, 1st Baron Lytton, the famous novelist, for whom with his descendants see extant peerage works, under Lytton, E.

The second son, William Henry Lytton Earle Bulwer, **Baron Dalling and Bulwer** of Dalling, co. Norfolk, so cr. 23 Mar. 1871; was b. 13 Feb. 1801; educ. Harrow and Trin. Coll. and Downing Coll. Camb.; served in 1st Life Guards, 1824 and in the 58th Foot; entered Diplomatic Service, 1827, was Sec. of Legation, at Brussels, 1835-37; Sec. of Embassy at Constantinople, 1837-38, St. Petersburg, 1838-39; and Paris 1839-43; was Envoy extra-ordinary and minister plenipotentiary at Madrid, 1843-48, but was dismissed from this post having given offence to the Queen of Spain by a lecture to her; apptd. Envoy and Minister at Washington, 1849-52, at Florence 1852-54, and Ambassador at Constantinople, 1858-65; sat as Liberal M.P. for Wilton, 1830-31; for Coventry, 1831-35, and for Marylebone, 1835-37, and for Tamworth, 1868-71; made P.C. 1845; cr. K.C.B. 1848, and G.C.B. 1851; and a peer as above, 1871. He m. 9 Dec. 1848, Hon. Georgiana Charlotte Mary, dau. of Henry Wellesley, 1st Baron Cowley and d.s.p.

23 May 1872. Lady Dalling and Bulwer d. 2 Aug. 1878.
ARMS—Quarterly 1 and 4, Ermine on a chief indented azure three ducal crowns or. (Lytton); 2 and 3, Or three mullets sable pierced gules on a chief wavy azure a dove reguardant or, in the beak an olive branch vert.
CRESTS—1, A horned wolf's head erased ermine crined and armed or. 2, A dove reguardant argent in the beak an olive branch vert.
SUPPORTERS—Dexter, A dragon vert semée of crosses pattée or. Sinister, A lion reguardant ppr. gorged with a plain collar or., pendent therefrom an escutcheon argent charged with a boar's head erased sable.
MOTTO—Adversis major par secundis.

DALTON

PEERAGE—U.K. Life, Baron Dalton of Forest and Frith, co. Palatine of Durham.
SURNAME—Dalton.
CR.—28 Jan. 1960. EXT.—13 Feb. 1962.
HISTORY—The history of the Dalton family is of some antiquity, going back to Sir Richard de Dalton, of Bispham, co. Lancs, with whom the pedigree, as compiled by William Flower, Norroy King of Arms in the Visitation of Yorks in 1563-64, begins. It continues by a generation to generation descent down to the father of Lord Dalton. The full pedigree is given in the Supplement to the B.L.G. of 1952. This Supplement itself had a very interesting history. When the 1952 edition of B.L.G. was more than half way to press, an article in the Sunday Express, gave an account of the work which was being done. As a result some 200 inquiries were received at the office of Burke, requesting inclusion in the B.L.G. As the work was so much advanced, it seemed better to put these articles into a Supplement, which appeared accordingly in 1954. Among those who wished to have an entry were members of the Dalton family. The future peer did not wish to be entered, but his pedigree was none the less included for the interest which it had. For earlier generations therefore the reader is advised to see the Dalton family history as given in 1954. The Rev. John Neale Dalton, Rector of Milton Keynes, co. Buckingham, b. 1806; m. 1838, his cousin, Elisa Maria, dau. of William Allies, of Worcester, by his wife, Mary, the eldest dau. of William Edward Dalton, of Stanmore. The Rev. J. N. Dalton, d. 1880, leaving with other issue, an elder son, The Rev. Canon John Neale Dalton, who was cr. C.V.O. 1901, C.M.G. 1881, and K.C.V.O. 1911, Canon and Steward of St. George's Chapel, Windsor, 1885-1931; was Tutor and Gov. to T.R.H. Prince Albert Victor, (later Duke of Clarence) and Prince George (later King George V.); Chaplain-in-Ordinary to Queen Victoria, 1891-97, and Clerk of the Closet to Queen Victoria, Edward VII and George V, was author of several theological works, and of The Cruise of H.M.S. Bacchante. He was b. 24 Sept. 1839; was M.A. Clare Coll. Camb.; m. 1886, Catherine Alicia, dau. of Charles Evan-Thomas, (see B.L.G. 1952, Evan-Thomas of Llwyn Madoc), and d. 28 July 1931, having had issue,

Edward Hugh John Neale Dalton, **Baron Dalton** of Forest and Frith, co. Palatine of Durham, so cr. as a life peer 28 Jan. 1960; b. 1887; educ. Eton and King's Coll. Camb., B.A. 1909, M.A. 1913; D.Sc. London Univ. 1921. Barrister-at-Law, Middle Temple 1914, Hon. Bencher, 1946; served in World War I 1914-18, Lt. R.G.A., in France and Italy (awarded Italian Medal for valour 1917); M.P. Peckham Div. of Camberwell, 1924-29, Bishop Auckland 1929-31 and 1935-39, a prominent Socialist politician, Under Sec. of State for Foreign Affairs 1929-31, Min. of Economic Warfare 1940-42, Pres. Board of Trade 1942-45; Chan. of The Exchequer, July 1945-Nov. 1947 (left after the incident of the 'leak' of pre-Budget information), Chan. of Duchy of Leicester June 1948-Feb. 1950, and Min. of Town and Country Planning, Feb. 1950-Oct. 1951, made P.C. 1940, m. 1914 Ruth, Labour M.P. Bishop Auckland Feb.-May 1929, dau. of T. Hamilton Fox and d. 13 Feb. 1962. She d. 15 Mar. 1966.
ARMS—of Dalton family, (entered in 1954 B.L.G. Supplement as Dalton formerly of Stanmore). Azure, semée of cross crosslets a lion rampant guardant or.
CREST—A griffin or demi-dragon, issuant vert wings ouvert.
MOTTO—Inter cruces triumphans in Cruce.
Lord Dalton's residence was 185a, Ashley Gardens, London, S.W.1.

DALZIEL OF KIRKCALDY

PEERAGE—U.K. Baron Dalziel of Kirkcaldy, of Marylebone, London.
SURNAME—Dalziel.
CR.—28 June 1921. **EXT.**—15 July 1935. Also baronetcy cr. 25 Jan. 1918.
HISTORY—James Dalziel, Jnr. who d. in 1904 had a second son, Sir James Henry Dalziel, Bt., and **Baron Dalziel** of Kirkcaldy, b. 24 April 1868; educ. Borgue Acad., co. Kirkcudbright, Shrewsbury High Sch. and King's Coll. London; Liberal M.P. for Kirkcaldy Burghs 1892-1921. Chm. and Managing Dir. of United Newspapers Ltd., (including *Daily Chronicle*, *Lloyd's News* and *Reynold's Newspaper*), in World War I, was Chm. of Cttee, in charge of German prisoners. He was cr. Kt. Bach. 1908, a Baronet 25 June 1918 and a peer as Baron Dalziel of Kirkcaldy, of Marylebone, co. London, 28 June 1921. He m. 12 July 1928, Amy Thackery, widow of Donald Maceae of Wicklow. She d. 26 June 1935. He d.s.p. 15 July 1935.
ARMS—Azure a portcullis between three thistles leaved and slipped or.
CREST—A stag lodged ppr. collared attired and resting the dexter foot on a thistle leaved and slipped or.
SUPPORTERS—On either side a stag guardant ppr. attired or and charged on the shoulder with a plate, thereon a thistle leaved and slipped also ppr.
MOTTO—Semper audax.

DALZIEL OF WOOLER

PEERAGE—U.K. Baron Dalziel of Wooler, of Wooler, co. Northumberland.
SURNAME—Dalziel.
CR.—4 July 1927. **EXT.**—18 April 1928. Also a baronetcy cr. 14 May 1919.
HISTORY—Davison Octavian Dalziel had a son, Sir Davison Alexander Dalziel, Bt., **Baron Dalziel** of Wooler. b. Oct. 1854; M.P. Brixton 1910-23, and 1924-27, founder of Dalziel's News Agency, Chm. the Pullman Car Co. etc., cr. a baronet 14 May 1919 and Baron Dalziel of Wooler, of Wooler, co. Northumberland, 4 July 1927; m. 1876, Harriet dau. of J. G. Dunning and d. 18 April 1928.

DANESFORT

PEERAGE—U.K. Baron Danesfort, of Danesfort, co. Kerry.
SURNAME—Butcher.
CR.—19 Feb. 1924. **EXT.**—30 June 1935.
HISTORK—Robert Butcher of Ickleford, co. Hertford, lord of the manor of Ravensden, co. Bedford, was father of, Thomas Butcher of Northampton who m. Elizabeth Ives and had issue, Vice Adm. Samuel Butcher, R.N. of Danesfort, co. Kerry, b. 30 Oct. 1770; served under Lord Howe on the Glorious First of June, 1794 at Porto Rico 1801, and on the Scheldt 1813, Post Capt. 1802, Rear Adm. 1837, Vice Adm. 1847, m. 4 Feb. 1806, Elizabeth Anne, dau. of R. T. Herbert, M.P. of Cahirnane and Currens, co. Kerry. She d. 25 Nov. 1866. He d. 8 May 1849. They had issue,
1. Robert, of Cork, b. 1 Dec. 1807, m. 1826 Rebecca, dau. of John Deaves of Cork and d. 1873 leaving issue.
2. Richard George, b. 1808, b. 1815.
3. Samuel, see below.
4. Thomas Arthur, b. 24 Dec. 1812, d. 1 Mar. 1840.
5. Richard George Herbert of Dublin, M.D., F.R.C.S., M.R.I.A., Pres. of Royal Coll. Surgeons (Ireland) b. 21 April 1816, m. 7 July 1840, Julia, dau of E. Carmichael and d 1891
6. Edward Robert (1819-31).
7. George (1820-39).
8. Arthur, Major Gen. R.M.L.I. b. 10 Mar. 1822; m. 14 June 1845, Jane, dau. of Col. Charles Cox, 72nd Regt. and d. 7 July 1883 leaving issue.
9. John Barlow, Capt. R.M.L.I., b. 15 Mar. 1827; m. 6 Sept. 1852 Jane Denning, dau. of Capt. Sir William Elliot, K.C.B., R.N. and d. 26 June 1888 leaving issue.
1. Elizabeth Jane, b. 2 Jan. 1810. d. unm. 7 Sept. 1872.
2. Hilaire Frances, b. 30 Nov. 1817; m. 3 Sept. 1855, Edward Claude Lefebure and had issue.
3. Helena, b. 22 April 1823. d. 24 Aug. 1839.
4. Elizabeth Anne (1825-26).
The third son, The Most Rev. the Rt. Hon. Samuel Butcher, P.C., D.D., Bishop of Meath, b. 9 Oct. 1811; Trin. Coll. Dublin, 1829, Scholar 1832, Fell. 1837-52, D.D. 1852 Prof. of Ecclesiastical History 1850, Regius Prof. of Divinity 1852-66, Rector of Ballymoney 1854-66, Bishop of Meath 1866-76, m.

23 Nov. 1847, Mary, dau. of John Leahy of Southill, Killarney. She d. 9 June 1886. He d. 29 July 1876. They had issue,

1. Samuel Henry, of Danesfort, co. Kerry, b. 16 April 1850, B.A. and Fell. Trin. Coll. Camb. 1873, M.A. 1876, Fell. Univ. Coll. Oxford 1876, Prof. of Greek, Edinburgh 1882, M.P. Cambridge Univ. 1906-10; m. 8 June 1876, Rose Julia, dau. of Most Rev. Richard Chevenix Chevenix-French, P.C., D.D. Archbishop of Dublin (Ashtown, B.) she d. 7 April 1902. He d.s.p. 29 Dec. 1910.
2. John George Bt. and **Baron Danesfort** (3cc below).
1. Elizabeth, b. 5 Feb. 1849; m. 26 Oct. 1875, 2nd Lord Monteagle and d. 27 April 1908, leaving issue.
2. Mary Frances, b. 10 April 1854; m. 22 June 1882, Sir George Walter Prothero K.B.E. and had issue (Ernle, B.).
3. Augusta Emily, b. 10 May 1856; m. 4 April 1895, Charles Crawley M.A. and had issue.
4. Eleanor Louisa Gertrude, b. 26 April 1860, d. unm. 10 May 1894.

The second son, Sir John George Butcher, b. 15 Nov. 1853; educ. Marlborough and Trin. Coll. Camb., Scholar; Bell Univ. Scholar 1872, 8th Classic and 8th Wrangler 1874, M.A. and Fell. 1875; Barrister-at-Law, Lincoln's Inn 1878, Q.C. 1897, Bencher 1903, Treasurer 1926, mem. of Gen. Council of Bar, Tory M.P. for City of York, 1892-1906, and 1910-23; cr. a Baronet 28 June 1918 and **Baron Danesfort** of Danesfort, co. Kerry 19 Feb. 1924. He m. 9 April 1898, Alice Mary dau. of J. E. L. Brandreth. She d. 16 June 1929. He d.s.p. 30 June 1935.

ARMS—Vert an elephant argent.
CREST—A branch of a cotton tree fructed ppr.
MOTTO—Be steady.
Lord Danesfort's seat was Riccall Hall, York.

DARTREY

PEERAGE—Ireland. Baron Dartrey of Dawson's Grove, co. Monaghan, 28 May 1770. Ireland. Viscount Cremorne, 19 June 1785. Ireland. Baron Cremorne of Castle Dawson, co. Monaghan, 20 Nov. 1797.
U.K. Baron Dartrey of Dartrey, co. Monaghan, 7 Sept. 1817.
U.K. Earl of Dartrey, 20 Sept. 1847.
SURNAME—Dawson.
CR.—As set out above. **EXT.**—Irish Baron of Dartrey and Viscounty of Cremorne, 1 Mar. 1813. Irish Barony of Cremorne, and U.K. Barony of Dartrey and U.K. Earldom of Dartrey, 9 Feb. 1933.
HISTORY—Thomas Dawson, of a Yorkshire family who settled in Ireland at the end of the 16th century, was a burgess of Armagh, tempore James I, and had a son, John Dawson of Armagh, who by his wife Annie Richardson had issue, with a dau. Margaret, who m. Nov. 1696, Richard Chapell, a son, Walter Dawson of Armagh, m. (1) Mary, dau. of Edward Dixie, and (2) 2 Dec. 1680, Anne, dau. of John Jeeves of Drogheda, and d. 1704 having by his first marriage,

1. Walter, his heir.

2. Thomas, of Termonmaguirke, co. Armagh, and ancestor of the Dawsons of Charlesfort.
3. Edward.
1. Margaret, m. — Colyer, of Donegal.
2. Mary, m. Francis Foster.
3. Elizabeth, m. — Fletcher.

The eldest son, Walter Dawson, of Dawson's Grove, co. Monaghan, m. Nov. 1672, Frances, dau. of Richard Dawson, an officer in Cromwell's Army, with whom he obtained the estate of Dawson's Grove, and d. 1718, having had issue,

1. Walter, d.s.p.v.p.
2. John, m. Eleanor, dau. of James Dawson, of New Forest, co. Tipperary, and d.s.p.v.p.
3. Richard, of whom below.
1. Mary.
2. Elizabeth.

The only surv. son, Richard Dawson, of Dawson's Grove, a banker and alderman of the city of Dublin, M.P. co. Monaghan, m. 25 Feb. 1723, Elizabeth, dau. of John Vesey, Archbishop of Tuam, and sister of Sir John Vesey, Bt., Bishop of Ossory, and d. 29 Dec. 1766, having by her (who d. 4 Sept. 1730), had issue,

1. John, b. Nov. 1724; d. 1742.
2. Thomas, **1st Baron Cremorne** and **1st Viscount Cremorne** (see below).
3. Richard, of Ardee, Louth, m. 22 Aug. 1758, Anne, dau. of Sir Edward O'Brien, Bt., of Dromoland, and d. 1782, having had issue,
   (1) Richard, M.P. co. Monaghan 1797-1807, . 16 April 1762; m. 22 May 1784, Catherine, dau. of Arthur Graham, of Hockley, and d. 3 Sept. 1807, having had,
      1a. Richard Thomas, **2nd Baron Cremorne** (see below).
      1a. Penelope, Catherine, m. Jean Fidelie D'Hersant, and d. Dec. 1837.
      2a. Anna Maria, d. unm. 27 April 1883.
      3a. Eliza, m. 1814, S. B. Isaac, of Holywood House, co. Down, and d. 23 June 1850.
      4a Louisa, m. 20 Oct. 1810, Charles Coote, of Bellamont Forest, and d. 3 Nov. 1879. He d. 1843.
   (2) Edward, Lt. Col. 28th Foot, b. 1767; d.s.p.
   (3) Thomas Vesey, Very Rev., Dean of Clonmacnoise, b. 6 Nov. 1768; m. 6 Nov. 1793, Anna Maria, dau. of B. T. Balfour, and d.s.p.
   (4) Lucius Henry, Capt. R.N., d. 1795.
   (1) Mary, m. 1783, Col. Windham Quin (Dunraven, E.), and d. 1831.
   (2) Henrietta Frances, m. 28 May 1793, Col. Charles Rawdon, and had issue.
1. Frances, b. 12 Aug. 1729; m. Windham Quin, of Adare, and had issue (Dunraven, E.).

The eldest surv. son, Thomas Dawson, **1st Baron and Viscount Cremorne**, b. 25 Feb. 1725; M.P. co. Monaghan 1749-68; cr. Baron Dartrey of Dawson's Grove, co. Monaghan, in the Irish Peerage, 28 May 1770; cr. Viscount Cremorne, in the Irish Peerage, 19 June 1785. He was further cr. 20 Nov. 1797, Baron Cremorne, of Castle Dawson, co. Monaghan (Irish

Peerage), with remainder to the heirs male of his body, but failing such remainder to his nephew (see below), in like manner. He m. (1) 15 Aug. 1754, Anne, dau. of Thomas Fermor, 1st Earl of Pomfret. She d. 1 Mar. 1769. He m. (2) 8 May 1770, Philadelphia Hannah, dau. of Thomas Freame, of Philadelphia, U.S.A., by Margaretta, dau. of William Penn, the founder of that city. By his first wife he had a son, Richard, who d. 3 Mar. 1778 at Cambridge, and a dau., likewise d. young; by his second wife he had with a dau. who d. young, a son, Thomas, who d. 9 Oct. 1787, aged 16. Viscount Cremorne, d.s.p.s. 1 Mar. 1813. Viscountess Cremorne d. 14 April 1826. The Viscounty of Cremorne and Barony of Dartrey became extinct, but the Barony of Cremorne was inherited by the Viscount's great nephew,

Richard Thomas Dawson, **2nd Baron Cremorne**, b. 31 Aug. 1788; M.P. co. Monagham 1812-13; m. 10 Mar. 1815, Anne Elizabeth Emily, dau. of John Whaley, of Whaley Abbey, co. Wicklow, (she m. 2ndly 5 July 1828, Major Gen. John Dawson Rawdon, and d. 11 April 1885). The Baron Cremorne had issue,

1. Richard, **3rd Baron Cremorne**, and **1st Earl of Dartrey** (see below).
2. Thomas Vesey, Lt. Col. Coldstream Guards, b. 1819; m. 30 Jan. 1851, Hon. Augusta Frederica Annie FitzPatrick, dau. of John Wilson, 1st Lord Castletown (she m. 2ndly Charles Magniac, of Colworth, co. Bedford, and d. 24 Feb. 1903), and was k. at battle of Inkerman, 5 Nov. 1854, leaving issue,
   (1) Vesey John, C.V.O., Major Gen., col. cmdg. Irish Guards, served in Egypt, b. 4 April 1853.
   (2) Douglas Frederick Rawdon, Sir, G.C.V.O., C.M.G., Comptroller in Lord Chamberlain's Dept. 1907, Sec. of the Order of the Garter 1904, Master of Ceremonies to the King 1904-07, Lt. Col. and Brev. Col. Coldstream Guards, G.S.O. (1st grade) War Office, formerly Mil. Attaché at Vienna and in Paris, had numerous foreign orders; served in Egypt 1882, in Sudan, and in Nile expedition 1884-85, b. 25 April 1854; m. 15 Dec. 1903, Aimée Evelyn, dau. of Gordon Pirie, and widow of Herbert Oakley.

The 2nd Baron Cremorne d. 21 Mar. 1827, and was s. by his elder surv. son, Sir Richard Dawson, **1st Earl of Dartrey**, **3rd Baron Cremorne**, b. 7 Sept. 1817; cr. Baron Dartrey of Dartrey, co. Monaghan, 20 Sept. 1847, and Earl of Dartrey 12 July 1866. He was cr. K.P. 22 Feb. 1855. Lord Lt. of co. Monaghan 1871-97. He m. 12 July 1841, Augusta, dau. of Edward Stanley of Cross Hall, co. Lancaster, (Derby, E.). She d. 9 Aug. 1887. He d. 12 May 1897, having had issue,

1. Vesey, **2nd Earl of Dartrey** (see below).
2. Edward Stanley, Capt. R.N., High Sheriff co. Monaghan 1899, b. 16 Aug. 1843; m. 27 April 1898, Lady Elizabeth Meade, dau. of 4th Earl of Clanwilliam, and d. 13 Oct. 1919, having had issue, Kaitilin Elizabeth Anne, b 24 July 1900.
3. Richard Maitland Westenra, High Sheriff, co. Devon 1909, Capt. 92nd Highlanders,

b. 30 Jan. 1845; m. 20 Aug. 1878, Jane Emily, dau. of Lt. Col. S. Long, of Bromley Hill, and d. 7 Aug. 1914, having had issue,
   (1) Richard Long, of Holne Park, Ashburton, co. Devon, Capt. Coldstream Guards, b. 23 June 1879; k. in action 20 Nov. 1914.
   (1) Emily Mary, b. 31 Dec. 1881; d. unm. 24 April 1903.
   (2) Norah Phoebe, b. 14 Sept. 1883.
4. Anthony Lucius, **3rd Earl of Dartrey** (see below).
1. Mary Eleanor Anne, m. 8 Feb. 1872, 5th Earl of Ilchester and had issue.

The eldest son, Vesey Dawson, **2nd Earl of Dartrey**, b. 22 April 1842; educ. Eton; Lt. Col Coldstream Guards; M.P. co. Monaghan 1865-68; and High Sheriff 1878; m. 29 Aug. 1882, Julia Georgiana Sarah, dau. of Sir George Orby Wombwell, 4th Bt., and had issue,

1. Richard George, b. 14 Nov. 1890; d. 30 July 1894.
1. Edith Anne, b. 29 Dec. 1883; m. (1) 28 Jan. 1905, C. Douglas-Pennant, son of 2nd Baron Penrhyn, who d.s.p., k. in action, 29 Oct. 1914. She m. (2) 14 Nov. 1916, C. A. Windham.
2. Mary Augusta, b. 13 July, 1887; m. 12 June 1913, Major G. A. C. Crichton (Erne, E.), and had issue.

The 2nd Earl of Dartrey d. 14 June 1920, and was s. by his brother, Anthony Lucius Dawson, **3rd Earl of Dartrey**, b. 12 May 1855; m. 2 Oct. 1878, Mary Frances, Baroness de Ros, and d. s.p.m. 9 Feb. 1933, leaving issue, three daus. (De Ros, B.).

ARMS—Quarterly 1 and 4, Azure, on a bend engrailed or, three martlets gules. 2 and 3, Azure, three torches erect two and one argent inflamed gules.

CREST—An estoile of six points or.

SUPPORTERS—Dexter, An Irish wolf-hound. Sinister, An elk, both ppr., collared and chained or.

MOTTO—Toujours propice.

The seat of the Earls of Dartrey was Dartrey, co. Monaghan.

DAVEY

PEERAGE—U.K. Life. Baron Davey of Fernhurst, co. Sussex.

SURNAME—Davey.

CR.—13 Aug. 1894. **EXT.**—20 Feb. 1907.

HISTORY—Peter Davey of Horton, co. Bucks and Torquay, formerly of Camberwell, co. Surrey, m. Caroline Emma, dau. of the Rev. William Race, Rector of Rampisham cum Wraxall, co. Dorset, and d. 23 Mar. 1879 having had issue, a third son, Sir Horace Davey, **Baron Davey**, b. 29 Aug. 1833; educ. Rugby and Univ. Coll. Oxford, Scholar 1852, double first Mods 1854, double first Finals, B.A. 1855 and 1856, Fell. 1856-64. Johnson's Maths Sch. 1857, Senior Maths Scholar 1858, Eldon Law Scholar 1859, M.A. 1859. Barrister-at-Law 1861, Q.C. 1875, Bencher 1878; Counsel to Oxford Univ. 1877-93, Liberal M.P. Christchurch 1880-85, and for Stockton 1888-92, Solicitor Gen. 1886, cr. Kt. Bach. 1886, P.C. 1893, apptd. a Lord Justice of

Appeal, 1893-94 and a Lord of Appeal in Ordinary 13 Aug. 1894 and cr. a life peer as Baron Davey of Fernhurst, co. Sussex, 13 Aug. 1894, F.R.S. 1895. He m. 5 Aug. 1862, Louisa Hawes, dau. of John Donkin of Ormond House, Old Kent Road, co. Surrey and d. 20 Feb. 1907.

ARMS—Ermine a chevron sable between three mullets pierced gules in the centre chief point a balance or.

CREST—A demi lion ppr. holding between the paws a mullet pierced gules and supporting under the sinister paw a sword point downwards also ppr. hilt and pommel or.

SUPPORTERS On either side a lion gorged with a double chain gold, therefrom pendent a mullet pierced gules, each holding in the paw a sword erect also ppr. hilt and pommel or.

Lord Davey's seat was Verdley Place, Fernhurst, co. Sussex.

DAVIDSON OF LAMBETH

PEERAGE—U.K. Baron Davidson of Lambeth, of Lambeth, co. London.
SURNAME—Davidson.
CR.—14 Nov. 1928. EXT.—25 May 1930.
HISTORY—Henry Davidson of Edinburgh (see B.L.G. 1952, Davidson of Ockley Manor, late of Muirhouse, where his ancestry is given from 1676) m. 1845 Henrietta, (d. 1881) dau. of John Campbell Swinton of Kimmerghame, co. Berwick and had issue with two other sons and a dau., an eldest son, The Most Rev. Randall Thomas Davidson, **Baron Davidson of Lambeth**, b. 7 April 1848; educ. Harrow and Trin. Coll. Oxford, B.A. 1871. M.A. 1875, D.D. 1890; ordained deacon 1874 and priest 1875; curate of Dartford, co. Kent, 1874-77, Res. Chaplain to Archbishop of Canterbury 1877-83; hon. Chaplain to Queen Victoria, 1882-83, Dean of Windsor, Registrar of the Order of the Garter and Res. Chaplain to Queen Victoria 1883-91; Clerk of the Closet to Queen Victoria 1891-1901, and to King Edward VII 1901-03; consecrated Bishop of Rochester 25 April 1891; translated to Winchester 1895 and was Archbishop of Canterbury 1903-28 when he resigned and was cr. Baron Davidson of Lambeth, of Lambeth, co. London, 14 Nov. 1928. He was the first of the Lords Spiritual of Canterbury to resign and become a Temporal Lord. He m. 12 Nov. 1878, Edith Murdoch (d. June 1936) second dau. of the Most Rev. and Right Hon. Archibald Tait, P.C. D.C.L., 91st Archbishop of Canterbury and d.s.p. 25 May 1930. He received the Royal Victorian Chain 1911, the Grand Cross of St. Saviour of Greece 1918, Grand Cordon of Order of the Crown of Belgium 1919, and 1st class Order of St. Sava of Serbia 1919. He was made P.C. cr. K.C.V.O. 1902 and G.C.V.O. 1904. He was one of the four Counsellors of State during the absence in India of King George V, 1911-12 and during the King's absence abroad 1925.

ARMS—Azure on a chevron or, between two mullets in chief and a pheon in base argent, a fleur-de-lis gules, in the chief point a martlet for difference.

Lord Davidson lived at 10 Cheyne Walk, S.W.3. His club was the Athenaeum. He wrote a few books including the *Life of Archbishop Tait*, (his father-in-law) in 2 vols. 1891.

**DAWNAY OF COWICK

PEERAGE—G.B. Baron Dawnay of Cowick.
SURNAME—Dawnay.
CR.—9 June 1796. EXT.—18 Feb. 1832.
HISTORY—John Christopher Burton Dawnay, 5th Viscount Downe, (in the Irish peerage), (see extant peerage works, Downe, V.) b. 15 Nov. 1764; sat as Whig M.P. for Petersfield, 1787-90; was cr. 9 June 1796, **Baron Dawnay** of Cowick, co. York, in peerage of Great Britain. He m. (1) a ygr. dau. and coheiress of Major John Scott of Balconie. She d. 1798. He m. (2) 31 Dec. 1815, Louisa Maria, dau. of George Welstead, of Apsley, co. Sussex. He d.s.p. 18 Feb. 1832, when the Barony of Dawnay became extinct but when he was s. in the Viscounty by his brother, William Henry Dawnay, 6th Viscount Downe etc.

DAWSON OF PENN

PEERAGE—U.K. Baron Dawson of Penn. Viscount Dawson of Penn, co. Buckingham.
SURNAME—Dawson.
CR.—Barony 8 Feb. 1920. Viscounty 30 Oct. 1936. EXT.—7 Mar. 1945.
HISTORY—Henry Dawson, F.R.I.B.A., of Purley, co. Surrey, had issue, Sir Bertrand Edward Dawson, **Baron and Viscount Dawson** of Penn, educ. Univ. Coll. London, and the London Hospital, M.D. 1893, B.Sc. 1888, M.R.C.S. 1890, F.R.C.P., 1903; Physician Extraordinary to Edward VII, 1907-10, and George V 1910-14, physician in ordinary 1914-36, to George V and Queen Mary, Pres. Royal Coll. of Physicians 1931, served in World War I, Capt. R.A.M.C. (T.F.) Col. A.M.S. and promoted Major Gen., mentioned in despatches. Cr. K.C.V.O. 1911, C.B. 1916, G.C.V.O. 1917, K.C.M.G. 1919, Baron Dawson of Penn, co. Buckingham, 9 Feb. 1920, and Viscount Dawson of Penn, 30 Oct. 1936, and made P.C. 1929. He m. 18 Dec. 1900, Minnie Ethel, O.B.E., dau. of Sir Alfred Yarrow, 1st Bt., and d. 7 Mar. 1945 having had three daus.

ARMS—Ermines on a pale argent a rod of Aesculapius gules on a chief engrailed or three martlets of the third.

CREST—Upon a mount vert, between two wings sable, as many torches in saltire inflamed ppr.

SUPPORTERS—On either side a wolf sable, muzzled, collared and chained, the chain reflexed over the back or.

MOTTO—Droit et avant.

DE BLAQUIERE

PEERAGE—Ireland. Baron De Blaquiere of Ardkill, co. Londonderry.
SURNAME—De Blaquiere.
CR.—30 July 1800. Also a baronetcy, dated 16 July 1784. EXT.—28 July 1920.
HISTORY—John Blaquiere or Jean de Blaquiere, of Greenwich, London, who is said to have been one of the French refugees of 1685, after the revocation of the Edict of Nantes, when he would have been aged nine, m. Mary Elizabeth, dau. of Pierre de Varennes, a

Frenchman who was a bookseller in the Strand, London, and d. 22 April 1753, aged 77, having had with other issue, a 5th son, John Blaquiere, **1st Baron de Blaquiere**, b. 15 May 1732; Lt. Col. 17th Dragoons; Sec. of Legation in France, 1771-72; Chief Sec. to the Lord Lt. of Ireland, 1772-77; M.P. for Old Leighlin, 1773-83, Carlingford, 1783-90, Charleville, 1790-97, and Newtownards, 1797-1800; he was later M.P. in the U.K. Parliament for Rye, 1801-02, and for Downton, 1803-06; was made P.C., of Ireland, 1772; cr. K.B. 1774, a baronet of Ireland, 16 July 1784, and a peer of Ireland as Baron De Blaquiere, of Ardkill, co. Londonderry, 30 July 1800. He was F.R.S. and F.S.A., 1703, and granted the office of Alnager, 1775, which was abolished in 1817. (For this office he arranged to receive in lieu on surrender to his son, £1,000 per year, and on the abolition this was commuted to a pension for the 2nd Baron). He m. 24 Dec. 1775, Eleanor, dau. of Robert Dobson, of Anne's Grove, co. Cork, and d. 27 Aug. 1812, having had issue,

1. John, **2nd Baron** (see below).
2. William, **3rd Baron** (see below).
3. George, in the Army, served at Corunna, b. 27 July 1782; d.s.p. 1826.
4. Peter Boyle, b. 27 April 1784; served in R.N. as a midshipman under Capt. Bligh of the *Bounty*, and was present at the battle of Camperdown. He settled in Canada, and was mem. of Legislative Council and Chancellor of Univ. of Toronto. He m. (1) 13 Sept. 1804, Eliza (who d. 9 June 1814), dau. of Denis O'Brien, of Newcastle, co. Limerick, and had issue by her. He m. (2) 26 Nov. 1818, Eliza, dau. of William Roper, of Rathfarnham Castle, co. Dublin. She d. 1881. He d. 23 Oct. 1860, having had further issue by her. By his first marriage he had.
 (1) Peter Townshend, Lt. 46th Regt., b. 15 Sept. 1805; d.s.p. 4 Aug. 1838.
 (2) George, Capt. 8th Madras N.I., b. 20 Oct. 1806; d.s.p. at Madras, 1834.
 (3) William, registrar and notary, Supreme Court, Bombay, 1844; b. 10 July 1810; m. 1 Jan. 1846, Rebecca, dau. of W. H. Cannon, of Reading, co. Berks, and d. 23 May 1882, leaving an only child, Elizabeth Sophia Josephine, d. 25 Dec. 1885.
 (4) John, Midshipman R.N., on *Acorn*, b. 24 June 1812; lost at sea, April 1828.
 (1) Eliza Cecilia, m. at Jersey, 19 Nov. 1844, Michael Elijah Treeve, 2nd son of Capt. Treeve, and grandson of Sir Elijah Impey, and d. 27 Nov. 1891.
 (2) Anna Maria, m. 6 Oct. 1831, Samuel Le Fevre, collector of customs at Barbados, and d. 4 April 1860.
 (3) Eleanor, m. 26 April 1832, Lt. Col. Le Fevre, H.E.I.C.S., and d. 15 June 1859.
By his second marriage, Peter Boyle de Blaquiere had issue,
 (5) Charles, b. 7 Nov. 1819; m. (1) 1 Sept. 1848, Agnes, widow of W. Lawson, who d. 1864, leaving issue,
  1a Peter Henry, b. 5 Aug. 1849; d. unm. April 1887.
  2a William, **6th Baron de Blaquiere** (see below).

  1a Louisa Agnes, m. 25 Dec. 1875 John Matheson, of Woodstock, Canada, barrister. He d. 1878.
 Charles de Blaquiere m. (2) 18 April 1865, Caroline Dora, dau. of Rev. William Bettridge, B.D., Rector of Woodstock, Canada, and d. at Woodstock, 16 July 1689, leaving no further issue.
 (6) Henry, b. 11 May 1821; m. 11 Oct. 1848, Margaret Lucretia, dau. of Col. Alexander Whalley Light, 25th Regt. and d.s.p. 27 Jan. 1889.
 (7) George, b. 13 Aug. 1834; m. Jan. 1882, Eliza, dau. of Charles Judd, of Kaurie Hall, Pukekaroro, N.Z., and d.s.p.
 (4) Louisa Emily, m. 3 Feb. 1846, A.A. Farmer, of Woodlands, Upper Canada, brother of W. F. G. Farmer, of Nonsuch Park, co. Surrey, and d. 8 May 1868, leaving issue.
 (5) Augusta Caroline, m. 3 Oct. 1848, A. H. Farmer, and had issue.
 (6) Georgiana Lucy, m. 26 May 1849, Lt. Col. H. D. Crofton, (Crofton, Bt.) and had issue.
 (7) Isabel Elise, m. 1 Sept. 1870, Gen. Sir William Pollexfen Radcliffe, and had issue.
 (8) Harriette Sophia, d. unm. 17 Aug. 1900.
1. Anna Maria, m. Viscount Kirkwall, and had issue, (Orkney, E.), and d. 1843.
2. Elizabeth, m. 1807, John Barnard Hankey, of Fetcham Park, co. Surrey, (B.L.G. 1952 Barnard-Hankey of Plush Manor), and d. 11 Jan. 1870.
3. Eleanor, m. 1822, Joseph Knight, and d. 23 July 1867.
The eldest son, John de Blaquiere, **2nd Baron De Blaquiere**, b. 5 Nov. 1776, a prisoner in France at the time of his father's death; and d. unm. 7 April 1844, when he was s. by his next brother,

William de Blaquiere, **3rd Baron De Blaquiere**, b. 27 Jan. 1778; entered the Army, and served in Flanders, at the Cape of Good Hope, and in India; Major Gen. 1813; Lt. Gen. 1825; Gen. 1841; F.R.S. 1805; m. 16 Sept. 1811, Harriet, dau. of 1st Marquess Townshend, and d. 12 Nov. 1851, "having committed suicide by shooting himself while suffering from smallpox" (*C.P.*), and having had issue by her (who d. 9 Nov. 1848),
1. John, **4th Baron** (see below).
2. William Barnard, **5th Baron** (see below).
1. Rose, b. 27 Oct. 1813 and d. 11 Feb. 1818.
The elder son, John de Blaquiere, **4th Baron De Blaquiere**, Capt. 3rd West India Foot, 1844, and Capt. 41st Foot, 1854, b. 2 July 1812; m. (1) 28 July 1849, Anna, dau. of John Christie. She d. 18 Feb. 1851. He m. (2) 25 Nov. 1852, Eleanor Amelia, dau. of 1st Baron Hylton, and d.s.p. 2 Jan. 1871. Lady De Blaquiere d. 11 Jan. 1894. The 4th Baron was s. by his brother,

William Barnard de Blaquiere, **5th Baron De Blaquiere**, b. 16 Dec. 1814; served in R.N., Capt. 1873; m. 25 Sept. 1862, Anna Maria, dau. of John Wormald, of Brockworth Manor, co. Gloucester, and d.s.p. 24 Nov. 1889. He was s. by his cousin, (see above),

William de Blaquiere, **6th Baron De Blaquiere**, b. 5 Sept. 1856; m. 25 Jan. 1888. Lucienne, dau. of George Desbarats, of

PLATE 8

BARON DESBOROUGH.

BARON DUNSANDLE AND CLAN CONAL.

BARON EMLY.

BARON ESTCOURT.

BARON EVERSLEY.

EARL FARQUHAR.

PLATE 9

DUKE OF FIFE.

BARON FITZMAURICE.

VISCOUNT FRANKFORT DE MONTMORENCY.

BARON GLANTAWE.

BARON GLENESK.

BARON GWYDYR.

Montreal, and d. 28 July 1920, having had issue,
1. John. Lt. Scottish Rifles, Jan. 1913; b. 1 Aug. 1889; k. in action, 10 Mar. 1915.
2. Alan Boyle, sub. Lt. R.N., b. 28 Mar. 1895; lost in H.M.S. *Laurentic*, 25 Jan. 1917.
1. Kathleen, b. 17 Feb. 1891; m. 21 Sept. 1911, 2nd Lord Dorchester, and had issue.

ARMS—Ermine a lion rampant sable charged on the shoulder with an estoile or.
CREST—A garb, ppr. banded or.
SUPPORTERS—Dexter, A lion sable, collared and chained, charged on the shoulder with an estoile or; Sinister, A tiger, ppr. ducally gorged and chained or.
MOTTO—Tiens la verité.
The seat of the peer was Brockworth Manor, Glos.

DE FREYNE OF ARTAGH

PEERAGE—U.K. Baron De Freyne of Artag.
SURNAME—French.
CR.—16 May 1839. **EXT.**—29 Sept. 1856.
HISTORY—Arthur French, of French Park, co. Roscommon, a member of the family whose history is given in extant peerage works under De Freyne, B., ffrench, B. and Ypres, E., had an eldest son, Arthur French, who was b. about 1786; sat as Whig M.P. for co. Roscommon, 1821-32; was cr. on 16 May 1839, Baron De Freyne of Artagh, co. Roscommon, but as he had no male issue, he was cr. on 5 April, 1851, Baron De Freyne of Coolavin, co. Sligo with a special remainder, to his brothers, John, Charles, and FitzStephen, failing the issue male of his own body. Lord Lt. of co. Roscommon, 1854-56. He m. 1818 Mary, dau. of Christopher McDermott, of Cregga, and d.s.p. 29 Sept. 1856, when the Barony of De Freyne of the first (1839) creation became extinct, and he was s. in the Barony of 1851 by his brother, The Rev. John French, 2nd Baron De Freyne, for whom see extant peerages under De Freyne, B.
ARMS—Ermine a chevron sable.
CREST—A dolphin embowed ppr.
SUPPORTERS—Dexter, an ancient Irish warrior, habited supporting with his dexter hand a battle axe, head downwards and bearing on his sinister arm a shield all ppr. Sinister, A female figure vested and scarf flowing argent all ppr.
MOTTO—Malo mori quam foedari.

DE MONTALT

PEERAGE—U.K. Earl De Montalt of Dundrum, co. Tipperary.
SURNAME—Maude.
CR.—9 Sept. 1886. **EXT.**—9 Jan. 1905.
HISTORY—Cornwallis Maude, 4th Viscount Hawarden, b. 4 April 1817; a representative peer for Ireland 1862; cr. 9 Sept. 1886, **Earl De Montalt** of Dundrum, co. Tipperary; m. 24 Mar. 1845, Clementina Elphinstone, eldest dau. and coheiress of Adm. the Hon. Charles Fleming, son of 11th Lord Elphinstone and d.s.p.m.s. 9 Jan. 1905, leaving issue seven daus.

(see extant peerages). The Earldom became extinct and the Viscounty (with the Barony of De Montalt, and a Baronetcy) were inherited by the 1st and last Earl De Montalt's cousin, Robert Henry Maude, 5th Viscount Hawarden.
ARMS—Quarterly 1 and 4, Azure a lion rampant argent; 2 and 3, Argent three bars gemelles sable, over all a lion rampant gules, charged on the shoulder with a cross-crosslet fitchée or.
CREST—A lion's gamb erased and erect ppr. holding an oak branch slipped vert, acorned or.
SUPPORTERS—Two lions rampant gules each charged on the breast with a cross-crosslet fitchée or.
MOTTO—Virtute securum.

NOTE. It is of interest that the arms of Maude impaled by Warner appear on one of the very rare 20th century hatchments, this being in Thorpe Morieux Church. Lady Leucha Diana Maude, 6th dau. of the Earl de Montalt was wife of Sir Courtenay Warner, 1st Bt., and is bur. with him at Thorpe Morieux.

DESART

PEERAGE—I. Baron Desart of Desart, co. Kilkenny. I. Viscount Desart.
I. Earl of Desart and Viscount Castlecuffe. U.K. Baron Desart.
SURNAME—Cuffe.
CR.—I. Barony 10 Nov. 1732. I. Viscounty 6 Jan. 1781. I Earldom etc. 20 Dec. 1793. U.K. Barony 12 May 1909. **EXT.**—4 Nov. 1934.
HISTORY—The family of Cuffe went from Somerset and Northampton to Ireland where on 28 Nov. 1598 Hugh Cuffe had a grant of 6,000 acres in co. Cork, and settled at Cuffe's Wood. He had issue only two daus., and the male line continued through his nephew, Maurice Cuffe, of Ennis, co. Clare, a merchant who d. in 1638 and whose sixth son, Joseph Cuffe, served under Cromwell and received large grants of land. He m. Martha, dau. of Col. Agmondesham Muschamp and had twenty children by her, of whom the eldest, Agmondesham Cuffe, was attainted by James II's Irish Parliament in 1689 but was restored by William III. He m. Anne, dau. of Sir John Otway of London, and d. 1727 leaving an eldest son,
    John Cuffe, **1st Baron Desart**, of Kilkenny, M.P., cr. Baron Desart, 10 Nov. 1733, m. (1) Margaret, only dau. and heir of James Hamilton, of Carnesure. She d.s.p. He m. (2) Dorothea, dau. of Gen. Gorges of Kilbrew, co. Meath and had with other issue,
    1. John, **2nd Baron** (see below).
    2. Otway, **3rd Baron** (see below).
Lord Desart d. 1749 and was s. by his eldest son, John Cuffe, **2nd Baron Desart**, m. 1752, Sophia, dau. and heir of Brettridge Badham, of Rockfield, co. Cork and had issue three daus. He d. 1767 being s. by his brother,
    Otway Cuffe, **3rd Baron Desart, 1st Viscount Desart**, 6 Jan. 1781, and **1st Earl** of Desart and Viscount Castlecuffe, 20 Dec. 1793. He m. 18 Aug. 1785, Lady Anne ,Browne, dau. of 2nd Earl of Altamont. He d. 9 Aug. 1804 having had issue with two daus. a son,

John Otway Cuffe, **2nd Earl of Desart,** b. 20 Feb. 1788; m. 7 Oct. 1817, Catherine (who m. 2ndly R. L. Price and d. 1874), dau. and co-heir of Maurice O'Connor, of Mount Pleasant, King's County, and d. 22 Nov. 1820, leaving an only son,

Otway O'Connor, **3rd Earl of Desart,** a representative peer, b. 12 Oct. 1818; m. 28 June 1842, Elizabeth Lucy, dau. of 1st Earl Cawdor, and d. 1 April 1865, having had with a third son, d.s.p. and a dau.,

1. William Ulick O'Connor, **4th Earl** (see below).
2. Hamilton John Agmondesham, **5th Earl** (see below).

The eldest son, William Ulick O'Connor Cuffe, **4th Earl of Desart,** b. 10 July 1845, m. (1) 1 June 1871, Maria Emma Georgiana (m. diss. by div. 1878), dau. of T. H. Preston, of Moreby, co. Yorks, and had issue, a dau. He m. (2) 27 April 1881, Ellen, dau. of Henri L. Bischoffsheim and d. 15 Sept. 1898, being s. by his brother,

Sir Hamilton John Agmondesham Cuffe, **5th Earl of Desart,** b. 30 Aug. 1848, Barrister 1872; Solicitor to the Treasury and Queen's Proctor 1894-1909, cr. K.P., K.C.B., and Baron Desart of Desart, co. Kilkenny, in the U.K. peerage, and made P.C. He m. 19 July 1876, Lady Margaret Lascelles, dau. of 4th Earl of Harewood and d. 4 Nov. 1934, leaving issue two daus.

ARMS—Argent on a bend dancettée sable, between two plain cotises azure each charged with three bezants, as many fleur-de-lis of the first.
CREST—A cubit arm erect, vested or, charged with two bendlets undée azure, cuffed ermine, hand ppr., holding a pole axe of the first, staff of the second.
SUPPORTERS—Two leopards reguardant ppr. each gorged with a collar indented sable charged with three fleur-de-lis argent and chained of the second.
MOTTO—Virtus repulsae nescia sordidae.

DESBOROUGH

PEERAGE—U.K. Baron Desborough of Taplow, co. Buckingham.
SURNAME—Grenfell.
CR.—30 Dec. 1905. EXT. 9 Jan. 1945.
HISTORY—Pascoe Grenfell, merchant of Penzance, son of John Grenfell, b. 1692; m. (1) 29 Nov. 1718, Mary Edwards, who d.s.p. 1719; m. (2) Mary, dau. of John Maugham, of Marazion and d. 1752 leaving with other issue, a second son,

Pascoe Grenfell of Marazion, Consul of Holland, b. 1729; m. 13 Dec. 1758, Mary, dau. of William Tremenheere and d. 27 May 1810 leaving with other issue, an eldest son, Pascoe Grenfell, D.C.L., M.P. for Marlow and afterwards for Penrhyn, b. 3 Sept. 1761; m. (1) 26 Aug. 1786, his cousin, Charlotte Grenfell, and by her (d. 2 May 1790) had issue with others, a second son, Charles Pascoe (see below).

He m. (2) 15 Jan. 1798, Hon. Georgiana St. Leger, dau. of 1st Viscount Doneraile and had further issue (Grenfell, B.). He d. 23 Jan. 1838 and was s. by his son,

Charles Pascoe Grenfell, of Taplow Court, M.P. Preston, b. 4 April 1790; m. 22 June 1819, Lady Georgiana Molyneux, dau. of 2nd Earl of Sefton and d. 21 Mar. 1867, leaving with other issue,

1. Charles William, M.P. Sandwich 1847-52, and later for Windsor, b 17 Mar. 1823; m. 20 July 1852, Georgina, dau. of W. S. Lascelles (Harewood, E.) and d.v.p. 4 May 1861, leaving with other issue,
   William Henry, **Baron Desborough** (see below).
2. Henry Riversdale, M.P. for Stoke-upon-Trent, Director and Gov. of the Bank of England, b. 5 April 1824; m. 25 July 1867, Alethea Louisa, dau. of H. T. Adeane, and d. 11 Sept. 1902, leaving with a dau. Maud,
   Edward Charles, cr. Baron St. Just.

Charles Pascoe Grenfell's grandson, Sir William Henry Grenfell, **Baron Desborough,** b. 30 Oct. 1855; educ. Balliol Coll. Oxford, B.A., Hon. Fell. 1928; M.P. for Salisbury 1880-82 and 1885-86, for Hereford 1892-93 and for Wycombe div. of Bucks 1900-05, High Sheriff, Bucks. 1890, Pres. Brit. Chamber of Commerce, and Pres. of the London Chamber of Commerce, cr. Baron Desborough, of Taplow, co. Bucks, 30 Dec. 1905, C.V.O. 1907, K.C.V.O. 1908, G.C.V.O. 1925 and K.G. 1928. He m. 17 Feb. 1887 Ethel Anne Priscilla, dau. of Hon. Julian Fane (Westmorland, E.) and a co-heir of the barony of Butler (Lucan, B.). They had issue two sons Julian and Gerald both k. in World War I and a third son, Ivo, d. 1926 as a result of a motor accident, and two daus. Monica Margaret and Alexandra Imogen. Lord Desborough d. 9 Jan. 1945.
ARMS—Gules on a fesse between three organ rests or a mural crown of the field.
CREST—On a mural crown gules a griffin passant or, holding in the beak a sprig of laurel ppr.
SUPPORTERS—On either side a griffin or collared gules supporting a spear ppr., flowing therefrom a banner of the second charged with an organ rest as in the arms.
The Grenfell seats were Taplow Court, Taplow, Bucks. and Panshanger, Hertford.

DE TABLEY

PEERAGE—U.K. Baron De Tabley of Tabley House, co. Chester.
SURNAME—Leicester, previously Byrne.
CR.—10 July 1826. EXT.—22 Nov. 1895.
HISTORY—Sir John Fleming Leicester, 5th Bt., was the son and heir of Sir Peter Byrne, afterwards Leicester, 4th Bt. (see extant peerage works), and was b. 4 April 1762; he s. his father in the baronetcy and the family estates 12 Feb. 1770; educ. Trin. Coll. Cambridge, M.A. 1784; was Whig M.P. for Yarmouth, Isle of Wight 1791-96, for Heytesbury 1796-1802, and for Stockbridge, 1807; High Sheriff co. Cheshire 1804-05. He was cr. 10 July 1826, **Baron De Tabley** of Tabley House, co. Chester, and m. 10 Nov. 1810, Georgina Maria, dau. of Lt. Col. Joseph Cottin, and d. 18 June 1827, having by her (who m. 2ndly her late husband's nephew, Rev. F. Leicester and d. 5 Nov. 1859) had issue,

1. George, **2nd Baron** (see below).
2. William Henry, Gren. Guards, b 4 July 1813; d. 1845.

The elder son, Sir George Fleming Leicester, afterwards Warren, **2nd Baron De Tabley**, b. 28 Oct. 1811; educ. Eton and Ch. Ch. Oxford; assumed the surname of Warren in lieu of that of Leicester, with the arms only of Warren, on 18 Feb. 1832, in compliance with the will of his cousin, the Dowager Viscountess Bulkeley, on coming into her Lancashire estates. He was apptd. a Lord in Waiting, 1853-58, and 1859-66; Treasurer of the Household 1868-72; made P.C. 1869; m. (1) 21 June 1832, Catharina Barbara, dau. of Jerome, Count De Salis-Saglio. She d. 20 Feb. 1869. He m. (2) 26 Jan. 1871, Elizabeth, dau. of Shalcross Jacson, of Newton Bank, co. Chester, and widow of James Hugh Smith-Barry, and d. 19 Ot. 1887. She d. 14 Mar. 1915. They had issue,
1. John Byrne Leicester, **3rd Baron** (see below).
2. Francis Peter Leicester, (1842-45).
1. Catherine Leicester, d. 9 May, 1881.
2. Meriel Leicester, m. 31 Jan. 1862, Allen A. Bathurst, (6th Earl Bathurst) and d. 6 July 1872, having had issue.
3. Eleanor Leicester, who assumed by deed poll, 24 May 1900, the surname of Leighton-Warren instead of Leig*k*ton, she having m. 1864, Sir Baldwyn Leighton 8th Bt., and d. 14 Aug. 1914.
4. Margaret Leicester, m. 1875, Sir Arthur Keppel Cowell-Stepney, 2nd Bt. and d. 1921 leaving issue.

The elder son, Sir John Byrne Leicester Warren, 7th Bt., and **3rd Baron De Tabley**, was b. 26 April 1835; educ. Eton and Ch. Ch. Oxford, B.A. 1859, and M.A. 1860; Barrister-at-Law, Lincoln's Inn, 1860; F.S.A. 1883. He was a poet (writing as G. F. Preston or William Lancaster), a scholar, numismatist and botanist. He d. unm. 22 Nov. 1895, when the barony became extinct, but the baronetcy passed to his cousin, Sir Peter Fleming Frederic Leicester, 8th Bt. (see extant peerages).
ARMS—Chequy or and azure, on a canton gules a lion rampant argent (i.e. Warren following the assumption mentioned above).
CREST—On a chapeau gules turned up ermine, a wyvern argent, wings elevated, chequy or and azure.
SUPPORTERS—Two wyverns argent, wings elevated chequy or and azure.
MOTTO—Tenebo.
The seat of the family was Tabley House, near Knutsford, co. Chester. The London residence was 62 Elm Park Road, S.W. The 3rd Baron's clubs were Travellers' and Athenaeum.

DE VESCI

PEERAGE—U.K. Baron De Vesci of Abbey Leix in Queen's County.
SURNAME—Vesey.
CR.—8 Nov. 1884. EXT.—6 July 1903.
HISTORY—John Robert William Vesey, 4th Viscount de Vesci, Baron Knapton in Ireland, and an Irish Baronet, was b. 21 May 1844; was cr. Baron de Vesci of Abbey Leix, Queen's County, 8 Nov. 1884; m. 4 June, 1872 Lady Evelyn Charteris, dau. of 10th Earl of Wemyss

and d.s.p.m. 6 July 1903, when the U.K. Barony of 1884 became extinct and he was s. in his Irish titles by his nephew, Yvo Richard Vesey, 5th Viscount De Vesci, (extant peerages).
ARMS—Or, on a cross, sable a patriarchal cross of the field.
CREST—A hand erect in armour holding a laurel branch all ppr.
SUPPORTERS—Two figures of Hercules each holding in his exterior hand a club over his shoulder, habited about the middle all ppr.
MOTTO—Sub hoc signo vinces.

DEWAR

PEERAGE—U.K. Baron Dewar, of Homestall, co. Sussex.
SURNAME—Dewar.
CR.—20 May 1919. EXT.—11 April 1930. Also a baronetcy cr. 23 June 1917.
HISTORY—Thomas Robert Dewar, **Baron Dewar**, was the fifth son of John Dewar, of Perth, and Pittendyne, Moneydie, co. Perth. (see extant peerages, Forteviot, B.). He was b. 6 Jan. 1864; educ. Perth and Edinburgh; Managing Director of the firm of John Dewar and Sons Ltd., Perth; keen follower of coursing, winning the Waterloo Cup at Altcar in 1915; mem. L.C.C. for West Marylebone, 1892-95; Lt. for the City of London, Sheriff, 1897-98; M.P. St. George's Div., Tower Hamlets, 1900-06; cr. Kt. Bach. 1902, a Baronet 23 June 1917, and a peer as Baron Dewar, of Homestall, co. Sussex, 20 May 1919, and d. unm. 11 April 1930.
ARMS—Per saltire or and azure, a seax erect ppr., surmounted by a saltire engrailed per saltire of the second and first, between two cinquefoils in fess also of the first.
CREST—Between two thistles, leaved and slipped ppr., a cock gules, armed and spurred argent, charged on the breast with a cinquefoil or.
SUPPORTERS—On a compartment of grass semée of thistles ppr.; Dexter, A goat sable; Sinister, A greyhound ppr., collared gules.
MOTTO—Gloria patri.
Lord Dewar's seat was The Homestall, Ashurst Wood, co. Sussex.

**DIGBY

PEERAGE—Great Britain. Viscount Coleshill, co. Warwick, and Earl Digby, co. Lincoln.
SURNAME—Digby.
CR.—Viscount, and Earl 1 Nov. 1790. EXT.—12 May 1856.
HISTORY—Henry Digby, 7th Baron Digby of Geashill, King's Co. in the peerage of Ireland (see extant peerages, Digby, B.) b. 21 July 1731; was M.P. for Luggershall, 1755-61; and for Wells, 1761-65; Under Sec. of State for the South, 1755-56; a Lord of the Admiralty, 1763-65; was cr. Baron Digby of Sherborne, co. Dorset, in the peerage of Great Britain, 13 or 19 Aug. 1765, with a special remainder, in event of his having no male issue, to the male issue of his father. On 1 Nov. 1790, he was cr. **Viscount Coleshill**, co. Warwick, and **Earl Digby**, co. Lincoln, with usual remainder. He m. (1) 5 Sept. 1763, Elizabeth,

dau. of Hon. Charles Feilding, (Denbigh, E.). She d.s.p. 19 Jan. 1765. He m. (2) 10 Nov. 1770, Mary, dau. of John Knowler, Recorder of Canterbury. She d. 26 Feb. 1794. He d. 25 Sept. 1793, having had issue, by his second marriage,

1. Edward, **2nd Earl** and 8th Baron (see below).
2. Robert, Rev., b. 10 April 1775; d. 25 Sept. 1830.
1. Charlotte Maria, m. 22 July 1796, William Wingfield-Baker and d. 15 May 1807, leaving issue. (see B.L.G. 1952, Wingfield-Digby of Sherborne Castle and Coleshill).

The elder son, Edward Digby, **2nd Earl** and 8th Baron Digby, b. 6 Jan. 1773; educ. Ch. Ch. Oxford, 1790; Lord Lt. of Dorset, 1808-56; d. unm. 12 May 1856, when the Earldom of Digby and the Viscounty of Coleshill, became extinct, but the English barony of Digby of Sherborne, and the Irish Barony of Digby were inherited by his cousin, Edward St. Vincent Digby, who thus became 9th Baron Digby.
ARMS—Azure a fleur-de-lis argent.
CREST—An ostrich, holding in the beak a horseshoe, all ppr.
SUPPORTERS—Two monkeys ppr. environed about the middle and lined or.
MOTTO—Deo non fortuna.
This article, as indicated by the asterisk, comes within the date of Burke's Extinct Peerage of 1883, but is mentioned therein only with a reference to the extant peerage.

DONINGTON

PEERAGE—U.K. Baron Donington of Donington Park, co. Leicester.
SURNAME—Abney-Hastings formerly Clifton, and finally Clifton-Hastings-Campbell.
CR.—4 May 1880. **EXT.**—31 May 1927.
HISTORY—Thomas Clifton, of Clifton and Lytham (1788-1851) had with other issue (for which see *B.L.G.* 1952, Clifton of Lytham), a third son, Charles Frederick (Clifton) Abney-Hastings, **1st Baron Donington** of Donington Park, co. Leicester, b. 17 June 1822; educ. Eton and Ch. Ch. Oxford, B.A. 1845 and M.A. 1848; m. 30 April 1853, Lady Elizabeth Maud Hastings, eldest dau. of 2nd Marquess of Hastings, and heiress of her brother, Henry, 4th Marquess, as Countess of Loudoun in her own right. She s. her brother as Countess of Loudoum, on 10 Nov. 1868, and in Nov. 1871 she became also suo jure Baroness Botreaux, Hungerford, Moleyns, and Hastings, by the termination of the abeyance of those four baronies in her favour. She d. 23 Jan. 1874, aged 40. In 1859 by Act of Parliament her husband and herself assumed the surname of Abney-Hastings in place of that of Clifton, together with the arms of Abney-Hastings, in compliance with the settlement effected by Sir Charles Abney-Hastings, 2nd Bt. in 1844, he being a relative of the Countess of Loudoun. Mr. Charles Frederick Abney-Hastings was cr. 4 May 1880, Baron Donington, of Donington Park, co. Leicester. He d. 24 July, 1895. They had issue, with others (for whom see extant peerage, under Loudoun, E.),

1. Charles Edward Rawdon-Hastings, formerly Abney-Hastings, 11th Earl Loudoun, and **2nd Baron Donington** (see below).
2. Gilbert Theophilus Clifton Clifton Hastings Campbell, **3rd Baron Donington** (see below).

The eldest son, Charles Edward Hastings Rawdon-Hastings, 11th Earl Loudoun and **2nd Baron Donington**, b. 5 Jan. 1855; m. 4 Feb. 1880, the Hon. Alice Elizabeth FitzAlan Howard, dau. of Lord Howard of Glossop, and d. 17 May 1920, being then s. in the Loudoun Earldom, and other titles, by his niece, Edith Maud, 12th holder of the title, Countess of Loudoun, and in the barony of Donington by his brother,

Gilbert Theophilus Clifton Clifton-Hastings-Campbell, **3rd Baron Donington**, who assumed the surname and arms of Clifton-Hastings-Campbell by royal licence 2 Jan. 1896. He was b. 29 May 1859; m. 12 July 1894, Maud, Kemble, dau. of Sir Charles Edward Hamilton, 1st Bt. and had issue four daus.,

1. Margaret Selina Flora Maud, b. 7 July, 1895; m. 15 July 1917, Sir Edward Orde MacTaggart-Stewart, 2nd Bt., and had issue.
2. Edith Winifred Lelgarde, b. 21 Jan. 1897; d. 11 Sept. 1908.
3. Irene Mary Egidia, b. 9 Feb. 1898; m. 17 Oct. 1927, Capt. R. St. Barbe Emmott, and had issue.
4. Alice Moira Stuarta, b. 2 Jan. 1909; d. 22 June 1916.

The 3rd Baron Donington d.s.p.m. 31 May 1927.
ARMS (of 1st Baron Donington)—Quarterly 1 and 4, Argent a maunch within a bordure engrailed sable (Hastings); 2 and 3, Or, on a chief gules, a demi-lion issuant argent (Abney).
CRESTS—1. A bull's head erased ermines attired and ducally gorged argent (Hastings). 2. A demi-lion or, the sinister paw resting on an antique shield charged with the arms of Hastings, as in the arms (Abney).
SUPPORTERS—Dexter, A man tiger affrontée or, the visage resembling the human face ppr. gorged with a chain gold, pendent therefrom an escutcheon, of the arms of Clifton, viz. sable on a bend argent three mullets gules. Sinister, A bear argent muzzled gules, gorged with a chain or, therefrom pendent an escutcheon of the arms of Clifton as on the dexter, holding between the forepaws the trunk of a tree erect ppr.
MOTTO—Tenebras meas.

DONOVAN

PEERAGE—U.K. Life. Baron Donovan of Winchester, co. Southampton.
SURNAME—Donovan.
CR.—11 Jan. 1964. **EXT.**—12 Dec. 1971.
HISTORY—Cornelius Donovan, of Newport, co. Monmouth, had issue, Timothy Donovan, of London, b. Oct. 1853; m. 18 Oct. 1883, Laura (who d. 15 July 1913), dau. of James McSheedy, of Cardiff, and d. 22 Dec. 1906, having had, Sir Terence Norbert Donovan **Baron Donovan**, b. 13 June 1898; served in the Home Civil Service 1919-32; served in World War I in France 1917-18, with Bedfordshire Regt., and in France and Germany 1918-19, with R.A.F.; Barrister-at-Law, Middle

Temple 1924; K.C. 1945; Bencher 1950; and Treasurer 1970; Barrister-at-Law, Southern Rhodesia, 1937; he was Labour M.P. for East Leicester 1945-50, and for N.E. Leicester Feb.-July 1950; apptd. a Judge of the High Court of Justice, King's Bench Div. 1950-60; a Lord Justice of Appeal 1960-64; and a Lord of Appeal in Ordinary 1964, and was cr. Kt. Bach. 1950, made P.C. and cr. a life peer as Baron Donovan, of Winchester, co. Southampton 11 Jan. 1964. He was Chm. of Royal Commission on Trade Unions and Employers' Orgs. 1965. He m. 13 April 1925, Marjorie Florence, dau. of Charles Murray, of Winchester, and d. 12 Dec. 1971, having had issue,

1. Hugh Desmond, b. 23 Feb. 1934; educ. Harrow and New Coll. Oxford, B.A. 1957; m. 26 July 1968, Margaret Mary, dau. of H. F. Arbuthnott, of Winterfold House, Chaddesley Corbett, Worcestershire (Arbuthnott, V.).
2. John, b. 3 July 1938; educ. Harrow and Univ. Coll. Oxford, B.A. 1962.
1. Susan Elizabeth, b. 24 May 1936; educ. Bedales and Lausanne Univ.; m. 1 Oct. 1960, Gerard Francis Horton, and had issue,
   (1) Francis Edmund Horatius, b. 1 July 1961.
   (2) Gerard Hugo Terence, b. 20 Feb. 1968.
   (1) Victoria Mary Claire, b. 23 April 1963.
   (2) Emily Lucia Chantal, b. 5 June 1965.

ARMS—Quarterly gules and ermine an open book ppr. garnished or.
CREST—A grenade sable fired ppr. winged azure.
SUPPORTERS—On either side, upon the stock of a tree sprouting a peregrine falcon rising ppr.
MOTTO—Happiness through service.
Lord Donovan's residence was in Lamb Building, Temple, E.C.4. His club was the Athenaeum.

DORCHESTER

PEERAGE—U.K. Baron Dorchester of Dorchester, co. Oxford.
SURNAME—Carleton.
CR.—(1) 21 Aug. 1786. EXT.—13 Nov. 1897.
(2) 2 Aug. 1899. EXT.—20 Jan. 1963.
HISTORY—At the Visitation of Cumberland in 1665 by Sir William Dugdale, the representative of the Carletons, Sir William Carleton of Carleton Hall, certified his descent through eighteen generations from a Baldwin de Carleton said to have been seated there at the end of the 11th century. Whatever the facts of this pedigree, the family had branches recorded in B.L.G. and also in Burke's Extinct Peerage. The connected account of this line begins with, Thomas Carleton of Carleton Hall, near Penrith, co. Cumberland, b. 1513; m. Mabelle, dau. and coheiress of Thomas Carlisle of Carlisle and d. 1586. He was, through his elder son, the great grandfather of Sir William Carleton mentioned above. His ygr. son, Lancelot Carleton, of Brampton Foot, Gilsland, co. Cumberland, was b. 1594, settled at Rosefad, near Enniskillen, m. Eleanor, dau.

of James Kirkby, of Kirkby, co. Lancs and d. 1 Oct. 1619, having had issue,
Lancelot Carleton, of Rossfad, who was k. in service of King Charles I. He m. Mary, dau. of William Irvine of Castle Irvine, Fermanagh and had two sons, Christopher, ancestor of the Carleton-L'Estranges of Market Hill, Fermanagh (see B.L.G.) and an elder son, Lancelot Carleton of Rossfad, High Sheriff, Fermanagh, c. 1683 and Donegal, 1686. He m. Mary, dau. and heiress of John Cathcart and d. c. 1689, having had with five other sons, a third son, Christopher Carleton, of Newry, co. Down, m. Catherine, dau. of Henry Ball, and d. ca. 1738, leaving with other issue, a third son,
Gen. Sir Guy Carleton, **1st Baron Dorchester,** K.B., was Lt. Gov. of Canada 1766-70, Gov. 1775-78 and C. in C. in America 1781-83, serving with distinction in the war with the American Colonies. He was granted a pension of £1,000 per annum for his own life and for the lives of his wife and two elder sons. He was cr. Baron Dorchester of Dorchester, co. Oxford (in the peerage of Great Britain). 21 Aug. 1786. He m. 21 May 1772, Maria, dau. of the 2nd Earl of Effingham. He d. 10 Nov. 1808. She d. 14 Mar. 1836. They had, with four other sons who d. young and two daus.,

1. Christopher, Lt. Col., b. 1775; m. 1797, Priscilla Martha, dau. and co-heiress of Capt. William Belford, and d.v.p. 1806, having had issue (with a dau. Maria who d. at sea with her mother, 1815) a son, Arthur Henry, **2nd Baron** (see below).
2. George, Lt. Col., b. 1781; m. 1805, Henrietta, dau. of Edward King, of Askham Hall, co. Westmorland and was k. at Bergen-op-Zoom, 8 Mar. 1814 having had issue, with three daus, Guy, **3rd Baron** (see below).
3. Richard, Rev., M.A., Rector of Nately-Scures, Hampshire, b. 1792; m. 1820, Frances Louisa, dau. and coheiress of Eusebius Horton of Catton Hall, Derbyshire and d. 1860 having had with a dau. d. unm.
Dudley Wilmot, **4th Baron** (see below).
The first Baron was s. by his grandson,
Arthur Henry Carleton, **2nd Baron Dorchester,** b. 1805; d. unm. 1826 being s. in the Barony by his cousin,
Guy Carleton, **3rd Baron Dorchester,** b. 1811; m. 1837, Anne, dau. of Thomas W. J. Wauchope and had issue, with a yr. dau., Maria Georgiana, who m. Timothy Fetherstonhaugh (see that family in B.L.G.), an elder dau., Henrietta Anne, cr. **Baroness Dorchester** (see below). The 3rd Baron d. 3 Dec. 1875 and was s. by his cousin,
Dudley Wilmot Carleton, **4th Baron Dorchester,** Col. Coldstream Guards b. 1822; m. 1854, Hon. Charlotte Hobhouse, dau. and co-heiress of 1st Baron Broughton. She d. 1914. He d.s.p. 18 Nov. 1897 when the Barony of the 1786, first creation became extinct.
A second creation of a Barony of Dorchester was granted however to the cousin of the 4th Baron, namely
Henrietta Anne Carleton, **Baroness Dorchester** (see above). She m. 1stly 1864, Francis Paynton Pigott, eldest son of Francis Pigott, M.P., Gov. of the Isle of Man, and assumed the additional surname of Carleton on his marriage. He d. 7 April 1883 leaving with an elder son who d. young and a dau. a yr. son,

Dudley Massey Pigott, **2nd Baron** (see below). She m. 2ndly 1887, Major Gen. Richard Langford Leir of Ditcheat, co. Somerset (see *B.L.G.*) who assumed by Royal Licence the additional surname of Carleton. He d. 1933. She was cr. 2 Aug. 1899, Baroness Dorchester, of Dorchester, co. Oxford. She assumed in 1899, by Royal Licence for herself and her issue, the name of Carleton only. She d. 2 Mar. 1925 being s. by her son,

Dudley Massey Pigott Carlton, **2nd Baron Dorchester**, b. 28 Feb. 1876, educ. Wellington, served in the Army, Lt. Col. 9th Lancers, in the S. African War, 1899-1900, in N. Nigeria 1902-03, in the Kano-Sokato Expedition and in World War I 1914-18, received foreign decorations and O.B.E.; m. 21 Sept. 1911, Hon. Kathleen de Blaquiere, only surv. child of 6th and last Baron de Blaquiere (in present work) and d. 20 Jan. 1963 having had issue, two daus. **ARMS**—Ermine on a bend sable three pheons argent.
CREST—A dexter arm embowed ppr., vested above the elbow gules, edged argent, the hand grasping an arrow in bend sinister, point downwards, also ppr.
SUPPORTERS—Two beavers ppr; the dexter gorged with a mural coronet, the sinister with a naval coronet, both or.
MOTTO—Quondam his vicimus armis.
The seat of the Baron Dorchester was Greywell Hill, Basingstoke, Hants.

DOUGLAS OF KIRTLESIDE

PEERAGE—U.K. Baron Douglas of Kirtleside.
SURNAME—Douglas.
CR.—17 Feb. 1948. **EXT.**—30 Oct. 1969.
HISTORY—Sir William Douglas, 1st Earl of Queensberry (see extant peerage, Queensberry, M.) had a third son, Sir Archibald Douglas, to whom he gave Dornock, co. Dumfries, and who had with other issue who s. him at Dornock, (see Queensberry M.),
Major James Douglas, who was granted land by Charles II, b. 1634 and d. in Jamaica (will dated 1663) having had with other issue,
Thomas Douglas, b. 1660, m. in Jamaica Lady Watson and d. 1717 having had with other issue,
Samuel Douglas, b. 1700; m. a dau. of Robert James, of Jamaica, and had issue,
Samuel Douglas, merchant of Kingston, Jamaica, b. ca. 1720; m. 1748, Isabella Moncrieffe of Kingston, Jamaica, and had issue,
Robert Douglas, b. 1750, father of Samuel Douglas, who was father of
The Rev. Robert Douglas, Rector of Odell, co. Bedford, b. 18 July 1836, m. April 1863, Annie, dau. of Thomas Johnson a silk merchant of Manchester and Bowden, co. Chester and d. 1912. She d. 1922. They had with other issue, an eldest son,
Prof. Robert Langton Douglas, of New York, M.A. New Coll. Oxford, b. 1 Mar. 1864; m. (1) 1891 (marr. diss. by div. 1901) Margaret Jane, dau. of Percival Henry Cannon and had issue with two other sons,
William Sholto, **Baron Douglas** (see below).
He m. (2) 1902 (m. diss. by div. 1927) Gwendolen Mary, dau. of Thomas Henchman of Sydney, Australia and had further issue by her. He m. (3) 1928, Jean, dau. of John Stewart of

Edinburgh and d. 1951 having had by her further issue. The eldest son,
Sir William Sholto Douglas, **Baron Douglas** of Kirtleside, was b. 23 Dec. 1893; m. (1) 1919 (m. diss. by div. 1932) Mary Howard; (2) 7 Sept. 1933 (m. diss. by div. 1952) Joan Leslie, dau. of Col. H. C. Denny, and (3) 28 Feb. 1955, Hazel, dau. of George Eric Maas Walker, and widow of Capt. W. E. R. Walker, by whom he had a dau. Katherine Anne, b. 26 July 1957. He was educ. Tonbridge and Lincoln Coll. Oxford, Scholar; served in World War I 1914-18 (despatches three times, M.C., D.F.C.) at first with R.F.A., then transferred to R.F.C., cmdg. 43 and 84 Fighter Squadrons; he transferred to R.A.F. on formation 1 April 1918. Air Vice Marshal 1942, Marshal of the R.A.F. 1946. He was A.O.C. in C. Fighter Command 1940-42, Middle East Command 1942-44, Coastal Command 1944-45. He received decorations from nine of the allied nations, was created C.B. (1940), K.C.B. (1941), G.C.B. (1946) and Baron Douglas of Kirtleside of Dornock, co. Dumfries, 17 Feb. 1948. He d. 30 Oct. 1969.
ARMS—Quarterly 1 and 4, Argent a heart gules imperially crowned ppr. on a chief azure three mullets argent (Douglas); 2 and 3, Azure a bend between six crosses fitchée or (Mar); all within a bordure engrailed gules, on a canton sinister sable an eagle displayed or.
CREST—A heart gules imperially crowned ppr. between two wings displayed or.
SUPPORTERS—Two horses azure, winged, crined and hooved or.
MOTTOES (above the shield) Forward and aloft; (below the shield) Jamais arrière.

DOVER

PEERAGE—U.K. Baron Dover of Dover, co. Kent.
SURNAME—Agar-Ellis.
CR.—20 June 1831. **EXT.**—10 Sept. 1899.
HISTORY—Henry Welbore Agar-Ellis, 2nd Viscount Clifden, who lived 1761 to 1836, had with other issue (see extant peerage works, Clifden, V.), an only son, George James Welbore Agar-Ellis, who was cr. 20 June 1831, **Baron Dover** of Dover, co. Kent, and who was b. 17 Jan. 1797; educ. Westminster and Ch. Ch. Oxford, B.A. 1816, M.A. 1819; was Whig M.P. for Heytesbury, 1818-20; for Seaford, 1820-26; for Ludgershall 1826-30; and for Okehampton 1830-31. In 1816, when he was 19 he was elected F.S.A. and F.R.S.; from 1829-1833 he was Harleian Trustee of the British Museum. He was made a P.C. in 1830 and was for some weeks in 1830-31 Chief Commissioner of Woods and Forests. He was also Trustee of the National Gallery from 1827 and Prs. of the Roy. Soc. of Literature 1832-33. He m. 7 Mar. 1822, Georgiana, dau. of George Howard, 6th Earl of Carlisle, and d.v.p. 10 July 1833. He had issue with two daus.,
1. Henry, **2nd Baron Dover** and 3rd Viscount (see below).
2. Leopold George Frederick, **4th Baron Dover** and 5th Viscount (see below).
The 2nd Viscount Clifden d. 13 July 1836 and was s. by his grandson, Henry Agar-Ellis,

2nd **Baron Dover**, to which he had s. on his father's death, and 3rd Viscount Clifden, who was b. 25 Feb. 1825. He m. 23 Sept. 1861, Eliza Horatia Frederica, dau. of F. C. W. Seymour, (Hertford, M.) and d. 23 April 1896, having had issue with two daus., an only son,

Henry George Agar-Ellis, **3rd Baron Dover** and 4th Viscount Clifden, b. 2 Sept. 1863; d. unm. 28 Mar. 1895, being then s. by his uncle,

Leopold George Frederick Agar-Ellis, **4th Baron Dover** and 5th Viscount Clifden, who was b. 13 May 1829; m. 8 Feb. 1864, Harriet, dau. of 3rd Baron Camoys, and d.s.p.m.s. 10 Sept. 1899, when the Barony of Dover became extinct, but the Viscounty of Clifden was inherited by his cousin, Thomas Charles Agar-Robartes, 6th Viscount Clifden, and son of 1st Baron Robartes, (see extant peerage works).

ARMS—(of 2nd Viscount Clifden), Quarterly 1 and 4, Or on a cross sable five crescents argent (Ellis); 2 and 3, Azure a lion rampant or (Agar).

CREST—A female figure naked ppr. with her hair flowing down to her waist.

SUPPORTERS—Two greyhounds sable, the dexter charged on the body with three crescents or in pale and the sinister with as many crosses recercelée disjointed argent.

MOTTO—Non haec sine numine.

DOVERCOURT

PEERAGE—U.K. Baron Dovercourt of Harwich, co. Essex.

SURNAME—Holmes.

CR.—18 Jan. 1954. **EXT.**—22 April 1961.

HISTORY—Sir Joseph Stanley Holmes, **Baron Dovercourt**, was b. 31 Oct. 1878, the son of Horace G. Holmes, J.P.; was educ. City of London School; Chartered Accountant 1901, member L.C.C. 1910-19, M.P. N.E. Div. of Derbyshire 1918-22, Harwich 1835-54, Chm. N.W. Building Soc., was knighted 1945, created Baron Dovercourt 18 Jan. 1954, and had Order of Merit of Chile; m. 1905 Eva Gertrude, dau. of Thomas Bowley and d. 22 April 1961.

ARMS—Sable a lion rampant or, charged with three bendlets gules, on a chief of the second a rose gules barbed and seeded ppr. between two crescents of the first.

CREST—A demi griffin, wings addorsed sable and charged with three bendlets gules, holding between the claws a crescent or.

SUPPORTERS—On either side a talbot or, each gorged with a cord gules suspended therefrom an escutcheon azure, that on the dexter charged with an ancient ship with one mast or, with turrets at the bow and stern and a tower affixed below the mast head, the sail furled argent and a pennon flying to the dexter gules, and that on the sinister charged with a portcullis or.

MOTTO—Justum et tenacem.

DOVERDALE

PEERAGE—U.K. Baron Doverdale, of Westwood Park, co. Worcester.

SURNAME—Partington.

CR.—6 Jan. 1917. **EXT.**—18 Jan. 1949.

HISTORY—Edward Partington, of Bury, had a son, Sir Edward Partington, **1st Baron Doverdale**, of Westwood Park, co. Worcester, so cr. 6 Jan. 1917 (also cr. Kt. Bach. 1912), b. 1836; educ. privately; three times Mayor of Glossop; mem. Derbyshire C.C.; first Freeman of Borough of Glossop; formed Kellner-Partington Pulp Co. 1889; for many years Pres. of the Paper-Makers Assen. of Great Britain, J.P. and D.L. co. Derby, J.P. and Alderman of Glossop; had Officer's Cross, Order of Francis Joseph of Austria; Dir. of District Bank; m. 18 April 1860, Sarah Alcock, dau. of Thomas Howorth and by her (who d. 17 Feb. 1917) had issue,

1. Herbert, J.P. co. Derby, b. 4 Sept. 1868; educ. Rossall; Mayor of Glossop 1916; m. 23 Nov. 1894, Mary Alice, M.B.E., J.P. co. Derby and Hon. Freeman of Glossop, dau. of Abel Harrison, of Glossop, and d.s.p.m. and v.p. 6 May 1916, leaving issue two daus.
2. Oswald, **2nd Baron** (see below).
1. Alice, m. 1890, Major R. B. Sidebottom.
2. Beatrice, m. 1891, C. E. Knowles, and d. 1897, leaving issue.
3. Lillie, J.P. co. Kent, m. 1897, R. B. Ward, of Ashford, co. Kent, and had issue.

The 1st Baron Doverdale d. 5 Jan. 1925, and was s. by his second son, Oswald Partington, **2nd Baron Doverdale**, b. 4 May 1872; educ. Rossall; entered family business, a mem. of Olive and Partington, a Dir. of Kellner-Partington Co., and Chm. of Barrow Paper Mills Ltd.; M.P. High Peak Div. of Derbyshire 1900-1910 and for Shipley Div. of Yorkshire 1915-18; Junior Lord of the Treasury and Liberal Whip 1909-1910; Alderman London C.C. 1913-20; m. (1) 6 Aug. 1902 (m. diss. by div. 1934), Clare Isabel, dau. of M. F. O. Murray, 1st Viscount Elibank, and had issue by her,

Edward Alexander, **3rd Baron Doverdale** (see below).

Aline Emily, b. 8 June 1907; m. 11 June 1936, Capt. K. W. Hogg, (Magheramore, B.).

He m. (2) 26 July 1934, Leslie, dau. of George B. Cornell, of New York and widow of James B. Tailer, of New York, and d. 23 May 1935, being s. by his son,

Edward Alexander Partington, **3rd Baron Doverdale**, b. 25 Feb. 1904; educ. Eton; m. 18 May 1933, Audrey Ailsa, dau. of Arthur Pointing, of 22 Westbourne Street, London, and Darling Point, Sydney, N.S.Wales, and d. 18 Jan. 1949.

ARMS—Sable, on a bend nebuly between four mullets of six points two in chief and as many in base argent, three Cornish choughs ppr.

CREST—Out of the battlements of a tower a goat's head ppr. charged on the neck with a mullet of six points and between two escallops sable.

SUPPORTERS—On either side a sacred ibis ppr.

The seat of Lord Doverdale was Westwood Park, Droitwich, co. Worcester. His town residence was 14 Arlington House, Arlington Street, London, S.W.1. His clubs were Brooks's and Carlton.

DOWNHAM

PEERAGE—U.K. Baron Downham, of Fulham, co. London.
SURNAME—Fisher.
CR.—16 Nov. 1918. **EXT.**—2 July 1920.
HISTORY—The Rev. Frederick Fisher, Rector of Downham, Isle of Ely, m. Mary, dau. of William Hayes, and they had an eldest son, William Hayes Fisher, **Baron Downham,** who was b. 1853 at Downham and baptized there; educ. Haileybury and Univ. Coll. Oxford, B.A. 1876, M.A. 1878; Barrister-at-Law, Inner Temple 1879; he sat as Conservative M.P. for Fulham 1885-1906, and 1910-1918 (before the division of the seat into East and West Fulham —it is now one seat as Fulham again); he held the following posts, Priv. Sec. to Sir Michael Hicks-Beach when Chief Sec. for Ireland 1886-87, and to A. J. Balfour when Chief Sec. 1887-82; a Junior Lord of the Treasury and Ministerial Whip 1895-1902; Fin. Sec. to the Treasury 1902-03; he was Chm. of the Royal Patriotic Commission 1904, Alderman, L.C.C. 1907-13; Chm. of Finance Cttee., 1907-11; Leader of the Municipal Reform Party 1909-10; made P.C. 1911; and was Parl. Sec. to Local Gov. Board 1915-17; and Pres. of the same 1917-18; Chan. of Duchy of Lancaster 1918:19; Chm. of the L.C.C. 1919, Chm. of the Eagle Insurance Co. and Pres. of the National Skating Asscn.; a K.G. St. J., and cr. a peer as Baron Downham, of Fulham, co. London, 16 Nov. 1918. He m. 1895, his cousin Florence, dau. of H. Fisher. She d. 30 Aug. 1923. He d.s.p.m. 2 July 1920 at his home in Buckingham Palace Gardens, London. He had issue a dau., Rachel Florence, m. 18 Feb. 1922 (m. diss. by div. 1931), Major Thomas McCully Creighton, M.D., son of C. E. Creighton, of Dartmouth, Nova Scotia. She assumed the name of Hayes Fisher in lieu of that of Creighton in 1945. She d. 30 April 1962 leaving issue.
Lord Downham's name is on a memorial stone of the baths at Fulham Broadway.
ARMS—None recorded.

DROGHEDA

PEERAGE—Ireland. Marquess of Drogheda. 5 July 1791.
U.K. Baron Moore of Moore Place. 17 Jan. 1801.
SURNAME—Moore.
CR.—as above. **EXT.**—29 June 1892.
HISTORY—Charles Moore, 6th Earl of Drogheda (see extant peerages, under Drogheda, E.), b. 29 June 1730; was M.P. for Canice (Irishtown) 1756-58; s. his father as 8th Earl of Drogheda 1759; P.C. of Ireland 1760; K.P. 1783, being one of the original Knights; served in the Army from 1744; Col. 18th Light Dragoons, later 18th Hussars 1762-1821; Master Gen. of the Ordnance, in Ireland 1770-97; Major Gen. 1770; Lt. Gen. 1777; Gen. 1793; Field Marshal 1821; Gov.

of Meath 1759-1822; Gov. of Kinsale 1764-70; Constable of Maryborough Castle 1765-1822; a Lord Justice of Ireland 1766-67; M.P. for Horsham 1776-80; Jnt. Postmaster Gen. 1797-1806; cr. **Marquess of Drogheda,** in Irish peerage, on 5 July 1791; and Baron Moore of Moore Place, co. Kent, in the U.K. peerage on 17 Jan. 1801; m. 15 Feb. 1766, Lady Anne, dau. of Francis Seymour-Conway, 1st Marquess of Hertford. She d. 4 Nov. 1784. He d. 22 Dec. 1822, having had issue, with four daus.,

1. Edward, **2nd Marquess** (see below).
2. Henry Seymour, m. 28 Sept. 1824, Mary Letitia, dau. of Sir Henry Parnell, Bt., later 1st Baron Congleton and d. Aug. 1825. She m. 2ndly 1830, E. H. Cole, of Stoke Lyne, co. Oxford, and d. 6 May 1881, having had issue,
   Henry Francis Seymour, **3rd Marquess** (see below).

The elder son, Edward Moore, **2nd Marquess of Drogheda** and 7th Earl of Drogheda, b. 23 Aug. 1770; was M.P. Queen's Co. 1790-91, when he was unseated on a petition, evidently because of insanity, which persisted to his death unm. on 6 Feb. 1837, when he was s. by his nephew,
Henry Francis Seymour Moore, **3rd Marquess of Drogheda** and 8th Earl of Drogheda, b. 14 Aug. 1825; educ. Eton and Trin. Coll. Dublin, B.A. 1845; P.C. of Ireland 1858; cr. K.P. 1868; Lord Lt. co. Kildare 1874-1892; m. 25 Aug. 1847, Mary Caroline, dau. of John Stuart-Wortley-Mackenzie, 2nd Baron Wharncliffe of Wortley, and d.s.p. 29 June 1892. She d. 17 Oct. 1826. The Marquessate of Drogheda then became extinct at his death and also the barony of Moore of Moore Place. He was s. in the Earldom and other honours by his cousin,
Ponsonby William Moore, 9th Earl of Drogheda, (see extant peerages).
ARMS—Azure on a chief indented or, three mullets pierced gules.
CREST—Out of a ducal coronet or, a Moor's head ppr. wreathed about the temples argent and sable.
SUPPORTERS—Two greyhounds argent.
MOTTO—Fortis cadere, cedere, non potest.
The seat of the Marquesses of Drogheda was Moore Abbey, Monasterevan, co. Kildare.

**DUFFUS

PEERAGE—Scotland. Lord Duffus.
SURNAME—Sutherland, later Dunbar.
CR.—8 Dec. 1650. **EXT.**—28 Aug. 1875.
HISTORY—William Sutherland of Duffus, co. Moray (for whose antecedents see extant peerage works, under Dunbar of Hempriggs, Bt.), had a son and heir, Alexander Sutherland, b. about 1621; knighted about 1643; and cr. by Charles II, on 8 Dec. 1650, **Lord Duffus.** The patent was lost and, as no record of it existed, the limitation of the grant was unknown, but from the action taken in 1826 (see below) it appears that it was taken to be to the heirs male of the body of the grantee. Lord Duffus was Gov. of Perth in the royal interest, but compelled to surrender to Cromwell, by whom he was fined £1,000 in 1654. In 1660 he was apptd. P.C. for Scotland. He m. (1) before 1644, Jean, dau. and coheir of Colin Mackenzie,

1st Earl of Seaforth, and widow of John Sinclair, Master of Berridale. She d. 31 Mar. 1648. He m. (2) 13 Jan. 1653, Jean dau. of Sir Robert Innes, Bt. of Innes. She d.s.p. 10 Mar. 1653. He m. (3) 1654, Margaret, dau. of James Stewart, Earl of Moray, and she d. Jan. 1667. He m. (4) about 1668, Margaret, dau. of William Forbes, Lord Forbes. She m. 2ndly in 1676, Sir Robert Gordon, Bt., of Gordonstoun. Lord Duffus, d. 31 Aug. 1674, having had with other issue, an only son by his third wife,

James Sutherland, **2nd Lord Duffus,** made P.C. 1686; k. William Ross, of Kindeace, who was his creditor, and fled to England, where he was able to get immunity for the murder, probably because he supported the Revolution of 1688. He m. about 1674, Margaret, dau. of Kenneth Mackenzie, 3rd Earl of Seaforth, and d. 24 Sept. 1705, having had, with other issue,

Kenneth Sutherland, **3rd Lord Duffus,** who served in the R.N., and who was captured by the French after a desperate resistance in which he was severely wounded, 29 June 1711. He took part in the 1715 Rising, and was accordingly attainted, although he had left Sweden in order to give himself up. After a short stay in the Tower of London, he was released in 1717 without having been brought to trial. He then joined the Russian Navy. He m. 30 Mar. 1708, Charlotte Christina, dau. of Eric de Siobladem, Gov. of Gottenburg, Sweden. She d. 1771. He d. 1734, leaving an only son,

Eric Sutherland, but for attainder **4th Lord Duffus,** bapt. 29 Aug. 1710; made claim to the title, but was disallowed, 1734. He served as Ensign in Disney's Regt. 1731, and as Capt. in Sutherland's Regt., 1759. He m. his cousin, Elizabeth, dau. of his paternal uncle, the Hon. Sir James Dunbar, formerly Sutherland, 1st Bt., by Elizabeth, dau. and heiress of Sir William Dunbar, 1st Bt., of Hempriggs, co. Caithness. She d. 21 July 1800. He d. 15 Mar. 1769. They had an only surv. son,

James Sutherland, **5th Lord Duffus,** b. 8 June 1747; served in the Army, Capt. 1771, in 26th Foot. He was restored by Act of Parliament 25 May 1826, to the title and dignity of Lord Duffus, "as would all other persons who would be entitled to s. after him." He d. unm. 30 Jan. 1827, and on his death it was assumed that the limitation was to heirs male of the body, and the title was therefore assumed by,

Benjamin Dunbar, styling himself **6th Lord Duffus,** who was cousin and heir male of the 5th Lord, and the only surv. son of Sir William Dunbar, 2nd Bt., of Hempriggs. He was b. 28 April 1761; became 3rd Bt., 12 June 1793; he petitioned the House of Lords in common with the heir general in June 1838, as to their rights to the peerage but no further proceedings were taken. He m. 10 Dec. 1784, Janet, dau. of George Mackay, of Bighouse, and d. 27 Jan. 1843, having had an eldest surv. son,

Sir George Sutherland Dunbar, 4th Bt., who never assumed the title of Lord Duffus. He did petition in June 1838, with his father for the title. He d. unm. 28 Aug. 1875, when the baronetcy was for a time dormant until it passed to his sister's son, whose son assumed the title. The Barony of Duffus, however, became extinct in 1875 with the extinction of the issue male of the grantee.

ARMS—Gules a boar's head erased between three mullets, two and one, and as many crosses crosslet fitchée one and two or (Sutherland).
CREST—A stag's head ppr. collared or.
SUPPORTERS—A talbot argent, collared gules, and a horse argent.
MOTTO—Butt sicker.

DUGAN OF VICTORIA

PEERAGE—U.K. Baron Dugan of Victoria, of Lurgan, co. Armagh.
SURNAME—Dugan.
CR.—7 July 1949. **EXT.**—17 Aug. 1951.
HISTORY—Charles Winston Dugan, of Axmantown Mall, Birr, King's Co. Ireland had a son, Sir Winston Joseph Dugan, **Baron Dugan** of Victoria, b. 8 May 1877; educ. Lurgan Coll. and at Wimbledon, entered the Army 1896, Major Gen. 1930, served in the S. African War, 1899-1902, and in World War I 1914-18 cmd. Royal Irish Regt., and a Brig. (wounded, despatches 6 times, D.S.O.) Brevet Lt. Col. and Col. cmd. 56 (1st London) Div. T.A. 1931-34, ret. 1934. Gov. of S. Australia, 1934-39, and of Victoria 1939-49; cr. D.S.O. 1915, C.M.G. 1918, C.B. (mil.) 1929; K.C.M.G. 1934, G.C.M.G. 1944, and Baron Dugan, of Victoria, of Lurgan, co. Armagh 7 July 1949. He m. 1912 Ruby Lilian D.G. St. J., dau. of Charles Abbott of Abbott Abbey, co. Cork and d.s.p. 17 Aug. 1951.
ARMS—Quarterly azure and ermine, in the 1st and 4th quarters a griffin's head erased or, gorged with a mural coronet gules.
CREST—Issuant from a mural coronet or, a demi-lion azure grasping in the dexter paw a sword ppr. pommel and hilt gold, the blade entwined by a serpent vert.
SUPPORTERS—Dexter, An emu; Sinister, An eagle, both ppr.

DUKESTON

PEERAGE—U.K. Baron Dukeston, of Warrington, co. Palatine of Lancaster.
SURNAME—Dukes.
CR.—1 April 1947. **EXT.**—14 May 1948.
HISTORY—Charles Dukes was b. 28 Oct. 1881; was Gen. Sec. of the Nat. Union of Gen. and Municipal Workers, 1934-46; M.P. Warrington 1923-24, and 1929-31; Pres. T.U.C. 1946; and mem. of Council from 1934; mem. of Consultative Cttee to Min. of Labour; a Dir. of Bank of England, 1947; cr. C.B.E. 1942, and **Baron Dukeston** of Warrington, in the county Palatine of Lancaster, 1 April 1947. He d. 14 May 1948.
Lord Dukeston's entry in Burke's Peerage for 1949 (first postwar edition) takes up just over 1½ inches. He had wished to take the title of Lord Dukes. His residences were Woodfield, Copperkins Lane, Amersham, co. Buckingham and 5 Endsleigh Gardens, W.C.1.

DUNEDIN

PEERAGE—U.K. Baron Dunedin of Stenton, co. Perth, and Viscount Dunedin, of the same.
SURNAME—Murray.
CR.—Barony 9 Mar. 1905. Viscounty 17 Feb. 1926 EXT.—21 Aug. 1942.
HISTORY—This family descends from Sir William Graham, of Kincardine, the ancestor of the Dukes of Montrose. He m. as his 2nd wife, Lady Mary Stewart, 2nd dau. of King Robert III of Scotland, and had by her five sons, of whom the third was William Graham, of Garvock. His grandson was k. at Flodden (1513), and had a son John, who d. 1545, leaving issue two sons The elder was ancestor of the Grahams of Garvock, and the second son, John bought Balgowan. His great-grandson, Thomas, who d. 1726, had nine sons, of whom Patrick, b. 1693, m. Janet Murray, of Murrayshall, and assumed the surname of Murray. His grandson was Andrew Murray, of Murrayshall, Advocate Sheriff of co. Aberdeen, b. 13 Aug. 1782; m. 3 Oct. 1808, Janet, only child of Oliver Thomson, of Leckie Bank, co. Fife, and d. 6 Feb. 1847, having had with other issue, a third son,
Thomas Murray, W.S. and Crown Agent for Scotland, m. 19 Dec. 1848, Caroline Jane, dau. of John Tod, of Kirkhill. She d. 17 April 1906. He d. 10 Mar. 1891. They had issue an only child,
Sir Andrew Graham Murray, **Baron Dunedin**, and **Viscount Dunedin**, b. 21 Nov. 1849; educ. Harrow and Trin. Coll. Cambridge, B.A. 1872, M.A. 1875; called to Scottish Bar 1874; Advocate Depute 1888-90; Sheriff of Perthshire 1890-91; Q.C. 1891; Solicitor Gen. for Scotland 1891-92; and 1895-96; M.P. Bute 1891-1905; Lord Advocate for Scotland 1896-1903; Lord Lt. Bute 1901-05; Sec. for Scotland 1903-05. He was made P.C. 1896; cr. Baron Dunedin, of Stenton, co. Perth, 9 Mar. 1905, and Viscount Dunedin, of Stenton, co. Perth, 17 Feb. 1926, K.C.V.O. 1908 and G.C.V.O. 1923. He was Lord Justice Gen. and Pres. of the Court of Session 1905-13; Hon. Bencher of Middle Temple 1910; Lord of Appeal in Ordinary 1913-32; and Chm. of the Political Honours Review Cttee 1923. He m. (1) 1 Oct. 1874, Mary Clementina, who d. 2 Dec. 1922, dau. of Sir William Edmonstone, 4th Bt., and (2) 12 July 1923, Jean Elmslie Henderson, dau. of George Findlay, of Aberdeen, and d. 21 Aug. 1942, having had issue by his first wife,
1. Ronald Thomas Graham, b. 1 Aug. 1875; educ. Eton; served in World War I, Major in Black Watch and as a Censor in India, m. 19 Feb. 1903, Evelyn, dau. of Sir David Baird, 3rd Bt., and d.s.p. 24 Sept. 1934.
1. Gladys Esme.
2. Marjorie, m. 5 Feb. 1907, Major E. L. C. Fielden, (Feilden, Bt.) and had issue.
ARMS—Quarterly 1 and 4, Or three piles sable within a double tressure flory, counterflory gules, on a chief sable a crescent between two escallops or (Graham); 2 and 3, Azure a cross patée between three mullets argent within a double tressure flory counterflory or (Murray); in the centre of the quarters a crescent gules for difference.
CREST—A buck's head couped ppr.

SUPPORTERS—Two doves ppr.
MOTTO—Macte virtute.

DUNSANDLE AND CLANCONAL

PEERAGE—Ireland. Baron Dunsandle and Clanconal, of Dunsandle, co. Galway.
SURNAME—Daly.
CR.—6 June 1845. EXT.—25 Nov. 1911.
HISTORY—Dermot O'Daly, of Killimur, co. Galway, in 1578 had a grant from Elizabeth I of the manor of Larha, co. Galway, and left issue a son, Donogh, who had a second son, James Daly, who m. Anastasia D'Arcy, granddau. of James Riveagh D'Arcy, vice-pres. of Connaught, tempore Elizabeth I and had, with other children, an eldest son, Denis Daly, of Carrownakelly, Justice of common pleas and P.C. tempore James II, m. Mary, dau. of Thomas Power, of Pask, co. Limerick, and had by her, with other issue, a third son, Denis Daly, of Carrownakelly and heir to his father, m. dau. and heiress of George French, of Frenchbrook, co. Mayo, and left issue by her, James Daly, of Carrownakelly, and Dunsandle, co. Galway, m. (1) Bridget, dau. of 21st Lord Athenry; she d.s.p. He m. (2) Catherine, dau. of Sir Ralph Gore, and sister of the Earl of Ross, and had, with other issue by her, an eldest son,
The Rt. Hon. Denis Daly, of Dunsandle, co. Galway, M.P. co. Galway, Muster Master Gen., b. 1747; m. 1780, Henrietta, only dau. and heiress of Robert Maxwell, Earl of Farnham, and she d. 6 Mar. 1852. He had issue by her,
1. James, **1st Baron Dunsandle and Clanconal** (see below).
2. Robert, Rt. Rev., D.D., Bishop of Cashel and Waterford, 1843-72, who d. unm. 16 Feb. 1872.
1. Henrietta, d. unm.
2. Catherine, m. John Godley, of Killigar, co. Leitrim, and had issue.
3. Charlotte, m. the Very Rev. H. Newman, Dean of Cork.
4. Elizabeth.
5. Emily, m. Sir Morgan Crofton, Bt., and d. 16 Feb. 1876, having had issue.
6. Mary, m. the Rev. Arthur Knox, and d. 24 April 1885.
The elder son, James Daly, **1st Baron Dunsandle and Clanconal**, so cr. as a peer of Ireland 6 June 1845, M.P. co. Galway, b. 7 April 1782; m. 5 Mar. 1808, Maria Elizabeth, dau. and coheir of the Rt. Hon. Sir Skeffington Smyth, Bt., by Margaret, dau. of Hyacinth Daly, of Dalystown, co. Galway, and d. 7 Aug. 1847, having had issue by her (who d. 2 Nov. 188)
1. Denis St. George, **2nd Baron Dunsandle and Clanconal** (see below).
2. Skeffington James, **3rd Baron** (see below).
3. Charles Anthony, Major 89th Regt., who d. 29 Dec. 1854 in camp before Sebastopol.
4. Bowes Richard, b. 1814; d. unm. 20 May 1888.
5. Robert, A.D.C. and State Steward to Lord Lt. of Ireland, b. 1818; m. 27 Dec. 1845, the Hon. Cecilia Maria, dau. of William A'Court, 1st Baron Heytesbury;

she d. 25 Dec. 1889; he d. 15 Jan. 1892. They had,
(1) James Frederick, **4th Baron** (see below).
(2) Cecil Robert, b. 21 April 1851; d. 28 July 1893.
(3) Charles William, Lt. Gren. Guards, b. 1856; d. 1883.
(1) Alice Rosa, m. 6 Aug. 1878, Lt. Col. H. E. Colville, Gren. Guards, and d. 23 Sept. 1880.
(2) Florence Maria.
(3) Elinor Gertrude.
1. Margaret Eleanor, d. unm. 2 May 1857.
2. Rosa Gertrude Harriet, m. 25 Sept. 1856, J. E. Venables Vernon, of Clontarf Castle, Dublin, and d. 31 Aug. 1859.
The eldest son, Denis St. George Daly, **2nd Baron Dunsandle and Clanconal,** b. 10 July 1810, Capt. 7th Hussars; m. 1864, Mary (d. 6 Dec. 1868), dau. of William Broderick, and d. 11 Jan. 1893, s.p.l., having by her had, Anne, b. 1865; m. 29 April 1887, Valentine Martyn. The 2nd Baron had also (C.P.) a son born before marriage in 1850, William, who s. to Dunsandle and became Sheriff of co. Galway 1901. The 2nd Baron was s. by his brother,
Skeffington James Daly, **3rd Baron Dunsandle and Clanconal,** b. 25 Dec. 1811; d. unm. 7 Sept. 1894, and was s. by his nephew,
James Frederick Daly, **4th Baron Dunsandle and Clanconal,** b. 29 Aug. 1849; educ. Eton; Asst. Priv. Sec. to Lord Beaconsfield 1874-80, Priv. Sec. to First Lord of the Treasury 1885-87; and d. unm. 25 Nov. 1911.
ARMS—Per fess argent and or, a lion rampant per fess sable and gules; in chief two dexter hands couped gules. (The following quarterings are mentioned: 1. Daly. 2. Power. 3. French. 4. Maxwell. 5. Calderwood. 6. Deniston. 7. Barry. 8. Cantillon).
CREST—In front of an oak tree ppr. a greyhound courant sable.
SUPPORTERS—Dexter, A lion rampant as in the arms; Sinister, A greyhound ppr. gorged with an Irish crown or.
MOTTO—Deo fidelis et regi.
The seats of the Lords Dunsandle were Dunsandle, Loughrea, co. Galway; and Thomastown Castle, co. Tipperary.

DU PARCQ

PEERAGE—U.K. Life. Baron du Parcq of Grouville, Island of Jersey.
SURNAME—du Parcq.
CR.—5 Feb. 1946. EXT.—27 April 1949.
HISTORY—Barnabe du Parc is believed to have emigrated from Brittany to Jersey with his wife Colette ca. 1488, and settled at Gouvay, in the parish of Grouville, Jersey. They had issue, Jean du Parc, of Grouville, one of the defenders of Castle Orgueil in 1531, b. 1500; m. Catherine, dau. of Jean Gibault, Constable of St. Lawrence, and d. 1565, leaving issue, Guillaume du Parc, of Grouville, b. 1530; m. Jeanne, dau. of Matthieu Hicques, and d. 1588, having had,
Jean du Parc, of Grouville, m. Marie, dau. of Richard Mallet (son of Richard Mallet,

Seigneur of La Malletière, and of La Hague, Jurat of the Royal Court) and d. 1604, leaving issue,
1. Jean du Parc, of La Malletière, b. 1593; d. 1625.
2. Richard, see below.
The younger son, Richard du Parcq, Constable of Grouville, 1655-60, bapt. 5 Oct. 1600, d. 1663, leaving by his wife, Marie, dau. of Richard Regnault, of La Ville-es-Renaults, Richard du Parcq, of La Ville-es-Renaults, Centenier of Grouville, 1666; b. 1646, m. Rachel, dau. of Amice Jeune, and d. 1680, leaving, Amice du Parcq, of La Ville-es-Renaults, Centenier of Grouville, 1716-17, d. 1748 leaving by his wife, Susanne Roissier,
1. Amice, of La Ville-es-Renaults, Centenier of Grouville, b. 1703; and d. 1746 leaving by his wife, Elizabeth, dau. of Hugh Hooper, a son, the Rev. Jean du Parcq, Rector of Grouville, b. 1735; d.s.p. 1787.
2. Richard, see below.
The younger son, Richard du Parcq, left Grouville for St. Helier, b. 1706; m. 1743, Jeanne, dau. of Philippe Lerrier, and d. 1763 leaving issue, Philippe du Parcq, of St. Helier, b. 1753; m. Sara, dau. of Jean de St. Croix, and sister of Aaron de St. Croix, described as negociant and armateur, Jurat of the Royal Court, and d. 1731, leaving issue, Richard du Parcq, of St. Helier, b. 1788; m. Esther, dau. of Clement Guilleaume, and d. 1873, leaving issue, Clement du Parcq, of St. Helier, b. 1823; m. Mary Sarah, dau. of Edward Pixley, and d. 1893, leaving issue,
Clement Pixley du Parcq, of St. Helier; b. 1 June 1853; educ. Victoria Coll. Jersey; m. 1878, Sophia, dau. of Peter Thomas Thoreau, of Claremont Lodge, St. Helier, Jersey, and d. 26 Feb. 1911. She d. 15 April 1940. They had issue,
Sir Herbert du Parcq, **Baron du Parcq,** b. 5 Aug. 1880; educ. Victoria Coll. Jersey, and Exeter and Jesus Colls. Oxford, Sch. 1899, Pres. Oxford Union 1902, B.A. 1903, M.A. and B.C.L. 1908, Hon. Fell. 1935; Barrister-at-Law, Middle Temple, 1906; K.C. 1926, Bencher, 1931; Recorder of Portsmouth, 1928-29, and of Bristol, 1929-32; a Justice of the High Court, King's Bench Div. 1932-38, knighted 1932; Lord Justice of Appeal, 1938-46; mem. of Permanent Court of Arbitration at the Hague, 1945; made P.C. 1938; cr. a Lord of Appeal in Ordinary, as a life peer, Baron du Parcq of Grouville, Island of Jersey, 5 Feb. 1946. He m. 8 Sept. 1911, Lucy, (d. 1965) dau. of John Renouf, of St. Helier, Jersey, and d. 27 April 1949. He had issue,
1. John Renouf, b. 9 June 1917; educ. Rugby and Exeter Coll. Oxford, M.A.; m. 16 Nov. 1940, Elizabeth Anne, dau. of Evan Skull Poole, of Oxted, co. Surrey, and had issue, Richard Poole and Elizabeth Jane.
1. Helen, m. (1) 1935 (m. diss. by div. 1948) William Farr and had issue. She m. (2) 1948 Alec Andrew Muir and had further issue.
2. Catherine Simonne, m. 1939, Leslie Twelvetrees, and had issue.

DUVEEN

PEERAGE—U.K. Baron Duveen, of Millbank, in the City of Westminster. (also a baronetcy, dated 15 Feb. 1927).
SURNAME—Duveen.
CR.—3 Feb. 1933. **EXT.**—25 May 1939.
HISTORY—Sir Joseph Joel Duveen, b. in Holland, of Dutch nationality, a dealer in works of art and a benefactor to the Tate and National Galleries, was cr. Kt. Bach. 1908, of The Elms, Hampstead Heath, London, b. 1843; m. 10 Feb. 1869, Rosetta, (d. 25 June 1922) dau. of Abraham Barnett of Hull, and d. 9 Nov. 1908, leaving issue, with seven other sons and four daus., an eldest son,
Sir Joseph Duveen, Bt. and **Baron Duveen,** b. 14 Oct. 1869; educ. Brighton Coll.; an art connoisseur and collector; Pres. of Duveen Bros. Inc., of Paris and New York; Dir. of Duveen Bros. Ltd., London; cr. Kt. Bach. 1919, a baronet 15 Feb. 1927, and a peer as Baron Duveen, of Millbank, in the city of Westminster, 3 Feb. 1933. He m. 31 July 1899, Elsie, (d. 1963) dau. of Gustav Solomon, of New York, and d. 25 May 1939, having had issue,
Dorothy, m. (1) 23 July 1931, (m. diss. by div. 1937) William Francis Cuthbert Garthwaite, eldest son of Sir William Garthwaite, 1st Bt. She m. (2) 1938 B. H. Burns.
Lord Duveen made many gifts to the nation of art treasures, and his benefaction to the British Museum enabled the Elgin Marbles to be splendidly exhibited.
ARMS—Argent on a bend azure, three bees volant or, a chief gules.
CREST—In front of a garb or banded azure, two trefoils in saltire slipped vert.
SUPPORTERS—On either side a lion guardant gules charged on the shoulder with a plate thereon a Chinese dragon azure.
MOTTO—Honor industriae praemium.
Lord Duveen's address was 15 East 91st Street, New York City. His clubs were The Arts and the Reform.

EDINBURGH

PEERAGE—U.K. Duke of Edinburgh, Earl of Ulster, and Earl of Kent.
SURNAME—None until 1917, but often given in older books as Guelph.
CR.—24 May 1866. **EXT.**—30 July 1900 .
HISTORY—H.R.H. Prince Alfred Ernest Albert, Duke of Saxe Coburg and Gotha, Duke of Saxony, Duke of Julich, Cleve and Berg, cr. **Duke of Edinburgh, Earl of Ulster** and **Earl of Kent,** in peerage of U.K. on 24 May 1866; was b. at Windsor Castle, 6 Aug. 1844, the second son of Queen Victoria. He s. his uncle Ernest, Duke of Saxe Coburg and Gotha, as reigning Duke of Saxe Coburg and Gotha, on 22 Aug. 1893. H.R.H. was a Prince of the United Kingdom of Great Britain and Ireland; he was K.G., K.T., K.P., P.C., G.C.B., G.C.S.I., G.C.M.G. and G.C.I.E., Adm. of the Fleet, Master of Trin. House, and Gen. in the Prussian Army, etc., etc. He m. 23 Jan. 1874, H.I.H. the Grand Duchess Marie Alexandrovna, only dau. of Alexander II Emperor of Russia. They had issue, with four

daus., (see extant peerages, royal lineage), an only son,
H.R.H. Prince Alfred, K.G., Hereditary Prince, b. at Buckingham Palace, 15 Oct. 1874; d.v.p. unm. 6 Feb. 1899.
H.R.H. Duke Alfred d. at Rosenau, 30 July 1900, when his U.K. titles became extinct and he was s. as Reigning Duke of Saxe Coburg and Gotha by his nephew the Duke of Albany (see the title as a suspended peerage in present work).
ARMS—The royal arms differenced by a label of three points argent, the centre point charged with St. George's Cross and each of the other points with an anchor azure; and in the centre of the said royal arms, an escutcheon of the arms of Saxony, namely, barry of ten or and sable a crown of rue in bend vert.
CREST—On a coronet composed of crosses pattée and fleur-de-lis a lion statant guardant or, crowned with the like coronet and differenced with a label of three points argent charged as in the arms.
SUPPORTERS—The Royal Supporters differenced with the like coronet and label.
The English seat of the Duke was Eastwell Park, Ashford, Kent.

EGERTON OF TATTON

PEERAGE—U.K. Baron Egerton of Tatton, co. Chester, cr. 15 April 1859 ext. 30 Jan. 1958. Earl Egerton of Tatton, co. Chester and Viscount Salford, co. Lancaster, both cr. 22 July 1897 and ext. 16 Mar. 1909.
SURNAME—Egerton.
CR. and **EXT.**—as above.
HISTORY—The family of Egerton has a connected descent from David le Clerc de Malpas, temp. Henry III. From their property of Egerton in Cheshire was derived their surname. Sir Ralph Egerton (see Extant Peerage, Grey Egerton Bt.) had an illegitimate son, Sir Thomas Egerton, b. 1540, by Alice Spark. He was a distinguished barrister and became Lord Chancellor, being cr. 21 July 1603, Baron Ellesmere, co. Salop, and 7 Nov. 1616, Viscount Brackley. His son John, 2nd Viscount, was cr. 27 May 1617, Earl of Bridgewater. His son, 2nd Earl, was ancestor of the Dukes of Bridgewater (see Burke's Extinct Peerage) and through his third son, The Hon. Thomas Egerton, of Tatton Park, co. Chester of the Barons Egerton of Tatton. He had issue, John Egerton, of Tatton, who m. Elizabeth, dau. of Samuel Barbour and had issue, Samuel Egerton, of Tatton Park, b. 28 Dec. 1711. He m. Beatrix, dau. and co-heiress of the Rev. John Copley, of Battly, and had issue an only dau., Beatrix, who m. Daniel Wilson but d.s.p.v.p. At his death 10 Feb. 1780 Mr. Egerton devised his estates to his sister, Hester Egerton, m. William Tatton but on inheriting her brother's properties resumed by royal sign manual her maiden name on 8 May 1780. She d. 9 July 1780 leaving (with a dau. Elizabeth Tatton m. Sir Christopher Sykes, Bt. and had issue, see below), a son and successor,
William Tatton Egerton, of Tatton and Wythenshaw, M.P. Chester, b. 1749, assumed the name and arms of Egerton, m. (1) 1773, Frances Maria, dau. of the Very Rev. John

Fountayne, Dean of York, and by her who d. 1777, he had issue, a son, William, d. young. He m. (2) 1780, Mary, dau. of Richard Wilbraham Bootle (see Skelmersdale, B.) and by her d. 1784, had issue with a dau., and a son, Thomas William, ancestor of Tatton of Wythenshaw (see *B.L.G.* 1952).

Wilbraham (see below).

He m. (3) 1786, Anna Maria, dau. of Sir George Armytage, Bt. She d. 1790. He m. (4) 1803, Charlotte Clara, dau. of T. W. Payler, who d.s.p. 1804, and d. 21 April 1806, being s. by his son,

Wilbraham Egerton of Tatton, M.P. co. Chester 18/2-31, High Sheriff 1808, b. 1 Sept. 1781; m. 11 Jan. 1806 his first cousin Elizabeth (d. 1853) yr. dau. of Sir Christopher Sykes, Bt. (see above), and had with other issue (see editions of *B.P.* up to 1958) an eldest son,

William Tatton Egerton, **1st Baron Egerton** of Tatton, M.P. for Lymington and for co. Chester, Lord Lieut. co. Chester, created Baron Egerton of Tatton, co. Chester 15 April 1859. He was b. 30 Dec. 1806; m. 18 Dec. 1830, Lady Charlotte Elizabeth Loftus, eldest dau. of 2nd Marquess of Ely, and had with other issue,

1. Wilbraham, **2nd Baron** and only Earl (see below).
2. Alan de Tatton, **3rd Baron** (see below).

Lord Egerton d. 21 Feb. 1883 and was s. by his elder surviving son, Wilbraham Egerton, **2nd Baron and Earl Egerton of Tatton**, M.A. Oxford, M.P. N. Cheshire 1858-68, and Mid-Cheshire 1868-83, Chancellor of the Order of St. John of Jerusalem in England, Prov. G.M. of Freemasons, co. Chester 1886-1900, and Prov. G.M. of Mark Masons. He was cr. Earl Egerton of Tatton, co. Chester and Viscount Salford, co. Lancaster, 22 July 1897. He was b. 1832; m. (1) 1857, Lady Mary Sarah, eldest dau. of 2nd Earl Amherst, by whom he had a dau. Gertrude Lucia, m. 8th Earl of Albemarle. Earl Egerton m. (2) 1894, Alice Anne, dau. of Sir Graham Montgomery, 3rd Bt. and widow of 3rd Duke of Buckingham and Chandos and d.s.p.m. 16 Mar. 1909, when the Earldom and Viscounty became extinct while the Barony was inherited by his brother, Alan de Tatton Egerton, **3rd Baron Egerton of Tatton**, M.P. Mid-Cheshire 1883-85 and Knutsford 1885-1906, b. 1845; m. 1867, Anna Louisa, dau. of Simon Watson Taylor, of Erles Park, co. Wilts and d. 1920 having had issue by her with two other sons who d. young a third and surviving son, Maurice Egerton, **4th Baron Egerton of Tatton**, served as Major Cheshire Yeo. and formerly as Lt. R.N.V.R., b. 4 Aug. 1874 and d. 30 Jan. 1958.

ARMS—Argent a lion rampant gules between three pheons sable.

CREST—On a chapeau gules turned up ermine, a lion rampant also gules, supporting an arrow palewise or, pheoned and flighted argent.

SUPPORTERS—Dexter, A griffin argent gorged with a ducal coronet azure and pendent therefrom a pheon sable; Sinister, A lion gules gorged with a plain collar argent and pendent therefrom a pheon also argent.

MOTTO—Sic donec

ELIBANK

PEERAGE—U.K. Viscount Elibank, of Elibank, co. Selkirk.
SURNAME—Murray.
CR.—3 July 1911. **EXT.**—5 Dec. 1962.
HISTORY—Montolieu Fox Oliphant Murray was 10th Baron Elibank in the Peerage of Scotland (cr. 18 Mar. 1643) and a baronet of Nova Scotia (cr. 16 May 1628). He was the eldest son of the 9th Baron Elibank, whose ancestry is given in the Extant Peerage under Elibank B. (see below). Lord Elibank was b. 27 April 1840, served in the Royal Navy as Cmdr., being present in the China Expedition of 1860 and in the suppression of the negro revolt in Jamaica, 1865; he was cr. **Viscount Elibank** of Elibank co. Selkirk, 3 July 1911. He m. 2 May 1868 Blanche Alice, dau. of Edward J. Scott of Southsea, Hants and d. 20 Feb. 1927 having had issue with five daus.,

1. Alexander William Charles Oliphant, Under Sec. of State for India, 1909-10 and Patronage Sec. to the Treasury 1910-12, b. 1870; m. 1894. Hilda Louisa Janey Wolfe, dau. of J. W. Murray (Murray of Blackbarony Bt. and was made P.C. 1911 and cr. Baron Murray of Elibank, 13 Aug. 1912 (U.K. peerage). He d.s.p. 13 Sept. 1920.
2. Edward Oliphant, Capt. Q.O. Cameron Highlanders, b. 1871; m. 1900 Mary Millard, dau. of H. C. Allhusen (see B.L.G. 1952) and was k. in S. African War, 1901, leaving issue one dau.
3. Charles Gideon, 11th Baron and **2nd Viscount** (see below).
4. Arthur Cecil, 12th Baron and **3rd Viscount** (see below).

The 10th Baron and 1st Viscount was s. by his third son, Charles Gideon Murray, 11th Baron and **2nd Viscount Elibank**, b. 1877, took a prominent part in imperial affairs, being Administrator of St. Vincent 1909-14, and Lucia, 1914-18. M.P. for St. Rollon Div. of Glasgow 1918-22; served in the S. African war and was hon. Col. of 8th Bn. Royal Scots, 1939-45; m. 1908 Ermine Mary Katharine, dau. of H. R. Madocks of Glanywern, Denbigh, and widow of Lt. Col. J. H. Aspinwall. He d.s.p. 11 Mar. 1951, being s. by his brother, Arthur Cecil Murray, 12th Baron and **3rd Viscount Elibank**, b. 1879; had career distinguished in military and political spheres, and as an author of many historical works; Lt. Col. 2nd King Edward's Horse which he helped to raise in 1914; served in the China Expedition 1900, on the N.W.F. India and in Chitral with 5th Gurkha Rifles 1903-07, served in World War I 1915-16 with 1st Canadian Inf. Div. in France (despatches, D.S.O.) M.P. co. Kincardine, 1908-23 and passed Bill through House of Commons to improve conditions of worn out horse traffic. He was cr. C.M.G. (1918) having served as Asst. Mil. Attaché Washington, 1917-18. He m. 1931 Faith Celli an actress, dau. of Francis H. Standing. She d. 1942. He d. 5 Dec. 1962 when the Viscounty became extinct and the Barony of Elibank with the Nova Scotia baronetcy were inherited by his kinsman, James Alastair Frederick Campbell Erskine-Murray.
ARMS—Quarterly 1 and 4, Or, a fetterlock azure; on a chief azure three mullets argent

(Murray of Blackbarony) 2, Gules, a chevron between three crescents argent (Oliphant); 3, Azure a martlet or between three mullets argent within a double tressure, flory counter flory argent (Elibank).
CREST—A lion rampant gules holding between the paws a battle axe ppr.
SUPPORTERS—Two horses argent bridled gules.
MOTTO—Virtute fideque.

**ELLENBOROUGH

PEERAGE—U.K. Viscount Southam of Southam, co. Gloucester.
U.K. Earl of Ellenborough, co. Cumberland.
SURNAME—Law.
CR.—22 Oct. 1844. **EXT.**—22 Dec. 1871.
HISTORY—Edward Law, 2nd Baron Ellenborough (see that title in extant peerages was b. 8 Sept. 1790; educ. Eton and St. John's Coll. Camb. M.A. 1809; was Tory M.P. for St. Michaels 1815-18; was Chief Clerk of the Pleas, King's Bench, 1812-38; made P.C. 1828; Lord Privy Seal, 1828-29; Pres. of the Board of Control, 1828-30, 1834-35, Sept.-Oct. 1841, and Mar.-June, 1858; Gov. of India, 1841-44, and was cr. 22 Oct. 1844, (after his return from India), as **Viscount Southam,** of Southam, co. Gloucester, and **Earl of Ellenborough,** co. Cumberland; also cr. G.C.B. 1844; was First Lord of the Admiralty, Jan.-July, 1846; m. (1) 11 Dec. 1813, Lady Octavia, dau. of Robert Stewart, 1st Marquess of Londonderry. She d.s.p. 5 Mar. 1819. He m. (2) 15 Sept. 1824, Jane Elizabeth, dau. of Adm. Sir Henry Digby, (Digby, B.). This marriage ended in a divorce which Lord Ellenborough obtained by Act of Parliament 8 April 1830. The reason was Lady Ellenborough's adultery with Prince von Schwarzenberg, with whom Lord Ellenborough fought a duel and from whom he obtained damages of £25,000 in a legal action. Lady Ellenborough m. 2ndly 1832, Karl Theodore Herbert, Baron de Venningen, and thirdly Sheikh Medjwal el Mizrab, Arab Gen. in Greek service. She d. 11 Aug. 1881. The Earl of Ellenborough had issue by his second marriage an only child,
Arthur Dudley, b. 1828, d. 1 Feb. 1830.
The Earl d.s.p.s. 22 Dec. 1871, when the Earldom and Viscounty became extinct, but the Barony of Ellenborough was inherited by his nephew,
Charles Edmund Law, afterwards Towry-Law, 3rd Baron Ellenborough.
ARMS—Ermine on a bend engrailed between two cocks gules, three mullets pierced or.
CREST—A cock gules chained around the neck and charged on the breast with a mitre or.
SUPPORTERS—Two eagles wings elevated sable, the dexter chained around the neck, and pendent therefrom on the breast, a mitre or; the sinister with a like chain, and pendent therefrom a covered cup of the second.
MOTTO—Compositum jus fasque animi.

ELTISLEY

PEERAGE—U.K. Baron Eltisley of Croxton, co. Cambridge.
SURNAME—Newton.

CR.—15 Jan. 1934. **EXT.**—2 Sept. 1942.
HISTORY—Samuel Newton, Merchant in Liverpool, bought land in N. Wales between 1730 and 1740. He had a son,
Samuel Newton, who sold the Welsh properties, and bought Croxton, co. Cambridge 1820; m. Jane Roger, and had issue,
George Newton, m. 1829, Charlotte, dau. of Gen. Onslow, of Staughton House, co. Huntingdon, and d.v.p. 1837, leaving issue with two daus., an only son,
George Onslow Newton, of Croxton Park, co. Cambridge, and of Pickhill House, co. Denbigh, J.P. and D.L. co. Cambridge, and High Sheriff 1864, J.P. and D.L. co. Huntingdon, b. 22 Feb. 1830; educ. Trin. Col. Camb. B.A.; m. (1) 7 June 1852, Mary (d. 1855), dau. of W. B. Portman, of Hare Park, and had issue,
1. Frances Mary, m. her cousin Samuel Charles Newton, and d. April 1877.
He m. (2) 24 June 1858, Cecilia Florence (d. 7 Feb. 1869), dau. of Edwyn Burnaby of Baggrave Hall, co. Leicester, and had with one son who d. in infancy,
2. Cecilia Florence, m. 19 Nov. 1885, 9th Earl of Dysart, and d.s.p. 23 Dec. 1917.
He m. (3) 27 July 1878, Lady Alice Laura Sophia Cochrane, D.G. St. J., 2nd dau. of 11th Earl of Dundonaid and d. 7 Dec. 1900, having had further issue by her (who d. 8 Dec. 1914),
1. George Douglas Cochrane, **Baron Eltisley** (see below).
2. Denzil Onslow Cochrane, M.V.O., Capt. Middlesex Regt., b. 27 Oct. 1880, d. 9 Jan. 1915, of wounds received in action.
3. Thomas Cochrane, b. 1 Jan. 1885; served in World War I 1914-18, Col., despatches, D.S.O. and O.B.E.; m. 26 April 1924, Helen, dau. of Augustus Thorne, and had issue.
4. William Alexander Cochrane, Lt. R.G.A., b. 1886; m. 14 Aug. 1917, Marion, dau. of Capt. Sanson, of Calgary, Canada, and had issue.
5. Basil Cochrane, C.M.G., British Min. at Prague, b. 1889.
The eldest son, Sir George Douglas Cochrane Newton, **Baron Eltisley,** b. 14 July 1879; educ. Eton and Trin. Coll. Camb.; Director of Edmundson's Electricity Corpn. and other cos.; High Sheriff cos. Cambridge and Huntingdon 1909; Chm. both co. councils 1919 and 1920; Chm. Nat. Council of Agriculture for England 1922-23; M.P. Cambridge 1922-34; Official Adviser to the Gov. on agricultural matters at Imperial Economic Conference at Ottawa 1932, and at World Monetary Conference, London 1933. He was cr. K.B.E. 1919, and Baron Eltisley, of Croxton, co. Cambridge, 15 Jan. 1934, and had the decoration of Comm. of the Order of Leopold of Belgium. He m. 24 Aug. 1905, Muriel Mary Georgiana, only child of Col. Jemmett Duke, 17th Lancers, and d. 2 Sept. 1942, having had issue,
Myra Alice, b. 26 Aug. 1906; m. 20 Oct. 1927 (m. diss. by div. 1952), Sir Gifford Wheaton Grey Fox, 2nd Bt., and had issue.
Lord Eltisley's seat was at Croxton Park, St. Neots, co. Cambridge, and his town house 105 Eaton Place, London, S.W.1. His clubs were Carlton and Boodle's.

EMLY

PEERAGE—U.K. Baron Emly of Tervoe, co. Limerick.
SURNAME—Monsell.
CR.—12 Jan. 1874. **EXT.** 24 Nov. 1932.
HISTORY—John Monsell, or Mounsell, of Melcombe Regis, co. Dorset, m. 25 Feb. 1568, Jane, dau. of John Pitt, of Causeway, and d. 1586, having had with three daus., one son, John Monsell, of London, afterwards of Court Browne Castle, near Askeaton, co. Limerick, who went to Ireland in 1612, bought land there, but returned to England in 1634. IIc m. 1608, Mary Ash, of Westcombe, co. Somerset and had issue by her three sons and three daus. His will dated 18 May 1637 was proved in the Prerogative Court, Ireland. He d. 16 June 1637, and his third son,
Ephraim Monsell, of co. Limerick, and of lands in Frome, Somerset, was b. 1627; m. (1) Miss Sambourne and had issue two sons; (2) Miss Hutchens, and had issue, a third son; (3). Abigail, dau. of John Craven, of Limerick, and had three sons and two daus. He sold his property in Somerset and bought lands in Limerick where he settled in 1644. His eldest surv. son by his first marriage,
Thomas Monsell, of Tervoe, and Newtown, near Carrigogunnell, co. Limerick, and later of lands in Poblebrien, co. Limerick, d. 1712 having had issue, (with two elder sons—John, a Major in the Army who d.s.p. and Samborne, b. 1676, entered in T.C.D. 1694) a third son, Samuel Monsell, of Tervoe, m. the dau. of William Webb, of Gerrane, co. Limerick, and had with four other sons, an eldest son, William Monsell, of Tervoe, b. 1706; educ. T.C.D. 1722; m. (1) the dau. of the Rev. Richard Burgh, of Dromkeen, by whom he had a son, Samuel, d. unm.; and m. (2) 1751, Dymphna, dau. of Rev. Stackpole Pery, (see Limerick, E.), by whom he had his heir, William Thomas Monsell, of Tervoe, Col. in the Army, b. 21 Dec. 1754; m. 1776, Hannah, dau. of Amos Strettell, of Dublin, and had issue with three other sons to four daus., an eldest son,
William Monsell, of Tervoe, b. 1778; m. 1810, Olivia, dau. of Sir John Allen Johnson-Walsh, of Ballykilcavan, and d.v.p. 1822, leaving an only son and heir,
William Monsell, **Baron Emily** of Tervoe, so cr. 12 Jan. 1874, was b. 21 Sept. 1812; educ. Winchester and Oriel Coll. Oxford; Sheriff of co. Limerick, 1835; M.P. co. Limerick 1847-74; made P.C. 1855; Clerk of the Ordnance 1852-57; Under Sec. for Colonies 1868-71; Postmaster Gen. 1871-73; Lord Lt. co. Limerick 1871-94; Chan. of the Royal Univ. of Ireland 1885-94; m. (1) 11 Aug. 1836, Lady Anna Maria Charlotte Wyndham-Quin, only dau. of 2nd Earl of Dunraven. She d.s.p.s. 7 Jan. 1855. He m. (2) 23 Feb. 1857, Berthe, dau. of Philippe Auguste, Comte De Montigny Boulainvilliers, of Perreux in Burgundy. She d. 4 Nov. 1890. He d. 20 April 1894, having had issue, a third but only surv. son, (by his second wife),
Thomas William Gaston Monsell, **2nd Baron Emily**, State Steward to the Lord Lt. of Ireland 1880-82; Gent. Usher to the Viceroy of Ireland 1882-85, but "removed from the Commission of the Peace in Nov. 1899 for making inflammatory and disloyal speeches"

(*C.P.*) He was b. 5 Mar. 1858; m. 5 Sept. 1881, Frances Vincent de la Poer, dau. of John Power, of Gurteen, M.P., (Foreign Titles section in Burke's Peerage previous to 1949, Count de la Poer, a title of the Papal States), and d. 24 Nov. 1932, having by her (who d. 5 Sept. 1925) had issue,
William John Francis, b. 11 July, 1883, at the Gentleman Usher's House, Upper Castle Yard, Dublin, and d.v.p. 19 Feb. 1886.
Mary Olivia Augusta, O.B.E., D.G. St. J., m. 1 June 1881, Edmund de la Poer, Count de la Poer, (see above ref.) and had issue.
ARMS—Argent on a chevron between three mullets sable, a trefoil, slipped or.
CREST—A lion rampant ppr., holding between the paws a mullet sable.
SUPPORTERS—On either side, a lion ppr. gorged with a collar vair pendent therefrom an escutcheon of the arms.
MOTTO—Mone sale.
The seats of the Lords Emly were: Tervoe, co. Limerick and Chateau de Drouilly, Montoire. The Club of the 1st Baron was the Athenaeum.

EMMOTT

PEERAGE—Baron Emmott, of Oldham, co. Lancaster.
SURNAME—Emmott.
CR.—2 Nov. 1911. **EXT.**—13 Dec. 1926.
HISTORY—George Emmott, of Wood Bank, Disley, co. Chester, had a son, Thomas Emmott, J.P., of Brookfield, Oldham, and Anchorsholme, Poulton-le-Fylde, co. Lancaster, cotton manufacturer, b. 18 May 1823; m. 11 Oct. 1854, Hannah, (d. 20 Sept. 1896), dau. of John Barlow, of The Oak, Chorley, co. Chester (Barlow, Bt., of Bradwall Hall), and d. 27 Dec. 1892, having had,
1. George Henry, Queen Victoria Prof. of Law, Liverpool Univ. 1896, and Dean of the Faculty of Law, 1903; b. 28 Sept. 1855; educ. Trin. Coll. Camb. M.A., and Barrister-at-Law, Inner Temple; m. 24 Aug. 1881, Elizabeth, dau. of J. B. Braithwaite, and d. 8 Mar. 1916, having had issue, two sons and three daus.
2. John Thomas, b. 2 Dec. 1856; d. 30 June 1883.
3. Alfred, **Baron Emmott** (see below).
4. Theodore, Rev., b. 11 June 1859; educ. Christ's Coll. Camb., M.A.; m. 15 Jan. 1903, Jemima, E. L. Pemell, of Weston-Super-Mare.
5. Charles, of Thorpe Hall, Barnard Castle, and North Bailey, Durham, b. 6 May 1861; m. 27 June 1891, Lady Constance Harriet Campbell, dau. of 8th Duke of Argyll, and d. 18 Feb. 1910, leaving issue.
6. William Rhodes, b. 6 July 1863; m. 1 Dec. 1886, Julia, dau. of James Jones, of Lechlade Manor, co. Gloucester.
The third son, Sir Alfred Emmott, **Baron Emmott**, b. 8 May 1858; educ. Grove House, Tottenham, and London University, B.A., partner and Managing Director, Emmott and Walshall, cotton spinners, of Oldham; Mayor of Oldham, 1891-92; M.P. Oldham 1899-1911; Parl. Under Sec. for the Colonies, 1911-14;

First Commissioner of the Office of Works, 1914-15; Dir. of the War Trade Dept., 1915-19; Pres. of the Oldham Chamber of Commerce, made P.C. 1908; cr. Baron Emmott, of Oldham, co. Lancaster, 2 Nov. 1911; G.C.M.G. 1914, and G.B.E. 1917. He m. 5 Oct. 1887, Mary Gertrude (J.P. co. London), dau. of J. W. Lees, of Waterhead, Oldham, and d.s.p.m. 15 Dec. 1926, leaving,

1. Mary Gwendolen, b. 1 Sept. 1888; m. 6 May 1913, Home Peel, son of Charles Peel, of Sunninghill, Ascot, co. Berks, and has issue.
2. Dorothy, b. 14 Jan. 1890.

ARMS—Per pale azure and sable, a fess argent cottised or between three plates each charged with a bull's head caboshed azure as many annulets sable.

CREST—In front of a demi-bull sable armed or, semée of annulets, gorged with a collar gemel argent and holding between the legs a plate, three escallops reversed or.

SUPPORTERS—On either side a bull reguardant argent semée of roses and collared gules.

MOTTO—Tenes le vraie.

ENNISDALE

PEERAGE—U.K. Baron Ennisdale of Grateley, co. Southampton.

SURNAME—Lyons.

CR.—6 July 1939. EXT.—17 Aug. 1963. Also a Baronetcy cr. 3 Mar. 1937.

HISTORY—John Edward Lyons, of Ennis, co. Clare had a son, Sir Henry Edward Lyons, Bt., and Baron Ennisdale, b. 29 Aug. 1877; Major Gen., served in the S. African War 1900-02, and in World War I 1915-19, being D.A.Q.M.G. headquarters S. Command 1918-19. He m. 17 Jan. 1905, Helen, dau. of Frank Bishop. He was cr. O.B.E. (1919), a Kt. Bach. (1933), a Bt. 3 Mar. 1937 and a peer as Baron Ennisdale of Grateley, co. Southampton, 6 July 1939. He d. 17 Aug. 1963.

ARMS—Quarterly argent and azure in the first and fourth quarters a lion rampant and in the second and third a phoenix all counterchanged.

CREST—A lion rampant azure, collared and chained, the chain reflexed over the back or, holding in the sinister paw a trefoil slipped vert.

SUPPORTERS—On either side a lion rampant azure collared and chained or the chain reflexed over the back holding in the sinister and dexter paw respectively a trefoil slipped vert.

MOTTO—Facta non verba.

Lord Ennisdale's residence was Baynards Park, Cranleigh, Surrey.

**ENNISHOWEN AND CARRICKFERGUS

PEERAGE—U.K. Baron Ennishowen and Carrickfergus, of Ennishowen, co. Donegal and Carrickfergus, co. Antrim.

SURNAME—Chichester.

CR.—18 Aug. 1841. EXT.—20 Oct. 1883.

HISTORY—George Hamilton Chichester, 3rd Marquess of Donegall, was b. 10 Feb. 1797; educ. Eton; and Ch. Ch. Oxford; served in the

7th Hussars, as Capt.; sat as Tory M.P. for Carrickfergus, 1818-20; Belfast, 1820-30; co. Antrim, (as a Whig) 1830-37; and for Belfast again 1837-38, until defeated as a Liberal candidate for that constituency. He was Vice Chamberlain of the Household, 1830-34, and 1838-41; made P.C. 1830; cr. G.C.H. 1831; and on 18 Aug. 1841, during the lifetime of his father, the 2nd Marquess of Donegall, Baron Ennishowen and Carrickfergus, of Ennishowen, co. Dongal and Carrickfergus, co. Antrim. He was Lord Lt. of Antrim, 1841-83; Capt. of the Yeomen of the Guard, 1848-52, and cr. K.P. 1857. He m. (1) 8 Dec. 1822, Lady Harriet Anne Butler, dau. of the 1st Earl of Glengall. She d. 14 Sept. 1860. He m. (2) 26 Feb. 1862 Harriet, dau. of Sir Bellingham R. Graham, 7th Bt., and widow of Lt. Gen. Sir Frederick Ashworth. By his first marriage he had two sons, who d. young or unm. and a dau., Harriet who m. the 8th Earl of Shaftesbury. His second wife d. 6 Mar. 1884. He d.s.p.m.s. 20 Oct. 1883. The Barony of Ennishowen expired, and he was s. in the Marquessate and his other honours by his brother, Edward Chichester,

4th Marquess of Donegall. (see extant peerage works).

ERNLE

PEERAGE—U.K. Baron Ernle, of Chelsea, co. London.

SURNAME—Prothero.

CR.—4 Feb. 1919. EXT.—1 July 1937.

HISTORY—Thomas Prothero, of Malpas Court, co. Monmouth, High Sheriff 1846, b. 1780; m. (1) 1809, Mary, dau. of John Collins, of Ingatestone, Essex, who d. 18 Dec. 1835. He m. (2) 1838, Sarah, dau. of William Pattman, of Ham, co. Kent. He d. 23 April 1853, having had by his first marriage four sons and four daus., of whom the fourth son, The Rev. Canon George Prothero, b. 18 Mar. 1818; educ. Brasenose Coll. Oxford, B.A. 1843, M.A. 1866; Vicar of Clifton-on-Teme 1847-53, Curate of Whippingham, Isle of Wight 1853-57, Rector thereof 1857, Chaplain in Ordinary to Queen Victoria from 1866, and Canon of Westminster from 1869; m. 1846, Emma, only dau. of Rev. William Money Kyrle, (B.L.G.), of Homme House, Co. Hereford, and d. 16 Nov 1894, having had issue,

1. George Walter, Sir. K.B.E., M.A. King's Coll. Cambridge, and Litt.D.Camb., Vice Pres. of the Royal Hist. Soc., Univ. Lecturer in History and Fell, of King's Coll. 1876-94, Prof. of History, Edinburgh 1894-99, Editor of the Quarterly Review 1899-1920, Rede Lecturer, Camb. 1903, Lowell Lecturer, Boston 1910, Chichele Lecturer, Oxford 1915, Pres. R.H.S. 1901-05, Gov. of Holloway Coll. 1916, Dir. of Historical Section, Foreign Office 1918, b. 14 Oct. 1848; m. 22 June 1882, Mary Frances, dau. of Most Rev. Samuel Butcher, Bishop of Meath, (Danesfort, B.). She d. 9 April 1934. He d. 10 July 1922.
2. Arthur William Edward, Adm. R.N., b. 18 April 1850; m. 4 Sept. 1894, Helen Lucy, dau. of G. B. Ellicombe, of Chudleigh, co. Devon, and d. 1 Jan. 1931. She d. 27 April 1932.

3. Rowland Edmund, **Baron Ernle** (see below).
4. Michael Ernle du Sautoy, I.C.S., 1881-1912, M.A. Univ. Coll. Oxford, Inspector of Schools, India, 1908-12, b. 18 Dec. 1857; m. 15 Jan. 1884, Kathleen Eleanor Gay, dau. of Lt. Col. J. G. French, I.M.S., and d. 22 Jan. 1923, leaving issue.
  1. Mildred, m. Jan. 1885, Robert Scott Hankinson, of Little Basset Wood, Southampton, and had issue.

The third son, Rowland Edmund Prothero, **Baron Ernle,** b. 6 Sept. 1851; educ. Marlborough and Balliol Coll. Oxford, M.A. 1878, Fell. of All Souls 1875-91; Barrister at Law, Middle Temple, 1878; Editor of the *Quarterly Review* 1894-99; Agent-in-Chief to the Duke of Bedford, 1898-1918; M.P. Univ. of Oxford 1914-19; mem. Departmental Cttee. on Home Production of Food 1915; Pres. of the Board of Agriculture and Fisheries 1916-19; Freeman of City of London 1917; he was cr. Baron Ernle, of Chelsea, co. London, 4 Feb. 1919. He m. (1) 15 Aug. 1891, Mary Beatrice, dau. of John Bailward, of Horsington Manor, co. Somerset. She d. 3 May 1899. He m. (2) 9 April 1902, Barbara Jane, dau. of Lt. Col. C. O. Hamley. She d. 26 Nov. 1930. He d.s.m.p.s. 1 July 1937, having had issue the following:

Rowland John, b. 23 June 1894; educ. Eton and R.M.C. Sandhurst; 7th Hussars, 17 Sept. 1913; served in World War I and d. unm. 8 Nov. 1918, of wounds received in action in Mesopotamia, and was bur. there, Beatrice Hope, m. 3 Feb. 1923, V. P. Gilpin, and had issue.

Lord Ernle wrote many books, including *The Psalms in Human Life* and *English Farming Past and Present.*

ESTCOURT

PEERAGE—U.K. Baron Estcourt of Estcourt, Shipton Moyne, co. Gloucester and of Darrington, W.R. Yorks.
SURNAME—Estcourt later Sotheron-Estcourt.
CR.—3 Aug. 1903. **EXT.**—12 Jan. 1915.
HISTORY—In B.L.G. 1952 appeared the article Oswald formerly Estcourt formerly of Pinkney, in which the descent of the Estcourt family is traced from Walter de la Estcourt who held a knight's fee in 1303 in Shipton, co. Gloucester to Edmund Estcourt of Estcourt who was born circa 1609. This Edmund bequeathed a trust of £20,000 to his dau. Anna Maria, who m. William Earle of Malmesbury, co. Wilts and all his landed estates to Thomas Estcourt, 2nd son of Matthew Estcourt of Cam, co. Gloucester, whose relationship to the line recorded in B.L.G. 1952 has not been established. There is an account of the line derived from Matthew Estcourt in B.L.G. 1937, Sotheron-Estcourt of Estcourt and Darrington Hall.

Matthew Estcourt of Cam, by his wife Esther Halling, had issue with two daus.,
1. Matthew, d.s.p.
2. Thomas (see below).
3. Edward.

4. Edmund, Rev. D.D., Rector of Long Newenton and Didmarton, d. 17 Sept. 1802 aged 51.

The second son, Thomas Estcourt, inherited the estates of Walter Estcourt under the latter's will 1750, was b. 27 Sept. 1748; M.P. Cricklade; m. 6 Oct. 1774, the Hon. Jane Grimston, elder dau. of 2nd Viscount Grimston and had issue by her (who d. 28 May 1856),
1. Thomas Grimston Bucknall (see below).
2. Edmund William, Rev. M.A. Oriel Coll. Oxford, Rector of Long Newton, co. Wilts, and Shipton Moyne, co. Glos., b. 28 April 1782; m. 13 Feb. 1811, Bertha Elizabeth (d. 16 June 1850), dau. of Thomas Wyatt, of Wargrave, co. Berks, and d. 28 May 1856, having had issue,
   (1) Edward Thomas, b. 12 Sept. 1813; d. 1 Mar. 1814.
   (2) Edgar Edmund, Rev. M.A. Exeter Coll. Oxford, Canon of Birmingham R.C. Cathedral, b. 7 Feb. 1816, d. unm. 17 April 1884.
   (3) Matthew Hale, M.A. Exeter Coll. Oxford, b. 8 July 1818. d. unm. 1 April 1858.
   (4) Charles Wyatt, of Gatcombe House, I. of W., b. 20 Oct. 1820; m. 14 Sept. 1847, Frances Emma Coker (d. 18 Aug. 1875), dau. of C. H. Dane of N. Curry, co. Somerset, and d. 8 Oct. 1866, having had with other issue,
     1a. Edmund Walter (see below).
     2a. Arthur Sotheron, b. 1853, d. 1891
     1a. Birtha Mary, b. 1848, d. 1922.
     2a. Alice Madeline, b. 1852, m. Jonathan Westall and d. 1929.
     3a. Edith Rose, b. 1856.
     4a. Caroline Triesley, b. 1858.
     5a. Ethel Caroline, b. 1859.
   (5) Arthur Harbottle, M.A. Exeter Coll. Oxford, Barrister-at-Law, Lincoln's Inn, Dep. Gov. of the I. of W., b. 3 Nov. 1822, d. unm. 21 May 1898.
   (1) Mary Jane, d. unm. 12 Mar. 1901.
1. Harriet Jane Bucknall, b. 9 Aug. 1776; d. unm. 25 July 1839.
2. Charlotte, d. 20 July 1861, aged 80.

Mr. Thomas Estcourt d. 2 Dec. 1818 and was s. by his eldest son, Thomas Grimston Bucknall Estcourt, J.P. and D.L., M.P. Devizes 1805-26 and later Univ. of Oxford, Barrister-at-Law, D.C.L. of Corpus Christi Coll. Oxford; b. 3 Aug. 1775, assumed the additional surname of Bucknall 1824; m. 12 May 1800, Eleanor, dau. of James Sutton, of New Park, co. Wilts, and by her (d. 23 June 1829) had issue,
1. Thomas Henry Sutton (see below).
2. James Bucknall Bucknall-Estcourt, Major Gen. and Adjt. Gen. in the Crimea, b. 12 July 1802; educ. Harrow and R.M.C.; m. Caroline, dau. of Rt. Hon. Reginald Pole-Carew, and d. 24 June 1855. His widow was raised by Royal Warrant to the rank of a wife of a K.C.B. and was Lady Bucknall-Estcourt.
3. Edmund Hilary Bucknall-Estcourt (see below).
4. Walter Grimston Bucknall-Estcourt, Cmdr. R.N., b. 16 May 1807, d. on coast of Africa, 16 Sept. 1845.
5. William John Bucknall-Estcourt, Rev., M.A., Rector of Long Newton, co. Wilts, Hon. Canon of Gloucester, b. 17 May 1812; m. Mary, dau. of the Rev. John

Drake, and d. 4 April 1884, leaving issue, Eleanor, m. 1876, Rev. Edmund Walter Estcourt, Rector of Long Newnton, and had issue, four sons and four daus.

6. Edward Dugdale Bucknall-Estcourt, of Newnton House, co. Glos., Barrister-at-Law, b. 6 Feb. 1818; d. 12 July 1864.
1. Eleanor Anne, m. Rt. Hon. Henry V. Addington and d. 1878.
2. Georgiana Charlotte.
3. Mary Ann Harriet Bucknall-Estcourt, d. 1885.

Mr. T. G. Bucknall-Estcourt d. 26 July 1853, being s. by his eldest son,

The Rt. Hon. Thomas Henry Sutton Sotheron-Estcourt, of Estcourt, co. Glos, and of Darrington Hall, Yorks, J.P. and D.L., M.P. Marlborough 1827-32, Devizes 1835-44, and North Wilts 1844-65; b. 4 April 1802; educ. Harrow and Oriel Coll. Oxford, M.A. 1826; m. 21 Aug. 1830, Lucy Sarah (d. 1 July 1870), only child of Frank Sotheron, of Kirklington, co. Notts, Adm. of the Blue and assumed 17 July 1839 the surname and arms of Sotheron only. On the death of his father he resumed his patronymic. Made P.C. 1852 and Pres. of Poor Law Board; Sec. of State for Home Dept. 1859. He d. 1876 and was s. at Estcourt by his brother,

The Rev. Edmund Hilary Bucknall-Estcourt, of Estcourt, M.A. Merton Coll. Oxford, Rector of Echington, co. Derby, b. 22 Nov. 1803; m. 15 April 1830 Anne Elizabeth, dau. of Sir John Lowther Johnstone 6th Bt. She d. 1882. He d. 25 Jan. 1894, having had issue with 8 daus., an only son,

George Thomas Sotheron-Estcourt, **Baron Estcourt**, of Estcourt, Shipton Moyne, co. Gloucester and of Darrington, W.R. Yorks, so cr. 3 Aug. 1903; b. 21 Jan. 1839; educ. Harrow and Balliol Coll. Oxford, B.A. and M.A. 1865, M.P. North Wilts 1875-85, s. to Darrington 1876 under the will of his uncle and assumed the additional surname of Sotheron. He m. 14 April 1863, Monica (d. 31 Mar. 1922), dau. of Rev. Martin Stepylton and d.s.p. 12 Jan. 1915. He was s. in the estates by his cousin and heir of entail, the Rev. Edmund Walter Sotheron-Estcourt (see above) for whose descendants see *B.L.G.* 1937.

ARMS—Quarterly 1 and 4, Ermine on a chief indented gules three mullets of six points, a bordure or charged with eight cinquefoils sable (Estcourt); 2 and 3, Gules, on a bend indented between six cross crosslets argent, three eagles displayed sable, a canton ermine (Sotheron).
CRESTS—1. Issuant from a mural crown per pale azure and gules a demi eagle with wings displayed or, on each wing a mullet of six points also azure (Estcourt); 2. An eagle with two heads displayed per pale argent and gules the wings semée of cross crosslets counterchanged murally crowned, beaked and membered, and charged on the body with a cinquefoil or, for difference (Sotheron).
SUPPORTERS—On either side an eagle reguardant wings expanded and inverted gorged with a chain pendant therefrom an escutcheon or, the dexter charged with the arms of Estcourt the sinister with those of Sotheron.
MOTTO—Deo gratias.

EVANS

PEERAGE—U.K. Baron Evans of Merthyr Tydfil, co. Glamorgan.
SURNAME—Evans.
CR.—1 July 1957. EXT.—26 Oct. 1963.
HISTORY—John Evans of Dowlais, co. Glamorgan, b. 1842; m. Sarah Powell and d. 5 Aug. 1905 having had issue, Harry Evans of Dowlais, b. 1873; m. Edith Gwendoline Rees and d. 1914 having had issue, Sir Horace Evans, **Baron Evans,** a very distinguished physician, being Physician to King George VI, 1949-52, to Queen Mary, 1946-53, and to Elizabeth II, 1952-63, b. 1 Jan. 1903; educ. Liverpool Coll., City of London School, London Hospital and London Univ., M.B. (1928) M.D. (1930), F.R.C.P. Lond., M.R.C.S. Eng., m. 15 June 1920, Helen Aldwyth, dau. of T. J. Davies and had issue two daus. He was cr. K.C.V.O. (1949), G.C.V.O. (1955) and Baron Evans of Merthyr Tydfil, co. Glamorgan, 1 July 1957. He d. 26 Oct. 1963.
ARMS—Tierce in pairle gules, azure and sable in chief a Cornish chough ppr. and in base two organ rests or.
CREST—Two lion's paws azure supporting a stag's head erased or.
SUPPORTERS—Dexter, A lion gules; Sinister, A dragon sable, each supporting between the forelegs a rod of Aesculapius or.
MOTTO—Servabo fidem.
BADGE—In front of two slips of foxglove addorsed, leaved and flowered ppr. a fleur-de-lis vert flowered or, the whole enfiled with a Baron's coronet also ppr.

EVERSHED

PEERAGE—U.K. Baron Evershed of Stapenhill, co. Stafford.
SURNAME—Evershed.
CR.—20 Jan. 1956. EXT.—3 Oct. 1966.
HISTORY—The family of Evershed has a connected pedigree from Thomas Evershed, of Ackley, co. Surrey, b. ca. 1485, given in the 1952 ed. of B.L.G. (Evershed of Albury House). Sydney Evershed of Albury House, Burton-on-Trent, co. Staffs (1825-1903) had a fourth son, Frank Evershed of Grayrigg, Winshill, Burton-on-Trent, who by his wife Florence Helen, dau. of Thomas Barnabas Lowe, of Bearwood Bank, Burton-on-Trent, had issue, Francis Raymond Evershed, **Baron Evershed,** a very distinguished lawyer, b. 1899; educ. Clifton and Balliol Coll. Oxford, B.A.; served in World War I as 2nd Lt. R.E., and in World War II in C.D., Barrister-at-Law, Lincoln's Inn, 1923, Bencher 1938, K.C. 1933, Judge of the High Court 1944, Lord Justice of Appeal, 1947, Master of the Rolls, 1949-62, U.K. mem. of the Permanent Court of Arbitration at the Hague, 1950, Chm. of the Pilgrim Trust, 1960. He was cr. Kt. Bach. (1944) made a P.C. (1947) and cr. Baron Evershed of Stapenhill co. Stafford, 20 Jan. 1956. He m. 1928 Cecily Elizabeth Joan, dau. of the Hon. Charles Alan Bennett, of Middle Meadow, Beaconsfield, co. Bucks and d. 3 Oct. 1966.
ARMS—Argent on a chief sable three mullets of six points or pierced.

CREST—A mullet of six points or pierced between a pair of wings displayed argent.
MOTTO—Sic itur ad astra.

EVERSLEY OF HECKFIELD

PEERAGE—U.K. Viscount Eversley of Heckfield, co. Southampton.
SURNAME—Shaw-Lefevre.
CR.—11 April 1857. EXT.—28 Dec. 1888.
HISTORY—William Shaw, of Wakefield, co. Yorks, m. Mary (d. 1770, aged 84), dau. of John Ambler, of York, and d. aged 74 in 1768, having had, with an elder son, John who d.s.p. and a dau. Priscilla who d. unm., a ygr. son, The Rev. George Shaw, B.A., F.R.S., Rector of Womersley, co. York, b. 1723; m. Mary, dau. of Edward Green, of Hindley, Felkirk, co. York. She d. aged 59 in 1782, and he d. 1812, having had, with two other sons who d. young, and a dau. Maria Priscilla, who m. Rev. Littleton Powys, brother of 1st Lord Lidford, an only surv. son, Charles Shaw-Lefevre, who assumed by Royal Licence, on his marriage, the additional name and arms of Lefevre, M.P. for Newtown, I. of W., 1796-1802; and for Reading, 1802-20, Barrister-at-Law, Lincoln's Inn, m. 3 Sept. 1789, Helena, only dau. and heir of John Lefevre, of Heckfield Place, co. Hants, and Old Ford, Middlesex. She d. 17 Aug. 1834. He d. 27 April 1823. They had issue,
1. Charles, **Viscount Eversley.**
2. John George, (see Eversley, Baron, in present work).
3. Henry Francis, b. 16 July 1802; m. (1) 20 Mar. 1827, Helen, dau. of Major Gen. J. G. Le Marchant (Le Marchant Bt.), She d. Feb. 1833, leaving three daus. He m. (2) 2 Dec. 1835, Elizabeth Emma, dau. of Rev. John Foster; she d.s.p. 1842. He d. 3 Dec. 1880.

The eldest son, Charles Shaw-Lefevre, **Viscount Eversley,** of Heckfield, co. Southampton, so cr. 11 April 1857; b. 22 Feb. 1794; educ. Winchester and Trin. Coll. Camb., B.A. 1815, M.A. 1819; Barrister-at-Law, Lincoln's Inn, 1819, Bencher, 1839; M.P. Downton 1830-31, for Hants, 1831-32, and North Hampshire, 1832-57; Speaker of the House of Commons, 1839-57; made P.C. 1839; on his retirement from the Speakership he was given a pension of £4,000 per year for life; Gov. of the I. of W., 1857-88; cr. G.C.B. 1885; m. 24 June 1817, Emma Laura, dau. of Samuel Whitbread, of Southill, co. Bedford, and had issue with three daus., three sons, all named Charles, all of whom died in infancy. She d. 20 June 1857. He d. 28 Dec. 1888.
ARMS—Sable a chevron argent, between two trefoils slipped in chief and a bezant in base surmounted by a cross patée or.
CREST—Six arrows interlaced saltirewise three and three ppr. within an annulet or.
SUPPORTERS—On either side a talbot, that on the dexter gules, that on the sinister sable, each charged on the shoulder with a mace erect or.
MOTTO—Sans charger.

EVERSLEY

PEERAGE—U.K. Baron Eversley, of Old Ford, London.
SURNAME—Shaw-Lefevre.
CR.—16 July 1906. EXT.—23 April 1928.
HISTORY—Sir John George Shaw-Lefevre, K.C.B., second son of Charles Shaw-Lefevre (see Eversley, Viscount in present work), was b. 24 Jan. 1797; educ. Trin. Coll. Camb., M.A., Senior Wrangler, 1819, Barrister-at-Law, Inner Temple, and Bencher; M.P. Petersfield, 1832-34; Under Sec. for the Colonies, 1833-34; Poor Law Commissioner, 1834-41, and Clerk of the Parliaments, 1856-75; m. 29 Dec. 1824, Rachel Emily, dau. of Ichabod Wright, of Mapperley Hall, co. Notts. She d. 10 Feb. 1885. He d. 20 Aug. 1879. They had with five daus., a son, George John Shaw-Lefevre, **Baron Eversley,** of Old Ford, London, b. 12 June 1831; educ. Eton and Trin. Coll. Camb., M.A.; Barrister-at-Law, Inner Temple, 1855; Bencher, 1882; M.P. for Reading, 1863-85, and for Central Bradford, 1886-95; Sec. to Board of Trade, 1868-71; Under Sec. for Home Affairs, 1871; Sec. to the Admiralty, 1871-74; and in 1880; First Commissioner of Works, 1880-84; Postmaster Gen. 1882, and 1884-85; First Commissioner of Works, 1892-93, Pres. of Local Gov. Board, 1894-95; mem. or pres. of many commissions; made P.C. 1880, cr. Baron Eversley, of Old Ford, London, 16 July 1906; m. 24 Mar. 1874, Constance Emily, dau. of Henry John Moreton, 3rd Earl of Ducie, and d.s.p. 19 April 1928. She d. 27 Feb. 1929.
ARMS—Sable a chevron argent, between two trefoils slipped in chief and a bezant in base surmounted by a cross patée or.
CREST—Six arrows interlaced saltirewise three and three ppr. within an annulet or.
SUPPORTERS—On either side a man habited as a forester winding a horn ppr.
MOTTO—Sans changer.
Lord Eversley's seat was at Abbotsworthy House, Kingsworthy, Winchester. His clubs were the Athenaeum and Reform.

FABER

PEERAGE—U.K. Baron Faber of Butterwick, co. Lincoln.
SURNAME—Faber.
CR.—29 Dec. 1905. EXT.—17 Sept. 1920.
HISTORY—The descent of the family from John Faber, b. 1671, is given in great detail in B.L.G. 1952 Faber of Worsall Grange. Edmund Beckett Faber, **Baron Faber** was b. 9 Feb. 1847, the eldest son of Charles Wilson Faber, of Northaw, co. Herts, by his wife, Mary eldest dau. of Sir Edmund Beckett, 4th Bt., and sister of 1st Baron Grimthorpe. He was educ. Eton and Trin. Coll., Camb.; M.P. for Andover Dis. of Hants 1901-05, J.P. and D.L., W.R. Yorks, Chm. English County Bakers' Asscn. and of *Yorkshire Post;* senior partner in Beckett & Co. Bankers, Leeds and York and a director of the London & N.W. Railway and Sun Insurance Co. cr. Baron Faber of Butterwick, co. Lincoln, 29 Dec. 1905 and d. 17 Sept. 1920 (see also Wittenham, B. in present work).
ARMS—Or on a pale ermine a rose gules, barbed and seeded ppr., a chief azure thereon two mullets argent.

CREST—The battlements of a tower or thereon two mascles interlaced fessways vert in front of a dexter cubit arm in mail armour, the hand ppr. grasping a rose gules stalked leaved and slipped ppr.
SUPPORTERS—On either side a boar sable semée of roses argent, tusked bristled unguled and gorged with a collar or.
MOTTO—Quisque faber fortunae suae.

FAIRFIELD

PEERAGE—U.K. Baron Fairfield, of Caldy in the county palatine of Chester.
SURNAME—Greer.
CR.—1 Feb. 1939. **EXT.**—4 Feb. 1945.
HISTORY—Sir Frederick Arthur Greer, **Baron Fairfield,** 2nd son of Arthur Greer, of Ballasalla House, I. of M., by his wife, Mary, dau. of John Moore, of St. Helens, Lancs., was b. 1 Oct. 1863; Barrister-at-Law, Gray's Inn, 1886; K.C. and Bencher, 1910; a Justice of the High Court, King's bench Div. 1919-27; and a Lord Justice of Appeal, 1927-38; Chm. of the Council of Legal Education, 1934; cr. Kt. Bach. 1919; made a P.C. 1927; and cr. a peer as Baron Fairfield, of Caldy in the county palatine of Chester 1 Feb. 1939; m. (1) 17 Aug. 1901, Katherine, (d. 19 Mar. 1937), dau. of Emanuel van Noorden of Orangebury, S. Carolina, U.S.A., and had issue,

    Louise Mary, m. 11 May 1929, Ronw Moelwyn Hughes, Q.C. and had issue.

He m. (2) 4 Sept. 1939, Mabel Lily, dau. of W. J. Fraser, and widow of C. W. Neele, and d. 4 Feb. 1945. She d. 1 June 1960.
ARMS—Or two pallets ermine surmounted by a bend azure, all within a bordure engrailed azure.
CREST—In front of a cubit arm, vested azure cuffed argent, the hand ppr. grasping a trefoil slipped vert a fasces fesswise also ppr.
MOTTO—Hoc securior.
Lord Fairfield lived at Fairfield House, Croft Drive East, Caldy, co. Cheshire.

FAIRHAVEN

PEERAGE—U.K. Baron Fairhaven of Loder, co. Cambridge.
SURNAME—Broughton.
CR.—20 Mar. 1929. **EXT.**—20 Aug. 1966.
HISTORY—Urban Hanlon Broughton, of Park Close, Englefield Green, co. Surrey, M.P. 1915-18, Director of many American industrial companies, b. 1857; m. 1895, Cara Leland, dau. of Henry Huttleston Rogers of New York. He d. 30 Jan. 1929 before he could be raised to the peerage which it was intended to grant to him. By Royal Warrant of King George V dated 2 May 1929, his widow was granted the same style and title as would have been hers had her husband lived to become a peer. She was therefore officially styled Lady Fairhaven until her death in 1939 but she was not accorded the rights and privileges or the precedence proper to a peer's widow. The elder son of the late Mr. Broughton, Urban Huttleston Rogers Broughton, was, however, created **Baron Fairhaven of Lode,** co. Cambridge, on 20 Mar. 1929. His younger brother

Henry Rogers Broughton was granted the right to hold and enjoy the rank, title and precedence of a younger son of a baron. The letters patent limited the descent of the barony to the heirs male of Lord Fairhaven lawfully begotten. In the *London Gazette* for 25 July 1961 it was announced that the Queen had been pleased to create Lord Fairhaven a baron again as Lord Fairhaven of Anglesey Abbey, co. Cambridge with special remainder to his yr. brother and the later's heirs male. Lord Fairhaven d. without male issue on 20 Aug. 1966 and the Barony created in 1929 became extinct while that created in 1961 devolved upon his ygr. brother. The history of the family and title is therefore found in the books dealing with extant peerages. "Into the intricacies of this most interesting double creation it is not my purpose to enter. I am only concerned with one thing, which is that it was found necessary to issue two letters patent. The original letters patent which created the Barony of Fairhaven could not be changed. They had passed the Great Seal and no change could be permitted. Therefore Lord Fairhaven had to have a duel personality, he was both Lord Fairhaven of Lode and Lord Fairhaven of Anglesey Abbey . . . it is all reminiscent of the law of the Medes and Persians 'which altereth not' " (*Ramshackledom*, p. 31).
ARMS—Argent two bars and in the dexter chief point a saltire couped gules.
CREST—In front of a bull's head erased, sable collared and chained or, three fleur-de-lis, gold.
SUPPORTERS—On either side a winged bull sable, each armed and gorged with a chain or, pendent therefrom an escutcheon charged with the arms of Broughton.
MOTTO—Si je puis.

FALCONER OF HALKERTON

PEERAGE—Baron, Scottish, Baron Falconer of Halkerton.
SURNAME—Keith-Falconer.
CR.—20 Dec. 1647. **DORMANT**—25 May 1966.
HISTORY—Alexander Falconer, eldest son of Sir Alexander Falconer, of Halkerton, was cr. 20 Dec. 1647, with remainder to his heirs male whatsoever, a Lord of Session as **1st Baron Falconer** of Halkerton. His kinsman, the **5th Baron Falconer,** (David Falconer) m. 1703, Catherine Margaret, dau. of William Keith, 2nd Earl of Kintore. His grandson by this marriage, Anthony Adrian Falconer, **8th Baron Falconer,** s. to the Earldom of Kintore on the death of his cousin, George Keith, 10th Earl Marischal, and but for an attainder, Earl of Kintore, on 23 May 1778. The **8th Baron Falconer** became 5th Earl of Kintore. From him descended the 10th Earl of Kintore, who d.s.p. 25 May 1966, when he was s. in the Earldom and the Scottish Barony of Keith of Inverurie and of Keith Hall by his sister, Ethel Sydney Baird, 11th holder of the title, Countess of Kintore, and Lady Keith, while the Barony of Falconer of Halkerton became dormant. See also under Kintore Baron, for details of the U.K. Barony of Kintore which also in 1966 became extinct.

For the full details of the lineage of Falconer of Halkerton, see under Kintore, E. in extant peerages.

ARMS—Azure a falcon displayed between three mullets argent on his breast a man's heart gules.

CREST—An angel in a praying posture or within an orle of laurel ppr.

SUPPORTERS—Two falcons ppr.

MOTTO—Vive ut vivas.

FARNBOROUGH

PEERAGE—Baron Farnborough, of Farnborough, co. Southampton.

SURNAME—May.

CR.—11 May 1886. **EXT.**—17 May 1886.

HISTORY—A remarkable degree of reticence is shown in the notice concerning Lord Farnborough in the usual peerage sources, in the Complete Peerage, and in the D.N.B., as regards any mention of his parentage. In the record of Middle Temple admissions, he is simply entered as Thomas Erskine May, of Catherine Street, City of Westminster, Gent. He was b. in London, 8 Feb. 1815; educ. Bedford Gram. Sch.; adm. to Middle Temple, 20 Jan. 1834, called to the Bar, at Middle Temple, 4 May 1838; a Bencher 1873; Reader, Middle Temple, autumn, 1880; was Examiner of petitions for Private Bills in Parliament, 1846; Taxing Master for both Houses of Parliament 1847-56; Clerk Asst. 1856-71; Librarian to House of Commons; Clerk of the House of Commons, 1871-86. He was cr. C.B. 1860; K.C.B. 1866; D.C.L. Oxford, 1874; made P.C. 1884; cr. a peer as **Baron Farnborough**, of Farnborough, co. Southampton, 11 May 1886. He m. 27 Aug. 1839, Louisa Johanna, dau. of George Laughton, of Fareham, co. Hants, and d.s.p. 17 May 1886, in his official residence in the House of Parliament, and was bur. at Chippenham, co. Cambridge. Lady Farnborough d. 2 Feb. 1901. From the Middle Temple Bench Book, where nothing about parentage is given, the following description of Lord Farnborough's coat of arms is taken: (in the Bench Book there is a somewhat cautionary remark as to arms being shown, without necessarily being official.):

Quarterly 1 and 4, Gules a fess between eight billets or; 2 and 3, Azure three garbs or; Impaling, Argent on a fess between three crosses crosslet fitchée sable a cinquefoil of the field. (Panel). The 1st and 4th quarters are then described as the arms of Thomas May, of Faunt, co. Sussex, temp. Edward IV (Vis. Leicester 1619), the 2nd and 3rd quarters are the feudal arms of the earldom of Buchan (i.e. Erskine).

**FARNHAM

PEERAGE—Ireland. Viscount Farnham, co. Cavan.

Ireland. Earl of Farnham, co. Cavan.

SURNAME—Maxwell.

CR.—Viscounty, 10 Jan. 1781. Earldom 22 June 1785. **EXT.**—23 July 1823.

HISTORY—Barry Maxwell, **3rd Baron Farn-**

ham, was the second son of John Maxwell **1st Baron Farnham,** and s. his elder brother in that dignity on 16 Nov. 1779. He was a Barrister-at-Law, King's Inns, Dublin, 1748; Bencher; 1757; M.P. for co. Cavan, 1756-60, for Armagh City, 1761-68; and for co. Cavan 1768-79; in 1771 he assumed the surname of Barry in lieu of that of Maxwell, when he inherited the estates of his maternal grandfather, but on succeeding to the peerage, he resumed the surname of Maxwell. He was Prothonotary of the Court of Common Pleas in Ireland, 1741-1800. He was cr. **Viscount Farnham,** 10 Jan. 1781, and **Earl of Farnham,** co. Cavan, on 22 June 1785, both in the Irish peerage. He was made a P.C. of Ireland 1796. He m. (1) 15 Jan. 1751, or 1757, Margaret, dau. of Robert King, of Drewstown, co. Meath. She d. 4 Dec. 1766. He m. (2) 5 Aug. 1771, Grace, dau. of Arthur Burdett, of Ballymaney, co. Kildare. The 1st Earl had a son, and two daus. by his first marriage, and two daus., by his second union. He d. 7 Oct. 1800. The only son,

John James Maxwell, **2nd Earl of Farnham,** b. 5 Feb. 1759; was M.P. for co. Cavan 1779-83, and again 1793-1800. He was a Representative Peer for Ireland, 1816-33. He m. 1784, Grace, dau. of Thomas Cuffe, of Grange, co. Kilkenny (she d. 10 Feb. 1856), and d.s.p. 23 July 1823, when the Earldom and Viscounty became extinct, but he was s. in the Barony of Farnham, by his cousin,

John Maxwell, **5th Baron Farnham.** (see extant peerage works).

ARMS—Quarterly 1 and 4, Argent a saltire sable, on a chief of the first, three pallets of the second; 2 and 3, Barry of six argent and gules.

CREST—A buck's head, erased ppr.

SUPPORTERS—Two bucks ppr.

MOTTO—Je suis pret.

FARQUHAR

PEERAGE—U.K. Baron Farquhar of St. Marylebone, 20 Jan. 1898.

U.K. Viscount Farquhar, 21 June 1917.

U.K. Earl, 30 Nov. 1922.

(Also a baronetcy cr. 25 Oct. 1892).

SURNAME—Townsend-Farquhar, later Farquhar.

CR.—as above. **EXT.**—30 Aug. 1923.

HISTORY—Horace Brand Townsend-Farquhar, later Farquhar, was b. 18 May 1844, the fifth son of Sir Walter Minto Townsend-Farquhar, 2nd Bt. (see under Farquhar Bt., in extant baronetage; the Townsend-Farquhar baronetcy became extinct on 30 June 1934 with the death of the 6th baronet.) His mother was Erica Catherine, only child (illegitimate) of Eric Mackay, 7th Baron Reay. He was Pres. of the London Municipal Soc. 1894-1901; M.P. West Marylebone 1895-98; was cr. a baronet 25 Oct. 1892; a peer as **Baron Farquhar** of St. Marylebone, 20 Jan. 1898, and **Viscount Farquhar** 21 June 1917, and **Earl Farquhar** 10 Nov. 1922; mem. L.C.C. for East Marylebone 1899-1901, and for West Marylebone, Mar. to June 1901; Master of the Household 1901-07, and Lord Steward of the Household 1915; Pres. of the Nat. Union of Conservative and Constitutional Asscns. 1913, Pres. of the Metropolitan Div. of the Nat. Union of these asscns. and Treasurer of the Conservative Party; cr. K.C.V.O. 1901, and G.C.V.O. 1902; made P.C. 1907. He m. 5 Jan. 1895, Emilie, dau. of Henry Packe, of Harleston, co. Northants, and widow of Sir Edward Scott, 5th Bt., and d. 30 Aug. 1923 when all his honours became extinct.

ARMS—Argent a lion rampant sable, armed and langued gules, between two sinister hands couped and apaumée in chief gules, and a crescent in base azure, and a crescent for difference.

CREST—An eagle rising ppr.

SUPPORTERS—On either side a greyhound ppr. gorged with a chain or, suspended therefrom an escutcheon argent, charged with a crescent azure.

MOTTO—Mente manuque.

Lord Farquhar's residences were 7, Grosvenor Square, W., Castle Rising, King's Lynn and White Lodge, Richmond Park, S.W. His clubs were Turf, Marlborough, and Carlton.

FARRER

PEERAGE—U.K. Baron Farrer, of Abinger, co. Surrey. (Also a Baronetcy cr. 22 Oct. 1883.)

SURNAME—Farrer.

CR.—22 June 1893. EXT.—16 Dec. 1964.

HISTORY—Henry Farrer of Worsthorne, Burnley, co. Lancs, m. 1610 Janet Jackson, and d. 1633, leaving issue, Robert Farrer, of Lower Graystoneleigh, Chipping, co. Lancs, bapt. 27 Sept. 1618; d. Jan. 1702/3 leaving by his wife Margaret, Richard Farrer, bapt. 30 April 1658; m. 20 April 1686, Elizabeth Guy, and d. 1742 leaving issue, Oliver Farrer, b. 1693; m. 24 June 1718, Janet Banks and d. 1731 leaving issue, James Farrer, bapt. 1719 at Clapham, co Yorks, and d. 1766 leaving by his wife Mary, dau. and heiress of Thomas Harrison, with other issue, a third son, James Farrer, bapt. 15 Sept. 1751; m. Frances, dau. and heiress of William Loxham, of Woodford, co. Essex, and d. 1820, having had with other issue, Thomas Farrer, b. 16 Dec. 1787; m. 18 Sept. 1876, Cecilia (d. 1867), dau. of Richard Willis, of Halsnead, co. Lancs and d. 23 Sept. 1833, having had with other issue, an eldest son,

Sir Thomas Henry Farrer, **1st Baron Ferrer**, B.A. Oxford, Barrister-at-Law, sometime Permanent Sec. to the Board of Trade, b. 24 June 1819; m. (1) 10 Jan. 1854, Frances (d. 1870), dau. of William Erskine and by her had issue with a dau. Emma Cecilia, m. Sir Horace Darwin, and another son, d. unm.,

1. Thomas Cecil, **2nd Baron** (see below).
2. Noel Maitland, B.A. Trin. Coll. Camb., Priv. Sec. to Permanent Sec. of the Board of Trade, b. 1867; m. 1904 Mabel Elizabeth, dau. of Ralph Elliot and widow of Sir Alexander Mackenzie, and d. 1929 leaving issue,
   Anthony Thomas, **5th Baron** (see below).

Thomas Henry Farrer m. (2) 1873, Katherine Euphemia, dau. of Hensleigh Wedgwood. He was cr. a Baronet 22 Oct. 1883 and **Baron Farrer**, of Abinger, Surrey, 22 June 1893. He d. 11 Oct. 1899 and was s. by his elder surviving son,

Thomas Cecil Farrer, **2nd Baron Farrer,** M.A. Balliol Coll. Oxford, Pres. Soc. of Genealogists 1922, b. 25 Oct. 1859; m. (1) 27 July 1892, Evelyn Mary, (d. 1898), dau. of Hon. Charles Spring Rice (see Monteagle, B.) and by her had issue, with two daus.,

1. Cecil Claude, **3rd Baron** (see below).

He m. (2), 9 Nov. 1903, Evangeline, dau. of Octavius Newry Knox, of Abinger Hammer, co. Surrey (see Ranfurly, E.), and by her had further issue, with a dau.,

2. Oliver Thomas, **4th Baron** (see below).

Lord Farrer d. 12 April 1940 and was s. by his elder son, Sir Cecil Claude Farrer, **3rd Baron Farrer,** O.B.E. (1917), b. 8 May 1893; educ. Eton and New Coll. Oxford; m. 30 Sept. 1919, Evelyn Hilda Perry, dau. of Edward Tipping Crook, of Woodlands Hall, Bridgnorth and d.s.p. 11 Mar. 1948 when he was s. by his half brother,

Oliver Thomas Farrer, **4th Baron Farrer,** b. 5 Oct. 1904; educ. Westminster and Trin. Coll. Cambridge, B.A. (1925); served in World War II 1939-45, W/Cdr. R.A.F.V.R., despatches; m. 23 Oct. 1931, Hon. Katharine Runciman, dau. of 1st Viscount Runciman, and d.s.p. 24 Jan. 1954 when he was s. by his cousin,

Anthony Thomas Farrer, **5th Baron Farrer,** b. 22 April 1910; m. 1931 (m. diss. by div.) Florence Elizabeth Florio and d. 16 Dec. 1964.

ARMS—Argent on a bend engrailed sable four horse shoes argent.

CREST—A quatrefoil within a horse shoe between two wings all argent.

SUPPORTERS—On either side a horse reguardant argent, gorged with a riband pendant therefrom an escutcheon both sable, charged with two horseshoes palewise argent.

MOTTO—Ferre va ferme.

FAUCONBERGE

PEERAGE—England. Barony by writ Faucomberge or Fauconberge.

SURNAME—Fauconberge or Faucomberge, Lane-Fox, Anderson-Pelham etc. etc.

CR.—By writ 24 June, 1295. ABEYANT— 7 Feb. 1948.

HISTORY—The first **Baron Fauconberge**, Sir Walter de Faucomberge of Rise and Withernwick in Holderness, was the son and heir of Sir Piers de Faucomberge. His descendants are given in extant peerages until the time of his descendant, Joane, **Baroness Fauconberge,** bapt. 18 Oct. 1406. She m. Sir William Nevill, Baron Fauconberge and cr. Earl of Kent, 1461. He d. 9 Jan. 1462/3. She d. 11 Dec. 1490, aged 84. The earldom of Kent became extinct with the earl's death without male issue, but the Barony of Fauconberge fell into abeyance between the three daus. of the Baroness, namely,

1. Joan, m. Edward Bechom, and d.s.p.
2. Elizabeth, m. Sir Richard Strangways, and had issue, James, Sir, a coheir to his grandmother.
3. Alice, m. John Conyers, and had issue, William Conyers, 1st Baron Conyers, coheir to his grandmother.

On 29 Sept. 1903, the abeyance of the Barony of Fauconberge was terminated in favour of

Marcia Amelia Mary Lane-Fox, Countess of Yarborough, and Baroness Conyers, (see that title) and she became **6th Baroness Fauconberge**. The barony fell into abeyance again on the death on 7 Feb. 1948 of her son, the 5th Earl of Yarborough. (see Conyers, Barony).
ARMS—(of Fauconberge) Or a fess azure in chief three pallets gules.

**FERRERS OF CHARTLEY

PEERAGE—England. Baron Ferrers of Chartley.
SURNAME(S)—Ferrers, Devereux, Shirley, Compton, and Townshend.
CR.—By writ 1299. ABEYANT—31 Dec. 1855.
HISTORY—This barony deemed to have been cr. by writ of summons to Parliament in 1299, passed for some generations in the family of Ferrers, until circa 1446, after which it passed into the Devereux family, thence to the Shirleys, Earl Ferrers, and to the wife of James Compton, 5th Earl of Northampton, the latter being summoned on 28 Dec. 1711, as Baron Compton. He m. 7 Mar. 1715-16, Elizabeth, **Baroness Ferrers** of Chartley, sister and heiress of Robert Shirley, Viscount Tamworth, and granddau. of 1st Earl Ferrers. The 5th Earl of Northampton had issue an only child,
Lady Charotte Compton, who s. her mother in the barony of Ferrers of Chartley and her father in the Barony of Compton (q.v.), She m. the 1st Marquess Townshend, which brought those baronies into the Townshend family. She d. 3 Sept. 1770. Her son, the
2nd Marquess Townshend, s. her in the baronies, but his elder son, the
3rd Marquess Townshend, d.s.p. 31 Dec. 1855, when the two baronies of Ferrers and of Chartley fell into abeyance between his sisters and their descendants, namely the Lady Harriet Anne Ferrers, and the Lady Elizabeth Margaret Boutlbee.

FEVERSHAM

PEERAGE—U.K. Earl of Feversham, of Rydale, co. York, and Viscount Helmsley of Helmsley, co. York.
SURNAME—Duncombe.
CR.—25 July 1868. EXT.—4 Sept. 1963.
HISTORY—The pedigree of this family begins with Thomas Duncombe who possessed properties in Buckinghamshire in the reign of Henry VIII. It is given in the extant peerage under Baron Feversham. The first Baron Feversham, descendant of Thomas Duncombe was so cr. as Baron Feversham of Duncombe Park, co. York, 14 July 1826. He was s. on his death 16 July 1841 by his eldest son, William Duncombe, 2nd Baron Feversham, b. 1798; m. 1823, Lady Louisa Stewart, dau. of the 8th Earl of Galloway and d. 11 Feb. 1867, leaving with other issue, an elder surviving son,
William Ernest Duncombe, 3rd Baron Feversham, and **1st Earl of Feversham**, b. 28 Jan. 1829; m. 7 Aug. 1851, Mabel Violet, 2nd dau. of the Rt. Hon. Sir James Robert Graham, 2nd Bt. and had with other issue, an eldest son,

William Reginald, Viscount Helmsley, b. 1 Aug. 1852; m. 23 Dec. 1876, Lady Muriel Frances Talbot, dau. of the 19th Earl of Shrewsbury and d.v.p. 24 Dec. 1881, leaving issue, with one dau.,
Charles William Reginald, **2nd Earl.**
Lord Feversham was M.P. for East Retford 1852-57 and for N.R. Yorks 1859-67, he was cr. Viscount Helmsley of Helmsley and **Earl of Feversham** of Ryedale, both co. York, 25 July 1868. He d. 13 Jan. 1915 and was s. by his grandson,
Charles William Reginald Duncombe, **2nd Earl of Feversham**, M.A. Ch. Ch. Oxford, M.P. for Thirsk Div. of N.R. Yorks, Lt. Col., Yorks Hussar Yeo., served in World War I, b. 8 May 1879; m. 19 Jan. 1904 Lady Marjorie Greville, dau. of 5th Earl of Warwick and was k. in action, 15 Sept. 1916, leaving with other issue, an elder son,
Charles William Slingsby Duncombe, 5th Baron Feversham and **3rd Earl of Feversham**, b. 2 Nov. 1906; educ. Eton; Col. Yorks Hussars, served in World War II, D.S.O. 1945, Lord in Waiting to George V and Edward VIII, Chm. Nat. Assoc. for Mental Health; m. 9 May 1936 Lady Anne Wood, dau. of 1st Earl of Halifax and d. 4 Sept. 1963, having had issue a dau. Clarissa. The Earldom and Viscounty then became extinct and the Barony devolved upon the last Earl's kinsman, Charles Antony Peter Duncombe, 6th Baron Feversham, a free lance journalist.
ARMS—Per chevron engrailed gules and argent, three talbot's heads erased counterchanged.
CREST—Out of a ducal coronet or, a horse's hind leg sable, the shoe argent.
SUPPORTERS—Dexter, A horse of a dark iron grey colour guttee d'or, ducally gorged of the last: Sinister, A lion argent, powdered with fleur-de-lis sable, his head adorned with a plume of six feathers argent and azure issuing out of a ducal coronet or.
MOTTO—Deo regi patriae.

FIELD

PEERAGE—U.K. Baron Field of Bakeham, co. Surrey.
SURNAME—Field.
CR.—23 April 1890. EXT.—23 Jan. 1907.
HISTORY—Sir William Ventris Field, **Baron Field** of Bakeham, co. Surrey, so cr. 23 April 1890, was the second son of Thomas Flint Field, of Fielden, in Barton-in-the-Clay, co. Beds. He was b. 21 Aug. 1813; was a student at the Middle Temple, 1843; Barrister-at-Law, Inner Temple, 1850; Q.C. 1864; Bencher, Inner Temple, 1864; Justice of the Queen's bench, 1875; cr. Kt. Bach., 1875; a Judge of the High Court of Justice, Queen's Bench Div., 1875-1890; made P.C. 1890. He m. 1864, Louisa, dau. of John Smith. She d. 24 May 1880, and he d.s.p. 23 Jan. 1907.
ARMS—Sable a chevron engrailed ermine between three garbs, on a chief or a dolphin naiant ppr.
CREST—Issuant from clouds ppr, a cubit arm erect vested gules., cuff argent, the hand ppr. grasping a spear in bend sinister or., the whole between two wings argent.
SUPPORTERS—On either side a female

figure ppr. vested argent, mantle azure, the dexter figure holding in the sinister hand a torch erect sable fired ppr. and the sinister figure holding in the dexter hand a like torch.
MOTTO—Sapientia donum Dei.
Lord Field's seat was at Bakeham, Virginia Water, Staines. His club was the Athenaeum.

FIFE

PEERAGE—U.K. Duke of Fife and Marquess of Macduff, 29 July 1889.
U.K. Earl of Fife, 13 July 1885.
Ireland. Earl Fife, and Viscount Macduff, 26 April 1759.
Ireland. Baron Braco of Kilbryde, co. Cavan, 28 July 1735.
U.K. Baron Skene of Skene, co. Aberdeen.
SURNAME—Duff.
CR.—As above. **EXT.**—29 Jan. 1912. (Irish titles possibly dormant.)
HISTORY—James Duff, **5th Earl of Fife**, was s. by his only son, Alexander William George Duff, 6th Earl of Fife, and 1st Duke of Fife etc. so cr. 29 July 1889. He was b. 10 Nov. 1849. He m. 27 July 1889, at Buckingham Palace, the Princess Louise Victoria Alexandra Dagmar, eldest daul of Albert Edward, Prince of Wales, by Alexandra, dau. of Christian IX, King of Denmark. He d.s.p.m. 29 Jan. 1912 and his titles as set out above then became extinct (the Irish titles may be dormant). He had, however, been cr. 24 April 1900, **Duke of Fife** and **Earl of Macduff** in the peerage of the U.K., with special remainder in favour of his 1st and other daus., by his wife, and their male issue. Accordingly he was s. in the U.K. Dukedom of Fife as cr. 1900 by his elder dau. (see extant peerages for present holder of title).
ARMS—Quarterly 1 and 4, Or a lion rampant gules; 2 and 3, Vert a fess dancettée ermine between a hart's head cabossed in chief, and two escallops in base, or.
CRESTS—A horse in full gallop argent covered with a mantling gules bestrewed with escutcheons or, each charged with a lion rampant of the second, on his back a knight in complete armour, with his sword drawn, ppr. on his sinister arm a shield charged as the escutcheons; on the helmet a wreath of the colours thereon a demi-lion rampant gules;.
SUPPORTERS—Two savages, wreathed about the head and waist with laurel and holding in their exterior hands branches of trees over their shoulders, all ppr.
MOTTOES—Over the crest—Deus juvat. Under the shield, Virtute et opera.

FINLAY

PEERAGE—U.K. Baron Finlay, of Nairn, co. Nairn.
U.K. Viscount Finlay, of Nairn, co. Nairn.
SURNAME—Finlay.
CR.—Barony, 19 Dec. 1916. Viscounty 27 Mar. 1919. **EXT.**—30 June 1945.
HISTORY—William Finlay, of Cherry Bank, Newhaven, Edinburgh, F.R.C.P.(E.), m. Ann, dau. of Robert Bannatyne, of Leith, and d. 8 June 1886, having had issue by her (who d.

1862), an eldest son, Sir Robert Bannatyne Finlay, **1st Baron Finlay** and **Viscount Finlay,** b. 11 July 1842; educ. Edinburgh Academy, and Edinburgh Univ., 1858-63, graduating in medicine, M.D. 1863; student, Middle Temple, 1865, Studentship 1867, Barrister-at-Law, Middle Temple, 1867; Q.C. 1882, Bencher 1884, M.P. Inverness Burghs, 1885-92 and 1895-1906, and for Edinburgh and St. Andrews Univs., 1910-16; Solicitor Gen. 1895-1900; Attorney Gen. 1900-06; Treasurer, Middle Temple, 1902; Lord Chancellor, 1916-19; Brit. Mem. of the Court of Arbitration at The Hague, 1920; elected a Judge of the Permanent Court of International Justice, set up by the League of Nations, 1921. He was cr. Kt. Bach. 1895, G.C.M.G. 1904; made P.C. 1905; cr. Baron Finlay, of Nairn, co. Nairn, 19 Dec. 1916, and Viscount Finlay, of Nairn, co. Nairn, 27 Mar. 1919. He m. 26 Aug. 1874, Mary, dau. of Cosmo Innes, of Inverleith House, Edinburgh, and she d. 11 June 1911. He d. 9 Mar. 1929, having had issue,
William Finlay, **2nd Baron Finlay** and **Viscount Finlay,** b. 15 Oct. 1875; educ. Eton and Trin. Coll. Camb.; Barrister-at-Law, Middle Temple, 1901; K.C. 1914; Bencher, 1924; Junior Counsel to Board of Inland Revenue, 1905-14; Judge of the High Court of Justice, 1924; Adviser to the Foreign Office during the Paris Peace Conference; Chm. of Wiltshire Quarter Sessions, 1937; cr. K.B.E. 1920; m. 25 April 1902, at the Temple Church, London, Beatrice Marion, dau. of Edward Kirkpatrick Hall, of Kevin, co. Nairn, and d. 30 June 1945, having had issue, Rosalind Mary, m. 15 April 1939 Vice Adm. J. O. C. Hayes, and had issue.
ARMS—Argent on a chevron vert between two roses in chief and a mullet in base gules two swords points downwards and conjoined at the pommels of the field, hilted and pommelled or.
CREST—A hand holding a dagger ppr.
MOTTO—Fortis in arduis.

FITZALAN OF DERWENT

PEERAGE—U.K. Viscount Fitzalan of Derwent, co. Derby.
SURNAME—FitzAlan Howard.
CREATION—28 April 1921. **EXT.**—17 May 1962.
HISTORY—Edmund Bernard FitzAlan Howard, **Viscount Fitzalan** of Derwent, 3rd son of the 14th Duke of Norfolk, was b. 1 June 1855; by Royal Licence 10 July 1876, in compliance with the will of the 17th Earl of Shrewsbury he assumed the surname and arms of Talbot only; m. 5 Aug. 1879, Lady Mary Bertie, eldest dau. of the 7th Earl of Abingdon by whom he had issue, with a dau. Mary Caroline Magdalen, a son,
Henry Edmund Fitzalan Howard, **2nd Viscount** (see below).
He was M.P. for Chichester 1894-1921, served in the S. African War, 1899-1901, Col. 11th Hussars (despatches, D.S.O.); held several political appointments and was Lord Lieut. of Ireland 1921-22; was Deputy Earl Marshal 1917-29. He was made P.C., created K.G., G.C.V.O., and Viscount Fitzalan of Derwent, co. Derby, 28 April 1921, and by

royal licence 9 June 1921 resumed his patronymic of FitzAlan Howard. He d. 18 May 1847 when he was s. by his only son,

Henry Edmund FitzAlan Howard, **2nd Viscount Fitzalan** of Derwent, b. 30 Oct. 1883, educ. Oratory School and New Coll. Oxford, served in World War I, 1914-16 (wounded), Capt. 11th Hussars, was awarded O.B.E. (1922); m. 9 May 1922 (m. diss. by div. 1955), Joyce Elizabeth Mary, dau. of Col. P. J. Langdall (see Mowbray, Seagrave and Stourton, B.) and d. 17 May 1962 having had issue, two daus.

ARMS—Quarterly 1, Gules on a bend, between six cross crosslets fitchée argent, an escutcheon or charged with a demi lion rampant pierced through the mouth by an arrow, within the royal tressure of Scotland gules, a crescent for difference (Howard with honourable augmentation after Flodden 1513); 2, Gules three lions passant guardant in pale or, in chief a label of three points argent (Brotherton); 3, Chequy or and azure (Warren); 4, Gules, a lion rampant or (FitzAlan). **CRESTS**—1, On a cap of maintenance ppr. a lion statant guardant with tail extended or ducally gorged argent. 2, Issuant from a coronet or, a pair of wings gules each charged with a bend between six crosses crosslet fitchée argent. 3, Upon a mound vert a horse passant argent holding in the mouth a slip of oak fructed ppr. **SUPPORTERS**—Dexter, A lion; Sinister, A horse, both argent, the latter holding in the mouth a slip of oak fructed ppr. and each charged on the shoulder with an escutcheon argent thereon a chief azure. **MOTTO**—Sola virtus invicta.

FITZGERALD OF KILMARNOCK

PEERAGE—U.K. Baron (Life) Fitzgerald of Kilmarnock, co. Dublin.
SURNAME—Fitzgerald.
CR.—23 June 1882. **EXT.**—16 Oct. 1889.
HISTORY—David Fitzgerald, merchant of Dublin, m. Catherine, the eldest dau. of David Leahy, of London and had issue, John David Fitzgerald, **Baron Fitzgerald** of Kilmarnock, co. Dublin, was b. 1816; Barrister-at-Law, King's Inns 1838, Q.C. 1847, Solicitor Gen for Ireland 1855-56, Attorney Gen. 1856-58 and 1859-60; M.P. Ennis 1852-60; apptd. Justice of Queen's Bench in Ireland 1860 and a Lord of Appeal in Ordinary 1882 being then cr. a life peer as Baron Fitzgerald of Kilmarnock, co. Dublin. He m. (1) 1846 Rose (d. 1850), dau. of John O'Donahoe of Dublin and had issue,

1. David, b. 14 Jan. 1847; B.A. Camb., Barrister-at-Law 1871 and of Irish Bar 1872.
2. John Donohoe, b. 20 Jan. 1848; B.A. Camb.; Barrister-at-Law; m. 7 Jan. 1881 Emma Ysolda, dau. of Sir Thomas Barrett Lennard, Bt. of Belhus, co. Essex and had issue,
3. Gerald, b. 12 Aug. 1849, B.A. Trin. Coll. Dublin; Barrister-at-Law.

Lord Fitzgerald m. (2) 3 May 1860, Jane Mary Matilda Southwell and had further issue,
4. Arthur Southwell, Lt. 3rd Bn. Essex Regt., b. 16 Feb. 1861.

5. Eustance Robert Southwell, b. 2 April 1863.
6. Edward Southwell, b. 13 May 1864; m. 22 Aug. 1884, Margaret Mary, dau. of Matthew P. D'Arcy of Killarney, co. Wicklow.
7. Evelyn Charles Joseph Southwell, b. 11 Mar. 1874.
1. Josephine Mary, m. 2 July 1885, G. S. Gunnis of Gordonbush, co. Sutherland.
2. Geraldine Mary Catherine.
3. Edith Margaret Mary.
4. Ismay Gertrude Mary.
5. Gertrude Amabel Mary.
6. Muriel Mary.

Lord Fitzgerald d. 16 Oct. 1889.
ARMS—Ermine a mascle or, over all a saltire gules.
CREST—On the Roman fasces lying fesswise ppr. a boar passant ermine fretty gules.
SUPPORTERS—Dexter, A griffin argent gorged with a collar and pendent therefrom an escutcheon azure charged with a trefoil also argent; Sinister, A boar argent gorged with a collar and pendent therefrom an escutcheon azure charged with a rose also argent.
MOTTOES—Crom a boo and Fortis et Fidelis.
Lord Fitzgerald's seat was Kilmarnock, co. Dublin.

FITZHARDINGE

PEERAGE—U.K. Baron FitzHardinge, of the city and county of the city of Bristol.
SURNAME—Berkeley.
CR.—5 Aug. 1861. **EXT.**—9 Dec. 1916.
HISTORY—This forms part of the long and somewhat tangled story of the great house of Berkeley (extant peerages and under Berkeley, E. of in present work). Frederick Augustus Berkeley, 5th Earl of Berkeley, who was b. 14 May 1745, was alleged to have m. on 30 Mar. 1785, Mary, dau. of William Cole, but this marriage was declared unanimously by the House of Lords, on 1 July 1811, not to be proved. By a subsequent marriage, which took place on 16 May 1796, the 5th Earl had further issue, but the second son of the union of 1785 was,

Maurice Frederick FitzHardinge Berkeley, **Baron FitzHardinge**, who was b. 3 Jan. 1788, and entered the R.N. 1802; Rear Adm. 1849, Vice Adm. 1856, Adm. of the Blue, 1862, and Adm. of the White, 1863. He was M.P. Gloucester 1831-57, a Lord of the Admiralty four times between 1833 and 1857; was cr. C.B. 1840; P.C. 1855; K.C.B. 1855; G.C.B. 1861; cr. on 5 Aug. 1861, Baron FitzHardinge of the city, and co. of the city of Bristol. Like his elder brother, William FitzHardinge Berkeley who was cr. Earl FitzHardinge on 17 Aug. 1841, he claimed the Barony of Berkeley as a barony appertaining to the Castle and Honour of Berkeley but this claim was not in either case agreed by the House of Lords. The 1st Baron FitzHardinge m' (1) 4 Dec. 1823, Charlotte, dau. of 4th Duke of Richmond, and she d. 20 Aug. 1833. He m. (2) 30 Sept. 1834 Charlotte, dau. of 1st Earl of Ducie, and d. 17 Oct. 1867, at Berkeley Castle, having had issue by his first marriage a son and heir, (and a second son (see below), with two daus.),

Francis William FitzHardinge Berkeley, **2nd Baron FitzHardinge** of Bristol, b. 16 Nov. 1826; educ. Rugby; Capt. Royal Horse Guards, 1853-57; M.P. Cheltenham, 1856-65; m. 24 Nov. 1867, Georgina, dau. of William Holme-Summer, of Hatchlands, East Clandon, co. Surrey, and d.s.p. 29 June 1896, when he was s. by his only brother,

Charles Paget FitzHardinge Berkeley, **3rd Baron FitzHardinge** of Bristol, b. 19 April 1830; educ. Rugby; M.P. Gloucester City, 1862-65; m. 6 Dec. 1856; Louisa Elizabeth, only dau. of Henry Lindow Lindow, formerly Rawlinson, of Gawcomb, co. Glos. She d. 15 Nov. 1902. He d.s.p. 5 Dec. 1916, when the Barony of FitzHardinge of Bristol became extinct.

FITZMAURICE

PEERAGE—U.K. Baron FitzMaurice of Leigh, co. Wilts.
SURNAME—Petty-FitzMaurice.
CR.—9 Jan. 1906. **EXT.**—21 June 1935.
HISTORY—Edmond George Petty Petty-FitzMaurice, **Baron FitzMaurice**, fourth son of the 4th Marquess of Lansdowne, (extant peerages), b. 19 June 1846; educ. Eton and Trin. Coll. Cambridge, B.A. 1868, and Pres. of the Union; Barrister-at-Law, Lincoln's Inn, 1871; M.P. Calne, 1868-85; Under Sec. of State for Foreign Affairs, 1882-85 and again 1905-08; served on many commissions at home and abroad; M.P. North Wilts, 1898-1905; Chancellor of the Duchy of Lancaster, 1908-09; F.B.A.; m. 23 Nov. 1889, Caroline, dau. of W. J. FitzGerald, of Litchfield, Connecticut, U.S.A., and this marriage was annulled 1894. He d.s.p. 21 June 1935. He was the author of several biographies of political figures. His seat was at Leigh House, Bradford, co. Wilts.
ARMS—Quarterly 1 and 4, Ermine on a bend azure, a magnetic needle pointing at a polar star or (Petty); 2 and 3, Argent a saltire gules a chief ermine (FitzMaurice).
CRESTS—1, A beehive beset with bees diversely volant ppr.
2, A centaur drawing a bow and arrow ppr., the part from the waist argent.
SUPPORTERS—On either side a Pegasus ermine bridled, crined, winged and unguled or each charged on the shoulders with a fleur-de-lis azure surmounted by a crescent gold for difference.
MOTTO—Virtute non verbis.

**FITZWALTER

PEERAGE—U.K. Baron FitzWalter of Woodham Walter, co. Essex.
SURNAME—Bridges.
CR.—17 April 1868. **EXT.**—6 Dec. 1875.
HISTORY—Brook Bridges, of Grove, co. Middlesex, auditor of the Imprest, bought the estate of Goodnestone Park, co. Kent and built the residence there. He m. Mary, dau. of Sir Justinian Lewen, and had with other issue an eldest son, Sir Brook Bridges, of Gooden-

stone Park, cr. a Baronet 19 April 1718; m. (1) 1707, Margaret, dau. of Sir Robert Marsham 4th Bt. and sister of the 1st Baron Romney (extant peerages, Romney, E.) by whom he had a son, Brook, and a dau. Margaret. He m. (2) Mary dau. of Sir Thomas Hales, Bt., and d. 16 Mar. 1727-28. The son and heir, Sir Brook Bridges, 2nd Bt., High Sheriff, co. Kent, 1733. He m. Anne, dau. of Sir Thomas Palmer, Bt., (after her death she m. 2ndly, the Hon. Charles Feilding, Denbigh, E.) and d. 23 May 1733, leaving an only child,

Sir Brook Bridges, 3rd Bt., b. posthumously; m. 1765, Fanny, dau. of Edmund Fowler, of Graces, co. Essex, (son of Christopher Fowler and Frances, his wife, who was the dau. of Henry Mildmay, of Graces, co. Essex, by Mary, his wife, the sister and coheir of Benjamin Mildmay, Baron Fitzwalter, through whom the claim to the said Barony came into the Bridges family, see below). Lady Bridges d. 16 Mar. 1825. Sir Brook Bridges d. Sept. 1791. They had issue, with others,

1. Brook William, 4th Bt. (see below).
2. Henry, b. 1 June 1769; who took the surname of Brook. He m. 1 July 1795, Jane, dau. of Sir Thomas Pym Hales, Bt., and d. 21 Sept. 1855, having had issue, with others,
   (1) Brook Henry, Barrister-at-Law, b. 1799; d. 1829.
   (2) Thomas Pym, Rev., Sir, 7th Bt.
   (1) Jane, d. unm. 1862.
   (2) Mary, d. unm. 1803.
   (3) Emilia, m. 1844, the Ven. William Brise Ady.
3. Brook Edward, b. 1779; m. 1809, Harriet, dau. of John Foote. She d. 1864. They had issue, with others,
   (1) Brook Edward, Rev., m. 1843, Louisa Anne, dau. of Sir John Osborn, 5th Bt., and d. 28 July 1869 leaving six daus., of whom the eldest, Frederica Harriet, m. 1872, the Rev. Henry Western Plumptre.
   (2) George Talbot, Rev., 8th Bt.
The eldest son, Sir Brook William Bridges, 4th Bt., was b. 22 June 1767; he assumed the Christian name of Brook by Act of Parliament; m. (1) 4 Aug. 1800, Eleanor, dau. and eventually coheiress of John Foote, of Lombard Street, London, a banker. She d. 29 Jan. 1806. He m. (2) 15 Dec. 1809, Dorothy Elizabeth, dau. of Sir Henry Hawley, 1st Bt., and d. 21 April 1829. She d. 1816. By his first marriage, the 4th Bt. had issue,
1. Brook William, Sir, 5th Bt., and **Baron FitzWalter** (see below).
2. Brook George, Rev. 6th Bt.
1. Eleanor, m. April 1828, Rev. Henry Western Plumptre, son of John Plumptre, of Fredville, co. Kent, (B.L.G. 1952 Plumptre of Fredville) and d. 1892, leaving issue.
The elder son, Sir Brook William Bridges, 5th Bt., and **Baron FitzWalter** of Woodham Walter, co. Essex, b. 2 June 1801; educ. Winchester and Oriel Coll. Oxford, B.A. 1822, M.A. 1827; was M.P. for East Kent, Feb.-July 1852, and 1857-68. In 1841 he claimed the Barony of FitzWalter which was held to have been cr. by writ of summons in 1295. Although the abeyance of the Barony was not terminated in his favour, he proved himself heir to a moiety, and probably to the entirety thereof

(C.P. view). On 17 April 1868, he was cr. a peer by letters patent as above. He m. 4 July 1834, his cousin, Fanny, dau. of Lewis Cage, of Milgate, in Bersted, co. Kent, (her mother having been Fanny, eldest dau. of Sir Brook Bridges, 3rd Bt.). She d. 28 Oct. 1874. The Baron FitzWalter d.s.p. 6 Dec. 1875. His Barony then became extinct, but he was s. in the baronetcy by his brother,

The Rev. Sir Brook George Bridges, 6th Bt., b. 12 Oct. 1802; m. 15 Nov. 1832, Louisa, dau. of Charles Chaplin, (Chaplin, V.), and d.s.p.l. April 1890, being s. in the baronetcy, by his kinsman,

The Rev. Sir Thomas Pym Bridges, 7th Bt., b. 22 Oct. 1805; m. 14 June 1831, Sophia Louisa, eldest dau. of Sir William Lawrence Young, 3rd Bt., and d. 28 Feb. 1895, having had issue, two daus. He was s. in the baronetcy by his cousin,

The Rev. Sir George Talbot Bridges, 8th Bt., member of the Society of Jesus, b. 10 May 1818; d. 27 Nov. 1899.

The descent of the Barony of FitzWalter (of 1295) went through Eleanor Bridges, wife of Rev. H. W. Plumptre, (see above), whose grandson, Henry FitzWalter Plumptre, became 20th Baron FitzWalter, on 30 Sept. 1924 when the abeyance had been terminated in his favour, and he received a writ of summons to Parliament on that date (for particulars of further succession, extant peerage works, under FitzWalter, B.).

ARMS—(of Lord FitzWalter of the 1868 creation). Azure three water bougets or within a bordure ermine.

CREST—Out of a ducal coronet or, a Moor's head in profile ppr., wreathed about the temples argent and gold, gorged with a collar of the first pendent therefrom a cross pattée of the third.

SUPPORTERS—Dexter, A bull sable, horned, hoofed, maned, ducally gorged, and line reflexed over the back argent; Sinister, A like bull semée of plates.

MOTTO—Je garderay.

FLECK

PEERAGE—U.K. Baron Fleck of Saltcoats, co. Ayr.
SURNAME—Fleck.
CR.—3 Feb. 1961. EXT.—6 Aug. 1968.
HISTORY—Alexander Fleck, m. 1843 Mary Spiers, and was father of Robert Fleck, merchant, b. 11 Dec. 1863 at Saltcoats, co. Ayr, m. 7 Dec. 1887 Agnes Hendry, dau. of James Duncan, and d. 15 Aug. 1934. She d. 1947. Their only child was, Alexander Fleck, **Baron Fleck,** who was b. 11 Nov. 1889; educ. Saltcoats Public School, Hillhead High School and Glasgow Univ., D.Sc. (1916); after service with Glasgow Univ. Staff and other bodies and companies, became in 1931, Managing Director General Chemicals Div. of I.C.I. He was Chm. Billingham Div. I.C.I. (1937-44), a Dir. I.C.I. (1944-51) and in 1953-60 Chm. of I.C.I. He was cr. K.B.E. (1955) and Baron Fleck of Saltcoats, co. Ayr, 3 Feb. 1961. He m. 11 July 1917, Isabella Mitchell, dau. of Alexander Kelly of Campbell-

town, co. Argyll. She d. 1955. He d. 6 Aug. 1968.
ARMS—Azure a pile argent goutée azure between two salmon hauriant respectant and inclined ppr., each holding in his mouth an annulet or, a thunderbolt ppr. inflamed gules.
CREST—A swan sejant holding in his mouth a philisopher's stone or. (videlicet pellettée of roundels azure and gules).
SUPPORTERS—Dexter, A countryman attired in a brown coat, doubled vert, his breeches grey, his stockings vert, boots sable, bonnet azure, his seed basket hung about his shoulders and sowing with his dexter hand; Sinister, A monk ppr. attired in a brown habit, holding in his sinister hand a mortar argent with pestle azure.
MOTTO—(Above the shield) Reflect and Resolve.

FLOREY

PEERAGE—U.K. Life, Baron Florey, of Adelaide in the Commonwealth of Australia and of Marston in the City of Oxford.
SURNAME—Florey.
CR.—4 Feb. 1965. EXT.—21 Feb. 1968.
HISTORY—Joseph Florey of Adelaide, South Australia, m. Bertha Mary Wadham, and was father (with three daus. d. unm. and another, Hilda Josephine, Mrs. Gardner) of, Sir Howard Florey, O.M., **Baron Florey** of Adelaide, etc. (see above), b. 24 Sept. 1898; educ. St. Peter's Collegiate School, Adelaide, Adelaide Univ. M.B., B.S. 1921, M.D. 1944, and Magdalen Coll. Oxford, Rhodes Scholar 1921, B.A. 1923, M.A., B.Sc. 1924, and John Lucas Walker Scholar, Cambridge 1924; received very many hon. degrees; Fellow Gonville and Caius Coll. Camb., Ph.D., M.A., held many teaching appointments in Pathology, Visiting Prof. to Australia and New Zealand 1944. Chancellor of Australian Nat. Univ. at Canberra 1965; F.R.S. 1941, Pres. 1960-65, received numerous awards from all over the world; m. (1) 19 Oct. 1926, Ethel Mary (d. 1966), dau. of J. H. Reed, of Adelaide. He was cr. Kt. Bach. 1944; O.M. 1965, and a life peer as Baron Florey of Adelaide in the Commonwealth of Australia and of Marston in the City of Oxford 4 Feb. 1965. He m. (2) 6 June 1967, Hon. Margaret Augusta Fremantle, dau. of 3rd Baron Cottesloe and formerly wife of D. A. Jennings, and d. 21 Feb. 1968. He left issue a son and a dau.
Charles du Vé, b. 11 Sept. 1934; educ. Rugby, Gonville and Caius Coll. Camb., B.A. 1956, M.B.B., C.H. 1960, Univ. Coll. Hosp. Medical Sch. and Yale Univ., M.P.H. 1963; m. 14 April 1966, Susan Jill, dau. of Cecil Hopkins of Nuneaton, co. Warwick.
Paquita Mary Joanna, b. 26 Sept. 1929; m. 29 Jan. 1965, John McMichael and had issue.
Lord Florey's residence was 4 Elsfield Road, Marston, Oxford.

FORREST

The above, as the name of a barony which has become extinct, occurs in some works. It is not given in the *Complete Peerage*, Vol. XIII where it would normally be found, as the alleged creation took place in 1918. Nor does it occur in the list of peerages created between 1917 and 1921, the dates of the publication of Burke's Peerage around the first World War. (There was no publication of Burke's Peerage between those dates.) The title as that of an extinct peerage does come in Debrett's older lists of peerages rendered extinct, and under the entry of Sir John Forrest in *Who Was Who* he is described as a Baron; likewise in the *Concise D.N.B.* 1901-1050, his entry reads: "Forrest, John, first Baron Forrest." Inquiry was made of the House of Lords by letter, but no written reply was received from the Clerk of the Journals. However, an assistant speaking for the Clerk advised that recourse should be had to *The Times;* being pressed the assistant agreed that while the Barony had been conferred, letters patent could not have been issued, and the patent had not passed the Great Seal. *The Times* kindly sent a copy of the entry from its columns for 8 Feb. 1918, which merely stated that The King had conferred a Barony of the United Kingdom on the Right Hon. Sir John Forrest, P.C., G.C.M.G., Treasurer of the Commonwealth of Australia in recognition of his long and distinguished services to the Empire. He d. in 1918, at sea.

FORSTER

PEERAGE—U.K. Baron Forster, of Lepe, co. Southampton.
SURNAME—Forster.
CR.—12 Dec. 1919. EXT.—15 Jan. 1936.
HISTORY—Thomas Forster, of Adderstone, co. Northumberland, d. before 1412, having had by his wife Elizabeth, dau. and heir of Roger de Etherstone, a son, Thomas Forster, of Adderstone, who m. Elizabeth Featherstonhaugh, of Stanhope, and had nineteen sons, of whom the eldest, Thomas Forster, of Adderstone, m. a dau. of the Hilton family of Hilton Castle, co. Durham. They are described in the 1883 Extinct Peerage as being Barons of the Bishopric of Durham, being termed Barons of Hilton, although no peerage title was ever bestowed, unless perhaps by a writ of summons in 1295. (Incidentally the account in the Extinct Peerage contains a most unusual criticism, more commonly to be found in the vols. of the *C.P.* than in Burke's older vols.) Thomas Forster was bur. at Bamburgh, and his eldest son, Sir Thomas Forster, of Adderstone, was Marshal of Berwick; he m. Dorothy, a dau. of Ralph Ogle, 3rd Baron Ogle (see Extinct Peerages 1883). She m. 2ndly Sir Thomas Grey of Horton. Sir Thomas Forster, d. 1526, being bur. in the choir of Bamburgh Church, and being s. by his son, Thomas Forster, of Adderstone, Sheriff of Northumberland 1563 and 1571; m. Florence, third dau. of Sir Thomas Wharton, 1st Baron Wharton (see extant peerages, Wharton, B.) and by her had issue.

However, the succession of the present pedigree goes through one of Thomas Forster's illegitimate children,
Ralph Forster, of Overgrass, Felton, co. Northumberland, b. 1552; and d. 1616, having had issue,
William Forster, of Newcastle-on-Tyne, m. 1 Jan. 1626, Prudence Clark, of Newcastle, and had a son,
The Rev. William Forster, M.A. and B.D., Christ's Coll. Camb., and Vicar of Standground, co. Hunts., 1662-79; b. Dec. 1630; m. Alice (d. 8 Jan. 1694), dau. of William Coveney and widow of Samuel Forster, of Nassington, co. Northampton; d. 8 Dec. 1679, having had issue, with three daus. (and an elder son, Rev. William, M.A. Emmanuel Coll. Camb., who d. 1719, leaving issue) a ygr. son,
John Forster, of Peterborough, b. 1672; m. Jane Bass of London, and d. 13 Dec. 1752, leaving issue with two daus.,
1. John, Rev. (see below).
2. James, serjeant-at-law, and chief justice of the Isle of Ely, m. Susan, dau. and coheir of Sir John Strange, Master of the Rolls and had issue, three daus.
3. William, of London, d. unm. 1791.
The eldest son, The Rev. John Forster, M.A. and D.D. Emmanuel Coll. Camb., Rector of Eleton, co. Huntingdon, and of Walsoken, co. Norfolk, chaplain to the Duke of Manchester, b. Aug. 1713; m. 1746, Jane, sister of William Jervis, of Windsor, and d. 1787, leaving with three daus. an only son,
John Forster, of Coxhoe Park, co. Durham, and of Southend, co. Kent, later of Great Carlton, co. Lincoln, m. Elizabeth (d. 25 Jan, 1837) 2nd dau. of Rev. Ralph Drake-Erockman, of Beachborough (*B.L.G.* 1952), co. Kent, and d. 1 Dec. 1884, having had with others a fourth son,
Capt. Henry Forster, R.H.A., b. Oct. 1789; served throughout the Peninsular War and was wounded at Waterloo; m. 1825 Harriet Elizabeth, dau. of Thomas FitzGibbon, of Ballysedda, co. Limerick. She d. 23 Oct. 1839. He d. 1855, having had with two daus.,
Major John Forster, of Exbury House, co. Hants, Great Carlton, Lincs, and Southend, co. Kent, b. 1 Aug. 1826; m. 18 Dec. 1861, Emily Jane, dau. of John Ashton Case, of Summerhill, and Ince Hall, co. Lancs., and d. 16 Sept. 1886, having had issue,
1. John, b. 1863, d. 1870.
2. Henry William, **Baron Forster** (see below).
3. Samuel Eustace, b. 31 Mar. 1867.
The second son, Sir Henry William Forster, **Baron Forster,** of Lepe, co. Southampton, b. 31 Jan. 1866; educ. Eton and New Coll. Oxford, B.A.; M.P. Conservative for Sevenoaks 1892-1918, and for Bromley, 1918-19; a Lord of the Treasury 1902-05; Fin. Sec. to the War Office and a mem. of the Army Council, 1915-19; served in World War I; made P.C. 1917; cr. Baron Forster, of Lepe, co. Southampton, 12 Dec. 1919; and G.C.M.G. 1920; K.G. St. J.; Gov. Gen. of Australia 1920-25; m. 3 June 1890, Rachel Cecily, G.B.E. 1926 and D.G. St. J., only dau. of 1st Baron Montagu of Beaulieu. He d.s.p.m.s. 15 Jan. 1936, having had issue,
1. John, b. 13 May 1893; 2nd Lt. K.R.R.C.; served in World War I, and was k. in action, v.p.unm. 14 Sept. 1914.

2. Alfred Henry, b. 7 Feb. 1898; Lt. 2nd Dragoons (Royal Scots Greys), served in World War I 1916-19, when he d.v.p. and unm. of wounds received in action, 10 Mar. 1919.

1. Dorothy Charlotte, m. (1) 10 June 1914, Capt. Hon. Harold Fox Pitt Lubbock, (Avebury, B.) and had issue. He was k. in action 4 April 1918. She m. (2) 5 April 1923, 1st Baron Wardington, and had further issue.

2. Emily Rachel, m. 22 Dec. 1915, (m. diss. by div. 1930) Capt. G. H. L. Fox-Pitt-Rivers, and had issue. (B.L.G. 1952, Pitt-Rivers, of Hinton St. Mary and Rushmore.).

ARMS—Argent, on a chevron vert, between three hunting horns sable, a martlet or.
CREST—A dexter arm embowed in armour grasping in the hand ppr. a broken tilting lance or, the rerebrace charged with a cross patée sable.
SUPPORTERS—Dexter, A second lieutenant of the King's Royal Rifle Corps; Sinister, A Lieutenant of the 2nd Dragoons (Royal Scots Greys) both ppr.
MOTTO—Sta saldo.
Lord Forster's seat was Lepe House, Exbury, Hants.

FRANCIS-WILLIAMS

PEERAGE—U.K. Life Baron Francis-Williams, of Abinger, co. Surrey.
SURNAME—Williams.
CR.—13 April 1962. **EXT.**—5 June 1970.
HISTORY—John Edmund Williams, of The White Cottage, Holmbury St. Mary, co. Surrey, was father of an only son, Edward Francis Williams, **Baron Francis-Williams**, b. 10 Mar. 1903; educ. Queen Elizabeth's Gr. Sch. Middleton; Editor of *The Daily Herald* 1936-40; Controller of Press Censorship and News, Min. of Information 1941-45; P.R Adviser to the Prime Minister (Mr. Attlee, later Earl Attlee) 1945-47; Gov. of B.B.C. 1951-52; author of seventeen books; m. 1926, Jessie Melville, dau. of E. Hopkin, of Leeds, and d. 5 June 1970, having had issue,

John Melville, b. 20 June 1931; educ. St. Christopher's Sch. Letchworth and St. John's Coll. Camb.; Barrister-at-Law, Inner Temple 1955; m. 1955 Jean Margaret, dau. of Harold Lucas, of Huddersfield, and had issue.

Elizabeth Frances, m. 1963, G. A. Thomson, and had issue.

He was cr. C.B.E. 1945, and a life peer as Baron Francis-Williams, of Abinger, co. Surrey, 13 April 1962. The style Lord Francis-Williams is curiously identical with that commonly given by courtesy to the sons of Dukes.
ARMS—None.
SEAT—Griffins, Abinger Hammer, Surrey. Club was Reform.

FRANKFORT DE MONTMORENCY

PEERAGE—Ireland. Baron Frankfort of Galway, co. Kilkenny, and Viscount Frankfort de Montmorency.

SURNAME—de Montmorency (Morres before 1815).
CR.—Barony, 31 July 1800. Viscounty, 22 Jan. 1816. **EXT.**—5 July 1917.
HISTORY—The earlier history of this family is given in extant peerage works under De Montmorency Baronets. Redmond or Reymond Morres, had an elder son, Lodge Evans Morres, later de Montmorency, **1st Baron Frankfort** and **1st Viscount Frankfort de Montmorency**, b. 26 Jan. 1747; M.P. for Innistoge 1768-70, for Bandon Bridge 1776-96, for Ennis 1796-97, and for Dingle 1798-1800; Chief Sec. to the Lord Lieut. 1795-1800; was cr. Baron Frankfort of Galway, co. Kilkenny, 31 July 1800, and Viscount Frankfort de Montmorency, 22 Jan. 1816; assumed by Royal Licence 17 June 1815, the surname of de Montmorency*; m. (1) Jan. 1777, Mary, dau. and heiress of Joseph Fade, of Dublin. She d.s.p. 7 Feb. 1787. He m. (2) 6 Aug. 1804, Catharine, (d. 12 Nov. 1851), dau. of George White, of Castle Bellingham, and d. 21 Sept. 1822, having had issue by her with three daus.,

Lodge Reymond de Montmorency, **2nd Viscount Frankfort de Montmorency**, b. 26 Nov. 1806; m. 12 Jan. 1835, Georgiana Frederica (d. 16 April 1885), dau. of Peter FitzGibbon Henchy, Q.C., LL.D., and d. 25 Dec. 1889, having had issue,

Reymond Hervey de Montmorency, **3rd Viscount Frankfort de Montmorency**, Major Gen. and a Representative Peer, b. 21 Sept. 1835; m. 25 April 1866, Rachel Mary Lumley Godolphin (d. 10 Mar. 1936), dau. of Field Marshal Sir John Michel, and d. 7 May 1902, having had issue,

1. Raymond Hervey Lodge Joseph, V.C., Capt. 21st Lancers, served in Sudan with Lord Kitchener in 1898, being awarded the V.C. and mentioned in despatches; b. 5 Feb. 1867, and was k. in action in S. Africa, 23 Feb. 1900. He d.s.p.

2. Willoughby John Horace, **4th Viscount Frankfort de Montmorency**.

1. Caroline Blanche Fane, b. 6 April 1871; d. 18 Oct. 1892.

2. Kathleen Louisa Michel, served in World War I 1914-18, Order of Leopold with bar, b. 21 Sept. 1873; d. 4 Oct. 1927.

3. Lily Rachel Mary, served in World War I, two medals, Order of Leopold and Medaille de la Reine Elizabeth of Belgium, and Reconnaissance Française, b. 13 April 1875.

The younger son, Willoughby John Horace de Montmorency, **4th Viscount Frankfort de Montmorency**, Capt. D.C.L.I., served in Burma 1891-92, in Tirah 1897-98, and in the Nile Exped. 1899; b. 3 May 1866; m. 1 Feb. 1916, Mrs. Mabel Augusta Pearson, who d. 13 Dec. 1946, ygst. dau. of C. L. Throckmorton. He d.s.p. 5 July 1917.
ARMS—Argent, a cross gules between four eagles displayed sable, a crescent for difference.
CREST—A peacock in its pride ppr.
SUPPORTERS—Two angels ppr. crined and winged or, vested argent.
MOTTO—Dieu ayde.

*Note.—The assumption of the name of De Montmorency was dealt with very trenchantly by J. H. Round in *Feudal England*, under the heading of The Montmorency Imposture. He pointed out that the head of the French house refused to admit the claim of the Morris family to be members of the house of Montmorency. Round's language on the subject is characteristically unrestrained, and he remarks that at the same time, "it must be remembered that they (i.e. the pretensions to Montmorency ancestry for the Morrises) have been formally and officially recognised by Sir W. Betham, as Deputy Ulster, (and) by the English Crown."

**FURNIVAL

PEERAGE—U.K. Baron Furnival of Malahide, in Ireland.
SURNAME—Talbot.
CR.—8 May 1839. EXT.—29 Oct. 1849.
HISTORY—Richard Wogan Talbot, 2nd Baron Talbot of Malahide, in the Irish Peerage (see extant peerages under that title), was cr. a peer of the United Kingdom as **Baron Furnival** of Malahide, co. Dublin, on 8 May 1839. He d.s.p.m.s. 29 Oct. 1849, when the U.K. Barony became extinct.

FURNIVALL

PEERAGE—England. Baron Furnivall.
SURNAME—Furnivall, Neville, Talbot, Howard, Petre.
CR.—1295. ABEYANT—24 Dec. 1968.
HISTORY—This barony is one of those held to have been cr. by writ of summons, in 1295, and as such transmissible through the female line. It went in the family of the first holders, the Furnivalls, from 1295 to 1383. The first **Lord Furnivall**, Sir Thomas de Furnivalle, of Sheffield, Worksop, Grassthorpe, etc., was the son and heir of Sir Thomas de Furnivall, who in 1270 had licence to build a stone castle (also to crenellate and fortify) at Sheffield. The first Lord's great-granddaughter, Joane de Furnivall m. before 1 July 1379 Thomas de Neville, second son of Sir John Neville of Raby, co. Durham. Their dau., Maud Neville, m. John Talbot, cr. Earl of Shropshire, but usually known as Earl of Shrewsbury, the famous soldier who d. at the battle of Castillon in France, 1453. He was reckoned as **Lord Furnivall**. From him the lordship of Furnivall passed through the Talbot family, Earls of Shrewsbury down to 1616, when the barony fell into abeyance between the daus. of Gilbert Talbot, 7th Earl of Shrewsbury. His third dau., Alethea, Dowager Countess of Arundel, reckoned as being **Baroness Furnivall,** and from her it passed to her son, Thomas Howard, Earl of Arundel, and so continued in the family of the Dukes of Norfolk, until at the death in 1777 of the 9th Duke of Norfolk, Edward Howard, **Lord Furnivall,** the barony fell into abeyance. It passed to the Petre family, and on 3 May 1913 the abeyance was terminated in favour of Mary Frances Katherine Petre, reckoned as 19th holder of the barony. **Baroness Furnivall** d. on 24 Dec. 1968, when the peerage again fell into abeyance, this time between her daus., who are the Hon. Rosamond Mary Dent, known in religion as

Sister Ancilla, O.S.B. and the Hon. Mrs. Hornby (Patricia Mary Petre). For a full account of the Furnivall history reference may be made to extant peerages.

GARDNER

PEERAGE—Ireland. Baron Gardner of Uttoxeter, cr. 23 Dec. 1800.
U.K. Baron Gardner of Uttoxeter, co. Stafford, 27 Nov. 1806.
SURNAME—Gardner.
CR.—As above, plus a baronetcy ct. 9 Sept. 1894, for the person who became the first peer.
HISTORY—This peerage is dormant, and as such shown in extant peerage works with the note that it has been dormant since the death of the **3rd Baron** in 1883. The history is curious. The second son of the **1st Baron** (the third Baron left no male issue) Francis ffarington Gardner, Rear Adm., left a considerable number of descendants, many of whom lived, or live, in India. The Rear Adm.'s grandson, Alan Hyde Gardner, is described in the C.P. as having assumed the title on the death of the 3rd Baron, but took no steps to establish his right. He was the son and heir of Stewart William Gardner, who d. 20 July 1882, by his cousin Jane Hurmozee Begum, the dau. of Col. Alan Gardner. Alan Hyde Gardner, the titular **4th Baron** was b. 1 July 1836, and m. 12 Mar. 1879, Jane, dau. of Ungun Sheko. He d. 9 July 1899. His only child and heir, Alan Legge Gardner, titular **5th Baron** was stated in newspapers of the period 1901-1904 to be preparing a claim to the Barony. The St. James's Gazette, under 13 Nov. 1901, stated that the titular 4th Baron had actually taken his seat in the Lords, sponsored by Lord Wemyss (C.P. vol. V. p. 620, with appropriate exclamation mark). It is also stated in the same vol. of C.P. that another claimant Alan Hyde Gardner, also a descendent of Rear Adm. Francis ffarington Gardner, and b. 1878, son of an artist at Norwich, had appeared. His line of descendants have to the knowledge of the present writer, considered a possible claim to the Barony. In the words of C.P. vol. referred to above, "Such a claim could obviously only be made good by showing the bastardy of the claimants given in the text." Such question would presumably turn upon the validity in English law of the marriages in India, i.e. whether they could be considered in English law not Christian but polygamous marriages.
ARMS—(of last Baron Gardner—as given in current peerage works). Or on a chevron gules between three griffins heads erased azure an anchor erect between two lions guardant counter passant chevronwise of the field.
CREST—A demi-griffin azure collared and lined and supporting in the claws an anchor or.
SUPPORTERS—Two griffins wings elevated azure beaked, membered and gorged with a naval coronet or each resting the interior hind foot on an anchor with cable, sable.
MOTTO—Valet anchora virtus.

GLADSTONE

PEERAGE—U.K. Viscount Gladstone, of the county of Lanark.
SURNAME—Gladstone.
CR.—15 Feb. 1910. EXT.—6 Mar. 1930.
HISTORY—Herbert John Gladstone, fourth and ygst. son of the statesman, William Ewart Gladstone, was b. at 12 Downing Street, 7 Jan. 1854; educ. Eton and Univ. Coll. Oxford 1872-76; History Lecturer at Keble Coll. Oxford 1877-80; Priv. Sec. to Prime Minister 1880; M.P. Leeds 1880-85; and West Leeds 1885-1910; Junior Lord of the Treasury 1881, Deputy Commissioner of the Office of Works 1885; Fin. Sec. to the War Office 1886; Under Sec. of State for the Home Dept. 1892-94; First Commissioner of Works 1894-95; Chief Liberal Whip 1899-1905; Home Sec. 1905-10; He was made P.C. 1894, and cr. **Viscount Gladstone**, of the county of Lanark, 15 Feb. 1910, G.C.M.G. 1910, G.C.B. 1914 and G.B.E. 1917; Gov. Gen. of the Union of S. Africa, and High Commissioner for S. Africa 1910-14; m. 2 Nov. 1901, Dorothy Mary, D.G. St. J., dau. of Sir Richard Paget, 1st Bt., and d.s.p. 6 Mar. 1930. His life was written by Sir C. E. Mallet in 1932.
ARMS—Argent, a savage's head affrontée distilling drops of blood, and wreathed about the temples with holly ppr. within an orle fleury gules, all within eight martlets in orle sable.
CREST—Issuant from a wreath of holly ppr. a demi griffin sable supporting between the claws a sword, the blade enfiled by a wreath of oak also ppr.
MOTTO—Fide et virtute.
Viscount Gladstone's residences were 2 Cleveland Square, St. James's, London, S.W. and Dane End, Ware, Herts. His clubs were National Liberal, Reform and Bath.

GLADSTONE OF HAWARDEN

PEERAGE—Baron Gladstone of Hawarden, of Hawarden, co. Flint.
SURNAME—Gladstone.
CR.—22 June 1932. EXT.—28 April 1935.
HISTORY—Henry Neville Gladstone, **Baron Gladstone** of Hawarden, was b. 2 April 1852, the third son of the statesman William Ewart Gladstone (for lineage see Gladstone, Bt., in extant peerages); educ. Eton and King's Coll. London; Fell. of King's Coll.; entered the firm of Ogilvy, Gillanders and Co., and served with corresponding Co. in India, Gillanders, Arbuthnot and Co. 1874-88; mem. of numerous cttees.; Alderman Flint C.C. 1916; Lord Lt. co. Flint; Treasurer Nat. Library of Wales, Pres. of Univ. Coll. of N. Wales at Bangor, and mem. of Welsh Church Governing Body; a Dir. of the P. and O. and B.I. Steamship Cos.; Lord of the manor of Hawarden; Constable of Flint Castle 1934; was cr. 22 June 1932, Baron Gladstone of Hawarden, of Hawarden, co. Flint; m. 30 Jan. 1890, Maud Ernestine, C.B.E., D.G. St. J., dau. of 1st and only Baron Rendel, and d.s.p. 28 April 1935.
ARMS—Quarterly 1 and 4 Argent a savage's head affrontée, distilling drops of blood, wreathed about the temples with holly ppr.

within an orle fleury gules all within eight martlets in orle sable; 2 and 3 Quarterly i and iv, Argent an eagle displayed with two heads sable; ii and iii, Argent three brands raguly sable fired ppr. on an inescutcheon argent, a human leg couped at the thigh sable (Glynne of Hawarden).
CREST—Issuant from a wreath of holly ppr. a demi-griffin sable, supporting between the claws a sword, the blade enfiled by a wreath of oak also ppr.
SUPPORTERS—Dexter, A hawk, wings elevated and addorsed sable, charged on the breast with a portcullis chained or. Sinister, An eagle's wings elevated and addorsed sable charged on the breast with two staves raguly saltirewise or, surmounted by a lotus flower ppr.
MOTTO—Fide et virtute.

GLANELY

PEERAGE—U.K. Baron Glanely, of St. Fagans, co. Glamorgan.
SURNAME—Tatem.
CR.—28 June 1918. Also a baronetcy 13 July, 1916. EXT.—28 June 1942.
HISTORY—Thomas Tatem, of Appledore, Devon, had a son, Sir William James Tatem, Bt., and **Baron Glanely**, b. 6 Mar. 1868; founder and Chm. of W. J. Tatem Ltd.; Chm. of Cardiff Shipowners' Asscn. 1907; High Sheriff, co. Glamorgan 1911-12; Dir. of many cos. and Pres. of several asscns. He was cr. a baronet 13 July 1916, and Baron Glanely, of St. Fagans, co. Glamorgan, 28 June 1918. He m. 14 Sept. 1897, Ada Mary, C.B.E. (who d. 17 April 1931), dau. of Thomas Williams, of Pengam, Cardiff, and d. 28 June 1942, having had issue, Thomas Shandon, b. 20 July 1898; d.v.p. 14 June 1905.
ARMS—Gyronny of six azure and argent, two crabs in fess ermine between in chief an escallop gules and in base an anchor cabled or.
CREST—A cubit arm vested azure cuffed argent, holding in the hand a telescope in bend sinister ppr.
SUPPORTERS—On either side a sea horse sable bezantée gorged with a mercantile crown or.
MOTTO—Fortis si jure fortis.
Lord Glaney's residences were: Exning House, Exning, Newmarket, and 12 Hill Street, Mayfair. His clubs were: Carlton, Junior Carlton, Bath and Royal Thames Yacht.

GLANTAWE

PEERAGE—U.K. Baron Glantawe, of Swansea, co. Glamorgan.
SURNAME—Jenkins.
CR.—18 July 1906. EXT.—27 July 1915.
HISTORY—Jenkin Jenkins, of Bath Villa, Morriston, co. Glamorgan, by Sarah, his wife, 4th dau. of John Jones, of Clydach and who d. 13 April 1902, had issue, Sir John Jones Jenkins, **Baron Glantawe**, of Swansea, co. Glamorgan, was cr. 18 July 1906. He was b. 10 May 1835; educ. privately; entered the Upper Forest Tinplate Works; Mayor of Swansea, 1869, 1879 and 1880; Liberal M.P.

for Carmarthen Boroughs, 1882-86, and as Liberal Unionist 1895-1900; cr. K.T. Bach. 1881; High Sheriff, co. Glamorgan, 1889; Chm. of Swansea Harbour Trust, and Dir. of several cos.; Hon. Freeman of Swansea, 1895; m. (1) 20 Jan. 1854, Margaret (d. 9 Mar. 1863) dau. of Josiah Rees, of Morriston. He m. (2) 10 May 1864, Catherine, dau. of Edward Daniel, of Morriston. She d. 29 June 1900. He d.s.p. m. 27 July 1915, leaving issue,

1. Olga Violet, m. 1895, Horace C. M. Daniell, and had issue.
2. Alina Kate Elaine, m. (1) 1920, Thomas Cooper Cooper-Smith, who d. 1926. She m. (2) 1st Viscount Bledisloe as his 2nd wife.

ARMS—Party per pale sable and gules on a chevron between two fleur-de-lis in chief and a lion's gamb erased in base argent a fleur-de-lis sable between two pellets.
CREST—A lion's gamb erect and erased argent holding a pellet charged with a fleur-de-lis and all between two fleur-de-lis argent.
SUPPORTERS—Dexter, A dragon; Sinister, A goat, both or, suspended round the neck of each on a riband, a shield per pale sable and gules thereon a fleur-de-lis argent.
MOTTO—Perseverance.
Lord Glantawe's seat was The Grange, Swansea. His clubs were Reform, National Liberal, Hurlingham, and Sports.

GLENESK

PEERAGE—U.K. Baron Glenesk, of Glenesk, co. Midlothian. (Also a baronetcy cr. 12 July 1887).
SURNAME—Borthwick.
CR.—16 Nov. 1895. EXT.—24 Nov. 1908.
HISTORY—This is described as a branch of the famous family of Borthwick of Borthwick (see that title in present work) who settled in Midlothian; one of the branch, Thomas Borthwick, was the prototype of Henry Morton in Sir Walter Scott's *Old Mortality*. The arms of this line certainly bear a very close resemblance to those of Borthwick of Borthwick. Thomas Borthwick, of Eddlestone, co. Peebles, m. Janet, dau. of Peter Blake, and widow of Archibald Kemp of Peebles, and had issue.

Peter Borthwick, M.P. for Evesham, 1835-38, and 1841-47, b. 13 Sept. 1804; m. 8 Jan. 1827, Margaret, dau. of John Colville, of Ewart, co. Northumberland, who d. 13 Nov. 1864, and d. 18 Dec. 1852, having had issue,

1. Algernon, Sir, Bt., and **Baron Glenesk** (see below).
2. George Colville, Major Gen. Imperial Ottoman Army, b. 15 June 1839; m. 4 May 1884, Sophie Schylowskála, dau. of Capt. Schylowskála, Russian Imperial Guard and d. Jan. 1896, leaving issue,
   Reginald, b. 18 April 1887.
   Jessie.
1. Harriet.

The elder son, Sir Algernon Borthwick, Bt., and **Baron Glenesk**, b. 27 Dec. 1830; J.P. Middlesex, M.P. for South Kensington, 1885-95; cr. a baronet 12 July 1887; and a peer, 16 Nov. 1895, as Baron Glenesk of Glenesk, co. Midlothian; m. 5 April 1870, Alice Beatrice dau. of Thomas Henry Lister of Armitage

Park, Sheffield, and d. 24 Nov. 1098, having had issue,

Oliver Andrev, b. 2 Mar. 1873; d. unm. 23 Mar. 1905. Lilias Margaret Frances, m. 15 Nov. 1893, 7th Earl Bathurst and had issue.

ARMS—Argent a cinquefoil sable, on a chief invected sable two cinquefoils of the field.
CREST—On a staff raguly fesswise sable a blackamoor's head in profile couped ppr.
SUPPORTERS—Two men in armour, each charged on the breast with a saltire and resting the exterior hands on battleaxes ppr.
MOTTO—Qui conducit.

GLENLYON

PEERAGE—U.K. Baron Glenlyon, of Glenlyon, co. Perth.
SURNAME—Murray.
CR.—17 July 1821. EXT.—8 May 1957.
HISTORY—Lord James Murray, the second son of John Murray, 4th Duke of Atholl was b. 29 May 1782; entered the Army, 1798; Major Gen. 1819; Lt. Gen. 1837; M.P. for Pertshire, 1807-12; a Lord of the Chamber, 1812-32; F.R.S 1818; K.C.H. 1820; cr. **Baron Glenlyon**, of Glenlyon, co. Perth, 17 July 1821; m. 19 May 1810, Emily Frances, dau. of Hugh Percy, 2nd Duke of Northumberland, and d. at Fenton's Hotel, in St. James's Street, London, on 12 Oct. 1837 being buried at Dunkeld, his widow d. 21 June 1844. They had with other issue, (extant peerages, under Atholl, D.), a son and heir, George Augustus Frederick John Murray, **2nd Baron Glenlyon**, b. 20 Sept. 1814. On the death of his uncle, the 5th Duke of Atholl, he s. to that dukedom, on 14 Sept. 1846, and became the 6th Duke of Atholl. From thereon the history of the Glenlyon Barony continues with that of the Dukes of Atholl, until the death unm 8 May 1957, of the 9th Duke, when the Glenlyon Barony became extinct, and the Dukedom passed to the 9th Duke's kinsman, George Iain, who became 10th Duke of Atholl, He is also among his other titles, Viscount Balwhidder Glenalmond and Glenlyon, the viscounty having been cr. in 1703, along with the Dukedom of Atholl, in the peerage of Scotland. (extant peerages, Atholl, D.).
ARMS—see under Atholl, in extant peerages.

GLENRAVEL

PEERAGE—U.K. Baron Glenravel, of Kensington, co. London. (Also a baronetcy cr. 26 July 1926).
SURNAME—Benn.
CR.—1 Feb. 1936. EXT.—13 June 1937.
HISTORY—The Rev. John Watkins Benn, M.A., Rector of Carrigaline and Douglas, co. Cork, 1814-1874, had with other issue, (see extant works, Benn of Rollesby, Bt.), and eldest son, Sir Arthur Shirley Benn, Bt., and **Baron Glenravel**, b. 20 Dec. 1858; educ. Clifton Coll. and abroad, and a student at Inner Temple, lived in Canada, and served in Canadian Garrison Artillery; Brit. Vice Consul, Mobile, Alabama; Managing Dir. of Hunter Benn and Co., Merchants and Timber Shippers; re-

turned to England, 1902; M.P. Conservative for Plymouth, 1910-18, and for Drake Div. of Plymouth, 1918-29, and for Park Div. of Sheffield, 1931-35; Chm. of Nat. Unionist Asscn. and Pres. of Asscn. of Brit. Chambers of Commerce, 1921-23; Chm. of Council of Federation of Chambers of Commerce of British Empire, 1928, Pres. 1931-34. He was cr. a baronet 26 July 1926, a peer as Baron Glenravel, of Kensington, co. London, 1 Feb. 1936 and a K.B.E. 1918. He m. 9 May 1888, Alys Maria (d. 4 June 1932) dau. of F. A. Luling, of Springhill, Alabama and d.s.p. 13 June 1937.

ARMS—Argent a chevron indented gules, between three lions rampant azure a trefoil slipped or.

CREST—A tiger passant argent, gorged with a collar dancettée gules, charged with a trefoil, as in the arms.

MOTTO—Courage sans peur.

GLENTANAR

PEERAGE—U.K. Baron Glentanar, of Glen Tanar, co. Aberdeen.

SURNAME—Coats.

CR.—29 June 1916. **EXT.**—28 June 1971.

HISTORY—The family of Coats, one of the most important in the history of British industry, has a connected descent from the mid 16th century in the region of Glasgow. The earlier history of the line is given in Coats Bt. (extant peerages). The fourth son of James Coats of Paisley, (see Coats, Bt.) had a fourth son, Thomas Coats, of Ferguslie and Maxwelton, co. Renfrew, b. 15 Oct. 1809; m. 13 Oct. 1840, Margaret, dau. of Thomas Glen, of Thornhill Johnstone, co. Renfrew, and d. 18 Oct. 1883, having by her (who d. 29 Jan. 1898) had with other issue,

1. James, of Ferguslie House, and Maxwelton, Paisley, b. 28 Nov. 1841; d. 22 Mar. 1912.

2. Thomas Glen Glen-Coats, Sir, 1st Bt., so. cr. 25 June 1894, b. 19 Feb. 1846; C.B., M.P. West Renfrewshire 1906-10; assumed the additional surname of Glen before his patronymic of Coats; m. 20 April 1876, Elsie Agnes, (d. 12 Mar. 1910) dau. of Alexander Walker of Montreal, Canada, and d. 12 July 1922, having had issue,
   (1) Thomas Coats Glen, 2nd Bt., B.A. Oxford, b. 5 May 1878; m. 5 April 1935, Louise, dau. of Emile Hugon, of Paris, and formerly wife of J. C. Newman, and d.s.p. 7 Mar. 1954, when the baronetcy became extinct.
   (2) Alexander Harold Glen, B.A. Oxford, b. 26 July 1883; m. 22 July 1924, Elizabeth Millar, dau. of Thomas Greenlees of Newark, Paisley, and d. 23 Oct. 1933, leaving two daus.,
      1a Margaret Elizabeth, b. 28 Jan. 1928.
      2a Winifred Lettice, b. 2 June 1929.
   (1) Marion Marjorie Winifred Glen, m. 1913, Major Edward H. T. Parsons, and d. 7 Sept. 1947, leaving issue.

3. George, **1st Baron Glentanar** (see below).

4. William Allan, of Dalskairth, co. Dumfries, b. 4 July 1853; m. 9 Oct. 1888,

Agnes Bunten, dau. of Sir John Muir, 1st Bt., and d. 31 Aug. 1926, leaving by her (who d. 1894),
   (1) Thomas Heywood, b. 23 Oct. 1889; m. (m. diss. by div. 1931), Olivia Violet, dau. of Hon. Lord Pitman, and d. 20 Dec. 1958 leaving issue.
      1a William David, Dir. J. & P. Coats, Ltd., 25 July 1924; educ. Eton; m. 8 Feb. 1950, Hon. Elizabeth L. G. MacAndrew, dau. of 1st Baron MacAndrew and had issue,
         1b Brian Glen Heywood, b. 1951; educ. Eton.
         2b Adrian James MacAndrew, b. 1955; educ. Eton.
         1b Frances Alice, b. 1958.

2.   2a Mark Alastair, b. 13 Feb. 1927; educ. Eton; m. 27 Nov. 1947 Rosemary Susan, dau. of Capt. Hon. F. W. Erskine, (Mar & Kellie, E.), and had issue,
         Nicholas James, b. 1952; educ. Eton.
         Virginia Jane, b. 1954.
      1a Jane Agnew, b. 26 Jan. 1921; m. (1) 14 May 1943 (m. diss. by div. 1955), N. P. Wood; m. (2) 25 Oct. 1958, A. M. Hamilton, by her first marr. she had issue,
         1b David Peter Kay, b. 1944.
         2b Alastair Norman, b. 1946.
         1b Jennifer Jane Fiona, b. 1947.
   (2) John Alexander, b. 1892; m. Sept. 1918, Audrey Gretchen, dau. of Charles Wilmot, of Belleville, Ontario and d. 20 June 1932. She d. 1942. They had issue,
      1a Vernon William, Mem. London Stock Exchange, and Company Dir., b. 20 July 1919; educ. Eton and Ch. Ch. Oxford; served in World War II, 1939-45, Bucks L.I. and Scots Guards; m. (1) (m. diss. by div. 1954), Catherine, dau. of Capt. H. V. Hinton, and m. (2) 2 Oct. 1954, Ethel dau. of Capt. F. R. Stephens, and widow of Brig. E. Bradney (B.L.G. 1952, Bradney of Tal-y-coed, co. Monmouth). He d. 17 Aug. 1960, having had by his first marriage,
         John William Rupert, b. 1950; educ. Eton.
         Alexandra Audrey, b. 1948.
      1a April Bunten, b. 21 April 1926; m. 25 May 1949 (marr. diss. by div. 1967), T. J. H. Bishop, and had issue,
         1b Peter Andrew Coats, b. 24 April 1950.
         2b Joel Alexander Muir, b. 1 Feb. 1962.
         1b Thais Mary, b. 5 Feb. 1952.
         2b Matile Henderson, b. 21 Sept. 1950.

5. Andrew, b. 27 May 1862; served in S. African War, 1899-1901, Glasgow Yeo. D.S.O.; m. 28 July 1903, Isabella Alice, dau. of Capt. G. F. Lyon, R.N. and d. 17 Feb. 1930.

1. Janet, b. 15 Feb. 1844; m. 1884, James Tait Black, of Underscar, Keswick and d. 15 Nov. 1918.

2. Catharine, b. 27 April 1851; m. James Boyd, of Carksey, co. Argyll and d. 8 Dec. 1928.
3. Margaret, d. unm. 1946.
4. Jeannie, m. George Barclay, of Thornhill, Johnstone, co. Renfrew, and d. 26 Jan. 1931.
5. Lily, d. unm. 12 Feb. 1954.

The third son, George Coats, **1st Baron Glentanar**, of Glen Tanar, co. Aberdeen, so cr. 29 June 1916; b. 11 Feb. 1849; m. 23 Dec. 1880, Margaret Lothian, eldest dau. of James Tait Black, of Underscar, Keswick. She d. 27 June 1935. He d. 26 Nov. 1918. Their children were,

    1. Thomas, **2nd Baron Glentanar** (see below).
    1. Charlotte Margaret Lothian, m. (1) 18 June 1904, Hon. William L. C. Walrond, M.P., (Waleran, B.) and had issue. He d. 2 Nov. 1915. She m. (2) 7 June 1920. Cmdr. H. W. A. Adams, R.N. who d. 30 Oct. 1966. She d. 25 Sept. 1962.
    2. Lilian Maud Glen, m. 23 Mar. 1909, 5th Duke of Wellington, and d. 3 May 1946, having had issue.

The only son, Sir Thomas Coats, **2nd Baron Glentanar**, b. 4 Dec. 1894; educ. Eton, Ch. Ch. Oxford and abroad; served in World War I, 1914-18, in France, with Worcestershire Regt. (despatches), formerly Black Watch, and Signal Service, R.E.; mem. Royal Co. of Archers (Sovereign's Bodyguard for Scotland), Hon. Bencher, Middle Temple, Hon. LL.D. Aberdeen, and Hon. Fell. Royal Coll. of Music; Chm. of Brit. Legion (Scotland) 1923-29; Commissioner for Scotland, Boy Scouts Asscn. 1923-53; D.L. and J.P. co. Aberdeen; Chm. A.T.C. Advisory Council for Scotland, 1941-45; and A.T.C. Scottish Welfare Council, 1942-45; m. 20 Dec. 1927 Grethe Dagbjørt, dau. of Thor Thoresen of Oslo, and had issue, Margaret Jean Dagbjørt, b. 11 Oct. 1928; m. 29 July 1950, Hon. James M. E. Bruce, son of 10th Earl of Elgin, and had issue. Lord Glentanar d. 28 June 1971.

ARMS—Or a stag's head erased gules between the attires a pheon azure, all between three mascles sable, within a bordure invected of the last.
CREST—An anchor erect ppr.
SUPPORTERS—Two stags gules attired or, between the attires a pheon azure.
MOTTOES—Be firm (above crest) and below arms—Non dormit qui custodit.

Lord Glentanar's seat was Glen Tanar, Aboyne, co. Aberdeen. His clubs were Carlton; Beefsteak; New (Edin.) and Royal Yacht Squadron (Cowes).

GLYN

PEERAGE—U.K. Baron Glyn of Farnborough, Co. Berks.
SURNAME—Glyn.
CR.—29 June 1953. **EXT.**—1 May 1960
Also a baronetcy cr. 21 Jan. 1934. —
HISTORY—The Rt. Rev. Edward Carr Glyn, eighth son of 1st Baron Wolverton, and Bishop of Peterborough 1897-1916 (see current peerages, Wolverton, B.) had a son, Sir Ralph George Campbell Glyn, Bt., and **Baron Glyn,**

b. 3 Mar. 1885; educ. Harrow and R.M.C.; served in World War I 1914-18 (despatches, M.C., Legion of Honour, American D.S.M., Order of St. Anne of Russia, and of White Eagle of Serbia); M.P. Clackmannan and E. Div. 1918-22, and Abingdon Div. of Berkshire 1924; cr. a Baronet 21 Jan. 1934 and Baron Glyn of Farnborough, co. Berks, 29 June 1953; m. 25 April 1921, Hon. Sibell, dau. of 2nd Baron Derwent, and widow of Brig. Gen. W. Long, and d. 1 May 1960.
ARMS—Argent, an eagle displayed with two heads sable, guttée d'or.
CREST—An eagle's head erased sable, guttée d'or, holding in the beak an escallop argent.
MOTTO—Fidei tenax.

GODDARD

PEERAGE—U.K. Life Baron Goddard of Aldbourne, co. Wilts.
SURNAME—Goddard.
CR.—19 July 1944. **EXT.**—29 May 1971.
HISTORY—Lord Goddard's father was Charles Goddard, of the well-known firm of solicitors, Peacock and Goddard. He was of 3, South Square, Gray's Inn, and m. Janet Gertrude, dau. of John Jobson, of Derby. She d. June 1934. He d. 22 May 1922. Their son, Sir Rayner Goddard, **Baron Goddard,** was b. 10 April 1877; educ. Marlborough where he was capt. of the rifle corps, and Victor ludorum, and Trinity Coll. Oxford, B.A. 2nd class hons. in Law 1898, and was awarded an Athletics Blue as a sprinter (he won the 100 yards at Oxford, in 1898, in 10⅘ sec.). He was called to the Bar at the Inner Temple, and Gray's Inn 1899 (he once—when the present writer was called to the Bar— referred to himself as being called, "in the middle ages"). He was K.C. 1923; Bencher, Inner Temple 1929; Recorder of Poole 1917-24, of Bath 1924-28, and of Plymouth 1928-32; his only active incursion into politics occurred in 1929 when he was persuaded to stand as an Independent Conservative against the sitting M.P. for South Kensington. He polled 6,000 votes in a three cornered fight, while the retiring member was returned with a majority of over 20,000 votes. In 1932 he was apptd. a Judge of the High Court, King's Bench Div., and cr. Kt. Bach. In 1938 he became a Lord Justice of Appeal and in 1944 a Lord of Appeal in Ordinary, being apptd. in 1946 Lord Chief Justice of England, a position which he held until 1958. He was made P.C. 1938; cr. a life peer as Baron Goddard, of Aldbourne, co. Wilts, and G.C.B. 1958. He was Hon. Sec. of the Barristers' Benevolent Asscn. 1912-17 and 1928-29. Many of Lord Goddard's judgments were famous, particularly in the criminal law with which he was much concerned in the later period of his judicial position. The famous case of Craig-Bentley at Croydon, in which the man who fired the shot which killed a policeman was not hanged, but the man who had not fired (Derek Bentley) was hanged, caused great discussion, and led to a very considerable correspondence following the publication of an article in *The Times* on the subject just after Lord Goddard's death. Lord Goddard was an advocate of strong treatment of criminals and as such was natu-

rally disliked by all so-called progressive persons. In another, and minor capacity, his judgment marked a distinct stage in the history and study of heraldry in England. On 21 Dec. 1954 Lord Goddard sat as Surrogate to the Earl Marshal, the Duke of Norfolk, in his own court in the Royal Courts of Justice in the Strand, at a sitting of the Court of Chivalry, revived after a lapse of nearly 2¼ centuries. The case was between the Manchester Corporation and the Manchester Palace of Varieties, and a full account of the whole proceedings, extending to 82 pages, is given verbatim in a pamphlet issued by the British Heraldry Society. Lord Goddard's judgment ran to nearly six pages, and was given by him on 21 Jan. 1955. He gave judgment in favour of the Manchester Corporation, but added: "If therefore it is laid down as a rule of this Court, as I would respectfully suggest to His Grace the Earl Marshal it should be, that leave must be obtained before any proceedings are instituted, it would I think prevent frivolous actions, and if this Court is to sit again it should be convened only where there is some really substantial reason for the exercise of its jurisdiction. Moreover, should there be any indication of a considerable desire to institute proceedings now that this Court has been revived, I am firmly of the opinion that it should be put upon a statutory basis, defining its jurisdiction and the sanctions it can impose." (For a discussion of the whole subject see the present writer's *The Story of Heraldry*, revised edition 1963). Lord Goddard m. 31 May 1906 Mary Linda, (d. 16 May 1928), dau. of Sir Felix Otto Schuster, 1st Bt., and had issue,

1. Pamela Mary Violet, b. 28 Dec. 1907; m. J. B. Maurice, M.R.C.S., L.R.C.P., and had issue, a son, Maurice Thelwall Rayner, b. 1938, and educ. Marlborough and Trin. Coll. Oxford, B.A.; and a dau. Rosanagh Mary Goddard, B.A. St. Anne's Coll. Oxford, m. J. P. Clay and had issue.
2. Janet Margaret, b. 26 Oct. 1900; m. 12 May 1934, Rt. Hon. Lord Justice Sir Eric Sachs, Lord Justice of Appeal, and had issue a son, Richard Edwin Goddard, and a dau. Katharine Frances Goddad (m. G. Pulay) and had issue.
3. Ruth Evelyn, b. 28 July 1912; m. 1937, A. S. Clayton, and had issue two sons, Christopher Sands and Stephen Charles Rayner.

Lord Goddard d. 29 May 1971.
His residence was Queen Elizabeth's Building, Temple. His clubs were Brooks's and Pratt's.

**GORDON OF DRUMEARN

PEERAGE—U.K. Life Baron Gordon of Drumearn, co. Stirling.
SURNAME—Gordon.
CR.—17 Oct. 1876. EXT.—21 Aug. 1879.
HISTORY—Edward Strathearn Gordon, **Baron Gordon** of Drumearn, was b. 10 April 1814, eldest son of Major John Gordon, 2nd Regt. of Foot, (described in *B.P.* as of the family of Gordon of Embo), by his wife, Catherine, dau. of Alexander Smith. He was educ. at the Academy, Inverness, and Edinburgh Univ.; Barrister, Scots Bar 1835;

Sheriff co. Perth 1858-66; sat as Conservative M.P. for Thetford 1867-68; and for Glasgow and Aberdeen Univs. 1869-76; was Solicitor Gen. for Scotland 1866-67, and Lord Advocate 1867-68, and again 1874-76; Q.C. 1868; Dean of Faculty 1869-74; P.C. 1874; apptd. on 17 Oct. 1876 a Lord of Appeal in Ordinary and cr. a peer for life as Baron Gordon of Drumearn, co. Stirling. He m. 1845, Agnes (d. 11 Oct. 1895), dau. of James MacInnes, of Auchenreoch, co. Stirling, and d. 21 Aug. 1879. They had issue,

1. John Edward.
2. Arthur.
3. Frederick.
4. Huntly Douglas.
1. Ella, m. Col. John James Gordon, Bengal Staff Corps.
2. Katherine.
3. Agnes Streathearn.

The baronetcy of Gordon of Embo (Nova Scotia), cr. 1631, became dormant 1936. The possible heir was Michael Gordon of Reading, following the death of the Rev. Dr. Alexander MacLennan Gordon of Kingston, Ontario, who was thought to be de jure 13th Bt.

GORT

PEERAGE—U.K. Viscount Gort.
SURNAME—Vereker.
CR.—8 Feb. 1946. EXT.—31 Mar. 1946.
HISTORY—Under Gort, Viscount, in extant peerages. The 6th Viscount Gort, in the Peerage of Ireland, was John Standish Surtees Prendergast Vereker, who held a barony and viscounty in the Irish peerage, and who was a very distinguished military commander. He had the V.C., G.C.B., G.B.E., D.S.O., M.V.O., M.C., etc. He had two sons both of whom d.v.p., and a dau. who m. 1st Viscount De L'Isle. When he d. 31 Mar. 1946, the U.K. Viscounty became extinct and the Irish titles passed to his brother, who thus became the 7th Viscount Gort in the Irish peerage.
ARMS—as under Viscount Gort in extant peerages.

GREENE

PEERAGE—U.K. Baron Greene of Holmbury St. Mary, co. Surrey.
SURNAME—Greene.
CR.—16 July 1941. EXT.—16 April 1952.
HISTORY—Cornelius Greene of Slyne, co. Lancaster, d. 14 Oct. 1669, having issue, Thomas Greene of Bolton Holmes, co. Lancs, d. 1714, being father of Cornelius Greene, who d. 1728 leaving issue, Richard Greene, b. 1727 who had issue, The Rev. Cornelius Greene, of Terwick, co. Sussex, who had issue The Rev. Cecil Greene, who by his wife Elizabeth Weguelin had a son, Arthur Weguelin Greene, a solicitor of Beckenham, co. Kent; educ. Lancing; m. Katherine Agnes, dau. of Octavius Tooks, of Gravesend, co. Kent. She d. Oct. 1939. He d. Aug. 1919. They had issue, Sir Wilfred Arthur Greene, **Baron Greene**, b. 30 Dec. 1883; educ. Westminster (King's Scholar 1896, More Scholar 1900, Capt. of School 1901) and Ch. Ch. Oxford, Craven and

Hertford Scholar, B.A. 1906, Fell. of All Souls 1907, Vinerian Law Scholar 1908; M.A. 1912; Barrister-at-Law, Inner Temple 1908, K.C. 1922, Bencher 1925, served in World War I 1914-18, Capt. 2/1st Bn. of Oxford and Bucks L.I. 1914-16, G.S.O. 5th Army 1917, and in 2nd Army 1917-18, M.C. 1918, O.B.E. 1919, Croix de Guerre (France) and Cavaliere of the Order of the Crown of Italy, a Lord Justice of Appeal 1935, Master of the Rolls 1937, a Lord of Appeal in Ordinary 1949-50, cr. Kt. Bach. 1935, made P.C. 1935 and cr. Baron Greene of Holmbury St. Mary, co. Surrey, 16 July 1941. He m. 28 May 1909, Nancy, dau. of Francis Wright of Nottingham and d. 16 April 1952.

GREY OF FALLODON

PEERAGE—U.K. Viscount Grey of Fallodon, co. Northumberland.
SURNAME—Grey.
CR.—27 July 1916. **EXT.**—7 Sept. 1933.
HISTORY—Under Grey of Fallodon, Bt. in extant peerage works. Sir Edward Grey, 3rd Bt., and **Viscount Grey of Fallodon,** was b. 25 April 1862; M.P. for Berwick Div. of Northumberland 1885-1916; Sec. of State for Foreign Affairs 1905-16; made P.C. 1902; cr. K.G. 1912; and Viscount Grey of Fallodon, co. Northumberland, 27 July 1916; m. (1) 20 Oct. 1885, Dorothy (d.s.p. 4 Feb. 1906), dau. of S. F. Widdrington, of Newton Hall, Northumberland; and (2) 4 June 1922, Pamela, (d. 18 Nov. 1918), dau. of Hon. Percy Scawen Wyndham, (Leconfield, B.), and widow of 1st Baron Glenconner. Viscount Grey d.s.p. 7 Sept. 1933, when the Viscounty became extinct and the baronetcy passed to his kinsman, Sir Charles George Grey, 4th Bt., etc.
ARMS—Gules, a lion rampant within a bordure engrailed argent, in the dexter chief point a mullet or.
CREST—A scaling ladder or, hooked and pointed sable.
MOTTO—De bon vouloir servir le Roy.

GREY DE RUTHYN

PEERAGE—England. Baron Grey de Ruthyn.
SURNAME—Butler-Bowdon (i.e. in 1966) previously Grey, Longueville, Yelverton, Gould, Rawdon, and Clifton.
CR.—30 Dec. 1324. **ABEYANT**—25 Oct. 1963.
HISTORY—Henry De Grey was granted in the 6th year of King Richard I, 1194, the manor of Thurrock, co. Essex, a grant which was confirmed by King John, who in a special charter allowed the said Henry de Grey to hunt the hare and the fox in any land belonging to the Crown, except the King's own demesne parks. In 1st year of Henry III, Henry de Grey had a grant of the manor of Grimston, co. Nottingham. He m. Isolda, niece and heiress of Robert Bardolf, of Codnor, co. Derby, and shared in the inheritance of her lands. He had issue,

1. Richard, of Codnor, ancestor of the Barons Grey, of Codnor, (Extinct Peerage, 1883).
2. John (see below).

3. William, of Landford, Nottingham, of Sandiacre, co. Derby, and of Cavendish, co. Suffolk, ancestor of the Barons Walsingham (see extant peerages).
4. Robert, from whom descended the Barons Grey of Rotherfield, who were attainted 1487, (see 1883 Extinct and Dormant Peerages).
5. Walter, Archbishop of York, 1216-55.
6. Henry.

The second son, Sir John de Grey, Sheriff cos. Buckingham and Bedford, 1239, and of co. Hereford, 1253, summoned in 1242 to attend the King in arms in Flanders, m. (1) Emma, dau. and heir of Sir Geoffrey de Glanville, and (2) Joane, widow of Pauline Peyvre (according to Dugdale), and d. 1265 when he was s. by his son, Reginald de Grey, 1st Baron Grey de Wilton, by writ of summons, 23 June 1295, to 26 Aug. 1307, Justice of Chester, 1281, m. Maud, dau. and heir of William, Lord Fitz-Hugh, and d. 1308, leaving with a dau. Joan, who m. Ralph, Lord Bassett, (see 1883 Extinct Peerage, under Baron Bassett, of Drayton) a son and successor, John de Grey, 2nd Baron Grey de Wilton, summoned to Parliament, 8 Jan. 1309 to 18 Sept. 1322, Justice of N. Wales, 1317 and Gov. of Caernarvon Castle, m. (1) Anne, dau. of William Ferrers. (see 1883 Extinct Peerage, Ferrers, B. of Groby), and by her had a son, Henry de Grey, 3rd Baron Grey de Wilton, from whom descended the Barons Grey de Wilton, attainted in 1604, (1883 Extinct Peerage, Barons Grey of Wilton, co. Hereford). The 15th and last Lord Grey de Wilton, Thomas de Grey, had a sister, Bridget Grey, m. Sir Rowland Egerton 1st Bt. of Egerton, so. cr. 5 April 1617 (extant peerages, Grey Egerton, Bt.) and was thus ancestor of the present Earl of Wilton (extant peerages). The 2nd Lord Grey de Wilton, m. (2) Maud, dau. of Ralph, 1st Baron Bassett, of Drayton and by her had issue, a son, Roger, of whom presently. The 2nd Lord Grey de Ruthyn, d. 28 Oct. 1323, and his son by his 2nd wife,

Roger de Grey, **1st Baron Grey de Ruthyn,** was summoned to Parliament as such from 30 Dec. 1324 to 15 Nov. 1351. He m. Elizabeth, dau. of John Hastings, 2nd Baron Hastings, of Bergavenny, (Hastings Baron, extant peerages), and d. 6 Mar. 1552/53, being s. by his eldest son,

Reginald de Grey, **2nd Baron Grey de Ruthyn,** aged 30 at his father's death, summoned to Parliament from 15 Mar. 1354, to 20 Mar. 1388, m. Eleanor, dau. of 2nd Lord Strange, of Blackmere (1883 Extinct Peerage), and d. July 1388, being s. by his eldest son,

Reginald de Grey, **3rd Baron Grey de Ruthyn,** aged 26 at time of father's death, summoned to Parliament, from 1389 to 1439, m. (1) Margaret, dau. of 7th Lord Roos, of Hamlake, (1883 Extinct Peerage), and by her had issue,

1. John, Sir, K.G., 1436, m. Constance, dau. of John Holland, Duke of Exeter (1883 Extinct Peerage), and d.v.p. 27 Aug. 1439, having issue,
   (1) Edmund, **4th Baron** (see below).
   (2) Thomas, Lord Richemount-Grey, so. cr. 25 June 1449, attainted 1461 and d.s.p.

He m. (2) circa, 1406, Joan, dau. and heir of Sir William de Astley, 4th Lord Astley, (1883 Extinct Peerage), and widow of Thomas

Raleigh, and by her had further issue.

2. Edward, ancestor in the male line of the Barons Grey of Groby, the Marquesses of Dorset, and the Dukes of Suffolk (1883 Extinct Peerage, all titles held by the Grey family). He m. Elizabeth, granddau. of William Ferrers, 5th Baron Ferrers of Groby, who d. in 1445, when the Barony of Ferrers of Groby devolved upon Elizabeth and Sir Edward Grey was summoned to Parliament in that dignity.

The 3rd Baron Grey de Ruthyn d. 20 Sept. 1440, and was s. by his grandson, Edmund de Grey, **4th Baron Grey de Ruthyn**, and 1st Earl of Kent, a Yorkist, cr. Earl of Kent, by Edward IV, 30 May 1465, and confirmed in the dignity by Henry VII, m. Lady Katherine Percy, dau. of 2nd Earl of Northumberland, and d. 1489, having had three sons and two daus., of whom the eldest surviving son,

George de Grey, **5th Baron Grey de Ruthyn**, and 2nd Earl of Kent, was sent into France as a commander 1491, to assist the Emperor Maximilian, and was Chief Commander against the Cornishmen in their rising, under Lord Audley, m. (1) Lady Anne Wydeville, dau. of 1st Earl Rivers, and widow of William Bourchier, son of Viscount Bourchier (1883 Extinct Peerage, Bourchier, B.), and widow of Sir Edward Wingfield, and by her who d. 30 July 1489, had issue,

1. Richard, **6th Baron** and 3rd Earl (see below).

He m. (2) Lady Katharine Herbert, dau. of 1st Earl of Pembroke, of 1st creation, and by her who d. before 8 May 1504 had further issue,

2. Henry, Sir, of Wrest, co. Bedford, **7th Baron** and 4th Earl (see below).
3. George, d. unm.
4. Anthony, of Branspeth, whose grandson Anthony, s. as 9th Earl of Kent, and was ancestor of Viscount Gooderich, of Gooderich Castle, co. Hereford, Earl of Harold, co. Bedford, Marquess of Kent, Duke of Kent, and Marquess de Grey (1883 Extinct Peerage).
1. Anne, m. Sir John Hussey, Lord Hussey, of Sleaford, (1883 Extinct Peerage).

The 2nd Earl of Kent d. 25 Dec. 1503, and was s. by his eldest son, Richard de Grey, **6th Baron Grey de Ruthyn**, and 3rd Earl of Kent, K.G., who served in France at the siege of Therouenne, with Henry VIII, b. 1481, m. (1) Elizabeth, dau. of Sir William Hussey, Lord Chief Justice, and sister of Lord Hussey, see above. He m. (2) Margaret, dau. of James Fynche, and widow of John Dawes and of Oliver Curteis. He d.s.p. 3 May 1524, when he was s. by his half brother,

Henry de Grey, **7th Baron Grey de Ruthyn** and 4th Earl of Kent, m. Anne (whose will was dated 6 Mar. 1564/5 and proved 26 May 1565) dau. of John Blennerhassett, of Southill, co. Bedford, and by her had issue, Henry, b. 1520, m. Margaret, dau. of John St. John, of Bletso, co. Bedford, and d.v.p. 1545, having had issue,

(1) Reginald, **8th Baron** and 5th Earl (see below).
(2) Henry, **9th Baron** and 6th Earl (see below).
(3) Charles, **10th Baron** and 7th Earl (see below).

The 7th Baron from the slenderness of his means declined to assume the peerage. He d.

24 Sept. 1562, when he was s. by his grandson, Reginald de Grey **8th Baron Grey de Ruthyn** and 5th Earl of Kent, m. Susan (who m. 2ndly 30 Sept. 1581, Sir John Wingfield, of Wingcoll, co. Lincoln) dau. of Richard Bertie, by Katherine, his wife, Baroness Willoughby de Eresby in her own right, widow of Sir Charles Brandon, 1st Duke of Suffolk. He d.s.p. 17 Mar. 1573, when he was s. by his brother,

Henry de Grey, **9th Baron Grey de Ruthyn,** and 6th Earl of Kent, one of the peers at the trial of Mary, Queen of Scots, 1587, b. 1541; m. Mary (d. 16 Nov. 1580) dau. of Sir George Cotton, and widow of 3rd Earl of Derby, and d.s.p. 31 Jan. 1514/15 when he was s. by his brother,

Charles de Grey, **10th Baron Grey de Ruthyn** and 7th Earl of Kent, m. Susan, (d. 1617) dau. of Sir Richard Cotton, of Bedhampton, co. Southampton, and had issue,

Henry, 11th Baron Grey de Ruthyn (see below).

Susan, m. 12 Aug. 1611. Sir Michael Longueville, of Wolverton, co. Bucks and d.v.p. (bur. 13 Dec. 1620, M. I. at Blunham, Co. Bedford) leaving issue,

Charles, **12th Baron Grey de Ruthyn** (see below).

The 10th Baron d. 26 Sept. 1623, s. by his only son,

Henry de Grey, **11th Baron Grey de Ruthyn** and 8th Earl of Kent, m. 1602, Lady Elizabeth Talbot (d. 7 Dec. 1651) dau. and coheir of 7th Earl of Shrewsbury and Waterford, and d.s.p. 21 Nov. 1639, when he was s. in the Earldom of Kent, by his kinsman Anthony Grey as 9th Earl, see above, and in the Barony by his nephew,

Charles Longueville, **12th Baron Grey de Ruthyn,** bapt. 21 April 1612; was confirmed in the Barony 5 Feb. 1640/41 and took his seat in the House of Lords, 10 Feb. 1641/42. He m. Frances (d. 22 May 1668) dau. and coheir of Edward Nevill, and d. 17 June 1643, having had issue an only dau. and heir,

Susan Longueville, **(13th holder) Baroness Grey de Ruthyn,** m. Sir Henry Yelverton, 2nd Bt., of Easton Maudiut, co. Northampton, M.P. co. Northampton 1660, and by him (who d. 30 Oct. 1670) had issue,

1. Charles, **14th Baron** (see below).
2. Henry, **15th Baron** (see below).
3. Christopher.
1. Frances, m. 1676, 1st Viscount Hatton, and d. 1684.

The Baroness d. 28 Jan. 1676, and was s. by her eldest son,

Sir Charles Yelverton, 3rd Bt. and **14th Baron Grey de Ruthyn,** b. 21 Aug. 1657, d. unm., of the s.p., 17 May 1679, being s. by his brother,

Sir Henry Yelverton, 4th Bt., **15th Baron Grey de Ruthyn,** and 1st Viscount Longueville, so cr. by patent 21 April 1690, was allowed at the coronation of James II, to carry the Golden Spurs; m. 11 July 1689 Barbara (d. 31 Jan. 1763, aged 98) dau. and coheir of Sir John Talbot, of Laycock, co. Wilts, (Shrewsbury, E.), and had issue two sons and five daus., of whom his successor was,

Sir Talbot Yelverton, 5th Bt., **16th Baron Grey de Ruthyn,** and 2nd Viscount Longueville, and 1st Earl of Sussex, so cr. in the last title, 26 Sept. 1717, carried the Golden Spurs at the coronation of George I, and officiated as

Deputy Earl Marshal at the coronation of George II. He m. Lucy, dau. of Henry Pelham, of Lewes, co. Sussex, and by her, who d. 1730, had issue,

1. George Augustus, Sir, and **17th Baron,** 2nd Earl etc. (see below).
2. Henry, **18th Baron** etc. (see below).

The 1st Earl of Sussex d. 27 Oct. 1731, being s. by his elder son,

Sir George Augustus Yelverton, 6th Bt., and **17th Baron Grey de Ruthyn,** and 2nd Earl of Sussex, a Lord of the Bedchamber to Frederick Prince of Wales, and to his son, afterwards George III, b. 27 July 1727; d. unm. 8 Jan. 1758, and was s. by his brother,

Sir Henry Yelverton, 7th Bt., **18th Baron Grey de Ruthyn,** and 3rd Earl of Sussex, b. 7 July 1728; m. (1) 17 Jan. 1757, Hester (d. 11 Jan. 1777) dau. of John Hall, of Mansfield, Woodhouse, co. Nottingham, and had issue, with a son, Talbot d. young, a dau. Barbara Yelverton, m. Oct. 1775, Edward Thoroton Gould, of Woodham Mansfield, and d.v.p. 8 April 1781, leaving issue,

1. Henry Edward, **19th Baron** (see below).
1. Barbara, d. unm.
2. Mary, m. 15 Oct. 1807, the Rev. and Hon. Frederick Powys, and d. 19 Jan. 1837, leaving issue (Lilford, B.).

The 2nd Earl of Sussex m. (2) 29 Jan. 1778, Mary (d.s.p. 9 July 1796), dau. of John Vaughan, of Bristol. He d. 22 April 1799, when his baronetcy, viscounty and earldom became extinct, but he was s. in the ancient barony by his grandson,

Henry Edward Gould, **19th Baron Grey de Ruthyn,** who assumed the surname of Yelverton on s. his grandfather, b. 8 Sept. 1780; m. 21 June 1809, Anna Maria (she m. 2ndly the Rev. and Hon. William Eden, 2nd son of 1st Baron Henley and d. 23 Oct. 1875), dau. of William Kelham, and d. 29 Oct. 1810, being s. by his only dau. and heir,

Barbara Yelverton, **(20th) Baroness Grey de Ruthyn,** b. 29 May 1810; m. (1) 18 Aug. 1831, George Augustus Francis Rawdon, 3rd Earl of Moira and 2nd Marquess of Hastings 1883 Extinct Peerage) and by him, who d. 13 June 1844 had issue,

1. Paulyn Reginald Serlo, 3rd Marquess of Hastings, d.v.m. unm. 17 Jan. 1851.
2. Henry Weysford Charles Plantagenet, **21st Baron** and 4th Marquess.
1. Edith Maud, s. her brother the 4th Marquess as Countess of Loudoun.
2. Bertha Lelgarde, **(22nd) Baroness Grey de Ruthyn.**
3. Victoria Mary Louisa, m. 31 Oct. 1859, John Forbes Stratford Kirwan, and d. 30 Mar. 1888, leaving issue.
4. Frances Augusta Constance, m. 30 July 1863, 4th Earl of Romney and d. 1 Sept. 1910 leaving issue.

The Marchioness of Hastings, (20th) Baroness Grey de Ruthyn, m. (2) 9 April 1845, Adm. Sir Hastings Reginald Henry, who assumed the surname of Yelverton, and had further issue,

5. Barbara, m. 23 Sept. 1872, 2nd Lord Churston and d. 1 Oct. 1924 leaving issue.

The Baroness d. 19 Nov. 1858, and was s. by her son, Henry Weysford Charles_ Plantagenet Rawdon, **21st Baron Grey de Ruthyn** and 4th Marquess of Hastings, b. 22 July 1842; m. 16 July 1864, Lady Florence Cecilia Paget (she m. 2ndly 9 June 1870, Sir George Chetwode, 4th Bt. and d. 3 Feb. 1907), dau. of 2nd Marquess of Anglesey, and d.s.p. 10 Nov. 1868. The Marquessate of Hastings and the Irish titles became extinct; the Scottish honours went to his eldest sister; his English baronies which descended to him from his brother, fell into abeyance between his sisters of the whole blood. The Barony of Grey de Ruthyn went into abeyance between his sisters cᶠ the whole blood and his half sister until Queen Victoria was pleased to terminate the abeyance in favour of the Marquess's second sister,

Bertha Lelgarde, Rawdon, **(22nd) Baroness Grey de Ruthyn,** b. 30 April 1835; m. 11 Dec. 1855, Augustus Wykeham Clifton, of Warton Hall, co. Lancaster, (B.L.G. 1952 Clifton of Clifton) and by him had issue,

1. Rawdon George Grey, **23rd Baron Grey de Ruthyn** (see below).
2. Cecil Talbot, **24th Baron** (see below).
1. Ella Cicely Mary, b. 22 Nov. 1856; m. 30 July 1879, Lancelot George Butler-Bowdon, of Barlborough House, Chesterfield, and d. 2 July 1912, leaving issue,

   John Lancelot Wykeham, **25th Baron Grey de Ruthyn** (see below).
2. Lelgarde Harry Florence, D. St. J. b. 16 Feb. 1870; m. 11 June 1895, Sir Alan Henry Bellingham, 4th Bt., and d. 15 Oct. 1939.

The Baroness was declared by the Cttee. of Privileges 1876 to be one of the coheirs of the Barony of Grey de Ruthyn, and the abeyance was terminated in her favour by letters patent 29 Dec. 1885; she d. 15 Dec. 1887, and was s. by her elder son, Rawdon George Grey Clifton, **23rd Baron Grey de Ruthyn,** b. 14 Nov. 1858; m. 1 Sept. 1892 Evelyn Isobel Ida Charlotte, (who d. 2 Oct. 1905), only dau. of James Foster, of Cranborne Hall, Windsor Forest, and had issue,

Reginald Francis Rawdon, b. 14 May d. 1 July 1893.

The 23rd Baron bore one of the Golden Spurs at the coronations of Edward VII and George V. He d. 29 Aug. 1912, and was s. by his brother,

Cecil Talbot Clifton, **24th Baron Grey de Ruthyn,** Hereditary Bearer of the Great Gold Spur at Coronations, b. 9 Jan. 1862; d.s.p. 21 May 1934, when the Barony fell into abeyance between his nephew John Lancelot Wykeham Butler Bowdon (see above) and his younger sister Lelgrade Harry Florence, (see above). In 1940 the Barony was called out of abeyance in favour of his nephew,

John Lancelot Wykeham Butler Bowdon. **25th Baron Grey de Ruthyn,** J.P. co. Derby, b. 25 Oct. 1883; educ. Mount St. Mary's Coll. Spinkhill; d. unm. 25 Oct. 1963, when the Barony again fell into abeyance between the representatives of the sisters of the Baroness, the 22nd holder of the title,

ARMS—(of last holder of barony). Quarterly of 8, 1st and 8th, Sable on a bend argent three mullets gules (Clifton); 2nd, Quarterly I and IV, Argent a maunche sable (Hastings); II and III, Argent a fess between three pheons sable (Rawdon); 3rd and 5th, Argent three lions rampant sable; a chief gules (Yelverton); 4th, Per saltire azure and or a lion rampant counter changed; 6th a fess dancettée ermine, between six cross crosslets argent (Longueville). 7th Barry of six argent and azure, inchief three torteaux (Grey de Ruthyn).

CREST—A dexter arm enbowed in armour-holding a sword ppr.

SUPPORTERS—Dexter, A wyvern or, collared and lined gules; Sinister, A lion reguardant gules.

MOTTO—Mortem aut triumphum.

GREY DE RADCLIFFE

PEERAGE—U.K. Baron Grey De Radcliffe, in the co. Palatine of Lancaster.

SURNAME—Egerton.

CR.—14 June 1875. EXT.—18 Jan. 1885.

HISTORY—Arthur Edward Holland Grey Egerton, 3rd Earl of Wilton, (see extant peerages), was b. 25 Nov. 1833; was M.P. for Weymouth and for Bath; served in 1st Life Guards, 1854-59; was cr. a peer of the U.K. as **Baron Grey De Radcliffe** in the co. Palatine of Lancaster, 14 June 1875. He m. 11 Aug. 1858, Lady Elizabeth Charlotte Louisa Craven, dau. of 2nd Earl of Craven. (She m. 2ndly, 14 Sept. 1886, A. V. Pryor, and d. 8 Mar. 1919). The 3rd Earl d.s.p. 18 Jan. 1885 when the Barony of Grey De Radcliffe became extinct and the earldom and the viscounty were inherited by the 3rd Earl's brother, Seymour John Grey Egerton, 4th Earl of Wilton, Viscount Grey De Wilton etc. (extant peerage works).

GUILLAMORE

PEERAGE—Ireland. Viscount Guillamore of Cahir-Guillamore and Baron O'Grady of Rockbarton, both co. Limerick.

SURNAME—O'Grady.

CR.—28 Jan. 1831. EXT.—15 Oct. 1955.

HISTORY—A comprehensive pedigree of the O'Grady family, described as one of the most ancient in North Munster, is given in B.L.G. of Ireland 1958 edition (O'Gray of Kilballyowen). Standish O'Grady, mentioned therein, had by his wife Honora, dau. and co-heiress of Jeremiah Hayes of Cahir, co. Limerick, a second son, Darby O'Grady, of Mount Prospect, co. Limerick, High Sheriff 1785, m. 1763, Mary, dau. of James Smyth of Limerick and had with other issue an eldest son,

Standish O'Grady, **1st Viscount Guillamore**, Lord Chief Baron of the Exchequer in Ireland, created Viscount Guillamore, of Cahir Guillamore, and Baron O'Grady of Rockbarton, both co. Limerick, 28 Jan. 1831; b. 1766; m. 1790, Katharine (d. 1853), dau. of John T. Waller of Castletown and had with other issue,

1. Standish, **2nd Viscount** (see below).
2. Waller, Barrister-at-Law, Q.C., m. 1823, Grace Elizabeth Massy, eldest dau. of 3rd Lord Massy, and d. 1849 having had with other issue,
   (1) Hugh Hamon Massy, b. 1825, m. 6 Aug. 1857, Zillah Selina Maria, dau. of W. H. Hutchinson, of Rockforest, co. Tipperary and d. 9 Dec. 1859, having had issue,
   1a Walter Massy, b. 14 Dec. 1858 and d.s.p. 1883.

2a Hugh Hamon Massy, **7th Viscount** (see below).
   (2) James Waller, Lt. R.N., b. 1832; m. 1865 Ada, dau. of W. C. Bruce (see Bruce of Stenhouse, Bt.) and d. 1898, leaving issue with two daus.,
   1a Richard, **8th Viscount** (see below).
   2a Standish Bruce, **9th Viscount** (see below).

The 1st Viscount d. 21 April 1840 and was s. by his eldest son, Standish O'Grady, **2nd Viscount Guillamore**, b. 1792; m. 1828, Gertrude Jane, dau. of the Hon. Berkeley Paget, and had with other issue,

1. Standish, **3rd Viscount** (see below).
2. Paget Standish, **4th Viscount** (see below).
3. Hardress Standish, **5th Viscount** (see below).
4. Frederick Standish, **6th Viscount** (see below).

The second Viscount d. 22 July 1848, when he was s. by his eldest son, Standish O'Grady, **3rd Viscount Guillamore**, b. 1832; m. 1853, Adelaide, dau. of Arthur Blennerhassett, of Ballyseedy, co. Kerry and d.s.p.m. 1860 being s. by his next brother,

Paget Standish O'Grady, **4th Viscount Guillamore**, b. 1835; m. 1869, Eliza, dau. of W. H. Feston, and d.s.p. 1877, when he was s. by his brother,

Hardress Standish O'Grady, **5th Viscount Guillamore**, b. 1841; d. unm. 1918 and was s. by his brother,

Frederick Standish O'Grady, **6th Viscount Guillamore**, b. 1847; m. (1) 1881 Mary Theresa Burdett (d.s.p. 1910), dau. of W. J. Coventry, and widow of G. S. T. de Windt and of J. H. Empson; m. (2) 1911, Gertrude Lily (d. 1952), dau. of J. Langford and by her had issue a dau. Kathleen Gertrude, m. Capt. G. C. Hearn. The 6th Viscount d.s.p.m. 11 Oct. 1927 and was s. by his cousin,

Hugh Hamon Massy O'Grady, **7th Viscount Guillamore**, Major Royal Sussex Regt., b. 1860; m. 1890, Mary Margaret Frances, dau. of Vere Hunt of High Park, co. Tipperary and d.s.p. 1930 being s. by his cousin, Richard O'Grady, **8th Viscount Guillamore**, b. 1867, d. unm. 1943 and was s. by his brother,

Standish Bruce O'Grady, **9th Viscount Guillamore**, Capt. 5th Bn. Royal Munster Fus., b. 1869, d. 15 Oct. 1955.

ARMS—Per pale gules and sable, three lions passant-guardant per pale argent and or, the centre lion charged on the side with a portcullis azure.

CREST—A horse's head erased argent charged with a portcullis azure.

SUPPORTERS—Two lions guardant per fess argent and or, each charged on the shoulder with a portcullis azure.

MOTTO—Vulneratus non victus.

GWYDYR

PEERAGE—Great Britain. Baron Gwydyr of Gwydyr, co. Carnarvon.

SURNAME—Burrell.

CR.—16 June 1796. (Also a baronetcy of Great Britain cr. 15 July 1766.) EXT.—13 Feb. 1915.

HISTORY—Peter Burrell, of Cuckfield, Sussex, settled at Langley Park, Beckenham, co. Kent, 1684. He m. Isabel, dau. of John Merrik, of Subbers, co. Essex, and had issue,

1. Peter, his successor.
2. Merrik, Sir, of West Grinstead, Sussex, M.P., and Gov. of the Bank of England, cr. a Baronet 15 July 1766, with remainder to his nephew, Peter Burrell. Sir Merrik d.s.p. 1787.

The elder son, Peter Burrell, of Beckenham, M.P., m. Amy, dau. of Hugh Raymond, of Saling Park, co. Essex and d. 16 April 1756, leaving issue,

1. Peter, surveyor gen. of crown lands, m. 1749, Elizabeth, dau. and heir of John Lewis, of Hackney, and had issue with four daus., an only son, Peter, who s. to the baronetcy of his great-uncle Sir Merrik Burrell.
2. William, M.P. Haslemere, m. Sophia, dau. and heir of Sir Charles Raymond, Bt. to whose baronetcy he succeeded. (See Burrell, Bt. in extant baronetage).

Mr. Peter Burrell was s. by his grandson, Sir Peter Burrell, 2nd Bt. (s. to the baronetcy of his great uncle as mentioned above), and **1st Baron Gwydyr** of Gwydyr, co. Carnarvon, so cr. 16 June 1796. He m. 28 Feb. 1779, Lady Priscilla Bertie, eldest dau. and heir of 3rd Duke of Ancaster and Kesteven, Marquess and Earl of Lindsey, Baron Willoughby de Eresby and Lord Great Chamberlain of England. On the death of her brother the 4th Duke of Ancaster, without issue, 8 July 1779, Lady Priscilla became suo jure Baroness Willoughby de Eresby. Lord Gwydyr d. 9 June 1820 and he and Baroness Willoughby de Eresby had issue, with a third son who d. unm. and a dau. m. 2nd Earl of Clare,

1. Peter Robert, **2nd Baron Gwydyr** (see below).
2. Lindsey Merrik Peter, b. 20 June 1786; m. 13 July 1807, Frances, dau. of James Daniell. She d. 1846. He d. 1 Jan. 1848. They had issue with seven daus. and three other sons who d. unm. or without male issue, a second son,
   Peter Robert, **4th Baron Gwydyr** (see below).

The first Baron Gwydyr was s. by his eldest son, Peter Robert Burrell, **2nd Baron Gwydyr**, P.C., who also s. his mother on 29 Dec. 1828 as 19th Baron Willoughby de Eresby and joint hereditary Great Chamberlain. He was b. 12 Mar. 1782; m. 1807, Clementine, dau. and heiress of James Drummond, Lord Perth, and had issue by her (who d. 26 Jan. 1865), with an eldest son, Frederick, d. unm.

1. Alberic, **3rd Baron Gwydyr** (see below).
1. Clementina, Dowager Lady Aveland, Baroness Willoughby de Eresby (23rd holder of title).
2. Elizabeth, d. unm. 1853.
3. Charlotte Augusta, m. 2nd Lord Carrington and d. 26 July 1879.

The 2nd Baron d. 22 Feb. 1865, and was s. by his son, Alberic Burrell, **3rd Baron Gwydyr**, and 20th Baron Willoughby de Eresby, Lord Great Chamberlain, and d. unm. 26 Aug. 1870, being s. in the Barony of Gwydyr by his cousin,
Peter Robert Burrell, **4th Baron Gwydyr**, Chm. of Quarter Sessions, co. Suffolk, b. 27 April 1810; m. (1) 10 Dec. 1840, Sophia,

only child of F. W. Campbell, of Barbreck, Scotland, and by her (d. 14 Mar. 1843) had issue,
Willoughby Merrik Campbell, **5th Baron Gwydyr** (see below).
He m. (2) 8 May 1856, Georgina, dau. of G. P. Holford, of Westonbirt, Glos. and she d. 24 Nov. 1892. By her Lord Gwydyr had further issue,
Cicely, b. 2 Jan. 1858.
Lord Gwydyr was High Sheriff, co. Suffolk 1858, high steward for Ipswich, Sec. to the Lord Great Chamberlain. He d. 3 April 1909, and was s. by his only son, Sir Willoughby Merrik Campbell Burrell, **5th Baron Gwydyr** and 6th Bt., Capt. Rifle Brig., hon. Col. 4th Bn. Suffolk Regt., F.R.G.S., b. 26 Oct. 1841; m. (1) 4 Sept. 1873, Mary, only child of Sir John Banks, K.C.B., of Golagh, co. Monaghan, and by her (who d. 26 June 1898), had issue,

1. Randulphus Clement Robert, b. 2 Nov. 1876; d. 13 Nov. 1882.
2. John Percy, b. 11 Feb. 1873; third sec. H.M. Diplomatic Service; d. unm. 17 Aug. 1902.
1. Catherine Mary Sermonia, m. 16 July 1902, Sir John Henniker Heaton, 2nd Bt., and had issue.

The 5th Baron Gwydyr m. (2) 4 June 1901, Anne, dau. of John Ord, of Overwhitton, co. Roxburgh, and d. 13 Feb. 1915. She d.s.p. 12 May 1910.

ARMS—Quarterly 1, Vert, three escutcheons argent, each charged with a bordure engrailed or (Burrell); 2, Or, fretty azure (Willoughby); 3, Argent, three battering rams barways in pale, ppr. headed and garnished azure (Bertie); 4, Vert, three eagles displayed in fess or (Gwynedd, Prince of Wales).
CRESTS—(1) A naked arm embowed ppr. holding a branch of laurel vert; (2) A Saracen's head couped and affrontée ppr. ducally crowned or.
SUPPORTERS—Dexter, A grey friar habited ppr. with his crutch and rosary or; Sinister, A savage wreathed about the temples and waist all ppr.
MOTTO—Animus non deficit aequus.

HAILEY

PEERAGE—U.K. Baron Hailey of Shahpur in the Punjab and Newport Pagnell, co. Buckingham.
SURNAME—Hailey.
CR.—15 July 1936. **EXT.**—1 June 1969.
HISTORY—George Hailey, yeoman of Arlesey, co. Bedford, d. 1712 leaving issue, George Hailey, Chief Constable of Clifton, co. Bedford, d. 1751, leaving issue, George Hailey, surgeon, of Shefford, co. Bedford, b. 1716, d. 1760, leaving issue, Thomas Hailey, of Pirton, co. Hertford, b. 1751, d. 7 Sept. 1809 leaving issue, William Hailey, M.R.C.S., of Oundle, Northants and Arlesey, co. Bedford, b. 13 June 1789 and d. 7 Feb. 1866 leaving issue, Hammett Hailey, M.R.C.S., of Rickford Lodge, Newport Pagnell, co. Buckingham. b. 25 May 1869; educ. Merchant Taylors' School and St. John's Coll. Oxford; m. 1 Jan. 1902, Rhoda, dau. of the Rev. S. Cotes, and d. 25 Dec. 1960. She d. 1943. They had with two other sons and three daus.,

Sir William Malcolm Hailey, **Baron Hailey**, described in *The Times* obituary notice as having "two careers of great distinction in public life. After spending close on 40 years as one of the most brilliant members of the Indian Civil Service of his day, he retired to take up the study of African colonial administration, and after the death of Lord Lugard was the foremost British authority on its manifold aspects. In India he had held a number of high posts culminating in the Governorship successively of the Punjab and the United Provinces. In the second phase of his public life he had strong formative influence on the new conceptions of colonial policy which marked postwar planning". He was b. 15 Feb. 1892; educ. Merchant Taylors' and Corpus Christi Coll. Oxford, Scholar, B.A. 1895, Hon. Fell. 1926, M.A. 1929, entered I.C.S. 1895, Gov. of Punjab 1924-28, and of United Provinces of Agra and Oudh, 1928-34. Chm. of Royal African Soc. 1946-58, and of many cttees. and asscns. He m. 18 Dec. 1896, Andreina Alesandra, dau. of Count Hannibale Balzani, of Rome, Italy. She d. 1939. They had issue, a son Alan Balzano, b. 1900 and k. on active service in the Middle East, Feb. 1943, and a dau. Gemma, d. unm. 1922. Lord Hailey was created C.I.E. (1911), C.S.I. (1915), K.C.S.I. (1922), G.C.I.E. (1928), G.C.S.I. (1932), G.C.M.G. (1938), Baron Hailey of Shahpur in the Punjab and Newport Pagnell co. Buckingham, 15 July 1936, was made P.C, 1949 and received O.M. 1956. He d. 1 June 1969.

HAIRE OF WHITEABBEY

PEERAGE—U.K. Life. Baron Haire of Whiteabbey, of Newtown Abbey, co. Antrim.
SURNAME—Haire .
CR.—1 May 1956. **EXT.**—7 Oct. 1966.
HISTORY—John Haire, a textile engineer of Portadown, co. Armagh, b. 1868; m. 1889, Mary, dau. of John Tedford of Laurelvale, co. Armagh. He d. 1928. She d. 28 Aug. 1956. They had issue,
1. Leonard, served in World War I, 1914-18, b. 28 Jan. 1895; m. 22 Aug. 1928, Emma Kathleen, dau. of Alexander Wilson, of Lurgan, co. Armagh and had issue, three sons.
2. John Edwin, **Baron Haire** (see below).
The younger son, John Edwin Haire, **Baron Haire** of Whiteabbey, b. 14 Nov. 1908; educ. Queen's Univ., Belfast, B.A. 1931, M.A. 1936, Diploma in Education 1931, Licentiate Guildhall Sch. of Music and Drama 1934; in World War II, served with R.A.F. 1941-46 (S/Ldr. R.A.F.) Coastal Cmd. and later Air Liaison Offr. to Admiralty 1943, Air Historian, Air Min. 1945-46; was. M.P. Wycombe 1945-51, mem. Parl. Delegation to Hungary 1946, to France 1946 and Berlin 1948. He m. 30 June 1939, Susanne Elizabeth, Ph.D., B.Litt., B.A., News Editor, Overseas Service, B.B.C., dau. of Dr. E. Kemeny of London. He was cr. a life peer as Baron Haire of Whiteabbey, of Newtownabbey, co. Antrim, 1 May 1965 and d. 7 Oct. 1966. He had issue,
1. Michael John Kemeny, b. 19 Dec. 1945; educ. St. Paul's and Univ. Coll. London.

2. Christopher Peter, b. 6 Feb. 1951, educ. Michael Hall, Forest Row, Sussex.
Lord Haire's seats were Whiteabbey, co. Antrim; Lynford Hall, Mundford, co. Norfolk. He also had property at Rockhill Castle, Kerryheel, co. Donegal.

HALDANE

PEERAGE—U.K. Viscount Haldane of Cloan co. Perth.
SURNAME—Haldane.
CR.—27 Mar. 1911. **EXT.**—23 Aug. 1928.
HISTORY—In the 1952 edition of Burke's Landed Gentry is a very long and detailed account of the family of Chinnery-Haldane of Gleneagles. Sir Richard Burdon Haldane, **Viscount Haldane**, was the fourth son of Robert Haldane, W.S., a cadet of the family. Viscount Haldane was born of Robert Haldane's second marriage, 27 July 1853, to Mary Elizabeth, (d. 20 May 1925), dau. of Richard Burdon-Sanderson, of Otterburn Dene, and of West Jesmond, co. Northumberland, and he was b. 30 July 1856 in Edinburgh; educ. Edinburgh Academy, Edinburgh Univ. M.A 1876, and Gottingen Univ.; Barrister-at-Law, Lincoln's Inn 1879; Q.C. 1890; Bencher 1893; Gray Scholar, and Ferguson Scholar, Gifford Lecturer, at St. Andrews 1902-04; M.P. Haddington 1885-1911; Sec. of State for War 1905-11; mem. of the Judicial Cttee. of the Privy Council 1911; Chancellor of the Univ, of Bristol 1911; Lord High Chancellor of Great Britain 1912-15; and again Jan. to Nov. 1924 in first Labour Gov.; made P.C. 1911; cr. Viscount Haldane of Cloan, co. Perth, 27 Mar. 1911; K.T. 1913; and O.M. 1915. He d. unm. 19 Aug. 1928. He was the author of several books, including his *Autobiography* published in 1929.
ARMS—Quarterly 1 and 4, Argent, a saltire engrailed sable (Haldane); 2, Argent, a saltire between four roses gules (Lennox); 3, Or, a bend chequy sable and argent (Menteith), in the centre of the quarters a crescent sable, all within a bordure or.
CREST—An eagle's head erased or.
SUPPORTERS—Two eagles' wings disclosed ppr. each charged on the neck with a crescent or.
MOTTO—Suffer.
Viscount Haldane's seat was at Cloan, Auchterarder, Perthshire.

HALDON

PEERAGE—U.K. Baron Haldon, of Haldon, co. Devon. (Also a baronetcy cr. 19 June 1782.)
SURNAME—Palk.
CR.—29 April 1880. **EXT.**—11 Jan. 1939.
HISTORY—Sir Robert Palk, 1st Bt., so cr. 19 June 1782, was the elder son of Walter Palk by his first wife, formerly Miss Abraham. Sir Robert was M.P. Ashburton 1767, and 1774-87, Gov. of Madras 1763, m. 11 Feb. 1761, Anne, dau. of Arthur Vansittart, (see Vansittart, B. in present work), and d. 29 April 1798 having had with three daus., an only son, Sir Lawrence Palk, 2nd Bt., M.P. co. Devon;

m. (1) Lady Mary Bligh, dau. of 3rd Earl of
Darnley. She d.s.p.s. 4 Mar. 1791. He m. (2)
1792, Lady Dorothy Elizabeth Vaughan, dau.
of 1st Earl of Lisburne, by whom (she d.
15 Feb. 1849) he had issue,
1. Lawrence Vaughan, Sir, 3rd Bt. (see
   below).
2. Robert John Malet, Barrister-at-Law
   b. 15 May 1794; m. 5 Aug. 1828, Harriet,
   dau. of George Hibbert, of Portland
   Place, and d. 1870, leaving issue,
   (1) Ashley, b. 1834, d. 1861.
   (2) Wilmot Henry, b. 1836; m. 1867,
       Elizabeth Alexandrina, Greig, dau. of
       John Mackenzie, of Golspie and d.
       13 June 1876, leaving issue,
       1a. Robert Wilmot Henry Malet,
           Barrister-at-Law, b. 1868; d. 10
           Oct. 1934.
       2a. John Wilmot Mackenzie, private
           in Black Watch b. 1874; d. 16
           Nov. 1916 of wounds received in
           action.
       3a. Wilmot Lawrence Lancelot, Lt.
           Durham L.I., formerly Midship-
           man R.N., b. 28 Aug. 1876.
       1a. Evelyn Beatrix Malet.
       2a Bessie Octavia Hibbert, m. 17
          June 1913, F. W. Hadden and
          had issue.
3. Wilmot Henry, Rev. B. A., b. 24 Oct.
   1796 and d. unm.
4. John, Major in the Army, b. 25 April
   1801; d. 4 Oct. 1838.
5. Edward, b. 1804; d. 22 Jan. 1821.
6. Arthur George, Rev., b. 1806, d. 1835.
1. Elizabeth Malet, b. 15 May 1818, Sir
   Horace Seymour, (Hertford, M.).
2. Mary, m. 27 Aug. 1835, 4th Earl of
   Lisburne.
The 2nd Bt. d. 20 June 1813, and was s. by
his eldest son, Sir Lawrence Vaughan Palk,
3rd Bt., M.P. Ashburton, b. 24 April 1793;
m. 9 Dec. 1815, Anna Eleanora, dau. of Sir
Bourchier Wrey, Bt., and widow of Edward
Hartopp, of Dalby House, co. Leicester. She
d. 25 Jan. 1846 leaving issue,
1. Lawrence, 1st Baron Haldon (see below).
2. Henry, Rev. B. C. L., Rector of Bridford
   and of Dunchideock, co. Devon, b. 25
   Feb. 1819; m. 17 Nov. 1846, Isabella
   Mary, dau. of James Pitman, of Dunchideock House, co. Devon, and d. 17
   April 1872.
3. Augustus, b. 1824.
1. Elizabeth Anna, m. 1848, Albany Bourchier Savile, of Holne Park, near Ashburton, and d. 1894.
2. Isabella, m. 1848, S. W. Gardiner, of
   Coombe Lodge, Oxford.
The 3rd Bt. d. 16 May 1860, and was s. by his
eldest son, Sir Lawrence Palk, 4th Bt., 1st
Baron Haldon, so cr. 29 April 1880; M.P.
South Devon 1854-68, and for East Devon
1868-80; b. 5 Jan. 1818; educ. Eton; m. 15
Nov. 1845, Maria Henrietta, dau. of Sir
Thomas Henry Hesketh, 4th Bt., and d. 22
Mar. 1883, having had by her (who d. 19 Dec.
1905),
1. Lawrence, Sir, 5th Bt., and 2nd Baron
   Haldon (see below).
2. Robert Henry, 23rd Fusiliers, b. 1848,
   d. 1878.
3. Walter George, Lt. R.H.A., d. 1 May
   1876.

4. Edward Arthur, 5th Baron Haldon (see
   below).
1. Annette Maria, m. 1873, Sir Alexander
   Baird, Bt. (Stonehaven, B.) and d. 1884,
   leaving issue.
2. Evelyn Elizabeth, m. 1882, Major Ernest
   Gambier-Parry and d. 1935, leaving
   issue. (B.L.G. 1952, Gambier-Parry of
   Highnam Court.)
The 1st Baron Haldon d. 22 Mar. 1883, and
was s. by his eldest son, Sir Lawrence Hesketh
Palk, 2nd Baron Haldon and 5th Bt. He was
b. 6 Sept. 1846; educ. Eton and Ch. Ch.
Oxford; was Lt. Scots Fusilier Guards; and
declared a bankrupt in 1891. He was also a
Lt. of Royal 1st Devons. He m. 7 Oct. 1868,
Constance Mary, dau. of 7th Viscount Barrington, of Ardglass, and had issue,
1. Lawrence William, 3rd Baron Haldon
   (see below).
2. Lawrence Charles Walter, D.S.O., Major
   and Temp. Lt. Col. Hampshire Regt.,
   b. 28 Sept. 1870; served in S. African
   War 1901-02 and in World War I,
   (despatches, D.S.O., Legion of Honour),
   k. in action 1 July 1916.
1. Florence Annette Georgina, b. 21 Oct.
   1871; d. unm. 22 April 1958.
2. Mary Evelyn, b. 28 Oct. 1875; educ. Univ.
   Coll. London; d. unm. 1 Feb. 1966.
The 2nd Baron Haldon d. 31 Dec. 1903. He
was s. by his elder son,
Sir Lawrence William Palk, 3rd Baron Haldon
and 6th Bt., b. 13 July 1869; educ. Eton;
Capt. 3rd Bn. Royal Fusiliers, served in S.
African War 1900-01; and in World War I
1914-18, Major, 13th Bn. Northumberland
Fusiliers. He m. (1) 10 Feb. 1893, Lidiana
Amalia Crezencia, (d. 26 Nov. 1928), dau. of
Col. Jacob William Maichle, in Russian
Imperial Army, and widow of D. F. Drew
of U.S.A., and had issue,
Lawrence Edward Broomfield, 4th Baron
Haldon (see below).
He m. (2) 25 Jan. 1929, Edith Castle, (d. 1
May 1930), dau. of William Ball Biggs of
Clifton, Bristol, and widow of E. C. Brightman,
of Cotham Park, Bristol, and d. 12 Jan. 1933,
when he was s. by his son,
Sir Lawrence Edward Broomfield Palk, 4th
Baron and 7th Bt., Capt. R. E., served in
World War I in Gallipoli, Egypt and Mesopotamia; b. 13 May 1896; educ. Beaumont;
he d. 16 Aug. 1938 and was s. by his kinsman,
Sir Edward Arthur Palk, 5th Baron Haldon,
and 8th. Bt., Lt. Col. and hon. Col. cmdg.
4th Bn. Devonshire Regt., b. 1854; m. 18 July
1883, Charlotte Frances, (d. 12 Jan. 1931),
dau. of Rev. Sir Frederick Shelley, 8th Bt. (see
extant peerages, Shelley, Bt.) and d.s.p. 11 Jan.
1939. The barony became extinct. The baronetcy passed to his kinsman,
Sir William Lawrence Launcelot Palk, 9th
Bt., who d. 27 Oct. 1945 when the baronetcy
also became extinct.
ARMS—Sable an eagle displayed argent
beaked and membered or, within a bordure
engrailed of the second.
CREST—On a semi-terrestrial globe of the
northern hemisphere ppr. an eagle rising
argent, beaked and membered or.
SUPPORTERS—Two native Indians ppr. girt
about the loins and turbaned argent.
MOTTO—Deo ducente.

Note. As late as the 1930s, the opening lineage of the Palks began with the statement that the family claimed descent from Henry Palk, tempore Henry VII, possessor of Ambrooke. In contrast may be read the statement in the C.P. under Haldon, that J. H. Round pointed out discrepancies in the older accounts and added that Robert Palk, the first baronet and real founder of the family, was the ygr. brother of Walter Palk, a clothier and yeoman farmer of Ashburton. The first baronet was admitted as a Servitor to Wadham Coll. Oxford, as son of Walter Palk, of Ashburton, described as "pleb." in 1736 and took deacon's orders, but went to India where he acquired a great fortune; the supporters of the arms granted to the first Lord Haldon bear witness to this fact.

HALIBURTON

PEERAGE—U.K. Baron Haliburton of Windsor in the Province of Nova Scotia, and Dominion of Canada.
SURNAME—Haliburton.
CR.—13 June 1898. EXT.—21 April 1907.
HISTORY—The Haliburtons who are described as having settled in America in the 17th century, are also described as cadets of the Scottish border family of Haliburton of Haliburton near Greenlaw in which they were tenants of the Earls of Dunbar. Thomas Chandler Haliburton, Judge of the Supreme Court of Nova Scotia, author of *Sam Slick*, m. Louisa, dau. of Capt. Neville, 2nd Life Guards and 19th Light Dragoons. They had issue, Sir Arthur Lawrence Haliburton, **Baron Haliburton** of Windsor in the Province of Nova Scotia and Dominion of Canada, so cr. 13 June 1898. He was b. 26 Sept. 1832; J.P. and D.L. London. D.C.L. King's Coll., Nova Scotia, served on Commissariat Staff, 1855-70, Dir. of Supplies and Transport at War Office 1878-88, Asst. Under Sec. for War 1888-95. P.U.S. 1895-97; cr. C.B. 1880, K.C.B. 1885, G.C.B. 1897. He m. 3 Nov. 1877, Mariana Emily, dau. of Leo Schuster and widow of Sir William Dickson Clay, 2nd Bt.
Lord Haliburton whose London home was 57 Lowdes Sq. S.W. and whose club was the Athenaeum, d. 21 April 1907.
ARMS—Argent, on a bend azure between two beavers sable three lozenges of the field, within a bordure ermine charged with four thistles leaved and slipped and as many maple leaves slipped alternately or.
CREST—A stag at gaze, gorged with a chaplet of maple leaves, between two branches of maple all ppr.
SUPPORTERS—On either side a wild cat guardant ppr., gorged with a chain or pendent therefrom an escutcheon azure charged with a maple leaf gold.
MOTTO—Watch weel.

**HAMILTON

PEERAGES—Scotland. Life. Duke of Hamilton, Marquess of Clydesdale, Earl of Arran, Lanark and Selkirk, Lord Aven, Machanshire, Polmont and Daer.
SURNAME—Douglas.

CR.—20 Sept. 1660. EXT.—18 April 1694.
HISTORY—The above mentioned titles occur in the family history of the Dukes of Hamilton and Brandon and of the Earls of Selkirk. They are of interest as an example of life peerages conferred long before the arguments advanced in the House of Lords over the famous Wensleydale life peerage. (cr. 16 Jan. 1856), when the House delivered itself of one of the strangest judgments, on the subject of life peerage, which it has ever brought forth. These titles were granted for life to William Douglas, 1st Earl of Selkirk, who thus became life Duke of Hamilton.

**HAMILTON OF WISHAW

PEERAGE—U.K. Baron Hamilton of Wishaw, co. Lanark.
SURNAME—Hamilton.
CR.—10 Sept. 1831. EXT.—22 Dec. 1868.
HISTORY—Robert Montgomery Hamilton, 8th Lord Belhaven and Stenton, was b. 1793; he s. to the Barony of Belhaven and Stenton on 29 Oct. 1814, on the death of his father, the 7th Lord. He was a Representative Peer for Scotland, 1819-32, and was cr. **Baron Hamilton** of Wishaw, co. Lanark in the U.K. peerage on 10 Sept. 1831. He was cr. K.T. 1861. He was High Commissioner to the Gen. Assembley of the Church of Scotland, 1831-41, 1847-51, 1853-57 and 1860-66. Lord Lt. of Lanark 1863-73. He m. 16 Dec. 1815, Hamilton, dau. of Walter Frederick Campbell, of Shawfield, and d.s.p. 22 Dec. 1868, when the Barony of Hamilton of Wishaw became extinct, and he was s. after some years of dormancy in the Scottish Barony by his kinsman, James Hamilton who then on 2 Aug. 1875 became oth Baron Belhaven and Stenton, (see extant peerage works, Belhaven and Stenton, B.).

HAMMOND OF KIRKELLA

PEERAGE—U.K. Baron Hammond of Kirk Ella in the town and county of the town of Kingston-upon-Hull.
SURNAME—Hammond.
CR.—5 Mar. 1874. EXT.—29 April 1890.
HISTORY—Anthony Hammond, of Selby, co. Yorks (1670-1729) had a son, Anthony Hammond, b. 1696, m. Mary Hayes and d. 1759 having had, William Hammond of Kirk Ella, E.R. Yorks, b. 1727 and d. 26 June 1793 had with eleven other children by his wife, Ann Bean, a ygst. son, George Hammond, Under Sec. of State for Foreign Affairs 1795-1806 and 1807-09, m. Margaret, dau. of Andrew Allen and had issue, Hammond, **Baron Hammond**, b. 25 June 1802; entered the Civil Service, 10 Oct. 1823; Under Sec. of State for Foreign Affairs 1854-73; P.C. 1866; cr. a peer as Baron Hammond of Kirk Ella etc. 5 Mar. 1874; m. 3 Jan. 1846, Mary Frances, dau. of Lord Robert Kerr, (Lothian, M.). She d. 14 June 1888. He d. 29 April 1890. They had issue,
1. Mary Georgina, b. 14 Jan. 1848.
2. Margaret Elizabeth, b. 26 Nov. 1851.
3. Katherine Cecilia, b. 2 April 1853.
ARMS—Argent, on a chevron pean, between three mullets sable, a sun in splend.our or.

CREST—Between a stag's attires a falcon rising ppr. each wing charged with a mullet or.
SUPPORTERS—On either side a falcon wings elevated ppr. gorged with a chain or pendent therefrom an escutcheon argent charged with a mullet sable.
MOTTO—Per tot discrimina rerum.
Seat. 25 Eaton Place, London S.W. Lord Hammond's club was the Athenaeum.

**HANMER OF HANMER AND FLINT

PEERAGE—U.K. Baron Hanmer of Hanmer and Flint, co. Flint.
SURNAME—Hanmer.
CR.—1 Oct. 1872. EXT.—8 Mar. 1881.
HISTORY—Sir John Hanmer, 3rd Bt., **Baron Hanmer** of Hanmer and Flint, co. Flint, was b. 22 Dec. 1809, the son of Lt. Col. Thomas Hanmer, who was the eldest son of Sir Thomas Hanmer, 2nd Bt. He was educ. Eton and Ch. Ch. Oxford; and s. his grand-father as 3rd Bt., on 4 Oct. 1828; was High Sheriff, co. Flint, 1832-33; sat as M.P. for Shrewsbury, 1832-37, for Hull, 1841-47; and for Flint Burghs, 1847-72; he was cr. a peer as above on 1 Oct. 1872. He m. 3 Sept. 1833, Georgiana, dau. of Sir George Chetwynd, 2nd Bt., and d.s.p. 8 Mar. 1881. Lady Hanmer d. 21 Mar. 1880. Lord Hanmer's barony became extinct at his death, but his baronetcy was inherited by his brother, Sir Wyndham Edward Hanmer, 4th Bt., (see extant peerage works).
ARMS—Argent, two lions passant guardant azure, armed and langued gules.
CREST—On a chapeau azure turned up ermine, a lion sejant guardant argent.
SUPPORTERS—Dexter, A swan argent; Sinister, A stork ppr., each holding in the beak a rose ppr. leaves vert.
MOTTO—Gardez l'honneur.
The seat of Lord Hanmer was Bettisfield Park, near Whitchurch, Salop.

HANNEN

PEERAGE—U.K. Life Baron Hannen, of Burdock, co. Sussex.
SURNAME—Hannen.
CR.—28 Jan. 1891. EXT.—29 Mar. 1894.
HISTORY—Sir James Hannen, **Baron Hannen,** b. 1821; educ. St. Paul's and Heidelberg Univ.; Barrister-at-Law, Middle Temple, 1848; Bencher; joined home circuit; junior counsel to Treasury, 1863; Judge of Court of Queen's Bench, 1868; cr. Kt. Bach, 1868; apptd. Serjeant-at-Law, 1868; P.C. 1872; Judge of Courts of Probate and Divorce, 1872; Pres. of Probate, Divorce and Admiralty Div. of High Court, 1875-91; apptd. a Lord of Appeal in Ordinary and a life peer, as Baron Hannen, of Burdock, co. Sussex, 28 Jan. 1891; D.C.L. Oxford, 1888; Pres. of Parnell Commission, 1888; arbitrator in matter of Behring Sea seal fisheries, 1892. He m. 4 Feb. 1847, Mary Elizabeth, (d. 1 Dec. 1872), dau. of Nicholas Winsland. He d. 29 Mar. 1894. having had issue,

1. James Chitty, B.A. Oxford; Barrister-at-Law, Registrar of Probate and Divorce Court, b. 1851; m. 8 April 1876, Lucy, dau. of C. Schaeffer, and d. 4 April 1903, leaving issue,
  James Archibald Winsland, B.A. Oxford, b. 14 Aug. 1878.
  Dorothy Margaret.
2. Henry Arthur, of the Hall, West Farleigh, co. Kent, J.P., Barrister-at-Law, b. 1 Mar. 1861; m. 30 Nov. 1896 Mabel, dau. of George Gould, and had issue,
  (1) Mabel Mary.
  (2) Gertrude Margaret.
1. Mary Lucy.
2. Margaret Ellen.

ARMS—Sable a demi-lion between three portcullises, within a bordure or.
CREST—A demi-lion sable gorged with a collar therefrom pendent from a chain an escutcheon or, charged with a portcullis sable.
MOTTO—His truth shall be thy shield.

**HATHERLEY

PEERAGE—U.K. Baron Hatherley of Down Hatherley, co. Gloucester.
SURNAME—Wood.
CR.—9 Dec. 1868. EXT.—10 July 1881.
HISTORY—Sir Matthew Wood, 1st Bt., b. 1768; d. 1843, had issue with others (see extant peerage works, under Wood of Hatherley House, Bt.), a second son, Sir William Page Wood, **Baron Hatherley** of Down Hatherley, co. Gloucester, b. 29 Nov. 1801; educ. Winchester, 1812-18, (being expelled, when a Prefect, for a revolt against the Head Master) and at Univ. of Geneva, 1818-20, and Trin. Coll. Camb. Scholar, 1820; B.A. and 24th Wrangler, and Fellow, 1824; M.A. 1827; LL.D. 1864; Barrister-at-Law, Lincoln's Inn, 1827; Q.C. 1845; D.C.L. Oxford, 1851; Hon. Student of Ch. Ch. Oxford, 1867, and a Vice Chancellor 1853-1868; sat as Liberal M.P. for Oxford, 1847-52; Vice Chancellor of the Co. Palatine of Lancaster, 1849-51; Solicitor Gen. Mar. 1851 to Feb. 1852, cr. Kt. Bach. 1851; a Lord Justice of Appeal, in Chancery, Mar. to Dec. 1868; made P.C. 1868, and Lord Chancellor, Dec. 1868 to Oct. 1872, being then cr. a peer, as Baron Hatherley of Down Hatherley, 9 Dec. 1868. He m. 5 Jan. 1830, Charlotte, dau. of Edward Moore, of Great Bealings, co. Suffolk, formerly Major in Bombay Army. Lady Hatherley d. 19 Nov. 1878. Lord Hatherley d.s.p. 10 July 1881.
ARMS—Quarterly argent and or, an oak tree, on a mount vert, fructed ppr. in the first and fourth quarters; a bull's head erased sable charged on the neck with a bezant in the second and third quarters; and, over all in pale, the mace of the Lord Mayor of London ppr.*
CREST—Out of a mural crown argent, a demi-wild man wreathed about the temples with oak, in the dexter hand, an oak tree eradicated and fructed, and in the sinister a club, all ppr.
SUPPORTERS—On either side a wild man wreathed about the temples and waist with oak, across the shoulder a wreath of ivy and holding a club, all ppr.
MOTTO—Defend the right.
*Sir Matthew Wood was twice Lord Mayor of London.

HAVERSHAM

PEERAGE—U.K. Baron Haversham, of Bracknell, co. Berks. (Also a Baronetcy, cr. 19 April 1858).
SURNAME—Hayter.
CR.—11 Jan. 1906. EXT.—10 May 1917.
HISTORY—John Hayter, of Winterbourne, Stoke, co. Wilts, m. by licence 10 Dec. 1782, Grace, dau. of Stephen Goodenough, of Codford, co. Wilts, and d. 25 Mar. 1827, having by her (who d. 30 July 1830) a ygst. son, The Rt. Hon. Sir William Goodenough Hayter, 1st Bt., so cr. 19 April 1858, b. 28 Jan. 1792, of South Hill Park, co. Berks, M.P. Wells 1837-65; Barrister-at-Law 1819, Q.C. 1839; Judge Advocate Gen. 1847. Made P.C. 1848; financial sec. 1849-50, and parl. sec. to the Treasury 1850-58; Bencher and in 1856 Treasurer of Lincoln's Inn; m. 18 Aug. 1832, Anne, dau. of William Pulsford, of Linsalde, co. Bucks, and d. 26 Dec. 1878, having by her (who d. 2 June 1889) had issue,
Arthur Divett, 2nd Bt., and **Baron Haversham** (see below),
Mary Pulsford, b. 29 Dec. 1833; m. 17 June 1857, Lt. Gen. William Rickman, of Barkham Manor, Wokingham, and d. 27 July 1906, leaving issue.
The son,
Sir Arthur Divett Hayter, 2nd Bt., and **Baron Haversham**, b. 9 Aug. 1835; educ. Eton and Brasenose Coll. Oxford, B.A. 1857, M.A. 1860; joined Gren. Guards; M.P. Wells 1865-68; for Bath 1873-85, and for Walsall 1893-95; a Lord of the Treasury 1880-82; Financial Sec. to War Office 1882-85; made P.C. 1894; Chm. of Public Accounts Cttee 1901-06; cr. Baron Haversham of Bracknell, co. Berks, 11 Jan. 1906; m. 7 Nov. 1866, Henrietta, dau. of Capt. Adrian John Hope, 4th Dragoon Guards and d.s.p. 10 May 1917. She d. 6 Sept. 1929.
ARMS—Azure an escallop between three bulls' heads couped or.
CREST—A bull's head erased sable semée of escallops or and pierced through the neck with a broken spear in bend sinister point upwards ppr.
SUPPORTERS—Dexter, A Roman senator habited ppr.; Sinister, A Roman soldier also habited and supporting with his exterior hand his shield ppr.
MOTTO—Via vi.
Seats were South Hill Park, Bracknell, Berks; Trevena, Tintagel, Cornwall; Linslade Manor, Leighton Buzzard, Bucks. Town house: 9 Grosvenor Square, W.

HENDERSON OF ARDWICK

PEERAGE—U.K. Baron Henderson of Ardwick of Morton Park, Carlisle.
SURNAME—Henderson.
CR.—22 January 1950. EXT.—26 Feb. 1950.
HISTORY—Joseph Henderson, **Baron Henserson** of Ardwick, of Morton Park, Carlisle, so cr. Jan. 1950, was first Labour Mayor of Carlisle 1927-28; an employee of L.N.E.R.; held office in N.U.R.; Pres. of N.U.R. 1933-36; was M.P. for Ardwick Div. of Manchester June-Oct. 1931 and 1935; a Lord of the Treasury 1945. He m. 1908 Janet Glendenning,

dau. of James Byers, of Rowanburnfoot, Canonbie, co. Dumfries, and d. 26 Feb. 1950, having had issue, one dau.,
Marjorie, b. 1910; m. 1937, George Taylor Irwin, and had issue a dau.
Janet Elizabeth, b. 1940.
ARMS—None.
SEAT—Rowanby, Eskdale Avenue, Morton Park, Carlisle.
The Baroness Henderson of Ardwick was Mayoress of the City of Carlisle 1927-28, and d. 17 Nov. 1962.

HENEAGE

PEERAGE—U.K. Baron Heneage of Hainton, co. Lincoln.
SURNAME—Heneage.
CR.—8 June 1956. EXT.—19 Feb. 1967.
HISTORY—John Heneage of Hainton, co. Lincoln, living 1398, m. (1) Alice, dau. of Walter Snettisham, co. Norfolk, and (2) Joan, dau. of Sir Anthony Browne, and d. 22 Sept. 1439, leaving with other issue of his first marriage, an eldest son,
John Heneage of Hainton, m. 1451 Eleanor, dau. and heiress of John Preston of South Reston, co. Lincoln, and had with other issue, an eldest son, John Heneage of Hainton, m. Katherine, dau. of Thomas Wynbish, of Nocton, Lincs. and d. 31 May 1530 aged 78, having had with other issue,
1. Thomas, Sir (see below).
2. John, m. Ann, dau. and heiress of Edward Cope of Denshanger and Helmdon, Northants, and d. 1557 leaving with other issue,
   (1) George, Sir, heir to his uncle (see below).
   (2) William, heir to his brother (see below).
The eldest son,
Sir Thomas Heneage of Hainton, a courtier of Henry VIII, by whom he was knighted and with whom he was present at the capture of Boulogne, m. Katherine, dau. of Sir John Shipwith of Ormsby, co. York and d. 21 Aug. 1553 leaving issue a dau. Elizabeth, his heiress who m. William 1st Lord Willoughby of Parham (1883 Extinct Peerage). At Hainton Sir Thomas was s. by his nephew,
Sir George Heneage of Hainton, M.P. Grimsby, a commander in Ireland against the rebels under Elizabeth I, a member of the royal household temp. Edward VI, Mary I and Elizabeth I, was knighted 1583. He m. twice but d.s.p. 16 Oct. 1595, being s. by his brother,
William Heneage of Hainton, m. (1) Anne, dau. and co-heiress of Ralph Fishbourne, and (2) Jane Brussels, Gentlewoman of the Privy Chamber to Elizabeth I. By his first marriage he had with other issue, an elder son,
Sir Thomas Heneage of Hainton, knighted by James I 1603, m. Barbara, dau. of Sir Thomas Guildford, Kt. of Hemstead. co. Kent and d. 5 June 1613, having had with other issue an eldest son,
Sir George Heneage of Hainton, knighted 1607, High Sheriff, co. Lincoln 1628, m. Elizabeth, dau. of Francis Tresham, of Rushton, co. Northampton and d. 7 Feb. 1659/60

having had with other issue, a 7th and surviving son,

George Heneage of Hainton, m. Faith, dau. of Sir Philip Tyrwhitt, of Stainfield, co. Lincoln and d. 15 July 1667 leaving issue,

George Heneage of Hainton, b. 16 Nov. 1651; m. (1) Mary, dau. and heiress of Thomas Kemp of Slindon, co. Sussex, and (2) Frances Moyser. He left with other issue by his first wife,

George Heneage, b. 3 Aug. 1674; m. (1) 1696, Mary, dau. and heiress of 6th Baron Petre and had with other issue,

1. George, his heir (see below).

He m. (2) 2 Aug. 1705, Elizabeth, dau. of Sir Henry Hemloke, Bt. and had with other issue,

2. Thomas Henry, m. (1) 1728 Anna Maria, dau. of Roboaldo Fieschi, Count de Lavagna, in Genoa and had issue, George Fieschi (see below). He m. (2) Katherine, dau. of J. F. Newport and had further issue.

George Heneage d. 31 Dec. 1731 and was s. by his eldest son,

George Heneage, of Hainton, b. 30 May 1698, m. Mary Bridget and d.s.p. 1745, being s. by his nephew,

George Fieschi Heneage, of Hainton, b. 7 Aug. 1730; m. 18 Sept. 1755, Hon. Katherine Petre, eldest dau. of 8th Baron Petre and d. 1782, having had with other issue, an eldest son,

George Robert Heneage, of Hainton, b. 21 Dec. 1768; m. 18 Aug. 1798 Frances Anne, dau. of Lt. Gen. George Ainslie and had issue,

1. George Fieschi, his heir (see below).
2. Edward Fieschi, b. 1802 whose great-great-grandson James Neil Heneage, b. 8 June 1945, was heir to the Hainton Estate.

George Robert Heneage d. 16 June 1833 and was s. by his eldest son,

George Fieschi Heneage, of Hainton, High Sheriff 1839, M.P. for Grimsby 1826-30, for Lincoln 1832-35 and 1852-62, b. 1800; m. 1833 Frances, dau. of Michael Tasburgh of Burghwallis, co. York and d. 11 May 1864 having had with other issue, an eldest son,

Edward Heneage, 1st Baron Heneage, M.P. Lincoln 1865-68, for Grimsby 1880-95, High Sheriff 1880, Chancellor of the Duchy of Lancaster 1886, b. 29 Mar. 1840; m. 9 June 1864, Lady Eleanor Cecilia Hare, dau. of 2nd Earl of Listowel, and with other issue,

1. George Edward, 2nd Baron (see below).
2. Thomas Robert, Rev., 3rd Baron (see below).

He was cr. Baron Heneage of Hainton, co. Lincoln 8 June 1896 and d. 10 Aug. 1922, being s. by his eldest son,

George Edward Heneage, 2nd Baron Heneage, B.A. Camb., Lt. Col. cmdg. 3rd Bn. Lincolnshire Regt. 1908-13, and cmdg. 10th Service Bn. Lincolnshire Regt. 1914-16, served in the S. African war 1902 and in World War I 1914-18, b. 1866; d. unm. 26 Jan. 1954 when he was s. by his only surviving brother,

The Rev. Thomas Robert Heneage, 3rd Baron Heneage, B.A. Trin. Hall, Camb. 1902, ordained deacon 1903; priest 1905, Curate of Spalding 1903-06, Rector of St. Mark, Victoria, B.C. 1909-12, Chaplain to Bishop of Columbia 1912-17, b. 24 July 1877; d. 19 Feb. 1967.

ARMS—Or, a greyhound courant sable, between three leopards' faces azure, a border engrailed gules.

CREST—A greyhound courant sable.
SUPPORTERS—On either side a greyhound sable, holding in the mouth an acorn leaved and slipped vert and gorged with a chain, pendant therefrom an escutcheon or, charged with a leopard's face azure.
MOTTO—Toujours firme.

HERRIES

PEERAGE—U.K. Baron Herries, of Caerlaverock Castle, co. Dumfries.
SURNAME—Constable-Maxwell.
CR.—10 Nov. 1884. EXT. 5 Oct. 1908.
HISTORY—Marmaduke Frances Constable-Maxwell, 11th Baron Herries in the peerage of Scotland, was cr. 10 Nov. 1884 a Baron of the United Kingdom peerage as **Baron Herries,** of Caerlaverock Castle, co. Dumfries. He d. 5 Oct. 1908, when the U.K. Barony became extinct and his Scottish barony devolved upon his elder dau. and heir of line, Gwendolen Mary, who m. 15 Feb. 1905 the 15th Duke of Norfolk. For full account of the Scottish barony see extant peerage under Norfolk, D.
ARMS—Quarterly 1, Argent, an eagle displayed with two heads sable beaked and membered gules, surmounted of an escutcheon of the first, charged with a saltire of the second, surcharged in the centre with a hedgehog or (Maxwell); 2, Quarterly I and IV, Argent a saltire sable in chief a label of three points gules (Maxwell); II and III Argent three hedgehogs sable (Herries); 3, Quarterly gules and vair, over all a bend or (Constable); 4, Azure, on a bend cotised argent, three billets sable (Haggerston).
CREST—A stag's head with ten tynes, argent.
SUPPORTERS—Two savages or wild men wreathed about the loins and holding clubs ppr.
MOTTO—Dominus dedit.
Seats were Everingham Park, near York; Caerlaverock Castle, co. Dumfries. Clubs were Athenaeum, Boodles, St. James's, Yorkshire and Hurlingham. (Caerlaverock Castle was the fortalice captured by King Edward I in 1300, an achievement which occasioned the making of the Caerlaverock Roll, so famous in heraldic history).

HEWART

PEERAGE—U.K. Baron Hewart, and Viscount Hewart, both of Bury, co. Lancs.
SURNAME—Hewart.
CR.—Barony, 24 Mar. 1922, Viscounty, 1 Nov. 1940. EXT.—23 July 1964.
HISTORY—Giles Hewart, of Colwyn Bay, N. Wales, J.P., formerly a draper, of Bury, co. Lancaster had with other children, eldest son, Sir Gordon Hewart, 1st Baron and 1st Viscount Hewart, b. 7 Jan. 1870; educ. Univ. Coll. Oxford, Scholar 1887, B.A. 1891, M.A. 1893; a journalist; Barrister-at-Law, Inner Temple 1902, K.C. 1912, Bencher 1917 and Treasurer 1938. M.P. for Leicester 1913-18 and East Div. of Leicester 1918-22, Solicitor Gen. 1916-19, Attorney Gen. 1919-22, Mem. of Cabinet 1921-22, Lord Chief Justice of England 1922-40 and Pres. of the War Com-

pensation Court 1922-29. He was cr. Kt. Bach. 29 Dec. 1916, made P.C. 1918 and cr. Baron Hewart of Bury, co. Lancaster 24 Mar. 1922, and Viscount Hewart of Bury, 1 Nov. 1940. He m. (1) 5 Oct. 1892, Sara Wood (d. 2 Nov. 1933), dau. of J. H. Riley, of Bury, and had issue with a dau. Katharine Mary, m. E. Hodgkin, a son, Hugh Vaughan, 2nd Viscount (see below).
Viscount Hewart m. (2) 29 Dec. 1934, Jean, dau. of J. R. Stewart of Wanganin, N.Z., and d. 5 May 1943, being s. by his second son, Hugh Vaughan Hewart, **2nd Viscount Hewart**, b. 11 Nov. 1896; educ. Manchester Gram. School, St. Paul's School and Univ. Coll. Oxford; served throughout World War I; d. 23 July 1964.

ARMS—Argent, on a fesse sable between two owls ppr. in chief and in base a cross patée sable, a fasces or.

CREST—In front of the trunk of a tree sprouting, thereon an owl ppr. three crosses patée fessewise or.

SUPPORTERS—On either side an owl ppr., charged with a fasces erect or.

MOTTO—Nulla retrosum.

HILL OF WIVENHOE

PEERAGE—U.K. Life. Baron Hill of Wivenhoe, co. Essex.

SURNAME—Hill.

CR.—21 Sept. 1967. **EXT.**—14 Dec. 1969.

HISTORY—James Edward Hill had a son, Edward James Hill, **Baron Hill** of Wivenhoe, so cr. 21 Sept. 1967, b. 20 Aug. 1899; educ. Napier Rd. Sch., East Ham, served in World War I 1914-18 with R.M. Engineers; Gen. Sec. United Soc. of Boiler Makers 1948-63, Pres. Amalgamated Soc. of Boilermakers, Shipwrights, Blacksmiths and Structural Workers, 1963-65, mem. of Gen. Council T.U.C. 1948-65; m. (1) Ethel (d. 1957) and (2) 1960 Hannah, Mrs. Crowther.
Lord Hill d. 14 Dec. 1969.

HIRST

PEERAGE—U.K. Baron Hirst, of Witton, co. Warwick.

SURNAME—Hirst (formerly Hirsch).

CR.—28 June 1934. **EXT.**—22 Jan. 1943. Also a baronetcy, 2 July 1925.

HISTORY—Hugo Hirst, formerly Hirsch, was b. 26 Nov. 1863; educ. at Munich; Chm of General Electric Co. Ltd., and mem. of the Cabinet Trade and Employment Panel and Board of Trade Advisory Council 1923-25; mem. of numerous cttees. and conferences; mem. of the Gov. Mission to Australia 1928-29; Master of the Glaziers Company 1928-29 and 1929-30; Pres. of Federation of British Industries 1936-37, Hon. mem. of the Inst. of Electrical Engineers; cr. a Baronet 2 July 1925, and a peer as Baron Hirst, of Witton, co. Warwick, 28 June 1934; m. 30 May 1892, Leontine, dau. of Herman Hirsch, and d. 22 Jan. 1943. She d. 22 Dec. 1938. They had issue,

1. Harold Hugh, b. 6 July 1893; served in World War I as Lt. 21st Bn. The Man-

chester Regt. attached to R.E. Signals; m. 9 May 1917, Carol Iris, M.B.E. (1946), dau. of Lewis Lindon, of Sussex Square, London, W., and d. 24 Feb. 1919, leaving issue by her (who m. 2ndly 1926 Maurice Dreyfus, m. diss. by div. 1938; she d. 20 Mar. 1966),

    Harold Hugh, b. 11 June 1919, P/O R.A.F.V.R., d. on active service 1941.

    Pamela Muriel Dorine, b. 6 April 1918; served in World War II as Junr. Cmdr. A.T.S.; granted rank, style and precedence as dau. of Baron, June 1943; m. (1) 1940, (m. diss. by div.), Capt. A. G. B. Gulyei, and (2) 1949, R. E. Goodale, and had issue, a son, Hugh Roy.

1. Muriel Elsie, D.J. St. J., m. 21 July 1919. Sir Leslie Carr Gamage, M.C., son of A. W. Gamage, of Holborn, and served. in World War I as V.A.D. She was k. in a car accident 27 Aug. 1969.
2. Irene Phyllis, C.B.E. 1961, m. 1922, G/C. T. F. D. Rose, R.A.F.V.R. and had issue.

ARMS—Or, on a fess ermine between in chief two roses gules barbed and seeded and in base upon a mount an oak tree ppr. a thunderbolt also ppr.

CREST—A stag's head ppr. collared and charged on the neck with three crescents interlaced or.

SUPPORTERS—Dexter, A horse. Sinister, A beaver each charged on the shoulder with a thunderbolt ppr.

HOBHOUSE

PEERAGE—U.K. Baron Hobhouse, of Hadspen, co. Somerset.

SURNAME—Hobhouse.

CR.—2 July 1885; **EXT.**—6 Dec. 1904.

HISTORY—Henry Hobhouse was the ygr. brother of John Hobhouse, (see extant peerages, Hobhouse, Bt.) was b. 1714; m. (1) 1738, Jane, dau. of James Banister. She d. 1756. He m. (2) 1761, Mary, dau. of Michael White, and by her who d. 1810 had a son, Thomas, who d. unm. Henry Hobhouse d. 1773, having had by his first marriage, with a dau. Jane, who m. 1774, John Freeman, of Letton, co. Hereford, a son and heir, Henry Hobhouse, of Hadspen House, co. Somerset, b. 1742; m. 1775, Sarah, dau. of the Rev. Richard Jenkyns, Canon of Wells, and d. 2 April 1792. She d. July 1777. They had issue, with a dau. Sarah, who d. unm. 1810, Rt. Hon. with a dau. Sarah, who d. unm. 1810, Rt. Hon. Henry Hobhouse, P.C., under Sec. of State for the Home Dept. 1817-27, of Hadspen House, b. 12 April 1776; m. 7 April 1806, Harriet, dau. of John Turton, of Sugnall Hall, co. Stafford, and d. 13 April 1854. She d. 7 May 1858. They had issue,

1. Henry, of Hadspen House, Somerset, M.A. Oxford, Barrister-at-Law, b. 13 July 1811; m. (1) 7 April 1853, the Hon. Charlotte Etruria Talbot, dau. of 3rd Lord Talbot de Malahide, and by her, who d. 17 April 1855, had issue,

    Henry, of Hadspen House, M.A., M.P. East Div. co. Somerset, b. 1 Mar. 1854; m. 12 Oct. 1880, Margaret

Heyworth, dau. of Richard Potter, of Standish House, co. Gloucester, and had issue,
Margaret Eliza, b. April 1855; m. 5 Sept. 1882 Thomas H. M. Bailward, of Horsington House, Somerset.
He m. (2) 1859, Frances, dau. of Very Rev. Thomas Gaisford, Dean of Christ Church, Oxford, and d. 11 Feb. 1862.

2. Edmund, Rt. Rev., LL.D., Bishop of Nelson, N.Z. 1858-65, b. 17 April 1817; m. (1) 1 Jan. 1858, Mary Elizabeth, dau. of Gen. the Hon. John Brodrick, and had issue two sons. She d. 12 Oct. 1864. He m. (2) 7 Jan. 1868, Anna, dau. of Dr. Williams, Warden of New Coll. Oxford.

3. Reginald, the Ven. Archdeacon of Bodmin, M.A., b. 15 Mar. 1818; m. 13 Aug. 1851, Caroline, dau. of Sir William Lewis Salusbury-Trelawney, 8th Bt., and by her (who d. 1889) had issue.

4. Arthur, Sir, **Baron Hobhouse** (see below).

1. Harriet, m. 31 Mar. 1834, the Rev. Canon Henry Jenkyns, D.D. of Durham, and d. 1876.

2. Catherine, d. unm. 4 April 1888, aged 80.

3. Eliza, d. unm. 7 Mar. 1887.

4. Eleanor, d. unm. 1842.

The fourth son, Sir Arthur Hobhouse, **Baron Hobhouse,** of Hadspen, co. Somerset, b. 10 Nov. 1819; educ. Eton and Balliol Coll. Oxford, M.A., Barrister-at-Law 1845; Q.C. 1862; Charity Commissioner 1866; Endowed Schools Commissioner 1869; Law mem. of Council of Gov. Gen. of India 1872; mem. of Judicial Cttee. of the Privy Council 1881; made P.C., cr. K.C.S.I. and C.I.E., and cr. a peer as Baron Hobhouse, of Hadspen, co. Somerset, 2 July 1885. He m. 10 Aug. 1848, Mary, dau. of Thomas Farrer, and sister of 1st Baron Farrer, of Abinger, and d. 6 Dec. 1904.
ARMS—Per pale azure and gules, three crescents argent issuant therefrom as many estoiles irradiated or.
CREST—Out of a mural crown, per pale azure and gules, an estoile or.
SUPPORTERS—Two horses sable, each charged on the shoulder with an estoile or.
MOTTO—Spero meliora.

HOBSON

PEERAGE—U.K. Life. Baron Hobson of Brent, co. Middlesex.
SURNAME—Hobson.
CR.—20 Jan. 1964. EXT.—17 Feb. 1966.
HISTORY—Edwin Hobson, of Leeds, b. 19 Feb. 1870; m. 4 Sept. 1898, Gertrude, dau. of Charles Rider of Leeds, and d. 13 Mar. 1940. She d. 29 June 1920. They had a son, Charles Rider Hobson, **Baron Hobson** of Brent, co. Middlesex, so cr. as life peer 20 Jan. 1964 He was b. 18 Feb. 1903; educ. Belle Vue Road Sch. Leeds, was a power station engineer 1927-45, mem. Willesden Borough Council 1931-45 and Alderman of Willesden 1945; M.P. North Wembley 1945-50, and Keighley 1950-59; Asst. Postmaster General 1947-51, Lord in Waiting 1964; m. 12 Sept. 1933, Doris Mary, dau. of Fred Spink of West Kensington and d. 17 Feb. 1966 having had issue, Marian

Elizabeth, B.A. 1963 Newnham Coll. Camb., b. 10 Nov 1941. Lord Hobson lived at 115, Dewsbury Road, London, N.W.10.

HOLDEN

PEERAGE—U.K. Baron Holden, of Alston, co. Cumberland.
SURNAME—Holden.
CR.—4 July 1908. EXT.—6 July 1951.
HISTORY—Isaac Holden, of Alston, co. Cumberland, d. 1826, having by his wife Mary Forest, of Alston, who d. 1850, had issue, Sir Isaac Holden, 1st Bt., of Oakworth House, Keighley, co. Yorks, M.P. for W.R. Yorks 1882-95, cr. a Baronet 1 July 1893; m. (1) 6 April 1832, Marion Love (d. 4 April 1847), and had with other issue,

1. Angus, Sir, 2nd Bt., and **1st Baron Holden** (see below).

2. Edward, father of Sir Isaac Holden, 5th Bt., who inherited the baronetcy in 1951 (see current peerages, Holden of Oakworth House, Bt.).

Sir Isaac m. (2) 5 April 1850, Sarah (d. 3 May 1890), dau. of John Sugden of Keighley, and d. 13 Aug. 1897 being s. by his son, Sir Angus Holden, 2nd Bt. and **1st Baron Holden,** M.P. for E. Bradford 1885-86, and for Buckrose Div. E.R. Yorks 1892-1900, cr. Baron Holden of Alston, c. Cumberland, 4 July 1908, b. 16 Mar. 1833; m. 23 May 1860, Margaret (d. 1913), dau. of Daniel Illingworth of Bradford and d. 25 Mar. 1912 having had with other issue a son,

Sir Ernest Illingworth Holden, 3rd Bt., and **2nd Baron Holden,** b. 8 Jan. 1876; m. (1) 19 May 1897, Ethel Eden (d. 26 May 1913), dau. of Major W. Cookson and had issue,

Angus William Eden, 4th Bt. and **3rd Baron** (see below).

Lord Holden m. (2) 17 Feb. 1914, Edith Isabel, dau. of B. G. S. Judd of Rickling, Essex, and had by her a dau. Donna Diana. He d. 30 Jan. 1937 being s. by his son, Sir Angus William Eden Holden, 4th Bt. and **3rd Baron Holden,** in Diplomatic Service, Legation to Holy See 1918, Embassy at Madrid 1921-24 and Berlin 1924-26, b. 1 Aug. 1898, and d. unm. 6 July 1951 when the Barony became extinct and the baronetcy was inherited by his kinsman, Sir Isaac Holden, 5th Bt. (see above).
ARMS—Or a chief azure over all a bend nebuly between two roses gules.
CREST—Issuant from a chaplet of oak vert, an eagle's head erased or gorged with a collar gemel azure.
SUPPORTERS—Two rams guardant ppr. armed and unguled sable, each charged on the shoulder with a rose gules barbed and seeded also ppr.
MOTTO—Extant recte factis praemia.

HOOD OF AVALON

PEERAGE—U.K. Baron Hood of Avalon, co. Somerset.
SURNAME—Hood.
CR.—22 Feb. 1892. EXT.—15 Nov. 1901.
HISTORY—Sir Arthur William Acland Hood,

Baron Hood of Avalon, b. 14 July 1824, second son of Sir Alexander Hood, 2nd Bt. (see extant peerage works, St. Audries, B.). He was Adm. R.N., served at siege of Sebastopol Dir. Gen. Naval Ordnance 1869-74; second Lord of the Admiralty 1877-80, and senior Lord of the Admiralty 1885-89; cr. G.C.B. 1889, and Baron Hood of Avalon, 22 Feb. 1892. He m. 2 Oct. 1855, Fanny Henrietta, third dau. of Sir Charles Fitzroy Maclean, 9th Bt., and d.s.p.m. 15 Nov. 1901. She d. 29 Aug. 1915. They had issue,

1. Emily Isabel, m. 19 April 1888, F. A. Mackinnon, and d. 18 May 1934, leaving issue (1952 *B.L.G.*).
2. Fanny Sophia m. 1895, Henry Allen, of Broadway Lodge, Glastonbury, and d. ca. 1940, leaving issue.

ARMS—Azure a fret argent on a chief or three crescents sable.

CREST—In front of an anchor in bend sinister or, a Cornish chough sable.

SUPPORTERS—Dexter, A figure representing Neptune; Sinister, A sagittarius, shooting backwards.

MOTTO—Zealous.

HORE-BELISHA

PEERAGE—U.K. Baron Hore-Belisha of Devonport, co. Devon.

SURNAME—Hore-Belisha.

CR.—14 Jan. 1954. **EXT.**—16 Feb. 1957.

HISTORY—Isaac David Belisha, son of David Belisha (b. 1789) of Manchester, was b. 1826 and m. as his second wife 1851, Bathsheba Benzaquen (d. 1904) and d. 1897 leaving with other issue, a second son, Jacob Isaac Belisha, Capt. the Royal Fusiliers, b. 1862; m. 1892, Elizabeth, dau. of John Leslie Miers of Euston Square, London, N.W.1, and d. 1894 leaving by her a son,

Leslie, **Baron Hore-Belisha** (see below). She m. 2ndly, 1912, Sir Charles F. A. Hore, K.B.E. (d. 1950) and d. 1926.

Leslie Hore-Belisha, **Baron Hore-Belisha**, b. 7 Sept. 1893; educ. Clifton and St. John's Coll. Oxford, M.A. (1919) and at Paris and Heidelberg; Barrister-at-Law, Inner Temple (1923); served in World War I with Royal Fusiliers, Public Schools Bn. and R.A.S.C. (Major, despatches); M.P. for Devonport Div. of Plymouth 1923-45; Minister of Transport 1934-37 with seat in the Cabinet Oct. 1936. In this Ministry he introduced the famous amber "Belisha" beacons. He was Sec. of State for War 1937-40 and had as unofficial adviser, Capt. Sir Liddell Hart; was Min. of Nat. Insurance in "Caretaker" Gov. May-July 1945. He m. 1944, Cynthia Sophie, dau. of C. Elliot (see Minto, E.). He was made P.C. 1935 and created Baron Hore-Belisha of Devonport, co. Devon, 14 Jan. 1954. He d. 16 Feb. 1957.

HORNE

PEERAGE—U.K. Baron Horne, of Stirkoke, co. Caithness.

SURNAME—Horne.

CR.—8 Oct. 1919. **EXT.**—14 Aug. 1929.

HISTORY—Donald Horne, of Langwell, co. Caithness, and of Athol Crescent, Edinburgh, who d. in 1870, had issue, James Horne, of Stirkoke, co. Caithness, b. 1822; was Major, Highland L.I. and Gordon Highlanders; m. 1855 and d. 1872, having had issue,

1. Donald Kenneth (1856-72).
2. Edward William, C.M.G., C.B.E., Col. Seaforth Highlanders, b. 1857; m. 1882, Marjorie, dau. of G. M. Cunningham, C.E., of Leithenhopes, co. Peebles, and had issue,
   James Kenneth (1889-1903),
   Margaret Isobel.
3. Henry Sinclair, Sir, **Baron Horne** (see below).
4. William Ogilvie, C.S.I., Commr. Land Revenues and Forests, Madras, b. 1 Nov. 1862; m. 27 Dec. 1900, Hope Helena, dau. of Henry Irwin, C.I.E., and had issue,
   (1) John Ogilvie, b. 1901.
   (2) Roderick Donald, b. 1905.
   (1) Joan Constance.
   (2) Elizabeth Harloe.
5. James, (1870-94).
6. George, b. 1872; m. Ethel Chesterton and went to Cape Colony.
1. Alice Mary, O.B.E. 1920, m. 25 Mar. 1884, Sir James Patten-MacDougall, K.C.B., Deputy Clerk Register and Keeper of Records for Scotland.
2. Edith Graham, m. 1897, Rev. G. H. Oakshott, D.D., of Yateley.
3. Maud Mary.
4. Jane Ogilvie, m. 1894, J. P. Rawlins, Punjab Police.
5. Constance Louisa, m. 1897, Surg. Col. J. H. Newman, I.M.S.
6. Gertrude Constance, d. 1872.

The third son, Sir Henry Sinclair Horne, **Baron Horne**, b. 19 Feb. 1861; educ. Harrow and Woolwich, entered R.A. 1880; Brev. Lt. Col. 1900; Brev. Col. 1906; Col. 1910; Major Gen. 1914; Lt. Gen. 1917; Gen. 1919; served in S. African War 1899-1902, and in World War I 1914-18, G.O.C. Div. Corps and Army. He was cr. C.B. 1914, K.C.B. 1916, K.C.M.G. 1918, G.C.B. 1919, and Baron Horne, of Stirkoke, co. Caithness, 8 Oct. 1919. He received thanks of Parliament and a grant of £30,000 along with his peerage. He held many foreign orders and decorations, was A.D.C. to King George V, and G.O.C. Eastern Command. He m. 1 July 1897, Kate, dau. of George McCorquodale, of Newton-le-Willows, co. Lancaster (see McCorquodale in present work) and d. 14 Aug. 1929, having had issue,

Kate, m. (1) 1 Feb. 1923 (m. diss. by div. 1940), Lt. Col. A. G. Hewson, M.C. and had issue. She m. (2) 15 May 1940, Capt. H. R. Hildreth, M.B.E.

ARMS—Or three bugle horns, stringed azure, a bordure of the last.

CREST—A bugle horn, stringed azure.

SUPPORTERS—Dexter, A gunner of the R.H.A.; Sinister, A private of the Seaforth Highlanders, both in field service uniform ppr.

MOTTO—Monitus munitus.

Lord Horne's seat was Priestwell House, East Haddon, Northants, with a London home at 23 Basil Mansions, S.W. His clubs were Naval and Military, Hurlingham and Ranelagh.

HORNE OF SLAMANNAN

PEERAGE—U.K. Viscount Horne of Slamannan.
SURNAME—Horne.
CR.—9 June 1937. EXT.—3 Sept. 1940.
HISTORY—Robert Horne, the eldest son of Robert Horne, of Brazietts, co. Dumbarton, was b. 7 Nov. 1763; and by Margaret, his wife, the dau. of Robert Stevenson, of Boghead, he had with other issue, George Horne, of Auckenkiln, co. Dumbarton, b. 10 Feb. 1801; by his wife Margaret Stevenson, had an eldest son, The Rev. Robert Stevenson Horne, Minister of the parish of Slamannan, co. Stirling, b. 27 May 1830; m. 3 Sept. 1856, Mary, dau. of Thomas Lockhead, of Toward, Argyll, and d. 30 April 1887, having had with other issue, a ygst. son,
Sir Robert Stevenson Horne, **Viscount Horne** of Slamannan, b. 28 Feb. 1871; educ. George Watson's Coll. Edinburgh, and Glasgow Univ. M.A., LL.B.; called to Scottish Bar, 1896; Lecturer in Philosophy, Univ. Coll. North Wales, 1895; Examiner in Philosophy at Aberdeen Univ. 1896-1900; K.C. 1910; served in World War I, with Royal Engineers, Lt. Col., Asst. Inspector Gen. of Transportation; Dir. of Dept. of Materials and Priority, Admiralty, and Dir. of Admiralty Labour Dept.; M.P. Hillhead Div. of Glasgow, 1918-37; Third Civil Lord of Admiralty; 1918-19; Min. of Labour, 1919-20; Pres. of the Board of Trade, 1920-21; Chancellor of the Exchequer, 1921-22; Chm. of Great Western Railway Co., 1934, and of South Wales Recovery and Expansion Cttee, 1936; made P.C. 1919; cr. K.B.E. 1918 G.B.E. 1920; and Viscount Horne of Slamannan, of Slamannan, co. Stirling, 9 June 1937. He was Chm and Dir. of many cos. He d. 3 Sept. 1940.
ARMS—Or a fess azure between in chief two bugle horns sable stringed gules, and in base a falcon's head erased sable.
CREST—A bugle horn sable stringed gules.
SUPPORTERS—Dexter, A mariner in the dress of the 14th century ppr. holding in his outer hand an astrolabe or; Sinister, Another mariner similarly attired, holding in his outer hand a sounding line and plummet ppr.
MOTTO—Monitus, munitus.

HORSBURGH

PEERAGE—U.K. Life. Baroness Horsburgh of Horsburgh, co. Peebles.
SURNAME—Horsburgh.
CR.—16 Dec. 1959. EXT.—6 Dec. 1969.
HISTORY—Dame Florence Gertrude Horsburgh, **Baroness Horsburgh** was the dau. of Henry Moncrieff Horsburgh (1858-92) C.A. of Edinburgh by his wife Mary Harriet. She was b. 13 Oct. 1889; educ. Lansdowne House, Edinburgh, and at St. Hilda's Folkestone; M.P. Dundee, 1931-45 and Moss Side Div. of Manchester 1950-59; Min. of Education 1951-54; a delegate to League of Nations, U.N. Assembly. Council of Europe Assembly, etc. She was cr. M.B.E. 1920, C.B.E. 1939, P.C. 1945, G.B.E. 1954 and a Life Peeress as Baroness Horsburgh of Horsburgh, co. Peebles, 16 Dec. 1959. She d. 6 Dec. 1969.

HOWTH

PEERAGE—Ireland. Baron Howth.
Ireland. Viscount St. Lawrence cr. 3 Sept. 1767.
Ireland. Earl of Howth, cr. 3 Sept. 1767.
U.K. Baron Howth of Howth, co. Dublin cr. 7 Oct. 1881.
SURNAME—St. Lawrence.
CR.—For the creation of the Irish Barony of Howth, authorities are unable to assign a date. The C.P. remarks "this is one of the Irish peerages by prescription, i.e. peerages which were recognized in 1489 by Henry VII, but of the date or mode of whose creation nothing certain is known."
EXT.—9 Mar. 1909 except possibly old Barony of Howth.
HISTORY—The account in the *C.P.* begins with a first Baron with a questioned date of 1440 on the ground that on his M.I. that date is mentioned where he is described as Baron Howth, but it is observed that this date may have been placed there by his descendant 100 years later. In old editions of Burke's Peerage a long line of Barons Howth is given with he line traced from Sir Armoricus or Amory Tristram, as 1st Baron Howth, and a line of descendants at variance with the line given in *C.P.* On the earlier history of the family, it may be enough to refer to J. H. Round, who in his work, *Peerage and Pedigree*, vol. ii., "The Geste of John de Courcy", regarded the story of Sir Amory Tristram as mythical. It seems clear that this family belonged to the baronage established in Ireland after the very partial conquest under Henry II. The following account of the line of descent is based on that accepted in the *C.P.* Nicholas St. Lawrence was son and heir of Adam St. Lawrence (who d. 1334) by Scholastica. Nicholas who d. 29 Sept. 1404, m. Alice, dau. of John Plunket of Beaulieu and had a son and heir,
Stephen St. Lawrence, who m. Elinor, dau. of Sir Robert Holywood, of Artain, and d. 1435 having had issue,
Christopher St. Lawrence, reckoned as **1st Baron Howth,** of Howth, co. Dublin, (see above) who did homage for his lands in 1437. In 1451 he had licence to search for a mine in his lordship of Howth. He was apptd. with his son Robert Howth, Esq, a Keeper of the Peace, co. Dublin, and was Constable of Dublin Castle for life 1461. It appears that he secured recognition of himself as being a Lord of Parliament. He m. before 1435 Anne Plunket, of Rathmore, co. Meath (she m. 2ndly Anthony Percy) and d. between 17 Sept. 1462 and 24 Jan. 1463/4, having an eldest son,
Sir Robert St. Lawrence (most of the lords Howth appear to have been knighted, and therefore henceforth this title will be mentioned only when specifically entered in the record of the family, Robert St. Lawrence, **2nd Baron Howth,** in 1472 elected a Knight of St. George (The Brotherhood of St. George lasted only 12 years and had a list of but 13 knights); was Lord Chancellor of Ireland 1483. He m. (1) before 1459, Alice, dau. and heir of Nicholas White of Killester, co. Dublin and (2) in England, 1478, Joan, dau. of Edmund Beaufort, Duke of Somerset, He d. in London 1486, being s. by his son and heir,

Nicholas St. Lawrence, **3rd Baron Howth,** said to have discovered and revealed to the English authorities, the designs of Lambert Simnel. He had a general pardon 1488, and was one of the 11 Irish barons who obeyed Henry VII's summons to attend his Court at Greenwich in 1489. He sat in the Irish Parl. in 1490 and 1493, and was knighted 1493/4. He commanded the billmen at the battle of Knockdoe, co. Galway, 19 Aug. 1504. Lord Chancellor of Ireland, 1509-1512. He m. (1) Janet, dau. of Christopher Plunkett, 2nd Lord Killeen, and (2) Anne, dau. of Thomas Berford, and widow of ———— Bermingham, of Ballydungan. He m. (3) Feb. 1504/5 Alice dau. of Robert Fitzsimons, and widow of Nicholas Cheevers. He d. 10 July 1526. His will was dated 1 Feb. 1504/5. His widow m. 3rdly ———— Plunket, of Loughcrew. The son and heir by the first marriage,

Christopher St. Lawrence, **4th Baron Howth,** aged 24 in 1526, previously knighted and Sheriff of co. Dublin. He m. before 1509, Anne, sister and heir of Richard Bermingham, of Ballydungan, the dau. of ———— Bermingham, by Anne, dau. of Thomas Berford, who became (see above) the 4th Baron's father's second wife. The 4th Baron d. 20 April 1542, having had issue,

1. Edward, **5th Baron** (see below).
2. Richard, **6th Baron** (see below).
3. Christopher, **7th Baron** (see below).

The eldest son, Edward St. Lawrence, **5th Baron Howth,** aged 34 in 1542; mem. of Council of Ireland, 1545/6; m. by dispensation, (m. sett. 19 Nov. 1528) Alison, dau. of James FitzLyons, of Aucheston, and d.s.p.m. 2 July 1549. His widow m. 2ndly, before 28 Feb. 1589, ———— Heron, and was granted lands by Elizabeth I at that date under name of Alison Heron, alias St. Lawrence, alias Howth. The children of the 5th Baron were,

1. Richard, only son, m. a dau. of ———— FitzSimon, of Dublin, and d.v.p. and s.p.
1. Anne, m. as his 2nd wife, Bartholomew Dillon, of Keppoch.
2. Alison, m. John Golding, and the eventual heir of the marriage was Alison Golding, who m. James Cusack, of Clonard, ancestor of the Cusacks of Abbeville, co. Dublin. "Among the descendants of these sisters the heir general of the first Peer is to be sought" (*C.P.*).

The 5th Baron was s. by his brother, Richard St. Lawrence, **6th Baron Howth,** admitted Lincoln's Inn, 1541. Received a pardon, 25 Sept. 1555; m. before Mar. 1550, Dame Catherine FitzGerald, natural dau. of 9th Earl of Kildare, and d.s.p. in autumn 1558, (I.P.M. Dublin, 1559) when he was s. by his brother,

Christopher St. Lawrence, **7th Baron Howth,** usually called the Blind Lord; admitted Lincoln's Inn, 1544; sat in Irish Parls. 1559 and 1585. Knighted 9 Feb. 1570 by Lord Deputy Sidney. In 1576 he was, however, for a while in prison in Dublin Castle, as being in conflict within the Pale with the Lord Deputy. On 8 July 1579, he was convicted of cruelty towards his wife, who had borne him 14 children, and also of illtreating his dau. Jane, to the extent that she died. His sentence was imprisonment and a fine of £1,000. He m. (1)

Elizabeth, dau. of Sir John Plunkett of Beaulieu, who was still living 20 Mar. 1564. He m. (2) Cecilia, 2nd dau. of Henry Cusack, Alderman, of Dublin, (she m. 2ndly John Barnewell, and 3rdly John Finglas and d. 1638). He d. 24 Oct. 1589, and was s. by his eldest son, (by his first marr.),

Nicholas St. Lawrence, **8th Baron Howth,** knighted 1588, aged 34 in 1589. He m. (1) Margaret, dau. of Sir Christopher Barnewall, of Turvey, co. Dublin, and (2) Mary, dau. of Sir Nicholas Whyte, of Leixlip, (widow of Robert Browne, and previously of Christopher Darcy) and d. about 11 May 1607 having by his first wife,

Christopher St. Lawrence, **9th Baron Howth,** Col. of Foot, knighted before 1600, and cmd. rear of vanguard at battle of Carlingford against rebel Earl of Tyrone, and pursued the fugitive Earl with 17 companies after the Mountjoy victory at Kinsale, 24 Dec. 1601. Later in 1608, he was a prisoner in Dublin and afterwards in London on suspicion of complicity with the Earls of Tyrone and Tyrconnell, but was apparently able to clear himself. He is reported to have been dangerously wounded in a brawl before his knighthood. He m. before 1597, Elizabeth, dau. of John Wentworth, of Horkesley, and Gosfield, co. Essex. He had separated from her by autumn 1605, and had to be ordered by the English Privy Council in 1608 to allow her £100 p.a. He sat in two Irish Parls. tempore James I. He d. 24 Oct. 1619, His widow m. 2ndly Sir Robert Newcomen, Bt. and d. 1627. The 9th Baron had issue,

1. Nicholas, **10th Baron** (see below).
2. Thomas, **11th Baron** (see below).
1. Margaret, m. (1) William FitzWilliam and (2) Michael Burford.

The 9th Baron Howth was s. by his elder son,

Nicholas St. Lawrence, **10th Baron Howth,** aged 22 in 1619; professed loyalty to the King in Dec. 1641; m. 1615, Jane, only surv. dau. and heir of George Montgomery, Bishop of Meath, and d.s.p.m.s. 1643/4 leaving four daus. (see below) and was s. by his brother,

Thomas St. Lawrence, **11th Baron Howth,** formerly of Stoke by Nayland, and in 1645 of Weston, co. Suffolk, who m. about 1628, Elenor, dau. of William Lynne, of Wormingford, and Little Horkesley, co. Essex, by his first wife, Audrey, dau. of Sir John Watts, sometime Lord Mayor of London. He d. 1649 (will dated 5 Aug., proved 3 Oct. 1649), and directed that he should be bur. at Howth. He was s. by his first son and heir,

William St. Lawrence, **12th Baron Howth,** bapt. 14 Sept. 1628 at Stoke by Nayland; educ. Colchester Gram. Sch. 1638; Custos Rotulorum of co. Dublin, 22 April 1661; sat in Irish Parl. 8 May 1661. He m. about 1650, Elizabeth, dau. of his uncle, Nicholas St. Lawrence, 10th Baron Howth, and widow of Col. FitzWilliam. He d. 17 June 1671, at Howth, aged 42. He was s. by his son and heir,

Thomas St. Lawrence, **13th Baron Howth,** b. 1659. He sat in the Irish Parl. of James II, 7 May 1689 and also in that of 5 Oct. 1692. On 2 Dec. 1697 he signed the declaration in favour of William III in defence of his person and government. He m. (sett. 20 Sept.), 23 Sept. 1687, Mary, eldest dau. of Henry Barnewell, 2nd Viscount Barnewell, of Kingsland by his 2nd wife, Mary, dau. of Richard

Nugent, Earl of Westmeath. She d. 16 Oct.
1715. He d. 30 May 1727. The 13th Baron
was s. by his eldest son,

William St. Lawrence, **14th Baron Howth,**
b. 11 Jan. 1688; M.P. for Ratoath, 1716-27;
sat in Irish House of Lords, 1727; made P.C.
of Ireland, 1729. He m. 2 Aug. 1728, (when
he was 40 and his bride 17) Lucy, ygr. dau.
of Lt. Gen. Richard Gorges, of Kilbrew, co.
Meath and d. 4 April 1748 at Dublin aged 60.
In his will dated 30 Jan. 1744, pr. 1748, he
directed that £350 should be spent on his
funeral and his monument. His widow m.
2ndly Nicholas Weldon of Knocks, co. Meath.
They had issue, an elder son,

Thomas St. Lawrence, **15th Baron Howth,**
and **1st Viscount St. Lawrence** and **1st Earl
of Howth,** b. 10 May 1730; educ. Trin. Coll.
Dublin, 1747; took his seat in Irish House
of Lords, 1751; Bencher of King's Inn,
Dublin, 1767. He was cr. Viscount St. Lawrence, and Earl of Howth, both in Irish
peerage, 3 Sept. 1767. He was made P.C. of
Ireland, 1768. He had a pension of £500 per
year in consideration of his own and his
ancestors' services. He m. 17 Nov. 1750,
Isabella, dau. of Sir Henry King, 3rd Bt.,
(Kingston, E.). She d. 20 Oct. 1794. He d.
29 Sept. 1801. They had,
1. William, **2nd Earl** (see below).
2. Henry, who d. unm. 1787.
3. Thomas, Rt. Rev., D.D. Bishop of Cork
   and Ross, 1807-41, b. 1755; m. Frances,
   eldest dau. and coheir of Rev. Henry
   Coghlan, D.D. and d. 10 Jan. 1831,
   leaving issue,
   (1) Thomas, Rev., m. 1818, Harriet, dau
       of Lt. Gen. John Gary, and d.s.p.
       1833.
   (2) Edward, Ven. Archdeacon of Ross,
       and Preb. of Cork, m. Elizabeth dau.
       of Sir Nicholas Colthurst, Bt. and
       d.s.p. 21 June 1842.
   (3) Robert Kingsborough, Rev., Rector
       of Moragh, b. 29 Sept. 1797; m.
       3 Sept. 1850, Elizabeth Anne, dau. of
       R. B. Townsend of Castle Townsend,
       co. Cork, and d.s.p. June 1886. His
       widow d. 13 Jan. 1885, aged 95.
   (1) Emma, m. 1805, Rev. W. L. Beaufort,
       LL.D., and d. 1865.
   (2) Isabella, m. 1808, Rt. Rev. Dr. John
       Leslie, Bishop of Kilmore, and d.
       1830 leaving issue.
   (3) Letitia, m. 1830, Rev. R. J. Rothe,
       and d. 1833.
   (4) Frances Elizabeth, m. 1836, R. M.
       Toghe, of Mitchelstown, co. West-
       meath and d. 1871.
1. Isabella, m. 1773, Dudley Cosby, Lord
   Sydney.
2. Elizabeth, m. 1786, Sir Paulus Aemilius
   Irving, Bt., and d. 1799.
3. Frances, m. 1808, Ven. Dr. James Phillott,
   Archdeacon of Bath, and d. 1842.

The 1st Earl was s. by his eldest son, William
St. Lawrence, **16th Baron Howth,** and **2nd Earl
of Howth,** b. 4 Oct. 1752; Trin. Coll. Dublin
1769; m. (1) 1 June 1777, Mary, dau. of
Thomas Bermingham, Earl of Louth and Lord
Athenry. She d.s.p.m. 20 July 1793. She left
issue,
1. Harriet, m. 1801, A. F. St. George, of
   Tyrone, co. Galway, and d. 1830 leaving
   issue.

2. Isabella, m. 1803, 3rd Earl Annesley
   (marr. dissolved in 1820) and d. 1827.
3. Matilda, m. Major William Burke, of
   Queensborough and d. 1849.
4. Mary, m. Clifford Trotter, and d. 1825.

The 2nd Earl m. (2) Margaret, dau. of William
Burke, of Keelogues, co. Galway, and d.
4 April 1822. She d. 19 Sept. 1856. They had
issue,
1. Thomas, **3rd Earl of Howth** (see below).
5. Catherine, m. 1828, Viscount Dungarvan,
   and d. 1879.
6. Elizabeth, m. 1831, Sir Edward Richard
   Borough, Bt., and d. 1863.

The 2nd Earl was s. by his only son, Thomas St.
Lawrence, **17th Baron Howth,** and **3rd Earl of
Howth,** b. 16 Aug. 1803; cr. K.P. 1835; Vice
Adm. of Province of Leinster, and Lord Lieut.
of co. Dublin, 1851-74; He m. (1) 9 Jan. 1826,
Lady Emily de Burgh, dau. of 13th Earl of
Clanricarde. She d. 5 Dec. 1842. They had issue,
1. William Ulick Tristram, **4th Earl** (see
   below).
1. Emily, m. 26 Oct. 1859, Thomas Gaisford, of Offington, Sussex, and d. 6 Nov.
   1868, leaving issue. (see B.L.G. of
   Ireland, 1958, Gaisford St. Lawrence of
   Howth Castle, see below).
2. Catherine Elizabeth, m. 1850, J. J.
   Wheble, of Bulmershe Court, co. Berks,
   and left issue.
3. Mary, d. 15 Nov. 1864.
4. Margaret, m. 20 June 1861, Sir Charles
   Compton W. Domvile, 2nd Bt. who
   d.s.p. 1884.

The 3rd Earl m. (2) 27 Feb. 1851, at Trin. Coll.
Camb., Henrietta Elizabeth Digby only dau. of
Peter Barfoot, of Midlington House, co.
Hants, and Landestown, co. Kildare. He d.
4 Feb. 1874 having had further issue,
2. Thomas Kenelm Digby, b. 12 Dec. 1855;
   Capt. 5th Dragoon Guards d. unm.
   8 May 1891.
5. Henrietta Eliza, m. 1881, Capt. Benjamin
   Lee Guiness, brother of Lord Ardilaun,
   and had issue.
6. Geraldine Digby.

The 3rd Earl was s. by his elder son, Sir William
Ulick Tristram St. Lawrence, **18th Baron
Howth** and **4th Earl of Howth,** b. 25 June
1827; educ. Eton; Capt. 7th Hussars, 1847-50;
High Sheriff, co. Dublin, 1854; State Steward
to the Viceroy of Ireland, 1855-58, and 1859-
66; sat as Liberal M.P. for borough of Galway,
1868-74; Vice Adm. of Province of Leinster.
He was cr. Baron Howth of Howth, co. Dublin.
in the Peerage of U.K. 7 Oct. 1881. He was cr,
K.P. 1884. He d. unm. aged 81 at Hotel
Metropole, Bournemouth, 9 Mar. 1909. He
was bur. at the old Abbey of St. Mary from
Howth Castle on 15 Mar. 1909. All his peerages
became extinct with the possible exception of
the old Barony of Howth.

In 1916 the total acreage of his family estates
was 10,754, worth £16,089 per year. Of these
8,784 were in Dublin and 1,970 in co. Meath.
The principal seat was Howth, co. Dublin. The
estates of the 4th Earl passed to his nephew,
Julian Charles Gaisford of Offington, Sussex,
which he sold in 1910, and who assumed by
Royal Licence, 1909 the additional name and
arms of St. Lawrence (see B.L.G. 1958, as
above mentioned). The seat of the Gaisford-
St. Lawrence family is Howth Castle, co.
Dublin.

ARMS—Gules two swords in saltire blades upwards ppr. hilts and pommels or between four roses argent barbed and seeded ppr.
CREST—A sea lion per fess argent and ppr.
SUPPORTERS—Dexter, A sea lion, as in the crest; Sinister, A mermaid ppr. holding in her exterior hand a mirror.
MOTTO—Qui pense.

HUDSON

PEERAGE—U.K. Viscount Hudson of Pewsey, co. Wilts.
SURNAME—Hudson.
CR.—5 Jan. 1952. EXT.—28 Aug. 1963.
HISTORY—Robert Spear Hudson of Bache Hall, co. Chester had issue, Robert William Hudson of Villa Paloma, Monaco; High Sheriff, Bucks, (1903), b. 1856; m. (1) Gerda Francesca, dau. of Robert Johnson. She d. 1932. He m. (2) 1932, Beatrice Sabina (d. 1950) dau. of Laurenzo Gaudengio of Lucca, and d. 1937 leaving issue by his 1st marriage, Robert Spear Hudson, b. 15 Aug. 1886; educ. Eton and Magdalen Coll. Oxford; was M.P. for Whitehaven Div. of Cumberland 1924-29, and for Southport, 1931-52, held several ministerial appointments including that of Minister of Agriculture and Fisheries, 1940-45, was Director of Willoughby's Consolidated Co. Ltd., from 1952, Pres. of the British Friesian Cattle Soc. 1954 and a Mem. of Council of the Roy. Agric. Soc. of England. He was made a P.C. 1938, appointed C.H. and cr. **Viscount Hudson** of Pewsey, co. Wilts, 5 Jan. 1952. He m. 1 Dec. 1918, Hannah (d. 24 April 1969) dau. of Philip Synge Physick Randolph of Philadelphia and d. 2 Feb. 1957 and was. s by the only son of the marriage,
Robert William Hudson, **2nd Viscount Hudson,** b. 28 April 1924; educ. Eton and Trin. Coll. Camb.; served with Life Guards in World War II, 1943-45, m. 14 Oct. 1948 (m. diss. by div. 1961) Marie Claire (d. 1969), dau. of Adrien Schmitt, of Paris and d. 28 Aug. 1963, having had issue a dau., Annabel Jocelyne, b. 1952; m. 9 Feb. 1970, A. J. Garton.
ARMS—Gules, a cross moline between two garbs and two dolphins in saltire or.
CREST—An East African crowned crane ppr.
SUPPORTERS—Dexter, A Friesian bull. Sinister, A sable antelope ppr. each gorged with a chain pendant therefrom a portcullis gold.
MOTTO—Animo non astutia.

HUNGARTON

PEERAGE—U.K. Baron Hungarton of Hungarton, co. Leicester.
SURNAME—Crawford.
CR.—7 Feb. 1951. EXT.—14 June 1966.
HISTORY—Robert Crawford, of Highfields Farm, Lowesby, co. Leicester, was father of Archibald Crawford, **Baron Hungarton** of Hungarton, co. Leicester, so cr. 7 Feb. 1951, b. 12 Sept. 1890; educ. Wyggeston Gram. Sch. Leicester; m. 14 Jan. 1914, Jean, dau. of David Johnstone of Castle Douglas, co. Kirkcudbright, and had issue, a son, David Robert, Sqd. Ldr. R.A.F., k. in action over

Germany 6 Feb. 1945, and a dau. Grace Hendry, m. 1941, E. J. Parker. Lord Hungarton was Man. Dir. Crawford, Prince and Johnston Ltd., Agric. Equipment Mfrs. of Lyston, Leics. He was a Lay Canon of Leicester Cathedral 1959. He d. 14 June 1966.
ARMS—Per chevron azure and argent, two cocks combatant of the second crested, wattled and membered gules, in base a fox's mask ppr.
CREST—In front of a garb or a horseshoe gules.
SUPPORTERS—On either side a bull sable armed and unguled or gorged with a collar vair, the dexter charged on the shoulder with a plate thereon a thistle slipped and leaved ppr. the sinister charged on the shoulder with a rose argent barbed and seeded also ppr.
MOTTO—Solum patriae.
Lord Hungarton lived at The Manor House, Hungarton, Leicester.

HUNSDON OF SCUTTERSKELFE

PEERAGE—U.K. Baron Hunsdon of Scutterskelfe, co. York.
SURNAME—Falkland.
CR.—15 May 1832. EXT.—12 Mar. 1884.
HISTORY—Lucius Bentinck Cary, 10th Viscount Falkland, was b. 5 Nov. 1803; served as Capt. 7th Foot; was a Lord of the Bedchamber to William IV 1830-37, the King being his father-in-law (see below). He was a Representative Peer for Scotland 1831-32, and was cr. on 15 May 1832 a peer of the United Kingdom, as **Baron Hunsdon** of Scutterskelfe, co. York; a Lord in Waiting, acting as Liberal Whip in the House of Lords 1837-40; Gov. of Nova Scotia 1840-46; Capt of the Yeomen of the Guard 1846-48; Gov. of Bombay 1848-53. He m. (1) 27 Dec. 1830, Amelia Fitz-Clarence, dau. of King William IV and 5th and ygst. sister of the Earl of Munster, these being the bastard children of the King by Dora, dau. of Francis Bland, of Kerry, known as Mrs. Jordan. She d. 2 July 1858. He m. (2) 10 Nov. 1859, Elizabeth Catherine, dau. of Major-Gen. Joseph Gubbins, of Stoneham, Hants, and widow of the 9th Duke of St. Albans. He d.s.p.s. 12 Mar. 1884, when the Barony of Hunsdon became extinct, and he was. s in the Viscounty by his brother, Plantaganet Pierrepoint Cary, 11th Viscount Falkland (see extant peerage works, Falkland, V.). The widow who d. 2 Dec. 1893, retained the style of the Dowager Duchess of St. Albans. By his first marriage the 10th Viscount had a son, Lucius William Charles Augustus Frederick Cary, styled Master of Falkland, who d.v.p. and s.p. 6 Aug. 1871 (details in extant peerages).

HURD

PEERAGE—U.K. Life. Baron Hurd of Newbury, co. Berkshire.
SURNAME—Hurd.
CR.—24 Aug. 1964. EXT.—12 Feb. 1966.
HISTORY—William Hurd, a Solicitor of North Hill, Highgate, London, b. 17 Jan.

1831; m. 1859 Elizabeth, dau. of Rev. Angier, and d. 1913. She d. 1910. Their children were, with other issue,

1. Percy Angier, Sir (see below).
2. Archibald, Sir. Kt. Bach. 1928, Hon. F.J.I., editor and author of many works, on staff of *Daily Telegraph* 1899-1928, Editor *Naval and Military Record* 1896-99, and Jt. Editor Brassey's *Naval Shipping Annual* 1921-28, b. 13 Aug. 1869; m. (1) 19 Sept. 1895, Anne Perrott (d. 14 Sept. 1946), dau. of Albert Groser; (2) Sept. 1947, Beatrice Maude, dau. of Alfred Stair and d. 20 June 1959. By his first wife he had two daus., Vivyen Groser, m. T. D. H. Bremner and Mary Barbara, m. Rt. Hon. Sir (Henry) Gordon Willmer (Lord Justice Willmer) and had issue.

The elder son, Sir Percy Angier Hurd, Kt. Bach. 1932, M.P. Frome 1918-23, London Editor *Montreal Star*, founder and editor *The Outlook*, and editor, *Canadian Gazette*, b. 18 May 1864; m. 5 Sept. 1893, Hannah, dau. of Rev. W. J. Cox, of Dundee and d. 5 June 1950. She d. 15 Feb. 1949. They had issue, with a yr. son Robert, an architect, d. unm. 1963, an elder son,

Sir Anthony Richard Hurd, **Baron Hurd,** b. 2 May 1901; educ. Marlborough and Pembroke Coll. Camb. B.A. 1922, M.A. 1926; farmed in Wiltshire and Berkshire from 1926, was Farming Editor of *The Field* 1924-37, and Agricultural Corres. of *The Times* 1932-58, Pres. Guild of Agric. Journalists, F.J.I., M.P. Newbury 1945-64, Agric. Adviser to Min. of Agriculture 1939-45; m. 26 Sept. 1928, Stephanie Frances, dau. of E. Moss Corner of Beaconsfield, Bucks. He was cr. Kt. Bach. 1959 and a life peer as Baron Hurd of Newbury, co. Berkshire 24 Aug. 1964. He d. 12 Feb. 1966, having had issue,

1. Douglas Richard, 1st Sec. H.M. Diplomatic Service, B.A. 1952, M.A. 1957, educ. Eton and Trin. Coll. Camb., b. 1930; m. 10 Nov. 1960, Tatiana Elizabeth Michele, dau. of A. C. B. Eyre (*B.L.G.* 1952, Crosthwaite-Eyre) and had issue three sons.
2. John Julian, b. 19 Mar. 1932, d. 3 June 1951.
3. Stephen Anthony, B.A. 1954, M.A. 1958, educ. Winchester and Magdalen Coll. Camb., b. 1933.

Lord Hurd's residence was Winterbourne Holt, Newbury, Berks.

HUTCHISON OF MONTROSE

PEERAGE—U.K. Baron Hutchison of Montrose.
SURNAME—Hutchison.
CR.—30 June 1932. EXT.—13 June 1950.
HISTORY—Alexander Hutchison, of Braehead, Kirkcaldy, had a son, Sir Robert Hutchison, **Baron Hutchison** of Montrose, of Kirkcaldy, co. Fife, so cr. 30 June 1932, was b. 5 Sept. 1873; joined 7th Dragoon Guards 1900; Capt. 11th Hussars 1905; Major 4th Dragoon Guards 1912; G.S.O. 3rd Grade, 1914, and 1st Grade 1915-17; served in S. African War 1900-02, and in World War I 1914-18; Major Gen. 1923; M.P. Kirkcaldy

1922-23 and Montrose 1924-32; Chief Liberal Whip 1926-30; was cr. D.S.O. 1915, C.B. 1918; K.C.M.G. 1919; and Baron Hutchison of Montrose, of Kirkcaldy, co. Fife, 30 June 1932. He m. (1) 26 April 1905, Agnes Begbie, only dau. of William Drysdale, of Kilrie, co. Fife. He m. (2) 28 April 1942, Alma, dau. of W. G. Cowes, of Buenos Aires, and widow of J. C. Drysdale, of Kilrie, co. Fife, and d. 13 June 1950. She m. as her third husband, 9 Dec. 1954, Brig. I. L. W. D. Laurie.
ARMS—Argent three arrows, points downwards meeting in base ppr., on a chief gules a martlet between a portcullis and a rose of the field.
CREST—A stag's head ppr.
MOTTO—Memor esto.

HYNDLEY

PEERAGE—U.K. Viscount Hyndley of Meads, co. Sussex and Baron Hyndley of Meads, co. Sussex.
SURNAME—Hindley.
CR.—Viscounty 2 Feb. 1948, Barony 21 Jan. 1931; also Baronetcy 22 Jan. 1927. EXT.—5 Jan. 1963.
HISTORY—Robert Hindley of Manchester, son of Henry Hindley of Manchester, b. 1741; m. Lettice Hardman and had with other issue,

William Hindley, m. Elizabeth, dau. of Hugh Johnson of Belfast and had issue,

The Rev. Hugh Johnson Hindley, Rector of Everton, co. Lancs, m. Elizabeth Mort and had issue,

The Rev. William Talbot Hindley, Vicar of Meads, co. Sussex, M.A. Camb. (1884), b. 12 Mar. 1845; m. 1869, Caroline, dau. of John Scott and had with other issue,

Sir John Scott Hindley, Bt., and **Viscount Hyndley,** b. 24 Oct. 1883; educ. Weymouth Coll., a great industrialist, being Managing Director of Powell Duffryn Ltd. 1931-46, and (after nationalization of coal mines) Chm. of National Coal Board 1946-51, a Director of the Bank of England 1931-45, Chm. of many boards and cttees; m. 1 July 1901, Vera, dau. of James Westall, of Coniscliffe Hall, Darlington, co. Durham, by whom he had two daus.,

1. Elizabeth Cairns, served in W.R.N.S. 1940-46.
2. Millicent Joyce, served in F.A.N.Y.

He was cr. Kt. Bach. (1921), a Baronet (1927), G.B.E. (1939), Baron Hyndley of Meads, co. Sussex, 21 Jan. 1931; and Viscount Hyndley of Meads, co. Sussex, 2 Feb. 1948. He d. 5 Jan. 1963.
ARMS—Azure, a stag lodged between three martlets argent.
CREST—A sinister and a dexter cubit arm in armour fess wise, grasping in the hands a scimitar ppr., pommel and hilt or, the blade transfixing a boar's head couped sable.
SUPPORTERS—On either side a hind ppr., that on the dexter gorged with a riband azure, pendant therefrom an escutcheon argent charged with a sword erect gules, and that on the sinister gorged with a like riband pendant therefrom an escutcheon gules charged with a spur the rowel upwards or.
MOTTO—Cor non jecur.
Lord Hyndley's residence was Meads Cottage, nr. Liphook, Hants.

ILKESTON

PEERAGE—U.K. Baron Ilkeston of Ilkeston, co. Derby.
SURNAME—Foster.
CR.—14 July 1910. **EXT.**—4 Jan. 1952.
HISTORY—Thomas Foster, of Beaulieu, co. Hants, b. 1705; d. 1780 having had issue,
Robert Foster, of Beaulieu, b. 1747; m. 1782 Catherine Farthing and had with other issue, an eldest son,
Thomas Foster, of Beaulieu, b. 1783; m. 1805, Hannah Smith, of Ashurst Lodge, and had with other issue, a fifth son,
Balthazar Foster, of Drogheda, co. Louth, b. 1813; m. 1839, Marian, dau. of J. Green, of Cambridge, and d. 1862 leaving with other issue,
Balthazar Walter Foster, **1st Baron Ilkeston,** M.P. for Chester 1885-86, and for Ilkeston Div. of Derby 1887-1910, Chm. Nat. Liberal Federation 1886-90, F.R.C.P. London, M.D. Erlangen Univ., held professorial appointment Queen's Coll. Birmingham, member of the Gen. Medical Council 1887-97, Vice Pres. and Gold Medallist, B.M.A. He was b. 17 July 1840; cr. Kt. Bach. 1886, made P.C. 1906 and cr. Baron Ilkeston, of Ilkeston, co. Derby, 14 July 1910. He m. 25 Aug. 1864, Emily Martha, dau. of W. L. Sargant of Birmingham, and d. 31 Jan. 1913, having had with one other son who d. young and three daus., a second son,
Balthazar Stephen Sargant Foster, **2nd Baron Ilkeston,** Barrister-at-Law, Inner Temple 1892, Stipendiary Magistrate of Birmingham 1910, b. 31 Aug. 1867; m. 20 Dec. 1901, Mildred Charlotte, dau. of Henry Peyton Cobb, M.P. and d. 4 Jan. 1952.
ARMS—Argent, a human heart gules between in chief two foxgloves leaved and slipped, and in base a caduceus ppr.
CREST—In front of a stag's head couped ppr. three human hearts in fess gules.
SUPPORTERS—On either side an elk reguardant ppr. pendant from the neck of each a bugle horn stringed gules.
MOTTO—Labore et virtute.

ILLINGWORTH

PEERAGE—U.K. Baron Illingworth, of Denton, W.R. co. York.
SURNAME—Illingworth.
CR.—4 June 1921. **EXT.**—23 Jan. 1942.
HISTORY—William Illingworth, of Illingworth, in Ovenden, co. York, was b. 1496, and d. 1543, having issue a second son,
John Illingworth, of Bingley, co. York, who d. 1593 leaving with other issue by his wife, Mary, a third son,
John Illingworth, of Harden, Bingley, who d. Jan. 1598 leaving by his wife, Agnes, a son,
Thomas Illingworth, of Harden, who m. 23 Nov. 1601, Elizabeth Morvell, and was father of,
Thomas Illingworth, of Harden, b. 1612; m. 23 June 1640, Elizabeth Ellis and had,
Robert Illingworth, of Allerton, co. York, and later of Harden and Bradford, b. 1643; m. 7 April 1667, Mary Wright, by whom he had,

Jonathan Illingworth, of Allerton, b. 1672; and d. 1745 having a third son,
Jonas Illingworth, of Allerton, b. 1720, had issue,
William Illingworth, of Moorhouse, Allerton, b. 1744; m. 12 Nov. 1760, Martha Wilinson, of Allerton, and had with other issue,
Phineas Illingworth, of Bradford, b. 17 Sept. 1763 m. 18 May 1788, Betty Booth, and d. 28 July, 1837. She d. 15 Jan. 1845. Their third son,
Daniel Illingworth, of Bradford, b. 12 Dec. 1792; m. Elizabeth Hill, and d. 18 June 1854, having a second son,
Henry Illingworth, of Ladye Royde Hall, Bradford, b. 6 Nov. 1829; m. 23 May 1860, Mary, the eldest dau. of Sir Isaac Holden (extant peerage works, Holden, Bt.), 1st Bt. and d. 23 Sept. 1895. She d. 29 Oct. 1908. They had issue,
1. Harry Holden, of Wydale, Brompton-le-Sawdon, co. York, b. 14 Oct. 1862; m. 10 Sept. 1890, Gertrude Elizabeth, dau. of William Harker, of Pateley Bridge, co. York, and d. 7 Feb. 1925, leaving issue,
   (1) Henry Cyril Harker, b. 25 Jan. 1896; served in World War I 1914-17, M.C., Major K.R.R.C.; m. 18 Dec. 1928, Lady Margaret Cynthia Lindsay, eldest dau. of 27th Earl of Crawford.
   (1) Violet Gertrude.
   (2) Mary Ethel Phyllis, m. 13 Mar. 1919, Brig. C. L. Rome, D.S.O., and had issue.
2. Albert Holden, **Baron Illingworth** (see below).
3. Percy Holden, Rt. Hon., P.C., b. 19 Mar. 1869; M.A., LL.B. Camb., Barrister-at-Law, Inner Temple 1894; served in S. African War 1900; M.P. Shipley Div. of York; Parl. Sec. to the Treasury, and Parl. Sec. to Chief Sec. for Ireland 1906-10; m. 16 Jan. 1907, Mary Mackenzie, dau. of George Coats, of Staneley, co. Renfrew, and d. 3 Jan. 1915, having had issue, three sons.
1. Marion Illingworth, m. 1 June 1881, Tom Mitchell, of The Park, Eccleshill, co. York, who d. 8 May 1915. She resumed her patronymic of Illingworth by deed poll 1913, and d. 17 May 1929, leaving issue.
2. Mary Gertrude, m. 12 June 1894, J. E. Darnton, and had issue. (He was the representative of the family of the Barons von Schunck, derived from the Spanish Netherlands, and whose lineage was given in pre-1949 editions of Burke's Peerage, Foreign Titles section).
The third son, Albert Holden Illingworth, **Baron Illingworth,** of Denton, W.R. Yorks, so cr. 4 June 1921, b. 25 May 1865; educ. London International Coll. and in French Switzerland; became partner in Daniel Illingworth and Sons, Spinners, a Dir. of A. H. Illingworth Ltd., of Bradford, and Chm. of Isaac Holden et Fils, S.A., Pres. Bradford Chamber of Commerce 1910; M.P. Heywood Div. of Lancashire 1915-18, and Heywood and Radcliffe Div. 1918-21; Postmaster Gen. 1916-21, made P.C. 1916; served on may cttees. and was Dir. of various cos.; m. (1) 18 April 1895 (m. diss. by div. 1926), Annie Elizabeth, dau. of Isaac Holden Crothers, of Le Chateau

Croix, Nord, France. He m. (2) 18 Nov. 1931, Margaret Mary Clare, dau. of William Basil Wilberforce, of Markington Hall, co. York. (B.L.G. 1952, Wilberforce of Markington.) He d. 23 Jan. 1942.

ARMS—Argent, on a fess flory counter flory gules, between three escallops sable, as many roses of the field, barbed and seeded ppr.

CREST—Upon a crescent argent a cock ppr.

SUPPORTERS—On either side a cock sable, combed, wattled and winged gules, gorged with a collar or pendant therefrom an escutcheon gold, charged with a fleur-de-lis sable.

MOTTO—Illingworth remembers.

INVERCHAPEL

PEERAGE—U.K. Baron Inverchapel of Loch Eck, co. Argyll.

SURNAME—Kerr.

CR.—5 April 1946. EXT.—5 July 1951.

HISTORY—John Kerr Clark of Crossbasket Castle, Hamilton, co. Lanark, b. 1836; m. 1870, Kate Louisa, dau. of Sir John Struan Robertson, K.C.M.G., and d. 1910, having had with other issue, a fifth son, Sir Archibald John Kerr Clark Kerr, **Baron Inverchapel**, assumed in 1911 the surname of Kerr after that of Kerr Clark, b. 17 Mar. 1882; educ. privately; entered the diplomatic service 1906 and served as secretary in several embassies, was Envoy Extraordinary and Minister Plenipotentiary to the Central American Republics, 1925-28, to Chile 1928-30 and to Sweden 1931-34, Ambassador to Iraq, 1935-38, to China 1938-42, to the U.S.S.R. 1942-46, and at Washington 1946-48. He was cr. K.C.M.G. 1935, G.C.M.G. 1942, made a P.C. 1944 and cr. Baron Inverchapel, of Loch Eck, co. Argyll, 5 April 1946. He m. 24 April 1929, Maria Teresa Dia Salas, dau. of Don Javier Diaz Lira of Santiago de Chile and d.s.p. 5 July 1951.

ARMS—Per pale, dexter gules, sinister per fesse sable and or, a fesse chequy argent and azure, surmounted of a chevron of the 5th, charged with three mullets of the 1st all between the sun in his splendour of the 3rd and a boar's head couped of the 4th armed gold and langued, gules in chief and, a crescent in the base counter-changed of the 4th and 1st.

CREST—The sun in his splendour or between two wings azure (Kerr); 2, A demi-huntsman attired ppr. blowing a horn sable garnished argent (Clark).

SUPPORTERS—Two naked athletes ppr. that on the dexter holding in his exterior hand a quill argent feathered gules, that on the sinister holding in his hand a discus argent.

MOTTOES—1, Above dexter crest, Late but hungry. 2, above sinister crest, Blast. 3, (on compartment) Concussus surgo.

INVERCLYDE

PEERAGE—U.K. Baron Inverclyde of Castle Wemyss, co. Renfrew.

SURNAME—Burns.

CR.—28 July 1897. EXT.—17 June 1957. Also a Baronetcy Burns of Wemyss Bay, co. Renfrew 24 June 1889.

HISTORY—John Burn of Courtown (which he sold) and of Stirth, both in co. Stirling, changed his name to Burns; m. 1741, Janet dau. of William Young of Risk, co. Stirling and had issue, The Rev. John Burns, D.D., b. 1744; m. 1775, Elizabeth, dau. of John Stevenson of Glasgow, and d. 1839 having had with other issue (including James, ancestor of the Burns of Kilmahew, B.L.G.) a yst. son, Sir George Burns, 1st Bt. of Wemyss Bay, co. Renfrew, so cr. 24 June 1889, b. 10 Dec. 1795; m. 10 June 1822, Jane, dau. of James Cleland LL.D. of Glasgow, and d. 2 June 1890, having had with other issue,

John Burns, **1st Baron Inverclyde** of Castle Wemyss, co. Renfrew, so cr. 28 July 1897, b. 24 June 1829; m. 27 Nov. 1860 Emily, dau. of G. C. Arbuthnot (see Arbuthnot, B.) and had issue with three daus.,

1. George Arbuthnot, **2nd Baron** (see below).
2. James Cleland, **3rd Baron** (see below).

The 1st Baron d. 12 Feb. 1901 and was s. by his elder son, George Arbuthnot Burns, **2nd Baron Inverclyde**, Lord Dean of Guild of City of Glasgow 1903-04, Chm. Cunard Steamship Co., b. 17 Sept. 1861; m. 6 April 1886, Mary, dau. of Hickson Fergusson of The Knowe, co. Ayr, and d.s.p. 8 Oct. 1905, being s. by his brother,

James Cleland Burns, **3rd Baron Inverclyde**, Pres. Chamber of Shipping of U.K. 1899, of Glasgow Shipowners' Assoc. 1900, of G. & J. Ltd., and of Burns Steamship Co. Ltd., Master of the Company of Shipwrights, 1918, Lord Lieut. co. Dumbarton, b. 14 Feb. 1864; m. 2 April 1891, Charlotte Mary Emily, dau. of Robert Nugent-Dunbar (see B.L.G.) and d. 16 Aug. 1919 having had issue with two daus.,

John Alan Burns, **4th Baron Inverclyde**, b. 12 Dec. 1897; educ. Eton and R.M.C., served in World War I, Lt. Scots Guards (wounded) and in World War II, Capt. Scots Guards, 1940, Pres. of many organizations, Master of Eglington Foxhounds 1932-35, and of Lanark and Renfrewshire Foxhounds, 1935-49; received many foreign decorations, was K. St. J., and a mem. of Royal Co. of Archers (Queen's Bodyguard of Scotland); m. (1) 23 Nov. 1926, Olive Sylvia, dau. of Arthur Sainsbury (from whom he obtained a divorce in Scottish Court, 1928) and m. (2) 21 Mar. 1929, June, an actress, only dau. of Walter Howard Tripp (from whom he obtained a divorce in Scottish Court, 1933). He d.s.p. 17 June 1957.

ARMS—Or, two mullets of six points pierced in chief and a hunting horn in base sable, garnished and stringed vert.

CREST—A dexter hand, ppr. holding a hunting horn sable garnished vert.

SUPPORTERS—On either side a sailor habited, that on the dexter resting his exterior hand on an anchor and that on the sinister resting his exterior hand on a rudder all ppr.

MOTTO—Ever ready.

INVERNAIRN

PEERAGE—U.K. Baron Invernairn, of Strathnairn, co. Inverness. (Also a baronetcy cr. 22 Jan. 1914.)

SURNAME—Beardmore.

CR.—15 Jan. 1921. EXT.—9 April 1936.

HISTORY—William Beardmore, of Parkhead, Glasgow, was father of an eldest son, Sir William Beardmore, Bt., and **Baron Invernairn**, b. 16 Oct. 1856; educ. High School, Glasgow, Ayr Academy, and School of Mines, South Kensington, M.Inst.C.E., entered the firm of William Beardmore and Co. Ltd., of Dalmuir, Scotland, becoming Chm. and Managing Dir. thereof; a Dir. of many other cos.; Pres. of the Iron and Steel Inst. 1917. He was cr. a baronet 22 Jan. 1914, and a peer as Baron Invernairn of Strathnairn, co. Inverness, 15 Jan. 1921. He m. 11 June 1902, Elspeth Stiven, eldest dau. of Tullis, of Glencairn, Rutherglen, and d.s.p. 13 April 1936. He was interested in exploration and supported Antarctic expeditions owing to which his name was given by Sir Ernest Shackleton to the Beardmore Glacier.

ARMS—Argent, a fess between three wolves' tails sable.

CREST—A wolf rampant reguardant sable.

SUPPORTERS—On either side a stag reguardant ppr. gorged with a collar pendent therefrom an escutcheon or, that on the dexter charged with a rose gules, barbed and seeded ppr. and that on the sinister charged with a thistle leaved and slipped also ppr.

BADGE—Two wolves' tails in saltire sable enfiled with a Baron's coronet or.

MOTTO—Providentiae me committo.

ISLINGTON

PEERAGE—U.K. Baron Islington, of Islington, co. London. (Also a baronetcy cr. 21 Sept. 1802.)

SURNAME—Dickson, later Dickson-Poynder.

CR.—27 April 1910. **EXT.**—6 Dec. 1936.

HISTORY—Archibald Dickson, of Scottish origins, of Pontefract, co. York, (his brother James Dickson, was M.P. for boroughs of Peebles, Lanark, Linlithgow, and Selkirk, and d. 1771) had with other issue,

1. William, of Sydenham House, Roxburgh, Adm. of the Blue, m. (1) Jane, dau. of Alexander Collingwood, of Unthank, Northumberland. She d. 12 April 1782. He m. (2) 1786, Elizabeth, dau. of James Charteris, and d. May 1803, having had with other issue, a second son by his first marriage,
   Archibald Collingwood, **2nd Bt.**, by special remainder (see below).
2. Archibald, **1st Bt.**, (see below).

The second son, Sir Archibald Dickson, **1st Bt.**, so cr. 21 Sept. 1802, with remainder, in default of his own male issue, to his nephew, Archibald Collingwood Dickson, (see above); Adm. of the Blue, of Hardingham, Norfolk; m. (1) Elizabeth (d. 1799) dau. of Richard Porter, and had an only dau.,
   Elizabeth, m. (1) 1791, her cousin, Capt. William Dickson, 22nd Regt., eldest son of Adm. William Dickson (see above). He d.s.p. 1795 and she m. (2) 2 Aug. 1804, Rear Adm. John Child Purvis, and d. 27 July 1856.

He m. (2) 2 Dec. 1800, Frances Anne, dau. of Rev. James Willis, of Norwich (she m. secondly Major Gen. E. J. O'Brien) and d.s.p.m. May 1803, when he was s. by his nephew,
Sir Archibald Collingwood Dickson, **2nd**

Bt., Rear Adm. of the Red, b. 30 June 1772; m. 17 Aug. 1797, Harriet, dau. of Adm. John Bourmaster, of Tichfield, Hants, and she d. 6 Jan. 1863. He d. 18 June 1827. They had issue,
1. William, Sir, **3rd Bt.** (see below).
2. Archibald, b. 24 Nov. 1802; d.s.p. in India, 1834.
3. John Collingwood, d. young.
4. Colpoys, Sir, **4th Bt.** (see below).
5. Alexander Collingwood Thomas, Sir, **5th Bt.** (see below).
6. John Bourmaster, Rear Adm. R.N., C.B., b. 29 April 1815; m. (1) 19 June 1855, Sarah Matilda, dau. of Thomas Poynder, of Hilmarton, Calne, Wilts. and had by her (who d. 6 Jan. 1863),
   (1) John Poynder, **6th Bt.**, and **Baron Islington** (see below).
   (1) Mary Harriet Isabella Cumberland, m. (1) 12 Jan. 1881, Frederick Amelius Beauclerk, (St. Albans, D.) who d. 22 May 1887 and she m. (2) Lt. Col. R. F. M. Johnstone, (Johnstone Bt.).
   (2) Caroline Matilda.
   (3) Isabella Emily, m. July 1890, Major Arthur Cotes, of Bowden House, Chippenham, Wilts.
   He m. (2) 4 Aug. 1868, Ellen, dau. of William Hamwood Frampton, of Hall House, Somerset, and d. 11 Feb. 1876.
7. George Collingwood, Capt. 24th Madras L.I., b. 15 Dec. 1817; m. 11 Dec. 1849, Henrietta Emma, eldest dau. of William Hamwood Frampton, of Hall House, Somerset who d. 3 Jan. 1914. He d. 1853 leaving two daus.
8. Francis Farhill Collingwood, Capt. Madras Fusiliers, b. 29 Sept. 1822; m. Frances Murtagh, dau. of Thomas Turner, of Arcot, India, and d. 1884, having had issue with four daus., a son, John Colpuys, who was b. 1849 and d. 1903.
1. Harriet Jane, m. 17 Aug. 1820, Adm. Thomas Wren Carter, C.B., and d. 21 Dec. 1859, leaving issue.
2. Mary Magdalen, m. 7 Dec. 1826, Lt. Gen. Claude Douglas, and d. 1847 leaving issue.
3. Augusta Caroline. d. Aug. 1833.

The eldest son, Sir William Dickson, **3rd Bt.**, Vice Adm. R.N., b. 16 June 1798; m. 26 June 1850, Laura Emmeline, only dau. of Col. Lewis Northey, Llanywathan. She m. 2ndly, 1869, H. B. P. Montgomery, and d. 1890. Sir William d.s.p. 5 Jan. 1868, and was s. by his brother,
Sir Colpoys Dickson, **4th Bt.**, Co. Bengal Army, b. 21 Aug. 1807; m. 1831, Emma, dau. of William Knyvett, and d. 21 May 1868, leaving a dau. Emma, and being s. by his brother,
Sir Alexander Collingwood Thomas Dickson, **5th Bt.**, Capt. R.N., b. 1 Aug. 1810; m. 15 Nov. 1837, Amelia Caroline Beauclerk Whimper, who d. 27 July 1882. Sir Alexander d.s.p. 22 June 1884, and was s. by his nephew,
Sir John Poynder Dickson-Poynder, **6th Bt.**, and **Baron Islington**, b. 31 Oct. 1866; educ. Harrow and Ch. Ch. Oxford; assumed by Royal Licence, 12 Jan. 1888, the additional surname and arms of Poynder, (on s. to his maternal uncle's property); High Sheriff, co. Wilts, 1890; M.P. Chippenham Div. Wilts,

1892-1910; mem. L.C.C. 1898-1904; served in S. African War, 1900-01, A.D.C. to Gen. Lord Methuen; Lt. 3rd Bn. Royal Scots, and Major, Hon. Col. Royal Wilts Yeo.; awarded D.S.O. 1900; Gov. of New Zealand, 1910-12; was cr. Baron Islington, of Islington, co. London, 27 April 1910; made P.C. 1911; cr. K.C.M.G. 1911, and G.C.M.G. 1913; Under Sec. of State for the Colonies, 1914-15; and for India, 1915-18; Chm. of Imperial Inst. 1914-22; cr. G.B.E. 1926; was K.J. St. J.; m. 30 Sept. 1896, Anne Beauclerk, D.G. St. J., dau. of Henry Robert Duncan Dundas, of Glenesk, and d.s.p.m. 6 Dec. 1936, having had issue,

Joan Alice Katharine, b. 11 Sept. 1897; m. 31 Jan. 1923 1st Baron Altrincham, and had issue.

ARMS—Quarterly 1 and 4, Pily counterpily of four traits or and sable, the points ending in crosses formée two in chief and one in base, in the centre chief point a castle of the second and in base two martlets of the first, a chief azure, thereon a key erect, the wards upwards and to the sinister gold, between a rose on the dexter side and a fleur-de-lis on the sinister argent (Poynder); 2 and 3, Azure, an anchor erect or encircled with an oak wreath vert between three mullets pierced or, on a chief of the second three pallets gules in the centre of the chief a mural crown argent. (Dickson).

CRESTS—1. Issuant out of the battlements of a castle argent charged with a cross flory gules, a dexter cubit arm vested sable, charged with a key as in the arms, cuff or, the hand ppr. holding a cross patée fitchée in bend also argent. (Poynder). 2. Over an armed arm brandishing a falchion ppr. a trident and spear in saltire or. (Dickson).

SUPPORTERS—Dexter, An eagle wings endorsed ppr. Sinister, A lion rampant gules, each gorged with a collar argent pendent therefrom a plate charged with a rose also gules.

MOTTO—Fortes fortuna juvat.

The seat of Lord Islington was Hartham Park, Corsham, Wilts.

ISMAY

PEERAGE—U.K. Baron Ismay of Wormington, Co. Gloucester.

SURNAME—Ismay.

CR.—14 Jan. 1947. EXT.—17 Dec. 1965.

HISTORY—William Ismay, of Milton, near Sittingbourne, co. Kent, m. Susanna, dau. of F. Richards, of Croydon, and d. 1879 having had with other issue, a second son, Sir Stanley Ismay, C.S.I. (1901), K.C.S.I. (1911) in the Indian C.S., Barrister-at-Law, mem. of the Viceroy's Legislative Council 1905-07, and Chief Comm. of Central Provinces and Berar 1906, Chief Judge, Mysore Chief Court 1908-14, b. 1 July 1848; m. 9 Nov. 1875, Beatrice Ellen, dau. of Col. Hastings Read, and d. 7 June 1914, having had with other issue, a yr. son, Sir Hastings Lionel Ismay, **Baron Ismay,** b. 21 June 1887; educ. Charterhouse and R.M.C.; joined Army 1905; 21st Cavalry, I.A. 1907; served on the N.W. Frontier of India 1908; in Somaliland 1914-14 (despatches) and in World War I (1914-18) and in Somaliland 1920 (despatches twice, D.S.O. and clasp); Asst. Sec. to Cttee. of

Imperial Defence 1926-30, G.S.O. (1) War Office, 1933-36, Dep. Sec. to Cttee. of Imperial Defence 1936-38, Chief of Staff to Min. of Defence 1940-46 (on the last appt. Sir Winston Churchill commented: "My personal and official connection with Gen. Ismay and his relations to the Chiefs of Staff Cttee. was preserved unbroken and unweakened from 1 May 1940 to 27 July 1945 when I laid down my charge"—*The Second World War,* vol 1, p. 507). He was promoted Maj. Gen. 1939, Lt. Gen. 1942 and Gen. 1944, and was Sec. Gen. of N.A.T.O. 1952-57; known to contemporaries by the nickname of "Pug", Lord Ismay was cr. C.B. 1931, K.C.B. 1940, C.H. 1945, G.C.B. 1946, Baron Ismay of Wormington, co. Gloucester, 14 Jan. 1947 and K.G. 1957; made P.C. 1951. He m. 4 Aug. 1921, Laura Kathleen, dau. of H. G. Clegg, of Wormington Grange, Broadway, Glos., and had issue three daus. He d. 17 Dec. 1965. His residence was Wormington Grange, Glos.

ARMS—Azure, a cross crosslet or, on a chief argent a maunch sable between two pairs of cavalry swords in saltire ppr.

CREST—Two cavalry swords in saltire ppr., in front of a crescent, between two annulets gules.

SUPPORTERS—Dexter, A private of the Somaliland Camel Corps; Sinister, A sowar of the Indian Cavalry, both in field service dress ppr.

MOTTO—Have no fear.

JACKSON

PEERAGE—U.K. Baron Jackson of Glewstone, co. Hereford.

SURNAME—Jackson.

CR.—6 July 1945. EXT.—2 May 1954.

HISTORY—George Jackson, J.P., of Edgbaston, Birmingham, m. Minnie Blay and had issue, William Frederick Jackson, **Baron Jackson,** a fruit grower and farmer, M.P. for cos. Brecon and Radnor, 1939-45, b. 29 Nov. 1893, educ. King Edward VI High School, Birmingham; served in World War I, sergeant 14th Roy. Warwickshire Regt. 1914-16 (invalided out); m. 19 April 1923, Hope Hardy Falconer, dau. of B. W. Gilmour, of Glasgow. They had an adopted son, George Andrew David. W. J. Jackson was created Baron Jackson of Glewstone, co. Hereford, 6 July 1945. He d. 2 May 1954. His residence was Glewstone, Bridstow, Ross-on-Wye, co. Hereford.

JACKSON OF BURNLEY

PEERAGE—U.K. Life. Baron Jackson of Burnley, of Burnley, co. Palatine of Lancaster.

SURNAME—Jackson.

CR.—19 Jan. 1967. EXT.—17 Feb. 1970.

HISTORY—Herbert Jackson (1879-1943), of Thompson Park, Burnley, co. Lancs., by his wife, Annie, dau. of Samuel Hiley of Todmorden, co. Lancs, had a son, Sir Willis Jackson, **Baron Jackson** of Burnley, b. 29 Oct. 1904; educ. Burnley Grm. Sch. and Manchester Univ., D.Sc. 1936, D.Phil. Oxford 1936;

F.R.S. 1953, held many professional appointments in electrical engineering and was mem. of numerous councils and cttees.; Pres. British Assoc. for the Advancement of Science 1966-67. He was cr. Kt. Bach. 1958 and a Life Peer as Baron Jackson of Burnley, of Burnley, co. Palatine of Lancaster, 19 Jan. 1967. He m. 28 Dec. 1938, Mary Elizabeth, dau. of R. O. Boswall and had issue, two daus., (1) Anne Boswall, m. D. G. Freeston and (2) Ruth Lesley. Lord Jackson d. 17 Feb. 1970.

ARMS—Quarterly per fess indented or and azure in the 1st and 4th quarters a rose gules barbed and seeded ppr, and in the 2nd and 3rd a thunderbolt or.
CREST—In front of a terrestrial globe ppr. a torch erect or, inflamed ppr.
SUPPORTERS—Dexter, An Indian habited in the court dress of Mysore; Sinister, A notable of the Eastern Region of Nigeria, habited in traditional robes and headdress both ppr.
MOTTO—Towards understanding.

JAMES OF HEREFORD

PEERAGE—U.K. Baron James of Hereford, co. Hereford.
SURNAME—James.
CR.—5 Aug. 1895. EXT.—18 Aug. 1911.
HISTORY—Philip Turner James, Surgeon, of Hereford, m. Frances Gertrude, dau. of John Bodenham, and was father of Sir Henry James, **Baron James** of Hereford, b. 30 Oct. 1828; educ. Cheltenham Coll., Barrister-at-Law, Middle Temple 1852, Q.C. 1869, Bencher 1870, Treasurer 1888, Solicitor Gen. 1873, Attorney Gen. 1873-74 and 1880-85, Attorney Gen. to the Prince of Wales (later Edward VII) and to the Duchy of Cornwall 1892-95 and Chancellor of the Duchy of Lancaster 1895-1902, mem. Judicial Cttee. of Privy Council 1896, M.P. Taunton 1869-85 and Bury 1885-95; cr. Kt. Bach. 1873, P.C. 1885, G.C.V.O. 1902 and Baron James of Hereford, co. Hereford, 5 Aug. 1895. He d. 18 Aug. 1911.

ARMS—Sable a fess argent guttée de poix, between three swords, two in chief, one in bend the point upwards one in bend sinister the point downwards and one in pale in base, point downwards ppr. pommel and hilts or.
CREST—A cubit arm erect ppr. pendent from the hand by a chain or an escutcheon ermine charged with a balance gold, the hand grasping a sword erect ppr. pommel and hilt of the second, the blade transfixing a boar's head couped ermine.
SUPPORTERS—On either side a lion, the dexter ermines and the sinister ermine, each gorged with a chain or and pendent therefrom an escutcheon gules charged with a balance gold.
MOTTO—Vim vi repellere licet.
Lord James of Hereford was a member of the following clubs: Brooks's, Athenaeum, Reform, National Liberal, Devonshire, Marlborough, Turf and Garrick.

JENKINS

PEERAGE—U.K. Life. Baron Jenkins of Ashley Gardens in the City of Westminster.
SURNAME—Jenkins.
CR.—6 April 1959. EXT.—6 April 1969.
HISTORY—James Jenkins, of Glansawdde, Llangadock, co. Carmarthen had a son, Sir John Lewis Jenkins, K.C.S.I., M.A. Oxford, entered I.C.S. 1879, mem. of Council of Gov. of Bombay 1909-10, and of Council of Gov. Gen. of India 1910-12; b. 22 July 1857; m. 1890 Florence Mildred, dau. of Sir Arthur Trevor, K.C.S.I., and d. 13 Jan. 1912 leaving issue with four other sons, and two daus., a third son, Sir David Llewelyn Jenkins, **Baron Jenkins**, b. 8 April 1899; educ. Charterhouse and Balliol Coll. Oxford, B.A. 1920, M.A. 1928; served in World War I 1918 and in World War II 1940-45; Barrister-at-Law, Lincoln's Inn 1923, K.C. 1938, Bencher 1945; Attorney Gen. Duchy of Lancaster, a Judge of the Chancery Div. of High Court of Justice 1947, Lord Justice of Appeal 1949, and a Lord of Appeal in Ordinary 1959. He was cr. Kt. Bach. 1947, P.C. 1949, and a Life Peer as Baron Jenkins of Ashley Gardens in the City of Westminster, 6 April 1959. He d. 6 April 1969.

ARMS—Paly of six gules and ermine, an orle of leeks or.
CREST—On a wreath argent and gules, issuant from a circlet of lotus flowers and leaves ppr. a lion passant or.
SUPPORTERS—Dexter, A wyvern argent; Sinister, A dragon gules.
MOTTO—Non sine jure.

JOWITT

PEERAGE—U.K. Baron Jowitt and Viscount Jowitt, of Stevenage, co. Hertford. Viscount Stevenage of Stevenage and Earl Jowitt.
SURNAME—Jowitt.
CR.—Baron 2 Aug. 1945. Viscount 20 Jan. 1947. Viscount Stevenage and Earl Jowitt 24 Dec. 1951. EXT.—16 Aug. 1957.
HISTORY—Richard Jowitt of Beeston, near Leeds, b. ca. 1661, had a son, Richard Jowitt, of Holbeck, co. Yorks. b. ca. 1691 had issue, John Jowitt, of Churwell, co. Yorks. b. 10 May 1721; m. 18 April 1747, Ann, dau. of Thomas Benson, of Gilderstone, nr. Leeds and d. 1775 leaving issue, Joseph Jowitt, of Churwell, b. 1 Oct. 1757; m. 30 May 1787, Grace, dau. of Thomas Firth, of Huddersfield, and d. 1803 having had issue, John Jowitt of Leeds, b. 3 May 1790; m. 29 Jan. 1829, Mary Ann, dau. of Thomas Norton, of Peckham Rye, co. Surrey, and d. 24 Dec. 1860 leaving issue,
The Rev. William Jowitt, M.A., Rector of Stevenage, co. Hertford, b. 2 July 1834, educ. at St. John's Coll. Oxford and Univ. Coll. Durham; m. 1866, Louisa Margaret, dau. of John Allen of Oldfield Hall, Altrincham, and d. 1912, having had issue,
Sir William Allen Jowitt, **Earl Jowitt**, b. 15 April 1885, educ. Marlborough and New Coll. Oxford, B.A. 1906, Barrister-at-Law, Middle Temple, 1909; K.C. 1922; M.P. for Hartlepools 1922-24, and for Preston 1929-31, and Ashton-under-Lyne 1929-45. A Liberal, he joined the

Second Labour Gov. in 1929, and became Attorney Gen. June 1929-Jan. 1932; was Solicitor-Gen. May 1940-Mar. 1942, held several Ministerial appts., Lord High Chancellor 1945-51. He was made Kt. Bach. 1929, a P.C. 1931; cr. Baron Jowitt 2 Aug. 1945, Viscount Jowitt, of Stevenage, co. Hertford, 20 Jan. 1947, Viscount Jowitt of Stevenage, co. Hertford, and Earl Jowitt, 24 Dec. 1951. He m. 19 Dec. 1913, Lesley, dau. of James Patrick McIntyre and d. 16 Aug. 1957 having had issue a dau.,

Penelope, b. 22 Jan. 1923; m. 1943, George Wynn-Williams, F.R.C.S., and had issue.

ARMS—Azure on a chevron argent, between two chaplets of oak in chief and a lion sejant guardant in base or, three bugle horns, stringed sable.

CREST—A lion sejant guardant gules, the dexter forepaw supporting an escutcheon of the arms.

SUPPORTERS—On either side a spaniel with a Chancellor's purse ppr., that on the dexter charged with a rose argent and that on the sinister with a rose gules both barbed and seeded also ppr., suspended from the neck by a cord or.

MOTTO—Tenax et fidelis.

Earl Jowitt's residence was at West Lodge, Bradfield St. George, nr. Bury St. Edmunds, Suffolk.

KEANE

PEERAGE—U.K. Baron Keane of Ghuznee in Afghanistan and Cappoquin, co. Waterford.

SURNAME—Keane.

CR.—23 Dec. 1839. EXT.—27 Nov. 1901.

HISTORY—Sir John Keane, 1st Bt., (see extant peerage works) had a second son, Sir John Keane, **Baron Keane** of Ghuznee etc., b. 6 Feb. 1781; entered the Army in 1793; served in Egypt, 1801-02; at Martinique, Lt. Col. 13th Foot, 1809, and in the Peninsular War, to 1814, present at battles of Vittoria, the Pyrenees, Nivelle, and in the American War, 1814, when he made a successful attack on New Orleans; Gov. of St. Lucia, 1818-25; C. in C. Jamaica, 1823-30; Major Gen. 1814; Lt. Gen. 1830; C. in C. Bombay 1833-39, leading the Afghanistan expedition and capturing Ghuznee, 23 July 1839. He was cr. K.C.B. 1815; G.C.H. 1831; and Baron Keane of Ghuznee in Afghanistan and Cappoquin, co. Waterford, 23 Dec. 1839, with a pension of £2,000 for himself and his two immediate successors in the peerage, and received the thanks both of the East India Co. and of Parliament (a full account of the expedition is given in ch. xxiii of vol. xii of Sir John Fortescue's *History of the British Army* 1839-1852 where the capture of Ghuznee or Ghazni is described in the words of Sir Robert Peel, as "the most brilliant achievement of our arms in Asia" since Ghuznee had been deemed impregnable, but was captured by Keane's forces by storm, Kandahar having been entered on 25 April 1839). Baron Keane m. (1) 1 Aug. 1806, Grace, 2nd dau. of Lt. Gen. Sir John Smith, R.A., and she d. 14 July 1838. Lord Keane m. (2) 20 Aug. 1840, Charlotte Maria, dau. of Col. Boland, and d. 26 Aug. 1844. His

widow m. as his 2nd wife, William Pigott of Dullingham, co. Cambridge and d. 8 Sept. 1884. By his first wife Lord Keane had issue,

1. Edward Arthur Wellington, **2nd Baron** (see below).
2. John Manly Arbuthnot, **3rd Baron** (see below).
3. George Disney, Adm. R.N., C.B., b. 26 Sept. 1817; m. 31 July 1881, Katharine Mary, dau. of Major Alexander McLeod, widow of Thomas L. Brooke, and d.s.p. 19 Oct. 1891.
4. Hussey Fane, Lt. Gen. C.B., b. 14 June 1822; m. 11 Jan. 1886, Lady Isabella Emma Elizabeth, dau. of 5th Earl of Orkney, and widow of S. L. Schuster, and d.s.p. 25 Oct. 1895.
1. Charlotte Emilia, d. 22 June 1859.
2. Georgiana Isabella, m. 16 July 1840, W. H. Penrose, of Lahene, co. Cork, and d. 14 April 1854.

The eldest son, Edward Arthur Wellington Keane, **2nd Baron Keane** of Ghuznee and Cappoquin, b. 4 May 1815; Major in 37th Foot, and A.D.C. to his father, in Afghanistan campaign; m. 13 April 1847, Louisa Caroline Lydia, dau. of S. Y. Benyon, of Stretchworth Park, and Denston Hall, co. Cambridge, and d.s.p.m. 25 July 1882, leaving issue,

Emily Julia Charlotte, b. 12 Jan. 1848; m. (1) 1866 (m. diss. by div. 1882) H. A. Herbert, M.P. of Muckross, co. Kerry, and had issue. She m. (2) 1897, H. H. Vignoles, and d. 2 July 1911.

The 2nd Baron was s. by his brother, John Manly Arbuthnot Keane, **3rd Baron Keane** of Ghuznee and of Cappoquin, b. 1 Sept. 1816; Lt. 33rd Foot, 1833; Major Rifle Brig. 1846-48; High Sheriff, co. Wexford, 1875. He m. (1) 11 May 1848, Mary Jane, dau. of Sir Hugh Palliser, (formerly Walters) 2nd Bt., and widow of William Lockhart. She d.s.p. 29 Oct. 1881. He m. (2) 6 May 1885, Francina Maria, dau. of Charles Lane, of Badgemore, co. Oxford, and widow of Rt. Rev. Thomas Baker, Morrell, Bishop Coadjutor, of Edinburgh, and she d. 20 Nov. 1901. The 3rd Baron d.s.p. 27 Nov. 1901.

ARMS—Gules three salmon naiant in pale argent; on a chief of honourable augmentation a representation of the fortress of Ghuznee all ppr.

CRESTS—1, A representation of the Kabul gate of the fortress of Ghuznee all ppr. and on an escroll above, the word "Ghuznee"; 2, A cat sejant ppr. supporting in his dexter paw a flag staff, thereon a union jack ppr.

SUPPORTERS—Dexter, A mounted Belochee soldier; Sinister, A mounted Afghan soldier, both ppr.

MOTTO—Deus mihi providebit.

The principal house of the Lords Keane was Castletown House, near Churchtown, co. Wexford.

KEITH

PEERAGE—Ireland. Baron Keith of Stonehaven Marischal, cr. 16 Mar. 1797.

Great Britain. Baron Keith of Stonehaven Marischal, co. Kincardine, cr. 15 Dec. 1801.

U.K. Baron Keith of Banheath, co. Dumbarton, 17 Sept. 1803.

U.K. Viscount Keith, 1 June 1814.

SURNAME—Elphinstone.

CR.—As above. EXT.—The Viscounty of Keith and the Barony of 1801 became extinct 10 Mar. 1823. The Irish Barony and the U.K. Barony of 1803, 11 Nov. 1867.

HISTORY—George Keith Elphinstone, fifth son of 10th Lord Elphinstone (see extant peerge works, Elphinstone, B.), was b. 7 Jan. 1745-46; served in R.N.; Rear Adm. 1794; Vice Adm. 1795; Adm. of the Blue 1801; of the White 1805; and of the Red 1810; was Whig M.P. for Dumbarton 1781-90; and for co. Stirling 1796-1801; F.R.S.; was Keeper of the Signet and Councillor of State for Scotland. He served with distinction against the French in 1793 off Toulon; commanded the expedition to Cape Town when it surrendered 1795, and received the surrender of the Dutch Fleet in 1796. He put down the Nore Mutiny, being Commander at Sheerness, was C.in.C. Mediterranean 1799-1802; and was C.in.C. of the Channel Fleet 1812. He was cr. K.B. 1794; and G.C.B. 1815; on 16 Mar. 1797, **Baron Keith** of Stonehaven Marischal, in the Irish peerage, and with a special remainder in default of his heirs male, to his daughter Margaret (see below). On 15 Dec. 1801, he was cr. a peer of Great Britain as Baron Keith of Stonehaven Marischal, co. Kincardine. On 17 Sept. 1803 he was cr. Baron Keith of Banheath, co. Dumbarton, with a special remainder to his daughter. He was further created **Viscount Keith**. He had several foreign knighthoods. He m. (1) 9 April 1787, Jane. dau. and coheiress of William Mercer, of Aldie, co. Perth, a Col. in the Army, this William Mercer being son and heir of the Hon. Robert Mercer, otherwise Nairne, second son of William, 2nd Lord Nairne (see Nairne, in extant peerage works). She d. 12 Dec. 1789. He m. (2) Hester Maria, dau. and coheiress of Henry Thrale, of Streatham, co. Surrey, a brewer and d. 10 Mar. 1823. His widow d. 31 Mar. 1857. By his first marriage he had an only dau.,

Margaret Mercer, **Baroness Keith,** 2nd holder of that title (see below).

By his second marriage he had,

Georgiana Auguste Henrietta, who m. (1) Hon. J. Villiers (Jersey E.) and (2) Lord William Osborne, brother of the 8th Duke of Leeds, and d.s.p. 21 Sept. 1892.

The only dau. of the first marriage,

Margaret Mercer Elphinstone, suo jure **Baroness Keith** of Stonehaven Marischal, in Irish peerage, and Baroness Keith of Banheath was b. 12 June 1788; m. 20 June 1817, Auguste Charles Joseph, Count de Flahault de la Billardrie, French Ambassador to Vienna and later to London. He d. 2 Sept. 1870. She s. on 7 Dec. 1837, as Baroness Nairne on the death of her cousin the 4th Baron Nairne. She had issue five daus., and d. 11 Nov. 1867, when her eldest dau. s. her as Baroness Nairne, but when the Baronies of Keith of Stonehaven and Keith of Banheath became extinct, the remainder evidently being only to heirs male of her body.

ARMS—Argent a chevron sable between three boars' heads erased gules.

CREST—A lady from the middle well attired ppr. holding in her dexter hand a tower argent and in her sinister a laurel branch ppr.

SUPPORTERS—Dexter, A savage ppr. wreathed head and middle with oak leaves vert,

in his exterior hand a club, resting on his right shoulder, on his breast a shield azure charged with three fleur-de-lis or, at his feet an anchor sable; Sinister, A stag ppr. attired and unguled or, collared azure, the collar charged with three cinquefoils argent and pendent therefrom a shield of the last with a chief gules charged with three pallets gold, the dexter hind foot resting on an anchor sable.

KEITH OF AVONHOLM

PEERAGE—U.K. Life. Baron Keith of Avonholm, of St. Bernards in the City of Edinburgh.

SURNAME—Keith.

CR.—4 Nov. 1953. EXT.—29 June 1964.

HISTORY—James Keith, Provost of Hamilton, co. Lanark, by his wife Helen Hamilton, had a son, Sir Henry Shanks Keith, G.B.E., of Avonholm, Hamilton, co. Lanark, Provost of Hamilton, 1901-08, and in 1919; b. 25 Dec. 1852. m. 16 June 1885, Elizabeth, dau. of John Hamilton of Mayfield, Bothwell, and d. 9 July 1944. She d. 1934. They had with other children, James Keith, **Baron Keith of Avonholm,** M.A., LL.B., b. 20 May 1886; served under Sudan Gov. 1917-19; Advocate, Scots Bar, 1911, K.C. 1926, Dean of Faculty of Advocates 1936-37, a Senator of Coll. of Justice, Scotland 1937-53, a Lord of Appeal in Ordinary 1953, served as chm. or pres. of many cttees and asscns., made P.C. 1953 and a Life Peer as Baron Keith of Avonholm of St. Bernards in the City of Edinburgh 4 Nov. 1953. He m. 7 July 1915, Jean Maitland, dau. of Andrew Bennett, and d. 29 June 1964. Their children were: (1) Henry Shanks, Advocate Scots Bar, 1950 and Barrister-at-Law, Grays Inn, 1951, m. Alison Brown and had issue.

1. Elizabeth Hamilton, m. R. A. Solley and had issue.
2. Helena Stewart, m. G. O. Mayne and had issue.

KELHEAD

PEERAGE—U.K. Baron Kelhead of Kelhead, co. Dumfries.

SURNAME—Douglas.

CR.—22 June 1893. EXT.—19 Oct. 1894.

HISTORY—Francis Archibald Douglas, styled Viscount Drumlanrig, eldest son of the 9th Marquess of Queensberry (see extant peerage works), b. 3 Feb. 1867; a Lord in Waiting to Queen Victoria; cr. a peer of the U.K. as **Baron Kelhead,** of Kelhead, co. Dumfries, 22 June 1893. Lt. 2nd Bn. Coldstream Guards; d. unm. vp. 19 Oct. 1894, in a shooting accident in Wiltshire, when the barony became extinct.

KELVIN

PEERAGE—U.K. Baron Kelvin of Largs.

SURNAME—Thomson.

CR.—23 Feb. 1892. EXT.—17 Dec. 1907.

HISTORY—James Thomson, son of a small farmer in Northern Ireland, was Prof. of

Mathematics at Glasgow Univ., and LL.D. He was b. 1786, m. Margaret, dau. of William Gardiner, and d. 1849 having had issue a second son, William Thomson, **Baron Kelvin** of Largs, b. 26 June 1824, at Belfast; educ. Glasgow Univ. and St. Peter's Coll. Camb., of which he became Fellow, 1845-52, and again 1872; was 2nd Wrangler, first Smith's prizeman and Hopkins' prizeman, and B.A. 1845; M.A. 1848; described in C.P. as "entitled to a greater number of letters after his name than any man of his time." He was Prof. of Natural Philosophy in Univ. of Glasgow, 1846-99; F.R.S. 1851; cr. Kt. Bach. 1866, for services in laying down the Atlantic Cable; Pres. Royal Soc. 1890-95, and was a Dir. of several manufacturing cos. He was cr. Baron Kelvin of Largs, 23 Feb. 1892, G.C.V.O. 1896; O.M. 1902, and P.C. 1902. He m. (1) 1852, his second cousin, Margaret, dau. of Walter Crum, of Thornliebank who d. 17 June 1870. He m. (2) 24 June 1874, in Madeira Frances Anna, dau. of Charles R. Blandy, of Madeira, and d.s.p. 17 Dec. 1907. His widow d. 16 Mar. 1916. Lord Kelvin had built a mansion at Netherhall, near Largs, and at his death was possessed of estates of some 2,000 acres, Netherhall being correctly described as a seat. Lord Kelvin's enormously successful career cannot be summarised in a few lines. It is sufficient to refer to the biography in D.N.B. where his numerous achievements were detailed. He was a man of very varied talents and, unlike many great inventors, a practical man of great application in numerous projects, so that it came easily to him to take up directorships in commercial cos. He was a man of great Christian faith. It has been pointed out that he had concluded from certain researches into the apparent rate of cooling of the earth's crust that the age of the earth must be in the region of 20 million years, but modern views are that this age is quite inadequate for the requirements of the evolutionary theory.

ARMS—Argent, a stag's head caboshed gules, on a chief azure a thunderbolt ppr. winged or, between two spur rowels of the field.

CREST—A cubit arm erect vested azure, cuffed argent, the hand grasping five ears of rye ppr.

SUPPORTERS—Dexter, A student of the Univ. of Glasgow, habited, holding in his dexter hand a marine voltmeter all ppr.; Sinister, A sailor habited, holding in the dexter hand a coil, the rope passing through the sinister, and suspended therefrom a sinker of a sounding machine, all ppr.

MOTTO—(Over the crest)—Honesty without fear.

KENMARE

PEERAGE—Ireland. Baron of Castlerosse and Viscount Kenmare, 12 Feb. 1798. Viscount Castlerosse and Earl of Kenmare 29 Dec. 1800. U.K. Baron Kenmare of Killarney, co. Kerry 12 Mar. 1856. Also a Baronetcy of Ireland, cr. 16 Feb. 1621/2.

SURNAME—Browne.

CR.—As above. EXT. 14 Feb. 1952.

HISTORY—Sir Valentine Browne, of Totteridge, co. Herts, Auditor Gen. of Ireland, d. 8 Feb. 1567 having had a son, Sir Valentine Browne, P.C., M.P. for Sligo 1588, received grants of land in Ireland; m. (1) Elizabeth, dau. of Robert Alexander, of London, and had by her a son, Valentine, Sir, knighted 23 April 1603, ancestor of the Brownes of Crafts, co. Lincoln. He m. (2) Thomasine, dau. of Robert Bacon, (see Bacon, Bt.) and d. 1588/9 having had by her with other issue, Sir Nicholas Browne, Kt., of Molahiffe, co. Kerry; m. Sheila, dau. of O'Sullivan Beare, and d. 12 Dec. 1606, having had with other issue, an eldest son, Sir Valentine Browne, 1st Bt., so cr. 16 Feb. 1621/2 and received from James I confirmation of all his lands including the lakes of Killarney. He m. (1) Lady Ellis Fitzgerald, dau. of the 15th Earl of Desmond (Extinct Peerage 1883); (2) Sheely, dau. of 1st Viscount Muskerry (Extinct Peerage, Clancarty, E.) and d. 13 Sept. 1633, being s. by his eldest son by his first marriage, Sir Valentine Browne, 2nd Bt., m. Mary, dau. of 1st Viscount Muskerry (and thus his stepaunt, being sister of his father's second wife), and d. 25 April 1640, having had with two daus. and a son John, who d. 15 Aug. 1706, an elder son,

Sir Valentine Browne, 3rd Bt., made a P.C. by James II, and after the latter's abdication, cr. **Baron of Castlerosse** and **Viscount Kenmare**, 20 May 1689. He is styled in some peerage works as 1st Viscount Kenmare but the honours derived from James II in exile from England were never acknowledged in law. Sir Valentine served as a Col. in James II's army and thus lost his estates. He was b. 1637; m. Jane, dau. and heiress of Sir Nicholas Plunket, of Balratty, co. Meath, and d. before 23 June 1694 being s. by his eldest son,

Nicholas Browne (styled sometimes **2nd Viscount Kenmare**) who served in the army of James II in exile and was attainted in consequence. He m. 1684, Helen (d. July 1700) the eldest dau. and heiress of his kinsman, Thomas Browne of Hospital, at Aney, co. Limerick, a yr. son of the 1st baronet. By his marriage he acquired large estates in cos. Kerry and Cork, but these were forfeited for his life. He d. April 1720 having had with other issue,

Valentine Browne (styled **3rd Viscount Kenmare**) who recovered the family estates; m. (1) 1720, Honoria (d. 1729), dau. of Thomas Butler (see Ormonde, D.) and had by her, with two daus.,

Thomas (styled **4th Viscount**) (see below). He m. (2) 1735, Mary, only dau. of Maurice Fitzgerald, of Castle Ishen, co. Cork, widow of the 5th Earl of Fingall, and later wife of 4th Baron Bellew (Extinct Peerage) and d. 30 June 1736 having begotten a dau. b. posthumously and being s. by his son,

Thomas Browne (soidisant **4th Viscount Kenmare**), m. 1750, Anne, only dau. of Thomas Cooke, of Painstown, co. Carlow and d. 9 Sept. 1795, having had with a dau., Catherine, a son,

Valentine Browne, **1st Earl of Kenmare**, who was cr. 12 Feb. 1798, Baron of Castlerosse and Viscount Kenmare and on 29 Dec. 1800, Viscount of Castlerosse and Earl of Kenmare. He was b. Jan. 1754; m. (1) 1777, Charlotte, dau. of 11th Viscount Dillon and had an only dau., Charlotte, m. Sir George Goold, 2nd Bt. (Current peerage works) and m. (2) 1785, Mary, dau. of Michael Aylmer, of co. Kildare and had further issue with two daus.,

1. Valentine, **2nd Earl** (see below).
2. Thomas, **3rd Earl** (see below).
3. William, b. 1 Nov. 1791; m. 29 April 1826, Anne Frances, dau. of Thomas Segrave and d. 4 Aug. 1876.
4. Michael, b. 18 May 1793, fought at Waterloo and wounded, d. 1825.

The 1st Earl d. 3 Oct. 1812, being s. by his eldest son, Valentine Browne, **2nd Earl of Kenmare**, P.C. Ireland, cr. Baron Kenmare of Castlerosse, co. Kerry in the peerage of the U.K., 17 Aug. 1841. He was b. 15 Jan. 1788; m. 1 July 1876, Augusta, dau. of Sir Robert Wilmot, 2nd Bt., and d.s.p. 31 Oct. 1853 when the U.K. Barony became extinct and he was s. in his Irish peerages by his brother,

Thomas Browne, **3rd Earl of Kenmare,** Capt. in the Army, served in the Peninsular War with the 40th Regt. with distinction, and was cr. Baron Kenmare of Killarney, co. Kerry in the U.K. peerage, 12 Mar. 1856. He was b. 15 Jan. 1789; m. 1822, Catherine, dau. and heiress of Edmund O'Callaghan, of Kilgory, co. Clare, and had issue with a dau. Ellen Maria (d. unm. 10 Dec. 1905),

Valentine Augustus, **4th Earl** (see below).

Mary Catherine, m. 4 Mar. 1851, Robert Berkeley, of Spetchley Park, co. Worcester and had issue (see B.L.G. 1952).

The 3rd Earl d. 26 Dec. 1871 being s. by his only son,

Sir Valentine Augustus Browne, **4th Earl of Kenmare**, K.P., P.C., M.P. co. Kerry 1852-71, Comptroller of H.M.'s Household 1856-58, High Sheriff co. Kerry 1851, b. 16 May 1825; m. 28 April 1858, Gertrude Harriet, dau. of Lord Charles Thynne (Bath, M.) and had issue,

1. Valentine Charles, **5th Earl** (see below).
2. Cecil Augustine, b. 1864, d. unm. 1887.
1. Margaret Theodora May Catherine, m. 1889 G. C. Douglas and d.s.p. 1940.

The 4th Earl d. 9 Feb. 1905 being s. by his only surv. son, Valentine Charles Browne, **5th Earl of Kenmare**, C.V.O. (1904), Master of the Horse 1903-05, mem. of the Senate of Southern Ireland 1921, Col. 3rd Bn. Roy. Munster Fus. and 8th Bn. Liverpool Regt., T/Major Roy. Munster Fus. 1914-15, b. 1 Dec. 1860; m. 26 April 1887, Elizabeth (d. 1944), dau. of 1st Baron Revelstoke and had issue, with two daus.,

1. Valentine Edward Charles, **6th Earl** (see below).
2. Maurice Henry Dermot, Lt. Coldstream Guards, b. 25 July 1894, k. in action 29 Sept. 1915.
3. Gerald Ralph Desmond, **7th Earl** (see below).

The 5th Earl d. 14 Nov. 1941 and was s. by his eldest son, Valentine Edward Charles Browne, **6th Earl of Kenmare**, B.A. Trin. Coll. Camb., a distinguished journalist writing a weekly page for the *Sunday Express*, and a Director of the *Sunday Express*, etc., served in World War I 1914 (wounded), Capt. the Irish Guards, b. 29 May 1891; m. (1) 16 May 1928 (m. diss. by div. 1938), Doris, dau. of Edward de Lavigne, and (2) 26 Jan. 1943, Enid Maude, dau. of Charles Lindeman of Sydney, Australia (and widow of Roderick Cameron, of Brig. Gen. F. H. Cavendish and of 1st Viscount Furness) and d.s.p. 20 Sept. 1943, being s. by his brother,

Gerald Ralph Desmond Browne, **7th Earl**

of Kenmare, b. 20 Dec. 1898; educ. Oratory School; served in World War I 1916-18, Major 1st Dragoons; made O.B.E. 1922, d. 14 Feb. 1952.

ARMS—Argent, three martlets in pale between two flaunches sable each charged with a lion passant-guardant of the field, armed and langued gules.

CREST—A dragon's head couped argent between two wings sable guttée d'eau.

SUPPORTERS—Two lynxes argent guttée de poix, plain collared and chained or.

MOTTO—Loyal en tout.

The seat of the Earl was Kenmare House, Killarney, co. Kerry.

KENRY

PEERAGE—U.K. Baron Kenry, co. Limerick.
SURNAME—Wyndham-Quin.
CR.—16 June 1866. **EXT.**—14 June 1926.
HISTORY—Edwin Richard Wyndham Wyndham-Quin, 3rd Earl of Dunraven and Mount-Earl, b. 19 May 1812; was cr. on 12 June 1866, **Baron Kenry**, co. Limerick in the peerage of the United Kingdom. He d. 6 Oct. 1871, being s. by his only son,

William Thomas Wyndham-Quin, 4th Earl of Dunraven and Mount-Earl, etc. and **2nd Baron Kenry**. He d.s.p.m. 14 June 1926, when the Barony of Kenry became extinct, but the Irish titles and the baronetcy passed to his cousin, Windham Henry Wyndham-Quin, who became 5th Earl of Dunraven, etc. and whose history with that of the ancestry of the 3rd Earl is given in extant peerages.

KESTEVEN

PEERAGE—U.K. Baron Kesteven of Casewick, co. Lincoln.
SURNAME—Trollope.
CR.—15 April 1868. **EXT.**—5 Nov. 1915.
HISTORY—Sir John Trollope, 6th Bt. (see extant peerages works, Trollope, of Casewick, Bt.) had with other issue, an eldest son, Sir John Trollope, 7th Bt., **1st Baron Kesteven,** b. 5 May 1800; educ. Eton; s. his father as 7th Bt. 28 April 1820; served as an officer in the 10th Hussars; High Sheriff co. Lincoln, 1825; M.P. South Lincolnshire, 1841-68; Pres. of the Poor Law Board, 1852; made P.C. 1852, and cr. Baron Kesteven of Casewick, co. Lincoln, 15 April 1868; m. 26 Oct. 1847, Julia Maria, dau. of Sir Robert Sheffield, 4th Bt., and d. 17 Dec. 1874, having had issue with two daus.,

1. John Henry, **2nd Baron** (see below).
2. Robert Cranmer, Major 3rd Bn. Northamptonshire Regt., b. 7 Nov. 1852 m. 22 Oct. 1885, Ethel Mary, dau. of Col. G. H. Warrington Carew, of Crowcombe Court, co. Somerset, and d. 25 Nov. 1908, leaving issue,

Thomas Carew, **3rd Baron** (see below).
Dorothy Nesta, of Casewick, Stamford, Lincs, who s. to the family estates in 1915, and was granted by royal warrant, 1916, the title and precedence of a Baron's dau., m. 17 Oct. 1918, Lt. Col. F. D. Bellew, and had

issue. They assumed by Royal Licence, the additional name and arms of Trollope.
3. Charles William, b. 24 Sept. 1855; d. 5 July 1897.

The eldest son, Sir John Henry Trollope, 8th Bt., and **2nd Baron Kesteven,** b. 22 Sept. 1851; educ. Eton and Magdalene Coll. Camb.; served in S. African War, 1900; m. 25 Mar. 1914, Amy Myddelton, dau. of C. G. Peacock, of Greatford Hall, Stamford, and widow of Edgar Lubbock. She d. 13 April 1941. He d.s.p. 23 July 1915, and was s. by his nephew.

Thomas Carew Trollope, 9th Bt., and **3rd Baron Kesteven,** b. 1 May 1891; served in World War I, Capt. Lincolnshire Yeo., and d. unm. 5 Nov. 1915, of wounds received in action on a transport off the Algerian coast. The Barony then became extinct and the baronetcy passed to his cousin, Sir William Henry Trollope, 10th Bt., (see extant peerages).

ARMS—Vert three stags courant argent, attired or, within a bordure of the second.
CREST—On a mount vert a stag courant argent attired or, holding in the mouth an oak leaf ppr.
SUPPORTERS—On either side a stag argent ducally gorged and attired or, holding in the mouth an oak leaf ppr.
MOTTO—Audio sed taceo.

KEYNES

PEERAGE—U.K. Baron Keynes, of Tilton, co. Sussex.
SURNAME—Keynes.
CR.—14 July 1942. **EXT.**—21 April 1946.
HISTORY—John Keynes and Anna Maynard Neville had issue, John Neville Keynes, b. 31 Aug. 1852; educ. Amersham Hall Sch., Univ. Coll. London, Fell. 1875, and Pembroke Coll. Camb., Fell. 1876; held appts. in Camb. Univ. in the Registrary, 1910-25; m. 1880, Florence Ada, dau. of Rev. John Brown, D.D., and d. 15 Nov. 1940, having had issue with one dau., an only son, John Maynard Keynes, **Baron Keynes,** b. 5 June 1883; educ. Eton and King's Coll. Camb., B.A. 1905, M.A. 1908, Fell. 1909; served in India Office, 1906-08, Act. Prin. Clerk, Treasury, 1917-19; mem. Treasury Cttee on Finance and Industry 1921-31; Prin. Representative of Treasury at Paris Peace Conf. and Deputy for Chan. of the Exchequer on Supreme Economic Council, 1919; Trustee of National Gallery, 1941; High Steward of Camb. 1943; F.B.A.; Dir. of Bank of England; Bursar of King's Coll. Camb.; Sec. Royal Economic Soc.; Editor of *Economic Journal* and author of many very influential books on economics; Chm. of Council for Encouragement of Music and Arts 1942; cr. C.B. (Civil) 1917 and Baron Keynes, of Tilton, co. Sussex, 14 July 1942. He m. 7 Aug. 1925, Lydia, a ballerina, dau. of Vassili Loppkoff, of Leningrad and d. 21 April 1946.
ARMS—None exemplified.
Lord Keynes's residences were Tilton, Firle, Sussex; 46 Gordon Square, London W.C. and King's Coll., Cambridge.

KILMUIR

PEERAGE—U.K. Viscount Kilmuir, of Creich, co. Sutherland.
SURNAME—Fyfe.
CR.—19 Oct. 1954. **EXT.**—27 Jan. 1967.
HISTORY—William Fyfe of Kirkton in Aberdeenshire, had with other issue by his wife, Hannah Ross, William Thomson Fyfe, Headmaster of Gram. Sch. Aberdeen, author of *Edinburgh under Sir Walter Scott*, b. 29 July 1857; educ. Aberdeen Gram. Sch. and King's Coll. Aberdeen, M.A.; m. (1) Helen Grey, and had issue with two other sons and two daus. a second son, Cleveland, Sir, C.B.E. (1935), Kt. Bach. (1943), Master of Co. of Farmers 1956-57, b. 1888; m. May Church and d. 1959 having had issue a son, He m. (2) 1898, Isabella, dau. of David Campbell, of Dornoch, co. Sutherland, and d. 30 Sept. 1939. She d. 28 Feb. 1942. They had issue,

Sir David Maxwell Fyfe, **Viscount Kilmuir,** b. 29 May 1900; educ. George Watson's Coll. and Balliol Oxford, B.A. (1922), Hon. Fell. (1954) and M.A. (1960); he served in World War I with the Scots Guards. Barrister-at-Law, Gray's Inn (1922); K.C. 1934, Bencher 1936; M.P. for West Derby 1935-00; Recorder of Oldham 1936-42; Solicitor Gen. 1942-45; Attorney Gen. May-Aug. 1945; negotiated Four Power Agreement for trial of German War Criminals and was Dep. Chief Prosecutor at Nuremburg 1945-46 when he was brilliantly successful in his cross examination of Herman Goering ("the most formidable witness I have ever examined" Lord Kilmuir in his book, *Political Adventure*, 1964). He was appointed Lord Chancellor, Oct. 1954, made P.C. 1945, cr. Kt. Bach. 1942; G.C.V.O. 1953, and Viscount Kilmuir of Creich, co. Sutherland, 19 Oct. 1954. He m. 15 April 1925, Sylvia Margaret, D.B.E. (1957), dau. of W. R. Harrison of Liverpool and d. 27 Jan. 1967 having had issue, three daus.
1. Lalage (1926-44, d. unm.).
2. Pamela Maxwell, b. 1928; m. (1) 1950, Clive Wigram (d. 17 Aug. 1956); m. (2) 26 Oct. 1957, C. G. Blackmore and had issue by both marriages.
3. Miranda Maxwell, b. 1938; m. 1960 M. O. Cormack and had issue.

Lady Kilmuir m. 2ndly, 1968, the 9th Earl de la Warr.
ARMS—Or a lion rampant gules armed and langued azure, on a chief of the second a water bouget between two mullets, a bordure invected argent.
CREST—A demi-lion rampant gules armed and langued azure between six ears of wheat or, three on each side.
SUPPORTERS—Dexter, A griffin or, gorged with a collar gules, charged with a water bouget between two mullets argent; Sinister, A dragon gules armed and langued vert, gorged with a collar of the same embordured invected argent.
MOTTO—Decens et honestum.

KING-HALL

PEERAGE—U.K. Life. Baron King-Hall of Headley, co. Southampton.
SURNAME—King-Hall.
CR.—19 Jan. 1966. **EXT.**—2 June 1966.

PLATE 10

BARON HALDON.

BARON HERRIES.

BARON HAVERSHAM.

EARL OF HOWTH.

BARON JAMES

PLATE 11

HONESTY WITHOUT FEAR

BARON KELVIN.

EARL OF KENMARE.

BARON KESTEVEN.

BARON KINNEAR.

BARON KNARESBOROUGH.

BARON LEITH

HISTORY—James Hall, M.D., Surg. R.N., b. 17 Sept. 1784; m. 1809, Mary, dau. of Lt. Francis Miller, R.N. and d. Mar. 1869 leaving issue, Adm. Sir William King-Hall, K.C.B., 1871, b. Mar. 1816, served in R.N. from 1829, Rear Adm. 1869, Vice Adm. 1875, C. in C. the Nore, 1877-79, Adm. 1879, m. (1) 20 June 1844, Louisa (d. 29 June 1875) dau. of James Forman of Coldstream, Berwickshire and (2) 6 July 1880, Charlotte, dau. of T. C. Simpson and widow of Thomas K. Tillotson and d. 29 July 1886. By his first marriage he had with other issue,

1. George Fowler, Sir (see below).
2. Herbert Goodenough King-Hall, Sir, K.C.B. 1916, C.V.O. 1908, C.B. 1907, D.S.O. 1894, b. 15 Mar. 1862; entered R.N. 1875, served in Egyptian War 1882, in operations on the Gambia 1894, in S. African War 1902 (despatches) Capt. 1900, Rear Adm. 1909, Vice Adm. 1915, Adm. 1918. cmdg. Orkneys and Shetlands 1918-19; m. 30 Mar. 1905, Lady Mabel Murray, dau. of Viscount Stormont (Mansfield E.) and d.s.p. 20 Oct. 1936.

The elder son, Adm. Sir George Fowler King-Hall, K.C.B. 1911, C.V.O. 1907, de. b. 14 Aug. 1850; entered R.N. 1863; Capt. 1891, Rear Adm. 1904, Vice Adml 1908, Adm. 1912; m. 5 April 1892, Olga Felicia (d. 14 Aug. 1950) dau. of R. J. C. R. Ker (B.L.G. of Ireland 1958, Ker of Portavo) and d. 10 Sept. 1939, having had issue with two daus., and a ygr. son,

Sir (William) Stephen King-Hall, Baron King-Hall, b. 1 Jan. 1893; educ. Lausanne and R.N.C., served in World War I, 1914-18, with Grand Fleet and 11th Submarine Flotilla, R.N. Staff Coll. 1920-21, Staff Coll. Camberley 1924, Intelligence Officer Mediterranean Fleet, 1925, Atlantic Fleet 1927, Admiralty Naval Staff 1928-29, Cmdr. R.N.; M.P. Ormskirk Div. 1939-45, well known as a writer of plays and on current affairs, founder of the King-Hall News Letter 1936 and of Hansard Soc. 1944, which published in 1954, symposium—*The Future of the House of Lords*, ed. S. D. Bailey—to which Lord King-Hall wrote the Foreword. He m. 15 April 1919, Kathleen Amelia (d. 16 May 1963) dau. of Francis Spencer and had three daus., Ann, Frances Susan, and Jane (m. Yves Barraud and had issue three sons). Cmdr. King-Hall was cr. Kt. Bach 1954 and a life peer as Baron King-Hall, of Headley, co. Southampton. He d. 2 June 1966.

His residence was The Penthouse, 162, Buckingham Palace Road, London, S.W.1.

KINGSTON OF MITCHELSTOWN

PEERAGE—U.K. Baron Kingston of Mitchelstown, co. Cork.
SURNAME—King.
CR.—17 July 1821. EXT.—8 Sept. 1869.
HISTORY—George King, 3rd Earl of Kingston, was b. 8 April 1771; educ. Eton and Exeter Coll. Oxford; was M.P. for Roscommon 1797-99; s. his father as 3rd Earl of Kingston on 17 April 1799; was Representative Peer for Ireland 1807-39; was cr. 17 July 1821,

Baron Kingston of Mitchelstown, co. Cork, in the U.K. peerage; m. 7 May 1794, Helena, dau. of Stephen Moore, 1st Earl of Mountcashell, and d. 18 Oct. 1839, having had issue, with two daus.,

1. Edward, styled Viscount Kingsborough, who was b. 1795 and d. unm. of typhus fever in the debtors' prison Dublin for a debt not his own but his father's in 1837. He wrote much on the antiquities of Mexico and had the theory that the American Indians were descended from the Ten Lost Tribes of Israel.
2. Robert Henry, 4th Earl and 2nd Baron (see below).
3. James, 5th Earl and 3rd Baron (see below).

The elder surv. son, Robert Henry King, 4th Earl of Kingston and 2nd Baron, b. 4th Oct. 1796; educ. Exeter Coll. Oxford, B.A. 1818; served in the 5th Foot, being an Ensign in the Army of Occupation in France; was Whig M.P. for co. Cork 1826-32; High Sheriff of co. Cork 1836; d. unm. 21 Jan. 1867, having been declared of unsound mind 1861. He was s. by his brother,

James King, 5th Earl of Kingston and 3rd Baron, b. 8 April 1800; educ. Trin. Coll. Dublin, and Barrister-at-Law, King's Inn, Dublin 1825, and Lincoln's Inn 1827. He m. 25 Aug. 1860, Anna, dau. of Matthew Brinckley, of Parsonstown, co. Meath, and d.s.p. 8 Sept. 1869, when the barony of Kingston of Mitchelstown became extinct and he was s. in the earldom of Kingston by his cousin,

Robert King, 6th Earl of Kingston, also 2nd Viscount Lorton, (see extant peerage works, Kingston, E.).

KINNEAR

PEERAGE—U.K. Baron Kinnear of Spurness, co. Orkney.
SURNAME—Kinnear.
CR.—5 Feb. 1897. EXT.—20 Dec. 1917.
HISTORY—Thomas Kinnear, a banker in Edinburgh, m. Janet Hutchison and had an eldest son, George Kinnear, a merchant in Edinburgh, m. Fearne, dau. of John Gardiner, M.D., Pres. of Royal Coll. of Physicians, Edinburgh and had issue a second son, John Gardiner Kinnear, of Glasgow, who m. Mary, dau. of Alexander Smith, banker of Edinburgh, and had with other issue, an eldest surv. son, Alexander Smith Kinnear, Baron Kinnear of Spurness, co. Orkney, b. 3 Nov. 1833; educ. Univs. of Glasgow and Edinburgh; Advocate Scottish Bar 1856; Q.C. 1881; Dean of the Faculty of Advocates 1881-82; a Senator of the College of Justice; a Lord of Session (Scotland) 1882-1913, under the style of Lord Kinnear; LL.D. Glasgow 1894, and Edinburgh. He was cr. Baron Kinnear of Spurness, co. Orkney 5 Feb. 1897, and made a P.C. 1911. He d. unm. 20 Dec. 1917.
ARMS—Sable on a bend or three martlets vert within a bordure engrailed of the second.
CREST—An anchor ppr. cabled or.
SUPPORTERS—On either side a seagull standing on a fasces all ppr.
MOTTO—Spem fortuna alit.

KINTORE

PEERAGE—U.K. Baron Kintore, of Kintore, co. Aberdeen.
SURNAME—Keith-Falconer.
CR.—5 July 1838. EXT.—25 May 1966.
HISTORY—The U.K. Barony was cr. for the 7th Earl of Kintore. On the death of his grandson, the 10th Earl, the Barony became extinct (see Kintore, E. in current peerages). See also Falconer of Halkerton, B. Dormant).

KIRKLEY

PEERAGE—U.K. Baron Kirkley, of Kirkley, co. Northumberland. (Also a baronetcy, cr. 24 June 1921.)
SURNAME—Noble.
CR.—21 Jan. 1930. EXT.—11 Sept. 1935.
HISTORY—John Noble, F.E.I.S., of Saville Place Academy, Newcastle-upon-Tyne, m. 1849 Mary Waddell, dau. of James Black, of West Boldon, co. Durham, and d. 30 June 1869, having had by her (who d. 29 Feb. 1884),
Sir William Joseph Noble, Bt. and **Baron Kirkley**, b. 13 Jan. 1863; a shipowner, and for 25 years a partner in Cairn, Noble and Co.; Vice Pres. Newcastle and Gateshead Chamber of Commerce, 1915-35; Dir. of Blackwell Colliery Co., and of Furness Withy and Co., Chm. of Cairn Line of Steamships, and of the Tyne Improvements Commission; was cr. a baronet 24 June 1921, and a peer as Baron Kirkley, of Kirkley, co. Northumberland, 21 Jan. 1930. He was Pres. of the Chamber of Shipping of the U.K., and first Hon. Pres. of the Baltic and White Sea Conference; he was a Kt. of the Order of St. Olav. He m. 30 Aug. 1888, Margaret, dau. of William Dixon, of Humshaugh, co. Northumberland, who d. 25 Sept. 1928. They had issue,
1. John Waddell, b. April 1889, d. in infancy.
2. William Black, Lt. 6th Bn. Northumberland Fusiliers, who was k. in action at St. Julien, Belgium, 26 April 1915.
1. Sheila Black, m. 1917, Frederick Williamson, Noble, F.R.C.S. and had issue.
2. Phyllis Margaret Black, m. 1920 Capt. Cecil Dodd, Devon Regt. and had issue. Marr. diss by div. 1938, and she assumed by deed poll the additional surname of Noble.
Lord Kirkley d.s.p.m.s. 11 Sept. 1935.
ARMS—Gules a lymphad in chief two bay leaves or.
CREST—In front of a dexter cubit arm vested azure, the hand grasping a sword ppr. pommel and hilt or, an anchor fesswise sable.
SUPPORTERS—On either side a sea lion ppr. charged on the shoulder with a laurel leaf or.
BADGE—A sprig of bay and a sprig of maple in saltire. ppr. enfiled by a circlet or.
MOTTO—Virtute et valore.
Lord Kirkley's seat was Kirkley Hall, Ponteland, Northumberland.

KITCHENER

PEERAGE—U.K. Baron Kitchener of Khartoum.
SURNAME—Kitchener.
CR.—1 Nov. 1898. EXT.—5 June 1916.
HISTORY—Sir Horatio Herbert Kitchener, the famous soldier and administrator, was cr. on 1 Nov. 1898 **Baron Kitchener** of Khartoum, following on his victory over the forces of the Mahdi at Omdurman, and avenging of the murder of Gen. Gordon. He was further cr. Viscount Kitchener of Khartoum, Baron Denton, Viscount Broome, and Earl Kitchener of Khartoum and of Broome, all these peerages being with special remainder which caused them after his death in 1916 to pass to his eldest brother. (see extant peerages). The Barony of Kitchener of Khartoum cr. in 1898 became extinct.
ARMS—See extant peerages under Earl Kitchener.

KNARESBOROUGH

PEERAGE—U.K. Baron Knaresborough, of Kirby Hall, co. York.
SURNAME—Meysey-Thompson.
CR.—26 Dec. 1905. EXT.—3 Mar. 1929.
HISTORY—Richard John Thompson, of Kirby Hall, co. York, b. 1771; m. 1803, Elizabeth, dau. of John Turton, of Sugnall Hall, co. Staffs, by his wife Mary, dau. and coheiress of Richard Meysey, of Shakenhurst, co. Worcester, and d. 3 Aug. 1858. His eldest son,
Sir Harry Stephen Meysey-Thompson, 1st Bt. so cr. 26 Mar. 1874, apparently assumed the additional surname of Meysey. He d. 17 May 1874, and was s. in the baronetcy by his eldest son,
Sir Henry Meysey Meysey-Thompson, 2nd Bt., **Baron Knaresborough** was allowed by Royal Licence to continue to use the additional name and arms of Meysey. He was b. 30 Aug. 1845; educ. Eton and Trin. Coll. Camb. B.A. 1868; M.P. Knaresborough 1880 (but on a petition the election was declared void); M.P. for the Brigg Div. of Lincolnshire, 1885-86, and for Handsworth Div. of Staffordshire 1892-1905; Dir. and later Chm. of the North Eastern Railway; cr. 26 Dec. 1905, Baron Knaresborough, of Kirby Hall, co. York. He m. 21 April 1885, Ethel Adeline, only child of Sir Henry Pottinger, 3rd Bt. She d. 18 Aug. 1922. He d.s.p.m.s. 3 Mar. 1929, having had,
Claude Henry Meysey, b. 5 April 1887; educ. R.M.C. Sandhurst; joined the Rifle Brigade, Adjutant 1913; Capt. 1914. Served in World War I and d. 17 June 1915, of wounds received in action at Ypres.
Lord Knaresborough had also four daus., for whom and for the succession of his nephew to the baronetcy, as Sir Algar de Clifford Charles Meysey-Thompson, 3rd Bt., see extant peerages under Meysey-Thompson, Bt.
ARMS—Per fess argent and sable, a fess counter-embattled between three falcons counterchanged belled and jessed or (Thompson).
CREST—An arm embowed in armour quarterly or and azure, the gauntlet ppr. holding a truncheon of a broken lance of the first.
SUPPORTERS—On either side a dragon sable winged and gorged with a wreath of oak fructed, all or.
MOTTO—Je veux de bonne guere.

KNIGHTLEY OF FAWSLEY

PEERAGE—U.K. Baron Knightley of Fawsley, co. Northampton. (Also a Baronetcy cr. 2 Feb. 1798).
SURNAME—Knightley.
CR.—23 Aug. 1892. **EXT.**—19 Dec. 1895.
HISTORY—In the account which follows, down to the particulars of the Sir Richard Knightley who was cr. a K.B. at the Coronation of Charles II, an endeavour has been made to work out the pedigree of this very anciently recorded family, from sources available, namely the Visitation of Northants in 1681, Metcalfe's Visitations of the same county, and also with reference to the article on the Knightleys of Fawsley by Lady Knightley and Oswald Barron in *The Ancestor*, Vol. 2, p. 1. It is not possible in all cases to give the exact relationship of the line, but undoubtedly this family was of a long recorded ancestry and possessed of landed property over many centuries, in Northants from 1416, and in Staffordshire for a considerable period before that date.

Roger Knightley of Gnosall, co. Stafford, m. and had issue, an eldest son,
Roger (or Robert) Knightley who had issue, three sons, John, Robert and Roger, of whom the eldest,
John Knightley, m. Elizabeth, dau. and heiress of Adam Burgh, of Burgh Hall, and Cowley, and had issue three sons, Richard, John and Edmond, of whom the eldest,
Richard Knightley, of Burgh Hall and Cowley, m. Elizabeth, dau. of . . . Gifford, and had issue,
Richard Knightley, who acquired the manor of Fawsley, in 1416, was M.P. co. Northampton, and m. Elizabeth Purefoy. He d. 1443, leaving a son,
Sir Richard Knightley, knighted in 1494, three times High Sheriff Northants, m. Eleanor, dau. of John Throgmorton, of Cowton, co. Warwick, and had issue,
1. Richard (see below).
2. John.
3. James and four daus.
The eldest son,
Sir Richard Knightley, of Fawsley, m. Jane Skenard or Skynnerton, dau. and heir of Henry Skenard, of Alderton, co. Northampton, and d. 1534 (altar tomb in Fawsley church) having had issue, (with a dau. Susan m. Sir William Spencer, of Althorp),
1. Richard, m. Jane, dau. of Sir John Spencer, of Althorp, and d. at Upton, in 1537 (altar tomb at Upton, nr. Northampton), three years after his father, leaving issue, five daus.
2. Thomas, m. a dau. of . . . Burnaby, of Watford, co. Northampton, and d.s.p. 18 Oct. 1516 (see below).
3. Edmond, Sir, Sergeant at Law, who built the great Hall at Fawsley; m. Ursula, dau. of Sir George Vere, and sister of John Vere, Earl of Oxford, and widow of Sir George Windsor. He d. 12 Sept. 1543, having had issue, six daus.
4. John, Rev., Rector of Byfield, and Dean of the Collegiate Church of St. Mary's Warwick, (see below).
5. Valentine (see below).
Thomas Knightley having d. during his father's lifetime, John, executed a deed dated 21 Mar.

1543, by which he released the family property to his ygr. brother Valentine, who on the death of the third brother, Sir Edmond, inherited Fawsley.
Sir Valentine Knightley, of Fawsley, was knighted at the Coronation of Edward VI, Feb. 1547. He was High Sheriff, Northants. He m. Anne (d. 1554), dau. of Sir Edward Ferrers, of Baddesley Clinton, co. Warwick, and d. 1566 (M.I. Fawsley Church) having had issue with four daus.
1. Richard, Sir (see below).
2. Edmond, of Grandborough, co. Warwick, who m. Alice, dau. of William Bury, and had issue, dying 1575.
3. Thomas, of Burghall, Staffs. m. Elizabeth, dau. of John Shukburgh.
4. Edward, of Offchurch, co. Warwick.
5. Berry, to whom his brother, Edmond, left his night gown.
The eldest son,
Sir Richard Knightley, of Fawsley, b. 1534; m. (1) Mary (d. 27 Sept. 1573) dau. of Richard Fermor, of Easton Neston, and (2) Elizabeth, dau. of Edward Seymour, Duke of Somerset, and had numerous children by both wives. He d. 1615. He had been fined £10,000 by the Court of Star Chamber for having acted on behalf of the Nonconformists (Puritans) in 1605. His son,
Sir Valentine Knightley, s. to Fawsley. He m. Anne dau. of Sir Richard Unton and was bur. 12 Dec. 1618 when Fawsley was inherited by his nephew,
Richard Knightley, M.P., of Burgh Hall, Staffs, and of Fawsley, High Sheriff, m. Jane dau. of Sir Edward Littleton, and d. 1650 aged 70, when the estate of Fawsley passed to another,
Richard Knightley (described as a nephew of Sir Richard Knightley who d. 1615) and his son, was,
Sir Richard Knightley, M.P., cr. K.B. at Coronation of Charles II, he having been a member of the Council of State which recalled the King; he m. a dau. of John Hampden, and had issue a son, Essex Knightley who d.s.p.m. when the estates passed to a kinsman and first cousin,
Lucy Knightley, of Fawsley, (son of Lucy Knightley a Hamburg merchant) who m. Jane Grey Benson, (descended from King Edward III through the Bourchiers, Earls of Bath, *Burke's Royal Families*, pedigree cliii)., dau. and heir of Henry Benson, and d. Aug. 1738, being s. by his son,
Valentine Knightley, of Fawsley, M.P. co. Northampton, 1748-54, b. 1 May 1718; m. 21 Dec. 1740, Elizabeth, dau. of Edward Dummer, of Swathling. She d. 11 Aug. 1760. He d. 2 May 1754. They had with other issue,
1. John, Sir, 1st. Bt. (see below).
2. Charles, Rev. B.C.L. Trin. Coll. Oxford, b. 29 Oct. 1753; m. 23 June 1779, Elizabeth, only dau. of Henry Boulton, of Moulton, co. Lincoln and d. 28 June 1787, having had with other issue,
(1) Charles, Sir, 2nd Bt. (see below).
(2) Henry, Rev. M.A. Ch. Ch. Oxford, b. 23 Jan. 1786; m. 1810, Jane Diana, dau. of Rev. Philip Scory, of Lockington Hall, co. Leicester and d. 9 Sept. 1813, leaving with other issue.
1a Valentine, Sir, 4th Bt. (see below).

2a Henry Charles, Rev. B.A. Camb., b. 22 Dec. 1823; m. 22 April 1851, Mary Maria, eldest dau. of Capt. S. Richmond, and d. 14 Aug. 1884, having had with other issue,

    1b Charles Valentine, Sir, 5th Bt. (see below).

    2b Henry Francis, Sir, 6th Bt. (see below).

The heir to the estates,

The Rev. Sir John Knightley, 1st Bt., so cr. 2 Feb. 1798, with special remainder in default of male issue to the heirs male of his deceased ygr. brother the Rev. Charles Knightley. The 1st Bt. was b. 17 Feb. 1746; m. 15 April 1779, Mary, only dau. and heiress of John Baines, of Layham, co. Suffolk, but d.s.p. 29 Jan. 1812. She d. 21 Oct. 1830. The baronetcy was inherited by the 1st Bt.'s nephew,

Sir Charles Knightley, 2nd Bt., M.P. for S. Northampton, 1834-52; b. 30 June 1781; m. 24 Aug. 1813, Selina Mary, dau. of F. L. Hervey, (Bristol, M.), and d. 30 Aug. 1864. She d. 27 July 1836. They had issue (with a dau. Sophia Selena, who m. the Hon. H. E. H. Gage, and had issue, the 5th Viscount Gage, [see that title, in extant peerage works]),

Sir Rainald Knightley, 3rd Bt., and **Baron Knightley**, of Fawsley, co. Northampton, so cr. 23 Aug. 1892, was b. 22 Oct. 1819; was M.P. for South Northants, 1852-92; m. 20 Oct. 1869, Louisa Mary, dau. of Gen. Sir Edward Bowater. Lady Knightley was D.G. St. J., and an extra Lady-in-Waiting to H.R.H. the Duchess of Albany. She d. 3 Oct. 1913. Lord Knightley d.s.p. 19 Dec. 1895. The barony became extinct and the baronetcy devolved upon the 3rd Bt.'s cousin,

The Rev. Sir Valentine Knightley, 4th Bt., b. 30 Sept. 1812; educ. Ch. Ch. Oxford, M.A., and d. unm. 28 April 1898, being s. by his nephew,

Sir Charles Valentine Knightley, 5th Bt., b. 22 July 1853; Barrister-at-Law, and C.C. Byfield Div. of co. Northampton; m. 26 April 1883, Juliet Claudine, dau. of T. W. Watson, of Lubenham, co. Leicester and d.s.p. 20 Mar. 1932, when he was s. by his brother,

The Rev. Sir Henry Francis Knightley, 6th Bt., who was b. 30 July 1854, Vicar of Wasperton, co. Warwick, 1883-96; m. 14 Feb. 1884, Florence Mary, dau. of Capt. Thomas Garratt, of Braunston House, Rugby. She d. 12 July 1927. He d.s.p.

ARMS—Quarterly 1 and 4, Ermine; 2 and 3, Paly of six or and gules, all within a bordure azure.

CREST—A buck's head, couped, argent, attired or.

SUPPORTERS—Two falcons, ppr.

MOTTO—Invita Fortuna.

The seat of the family was Fawsley Park, Daventry, co. Northampton.

KYLSANT

PEERAGE—U.K. Baron Kylsant, of Carmarthen, co. Carmarthen and of Amroth, co. Pembroke.

SURNAME—Philipps.

CR.—14 Feb. 1923. EXT.—5 June 1937.

HISTORY—The Rev. Sir James Erasmus Philipps, 12th Bt. of Picton, co. Pembroke, (see extant peerages under St. Davids, V.) had a third son,

Owen Cosby Philipps, **Baron Kylsant,** b. 25 Mar. 1863; after having served an apprenticeship with a firm of shipowners and brokers he founded a shipping company of his own on the Clyde. From then on he was extremely active in the shipping industry. He was Chm. and Managing Dir. of the Royal Mail Steam Packet Co. 1902, and later of the White Star and Union Castle Lines, with their associated cos. He assumed control of Harland Wolff of Belfast on the death of Lord Pirrie in 1924, and in 1927 he acquired for £7 million the entire share capital of the Ocean Steam Navigation Co. (whose fleet was known as the White Star Line). He was a mem. of many Gov. Cttees, and Pres. of the Federation of Chambers of Commerce of the British Empire. He was High Sheriff of co. Pembroke, 1904; M.P. for Pembroke Boroughs, 1906-10, for Chester, 1916-18, and for the City of Chester Div. 1918-22. He was sub-prior of the Priory of Wales, Order of St. J. of Jerusalem, 1922-30; Lord Lt. of the County of the town of Haverfordwest, 1924-31, and Vice Adm. of N. Wales and co. Carmarthen; he was cr. K.C.M.G. 1909, G.C.M.G. 1918-31; appointed K.J. St. J. 1925-31, and cr. Baron Kylsant, of Carmarthen, co. Carmarthen and of Amroth, co. Pembroke, 14 Feb. 1923. He m. 16 Sept. 1902, Mai Alice Magdalen, C.B.E., D.J. St. J., dau. of Thomas Morris, of Coomb, co. Carmarthen and d.s.p.m. 5 June 1937, leaving three daus.,

1. Nesta Donne, m. 17 Sept. 1923 10th Earl of Coventry and had issue.
2. Olwen Gwynne, m. 21 Feb. 1925, 7th Baron Suffield.
3. Honor Chedworth, m. 2 June 1927, 2nd Baron Faringdon (m. annulled 1931).

Further details in extant peerages.

Lord Kylsant was arrested and tried at the Old Bailey on charges of publishing false annual reports for 1926-27 and a false prospectus in 1928 in connection with an issue of debenture stock. On the first charge he was found not guilty, but the prospectus was held to be false as he had kept up the payment of dividends from non-recurring sums available and from reserves. He was sentenced to 12 months imprisonment in the second division. R. v. Kylsant (1932) 1 K.B. 442 is a classic case in a section of Company Law.

ARMS—Argent a lion rampant sable, ducally gorged and chained or.

CREST—A lion as in the arms.

SUPPORTERS—Dexter, A knight in chain armour ppr. garnished or, resting the exterior hand on the hilt of his sword, and bearing on a white surcoat a lion rampant sable, ducally gorged and chained gold, a mullet for cadency; Sinister, A similar knight bearing on a white surcoat three cocks gules, two and one, armed, jelloped and wattled or.

MOTTO—Ducit amor patriae.

Lord Kylsant's seats were—Coomb, Llangain, Carmarthenshire and Amroth Castle, Amroth, Pembrokeshire.

LAMBOURNE

PEERAGE—U.K. Baron Lambourne, of Lambourne, co. Essex.
SURNAME—Lockwood.
CR.—19 June 1917. EXT.—26 Dec. 1928.
HISTORY—The Rev. Richard Lockwood, Rector of Tiffield, 1527, and of Dingley, co. Northampton, 1530, who d. 1535, left a son, Richard Lockwood, of Dingley, who d. 1598, having had issue (with a ygr. son, John, Vicar of Towcester, who fought for Charles I at Naseby and was wounded), an elder son, Richard Lockwood, of Newington m. Mary, dau. of James Reading, and d. 1632 (bur. at Bermondsey) leaving issue,
Richard Lockwood, of Gayton, co. Northampton, and of Dews Hall, co. Essex, High Sheriff, co. Northampton 1695, who acquired the estate of Lambourne, co. Essex, by his marriage with Susannah, only dau. and heiress of Edward Cutts, of Lambourne. He was bur. at Gayton. She d. 1709, They had issue, a ygr. son,
Richard Lockwood, b. 1672; educ. Westminster; M.P. Hindon, Aug. 1713-Jan. 1714, for London city May 1722-July 1727, and for Worcester city 1734-41; said to have acquired Dews Hall, in 1722, though in *The Record of Old Westminsters, Vol. 2*, his father is described as of that property; m. Matilda, dau. of George Vernon, of Sudbury, co. Derby, and d. 30 Aug. 1756, aged 80, having had issue,
1. Richard, of Lambourne, Verderer of Waltham Forest, b. 1712; educ. Westminster, adm. 1720; m. 1749, his cousin, Anne Catharina Vernon, sister of George Vernon, 1st Baron Vernon and d.s.p. 24 Mar. 1797.
2. John, b. 1717; educ. Westminster, adm. 1724; m. 19 April 1755, Matilda, dau. of Edward Conyers, of Copped Hall, co. Essex, and d. 14 Jan. 1777, having had an only dau., Mathilda, who m. 14 April 1788 H. C. Cotton, and d. 1848, having had issue, (Combermere, V.).
3. Edward (see below).
4. Henry, adm. Westminster April 1727, aged 8; d. of yellow fever in Jamaica, about 1739.
5. Thomas, adm. Westminster Sept. 1731, aged 7; m. (1) 13 April 1762, Bridget, dau. of Robert Morris, of Tredegar, co. Glamorgan (Morris, Bt. of Claremont) and had issue. He m. (2) 24 Feb. 1772, Jane Waller, and d. 15 May 1805 having had issue,
Thomas, of Dan-y-graig, co. Glamorgan, m. 16 June 1789, Charlotte ygr. dau. of Lord George Manners-Sutton (see Rutland, D. and in present work, Canterbury, V.). She d. 1827. They had issue,
Robert Manners, adm. Westminster 4 Feb. 1807, and left 1809; Ensign 52nd Foot, 1813; Lt. 1814; Lt. Rifle Brig. 1816; Lt. 89th Foot, 1818; Capt. 22nd Foot, 1821; 80th Foot, 1822; British half pay, Portuguese and Spanish Service, 1822; 94th Foot, 1833; ret. 1833; m. 23 Dec. 1821, Lady Julia Gore, ygst. dau. of 2nd Earl of Arran, and d. 28 Nov. 1865. She d. 21 Aug. 1891, aged 91, leaving issue.
6. William, adm. Westminster, May 1733, aged 8; Oriel Coll. Oxford, 1743 B.A. 1747;

Fell. 1748; M.A. 1750; adm. Inner Temple, 1743; Rector of Fyfield, co. Essex, 1753-1803; m. 24 April 1760, Mary Bennett, of Chelmsford, co. Essex, and had issue.
The third son,
The Rev. Edward Lockwood, b. 6 Jan. 1720; adm. Westminster April 1727; St. John's Coll. Oxford, B.A. 1740, M.A. (from All Souls Coll.) 1744; Rector of Hanwell, co. Oxon, and of St. Peter's, Northampton, from 1750; m. (1) 29 Aug. 1752, Lucy, dau. of the Rev. William Dowdeswell, Rector of Kingham, co. Oxford (A.Q.S. at Westminster in 1703); (2) 23 Feb. 1770, Elizabeth, dau. of Joseph Percival, of Stapleton, co. Gloucester; and (3) 3 Nov. 1772, Judith, dau. and coheiress of John Bedingfeld, of Bedston, St. Andrews, co. Norfolk, and widow of Sir John Rous, 5th Bt. (Stradbrooke, E.). The Rev. Edward Lockwood d. 22 Jan. 1802, having had issue of his first marriage,
1. William Joseph (see below).
2. Edward Lockwood-Perceval, who assumed the additional surname of Perceval, adm. Westminster 26 Jan. 1773, and left 1779; Univ. Coll. Oxford, 1779, aged 17, B.A. 1783. All Souls Coll.; B.C.L. 1786; m. 15 June 1790, Louisa Bridget, dau. of Lord George Manners-Sutton (Portland, D. and in present work, Canterbury, V.). She d. 5 Feb. 1800. He d. 6 July 1804, leaving issue, a 2nd son,
George Harvey Lockwood-Perceval, b. 1 Feb. 1793; at Westminster Sch. 1803-1806; R.M.C. Great Marlow; Ensign 2nd Foot Guards, 1809; Lt. and Capt. 1813; d. 11 Nov. 1815.
3. John Cutts, Rev., adm. Westminster, 1774, left 1780; Ch. Ch. Oxford, matric 1781, aged 18, B.A. 1784; M.A. 1787; Vicar of Yoxford, co. Suffolk, 1793-1816; Rector of Topcroft, co. Norfolk, 1797-1816; Vicar of Croydon, co. Surrey, from 1816; Rector of Coulsdon, from 1820; m. 3 Mar. 1795, Amelia, dau. of Thomas Boddginton, of Clapton, co. Middlesex, and d. 1830, leaving issue, an only son,
John William, Rev., b. 1800; adm. Westminster 1812; left 1816; Ch. Ch. Oxford, B.A. 1821, M.A. 1823; ordained 1826; Vicar of Chalgrove, co. Oxford, 1832; Rector of St. Luke's Chelsea, 1832-36; Rector of Kingham, co. Oxford, from 1836; m. 3 Oct. 1832, Alicia, dau. of Samuel Davis, of Birdhurst, co. Surrey, a Dir. of H.E.I.C.S., and Accountant-Gen. in Bengal; d. 29 Nov. 1879, having had issue,
  1a Henry Boileau, b. 21 Mar. 1840; adm. Westminster, 1853; Q.S. 1855; left 1856; cadet H.E.I.C.S. Bengal 1858; Cornet, 1858; Lt. 4th European Bengal Cavalry, 1858; Capt. 1864; ret. 1875; Gen. Inspector under Local Gov. Board; m. (1) May 1886; (2) 9 Nov. 1912, Frances, eldest dau. of Giffard Rainsford, M.D., of Gloucester Place, Hyde Park, London, and d. 21 Feb. 1919.
  2a Samuel Davis, b. 3 May 1842 (described in *Record of Old*

Westminsters, as 4th son); adm. Westminster, 12 June 1857; but left 1857 (Dec.); Cadet H.E.I.C.S. Bengal, 1859; Cornet, unposted, Cavalry 1859; Lt. 13th Cavalry, 1861; on furlough, 1865; resigned 1867; matric. St. Mary Hall, Oxford 1866; B.A. 1868; ordained 1869; Curate of Kingham, co. Oxford, 1870-71; Rector of Wood Eaton, co. Oxford, 1871-80, and of Kingham, from 1880; m. 30 May 1871, Sophia Theresa, dau. of the Rev. Philip Wynter, D.D., Pres. of St. John's Coll. Oxford, and d. 28 Nov. 1911.

3a Richard Bernard, b. April 1844; adm. Westminster 7 June 1860, left Dec. 1860; Cadet Indian Army, 1860; Cornet 20th Hussars, 1861; Lt. 1864; Capt. 3rd Punjab Cavalry 1873; d. unm. 9 June 1879.

4a Charles Vernon, b. 26 April 1847; adm. Westminster 12 June 1862; left 1864; m. and d. at Madeira, 18 June 1882.

1. Anne, m. (1) George Drake and (2) George Fuller and d.s.p.
2. Frances Dorothy, m. 26 July 1789, Charles Drummond, of London, a banker and d. 24 Feb. 1831, leaving issue, (Perth, E.).

The eldest son,

William Joseph Lockwood, of Dews Hall, co. Essex, b. 1760; adm. Westminster Sch. 1 Feb. 1773; left Aug. 1774; was shot blind at Westminster Sch. in a battle against the mob, (according to Burke's L.G. 1846, p. 757, quoted in *Record of Old Westminsters, Vol. 2*); m. 1 July 1787, Elizabeth only dau. of Capt. Sir Edward Joseph Jekyll, R.N., and d. 9 Oct. 1801, having by her (who d. 12 May 1790) had issue, an only son,

William Joseph Lockwood, of Dews Hall, and Bishop's Hall, co. Essex, Capt. Coldstream Guards, and Verderer, of Epping Forest; m. 13 June 1816, Rachel, dau. of Sir Mark Wood, 1st Bt., of Gatton, co. Surrey. She d. 1874. He d. 16 Sept. 1854. Their issue were,

1. William Mark (see below).
2. George, Capt. 8th Hussars, A.D.C. to Lord Cardigan, k. in action in the charge of the Light Brigade at Balaclava, 25 Oct. 1854.
1. Helen Maria, d. unm. 9 Feb. 1899.
2. Georgiana Matilda Josephine, m. 16 May 1855, Adm. Sir George Ommaney Willes, G.C.B. She d. 1912.

The elder son,

Lt. Gen. William Mark Lockwood, afterwards Wood, a surname which he assumed in 1828 under the will of his maternal uncle, Sir Mark Wood, 2nd Bt. who d.s.p. He was b. 11 Mar. 1817, was of Bishop's Hall, co. Essex, J.P. and D.L. that county and High Sheriff co. Monmouth, 1847; served in the Crimean War, Coldstream Guards and Col. 67th Regt. He m. 13 June 1846, Amelia Jane, (d. 17 Oct. 1898) dau. of Sir Robert Williams, 9th Bt., (Williams-Bulkeley, Bt.), and d. 18 Mar. 1883, having had,

1. Amelius Richard Mark, **Baron Lambourne** (see below).

2. William Robert Percival Lockwood, the surname which he resumed in 1887, in lieu of Wood, of Rose Court, Havering, Romford, co. Essex, b. 9 Aug. 1851; Capt. 4th Bn. Oxford L.I.; m. 6 June 1876, Chinty Mary Catherine, dau. of Gen. Corbet Cotton (Combermere, V.) and had issue,
   (1) Richard William Mark, 2nd Lt. Coldstream Guards, b. 28 Mar. 1891; k. in action 20 Sept. 1914.
   (1) Gwendoline Yolande Matilda, m. 3 June 1902, William Lowther Lysley, of Pewsham, Chippenham, co. Wilts.
   (2) Rachel Jannette Augusta.
   (3) Chinty Helen Charlotte, m. 18 Nov. 1909, Charles Farquhar de Paravicini, and had issue (see B.L.G. Supplement 1954 De Paravicini).
   (4) Oilve Eleanor Isobel, m. 20 May 1916. Capt. C. Lambton, and had issue, (Durham, E.).
1. Amy Rachel.

The elder son,

Amelius Richard Mark Lockwood, **Baron Lambourne**, b. 17 Aug. 1847; assumed surname of Lockwood in lieu of that of Wood in 1876; educ. Eton; joined, Coldstream Guards, 1866; A.D.C. to Gen. Newton cmdg. Dublin Div.; served on staff of Lord Lt. of Ireland; ret. as Capt. and Lt. Col. 1883; M.P. for E. Epping Div. of Essex, 1892-1917; Prov. Grand Master of Essex Freemasons, 1902; P.C. 1905; Vice Pres. R.S.P.C.A., Lord Lt. of Essex, 1919; cr. C.V.O. 1905; a peer as Baron Lambourne, of Lambourne, co. Essex, 19 June 1917; and G.C.V.O. 1927; m. 20 July 1876, Isabella, (d. 22 Sept. 1923), dau. of Sir John Ralph Milbanke-Huskisson, 8th Bt., (Milbanke, Bt.), and d.s.p. 26 Dec. 1928.

ARMS—Argent an oak tree vert, eradicated and fructed ppr. between three martlets sable.

CREST—Upon waves of the sea a frigate under sail ppr.

SUPPORTERS—On either side a sailor of the early 19th century ppr. cap and jacket vert, lapels, cuffs and trousers argent.

MOTTO—Tutus in undis.

The seat of Lord Lambourne was Bishop's Hall, Romford, Essex.

LAMBURY

PEERAGE—U.K. Baron Lambury of Northfield, co. Warwick.

SURNAME—Lord.

CR.—20 Mar. 1962. **EXT.**—13 Sept. 1967.

HISTORY—William Lord, of Coventry, co. Warwick, b. 1867; educ. Old Bablake Sch. Coventry; m. 1888 Emma, dau. of George Swain of Coventry, and d. 26 Nov. 1911. She d. 9 May 1938. They had issue, with a dau., Annie Florence (m. Benjamin Blunderstone and d. 1963, leaving one son) a son,

Sir Leonard Percy Lord, **Baron Lambury,** b. 15 Nov. 1896; educ. Bablake Sch. Coventry; M.I.M.E., apprenticed at Courtaulds, Coventry; Man. Dir. Morris Motors Ltd. 1932-36, Works Dir. Austin Motor Co. 1938-41, Dep. Chm. and Jt. Man. Dir. 1941-45, Chm. and Man. Dir. 1945, Dep. Chm. and Man. Dir. British Motor Corp. 1951. Chm. and Man. Dir. 1952-58, Exec. Chm. 1958-61, Vice Pres.

1961, Pres. Dir. and Consultant 1963. He m. 16 July 1921, Ethel Lily, dau. of George Horton of Coventry. He was cr. K.B.E. 1954 and Baron Lambury of Northfield, co. Warwick 20 Mar. 1962. He d. 13 Sept. 1967. He had issue three daus.

1. Joan Marguerite m. 1951 (m. diss. by div. 1965) M. L. Breeden and had issue; she m. 2ndly A. J. Macdonald;
2. Patricia Anne, m. 1951 (m. diss. by div. 1968) Cmdr. M. J. Howard-Smith, R.N. and had issue;
3. Pauline Ruth, m. 1954 John Pither and had issue.

ARMS—Vert a lion rampant or, on a chief gules three winged wheels of the second.
CREST—A representation of a 15th century church tower and spire between two smaller like towers and spires ppr.
SUPPORTERS—Dexter, A bay horse ppr; Sinister, A Hereford bull ppr.

Lord Lambury lived at Warren's Gorse, Cirencester, co. Gloucester.

LAMINGTON

PEERAGE—U.K. Baron Lamington of Lamington, co. Lanark.
SURNAME—Cochrane-Baillie.
CR.—3 May 1880. EXT.—20 Sept. 1951.
HISTORY—Adm. of the Fleet, Sir Thomas John Cochrane, grandson of the 8th Earl of Dundonald (see current peerages) b. 5 Feb. 1789; m. (1) 6 Jan. 1872, Matilda, dau. of Lt. Gen. Sir Charles Lockhart Ross, 7th Bt. She d. 4 Sept. 1819. He m. (2) 8 Jan. 1853, Rosetta (d. 1901) dau. of Sir J. D. Wheeler-Cuffe, 1st Bt., and d. 19 Oct. 1872. (Lady Cochrane, Sir Thomas's first wife was the granddau. of Adm. Sir John Lockhart Ross, 6th Bt., by Elizabeth Dundas, his wife, the heiress of Lamington, and also heiress of her mother, Henrietta, dau. and heiress of Sir James Carmichael of Bonnington by Margaret his wife, dau. and heiress of William Baillie of Lamington. She assumed the additional surname of Wishart and d. 4 Sept. 1819). Sir Thomas Cochrane's eldest son by his first marriage therefore bore the following surnames,

Alexander Dundas Ross Cochrane-Wishart-Baillie, **1st Baron Lamington**, so cr. 3 May 1880, b. 24 Nov. 1816; M.P. Bridport 1841-52, co. Lanark 1857, Honiton 1959-68 and Isle of Wight 1870-80, m. 4 Dec. 1844, Annabella Mary Elizabeth, dau. of A. R. Drummond of Cadlands, Southampton, (Perth, E.) and d. 15 Feb. 1890, having had issue, with three daus., an only son,

Sir Charles Wallace Alexander Napier Cochrane-Baillie, **2nd Baron Lamington**, G.C.M.G., G.C.I.E., M.P. St. Pancras 1886-90, Gov. of Queensland 1895-1901, and of Bombay 1903-07, b. 29 July 1860; m. 13 June 1895, Mary Haughton, dau. of only Baron Newlands and d. 16 Sept. 1940, having with one dau., Grisell m. Capt. E. G. G. Hastings R.N. (Huntingdon, E.), an only son,

Victor Alexander Brisbane William Cochrane-Baillie, **3rd Baron Lamington**, b. 23 July 1896, educ. Eton and Ch. Ch. Oxford, served in World War I, 1914-17 (wounded twice, despatches, M.C., Capt. Scots Guards)

m. 8 June 1922, Riette, dau. of D. A. Neilson and d. 20 Sept. 1951.
ARMS—Quarterly 1 and 4, Azure nine estoiles of six points wavy, three, three, two and one (Baillie); 2 and 3, Argent a chevron gules between three boars' heads erased azure langued gules, on a chief wavy azure a sphinx couchant of the field.
CRESTS—(1) (On the dexter side) Issuing out of a naval crown or, a dexter arm embowed vested azure cuffed argent the hand holding a flagstaff ppr. thereon hoisted the flag of a rear adm. of the white, being argent a cross gules and thereon the words 'St. Domingo' in letters of gold. (2) (In the centre) A boar's head erased ppr. (3) A horse passant argent.
SUPPORTERS—On either side a boar ppr. gorged with a collar or pendent therefrom an escutcheon of the arms of Baillie.
MOTTO—Quid clarius astris.

The seat of Lord Lamington was Lamington, co. Lanark.

LANG OF LAMBETH

PEERAGE—U.K. Baron Lang of Lambeth, of Lambeth, co. Surrey.
SURNAME—Lang.
CR.—2 April 1942. EXT.—5 Dec. 1945.
HISTORY—A connected genealogy of the Lang family of this line is not available, but the following details are gleaned from the authoritative biography of the Archbishop Lord Lang of Lambeth, *Cosmo Gordon Lang*, by J. G. Lockhart, 1949. There it is stated (page 1, chapter 1) that John Marshal Lang, the Archbishop's father, was "of good Scottish stock, stemming back on one side to a certain David Marshal, a surgeon in the Royal Navy in the early years of the 18th century. When David left the Service, he settled down on a property at Neilsand, in Lanarkshire. He and his wife, Anna Weir, had one son, also David, who in turn had another son, John, grandfather of the Minister of Fyvie" (i.e. John Marshall Lang). "This John Marshall married Elizabeth Stobie, of Luscar in Fife, a property which had been in the Stobie family since the reign of Charles II. A Stobie fought at Bothwell Brig. (on the Covenanting side), . . . John and Elizabeth Marshall had one child, a daughter, Anna, by name, who was born in 1807, and married Gavin Lang, Minister of the Parish of Glassford, a windswept village between Hamilton and Strathaven in the Middle Ward of Lanarkshire. Of the Langs nothing seems to be known, beyond the solitary fact that Gavin's father was a West India merchant."

The Very Rev. John Marshall Lang, was the second son of the Rev. Gavin Lang and Anna Robertson (so named in other references) Marshall of Nielsand. He was b. 14 May 1834; m. 1861 (in J. G. Lockhart the date is given as 1859) Hannah Agnes, dau. of the Rev. P. Hay Leith, D.D., Min. of Hamilton, and had issue, six sons and a dau. He was cr. C.V.O., was D.D., LL.D., Principal of Aberdeen Univ., and lived at Chanonry Lodge, Old Aberdeen. He d. 2 May 1909, and his third son was,

Cosmo Gordon Lang, **Baron Lang** of Lambeth, b. 31 Oct. 1864; educ. Glasgow Univ.

and Balliol Coll. Oxford, B.A. 1885; M.A. 1888; Fell. All Souls, Oxford, 1889-93, and 1896-1928, Visitor, 1928-42; Fell. Magdalen Coll. Oxford, 1893-96; was a student of the Inner Temple, 1883-89; was received into the Church of England and confirmed by the Bishop of Lincoln, 1889; went to Cuddesdon Theological Coll. was ordained deacon 1890, became curate of Leeds Parish Church, 1890-93; ordained priest, 1891; Examining Chaplain to Bishop of Lichfield, 1893-95; Fell. and Dean of Divinity of Magdalen Coll. Oxford, 1893-96; Vicar of St. Mary's Oxford 1894-96; Examining Chaplain to Bishop of Oxford, 1894-1901; Vicar of Portsea, and Chaplain to Kingston Prison, 1896-1901; Hon. Chaplain to Queen Victoria, 1899-1901; Canon and Treasurer of St. Paul's 1901-09; consec. Bishop of Stepney, 1901; enthroned as 89th Archbishop of York, 1909, and trans. as 95th Archbishop of Canterbury 1928. He resigned the see 1942. Apptd. Lord High Almoner, 1933; was mem. Council of State 1928-29; a Prin. Trustee of Brit. Museum, 1928-42; made P.C. 1909; given Royal Victorian Chain, 1923; cr. G.C.V.O. 1937 and Baron Lang of Lambeth, of Lambeth, co. Surrey, 2 April 1942, following the precedent by which Archbishop Davidson had been cr. a temporal lord. He d. unm. 5 Dec. 1945.

For an interesting comment on the career of the Archbishop during the abdication crisis of Edward VIII's reign there is the Duke of Windsor's own statement (contained in his book, *A King's Story*, 1951, in which, after referring to the opposition of the then Prime Minister and other senior Ministers to his projected marriage, he wrote: "Behind them, I suspected, was a shadowy, hovering presence, the Archbishop of Canterbury. Curiously enough, I did not once see him throughout this period. He stood aside until the fateful fabric had been woven and the crisis was over. Yet from beginning to end I had a disquieting feeling that he was invisibly and noiselessly about." (p. 331).

ARMS—Parted per pale and per fess, the latter indented argent and sable, in the first quarter a book expanded ppr. leaved gules and in the fourth quarter two dock leaves vert.
CREST—A tower argent masoned sable.

LATHOM

PEERAGE—U.K. Earl of Lathom, co. Lancaster.
SURNAME—Bootle-Wilbraham.
CR.—3 May 1880. EXT.—6 Feb. 1930.
HISTORY—Edward Bootle-Wilbraham, was cr. 30 Jan. 1828, Baron Skelmersdale, (see that title in extant peerages), and had, with other issue by his wife, Mary Elizabeth, dau. of Rev. Edward Taylor, an eldest son, Richard, M.P. b. 1801, and d.v.p. 5 May 1844, leaving by his wife, Jessy, dau. of Sir Richard Brooke, 6th Bt., an only son,
Edward, **1st Earl of Lathom** (see below).
The 1st Baron Skelmersdale d. 3 April 1853, and was s. by his grandson,
Edward Bootle-Wilbraham, **1st Earl of Lathom,** and 2nd Baron Skelmersdale, was b. 12 Dec. 1837; educ. Eton and Ch. Ch. Oxford, was a Lord in Waiting 1866-68, and

Capt. of the Yeomen of the Guard, 1874-80; was made P.C. 1874, cr. Earl of Lathom, co. Lancaster, 3 May 1880, and G.C.B. 1892. He m. 16 Aug. 1860, Alice, dau. of George Villiers, 4th Earl of Clarendon, and by her (who was k. in a carriage accident, 23 Nov. 1897) had with other issue,
Edward George Bootle-Wilbraham, **2nd Earl of Lathom,** and 3rd Baron Skelmersdale, b. 26 Oct. 1864; educ. Eton; Major Royal Horse Guards, 1896-97; m. 15 Aug. 1889, Wilma, dau. of William Pleydell-Bourverie, 5th Earl of Radnor, and d. 15 Mar. 1910, having had by her (who m. 2ndly, 1912, Lt. Gen. Sir Henry Merrick Lawson, and d. 10 Feb. 1931) with three daus.,
Edward William Bootle-Wilbraham, **3rd Earl of Lathom,** and 4th Baron Skelmersdale, b. 16 May 1895; educ. Eton; served in World War I, 1914-18, Capt. Lancs. Hussars, and was A.D.C. to Gov. of Bombay, 1916-18; m. 2 Nov. 1927, Marie Xenia, dau. of E. W. de Tunzelman, of Singapore, and formerly wife of William Morrison, and d.s.p. 6 Feb. 1930, when the earldom became extinct and the Barony of Skelmersdale passed to his kinsman, Capt. Arthur George Bootle-Wilbraham, who became 5th Baron Skelmersdale.
ARMS—Quarterly 1 and 4, Argent three bendlets wavy azure (Wilbraham); 2 and 3, Gules, on a chevron engrailed between three combs argent, as many crosses patée fitchée of the field (Bootle).
CRESTS—1, A wolf's head erased argent (Wilbraham); 2, A demi-lion reguardant ppr. holding between his paws an escutcheon gules, charged with a cross flory argent (Bootle).
SUPPORTERS—Dexter, A wolf argent gorged with a collar azure pendent therefrom an escutcheon, the field azure, charged with two bars argent, a canton sable thereon a wolf's head erased silver, being the ancient arms of Wilbraham; Sinister, A wolf ppr. collared or, and therefrom pendent an escutcheon as the dexter.
MOTTO—In portu quies.
The Earls seat was Lathom House, Ormskirk, Lancashire. His town residence was 21 Eaton Terrace, London, S.W.

LAUDERDALE

PEERAGE—U.K. Baron Lauderdale, of Thirlestane, co. Berwick.
SURNAME—Maitland.
CR.—22 Feb. 1806. EXT.—22 Mar. 1863.
HISTORY—James Maitland, 8th Earl of Lauderdale, (see extant peerage works), was b. 26 Jan. 1759; was educ. Trin. Coll. Oxford, the Univs. of Edinburgh, Glasgow and Paris; a student of Lincoln's Inn, and a Mem. of the Faculty of Avocates, 1780; sat as M.P. for Newport, Cornwall, 1780-84; and for Malmesbury, 1784-89; was a Representative Peer for Scotland, 1790-96; was cr. a peer of the U.K. as **Baron Lauderdale** of Thirlestane, co. Berwick, 22 Feb. 1806; made P.C. 1806, (and resworn 1826); cr. K.T. 1821. He m. 15 Aug. 1782, Eleanor, dau. of Anthony Todd, and d. 15 Sept. 1839. She d. 16 Sept. 1856. Their children were: (with two daus. and other issue),
 1. James, 9th Earl and **2nd Baron** (see below).

2. Anthony, 10th Earl and **3rd Baron** (see below).

The elder son,

James Maitland, 9th Earl of Lauderdale, and **2nd Baron Lauderdale** of Thirlestane, b. 12 Feb. 1784; educ. Eton and Edinburgh Univ.; sat as Whig M.P. for Camelford, 1806-07, for Richmond, 1818-20, and as a Tory for Appleby, 1826-32; was Lord Lt. of Berwickshire, 1841-60; d. unm. 22 Aug. 1860, being s. by his brother,

Anthony Maitland, 10th Earl of Lauderdale, and **3rd Baron Lauderdale** of Thirlestane, b. 10. June 1785; served in the R.N., and was severely wounded in action against Boulogne flotilla, Aug. 1801; Adm. of the Red, 1862; Whig M.P. for Haddington Burghs, 1813-18, and as Tory for Berwickshire, 1826-32; cr. C.B. 1816; K.C.M.G. 1820; K.C.B. 1832; and G.C.B. 1862. On his death unm. 22 Mar. 1863, the barony of Lauderdale of Thirlestane became extinct and he was s. in the Earldom and his other titles, by his first cousin,

Thomas Maitland, 11th Earl of Lauderdale, etc.

LAWRENCE OF KINGSGATE

PEERAGE—U.K. Baron Lawrence of Kingsgate, of Holland House, Kingsgate, co. Kent.
SURNAME—Lawrence.
CR.—23 July 1923. EXT.—17 Dec. 1927.
HISTORY—Lord Lawrence of the Punjab, and of Gratley, co. Southampton, had with other issue (see extant peerages, Lawrence, B. and Lawrence of Lucknow, Bt.) a third son,

Charles Napier Lawrence, **Baron Lawrence** of Kingsgate, of Holland House, Kingsgate, co. Kent, so. cr. 23 July 1923, was b. 27 May 1855; educ. Marlborough; Dir. of L.N.W.R. from 1884, Chm. 1921-23; First Chm. of London Midland and Scottish Railway, 1923-24; Chm. of Antofagasta and Bolivia Railway; Chm. of North British and Mercantile Insurance Co.; served on several Royal Commissions; m. 22 June 1881, Catherine, dau. of F. W. Sumner, of New York, and niece of James Gerard, sometime American Ambassador in London. Lord Lawrence d.s.p. 17 Dec. 1927. His widow d. 7 Nov. 1934.
ARMS—Ermine on a cross raguly gules an eastern crown or, on a chief azure two swords in saltire ppr. pommels and hilts gold between as many leopards' heads argent.
CREST—Out of an eastern crown or, a cubit arm entwined by a wreath of laurel and holding a dagger all ppr.
SUPPORTERS—On either side a Bengal tiger reguardant ppr. gorged with an eastern crown or, and charged on the shoulder with a lotus flower ppr.
MOTTO—Be ready.

LAWSON

PEERAGE—U.K. Baron Lawson, of Beamish, co. Durham.
SURNAME—Lawson.
CR.—17 Mar. 1950. EXT.—3 Aug. 1965.
HISTORY—John Lawson of Whitehaven, co. Cumberland, was father of John James

Lawson, **Baron Lawson**, b. 16 Oct. 1881, began working life in 1893 at Boldon Colliery, co. Durham, served in World War I with R.F.A.; M.P. for Chester-le-Street Div. of co. Durham 1919-49; was Dep. Regnl. Commr. C.D. Northern Region 1939-44, Vice Chm. British Council, 1944 and Sec. of State for War 1945-46. He was made P.C., 1945, was K. St. J., and created Baron Lawson of Beamish, co. Durham, 17 Mar. 1950. He m. 1906, Isabella, dau. of Robert Scott, and d. 3 Aug. 1965, leaving three daus.,

1. Irene, b. 1909; m. 1935, C. F. C. Lawson and had issue.
2. Edna, b. 1912; m. D. Brown and had issue,
3. Alma, b. 1920.

LEE OF FAREHAM

PEERAGE—U.K. Baron Lee of Fareham and Viscount Lee of Fareham, of Bridport, co. Dorset and of Chequers, co. Buckingham.
SURNAME—Lee.
CR.—Barony 9 July 1918. Viscounty 28 Nov. 1922. EXT.—21 July 1947.
HISTORY—The Rev. Melville Lauriston Lee, Rector of Bridport, co. Dorset, m. Emily Winter, dau. of Thomas Dicker, of Lewes, and d. 1870. She d. 2 Sept. 1918. They had issue, with others, a ygr. son,

Sir Arthur Hamilton Lee, **Baron Lee** of Fareham, and **Viscount Lee** of Fareham, b. 8 Nov. 1868; educ. Cheltenham and R.M.A. Woolwich; joined R.A. 1888; Adj. Hong Kong Vols. 1889-90; Adj. R.A. Isle of Wight Western Defences, 1891-93; Prof. of Strategy and Tactics, Royal Mil. Coll. Kingston, Canada, 1893-98; organised Mil Survey of the Canadian Frontier, 1894-96; served with the U.S. Army in the Spanish American War, 1898 as Brit. Mil. Attaché, received American War Medal; Capt. 1898; Mil. Attaché, and Lt. Col., Washington, 1899; Brev. Major, 1900, and retired from Army; M.P. Fareham Div. Hampshire, 1900-18; Civil Lord of the Admiralty, 1903-05; served on many commissions and cttees; served in World War I, 1914-15, (despatches twice, Col.,), Parl. Mil. Sec. to Ministry of Munitions, 1915-16, and Pers. Mil. Sec. to Sec. of State for War, 1916; Dir. Gen. of Food Production, 1917-18; was cr. K.C.B. 1916; Baron Lee of Fareham, of Chequers, co. Buckingham, 9 July 1918; G.B.E. 1918; P.C. 1919; Viscount Lee of Fareham, of Bridport, co. Dorset, 28 Nov. 1922; G.C.S.I. 1925; G.C.V.O. 1929; K.J. St. J.; was Min. of Agriculture and Fisheries, 1919-21; First Lord of the Admiralty, 1921-22; Pres. of Royal Hospital and Home for Incurables, Putney, and holder of many other similar posts. He m. 23 Dec. 1899, Ruth, D.G. St. J., dau. of J. G. Moore, of New York, and d.s.p. 21 July 1947. Lord and Lady Lee gave in Oct. 1920, the estate of Chequers to the nation as a residence for Prime Ministers.
ARMS—Argent two chevronels between three leopards' faces sable, in the centre point an inescutcheon chequy or and purpure.
CREST—On a naval coronet or a leopard's face sable.
SUPPORTERS—Dexter, A female figure ppr. habited argent, holding in her exterior hand a

sheaf of wheat also ppr; Sinister, A like figure charged on the breast with a Latin cross gules and holding in her exterior hand a grenade fired or.

MOTTO—Pro patria omnia.

LEEDS

PEERAGE—Scotland—Viscount Oseburne (i.e. Osborne) of Dunblane, 2 Feb. 1672/3.
England—Baron Osborne of Kiveton, co. York and Viscount Latimer of Danby co. York. 15 Aug. 1673.
England—Earl of Danby, co. York 27 June 1674. Marquess of Carmarthen 9 April 1689. Duke of Leeds, 4 May 1694.
United Kingdom—Baron Goldolphin, 14 May 1832. (Also a Baronetcy cr. 13 July 1620).

SURNAME—Osborne.

CR.—As above. All EXT.—20 Mar. 1964.

HISTORY—"Each age in our history has contributed to the growth of the peerage. As each social class has arisen to respect ability and wealth it has claimed its perquisites, and among these has been the coronet. The Osbornes were a family of merchants in London, and the second man on their pedigree roll was Sir Edward Osborne, Lord Mayor of London in 1583. From then on they did not lack a title in any generation, and the Lord Mayor's great-grandson became the first Duke of Leeds".

Sir Edward Osborne, knighted 1583/4, on becoming Lord Mayor of London, was the son of Richard Osborne and m. Anna, dau. of Sir William Hewett, Lord Mayor of London 1559. (He had saved his master's daughter from the Thames and eventually married her.) He d. 1591 having had with other issue, an elder son,

Sir Hewett Osborne, Kt., of Kiveton, co. York, knighted by the Earl of Essex in Ireland, 1599. He was bapt. 13 Mar. 1566/7, m. Joice, dau. of Thomas Fleetwood, Master of the Mint, and d. Sept. 1599 having had issue, an only son,

Sir Edward Osborne, 1st Bt., so cr. 13 July 1620, b. 1596; m. (1) 1618 Margaret (d. 7 Nov. 1624) dau. of 1st Viscount Fauconberg, and had issue by her, a son Edward, who d. young, being killed by the fall of some chimneys at his home, 1638. Sir Edward m. (2) Anne, widow of William Middleton and dau. of Thomas Walmsley (by Eleanor, his wife, sister of the Earl of Danby and dau. of Sir John Danvers, by Elizabeth his wife, dau. and co-heir of 4th Lord Latymer). Sir Edward d. 9 Sept. 1647 having had by his second marriage an only son,

Sir Thomas Osborne, 2nd Bt., and 1st Duke of Leeds, K.G., a prominent statesman in the reigns of Charles II and William III. Lord High Treasurer of England, 1673-79, and Lord Pres. of the Council 1689-95. He received the grant of every rank in the peerage. He was cr. Viscount Oseburne of Dunblane in the peerage of Scotland, 2 Feb. 1672/3; Baron Osborne of Kiveton and Viscount Latimer of Danby, co. York in the peerage of England, 15 Aug. 1673, and Earl of Danby 27 June 1674; Marquess of Carmarthen 9 April 1689 and Duke of Leeds, 4 May 1694, these three dignities being also in the peerage of England.

In 1675 he was cr. K.G. The Duke m. 1651, Bridget (d. 1704) dau. of Montague Bertie, 2nd Earl of Lindsey, and d. 26 July 1712, having had with other male issue who d. young, and five daus., a surviving son,

Peregrine Osborne, 2nd Duke of Leeds, summoned to the House of Lords as Baron Osborne of Kiveton in his father's lifetime and became on 5 Dec. 1674 Viscount Osborne of Dunblane his father having surrendered that dignity in his favour in Aug. 1673. He m. 25 April 1682 Bridget, only dau. and heiress of Sir Thomas Hyde, Bt., and d. 25 June 1729 having had with other issue, a second and surviving son,

Peregrine Hyde Osborne, 3rd Duke of Leeds, having been previously summoned to Parliament as Lord Osborne, b. 11 Nov. 1691; m. (1) 16 Dec. 1712 Elizabeth (d. 1713) dau. of Robert Earl of Oxford; (2) 17 Sept. 1719 Anne (d. 1722), dau. of 6th Duke of Somerset, by whom he had no surviving children, and (3) 9 April 1725, Juliana, dau. and co-heiress of Roger Hele. The Duke d. 9 May 1731, being s. by the only son of his first marriage,

Thomas Osborne, 4th Duke of Leeds, K.G., b. 6 Nov. 1713; m. 21 June 1740 Mary, dau. and sole heiress of 2nd Earl of Godolphin and d. 23 Mar. 1789 being s. by his only son,

Francis Goldolphin Osborne, 5th Duke of Leeds, K.G., Foreign Sec. b. 29 Jan. 1751; m. (1) 29 Nov. 1773, Amelia, Baroness Conyers, only dau. of 4th Earl of Holderness and Baron Conyers, and had issue,

1. George William Frederick, 6th Duke (see below).
2. Francis Godolphin, 1st Baron Godolphin of Farnham Royal co. Buckingham which he was cr. 14 May 1832 in the peerage of the U.K. He was b. 18 Oct. 1777; m. 31 Mar. 1800, Hon. Elizabeth Eden, dau. of 1st Baron Auckland and d. 15 Feb. 1850 having had with other issue (d.s.p.),
   (1) George Godolphin, 2nd Baron Godolphin, 8th Duke of Leeds (see below).
   (2) William Godolphin m. 3 times but d.s.p. 28 Dec. 1888.
   (3) Sydney Godolphin, Rev. B.A., b. 5 Feb. 1808; m. 29 May 1834, Emily Charlotte dau. of Pascoe Grenfell (see Desborough, B.) and d. 9 May 1889, having had with other issue, d. unm. or d.s.p. an eldest son,
   Francis D'Arcy Godolphin, Sir, 12th Duke of Leeds (see below).

The first marriage of the 5th Duke was diss. by Act of Parliament, May 1779. Baroness Conyers then m. John Byron, father of the poet by a second marriage. The Duke m. (2) 11 Oct. 1788, Catherine, dau. of Thomas Anguish by whom he had a son, Sidney Godolphin (b. 1789, d. 1861) and a dau. The 5th Duke d. 31 Jan. 1799 being s. by his eldest son,

George William Frederick Osborne, 6th Duke of Leeds, Master of the Horse, 4 May, P.C. 10 May, and K.G. 10 May, all in 1827. He was b. 21 July 1775, s. his mother on her death in 1784 as 10th Baron Conyers; m. 17 Aug. 1797, Charlotte, dau. of 1st Marquess Townshend and had issue,

1. Francis Godolphin D'Arcy, 7th Duke (see below).

2. Conyers George Thomas William, b. 6 May 1812, d. unm. 16 Feb. 1831 being k. accidently while wrestling at Oxford.
1. Charlotte Mary Anne Georgiana, m. 22 May 1826, Sackville Lane Fox and d. 17 Jan. 1836, having had with other issue, Sackville George Lane Fox who eventually became 12th Baron Conyers (see current peerages Yarborough, E.), The 6th Duke d. 10 July 1838 and was s. by his only s. son,
Francis Godolphin D'Arcy Osborne, **7th Duke of Leeds,** b. 21 May 1798; summoned to the House of Lords on 23 June 1838 as Baron Osborne. He m. 24 April 1828, Louisa Catherine, dau. of Richard Caton of Maryland, and widow of Sir F. Bathurst-Hervey, Bt. She d. 1874. The 6th Duke d.s.p. 4 May 1859 when the Barony of Conyers devolved upon his nephew Sackville George Lane Fox (see above), but all his other honours were inherited by his first cousin and heir male,
George Godolphin Osborne, **2nd Baron Godolphin** and **8th Duke of Leeds.** He was b. 16 July 1802; m. 21 Oct. 1824, Harriette Emma Arundel Stewart and d. 8 Aug. 1872, having had issue with four daus.,
 1. George Godolphin, **9th Duke** (see below).
 2. Francis George Godolphin, Rev. M.A. Camb. b. 6 April 1830; m. 4 July 1854, Matilda Rich and d. 6 Mar. 1907, having had issue a dau. Harriet.
 3. D'Arcy Godolphin, Major 87th Foot, b. 14 June 1834; m. 6 Dec. 1887, Annie Allhusen, widow of Robert Laycock, and d.s.p. 20 Mar. 1895.
 4. William Godolphin, b. 28 Aug. 1835; m. 8 Sept. 1859, Mary Catherine dau. of John Headley, and d. 26 Dec. 1885, having had issue with a dau. Charlotte, a son William D'Arcy Godolphin (1860-87).
The 8th Duke was s. by his eldest son,
George Godolphin Osborne, **9th Duke of Leeds,** b. 11 Aug. 1828, m. 16 Jan. 1861, Fanny Georgiana, dau. of 4th Baron Rivers. She d. 26 Oct. 1896, he d. 23 Dec. 1895. They had issue with one other son d. in infancy and five daus.,
 1. George Godolphin, **10th Duke** (see below).
 2. Francis Granville Godolphin, Capt. R.N., b. 11 Mar. 1864; m. 25 Nov. 1896, Blanche Ruth Tatton, dau. of Adm. W. S. Grieve (see B.L.G. 1952 Tatton Brown of Westgate Wood) and d. 17 Oct. 1924.
 3. Albert Edward Godolphin, b. 10 April 1866; d. unm. 30 June 1914.
The 9th Duke was s. by his eldest son,
George Godolphin Osborne, **10th Duke of Leeds,** M.P. Brixton 1887-95, Capt. R.N.V.R., Lt. Yorkshire Hussars, A.D.C. to George V 1921-22, b. 18 Sept. 1862; m. 12 Feb. 1884, Lady Katherine Lambton, dau. of 2nd Earl of Durham. She d. 1952. The Duke d. 10 May 1927, having had issue with four daus., a son,
John Francis Godolphin Osborne, **11th Duke of Leeds,** b. 12 Mar. 1901; educ. Eton and Jesus Coll. Camb.; m. (1) 27 Mar. 1933 (m. diss. by div. 1948) Irma Amelia, dau. of Iskender de Malkhozouny of Paris, formerly m. to Paul Brewster; m. (2) 21 Dec. 1948 (m. diss. by div. 1955) Audrey, dau. of Brig. Desmond Young and formerly m. to A. E. B.

Williams; m. (3) 22 Feb. 1955, Caroline Fleur, dau. of Col. H. M. Vatcher and d. July 1963, leaving by his second marriage a dau. Camilla Dorothy Godolphin, b. 14 Aug. 1950. He was s. by his kinsman,
Sir Francis D'Arcy Godolphin Osborne K.C.M.G., **12th Duke of Leeds,** formerly Envoy Extra. and Min. Plen. at Washington (1931-35) and with the Holy See (1936-47), b. 16 Sept. 1884, d. 20 Mar. 1964.
ARMS—Quarterly 1 and 4, Quarterly ermine and azure, overall, a cross or (Osborne). 2, Gules an eagle with two heads, displayed between three fleur-de-lis argent; 3, Sable a lion rampant argent on a canton of the last a cross gules.
CRESTS—1. An heraldic tiger passant, or, tufted and maned sable (Osborne). 2. A dolphin, embowed sable (Godolphin).
SUPPORTERS—Dexter, A griffin or; Sinister, An heraldic tiger argent, each gorged with a ducal coronet azure.
MOTTO—Pax in bello.
The residences of the 11th Duke were Melbourne House, St. John, Jersey, C.I. and La Falaise, Roquebrune, Cap Martin, A.M. France.

LEIGHTON

PEERAGE—U.K. Baron Leighton of Stretton, co. Salop. (Also a Baronetcy cr. 11 Feb. 1886.)
SURNAME—Leighton.
CR.—24 Jan. 1896. **EXT.**—25 Jan. 1896.
HISTORY—Sir James Boniface Leighton, of Greenford, co. Middlesex, and Thearne, co. York, Physician to the Tzar and Tzarina of Russia, and Physician Gen. to the Imperial Fleet of Russia, was b. 1769; cr. Kt. Bach. at St. James's Palace, 27 Oct. 1830; m. Frances, dau. of Edward I'Anson, of London, and d. 7 Mar. 1843, having by her (who d. Jan. 1853 aged 83) with other issue, an only son,
Frederick Septimus Leighton, M.D., of Kensington Park Gardens, London, m. 24 June 1826, Augusta Susan, dau. of George Augustus Nash, of Edmonton, co. Middlesex, by Lydia Watson, his wife, and d. 24 Jan. 1892, aged 92, having had by her (who was b. 28 Dec. 1805),
 1. Frederick, Sir, Bt. and **Baron Leighton** (see below).
 1. Alexandra, b. 23 Dec. 1828; bapt. at St. Petersburg 29 Jan. following, the Empress of Russia being godmother; m. 7 Mar. 1857, Major Sutherland Orr, 3rd Regt. Nizam's Cavalry, Hyderabad contingency.
 2. Augusta Winnburg, b. 10 Sept. 1835; m. 9 May 1859, Arthur Matthews, of Florence, Italy. He d. Dec. 1882.
The only son,
Sir Frederic Leighton, **Baron Leighton** of Stretton, co. Salop, b. 3 Dec. 1830; studied painting at academies of Berlin, Florence and Frankfort; exhibited first picture at Royal Academy, 1855; Assoc. R.A. 1864; R.A. 1869; Pres. of Royal Academy, 1878-96; cr. Kt. Bach. at Windsor, 1878; Hon. Col. Artists' Rifles Volunteers; D.C.L. Hon. Oxford, LL.D. Cambridge, and Edinburgh, and Dublin; Assoc. Institute de France, mem.

of several foreign academies, and knight of several foreign orders; cr. a Baronet 11 Feb. 1886; and a Peer 24 Jan. 1896, the letters patent bearing date the day before his death, thus creating the unique distinction of a peerage which endured but for a day, as he d. unm. 25 Jan. 1896. His title was chosen from the ancient possession of the Leightons, (see extant peerages Leighton Bt.) of Stretton, which was acquired in 1383 by John Leighton, but the C.P. adds that Lord Leighton's line had not established descent from this family. In William Gaunt's *Victorian Olympus* there is a full account of Lord Leighten's career.

ARMS—Quarterly per fess raguly or and gules, in the second and third quarters a wyvern of the first.

CREST—Upon a staff raguly fesswise sable, a wyvern ppr. gorged with a chain or, suspended therefrom an escutcheon argent, issuant from the base flames of fire ppr.

MOTTO—Dread shame.

LEITH OF FYVIE

PEERAGE—U.K. Baron Leith of Fyvie, co. Aberdeen.

SURNAME—Forbes-Leith.

CR.—18 Dec. 1905. EXT.—14 Nov. 1925.

HISTORY—Rear Adm. John James Leith, R.N., son of Gen. Alexander Leith-Hay (see Forbes-Leith of Fyvie, Bt. in extant peerages), b. 22 Oct. 1788; m. 27 June, 1843, Margaret, only surv. child of Alexander Forbes, of Blackford, co. Aberdeen, and d. 25 Oct. 1854. She d. 12 April 1899. They had with other issue an eldest son,

Alexander John Forbes-Leith, **Baron Leith** of Fyvie, co. Aberdeen, so. cr. 18 Dec. 1905; b. 6 Aug. 1847; educ. Berlin, St. Cyr, and Dr. Burney's Naval Acad. Gosport, Hampshire; entered R.N. as cadet on board H.M.S. *Britannia*, 1860, and was midshipman on H.M.S. *Zealous*, 1861, served in the operations in New Zealand in 1864-65, and was also awarded the Royal Humane Soc. Medal for saving a boy from drowning (later saving three men from drowning); Lt. R.N. 1869 ret. 1872; held several business appointments in U.S.A., being Pres. of the Joliet Steel Co., of the Illinois Steel Co., and organiser of the Federal Steel Co. He m. 19 Oct. 1871, Marie Louise, dau. of Derick Algernon January, of St. Louis, U.S.A., and d. 14 Nov. 1925. She d. 9 June 1930. They had issue,

Percy, b. 13 Mar. 1881; educ. Eton and R.M.C. Sandhurst; 2nd Lt. 1st Royal Dragoons, 1900, and served in S. African War, where he d. unm. 31 Dec. 1900.

Ethel Louise, O.B.E., b. 10 Aug. 1872; m. 22 July 1921, Col. Sir Charles Rosedew Burn, 1st Bt., who assumed by Royal Licence, 1925, under the will of Lord Leith of Fyvie, the name and arms of Forbes-Leith (see Forbes-Leith, Bt., in extant peerages).

ARMS—Quarterly 1 and 4, Or a cross crosslet fitchée sable between three crescents in chief and as many fusils in base gules (Leith); 2, Quarterly I and IV, Azure on a chevron between three bears' heads couped argent muzzled gules, a man's heart ppr. between two daggers of the first pommelled or (Forbes of Blackford); II, Azure a fess chequy argent and of the first between three boars' heads erased or, within a bordure indented of the second (Gordon of Badenscoth); III, Argent a fir tree growing out of a mount in base vert, surmounted by a sword in bend supporting on the point an imperial crown ppr.; in sinister chief and dexter base a lion's head erased azure (Gregory); 3, Per fess azure and argent, in chief three bears' heads couped of the second muzzled gules and in base as many unicorns' heads erased sable (Forbes of Ballogie).

CRESTS—1. A cross crosslet fitchée sable (motto over—Trustie to the end) 2. A boar's head and neck couped argent muzzled azure (motto over—Spe expecto).

SUPPORTERS—On either side an opinicus sable, beaked and armed gules, winged and crowned with an antique coronet or.

MOTTO—(below the arms) Spes forti viro.

The seat of Lord Fyvie was Fyvie Castle, Fyvie, co. Aberdeen with a residence at Lupton, Churston Ferrers, S. Devon.

LEITRIM

PEERAGE—Ireland. Baron Leitrim of Manor Hamilton, co. Leitrim. Viscount Leitrim, Earl of Leitrim.

U.K. Baron Clements of Kilmacuran, co. Donegal.

SURNAME—Clements.

CR.—Baron Leitrim 11 Oct. 1783. Viscount Leitrim 3 Dec. 1793. Earl of Leitrim 30 Sept. 1795. Baron Clements 20 June 1831.

EXT.—9 June 1952.

HISTORY—Richard Clements of Croft, co. Leicester, d. Feb. 1571/72 leaving with other issue, by Elizabeth his wife,

Robert Clements of Croft, m. (1) Alice (d. 1585) and (2) Margaret and d. 1606 having, with other issue by his first wife,

Richard Clements of Cosby, co. Leicester, m. 2 Mar. 1594/95, Agnes Fellows and d. July 1617 having had with other issue by her (who d. 1619),

Robert Clements of Huncote, co. Leicester and Ansley, co. Warwick, b. 1595; emigrated to New England in 1642; by his first wife Lydia he had with other issue,

Daniel Clements of Rathkenny, co. Cavan, a cornet in the New Model Army who d. 1680 having had by his wife, Elizabeth, an only son,

Robert Clements of Rathkenny, Deputy Vice Treasurer of Ireland, m. Miss Sandford of Moyglare and had with others,

1. Theophilus Clements, of Rathkenny, M.P. Cavan 1713-29, Teller of the Exchequer in Ireland, m. Elizabeth, dau. of Francis Burton of Buncraggy, co. Clare, and d.s.p. before 6 Aug. 1729.
2. Nathaniel (see below).

The yr. son,

The Rt. Hon. Nathaniel Clements, s. to representation of the family, M.P. for Dunleek and later for Cavan and Leitrim, one of the Tellers of the Exchequer and Deputy Vice Treasurer of Ireland; m. 31 Jan. 1729, Hannah, dau. of the Very Rev. William Gore, Dean of Down, and had issue,

1. Robert, **1st Earl of Leitrim** (see below).
2. Henry Theophilus, Rt. Hon., from whom the Clements of Ashfield.

1. Elizabeth, m. 19 Mar. 1750, 2nd Baron Conyngham (see Conyngham, M.).
2. Hannah, m. 1752, George Leslie Montgomery, M.P. for Ballyconnell, co. Cavan and d. Jan. 1786 leaving issue.
3. Catherine, m. 27 Dec. 1767, 1st Baron Clarina (see that title).
4. Alicia, m. 22 Aug. 1773, Ralph Gore, Earl of Ross (extinct).

Nathaniel Clements d. 1777. His wife d. 1781. The elder son,

Robert Clements, **1st Earl of Leitrim**, b. 25 Nov. 1732; cr. a peer of Ireland as Baron Leitrim of Manor Hamilton, co. Leitrim, 11 Oct. 1783; cr. Viscount Leitrim 3 Dec. 1793, and Earl of Leitrim, 30 Sept. 1795. At the Union in 1800/01 he was one of the original representative Irish peers. He m. 31 May 1765, Elizabeth, dau. of 1st Earl of Massareene, and by her (who d. 29 May 1817) had with others,

Nathaniel, **2nd Earl** (see below).
Caroline, m. 27 May 1802, 2nd Viscount Sydney (Townshend, M.).

The 1st Earl d. 27 July 1804 and was s. by,

Nathaniel Clements, **2nd Earl of Leitrim**, K.P., b. 9 May 1768, cr. **Baron Clements** of Kilmacrenan, co. Donegal in the U.K. peerage, 20 June 1831, was a trustee of the linen manufacture and port searcher at Dublin, m. Mary (d. 5 Feb. 1840) eldest dau. and coheir of William Bermingham, of Ross Hill, co. Galway, and by her had issue,

1. Robert Bermingham, M.P., co. Leitrim 1826-30, and 1832-39, b. May 1805, d. unm. 24 Jan. 1839.
2. William Sydney, **3rd Earl** (see below).
3. Charles Sheffington, M.P. co. Leitrim 1847-52, Capt. in the Army b. 1807; d. unm. 29 Sept. 1877.
4. George Robert Anson, R.N., d. unm. 5 Dec. 1837.
5. Francis Nathaniel, Rev., Vicar of Norton and hon. Canon of Durham, b. 1812; m. (1) 3 Dec. 1838, Charlotte, dau. of the Rev. Gilbert King of Langfield, co. Tyrone. She d. 23 Oct. 1868. He m. (2) 6 Jan. 1870, Amelia (d.s.p. 1911), dau. of Sir William Verner, 1st Bt., and d. 27 May 1870, having had issue by his first wife with six daus., one son,
   Robert Bermingham, **4th Earl** (see below).
1. Maria, m. 24 July 1828, the Rev. and Hon. E. S. Keppel and d.s.p. 8 Jan. 1885.
2. Elizabeth Victoria, d. 28 Jan. 1892, aged 89.
3. Caroline, m. 21 Mar. 1833, John Ynyr Burges, of Parkanaur, co. Tyrone and Eastham, co. Essex, and d. 12 Oct. 1869 leaving issue.

The 2nd Earl d. 31 Dec. 1854 and was s. by,

William Sydney Clements, **3rd Earl of Leitrim**, Lt. Col. 52nd Foot, M.P. for Leitrim 1839-47, b. 1806; murdered 2 April 1878*, being s. by his nephew,

Robert Bermingham Clements, **4th Earl of Leitrim**, Lt. R.N., b. 5 March 1847, m. 2 Sept. 1873, Lady Winifred Coke (Leicester, E.) and had issue,

1. Charles, **5th Earl** (see below).
2. Robert Clements, 1888-90.
3. Francis Patrick, R.N. 1898-1906, b. 13 Sept. 1885, d. unm. about 20 May 1907.

1. Winifred Edith, m. 21 Jan. 1899, A. H. Renshaw (Renshaw Bt.).
2. Mary Hilda, m. 5 July 1905 4th Baron Rayleigh.
3. Maude, m. (1) 19 Jan. 1899, Major H. W. Vivian (Swansea, B.), she m. (2) C. F. Roundell (B.L.G.).
4. Lily, b. 1 Jan. and d. 12 Feb. 1882.
5. Kathleen, m. (1) 2 Mar. 1910, G. Keith-Falconer Smith (B.L.G. m. (2) Cmdr. R. G. Studd, R.N. (Studd, Bt.).

The 4th Earl d. 5 April 1892 being s. by his eldest son,

Charles Clements, **5th Earl of Leitrim**, b. 23 June 1879, served in S. African war 1900-02 and in World War I 1915-17, Major 11th Bn. Royal Inniskilling Fusiliers, formerly Lt. 9th Lancers, Asst. Priv. Sec. to the Sec. of State for the Colonies, 1917; m. (1) 22 Oct. 1902 (m. diss. by div.) Violet Lina, only dau. of R. Henderson of Sedgwick Park, Horsham, co. Sussex (B.L.G.) and (2) 29 April 1939, Hon. Mrs. Anne Mary Challoner Borrett, dau. of Hon. W. A. Vanneck, (Huntingfield, B.) and d. 9 June 1952.

ARMS—Quarterly 1 and 4, Argent two bends wavy sable, on a chief gules three bezants (Clements); 2 and 3, Per pale indented or and gules (Bermingham).
CREST—A hawk ppr.
SUPPORTERS—Dexter, A buck ppr. in its mouth a trefoil; Sinister, A buck ppr. plain collared or.
MOTTO—Patriis virtutibus.
The Earl of Leitrim's seat was Mulroy, co. Donegal.

*The murder of the 3rd Earl took place at Craatlaghwood, near Milford, co. Donegal, and the Earl's clerk and coachman were also killed. The murder is thought to have been one of those agrarian crimes described by Conan Doyle in his short story, *The Green Flag*. The C.P. adds that at the Earl's funeral the mob, full of drink, crowded into the cemetery and tried to drag the coffin from the hearse.

LINCOLNSHIRE

PEERAGE—U.K. Earl Carrington and Viscount Wendover, of Cheping Wycombe, co. Buckingham, cr. 16 July 1895. Marquess of Lincolnshire, 26 Feb. 1912.
SURNAME—Wynn-Carrington formerly Carrington (and Carington).
CR.—as above. **EXT.**—13 June 1928.
HISTORY—Charles Robert Carrington, later Wynn-Carrington, 3rd Baron Carrington (see extant peerages), b. 16 May 1843; educ. Eton and Trin. Coll. Camb., B.A. 1863; M.P. Wycombe, 1865-68; Capt. Royal Horse Guards, 1869; on the death of his mother he inherited a part in the office of Hereditary Great Chamberlain of England, (see under Willoughby de Eresby, extant peerages), and by Royal Licence 21 Aug. 1880, he and his two brothers were authorised to continue using the name Carington, in place of that of Carrington, the original family surname having been Smith. He was made P.C. 1881, cr. G.C.M.G. 1885, **Earl Carrington** and Viscount Wendover, of Cheping Wycombe, co. Buckingham, 16 July 1895, and Marquess of Lincolnshire,

26 Feb. 1912. By royal licence he took the name of Wynn-Carrington in lieu of that of Carington, 24 April 1896. He was Gov. of New South Wales, 1885-90; Lord Great Chamberlain at the Coronation of George V. He was cr. K.G. 1906. He m. 16 July 1878, Cecilia Margaret, dau. of Charles Harbord, 5th Baron Suffield, and d. 13 June 1928 having had issue with five daus. a son,

Albert Edward Charles Robert, b. 24 April 1895; educ. Eton; served in World War I, Lt. Royal Horse Guards, and d. 19 May 1915, of wounds received in action.

The Marquessate, earldom and viscounty became extinct, and the Barony of Carrington devolved upon the Marquess's brother, who became 4th Baron Carrington.

ARMS—Quarterly of six: 1, Or a chevron cottised between three demi griffins the two in chief respectant sable; 2, Vert three shields argent each charged with a bordure engrailed or; 3, Argent three battering rams ppr. headed azure; 4, Or fretty azure; 5, Vert three eagles displayed in fess or; 6, or, Three bars wavy gules.

CREST—An elephant's head erased or, eared gules, charged on the neck with three fleur-de-lis, two and one azure.

SUPPORTERS—Two griffins wings elevated sable, the dexter charged with three fleur-de-lis palewise or, the sinister with three trefoils slipped palewise of the last.

MOTTO—Tenax in fide.

The Marquess had seats at Gwydyr Castle, North Wales, and Daws Hill, High Wycombe, Bucks.

LINDGREN

PEERAGE—U.K. Life. Baron Lindgren, of Welwyn Garden City, co. Hertford.
SURNAME—Lindgren.
CR.—9 Feb. 1961. EXT.—8 Sept. 1971.
HISTORY—George William Lindgren, of Islington, London, N.1., b. 28 Aug. 1870; m. 8 Jan. 1900, Emily Maude, dau. of George Hiom, of Tottenham, London, N., and d. 25 April 1946. She d. 1 Feb. 1961. They had issue,
1. George Samuel, Baron Lindgren (see below).
2. Frederick William, O.B.E. 1967, C.A., of King's Keep, Putney Hill, London, S.W.15. b. 1902; m. 1928, Nellie Ada Mary, dau. of H. W. Davies, of Holloway, London, N. She d. 1943.
1. Elsie Henrietta.

The elder son,

George Samuel Lindgren, Baron Lindgren, of Welwyn Garden City, co. Hertford, so cr. as a life peer 9 Feb. 1961, also O. St. J. 1965, b. 11 Nov. 1900; educ. Hungerford Road, Elem. Sch.; clerk in L.N.E.R. and mem. Nat. Executive Cttee of Railway Clerks, Asscn. 1933-46; M.P. for Wellingborough Div. of Northants, 1945-59; Parl. Sec. to Min. of Nat. Insurance, 1945-46; to Min. of Civil Aviation, 1946-50; and to Min. of Local Gov. and Planning, 1950-51; mem. Welwyn Garden City U.D.C. 1928-46; Chm. London Trades Council, 1938-42; Dep. Regional Commsr., W. Midlands, 1942-45; and Treasurer, Transport Salaried Staff Asscn. 1956-61; Prl. Sec. to Min. of Power, 1966. He m. 10 July 1926,

Elsie Olive, dau. of Frank Reed, of Chishall, nr. Royston, co. Hertford, and d. 8 Sept. 1971, leaving issue,

Graham Alastair, b. 1928; educ. Welwyn Garden City Grm. Sch.; m. 1953, Gwendolyne Mary, dau. of A. W. Miller, and had issue, a son Derek Andrew, b. 1969.

ARMS—None.

Seat was 4 Attimore Close, Welwyn Garden City, Herts.

LINDLEY

PEERAGE—U.K. Life. Baron Lindley, of East Carleton, co. Norfolk.
SURNAME—Lindley.
CR.—10 May 1900. EXT.—13 Dec. 1921.
HISTORY—George Lindley, of Catton, Norwich, had issue,
John Lindley, LL.D., Ph.D., F.R.S., of Acton Green, co. Middlesex, Prof. of Botany at Univ. Coll. London, b. 5 Feb. 1799; m. 1823, Sarah, dau. of Anthony George Freestone, of St. Margaret's, South Elmham, Suffolk, and d. 1865. She d. 1869. They had issue,
1. George, b. 1824; d. 1831.
2. Nathaniel, Baron Lindley (see below).
1. Sarah, m. 27 April 1852, the Hon. Sir Henry Pering Pellew, Crease, Judge of the High Court, British Columbia.
2. Barbara, m. 1867, the Rev. Edmund Thompson, M.A., Fell. of Christ's Coll. Camb., Rector of Clipstone.

The second son,

Sir Nathaniel Lindley, Baron Lindley, b. 29 Nov. 1828; educ. Univ. Coll. London; Barrister-at-Law, Middle Temple, 1850, Q.C. 1872, Bencher, 1874 ,Treasurer, 1892, Serjeant-at-Law 1875 (being the last appointed, as this order was abolished in 1877); Justice of Common Pleas, 1875, Judge of the High Court, 1875-80, Common Pleas Div. and in 1880-81, of Queen's Bench; Lord Justice of Appeal, 1881-97, Master of the Rolls, 1897-1900, and a Lord of Appeal in Ordinary, 1900-05; cr. Kt. Bach. 1875, made P.C. 1881; and cr. a life peer as Baron Lindley, of East Carleton, co. Norfolk, 10 May 1900. He m. 5 Aug. 1858, Sarah Katherine, (d. 8 Feb. 1912) dau. of Edward John Teale, of Leeds, and d. 9 Dec. 1921 having had issue,
1. John Edward, Major Gen. and Col. 1st Dragoons, Commandant Sch. of Instruction, Imp. Yeo., 1901-03, Brig. Gen. 3rd Cav. Brig., Irish Command, 1907-10, cmdg. Welsh Div. Territorial Force, 1914-15, served in S. African War, 1899-1900, and in World War I, 1914-15; b. 15 Sept. 1860; m. 28 Sept. 1887, Isabel, dau. of F. M. Nichols, of Lawford Hall, Essex, and d. 7 April 1925, leaving issue,
Mary Katharine, m. 30 June 1910, Hon. Robert Bruce, 10th Hussars, and has issue, (Elgin, E.).
2. Walter Barry, M.A. Univ. Coll. Oxford, Barrister-at-Law, Lincoln's Inn, Judge of Devon and Somerset County Court, 1912, and Deputy Chm. Quarter Sessions, Somerset, b. 31 Dec. 1861 m. 26 Feb. 1908, Hilda Mary, dau. of Capt. C. M. Fox, of Corfe House, Taunton.

3. Lennox Hannay, M.A., M.B. Oxford, served in R.A.M.C. as Capt. 12 Ambulance Train, B.E.F., physician to Shah of Persia at Teheran, had 1st class of the Persian Order of the Lion and Sun, b. 14 May 1868; m. (1) 1898, Karimeh, (d. 18 Sept. 1911) otherwise Caroline Grevotte, and had issue,

(1) Nathaniel Alexander, Norfolk T.A.A., F/O R.A.F., b. 14 Sept. 1901; m. 1 June 1931, Barbara Constance, dau. of Sir Cuthbert Slade, 4th Bt., and had issue, John Alexander, b. 20 Oct. 1932.

(2) Walter John Hugh, F/Lt., R.A.F., b. 26 Mar. 1906;

(1) Rachel Isabel, m. 12 Aug. 1925, Lionel Marmion Dymoke (B.L.G. 1952, Dymoke of Scrivelsby).

L. H. Lindley m. (2) 21 June 1913, Adelaide Rosa, dau. of Roger Kerrison, of Glevering Hall, co. Suffolk, and widow of Col. G. C. H. Parlby, R.A.

4. Percy Hooker, twin, b. 14 May 1868; d. 1871.

5. Francis Oswald, Rt. Hon. Sir, P.C., G.C.M.G., C.B., C.B.E., Ambassador, Vienna, 1920-21; Athens, 1922-23; Oslo, 1929-30, Lisbon, 1929-31, and Tokyo, 1931-34; b. 12 June 1872; B.A. Magdalen Coll. Oxford; m. 12 Jan. 1903, Hon. Etheldreda Mary Fraser dau. of 13th Lord Lovat and had issue, four daus.

1. Jessie Louisa.
2. Annie Clayton, m. 1886, Sir William Gull, 2nd Bt.
3. Mary Beatrice, d. unm. 1895.
4. Constance Mary, m. 1909, Major C. F. Gurney.

ARMS—Argent on a chief nebuly azure a quatrefoil between two griffins' heads, all argent.
CREST—In front of a pelican in her piety argent, vulning herself ppr. and charged with a pheon point downwards, three quatrefoils fesswise or.
SUPPORTERS—Dexter, A griffin, wings elevated argent; Sinister, A pelican wings elevated also argent, vulned and each standing on a fasces ppr.
MOTTO—Sis fortis.
Lord Lindley's residence was The Lodge, East Carleton, near Norwich. His club was the Athenaeum.

LINGEN

PEERAGE—U.K. Baron Lingen of Lingen, co. Hereford.
SURNAME—Lingen.
CR.—3 July 1885. **EXT.**—22 July 1905.
HISTORY—Lingen is a small village about two miles from Wigmore, co. Hereford, and the present family took its name from the place. References to the connection of the family with the place are given from the Rev. R. W. Eyton, in his *Antiquities of Shropshire* (vol. v pp. 73-78, and xi pp. 332-34.). From the 12th century, the family is traced (in old editions of Burke's Peerage) as follows:
Ralph de Lingen, soon after 1189 was s. by a son, and in due time by a grandson and a

great-grandson, all named John of Lingen. To his descendant Sir Ralph de Lingen, M.P. co. Hereford, 1373, is attributed a son and heir,
Sir Ralph Lingen, of Sutton and Lingen. Sutton was a property of the family for a long time. (In 1722 Thomas Lingen, of Sutton, m. Anne Burton, and their son, Robert Lingen s. his uncle, at Longner, nr. Shrewsbury, Salop and took the surname of Burton, by Act of Parliament, 1748, see B.L.G. 1952, Burton of Longner Hall.) The vols. of *The Ancestor*, usually a scourge to genealogical pretension refer to Lingens as among old families. (Vol. i, p. 249: "the old Herefordshire families of Hopton, Lingen and Hill have already emerged as tenants by knight service," this referring to the early 14th century. Again in vol. xii, there is quotation of a crest, Lyngeyn: "beryth to his crest a bundell of lykes in a crowne of gold manteled geules doubled silver" which has a certain resemblance to the crest of Lord Lingen). Sir Ralph Lingen of 1373 m. Margery, sis. of Sir Robert Pembrugge, of Tong Castle, co. Salop, and had issue, a son and heir,
Sir Ralph Lingen, of Sutton and Lingen, by his wife Jane, dau. of John Russell, had issue,
Sir John Lingen, of Sutton and Lingen, Sheriff co. Hereford, 1469, 1486, and 1496. He m. Elizabeth, dau. and coheir of Sir John Burgh, and d. 1506. His widow d. 1522, and they were both bur. at Aymestry. Their son and heir,
Sir John Lingen, of Sutton and Lingen, Sheriff co. Hereford, 1506 and 1517; m. 1512, Eleanor, dau. and heir of Thomas Milewater, of Stock Edith. Sir John Lingen thus became jure uxoris, lord of Stock Edith. He d. 1530, leaving with a dau. who m. John Wigmore, of Lucton, a son and successor,
John Lingen, of Stock Edith, Sheriff co. Hereford, 1544; m. 1530, Margaret, dau. of Sir Thomas Englefield, Speaker of the House of Commons, in 1496 (the descendant of Sir Thomas became baronet, in 1612—see Burke's Extinct Baronetcies) John Lingen d. 11 Feb. 1546, and was s. by his eldest son,
John Lingen, of Stoke Edith and of Sutton, M.P. co. Hereford, 1554; m. Isabel, dau. of John Breynton of Stretton-Sugwas, and d. 3 May 1554, being bur. in St. Dunstan's in the West, Fleet Street, London having had issue an only dau.,
Jane, Lingen, who m. William Shelley, of Michelgrove, co. Sussex. She founded Lingen's Almhouses, outside the Eigne gate of the city of Hereford, and Shelley's School in the parish of Marden. She was imprisoned for a time, on account of harbouring a Catholic priest and her husband was attainted in 1583. She d.s.p. 1610, having inherited a great estate from her father and a small revenue by her own efforts. She was s. by her first cousin,
Edward Lingen, of Sutton, Sheriff co. Hereford, son of William, one of Jane Lingen's father's brothers (He had m. Cecil dau. of Thomas Anthony Ingram). He m. Blanche, dau. of Sir Roger Bodenham, of Rotherwas, co. Hereford, and had with three daus. and a ygr. son, John, a Captain in the royal army, who was k. at Ledbury, three surviving sons,

1. Henry, Sir, knighted by Charles I, on 31 July 1645; he was a very strong royalist and fought for the royal cause. He sat as M.P. for the city of Hereford, in the first parliament of Charles II, (1660-61).

He m. Alice, dau. of Sir Walter Pye, of
The Mynde, co. Salop, and d. 1662. Of
his sons, all d.s.p. He had seven daus.,
and among them his estates, greatly
reduced by fines imposed on him by the
Parliamentarians, were divided, and
passed to other families.

2. Roger of Radbrook, co. Gloucester, the
ultimate male line representative, whose
descendant became ancestor of the
Burtons of Longner mentioned above.
3. Thomas (see below).

The third son,
Thomas Lingen, of Leighton Court, was
bapt. 13 Sept. 1618; m. Katherine, dau. of
Mathew Meysey, of Shakenhurst, co.
Worcester, and widow of John Fox, of Leighton
Court. He d. 1696, being s. by his only surv.
son,
Thomas Lingen, of Leighton Court, b.
1665; m. (lic. dated 17 Nov. 1690) Mary, dau.
of Thomas Bury, of Sownsnett, and widow of
Francis Meysey, of Shakenhurst and had,
with other issue who d. young, an elder son and
successor.,
Henry Lingen, of Worcester, b. 1695; m.
Elizabeth Weston and had an only son,
The Rev. Ralph Lingen, M.A., and Fellow
of Wadham Coll. Oxford, Rector of Castle
Frome, co. Hereford, and Rock, co. Worcester,
b. 1730; m. Elizabeth, dau. of Robert Gomery,
of Rock, and had issue,

1. Henry, Rev., of Abberley, co. Worcester,
M.A. and Fellow of Wadham Coll.
Oxford, b. 1765; m. Ann, dau. of William
Wharton, of Abberley, and had five sons
and two daus. all of whom d.s.p. except
Francis of The Bower, Rock, and
Thomas, of Lincome, near Stourport,
both of whom m. and left issue.
2. Thomas, a merchant of Birmingham b.
1771; m. Ann Palmer, dau. of Robert
Wheeler, of Birmingham, and d. 1848,
leaving an only son,
Ralph Robert Wheeler, **Baron Lingen**
(see below).
3. Francis, d.s.p.
1. Ann, d.s.p.
2. Mary, m. Rev. John Seager, Rector of
Welsh Bucknor and had issue.

Sir Ralph Robert Wheeler Lingen, was b. at
Birmingham, 19 Feb. 1819; educ. Bridgnorth
Sch. and Trin. Coll. Oxford, Scholar 1837;
Ireland Scholar 1838; Hertford Scholar 1839;
1st Class Classics, 1840; B.A. 1841; Fell. of
Balliol Coll. 1841-50; Latin Essay, 1843;
Asst. Master, Rugby 1843; Eldon Scholar,
1848; M.A. 1846; Barrister-at-Law, Lincoln's
Inn, 1847; Ch. Sec. to the Educational Cttee of
the Privy Council, 1850-70; Per. Sec. to the
Treasury, 1870-75. He was cr. C.B. 1870;
K.C.B. 1879; and **Baron Lingen**, of Lingen,
co. Hereford, 3 July 1885. He m. 4 Dec. 1852,
at Putney, Emma fourth dau. of Robert
Hutton, of Putney Park, co. Surrey, M.P.
Dublin. She d. 31 Jan. 1908. He d.s.p. 22 July
1905. His will was proved at over £64,000.
His residence was 13 Wetherby Gardens, South
Kensington, S.W.
ARMS—Barry of six or and azure, on a bend
gules three roses argent.
CREST—Out of a ducal coronet or a garb vert.
SUPPORTERS—Two mastiffs, collared and
chained or, each charged with a rose argent.
MOTTO—Dominus providebit.

LISMORE

PEERAGE—Ireland. Baron Lismore of Shan-
bally, co. Tipperary, cr. 27 June 1785.
Ireland. Viscount Lismore of Shanbally, co.
Tipperary, cr. 30 May 1806.
U.K. Baron Lismore of Shanbally Castle,
co. Tipperary, cr. 6 July 1838.
SURNAME—O'Callaghan.
CR.—as above. **EXT.**—29 Oct. 1898.
HISTORY—Timothy O'Callaghan, of Blan-
tyre, co. Cork had a son,
Cornelius O'Callaghan, M.P. for Fethard,
and a lawyer, who m. Maria, dau. of Robert
Jolley, and had issue, with two elder sons who
d.s.p., a ygst son,
Thomas O'Callaghan, of Shanbally, co.
Tipperary, m. (1) 1740, Sarah, dau. of John
Davis, of Carrickfergus, and (2) Hannah, dau.
of Chief Justice Rogerson, and widow of
Anthony Jephson, (by whom he had a dau.
Elizabeth m. twice, first to Robert Longfield,
and 2ndly to William Colthurst). By his first
wife he had an only son,
Cornelius O'Callaghan, b. 7 Jan. 1740/41;
sat as M.P. for Fethard, from 1761 to 1785; and
was cr. 27 June 1785, **Baron Lismore** of Shanbally, co. Tipperary, in the Irish peerage. He
m. 13 Dec. 1774, Frances, dau. of Rt. Hon.
John Ponsonby, (Bessbrough, E.), and sister
of 1st Baron Ponsonby of Imokilly. She d.
18 Feb. 1757. He d. 12 July 1797. They had
issue,

1. Cornelius, **2nd Baron** and **1st Viscount
Lismore** (see below).
2. Robert William, Sir, Lt. Gen., Col. 39th
Foot, and K.C.B., b. Oct. 1777; d. unm.
9 June 1849.
3. George, b. 9 Sept. 1787; d. unm. 13 Mar.
1856.
1. Louisa, m. 18 July 1807, William Cavendish, and d. 18 April 1863, leaving issue,
(Devonshire, D.).
2. Elizabeth, m. John Hyde, of Castle Hyde,
Ireland and d. 1824.
3. Mary, m. 1849, Rev. Thomas Scott, M.A.
of Barmeen, co. Dublin.

The eldest son,
Cornelius O'Callaghan, **2nd Baron Lismore,**
was cr. 30 May 1806, **Viscount Lismore,** of
Shanbally, co. Tipperary; made P.C. of
Ireland, 1835; and cr. Baron Lismore of
Shanbally Castle, co. Tipperary, in the U.K.
peerage, on 6 July 1838. He was b. 2 Oct.
1775; Lord Lt. of Tipperary, 1851 to 1857. He
m. 11 Aug. 1808, Eleanor, dau. of John Butler,
Earl of Ormonde and Ossory, from whom he
was divorced by Act of Parliament in 1826. He
d. 30 May 1857. She d. 27 Sept. 1859. They had,
1. Cornelius, 12th Lancers, b. 1809; d.
un. 16 Aug. 1849.
2. William Frederick, Capt. 44th Foot, d.
unm. in India, 1836.
3. George Ponsonby, **2nd Viscount** (see
below).
1. Anne Maria Louisa, m. 10 May 1841,
3rd Baron Dunalley.

The third and only surv. son,
George Ponsonby O'Callaghan, **2nd Viscount Lismore,** was b. 16 Mar. 1815; served in
the 17th Lancers; High Sheriff, co. Tipperary,
1853; Lord Lt. co. Tipperary 1857-85. He m.
25 July 1839, Mary, dau. of George Norbury,
of Fulmer, co. Buckingham, and by her (d.
15 April 1900), had issue,

PLATE 12

VISCOUNT LLANDAFF.

BARON LISTER.

BARON LLANGATTOCK.

EARL OF LONDESBOROUGH.

BARON LUDLOW.

BARON MACNAGHTEN.

PLATE 13

BARON MASHAM.

VISCOUNT MILNER.

EARL MOUNT CASHELL.

BARON MOUNT STEPHEN.

BARON MUNCASTER.

BARON NEWLANDS.

1. George Cornelius Gerald, b. 3 Nov. 1846; m. 24 Dec. 1874, at Umballa, India, Rosina, dau. of the Rev. W. H. Williams, and widow of E. C. Follett. He d.s.p.v.p. Mar. 1885.
2. William Frederick Ormonde, M.P. co. Tipperary, b. 14 Nov. 1852; d.v.p. 20 April 1877.

The 2nd Viscount d. 29 Oct. 1898.

ARMS—Argent, in base, a mount vert, on the sinister side a hurst of oak trees, therefrom issuant a wolf passant towards the dexter ppr.
CREST—A naked dexter arm embowed, holding a sword bendwise, entwined with a snake all ppr.
SUPPORTERS—Two stags ppr.
MOTTO—Fidus et audax.

The seat of the family was at Shanbally Castle, Clogheen, co. Tipperary with a London residence at 31 Old Burlington Street, W. The 2nd Viscount's clubs were Travellers' and Kildare Street, Dublin.

LISTER

PEERAGE—U.K. Baron Lister of Lyme Regis, co. Dorset. (Also a baronetcy cr. 26 Dec. 1883.)
SURNAME—Lister.
CR.—6 Feb. 1897. **EXT.**—10 Feb. 1912.
HISTORY—John Lister, of Stoke Newington, co. Middlesex, a wine merchant, b. 14 Dec. 1737; m. 10 Oct. 1764, Mary Jackson (d. 1 Mar. 1808), and d. 9 Feb. 1836, having had issue,
1. Joseph Jackson (see below)
1. Mary, b. 1766; d. unm. 1847.
2. Elizabeth, b. 1768; m. 1789, T. B. Beck, of Dover, co. Kent, and d. 24 Feb. 1857, leaving issue.

The only son,

Joseph Jackson Lister, of Upton House, Upton Lane, West Ham, co. Essex, a wine merchant; a mem. Soc. of Friends; had a keen interest in optics, and became F.R.S., is credited with discovery of principle on which modern microscopes are made; b. 11 Jan. 1786; m. 14 July 1818, Isabella, dau. of Anthony Harris, of Maryport, co. Cumberland and d. 24 Oct. 1869, having by her (who d. 3 Sept. 1864) had issue,
1. John, b. 1822; d. unm. 1846.
2. Joseph, Sir, Bt. and **Baron Lister** (see below).
3. William Henry, b. 1828; d. unm. at sea 28 Oct. 1859.
4. Arthur, of Highcliff, Lyme Regis, and of Leytonstone, co. Essex, J.P., F.R.S., b. 17 April 1830; m. 2 May 1855, Susanna, dau. of William Tindall, of East Dulwich, co. Surrey, and had issue.
1. Mary, m. 21 Aug. 1845, Rickman Godlee, and had issue.
2. Isabella Sophia, m. 1848, Thomas Pim, and d. 1870 leaving issue.
3. Jane, m. 1858, Smith Harrison, of Elmhurst, Woodford, co. Essex, and had issue.

The second son,

Sir Joseph Lister, **Baron Lister**, was b. 5 April 1827; educ. at two Quaker Schools, and Univ. Coll. London, B.A. 1847, M.B. 1852; and Univ. Coll. Hospital; F.R.C.S. 1852;

F.R.C.S. Scot. 1855; F.R.S. 1860, Treasurer, R.S. 1893-95, and Pres. 1895-1900; mem. of Gen. Medical Council, 1876-77; LL.D. Edinburgh 1878; cr. a baronet 26 Dec. 1883; a peer as Baron Lister, of Lyme Regis, co. Dorset, 6 Feb. 1897. He m. 23 April 1856, Agnes, dau. of James Syme, Prof. of Clinical Surgery, in Edin. Univ. She d. 12 April 1893. He d.s.p. 10 Feb. 1912. He was the first surgeon to receive a peerage, and the second man to receive one for his scientific attainments. His *Collected Papers* were published by the Clarendon Press, in 1909.

ARMS—Ermine on a fess invected sable three mullets argent, in chief a club in pale entwined with a serpent all ppr.
CREST—In front of a stag's head erased ppr. three mullets argent.
SUPPORTERS—On either side a stag ppr. gorged with a chain or pendent therefrom an escutcheon charged with a cubit arm erect holding a staff entwined by a serpent both ppr.
MOTTO—Malo mori quam foedari.

Lord Lister's residence was 12 Park Crescent, Portland Place, W. His club was the Athenaeum.

LLANDAFF

PEERAGE—U.K. Viscount Llandaff, of Hereford, co. Hereford.
SURNAME—Matthews.
CR.—5 Aug. 1895. **EXT.**—3 April 1913.
HISTORY—William Mathew, of Burghill and Pipe, co. Hereford, who d. 1681, is supposed to have been of the same family as the Francis Mathew, of Thomastown, who in 1783, 1793, and 1797 respectively became Baron, Viscount and Earl of Landaff in the Irish peerage, and whose titles became extinct in 1833. Whatever the truth of this assertion, the pedigree from William Mathew is as follows. By his wife, Alicia he had, with a dau. Anne, who m. (1) Thomas Payne and (2) Theophilus Meyricke, one son,

Humphrey Mathews, who m. Margaret Rawlins, and d. 1700 having had with two ygr. sons, Humphrey and Edward, an eldest son,

William Mathews, of Brynans Bridge, Burghill, b. 1688; m. 19 July 1718, Mary, dau. of John Ashman, and d. 9 April 1726, having had with three daus. (Mary, Margaret and Anne, the last named m. John Kemmett, of Tewkesbury),

William Mathews, of Burton Court, and Llangarren, High Sheriff, co. Hereford, 1777, b. Feb. 1722; m. 18 Sept. 1750, Jane, dau. and eventual heir of Philip Hoskyns, of Bernithen Court, She d. May 1768. He d. 29 Aug. 1799, having had with a son, William (who d. young), an elder son,

John Mathews, of Burton Court, Bernithen Court, and Belmont, co. Hereford, M.P. co. Hereford, 1803-06; m. 9 Nov. 1778, Elizabeth, dau. and heir of Arthur Ellis, and d. 15 Jan. 1826, having had by her,
1. William Hoskyns, b. 7 April 1780; d. unm. 3 Jan. 1804.
2. John Holder, b. 23 Jan. 1783; d. unm. 1 Feb. 1849.
3. Charles Skinner, b. 26 Mar. 1785; d. unm. 3 Aug. 1811.

4. Arthur, Rev., Fell. Brazenose Coll. Oxford, Canon of Hereford, b. 7 Feb. 1788; d. unm. 23 Sept. 1840.
5. Henry (see below).
6. Alfred, b. 25 Jan. 1792; Capt. R.N.; m. Emily Rosetta, dau. of Rev. J. Bernard, of Crowcombe Court, Somerset, and d.s.p. 1873.
7. Edward d. an infant, 1794.
8. Frederick Hoskyns, b. 14 Sept. 1798; d. unm. 1883.
1. Elizabeth, d. unm. Dec. 1860.
2. Eleanora, d. unm. 21 Jan. 1861.
3. Jane, d. unm. 22 Jan. 1861.
4. Mary, m. (1) Henry Hatsell, of Marden Park, and (2) Richard White of Acton Hill, and d. 1 Aug. 1860.
5. Anne, m. A. Robertson, M.D., of Northampton, and d.s.p. 14 April 1864.
6. Charlotte, d. unm. 28 Feb. 1874.

The fifth son,

Henry Mathews, of Belmont, co. Hereford, Fell. King's Coll. Camb., Puisne Judge of Ceylon, author of *The Diary of an Invalid*, b. 21 June 1789; m. Aug. 1821, Emma, dau. of William Blount, of Orleton, co. Hereford. She d. 30 July 1861. He d. 20 May 1828. They had issue,

1. Henry, **Viscount Llandaff** (see below).
1. Mary, m. 24 Sept. 1842, Julien Francois Bertrand de la Chere, who d. 15 Aug. 1879. She d. 15 Aug. 1890, having had issue,
   (1) Henri, Cmdr. 13th Dragoons, Chev. Legion d'Hon. d.s.p. 1886.
   (2) Eugenè Gaston.
   (1) Marie Sophie, m. 1883, Baron de Cassin, of the Chateau du Guè Pean and had issue.
   (2) Winifred Berthe.
   (3) Alice, m. 20 Oct. 1888, Alfred Hornyold, and had issue.
2. Helen, a sister of charity, d. 16 July 1894.

The only son,

Henry Mathews, **Viscount Llandaff,** b. 13 Jan. 1826 in Ceylon; educ. Univ. of Paris, graduating 1844; and London Univ. B.A., 1847 and LL.B. 1849; Barrister-at-Law, Lincoln's Inn, 1850; Sec. to Earl Marshal, 1864-69; Q.C. 1868; M.P. for Dungarvan, 1868-74; and for East Birmingham, 1886-95; mem. of Senate for London Univ., 1885; P.C. 1886; Home Sec. 1886-92. He was cr. Viscount Llandaff, of Hereford, co. Hereford, 5 Aug. 1895. He d. unm. 3 April 1913.

ARMS—Or a lion rampant reguardant between two flaunches sable, on each flaunch a mullet argent.
CREST—On a mount vert, a heathcock, in the beak a sprig of broom ppr.
SUPPORTERS—On either side, a unicorn sable, gorged with a wreath of oak fructed supporting a fasces, both ppr.
MOTTO—Y ffynno Duw y fydd (What God willeth shall be.)

LLANGATTOCK

PEERAGE—U.K. Baron Llangattock, of the Hendre, co. Monmouth.
SURNAME—Rolls.
CR.—30 Aug. 1892. EXT.—31 Oct. 1916.

HISTORY—John Rolls, of The Grange, co Surrey, High Sheriff, co. Monmouth, 1794, was b. 1735; m. 21 Oct. 1767, Sarah, dau. of Thomas Coysh, of Camberwell, niece and heir of Henry Allen, and d. 8 Sept. 1801, having by her (who d. 7 Sept. 1801) had an only surv. son,

John Rolls, of Bryanston Square, London, of The Grange, co. Surrey, and of The Hendre, co. Monmouth, b. 20 Oct. 1776; m. 27 Jan. 1803, Martha, only dau. and heir of Jacob Barnett and d. 31 Jan. 1837 having by her had issue, with a ygr. son and three daus., an elder son,

John Etherington Welch Rolls, of The Hendre, High Sheriff, 1842, b. 4 May 1807, m. 26 Feb. 1833, Elizabeth Mary, dau. of Walter Long, of Preshaw House, co. Hants. and d. 27 May 1870, having had issue with six daus. an only son,

John Allan Rolls, **1st Baron Llangattock,** b. 19 Feb. 1837; educ. Eton and Ch. Ch. Oxford; Capt. Royal Glouc. Hussars; High Sheriff co. Monmouth, 1875; M.P. co. Monmouth, 1880-85; Mayor of Monmouth, 1896-99; cr. Baron Llangattock, of The Hendre, co. Monmouth, 30 Aug. 1892; m. 20 Oct. 1868, Georgiana Marcia, D.G. St. J., dau. of Col. Sir Charles FitzRoy Maclean, 9th Bt., and d. 24 Sept. 1912. She d. 1 April 1923. They had issue,

1. John Maclean, **2nd Baron** (see below).
2. Henry Allen, Lt. Royal Monmouthshire eng. mil. b. 5 Aug. 1871; d. unm. 26 June 1916.
3. Charles Stewart, M.A., Camb., F.R.G.S., F.R.Met.S., Assoc.M.I.M.E., the first airman to cross and recross the English Channel, and one of the founders of the firm of Rolls Royce, b. 27 Aug. 1877; d. unm. 12 July 1910, k. in the wreck of his plane at Bournemouth.
1. Eleanor Georgiana, m. 23 April 1898, Sir John Courtown E. Shelley, 6th Bt.; they assumed by Royal Licence 1917, the additional name and arms of Rolls. (extant peerages, De Lisle V.).

The eldest son,

John Maclean Rolls, **2nd Baron Llangattock,** b. 25 April 1870; educ. Eton and Ch. Ch. Oxford, B.C.L., and B.A. 1895, M.A.; Barrister-at-Law, Inner Temple, 1896; High Sheriff co. Monmouth, 1900; Mayor of Monmouth, 1906; served in World War I, Major 4th Welsh Brig. R.F.A., and d. unm. of wounds received in action, 31 Oct. 1916.

ARMS—Quarterly 1 and 4, Argent on a fess dancettée with plain cotises sable between three billets sable, each charged with a lion rampant or, as many bezants; 2 and 3, Gules an eagle displayed, barry of six, erminois and azure.
CREST—Out of a wreath of oak a dexter cubit arm vested or, cuffed sable the arm charged with a fess dancettée double cotised sable, charged with three bezants, in the hand ppr. a roll of parchment argent.
SUPPORTERS—Dexter, A lion rampant ppr. suspended from a chain round the neck or a shield argent, charged with a rock gules; Sinister, A tiger ppr. suspended from a chain round the neck or, a shield or, in base on waves of the sea ppr. an ancient galley with sails furled sable.
MOTTO—Celeritas et veritas.

The seats of the family were—The Hendre, near Monmouth; Llangattock Manor, Monmouth. Town residence was South Lodge, Rutland Gate, S.W.

LLEWELLIN

PEERAGE—U.K. Baron Llewellin of Upton, co. Dorset.
SURNAME—Llewellin.
CR.—12 Sept. 1945. EXT.—24 Jan. 1957.
HISTORY—William Llewellin, of Hill Grange, Abergavenny, co. Monmouth, by his wife Margaret (née Coffin) had issue,
William Llewellin, b. 4 Jan. 1856; educ. Sherborne and Univ. Coll. Oxford; bought Upton House, co. Dorset from the Tichborne family; High Sheriff Monmouth 1901, and Dorset 1919; m. (1) 23 Jan. 1889, Frances Mary (d. 24 May 1907) dau. of L. D. Wigan (B.L.G. 1952, Wigan of Towbury Hill) and (2) 29 Oct. 1908 Ada Elizabeth, dau. of Henry Wigan of Winchmore Hill, N.21., and d. 4 July 1927. By his first marriage he had an elder son, William Wigan; a dau. Mary Margaret, and a ygr. son,
John Jestyn Llewellin, **Baron Llewellin,** b. 6 Feb. 1893; educ. Eton and Univ. Coll. Oxford, B.A. 1917, M.A. 1920, Barrister-at-Law, Inner Temple, 1921; served in World War I 1914-18 (R.G.A., wounded, M.C. 1917) Lt. Col. and Brev. Col. 1932-38, Dorset Heavy Bde., R.A., awarded T.D.; M.P. Uxbridge Div. of Middlesex, 1929-45, Civil Lord of the Admiralty, 1937-39 Min. Resident in Washington for Supply and Chm., British Supply Council 1942-45, cr. O.B.E., 1926, C.B.E. 1939, made P.C. 1941, and cr. Baron Llewellin of Upton, co. Dorset, 12 Sept. 1945. He d. 24 Jan. 1957.
ARMS—Gules three chevronels couped ermine between as many spear heads or.
CREST—A lamb passant argent supporting with the dexter forefoot a flagstaff in bend sinister ppr. therefrom flowing a banner gules charged with a spear head or between two wings gules on each a like spear head.
SUPPORTERS—Dexter, A farmer holding in the exterior hand a hay fork; Sinister, An officer of the Merchant Navy holding in the exterior hand a pair of binoculars all ppr.
MOTTO—Dew Fo-o-fy Rhann.
Lord Llewellin's seat was Upton House, Poole, Dorset.

LOCHEE

PEERAGE—U.K. Baron Lochee, of Gourie, co. Perth.
SURNAME—Robertson.
CR.—22 May 1908. EXT.—13 Sept. 1911.
HISTORY—Edmund Robertson of Kinnaird, Inchture, co. Perth had an eldest son,
Edmund Robertson, **Baron Lochee** of Gourie, co. Perth, so cr. 22 May 1908. He was b. 28 Oct. 1845; educ. St. Andrews and Lincoln Coll. Oxford, Sch. 1866-70, B.A. 1870 (1st Class classics) Fell. of Corpus Christi Coll. 1870, M.A. 1874, (Vinerian Law Sch.) Barrister-at-Law, Lincoln's Inn 1871, Jt. Examiner in Jurisprudence and Legal and

Court History 1884 and in Roman and Inter. Law, the Inns of Court 1884. Examiner in Eng. Court History at London Univ. 1877-82, Public Examiner in Jurisprudence, Oxford 1877-79, Q.C. 1895, Reader of Lincoln's Inn and Bencher 1898. M.P. Dundee 1885-1908, Civil Lord of the Admiralty 1892-95. Parl. Sec. to the Admiralty 1905-08, D.L. co. and city of Dundee, Reader in Law and Equity, Inns of Court. He d. 13 Sept. 1911.
Lord Lochee's residence was 69a Pall Mall, London S.W. His club was Reform.

LONDESBOROUGH

PEERAGE—U.K. Earl of Londesborough, and Viscount Raincliffe of Raincliffe, both in N.R. Yorks.
SURNAME—Denison.
CR.—1 July 1887. EXT.—17 April 1937.
HISTORY—Lord Albert Denison, formerly Conyngham, the second surv. son of the 1st Marquess of Conyngham was cr. Baron Londesborough, 4 Mar. 1850. He had with other issue (see extant peerages, Londesborough, B.), an eldest son,
William Henry Forester Denison, 2nd Baron Londesborough and **1st Viscount Raincliffe** and **1st Earl of Londesborough,** b. 19 June 1834; educ. Eton; sat as Liberal M.P. for Beverley, 1857-59, and for Scarborough, 1859-60 and on joining the Conservatives, he was cr. Viscount Raincliffe of Raincliffe, N.R. Yorks, and Earl of Londesborough, N.R. Yorks, 1 July 1887; m. 10 Sept. 1863, Edith Frances Wilhelmina, dau. of Henry Somerset, 7th Duke of Beaufort, and d. 19 April 1900, leaving with four daus., an only son,
William Francis Henry Denison, 3rd Baron Londesborough, and **2nd Earl of Londesborough,** cr. K.C.V.O. 1907; b. 30 Dec. 1864; m. 11 Aug. 1887, Lady Grace Adelaide Fane, dau. of 12th Earl of Westmorland, and d. 30 Oct. 1917, leaving issue with one dau.,
  1. George Francis William Henry, **3rd Earl** (see below).
  2. Hugo William Cecil, **4th Earl** (see below).
The elder son,
George Francis William Henry Denison, 4th Baron Londesborough and **3rd Earl of Londesborough,** b. 17 July 1892; d. unm. 12 Sept. 1920, being s. by his brother,
Hugo William Cecil Denison, 5th Baron Londesborough and **4th Earl of Londesborough,** b. 13 Nov. 1894; educ. Wellington; served in World War I, 1914-18, Capt. 1st Life Guards; m. 4 Sept. 1935, Marigold Rosemary Joyce, dau. of Edgar Lubbock, (Avebury, B.) and d. 17 April 1937, having had issue a dau. At his death the Earldom and Viscounty became extinct, while the Barony of Londesborough, passed to his cousin Ernest William Denison, who became 6th Baron Londesborough.
ARMS—Quarterly 1 and 4, Ermine, a bend azure, cottised sable, between a unicorn's head erased in chief, and a cross crosslet fitchée in base gules (Denison); 2 and 3, Argent a shakefork between three mullets one and two sable (Conyngham).
CRESTS—1. Issuant from clouds an arm in bend ppr. vested gules, cuffed ermine and

charged with a covered cup or, the forefinger pointing to an estoile radiated gold, (Denison); 2. A unicorn's head erased argent, maned, and armed or (Conyngham).

SUPPORTERS—Dexter, A horse argent maned, unguled and charged on the shoulder with an eagle displayed or; Sinister, A stag argent attired, unguled and charged on the shoulder with a griffin's head erased or, both charged on the body with a crescent sable.

MOTTO—Adversa virtute repello.

The Earl's seat was Blankney Hall, Lincoln.

LOREBURN

PEERAGE—U.K. Baron Loreburn, of Dumfries, co. Dumfries. Earl Loreburn, of Dumfries, co. Dumfries.

SURNAME—Reid.

CR.—Barony, 8 Jan. 1906. Earldom 4 July 1911. **EXT.**—30 Nov. 1923.

HISTORY—James Reid, a merchant in Edinburgh, had a ygst. son, John Reid, an Advocate of the Scots Bar, who m. Helen, dau. of George Cunningham, Inspector Gen. of Customs, and had issue,

Sir James John Reid, of Mouswald Place, Dumfries, Chief Justice of the Ionian Islands, who m. Mary Dalziel, dau. of Robert Threshie, of Barnbarroch, co. Kirkcudbright, and had issue,

Sir Robert Threshie Reid, **Baron Loreburn,** and **Earl Loreburn,** b. 3 April 1846; educ. Cheltenham Coll. and Balliol Coll. Oxford, Scholar, B.A.; Barrister-at-Law, Inner Temple, 1871; Q.C. 1882, and Bencher 1890; M.P. Hereford, 1880-85; and Dumfries Burghs, 1886-1905; Solicitor Gen. 1894; Attorney Gen. 1894-95; Lord High Chancellor, 1905-12; made P.C. 1905; cr. Kt. Bach. 1894; Baron Loreburn, of Dumfries co. Dumfries, 8 Jan. 1906; Earl Loreburn of Dumfries, co. Dumfries, 4 July 1911, and G.C.M.G. 1899. He m. (1) 26 Jan. 1871, Emily Douglas, dau. of Capt. A. C. Fleming, who d. 23 Aug. 1904. He m. (2) 3 Dec. 1907, Violet Elizabeth, dau. of William F. Hicks Beach, of Witcombe Park, co. Gloucester (St. Aldwyn, E.). He d.s.p. 30 Nov. 1923.

ARMS—Azure a lion rampant argent, on a chief engrailed or a book expanded ppr. between two keys in saltire, and two swords in saltire gules.

CREST—A cubit arm holding a book, leaves expanded ppr.

SUPPORTERS—On either side a collie dog ppr.

MOTTO—Pro virtute.

LUDLOW

PEERAGE—U.K. Baron Ludlow of Heywood, co. Wilts.

SURNAME—Lopes (previously Franco).

CR.—26 July 1897. **EXT.**—8 Nov. 1922.

HISTORY—Sir Manasseh Massey Lopes, 1st Bt., d.s.p. 26 Mar. 1831 when he was s. by a special remainder in the patent by his nephew, Ralph Franco, who on s. his uncle assumed by Royal Licence, in compliance with the will of his uncle, the surname of Lopes only, and the arms of Lopes quarterly with those of Franco.

Sir Ralph Lopes, 2nd Bt., as he then became, had issue, with an eldest son, Sir Massey Lopes, 3rd Bt., (ancestor of the Barons Roborough, see extant peerage works), a third son,

The Rt. Hon. Sir Henry Charles Lopes, **1st Baron Ludlow,** b. 3 Oct. 1828; educ. Winchester and Balliol Coll. Oxford, B.A. 1849; Barrister-at-Law, Inner Temple, 1852; Q.C. 1869; Bencher, 1870; Treasurer, 1890-91; Recorder of Exeter, 1867-76; was Conservative M.P. for Launceston, 1868-74; and for Frome, 1874-76; a Judge of the High Court of Justice, Common Pleas Div., 1876-80; Lord Justice of Appeal, 1885-97; cr. Kt. Bach. 1876; P.C. 1885; cr. Baron Ludlow of Heywood, co. Wilts, 26 July 1897; m. 20 Sept. 1854, Cordelia Lucy, dau. of Erving Clark, of Efford Manor, nr. Plymouth. She d. 22 Dec. 1891. He d. 25 Dec. 1899. They had issue,

1. Henry Ludlow, **2nd Baron Ludlow** (see below).
1. Susan Ludlow Cordelia, m. 1 June 1901, Archibald Bence-Jones, M.A., Barrister-at-Law, of 56 Upper Berkeley Street, London, W.1. and d. 20 April 1938, leaving issue, (see Burke's Landed Gentry of Ireland, 1958).
2. Cordelia Lucy, m. 18 July 1896, Sir John Hanham, 9th Bt., and d. 18 April 1945, leaving issue. (Hanham, Bt.).
3. Ethel Maud, d. unm. 11 Dec. 1943.
4. Ernestine Frances, m. 20 Nov. 1897, her cousin, George Lopes, of Sandridge Park, Melksham, and d.s.p. Sept. 1938.
5. Bertha Susan, m. 17 Dec. 1898, 1st Viscount Bledisloe, and d. 6 May 1926 (Bledisloe, V.).

The only son,

Henry Ludlow Lopes, **2nd Baron Ludlow,** b. 30 Sept. 1865; educ. Eton and Balliol Coll. Oxford, B.A. 1888; M.A. 1894; Barrister-at-Law, Middle Temple, 1890; Counsel to the Treasury, the Great Western Railway, and the Post Office on the Western Circuit; Pres. and Chm. of the Cancer Hospital; Treasurer of St. Bartholomew's Hospital; mem. L.C.C. East Marylebone, 1904-07; served in World War I, as Staff Capt.; m. (1) 25 Mar. 1903, Blanche, dau. of William Holden, of Palace House, co. Lancs., and widow of Frederick George Ellis, 7th Baron Howard de Walden, She d. 8 April 1911. He m. (2) 25 Sept. 1919, Alice Sedgwick, D.G. St. J., dau. of James Mankiewicz, of Pembridge Square, London, W., and widow of Sir Julius Wernher, 1st Bt. (Wernher, Bt.) and d.s.p. 8 Nov. 1922.

ARMS—Quarterly 1 and 4, Azure on a chevron, between three eagles rising or, as many bars gemelle gules, on a chief of the second five lozenges of the field. (Lopes); 2 and 3, In a landscape field a fountain, thereout issuing a palm tree, all ppr. (Franco).

CRESTS—1. a Lion sejant erminois, gorged with a collar gemelle gules, resting the dexter paw on a lozenge azure (Lopes); 2. A dexter arm couped and embowed, habited purpure, purfled and diapered or, cuffed argent, holding in the hand ppr. a palm branch vert. (Franco).

SUPPORTERS—On either side a Pegasus sable, winged and gorged with a collar gemelle or standing on a fasces ppr.

MOTTOES—Quod tibi, id, alii (Lopes). Sub pace, copia (Franco).

The seats of Lord Ludlow were Heywood, Westbury, Wilts, and Lamport, Northampton.

LUGARD

PEERAGE—U.K. Baron Lugard, of Abinger, co. Surrey.
SURNAME—Lugard.
CR.—16 Mar. 1928. EXT.—11 April 1945.
HISTORY—John Lugard was Capt. 6th Inniskillin Dragoons and later Adjutant and Sec. of the Duke of York's Royal Military Asylum, Chelsea, b. 1761; served in the Netherlands, 1793-95; m. 1803, Jane Llewellyn Trewman, dau. of Robert Trewman, of Exeter, and d. 30 Sept. 1843, leaving issue,

1. Frederick Grueber, Rev., M.A., Army Chaplain in East India Co.'s service, later Vicar of Norton-juxta-Kempsey, near Worcester, 1873-93, b. 19 Aug. 1808; m. (1) 1834, Grace Price Morgan, and had issue. He m. (2) 1848, Emma Cameron, and had issue, two daus. He m. (3) Mary Jane (d. 12 June 1865) dau. of Rev. John G. Howard, and d. 31 May 1900 having by his third wife had issue, with two daus.,
   (1) Frederick John Delatry, **Baron Lugard** (see below).
   (2) Edward James, D.S.O., O.B.E., Major I.A., b. 23 Mar. 1865; m. 4 July 1893, Charlotte Eleanor, dau. of Rev. G. B. Howard and had issue.
2. Edward, Gen. Sir, P.C., G.C.B., 31st Foot, served in the Afghan War, 1842, in the Sikh Wars, 1845-46, and 1848-49, in Persia 1857, and in the Indian Mutiny when he cmd. a division at the capture of Lucknow, Under Sec. of State for War, 1861-71; b. 8 May 1810; m. (1) 1837, Isabella Mowbray, (d. 1868), dau. of Henry Hart, and (2) Matty, dau. of J. Fulbrow, and d. 31 Oct. 1898.
3. Henry Williamson, Lt. Col. R.E. in China, 1857, where he d. on active service, 1 Dec. 1857.

Frederick John Delatry Lugard **Baron Lugard,** was b. 22 Jan. 1858 at Fort St. George, Madras; educ. Rossall and the Royal Military College, Sandhurst; joined the Norfolk Regt. 1878; had a very distinguished career as soldier and administrator; served in the Afghan War 1879-80; the Sudan 1885 (despatches); Burma, 1886-87 (despatches 3 times), D.S.O. 1887; cmd. an expedition against slave traders on Lake Nyasa, 1888 (wounded); served in Uganda under the Imperial British East Africa Co. 1889-92; in command Royal Niger Co. Exped. to Borgu, West Africa, 1894-95; cmd. exped. into Ngamiland 1896-97; H.M. Commissioner for hinterland of Nigeria and Lagos, and Commandant with rank of Brig. of the force which he raised, the West African Frontier Force, 1897-99; High Commissioner and C. in C. of Northern Nigeria, 1900-06; served in Kano and Sokoto Exped. 1903; ret. from Army with rank of Lt. Col. and Brev. Col. 1905; Gov. and C. in C. of Hong Kong, 1907-12; Gov. of Northern and Southern Nigeria, 1912-13; Gov. Gen. of Northern Nigeria, 1914-19; was cr. C.B. 1895; K.C.M.G. 1901; G.C.M.G. 1911; made P.C. 1920, and cr. Baron Lugard, of Abinger, co. Surrey, 16 Mar. 1928. He m. 11 June 1902, Flora Louise, D.B.E., author of several books, and a special correspondent of *The Times* in Africa, Australia, Canada and the Klondike, and dau. of Major Gen. George Shaw. She d. 25 Jan. 1929.

He d. 11 April 1945. Lord Lugard who wrote in 1893, *The Rise of Our East African Empire* and *The Dual Mandate in British Tropical Africa,* was a Gold Medallist of the Royal Geographical Society and of the African Society.
ARMS—Gules an eastern crown between three wolves' heads couped or, each gorged with a collar gemel of the field.
CREST—A wolf's head erased or, in the mouth a flag staff bendwise ppr. therefrom flowing to the dexter a banner gules charged with an eastern crown gold.
SUPPORTERS—On either side a wolf ppr. gorged with an eastern crown or.
MOTTO—Fide et fortitudine.
Lord Lugard's residence was Little Parkhurst, Abinger Common, Surrey. His club was the Athenaeum.

LYONS

PEERAGE—U.K. Baron Lyons.
U.K. Viscount Lyons—both of Christchurch, co. Hants.
(Also a baronetcy cr. 29 July 1840.)
SURNAME—Lyons.
CR.—Barony 25 June 1856. Viscounty 24 Nov. 1881. EXT.—5 Dec. 1887.
HISTORY—In 1622 William Lyons bought from Lord Dunsany some 3000 acres in King's Co. and m. Margaret Moore, of Crogham, who was great aunt of the 1st Earl of Charleville and cousin of the Earl of Drogheda. William Lyons d. 1633 leaving,
Charles Lyons, temp. Charles II was father of Henry Lyons of River Lyons, who m. Anne, sister of Robert, Earl of Belvedere, and of John Lyons a Major in the army of William III and Queen Anne. He obtained with his wife, Elizabeth, a dau. of Henry Williams, Deputy Gov. of Antigua, considerable property in that island. Their third son,
Samuel Lyons settled at Antigua and had issue,
Henry Lyons of Antigua and of Philadelphia who m. 24 Aug. 1690, Sarah dau. of Samuel Winthrop (grandson of John Winthrop, 1st Gov. of New England) and was grandfather of,
John Lyons, of Lyons in Antigua and Sturtlow House, co. Huntingdon, b. 31 Aug. 1731; m. 1 Feb. 1753, Jane, dau. of Col. S. Harman of Harmans, Antigua and St. Austins, co. Hants, and had issue,
John Lyons, of Lyons in Antigua and St. Austins, co. Hants. m. (1) 1784, Catharine, dau. of Main Swete Walrond of Montrath, co. Devon, by Sarah his wife, sister and heir of William Lyons, and had issue,

1. John, Vice Adm. R.N., b. 1 Sept. 1787; m. (1) Caroline, dau. of Major Bowen and (2) 31 Aug. 1865 Anna Maria, widow of Col. J. L. Mowatt R.A. and d. 15 Dec. 1872.
2. Theodore, d. unm. 1825.
3. Henry, Lt. R.A., k. at Copenhagen, 1807.
4. Edmund, **1st Baron Lyons** (see below).
5. George Rose, H.E.I.C.S. d. 1828.
6. William Mills, b. 1797; m. Mary dau. of J. Adams.
7. Maine Waldrond, mortally wounded at Navarino 1827.

8. Humphrey Lt. Gen. I.A., b. 8 July 1802; m. 4 Nov. 1837, Eliza, dau. of Henry Bennett of Fir Grove, Liverpool and had issue.
9. Charles Bethel, m. Henrietta, widow of Capt. Sockett.
1. Anne, d. unm.
2. Catherine d. 1857.
3. Caroline m. Henry Pearson.
John Lyons m. (2) 17 May 1804, Elizabeth (d. 1821) dau. of William Robbins and had further issue,
10. Samuel Athill, Col. I.A. m. 1820 Sophia dau. of Col. Logie and had issue.
11. Edward Robbins, Capt. H.E.I.C.S. d. unm. 1849.
4. Frances Walrond.
The fourth son,
Sir Edmund Lyons, 1st Bt, and **1st Baron Lyons**, b. 21 Nov. 1790, served in R.N., Capt. 1814, Vice Adm. of the White; escorted Louis XVIII to France on the *Rinaldo*. In 1855 in command of the Mediterranean Fleet and served in Crimean War with distinction. He was cr. G.C.B., G.C.M.G., K.C.H., a Bt., 29 July 1814, and a peer as Baron Lyons 25 June 1856 of Christchurch, co. Hants. He m. 18 July 1814, Augusta Louisa (d. 10 Mar. 1852) dau. of Capt. Josiah Rogers R.N. and d. at Arundel Castle, Sussex, 23 Nov. 1858 having had issue,
1. Richard Bickerton Pemell, **1st Viscount** and **2nd Baron Lyons** (see below).
2. Edmund Mowbray, b. 27 June 1819, Capt. R.N. served in the Crimean War with distinction and d. unm. 1855, k. in action.
1. Anna Theresa Bickerton, m. at Athens, 24 Dec. 1839, Philip Hartman Veit, Baron von Wurtzburg of Bavaria.
2. Auguata Mary Minna Catherine, m. 19 June 1839, 14th Duke of Norfolk.
The elder son,
Sir Richard Bickerton Pemell Lyons, 2nd Bt., **2nd Baron Lyons** and **Viscount Lyons** was b. 26 April 1817; was cr. K.C.B. 1860; G.C.B. 1862; G.C.M.G. 1879; and Viscount Lyons of Christchurch, co. Hants 24 Nov. 1881; Envoy Extraordinary and Minister Plenipotentiary at Florence 1858 and at Washington 1858-65; made P.C. 1865 M.A. and D.C.L. Oxford. He d. 5 Dec. 1887.
ARMS—Sable on a chevron between three lions sejant guardant argent as many castles, triple towered of the field.
CREST—On a chapeau gules doubled ermine a Sea-lion's head erased argent, gorged with a naval crown azure holding in the mouth a flag staff in bend sinister ppr. therefrom flowing a banner azure having inscribed thereon "Marach" in letters of gold.
SUPPORTERS—On either side, a lion guardant sable charged on the shoulder with a castle triple towered argent.
MOTTO—Noli irritare leones.

MABANE

PEERAGE—U.K. Baron Mabane, of Rye, co. Sussex.
SURNAME—Mabane.
CR.—15 June 1962. **EXT.**—16 Nov. 1969.
HISTORY—Sir William Mabane, Baron

Mabane, was the son of Joseph Greenwood Mabane, of Leeds, b. 1863, m. 1884, Margaret, (d. 1901) dau. of Robert Steele, of Leeds, and d. 22 Mar. 1923, having had issue, a son, as above and a dau. Mary Isabel, m. Archibald Allison Armstrong and had issue two daus. The son,
Sir William Mabane, **Baron Mabane**, b. 12 Jan. 1895; educ. Woodhouse Grove Sch. and Gonville and Caius Coll. Camb., B.A. 1920, M.A. 1923; served in World War I, 1914-18 (wounded, despatches) Capt. 13th Yorks Regt., M.P. Huddersfield 1931-45, held several ministerial Appointments including Min. of State, Foreign Office 1945, was Chm. Civil Defence Comm. 1951; m. (1) 1918 (m. diss. by div. 1926) Louise (d. 1947) dau. of E. Tanton and (2) 31 Mar. 1944, Stella Jane, dau. of J. Duggan of Buenos Aires. Lord Mabane d. 16 Nov. 1969.
ARMS—Azure between two chevronels or three roses argent, barbed and seeded ppr., all between in chief two goats' heads erased silver armed gold, and in base a portcullis chained of the second.
CREST—Upon a rock sable, a cormorant or resting the dexter claw upon a heart gules.
SUPPORTERS—Dexter, A lion or; Sinister, A goat argent; each supporting a banner argent the poles gules steeled ppr., the dexter charged with a caduceus sable.
MOTTO—Dictum meum pactum.

MAENAN

PEERAGE—U.K. Baron Maenan of Ellesmere, co. Salop.
SURNAME—Taylor.
CR.—29 June 1948. **EXT.**—22 Sept. 1951.
HISTORY—The Ven. William Francis Taylor, D.D. Archdeacon of Liverpool, B.A. Trin. Coll. Dublin, 1847, M.A. 1850. LL.B. 1855 adm. Oxford ad eundem 8 May 1856, B.D. and D.D. 1871, perp. curate St. John's Liverpool 1851-61, and St. Silas Liverpool 1961-70, Vicar of St. Chrysostom, Everton, 1870, Hon. Canon Liverpool 1880, had issue,
Sir (William) Francis Kyffin Taylor, G.B.E., **Baron Maenan**, b. 9 July 1854; educ. Exeter Coll. Oxford, B.A. 1877; Barrister-at-Law, Inner Temple, 1879; Q.C. 1895, Bencher 1905, Treasurer 1926 and Master of the Garden 1928; mem. of the Bar Council, 1900; J.P. and D.L. and Chm. Quarter Sessions, Salop, Recorder of Bolton, 1901; Comm. of Assize 1919-20, 1925 and 1929; served on many cttees. as Chm. or mem.; Presiding Judge, Court of Passage, Liverpool, 1903-48, Judge of Appeal in Isle of Man 1918-21; Vice Pres. of War Compensation Court 1920-21; was cr. K.B.E. (Civil) 1918 G.B.E. (Civil) 1929, and Baron Maenan, of Ellesmere, co. Salop, 29 June 1948, m. 1883, Mary Fleming, dau. of Robert Crooks of Rosemount, Liverpool, and d. 22 Sept. 1951 having had issue,
Ermine Mary Kyffin, b. 1884; m. 1917 A. G. Evans, M.D. and had issue.
ARMS—Per fess raguly argent and sable, a lion rampant counterchanged, on a chief invected gules a fleur-de-lis between two boars' heads couped and erect or.
CREST—A lion rampant per fess raguly sable and argent holding between the forepaws a

pheon and resting the dexter hind leg on three fusils conjoined or.

SUPPORTERS—Dexter, A lion sable charged on the shoulder with three lozenges conjoined in fess argent; Sinister, A lion argent charged on the shoulder with three lozenges conjoined in fess sable.

MOTTO—Cenfigena-ladd-el-hunan.

MACDONALD OF EARNSCLIFFE

PEERAGE—U.K. Barony. Macdonald of Earnscliffe in the Prov. of Ontario and Dominion of Canada.

SURNAME—Macdonald.

CR.—14 Aug. 1891. **EXT.**—5 Sept. 1920.

HISTORY—John Macdonald, merchant and provost, of Rogart Dornoch, co. Sutherland, m. 18 Aug. 1778, Jean Macdonald, and had issue four sons and three daus., of whom the second son,

Hugh Macdonald, of Dornoch, settled at Kingston, Canada, in 1820. He was b. 12 Dec. 1782; m. 21 Oct. 1811, Helen, dau. of Capt. James Shaw, and had issue by her (she d. 24 Oct. 1862) with two other sons who d. young, and two daus., an only surv. son,

The Rt. Hon. Sir John Alexander Macdonald, who was b. 11 Jan. 1815, in Glasgow; educ. Grammar Sch., Kingston, Ontario; Barrister 1836; Q.C. 1846; mem. of House of Assembly, for Kingston, 1844; Attorney Gen. 1854-62 and 1864-67; Prime Minister of Canada, 1857-62, and Prime Minister of the Dominion of Canada, 1867-73 and 1878-91, he being the first to hold that office, and having made the confederation of British North America possible. He m. (1) his cousin, Isabella, dau. of Alexander Clark, of Dalnavert, co. Inverness, by whom (she d. 28 Dec. 1857) he had issue, an only surv. son,

Hugh John, Sir, b. 13 Mar. 1850; Barrister, Attorney Gen., Q.C. 1899, M.P. 1891 and 1896; Minister of Interior, 1896; Prime Minister of Prov. of Manitoba, 1899; Police Magistrate of City of Winnipeg, 1911; served in Canadian Militia during Fenian Raids, the Red River Exped. and the N.W. Rebellion of 1885; m. (1) June 1876, Mary Jane Agnes, dau. of W. A. Murray, of Toronto, and widow of J. L. King, M.D. She d. 1881, leaving one dau., Isabel. He m. (2) 23 April 1883, Agnes Gertrude, dau. of Salter Jehosaphat Van Koughnet, K.C., of Toronto, and had a son, John Alexander, b. 7 Aug. 1884; d. unm. 26 April 1905.

Sir John m. (2) 16 Feb. 1867 Susan Agnes, dau. of the Hon. T. J. Bernard, of Jamaica, and d. 6 June 1891. In consideration of her husband's services, his widow was cr. 14 Aug. 1891, **Baroness Macdonald** of Earnscliffe in the Prov. of Ontario and Dominion of Canada. As the only issue of the second of Sir John's marriages, was a dau., Mary Theodora Margaret, b. 8 Feb. 1869, the peerage became extinct on the death of his widow, on 5 Sept. 1920. Sir John was made P.C. 1879; cr. K.C.B. 1867, G.C.B. 1884; and he was a Knight Grand Cross of the Order of Isabella the Catholic of Spain. He was also D.C.L. of Oxford, and LL.D. of Queen's Univ., Canada. Lady Macdonald's seats were: Earnscliffe,

Ottawa; Les Rochers, Riviere du Loup, Quebec; and Ketosin, National Park, Banff, N.W. Territories. Her club was The Ladies Empire, 69 Grosvenor Street, London, W.

MACDONNELL

PEERAGE—U.K. Baron MacDonnell, of Swinford, co. Mayo.

SURNAME—MacDonnell.

CR.—2 July 1908. **EXT.**—9 June 1925.

HISTORY—Antony MacDonnell of Palmfield, co. Mayo was father of Mark Garvey MacDonnell whose eldest son was,

Sir Anthony Patrick MacDonnell, **Baron MacDonnell** of Swinford, co. Mayo b. 7 Mar. 1844; educ. Queen's Coll. Galway, M.A., D.Litt; entered Bengal C.S. 1865, Sec. to Government of Bengal 1884 and to Gov. of India, Home Department 1887, Chief Commissioner of Burma 1889, and of Central Provinces 1890-93 was Acting Gov. of Bengal 1893, Mem. of Gov. General's Council 1893-95, Lt. Gov. of N.W. Provinces and Oudh 1895-1901, and Under Sec. to the Lord Lt. of Ireland 1902-08; cr. C.S.I. 1888, K.C.S.I. 1893, G.C.S.I. 1897 and K.C.V.O. 1903; apptd. P.C. (Grt. Britain) 1902 and Ireland 1903 and cr. Baron MacDonnell of Swinford, co. Mayo 2 July 1908. He m. Nov. 1878, Henrietta, dau. of Ewen MacDonell of 59 Nevern Square, London S.W. and d. 9 June 1925 having had issue,

Anne Margaret.

ARMS—Quarterly indented, 1st, or a lion rampant gules, armed and langued azure; 2nd, or an arm in armour embowed couped at the shoulder, the hand holding a cross crosslet fitchée vert; 3rd, argent a ship in full sail sable, and 4th, per fess wavy azure and vert a dolphin naiant ppr., in the centre point over all on a star of five points of the second a trefoil slipped of the first.

SUPPORTERS—Dexter, A sambur deer ppr.; Sinister, An Irish deerhound ppr.

CREST—An arm in armour embowed couped at the shoulder the hand holding a cross crosslet fitchée vert.

MOTTO—Tout jour prest.

MACMILLAN

PEERAGE—U.K. Life Baron Macmillan, of Aberfeldy, co. Perth.

SURNAME—Macmillan.

CR.—3 Feb. 1930. **EXT.**—5 Sept. 1952.

HISTORY—Alexander Macmillan, of Aberfeldy, co. Perth, had issue,

The Rev. Hugh Macmillan, D.D., LL.D., b. 17 Sept. 1833; m. June 1859, Jane (d. 14 Jan. 1922) dau. of William Pattison, of Edinburgh, and d. 24 May 1903, leaving issue with five daus., an only son,

Sir Hugh Pattison Macmillan, **Baron Macmillan**, b. 20 Feb. 1873; educ. Edinburgh Univ., M.A. 1893; and Glasgow Univ., LL.B. 1896; Advocate of the Scots Bar, 1897; K.C. 1912, Hon. Bencher, Inner Temple, 1924; Examiner in Law, Glasgow Univ. 1899-1904; Editor of the *Juridical Review*, 1900-07; Asst. Director of Intelligence, Min. of

Information, 1918; Senior Legal Assessor, Edinburgh, 1920, Standing Counsel, Convention of Royal Burghs, Scotland, 1923; Lord Advocate for Scotland (non-political) 1924; Chm. Royal Commission on Lunacy, 1924; apptd. 3 Feb. 1930 a Lord of Appeal in Ordinary, and cr. a Baron for life as Baron Macmillan, of Aberfeldy, co. Perth; made a P.C. 1924, and cr. G.C.V.O. 1937; chm. of very many commissions and committees, Pres. of the *Commission permanente de conciliation* between the Netherlands and Norway, apptd. by French Gov. a córresponding mem. on Foreign and International Law; mem. of Worshipful Co. of Glaziers, and Freeman of City of London; F.R.S.E., F.S.A. Scot., Pres. of Gen. Advisory Council of B.B.C., 1937; m. 27 July 1901, Elizabeth Katharine Grace, dau. of William Johnstone Marshall, M.D., of Greenock, and d. 5 Sept. 1952.

ARMS—Or a lion rampant sable, armed and langued gules, on a chief ermine three mullets azure.

CREST—A dexter and a sinister hand ppr. grasping a two handed sword argent hilted and pomelled or.

SUPPORTERS—Two cats-a-mountain guardant ppr.

MOTTO—Miseris succurrere disco.

Residences were at 44 Millbank, Westminster, S.W.1 and Moon Hall, Ewhurst, Surrey. His clubs were Athenaeum, Carlton and New (of Edinburgh).

MACNAGHTEN

PEERAGE—U.K. Life. Baron Macnaghten of Runkerry, co. Antrim.

SURNAME—Macnaghten.

CR.—25 Jan. 1887. **EXT.**—17 Feb. 1913.

HISTORY—Edward Macnaghten, **Baron Macnaghten,** was b. 3 Feb. 1830, the second son of Sir Edmund Charles Workman-Macnaghten, 2nd Bt. (see Macnaghten Bt., in extant peerages). He was educ. Queen's Coll. Belfast and Trin. Coll. Camb., B.A. 1852; Fellow, 1853; M.A. 1856; Barrister-at-Law, Lincoln's Inn, 1857; Q.C. 1880; Bencher and Treasurer, 1907; M.P. co. Antrim, 1880-85, and North Antrim 1885-87; made P.C. 1887, and apptd. Lord of Appeal in Ordinary, being then cr. a Baron for life as Baron Macnaghten of Runkerry, co. Antrim, 25 Jan. 1887. He s. his brother as 4th Bt., on 21 July 1911. He m. 18 Dec. 1858, Frances Arabella (d. 22 Oct. 1903) dau. of the Rt. Hon. Sir Samuel Martin, of Crindle, co. Londonderry, one of the Barons of the Exchequer, 1850-74. He d. 17 Feb. 1913, having had issue, five sons and seven daus., of whom the three eldest sons s. him in turn in the baronetcy. (see Macnaghten, Bt.).

ARMS—Quarterly 1 and 4, Argent an arm issuant from the sinister ppr. the hand grasping a cross crosslet fitchée azure; 2 and 3, Argent a tower gules, all within a bordure ermine.

CREST—A tower gules.

SUPPORTERS—Two roebucks ppr., each gorged with a double chain or, pendent therefrom an escutcheon argent, charged with two fasces in saltire of the second.

MOTTO—I hope in God.

MAGHERAMORNE

PEERAGE—U.K. Baron Magheramorne, of Magheramorne, co. Antrim.

SURNAME—McGarel-Hogg.

CR.—5 July 1887. **EXT.**—21 April 1957.

HISTORY—The family of Hogg went from Scotland or Northern England to Northern Ireland in the second half of the 17th century when William Hogg m. 11 June 1686, Elizabeth Wilson, as his second wife, and d. 1716 leaving issue by her, from whom descended the baronets Hogg (see current peerages). The first Baronet, Sir James Weir Hogg, P.C., Barrister-at-Law who was so cr. 20 July 1846, was Registrar of the Supreme Court of Judicature and Vice Admiralty Court at Calcutta. He had with other issue (Hogg Bt.) an eldest son,

Sir James MacNaghten McGarel-Hogg, 2nd Bt., and **1st Baron Magheramorne**, K.C.B., who assumed by Royal Licence, 8 Feb. 1877, the surname of McGarel in addition to and before that of Hogg, with the additional arms of McGarel, this being in accordance with the will of his brother-in-law, Charles McGarel of Magheramorne. He was cr. K.C.B., and a peer as Baron Magheramorne, of Magheramorne, co. Antrim, 5 July 1887. He was b. 3 May 1823; m. 21 Aug. 1857, Hon. Caroline Elizabeth Pennant dau. of 1st Baron Penrhyn, and had issue, with a dau. Edith, m. Hon. Arthur Saumarez, 2nd son of 3rd Baron de Saumarez,

1. James Douglas, **2nd Baron** (see below).
2. Douglas Stuart, **3rd Baron** (see below).
3. Ronald Tracy, **4th Baron** (see below).
4. Archibald Campbell, b. 1866, d. unm. 1945.
5. Gerald Francis, b. 1868; d. unm. 1942.

The first Baron Magheramorne d. 27 June 1890 being s. by his eldest son,

James Douglas McGarel-Hogg, **2nd Baron Magheramorne,** Capt. 1st Life Guards, A.D.C. to Lord Lieut. of Ireland, b. 16 Jan. 1861; m. 23 Oct. 1889, Lady Evelyn Ashley, dau. of 8th Earl of Shaftesbury and had issue a dau. Norah Evelyn, m. 1919 Lt. Col. E. J. Groves (who took additional surname of McGarel) and d. 30 Jan. 1967 leaving issue (B.L.G. 1952, Groves formerly of Holehird). Lord Magheramorne d. 10 Mar. 1903 being s. by his brother,

Dudley Stuart McGarel-Hogg, **3rd Baron Magheramorne,** b. 3 Dec. 1863; d. unm. 14 Mar. 1946, being s. by his brother,

Ronald Tracy McGarel-Hogg, **4th Baron Magheramorne,** b. 28 July 1865; d. unm. 15 April 1957. The peerage then became extinct while the baronetcy was inherited by his kinsman, Sir Kenneth Weir Hogg, 6th Bt.

ARMS—Quarterly 1 and 4, Argent three boar's heads erased azure langued gules between two flaunches of the second each charged with a crescent of the field (Hogg); 2 and 3, Or a fesse vairé ermine and purpure, cotised sable, between three greyhounds' heads of the last collared argent with line reflexed gold (McGarel).

CRESTS—Out of an Eastern crown argent an oak tree fructed ppr. and pendent therefrom an escutcheon azure charged with a dexter arm, embowed in armour, the hand grasping an arrow in bend sinister, point downwards all ppr. (Hogg). 2. Upon a mount vert in front of a branch of oak erect ppr. a greyhound sejant sable, collared and line reflexed over the back or (McGarel).

SUPPORTERS—Two falcons ppr. each gorged with a collar vair pendent therefrom an escutcheon, that on the dexter charged with the arms of Hogg, that on the sinister with the arms of McGarel.
MOTTO—Dat gloria vires (Hogg). Fide et fiducia (McGarel).

MALCOLM OF POLTALLOCH

PEERAGE—U.K. Baron Malcolm of Poltalloch, co. Argyll.
SURNAME—Malcolm.
CR.—9 June 1896. EXT.—6 Mar. 1902.
HISTORY—John Malcolm, 14th laird of Poltalloch, (see B.L.G. 1952, Malcolm of Poltalloch), had with other issue, an eldest son and heir,
John Wingfield Malcolm, 15th laird of Poltalloch, and **Baron Malcolm** of Poltalloch, who was b. 16 May 1833; educ. Eton and Ch. Ch. Oxford, B.A., 1856, M.A. 1865; Conservative M.P. for Boston, 1860-80, and for co. Argyll, 1886-92; cr. C.B. 1892; and a peer on 9 June 1896. He m. (1) 25 July 1861. Alice Frederica, dau. of George Ives Irby, (4th Baron Boston). She d.s.p. 12 Oct. 1896. He m. (2) 3 Nov. 1897 Marie Jane Lilian, widow of H. Gardner Lister, of U.S.A. She d. 26 Aug. 1927. He d.s.p. 6 Mar. 1902. His peerage became extinct but he was s. at Poltalloch by his brother, Edward Donald, who became 16th laird of Poltalloch.
ARMS—Argent on a saltire azure between four stags' heads erased gules five mullets or.
CREST—A tower argent.
SUPPORTERS—On either side a stag at gaze ppr. collared and chains reflexed over the back or.
MOTTOES—(over the crest) In ardua tendit. (below the arms) Deus refugium nostrum.
The seat of Lord Malcolm was Poltalloch, Kilmartin, Argyll. His clubs were New (Edinburgh) and Naval and Military.

MAMHEAD

PEERAGE—U.K. Baron Mamhead, of Exeter, co. Devon.
SURNAME—Newman.
CR.—5 Dec. 1931. EXT.—2 Nov. 1945.
HISTORY—Sir Robert Hunt Stapylton Dudley Lydston Newman, 4th Bt. (see extant works, Newman of Mamhead Bt.), **Baron Mamhead**, was b. 27 Oct. 1871; s. his father as 4th Bt., 29 Nov. 1892; M.P. for Exeter, 1918-29, and 1929-31 sitting formerly as Conservative, and latterly as an Independent; J.P., C.C., D.L. for Devon; cr. Baron Mamhead, 5 Dec. 1931; d. unm. 2 Nov. 1945, when his barony became extinct and he was s. in the baronetcy by his cousin, Sir Ralph Alured Newman, 5th Bt., (see current works).
ARMS—Azure three demi-lions couped argent, powdered with cross crosslets sable.
CREST—A lion rampant per chevron azure gutté d'eau and argent gutté de sang.
SUPPORTERS—Dexter, A stag ppr.; Sinister, A pegasus argent winged, maned, tailed and tufted or; each gorged with a mural crown gold.
MOTTO—Ubi amor ibi fides.

Lord Mamhead's seat was Mamhead Park, Exeter.

MANVERS

PEERAGE—Great Britain. Baron Pierrepont of Holme Pierrepont and Viscount Newark, of Newark-on-Trent, both co. Nottingham. U.K. Earl Manvers.
SURNAME—Pierrepont (previously Medows).
CR.—Barony and Viscounty, 23 July 1796. Earldom. 9 April 1806. EXT.—13 Feb. 1955.
HISTORY William Medowe, of Rushmere, co. Suffolk, whose will was dated 14 Sept. 1541, and proved 9 Oct. 1542, had issue by Isabel, his wife,
William Medowe, of Rushmere, (will dated 24 Aug. and proved 22 Oct. 1580) by his wife, Margaret, had issue,
1. William, of Coddenham, later of Witnesham Hall, co. Suffolk, m. Gryssell, dau. of John Wynter, of Witnesham Hall, E. Suffolk, and from this marriage came the families of Meadows of Witnesham, and Meadows-Theobald, of Claydon. He d. 19 Jan. 1637, aged 78.
2. Daniel, see below.
The ygr. son,
Daniel Medows, of Chattisham Hall, E. Suffolk, b. at Rushmere 1577, bought in 1630, the lordship of Witnesham, from Sir Robert Hitcham, Bt., m. at Stowmarket, Elizabeth (bur. 28 Dec. 1678), dau. and eventual co-heir of Robert Smith, of Wickham Market, and d. 1651 having had with other issue,
Sir Philip Medows, Knight Marshal of the King's Palace, and ambassador to the courts of Denmark and Sweden, b. 1625; m. 1661, Constance, second dau. and coheir of Francis Lucy, ygst. brother of Sir Thomas Lucy, of Charlecote, and d. 16 Sept. 1718, being s. by his son,
Sir Philip Medows, Knight Marshal of the King's Palace, m. Dorothy Boscawen, sister of 1st Viscount Falmouth, and d. 3 Dec. 1757, having had issue with four other daus.,
1. Sydney, who s. his father as Marshal of the Palace, m. Jemima, dau. of Hon. Charles Montague, 5th son of 1st Earl of Sandwich, and d.s.p. 1792.
2. Edward, an Offr. of Dragoons.
3. Philip (see below).
1. Mary, Maid of Hon. to Queen Caroline, wife of George II, d. unm.
The third son,
Philip Medows, Dep. Ranger, of Richmond Park, m. ¬1734, Frances, dau. of William Pierrepont styled Earl of Kingston, also Marquess of Dorchester, the eldest son of Evelyn, Marquess of Dorchester, and afterwards cr. Duke of Kingston, (1883 Extinct Peerage) and had issue,
1. Evelyn Philip, of Conbolt, co. Hants. who was the principal legattee under the will of Elizabeth, Duchess of Kingston, was b. 3 Dec. 1736; m. (1) Margaret, dau. of Capt. William Cramond, described as of the Auldbar family; m. (2) 25 May, 1811 Harriot Maria, dau. of James Norie, of London, but by her had no issue. She m. (2) Col. Sir Alexander Dickson, K.C.B., and (3) Sir John Campbell. Evelyn Philip d. 4 July 1826.

2. Charles, **1st Earl Manvers,** heir to his uncle, the Duke of Kingston (see below).
3. William, Rt. Hon., Sir, P.C. Ireland, K.B. Gen. Gov. of Madras, b. 31 Jan. 1739; m. 1770, Frances Augusta, dau. of Robert Hammerton, of Hammerton, co. Tipperary, and d.s.p. 1813.
4. Edward, Capt. R.N., m. 1785, Mary, dau. of John Brodie, and d. 1813.
1. Frances, a Maid of Honour, m. 3 Sept. 1768, Col. Alexander Campbell, and d. 1770, leaving issue.

The eldest surv. son,
Charles Medows, later Pierrepont, **1st Earl Manvers,** b. 14 Nov. 1737; s. to the estates of his uncle, the Duke of Kingston, when the latter d. in 1773, upon which the Dukedom of Kingston, (with other titles, e.g. Viscount Newark, Earl of Kingston, and Marquess of Dorchester) became extinct. Mr. Medows then assumed by royal sign manual in 1788, the surname and arms of Pierrepont in lieu of those of Medows. He was M.P. for co. Nottingham from 1778 to 1796. On 23 July 1796 he was cr. Baron Pierrepont of Holme Pierrepont and Viscount Newark of Newark-on-Trent, and was further cr. on 9 April 1806, Earl Manvers. He m. 1774, Anne Orton, (d. 24 Aug. 1832) yst. dau. of William Mills, of Richmond, and had issue,
1. Evelyn Henry Frederick, b. 1775; d. 1801.
2. Charles Herbert, **2nd Earl Manvers** (see below).
3. Henry Manvers, of Conbolt Park, co. Hants, P.C., Envoy to the Court of Denmark, b. 18 Mar. 1780; m. 1818, Sophia, (d. 1823), dau. of 1st Marquess of Exeter, and d. 10 Nov. 1851, having by her had an only child, Augusta Sophia Anne, m. 9 July 1844, Lord Charles Wellesley, and d. 13 July 1893, aged 73 leaving issue.
4. Philip Sydney, of Evenley Hall, co. Northampton, b. 13 June 1786; m. 10 Aug. 1810 Georgiana (d. 14 Oct. 1872), dau. and heiress of Herbert Gwynne Browne, of Imley Park, co. Merioneth, and widow of Pryce Edwards, of Talgarth, and d.s.p. 15 Feb. 1864.
1. Frances Augusta, m. (1) 20 Oct. 1802, Adm. William Bentinck, who d. 21 Feb. 1813; she m. (2) 30 July 1821, H. W. Stephens, and d. 10 Feb. 1847.

The first Earl Manvers d. 17 June 1816, and was s. by his eldest surv. son,
Charles Herbert Pierrepont, **2nd Earl Manvers,** b. 11 Aug. 1778; m. 23 Aug. 1804, Mary Letitia, dau. of A. H. Eyre, of Grive, co. Nottingham. She d. 7 Sept. 1860. They had issue,
1. Charles Evelyn, styled Viscount Newark, b. 2 Sept. 1805; m. 16 Aug. 1832, Emily (d. 1851) 2nd dau. of Lord Hatherton, and d.s.p. 23 Aug. 1850.
2. Sidney William Herbert, **3rd Earl** (see below).
1. Mary Frances, m. 21 Aug. 1845, Edward C. Egerton, brother of Lord Egerton, and d. 12 June 1905 leaving issue.
2. Annora Charlotte, m. 18 Aug. 1853, Charles Watkin Williams Wynn, and d. 22 Mar. 1888, leaving issue.

The second Earl d. 27 Oct. 1860, and was s. by his only surv. son,

Sidney William Herbert Pierrepont, **3rd Earl Manvers,** M.P. South Nottingham, 1852-60, B.A. Oxford, b. 12 Mar. 1825; m. 15 June 1852, Georgine Jane Elizabeth Fanny de Franquetot (d. 28 July 1910), dau. of Augustin Louis Joseph Casimir Gustave de Franquetot, Duc de Colgny, and by her had issue,
1. Charles William Sidney, **4th Earl Manvers** (see below).
2. Evelyn Henry, b. 23 Aug. 1856; m. 1 June, 1880, Sophia, (who d. as a result of an accident, 5 June 1941), dau. of William Arkwright, of Sutton Scarsdale, co. Derby, and d. 4 June 1926, having had issue,
   (1) Gervas Evelyn, **6th Earl Manvers** (see below).
   (1) Eva Mary, b. 23 Oct. 1882; was granted with her sister the rank of daus. of an earl by George VI, Aug. 1940; m. 4 July 1906, E. M. Scott-MacKirdy, and had issue,
   (2) Clare Isma, Mayor of Chelsea, 1939-41, C.C. Dorset, 1949; b. 2 Sept. 1884; m. 20 Sept. 1919, Fred Somerset Hartnell.
   (3) Ida Helen, b. 27 Jan. 1886; d. 6 Aug. 1894.
3. Henry Sydney, b. 18 Aug. 1863; d. 4 Mar. 1882.
1. Emily Annora Charlotte, b. 16 Mar. 1853; m. 24 Sept. 1878, 4th Earl Beauchamp, and d. 11 May 1935 having had issue.
2. Mary Augusta, b. 21 Dec. 1865; m. 4 April 1899, John Peter Grant, of Rothiemurchus, (B.L.G. 1952) and d. 6 Mar. 1917 leaving issue.

The third Earl d. 16 Jan. 1900, and was s. by his eldest son,
Charles William Sidney Pierrepont, **4th Earl Manvers,** M.P. for Newark, 1885-95, Lt. Gren. Guards, Hon. Col. 8th Bn. Sherwood Foresters, b. 2 Aug. 1854; m. 28 Sept. 1880, Helen, dau. of Sir Michael Shaw-Stewart, 7th Bt.; she d. 11 Mar. 1939. They had issue,
1. Evelyn Robert, **5th Earl** (see below).
1. Cicely Mary, b. 4 Nov. 1886; m. 6 Oct. 1915, Lt. Col. F. H. Hardy, and d. 24 Oct. 1936.
2. Alice Helen, b. 30 Aug. 1889.
3. Sibell, b. 19 May 1892; m. 10 April 1923, H. D. Argles.

The fourth Earl d. 17 July 1926, and was s. by his only son,
Evelyn Robert Pierrepont, **5th Earl Manvers,** b. 25 July 1888; d. unm. 6 April 1940, being s. by his cousin,
Gervas Evelyn Pierrepont, **6th Earl Manvers,** b. 15 April 1881; educ. Winchester and Cooper's Hill; C.C. for London, Brixton Div. 1922-46; Dep. Chm. 1938-39; and for Notts., 1940-46; served in World War I, 1914-19 (despatches and M.C.) Order of Crown of Belgium and Croix de Guerre; m. 5 Feb. 1918, Marie-Louise Roosevelt, dau. of Sir Frederick W. L. Butterfield, and d. 13 Feb. 1955, having had issue,
1. Evelyn Louis Butterfield, b. 8 May 1924; d. 29 Sept. 1928.
1. Mary Helen Venetia, b. 22 May 1920; d. 21 Feb. 1930.
2. Frederica Rozelle Ridgway, b. 17 Nov. 1925, served in World War II, 1943-45, as leading stoker, W.R.N.S.

ARMS—Argent semée of cinquefoils gules, a lion rampant sable.
CREST—A lion rampant sable, between two wings erect argent.
SUPPORTERS—Two lions sable, armed and langued gules.
MOTTO—Pie repone te.
The Earl's seat was at Thoresby Park, Ollerton, co. Nottingham. His town house, was 14 South Terrace, Thurloe Square, S.W.7.
The Duchess of Kingston referred to above was the subject of the famous trial for bigamy before the House of Lords in 1776. She had been married to Augustus John Hervey, who later became 3rd Earl of Bristol. The marriage to the Duke of Kingston was bigamous, though publically celebrated. There is a full report of the case in *Tried by their Peers* by Rupert Furneaux, 1959, and see also, the Marquess of Bristol in extant peerages. The Duke of Kingston had left a will by which his so-called widow was to receive his personal estate without reservation, and a life interest in his real estate, which at her death, was to pass to Charles Medows, later 1st Earl Manvers. The elder nephew, Evelyn Medows was disinherited, and it was from this fact that the trial for bigamy developed.

MARKS

PEERAGE—U.K. Baron Marks, of Woolwich, co. Kent.
SURNAME—Marks.
CR.—16 July 1929. EXT.—24 Sept. 1938.
HISTORY—Michael Marks, of Wellington, co. Somerset, who d. about 1864 was father of,
William Marks, of Myrtle Cottage, Eltham, co. Kent, b. 23 Jan. 1834; m. 22 Sept. 1857, Amelia Adelaide, dau. of Thomas Croydon, of Bristol, and d. 4 Feb. 1918. She d. 27 Feb. 1916. They had issue, with a ygr. son and two daus., an elder son,
Sir George Croydon Marks, **Baron Marks,** b. 9 June 1858; educ. Royal Arsenal Sch., Woolwich, and King's coll. London; M.I.M.E., A.M.I.C.E., apprenticed as an engineer at the Royal Arsenal, Woolwich, and practised as a consultant engineer from 1887; he founded and became the senior partner in the firm of Marks and Clerk; was M.P. for Launceston Div. of Cornwall, 1906-18, and for Northern Div. of Cornwall 1918-24, sitting as a Liberal; cr. Kt. Bach. 1911, and Baron Marks, of Woolwich, co. Kent, 16 July 1929, the month following his adherence to the second Labour Gov. He was cr. C.B.E. 1917. He m. 30 July 1881, Margaret, dau. of Thomas Maynard, of Bath. He d.s.p. 24 Sept. 1938.
ARMS—Argent on a chevron gules two martlets respectant or, on a chief sable, a greyhound courant of the field.
CREST—A winged lion sejant gules, resting the dexter paw on a closed book gold.
SUPPORTERS—On either side a winged lion rampant gules, charged on the shoulder with an open book or.
MOTTO—Animo et labore.

MARSHALL OF CHIPSTEAD

PEERAGE—U.K. Baron Marshall of Chipstead, of Chipstead, co. Surrey.
SURNAME—Marshall.
CR.—14 Jan. 1921. EXT.—29 Mar. 1936.
HISTORY—William Marshall, of London, d. 25 Feb. 1889, leaving issue, with an elder son, and a dau., by his wife, Mary Ann Jones, (d. 28 Aug. 1886), a second son,
Horace Brooks Marshall, of Brixton, co. Surrey, b. 29 Dec. 1829; m. Ellen (d. 1889), dau. of Thomas Grimwood, of Bredfield, co. Suffolk, and d. 1 Sept. 1896, having had issue an only son,
Sir Horace Brooks, **Baron Marshall** of Chipstead, b. 5 Aug. 1865; educ. Dulwich Coll. and Trin. Coll. Dublin, B.A. 1887, M.A. 1891; entered firm of Horace Marshall and Son, Newspaper agents and distributors, 1886, and became sole owner 1896; Lt. for City of London, Sheriff 1901-02; Grand Treasurer of the Freemasons of England, 1901-02; Alderman, City of London, 1909; Master of the Stationers' Co., 1917, and of the Spectacle Makers' Co., 1918-20; Lord Mayor of London, 1918; was cr. Kt. Bach. 1902, made P.C. 1919; K.C.V.O. 1920; cr. Baron Marshall of Chipstead, of Chipstead, co. Surrey, 14 Jan. 1921. He was also K.G. St. J., and possessed the following foreign orders, Leg. d'Hon. of France, of the Crown, (Italy), the Crown (Rumania), Crown (Belgium), George I (Greece), St. Olaf, (Norway), Red Cross (Japan), Excellent Crop (China) and Timsal, (Persia). *The Times* considered that probably no civilian, not being a courtier, had so many foreign decorations of exalted classes. Lord Marshall m. 12 Feb. 1889, Laura, D.G. St. J., dau. of George Siggs, of Streatham Hill, co. Surrey. She d. 8 May 1921. He d. 29 Mar. 1936, having had issue,
1. Horace Brooks, b. 8 Mar. 1892; d. an infant 1893.
1. Laura Ellen, m. 18 Oct. 1917, Joseph Arthur Rank, 1st Baron Rank (extant peerages), and had issue.
2. Gwendoline Brooks, D.G. St. J., m. 26 Oct. 1933, J. R. Tidsley.
ARMS—Or a pale vert on a chief flory gules three antelopes' heads erased of the field.
CREST—In front of a roll of paper ppr. a stag's head erased or.
SUPPORTERS—Dexter, A dragon gules; Sinister, An antelope ppr. both collared or.
MOTTO—Facta non verba.
Lord Marshall's seat was at Shalden Park, Chipstead, Surrey.

MASHAM

PEERAGE—U.K. Baron Masham of Swinton, co. York.
SURNAME—Cunliffe-Lister.
CR.—15 July 1891. EXT.—4 Jan. 1924.
HISTORY—Ellis Cunliffe, was the eldest son of John Cunliffe, of High House, Addingham, co. York, and was b. after 1772; he m. as his first wife, 1 April, 1795, his cousin Ruth Myers, niece and heiress of Samuel Lister, of Manningham Hall, co. York. He m. (2) 1809, Mary, dau. of William Kay, of Cottingham. He assumed the additional surname of Lister,

1809, under the will of Samuel Lister aforesaid, and the further additional surname of Kay, in 1842 upon the death of the said William Kay. He m. (3) 1844, Eliza Mellifont, dau. of Richard Talbot, of Malahide, and d. 24 Nov. 1853, having with other issue by his second wife, a fourth son, (for earlier ancestry and other issue see extant peerage works, under Swinton, E.),

Samuel Cunliffe-Lister, of Swinton Park, Masham, co. York, **1st Baron Masham**, b. 1 Jan. 1815; High Sheriff Yorks, 1887; cr. Baron Masham of Swinton, co. York, 15 July 1891; m. 6 Sept. 1854, Anne, dau. of John Dearden, of Hollins Hall, and d. 2 Feb. 1906. He bought the Swinton estates and the nearby Jervaulx Estate, the former purchase in 1882 from George Danby Affleck, the devisee of Mrs. Danby-Vernon-Harcourt, of Swinton Park (Vernon, B.). He was the inventor of the mechanical woolcomb, a silk comb for utilization of silkwaste, and a velvet loom, and by these efforts he ultimately acquired a very large fortune. A statue was set up to him in Bradford during his lifetime. He had issue with five daus. (see Swinton, E.),

1. Samuel Cunliffe, **2nd Baron Masham** (see below).
2. John Cunliffe, **3rd Baron Masham** (see below).

The elder son,

Samuel Cunliffe Cunliffe-Lister, **2nd Baron Masham**, b. 2 Aug. 1857; educ. Harrow and St. John's Coll. Oxford, B.A. 1878; d. unm. 24 Jan. 1917, and was s. by his brother,

John Cunliffe Cunliffe-Lister, **3rd Baron Masham**, b. 9 Aug. 1867; m. 7 April, 1906, Elizabeth Alice, dau. of W. R. Brockton, of Farndon, Newark-on-Trent, and d.s.p. 4 Jan. 1924. She d. 28 May 1924.

ARMS—Quarterly 1 and 4, Ermine on a fess sable three mullets or; 2 and 3, Sable three conies courant argent.
CRESTS—1. A stag's head erased per fess, ppr. and or, attired sable (Lister). 2. A greyhound sejant argent, charged with a pellet and collared sable (Cunliffe).
SUPPORTERS—Dexter, A stag or, gorged with a collar sable, pendent therefrom an escutcheon of the Lister arms; Sinister, A greyhound argent gorged with a collar sable, therefrom pendent an escutcheon of the Cunliffe arms.
MOTTO—Retinens vestigia famae.
Lord Masham's seat was Swinton Park, near Bedale, Yorkshire.

MATHERS

PEERAGE—U.K. Baron Mathers, of Newtown St. Boswells, co. Rosburgh.
SURNAME—Mathers.
CR.—30 Jan. 1952. **EXT.**—26 Sept. 1965.
HISTORY—George Mathers, J.P., b. 21 June 1862; m. 11 June 1885, Annie, dau. of James Barclay, Seaforth Highlanders, of Newtown St. Boswells, by his wife Agnes Davidson. She d. 24 May 1920. He d. 13 Nov. 1935, leaving issue,

George Mathers, **Baron Mathers**, b. 28 Feb. 1886; educ. Newton St. Boswells Sch., and evening classes, Carlisle and Edinburgh; Pres. Carlisle Trades Council and Labour

Party, 1917-20; mem. Carlisle City Council, 1919; M.P. W.Edinburgh, 1929-31, Linlithgowshire 1935-50, and W. Lothian, 1950-51; Parl. Priv. Sec. to Parl. Under Sec. of State for India and to Under Sec. of State for Colonies, 1929; Comptroller of H.M. Household, 1944-45; Treasurer, 1945-46; Dep. Chief Whip, 1945-46; Lord High Commissioner to Gen. Assembly of Church of Scotland, 1946-48 and 1951; made P.C. 1947, and cr. Baron Mathers of Newtown St. Boswells, 30 Jan. 1952; m. (1) 6 June 1916, Edith Mary (d.s.p. 5 June 1938) dau. of William Robinson, of Carlisle, and (2) 31 Jan. 1940, Jessie Newton, dau. of George Graham, J.P., of Peebles and Edinburgh, and d. 26 Sept. 1965.
Lord Mathers was D.L. Edinburgh, and his residence was 18 Manor Place, Edinburgh. His club was the Royal Empire Society.

McCORQUODALE OF NEWTON

PEERAGE—U.K. Baron McCorquodale of Newton, in the co. Palatine of Lancaster.
SURNAME—McCorquodale.
CR.—2 Sept. 1955. **EXT.**—25 Sept. 1971.
HISTORY—Archibald McCorquodale, m. 1757, Anne MacCallum, and had a second son,

Hugh McCorquodale, m. 19 Sept. 1803, Lucia, dau. of George Hall, of Dundee, and d. 1848 having had with other issue,

George McCorquodale, of Newton-le-Willows, co. Lancaster and of Gadlys, co. Anglesey, High Sheriff co. Lancaster, 1882, and of Anglesey, 1889, founded the firm of McCorquodale printers to do railway printing at Newton-le-Willows in 1846. From this developed the McCorquodale Group of Cos., one of the biggest commercial jobbing printing organizations in Europe; he was b. 10 May 1817; m. (1) 24 Dec. 1844, Louisa Kate, dau. of Frederick Honan. of co. Limerick, and had by her (who d. 1870) five sons, and seven daus. of whom,

1. Hugh, b. 1845; d. unm. 1868.
2. George Frederick, of Dalchroy, co. Moray, b. 5 Nov. 1853; educ. Clifton; m. July 1879, Mary Augusta Walcott, dau. of Lt. Col. Sir Edmund Y. W. Henderson, Commissioner of the Metropolitan Police, and d. 6 May 1936, having by her (who d. Feb. 1935) had issue,
   Edmund George, b. 23 July 1881; educ. Harrow and Trin. Coll. Camb.; d. unm. 24 May 1904.
   Mary Douglas, B.E.M. (Civil) 1945, b. 2 Aug. 1880; m. 16 Dec. 1904, Capt. J. L. Wood, D.S.O., who d. of wounds received in action, 11 June 1915. She d. 5 Dec. 1968, leaving issue, one son.
3. Alexander Cowan, of Cound Hall, co. Salop, High Sheriff of that county 1912, b. 10 Mar. 1858; m. 1886, Maggie Janet, dau. of Alexander Cox of Hafod Elroy, co. Derby, and d. 10 Jan. 1941, having by her (who d. 1945) had issue,
   Alexander George, of Cound Hall, co. Salop, (see B.L.G. 1952) which he sold; b. 7 Aug. 1897; educ. Harrow;

m. (1) 23 April 1927 (m. diss. by div. 1932), (Mary) Barbara Hamilton, only dau. of Major Bertram Cartland, of Littlewood House, Poolbrook, nr. Malvern (she m. 2ndly 1936, Hugh McCorquodale, see below, and is famous as the author of a very large number of romantic novels—see her entry in Who's Who). By his first marriage Alexander George McCorquodale had issue,

     Raine, Countess of Dartmouth, Westminster City Councillor, 1954-65, mem. L.C.C. Lewisham West, 1958 65; mem. G.L.C. Richmond, 1967; Chm. G.L.C. Historical Buildings Board, 1968; b. 9 Sept. 1929; m. 21 July 1948, 9th Earl of Dartmouth, and had issue.

A. G. McCorquodale m. (2) 27 Dec. 1945, Margaret T. E. Cavendish, dau. of G. C. P. Browne, (Kilmaine, B.) and formerly wife of M. B. Shelley, and d. 6 Nov. 1964. She d. 5. Jan. 1966.

Marjorie, F.R.G.S., b. 1 June 1887; m. (1) 26 Nov. 1914, Capt. A. Y. G. Thomson, M.C., who was k. in action, 30 Nov. 1917. She m. (2) 9 June 1923, Lt. Col. H. G. Sotheby, (B.L.G. 1952, Sotheby of Ecton).

4. Norman (see below).

5. Harold of Forest Hall, Ongar, co. Essex, and Saluscraggie, Helmsdale, co. Sutherland, b. 27 April 1865; educ. Harrow and Ch. Ch. Oxford; m. 15 Nov. 1893, Grace, dau. of Major Bevil Granville, of Wellesbourne, co. Warwick (B.L.G. 1952), and d. 27 Sept. 1943, leaving issue,

(1) Kenneth, M.C., T.D., Major Lovat Scouts, Yeo., b. 18 Nov. 1894; educ. Harrow and Jesus Coll. Camb.; m. 16 Oct. 1923, Ellen Viva, dau. of Lt. Col. Martin, of Isle of Skye and had issue,

     1a Alastair, a distinguished athlete, b. 5 Dec. 1925; educ. Harrow; m. 26 July 1947, Rosemary, dau. of Major H. B. Turnor, (B.L.G. 1952, Turnor of Stoke Rochford), and had issue,

         Neil Edmund, b. 1951; educ. Harrow.

         Sarah, b. 1948; m. 1969, Geoffrey Neil Van Cutsem, (B.L.G. 1952, Van Cutsem formerly of St. John's).

     2a Ian, b. 6 and d. 8 Sept. 1929.

     1a Jean, b. 1931; m. 1956, 2nd Baron Denham and had issue.

(2) Hugh, M.C. Cameron Highlanders; b. 1 April 1898; educ. Harrow and R.M.C. Sandhurst; m. 28 Dec. 1936, Barbara Hamilton, C. St. J., dau. of Major Cartland (see above) and d. 29 Dec. 1963, leaving issue,

     1a Ian Hamilton, b. 11 Oct. 1937; educ. Harrow and Magdalene Coll. Camb.

     2a Glen, stockbroker, b. 31 Dec. 1939; educ. Harrow and Ch. Ch. Oxford, B.A.

(3) Donald, b. 4 April 1902; educ. Harrow and R.M.C. Sandhurst; served in World War II, cmdg.

K.D.G. 1940-42, Col. 1942, (despatches, O.B.E. 1942) m. 30 Oct. 1928, Diana Margaret, dau. of F. W. Tennant, of Spofforth Grange, co. York, and had issue,

     John, b. 24 Feb. 1930; educ. Harrow; m. (1) 28 Mar. 1953 (m. diss. by div. 1959) Rosemary Anne Fowler, and had issue,

         1b Rosamond Diana, b. 9 June 1954.

     He m. (2) 18 Sept. 1961, Susan Elizabeth Jardine, dau. of J. A. Pick, and had further issue,

         1b Angus, b. 10 Dec. 1964.

         2b Charlotte Grace, b. 2 Jan. 1963.

     Agnes Jill, b. 3 Dec. 1934;

(4) Angus, b. 13 Dec. 1905; educ. Harrow and R.M.C. Sandhurst; served in World War II, (despatches, Major Coldstream Guards); m. 5 Dec. 1934, his cousin Pamela Constance, dau. of Norman McCorquodale, (see below) and was k. in action at Dunkirk, 31 May 1940, leaving issue,

     Colin Norman, b. 26 May 1938; educ. Harrow and Ch. Ch. Oxford.

     Rona Helena, b. 25 Mar. 1936; m. 1958, David Lowsley-Williams, of Chavenage, Tetbury, co. Glos. and had issue,

         1b David George Savile, b. 19 April 1959.

         1b Caroline, b. 13 Jan. 1962.

         2b Joanna, b. 13 Nov. 1963.

(1) Janet, b. 1895; m. 1921, Col. G. J. Edwards, D.S.O., M.C., and d. 1940 leaving issue, two daus.

1. Edith Beatrice Emilie, m. Thomas Barrington Donnelly, and d. 7 June 1960.
George McCorquodale, of Newton-le-Willows, (see above) m. (2) 3 Jan. 1872, Emily, dau. of Rev. Thomas Sanderson, D.D., Vicar of Great Doddington, co. Northampton, and d. 1895, having by her had further issue, with one dau.,

6. Hugh Stewart, b. 1875; educ. Harrow and Trin. Coll. Camb., B.A. 1897; served in S. African War, Lt. Thorneycroft's Mounted Infantry, and was k. in action at Spion Kop, 29 Jan. 1900.
The fourth son,
Norman McCorquodale, O.B.E. 1920, of Winslow Hall, co. Buckingham, High Sheriff of that county, 1909; b. 24 Oct. 1863; educ. Harrow and Pembroke Coll. Oxford; m. 7 Jan. 1897, Constance Helena, dau. of E. C. Burton, of The Lodge, Daventry, and d. 3 Jan. 1938 having by her issue (she d. 16 Aug. 1939),

1. Norman Duncan, b. 19 Nov. 1898; educ. Harrow and R.M.C. Sandhurst; served in World War II, 1939-45 (despatches, M.C.); mem. of the Royal Co. of Archers, (Sovereign's Bodyguard for Scotland), m. 19 April 1923, Barbara Helen, dau. of Capt. Jersey de Knoop, of Calveley Hall, co. Chester, and had issue,

(1) Euan Norman Jersey, mem. Royal Co. of Archers, Capt. 8th K.R.I. Hussars, b. 22 Oct. 1929; educ. Eton; m. (1) 7 Dec. 1955 (marr. diss. by div. 1965), Ann Sybella Sarah Penelope, dau. of

Brig. Archer Francis Lawrence Clive, (B.L.G. 1952, Clive of Perrystone Court) and had issue,
   David Norman Berkeley, b. 1960.
   Joanna, b. 1957.
He m. (2) 24 April 1969, Sally Seabourne, dau. of Col. W. D. Seabourne May, of Whitchurch, co. Hants.
(1) Helen Barbara Margaret, b. 20 July 1924; m. 12 Nov. 1942, W. G. Gordon, D.F.C., T.D., and had issue three sons and three daus.
(2) Mary Pamela, b. 31 May 1932, m. 10 April 1956, Capt. Fergus Michael Claude Bowes-Lyons, (Strathmore, E.), and had issue.
2. Malcolm Stewart, **Baron McCorquodale** (see below).
3. George, Capt. 99th Royal Bucks. Yeo., Field Regt. R.A., T.A., b. 10 Dec. 1904; educ. Harrow and Ch. Ch. Oxford, M.A., m. 3 Oct. 1933, Hon. Charlotte Enid Lawson-Johnston, dau. of 1st Baron Luke, and had issue,
(1) Duncan Hugh, 1936-42.
(2) Hamish Norman, A.C.A., b. 6 Feb. 1945; educ. Harrow.
(1) Laura Jane, b. 5 Jan. 1935; m. 27 April 1957; Hugh Dudley Wilbraham, son of Capt. Ralph Venables Wilbraham, (B.L.G. 1952, Wilbraham of Delamere) and had issue.
(2) Christina, b. 8 May 1943.
(3) Lucy Enid, b. 4 May 1948.
1. Mary Rosamond, b. 19 Oct. 1897; m. 24 April 1924; the Rev. Canon J. S. Gibbs, M.C., (Aldenham, B.), and d. after a car accident, 17 Feb. 1966, leaving issue.
2. Pamela Constance, b. 10 April 1910; m. her cousin Angus McCorquodale, (see above), and d. 8 Jan. 1944.
The second son,
Sir Malcolm Stewart McCorquodale, **Baron McCorquodale**, of Newton, b. 29 Mar. 1901; educ. Harrow and Ch. Ch. Oxford, B.A. 1922, M.A. 1924; Conservative M.P. for Epsom, 1947-55; and National Conservative M.P. for Sowerby, Div. of Yorks, 1931-45; in 1939 Parl. Priv. Sec. to Pres. of Board of Trade, and 1942-45, Parl. Sec. to Min. of Labour (then Ernest Bevin); and was in charge of man power recruitment; was Chm. of Cttee which worked out the plans for demobilization; served in World War II, 1940-41, as F/Lt. R.A.F.V.R.; Chm. of Govs. of Harrow Sch.; Pres. of Brit. Employers' Confederation; Chm. of Management Cttee. of King Edward's Hospital; Chm. McCorquodale and Co. Ltd., and assoc. cos., and Dir. of Bank of Scotland. He m. (1) 6 Oct. 1931, Winifred Sophia Doris, dau. of J. O. M. Clark, of Glasgow, and by her (who d. 16 Nov. 1960) had issue,
1. Pamela Susan, b. 23 May 1934; m. 2 Feb. 1956, Capt. W. F. E. Forbes, Coldstream Guards, son of Lt. Col. William Forbes of Callendar, (see B.L.G. 1952, Forbes of Callendar), and had two adopted daus.,
(1) Emma Sophia, b. Oct. 1964.
(2) Rosanna Mary, b. Sept. 1967.
2. Prudence Fiona, b. 27 June 1936; m. 4 Jan. 1962, Carel Maurits Mosselmans, T.D., son of Adriaan Willem Mossel-

mans, of The Hague, Netherlands, and had issue,
(1) Michael Ludowick Stewart, b. 27 Nov. 1962.
(2) Julian Frederick Willem, b. 2 Sept. 1964.
Lord McCorquodale m. (2) 26 Jan. 1962, Hon. Daisy Yoskyl Consuelo, dau. of 2nd Viscount Cowdray (see that title in extant peerage works), and widow of Hon. Robert Brampton Gordon, (Cranworth, B.) and of Lt. Col. Alastair Monteith Gibb, Royal Wilts Yeo. Lord McCorquodale d. 25 Sept. 1971.
ARMS—Argent a stag salient gules attired or, surmounted of a fess wreathed of the second and third, within a bordure engrailed or.
CREST—A stag at gaze ppr. attired gules.
SUPPORTERS—On either side, a stag guardant ppr. attired gules, gorged with a collar engrailed azure.
MOTTO—(over crest) Vivat rex.
Lord McCorquodale's seat was Cotswold Park, Cirencester, co. Gloucester. His London home was 30 Jay Mews, S.W.7. His clubs were Carlton and R.A.C.

McENTEE

PEERAGE—U.K. Baron McEntee, of Walthamstow, co. Essex.
SURNAME—McEntee.
CR.—26 June 1951. **EXT.**—11 Feb. 1953.
HISTORY—Dr. William Charles McEntee, Resident Medical Officer at a dispensary in Dublin, b. circa 1844; m. Kate, dau. of Valentine Burchell, She d. circa 1877. He d. circa 1876, leaving issue, with a son Henry Hugh, and a dau. Alicia, an elder son,
Valentine La Touche McEntee, **Baron McEntee**, b. 16 Jan. 1871; educ. Elem. Sch. and private tuition; M.P. West Div. of Walthamstow, 1922-24, and 1929-50; Mayor of Walthamstow 1929-30 and 1951-52; Parl. Priv. Sec. to Parl. Sec. Min. of Works, 1942-45; Chm. Kitchen Cttee. House of Commons, 1945-50; cr. C.B.E. 1948, and Baron McEntee, of Walthamstow, co. Essex, 26 June 1951; m. (1) 1892, Elizabeth (who d.) dau. of Edward Crawford, a bookbinder of Dublin, and (2) June 1920, Catherine, dau. of Charles Windsor, civil servant, of Walthamstow, and d. 11 Feb. 1951.
Lord McEntee's residence was 57 Hillcrest Road, Walthamstow, E.17.

MELFORT

PEERAGE—Scotland. Earl of Melfort, Viscount of Forth, Lord Drummond of Riccartoun, Castlemains and Gilstoun. cr. 21 Aug. 1686. Also Scotland Viscount of Melfort and Lord Drummond of Geillestoun, cr. 14 April 1685.
SURNAME—Drummond.
CR.—as above. **DORMANT.**—28 Feb. 1902.
HISTORY—John Drummond, the second son of the 3rd Earl of Perth (see extant peerages, Perth, E.) b. circa 1650; was cr. as above mentioned, in each case with a special remainder to the heirs male of his body by his

second marriage, failing whom to heirs male of his body whatsoever. He followed James II into exile in France, and there was cr. by James II as Baron of Cleworth, (7 Aug. 1689) and Duke of Melfort, Marquess of Forth, Earl of Isla and Burntizland, Viscount of Rickerton, Lord Castelmains and Galston (17 April 1692) with special remainder as in the creations made while James II was on the throne. He was outlawed on 23 July 1694, and attainted by Act of Parliament 2 July 1695, by which all his honours became forfeited. After James's death he was recognised by Louis XIV as a French peer, le Duc de Melfort. The descendants of the Earl of Melfort continued abroad until, on 28 June 1853, the attainder was reversed, and George Drummond, the great-great-grandson of the 1st Earl of Melfort was declared in England to be entitled to the dignities of Earl of Perth (cr. 1605) Earl of Melfort (1686 as above) Viscount Forth (1686) Lord Drummond (1488), and Lord Drummond of Riccartoun, Castlemains and Gilstoun (1686). He s. to the Earldom of Perth as 14th Earl, but on his death s.p.m.s. 28 Feb. 1902, the Earldom of Melfort etc. became dormant. He was s. as 15th Earl of Perth by his kinsman, William Huntly Drummond, Viscount Strathallan, (see extant peerage works).

**MELROSE

PEERAGE—U.K. Baron Melrose (sometimes styled Melros) of Tyninghame, co. Haddington.
SURNAME—Hamilton.
CR.—24 July 1827. EXT.—1 Dec. 1858.
HISTORY—The 9th Earl of Haddington (see that title in extant peerages)—Sir Thomas Hamilton, K.T., P.C.—was b. 21 June 1780; educ. Univ. of Edinburgh, and Ch. Ch. Oxford B.A. 1801; M.A. 1815; was Tory M.P. for St. Germans, 1802-06, for Cockermouth, Jan.-April 1807; for Callington 1807-12; for St. Michael, 1814-18; for Rochester, 1818-26, and for Yarmouth, Isle of Wight, 1826-27; P.C. 1814; Commissioner for Indian Affairs, 1809; and 1814-22; cr. (v.p.) Baron Melrose (Melros) of Tyninghame, co. Haddington, 24 July 1827 in peerage of U.K. He was Lord Lt. of Ireland 1834-35; First Lord of the Admiralty 1841-46; F.R.S. 1844; an Elder Brother of Trinity House, 1844-59; Lord Privy Seal, 1846; cr. K.T. 1853; he m. 13 Oct. 1802, Maria, dau. of George Parker, 4th Earl of Macclesfield, and d.s.p. 1 Dec. 1858, when the barony of Melrose (Melros) became extinct, and he was s. in his other honours by his cousin,
George Baillie, afterwards Baillie-Hamilton, 10th Earl of Haddington (see extant peerages).

MERRIMAN

PEERAGE—U.K. Baron Merriman of Knutsford in the co. Palatine of Chester.
SURNAME—Merriman.
CR.—27 Jan. 1941. EXT.—18 Jan. 1962.
HISTORY—Charles Anthony Merriman, M.R.C.S., of Heath House, Knutsford, Cheshire was a member of a family chronicled in great detail in B.L.G. 1952 ed. (Merriman formerly of Mildenhall) where the ancestry is traced to the beginning of the 17th century. He had, with other issue, a fifth son,
Frank Merriman, of Hollingford House, Knutsford, co. Chester, b. 18 July 1852; educ. Sandbach Grm. Sch.; m. 8 July 1879, Mariquita, dau. of J. P. Boyd and d. 25 Feb. 1920 leaving, with other issue (see B.L.G. 1952) by her (d. 15 Aug. 1930), an elder dau.,
Sir Frank Boyd Merriman, Baron Merriman, b. 28 April 1880; educ. Winchester; Barrister-at-Law Inner Temple, 1904, Bencher 1927 and Dep. Treasurer to King George VI, 1949; K.C. 1919, Recorder of Wigan 1920-28; M.P. for Rusholme Div. of Manchester 1924. 28; Solicitor Gen. 1928-29 and 1932-33; Pres. of the Probate, Divorce and Admiralty Div. of the High Court, 1933. He served in World War I, 1914-18, (Major Manchester Regt. and D.A.A.G., despatches 3). He was awarded O.B.E. 1918, created Kt. Bach. 1928, made P.C. 1933, created Baron Merriman of Knutsford in the co. Palatine of Chester 27 Jan. 1941 and G.C.V.O. 1950. He m. (1) 11 Sept. 1907, Eva Mary (d. 1 May 1919) dau. of the Rev. H. L. Freer and had issue two daus. He m. (2) 18 Dec. 1920 Olive McLaren, (d. 14 Mar. 1952) dau. of F. W. Carver. He m. (3) 1 Jan. 1953, Jane Lamb, dau. of James Stormouth of Belfast and d. 18 Jan. 1962.
ARMS—Argent on a chevron cottised sable, between three Cornish choughs ppr. as many crescents of the field.
CREST—A serpent nowed, therefrom issuant a dexter arm embowed in armour ppr. garnished or, the hand grasping a short sword also ppr. pommel and hilt gold.
SUPPORTERS—Dexter, A Welsh corgi; Sinister, A springer spaniel both ppr.
MOTTO—Terar dum prosim.
(The Merriman pedigree as shown in B.L.G. 1952 is a very fine example of the way in which a mercantile middle class family can be traced and documented in English records. Lord Merriman expressed to the author his surprise at the degree of attention given to the pedigree in a review of the 1949 B.P. in the Times Literary Supplement, but this was on account of the wealth of information which the pedigree contained.)

MILDMAY OF FLETE

PEERAGE—U.K. Baron Mildmay of Flete.
SURNAME—Mildmay.
CR.—20 Nov. 1922. EXT.—12 May 1950.
HISTORY—Henry Bingham Mildmay of Shoreham Place, co. Kent, and of Flete, co. Devon, b. 1828, d. 1905 leaving with other issue (see extant peerages, St. John Mildmay, Bt.) an eldest son,
Francis Bingham Mildmay, Baron Mildmay of Flete, of Totnes, co. Devon, so cr. 20 Nov. 1922; b. 26 April 1861; educ. Eton and Trin. Coll. Camb. B.A. 1885, M.P. Totnes Div. of Devonshire 1885-Nov. 1918 and for Totnes Div. Dec. 1918-1922; a Dir. of Great Western Railway, Lord Lt. of Devonshire 1928, a mem. of Cttee for review of Political Honours Commission 1923-24, served in S. African War 1900 and in World War I 1914-18 on Gen. Staff in France, Flanders and Germany

(despatches 4 times), Major and Hon. Lt. Col. W. Kent Yeo. Had T.D., was made P.C. 1916 and was cr. a peer 1922. He m. 1906, Alice O. St. J., dau. of Charles Seymour Grenfell, of Elibank, Taplow and had issue,
Anthony Bingham, **2nd Baron Mildmay,** of Flete (see below).
Helen Winifred, b. 17 Aug. 1907; m. 1945 Lt. Cmdr. R. J. B. White, later Mildmay-White, and had issue.
The first Lord Mildmay d. 8 Feb. 1947, and was s. by his only son,
Anthony Bingham Mildmay, **2nd Baron Mildmay** of Flete, b. 14 April 1909; educ. Eton and Trin. Coll. Camb. B.A. 1930; served in World War II, (despatches), Capt. Welsh Guards; Gov. of Royal Vet. Coll., and on Council of the Roy. Agric. Soc. of England. d. unm. 12 May 1950, in an accident while bathing.
ARMS—Argent three lions rampant azure armed and langued gules.
CREST—A lion rampant guardant azure.
SUPPORTERS—On either side a lion guardant azure charged on the shoulder with a mullet and supporting between the forelegs a branch of oak fructed or.
Lord Mildmay's seats were, Flete, Ermington, Devon and Shoreham Place, Sevenoaks, Kent.

MILNER

PEERAGE—U.K. Baron Milner of St. James's London and Capetown in the Colony of Good Hope. U.K. Viscount Milner.
SURNAME—Milner.
CR.—Barony, 27 May 1901. Viscounty 15 July 1902. EXT.—16 May 1925.
HISTORY—Charles Milner, M.D. m. Mary Ierne, dau. of Major Gen. Ready, Gov. of the Isle of Man and had issue,
Sir Alfred Milner, **Baron and Viscount Milner,** b. 23 Mar. 1854 at Giessen in Germany; educ. St. Peter's Tubingen, King's Coll. London and Balliol Coll. Oxford, Hertford Scholar 1874, Jenkyns Exhibitioner 1875-77, Fell. New Coll. Oxford 1876, Pres. Oxford Union Soc., Craven Sch. 1877, Eldon Sch. and Derby Sch. 1878; M.A. 1879, Barrister-at-Law, Inner Temple 1881, sub. editor *Pall Mall Gazette* 1882-85, Priv. Sec. to G. J. Goshen, Chancellor of the Exchequer 1887-89, under sec. for Finance in Egypt 1889-92, Chm. Board of Inland Revenue 1892-97, Gov. of Cape of Good Hope 1897-1901, High Commissioner for S. Africa 1897-1905, Gov. of Transvaal and Orange River Colony 1901-05, Min. without Portfolio and mem. of War Cabinet 1916-18, Sec. of State for War 1918-19, Sec. of State for the Colonies 1919-21; was made P.C. 1901, cr. C.B. 1894, K.C.B. 1895, G.C.M.G. 1897, G.C.B. 1901, Baron Milner of St. James's, London and Capetown in the Colony of the Cape of Good Hope, 27 May 1901 and Viscount Milner, 15 July 1902. He m. 26 Feb. 1921, Violet Georgina L.G. St. J., Chev. of Leg. d'Hon., Editor, *The National Review* 1932, dau. of Adm. Frederick Augustus Maxse and widow of Lord Edward Herbert Gascoyne-Cecil of Great Wigsell, Bodiam, co. Sussex. He d. 16 May 1925.

ARMS—Per chevron vert and or, two snaffle bits erect in chief or and a stag's head erased in base ppr.
CREST—In front of a stag's head erased ppr. gorged with a bar gemel, a snaffle bit fesswise or.
SUPPORTERS—On either side a springbok gorged with a wreath of oak fructed ppr.
MOTTO—Acer non effrenus.
Lord Milner's residences were Sturry Court, Sturry, Kent and 47 Duke Street, St. James's, London S.W.

MILLTOWN

PEERAGE—Irish Earldom of Milltown, cr. 10 May 1763.
Irish Viscounty of Russborough, cr. 8 Sept. 1760.
Irish Barony of Russborough, cr. 5 May 1756.
SURNAME—Leeson.
CR.—see dates as above. DORMANT—since 24 Mar. 1891, the date of death of the 7th Earl of Milltown.
HISTORY—This is a case of a peerage, to the succession of which no claim has been made out. The full account of the history of this peerage is given in current peerage works, evidently with the idea that an heir to the peerage exists and may come forward to prove a claim, but no indication is given as to the line from which this heir may come.
ARMS—Gules a chief argent on the lower part a cloud the rays of the sun issuing therefrom, ppr.
CREST—A demi lion rampant gules, holding between the paws the sun or.
SUPPORTERS—Dexter, A horse; Sinister, A talbot dog both argent.
MOTTO—Clarior e tenebris.

MITCHISON

PEERAGE—U.K. Life. Baron Mitchison of Carradale, co. Argyll.
SURNAME—Mitchison.
CR.—5 Oct. 1964. EXT.—14 Feb. 1970.
HISTORY—Gilbert Richard Mitchison, **Baron Mitchison** was the elder son of Arthur Maw Mitchison by his wife Mary Emmeline Russell. He was b. 23 Mar. 1894; educ. Eton and New Coll. Oxford, M.A., served in World War I 1914-18, Major G.S.O. 2; Barrister-at-Law, Inner Temple 1917, Q.C. 1946; M.P. Kettering Div. of Northants 1945-64; cr. C.B.E. 1953 and a Life Peer as Baron Mitchison, of Carradale co. Argyll, 5 Oct. 1964. He m. 11 Feb. 1916, Naomi Mary Margaret (author Naomi Mitchison) dau. of J. S. Haldane (B.L.G.) 1952 Chinnery-Haldane of Gleneagles) and had issue,
1. Denis Anthony, b. 6 Sept. 1919; educ. Abbotsholme Sch., Trin. Coll. Camb., M.B., B. Chir. 1943; and Univ. Coll. Hosp., M.R.C.S., Eng. and L.R.C.P. Lond. 1943; Prof. of Bacteriology, Royal Post Graduate Med. Sch. of London; m. 9 Sept. 1940, Ruth Sylvia, M.B., B. Chir. Camb., M.R.C.S. Eng., and L.R.C.P. Lond., dau. of Hubert A. Gill, of Croy-

don, co. Surrey, and had issue, two sons and two daus.
2. John Murdoch, b. 11 June 1922; educ. Winchester and Trin. Coll. Camb., B.A. 1943, M.A. 1946, Ph.D. 1950, Fell. 1950-54, Prof. of Zoology, Edin. Univ. 1964; m. 21 June 1947, Rosalind Mary, dau. of E. W. Wrong, of Toronto, Canada, and had issue, a son and three daus.
3. Nicolas Avrion, F.R.S., b. 5 May 1928; m. 30 July 1957, Lorna Margaret, dau. of Major Gen. J. S. S. Martin, I.M.S. and had issue, two sons, and three daus.
1. Sonja Lois, B.A. Lady Margaret Hall, Oxford; m. 21 Mar. 1959, John Godfrey, and had issue two daus.
2. Valentine Harriet Isobel Dione, B.A. Somerville Coll. Oxford, m. 12 Jan. 1955, Mark Arnold-Forster, (B.L.G. 1952), and had issue three sons, and two daus.
Lord Mitchison d. 14 Feb. 1970.
His residence was Carradale House, Carradale, Campbelltown, co. Argyll.

MONCKTON

PEERAGE—U.K. Baron Monckton, of Serlby, co. Nottingham.
SURNAME—Monckton-Arundell.
CR.—4 July 1887. EXT.—1 Jan. 1971.
HISTORY—The lineage of the Monckton family is found in extant peerages under Galway, Viscount, and Monckton of Brenchley, Viscount. The 7th Viscount Galway, in the peerage of Ireland, George Edmund Milnes Monckton-Arundell, b. 18 Nov. 1844; educ. Ch. Ch. Oxford M.A.; was M.P. North Notts, 1872-85; was A.D.C. to Queen Victoria, 1897-1901; to King Edward VII, 1901-10; and to King George V, 1910-20; was cr. Baron Monckton, of Serlby, co. Nottingham, 4 July 1887, in the peerage of the U.K.; m. 24 July 1879, Vere, L.J. St. J., dau. of Ellis Gosling, of Busbridge Hall, Surrey; she d. 3 Jan. 1921. He d. 7 Mar. 1931. Their issue were,
Their issue were,
 George Vere Arundell, 8th Viscount Galway, and 2nd Baron Monckton (see below).
 Violet Frances, O. St. J., m. 1904, Lt. Col. G. H. J. Skeffington Smyth, who assumed the surname of FitzPatrick in 1938, and d. 24 Oct. 1930 leaving issue.
The only son,
 George Vere Arundell Monckton-Arundell, 8th Viscount Galway and 2nd Baron Monckton, b. 24 Mar. 1882; educ. Ch. Ch. Oxford, M.A.; served in World War I, (despatches, D.S.O., O.B.E.); cr. G.C.M.G. 1935; P.C. 1937; Col. Life Guards; m. 24 June 1922, Hon. Lucy Emily Margaret White, dau. of 3rd Baron Annaly, and d. 27 Mar. 1943, leaving issue.
1. Simon George Robert, 9th Viscount Galway, and 3rd Baron Monckton (see below).
2. Mary Victoria, m. 1947, D. H. Fetherstonhaugh, (Fetherstonhaugh of Kirkoswald, (B.L.G.)) and had issue.
2. Celia Ella Vere, m. 1959, Sir Joshua Francis Rowley, 7th Bt. and had issue.
3. Isabel Cynthia.
The only son,

Simon George Robert Monckton-Arundell, 9th Viscount Galway, and 3rd Baron Monckton, b. 11 Nov. 1929; educ. Eton; Major the Life Guards; m. 4 Nov. 1953, Lady Teresa Jane Fox-Strangways, only dau. of 7th Earl of Ilchester, and d. 1 Jan. 1971, when the Barony of Monckton became extinct and the Viscounty devolved upon the 9th Viscount's heir and kinsman,
 William Arundell Monckton, 10th Viscount Galway (see extant peerages).
ARMS—Quarterly 1 and 4, Sable six swallows, three, two and one, argent; (Arundell); 2 and 3, Sable on a chevron between three martlets or as many mullets of the field (Monckton).
CRESTS—1. On a chapeau azure, turned up ermine, a swallow argent (Arundell). 2. A martlet or (Monckton).
SUPPORTERS—Two unicorns ermine, crined, armed, and unguled, each gorged with an Eastern diadem or.
MOTTO—Famam extendere factis.
The seats of Lord Monckton were Serlby Hall, Bawtry, co. Nottingham and Bishopfield House, Bawtry, Doncaster.

MONSLOW

PEERAGE—U.K. Life Baron Monslow of Barrow-in-Furness.
SURNAME—Monslow.
CR.—15 June 1966. EXT.—12 Oct. 1966.
HISTORY—Walter Monslow was organizing Sec. of Assoc. Soc. of Locomotive Engineers and Firemen, Labour M.P. Barrow-in-Furness 1945-66, Min. of Civil Aviation 1949-50 and Min. of Food, 1950-51, cr. a life peer 15 June 1966 and d. 12 Oct. 1966.

MORLEY OF BLACKBURN

PEERAGE—U.K. Viscount Morley of Blackburn, co. Lancaster.
SURNAME—Morley.
CR.—2 May 1908. EXT.—23 Sept. 1923.
HISTORY—John Morley, Viscount Morley, second son of Jonathan Morley, a Surgeon of Blackburn, co. Lancaster, was distinguished as a politician and as a writer. He wrote lives of Gladstone, Cobden, Voltaire, Diderot, Walpole and Cromwell, and was Editor of the English Men of Letters and Twelve English Statesmen series. He is also said to have been the first peer to have had no coat of arms. He was b. 24 Dec. 1838; educ. Cheltenham Coll. and Lincoln Coll. Oxford, B.A. 1859; Hon. Fell. of All Souls, Barrister-at-Law, Lincoln's Inn, 1873; Editor of the Pall Mall Gazette, and of The Fortnightly Review; M.P. for Newcastle-on-Tyne, 1883-95; and for Montrose Burghs, 1896-1908; Chief Sec. for Ireland, with a seat in the Cabinet, 1886, and 1892-95; made P.C. 1886; Bencher, Lincoln's Inn, 1893; Sec. of State for India, 1905-10; Lord Pres. of the Council, 1910-14; cr. O.M. 1902; and Viscount Morley of Blackburn, co. Lancaster, 2 May 1908. He m. Mary, a widow, of one Ayling, and d.s.p. 23 Sept. 1923. She d. Nov. 1923.

Viscount Morley's residence was Flowermead, Wimbledon Park, S.W. He was cremated and the ashes bur. in Putney Vale Cemetery as were those of his widow. His club was the Athenaeum.

MORRIS

PEERAGE—U.K. (Life) Baron Morris of Spiddal, co. Galway.
SURNAME—Morris.
CR.—5 Dec. 1889. **EXT.**—8 Sept. 1901.
HISTORY—Sir Michael Morris, 1st Bt., **Baron Morris** of Spiddal, co. Galway, and later Baron Killanin of Galway, co. Galway, son of Martin Morris, of Spiddal and Galway, b. 14 Nov. 1826; educ. Trin. Coll. Dublin, B.A., and Senior Moderator in ethics and logic, 1847; Barrister-at-Law, King's Inn, 1849; Recorder of Galway, 1857-65; Q.C. 1863; made P.C. Ireland 1866, and Bencher, King's Inn, 1866; Independent Conservative M.P. for Galway, 1865; Solicitor Gen. for Ireland, July 1866, and Attorney Gen. for Ireland, Nov. 1866; Judge of the Court of Common Pleas, 1867, Lord Chief Justice 1876, and Lord Chief Justice of Ireland, 1887; a Lord of Appeal in Ordinary, 1889-1900; made a Baronet, 14 Sept. 1885; a life peer as Baron Morris of Spiddal, co. Galway, 5 Dec. 1889, as Lord of Appeal in Ordinary; he was further cr. Baron Killanin of Galway, co. Galway, as an hereditary peer, 15 June 1900. He m. 18 Sept. 1860, Anna, (d. 17 Oct. 1906), dau. of the Hon. George Henry Hughes, Baron of the Court of Exchequer in Ireland, and d. 8 Sept. 1901, when his life peerage ceased he was s. in the baronetcy and the hereditary barony of Killanin by his eldest son,
    Martin Henry FitzPatrick Morris, 2nd Bt. and 2nd Baron Killanin, for whom see extant peerage works, under Killanin, B.
ARMS—Ermine a fess indented sable, in base a lion rampant sable armed and langued gules.
CREST—On a fasces ppr. a lion's head erased gutté de sang.
SUPPORTERS—On either side a lion gules gorged with a chain or pendent therefrom an escutcheon ermine charged with a sword erect ppr. pomel and hilt gold and standing on a fasces also ppr.
MOTTO—Si Deus nobiscum quis contra nos?

MORRISON OF LAMBETH

PEERAGE—U.K. Life. Baron Morrison of Lambeth, of Lambeth, co. London.
SURNAME—Morrison.
CR.—2 Nov. 1959. **EXT.**—6 Mar. 1965.
HISTORY—Herbert Stanley Morrison, **Baron Morrison** of Lambeth, was b. 3 Jan. 1888, the son of Henry Morrison of Brixton, a police constable; educ. at Elementary sch., and on leaving school he became a shop assistant. He had a very distinguished career in the Labour Party, in local and national politics. He was Sec. of the London Labour Party 1915-45 and was a mem. of the L.C.C. 1922-45, being largely the architect of the Party's gaining control of the L.C.C. of which he was Leader from 1934-40. Morrison was M.P., S. Div. of

Hackney 1923-24, 1929-31 and 1935-45, and for E. Div. of Lewisham 1945-50 and S. Div. of Lewisham 1950-59. Home Sec. 1940-45, Lord Pres. of the Council and Leader of the House of Commons 1945-51, Foreign Sec. Mar.-Oct. 1951. He was defeated in 1955 by Hugh Gaitskill in contest for the leadership of the Labour Party. He was made P.C. 1931 cr. C.H. 1951 and a Life Peer as Baron Morrison of Lambeth, of Lambeth, co. London. He m. (1) 15 Mar. 1919, Margaret, dau. of Howard Kent and had issue a dau., Mary Joyce who m. (1) Hon. H. Williams son of Lord Williams of Barnburgh (see that title) and (2) G. N. Mandelson. Mrs. Morrison d. 11 July 1953. Lord Morrison m. (2) 6 Jan. 1955, Edith, dau. of John M. Meadowcroft and d. 6 Mar. 1965.

MOULTON

PEERAGE—U.K. Life. Baron Moulton of Bank, co. Southampton.
SURNAME—Moulton.
CR.—1 Oct. 1912. **EXT.**—9 Mar. 1921.
HISTORY—The Rev. James Egan Moulton, a Wesleyan Minister, had a third son,
    Sir John Fletcher Moulton, **Baron Moulton** of Bank, co. Southampton, b. 18 Nov. 1844; educ. Kingswood Sch. near Bath and St. John's Coll. Camb. Senior Wrangler and First Smith's Prizeman 1868, M.A., Fell. Christ's Coll. Camb. 1868-73; Barrister-at-Law, Middle Temple 1874, Q.C. 1885, Bencher and Treasurer Middle Temple, 1910, M.P. Clapham Div. of Battersea 1885-86, for South Hackney 1894-95 and for Launceston Div. of Cornwall 1898-1906, Lord Justice of Appeal 1906, made P.C. and cr. Kt. Bach. 1906, Lord of Appeal in Ordinary, Oct. 1912 and cr. a life peer. He was Dir. Gen. of Explosive Supplies in Ministry of Munitions, 1915, F.R.S. and F.R.A.S. He m. (1) 24 April 1875, Clara, widow of R. W. Thompson and by her, who d. 13 July 1888, had issue,
    Hugh Fletcher, B.A. Camb. 5th Wrangler 1898, Barrister-at-Law, Middle Temple, served in World War I 1914-18, Major R.G.A., M.P. Salisbury Div. of Wiltshire 1923-24, wrote life of his father 1922. b. 1 April 1876, m. 30 July 1902, Ida, dau. of G. B. Houghton.
He m. (2) 20 May 1901, Mary May, dau. of Major Henry Davis, of Naples. She d. 25 Jan. 1909 leaving a dau.
    Sylvia May Fletcher, b. 15 June 1902; B.A. Camb., and Barrister-at-Law, Middle Temple.
Lord Moulton d. 9 Mar. 1921.
ARMS—Gules four bars per pale argent and or, two flaunches or each charged with a sun gules.
CREST—Upon a mount a lamb statant ppr. holding in the mouth a trefoil slipped vert, the whole between four ears of wheat stalked and leaved two on either side also ppr.
Lord Moulton was member of the following clubs: Athenaeum, Reform, National Liberal, Savage, Garrick, Hurlingham, Royal Automobile and Ranelagh.

MOUNT CASHELL

PEERAGE—Ireland. Baron Kilworth of Moore Park, co. Cork, 14 July 1764.
Ireland. Viscount Mount Cashell, of the city of Cashell, 22 Jan. 1766.
Ireland. Earl Mount Cashell, of Cashell, 5 Jan. 1781.
SURNAME—Moore.
CR.—Dates as above. **EXT.**—1 April 1915.
HISTORY—Richard Moore, of Clonmel, High Sheriff, co. Waterford, 1666, and Tipperary, 1675, d. 1690, (will proved 10 Sept. 1690) leaving issue by his wife, Margaret,

1. Stephen (see below).
2. Thomas, of Chancellorstown, co. Tipperary, m. Eleanor, dau. of Richard Covert, of Cork, Alderman, (she m. 2ndly James Harrison, of Cloghford, co. Tipperary). His will was proved 2 Mar. 1702/3. He had the following issue,
   (1) Stephen, ancestor of Moore, of Barn, co. Tipperary.
   (2) Guy, of Abbey, co. Tipperary, b. 1691; High Sheriff, co. Tipperary, 1722; m. 1717, Mary, dau. and heiress of Chidley Coote, and had issue, (Waterpark, B.).
   (3) Robert, of Ardmoyle, and Mooremount, m. Elinor, the ygr. dau. of Chidley Coote, and had issue.
   (4) Thomas, of Moore Hall, co. Cork, and of Marlfield, co. Tipperary, m. 1721, Mary, dau. of Richard Moore, of Cashell and d. 1752, having had issue,
      1a Stephen, High Sheriff, co. Tipperary, 1757; m. 12 Feb. 1751, Alicia, ygr. dau. of Sir Robert Maude, Bt.
      2a Richard, b. 1725.
      1a Elizabeth, m. Sir Arthur Newcomen, Bt.
      2a Sophia, Mrs. Preston.
      3a Anne, m. Sir James May, Bt.,
      4a Mary, d. young.
   (5) Covert.

The elder son,
Stephen Moore, of Kilworth, co. Cork, which he bought. He lent £3,000 to William III, a loan never repaid. He was appointed by William III as Gov. of Tipperary, and Col. of the local militia. He m. Bridget Croke and d. 1703, having had with an only dau., Margaret (who m. 1698 George King, of Kilpeacon, co. Limerick, who d.s.p.) an only son,
Richard Moore, of Cashell, co. Tipperary, m. 22 Mar. 1692, Elizabeth, eldest dau. of William Ponsonby, Viscount Duncannon, and d.v.p. 1699, leaving by her (who m. 2ndly, Thomas Newcomen),

1. Stephen, **1st Viscount Mount Cashell** (see below).
1. Mary, m. 1721, Thomas Moore, of Moore Hall, and Marlfield, (see above).
2. Elizabeth, m. William Chartres.

The only son,
Stephen Moore, was cr. 14 July 1764, Baron Kilworth, of Moore Park, co. Cork, and on 22 Jan. 1766, **Viscount Mount Cashell,** of the City of Cashell, both in the peerage of Ireland. The 1st Viscount m. Alicia, dau. of Hugh Colville, and d. 1766, having had issue,

1. Richard, b. 1725; d. unm. 1761.
2. Stephen, **2nd Viscount and 1st Earl** (see below).

3. William, m. Anne, dau. and coheir of D. Fowkes, and d. 21 Nov. 1810, leaving issue,
   (1) Stephen, of Saperton, d. 11 Sept. 1838.
   (2) William, of Moore Hill, and Saperton, m. 1812, Mary, dau. of the Rev. the Hon. Robert Moore, She d. 18 Mar. 1834. He d. 4 Mar. 1849, having had,
      William, of Moore Hill, co. Waterford, b. 14 Jan. 1816; m. Aug. 1845, Jane, dau. of Charles Gooden and d. 21 Nov. 1856.
      Helena Anne, m. 19 Sept. 1839, Robert Perceval Maxwell, of Finnebrogue, co. Down, and d. 23 Jan. 1888, leaving issue.
   (1) Elizabeth.
4. Robert, Rev., m. Isabella, only dau. of Richard Odell, of Odell Lodge, co. Waterford, and d. 1817, having had, with other issue deceased, three daus.,
   (1) Mary, m. her cousin, William Moore, see above.
   (2) Harriet.
   (3) Louisa, d. 13 Nov. 1853.
1. Sarah, m. 21 Sept. 1750, Henry Sandford, of Castlerea, and d. 3 Oct. 1764, leaving issue.
2. Mary, m. 12 Oct. 1761, the 4th Earl of Inchiquin and d.s.p. 1793.
3. Elizabeth, m. the Hon. Ponsonby Moore, brother of the 1st Marquess of Drogheda.
4. Catherine, m. 1st Lord Hartland, and d. 1834.

The eldest surv. son,
Stephen Moore, 2nd Baron Kilworth, 2nd Viscount Mount Cashell and **1st Earl Mount Cashell,** being cr. the last on 5 Jan. 1781. He m. 1769, Helena, dau. of the 2nd Earl of Moira, and d. 14 May 1790, having had issue,

1. Stephen, **2nd Earl** (see below).
2. John, b. 19 June 1772.
3. William, b. 7 April 1775.
1. Helena, m. 6 May 1794, George King, 3rd Earl of Kingston and had issue.

The eldest son,
Stephen Moore, **2nd Earl Mount Cashell,** b. 19 Mar. 1770; m. 12 Sept. 1791, Margaret, dau. of Robert King, 2nd Earl of Kingston, (she m. 2ndly, G. W. Tighe, and d. 1835), and d. Oct. 1822, having had issue,

1. Stephen, **3rd Earl** (see below).
2. Robert, Lt. Col. b. 11 July 1793; d. 4 Nov. 1856.
3. Edward, George, Rev., Canon of Windsor, and Rector of West Ilsley, co. Berks, b. 18 Aug. 1798; m. 27 Mar. 1827 Anne Matilda, dau. of Robert George William Tefusis 17th Baron Clinton, and d. 8 Feb. 1876. She d. 24 Feb. 1876. They had issue,
   (1) Edward George Augustus Harcourt, **6th Earl Mount Cashell** (see below).
   (2) Charles Robert, b. 11 Aug. 1831; d. 2 Feb. 1853.
   (1) Louisa Fanny Matilda, d. unm. 11 Aug. 1902. With her sister Mary given the precedence as earl's daughters 10 Aug. 1899.
   (2) Mary Augusta Georgiana, m. 24 Nov. 1864, Algernon Gilliat, of Fern Hill, co. Berks, and d. 23 April 1903, leaving issue.

4. Richard Francis, H.E.I.C.S., b. 26 July 1802; d. 15 Nov. 1873.
1. Helena Eleanor, m. 9 Feb. 1813, Sir Richard Robinson, Bt. of Rokeby Hall, and d. 23 Sept. 1859.
2. Jane Eliza, m. 17 June 1819, Rt. Hon. William Yates Peel, son of Sir Robert Peel, 1st Bt. (Peel of Drayton Manor, Bt.).
3. Elizabeth Anne, d. 6 Sept. 1892, aged 88.
The eldest son,
Stephen Moore, **3rd Earl Mount Cashell,** b. 20 Aug. 1792; m. 31 May 1819, Anna Maria, dau. of Samuel Wyse, Canton of Berne, Switzerland, She d. 4 July 1876. He d. 10 Oct. 1883. They had issue,
1. Stephen, **4th Earl** (see below).
2. Charles William More Smyth, **5th Earl** (see below).
3. George Francis, b. 19 April 1832; m. 15 Aug. 1865, Jane (d. 13 July 1868) dau. of George Mainwaring Dance, and d. 24 Jan. 1881.
1. Jane, d. unm. 8 Aug. 1907.
2. Helena Adelaide, m. 15 Nov. 1849, Rev. Edward Henry Newenham, of Coolmore, co. Cork, and had issue.
3. Anna Maria Isabella, m. (1) 27 July 1848, R. P. H. Jodrell, who d.s.p. 1855 (Jodrell, Bt.) and (2) 30 April 1856, J. H. Freme, of Wrentnall House, co. Shropshire.
4. Catherine Louisa, m. 10 Aug. 1858, Richard Spread Morgan, of Bridestown, co. Cork, and d. 18 May 1886, leaving issue.
The eldest son,
Stephen Moore, **4th Earl Mount Cashell,** b. 11 Mar. 1825; d. unm. 9 Nov. 1889, being s. by his brother,
Charles William Moore, **5th Earl Mount Cashell,** High Sheriff co. Waterford, 1862; b. 17 Oct. 1826; m. (1) 18 Jan. 1848, Charlotte Mary, only child of Richard Smyth, of Ballynatray, co. Waterford. She d. 17 Jan. 1892. They had issue,
1. Richard Charles More, b. 26 Sept. 1839; m. 16 Oct. 1884, Helen Stirling, dau. of Rev. William Markellar, of Edinburgh, and d.v.p. 3 Jan. 1888, leaving issue,
   Claude Stephen William Richard, 1887-90.
1. Harriette Gertrude Isabella, m. 17 Oct. 1872, Col. J. H. Graham Smyth, formerly Holroyd. They assumed by Royal Licence, 3 June 1892, on s. to the estates of Ballynatray, the surname and arms of Smyth. They had issue.
2. Helena Anna Mary, d. unm. 6 Nov. 1876.
3. Charlotte Adelaide Louisa Riversdale, m. 27 Aug. 1898, Brooke Wellington Brasier.
The 5th Earl m. (2) 17 Oct. 1893, Florence, dau. of Henry Cornelius, of Ross-na-Clonagh, Queen's Co. He assumed by Royal Licence 29 July 1858, the surname and arms of Smyth only but relinquished that surname when he s. to the peerage. He d. 20 Feb. 1898 being s. by his cousin,
Edward George Augustus Harcourt Moore, **6th Earl Mount Cashell,** b. 27 Nov. 1829; M.A. St. John's Coll. Camb.; d. unm. 1 April 1915.
ARMS—Sable a swan argent, membered and beaked, within a bordure engrailed or.

CREST—A goshawk wings addorsed preying on a coney all ppr.
SUPPORTERS—Dexter, A leopard; Sinister, A rhinoceros, both ppr. collared and chained or.
MOTTO—Vis unita fortior.

MOUNTMORRES

PEERAGE—Ireland. Baron Mountmorres, of Castlemorres, co. Kilkenny. Viscount Mountmorres.
SURNAME—De Montmorency (Morres).
CR.—Barony, 4 May 1756. Viscounty, 29 June 1763. **EXT.**—15 Oct. 1951.
HISTORY—The family of De Montmorency is that of the Baronets of the name, whose history occurs in extant peerage works. It begins with Roderick Morres, of Knockagh, co. Tipperary, whose son was cr. a baronet Sir John Morres, 28 Mar. 1631. It appears that the surname of de Montmorency, described as the ancient surname of the family, was simply assumed in 1815 (see article in present volume on the extinct peerage, Viscount Frankfort de Montmorency) and this surname was taken by the remaining branches of the family.
The line of the baronets is given in extant peerage works under De Montmorency, and the descent of the baronets and their collaterals down to Frances Morres, of Castle Morres, whose eldest son,
Hervey Morres, (de Montmorency) was cr. 4 May 1756, Baron Mountmorres of Castle Morres, and on 29 June 1763, **Viscount Mountmorres,** both titles in the peerage of Ireland. The 1st Viscount was m. (1) 3 Nov. 1742, to Letitia (who d. 9 Feb. 1754) dau. of 1st Earl of Bessborough, and by her had issue, (with two daus.), a son,
1. Hervey Redmond, **2nd Viscount** (see below).
He m. (2), July 1755, Mary, dau. of William Wall, of Coolnmuckty Castle, co. Waterford, and had further issue,
2. Francis Hervey, **3rd Viscount** (see below).
3. William Mary, b. 1760; m. Ann Clacke, and was drowned in 1809, leaving a dau.
The 1st Viscount d. 6 April 1776, and was s. by his eldest son,
Hervey Redmond Morres, **2nd Viscount Mountmorres,** who inherited the baronetcy of the family on the death in 1795 of Sir Nicholas Morres, 9th Bt. thus becoming 10th Bt., He d. unm. 17 Aug. 1797, and was s. by his half brother,
Sir Francis Hervey Morres (de Montmorency) 11th Bt., and **3rd Viscount Mountmorres,** b. 1 Sept. 1756; m. 24 April 1794, Anne (d. 21 July 1823), dau. of Joseph Reade, of Castle Hoyle, and had issue with three daus.,
Hervey, **4th Viscount** (see below).
The 3rd Viscount resumed the surname of De Montmorency by Royal Licence, and d. 23 Mar. 1833, being s. by his only son,
Hervey de Montmorency, **4th Viscount Mountmorres,** and 12th Bt., Dean of Athenry, b. 20 Aug. 1796; m. 5 July 1831, Sarah (d. 22 Feb. 1877) dau. of William Shaw, of Temple Hill, and had issue with two daus.,
1. William Browne, **5th Viscount** (see below).

2. Francis Raymond, Barrister-at-Law, b. 6 May 1835; m. 1 June 1865, Elizabeth Hester, dau. of Lt. Col. J. R. Mathews, of White Abbey, co. Antrim, and d.s.p. 27 Sept. 1910.
3. Albert Bouchard, b. 18 Mar. 1840, Col. R.A.; d. unm. 19 May 1899.
4. Arthur Hill Trevor, B.A. Dublin, M.D., L.R.C.S.I.; b. 19 Feb. 1846; m. 28 Mar. 1878, Caroline, dau. of Rev. George Kemmis, of St. Helen's, Blackrock, and d. 1 Jan. 1910, leaving issue with three daus.,

Arthur Hervé Alberic Bouchard, **7th Viscount** (see below).

The 4th Viscount d. 23 Jan. 1872, and was s. by his eldest son,

William Browne de Montmorency, **5th Viscount Mountmorres,** and 13th Bt., b. 21 April 1832; m. 12 Nov. 1862, Harriet (d. 20 Feb. 1923) dau. of George Broadrick, of Hamphall Stubbs, co. York, and granddau. of Sir Richard Fletcher, 1st Bt., of Carrow, and had issue with two daus. who d. unm.,

1. Hervey Ramond, b. 26 Mar. 1865, d. 2 June 1865.
2. William Geoffrey Bouchard, **6th Viscount** (see below).
3. Arthur Alberic, Midshipman, R.N., b. 25 Oct. 1874; drowned 15 July 1891.

The 5th Viscount was murdered at Rusheed, Ballincode, co. Galway, 25 Sept. 1880, and was s. by his elder surv. son,

The Rev. William Geoffrey Bouchard de Montmorency, **6th Viscount Montmorres,** and 14th Bt., Clerk in Holy Orders, formerly Lt. R.N.V.R., b. 23 Sept. 1872; educ. Radley, Paris Univ. and Balliol Coll. Oxford; Dir. Tropical Inst. Liverpool Univ. 1904-08; ordinaed Deacon, 1913, and Priest 1914; Vicar of Swinton, Lancs, 1917-25; and of St. Mark's South Farnborough, 1925-33; Rector of St. Paul's, Wokingham, co. Berks, 1935; Chaplain, R.N.V.R., m. (1) 27 Sept. 1893, Bessie Louise Cameron, dau. of S. T. Rowe, of Trecarrel, Redruth, and by her who d. 15 Oct. 1931, had issue,

Marjorie Evelyn Louise, b. 15 Oct. 1897; m. 24 Oct. 1918, Sir Roger B. Hulton 3rd Bt. and had issue.

The 6th Viscount m. (2) 10 April 1934, Tempe Irene (d. 4 Mar. 1937) dau. of C. F. Cross, and d.s.p.m. 2 Dec. 1936 being s. by his cousin,

The Rev. Arthur Hervé Alberic Bouchard de Montmorency, **7th Viscount Mountmorres,** and 15th Bt., b. 6 Feb. 1879; educ. Trin. Coll. Dublin, B.A. 1907, M.A. 1912; clerk in Holy Orders, incumbent of Omeath, co. Louth, 1922-39; Rector of Lanham and Vicar of Terriard, co. Hants, 1939-48; mem. Alton R.D.C. 1939-43; served in the S. African War, (medal with two clasps), and in World War I, 1915-16, as Chaplain to the Forces, hon. Chaplain from 1916; m. 15 April 1914, Katherine Sophia Clay, dau. of T. A. Warrand, of Bridge of Allan, and had issue,

1. Sheila Marguerite Evelyn, served in World War II in C.D.; m. 9 Dec. 1950, Robert Vernon Smith, and had issue, two sons.
2. Carole Madge Warrand, served in World War II in the W.A.A.F., m. 6 Dec. 1947, D. O. Morris, and had issue, a son and a dau.

The 7th Viscount d. 15 Oct. 1951, when the

Viscounty and Barony became extinct and the baronetcy passed to his kinsman, Sir (Hervey) Angus de Montmorency, 16th Bt., for whom see extant peerage.

ARMS—Or a cross gules, between four eagles displayed azure.
CREST—Out of a ducal coronet a peacock in its pride ppr.
SUPPORTERS—Two angels ppr. hair and wings or, vested argent.
MOTTO—Dieu ayde.

MOUNT STEPHEN

PEERAGE—U.K. Baron Mount Stephen, of Mount Stephen, in the Province of British Columbia and Dominion of Canada, and of Dufftown, co. Banff.
SURNAME—Stephen.
CR.—23 June 1891. **EXT.**—29 Nov. 1921.
HISTORY—William Stephen, of Hillside, and of Dufftown, co. Banff, b. 1769; d. 1852, having had by his wife, Elizabeth Cameron, (who d. 7 June 1845, aged 69) with other issue,

William Stephen, of Dufftown, and later of Montreal, Canada, b. 25 Mar. 1801; m. 22 Nov. 1828, Elspet, dau. of John Smith, of Knockando, co. Elgin, and had with other children,

Sir George Stephen, Bt., and **Baron Mount Stephen,** b. 5 June 1829, in Scotland; entered business in Montreal in 1850, and became a successful cloth manufacturer; with a group of colleagues he completed the St. Paul and Pacific and Canadian Pacific Railways; Pres. of Canadian Pacific Railway Co., 1880-88; settled in England 1893. He was cr. a baronet 3 Mar. 1886, and a peer as Baron Mount Stephen, of Mount Stephen, in the Province of British Columbia and Dominion of Canada, and of Dufftown, co. Banff, 23 June 1891. He m. 8 Mar. 1853, Charlotte Annie, dau. of Benjamin Kane. She d.s.p. 10 April 1896. He m. (2) Gian, L.G. St. J., dau. of Capt. Robert George Tufnell, R.N. He d. 29 Nov. 1921.

ARMS—Or on a mount in base vert a maple tree ppr., in chief two fleurs-de-lis azure.
CREST—A horse's head erased argent, bridled ppr. holding in the mouth a sprig of three maple leaves vert, and charged on the neck with a fleur-de-lis azure.
SUPPORTERS—On either side a horse reguardant argent bridled ppr. holding in the mouth a sprig of three maple leaves vert and charged on the shoulder with a fleur-de-lis azure.
MOTTO—Contra audentior.

Lord Mount Stephen's seats were Grand Metis, Quebec, Canada; Brocket Hall, Hatfield, Herts. His town residence was 17 Carlton House Terrace, S.W. His Clubs were Carlton, St. James's, Marlborough, Arthur's and Travellers.

MOUNT TEMPLE

PEERAGE—U.K. Baron Mount Temple, of Lee, co. Southampton.
SURNAME—Ashley.
CR.—13 Jan. 1932. **EXT.**—3 July 1939.

HISTORY—Wilfrid William Ashley, **Baron Mount Temple,** son of the Rt. Hon. Anthony Evelyn Melbourne Ashley, and grandson of the 7th Earl of Shaftesbury, (see extant peerages), b. 13 Sept. 1867; educ. Harrow and Magdalen Coll. Oxford; M.P. for Blackpool, 1906-18, for Fylde Div. of Lancs. 1918-22, and for New Forest and Christchurch Div. of Hants, 1922-32; High Steward of Romsey, hon. Lt. Col. Gren. Guards, Major 3rd Bn. Hampshire Regt., and Lt. Col. cmdg. 20th Bn. King's Liverpool Regt.; Chm. Anti-Socialist Union, and Pres. of Anglo-German Fellowship; Parl. Sec. to Min. of Transport, 1922-23, Under Sec. of State for War, 1923-24; and Min. of Transport, 1924-29, in which position he reorganized the ministry and planned the roundabout system; made P.C., 1924, and cr. Baron Mount Temple, of Lee, co. Southampton, 13 Jan. 1932. He m. (1) 4 Jan. 1901, Amalia Maud, (d. 5 Feb. 1911), only child of Rt. Hon. Sir Ernest Cassel, P.C., G.C.B., G.C.M.G., G.C.V.O., and had issue,

1. Edwina Cynthia Annette, C.I., G.B.E., D.C.V.O., D.G. St. J., b. 28 Nov. 1901; m. 18 July 1922, Adm. of the Fleet the 1st Earl of Mountbatten, of Burma (extant peerages) and d. 21 Feb. 1960, leaving issue.
2. Ruth Mary Clarisse, m. (1) 12 May 1927, (marr. diss. by div. 1940) Capt. A. S. Cunningham-Reid, and had issue. She m. (2) 3 Sept. 1940, (marr. diss. by div. 1943), Laurie Gardner, and m. (3) 15 June 1944, (marr. diss. by div.) 4th Baron Delamere.

Lord Mount Stephen m. (2) 29 Aug. 1914, Muriel Emily, dau. of Rev. W. Spencer, and formerly wife of Rear Adm. Hon. A. L. O. Forbes-Sempill (Sempill, B.). She d. 24 June 1954. Lord Mount Temple d.s.p.m. 3 July 1939.
ARMS, CREST and **MOTTO**—as for Earl of Shaftesbury.
SUPPORTERS—Dexter, A bull sable armed, unguled and charged on the shoulder with a crescent or; Sinister, A horse reguardant argent. maned, tailed and unguled or, charged on the shoulder with a crescent sable.
Lord Mount Stephen's seats were Broadlands, Romsey, Hants.; Classiebawn Castle, co. Sligo.

MUIR MACKENZIE

PEERAGE—U.K. Baron Muir Mackenzie, of Delvine, co. Perth.
SURNAME—Muir Mackenzie.
CR.—29 June 1915. **EXT.**—22 May 1930.
HISTORY—Sir John William Pitt Muir Mackenzie, 2nd Bt., (see extant peerages, Muir Mackenzie of Delvine, Bt.), had with other issue, a fourth son,
Sir Kenneth Augustus Muir Mackenzie, **Baron Muir Mackenzie,** b. 26 June 1845; educ. Charterhouse and Balliol Coll. Oxford, B.A. 1868, M.A. 1873; Barrister-at-Law, Lincoln's Inn, 1873; Q.C. 1887; Bencher, 1891; Perm. Sec. to Lord Chancellor, 1880-1915; Clerk to the Crown in Chancery, 1885-1915; cr. C.B. 1893; K.C.B. 1898; G.C.B. 1911, and Baron Muir Mackenzie, of Delvine, co. Perth, 29 June 1915; made P.C. 1924. m. 26 Feb. 1874, Amelia, dau. of William Graham, M.P. and

d.s.p.m.s. 22 May 1930. She d. 18 Dec. 1900. They had had issue,
1. William Montagu, Barrister-at-Law, b. 12 May 1876; d. unm. 18 July 1901.
1. Margaret Mary, b. 29 May 1879; m. 3 Jan. 1907, Donnell Post, and d. 10 Aug. 1958, leaving issue.
2. Dorothea Frances, b. 4 April 1881; m. 5 Mar. 1907, Mark Hambourg, the pianist and had issue.
3. Magdalen, b. 26 April 1884; m. 10 July 1905, Rt. Hon. Sir Henry Robert Clive, and had issue.
ARMS—None matriculated at the Lyon Office since 1st Bt did so on 30 Dec. 1830.

MUNCASTER

PEERAGE—Ireland. Baron Muncaster in Ireland. U.K. Baron Muncaster, of Muncaster, co. Cumberland.
SURNAME—Pennington.
CR.—Irish Barony 21 Oct. 1783. U.K. Barony 11 June 1898. (Also a baronetcy cr. 21 June 1676.) **EXT.**—30 Mar. 1917.
HISTORY—Joseph Pennington, of Pennington, co. Lancaster, and of Muncaster, co. Cumberland, d. about 1640 having had by his wife, Isabel, dau. of Alvery Copley, of Botley, co. York, and widow of Sir Robert Savile, of Hawley, co. York, (with a dau. Bridget, m. Sir William Huddlestone, of Millum Castle, Cumberland), a son and successor,
William Pennington, of Muncaster, m. Catherine, dau. of Richard Sherborne, of Stonyhurst, co. Lancaster, and d. Aug. 1652, having had issue,
1. Joseph, his heir (see below).
2. Alan, M.D., of Chester, living 1665; m. Bridget, dau. of John Aleworth, of Somerset and had issue,
   William, b. 1659.
3. Richard, of Salford, co. Lancaster, Barrister-at-Law, Gray's Inn, m. Anne, dau. of Robert Blundell, of Ince Blundell, co. Lancs.
4. William.
1. Isabel, unm. in 1695.
2. Catharine, m. Sir Jeffrey Shakerley, of Shakerley (see Shakerley Bt.).
3. Elizabeth, m. Sir Robert Bradshaigh, Bt., of Haigh, co. Lancs.
The eldest son,
Joseph Pennington, of Muncaster, m. Margaret, dau. of John Fleetwood, of Penwortham, co. Lancs, and had issue,
Sir William Pennington, 1st Bt., so cr. 21 June 1676. Lord Lt. of Cumberland, 1686, Vice Adm. of Cumberland and Westmorland 1710; m. Isabel, dau. of John Stapleton, and d. 1 July 1730, having had issue,
1. Joseph, Sir, 2nd Bt. (see below).
1. Elizabeth, m. (1) John Archer, of Oxenholme, Westmorland, and (2) Thomas Strickland, of Sizergh.
2. Margaret.
The only son,
Sir Joseph Pennington, 2nd Bt., M.P. for co. Cumberland, m. Hon. Margaret Lowther, dau. of 1st Viscount Lonsdale, (Lonsdale, E.) and d. 1744, having had issue, with an eldest son who d.v.p. 1734,
1. John, Sir, 3rd Bt. (see below).

2. Lowther, d. at Cambridge, 1733.
3. Joseph, Sir, 4th Bt. (see below).
1. Catherine, m. 1731, Robert Lowther, Gov. of Barbados.

The eldest surv. son,

Sir John Pennington, 3rd Bt., M.P. co. Cumberland, Lord Lt. co. Westmorland, d.s.p. 24 Mar. 1768, and was s. by his brother,

Sir Joseph Pennington, 4th Bt., m. Sarah, dau. and heiress of John Moore, of Somerset, and d. 1793, having had issue,

1. John, 5th Bt. and **1st Baron Muncaster** (see below).
2. Joseph, an officer in sea service, d. in America.
3. Lowther, **2nd Baron** (see below).
1. Jane.
2. Margaret.
3. Catherine, m. Humphrey Osbaldeston, of Hunmanby, co. York.

The eldest son,

Sir John Pennington, 5th Bt., and **1st Baron Muncaster**, so cr. 21 Oct. 1783, in the peerage of Ireland, b. about 1740; the peerage had special remainder to his brother Lowther Pennington. He m. Penelope (d. 13 Nov. 1806) dau. of James Compton, and d. 8 Oct. 1813, leaving a dau. Maria Frances Margaret, m. 1811, 24th Earl of Crawford and Balcarres, and d. 1850. The 1st Baron was s. under the special limitation by his brother,

Sir Lowtner Pennington, 6th Bt., and **2nd Baron Muncaster**, Gen. officer in the Army, and Col. of one of the royal veteran bns. He m. 13 Jan. 1802, Esther, dau. of Thomas Barry, of Clapham, co. Surrey, and widow of James Morrison. She d. 7 Oct. 1827. He d. 29 July 1818. The only son,

Sir Lowther Augustus John Pennington, 7th Bt. and **3rd Baron Muncaster**, b. 14 Dec. 1802; m. 15 Dec. 1828, Frances Catherine, dau. of Sir John Ramsden Bt., She d. 30 Jan. 1853. He d. 30 April 1838. They had issue,

1. Gamel Augustus, **4th Baron** (see below).
2. Josslyn, b. 1833, d. an infant.
3. Josslyn Francis, **5th Baron** (see below).
4. Alan Joseph, served in R.N. at Sebastopol, and later was Lt. Rifle Brigade, b. 5 April 1837; m. 9 Dec. 1880, Anna Eleanora (d. 5 Fec. 1934) dau. of Edward Hartopp, of Dalby Hall, co. Leicester. He d.s.p. 14 June 1913.
1. Fanny Caroline, d. at Vevey, 12 July 1864.
2. Rachel Matilda, d. young.
3. Louisa Theodosia, m. 1858, Edgar Atheling Drummond, and d. 1886 (Perth, E.),

The eldest son,

Sir Gamel Augustus Pennington, 8th Bt. and **4th Baron Muncaster**, b. 3 Dec. 1831; m. 2 Aug. 1855, Lady Jane Louisa Octavia, Grosvenor, 8th dau. of 2nd Marquess of Westminster (Westminster, D.), by whom he had an only child, Margaret Susan Elizabeth, who d. 8 July 1871, aged 11. He d. at Castellamare, near Naples, 13 June 1862, Lady Muncaster m. 2ndly 1863, Hugh Barlow Lindsay (Crawford, E.). The 4th Baron was s. by his next surv. brother,

Sir Josslyn Francis Pennington, 9th Bt., and **5th Baron Muncaster**, b. 25 Dec. 1834; Lord Lt. co. Cumberland, and Pres. of Terr. Force Asscn. of Cumberland. J.P. and D.L., E.R. Yorks; M.P. for West Cumberland, 1872-80; and for Egremont Div. of Cumberland, 1885-

92; Capt. Rifle Brig., served in the Crimean War; was cr. a peer of the United Kingdom, 11 June 1898, as Baron Muncaster, of Muncaster, co. Cumberland. He m. 9 April 1863, Constance, dau. of Edmund L'Estrange, related on the female side to the Earls of Scarborough. She d. 13 July 1917. He d.s.p. 30 Mar. 1917.

ARMS—Or five fusils conjoined in fess azure.
CREST—A mountain cat passant guardant ppr.
SUPPORTERS—Dexter, A lion guardant ppr. charged on the breast with an oak branch vert; Sinister, A horse reguardant ppr. bridled or.
MOTTOES Vincit amor patriae. (and over the crest) Firm, vigilant, active.

The seat of the Lords Muncaster was Muncaster Castle, Ravenglass, Cumberland.

MURRAY OF ELIBANK

PEERAGE—U.K. Baron Murray of Elibank, of Elibank, co. Selkirk.
SURNAME—Murray.
CR.—13 Aug. 1912. **EXT.**—13 Sept. 1920.
HISTORY—The 10th Baron Elibank, and 1st Viscount Elibank, (see extant peerages, Elibank, B.), had an eldest son,

Alexander William Charles Oliphant Murray, **Baron Murray** of Elibank, b. 12 April 1870; M.P. for Midlothian, 1900-04, for Peebles and Selkirk, 1906-10, and for Midlothian 1910-12; Comptroller of the Household and Scottish Whip, 1905-09, Under Sec. of State for India, 1909-10, and Patronage Sec. to the Treasury, 1910-12; a partner with Lord Cowdray in the firm of S. Pearson and Son Ltd.; Hon. Dir. of Recruiting for Munition Workers, 1915; P.C. 1911, and cr. Baron Murray of Elibank, of Elibank, co. Selkirk, 13 Aug. 1912. He m. 1 Aug. 1894, Hilda Louisa Janey Wolfe, ygr. dau. of James Wolfe Murray, of Cringletie, co. Peebles, (Murray, Bt., of Blackbarony), and d.s.p.v.p. 13 Sept. 1920. (His ygr. brother, Charles Gideon Murray, s. to the titles of the 1st Viscount as 11th Baron Elibank, and 2nd Viscount Elibank (see extant peerages, and article, Elibank V. in present volume).
ARMS—as for Elibank, V.

NEWLANDS

PEERAGE—U.K. Baron Newlands, of Newlands, and Barrowfield, in the county of city of Glasgow, and of Mauldslie Castle, co. Lanark.
SURNAME—Hozier.
CR.—19 Jan. 1898. **EXT.**—5 Sept. 1929. (Also a baronetcy cr. 12 June 1890.)
HISTORY—William Hozier, of Partick and Thornwood, co. Lanark, had a son,

James Hozier, in the magistracy of Glasgow, who s. to Partick and Thornwood, and later acquired Newlands, Barrowfield, and Whifflet. He m. Helen Robertson, of Lauchope, and d. 21 May 1797, having had issue,

1. William (see below).
2. James, Capt. 34th Regt., m. 1792, Hon. Christiane de Moleyns, dau. of 1st Baron Ventry, and had issue.

1. Elizabeth, m. John Graham of Kittochside, and had issue.
2. Catherine, b. 26 Sept. 1772; m. 11 June 1805, John Roberton, of Lauchope and had issue.
3. Helen, m. James Towers, and had issue.
4. Ann, m. James Hamilton, and had issue.

The elder son,

William Hozier, of Newlands and Barrowfield, b. 9 Jan. 1760; acquired Tannochside, co. Lanark; m. (1) 4 Jan. 1791, Jean (d. 28 Aug. 1792), dau. of John Campbell of Clathie and Killermont, and had issue, a son, James, (see below). He m. (2) Lilias, dau. of John Wallace of Cessnock and Kelly. She d. 2 Dec. 1841. By her he had a second son, John Wallace Hozier, who was b. 1795, educ. St. John's Coll. Camb., served as a Cornet, Royal Scots Greys, and d. unm. 30 Jan. 1826. William Hozier, d. 7 June 1841, being s. by his elder son,

James Hozier, of Newlands and Mauldslie Castle, co. Lanark, Convener of the county of Lanark, b. 14 Nov. 1791; m. 11 May 1824, Catherine Margaret, dau. of Sir William Feilden, 1st Bt., and had issue. She d. 27 April 1870. He d. 12 Jan. 1878, having had,

1. William Wallace, **1st Baron Newlands** (see below).
2. John Wallace, 1830-33.
3. John Wallace, b. 14 Feb. 1834; educ. Harrow and Balliol Coll. Oxford; Lt. Col. cmdg. Royal Scots Greys, and priv. sec. to Rth. Hon. Sydney Herbert, Sec. of State for War. He d. unm. 30 Sept. 1905.
4. Henry Montague, Sir, K.C.B., of Stonehouse, co. Lanark, b. 20 Mar. 1838; was Sec. of Lloyd's; served in Royal Artillery, at the capture of the Taku Forts in the second Chinese war (1857) and throughout the Abyssinian campaign, on the staff of Lord Napier of Magdala (1867); served in the 2nd Life Guards, and 3rd Dragoon Guards, and was attached to the Prussian Army in the war of 1866 with Austria, and was Asst. Mil. Attaché in the Franco-Prussian War, 1870-71; received Knight's Iron Cross, of Germany; m. 28 Sept. 1878, Lady Henrietta Blanche Ogilvy, dau. of 7th Earl of Airlie, and d. 28 Feb. 1907, having had issue,
   (1) William Ogilvy, Lt. R.N., b. 2 April 1888.
   (1) Kitty Ogilvy, b. 15 April 1883; d. unm. 5 Mar. 1900.
   (2) Clementine Ogilvy b. 1 April 1885; 12 Sept. 1908, Rt. Hon. Winston Churchill, later Sir Winston K.G. (Marlborough, D.). (Of this union Sir Winston wrote at the end of his book, *My Early Life*, "September, 1908, when I married and lived happily ever afterwards.").
   (3) Margaret Nellie Ogilvy, b. 3 April 1888; m. 4 Dec. 1915; m. Col. B. H. A. Romilly, D.S.O.
1. Catherine Haughton, 1826-31.
2. Jean Campbell, m. 21 Mar. 1861, Lt. Gen. Randle Joseph Feilden, C.M.G. of Wilton Park, co. Lancaster, and d. 20 Mar. 1909, leaving issue.
3. Mary Haughton Georgiana.

The eldest son,

William Wallace Hozier, **1st Baron Newlands,** cr. a Baronet, 12 June 1890; and cr. a

peer as Baron Newlands, of Newlands and Barrowfield, in the county of the city of Glasgow, and of Mauldslie Castle, co. Lanark, 19 Jan. 1898; b. 24 Feb. 1825; Vice Lt. and Convener of Lanarkshire, Chm. of first Lanarkshire C.C., J.P. and D.L. for the county of the city of Glasgow, J.P. for co. Argyllshire; Lt. Col. of the auxiliary forces, served as Lt. Royal Scots Greys, as Capt. and Adjt. Lanarkshire Regt., Yeo. Cav. and Lt. Col. cmdg. 4th Bn. Lanarkshire Rifle Vol.s; m. Aug. 1849, Frances Anne, dau. of John O'Hara, of Raheen, by his wife, Arabella, Lady O'Donel, dau. of Sir John Blake, Bt., of Menlough Castle, and d. 30 Jan. 1906. She d. 13 Jan. 1891. They had issue,

1. James Henry Cecil, **2nd Baron Newlands** (see below).
1. Arabella Rose Evelyn, m. 3 April 1879, Sir William James Gardiner Baird, 8th Bt. of Saughton Hall, and d. 18 June 1916, leaving issue.
2. Catherine Rose, m. 5 Mar. 1912, Sir W. Algernon Law, (Ellenborough, B.) and d. 31 July 1930.
3. Mary Haughton, m. 13 June 1895, 2nd Baron Lamington, and had issue.

The eldest son,

James Henry Cecil Hozier, **2nd Baron Newlands,** b. 4 April 1851; M.P. South Lanarkshire, 1886-1906; served in Foreign Office, 1874-78; Priv. Sec. to Marquess of Salisbury, when Foreign Sec. 1878-80 and again when Prime Min. 1885-86; Lord Lt. co. Lanark 1915-21; Lt. Royal Co. of Archers, The Sovereign's Bodyguard for Scotland, a Public Works Loan Commissioner, received Freedom of Glasgow, 1917; Grand Master mason of Scotland, 1899-1903; m. 24 May 1880, Lady Mary Cecil, dau. of 3rd Marquess of Exeter, and d.s.p. 5 Sept. 1929. She d. 12 Aug. 1930.

ARMS—Vair, on a chevron gules three bezants, a chief gyronny of eight or and sable.

CREST—A bloodhound sejant ppr.

SUPPORTERS—On either side a dapple grey horse, gorged with a riband, suspended therefrom an escutcheon gules, charged with three bezants in chevron.

MOTTO—Aye ready.

The seats of Lord Newlands were—Mauldslie Castle, Carluke, co. Lanark, and Barrowfield Lodge, Brighton. Town residence was 26 Grosvenor Square, London, W. Clubs were: Carlton, Athenaeum; St. James's; White's; Bachelors; Garrick; Royal Automobile; Pratt's; New (Edinburgh) and Western (Glasgow).

NICHOLSON

PEERAGE—U.K. Baron Nicholson, of Roundhay, co. York.

SURNAME—Nicholson.

CR.—11 July 1912. **EXT.**—13 Sept. 1918.

HISTORY—William Nicholson, whose grandfather came to Yorkshire from Northumberland in 1680, m. (1) 1761, Hanna Slater, of Craven co. York, and had

1. Thomas (see below).

He m. (2) Grace, dau. of John Whitaker, and d. 1812 having had further issue,

2. Stephen, s. his brother (see below).

1. Mary, m. Thomas Phillips, of Leeds, and had an eldest son, William Nicholas Phillips, s. his uncle (see below).
The elder son,
Thomas Nicholson, of Roundhay Park, Leeds, was a banker in Leeds and in London, m. Elizabeth, dau. of William Jackson, of London, and d.s.p. 14 Jan. 1821 being s. by his half brother,
Stephen Nicholson, of Roundhay Park, b. Jan. 1779; m. Dec. 1807, Sarah, dau. of Matthew Rhodes, of Campbell, near Leeds and was s. by his nephew,
William Nichol Phillips, afterwards Nicholson, as by Royal Licence 13 Oct. 1827 he assumed the name and arms of Nicholson. He was b. 12 Dec. 1803; was of Roundhay Park, J.P., and D.L., W.R. Yorks, M.A. Cambridge; m. 2 Oct. 1827, Martha, dau. and coheir of Abram Rhodes, of Wold Newton Hall, Yorks, and had with other issue,
Sir William Gustavus Nicholson, **Baron Nicholson**, b. 2 Mar. 1845; joined R.E., Lt. 1865; Capt. 1878; Brev. Major 1881, Brev. Lt. Col. 1887; Col. 1891; Major Gen. 1899; Lt. Gen. 1901; Gen. 1906; and Field Marshal, 1911 served in the Punjab, 1872; in the Afghan War, 1878-80 (despatches); in the Egyptian Exped. 1882; in Burmese Exped. 1886-87; (despatches); Mil. Sec. to C. in C. in India, 1890-93; Chief Engineer, 1894; Dep. Adjt. Gen., Punjab, 1895-98; served in Tirah Exped. 1897-98, (despatches, K.C.B.); in the S. African War, 1899-1900 (despatches twice); Adj. Gen. in India, 1898-99; Dir. Gen. of Mobilization and Mil. Intelligence, 1901-04; Chief Mil. Attaché with Japanese Army in Manchuria (Japanese War Medal, and Cordon of the Rising Sun); mem. of Cttee of Imperial defence, 1912; cr. C.B. 1891; K.C.B. 1898; G.C.B. 1908; K.J. St. J.; and cr. Baron Nicholson of Roundhay, co. York, 11 July 1912. He m. 1871, Victoire M.U., dau. of D. Dillon. Lord Nicholson who was Chief of the Imperial Gen. Staff 1908-12, d.s.p. 13 Sept. 1918.
ARMS—Barry of six ermine and gules, on a chief azure a cross patée argent between two suns in splendour ppr.
CREST—On a branch of a tree fessways ppr. a lion's head erased at the neck or and charged with a cross patée gules.
MOTTO—Providentia Dei.

NORMAN

PEERAGE—U.K. Baron Norman of St. Clere, co. Kent.
SURNAME—Norman.
CR.—13 Oct. 1944. EXT.—4 Feb. 1950.
HISTORY—A full account of the history of the Norman family is given in the 1952 edition of B.L.G., under the articles of Norman of the Rookery, and its derivative, Norman of Moor Place. Frederick Henry Norman, of Moor Place, Much Hadham, co. Hertford, 4th son of George Warde Norman, of Bromley Common, co. Kent, (Norman of the Rookery), and was b. 23 Jan. 1839; educ. Eton and Trin. Coll. Camb. B.A., 1861, M.A. 1865; Barrister-at-Law, Inner Temple, 1863, High Sheriff of Herts 1899; m. 15 Nov. 1870, Lina Susan Penelope, (who d. 2 Jan. 1950) only dau. of Sir Mark Wilks Collet, 1st Bt. of St. Clere,

Kemsing, nr. Sevenoaks co. Kent, (B.P. 1939 edit.), and d. 6 Oct. 1916, leaving with other issue, (Norman of Moor Place,) an elder son,
Montagu Collet Norman, **Baron Norman**, of St. Clere, co. Kent, so cr. 13 Oct. 1944. b. 6 Sept. 1871; educ. Eton and King's Coll. Camb.; served in S. African War, 1900-01, Capt. 4th Bn. Bedfordshire Regt., mentioned in despatches and D.S.O. 1900; partner in firm of Brown Shipley and Co., London and Brown Bros., New York, 1900; a Dir. of Bank of England, 1907-19, Dep. Gov. 1918-20, and Gov. 1920-44; Chm. of Bankers' Industrial Development Co. Ltd., from 1930; a Dir. of Bank of International Settlements; made a P.C. 1923, and a peer as above; m. 21 Jan. 1933, Priscilla Cecilia Maria Worsthorne, J.P. co. London, dau. of Major Robert Reyntiens, Belgians, by his wife, Lady Alice Josephine Norris, dau. of 7th Earl of Abingdon, and d. 4 Feb. 1950.
ARMS—Argent on a bend gules three stags' heads cabossed of the field, a chief sable thereon three bezants.
CREST—A stag's head erased ppr., charged with a fess or thereon a torteau.
SUPPORTERS—On either side a hind ppr. holding in the mouth a sprig or, oak leaved and fructed ppr.
MOTTO—Aere perennius.
Lord Norman's residences were St. Clere, Kemsing, Kent, and Thorpe Lodge, Campden Hill, W.8. His club was the Athenaeum.

NORMANBROOK

PEERAGE—U.K. Baron Normanbrook of Chelsea, co. of London.
SURNAME—Brook.
CR.—24 Jan. 1964. EXT.—15 June 1967.
HISTORY—George Brook, a cabinet maker of Bradford, had issue,
Frederick Charles Brook, of Bristol, District Inspector, Min. of Health, b. 3 June 1867; m. 26 Dec. 1894, Annie, dau. of Thomas Smith, of Bradford, co. Yorks, and d. 4 Feb. 1937. She d. 1921. They had issue, with a dau. Elsie, d. 1939.
Sir Norman Craven Brook, **Baron Normanbrook**, b. 29 April 1902, educ. Wolverhampton Grm. Sch. and Wadham Coll. Oxford, B.A. 1925, M.A. 1949, entered Home Civil Service, 1925, Addt. Sec. to Cabinet 1945-46, Sec. to Cabinet 1947-62, Jt. Perm. Sec. to Treasury and Head of Civil Service 1956-62, Chm. of B.B.C. 1964; m. 30 Nov. 1929, Ida Mary, dau. of E. A. Goshawk; was cr. C.B. 1942, K.C.B. 1946; G.C.B. 1951, made P.C. 1953 and cr. Baron Normanbrook, of Chelsea, co. of London, 24 Jan. 1964. He d. 15 June 1967.
ARMS—Gules two pens in saltire within an orle of plummets and roses argent barbed and seeded ppr. alternately.
CREST—In front of and surrounding a book bound gules clasped and garnished or, a chaplet of roses as in the arms.
SUPPORTERS—Dexter, A crow ppr.; Sinister, A goshawk ppr. belled and jessed or.
MOTTO—Tuta silentio merces.

NORMAND

PEERAGE—U.K. Life. Baron Normand of Aberdour, co. Fife.
SURNAME—Normand.
CR.—6 Jan. 1947. **EXT.**—5 Oct. 1962.
HISTORY—Andrew Normand, a seaman, was drowned in the Firth of Forth in 1754 having had issue by his wife Margaret White,
James Normand of Dysart, co. Fife, b. 1754 and d. 25 Mar. 1843, having had nine children of whom,
James Normand of Blairhill, Dysart and Whitehill, Aberdour, co. Fife, b. 1798 and d. 1874 having had a son,
Patrick Hill Normand of Whitehill, Aberdour, b. 27 Dec. 1843; m. 1870 Ellen, dau. of George Prentice of Thornton, co. Fife and d. 15 Oct. 1910 having had with other children,
Wilfred Guild Normand, **Baron Normand,** b. 6 May 1884; educ. Fettes, Oriel Coll., B.A. 1906, M.A. 1934, in Paris and Edin. Univ. LL.B. 1910; served in World War I 1915-18; Advocate, Scots Bar, 1910, K.C. 1925, Hon. Bencher, Middle Temple, 1934; Solicitor Gen. for Scotland 1929, and 1931-33, Lord Advocate 1933-35, Lord Justice Gen. of Scotland, and Lord Pres. of the Court of Session 1935-47, Lord of Appeal in Ordinary 1947-53, M.P. for W. Div. of Edinburgh 1931-35; was made P.C. 1933, cr. a Life Peer as Baron Normand of Aberdour, co. Fife, 6 Jan. 1947. He m. (1) 22 July 1913, Gertrude, dau. of William Lawson, and had issue a son, William and a dau. Patricia Drake (m. D. W. Gourlay). Mrs Normand d. 8 Nov. 1923. He m. (2) 27 April 1927, Marion, dau. of David Cunningham and d. 5 Oct. 1962.
ARMS—Sable a lion rampant or armed and langued gules, on a chief engrailed of the second seven billets azure a border of the third.
CREST—A paschal lamb ppr. enhaloed gules with the appropriate cross or sustaining in its dexter hoof a banner azure charged with St. Andrew's cross argent.
SUPPORTERS—Two lions or armed and langued gules each powdered with seven billets azure.
MOTTO—Auxilium ab alto.

NORTH

PEERAGE—England. Baron North of Kirtling, co. Cambridge.
SURNAME—North.
CR.—(by writ of summons), 17 Feb. 1553-54.
ABEYANT—19 Dec. 1941.
HISTORY—This peerage was first held by Sir Edward North, a lawyer, who was M.P. for co. Cambridge, and Joint Clerk of the Parliament, King's Serjeant-at-Law, 1536, Chancellor of the Court of Augmentations, 1538, and summoned to the Lords on 17 Feb. 1553-54, as Baron North of Kirtling, co. Cambridge. He was the great-great-grandson of Robert North who had lived in the time of Henry V. From the first Baron North the history of the family is traced in the extant peerage works, through several generations of distinction, to the 5th Lord, whose second son was cr. 27 Sept. 1683, Baron of Guilford, co. Surrey, and from whom came the Earls of Guilford, (so cr. 8 April 1752). Francis North, the first Earl of Guilford became the 7th Baron North, but on the death of the 9th Lord North, who was also 3rd Earl of Guilford, the barony of North fell into abeyance between his three daus., while the Barony of Guilford, and the Earldom of Guilford devolved on the heir male, his brother Francis North, 4th Earl of Guilford, (see extant peerages, Guilford, E.). Susan North, Baroness North, 10th holder of the title, m. Col. the Rt. Hon. J. S. Doyle, who took the name of North in lieu of Doyle. On the Baroness's death on 5 Mar. 1884, her son,
William Henry John North, **11th Baron North,** b. 5 Oct. 1836; m. 12 Jan. 1858, Frederica, dau. of Cmdr. Richard Howe Cockerell, and d. 8 April 1932, having had issue, with one other son and four daus., an elder son,
William Frederick John North, **12th Baron North,** b. 13 Oct. 1860; m. 7 Nov. 1885, Arabella Valerie Keppel, (d. 3 Aug. 1965), dau. of Charles North, of Rougham Hall, co. Norfolk, (Guilford, E.). and d. 10 Dec. 1938, having had issue,
1. Dudley William John, M.C., served in World War I, b. 9 Aug. 1891; m. 8 Aug. 1914, Dorothy, dau. of Capt. J. R. Donne, and d. 29 Mar. 1936, leaving issue,
   (1) John Dudley, **13th Baron** (see below).
   (1) Dorothy Anne, b. 4 May 1915; m. (1) 17 Sept. 1937, (m. diss. by div. 1950), Major R. A. C. Graham, and had issue,
   1a Penelope Virginia, b. 25 June 1940. She m. (2) 23 Sept. 1950, Major J. E. R. Bowlby, and had further issue,
   2a Gina Anne, b. 17 Feb. 1954.
   (2) Susan Silence, b. 19 Jan. 1920; m. Feb. 1943, F. G. Beauchamp, M.B. and had issue,
   1a Susan Donne, b. 14 Mar. 1944; m. 4 Nov. 1965 (m. diss. by div. 1969), Hon. N. C. Cavendish, (Chesham, B.).
   2a Sally North, b. 18 June 1945; m. 1 Dec. 1966, M. R. Parkin.
   3a Elizabeth Silence, b. 9 Nov. 1950.
1. Dudleya Susan, M.B.E. b. 22 May 1895.
The 12th Baron was s. by his grandson,
John Dudley North, **13th Baron North,** served in World War II, b. 7 June 1917; m. 1940, Margaret, dau. of W. H. Glennie, of Cape Province, S. Africa, and was k. in action 19 Dec. 1941, when his ship H.M.S. *Neptune,* was sunk in the Mediterranean. The Baroness m. 2ndly 1943, Lt. W. B. James, U.S. Marine Corps. The Barony fell into abeyance between the two sisters of the 13th Baron, both of whom had been granted by King George VI the title, rank and precedence of the daus. of a baron.
ARMS—Az. a lion passant, or, between three fleurs-de-lis, arg.
CREST—A dragon's head erased sa. ducally gorged and chained or.
SUPPORTERS—Two dragons, wings elevated, sa. ducally gorged and chained, or.
MOTTO—Animo et fide.

NORTHBROOK

PEERAGE—U.K. Viscount Baring, of Lee, co. Kent, and Earl of Northbrook, of Stratton, Southampton.
SURNAME—Baring.
CR.—10 June 1876. **EXT.**—12 April 1929.

HISTORY—Francis Thornhill Baring, 1st Baron Northbrook, and a baronet (see extant peerages, Northbrook, B.), was b. 1796 and d. 1866, being s. by his eldest son,

Thomas George Baring, 2nd Baron Northbrook, and cr. **Earl of Northbrook,** of Stratton, Southampton, and Viscount Baring of Lee, co. Kent, 10 June 1876. He was b. 22 Jan. 1826. He was High Steward of Winchester; M.P. for Penryn and Falmouth, 1857-66; a Lord of the Admiralty, 1857-58; Under Sec. of State for War, 1861; for India, 1861-64; and for Home Affairs, 1864-66; Sec. to the Admiralty, 1866; Under Sec. for War, 1868-72; First Lord of the Admiralty, 1880-85; and Viceroy and Gov. Gen. of India, 1872-76; P.C., cr. G.C.S.I., was F.R.S.; m. 6 Sept. 1848, Elizabeth Harriet, dau. of Henry Charles Sturt, of Crichel, co. Dorset, (Alington, B.). and d. 15 Nov. 1904. She d. 3 June 1867. They had issue,

1. Francis George, **2nd Earl** and 3rd Baron Northbrook (see below).
2. Arthur Napier Thomas, R.N., b. 3 June 1854; lost in the *Captain* at sea, 7 Sept. 1870.
1. Jane Emma, C.I., C.B.E., m. 29 June 1890, Col. the Hon. Sir Henry G. L. Crichton, (Erne, E.) and d. 17 Jan. 1936.

The elder son,

Francis George Baring, **2nd Earl of Northbrook,** and 3rd Baron Northbrook, High Steward of Winchester, 1906, M.P. for Winchester, 1880-85, and for N. Bedford, 1886-92, b. 6 Dec. 1850; m. (1) 26 June 1894, Ada Ethel Sophie, who d.s.p. 22 July 1894, dau. of Col. C. Davidson, and m. (2) 10 June 1899, Florence Anita Eyre, C.B.E., dau. of Eyre Coote, of West Park, co. Hants (Coote, Bt.) and widow of Sir Robert John Abercromby, 7th Bt., She d. 4 Dec. 1946. The 2nd Earl d.s.p. 12 April 1929, when the earldom and viscounty became extinct and the baronetcy and the barony of Northbrook devolved upon his kinsman, Francis Arthur Baring, who became Bt. and 4th Baron Northbrook (extant peerages Northbrook, B.).

ARMS—Azure a fess or; in chief a bear's head ppr. muzzled and ringed gold.

CREST—A mullet erminois, between two wings argent.

SUPPORTERS—Two bears ppr. muzzled or, gorged with a chain of the last, therefrom pendent an escutcheon; that on the dexter charged with a portcullis gu. and that on the sinister with a palm tree on a mount proper.

MOTTO—Probitate et labore.

NORTHCLIFFE

PEERAGE—U.K. Baron Northcliffe, of the Isle of Thanet, co. Kent.
U.K. Viscount Northcliffe, of St. Peter, co. Kent.

SURNAME—Harmsworth.

CR.—Barony 27 Dec. 1905. Viscounty 14 Jan. 1918. (Also a baronetcy cr. 23 Aug. 1904.)

HISTORY—Alfred Harmsworth, Barrister-at-Law of the Middle Temple of a yeoman family in Hampshire, m. Geraldine Mary, dau. of William Maffett, of Pembroke Place, Dublin, and had, with other issue, (see extant peerages, under Rothermere, V.) an eldest son,

Sir Alfred Charles William Harmsworth, Bt. and **Viscount Northcliffe,** also Baron Northcliffe, b. 15 July 1865 at Chapelizod, co. Dublin; educ. Stamford Grammar Sch. and privately; entered journalism and made the greatest revolution in it since its origins, by producing the popular newspaper and magazine to suit the needs of the newly educated classes; started *The Daily Mail* in 1896, and *Answers, The Ladies' Mirror* (which became *The Daily Mirror*); acquired *The Evening News* in 1894, and from 1908 to his death was the principal proprietor of *The Times.* In World War I, he was Chm. of the British Mission to the U.S.A., May to Nov. 1917, and Dir. of Propaganda in enemy countries, Feb. to Nov. 1918. He was cr. a baronet 23 Aug. 1904; Baron Northcliffe, of the Isle of Thanet, 27 Dec. 1905; and Viscount Northcliffe, of St. Peter, co. Kent. He m. 11 April 1888, Mary Elizabeth, G.B.E., D.G. St. J., dau. of Robert Milner, of Kidlington, co. Oxford. He d.s.p. 14 Aug. 1922. His widow m. 2ndly 4 April 1923, Sir Robert Arundell Hudson,

ARMS—(They are the same as those now borne by Viscount Rothermere, Viscount Northcliffe's nephew.) Azure two rolls of paper in saltire or banded in the centre gules between four bees volant or.

CREST—A cubit arm erect, the hand holding a roll of paper fesswise ppr. between two ostrich feathers or.

SUPPORTERS—On either side a gladiator fully habited and accoutred, the dexter holding in the exterior hand a sword, and the sinister on the exterior arm a shield all ppr.

MOTTO—Bene qui sedulo.

NORTHCOTE

PEERAGE—U.K. Baron Northcote, of Exeter, co. Devon.

SURNAME—Northcote.

CR.—20 Jan. 1900. EXT.—29 Sept. 1911. (Also a baronetcy cr. 23 Nov. 1884.)

HISTORY—The 1st Earl of Iddesleigh, (see extant peerage works) had a second son,

Sir Henry Stafford Northcote, **Baron Northcote,** b. 18 Nov. 1846; educ. Eton and Merton Coll. Oxford, B.A. 1869, and M.A. 1873; clerk in the Foreign Office, 1868; sec. to British mems. of the claims commission at Washington relating to the *Alabama,* 1871-73; priv. sec. to his father when the latter was Chancellor of the Exchequer, 1877-80; Conservative M.P. for Exeter, 1880-90; financial sec. to War Office, 1886-87; surveyor gen. of ordnance, 1886-87; Gov. of Bombay, 1899-1903; Gov. Gen. of Australia, 1903-07; cr. C.B. 1880; a baronet, 23 Nov. 1887; a baron as Baron Northcote of Exeter, co. Devon, 20 Jan. 1900 and G.C.I.E. 1900; and G.C.M.G. 1904. He m. 2 Oct. 1873, Alice, C.I. D.G. St. J., adopted dau. of Lord Mount Stephen (see in present work). He d.s.p. 29 Sept. 1911.

ARMS—Quarterly 1 and 4, Argent a fess between three crosses moline, sable; 2 and 3, Argent three crosses-crosslet in bend sable, a crescent for differenee.

CREST—On a chapeau gules turned up ermine a stag trippant argent, on the shoulder a crescent for difference.

SUPPORTERS—Two stags ppr. pendent from the neck of each by a gold chain an escutcheon ermine thereon a pine cone or and charged on the shoulder with a crescent for difference.
MOTTO—Christi crux est mea lux.

NORTHWICK

PEERAGE—Great Britain. Baron Northwick of Northwick Park, co. Worcester.
SURNAME—Rushout.
CR.—26 Oct. 1797. (Also a baronetcy cr. 17 June 1661.) EXT.—11 Nov. 1887.
HISTORY—John Rushout from France settled in England temp. Charles I as a London merchant. He m. Anne dau. of Joas Godschalch and had an only surv. son,
Sir James Rushout 1st Bt., of Milnst Maylands, co. Essex, cr. a baronet 17 June 1661. He m. Alice, dau. and heiress of Edward Pitt of Harrow on the Hill, Middlesex, and widow of Edward Palmer. He d. 1698 having had with other issue,
1. (Sir) James, 2nd Bt. (see below).
2. John, Rt. Hon. Sir, 4th Bt. (see below).
The elder surv. son,
Sir James Rushout, 2nd Bt., m. Arabella, dau. of Sir Thomas Vernon d. 1705, being s. by his only son,
Sir James Rushout who d.s.p. 1711 and was s. by his uncle,   —
The Rt. Hon. Sir John Rushout 4th Bt., Treasurer of the Navy, of Northwick co. Worcester, m. Lady Anne, dau. of George Compton, 4th Earl of Northampton, and had issue,
John, Sir, 5th Bt. and 1st Baron (see below).
Elizabeth, m. Richard Myddlelton of Chirk Castle, co. Denbigh.
The only son,
Sir John Rushout, 5th Bt., and 1st Baron Northwick, of Northwick Park, co. Worcester, so cr. 26 Oct. 1797, was b. 23 July 1738; educ. Eton and Ch. Ch. Oxford, M.P. Evesham 1761-96, F.S.A. 1799. He m. 3 June 1766, Rebecca (d. 3 Oct. 1818) dau. of Humphrey Bowles of Wanstead, co. Essex, and d. 20 Oct. 1800 having had issue,
1. John, 2nd Baron (see below).
2. George, Rev. b. 30 July 1772, by Royal Licence 29 June 1817 took the surname of Bowles in addition to, and after the surname of Rushout, m. 1803 Caroline (d. 1818) dau. of John Stewart, 7th Earl of Galloway and d. Oct. 1842 leaving,
(1) George, 3rd Baron (see below).
(1) Caroline.
(2) Georgiana.
(3) Harriot.
1. Anne, d. 4 April 1849.
2. Harriet, m. 13 Feb. 1808, Sir Charles Cockerell, later Rushout, Bt. and d. 30 Oct. 1851.
3. Elizabeth, m. (1) 24 June 1797, Sydney Bowles, and (2) 7 Aug. 1819 John Wallis Graeve and d. 15 Jan. 1862.
The elder son,
Sir John Rushout 6th Bt., and 2nd Baron Northwick, b. 16 Feb. 1770; Gov. of Harrow School 1801-59; F.S.A. 1800, formed a splendid collection of over 1500 pictures at Northwick; in 1831 had dispute with local magistrates over removal of a threshing machine, a matter on

which he wrote a 55 page pamphlet. He d. unm. 20 Jan. 1859 and was s. by his nephew,
Sir George Rushout, 7th Bt., and 3rd Baron Northwick, b. 30 Aug. 1811 educ. Harrow and Ch. Ch. Oxford, B.A. 1833, M.A. 1826; served in 1st Life Guards, Cornet 1833, Lt. 1837, Capt. 1842; Gov. of Harrow Sch. and of Cheltenham Coll.; sat as Conservative M.P. for Evesham 1837-41 and for East Worcestershire 1847-59, fought one of the last duels to occur in England (8 May 1838) over a dispute over his 1837 election, with Peter Borthwick, father of Lord Glenesk; m. 15 April 1869, Elizabeth Augusta, dau. of William Bateman-Hanbury, 1st Baron Bateman of Shobdon, and widow of Major G. D. Warburton. He d.s.p. 11 Nov. 1887. Lady Northwick d. 29 May 1912. They had had issue,
Caroline, b. 15 July 1870, d.v.p. 17 Sept. 1878.
ARMS—Sable two lions passant guardant within a bordure engrailed or.
CREST—A lion passant guardant or.
SUPPORTERS—Two angels ppr. winged and crined or habited argent, semée of fleurs-de-lis and mullets gold, round the waist sashes azure, holding in their exterior hands palm branches vert.
MOTTO—Par ternis suppar.
The seats of the family were Northwick Park, Moreton-in-the-Marsh, co. Worcester, Burford House, Tenbury, co. Worcester.

NOVAR

PEERAGE—U.K. Viscount Novar, of Raith, co. Fife.
SURNAME—Munro-Ferguson.
CR.—6 Dec. 1920. EXT.—30 Mar. 1934.
HISTORY—In B.L.G. 1952 (Munro-Ferguson of Novar) is given the ancestry of the Ferguson family of Raith. Col. Robert Munro Ferguson, of Raith, co. Fife, and Novar, Ross-shire, had with other issue (see B.L.G. 1952) an eldest son,
Sir Ronald Craufurd Munro-Ferguson, Viscount Novar, of Raith, co. Fife, b. 6 Mar. 1860; educ. R.M.C. Sandhurst; joined 1st Fifeshire Light Horse, 1875; joined Gren. Guards, 1879; ret. 1884; sat as Liberal M.P. for Ross and Cromarty, 1884-85; and for the Leith Burghs, 1886-1914; Priv. Sec. to the Sec. of State for Foreign Affairs, 1886, and 1892-94; a Junior Lord of the Treasury, 1894-95; Provost of Kirkcaldy, 1906-14; P.C. 1910; Gov. Gen. of Australia, 1914-20; Sec. of State for Scotland, 1922-24; Chm. of Political Honours Cttee, 1925; Vice Lt. of Fife, 1926. He was cr. G.C.M.G. 1914; Viscount Novar, of Raith, co. Fife, 6 Dec. 1920; K.T. 1926; he m. 31 Aug. 1889, Helen Hermione, G.B.E., 1918, dau. of Frederick Temple Hamilton-Temple,-Blackwood, 1st Marquess of Dufferin and Ava and d.s.p. 30 Mar. 1934.
ARMS—Argent a lion rampant azure between three buckles gules, a chief chequy of the first and second.
CREST—A demi-lion ppr, holding between the paws a buckle gules.
SUPPORTERS—Dexter, An emu; Sinister, An eagle, both ppr.
MOTTO—Virtutis fortuna comes.
Viscount Novar's seats were—Novar, Ross-shire; Raith, Kirkcaldy.

NUFFIELD

PEERAGE—U.K. Baron Nuffield of Nuffield, co. Oxford and Viscount Nuffield.

SURNAME—Morris.

CR.—13 Jan. 1934, Barony, 24 Jan. 1938 Viscounty. (Also a Baronetcy cr. 27 Mar. 1929.) **EXT.**—22 Aug. 1963.

HISTORY—The ancestry of this family illustrates the comparative richness of English records. On the history of the Morrises the Complete Peerage Vol. 13 has this to say: "The earliest reference to the Morris family in Oxfordshire which has come to light is that of William Morice, who held land in Swarford of the Manor of Hook Norton in 1278. He was s. there by Thomas Morice who held other land at Sandford in the hundred of Wootton in 1316, being s. in turn by Stephen Morice, who was assessed for the subsidy of 1327 on his land in Swarford. Entries of the name occur in the court Rolls of the Manor of Witney from 1352 and in those of the manors of the Abbot of Eysham from 1389 onwards, after which the rolls show a succession of John, David, John and John Morris at South Leigh, holding their copyhold land of Eysham manor down to the year 1524. These are the probable ancestors of the Morris family at Kiddington. The pedigree (i.e. from 1586) is a good example of the value of our public records as the source of information for the history of a typical yeoman family who were tenants and not landowners".

Also, "The ancestry of the former William Morris who once kept a cycle shop can be traced from father to son without a break right back to 1586. There they are eleven generations of Morrises, always living in Oxfordshire, and working on the land which they rented and did not own" (L.G. Pine, *Trace Your Ancestors* p. 9). The Morris genealogy was worked out by Alfred Trego Butler, Windsor Herald 1931-46.

John Morris of Kiddington, b. ca. 1560, m. 15 Oct. 1582, Elizabeth, dau. of Robert Offylde, of Over Kiddington and d. Dec. 1606, leaving a son,

John Morris of Combe Longa, co. Oxford, b. 1594; m. Jane Hurst, of Combe, and d. 1649, having with other issue, an eldest son,

Richard Morris of Combe Longa, and of Wootton, and Stonesfield who had issue,

William Morris, of Fowler, in Charlbury, co. Oxford, b. May 1656 and d. May 1716 having had by Jane his wife, four sons, of whom the third,

Thomas Morris, of New Woodstock, b. 1698 and d. 1760 leaving by his wife Anne Prior, three daus., two elder sons, William and Thomas of New Woodstock (d. 1797 aged 51), leaving issue, a yst son,

John Morris of Tackley, and later of Dornford in Wootton, co. Oxford, b. 1752; m. 9 Nov. 1777, Sarah, dau. of Gabriel Nixon and d. 1797 having had issue (with (1) John, b. 1781, (2) Thomas d.s.p. 1839, a dau. Sarah, m. 1816 Richard Morris of High Lodge, Ascot-under-Wychwood co. Oxford) a yst. son,

Gabriel Morris, of Wootton and later of Witney, co. Oxford, b. 1794; m. 5 Oct. 1816, Hannah, dau. of William Long of Witney, and d. May 1829. She d. Sept. 1850. They had with other children,

William Morris of Witney, b. 1817 and d. 4 Oct. 1887, leaving by Anne his wife (dau. of

Thomas Causby of Witney, and widow of William Edginton),

Frederick Morris of Oxford, b. 31 Aug. 1849, m. 7 Nov. 1876, Emily Ann (d. 8 Jan. 1934) dau. of Richard Pether, of Cowley, Oxford and d. 1 Jan. 1916 leaving issue,

1. William Richard, Sir, **Viscount Nuffield** (see below).
1. Emily Ann, m. 25 June 1903, F. A. Yockney, of Rainbow House, Boars Hill, Oxford, and d. 19 Aug. 1957 leaving issue.
2. Alice.

The only son,

Sir William Richard Morris, Bt., Viscount Nuffield, was described by *The Times* in its obituary notice (22 Aug. 1963) as a great industrialist and princely giver. "With the death of Lord Nuffield . . . British public life is left the poorer by the loss of a great industrialist who revolutionized the motor industry in this country and a philanthropist whose munificent benefactions must make his name remembered with those of Carnegie and Rockefeller. By the time he was 80 it was estimated that he had given away over £27 million". Among his minor benefactions was £50,000 to enable the completion of the *Complete Peerage*. He was b. 10 Oct. 1877, educ. at elementary schools and placed at the age of 16 in a bicycle shop to learn the trade but after 9 months he borrowed £4 with which he started a bicycle shop in Oxford in 1893. From bicycles to motor cycles, and then to the manufacture of cars. He was Chm. of Morris Motors Ltd., and its associated cos. from 1919-52. He was cr. O.B.E. 1918, a Baronet 27 Mar. 1929, G.B.E 1941, C.H. 1958, a peer as Baron Nuffield of Nuffield, co. Oxford 13 Jan. 1934 and Viscount Nuffield 24 Jan. 1938. He was elected F.R.S. in 1939 and received hon. D.C.L. 1931 and M.A. Oxford 1937, together with very many other honours and distinctions. He m. 9 April 1904, Elizabeth Maud, dau. of William Jones Anstey, a furrier, of Oxford and d.s.p. 22 Aug. 1963.

ARMS—Ermine on a fess or between in chief two roses gules barbed and seeded ppr. and in base a balance or, three pears sable.

CREST—A demi-bull gules, armed and unguled or, resting the sinister hoof on a winged wheel gold.

SUPPORTERS—On either side a beaver vert, the tail scaly argent and azure gorged with a collar pendent therefrom an escutcheon or, charged with three pears slipped sable.

BADGE—Two spriggs of speedwell in saltire enfiled with a baron's coronet ppr.

MOTTO—Fiat justitia.

O'BRIEN

PEERAGE—U.K. Baron O'Brien of Kilfenora, co. Clare.

SURNAME—O'Brien.

CR.—16 June 1900. **EXT.**—7 Sept. 1914. (Also a baronetcy cr. 28 Sept. 1891.)

HISTORY—Torlogh or Terence O'Brien, m. Elizabeth, dau. of Henry O'Brien, of Ballycorick, co. Clare, and had issue an elder son,

Torlogh or Terence O'Brien, of Cross (later called Elmvale), m. Eleanor, dau. of Mortogh O'Hogan and had issue with an elder son, John, of Elmvale who d.s.p., a ygr. son,

James O'Brien, of Limerick, and of Elmvale, co. Clare, m. Feb. 1791, Margaret, dau. of Peter Long, of Waterford, and d. 21 Feb. 1806, having by her (who m. 2ndly Cornelius O'Brien and d. 1839), had issue,

1. John (see below).
2. Peter of Limerick, b. Sept. 1797; m. Emily, dau. of Edward Shiel, and d.s.p. 1855.
3. Terence, b. 1802; d. unm. 1820.
4. James, a Judge of the Court of Queen's bench in Ireland; b. 1806; Barrister-at-Law, King's Inns, 1830; Q.C. 1841; Serjeant, 1848; M.P. Limerick, 1854-58; Judge, 1858; m. 1836, Margaret, dau. of Thomas Segrave, and d. 1882, leaving issue.

The eldest son,

John O'Brien, of Elmvale, and of Ballynalacken, co. Clare, High Sheriff, co. Clare 1836, and M.P. for city of Limerick, 1841-52; b. 1794; m. 1827, Ellen, dau. of Jeremiah, Murphy, of Hyde Park, co. Cork, She d. 19 Dec. 1866. He d. 6 Feb. 1855. They had issue,

1. James, of Ballynalacken Castle, co. Clare, High Sheriff, 1858, b. 1832; m. 1865, Georgina, dau. of G. Martyn, and widow of Francis Macnamara Calcutt.
2. Jerome, 28th Regt., m. Elizabeth, dau. of Robert Clarke, and had issue.
3. John, a Cistercian monk, d. 1889.
4. William, Indian R.H.A., d. unm.
5. Peter, Sir, Bt. and **Baron O'Brien** (see below).
6. Terence.
1. Margaret, m. James Martin, of Dublin.
2. Ellen, m. Robert Daniell, of New Forest, Westmeath.
3. Catto, a nun.
4. Anne, a nun.

The fifth son,

Sir Peter O'Brien, Bt., and **Baron O'Brien** of Kilfenora, co. Clare, b. 29 June 1842; M.A. Trin. Coll. Dublin, Visitor and Hon. LL.D.; Barrister, King's Inns, 1865; Q.C. 1880, Bencher, 1884; for some years acted as Registrar for his uncle, Mr. Justice O'Brien; senior Crown Prosecutor for Dublin 1883; Serjeant-at-law, 1884; Solicitor Gen. for Ireland, 1887-88, and Attorney Gen. 1888-89; made P.C. 1888; Lord Chief Justice of Ireland, 1889, and cr. a baronet 28 Sept. 1891, and a peer as Baron O'Brien of Kilfenora, co. Clare, 16 June 1900. He retired 1913. He m. 8 Aug. 1867, Annie, dau. of Robert Clarke, of Bansha, co. Tipperary, and d. 7 Sept. 1914, having had issue,

1. James, d. young.
1. Annie Georgina.
2. Ellen Mary, d. unm. 13 Oct. 1930.

ARMS—Gules, three lions passant guardant in pale per pale or and argent a chief of the second.

CREST—An arm embowed vested azure, brandishing a sword argent, hilt and pommel or, and charged with a fasces in pale ppr.

MOTTO—Vigueur de dessus.

OLIVIER

PEERAGE—U.K. Baron Olivier, of Ramsden, co. Oxford.

SURNAME—Olivier.

CR.—9 Feb. 1924. EXT.—15 Feb. 1943.

HISTORY—Laurent Olivier, of Nay, France, b. about 1520, had a son, Bernard Olivier, of Nay (b. 1550) whose son, Peter Olivier, b. about 1575, had a son, Isaac Olivier, b. 1600; m. 1630, Isabeau de Masselin, and d. 1671, having an elder son,

The Rev. Jourdain Olivier, b. 1643; m. 1677, Anne Day, and had with other issue, an eldest son,

The Rev. Jerome Olivier, b. 1687; m. 21 May 1721, Julie, dau. of Joseph de la Motte, and had issue,

Daniel Josias Olivier, merchant in London, b. 1722; m. 1750, Susannah, dau. of J. Massé. She d. 1803. He d. 1782, having had with other issue who d. young,

The Rev. Daniel Stephen Olivier, Rector of Clifton, co. Bedford, b. 16 June 1755; m. (1) 30 Mar. 1786, Margaret Harriet, dau. of Rev. Henry Arnold, D.D. She d. 1816. He m. (2) Miss Enderby who d.s.p. 1827. He d. 28 Dec. 1826, having had by his first marriage a second son,

Henry Stephen Olivier, of Potterne Manor House, co. Wilts, High Sheriff, 1843, Lt. Col. in the Army, b. 14 Aug. 1796; m. 11 Dec. 1823, Mary, dau. of Rear Adm. Sir Richard Dacres, G.C.B., and d. 1866, having had with other issue,

The Rev. Henry Arnold Olivier, of Shapley Hill, Winchfield, co. Hants, Rector of Poulshot, co. Wilts, b. 18 Feb. 1826; m. Anne Elizabeth Hardcastle (d. 1912) dau. of A. Arnould, M.D., and d. 1912, having had with four daus.,

1. Henry Dacres, of Shapley Hill, Winchfield, co. Hants, Lt. Col., b. 1850; d. 30 Mar. 1935.
2. Sydney Haldane, **Baron Olivier** (see below).
3. Herbert Arnould, portrait painter, b. 1861; m. 1903, Margaret Barclay, dau. of Sir William Peat and had issue.
4. Gerard Kerr, Rev., M.A. Oxford, Rector of Letchworth, co. Hertford, 1918-24, and of Addington, co. Buckingham, 1924-30, b. 1869; m. (1) 1898 Agnes Louise, dau. of I. A. Crookenden, and had issue, Laurence Kerr, later, and Baron Olivier, so cr. as a Life Peer in 1970 and gazetted 9 Mar. 1971, as Baron Olivier, of Brighton, co. Sussex. (see the 1952 edition of B.L.G. where under Olivier of Notley Abbey, the above pedigree with greater lateral detail is given).

The Rev. G. K. Olivier m. (2), 1924, Isobel Buchanan, dau. of Thomas Ronaldean and d. 30 Mar. 1939.

The second son,

Sir Sydney Haldane Olivier, **Baron Olivier,** b. 16 April 1859; educ. Lausanne, Kineton Sch., Tonbridge, Corpus Christi Coll. Oxford, B.A. 1881, and in Germany; entered Colonial Office, 1882; Acting Colonial Sec. British Honduras 1890-91; Auditor Gen. of the Leeward Islands, 1895-96; Sec. to the West India Royal Commission, 1897; Colonial Sec. Jamaica, 1899-1904; acting Gov. 1900, 1902, and 1904; Prin. Clerk, West African and West Indian Depts., Colonial Office, 1904-07; Gov. of Jamaica, 1907-13; Per. Sec. to Board of Agriculture and Fisheries, 1913-17; retired from Public Service, 1920; Sec. of State for India in first Labour Gov. 1924. He was cr. C.M.G. 1898; K.C.M.G. 1907, C.B. 1917 and

made P.C. 1924, and cr. 9 Feb. 1924, Baron Olivier, of Ramsden, co. Oxford. He m. 21 May 1885, Margaret, dau. of Homersham Cox, and d. 15 Feb. 1943, having had issue,
1. Margery.
2. Brynhild, m. (1) 1912, (m. diss. by div. 1924), A. E. Popham, and had issue. She m. (2) 1924, F. R. N. Sherrard, and d. 13 Jan. 1935 leaving issue.
3. Daphne, m. 1925, Cecil Harwood, and d. 14 July 1950, leaving issue.
4. Noel Olivier, M.D. m. 1920, W. A. Richards, F.R.C.S., and had issue.
Lord Olivier was the author of several works, including *Jamica the Blessed Island*, and *Poems and Parodies*.
ARMS—(of Life Peer only). Argent on a mount in base vert charged with a plough or, an olive tree fructed proper over all two bars gemel in fess each engrailed on the upper and inverted on the lower edge azure.
CREST—A swan rousant argent membered or, gorged with a baron's coronet proper, affixed thereto a chain reflexed over the back, the terminal ring encircling the sinister leg or, and holding in the beak an olive branch fructed proper.
MOTTO—Sicut oliva virens laetor in aede Dei. (This coat of arms, to which no supporters are attached at present, includes an olive tree as representing the name of Lord Olivier and a plough which is an allusion to his wife, Miss Joan Plowright. The motto is described as a family one and is usually translated in English as "I rejoice in the House of the Lord even as the olive tree flourishes".)

ORFORD

PEERAGE—U.K. Earl of Orford.
SURNAME—Walpole.
CR.—10 April 1806. **EXT.**—27 Sept. 1931.
HISTORY—Amid the great cloud of legend and downright myth which was given until quite recently in peerage works on the history of the Walpoles, there is one item of fact, namely the derivation of the family name from Walpole in Norfolk. (There are other places called Walpole, e.g. in Suffolk.) The head of the family (in 1971) was the 7th Baron Walpole of Wolterton, and 9th Baron Walpole of Walpole, peerages to which he s. in 1931. The pedigree as given in modern peerage works, under Walpole, B. begins with a respectable (probably) yeoman, Thomas Walpole, of Houghton in Norfolk. Five generations of a very normal pedigree, but without dates, take the descent to Sir Edward Walpole, K.B., (so cr. 23 April 1661, the date of the Coronation of King Charles II). The son of the Thomas Walpole mentioned above, Edward Walpole, m. Lucy, dau. of Sir Terry Robsart, of Sidestone, co. Norfolk, and their son, John Walpole was the cousin and heir of Amy Robsart, the dau. of Sir John Robsart, and wife of Robert Dudley, Earl of Leicester. Amy Dudley's death in curious circumstances provided the background to Sir Walter Scott's *Kenilworth*, and to numerous calumnies tempore Elizabeth I, reflected in the famous Ballad of Cumnor Hall, retold by the poet Mickle.
The Sir Edward Walpole, of 1661 was M.P. in the Restoration Parliament. His elder son

was Robert Walpole, M.P. for Castle Rising, co. Norfolk, 1689-1700. He had, with other children, an eldest son, Robert, and a younger son, Horatio, from the latter of whom descended the line of the present (1971) holder of the two baronies.
The elder son, was the celebrated Sir Robert Walpole, whose biography is part of the history of England, and who is reckoned as the first of her line of Prime Ministers. He was cr. on 6 Feb. 1742, Baron of Houghton, Viscount Walpole, and **Earl of Orford**. He was s. in these honours by his eldest son, by his grandson, and by his youngest son, the last named being not only **4th Earl of Orford**, but also the famous literary man, Horace Walpole, whose works, such as *The Castle of Otranto*, and the *Catalogue of Royal and Noble Authors*, have always found a place in English literary history. On his death unmarried on 2 Mar. 1797, the three peerages enumerated above became extinct. But his elder brother, the **2nd Earl of Orford** had been cr. 1 June 1723, Baron Walpole, of Walpole, co. Norfolk. This latter barony was limited by special remainder in default of male issue to the descendants of the 2nd Earl's grandfather. Therefore at the death of Horace Walpole, 4th Earl of Orford, of the first creation, the barony of Walpole of Walpole, devolved upon the 4th Earl's first cousin, Horatio Walpole, who was the eldest son of Horatio Walpole, brother of Sir Robert Walpole. This last named Horatio Walpole had been cr. on 4 June 1756, Baron Walpole, of Wolterton, co. Norfolk.
The first cousin of the 4th Earl of Orford of the first creation, Horatio Walpole thus became, in succession to his father, 2nd Baron, and in succession to his cousin, 4th Baron. He was also cr. on 10 April 1806, **Earl of Orford**, of the second creation. He was b. 12 June 1723; m. 12 May 1748, Lady Rachel Cavendish (d. 8 May 1805) dau. of the 3rd Duke of Devonshire, and d. 24 Feb. 1809, having had with other issue who d. unm. or without leaving children, an eldest son,
Horatio Walpole, **2nd Earl of Orford**, b. 24 June 1752; m. (1) 27 July 1781, Sophia, dau. of Charles Churchill. She d. 1797. He m. (2) 28 July 1806, Catherine Tunstall, widow of Rev. Edward Chamberlayne, and d. 15 June 1822, when he was s. by the son of his first marriage,
Horatio Walpole, **3rd Earl of Orford**, b. 14 June 1783; m. 23 July 1812, dau. of William Augustus Fawkener, of Brereton Hall, co. Salop, and d. 29 Dec. 1858, having had with other issue (a second son, Henry who d.s.p. and two daus.),
1. Horatio William, **4th Earl** (see below).
2. Frederick, Cmdr. R.N., M.P. for N. Norfolk, b. 18 Sept. 1822; m. 12 Feb. 1852 Laura Sophia Frances, only dau. of Francis Walpole, and granddau. of Hon. Robert Walpole, and d. 1 April 1876, having had issue,
   (1) Robert Horace, **5th Earl** (see below).
   (2) Clare Horatio, b. 21 Nov. 1858; m. Ann Gardner, of Nelson, Virginia, U.S.A. and d. 6 May 1906 leaving issue,
      Amye, m. Hugh W. Davis, and d. 13 April 1967, leaving issue.
The 3rd Earl of Orford was s. by his eldest son,
Horatio William Walpole, **4th Earl of Orford**, b. 18 April 1813; m. 11 Nov. 1841,

Harriet Bettina Frances, only child of Hon. Sir Fleetwood Broughton Reynolds Pellew, (Exmouth, V.), and d. 7 Dec. 1894, having had issue two daus. and being s. by his nephew,

Robert Horace Walpole, **5th Earl of Orford**, b. 10 July 1854; Lt. R.N. and Capt. 4th Bn. Norfolk Regt.; served on several special embassies and missions, m. (1) 17 May 1888, Louisa Melissa, dau. of D. C. Corbin, of New York, She d. 4 May 1909. He m. (2) 15 Sept. 1917, Emily Gladys, dau. of the Rev. Thomas Henry Royal Oakes, Rector of Thurgarton, Norwich. By his first marriage he had issue a son, Horatio Corbin, who d. in 1893 aged two, and a dau. By his second marriage he had two more daus. He d.s.p.m.s. 27 Sept. 1931, when the Earldom of Orford, of the second creation became extinct and the baronies of Walpole of Walpole, and Walpole of Wolterton were inherited by his cousin,

Robert Henry Montgomerie Walpole, see above, and for full details, under Walpole, B. in extant peerages.

ARMS—Or on a fess between two chevronels sable, three cross crosslets of the field.
CREST—The bust of a man in profile couped at the shoulder ppr. ducally crowned or, from the coronet flowing a long cap turned forwards, gules, tasselled and charged with a catherine wheel, gold.
SUPPORTERS—Dexter, An antelope; Sinister, A stag both argent attired ppr. unguled or, each gorged with a collar chequy of the last and azure, chained gold.
MOTTO—Fari quae sentiat.
The seats of the Earls of Orford were— Wolterton Park, Norwich, and Nannington and Waborne Halls, Norfolk. The residence was Barnaline Lodge, Kilchteran, co. Argyll.

**ORMONDE

PEERAGE—England. Baron Butler, of Lanthony, co. Monmouth.
Ireland. Marquess of Ormonde.
SURNAME—Butler.
CR.—Barony 20 Jan. 1801. Marquessate 1816. **EXT.**—10 Aug. 1820.
HISTORY—In the 1883 Extinct Peerage there is a reference to this peerage in the index as being mentioned on p. 94, but no entry appears.

The two peerages were conferred on Walter Butler, the 18th Earl of Ormonde, who was b. 5 Feb. 1770, and who d.s.p. 10 Aug. 1820, when the two peerages became extinct and he was s. in the earldom and other honours by his brother,

James Butler, 19th Earl of Ormonde, who was given a barony of the U.K. as Baron Ormonde of Llanthony, co. Monmouth, on 17 July 1821, and also cr. a Marquess of Ormonde in the Irish peerage on 29 Oct. 1825. For other details see Ormonde, M. in extant peerage works.

**OVERSTONE

PEERAGE—U.K. Baron Overstone, of Overstone and Fotheringay, both co. Northampton.
SURNAME—Loyd.
CR.—5 Mar. 1850. **EXT.**—17 Nov. 1883.
HISTORY—William Loyd, of Court Henry,

co. Carmarthen, had with other issue, an eldest son, (for other descendants see B.L.G. 1952, Loyd formerly of Monk's Orchard), Lewis Loyd, a banker, of Overtsone Park, co. Northampton, and London. He was b. 1 Jan. 1768. He m. (1) 11 Nov. 1793, Sarah, dau. of John Jones, of Manchester, and m. (2) Mary, widow of — Champion, and d. 13 May 1858, leaving an only son, by his first marriage.

Samuel Jones Loyd, **Baron Overstone**, of Overstone, and Fotheringay, co. Northampton, so cr. 5 Mar. 1859; b. 25 Sept. 1796; educ. Trin. Coll. Camb. M.A.; M.P. for Hythe, 1819-26; m. 10 Aug. 1829, Harriet (d. 6 Nov. 1864) dau. of Ichabod Wright, of Mapperley Hall, co. Nottingham (B.L.G. 1952, Osmaston of Lowfold) and d. 17 Nov. 1883, having had issue,

Henry Jones, b. 20 Dec. 1832; d.v.p. 31 Mar. 1833.
Harriet Sarah, m. 17 Nov. 1858, Baron Wantage (see that title in present work) and d.s.p. 9 Aug. 1920.

ARMS—Per bend sinister ermine and argent an eagle with two heads displayed within a bordure sable bezantée.
CREST—A buck's head ppr. attired or, erased sable, charged on the neck with a fess engrailed of the third thereon three bezants.
SUPPORTERS—Dexter, A stag ppr. attired, ducally gorged and chain reflexed over the back and charged on the shoulder with a cross clechée or; Sinister, An eagle, wings elevated sable, beaked and membered or, ducally gorged, chain reflexed over the back, and charged on the breast with a cross clechée voided gold.
MOTTO—Non mihi sed patriae.

OVERTOUN

PEERAGE—U.K. Baron Overtoun, of Overtoun, co. Dumbarton.
SURNAME—White.
CR.—23 June 1893. **EXT.**—15 Feb. 1908.
HISTORY—James White, of Overtoun, co. Dumbarton, the son of John White, of Shawfield, m. 7 Sept. 1836, Fanny, dau. of Alexander Campbell, of Barnhill, co. Dumbarton, and d. 8 Mar. 1884, having by her (who d. 18 Jan. 1891) had issue with six daus., an only son,

John Campbell White, **Baron Overtoun**, of Overtoun, co. Dumbarton, so cr. 23 June 1893; F.R.G.S., M.A. Glasgow, 1864; joined his father's chemical firm at Shawfield, 1867; J.P. and D.L. co. Dumbarton, and J.P. co. Lanark; was a generous donor to the United Free Church after 1904, and to the United Free Church mission in Livingstonia; b. 21 Nov. 1843; m. 18 Sept. 1867, Grace Eliza, eldest dau. of James H. McClure, Solicitor of Glasgow, and d. 15 Feb. 1908.

ARMS—Or an eagle displayed between three quatrefoils two and one, on a chief engrailed azure a bezant between two garbs of the first.
CREST—An arm embowed ppr. the hand grasping two branches of laurel in orle vert fructed or.
SUPPORTERS—On either side an eagle wings elevated azure each charged on the breast with a quatrefoil and standing on a garb or.
MOTTO—(over the crest) Virtute.
Lord Overtoun's seat was Overtoun, co. Dumbarton.

PLATE 14

BARON NORTH.

EARL OF NORTHBROOK.

BARON NORTHCOTE.

VISCOUNT NORTHCLIFFE.

BARON O'BRIEN.

EARL OF ORFORD.

PLATE 15

BARON OVERTOUN.

BARON PECKOVER.

VISCOUNT PIRRIE.

BARON PLAYFAIR.

EARL RAVENSWORTH.

BARON RATHMORE.

OXENBRIDGE

PEERAGE—U.K. Viscount Oxenbridge of Burton, co. Lincoln.
SURNAME—Monson.
CR.—13 Aug. 1886. **EXT.**—16 April 1898.
HISTORY—Sir William John Monson, a baronet, 7th Baron Monson, (see extant peerage works), was cr. on 13 Aug. 1886, **Viscount Oxenbridge**, of Burton, co. Lincoln. He was b. 18 Feb. 1829; he was P.C., A.D.C. to Queen Victoria, Treasurer of the Royal Household, 1874; Capt. of the Yeomen of the Guard, 1880-86; Master of the Horse to Queen Victoria, 1892-94; sat as M.P. for Reigate 1858-62; m. 7 Aug. 1869, the Hon. Maria Adelaide, Maude, 2nd dau. of 3rd Viscount Hawarden (extant peerages), and sister of only Earl de Montalt (see that article in present work) and widow of 2nd Earl of Yarborough. Viscountess Oxenbridge d. 24 Dec. 1897. Viscount Oxenbridge d.s.p. 16 April 1898, when the Viscounty became extinct but he was s. in the Barony of Monson and the baronetcy by his brother,
Debonnaire John Monson, 8th Baron Monson,
ARMS—see Monson, B. in extant peerages.

PARKER OF WADDINGTON

PEERAGE—U.K. Life. Baron Parker of Waddington.
SURNAME—Parker.
CR.—4 Mar. 1913. **EXT.**—12 July 1918.
HISTORY—Edmund Parker is the name with which the pedigree of this family begins in Dugdale's Visitation of Yorkshire in 1665. He was the son of Giles Parker, of Horricksford and m. Elizabeth, the dau. and heir of John Redmayne, by Elizabeth his wife, dau. and heir of Robert Parker, of Browsholme in the forest of Bolland, co. York. He d. 1546 having had sixteen children, of whom,
Robert Parker, of Brownsholme, co. York, was Bowbearer of Bolland Forest, living 1591; m. 1554 Elizabeth, dau. of Edmund Chadderton, of Nuthurst, co. Lancs, and sister of William Chadderton, Bishop of Chester and Lincoln, and had, with other issue, an eldest surv. son,
Thomas Parker, Bowbearer of the Forest of Bolland, m. Bridget, dau. and coheir of James Tempest, of Rayne in Craven, co. York, and d. 12 Mar. 1634, having had, with other issue, an eldest son,
Edward Parker, of Browsholme, b. 3 Aug. 1602; m. 28 Jan. 1629, Mary, dau. of Richard Sunderland, of High Sunderland, co. York, and by her (who d. 1673) had issue,
1. Thomas (see below).
2. Robert of Carlton in Craven and Marley Hall, was Bowbearer at Waddington W.R. York, 1633; m. Jane, dau. of William Rookes, of Royds Hall and d.s.p. He founded the hospital at Waddington for poor widows.
3. Edward, Barrister-at-law, bapt. at Waddington 1 May 1636; m. Jane, dau. of Thomas Boteler, of Hatton Garden.
4. Richard bapt. at Waddington, 14 Nov. 1637.
5. Roger, bapt. at Waddington, 20 Jan. 1638, who had issue.

1. Mary, b. 17 May 1641; m. Thomas Heber, of Holling Hall, co. Yorks.
Edward Parker d. 1667 and was bur. at Waddington, being s. by his eldest son,
Thomas Parker, of Browsholme, bapt. at Waddington, 1 May 1631; m. Margaret dau. of Radcliffe Assheton, of Cuerdale, co. Lancs., and d. 1 Aug. 1695, having had issue, with an elder son, Edward, of Browsholme, a ygr. son,
Robert Parker, of Alkincoats, b. 1662; bought that estate, m. 1696 Ellen, dau. of Miles Whitaker, and d. 1714, having had with others an eldest son,
Thomas Parker, of Alkincoats, b. at Waddington 7 Dec. 1696, m. Alice dau. and heir of John Blakey, of Lanehead, and had issue,
Robert Parker, of Alkincoats, educ. Emmanuel Coll. Camb., who m. his cousin, Elizabeth, only dau. of John Parker, of Browsholme, and had, with other issue, a second son,
John Parker, afterwards Toulson, of Skipwith, co. York, m. 1804, Hester Arthur, dau. of John Arthur Worsop, of Howden, co. York, and had issue, with others, a second son,
The Rev. Richard Parker, Rector of Wellcum-Claxby, co. Lincoln, b. 20 Jan. 1809; m. (1) 14 Oct. 1841, Harriet Emma, (d. 6 April 1849), dau. of George Gowan H.E.I.C.S., and had, with other issue,
1. George Arthur, Sir, Judge of the High Court, Madras, 1886; educ. Uppingham, and Trin. Hall. Camb.; b. 1843; d. unm. 1900.
He m. (2) 22 May 1855, Elizabeth (d. 12 May 1904), dau. of R. A. Coffin, of Worthing, co. Sussex, and d. 23 Feb. 1887, having had further issue, of whom,
2. Robert John, **Baron Parker** of Waddington (see below).
3. Edmund Henry, Dir. of Barclay and Co., Bankers, b. 1858; m. 1888, Ellen, dau. of Clement Francis, of Guy Hall, Cambridge, and had issue.
The second mentioned son,
Sir Robert John Parker, **Baron Parker** of Waddington, b. 25 Feb. 1857; educ. Eton and King's Coll. Cambridge, B.A. 1880; Fellow, 1881; M.A. 1883; Barrister-at-Law, Lincoln's Inn, 1883; Junior Counsel to the Treasury, 1900; Judge of the High Court, Chancery Div. 1906-13; P.C. 1913; cr. Kt. Bach. 1906; apptd. 4 Mar. 1913, a Lord of Appeal in Ordinary, and cr. a peer for life as Baron Parker of Waddington, of Waddington, co. York. He m. 9 Sept. 1884, Constance, dau. of John Trevor Barkley, and d. 12 July 1918, having had issue,
1. Trevor Tempest, Cmdr. R.N., D.S.C., b. 14 Dec. 1890. m. 1917, Marie Louise Kleinwort, and had issue.
2. John Stanley, b. 23 Dec. 1892, served in World War I. m. May 1921, Marion Blanche Taberer, and had issue.
3. Hubert Lister, b. 28 May 1900; Barrister-at-law, Lincoln's Inn, 1924, m. 1924, Loryn Bowser, of Kentucky, U.S.A.
1. Vivien, b. 1885; m. T. B. Hart.
2. Gwendoline, b. 1887; m. 1908 Sir George Schuster and had issue.
ARMS—Vert a chevron between three stags' heads cabossed or.
CREST—A stag trippant ppr. gorged with a collar vert.

SUPPORTERS—On either side a bowman of the 15th century habited and accoutred ppr.
MOTTO—Nec fluctu nec flatu movetur.
Lord Parker of Waddington's residences were Aldworth, Haslemere, Surrey, and 28 Wellington Court, Knightsbridge, S.W. His clubs were Athenaeum, and United University.

PASSFIELD

PEERAGE—U.K. Baron Passfield, of Passfield Corner, co. Southampton.
SURNAME—Webb.
CR.—22 June 1929. **EXT.**—13 Oct. 1947.
HISTORY—Charles Webb, of London, by his wife Elizabeth Mary, dau. of Benjamin Stacey, was father of,
Sidney James Webb, **Baron Passfield**, b. 13 July 1859, in London, where he was baptized. He was educ. abroad and at London Univ., LL.B.; Barrister-at-Law, Gray's Inn, 1885; a clerk in War Office, 1878-79; a Surveyor of Taxes, 1879-81; a clerk in the Colonial Office, 1881-91; mem. L.C.C. for Deptford, 1892-1910; mem. of Senate 1901-10, and Prof. of Public Administration at London Univ. (Sch. of Economics and Political Science) 1912-27; M.P. (Labour) for the Seaham Div. of Durham, 1922-29; P.C. 1924; Pres. of Board of Trade, 1924; Sec. of State for Dominion Affairs and for the Colonies 1929-30, also Sec. of State for the Colonies, 1930-1931. He m. 23 July 1892, Martha Beatrice, 8th dau. of Richard Potter, a wealthy industrialist, and granddau. of Richard Potter. With her he wrote extensively on social and political matters, including *The History of Trade Unionism*, and *English Local Government* (9 vols.). They visited Russia in 1932, and published their impressions in *Soviet Communism: A New Civilization?*, a work which did much to encourage the pathetic left wing view of pre-1939 Russia as a democracy. He was cr. Baron Passfield, of Passfield Corner, co. Southampton, 22 June 1929, partly in order to strengthen the very small Labour representation in the House of Lords; cr. also 1944, O.M. At the time of his elevation to the peerage Beatrice Webb publically announced that she would be known as Lady Passfield. She d. 1943. He d. 13 Oct. 1947. Their ashes were bur. in Westminster Abbey. Lord Passfield was the originator of the London Sch. of Economics. He was Hon. D.Sec.(Econ.). London.
His seat was Passfield Corner, Liphook, Hants. His club the Athenaeum.

PAUNCEFOTE

PEERAGE—U.K. Baron Pauncefote of Preston, co. Gloucester.
SURNAME—Pauncefote (originally Smith).
CR.—18 Aug. 1899. **EXT.**—24 May 1902.
HISTORY—Abel Smith of Stoke, co. Nottingham, was the ygst. son of Thomas Smith and by his wife Jane, dau. of George Beaumont, had issue,
1. George, Sir, (see below).
2. John, of London, bapt. 5 May 1716; by his wife, Elizabeth Greenhead, of Chelsea, had an only son,

Thomas of Foel Alt, co. Cardigan, and Gedling, co. Nottingham m. Mary, dau. of James Bigsby of Nottingham and with other issue had a third son,
Robert, s. his cousin (see below).
3. Abel, ancestor of Lord Carrington.
The eldest son,
Sir George Smith, 1st Bart, so cr. 31 Oct. 1757; m. (1) Mary, only dau. and heiress of Major W. Howe of Beckingham co. Lincoln by his wife Elizabeth, the dau. and eventual heir of William Pauncefote, of Carnwalls co. Gloucester. She d. 1761, leaving issue. He m. (2) 1768, Catherine, dau. of the Ven. William Vyse, Archdeacon of Lichfield. She d.s.p. The son by the first marriage,
Sir George Pauncefote, 2nd Bt., of Stoke Hall, co. Nottingham, s. to the Pauncefote estates on the death of his cousin, Robert Bromley and at the latter's request assumed the arms and surname of Bromley in lieu of that of Smith, by Royal Licence of 17 Feb. 1778, and by further Royal Licence of 6 April 1803 he assumed the name and arms of Pauncefote. He was b. 18 Aug. 1753; m. 8 Jan. 1778, Hon. Esther Curzon, dau. of Assheton, Viscount Curzon. By her he had an only son (Bromley, Bt.). He d. 17 Aug. 1808 and by his will devised the estate of Preston Court, co. Gloucester, to his cousin,
Robert Smith subsequently Pauncefote who assumed by Royal Licence 29 Jan. 1809, the name and arms of Pauncefote in compliance with his cousin's will. He was b. 1788; educ. Worcester Coll. Oxford, B.A.; m. Emma (d. 28 June 1853) dau. of Robert Smith and d. 1843 having had issue,
1. Robert, b. 1 Feb. 1819, d. unm. 18 Nov. 1847.
2. Bernard, b. 14 Jan. 1826, served Madras C.S.; m. 5 July 1847, Eliza Louisa, dau. of Henry Philips of London and d. 1 Feb. 1894 having had issue,
   (1) Bernard, b. 28 June 1848; m. 20 Aug. 1873, Emily de Courcy, dau. of Rev. Robert Baker, and d.s.p. 20 Sept. 1882.
   (1) Eleanor.
   (2) Clara.
   (3) Evelyn Louisa.
3. Julian, **Baron Pauncefote** (see below).
1. Clara, m. Aug. 1842, Adm. W. C. Popham of Stourfield, co. Hants and had issue. He d. 1864.
2. Matilda Theodora, m. Sept. 1842, Baron Charles John Lachmann-Falkeran of Falkeran, Silesia and had issue.
The third son,
Sir Julian Pauncefote, **Baron Pauncefote** of Preston, co. Gloucester, so cr. 18 Aug. 1899, and cr. G.C.B., G.C.M.G., and made P.C. was b. 13 Sept. 1828; m. 14 Sept. 1859, Selina Fitzgerald, dau. of Major William Cubitt, of Catfield, Norfolk and had issue,
1. Reginald, d. young.
1. Selina Maud.
2. Violet Sibyl.
3. Lilian, m. 24 Feb. 1900, Robert Bromley, eldest son of Sir Henry Bromley, 5th Bt., and had issue.
4. Audrey Olivia.
Lord Pauncefote was Barrister-at-Law 1852, Attorney Gen. of Hong Kong 1863-73, Chief Justice of Leeward Islands 1874, Asst. Under Sec. of State for Colonies 1874-76 and for

Foreign Affairs 1876-82. P.U.S. 1882-89; Min. Plenipotentiary to U.S.A. 1889-93 and Ambassador Extra. and Plenipotentiary 1893. He d. 24 May 1902.

ARMS—Gules three lions rampant two and one argent, in the centre chief a sprig of oak or.

CREST—A lion rampant argent ducally crowned and holding between the paws an escutcheon or, thereon a wolf's head ppr.

SUPPORTERS—Two lions argent, each gorged with a gold chain pendent therefrom an escutcheon gules thereon a wolf's head argent.

MOTTO—Pensez forte.

PECKOVER

PEERAGE—U.K. Baron Peckover, of Wisbech, co. Cambridge.

SURNAME—Peckover.

CR.—20 July 1907. **EXT.**—21 Oct. 1919.

HISTORY—Edmund Peckover, of Charlton, co. Northampton, was at first a trooper in Cromwell's army, but when he joined the Society of Friends, he obtained his discharge from the service. This discharge, dated 6 Aug. 1655, was right into the 20th century held by the family in its archives. He settled at Fakenham in Norfolk, purchasing land in 1670, which again was in possession of his descendants in the 20th century. By his wife, Margaret, dau. of W. Munke, of Fakenham, who d. 1681, he had issue,

Joseph Peckover, of Fakenham, m. Catherine, dau. of James Long, of Swainsthorpe. She d. 16 Sept. 1726. They had issue with two older sons who d.s.p.m. a third son,

Joseph Peckover, of Fakenham, who m. Ann, dau. of Richard Wright, of Norwich, and by her (who d. 15 June 1744) had issue with others, an eldest son,

Richard Peckover, of Fakenham, b. 27 Jan. 1730; m. 4 April 1753, Jane, dau. and only child of Daniel Jessup, of Theberton, co. Suffolk, through whom the estates in Theberton and Badingham, co. Suffolk, came into the family. He d. 1 Sept. 1757. She d. April 1796. They had, with two other sons, who d. unm., a second son,

Jonathan Peckover, of Bank House, Wisbech, b. 23 Jan. 1755; m. 22 Oct. 1789, Susanna, dau. of William Payne, of Newhill Grange, York. He d. 18 Dec. 1833. She d. 3 Nov. 1853, having had, with other issue, a fourth son,

Algernon Peckover, of Dibalds Holme, Wisbech, b. 25 Nov. 1803; m. 26 Mar. 1828, Priscilla, dau. of Dykes Alexander, of Ipswich, banker. She d. 1 July 1883. He d. 10 Dec. 1893, having had issue,

1. Alexander, **Baron Peckover** (see below).
2. Jonathan, b. 16 June 1835; d. unm. 8 Feb. 1882.
1. Susanna, d. unm. 18 Oct. 1903.
2. Priscilla Hannah.
3. Jane, d. unm. 15 April 1909.
4. Katherine Elizabeth, m. 1867, Christopher Bowly, and d. 1869.
5. Algerina.
6. Wilhelmina, d. unm. 10 Dec. 1910.

The eldest son,

Alexander Peckover, **Baron Peckover**, b. 16 Aug. 1830; educ. Grove House Sch. Tottenham; entered firm of Gurney, Peckover

and Co. 1847; partner 1877; retired 1894; Lord Lt. Cambridgeshire 1894-1907; Pres. of Addenbrooke's Hospital, to which he gave an operating theatre; Vice Pres. of Hakluyt, Biblical, Archaeological and British Numismatic Socs.; F.S.A., F.R.G.S., F.L.S. He was cr. Baron Peckover, of Wisbech, co. Cambridge, 20 July 1907. He m. 8 April 1858, Eliza, only child of Joseph Sharples, Banker, of Hitchin, co. Herts, and d.s.p.m. 21 Oct. 1919 She d. 7 Aug. 1862. They had issue,

1. Elizabeth Josephine, m. 1893, J. D. Penrose, of Watford, and had issue.
2. Alexandrina.
3. Anna Jane.

ARMS—Per pale gules and sable a garb or, on a chief nebuly of the last, three lions rampant azure.

CREST—A lion rampant azure, holding in the dexter paw a sprig of oak, leaved fructed and slipped ppr. and resting the sinister forepaw on an escutcheon charged with the arms.

SUPPORTERS—On either side a woodpecker close ppr.

MOTTO—In Christo speravi.

Lord Peckover's residence was Bank House, Wisbech.

PENZANCE

PEERAGE—U.K. Baron Penzance, of Penzance, co. Cornwall.

SURNAME—Wilde.

CR.—6 April 1869. **EXT.**—9 Dec. 1899.

HISTORY—Sir James Plaisted Wilde, **Lord Penzance**, was the second son of Edward Archer Wilde, and the nephew of the 1st Baron Truro, (see that title in present work). He was b. 12 July 1816; m. 20 Feb. 1860, Lady Mary Pleydell-Bouverie, dau. of 3rd Earl of Radnor. She d. 24 Oct. 1900. Lord Penzance, was educ. Winchester and Trin. Coll. Camb., M.A. 1842; Barrister-at-Law, Inner Temple, 1839; Bencher, 1856; Counsel to Commissioners of Customs, 1840; Q.C. 1855; counsel to Duchy of Lancaster, 1859; made baron of Exchequer, invested with the coif and cr. Kt. Bach. 1860; transferred to Court of Probate and Divorce, 1863; was cr. a peer as Baron Penzance, of Penzance, co. Cornwall, 6 April 1869; retired from the Bench in 1872 owing to ill-health, but undertook office of judge under Public Worship Regulation Act, 1874; Dean of Arches, Court of Canterbury, Master of Faculties, and official principal of Chancery Court of York, 1875; ret. from Bench finally 1899. He served on many commissions. He d.s.p. 9 Dec. 1899.

ARMS—Ermine on a cross sable, a plate; on a chief of the second three martlets argent.

CREST—A hart lodged holding in its mouth a rose ppr.

SUPPORTERS—On either side a bull reguardant argent, gorged with a collar vair and chain reflexed over the back.

MOTTO—Veritas victrix.

Seat was Eashing Park, Godalming, Surrey. His club was Brooks's.

PERCY OF NEWCASTLE

PEERAGE—U.K. Baron Percy of Newcastle, of Etchingham, co. Sussex.
SURNAME—Percy.
CR.—12 Feb. 1953. **EXT.**—3 April 1958.
HISTORY—Lord Eustace Sutherland Campbell Percy, seventh son of the 7th Duke of Northumberland, was b. 21 Mar. 1887; educ. Eton and Ch. Ch. Oxford, B.A. 1907, and M.A. 1913; 3rd Sec. Diplomatic Service, 1911-19; M.P. Hastings, 1921-37, Parl. Sec. to Board of Education, 1923, and to Min. of Health, 1923-24, Pres. of Board of Education, 1924-29, Min. without Portfolio, 1935-36, Rector of King's Coll. Newcastle, 1937-52, Chm. Royal Comm. on Mental Patients, 1954, and Pres. of the Royal Inst. 1941; made a P.C. 1924, and cr. a peer as **Baron Percy** of Newcastle, of Ethingham, co. Sussex, 12 Feb. 1953; m. 4 Dec. 1918, Stella Katherine, dau. of Major Gen. Lawrence Drummond, (Perth, E.), and d. 3 April 1958, having had issue,
1. Mary Edith, b. 24 Oct. 1919; educ. Bristol Univ.
2. Dorothy Anne, b. 21 Sept. 1926; educ. Durham Univ. M.B. 1949; m. 23 Mar. 1957, Major T. R. H. Eustace, and had issue.

ARMS—As under Northumberland, D., but no Suppoiters were recorded by 1957.

PERRY

PEERAGE—U.K. Baron Perry, of Stock Harvard, co. Essex.
SURNAME—Perry.
CR.—28 Jan. 1938. **EXT.**—17 June 1956.
HISTORY—Alfred Thomas Perry, of Bristol, m. Elizabeth, dau. of the Rev. Henry Wheeler, and had a son,
Sir Perceval Lea Dewhurst Perry, **Baron Perry**, b. 18 Mar. 1878, at Bristol, educ. King Edward's Sch. Birmingham; Fell. of the Chartered Inst. of Secretaries, 1904; Pres. of Motor Trade Asscn., 1914-16; Director of Food Production Dept., 1916; of Agricultural Machinery Dept., Ministry of Munitions, 1917-18; Hon. Pres. of Slough Estates Ltd., Dir. Ford Motor Co. and of Firestone Tyre and Rubber Co., Business Adviser, Min. of Food, 1939-40; was F.R.G.S., and had orders of Kt. Cmdr. George I of the Hellenes, Offr. Legion of Honour, Cmdr. of Leopold of Belgium, and Liberty Medal of King Christian Xth of Denmark, 1947; Hon. LL.D. Birmingham, 1937; cr. C.B.E. 1917, K.B.E., 1918, and a peer as Baron Perry of Stock Harvard, co. Essex, 28 Jan. 1938. He was author of *O.K. Verses* 1906, *American Invasion*, 1912, *New Songs*, 1925, *Island of Enchantment*, 1926, *International Trade Balance*, 1932, also some pamphlets and papers. He m. 26 Dec. 1902, Catherine, dau. of John Meals, of Hull, and d. 17 June 1956.
Sir Compton Mackenzie's autobiography (*Octaves*) contains several references to Lord Perry, particularly in *Octave V*, regarding the lease of the island of Herm in the Channel Islands. On p. 257 of *Octave V* Sir Compton tells of Lord Perry's account of a kitten which grew into a cat and then cost him 1/6 (modern $7\frac{1}{2}$ n.p.) per week for its food.

ARMS—Or on a bend sable, between two escallops gules, three crosses patonce of the field.
CREST—A pied wagtail ppr.
SUPPORTERS—On either side a hippocampus ppr. gorged with a collar or charged with four pearls ppr.
MOTTO—Look Beyond.
BADGE—A pear slipped and leaved ppr. enfiled with a circlet or, charged with four pearls also ppr.
Lord Perry's residences were Nassau, Bahamas and 16 Berkeley Street, W.1. His clubs were Brooks's, Reform and Portland.

PETHICK-LAWRENCE

PEERAGE—U.K. Baron Pethick-Lawrence, of Peaslake, co. Surrey.
SURNAME—Pethick-Lawrence.
CR.—16 Aug. 1945. **EXR.**—10 Sept. 1961.
HISTORY—Joseph Lawrence, of St. Ives, co. Cornwall, had issue,
Thomas Lawrence, of St. Agnes, co. Cornwall, bapt. 13 April 1727; m. 1759, Jane, (d. Feb. 1811) dau. of Anthony Rowse, of Illogan, co. Cornwall, and d. Aug. (bur. 13 Aug.) 1811, leaving issue,
Thomas Lawrence, of St. Agnes, co. Cornwall, bapt. 12 Feb. 1760; m. 1 April 1788, Mary, (d. 12 April 1850), dau. of John Tonkin, of St. Agnes and d. 13 Mar. 1812, leaving with other issue,
William Lawrence, of Tavistock Square, London, Alderman of the Ward of Bread Street, London, from 1848, J.P. Middlesex and the City of Westminster, Sheriff of London, and Middlesex, 1848-49; b. 4 Feb. 1789; m. 21 Sept. 1817, Jane, (d. 14 Feb. 1874) dau. of James Clarke, of Wymeswold, near Loughborough, co. Leicester, and d. 25 Nov. 1855, having had issue,
1. William, Sir, Alderman of the Ward of Bread Street, London, from 1855; D.L. Middlesex and City of Westminster, M.P. for London, 1865-74; and 1880-85; Sheriff of London and Middlesex, 1857-58, and Lord Mayor of London, 1863-64, b. 2 Sept. 1818; d. unm. 18 April 1897.
2. James Clarke, Sir, Bt., Alderman of the Ward of Wallbrook, London from 1860, M.P. for Lambeth 1868-85; J.P. for Surrey, Middlesex, and the City of Westminster, Sheriff of London and Middlesex, 1862; Lord Mayor of London, 1868-69; b. 1 Sept. 1820, cr. a Baronet 16 Dec. 1869; m. 17 Mar. 1887 Agnes Harriette (d. 9 Nov. 1944), dau. of Michael Castle, of Hatherleigh House co. Gloucester, and d. 21 May 1897, when his baronetcy became extinct, he leaving issue a dau.,
   Theodora Agnes Clarke Durning-Lawrence, b. 11 Dec. 1889; assumed by Royal Licence, 14 July 1914, the surname of Durning in addition to, and before that of, Lawrence.
3. Alfred, b. 29 Oct. 1824; d. Nov. 1825.
4. Alfred (secundus) (see below).
5. Frederick, b. 4 April, 1828; d. unm. 31 May 1864.
6. Joseph, b. 9 and d. 30 April 1830.

7. Edwin Durning-Lawrence, Sir, Bt., of King's Ride, Ascot, co. Berks, b. 2 Feb. 1837; B.A., LL.D. London, Barrister-at-Law Middle Temple, 1867; J.P. Berks, M.P. Truro, 1895-1906; assumed by Royal Licence, 2 Feb. 1898, surname of Durning in addition to and before that of Lawrence, cr. a baronet 11 Mar. 1898; m. 11 June 1874, Edith Jane, (d. 27 April 1929), dau. and coheir of J. B. Smith, of King's Ride, Ascot, co. Berks, M.P. (by Jemima, his wife, dau. and coheir of William Durning, of Liverpool) and d. 21 April 1914, when his baronetcy became extinct, he having had issue,

Edwin Smith, b. 23 and d. 25 Aug. 1878.

Sir Edwin is mentioned in Sir Sidney Lee's Life of Shakespeare. "The Baconians found an English champion in Sir Edwin Durning-Lawrence who pressed into his service every manner of misapprehension in his Bacon is Shakespeare, (1900) of a penny abridgment of which he claimed to have circulated 300,000 copies during 1912. Sir Edwin . . . credited Bacon with the composition not only of Shakespeare's works but of almost all the great literature of his time." (op. cit. p. 652).

1. Jane, b. 10 Sept. 1822; d. unm. 2 May 1897.
2. Emma, b. 6 Aug. 1832; d. unm. 4 Feb. 1874.
3. Caroline, b. 11 Dec. 1834; d. unm. 24 June 1853.

The fourth son,

Alfred Lawrence, of 42 Gloucester Gardens, Bayswater, W.2., a Commr. of Lieutenacy for London, b. 19 July 1826; m. 27 Oct. 1858, Mary Elizabeth, (d. 13 June 1903) dau. of Henry Ridge, of Upper Clapton, co. Middlesex, and d. 9 June 1875, leaving issue,

1. Henry.
2. Frederick William, **Baron Pethick-Lawrence** (see below).
1. Ellen Mary.
2. Annie Jane.
3. Caroline Aspland.

The second son,

Frederick William Pethick-Lawrence, **Baron Pethick-Lawrence**, b. 28 Dec. 1871; educ. Eton and Trin. Coll. Camb., B.A. 1894, M.A. 1896; Fell. 1897-1903; Barrister-at-Law, Inner Temple, 1899; Dunkin Prof. at Manchester Coll. Oxford, 1900, Chm. of Consolidated Newspapers 1901-06; mem. of Fabian Soc., M.P. for West Div. of Leicester 1923-31; and for E. Div. of Edinburgh, 1935-45; Fin. Sec. to the Treasury, 1929-31, Vice Chm. of Parl. Labour Party 1943; Sec. of State for India and Burma, 1945-47; mem. of various commissions anc cttees; mem., of Political Honours Scrutiny Cttee; author of several books, made P.C. 1937, cr. a peer as Baron Pethick-Lawrence, of Peaslake, co. Surrey, 16 Aug. 1945; assumed the additional surname of Pethick before that of Lawrence on his marriage; m. 2 Oct. 1901, Emmeline (author of My Part in a Changing World, 1938) dau. of Henry Pethick, of Weston-super-Mare, Somerset and d. 10 Sept. 1961.

ARMS—Ermine on a cross raguly gules, between in the first and fourth quarters a fasces erect encircled by a wreath of oak ppr., a pair of compasses extended or.

CREST—A wolf's head erased argent crusilly and charged with a pair of compasses extended sable.
MOTTO—Per ardua stabilis.
Lord Pethick-Lawrence's residences were Fourways, Gomshall, nr. Guildford, Surrey, and 11, Old Square, Lincoln's Inn, W.C.2. His club was Royal Aero.

PIRBRIGHT

PEERAGE—U.K. Baron Pirbright, of Pirbright, co. Surrey.
SURNAME—De Worms.
CR.—15 Nov. 1895. EXT.—9 Jan. 1903.
HISTORY—Solomon Benedict de Worms, b. Feb. 1801, the son of Benedict Worms, of Frankfort-on-the-Main, by his wife, Jeanette, eldest dau. of Mayer-Amschel Von Rothschild, and sister of Baron Nathan Mayer de Rothschild, of London (see that family in extant peerage works). He was cr. a hereditary baron of the Austrian Empire by Imperial Letters Patent dated at Vienna, 23 April 1871. By Royal Licence, 10 Aug. 1874, Queen Victoria granted him and his descendants permission to use the title in Britain. He m. 11 July 1827, Henrietta, eldest dau. of Samuel Moses Samuel, of Park Crescent, London, and d. 20 Oct. 1882. She d. 24 Jan. 1845. They had issue,

1. George, 2nd Baron de Worms, of Milton Park, Egham, D.L. and J.P. for Surrey, Middlesex, and Westminster, Knight Grand Commander of the Imperial and Royal Austrian order of Francis Joseph F.S.A., and Vice Pres. Roy. Soc. of Lit., b. 16 Feb. 1829; m. 18 April 1860, Louisa, dau. of Baron de Samuel, and d. 1902 having had issue,
   (1) Anthony Denis Maurice George, 3rd Baron de Worms, Fell. Roy. Soc. of Lit., and Roy. Philatelic Soc., b. 4 Jan. 1869; m. 1901, Louisa, dau. of Moritz A. Goldscmidt of 66 Mount Street, Grosvenor Square, London, W., and had issue two sons and a dau.
   (2) Percy George, b. 3 Nov. 1873; m. 1900, Nora, only dau. of Sir Harry S. Samuel, M.P. and had issue a son and a dau.
   (1) Henrietta Emmy Louisa Amelia, b. 17 Aug. 1875.
2. Anthony Mayer, b. 12 Oct. 1830; m. 1 July 1860, Emma Augusta, dau. of Baron Frederick Von Schey, of Vienna, and d. 2 Nov. 1864, leaving issue three daus.
3. Henry, cr. **Baron Pirbright** (see below).
1. Ellen Henrietta, b. 13 Jan. 1836; m. 25 Mar. 1857, Adolf Landauer, of Vienna, and had issue, a son and four daus.

The third son,

Henry de Worms, **Baron Pirbright**, of Pirbright, co. Surrey, so cr. 15 Nov. 1895; was b. 20 Oct. 1840; J.P. and D.L. for Middlesex and Westminster; M.P. for Greenwich, 1880-85, and for East Toxteth Div. of Liverpool, 1885-95, Parl. Sec. to Board of Trade, 1885-88, and Under Sec. of State for the Colonies, 1888-92; Barrister-at-Law, Inner Temple, 1863; Fell. of King's Coll. London; made P.C.; F.R.S.; and cr. a peer as Baron Pirbright, of Pirbright, co. Surrey, 15 Nov. 1895. He m.

(1) 5 May 1864, Fanny, dau. of Baron Von Todeschi, of Vienna, and by her had issue,
1. Alice Henrietta Antoinette Evelina, b. 2 April 1865; m. (1) 28 April 1886, J. H. B. Warner, of Quorn Hill, co. Leicester who d.s.p. 1891. She m. (2) 1892, D. M. Morison, who d. 23 Feb. 1924, leaving issue.
2. Dora Sophia Emmy, b. 9 June 1869.
3. Constance Valerie Sophie, b. 28 April 1875; m. 4 Nov. 1895 Count Maximilian Carl Friedrich von Loewenstein Scharffeneck, herditary chamberlain at Court of Bavaria, and had issue.
Lord Pirbrihgt m. (2) 25 Jan. 1887. Sarah, D.G. St. J., only dau. of Sir Benjamin Samuel Phillips, and d.s.p.m. 9 Jan. 1903. She d. 2 Nov. 1914.
ARMS—(Described as granted in Austria in 1871, and allowed by Royal Licence in College of Arms, 1874). Quarterly 1 and 4, Azure a key in bend wards upwards or; 2 and 3, Or an eagle displayed sable, over all an escutcheon gules, a dexter arm fesswise, couped at the wrist ppr., the hands grasping three arrows, one in pale and two in saltire, or barbed and flighted argent.
CREST—Out of a ducal coronet five ostrich feathers or, gules, or, azure and or.
MOTTO—(in letters gules), Vinctus non victus.
SUPPORTERS—(as for 3rd Baron de Worms) On a bronze compartment, on either side a lion gold, collared and chained or.
ARMS—(as set out in peerages circa 1903 for Lord Pirbright). Quarterly 1 and 4, Azure a key bendwise or; 2 and 3, Or an eagle displayed sable, Over all an escutcheon of pretence gules charged in fess with a hand couped at the wrist grasping three arrows, two in saltire and one in pale points upwards ppr.
CREST—Out of a ducal coronet or a plume of five ostrich feathers, or, gules, or, azure, and or.
SUPPORTERS—On either side a lion or, gorged with a collar azure, chain reflexed over the back gold, pendent from the collar an escutcheon argent charged with an oak branch vert thereon a squirrel sejant ppr.

PIRRIE

PEERAGE—U.K. Baron Pirrie, of Belfast. Viscount Pirrie, of Belfast.
SURNAME—Pirrie.
CR.—Barony, 17 July 1906. Viscounty, 9 July 1921. EXT.—6 June 1924.
HISTORY—William Pirrie, of Conlig House, by his wife Elizabeth, dau. of William Morrison, had three sons and four daus., of whom the second son,
James Alexander Pirrie, of Little Clandeboye, co. Down, m. Eliza, dau. of Alexander Montgomery, of Dundesart, co. Antrim. She d. 1895. He d. 1849, having had with a dau., Eliza who m. Thomas Andrews, an only son,
Sir William James Pirrie, **Baron and Viscount Pirrie**, b, 31 May 1847; in Quebec; educ. the Belfast Royal Academical Inst.; entered Harland and Wolff's shipbuilding and engineering works, 1862, and became a partner in 1874, Chm. thereof 1895; became a leading shipbuilder and shipowner, and most of the White Star fleet were built by Harland and Wolff including the *Titanic*. He had interests in

banking, railways, insurance and oil. He was Lord Mayor of Belfast, 1896 and 1897; P.C. 1897; High Sheriff co. Antrim, 1898, and co. Down, 1899. He was cr. Baron Pirrie, of Belfast, 17 July 1906, and K.P. 1908, also Viscount Pirrie, of Belfast 9 July 1921. He was Comptroller of the Household of the Lord Lt. of Ireland, 1907-13; His Majesty's Lt. for City of Belfast, 1911; mem. of War Office Supply Board, 1916; made P.C. 1918; Comptroller Gen. of Merchant Shipbuilding 1918, to organize production of merchant ships. He was a mem. of the Senate of Northern Ireland, 1921. He m. 17 April 1879, Margaret Montgomery, dau. of John Carlisle, and d.s.p. 6 June 1924, of pneumonia while voyaging off Cuba. He was Hon. LL.D. Royal Univ. of Ireland 1899, and Hon. D.Sc. Trin. Coll. Dublin 1903. He was bur. 23 June 1924 in Belfast. Lady Pirrie d. 19 June 1935. On her husband's death she was apptd. Pres. of Harland and Wolff, and was the first woman Hon. Freeman of Belfast and first woman magistrate for Belfast.
ARMS—Argent a saltire gules between in chief and in base a bugle horn stringed sable and in fess two seahorses respecting one another ppr.
CREST—A falcon's head erased per saltire argent and gules.
SUPPORTERS—On either side upon an anchor fesswise ppr. a falcon argent beaked, membered and collared sable, belled or.
MOTTO—Deeds not words.
Lord Pirrie's residences were Witley Park, Godalming, Surrey, and 24 Belgrave Square, S.W. His clubs were Reform, Kildare Street, Dublin and Ulster, Belfast.

PLAYFAIR

PEERAGE—U.K. Baron Playfair, of St. Andrews, co. Fife.
SURNAME—Playfair.
CR.—3 Sept. 1892. EXT.—26 Dec. 1939.
HISTORY—Robert Playfair, of the parish of Bendochy, co. Perth where he was a landowner, by his wife, Christian Ritchie, had two sons, (the elder Patrick was ancestor of the famous Prof. John Playfair lived 1748-1819, and the Playfairs of Dalmarnock, co. Lanark, and of Ardmillan co. Ayr), of whom the ygr.,
James Playfair, b. 1646, had with others a son,
James Playfair, of Coultie, in the parish of Bendochy, who by his wife, Janet Roger, had issue,
George Playfair, of Knowhead, m. his cousin Jean Roger (d. 1804, aged 93) and had issue,
The Rev. James Playfair, D.D. St. Andrews 1779, Principal of St. Andrew's Univ., and Historiographer Royal for Scotland, and for many years to the Prince Regent, also Min. of Church of St. Leonards, Fife, 1800, who m. Margaret, dau. of George Lyon, of Ogil, co. Forfar, and sister of the Rev. James Lyon, D.D., Minister of Glamis, and d. May 1819, having had issue,
1. George (see below).
2. William Davidson, Col. I.A., m. 3 Nov. 1812, Anne, dau. of John Ross, of Edinburgh, and d.v.p. 1852, aged 69, having had issue.

3. Hugh Lyon, Sir, K.C.B., b. 20 Feb. 1787; studied at St. Andrews Univ.; entered Bengal Horse Artillery, 1804 and saw much service in India, retired, 1834; was Provost, St. Andrews, 1842-61; revived the Royal and Ancient Golf Club, was made LL.D. St. Andrews, 1856 and knighted, 1856; m. 10 July 1809, Jane, dau. of William Dalgelish, of Scotscraig co. Fife, and d. 19 Jan. 1861, leaving issue.
The eldest son,
George Playfair, of St. Andrews, M.D., Chief Insp. Gen. of Hospitals, Bengal, b. 4 Jan. 1782; m. 8 Nov. 1814, Janet (d. 1862) dau. of John Ross, of Edinburgh, and d. 26 Nov. 1846, having had issue,
1. George Ranken, late Prim. of the Medical Coll. Agra, b. 13 Nov. 1816; m. 30 Oct. 1849, Fanny, dau. of Gen. Home. She d. 10 Jan. 1893. He d. 1885. They had issue.
2. Lyon, Baron Playfair (see below).
3. Robert Lambert, Sir, author and administrator, b. 1828; entered Madras Artillery, 1846; Capt. 1858; trans. Madras Staff Corps, 1861; Major, 1866; ret. as Lt. Col. 1867; Asst. Political Res. at Aden, 1854-62; F.R.G.S. 1860; political agent at Zanzibar, 1862 and consul 1863; consul gen. for Algeria, 1867; for Algeria and Tunis, 1885; for Algeria and Northern coast of Africa, 1889-96; cr. K.C.M.G. 1886; he wrote numerous works, including bibliographies of Algeria, 1851-87 (publ. 1888), of Tripoli and Cyrenaica, (1889), and of Morocco, (1892), with books of travel, handbooks for travellers, and other books; he m. 1851, Agnes, dau. of Gen. Webster, of Balgarvie, co. Fife, and d. Feb. 1899, having had issue.
4. William Smoult, obstetric physician, b. 27 July 1836; M.D. Edinburgh, 1856; Prof. of Surgery, at Calcutta Medical Coll. 1859-60; M.R.C.P. 1863; F.R.C.P. 1870; Prof. of Obstetric Medicine in King's Coll. and obstetric physician, to King's Coll. Hospital, 1872-1898; Hon. LL.D. St. Andrews, 1885, and Edinburgh, 1898; author of *Science and Practice of Midwifery*, 1876, and with Sir T. C. Allbutt, of *System of Gynaecology*, 1896. He m. 26 April 1864, Emily (d. 21 Nov. 1916) dau. of James Kitson, of Elmet Hall, Leeds (Airedale, B.) and d. 13 Aug. 1903, leaving issue.
Nigel Ross, Sir, b. 1874, actor manager; educ. Harrow and Univ. Coll. Oxford; on professional stage, 1902-18, largely in good humoured comedy; among his scholarly and finished productions at the Lyric Theatre, Hammersmith, from 1920-34, among the plays of 18th century comedy and 20th century satire, was the revival of the *Beggar's Opera*, in 1920. He was knighted 1928 and d. 1934.
1. Ann, m. Capt. Hickey, and d. 6 Oct. 1861 leaving issue a dau.
2. Jessie Macdonald, m. April 1840, as his 3rd wife, the Col. J. S. H. Weston, of West Horsley Place, co. Surrey, and had issue.
3. Agnes, d. unm. 18 Jan. 1871.
The second son,

Sir Lyon Playfair, 1st Baron Playfair, b. at Chunar, India, 21 May 1818; educ. St. Andrews, and studied chemistry at Glasgow under Thomas Graham, to whom he was asst. at Univ. Coll. London; Ph.D. Giessen.; hon. Prof. of Chemistry to Royal Inst. of Manchester, 1842-45; chemist to Geological Survey and Prof. in New Sch. of Mines, Jermyn Street, London, 1845; F.R.S. 1848; Pres. of Chemical Soc. 1857-59; took part in organizing Great Exhibition, 1851; Prof. of Chemistry at Edinburgh, 1858-69; sat as Liberal M.P. for Univs. of Edinburgh and St. Andrews, 1868-85; was Postmaster Gen. 1873; Chm. of Ways and Means, and Deputy Speaker of House of Commons, 1880-83; and Vice Pres. of Cttee of Council on Education 1886; sat as Liberal M.P. for South Leeds, 1885-92; a lord in Waiting to Queen Victoria, 1892-95; was cr. C.B. 1851; K.C.B. 1883, a peer as Baron Playfair of St. Andrews, co. Fife, 3 Sept. 1892 and G.C.B. 1895, made P.C. He m. (1) 28 July 1846, Margaret Eliza (d. 13 Aug. 1855) dau. of James Oakes, of Eiddings House, Alfreton, by whom he had,
1. George James, 2nd Baron (see below).
1. Jessie Anne, b. 8 July 1847; m. (1) 5 Jan. 1869, Capt. Edmund Peel, of Tamworth, 14th Hussars. He d. 9 June 1885, leaving issue. She m. (2) Gen. Sir R. M. Stewart, G.C.B., R.A., and d. 24 May 1927.
Lord Playfair m. (2) 17 Dec. 1857, Jean Ann, dau. of Crawley Millington, of Crawley House, and had by her (d. 1877) further issue,
2. Ethel Mary Lyon, b. 6 Jan. 1862; m. 1886, Major Frederick William Bloomfield of El Biar, Algeria, and had issue.
Lord Playfair m. (3) 3 Oct. 1878, Edith, dau. of Samuel Hammond Russell, of Boston, U.S.A., and d. 29 May 1898. The widow m. 2ndly 25 June 1901, R. F. Crooks, and d. 14 Jan. 1932.
The only son,
George James Playfair, 2nd Baron Playfair, Brig. Gen., b. 31 Mar. 1849; served with R.A., Col., and Brig. Gen. in cmd. of Coast Defences, 1903-06 and Hon. Col. 2nd Highland Brigade, R.F.A., 1903-29 (T.D.); served with the Turkish Army in the war of 1877, against Russia, at the battles before Plevna, and Shipka Pass. He m. (1) 4 Jan. 1877, Lucy Osborne, dau. of T. G. Matthews, of Portishead and Bristol. She d. 8 Oct. 1877. They had issue,
Lucy Jessie Lyon, m. 21 Nov. 1907, Major Lionel Culme Soltau-Symons, D.S.O., Durham L.I., ygst. son of George William Culme Soltau-Symons, of Chaddlewood, co. Devon. He d. 8 April 1944.
Lord Playfair m. (2) 12 Jan. 1888, Augusta Mary, dau. of H. T. Hickman, of Chorlton House Leamington and d. 26 Dec. 1939, having had issue,
Lyon George Henry Lyon, Capt. R.F.A., b. 19 Oct. 1888; k. in action, 20 April 1915.
ARMS—Vert a lion rampant argent on a chief or a fleur-de-lis gules, between two castles ppr.
CREST—On a cap of maintenance gules, turned up ermine, a pelican vulning itself ppr.
SUPPORTERS—On either side a lion reguardant argent, gorged with a wreath of bay leaves ppr. and charged on the shoulder with an escutcheon vert, thereon a thistle leaved and slipped or.
MOTTO—Dum spiro spero.

Lord Playfair's seat was Heydon Hall, Norwich. His club was Naval and Military.

PLENDER

PEERAGE—U.K. Baron Plender, of Sundridge, co. Kent. (Also a baronetcy cr. 16 July 1923.)
SURNAME—Plender.
CR.—20 Jan. 1931. **EXT.**—19 Jan. 1946.
HISTORY—Robert Plender, b. 1722; m. 1751, Margaret Thomson, and d. at Alnham, co. Northumberland 1788, having had a son,
William Plender, b. 1769; m. 1789, Mary Storey and d. at Newbrough, co. Northumberland, 1831, having had issue,
William Plender, b. 1794; m. 1829, Mary Hedley, and d. at Tynemouth 1878, leaving issue,
William Plender, of The Oaks, Dalston, co. Northumberland, b. 27 Jan. 1833; m. 1 Nov. 1860, Elizabeth Agnes Smallpiece, dau. of John Edward Smallpiece Vardy, and d. at Dalston, 7 Oct. 1911, having by her who d. 22 May 1917, had issue,
1. William, Sir, Bt. and **Baron Plender** (see below).
2. George Vardy, b. 1865; m. 1900, Adela Aguilla of San José, Costa Rica, and d. 1901.
3. John Edward, b. 1870; m. 1916, Emily Florence Jane, widow of T. W. Bagnall.
4. Robert, b. 1872 and d. 1886.
5. Thomas Turner, b. 1876; m. Annie Appleton and had issue.
1. Elizabeth, d. 27 April 1925.
2. Mary, d. 1909.
3. Sarah Hedley, d. 1877.
4. Edith.
The eldest son,
Sir William Plender, Bt., and **Baron Plender**, b. 20 Aug. 1861; Senior Partner in the international firm of Deloitte, Plender, Griffiths and Co., Chartered Accountants; Pres. of Inst. of Chartered Accountants, 1910-12 and 1929-30; mem. and Chm. of numerous commissions; Treasury Controller of German, Austrian and Turkish Banks, 1914-18; Hon. Financial Adviser to Board of Trade, 1918; cr. Kt. Bach. 1911; a baronet 16 July 1923; High Sheriff, co. London, 1927-28; and of co. Kent, 1928-29; Pres. of Fourth International Congress on Accounting, London, 1933; Lt. for City of London; Chm. of Gov. Body, City of London, Coll. 1935; Chm. of German Debts Cttee 1935; Hon. Treas. Royal Geographical Soc.; Hon mem. Inst. of Journalists; Gov. of St. Thomas's Hospital. He was cr. G.B.E. 1918; and Baron Plender, of Sundridge, co. Kent, 20 Jan. 1931. He m. (1) 8 Oct. 1891, Marian Elizabeth D.G. St. J., who d. 31 Dec. 1930. He m. (2) 27 April 1932, Mabel Agnes, D. St. J., dau. of Peter George Laurie, and widow of G. N. Stevens, and d.s.p. 19 Jan. 1946.
ARMS—Vert a chevron engrailed ermine between in chief a fleur-de-lis and in base a trefoil slipped argent.
CREST—Issuant from a baron's coronet or, a dexter cubit arm, habited azure, charged with a fleur-de-lis gold holding in the hand a scroll ppr.
SUPPORTERS—Dexter, A stag; Sinister, A lion ppr. each collared and chained, the chain

reflexed over the back or, and charged on the shoulder with a rose gules and a thistle, both leaved and slipped ppr. in saltire.
MOTTO—Prompte et consulto.
Lord Plender's residences were Ovenden, Sundridge Sevenoaks, Kent; and 51 Kensington Court, W.8. His clubs were, Brooks's, Garrick, Athenaeum, Beefsteak, City of London, Reform, and Arts.

PLUMER

PEERAGE—U.K. Baron Plumer, of Messines and of Bilton, co. York. U.K. Viscount Plumer of the same.
SURNAME—Plumer.
CR.—Barony 4 Oct. 1919. Viscounty 24 June 1929. **EXT.**—24 Feb. 1944.
HISTORY—Thomas Plummer, of Bedale, co. York, m. 3 Feb. 1638/39 Dorothy Brockell, of Bedale, and had, with other issue,
William Plummer, of Bedale, b. 1641; and d. 1714, having had with other issue,
Thomas Plummer, of Bedale, who was bapt. 1 June 1684, and who, by his second wife, Alice, dau. of Francis Hall, of East Lilling, co. York, whom he m. 14 Dec. 1710, had at his death on 17 Mar. 1781, had with other issue,
Sir Thomas Plumer, Master of the Rolls, b. 10 Dec. 1753; m. 26 Aug. 1794, Marianne, dau. of John Turton, and d. 25 Mar. 1824, having had with others,
Thomas Hall Plumer, of Canons, co. Middlesex, b. 24 Aug. 1795; m. May 1822, Anne Headland, and d. 24 Dec. 1852, having had with others, a second son,
Hall Plumer, of Malpas Lodge, Torquay, b. 15 Sept. 1827; m. 18 May 1854 Louisa Alice Hudson, (d. 17 Nov. 1903) dau. of Henry Turnley, of Kensington, and d. 14 June 1888, having had with other issue,
Herbert Charles Onslow Plumer, **Baron and Viscount Plumer**, b. 13 Mar. 1857; educ. Eton and R.M.C. Sandhurst; joined 65th Foot, 1876; Capt. York and Lancaster Regt. 1882; served in the Sudan, 1884; D.A.A.G. Jersey, 1890-93; Major, 1893; served in Matabeleland, 1896; Brev. Lt. Col. 1897; served in S. African War, 1899-1902, in command Rhodesian Field Force, (wounded); Brev. Col. 1900; Major Gen. 1902; Gen. Officer cmdg. 5th Div. Irish Command, 1906-09; Lt. Gen. 1908; G.O.C. Northern Cmd. 1911-14; served in World War I, 1914-18; Gen. 1915; Cmd. 2nd Army, in France, 1915-17; Commanded Brit. Forces in Italy, 1917-18; and again the 2nd Army in France, 1918-19; commanded Army of the Rhine, 1918-19; Field Marshal, 1919. He was cr. C.B. 1900; K.C.B. 1906; G.C.M.G. 1916; G.C.V.O. 1917; G.C.B. 1918; and received thanks of Parliament, with £30,000 for his services in World War I. He was cr. Baron Plumer, of Messines and of Bilton, co. York, 4 Oct. 1919; and Viscount Plumer, 24 June 1929. Gov. of Malta, 1919-24; High Commissioner and C. in C. Palestine, 1924-28; and High Commissioner for Transjordan, 1928. He was K.J. St. J., and had several foreign orders. He m. 22 July 1884, Annie Constance, O.B.E., D.G. St. J. dau. of George Goss, of Park Crescent, London. He d. 16 July 1932. She d. 1941. They had issue,

1. Thomas Hall Rokeby, **2nd Viscount Plumer** (see below).
1. Eleanor Mary, b. 22 July 1885; M.A., and Warden of St. Andrew's Hall, Reading, 1927-31.
2. Sybil Margaret, O.B.E. 1920; b. 21 Feb. 1887; m. 1916, Major A. S. Orpen, O.B.E. and had issue.
3. Marjorie Constance, b. 21 April 1889; m. 1920, Major W. H. Brooke, and d. 1965 leaving issue.

The only son,
Thomas Hall Rokeby Plumer, **2nd Viscount Plumer**, b. 17 May 1890; educ. Eton; joined Canadian Expeditionary Force, and served in World War I, with Canadian Army Service Corps; Capt. 1916; Asst. Prov. Marshal, 1917; awarded M.C. and Croix de Guerre; m. 26 July 1919, Anne Monica Georgiana, dau. of Brig. Gen. Henry Tempest-Hicks, C.B., and d. 24 Feb. 1944. She d. 2 May 1963. They had issue,

1. Anne Cynthia Veronica Tempest, b. 22 April 1921; m. 1952, J. F. M. Leapman, and had issue.
2. Daphne Mary Crystal, b. 29 Jan. 1929; m. 1949, Lt. F. H. Lowry-Corry R.N. (Belmore, E.) and had issue.
3. Rosemary Diana, b. 29 Jan. 1929.

ARMS—Gules on a chevron between in chief two lion's heads erased and in base a sword argent, pommel and hilt or, and enfiled with a wreath of laurel ppr., three ravens sable.
CREST—A demi-lion ppr. holding in the dexter paw a plume of four ostrich feathers or.
SUPPORTERS—Dexter, A private of the York and Lancaster Regt.; Sinister, A trooper of the Rhodesian Field Force, each holding in the exterior hand a rifle ppr.
MOTTO—Consulto et audacter.

PONTYPRIDD

PEERAGE—U.K. Baron Pontypridd, of Cardiff, co. Glamorgan.
SURNAME—Thomas.
CR.—8 Feb. 1912. **EXT.**—14 Dec. 1927.
HISTORY—Daniel Thomas, of Llwyngrant, Penylan, Cardiff, had an eldest son,
Sir Alfred Thomas, **Baron Pontypridd**, b. 16 Sept. 1840, at Llwyngrant and educ. at Penygroes Llanedarne Sch. and Weston Sch. Bath; entered his father's business, that of a contractor and owner of lime works, and assisted in the construction of the Rhondda Fach branch of the Taff Vale Railway, but ultimately gave himself over entirely to public works. He was Mayor of Cardiff 1881; Hon. Freeman, 1886; M.P. East Glamorganshire 1885-1911; Pres. of Baptist Union, 1886; Chm. of Welsh Parl. Party 1897-1910; Pres. of Univ. Coll. Cardiff, 1901-06, Pres. of Welsh Nat. Museum; cr. Kt. Bach. 1902; and Baron Pontypridd, of Cardiff, co. Glamorgan, 8 Feb. 1912. He d. unm. 14 Dec. 1927.
His residence was Bronwydd, Cardiff. His clubs were Reform, National Liberal and Devonshire.
ARMS—Per fess wavy azure and argent, in base ten barrulets also wavy of the first over all the arch of a bridge ppr. charged on either side with three pellets.

CREST—Upon a rock an eagle with wings elevated and endorsed emitting flames from the mouth all ppr.
SUPPORTERS—On either side a man's figure vested as a Welsh bard that on the dexter holding in the exterior hand a scroll inscribed HEN-WLAD-FY-NHADAU, ppr. that on the sinister supporting in the exterior hand a harp or.

PORTAL OF HUNGERFORD

PEERAGE—U.K. Viscount Portal of Hungerford, of Hungerford, co. Berkshire.
SURNAME—Portal.
CR.—28 Jan. 1946. **EXT.**—22 April 1971.
HISTORY—The Portal family is of French extraction, tracing its descent from Louis Portal, who was alive in 1456. This man's direct descendant was Jean Francois Portal, of Poitiers, who was forced to leave France owing to the anti-Protestant persecution in 1699, and he took refuge in London. There is a full account of the lineage in extant peerage works, under Portal, Baron. Edward Robert Portal, of Sulham House, Pangbourne, a Barrister-at-Law, of the Inner Temple, 1880; b. 22 April 1854. He m. (1) 17 Jan. 1878, Rose Leslie, dau. of J. M. Napier, and by her had issue (see Portal, B.). He m. (2) 10 Aug. 1892, Ellinor Kate, dau. of Capt. C. W. Hill, 69th Regt., and d. 26 Mar. 1953, having by her (who d. 25 Nov. 1946) had further issue, with others, an eldest son,
Sir Charles Frederick Algernon Portal, **Baron Portal and Viscount Portal**. He was b. 21 May 1893; educ. Winchester and Ch. Ch. Oxford; joined R.F.C. 1915; and R.A.F. on its formation 1918; served in World War I, 1914-19, (despatches, M.C., D.S.O. 1917, and bar, 1918); from 1930-34 was on staff of Dir. of Operations and Intellig. Air Ministry; cmd. British Forces, in Aden, 1934-35; R.A.F. Instructor, Imperial Defence Coll. 1935-37; Air Vice Marshal, 1937; Dir. of Organization Air Ministry, 1937-38; Air Mem. for Personnel, Air Council, 1939-40; Air Marshal, 1939; A.O.C. in C. Bomber Command, Mar.-Oct. 1940; Chief of Air Staff 1940-45; Air Chief Marshal, 1940; Marshal of the R.A.F. 1944; was Controller of Atomic Energy, Min. of Supply, 1946-51; Chm. British Aluminium Co. Ltd. 1953-59; and of other cos.; Chm. King Edward VII Hosp. Midhurst, Sussex, 1950-68; Freedom of City of London conferred, 1946; m. 22 July 1919, Joan Margaret, dau. of Sir Charles G. E. Welby, 5th Bt., and had issue,
1. Richard, b. and d. 12 Sept. 1921.
1. Rosemary Ann, **Baroness Portal**, b. 12 May 1923 (see below).
2. Mavis Elizabeth Alouette, b. 13 June 1926.

He was cr. C.B. 1939, K.C.B. 1940, G.C.B. 1942, O.M. 1946, and K.G. 1946. He was cr. Baron Portal of Hungerford, of Hungerford, co. Berkshire 17 Sept. 1945 and cr. Viscount Portal of Hungerford, of Hungerford, co. Berkshire, 28 Jan. 1946. The Viscounty followed the usual limitations, but the Barony had a special remainder to his eldest dau. (in default of male issue), and the heirs male of her body, and in default of such issue, to every other dau. successively in order of seniority of age and priority of birth, and the heirs male of their bodies.

Viscount Portal d.s.p.m.s. 22 April 1971, and the Viscounty then became extinct, but in the Barony he was s. by his elder dau.,

Rosemary Ann Portal, (2nd holder of the title) **Baroness Portal** of Hungerford (see extant peerage works).

ARMS—Argent a lion rampant sable between a fleur-de-lis azure and a rose gules barbed and seeded ppr. on a chief of the third an astral crown or.

CREST—Issuant from an astral crown or a portal between two towers ppr.

SUPPORTERS—Dexter, A pilot of the R.A.F.; Sinister, A mechanic of the R.A.F. both in service dress ppr.

MOTTO—Armet nos ultio regum.

Viscount Portal's residence was West Ashling House, Chichester. His club was Travellers.

PORTER

PEERAGE—U.K. Life Baron Porter of Longfield, co. Tyrone.

SURNAME—Porter.

CR.—28 Mar. 1938. EXT.—13 Feb. 1956.

HISTORY—Hugh Porter, of Belfast and Cambridge, b. 7 Feb. 1877; educ. Emmanuel Coll. Cambridge, Hon. Fell. 1937; had a son, Sir Samuel Lowry Porter, who was Barrister-at-Law, Inner Temple, 1905; K.C. 1925; served in World War I, Capt. on Gen. List, M.B.E.; Recorder of Newcastle-under-Lyme, 1928-32, and of Walsall, 1932-34; apptd. a Judge of the High Court, King's Bench Div. 1934, and knighted 1934, apptd. a Lord of Appeal in Ordinary, 1938, and cr. a life peer as **Baron Porter** of Longfield, co. Tyrone, 28 Mar. 1938. He was made a P.C. 1938, and cr. G.B.E. 1951. He d. 13 Feb. 1956.

PORTSEA

PEERAGE—U.K. Baron Portsea, of Portsmouth, co. Southampton. (Also a baronetcy cr. 7 July 1916.)

SURNAME—Falle.

CR.—12 Jan. 1934. EXT.—1 Nov. 1948.

HISTORY—The name of Falle is found early in records in Jersey. The connected pedigree runs from John Falle of St. Saviour, Jersey, b. about 1475, son of John Falle, of Maufant, and brother of Laurence Falle, of Maufant, Prévôt of St. Saviour in 1500. John Falle, d. 1557, having a second but surv. son,

Nicodème Falle, b. circa 1505; m. Clemence dau. and coheir of John Dirvault, of St. Saviour, and d.v.p. about 1542, leaving issue,

Richard Falle, of Maufant and St. Saviour, bapt. 22 Nov. 1530; m. 1564, Catherine, (d. 1597), dau. of Lucas Falle, and d. 1576, leaving a son,

Jean Falle, of Maufant and St. Saviour, bapt. 16 April 1568; m. Jan. 1620 Mary, (d. Feb. 1624), dau. of William Poingdestre, and d. about 1645, leaving,

Laurens Falle, of Maufant, bapt. 26 May 1622; m. (1) 1642, Suzanne, dau. of John de la Lande, who d. 1667. He m. (2) 16 Mar. 1667, Mary du Parcq, and d. 1670 leaving by his first wife,

Elie Falle, of Maufant, bapt. 6 July 1645; m. 11 Sept. 1667; Suzanne, dau. of John Ahier, of Ville Pâtiér, St. Saviour. She d. 1688. He d. 1702, leaving,

Elie Falle, of Maufant, and of Grouville, bapt. 11 April 1675; m. 26 June 1706, Elizabeth, dau. of John Aubin, of St. Martin, and d. 1748, leaving,

Elie Falle, of Maufant and Grouville, bapt. 20 May 1707; m. 22 Feb. 1729 Elizabeth, dau. of Julian Brée (by Jeanne, his wife, dau. of Edmond Estur, and Elizabeth his wife, sister of the Rev. Philip Falle, M.A., Oxford, the historian of Jersey). He d. 1826, leaving a son,

Elie Falle, of Hamble St. Saviour, and of Trinity, Capt. Royal Jersey Militia. bapt. 28 Mar. 1756; m. as his second wife, 1782, Elizabeth, dau. and co-heir of Joshua Blampied, of Trinity, and d. 1838 having had issue with a fourth but second surv. son,

Joshua Falle, of Hamble, b. 1791; m. 1819, Esther, dau. of George Bertram of Grafford, St. Martin, Jurat of the Royal Court of Jersey. He d. 8 Feb. 1871. She d. 1876. They had an only son,

Joshua George Falle, of Hamble, and Plaisance, Connétable of St. Helier, 1864-73; Jurat of the Royal Court, 1873-1903; b. 27 Nov. 1820; m. 16 June 1855; Mary Elizabeth (who d. 18 May 1917) dau. and coheir of Francis Godfray, of Bagatelle, Jersey, and d. 15 Feb. 1903, leaving an only son,

Sir Bertram Godfray, Falle, Bt. and **Baron Portsea** of Portsmouth, co. Southampton, b. 21 Nov. 1859; educ. privately, at Victoria Coll. Jersey, Pembroke Coll. Camb., M.A. 1886, LL.M. 1886, and at Univ. of Paris, B. en droit, 1901; Barrister-at-Law, Inner Temple, 1885; Enroller of Deeds, Office of Works, 1898; Judge of Native Court, in Egypt, 1901-03; Conservative M.P. for Portsmouth, 1910-18 and for N. Div. Portsmouth, 1918-34 served in Royal Jersey Artillery, and in World War I, Major R.F.A. He was cr. a baronet 7 July 1916; and a peer as Baron Portsea, of Portsmouth, co. Southampton, 12 Jan. 1934. He m. 18 Jan. 1906, Mary Hubbard, dau. of Russell Sturgis, of Boston, U.S.A. and Carlton House Terrace, London, and widow of Lt. Col. L. R. Seymour. He d. 1 Nov. 1948.

ARMS—Quarterly 1 and 4, Argent on a chevron between three martlets sable as many fleurs-de-lis of the field (Falle); 2 and 3, Argent a griffin segreant sable within a bordure of the last charged alternately with four plates and as many escallops or (Godfray).

CREST—A talbot guardant argent.

SUPPORTERS—Dexter, A talbot guardant argent, gorged with a collar sable, charged with three fleurs-de-lis also argent; Sinister, A griffin sable, charged on the neck with an escallop or, between two plates within a collar gemel gold.

MOTTO—Remembrez.

QUEENBOROUGH

PEERAGE—U.K. Baron Queenborough, of Queenborough, co. Kent.

SURNAME—Paget.

CR.—18 Jan. 1918. EXT.—22 Sept. 1949.

HISTORY—Lord Alfred Henry Paget, who

d. 1888 was the fifth son of the 1st Marquess of Anglesey (see extant peerages), and had issue, a sixth son,

Sir Almeric Hugh Paget, **Baron Queenborough,** b. 14 Mar. 1861; educ. Harrow and Corpus Christi Coll. Camb., Hon. Fell.; High Sheriff co. Suffolk, 1909; M.P. Cambridge, 1910-17 when he resigned his seat; he lived for many years in America, where he had considerable interests, and he was director of several commercial concerns; he was Gov. of Guy's Hospital; Pres. Miller Gen. Hospital at Greenwich; mem. of Council of Royal Zoological Soc., and Pres. of Royal Society of St. George, K.J. St. J.; cr. G.B.E. 1926, and Baron Queenborough, of Queenborough, co. Kent, 18 Jan. 1918; m. (1) 12 Nov. 1895, Pauline, dau. of Hon. William C. Whitney, Sec. of U.S. Navy, and by her (who d. 22 Nov. 1916) had issue,

1. Olivia Cecilia, m. (1) 1919, (m. diss. by div. 1925), Hon. Charles J. F. Winn, (St. Oswald, B.), and had issue. She m. (2) 1925, A. T. F. Wilson-Filmer, (m. diss. by div. 1931), and m. (3) 1931, Sir Adrian Baillie, (m. diss. by div. 1944) and had issue.
2. Dorothy Wyndham.

Lord Queenborough m. (2) 19 July 1921, Edith, (d. Jan. 1933) dau. of W. S. Miller, of New York, and d. 22 Sept. 1949, having had further issue,

3. Audrey Elizabeth, b. 1922; m. (1) 1945, Cmdt. Christian Martell, D.F.C., French Air Force, who was k. in an aircraft accident 1945; she m. (2) 1946, A. R. Nelson, (m. diss. by div. 1956) and had issue. She m. (3) 1956 Lt. Cmdr. C. P. H. Lucy, R.N.
4. Enid Louise, b. 1923; m. 1947 Capt. Comte Rolland de la Paype, Armée de l'Air, (m. diss. by div.), and had issue.
5. Cicilli Carol, b. 1928; m. 1949, Capt. R. V. J. Evans and had issue.

ARMS—Sable on a cross engrailed between four eagles displayed argent five lions passant guardant of the field.
CREST—A demi-heraldic tiger sable, maned, tufted and ducally gorged argent.
SUPPORTERS—On either side a sailor habited in the costume of the period (1840) ppr. supporting with the exterior hand a flag argent thereon a cross patée gules, within a bordure azure.
MOTTO—Per il suo contrario.
Lord Queenborough's seat was Camfield Place, Hatfield, co. Hertford.

QUIBELL

PEERAGE—U.K. Baron Quibell, of Scunthorpe, co. Lincoln.
SURNAME—Quibell.
CR.—7 July 1945. **EXT.**—16 April 1962.
HISTORY—David John Quibell, of Scunthorpe, co. Lincoln, had a son,

David John Kinsley Quibell, **Baron Quibell,** of Scunthorpe, co. Lincoln, so cr. 7 July 1945. He was b. 21 Dec. 1878; educ. Messingham C. of E. Sch.; a builder and contractor, Past Pres. of Scunthorpe Co-op Soc., Chm. Scunthorpe U.D.C. 1914-15 and 1934-35; Chm. Stewart & Arnold Ltd., M.P. for Brigg Div. of

co. Lincoln 1929-31, and 1935-45, Mayor of Scunthorpe 1953. He m. (1) 12 Sept. 1900, Edith Jane, dau. of J. Foster and by her, who d. 14 Mar. 1953, had issue, a dau. Edith Ellen who m. Eric Bennard. He m. (2) 27 May 1954 Catherine Cameron, dau. of J. C. Rae, and d. 16 April 1962.
ARMS—Per fess vert and argent, in chief two garbs or, and in base an arch throughout gules, masoned sable.
CREST—In front of a pair of dividers pilewise or a trowel erect argent, hafted gules.
SUPPORTERS—Dexter, A grey horse ppr.; Sinister, A bulldog ppr. collared gules suspended therefrom a bell or.
MOTTO—Per ardua ad palmas.

QUICKSWOOD

PEERAGE—U.K. Baron Quickswood, of Clothall, co. Hertford.
SURNAME—Gascoyne-Cecil.
CR.—25 Jan. 1941. **EXT.**—10 Dec. 1956.
HISTORY—Lord Hugh Richard Heathcote Gascoyne-Cecil, fifth son of third Marquess of Salisbury, b. 14 Oct. 1869; educ. Eton and Univ. Coll. Oxford, B.A. 1891, M.A. 1894, Fell. Hertford Coll. 1891-1936, and Hon. Fell., also Hon. Fell. New Coll. Oxford, 1944; served in World War I, Lieut. R.F.C.; Asst. Sec. to Sec. of State for Foreign Affairs, (the latter being his father) 1891-92; M.P. Greenwich, 1895-1906, and Oxford Univ. 1910-37; mem. House of Laity, Church Assembly, 1919-45; Provost of Eton, 1936-44; cr. P.C. 1918 and cr. **Baron Quickswood,** of Clothall, co. Hertford, 25 Jan. 1941. He d. 10 Dec. 1956.
ARMS—Quarterly 1 and 4, Barry of ten argent and azure, over all six escutcheons, three, two and one, sable, each charged with a lion rampant of the first (Cecil); 2 and 3, Argent on a pale sable a conger's head erased and erect or charged with an ermine spot (Gascoyne) an annulet for difference.
CRESTS—1. Six arrows in saltire or, barbed and feathered argent, banded gules buckled and garnished gold, surmounted by a morion ppr. (Cecil); 2. A conger's head erased and erect or, charged with an ermine spot.
MOTTO—Sero sed serio.

RADSTOCK

PEERAGE—Ireland. Baron Radstock, of Castle Town, Queen's County.
SURNAME—Waldegrave.
CR.—20 Dec. 1800. **EXT.**—17 Sept. 1953.
HISTORY—John Waldegrave, 3rd Earl Waldegrave, had a second son,

Sir William Waldegrave, **1st Baron Radstock,** Adm. of the Red, and previously Vice Adm. of the Blue, distinguished in the defeat of the Spanish Fleet off Cape St. Vincent, 14 Feb. 1797, cr. G.C.B., and on 20 Dec. 1800, cr. Baron Radstock, of Castle Town, Queen's County, in the peerage of Ireland, was b. 9 July 1753; m. 28 Dec. 1785, Cornelia, dau. of David van Lennap, chief of the Dutch Factory at Smyrna. She d. 1839. He d. 20 Aug. 1825, having had with other issue, (the male lines of which have become extinct, see extant peerages under Waldegrave, E.), an elder son,

Granville George Waldegrave, **2nd Baron Radstock,** C.B., Vice Adm. of the Red, b. 24 Sept. 1786; m. 7 Aug. 1823, Esther Caroline, dau. of James Puget, of Totteridge, co. Hertford. She d. 16 Mar. 1874. He d. 11 May 1857, leaving issue,
1. Granville Augustus William, **3rd Baron** (see below).
1. Elizabeth Cornelia, d. unm. 16 April 1903.
2. Caroline Esther, m. 15 June 1852, Sir Thomas W. B. P. Beauchamp, 4th Bt. of Langley Park, Norfolk (extant peerages), and d. 3 July 1898, leaving issue.
The only son,
Granville Augustus William Waldegrave, **3rd Baron Radstock,** b. 10 April 1833; M.A. Oxford, Lt. Col. cmdg. West Middlesex Rifles, 1860-66; m. 16 July 1858, Susan Charlotte, dau. of John Hales Calcraft, of Rempstone. She d. 8 Dec. 1892. He d. 8 Dec. 1913. They had issue, with five daus.,
1. Granville George, **4th Baron** (see below).
2. Montague, **5th Baron** (see below).
3. John, LL.B. Camb. and Barrister-at-Law, b. 30 Dec. 1868; d. whilst serving with Imperial Yeo. in S. African war, 4 April 1901.
The eldest son,
Granville George Waldegrave, **4th Baron Radstock,** C.B.E. B.A. Trin. Coll. Camb., b. 1 Sept. 1859; d. unm. 2 April 1937, being s. by his brother,
Montagu Waldegrave, **5th Baron Radstock,** b. 15 July 1867; educ. Trin. Coll. Camb., B.A. 1889; m. 15 July 1898, Constance Marian, dau. of James C. J. Brodie, of Lethen, co. Nairn, (B.L.G. 1952) and 17 Sept. 1953, having had issue, with three daus., an only son,
John Montague Granville, b. 29 Aug. 1905; served in World War II, 1939-44, Cmdr. R.N. and D.S.C.; m. 29 June 1940, Lady Hersey Margaret Boyle, dau. of 8th Earl of Glasgow, and was k. on active service, in H.M.S. *Penelope,* v.p. 18 Feb. 1944. He left issue,
1. Horatia Marion, b. 1 Aug. 1941.
2. Griselda Hyacinthe, b. 6 June 1943; m. 1967 C. D. S. Drace Francis and had issue.
ARMS—Per pale argent and gules a crescent sable for difference.
CREST—Out of a ducal coronet or, a plume of five ostrich feathers, per pale argent and gules, a crescent sable for difference.
SUPPORTERS—Dexter, A talbot reguardant sable, eared and navally gorged or; Sinister, An eagle reguardant wings expanded and elevated holding in the dexter claw a thunderbolt all ppr.
MOTTO—St. Vincent.

RAMSDEN

PEERAGE—U.K. Baron Ramsden of Birkenshaw, W.R. co. Yorks.
SURNAME—Ramsden.
CR.—17 June 1945. **EXT.**—9 Aug. 1955.
HISTORY—Squire Ramsden, b. 1803 d. 1859 having, by Mary Anne (d. 1891) his wife, had issue,
James Ramsden, of The Wheatleys, Gomersal, nr. Leeds, co. York, b. 17 Dec. 1852; m.

1882, Mary Jane Hargreaves, (d. 22 Aug. 1885) and d. 4 Aug. 1931, leaving an only child,
Sir Eugene Joseph Squire Hargreaves Ramsden, **Baron Ramsden,** b. 2 Feb. 1883; served in World War I, 1915-18; M.P.N. Div. Bradford, 1924-29; and 1931-45; Chm. Exc. Cttee. Nat. Union of Conservative and Unionist Asscns. 1938-43, Chm. of several commissions etc., Chm. Crosthwaite Furnaces and Scriven Machine Tools, Dir. of several cos., and a principal of James Ramsden Ltd.; made O.B.E. 1919, cr. Kt. Bach. 1933; cr. Baronet, 1 July 1938, and Baron Ramsden, of Birkenshaw, W.R. Yorks, 17 June 1945; m. 22 May 1919, Margaret, S.S. St. J., dau. of Frank Eugene Withey, of Michigan, U.S.A. and widow of Major George Farwell, U.S. Army, and d. 9 Aug. 1955.
ARMS—Gules in chief two roses argent, barbed and seeded ppr. and in base a ram's head caboshed or.
CREST—A ram's head caboshed, the horns enchained or.
SUPPORTERS—Dexter, A grey parrot; Sinister, A Cairn terrier, both ppr.
MOTTO—Fortiter in re.
Lord Ramsden's residences were—The Wheatleys, Gomersal, nr. Leeds, co. York and Trem-y-Mor, St. David's, co. Pembroke. His clubs were Carlton, and Union.

RANELAGH

PEERAGE—Ireland. Baron Jones of Navan, co. Neath. Ireland. Viscount Ranelagh, both cr. 25 Aug. 1628.
Ireland. Earl of Ranelagh 11 Dec. 1677.
SURNAME—Jones.
CR.—As above. **EXT.**—13 Nov. 1885.
HISTORY—David Jones of Chepstow, (brother to William Jones, of Treowen, ancestor of Herbert of Llanarth, co. Mon.) m. Ursula, dau. of Wartle Wynwood, of Beston, co. Glos. and had issue,
1. Henry (see below).
2. Richard of Claypit, co. Monmouth, had issue,
The elder son,
Henry Jones of Middleton, co. Lancs. m. a dau. of H. Daniel of Acton, co. Suffolk, and had issue,
1. Roger, Sir, an alderman and Sheriff of London, knighted at Whitehall 8 July 1604.
2. Thomas (see below).
The yngr. son,
Thomas Jones, Bishop of Meath and Archibishop of Dublin, 1584 and 1605, also Lord Chancellor of Ireland 1605-19, m. Margaret, dau. of Adam Purdon, of Lurgan-Race, co. Louth and widow of John Douglas and d. 1619 having had issue (with 2 daus. Margaret m. Gilbert Domvile and Jane m. Henry Piers) an only son,
Sir Roger Jones, **Baron Jones** and **Viscount Ranelagh,** knighted at Drogheda 24 Mar. 1606/07, was M.P. for Trim. 1613-15. P.C. (Ireland) 1620, Vice Pres. Connaught 1626 and apptd. Chief Leader of the Army and Forces there; cr. 25 Aug. 1628, Baron Jones of Navan, co. Meath, and Viscount Ranelagh in Irish peerage. He m. (1) Frances (d. 13 Nov. 1620) dau. of Gerald Moore, 1st Viscount

Drogheda and (2) Catherine, dau. of Sir Henry Longuevile and d. 1643 (M.I. to him and his father in St. Patrick's, Dublin). He had issue,

1. Arthur, **2nd Viscount** (see below).
2. Thomas, had an eldest son, Roger who had issue, Charles, m. Elizabeth dau. of James Douglas of Haddington and had issue, Charles Wilkinson **4th Viscount** (see below).

The elder son,

Arthur Jones, **2nd Viscount Ranelagh** was M.P. for Sligo 1634-35 and for Weobley, co. Hereford, 1640-44, served as Capt. in the Parliamentary Army made P.C. Ireland 1660. He m. 1630 Katherine, dau. of Richard Boyle, 1st Earl of Cork, and d. 7 Jan. 1669/70 having had issue an only son,

Richard Jones, **3rd Viscount Ranelagh** and **1st Earl of Ranelagh**, b. 8 Feb. 1640/41; a pupil of John Milton, studied at Oxford 1656 and travelled on Continent with a tutor 1657-60; was M.P. for Roscommon 1661-66 and Gov. of Roscommon Castle 1661, one of the first Fellows of the R.S. 1663; Chan. of the Exchequer in Ireland 1668-74, M.P. for Plymouth 1685-87, Newtown 1689-95, Chichester 1695-98, Marlborough 1698-1700 and West Looe, 1701-03; Gentleman of the Bedchamber 1679, cr. on 11 Dec. 1677 Earl of Ranelagh in the Irish peerage, made P.C. Ireland 1668 and England 1691-/2; Paymaster Gen. of the Army 1685-1702 and convicted in Feb. 1702/3 of misappropriation of £72,000 in the above mentioned office. He was expelled from the Commons but was apptd. a Gov. of Queen Anne's Bounty in 1704. He m. (1) 28 Oct. 1662, Elizabeth dau. of Francis Willoughby, 5th Baron Willoughby of Parham. She d. 1 Aug. 1695, having had with other issue,

Edward, b. 2 Oct. 1675 and d.v.p. bur. 29 Mar. 1678.

He m. (2) 9 Jan. 1695/6 Margaret Dow, Baroness Stowell, 4th dau. of James Cecil, 3rd Earl of Salisbury and d.s.p.m.s. 5 Jan. 1711/12 being bur. in Westminster Abbey. By his first marr. he had also three daus.,

1. Elizabeth, Countess of Kildare d.s.p. 10 April 1758 aged 93.
2. Frances, Countess of Corringsly, disinherited by her father because of her marriage and d. 19 Feb. 1714 leaving issue.
3. Catherine, d. unm. 12 April 1740.

At the death of the 3rd Viscount his Earldom of Ranelagh became extinct. The title of Ranelagh was granted as an Irish Barony to Sir Arthur Cole Bt., in 1715. He d.s.p. 1754, when his barony of Ranelagh became extinct. The Viscounty of Ranelagh remained dormant during this time but in 1759 the cousin of the 3rd Viscount established his claim and took his seat in the House of Lords (Irish) on 16 Oct. 1759. He was,

Charles Wilkinson Jones **4th Viscount Ranelagh** (see above). He was Constable of Athlone Castle 1765-97. He received grants and pensions of some £13,000. He m. 6 Jan. 1761, Sarah (d. 1812) dau. of Thomas Montgomery and d. 20 April 1797. They had issue,

1. Charles **5th Viscount Ranelagh** (see below).
2. Thomas **6th Viscount** (see below).

3. Richard, Major, b. 24 Mar. 1764; m. 14 Sept. 1785, Sophia, dau. of John Gildard of Blackley Hurst, co. Lancs, and d.s.p.
4. Benjamin, Lt. Col. d. unm. 1770.
5. John, Major 13th Hussars, m. Eliza (she d. in childbed), dau. of Major Cane of Dublin.
6. Alexander Montgomery, Vice Adm. R.N., b. 1778, m. Caroline, dau. of Thomas Palmer, of Hambledon, co. Hants. She d. 1858. He d. 1862 their issue were,
   (1) Alexander Montgomery, M.A. Trin. Coll. Camb. b. 13 Sept. 1812 d. unm. 5 April 1883.
   (2) Robert Molesworth, b. 1814 d. 1856.
   (3) Henry Herbert Montgomery (1831-51).
   (1) Caroline Sarah, m. 1834 Viscount Henry de Vismes, 2nd son of Elisée William Count de Vismes and d. 1877.
   (2) Mary m. 1860 Rev. J. Williams.

The eldest son,

Charles Jones, **5th Viscount Ranelagh**, b. 29 Oct. 1761, educ. Trin. Coll. Dublin and served in R.N., Capt., d. unm. 20 Dec. 1800 on board the ship which he commanded, the frigate *Doris* in Plymouth Sound, He was s. by his brother,

Thomas Jones, **6th Viscount Ranelagh**, b. 3 Feb. 1763, served in the 66th Foot, being Major, m. (1) 21 Aug. 1804 at Fulham, co. Middlesex, Caroline Elizabeth Stephens, bastard dau. and heiress of Sir Philip Stephens 1st and only Bt. Viscountess Ranelagh d. 17 June 1805 in childbed s.p.s. (bur. at Fulham). He m. (2) 13 Sept. 1811, Caroline Louisa Thompson, bastard dau. of Col. Lee of Yorkshire and d. 4 July 1820 at Ranelagh House (commemorated by modern Ranelagh Gardens), his seat at Fulham where he was bur. By his 2nd wife he had issue,

Thomas Heron, **7th Viscount** (see below).
Barbara, m. 26 July 1834, Count John Bernard von Reckberg (Austrian Empire).

The 2nd Viscountess Ranelagh d. 25 Nov. 1866 at Mayfield, Sussex aged 77.

The only son,

Thomas Heron Jones, **7th Viscount Ranelagh**, b. 9 Jan. 1812 at Fulham; educ. Dr. Robert's Sch., in Whitehead's Grove, Chelsea. As a minor he was present at the siege of Antwerp and later served as a volunteer in the Spanish War of Succession under Sir De Lacy Evans on behalf of the Carlists; served in 1st Life Guards; Lt. Col. 2nd South Middlesex Volunteers, was cr. K.C.B. (Civil) 1881. He d. unm. 13 Nov. 1885, at 18 Victoria Mansions, Victoria Street, Westminster, and was bur. with military honours on 21 Nov. at Fulham where there are M.I.s to the family in the churchyard and in the parish Church of All Saints.

ARMS—Azure a cross between four pheons points downwards or.

CREST—A dexter arm embowed in armour the hand in a gauntlet ppr. grasping a dart or.

SUPPORTERS—Two griffins erminois.

MOTTO—Caelitus mihi vires.

In 1883 the family estates consisted of 3,043 acres in Norfolk worth £5,691 a year. The seats were Mulgrave House (or Ranelagh House) Fulham, Middlesex, and Horsham St. Faith, near Norwich.

The town residence was 18 Albert Mansions, Victoria Street, Westminster. The 7th Viscount's club was the Carlton.

RANKSBOROUGH

PEERAGE—U.K. Baron Ranksborough, of Ranksborough in the county of Rutland.
SURNAME—Brocklehurst.
CR.—3 July 1914. **EXT.**—28 Feb. 1921.
HISTORY—Oliver Brocklehurst, of Glossop, co. Derby, d. 1566, leaving by his wife Joanna, a son,
George Brocklehurst, settled at Gap House, Taxal, admitted to copyhold property within the manor and forest of Macclesfield, 1623, and d. 1688, having had (with a dau. Elizabeth who m. 1623, John Pownall), a son,
George Brocklehurst, of Kettlesham, admitted as a customary tenant of his father's holdings in Macclesfield, in 1651. He d. 1678 having had issue,
1. George, of Gap House, d. 1748, whose descendant sold that property in 1822, to Thomas Brocklehurst, of The Fence, (see below).
2. William (see below).
The second son,
William Brocklehurst of the Lower House, Hurdsfield, which he bought in 1709, an alderman of Macclesfield, d. 1715, having had issue, with two other sons and a dau.
1. John (see below).
2. William, of Lea Hall, Mottram St. Andrew, whose line became extinct.
1. Sarah, b. 1715; d. unm. 1747.
The elder son,
John Brocklehurst, of Macclesfield, bapt. Nov. 1714; m. 1741, Rebecca, dau. of John Bridges, of Sheffield, and d. 1796, having had issue, with a dau., Ann, who m. Philip Stockdale, an only surv. son,
John Brocklehurst, of Macclesfield, and Lea Hall, co. Chester, b. 5 Aug. 1754; m. 27 Mar. 1783, Sarah, dau. and heiress of Peter Pownall, of Pownall Green, Bramhall, co. Chester. She d. July 1843. He d. 16 June 1839. They had issue,
1. William, of Tytherington, Cheshire, and Swythamley Hall, co. Stafford, a banker in Macclesfield, b. 20 Feb. 1784; m. Oct. 1812, Ann, dau. of William Coare, of Islington, co. Middlesex. She d. 19 Feb. 1847. He d. 13 Sept. 1859.
2. John (see below).
3. Thomas, of The Fence, banker in Macclesfield, b. 21 Jan. 1791; m. 12 Aug. 1823, Martha Mary, dau. of Thomas Unett, of Market Drayton, co. Salop, and d. 1870, having had issue, six sons and four daus.
1. Mary, of Jordan's Gate, Macclesfield, d. unm. May 1852.
The second son,
John Brocklehurst, of Hurdsfield House, co. Chester, M.P. Macclesfield, 1832-68, b. 30 Oct. 1788; m. 1814, Mary, dau. of William Coare, and d. 1870. She d. 1 Feb. 1848. They had issue, with four daus.,
1. William Coare, of Butley Hall, and Tytherington, Cheshire, M.P. Macclesfield, 1868-80, and 1885-86, Pres. of the

Macclesfield Chamber of Commerce, b. 9 Feb. 1818; m. 24 May 1849, Mary, dau. of William Worthington, of Brockhurst Hall, Northwich, co. Chester, and d. 3 June 1900, leaving issue, (B.L.G.).
2. Henry (see below).
3. Peter Pownall, of Hurdsfield House, b. April 1821; d. unm.
4. Philip Lancaster, Sir, cr. Bt. 27 Aug. 1903. (see Brocklehurst, Bt.).
The second son,
Henry Brocklehurst, of Foden Bank, Macclesfield, b. 28 Aug. 1819; m. 4 May 1848, Anne, dau. of John Fielden, of Centre Vale, Todmorden, M.P. Oldham, and d. 1870 having had issue, with others (see extant baronetcies, Brocklehurst), an eldest son,
John Fielden Brocklehurst, **Baron Ranksborough,** b. 13 May 1852; educ. Rugby and Trin. Coll. Cambridge, B.A. 1873; joined Royal Horse Guards, 1874; served in the Egyptian Campaign, 1882, being present at battles of El Magfar, Mahsama, Kassassin, and Tel-el-Kebir, and in the Sudan Expedition, 1884-85; Brev. Lt. Col. 1891; cmd. Royal Horse Guards, 1894-99, Col. 1899; served in the S. African War, 1899-1901, Major Gen. cmdg. 3rd Cavalry Brig.; Lord Lt. Rutland 1906-1921; was Equerry to Queen Victoria, 1899-1901, to Queen Alexandra 1901-10, Extra Equerry to Queen Alexandra 1910-1921, and a Lord in Waiting to King George V, 1915. He m. 23 Feb. 1878, Louisa Alice, dau. of Hon. Laurence Parsons, (Rosse, E.). He was cr. M.V.O. 1897, C.B. 1900, C.V.O. 1901, and Baron Ranksborough, of Ranksborough, in the county of Rutland, 3 July 1914. He d. 28 Feb. 1921. Lady Ranksborough d. 28 Oct. 1937.
ARMS—Per pale argent and sable, three chevronels engrailed between as many brocks all counterchanged.
CREST—A brock sable holding in the mouth a slip of oak fructed ppr. in front of a mount vert thereon two oak trees also ppr.
SUPPORTERS—On either side a Roman soldier reguardant resting the exterior hand on a shield all ppr.
MOTTO—Veritas me dirigit.
Lord Ranksborough's seats were Ranksborough, Oakham, Rutland, and Kingston Hill Place, S.W. His clubs were Carlton, Brookes's and Turf.

RATHMORE

PEERAGE—U.K. Baron Rathmore, of Shanganagh, co. Dublin.
SURNAME—Plunket.
CR.—14 Nov. 1895. **EXT.**—22 Aug. 1919.
HISTORY—David Robert Plunket, **Baron Rathmore,** was b. 3 Dec. 1838, third son of John Plunket, 3rd Baron Plunket (see that title in extant peerages). He was educ. Trin. Coll. Dublin, M.A., LL.D. 1875; Barrister-at-Law, King's Inns, Dublin 1862; Q.C. 1868; Law Adviser to Irish Gov., 1868; Solicitor-Gen. for Ireland, 1875-77; Paymaster Gen. 1880; First Commissioner of Works, 1885-86; and 1886-92; M.P. Dublin Univ. 1870-95; cr. Baron Rathmore, of Shanganagh, co. Dublin, 14 Nov. 1895. He d. 22 Aug. 1919.

ARMS—Sable a bend between a tower in sinister chief and a portcullis in dexter base, all or, a mullet for difference.
CREST—A horse passant argent, charged on the side with a portcullis sable.
SUPPORTERS—Dexter, An antelope or; Sinister, A horse argent each gorged with a plain collar sable, pendent therefrom a portcullis of the last and charged on the body with a mullet for difference.
MOTTO—Festina lente.
Lord Rathmore's residence was Southfields House, Wimbledon Park, S.W.

RAVENSWORTH

PEERAGE—U.K. Earl of Ravensworth and Baron of Eslington, co. Northumberland.
SURNAME—Liddell.
CR.—2 April 1874. EXT.—7 Feb. 1904.
HISTORY—This family originates in Durham, where in the 16th century the earliest progenitor from whom the line of descent is traced (see extant peerages, under Ravensworth, B.) was Thomas Liddell, whose son, Thomas Liddell was an Alderman of Newcastle-upon-Tyne, who acquired by purchase Ravensworth Castle in 1607. His eldest son was Thomas Liddell of Ravensworth Castle, whose son, Sir Thomas Liddell, a royalist was cr. by Charles I a baronet, 2 Nov. 1642. From him descended the present Barons Ravensworth, who also hold the baronetcy conferred upon him. The 4th Bt., Sir Henry Liddell, was cr. Baron Ravensworth, of Ravensworth Castle, 29 June 1747, but this peerage became extinct when he d.s.p.m. 30 Jan. 1784. The baronetcy then passed to his nephew, Sir Henry George Liddell, 5th Bt. (b. 1749-91) whose elder son,
Sir Thomas Henry, 6th Bt., was cr. Baron Ravensworth, 17 July 1821. He d. 7 Mar. 1855, having had with other issue (extant peerages, Ravensworth, B.),
1. Henry Thomas, 7th Bt., and 2nd Baron Ravensworth, and **1st Earl of Ravensworth** (see below).
2. Robert, Rev., M.A., Vicar of St. Paul's Knightsbridge, 1851-81, b. 1808; m. 1836, Emily Ann Charlotte, dau. of Rev. the Hon. G. V. Wellesley, (Wellington, D.), and d. 1888, leaving with other issue, Arthur Thomas, 5th Baron.
The eldest son,
Sir Henry Thomas Liddell, 7th Bt., 2nd Baron Ravensworth, was cr. **Earl of Ravensworth**, and **Baron of Eslington**, 2 April 1874; b. 10 Mar. 1797; M.P. for Northumberland, for Durham, and for Liverpool in succession; m. 9 Nov. 1820, Isabella Horatia, dau. of Lord George Seymour (Hertford, M.). and d. 19 Mar. 1878, having had issue, with eight daus.,
1. Henry George, **2nd Earl of Ravensworth** (see below).
2. Atholl Charles John, **3rd Earl of Ravensworth** (see below).
The elder son,
Sir Henry George Liddell, 8th Bt., 3rd Baron Ravensworth, and **2nd Earl of Ravensworth**, M.P. for S. Northumberland, 1852-78, b. 8 Oct. 1821; m. (1) 8 Dec. 1852, Mary Diana, only child of Capt. Orlando Gunning Sutton, R.N., and she d. 8 Dec. 1890. He m.

(2) 7 Sept. 1892, Emma Sophia Georgiana, (she m. 3rdly 1904, J. W. Wadsworth), dau. of Hon. Richard Denman (Denman, B.) and widow of Major O. B. C. Resswell, and d.s.p.m. having had issue two daus. by his first marriage. He was s. by his brother,
Sir Atholl Charles John Liddell, 9th Bt., 4th Baron Ravensworth and **3rd Earl of Ravensworth**, b. 6 Aug. 1833; m. 19 May 1866, Caroline Cecilia, (who m. 2ndly the 4th Earl of Mount Edgecumbe), dau. of Hon. George Edgecumbe (Mount Edgecumbe E.) and d.s.p. 7 Feb. 1904. The Earldom of Ravensworth and the Barony of Eslington, then became extinct, but the baronetcy and the Barony of Ravensworth passed to the cousin of the 3rd Earl, namely (see above),
Arthur Thomas Liddell, who became 5th Baron Ravensdale, and ancestor of the present Barons Ravensworth.
ARMS—Argent fretty gules on a chief of the last three leopards' faces or.
CREST—A lion rampant sable billettée and crowned with an eastern crown or.
SUPPORTERS—Two leopards or, semée of golps and gorged with mural crowns purpure.
MOTTO—Fama semper vivit.
The Earl's seats were—Ravensworth Castle, Gateshead; Eslington Park, Alnwick.

RAWLINSON

PEERAGE—U.K. Baron Rawlinson, of Trent, co. Dorset.
SURNAME—Rawlinson.
CR.—6 Oct. 1919. EXT.—25 April 1925.
HISTORY—Sir Henry Creswicke Rawlinson, 1st Bt., (see extant peerage works, Rawlinson, Bt.) had issue,
1. Henry Seymour, Sir, 2nd Bt. and **Baron Rawlinson** (see below).
2. Alfred, Sir, 3rd Bt.
Sir Henry d. 5 Mar. 1895, and was s. in the baronetcy by his elder son,
Sir Henry Seymour Rawlinson, 2nd Bt. and **Baron Rawlinson**. He was b. 20 Feb. 1864; educ. Eton and R.M.C. Sandhurst; joined 60th K.R.R. 1884; served in the Burma campaign, 1886-87 (despatches), with the Mounted Infantry; Capt. 1911; entered Staff Coll. Camberley, 1892; transferred to Coldstream Guards, 1892; D.A.A.G. Egypt, 1898; served in the Nile Exped. 1898, present at battles of Atbara and Khartoum, (despatches); Major and Brev. Lt. Col. 1899; D.A.A.G. Natal, 1899; in the A. Sfrican War, 1899-1902, in Ladysmith during the siege, and commanded a mobile column 1901-1902 (despatches five times); Brev. Col. 1902; Brig. Gen. 1903; Commandant Staff Coll. Camberley, 1903-06; Major Gen. 1909; temporary Dir. of Recruiting, 1914; served in World War I, as commander of 4th Army Corps, 1914-15; Army Commander 4th Army, 1915-18; Lt. Gen. 1916; Gen. 1917; mem. of Army Council, 1918-19; commanded Forces in N. Russia, Aug. to Nov. 1919; Gen. Officer cmdg. at Aldershot, 1919-20. He was cr. C.B. 1902, K.C.B. 1915; G.C.V.O. 1917; K.C.M.G. 1918; G.C.B. 1919; received thanks of Parliament with grant of £30,000 at end of World War I, and on 6 Oct. 1919, was cr. Baron Rawlinson, of Trent, co. Dorset. He was cr. G.C.S.I. 1924, and was

K.G. St. J. He m. 6 Nov. 1890, Meredith Sophia Frances dau. of Coleridge John Kennard, of Fernhill, co. Hants, and d.s.p. 28 Mar. 1925.
ARMS—Sable three swords palewise ppr., the centre one point downwards, the other two points upwards ppr. pommels and hilts gold, a chief embattled or, thereon an eastern crown gules.
CREST—Issuant from an eastern crown or, a cubit arm in armour the hand in a gauntlet encircled with a wreath of laurel and grasping a sword in bend, all ppr., pommel and hilt gold.
SUPPORTERS—Dexter, A British infantryman in the service garb of 1918; Sinister, An Anzac in service dress, all ppr.
MOTTO—Festina lente.

REAY

PEERAGE—U.K. Baron Reay, of Durness, co. Sutherland.
SURNAME—Mackay.
CR.—8 Oct. 1881. EXT.—1 Aug. 1921.
HISTORY—Sir Donald James Mackay, K.T. 11th Baron Reay, of Reay, co. Caithness, in the peerage of Scotland, and **Baron Reay**, of Durness, co. Sutherland, in the peerage of the United Kingdom, a baronet of Nova Scotia, and Baron Mackay, of Ophemert in Holland, b. 22 Dec. 1839; the son of the 10th Baron Reay, who was minister of state, vice pres. of the Privy Council and Grand Cross of the Netherland Lion in the Kingdom of the Netherlands. The 10th Baron Reay d. 6 Mar. 1876, and was s. by son, who was naturalized a British subject in 1877, by Act of Parliament, (40 and 14 Vict. cap. 1), and was then cr. 8 Oct. 1881 a peer of the United Kingdom as mentioned above. He was made P.C. and cr. K.T.; was D.L. cos. Berwick and Selkirk, Rector of St. Andrew's Univ. 1884; Gov. of Bombay, 1885-90; Under Sec. of State for India, 1894-95; Chm. London Sch. Board, 1897-1904; first Pres. of Brit. Academy 1902-07; Foreign Mem. of French Academy of Political Science. He m. 5 June 1877, Fanny Georgiana Jane, C.I., dau. of Richard Hasler, of Aldingbourne, co. Sussex, and widow of Capt. Alexander Mitchell M.P., of Stow, co. Midlothian. He d. 1 Aug. 1921, when the U.K. Barony became extinct and the other honours passed to his cousin, Eric Mackay, 12th Baron Reay, (see extant peerages, Reay, B.).
ARMS—Azure on a chevron between three bears' heads couped argent, muzzled gules, a roebuck's head erased, between two hands, issuant from the ends of the chevron, each holding a dagger, all ppr.
CREST—A dexter cubit arm erect, holding a dagger, in pale all ppr. pommel and hilt or.
SUPPORTERS—Dexter, A pikeman armed at all points; Sinister, A musketeer, both ppr.
MOTTO—Manu forti.
The 11th Baron's seats were—Ophemert, Netherlands; Carolside, Warlston; Laidlawstiel, Galashiels. His town residence was 6, Great Stanhope Street, W. His clubs were Athenaeum; Travellers' and St. James's.

REDESDALE

PEERAGE—U.K. Baron Redesdale, of Redesdale, co. Northumberland.
U.K. Earl of Redesdale, co. Northumberland.
SURNAME—Freeman-Mitford.
CR.—Barony 15 Feb. 1802. Earldom 3 Jan. 1877. EXT.—2 May 1886.
HISTORY—John Mitford, of Newton House, and Exbury, co. Hants d. 16 May 1761, having had with other issue (see extant peerages, Redesdale, B.) a second son,
Sir John Mitford, later Freeman-Mitford, **Baron Redesdale**, of Redesdale, co. Northumberland, b. 18 Aug. 1748; Barrister-at-Law, 1777; M.P. for Beeralston, 1788-89, and for E. Looe, 1799-1802; K.C. 1789; cr. Kt. Bach. 1793; Solicitor Gen. 1793-99, and Attorney Gen. 1799-1801; P.C. 1801; Speaker of the House of Commons, 1801-02; Lord Chancellor of Ireland, 1802-06 cr. Baron Redesdale, of Redesdale, co. Northumberland, 15 Feb. 1802; m. 6 June 1803, Frances Perceval, third dau. of 2nd Earl of Egmont. She d. 22 Aug. 1817. Lord Redesdale s. to the estates of Thomas Edwards-Freeman, of Batsford Park, co. Gloucester, and assumed by Royal Licence 28 Jan. 1809, the additional name and arms of Freeman. He d. 16 Jan. 1830, having had issue with three daus.,
John Thomas Freeman-Mitford, **2nd Baron Redesdale,** and **1st Earl of Redesdale,** so cr. 3 Jan. 1877, was b. 9 Sept. 1805; educ. New Coll. Oxford, M.A.; Chm. of Cttees. and Speaker of the House of Lords, 1851-86; d. unm. 2 May 1886, when both peerages became extinct and he was s. in his estates by his cousin, Algernon Bertram Freeman-Mitford, Baron Redesdale, of Redesdale, co. Northumberland, so cr. 22 July 1902 (see extant peerages, Redesdale, B.).
ARMS—Quarterly 1 and 4, Argent a fess between three moledewarps sable (Mitford); 2 and 3, Azure three fusils in fess or, for distinction a canton ermine, (Freeman).
CRESTS—1. Two hands couped at the wrist ppr. grasping a sword erect argent at the point, hilt or, the blade enfiled with a boar's head erased sable (Mitford). 2. A demi-wolf argent supporting between the paws a fusil or, for distinction gorged with a collar dancettée gules (Freeman).
SUPPORTERS—Two eagles rising sable each gorged with a wreath of shamrock ppr. and each beaked, membered and charged on the breast with a fusil or.
MOTTO—Aequabiliter et diligenter.

RENDEL

PEERAGE—U.K. Baron Rendel of Hatchlands, co. Surrey.
SURNAME—Rendel.
CR.—30 Mar. 1894. EXT.—4 June 1913.
HISTORY—James Meadows Rendel, F.R.S. and engineer had a third surviving son,
Stuart Rendel, **Baron Rendel** of Hatchlands, co. Surrey, b. 2 July 1834; educ. Eton and Oriel Coll. Oxford, B.A. 1856, M.A. 1859, Barrister-at-Law, 1861; mem. Lord Armstrong's engineering firm and its managing partner in London, M.P. Montgomeryshire

PLATE 16

BARON REAY.

BARON RENDEL.

BARON RIBBLESDALE.

MARQUESS OF RIPON.

BARON ROBERTSON.

EARL ROBERTS.

PLATE 17

BARON ROSMEAD.

BARON SANDERSON.

BARON SANDHURST.

EARL OF SHEFFIELD.

BARON SHERARD.

BARON STALBRIDGE.

1880-94, Pres. Univ. Coll. of Wales, Officer of Order of Crown of Italy, Kt. of Order of Charles XII of Spain, cr. Baron Rendel of Hatchlands, co. Surrey, 30 Mar. 1894. He m. 1 Oct. 1857 Ellen Sophy (d. 20 May 1912), dau. of W. E. Hubbard, of Horsham, co. Sussex (Addington, B.) and d. 4 June 1913, leaving issue four daus.,
1. Rose Ellen, O.B.E., m. (1) 1886, H. C. Goodhart, who d. 1895, having had issue. She m. (2) 1902, W. C. Cooper, and d. 1927.
2. Maud Ernestine, C.B.E., D.G. St. J., m. 1890, 1st Baron Gladstone of Hawarden.
3. Grace Daphne, m. 1899, Lt. Col. E. M. Dunne, and had issue.
4. Clarice Margaret, S.S. St. J.
ARMS—Per fess nebuly sable and argent a pale counterchanged, in chief a staff raguly couped and erect between two demi lions rampant erased and in base a demi lion rampant erased between two staffs raguly couped and erect all counterchanged.
CREST—In front of a rock ppr. thereon a wolf passant azure, collared argent and supporting a flag staff ppr. therefrom flowing to the sinister a banner sable, charged with a demi lion rampant erased of the second, a staff raguly couped in fess vert.
SUPPORTERS—On either side a wolf azure collared argent holding in the mouth a staff raguly of the second, and charged on the shoulder with a plate thereon a demi lion rampant erased sable.
MOTTO—Labore et consilio.

RHAYADER

PEERAGE—U.K. Baron Rhayader, of Rhayader, co. Radnor.
SURNAME—Leif-Jones.
CR.—25 Jan. 1932. EXT.—26 Sept. 1939.
HISTORY—John Jones, of Rhayader, co. Radnor who d. 1829 had issue,
The Rev. Thomas Jones, of Morriston, co. Glamorgan, b. 17 July 1819; m. (1) Mar. 1851, Jane, dau. of John Jones, of Dowlais, who d. 1867. He m. (2) Feb. 1870, Anne Howell, and d. 24 June 1882, having had with other issue by his first wife, a son,
Leifchild Stratten Leif-Jones, **Baron Rhayader**, b. 16 Jan. 1862; educ. at the Scotch Sch. Melbourne, and Trin. Coll. Oxford, B.A. 1885, M.A. 1889, and Sch. 1st Class Maths 1885; sat as Liberal M.P. for North Westmorland, 1905-10, for Rushcliffe Div. of Notts, 1910-18, and for Camborne Div. of Cornwall, 1923-24 and 1929-31; P.C. 1917; assumed by deed poll 11 Jan. 1932, the additional surname of Leif before that of Jones, and was cr. Baron Rhayader, of Rhayader, co. Radnor, 25 Jan. 1932. He d. 26 Sept. 1939.
ARMS—Azure on a pile between two fleurs-de-lis or a chaplet of laurel ppr.
CREST—Upon three mullets of eight points argent a griffin's head erased per pale or and of the first.
SUPPORTERS—Dexter, A griffin reguardant or, winged azure, the wings semée of saltires argent; Sinister, A like griffin the wings semée of cross crosslets fitchée also argent.
MOTTO—Cum lege libertas.

RHONDDA

PEERAGE—U.K. Baron Rhondda, of Llanwern, co. Monmouth, and Viscount Rhondda, of Llanwern, co. Monmouth.
SURNAME—Thomas.
CR.—Barony, 28 Jan. 1916, and Viscounty, 19 June 1918. EXT.—20 July 1958.
HISTORY—John Thomas of Cefn Llwyn, Magor, co. Monmouth, and of Pen-y-yard, co. Glamorgan, b. 1770; m. Jane Pritchard, of Pen-y-Rhol, Talgarth, co. Brecon, and d. April 1812, leaving issue,
Samuel Thomas of Merthyr Yscyborwen, co. Glamorgan, b. 17 Jan. 1800; m. 7 Sept. 1841 Rachel dau. of Morgan Joseph (or Watkin), of Mount Pleasant, She d. 21 Mar. 1896. He d. 24 April 1879. They had issue,
1. John Howard, of Yscyborwen, and Moyles Court, Ringwood, co. Hants, b. 7 Jan. 1853; m. 10 Nov. 1880, Rose Helen, dau. of George Augustus Haig, of Penithon, co. Radnor, (B.L.G. 1952) and d. 11 May 1919 having had issue.
2. David Alfred, **Baron and Viscount Rhondda** (see below).
3. Samuel Morton, Major 3rd Bn. Welsh Regt.; b. 24 Dec. 1859; m. 27 July 1882, Mary Hamilton, dau. of Joseph Evans, of Merthyr Tydfil, and had issue.
1. Mina Williams, m. 24 Sept. 1892, Lt. Col. F. R. Howell, 3rd Bn. Welsh Regt. and had issue.
2. Louisa Mary.
The second son,
David Alfred Thomas, **1st Baron and Viscount Rhondda**, b. 26 Mar. 1856; M.A. Caius Coll. Camb.; D.L. and J.P. co. Glamorgan; M.P. Merthyr Burghs, 1888-1910, and Cardiff 1910; Pres. of Local Gov. Board, 1916-17, and Food Controller, 1917-18; cr. Baron Rhondda of Llanwern, co. Monmouth, 28 Jan. 1916, made P.C. 13 Dec. 1916, and cr. Viscount Rhondda, of Llanwern, co. Monmouth, 19 June 1918. He m. 27 June 1882, Sybil Margaret, D.B.E. (1920). She d. 11 Mar. 1941. He* d.s.p.m. 3 July 1918 when his Barony became extinct, but the Viscounty passed owing to special remainer, failing heirs male of his body, to his only child,
Margaret Haig Thomas, **2nd Viscountess Rhondda**, J.P., b. 12 June 1883; educ. St. Leonard's Sch. St. Andrew's and Somerville Coll. Oxford; editor of *Time and Tide* and Chm. Time and Tide Publishing Co.; mem. of Court of Governors of London Sch. of Economics; Pres. of Univ. Coll. of S. Wales, and of Monmouthshire, 1950-55; m. 9 July 1908, (m. diss. by div., 1923), Sir Humphrey Mackworth, 7th Bt. who d. 1948. She d. 20 July 1958. She had reassumed the surname of Thomas. She wrote: *D. A. Thomas, Viscount Rhondda*, 1921, *Leisured Women*, 1928; *This was my World*, 1933; and *Notes on the Way*, 1937. Her residences were Churt, Halewell, Shere, Surrey; 70 Arlington House, St. James's, S.W.1.
Viscountess Rhondda's Case in 1922 is important and is included in most legal works which deal with the Constitution, and with the House of Lords. "It was argued that the disqualification of a peeress in her own right from sitting in the House of Lords was part of the general disqualification of women from public office which had been removed by the

Sex Disqualification (Removal) Act, 1919. The claim was disallowed by the Committee of Privileges. The decision could rest either on the ground that, if Parliament had intended to introduce such an important constitutional change as an alteration of the composition of the Legislature, it would have done so expressly; or on the ground that the exclusion of women from the House of Lords is not an incapacity on the part of women but is a characteristic inherent in the legal nature of a peerage. The latter view was that of Lord Birkenhead, then Lord Chancellor." *Principles of English Law and the Constitution.* by O. Hood Phillips, 1939, p. 255. It may be added that while the judgment of Lord Birkenhead is full of valuable information on the nature of peerage, the conclusion reached is contrary to common sense and good judgment, a condition not unusual in the law's dealings with the subject of peerage.

ARMS—Per pale ermine and ermines three chevronels gules between as many eagles displayed or, collared of the third.

SUPPORTERS—Dexter, A miner resting the exterior hand upon a shovel; Sinister, A like miner holding in the interior hand a safety lamp and in the exterior hand a pickaxe over the shoulder, all ppr.

CREST—(of Lord Rhondda) An eagle party per pale ermine and ermines perched with wings displayed and charged on the breast with three chevronels gules.

MOTTO—Diligentia absque timore.

*NOTE. H. G. Wells, thus referred to Lord Rhondda (in describing the aftermath of the first World War): "Everywhere men who would have been regarded as shady adventurers before 1914 had acquired power and influence while better men toiled unprofitably. Such men as Lord Rhondda, the British food controller, killed themselves with hard work while the war profiteer waxed rich and secured his grip upon press and party organization." (This was in the 1920 *Outline of History*, p. 578 but in the edition of the same work published in 1951 and revised and brought up to date by Raymond Postgate, the reference to Lord Rhondda was omitted).

RIBBLESDALE

PEERAGE—Great Britain. Baron Ribblesdale of Gisburne Park, co. York.

SURNAME—Lister.

CR.—28 Oct. 1797. **EXT.**—21 Oct. 1925.

HISTORY—Thomas Lister, of Gisburne Park, co. York, M.P. 1710-45; b. 8 Oct. 1688; m. 1716, Catherine dau. and coheir of Sir Ralph Assheton, Bt. of Whalley Abbey, co. Lancaster, and had issue, with a ygr. son Nathaniel whose grandson Thomas Henry Lister was author of *Granby*, an elder son,

Thomas Lister, M.P., b. 19 Jan. 1723; m. Beatrix, dau. of Jessop Hulton, of Hulton Park, co. Lancaster, and d. 8 Nov. 1761, leaving with a dau. Beatrix who m. Thomas Parker of Brownsholme, co. York, an only son,

Thomas Lister, **1st Baron Ribblesdale**, of Gisburne Park, co. York, so cr. 26 Oct. 1797; b. 22 Mar. 1752; m. 1789, Rebecca, dau. of Joseph Feilding, and d. 22 Sept. 1826, having had with two daus., an only son and successor,

Thomas Lister, **2nd Baron Ribblesdale,** b. 23 Jan. 1790; m. 9 Feb. 1826 Adelaide, dau. of Thomas Lister, of Armitage Park, co. Stafford (she m. secondly 1835 Lord John Russell, afterwards Earl Russell, and d. 1 Nov. 1838) and d. 10 Dec. 1832, having had with three daus., an only son,

Thomas Lister, **3rd Baron Ribblesdale,** Officer Royal Horse Guards, b. 28 April 1828; m. 7 May 1853, Emma, dau. of Col. William Nure, of Caldwell, M.P. She d. 5 July 1911. He d. 25 Aug. 1876. They had issue,

1. Thomas, **4th Baron Ribblesdale** (see below).
2. Martin, British Resident in Straits Settlements, b. 25 July 1857; d. 24 Feb. 1897.
3. Reginald, Sir, K.C.M.G., C.V.O., in Diplomatic Service 1886-1912, Min. plen. at Paris, 1906-08, and at Tangier, and Consul Gen. in Morocco, 1908-12; b. 19 May 1865; d. unm. 10 Nov. 1912.
1. Beatrix.
2. Adelaide.

The eldest son,

Thomas Lister, **4th Baron Ribblesdale,** b. 29 Oct. 1854; Capt. Rifle Brig.; a lord-in-waiting to Queen Victoria, 1880-85; Master of the Royal Buckhounds 1892-95; Trustee of the National Gallery and National Portrait Gallery; m. (1) 7 April 1877, Charlotte Monckton, dau. of Sir Charles Tennant (Glenconner B.). She d. 2 May 1911, having had issue,

1. Thomas, D.S.O., Capt. 10th Hussars, served in S. African War, 1899-1902 (wounded, despatches twice), and in Somaliland, 1903-04; b. 2 May 1878; k. in action at Jidballi, Somaliland, 10 Jan. 1904.
2. Charles Alfred, b. 26 Oct. 1887; educ. Eton and Balliol Coll. Oxford, Attaché Diplomatic Service, 1910, 3rd Sec. 1912; served at Rome, and Constantinople; was 2nd Lt. Middlesex Hussars, 1914, and in Royal Naval Div. served in the Dardanelles campaign, and was three times wounded. He d. 28 Aug. 1915, of wounds received in action.
1. Barbara, b. 30 May 1880; m. 1905, Lt. Col. Sir M. R. H. Wilson, 4th Bt., and had issue.
2. Laura, b. 12 Jan. 1892; m. 15 Oct. 1910, 14th Lord Lovat, and d. 24 Mar. 1965, leaving issue.
3. Diana, b. 7 May 1893; m. (1) 1913, P. L. Wyndham, who was k. in action 15 Sept. 1914. She m. (2) 1918, Capt. A. E. Capel, and had issue. She m. (3) 1923, 14th Earl of Westmorland, and had issue.

The 4th Baron Ribblesdale, m. (2) 1919, Ava, dau. of Edward Willings, of Philadelphia and formerly wife of Col. Jacob Astor, and d.s.p.m.s. 21 Oct. 1925.

ARMS—Ermine on a fess sable three mullets or.

CREST—A stag's head erased per fess, ppr. and gules, attired or, differenced with a crescent.

SUPPORTERS—Dexter, A stag reguardant sable, attired and hoofed or, charged on the body with an eagle displayed or gorged with a collar of SS and portcullises gold; Sinister, A bay horse, bridled, saddled and supporting a

staff ppr. headed or, with a banner vert fringed and charged with the letters, Y.L.D. gold (meaning York Light Dragoons).
MOTTO—Retinens vestigia famae.
Lord Ribblesdale's seat was Gisburne Park, Clitheroe, Yorks.

RIDDELL

PEERAGE—U.K. Baron Riddell, of Walton Heath, co. Surrey.
SURNAME—Riddell.
CR,—28 Jan. 1920. EXT.—5 Dec. 1934. (Also a baronetcy cr. 31 Jan. 1918.)
HISTORY—James Riddell of Duns, co. Berwick, who d. in 1867 had by his wife, Isabel Young, a son,
  Sir George Allardice Riddell, Bt., and **Baron Riddell,** b. 25 May 1865 at Duns; educ. in London; admitted a solicitor 1888; retired 1903, and entered journalism; became Chm. of George Newnes Ltd., C. Arthur Pearson Ltd. and News of the World Ltd, and was a Dir. of Country Life Ltd., Newnes and Pearson Printing Co. Ltd., and W. H. Collingridge and Co. Ltd.; cr. Kt. Bach. 1909; was Liaison Officer between Gov. and the Press during World War I, 1914-18, and at Versailles Conference, 1919; was cr. a baronet 31 Jan. 1918; represented the British Press at the Peace Conferences 1919-22; and later at other international conferences; was cr. Baron Riddell, of Walton Heath, co. Surrey 28 Jan. 1920. He was the Founder of the London Sch. of Printing, Pres. of the Advisory Council of London Sch. of Printing and Kindred Trades, 1922-24; Chm. of the Newspaper Proprietors' Asscn., and was an hon. member of the British Medical Asscn., hon. Fell. of the British Sch. of Obstetricians and Pres. of the Medico-Legal Society. He wrote extensively, including *Lord Riddell's War Diary,* 1914-18 pub. 1933, and *Lord Riddell's Intimate Diary of the Peace Conference and After,* also pub. 1933, the profits from which were given to the Newspaper Press Fund, which with many other charities benefited from his will. He wrote also, *Some Things That Matter,* 1922, *More Things That Matter,* 1925, *Dame Louisa Aldrich-Blake,* 1926, *Looking Round,* 1928, *Medico-Legal Problems,* 1929. He m. 2 Nov. 1900, Annie Molison, dau. of David William Allardice, of Valparaiso, Chile, and Rockferry, co. Chester, and d.s.p. 5 Dec. 1934.
ARMS—Per chevron azure and gules, in chief two ears of rye leaved and slipped and in base an ancient printing press or.
CREST—Issuant out of a bank of clouds, a carrier pigeon volant holding in the beak an open scroll all ppr.
SUPPORTERS—On either side a printer of the time of Caxton ppr.
BADGE—An ear of rye leaved and slipped and enfiled by a circlet or.
MOTTO—Knowledge is power.

RIPON

PEERAGE—G.B. Baron Grantham of Grantham in co. Lincoln. 7 April 1761.
U.K. Earl of Ripon, 13 April 1833.
U.K. Viscount Goderich, 28 April 1827.

U.K. Earl de Grey (of Wrest), 25 Oct. 1816.
U.K. Marquess of Ripon, 23 June 1871. (Also a baronetcy cr. 13 Feb. 1689/90.)
SURNAME—Robinson.
CR.—Dates as above. EXT.—22 Sept. 1923.
HISTORY—William Robinson, was an eminent Hamburg merchant, and was Lord Mayor of York, 1581 and 1594; M.P. York, 1584 and 1588; m. (1) a dau. of John Redman, of Tulworth, co. York, and had issue,
  1. William, his successor (see below).
He m. (2) a dau. of Thomas Harrison, of York, and had further issue,
  2. Thomas, who inherited his father's estate in Richmondshire, and d.s.p. 1625.
William Robinson d. 1616 aged 94 and was bur. at St. Crux, York. His elder son,
  William Robinson, of Newby, co. York, Sheriff of York, 1607, and Lord Mayor, 1619; s. in 1616 to his father's property in and near the city of York, and in 1625 to his half brother's estate. He m. Margaret, dau. of Sir Henry Jenkins, of Grimstone, co. York, and d. 1626 (will proved 20 Oct. 1626) having had with other issue, a son and heir,
  Sir William Robinson, of Newby, M.P. York 1628, knighted by Charles I at Edinburgh, 1633; High Sheriff, co. York, 1639; m. (1) Mary, one of the coheirs of Sir William Bamborough, Bt., of Housam, co. York by whom he had one son, William who d. at Paris under age. He m. (2) Frances, dau. of Sir Thomas Metcalfe, of Napps, co. York and d. 1658 having had by her with three daus.,
  1. Metcalfe, Sir, his heir (see below).
  2. Thomas, m. Elizabeth, dau. of Charles Tancred, of Arden, co. York, and was bur. 16 July 1678, leaving with other issue, an elder son,
    William, Sir, 1st Bt., heir to his uncle (see below).
The elder surv. son,
  Sir Metcalfe Robinson, Bt. of Newby, so cr. 30 July 1660, M.P. for York, 1660, 1661-79, and 1685-87. He m. Margaret, dau. of Sir William D'Arcy, of Wilton Castle, co. Durham, and d.s.p.s. 6 Feb. 1688/89, when his title became extinct and his estates were inherited by his nephew,
  Sir William Robinson, 1st Bt., of Newby, b. 1655; cr. a baronet 13 Feb. 1689/90, High Sheriff co. York, 1689, M.P. for Northallerton, 1689/95, and for City of York, 1698-1722. He m. 8 Sept. 1699, Mary, dau. of George Aislabie, of Studley Royal, co. York, and had the following issue,
  1. Metcalfe, Sir, 2nd Bt., d. unm. 2 Dec. 1738.
  2. Tancred, Sir, 3rd Bt., Rear Adm. of the White, Lord Mayor of York, 1718 and 1738. He m. 1713, his cousin, Mary, only dau. and heir of Rowland Norton, of Disforth, co. York, by his wife, Margaret, dau. of Thomas Robinson, of York, (see above). She d. 1748. He d. 1754 having had issue,
    (1) William, Sir, 4th Bt., b. 1713; m. Dorothy, dau. of John Thornhill, of Stanton, co. Derby, and d.s.p. 4 Mar. 1770.
    (2) Norton, Sir, 5th Bt., (see below).
    (3) Thomas, d.s.p. April 1740.
    (1) Mary, m. Thomas Pierce, of Pierceburgh, co. York.
    (2) Elizabeth, d. unm.

(3) Alethea, d. unm. 1767.

(4) Margaret.

3. William, Col. of Marines, d.s.p. at Port Royal, Jamaica, 17 June 1741.

4. Thomas, **1st Baron Grantham** (see below).

5. John, Major of Marines, d.s.p. at Jamaica, 1742.

1. Anne, m. Thomas Worsley, of Hovingham, co. York, and d. 15 Jan. 1768.

Sir William, 1st Bt. d. 22 Dec. 1736. His fourth son,

Thomas Robinson, **1st Baron Grantham,** so cr. 7 April 1761 as Baron Grantham in the co. of Lincoln, was M.A. Trin. Coll. Camb., 1719; Sec. of Embassy, at Paris, 1723-30; envoy to Vienna, 1730-48; junior lord of trade, 1748-49; master of the wardrobe, 1749-54; and 1755-60; Sec. of State for the south 1754-55, and in 1755 one of the regents for the realm; M.P. for Thirsk, 1727-34, and for Christchurch, 1749-61; made P.C. and cr. K.B., m. 13 July 1737, Frances, dau. of Thomas Worsley, of Hovingham, co. York, and by her (who d. 1760) had issue,

1. Thomas, **2nd Baron Grantham** (see below).

2. Frederick, b. 11 Oct. 1746; m. 1785, Catherine Gertrude, dau. of James Harris, M.P. and sister of 1st Earl of Malmesbury and d.s.p. 1792.

1. Theresa, m. 1769, 1st Lord Borington, and d. 1775 leaving issue.

The 1st Baron Grantham, d. 30 Sept. 1770, being s. by his elder son,

Thomas Robinson, **2nd Baron Grantham,** b. 30 Nov. 1738; M.A. Christ's Coll. Camb.; M.P. Christchurch, 1761-70; junior lord of trade, 1766; P.C. 1770; vice-chamberlain of the household, 1770-71; ambassador to Madrid, 1771-79; pres. of the Board of Trade, 1780-82; sec. of state for foreign affairs, 1782-83; m. 17 Aug. 1780, Mary Jemima, 2nd dau. and coheir of 2nd Earl of Hardwicke. Her only sister, Amabel Yorke, Baroness Lucas in her own right, was cr. **Countess de Grey,** on 25 Oct. 1816, with remainder to her sister Mary Jemima Robinson, Baroness Grantham, and her male heirs. Lady Grantham d. 7 Jan. 1830. Lord Grantham d. 20 July 1786. They had issue,

1. Thomas Philip, **3rd Baron Grantham,** and **2nd Earl de Grey.**

2. Frederick John, **1st Viscount Goderich,** and **1st Earl of Ripon,** b. 1 Nov. 1782; he was First Lord of the Treasury, 1827-28; cr. Viscount Goderich, 28 April 1877; was Sec. of State for the Colonies and Lord Privy Seal; cr. Viscount Goderich, 28 April 1827, and cr. Earl of Ripon, 13 April 1833. He m. 1 Sept. 1814, Sarah Albinia Louisa, only dau. and eventual coheir of the 4th Earl of Buckinghamshire, and d. 28 Jan. 1859 having by her (who d. 9 April 1867) had issue,

George Frederick Samuel, **2nd Earl of Ripon, 3rd Earl de Grey,** and **1st Marquess of Ripon** (see below).

Eleanor Henrietta Victoria, d. young, 31 Oct. 1826.

The 2nd Baron Grantham, was s. by his elder son,

Thomas Philip (Robinson), later De Grey, **2nd Earl de Grey,** and **3rd Baron Grantham,** b. 8 Dec. 1781; s. to the baronetcy on the death of his kinsman, the 5th Baronet Sir Norton Robinson in 1792 (see above), and in 1833 s.

his maternal aunt as 2nd Earl de Grey. He had previously taken in lieu of his surname of Robinson that of Weddell; on s. to the Earldom of De Grey he assumed the name and arms of De Grey. He m. 20 July 1805, Lady Henrietta Frances Cole, dau. of 1st Earl of Enniskillen. She d. 2 July 1848. They had two surv. daus.,

1. Anne Florence, Baroness Lucas (see extant peerages).

2. Mary Gertrude, m. 6 July 1832, Henry Vyner, and d. 11 July 1892, leaving issue, (Lucas, B.).

The 2nd Earl de Grey was Lord Lt. of Ireland and Lord Lt. co. Bedford. He d. 14 Nov. 1859, being s. in the barony of Lucas by his elder dau., and in his other titles by his nephew,

George Frederick Samuel Robinson, **3rd Earl de Grey, 2nd Viscount Goderich, 4th Baron Grantham,** and **1st Marquess of Ripon.** He s. his father as **2nd Earl of Ripon** in 1859; his uncle as 3rd Earl de Grey, 1859 and was cr. Marquess of Ripon 23 June 1871. He was b. 24 Oct. 1827; was M.P. for Hull, 1852-53, Huddersfield, 1853-57; and for the W.R. York 1857-59; Lord Lt. N.R. Yorks, 1873-1906, Mayor of Ripon, 1895 held many political posts, and was Lord Pres. of the Council, 1868-73; Gov. Gen. and Viceroy of India 1880-84; First Lord of the Admiralty, 1886; Lord Privy Seal, 1905-08; m. 8 April 1851, his cousin, Henrietta Ann Theodosia, C.I., dau. of Capt. Henry Vyner of Gautby Hall, co. Lincoln (Lucas, B.). and d. 9 July 1900 having had issue by her (d. 28 Feb. 1907) with a dau., d. an infant, an only son,

Sir Frederick Oliver Robinson, **2nd Marquess of Ripon, 4th Earl de Grey** of Wrest, co. Bedford, **3rd Earl of Ripon,** co. York, **3rd Viscount Goderich** of Nocton, and **5th Baron Grantham** of Grantham co. Lincoln, and a baronet, cr. G.C.V.O.; b. 29 Jan. 1852; treasurer to Queen Alexandra, 1901; a trustee of the Wallace Collection 1912; M.P. Ripon, 1874-80; m. 7 May 1885, Constance Gladys, dau. of 1st Lord Herbert of Lea, (Pembroke and Montgomery, E.) and widow of 4th Earl of Lonsdale. He d. 22 Sept. 1923.

ARMS—Vert a chevron between three stags in gaze or.

CREST—Out of a coronet composed of fleurs-de-lis, or, a mount vert thereon a stag at gaze gold.

SUPPORTERS—On either side a greyhound reguardant sable.

MOTTO—Qualis ab incepto.

The Marquess of Ripon's seat was Studley Royal, near Ripon, co. York. He had also a residence at Coombe Court, Kingston Hill, Surrey. His clubs were White's, Turf, Marlborough, Hurlingham, Yorkshire and Orleans.

ROBERTS

PEERAGE—U.K. Earl Roberts of Kandahar, in Afghanistan and Pretoria in the Transvaal Colony, and of the City of Waterford, and Viscount St. Pierre, both cr. 11 Feb. 1901. Also U.K. Baron Roberts of Kandahar in Afghanistan and of the City of Waterford, 20 Feb. 1892.

SURNAME—Roberts and later Lewin.

CR.—as above. EXT.—Barony and Baronetcy, 14 Nov. 1914, Viscounty and Earldom 21 Feb. 1955.

HISTORY—Thomas Roberts, of the city of Waterford, m. Sarah, dau. of John Bowles, of Waterford, and d. before 18 Nov. 1775, leaving with another son, Benjamin, a son,
John Roberts, of Waterford, an architect, b. 1712; m. Mary Susannah, dau. of Francis Sautelle, of Waterford, of a French refugee family. She d. 21 Jan. 1800, aged 84. He d. 23 May 1796. They had five sons of whom the eldest,
The Rev. John Roberts, Rector of Kill St. Nicholas, co. Waterford, and Ballymacward, co. Galway, J.P. co. Waterford, and Provost of the diocese of Kilmacduagh, B.A. Trin. Coll. Dublin, b. 24 Jan. 1745, m. 23 Jan. 1771, Anne, dau. of Rev. Abraham Sandys, minor canon of St. Patrick's Cathedral, Dublin. She d. 7 May 1833, aged 78. He d. before 12 May 1815. They had with other issue,
  1. John, of Waterford, b. 14 April 1773; m. 18 May 1796, Grace, dau. of William Dobbyn. She d. 1854. He d. 2 Feb. 1837, leaving issue.
  2. Thomas, Capt. R.N., b. 12 Jan. 1778; m. 25 June 1804, Katherine, (d. 24 Jan. 1867) dau. of Major James Hackett and d. 16 Feb. 1855, leaving issue.
  3. Abraham, Sir, (see below).
  4. Samuel, Sir, C.B., of Belmont, co. Waterford, Capt. R.N., b. 2 July 1785; m. 30 May 1818, Rosamund, (d. 3 Nov. 1844) dau. of Benjamin Roberts, of Waterford, and d.s.p.s. 16 Dec. 1848.
The third son,
Gen. Sir Abraham Roberts, G.C.B., Col. 101st Regt., served in India and throughout the first Afghan War, b. 11 April 1784; m. (1) 20 July 1820, Frances Isabella (d. 14 May 1827) dau. of George Poyntz Rocketts, B.C.S., and had issue,
  1. George Rocketts, Major Gen. B.S.C., b. 8 Feb. 1827; m. 6 Mar. 1857, Harriett, (d. 13 Feb. 1908) dau. of Capt. Thomas Roberts, Bengal Army, and d. 22 Mar. 1915, leaving issue.
  1. Frances Eliza m. 20 Oct. 1842, Gen. Charles Grant, C.B., Bengal Artillery, and d. 15 Oct. 1853 leaving issue.
  2. Maria Isabella, m. 20 Oct. 1842, Col. W. M. G. M. Welwood, and d. 25 Dec. 1886, leaving issue. (B.L.G. 1952, Maconochie-Welwood, of Kirnewton and Garvock).
Sir Abraham m. (2) 2 Aug. 1830, Isabella (d. 7 Mar. 1882) dau. of Abraham Bunbury, of Kilfeacle, co. Tipperary, and widow of Major H. G. Maxwell, of Ardwell, and d. 28 Dec. 1873, having by her had further issue,
  2. Frederick Sleigh, **Earl Roberts** (see below).
  3. Harriet Mercer, d. unm. 8 Oct. 1880.
The second son,
Sir Frederick Sleigh Roberts, Bt., **Baron Roberts**, and **Viscount St. Pierre** and **Earl Roberts**, was b. 30 Sept. 1832; 2nd Lt. Bengal Infantry, 1851; he served in the Army throughout the Indian Mutiny, 1857-58 on the N.W. Frontier, 1863, in the Abyssinian war, 1868, with Lushai Exped. Force, 1871-72; (despatches, and C.B.); cmd. the Kabul Field Force, in advance to and occupation of Kabul, 1879, the Kabul-Kandahar Force, 1880, and the Army in Burma, 1886; he was Field Marshal and C. in C. of the Forces in S. Africa, 1899-1900; he was awarded the V.C.

(1858) and cr. C.B. 1872; K.C.B. 1879, G.C.B. 1880, G.C.I.E. 1887; G.C.S.I. 1893; P.C. 1895, K.P. 1897, K.G. 1901, and O.M. 1902. He was cr. a baronet, 15 June 1881 and a peer as Baron Roberts of Kandahar in Afghanistan and of the city of Waterford, (the title being derived from his services in Afghanistan and his family's long connection with Waterford), 20 Feb. 1892. In recognition of his victories in S. Africa he was cr. Viscount St. Pierre and Earl Roberts of Kandahar in Afghanistan and Pretoria, in the Transvaal Colony, and of the City of Waterford, with special remainder in default of male issue, to his elder dau., and the heirs male of her body; and in default of such issue to his ygr. dau. successively and the heirs male of her body, and in default of such issue to every other ygr. dau. successively and the heirs male of their bodies. Earl Roberts also received a grant of £100,000 for his services. He was author of *The Rise of Wellington*, and *Forty One Years in India*. He was educ. Eton, Sandhurst and Addiscombe; m. 17 May 1859, Nora Henrietta, C.I., R.R.C. (who d. 21 Dec. 1920) dau. of Capt. John Bews, by whom he had issue,
  1. Frederick Henry, b. and d. Aug. 1869.
  2. Frederick Hugh Sherston, V.C., Lt. K.R.R.C., b. 8 Jan. 1872, served in the Waziristan Exped. 1894-95 (despatches), with the Chitral Relief Force, 1895, Nile Exped. 1898, present at battle of Khartoum, and in S. Africa, 1899. He d. of wounds received at the battle of Colenso, 17 Dec. 1899, and was awarded posthumously the V.C. for his conspicuous bravery.
  1. Nora Frederica, b. 10 Mar. 1860; d. 3 Mar. 1861.
  2. Eveleen Sautelle, b. 18 July 1868; d. 8 Feb. 1869.
  3. Aileen Mary, **Countess Roberts, 2nd** holder of title.
  4. Ada Edwina Stewart, **Countess Roberts, 3rd** holder of title.
Earl Roberts d. 14 Nov. 1914, at the H.Q. of the British Army in France, and the baronetcy and barony became extinct, while he was s. in the Viscounty and Earldom by his elder surv. daughter,
Aileen Mary Roberts, **Countess Roberts, 2nd** holder of title, D.B.E. 1918, Chm. Lord Roberts Memorial Workshops, b. 20 Sept. 1870 and d. unm. 9 Oct. 1944, being s. by her sister,
Ada Edwina Stewart Lewin, **Countess Roberts, 3rd** holder of title, b. 28 Mar. 1875; Acting Cmdt. Ascot Aux. Mil. Hospital during World War I, 1914-19, O.B.E. 1918, Vice Pres. Wilts Red Cross, and a mem. of cttees of Lord Roberts Memorial Workshops, during World War II, 1939-45; m. 26 Feb. 1913, Brig. Gen. Henry Frederick Elliott Lewin, C.B., C.M.G., R.A., son of Cmdr. W. H. Lewin, R.N., and d. 21 Feb. 1955. He d. 1 Dec. 1946. They had issue,
Frederick Roberts Alexander, Lt. Irish Guards, b. 18 Jan. 1915, served in World War II, 1939-40, k. in action in Norway, May 1940.
ARMS—(of Earl Roberts). Azure three estoiles or, on a chief wavy or an eastern crown gules.
CREST—A lion rampant or, armed and langued gules charged on the shoulder with an eastern crown, as in the arms, and holding in

the dexter paw a sword blade wavy argent pommel and hilt gold.
SUPPORTERS—Dexter, A Highlander of the 92nd Regt.; Sinister, A Gurkha, both habited, and holding in their exterior hands a rifle, all ppr.
MOTTO—Virtute et valore.
The Earl's clubs were United Service, Athenaeum and Marlborough.

ROBERTSON

PEERAGE—U.K. Life. Baron Robertson, of Forteviot, co. Perth.
SURNAME—Robertson.
CR.—14 Nov. 1899. **EXT.**—2 Feb. 1909.
HISTORY—The Rev. Robert John Robertson, of Forteviot, co. Perth by Helen Saunders, his wife, dau. of the Rev. James Bannerman, of Cargill, co. Perth had issue,
James Patrick Bannerman Robertson, **Lord Robertson,** b. 10 Aug. 1845; educ. Edinburgh Univ. M.A., LL.D.; Advocate, Scots Bar, 1867; Q.C. 1885; Solicitor Gen. for Scotland 1885-86; and 1886-88; P.C. 1888; Lord Advocate, 1888-91; M.P. for Buteshire, 1885-91; Lord Justice Gen. 1891-99; Chm. of Commission on Irish Univ. Education, 1901; apptd. a Lord of Appeal in Ordinary, and a life peer as Baron Robertson, of Forteviot, co. Perth, 14 Nov. 1899. He m. 10 April 1872, Philadelphia Mary Lucy, dau. of W. N. Fraser, of Tornaveen, co. Aberdeen, and d. 2 Feb. 1909. She d. 25 Jan. 1907. They had issue,
1. Robert Bannerman Fraser, b. 14 Feb. 1873; educ. Winchester and Ch. Ch. Oxford, Barrister-at-Law, Inner Temple; Capt. 21st Lancers, served with Imperial Yeomanry in S. African War, 1900-01, (despatches and wounded) and in World War I, 1914-18, with 9th Lancers, (wounded and taken prisoner) and subsequently as G.S.O. War Office.
2. Hugh, 2nd Lt. 14th Hussars, b. 27 Sept. 1879; served in S. African War, 1900-01, and d. unm. 1 Feb. 1901.
1. Philadelphia Sybil, m. 15 June 1904, Charles Lachlan Maclean, (Maclean of Dowart, Bt.) and d. 12 Feb. 1945 having had issue.
ARMS—(recorded in Lyon Office, 1892). Gules a fess ermine between two wolves' heads erased in chief and a banner displayed bendwise in base argent, thereon a canton azure, charged with a saltire of the third.
CREST—A dexter cubit arm erect ppr. charged with an ermine spot, the hand holding an imperial crown also ppr.
MOTTO—Virtutis gloria merces.

ROBINS

PEERAGE—U.K. Baron Robins of Rhodesia and Chelsea.
SURNAME—Robins.
CR.—10 July 1958. **EXT.**—21 July 1962.
HISTORY—The family of Robins has been known in Northants since the 14th century. Richard Robins b. 1570, of Long Buckby, co. Northampton, m. 1596 Dorothy, dau. of John

Newport, of Harringham, co. Warwick and had with other issue, with whom the Northamptonshire Robins became extinct, a yr. son,
Col. Obedience Robins, who went to Virginia in 1621, being a shareholder in the Virginia Co., and moved to Northampton County, 1628; was mem. of the Governor's Council 1655-59. He was b. 1600; m. 1634, Grace O'Neill and d. 1662 having had issue,
Col. John Robins, of Salt Grove, Northampton County, Virginia, had grants of land there by patent, b. 6 Jan. 1636; m. 1662, Esther, dau. of Col. Nathaniel Littleton, of Accomac Co. Virginia, and d. 1709 having had issue,
Thomas Robins, of Chincoteague, Virginia, b. 1677; m. 1699, Elizabeth, dau. of Huguenot, Pierre Bowdoin, and d. 1728 leaving issue,
Thomas Robins, of Worcester Co. Maryland, b. 1702; m. 1738, Leah, dau. and heiress of Elias Whalley, of South Point, Maryland and d. 1765 leaving issue,
Thomas Robins of South Point, Maryland, b. 1740; m. 1768, Isabella, dau. of the Rev. William McClenachan, of Co. Armagh, Ireland and d. 1815 leaving issue,
Edward Robins of South Point, Maryland, b. 1769; m. 1792, Elizabeth dau. of Benjamin Purnell, of Worcester Co., Maryland, and d. 1857, having had issue,
Thomas Robins, of South Point, Maryland, moved in 1876 to Philadelphia. Pres. of the Philadelphia Nat. Bank, 1852-79, b. 1797; m. 1819 Eliza, dau. of the Rev. James Wiltbank and d. 1882 leaving issue,
The Rev. James Wiltbank Robins of Philadelphia, M.A., D.D., b. 30 Sept. 1831; m. 1856, Helen Hamilton, dau. of R. M. Patterson, M.D., and d. 1918 having had other issue, (see B.L.G. 1939 *American Supplement* and 1947 *Burke's Distinguished Families of America*),
Major Robert Patterson Robins, of Philadelphia, M.A., M.D., Major U.S. Army, served in the Spanish American War, 1898, b. 1857; m. 1883 Mary Routh (d. 1949) dau. of Thomas de la Roche Ellis of Elliston, Louisiana, and d. 6 Aug. 1905 leaving issue with a dau. Helen, a son,
Sir Thomas Ellis Robins, **Baron Robins,** b. 31 Oct. 1884; educ. the Blight Sch., Philadelphia, Univ. of Pennsylvania, B.A. (1904) and Ch. Ch. Oxford (Rhodes' Scholar); Priv. Sec. to Earl Winterton, M.P. 1909-14; naturalized as British subject, 1912; Gen. Man. The British S. Africa Co. 1928-33 and resident Director in Africa 1934-57; Dir. Anglo-American Corp. of S. Africa, and of many other cos. in S. Africa and Rhodesia. He served in World War I, 1914-18, cmdg. City of London Yeo., and on staff in Egypt, Gallipoli and Palestine (despatches twice, D.S.O. 1919); served in S. Rhodesia Forces 1930-39 (E.D. 1933), and in World War II, 1939-45, cmd. 1st Bn. the Rhodesia Regt. 1940-43, then G.S.O.I. Intelligence, G.H.Q. India 1943-46. He took a prominent part in Boy Scout Movement and held rank of Grand Master of English Freemasons in Rhodesia. He was created Kt. Bach. 1946, K.B.E. 1954 and Baron Robins of Rhodesia and Chelsea, 10 July 1958. He m. 31 Oct. 1912, Mary St. Quintin, dau. of Philip Wroughton of Woolley Park, Wantage, co. Berks (see B.L.G. 1952), and had issue two daus. He d. 21 July 1962.

ROB

ARMS—Per pale argent and sable two flaunches counter changed, a dolphin palewise head downwards affrontée also counter-changed between two fleurs-de-lis each per pale of the first and second.
CREST—A robin gorged with a necklace of copper beads ppr. between two spur rowels upwards or.
SUPPORTERS—Dexter, An American bald headed eagle wings inverted and addorsed ppr. semée of mullets of six points argent; Sinister, A lion or.
BADGE—A robin gorged with a necklace of diamonds ppr.
MOTTO Esse quam videri.

ROBINSON

PEERAGE—U.K. Baron Robinson of Kielder Forest, co. Northumberland, and of Adelaide in the Commonwealth of Australia.
SURNAME—Robinson.
CR.—15 July 1947. **EXT.**—5 Sept. 1952.
HISTORY—William Robinson, of Perth, W. Australia by his wife, Annie, had issue,
Sir Roy Lister Robinson, **Baron Robinson,** b. 8 Mar. 1883; educ. St. Peter's Coll. Adelaide, Sch. of Mines and Univ. of Adelaide, B.Sc. 1902, and Magdalen Coll. Oxford, B.A. 1908; F.S.A.S.M. Adelaide; Asst. Insp. (1909), Insp. 1910, Suptg. Insp. 1912, Board of Agric. and Fisheries; during World War I with Min. of Munitions and Agric., 1914-18; Tech. Commr. 1919-32, Vice-Chm. 1929-32, Chm. 1932-52 Forestry Commn.; cr. O.B.E. 1918, Kt. Bach., 1931, and a peer as Baron Robinson of Kielder Forest, co. Northumberland, and of Adelaide in the Commonwealth of Australia, 15 July 1947; m. 26 Nov. 1910, Charlotte Marion Cust, yr. dau. of Henry Cust Bradshaw, of Fair Oak Park, co. Hants, and d. 5 Sept. 1952, having had issue,
1. Michael Lister, D.S.O., D.F.C., b. 8 May 1916; educ. Downside; served in World War II, W/Cdr. R.A.F., had Belgian Croix de Guerre avec palme; k. in action 10 April 1942.
1. Teresa, b. 31 Oct. 1914; m. 23 Dec. 1939, W/Cmdr. Paul Henry Mills Richey, D.F.C., R.A.F. and had issue.
2. Magdalen Mary, b. 10 Jan. 1921; m. 16 Aug. 1941, J. J. B. Hunt, M.C., and had issue.

ROBSON

PEERAGE—U.K. Life. Baron Robson, of Jesmond, co. Northumberland.
SURNAME—Robson.
CR.—7 Oct. 1910. **EXT.**—11 Sept. 1918.
HISTORY—Sir William Snowdon Robson, **Baron Robson,** was b. 10 Sept. 1852, the third but only surv. son of Robert Robson, J.P. of Newcastle-upon-Tyne, who d. 1896, by his wife, Jane, dau. of William Snowdon. William Snowdon Robson was educ. privately and at Gonville and Caius Coll. Camb., B.A. 1877, and M.A. 1879; Barrister-at-Law, Inner Temple, 1880; Q.C. 1892; Bencher 1899. He was Liberal M.P. for Bow and Bromley Div. of Tower Hamlets, 1885-86, and for South

ROC

Shields, 1895-1910; Recorder of Newcastle-upon-Tyne, 1895-1905; Solicitor Gen. 1905-08; Attorney Gen. 1908-10; P.C. 1910; apptd. Lord of Appeal in Ordinary, 7 Oct. 1910, and a life peer as Baron Robson, of Jesmond, co. Northumberland. He resigned office of Lord of Appeal in 1912. He was cr. Kt. Bach. 1905, and G.C.M.G. 1911. He m. 26 May 1887, Catherine Emily, dau. of Charles Burge, of Park Crescent, W., and d. 11 Sept. 1918, having had issue,
1. Harold Burge, B.A. Oxford, J.P. Northumberland, Barrister-at-Law of Inner Temple, served in World War I, (despatches, Croix de Guerre, Capt. Northumberland Hussars); b. 10 Mar. 1888; m. (1) 27 Mar. 1912, (m. diss. by div. 1920). Ysolt, dau. of Col. Herman Le Roy-Lewis, of Westbury House, Petersfield, co. Hants, and had issue,
(1) William Michael, b. 31 Dec. 1912; m. 1 Feb. 1939, Aubrey Isobel Wales, dau. of Major W. H. Dick, and had issue.
He m. (2) 26 Jan. 1922, Iris Emmeline, dau. of Reginald Abel Smith and d. 13 Oct. 1964, having had further issue,
(2) Nigel John, b. 25 Dec. 1926; m. 1957, Anne, dau. of S. D. Gladstone, and had issue.
1. Kathleen, b. 22 June 1890; m. 20 Jan. 1923, Lt. Col. C. H. Gay.
2. Violet, b. 27 June 1892; m. 24 April 1913, Sir Charles Travis Clay, C.B., Librarian of House of Lords and had issue.
3. Diana, b. 7 May 1896.
ARMS—Azure a chevron ermine between in chief two boars' heads erased and on a mount issuant from the base a cross patonce or.
CREST—Issuant from a crescent or a boar's head couped at the neck azure.
SUPPORTERS—On either side, a cock robin ppr.
MOTTO—Fac et spera.

ROCHE

PEERAGE—U.K. Life. Baron Roche, of Chadlington, co. Oxford.
SURNAME—Roche.
CR.—14 Oct. 1935. **EXT.**—22 Dec. 1956.
HISTORY—John Roche, M.D., of Cork and of Norwich, b. 1888, had issue,
William Brock Roche, of Ipswich and Seaton, co. Devon, m. Mary (d. 19 June 1928) dau. of William Fraser and d. July 1925, having with other issue,
Sir (Alexander) Adair Roche, **Baron Roche,** b. 24 July 1871; educ. Ipswich Sch. and Wadham Coll. Oxford, Hon. Fell. 1917; Barrister-at-Law, Inner Temple, 1896; K.C. 1912; Bencher, 1917; Treasurer, 1939; Hon. Legal Adviser to Dept. of Foreign Trade, 1914-17; apptd. Judge of the High Court, King's Bench, 1917 and knighted, 1917; cr. Lord of Appeal in Ordinary, 1935, and a Life peer as Baron Roche, of Chadlington, co. Oxford 14 Oct. 1935. Made P.C. 1934; m. (1) 22 Mar. 1902, Elfreda Gabriel, ygst. dau. of John Fenwick, Spencer House, Wimbledon Common, and d. 22 Dec. 1956, having had issue,

235

1. John Fenwick Adair, b. 19 Jan. 1903; educ. Rugby and Wadham Coll. Oxford, B.A. 1924; m. 27 Dec. 1928, Ethel Meverell, dau. of K.C. Bayley, of Durham, (Laurie, Bt.) and had issue, two daus.
2. Thomas Gabriel, b. 11 May 1909; educ. Rugby and Wadham Coll. Oxford, Barrister-at-Law, Inner Temple, 1932; served in World War II, 1939-45, (despatches), Lt. Col. 92nd and 365th Field Bde. R.A.
1. Helen Patricia, m. 14 Mar. 1931; S/Ldr. Edward Garmondsway Waldy, R.A.F., son of W. Waldy, J.P., of Darlington, co. Durham, and had issue.

Lord Roche resigned the office of Lord of Appeal in Ordinary in 1938.
ARMS—Gules three roach naiant in pale and in chief as many cinquefoils argent.
CREST—Upon a rock a sea eagle affrontée, wings expanded ppr., holding in the beak a roach argent.
SUPPORTERS—Dexter, A Foxhound; Sinister, A Labrador retriever, both ppr.
MOTTO—Mon Dieu est ma roche.
Lord Roche's residence was Chadlington, co. Oxford. His club—Athenaeum.

ROE

PEERAGE—U.K. Baron Roe, of the Borough of Derby.
SURNAME—Roe.
CR.—5 Jan. 1917. **EXT.**—7 June 1923.
HISTORY—Thomas Roe, of Derby, J.P., Alderman, and Mayor of Derby, 1863-65; b. June 1805; m. 1829, Deborah, dau. of Absalom Oakley, of Derby. She d. 15 Mar. 1850 aged 39. He d. 21 Jan. 1879. They had issue,
1. Thomas, **Baron Roe** (see below).
2. Charles, d. unm. 2 Sept. 1908, aged 63.
1. Sarah, m. 9 Feb. 1860, Reuben Eastwood.
2. Eliza, m. 16 May 1872, James W. Newbold.
The elder son,
Sir Thomas Roe, **Baron Roe**, of the Borough of Derby, so cr. 5 June 1917, b. 13 July 1832, at Derby, and educ. there, entered Messrs. Roe and Son Ltd., 1854; elected mem. of Derby Corporation 1858, and retained a connection with that body unbroken for the rest of his life; Mayor of Derby, 1867-68; 1896-97, and 1910-11; given hon. freedom of the borough, 1908; Liberal M.P. for Derby, 1883-95 and 1900-1916; cr. Kt. Bach. 1894; Pres. of the Urban District Councils Assoc. of England and Wales, J.P. Derbyshire, and Senior Grand Warden of England (Freemasons). He was m. 28 Aug. 1903, Emily, dau. of Matthew Kirtley, of Derby. She d. 31 July 1909, and he d.s.p. 7 June 1923.
Lord Roe's residence was Litchurch, Derby. His clubs were Reform and National Liberal.

ROKEBY

PEERAGE—Ireland. Baron Rokeby of Armagh.
SURNAME—Robinson.
CR.—26 Feb. 1777. (Also a baronetcy cr. 10 Mar. 1730.) **EXT.**—25 May 1883.

HISTORY—William Robinson of Brignal bought the estate of Rokeby, N.R. Yorks (which will always be associated with Sir Walter Scott's poem of that name) in 1610 from Sir Thomas Rokeby and m. Mary, dau. of Thomas Hall of Thornton, co. York. He had issue,
Thomas Robinson, Barrister-at-Law, Gray's Inn, Col. in Parliament forces and k. near Leeds leaving by his wife, Frances dau. of Leonard Smelt of Kirkby Fleetham,
1. William s. his grandfather (see below).
2. Leonard, Sir, Chamberlain to the City of London, m. Deborah, dau. of Sir James Collet and d. 1696 having had an only son,
Thomas, d. 1700. His only son, Matthew, of Edgley, co. York, m. Elizabeth, dau. of Thomas Drake of Cambridge and d. 1778 leaving issue,
(1) Matthew, **2nd Baron Rokeby** (see below).
(2) Morris, Six Clerks Office, Canterbury, m. Jane, dau. of John Greenland of Lovelace, co. Kent and d. 17 Oct. 1777, having had,
1a Morris, **3rd Baron** (see below).
2a Matthew, **4th Baron,** who assumed the additional surname and arms of Montague 1776 (see below).
(3) Robert, d. in China, unm.
(4) William, Rev. m. Mary, dau. of Adam Richardson of Kensington and had,
1a Matthew, Rev. m. Mary Anne Parsons and d.s.p. 1827.
1a Sarah Elizabeth, m. Samuel Truman and d. 1834 leaving issue.
2a Mary, m. Sir Samuel Egerton Brydges Bt., and d. 1844 having had issue.
(5) John, Fell. Trin. Hall, Camb.
(6) Charles, Recorder of Canterbury, m. Mary, 2nd dau. of John Greenland and widow of R. Dukes and had an only dau.,
Sarah, m. W. Hangham.
William Robinson of Rokeby, d. 1643, being s. by his grandson,
William Robinson, of Rokeby m. Mary, dau. and coheir of Francis Layton of Bawden and was s. by his only son,
Thomas Robinson, m. Grace, dau. of Sir Henry Stapylton Bt., of Myton co. York and he d. 1719 being s. by his only son,
William Robinson of Rokeby and of Merton Abbey, co. Surrey, b. 1675; m. Anne (d. 1730) dau. of Robert Walters of Cundall, N.R. Yorks and d. 1720, having had issue,
1. Thomas, Sir, 1st Bt., so cr. 10 Mar. 1730 with special remainder to his brothers and after them to his cousin, Matthew Robinson of Edgley, Yorks. He m. twice but d.s.p. 1777. He sold Rokeby estate in 1770 where he had rebuilt the house and incurred great expenditure.
2. William, Sir, 2nd Bt., d. unm. 1785, the baronetcy passing to his brother the 1st Baron Rokeby.
3. Henry, Major, k. at Cartagena 1741.
4. Richard, **1st Baron Rokeby** (see below).
5. Septimus, Sir, Gentleman Usher of the Black Rod, d. unm. 1765.
1. Anne, m. (1) Robert Knight and (2) James Cresset.

2. Grace, m. Very Rev. William Friend D.D. Dean of Canterbury.
The fourth son, (described in C.P. as sixth), Most Rev. Richard Robinson, Archbishop of Armagh, **1st Baron Rokeby** of Armagh in Irish peerage, so cr. 26 Feb. 1777, also 3rd Bt., was b. circa 1708, educ. Westminster 1720-26, King's Scholar 1722; Ch. Ch. Oxford B.A. 1730, M.A. 1733, B.D. and D.D. 1748; Chaplain to the Archbishop of York and in 1751 to the Duke of Dorset when Lord Lt. of Ireland; consecrated Bishop of Killala 1751, trans. to Leighlin and Ferns 1759. Kildare 1761, Dean of Ch. Ch. Dublin 1761, Archbishop of Armagh 1765-1794. Made P.C. of Ireland 1765, Lord Almoner and Vice Chancellor of Univ. of Dublin 1765-91. His peerage was cr. with special remainder, failing the heirs male of his body, to his brothers, in like manner and failing these as with the baronetcy to his cousin, Matthew Robinson of West Layton, N.R. Yorks. Lord Rokeby was Prelate of the newly founded Order of St. Patrick 1783. He became 3rd Bt. 1785. He d. unm. 10 Oct. 1794 and was s. in the barony and the baronetcy by his cousin,

Sir Matthew Robinson-Morris, formerly Robinson, **2nd Baron Rokeby** and 4th Bt. who was son and heir of Matthew Robinson (b. 1694, d. 1778) of Edgeley and West Layton, co. York, by Elizabeth Drake (see above), by Sarah dau. of Thomas Morris of Mount Morris in Horton, otherwise Monks Horton, co. Kent. The 2nd Baron took the name of Morris on inheriting through his mother the Morris estates in 1746. He was b. 1713; educ. Westminster and Trin. Hall Camb. LL.B. 1734, Fell. 1734-1800; adm. Lincoln's Inn 1730, F.R.S. 1746, sat as Whig M.P. for Canterbury 1747-61. He d. unm. 30 Nov. 1800 and was s. by his nephew.

Morris Robinson, **3rd Baron Rokeby** and 5th Bt., b. 14 July 1757; mem. Middle Temple, M.P. Boroughbridge 1790-96 and d. unm. May 1829 being s. by his brother,

Matthew Montagu formerly Robinson, **4th Baron Rokeby** and 6th Bt., b. 23 Nov. 1762; who took by Royal License on 3 June 1776, the name and arms of Montagu in lieu of those of Robinson in accordance with the will of his paternal aunt, Elizabeth, widow of Edward Montagu, grandson of the 1st Earl of Sandwich; was M.P. for Bossiney 1786-90, Tregony 1790-96 and St. Germans 1806-12. He m. Elizabeth, dau. and heir of Francis Charlton and d. 1 Sept. 1831, having had issue,
1. Edward, **5th Baron** (see below).
2. John, Lt. Col. Coldstream Guards d. 12 Dec. 1848.
3. Henry, **6th Baron** (see below).
4. Spencer Dudley, b. 1807; m. (1) 1842, Anna Louisa (d. 1865) dau. of Sir C. W. Flint and widow of J. Jekyll and had issue,
   (1) Emily Jane, m. 1865, Rev. J. Climenson.
   He m. (2) 1868, Henrietta Elizabeth Harriet, dau. of C. R. Pemberton and had issue,
   (2) Henrietta Mary.
1. Elizabeth, m. C. O. Bowles and d. 1875.
2. Catherine, m. 1831 Mr. Serjeant Goulburn and d. 1865.
3. Jane, m. 1811 Rt. Hon. Henry Goulburn and d. 1857.

4. Mary, m. 1820, Lt. Col. Ellison and d. 1877.
5. Eleanor, m. 1822 J. N. Fazakerly and d. 1847.
6. Caroline m. 1843 Lord William Godolphin Osborne (Leeds, D.) and d. 1867.
7. Emily d. 24 Nov. 1832.
The eldest son,
Edward Montague, **5th Baron Rokeby** and 7th Bt., b. 6 July 1787 d. unm. 7 April 1847 and was s. by his brother,
Henry Montagu, **6th Baron** and 8th Bt., b. 2 Feb. 1798, Ensign 3rd Regt. Foot Guards Scots Guards 1814. Lt. Col. cmdg. Regt. 1854, Major Gen. 1854, Lt. Gen. 1861, Gen. 1869, ret. 1877; served at Quatre Bras and Waterloo and in the Crimea where he cmd. the Guards Brigade and 1st Div. 1855. cr. K.C.B. 1856, G.C.B. 1875. He m. 18 Dec. 1826, Magdalen, dau. of Lt. Col. Thomas Hurley and widow of T. Croft. She d. 7 Dec. 1868. He d. 25 May 1883. They had issue,
1. Edmund (1835-52).
1. Mary m. 1855 14th Marquess of Winchester.
2. Harriet, m. 1855 L. S. W. Dawson-Damer.
3. Magdalen, m. 1856 Very. Rev. and Hon. Gerald Wellesley, Dean of Windsor.
4. Elizabeth.
ARMS—Quarterly 1 and 4, Argent three lozenges conjoined in fess gules, within a bordure sable and for difference a mullet on a mullet (Montagu); 2 and 3, Or an eagle displayed vert (Monthermer).
CREST—A griffin's head couped or beaked and wings elevated sable a mullet for difference.
SUPPORTERS—On either side a roebuck ppr. ducally gorged and chained or, the dexter charged on the shoulder with a mullet argent, the sinister charged on the shoulder with a quatrefoil gules.
MOTTO—Solo Deo Salus.
The seats were Hazlewood, King's Langley, Herts; Denton Hall, nr. Newcastle-on-Tyne and Eryholme co. York. Town House—Montagu House, 22 Portman Square. Club—United Service.
4th Baron Rokeby by Roy. Lic. 21 Dec. 1776 allowed to quarter Monthermer with Montagu —Montagu orig. Ladde (C.P. vol. ix) invented a descent from Montagu Earls of Salisbury and adopted arms (with a border for difference) but even appropriated their quartering of Morthermer.

ROMER

PEERAGE—U.K. Life. Baron Romer of New Romney, co. Kent.
SURNAME—Romer.
CR.—5 Jan. 1938. **EXT.**—19 Aug. 1944.
HISTORY—The composer Frank Romer by his wife Mary Lydia Cudworth had issue, a second son,
Rt. Hon. Sir Robert Romer, P.C., Kt. Bach. 1890, G.C.B. 1901, F.R.S., a Lord Justice of Appeal, 1899-1906, was b. 28 Dec. 1840; educ. private schools and Trin. Hall, Camb., Scholar, M.A., Senior Wrangler, Maths Tripos, 1863, and Smith's Prizeman; Prof. of Mathematics, Queen's Coll. Cork,

1865-66; Fell. Trin. Hall, 1867; Barrister-at-Law, Lincoln's Inn, 1867; Q.C. 1881; Bencher; P.C. 1899; a Judge of the High Court of Justice, Chancery Div. 1890-99. He m. 1864, Betty (d. 1916) dau. of Mark Lemon, (the first Editor of *Punch* 1841-70, b. 1809, d. 1870), and d. 19 Mar. 1918, having had issue,

Sir Mark Lemon Romer, **Baron Romer,** b. 9 Aug. 1866; educ. Rugby and Trin. Hall, Camb.; Barrister-at-Law, Lincoln's Inn, 1890; K.C. 1906; Bencher, 1910; a Judge of High Court of Justice, Chancery Div. 1922; and cr. Kt. Bach.; a Lord Justice of Appeal, 1929; made P.C., 1929; a Lord of Appeal in Ordinary, 1938, and a life peer as Baron Romer, of New Romney, co. Kent, 5 Jan. 1938; m. 12 July 1893, Hon. Anne Wilmot Ritchie, dau. of 1st Baron Ritchie, of Dundee and d. 19 Aug. 1944, having by her (who d. 3 Mar. 1948) had issue,

1. Mark Lemon Ritchie, b. 1894; served in World War I, Capt. K.R.R.C. and d. 1916, of wounds received in action.
2. Charles Robert, Rt. Hon. Sir, P.C., b. 19 Jan. 1897; educ. Rugby; Barrister-at-Law, Lincoln's Inn, 1921; K.C. 1937; Bencher, 1943; served in World War I, 1914-18, Capt. K.R.R.C., (wounded, despatches, twice, and O.B.E. Mil. 1919); apptd. Judge of High Court of Justice, Chancery Div., 1944, and a Lord Justice of Appeal, 1951-60; m. (1) 8 July 1919, Lorna, dau. of Brig. K. J. Buchanan, and had issue,
   (1) Veronica Ritchie, m. 1944, J. H Whitaker.
   He m. (2) 31 July 1925, Frances Evelyn Lebeau, dau. of Alfred Kemp, of The Cottage, Epping, and had further issue,
   (1) Mark Lemon Robert, b. 12 July 1927; m. 1953, Philippa Maynard, dau. of M. Tomson, of Hitchin, co. Hertford and had issue.
   (2) Ian Lebeau Ritchie, b. 26 Dec. 1929; m. 1952, Elizabeth dau. of J. Dales, and had issue.

ROOKWOOD

PEERAGE—U.K. Baron Rookwood, of Rookwood Hall, co. Essex. (Also a Baronetcy (of G.B.) cr. 12 May 1748.)
SURNAME—Selwyn-Ibbetson.
CR.—18 June 1892. EXT.—15 Jan. 1902.
HISTORY—Henry Ibbetson, of Reed Hall, co. York, had a ygr. son,

Sir Henry Ibbetson, Bt., who raised a corps of 100 men at his own expense during the 1745 rebellion, and, in consideration thereof, was cr. a Baronet, 12 May 1748. High Sheriff, co. York, 1748. He m. 1741, Isabella, dau. of Ralph Carr, of Cocken, and had issue with six daus.,

1. James, Sir, 2nd Bt.
2. Henry, m. Grace Norton, and had issue two daus.
3. Carr, Capt. of Dragoons, m. Miss Fletcher, niece of Sir Hugh Palliser, Bt.
4. Denzill, k. on 2 Feb. 1776, in a shooting party by the accidental discharge of his gun.

Sir Henry Ibbetson d. 1761, and was s. by his eldest son,

Sir James Ibbetson, 2nd Bt., m. 1768, Jane, dau. of John Caygill, of Shaw, co. York, (by his wife Jane, sister of Charles Selwyn, of Down Hall, co. Essex) and d. 4 Sept. 1795, having had with other issue,

1. Henry Carr, 3rd Bt. (see below).
2. Charles, 4th Bt. (see below).
3. James, k. by a fall from his horse, 1801.
4. John Thomas, 6th Bt. (see below).

The eldest son,

Sir Henry Carr Ibbetson, 3rd Bt., High Sheriff, co. York, 1803; m. 14 Nov. 1803, Alicia Mary, dau. of William Fenton Scott, of Woodhall. She d. 1858. He d.s.p. 5 June 1825. He was s. by his brother,

Sir Charles Ibbetson, 4th Bt., b. 26 Sept. 1779; resumed in 1825 his surname of Ibbetson, which he had relinquished for that of Selwyn by Royal Sign Manual 1817, when he had s. to the estates of his maternal great uncle Thomas Selwyn, of Down Hall, co. Essex. He m. 4 Feb. 1812, Charlotte Elizabeth, dau. of Thomas Stoughton, of Ballyhorgan, co. Kerry, and had issue,

1. Charles Henry, 5th Bt. (see below).
2. Frederick James, Lt. Queen's Bays, b. 1822; d. unm. 1853.
1. Laura, of Denton Park, Otley, co. York, m. 1845 Marmaduke Wyvill, of Constable Burton, co. York.

Sir Charles d. 9 April 1839, and was s. by his elder son,

Sir Charles Henry Ibbetson, 5th Bt., b. 24 July 1814; m. 28 Dec. 1847, Eden, dau. of J. T. Thackrah, and widow of Perceval Perkins, of Usworth Place, Devon. (She m. 3rdly 1867, Sir Henry John Selwyn-Ibbetson, 7th Bt. and Baron Rookwood, see below), and d.s.p. 6 July 1861, when he was s. by his uncle,

Sir John Thomas Selwyn, 6th Bt., b. 1789; he acquired the Selwyn estates when his brother Charles (see above) had inherited the baronetcy in 1825, and in consequence he assumed the surname of Selwyn in lieu of that of Ibbetson. He m. 1825 Isabella, dau. of Gen. John Leveson Gower, of Bill Hill, co. Berks. She d. 1858. He d. 20 Mar. 1869, leaving issue, with two daus., an only son and successor,

Sir Henry John Selwyn-Ibbetson, 7th Bt., and **Baron Rookwood,** b. 26 Sept. 1826; resumed the surname of Ibbetson, in conjunction with that of Selwyn. He was M.A. Camb., M.P. for South Essex, 1865-68 and for N.W. Essex, 1868-92, Under Sec. of State for the Home Department, 1874-78; and Financial Sec. to the Treasury, 1878-80; was cr. Baron Rookwood, of Rookwood Hall, co. Essex, 18 June 1892; m. (1) 8 Jan. 1850, Hon. Sarah Elizabeth Copley, dau. and coheir of Lord Lyndhurst, who d.s.p. 25 June 1865; he m. (2), 9 July 1867, Eden, dau. of George Thackrah, widow of his cousin, Sir Charles Ibbetson, 5th Bt. (see above), and she d.s.p. 1 April 1899. He m. (3) 5 Sept. 1900, Sophia Harriet, dau. of Major Digby Lawrell, and d.s.p. 15 Jan. 1902.
ARMS—Quarterly 1 and 4, Gules on a bend cottised argent, between two toisons d'or, three escallops of the field (Ibbotson); 2 and 3, Argent on a bend cottised sable, three annulets or (Selwyn).
CREST—A unicorn's head argent, powdered with escallops, horned, maned and erased gules (Ibbotson); Two lions' gambs ermine erased argent, supporting a torch in pale or, fired ppr. (Selwyn).

SUPPORTERS—Two rooks, wings addorsed sable, suspended from a chain round the neck of each a toison d'or.
MOTTO—Vixi liber et moriar.
Lord Rookwood's seat was Down Hall, Essex. His London residence was 62, Prince's Gate, S.W., and his clubs the Carlton and Travellers.

ROSMEAD

PEERAGE—U.K. Baron Rosmead, of Rosmead in co. of Westmeath and of Tafekberg, in S. Africa. (Also a baronetcy cr. 6 Feb. 1891.)
SURNAME—Robinson.
CR.—11 Aug. 1898. **EXT.**—26 May 1933.
HISTORY—Christopher Robinson, M.D., bur. at St. Audoen's, Dublin, 17 Jan. 1688-89, son of Bryan Robinson had issue by his wife, Mary, with a dau. Mary bur. 6 Mar. 1682-83, a son,
Bryan Robinson, M.B. Trin. Coll. Dublin, 1709, M.D. 1711, anatomy lecturer and Regius prof. of physic, 1745-54, d. Jan. 1754, having had issue,
1. Christopher (see below).
2. Robert, M.D., m. Elizabeth, only child of Thomas Lyster, of Lysterfield, co. Roscommon, and left issue, an only child, Elizabeth Robinson Lyster, (d. 1844) who m. 1785, Frederick Trench, of Woodlawn, co. Galway, cr. Baron Ashtown, 1800.
3. Bryan, B.A. Trin. Coll. Dublin 1737.
The eldest son,
Christopher Robinson, b. 1716; Barrister-at-Law, King's Inns, 1737, K.C. 1744; a Justice of the King's Bench 1758; m. May 1758, Elizabeth, dau. of Rev. Harstonge Martin, of Kilkenny, and d. Jan. 1781, having had three sons, of whom the only surv. was,
The Rev. Christopher Robinson, B.A. Trin. Coll. Dublin, 1783; M.A. 1786; Rector of Ahern, Diocese of Cloyne, 1789-1806, and later of Granard; m. 1786, Elizabeth, dau. of Rt. Hon. Sir Hercules Langrishe, 1st Bt., and d. 1837, having had with other issue,
1. Hercules, his heir (see below).
2. Bryan, Sir, b. 1808; Barrister, 1831; Judge of the Supreme Court of Newfoundland, 1858-77, knighted 1877; m. 1834, Selina, dau. of Arthur Holdsworth Brooking, of Brixham, co. Devon, and d. 6 Dec. 1887, having had with other issue, a son, Bryan Christopher, b. 1848.
The 2nd, but elder surv. son,
Adm. Hercules Robinson, of Rosmead, co. Westmeath, High Sheriff, 1842; b. 16 Mar. 1789; m. 22 June 1822, Frances Elizabeth, only child of Henry Widman Wood, and d. 15 May 1864, having had issue,
1. Henry, Sir, K.C.B., local gov. inspector in Ireland 1848-76; asst. under-sec and clerk of council in Ireland, 1876-79; vice-pres. local gov. board of Ireland, 1879-91; b. 1823; m. 12 Jan. 1853, Hon. Eva Annesley, dau. of 10th Viscount Annesley and d. Mar. 1893, leaving issue.
2. Hercules George Robert, **Baron Rosmead** (see below).
3. Loftus Christopher Hawker, Capt. R.N., m. Sarah, dau. of James Robinson.

4. Widman, d. in infancy.
5. William Cleaver Francis, Sir, G.C.M.G., F.R.G.S., Pres. of Montserrat 1862, Gov. of Falkland Islands, 1866, Prince Edward's Island, 1870-73, Western Australia, 1874, Straits Settlements, 1877-80, Western Australia 1880-82, South Australia, 1882-89, and of Western Australia, 1889-95, b. 14 Jan. 1834; m. 7 April 1862, Olivia Edith Dean, dau. of Most Rev. Thomas Stewart Townsend, Bishop of Meath, and d. 2 May 1897, leaving issue.
6. Frederick Charles Bryan, Vice Adm. R.N., F.R.G.S., C. in C. East Indian Station, A.D.C. to Queen Victoria, b. 1836; m. (1) 1864, Williamina, dau. of William Bradley; and (2) 1889, Alice, dau. of Col. Blackburn Tew, and d. 1896, leaving issue. His widow m. 2ndly R. E. Welby, (Welby, Bt.).
1. Frances Elizabeth.
The second son,
The Rt. Hon. Sir Hercules George Robert Robinson, **1st Baron Rosmead**, b. 19 Dec. 1824; Lt. Royal Irish Fusiliers; 1854 Pres. of Montserrat; Lt. Gov. St. Kitts, 1855-59; Gov. of Hong Kong, 1859-65; of Ceylon, 1865-72; of N.S. Wales, 1872-79; New Zealand, 1879-80; Gov. of Cape Colony, and H.M. Commissioner for S. Africa, 1881-89; Gov. and C. in C. Cape of Good Hope and High Comm. for S. Africa, 1895-97. He was made P.C. 1883; cr. Kt. Bach. 1859; K.C.M.G. 1869, G.C.M.G. 1875; a baronet 6 Feb. 1891; and Baron Rosmead of Rosmead, co. Westmeath, 11 Aug. 1896. He m. 24 April, 1846, Hon. Nea Annesley, dau. of 10th Viscount Annesley and d. 28 Oct. 1897. She d. 13 Jan. 1904. They had issue,
1. Hercules Arthur Temple, 2nd Bt. and **2nd Baron Rosmead** (see below).
1. Eleanor Frances Alti Maria, m. (1) 9 June 1870 (m. diss. 1883) Col. E. B. St. John and had issue, (St. John, B.) and (2) Major George Stevenson, and d. 24 Nov. 1893, leaving issue.
2. Nora Augusta Maud, m. (1) 7 Aug. 1878, A. K. Finlay, who d.s.p. 1883. She m. (2) 1887 C. R. Durant, and had issue.
3. Nerida Leeta, m. 1887, Col. Charles Tyrwhitt Dawkins, and had issue.
The only son,
Sir Hercules Arthur Temple Robinson, 2nd Bt. and **2nd Baron Rosmead**, b. 6 Nov. 1866; Major and hon. Lt. Col. 5th Bn. Royal Fusiliers, formerly Lt. Royal Irish Fusiliers, served in S. Africa in 1888, and in 1900 (despatches); m. 10 Oct. 1891, Hon. Edith Louisa Handcock, dau. of 4th Lord Castlemaine, and d. 26 May 1933. She d. Jan. 1936. They had issue,
1. Hercules Edward Joseph, 2nd Lt. 8th Bn. the Buffs, East Kent Regt., b. 1 Sept. 1895; d. 26 Sept. 1915, of wounds received in action.
1. Edith Norah Florence, b. 16 Oct. 1893.
2. Nea Kathleen Elizabeth Clare, b. 27 Nov. 1898; m. 6 June 1929, A. F. Garton-Ovenden, (m. diss. by div. 1931). By deed poll 1939 she resumed surname of Robinson.
ARMS—Vert a chevron engrailed between three stags at gaze or each charged with a fleur-de-lis azure.

CREST—Out of a crown vallery or, a mount vert thereon a stag as in the arms.
SUPPORTERS—Dexter, An ostrich; Sinister, A kangaroo, both reguardant ppr.
MOTTO—Legi regi fides.

ROSS

PEERAGE—U.K. Baron Ross of Hawkhead, co. Renfrew.
SURNAME—Boyle.
CR.—11 Aug. 1815. EXT.—23 April 1890.
HISTORY—George Boyle, 4th Earl of Glasgow, a Representative peer for Scotland, 1790-1815, was b. 1765. He was cr. a peer of the United Kingdom, as **Baron Ross** of Hawkhead, co. Renfrew, 11 Aug. 1815. At his death in 1843, he was s. by his ygr. but surv. son,
James Boyle, as 5th Earl of Glasgow, and **2nd Baron Ross.** He assumed by Royal Licence, in 1822, the additional surname of Carr, and on his death in 1869, was s. by his half brother,
George Frederick Boyle, 6th Earl of Glasgow, and **3rd Baron Ross,** who d. 23 April 1890, without male issue, when the Barony of Ross became extinct, and he was s. in his Scottish titles, by his kinsman,
David Boyle, 7th Earl of Glasgow, from whom descend the present line. (For ancestry and full details, see extant peerage works, Glasgow, E.)
ARMS—as under Earl of Glasgow.

**ROSSIE

PEERAGE—U.K. Baron Rossie of Rossie, co. Perth.
SURNAME—Kinnaird.
CR.—20 June 1831. EXT.—7 Jan. 1878.
HISTORY—George William Fox Kinnaird, 9th Baron Kinnaird of Inchture in the peerage of Scotland, who was b. 14 April 1807; educ. Eton; became Grand Master of Free Masons of Scotland, 1830-32; was cr. 23 June 1831, **Baron Rossie,** of Rossie, co. Perth in the U.K. peerage; was Master of the ·Buckhounds, 1839-41; made P.C. 1840; cr. K.T. 1857; m. 14 Dec. 1837, the Hon. Frances Anna Georgiana, dau. of William Frances Spencer Ponsonby, 1st Baron De Mauley of Canford. She d. 20 Mar. 1910. He d.s.p.m.s. 7 Jan. 1878. His two sons both d. young. His only dau. Olive Barbara, m. Howard R. A. Ogilvy, later 10th Bt.
Since the 9th Baron Kinnaird, and only Baron Rossie, had no surv. son, his barony of Rossie became extinct, but he had been cr. 1 Sept. 1860, Baron Kinnaird of Rossie, co. Perth in the U.K. peerage with a special remainder to his brother, Arthur FitzGerald Kinnaird, who accordingly s. him as 10th Baron Kinnaird in the Scottish peerage, and as 2nd Baron Kinnaird of Rossie, in the

U.K. peerage, for whom and his descendants see extant peerage works, under Kinnaird, B.

ROTHERHAM

PEERAGE—U.K. Baron Rotherham, of Broughton, co. Lancaster.
SURNAME—Holland.
CR.—18 July 1910. EXT.—24 Jan. 1950. Also a baronetcy cr. 18 July 1907.
HISTORY—William Holland, of Higher Broughton, Manchester, J.P., m. Ellen, dau. of Samuel Robinson, of Manchester, and d. 1892, having a second son,
Sir William Henry Holland, 1st Bt., and **1st Baron Rotherham,** b. 15 Dec. 1849; a partner in W. Holland and Sons; was Liberal M.P. for North Salford, 1892-95, and for Rotherham, 1899-1910; Pres. of the Manchester Chamber of Commerce, 1896-98; cr. Kt. Bach., 1902, a baronet. 18 July 1907, and Baron Rotherham, of Broughton, co. Lancaster, 18 July 1910. He m. 30 Sept. 1874, Mary, dau. of James Lund, of Malsis Hall, co. York, and d. 26 Dec. 1927. · She d. 15 Aug. 1931. They had issue,
  1. Stuart Lund, 2nd Bt. and **2nd Baron** (see below).
  1. Eirene, b. 19 Oct. 1875; m. 21 Sept. 1895, Harry Sowler, of Chorlton Hall, Malpas, co. Chester, and had issue.
  2. Margaret, m. (1) 25 April 1899, Lt. Col. H. K. Harley, D.S.O., and had issue. He d. 9 Jan. 1920. She m. (2) 9 Aug. 1910, William Murray Leslie, M.D., F.R.C.S., Barrister-at-Law, of Grayswood House, near Haslemere, co. Surrey, and had issue.
The only son,
Sir Stuart Lund Holland, 2nd Bt. and **2nd Baron Rotherham,** b. 25 Oct. 1876; educ. Harrow and Exeter Coll. Oxford; 6th Inniskilling Dragoons, 1900; served in the S. African War, 1901-02; Capt. 1906; Res. of Officers, 1911; served in World War I, 1914-19 with his Regt. and from 1 Nov. 1917, as Asst. Provost Marshal (despatches); was Asst. Admin. Min. of Munitions, 1920-21, and Inspector Min. of Pensions, 1922. He m. 25 Oct. 1909, Miriam Agnes, dau. of Henry William Wright, and d. 24 Jan. 1950. Lady Rotherham d. 1971 (Obituary, D.T. 2/12/71).
ARMS—Azure three fleur-de-lis in pale or between two lions rampant double queued argent.
CREST—A demi lion rampant double queued argent supporting a pennon of the arms erect.
SUPPORTERS—On either side a winged stag argent and unguled or, wings expanded azure each charged with a fleur-de-lis gold.
MOTTO—Da robur fer auxilium.

ROUNDWAY

PEERAGE—U.K. Baron Roundway, of Devizes, co. Wilts.
SURNAME—Colston.
CR.—30 June 1916. EXT.—29 Mar. 1944.

HISTORY—The famous Bristol philanthropist Edward Colston (1636-1721) in his will referred to "my cousin Mary now the wife of Thomas Edwards the younger" and five lines later to "my said niece Mary Edwards" with several other mentions of the latter, the cousin and niece being evidently the same person. Mary Edwards was a principal beneficiary of Edward Colston's will. So were her daughters, Mary (left £8000 under the will) and Sophia (£5000) The details above are taken from *Edward Colston: A Chronological Account of his Life and Work* by H. J. Wilkins, D.D., 1920. The ygr. dau. of Mary Edwards,

Sophia Edwards, of Filkin's Hall, m. Alexander Ready, of the Inner Temple, in 1734; he assumed the surname of Colston, and they had issue, a son and heir,

The Rev. Alexander Colston, of Filkin's Hall, educ. Trin. Coll. Oxford, 1759-63, B.A., Rector of Broadwell and Henbury, co. Gloucester. He m. (1) Louisa Minshull, dau. of Paul George Elers, of Black Burton, co. Wilts, and had issue, with three other sons and three daus.,

Edward Francis, his heir (see below).

He m. (2) Susannah, dau. of the Rev. Hook, of Gloucester, but she d.s.p. The eldest son,

Edward Francis Colston, of Filkin's Hall, b. 1769; m. (1) 1792, Arabella, dau. of Michael Clayfield, of Bristol. She d. 24 Feb. 1812. He m. (2) 18 Oct. 1814, Harriet, dau. of Robert Davies, of Farthingville, co. Cork. By his first wife he had two sons and four daus. of whom the elder son,

Edward Francis Colston, of Filkin's Hall, and of Roundway Park, co. Wilts, b. 15 April 1795; m. 1 Nov. 1819, Marianne, only dau. and heir of William Jenkins, of Shepton Mallet, co. Somerset, and d. 9 April 1847, having by her (who d. 2 Oct. 1865) had issue,

1. Edward, his heir (see below).
2. William Jenkins Craig, M.A. St. John's Coll. Oxford, b. 1824; d. unm. 1854.
3. Samuel Hunt, b. 23 Oct. 1825; d. unm. 22 Sept. 1854.
1. Arabella Sarah, m. 16 May 1855, Christopher Darby Griffith, of Padworth Park, co. Berks, and d. 13 Mar. 1891, leaving issue.

The eldest son,

Edward Colston, of Roundway Park, an officer in 1st Life Guards, 15th Hussars, and Royal Gloucestershire Hussars, b. 1 Oct. 1822; m. 20 June 1848, Louisa Ruperta, dau. of Rev. Edward Murray, (Atholl, D.), and d. 20 Dec. 1864, having had by her (who d. 20 Nov. 1900),

1. Edward Gloucester Murray, b. 15 April 1849; d. 26 Feb. 1859.
2. Charles Edward Hungerford Atholl, **1st Baron Roundway** (see below).
1. Amy Ruperta, m. 20 June 1872, Sir Christopher William Baynes, 4th Bt., and had issue.
2. Lilian Ann.

The second son,

Charles Edward Hungerford Atholl Colston, **1st Baron Roundway**, b. 16 May 1854; educ. Eton and Ch. Ch. Oxford, B.A. 1874; High Sheriff co. Wilts, 1885; Conservative M.P. for South Gloucestershire, 1892-1906; Chm. of Wiltshire Quarter Sessions; was cr. Baron Roundway, of Devizes co. Wilts, 30 June 1916; m. 13 Feb. 1879, Rosalind Emma, dau.

of Col. Charles Edward Gostling Murray, of Whitton Park, co. Middlesex, and d. 17 June 1925. She d. 8 Nov. 1938. They had issue an only son,

Edward Murray Colston, **2nd Baron Roundway**, b. 31 Dec. 1880; educ. Eton Grenadier Guards, 1900; served in S. African War, 1901-02, (wounded) Capt. 1908; served in World War I, 1914-19, (wounded, despatches five times), Major 1915; G.S.O.2 1915-16; Cmdt. of Imperial Sch. of Instruction in Egypt, 1915-17; Brev. Lt. Col. 1917; temp. Brig. Gen. cmdg. 233rd Infantry Brig. 1917-19, Lt. Col. 1920, and Col. 1924. Ret. with the rank of Brig. Gen. 1932; cr. M.V.O. 1908; D.S.O. 1916; and C.M.G. 1918; m. 28 April 1904, Blanche Gladys, only dau. of George Duddell, of Queen's Park, Brighton, and Hong Kong, and d. 29 Mar. 1944, having had issue,

Lydia Betty Mary, b. 13 May 1910.

ARMS—Argent two dolphins hauriant respectant and ingulphant of the flukes of an anchor reversed, all ppr., on a chief azure three mullets of the field.

CREST—A billet barry wavy of four argent and azure thereon a dolphin naiant ppr.

SUPPORTERS—Dexter, A dark brown horse; Sinister, A harrier hound, each charged on the shoulder with a sickle argent.

MOTTO—Go and do likewise.

Seat was Roundway Park, Devizes, co. Wilts.

ROWLEY

PEERAGE—U.K. Life. Baron Rowley, of Rowley Regis, co. Stafford.

SURNAME—Henderson.

CR.—27 May 1966. EXT.—28 Aug. 1968.

HISTORY—The Rt. Hon. Arthur Henderson, P.C., prominent Labour Party member and politician, had two sons, the elder being Baron Henderson and the younger,

Arthur Henderson, **Baron Rowley**, b. 27 Aug. 1893; educ. Central Sch. Darlington, Queen's Coll. Taunton, and Trin. Hall, Camb.; M.A. LL.B., served in World War I, 1914-18, and in II as Major 1941; Barrister-at-Law, Middle Temple 1921, K.C. 1939, formerly standing counsel to Labour Party, author of *Trade Unions and the Law*, and jt. author of *Industrial Law and Housing Law*. He was M.P. South Div. of Cardiff 1923-24, and 1929-31, Kingswinford Div. of Staffs 1935-50, Rowley Regis and Tipton 1950-66, was Sec. of State for Air 1947-51 and served on many cttees; m. 27 Aug. 1958, Mary Elizabeth, dau. of E. V. Barnes, of Stratford-on-Avon, and widow of Harold Gliksten. He was made P.C. 1947 and cr. a life peer as Baron Rowley of Rowley Regis, co. Stafford and d. 28 Aug. 1968.

Lord Rowley's residence was 710, Hood House, Dolphin Square, London, S.W.1.

ROWTON

PEERAGE—U.K. Baron Rowton, of Rowton Castle, co. Salop.

SURNAME—Lowry-Corry.

CR.—6 May 1880. EXT.—9 Nov. 1903.

HISTORY—The Rt. Hon. Henry Thomas Lowry-Corry, second son of the 2nd Earl of

Belmore, (see extant peerages), had issue, a second son,

Sir Montagu William Lowry-Corry, P.C., K.C.V.O., C.B., D.L. Salop, B.A. Camb.; Barrister-at-Law; Priv. Sec. to the Earl of Beaconsfield, 1866-68, and 1874-80; b. 8 Oct. 1838; cr. a peer as Baron Rowton, of Rowton Castle, co. Salop, 6 May 1880; d. unm. 9 Nov. 1903.

ARMS—Quarterly 1 and 4, Gules a saltire argent, in chief a rose or. (Corry); 2 and 3, Sable a cup argent, with a garland between two laurel branches, all issuing out of the same, vert (Lowry).

CRESTS—1. A cock ppr. charged with a crescent gules, (Corry). 2. A garland between two laurel branches vert (Lowry).

SUPPORTERS—On either side a stag ppr. semée of mullets argent gorged with a collar and line reflexed over the back or.

MOTTO—Loyal au mort.

ROYDEN

PEERAGE—U.K. Baron Royden, of Frankby, in the co. Palatine of Chester.

SURNAME—Royden.

CR.—28 Jan. 1944. EXT.—6 Nov. 1950.

HISTORY—Sir Thomas Royden, 2nd Bt., son of Sir Thomas Bland Royden, 1st Bt., (see extant peerages, Royden, Bt.) was b. 22 May 1871; educ. Winchester and Magdalen Coll. Oxford, M.A.; High Sheriff co. Hampshire, 1917; M.P. Bootle, 1918-22; Dir. of Cunard Steamship Co., Cunard White Star and other cos.; was cr. **Baron Royden,** of Frankby in the co. Palatine of Chester, 28 Jan. 1944; was C. St. J., and cr. C.H. 1919; m. 20 April 1922, Quenelda Mary, dau. of Harry Clegg, (Forres, B.), and widow of Charles J. Williamson, and d.s.p. 6 Nov. 1950, when the barony became extinct but the baronetcy passed to his brother, Sir Ernest Bland Royden, 3rd Bt.

ARMS—Vert three stag's heads erased in pale between two bugle horns stringed in fess all or.

CREST—A stag's head erased or, collared gemel and holding in the mouth a riband vert, suspended therefrom an escutcheon of the arms of Royden.

SUPPORTERS—On either side a stag per fess or and vert gorged with a collar gemel of the last.

MOTTO—Au Roy donne devoir.

Lord Royden's seats were Brockwood Park, Alresford, Hampshire, and Tillypronte, Tarland, co. Aberdeen.

RUFFSIDE

PEERAGE—U.K. Viscount Ruffside, of Hexham, co. Northumberland.

SURNAME—Brown.

CR.—14 Dec. 1951. EXT.—5 May 1958.

HISTORY—James Clifton Brown, of Holmbush, co. Sussex (Brown Bt. in extant peerages), had a 4th son,

Douglas Clifton Brown, **Viscount Ruffside,** b. 16 Aug. 1879; educ. Eton and Trin. Coll. Camb., B.A. 1901, M.A. 1905; M.P. Hexham Div. of Northumberland, 1918-23, and 1924-51; Dep. Chm. of Ways and Means Cttee. 1938-43,

Chm. 1943-51; Dep. Speaker of House of Commons, 1938-43, and Speaker 1943-51; Hon. Doctor Caen Univ. 1948, Liveryman of the Vintners' Co. and Freeman of City of London, Grand Cross of Legion of Honour, D.L. and J.P. co. Durham; made P.C. 1941, and cr. Viscount Ruffside, of Hexham, co. Northumberland, 14 Dec. 1951. He m. 24 June 1907, Violet Cicely Kathleen, only dau. of Frederick Eustace Arbuthnott Wollaston, of Shenton Hall, co. Leicester (B.L.G. 1952), and d. 5 May 1958, leaving issue,

Audrey Pellew Clifton, b. 19 May 1908; m. 22 Dec. 1931, H. B. H. Hylton-Foster, Q.C.

ARMS—Gules a chevron, between two bears' paws erased in chief and four hands conjoined in saltire in base; a chief engrailed of the last, thereon an eagle displayed sable.

CREST—A bear's paw as in the arms issuant out of a wreath of oak vert, holding a sinister hand ppr.

MOTTO—Est concordia fratrum.

Residence was Ruffside Hall, Shotley Bridge, co. Durham.

RUNCORN

PEERAGE—U.K. Life. Baron Runcorn of Heswall, co. Palatine of Chester.

SURNAME—Vosper.

CR.—20 April 1964. EXT.—20 Jan. 1968.

HISTORY—Thomas Vosper of Mossley Hall, Liverpool and Rhaggat Hall, Carrog, nr. Corwen, Wales, who according to his own account came from a family formerly living in Cornwall and Devon, was in business in Liverpool. He was b. 23 Dec. 1843; m. 1872 Christina, dau. of H. Fernie of Toxteth Park, Liverpool. He d. Dec. 1904. She d. 1920. They had, with an elder son, Harold Fernie (d.s.p. 1932) and a dau. Mabel Fernie, d. unm. 1944, the following,

1. Gerald Linn (see below).
2. Frank Symonds, b. 1877; educ. Marlborough; m. Ellen Dobell and d.s.p. 1950.
3. Norman, M.C., J.P., b. 28 Mar. 1880; educ. Marlborough; m. 1911 Jessie dau. of Hugh Brown, of Mossley Hill, Liverpool, and d. June 1948 having had issue with two daus., a son Norman Lyn, b. 9 Sept. 1915; educ. Marlborough; m. 24 April 1951, Amice Hubbach, dau. of Dr. J. H. Anderson.

The eldest surv. son,

Gerald Linn Vosper, partner in Wilson, Vosper and Coltart, Ships Stores and Export Merchants, Liverpool, b. 25 Feb. 1875; educ. Marlborough; m. 18 June 1902, Margery (d. 1961) dau. of Sir William Forwood and d. 2 Oct. 1956 leaving issue,

Dennis Forwood Vosper, **Baron Runcorn** b. 2 Jan. 1916; educ. The Leys, Hoylake, co. Chester, Marlborough and Pembroke Coll. Oxford, B.A. 1937; served in World War II with Cheshire Regt. 1939-46; partner in Wilson, Vosper and Coltart; M.P. Runcorn Div. of Cheshire 1950-64, Conservative Whip 1950-54, Lord Commr. of the Treasury 1951-54, Min. of Health, 1957; Min. of State, Home Office, 1960-61, Chm. Nat. Assistance Board 1964. He m. (1) 26 July 1940 (m. diss. by div. 1966), Margaret Eva, dau. of S. G. Ashford (2)

16 Dec. 1966, Helen Norah, dau. of Sir (Joseph) Crosland Graham. He was awarded T.D. 1950, made P.C. 1957, and cr. a life peer as Baron Runcorn of Heswall, co. Palatine of Chester and d. 20 Jan. 1968.
ARMS—Per chevron azure and gules on a chevron between in chief two garbs and in base a portcullis chained or, a cross moline sable.
CREST—Out of a tower triple towered or a stag's head ppr. attired of the first, in the mouth a hatchet, the haft gold, the blade ppr.
SUPPORTERS—On either side a beaver ppr. each gorged with a collar or, attached thereto a line reflexed over the back gules.
MOTTO—Diligence and service.
Lord Runcorn's residence was Plaish Hall, nr. Church Stretton, Salop.

RUSHCLIFFE

PEERAGE—U.K. Baron Rushcliffe, of Blackfordby, co. Leicester.
SURNAME—Betterton.
CR.—24 Jan. 1935. **EXT.**—18 Nov. 1949.
HISTORY—Henry Inman Betterton, of Woodville, co. Leicester, b. 12 Sept. 1844; m. 1 June 1870, Agnes, dau. of Samuel Bucknall, and d. 11 Dec. 1895, leaving issue. with two other sons and two daus., an eldest son,
Sir Henry Bucknall Betterton, Bt. and **Baron Rushcliffe**, b. 15 Aug. 1872; educ. Rugby and Ch. Ch. Oxford, B.A. 1893; Barrister-at-Law, Inner Temple, 1896; Conservative M.P. for Rushcliffe Div. of Nottinghamshire, 1918-34; Parl. Sec. to Min. of Labour, 1923-24, and 1924-29; P.C. 1931; Min. of Labour, 1931-34; Chm. of Unemployment Assistance Board, 1934-41; mem. of Political Honours Scrutiny Cttee.; was cr. O.B.E., 1918, C.B.E. 1920, G.B.E., 1941; cr. a baronet 30 July 1929; and Baron Rushcliffe, of Blackfordby, co. Leicester, 24 Jan. 1935; m. (1) 19 Dec. 1912, Violet, (d. 5 Oct 1947) dau. of J. G. Gilliat, Gov. of Bank of England, and (2) 24 April 1948, Inez Alfreda, formerly wife or Sir Harold Snagge and dau. of Alfred Lubbock, (Avebury, B.). He d. 18 Nov. 1949, having had issue by his first wife,
1. Averil Diana, b. 26 April 1914; m. (1) 9 Feb. 1939, Major R. Wyndham-Quin Going, who was k. in action June 1944, by whom she had issue. She m. (2) 28 June 1946, Brig. C. W. P. Richardson and had further issue.
2. Claudia Violet, b. 11 Oct. 1917; m. 28 April 1937, Lt. Col. F. H. Allhusen (B.L.G. 1952) and had issue.
ARMS—Argent three pheons sable on a chief gules a portcullis chained or between two cinquefoils ermine.
CREST—A pheon sable between two stags' attires or.
MOTTO—Constantia et labore.
Lord Rushcliffe's seat was The Gables, Hatchington Hill, Seaford, Sussex.

RUSSELL OF KILLOWEN

PEERAGE—U.K. Life Baron Russell of Killowen.
SURNAME—Russell.
CR.—7 May 1894. **EXT.**—10 Aug. 1900.

HISTORY—Arthur Russell of Scafield House, Killowen, co. Down had issue,
Sir Charles Russell, **Baron Russell** of Killowen, b. 10 Nov. 1832; educ. Castleknock Coll. and Trin. Coll. Dublin, Barrister-at-Law, Lincoln's Inn, 1859, Q.C., and Bencher 1872; Treasurer 1893; M.P. Dundalk 1880-85 and S. Div. Hackney 1885-94; Attorney Gen. Feb.-July 1886, and 1892-94; apptd. Lord of Appeal in Ordinary and cr. a Life peer as Baron Russell of Killowen and Lord Chief Justice of England July 1894; cr. K.B. 1886 and G.C.M.G. 1893; m. 1858, Ellen, dau. of J. S. Mulholland, M.D. of Belfast and d. 10 Aug. 1900 having had, with other issue, a fourth son,
Frank Russell, cr. Lord Russell of Killowen, a life peer of the second creation (see next article).
For earlier and complete lineage see Russell of Littleworth Corner, Bt. in extant peerages.
ARMS—Argent a lion rampant gules on a chief sable three escallops of the field, the whole within a bordure engrailed vert.
CREST—A goat passant argent armed or charged on the body with three trefoils slipped fesswise vert.
SUPPORTERS—Dexter, A goat or semée of trefoils slipped vert and gorged with a collar gemel gules; Sinister, A lion reguardant or, semée of escallops gules and gorged with a like collar.
MOTTO—Che sara sara.
Lord Russell's seat was Tadworth Court, Epsom, Surrey.

RUSSELL OF KILLOWEN

PEERAGE—U.K. Life Baron Russell of Killowen.
SURNAME—Russell.
CR.—18 Nov. 1929. **EXT.**—20 Dec. 1946.
HISTORY—Lord Russell of Killowen, whose life peerage was cr. 1894 and extinct 1900, (see preceding article), had a fourth son,
Frank Russell, **Lord Russell** of Killowen, of Killowen, co. Down, so cr. as a life peer 18 Nov. 1929, b. 2 July 1867; educ. Beamont Coll. (Old Windsor) and Oriel Coll. Oxford; Barrister-at-Law, Lincoln's Inn, 1893; K.C. 1908; Bencher 1913; apptd. a Judge of High Court of Justice, Chancery Div., 1919; Lord Justice of Appeal, in Ordinary 18 Nov. 1929; Treasurer, Lincoln's Inn, 1936. He m. 17 Feb. 1900, Mary Emily, dau. of Charles Thomson Ritchie, 1st Baron Ritchie of Dundee, and d. 20 Dec. 1946 having had issue, (see Russell of Littleworth Corner, Bt. in extant peerages).
ARMS—Argent a lion rampant gules on a chief sable three escallops of the field, the whole within a bordure engrailed vert.
CREST—A goat passant argent armed or, charged with three trefoils slipped fesswise vert.
MOTTO—Che sara sara.

RUTHERFORD OF NELSON

PEERAGE—U.K. Baron Rutherford of Nelson, of Cambridge, co. Cambridge.
SURNAME—Rutherford.
CR.—22 Jan. 1931. **EXT.**—19 Oct. 1937.

HISTORY—James Rutherford, a farmer of New Plymouth, Taranaki, New Zealand, who d. 1928 had by his wife, Martha Shuttleworth, (who d. 16 July 1935) twelve children, of whom, Sir Ernest Rutherford, **Baron Rutherford** of Nelson, was b. 30 Aug. 1871; educ. at Nelson Sch., Canterbury Coll. Christchurch, (Univ. of New Zealand, by means of scholarships from primary and secondary sch. at Nelson), M.A. 1893, B.Sc. 1894, and Trin. Coll. Camb., 1897, Research degree and Coutts-Trotter Studentship, M.A.; Macdonald Prof. of Physics at McGill Univ. Montreal, 1898-1907, where the bulk of his work was done on radio-activity, after research at Cambridge under J. J. Thomson; Langworthy Prof. and Dir. of Physical Laboratory in Manchester Univ., 1907-19; Cavendish Prof. of Experimental Physics at Cambridge and Fell. of Trin. Coll. 1919; Prof. of Natural Philosophy at Royal Inst., 1921; Pres. of British Association, 1923; F.R.S. and Pres. thereof 1925-30; Chm. of Advisory Council, Dept. of Scientific and Industrial Research, 1930. He was cr. Kt. Bach. 1914; O.M. 1925; and Baron Rutherford of Nelson of Cambridge, co. Cambridge, 22 Jan. 1931. He m. 28 June 1900, Mary Georgina, dau. of A. C. Newton, of Christ-church, N.Z., and d.s.p.m. 19 Oct. 1937, leaving issue,

    Eileen Mary, b. 1901; m. 6 Dec. 1921, Ralph Howard Fowler, and d. 23 Dec. 1930.

Lord Rutherford developed the nuclear theory of the atom ("splitting the atom") between 1906 and 1914, and it has been said of him that "unsurpassed in influence upon contem-poraries, he directly inspired many of the spectacular discoveries of the years after 1933." (D.N.B.). He received the Nobel Prize in 1908 for Chemistry.

ARMS—Per saltire arched gules and or two inescutcheons voided of the first in fess within each a martlet sable.

CREST—Upon a rock a kiwi ppr.

SUPPORTERS—Dexter, A figure representing Hermes Trismegistus; Sinister, A Maori holding in the exterior hand a club all ppr.

MOTTO—Primordia quaerere rerum.

(In the arms of the Atomic Energy Authority, the crest is made up of the sun signifying the benign power of the atom, and a shield on the sun which has for its charge a martlet, the latter being taken from the arms of Lord Rutherford.)

ST. AUDRIES

PEERAGE—U.K. Baron St. Audries, of St. Audries, co. Somerset.

SURNAME—Fuller-Acland-Hood.

CR.—22 June 1911. **EXT.**—16 Oct. 1971.

HISTORY—Sir Alexander Fuller-Acland-Hood, 4th Bt. (see that title in extant peerage works), **1st Baron St. Audries**, was b. 26 Sept. 1853; he s. his father as the 4th Bt. in the Baronetcy of Hood (which was cr. 13 April 1809) and his kinsman Sir Edward Dolman Scott, as 6th Bt. in the baronetcy of Bateman, of Hartington, co. Derby (cr. 15 Dec. 1806, with remainder in default of male issue, to the male issue of the daughter of the first baronet, Sir Hugh Bateman, in order of birth). Sir Alexander, thus being both 4th Bt. of the

Hood creation and 6th Bart. of the Bateman creation, was also cr. a peer as Baron St. Audries, of St. Audries, co. Somerset, 22 June 1911. He m. 26 July 1888, Hon. Mildred Rose Evelyn De Moleyns, dau. of 4th Baron Ventry. She d. 11 Oct. 1949. He d. 4 June 1917. They had issue,

1. Alexander Peregrine, **2nd Baron St. Audries** (see below).
2. Arthur John Palmer, b. 11 Feb. 1906; educ. Wellington and Trin. Coll. Camb., B.A. 1927, M.A. 1931; Barrister-at-Law, Gray's Inn, 1929; served in World War II, 1939-45, R.A. 1940; Capt. Intell. Corps, 1943; Major J.A.G.S. Dept., 1945-50, D.J.A. 1950-54; and Asst. J.A.G. 1954-61; m. 1 June 1939, Phyllis Lily Frances, dau. of D. B. I. Hallett, M.A., B.M.B. Ch., and d. 2 Nov. 1964, having had issue,
   (1) Elizabeth Periam, b. 2 Mar. 1940; educ. Cheltenham Ladies' Coll. and Girton Coll. Camb., M.A.
2. (2) Mary Mildred, b. 31 Oct. 1941; educ. Cheltenham Ladies' Coll.; m. 23 Sept. 1961, T. S. Hodder-Williams, who d. 9 Aug. 1969.
   (3) Sylvia, b. 30 Jan. 1944; educ. Chel-tenham Ladies' Coll.
1. Audrey Mildred, b. 30 April 1889.
2. Maud Isabel, b. 22 Nov. 1892.

The elder son,

Sir Alexander Peregrine Fuller-Acland-Hood, Bt., and **2nd Baron St. Audries**, b. 24 Dec. 1893; educ. Eton and Magdalen Coll. Oxford, M.A.; served in World War I Lt. Somerset L.I., 1914-17 and 2nd Lt. Gren. Guards, 1918-19; C.C. 1937-52; Somerset; C. St. J., and patron of three livings; he d. 16 Oct. 1971, when the barony of St. Audries became extinct. The heir to the baronetcies was his kinsman, Alexander William Fuller-Acland-Hood, who was b. 5 Mar. 1901, and who became a naturalized American citizen in 1926.

ARMS—Quarterly 1 and 4, Azure a fret argent, on a chief or three crescents sable (Hood); 2, Chequy argent and sable, a fess gules (Acland); 3, Argent three bars and a canton gules (Fuller).

CRESTS—1, A Cornish chough ppr. in front of an anchor in bend sinister or (Hood). 2. A sinister arm fesswise couped below the shoulder vested azure, the hand in a falconer's glove thereon a falcon argent, armed, legged and belled or (Acland). 3. Issuant from a ducal coronet gules a lion's head argent (Fuller).

SUPPORTERS—Two centaurs ppr.

MOTTO—Zealous.

Lord St. Audries's seat was Fairfield, Stog-ursey, Bridgwater, Somerset. His club was the Travellers.

ST. HELIER

PEERAGE—U.K. Baron St. Helier, of St. Helier, Jersey.

SURNAME—Jeune.

CR.—23 Feb. 1905. **EXT.**—9 April 1905.

HISTORY—The history of this Jersey family is given in B.L.G. 1952, (Symons-Jeune, formerly of Watlington Park). The Rt. Rev. Francis Jeune, Bishop of Peterborough, by his

wife Margaret Dyne, only child of Henry
Symons, of Axbridge, co. Somerset, had an
eldest son,
Sir Francis Henry Jeune, **Baron St. Helier**,
b. 17 Mar. 1843; educ. Harrow and Balliol
Coll. Oxford, B.A. 1865, M.A. 1874; Pres. of
Oxford Union, 1864; Barrister-at-Law, Inner
Temple, 1868; Fell. of Hertford Coll. 1874;
Q.C. 1888; Bencher, 1891; Judge of the Pro-
bate, Divorce and Admiralty Div. of High
Court, 1891; P.C. 1892; Pres. of the Probate,
Divorce and Admiralty Div. and Judge
Advocate Gen. 1892-1905; cr. Kt. Bach.
1891; K.C.B. 1897; G.C.B. 1902; and Baron
St. Helier, of St. Helier, Jersey, 23 Feb. 1905.
He m. 17 Aug. 1881, Susan Mary Elizabeth,
dau. of Keith William Stewart-Mackenzie, of
Seaforth, and widow of Col. the Hon. John
Constantine Stanley. He d.s.p.s. 9 April 1905,
having had issue,
Christian Francis Seaforth, Lt. Gren.
Guards, b. 10 Aug. 1882; d. unm. 19 Aug.
1904.
Lady St. Helier was cr. C.B.E. (1920) and
D.B.E. (1925), and d. 25 Jan. 1931.
ARMS (of Jeune)—Sable a stag trippant or
attired argent.
CREST—The attires of a stag argent.
MOTTO—Faire sans dire.

ST. MAUR

PEERAGE—U.K. Earl St. Maur, of Berry
Pomeroy, co. Devon.
SURNAME—Seymour.
CR.—19 June 1863. **EXT.**—28 Nov. 1885.
HISTORY—Edward Adolphus Seymour, 12th
Duke of Somerset, b. 20 Dec. 1804; m. 10
June 1830, Jane Georgiana, dau. of Thomas
Sheridan, and granddau. of Richard Brinsley
Sheridan, the playwright. She d. 14 Dec. 1884.
They had issue, with three daus. (see Somerset,
D. in extant peerages), two sons,
1. Edward Adolphus Ferdinand, styled
Earl St. Maur, who was b. 17 July 1835,
and summoned to the House of Lords in
his father's Barony of Seymour, 1863,
d.v.p. unm. 30 Sept. 1869.
2. Edward Percy, Attaché in turn to British
Embassies at Vienna, Madrid and Paris,
b. 19 Aug. 1841, and d.v.p. unm. 20
Dec. 1865.
The 12th Duke was cr. on 19 June 1863, a
peer of the U.K. as **Earl St. Maur** of Berry
Pomeroy, co. Devon, but on his death s.p.m.s.
on 28 Nov. 1885, the U.K. earldom became
extinct, and he was s. in the Dukedom and his
other honours by his brother,
Archibald Henry Algernon Seymour, 13th
Duke of Somerset (see extant peerages).

SANDERSON

PEERAGE—U.K. Baron Sanderson, of Armthorpe, co. York.
SURNAME—Sanderson.
CR.—20 Dec. 1905. **EXT.**—24 Mar. 1923.
HISTORY—Richard Sanderson, of Armthorpe, near Doncaster, a merchant and
banker of London, M.P. for Colchester,
1829-30, and 1832-47, b. 1784; m. 12 Feb.

1833, Hon. Charlotte Matilda Manners-Sutton,
dau. of 1st Viscount Canterbury. She d. 14 May
1898. He d. 29 Oct. 1857. They had issue,
1. Richard Manners, b. 11 Feb. 1835; m.
6 Sept. 1870, Matilda Anne Adelaide
Eliza, dau. of W. J. Walker, and d. 1885
leaving issue.
2. Thomas Henry, **Baron Sanderson** (see
below).
3. Percy, Sir, K.C.M.G., Consul Gen. for
States of New York, Delaware, New
Jersey, Rhode Island and Connecticut,
1894-1907 b. 7 July 1842.
4. Algernon Robert, Lt. 101st Bengal Inf.,
b. 18 Oct. 1844; k. in action in the
Umbeyla Pass, 1863.
5. Edward Manners, Rev., Hon. Canon of
Liverpool, M.A. Trin. Coll. Camb., b.
2 Oct. 1847; m. 23 June 1875, Eveline,
dau. of Rev. Canon George Venables,
and had issue.
1. Charlotte Louisa Gertrude.
2. Lucy Fanny Mary.
3. Matilda Amy Frances.
The second son,
Sir Thomas Henry Sanderson, **Baron
Sanderson**, b. 11 Jan. 1841; educ. Eton; a
Junior Clerk in Foreign Office, 1859; was a
Priv. Sec. to Under Sec. of State for Foreign
Affairs, 1866, and to the Sec. of State for
Foreign Affairs, 1866-69, 1874-78, and 1880-
85; promoted Senior Clerk, 1885; Asst. Under
Sec. for Foreign Affairs, 1889-94; P.U.S.
Foreign Affairs, 1894-1906; Chm. Royal Society
of Arts, 1911-13; cr. C.B. 1880; K.C.M.G.
1887; K.C.B. 1893; G.C.B. 1900; I.S.O. 1902;
and cr. Baron Sanderson, of Armthorpe, co.
York, 20 Dec. 1905. He d. unm. 24 Mar. 1923.
ARMS—Paly of six argent and azure on a
bend engrailed plain cotised sable a rose of the
first, barbed and seeded ppr. between two
annulets or.
CREST—A wolf's head erased ppr. gorged with
a collar azure, thereon three roses argent
barbed and seeded of the first.
SUPPORTERS—On either side a talbot or
supporting a flagstaff erect ppr. flowing therefrom a banner azure, charged with a rose
argent barbed and seeded of the second.
MOTTO—Da pacem Domine.

SANDERSON

PEERAGE—U.K. Baron Sanderson, of Hunmanby, co. York.
SURNAME—Furniss.
CR.—18 June 1930. **EXT.**—25 Mar. 1939.
HISTORY—Henry Furniss, of Whirlow
House, near Sheffield, d. Sept. 1872, leaving
issue,
Thomas Sanderson Furniss, of Higham
House, Stratford St. Mary, co. Suffolk, b.
15 Nov. 1833; m. 15 Sept. 1858, Mary (d.
6 Feb. 1899), dau. of Edward Fisher Sanderson,
of New York, and of Endcliffe Grange,
Sheffield, and d. 3 Feb. 1912, having had issue,
1. Henry Sanderson, **Baron Sanderson** (see
below).
2. Thomas Sanderson, b. 11 May 1872; m.
16 April 1907, Beatrice Mary, dau. of
Major F. E. Walter, (B.L.G. 1952,
Walter of Bear Wood) and d. 6 Jan.
1935 leaving issue, Thomas Walter
Sanderson, b. 1 Sept. 1911.

1. Mary Ann, b. 12 April 1860; d. unm. 30 Jan. 1906.
2. Julia Maud, b. 28 June 1870; m. 30 Nov. 1904, Rev. A. J. Brewster.

The elder son,

Henry Sanderson Furniss, **Baron Sanderson,** of Hunmanby, co. York, so cr. 18 June 1930, b. 1 Oct. 1868; educ. privately and Hertford Coll. Oxford, M.A.; Tutor and Lecturer at Ruskin Coll. Oxford, 1907-16; Principal of Ruskin Coll. 1916-25; author of books and periodicals, and editor of *The Industrial Outlook*, 1917; m. 23 Jan. 1902, Averil Dorothy, J.P. co. London, dau. of Henry Frederick Nicholl, of Bear Place, Twyford, co. Berks., and d. 25 Mar. 1939.

SANDFORD

PEERAGE—U.K. Baron Sandford, of Sandford, co. Salop.
SURNAME—Sandford.
CR.—20 Jan. 1891. **EXT.**—31 Dec. 1893.
HISTORY—In B.L.G. 1952 there is a long account of this anciently recorded family, Sandford formerly of Sandford. The ancestry is there traced to the early 12th century. A member of this family, Sir Daniel Keyte Sandford, M.P. for Paisley, 1834-35, Prof. of Greek, at Glasgow Univ., b. 1798; m. 2 July 1823, Cecilia Catherine, only dau. of John Charnock, and d. 4 Feb. 1838 leaving issue, with others (for whom see B.L.G. above mentioned), an eldest son,

Sir Francis Richard John Sandford, **Baron Sandford,** of Sandford co. Salop, so cr. 20 Jan. 1891; b. 14 May 1824; P.C.; cr. K.C.B., Sec. to the Royal Commissioners for the International Exhibition, 1862; Asst. Under Sec. of State for the Colonies; Sec. for the Education Dept. for England, 1870; of the Scotch Education Dept. 1872; a Charity Commissioner, 1884; one of the Cttee of Council on Education in Scotland; m. 1 Aug. 1849, Margaret Buchanan, 5th dau. of Robert Finlay, 2nd laird of Boturich, co. Dumbarton, (B.L.G. 1952, Finlay of Boturich), and d.s.p. 31 Dec. 1893. She d. 16 April 1905.
ARMS—Quarterly per fess indented ermine and azure.
CREST—A falcon wings endorsed preying on a partridge all ppr.
MOTTO—Nec temere nec timide.

SANDHURST

PEERAGE—U.K. Viscount Sandhurst, of Sandhurst, co. Berks.
SURNAME—Mansfield.
CR.—1 Jan. 1917. **EXT.**—2 Nov. 1921.
HISTORY—The 1st Baron Sandhurst, b. 1819, d. 1876, a distinguished soldier, had an eldest son,

William Mansfield, 2nd Baron Sandhurst, and **Viscount Sandhurst,** b. 31 Aug. 1855; Lt. Coldstream Guards; a Lord in Waiting, 1880-85; Under Sec. of State, for War, 1886, and again 1892-95; Gov. of Bombay, 1895-1900; Lord Chamberlain of the Household,

1912-21; P.C. 1907; cr. G.C.S.I., G.C.V.O., G.C.I.E., and Viscount Sandhurst, of Sandhurst, co. Berks, 1 Jan. 1917; had several foreign orders, and was K. St. J.; m. (1) 20 July 1881, Lady Victoria Alexandrina Spencer, C.I., dau. of 4th Earl Spencer, and by her (who d. 13 Mar. 1906) had issue,
Robert, b. 4 and d. 5 Sept. 1882.
Elizabeth, b. 9 June, and d. 17 Oct. 1884.
He m. (2) 5 July 1909, Eleanor Mary Caroline O.B.E., dau. of Matthew Arnold, and widow of Hon. Armine Wodehouse, (Kimberley, E.), and d.s.p. 2 Nov. 1921, when the Viscounty became extinct but the Barony of Sandhurst was inherited by his brother (see extant peerages, Sandhurst, B.) who became 3rd Baron Sandhurst.
ARMS—Argent on a chevron embattled azure, between three maunches sable, an eastern crown or; on a chief engrailed of the third, a lion of the fourth combatant, with a tiger cowed ppr.
CREST—Out of an eastern crown argent, a griffin's head sable, beaked or, between two branches a laurel, ppr.
MOTTO—Steadfast.
(Supporters now shown in extant peerages under Sandhurst, B. are a later grant, later than the time of the Viscount Sandhurst.)

SANKEY

PEERAGE—U.K. Baron Sankey, of Moreton, co. Gloucester, and Viscount Sankey.
SURNAME—Sankey.
CR.—Barony 21 June 1929. Viscounty, 30 Jan. 1932. **EXT.**—6 Feb. 1948.
HISTORY—Thomas Sankey, of Moreton, co. Gloucester, by his wife Catalina, dau. of James Dewsbury of Manchester, had with other issue,

Sir John Sankey, **Baron and Viscount Sankey,** b. 26 Oct. 1866; educ. Lancing and Jesus Coll. Oxford, Scholar, M.A., B.C.L.; Barrister-at-Law, Middle Temple, 1892; K.C. 1909; Chancellor of the Diocese of Llandaff, 1909-14; a Judge of the High Court of Justice, King's Bench, Div., 1914-28; Bencher, Middle Temple, 1914; a Lord Justice of Appeal, 1928-29; Lord High Chancellor, 1929-35; cr. Kt. Bach. 1914, made P.C. 1928; and cr. Baron Sankey, of Moreton, co. Gloucester, 21 June 1929; and Viscount Sankey, 30 Jan. 1932. Treasurer Middle Temple, 1936, G.B.E. 1917, K.G. St. J. He adhered to the Labour party in 1929 and joined the National Government with Ramsey Macdonald and others in 1931. He d. 6 Feb. 1948.
ARMS—Gules a fess ermine between in chief two martlets and in base a salmon naiant or.
CREST—In front of a dexter cubit arm vested gules and cuffed ermine, the hand grasping by the beam a pair of scales ppr. a martlet as in the arms.
SUPPORTERS—On either side a lion sable, gorged with a collar or, suspended therefrom on the dexter an escutcheon azure, charged with a Pascal Lamb of the second and on the sinister an escutcheon vert charged with a stag trippant gold.

SCHUSTER

PEERAGE—U.K. Baron Schuster, of Cerne, co. Dorset.
SURNAME—Schuster.
CR.—28 June 1944. **EXT.**—28 June 1956.
HISTORY—Samuel Schuster, of Weaste Lodge, Eccles, Manchester, b. 5 Feb. 1805; m. 6 June 1838, Fredericke Speyer, of Belton Lodge, Torquay, and d. 29 Aug. 1868, leaving issue,

Frederick Leo Schuster, of Heysham House, The Park, Cheltenham, b. 10 Mar. 1839; m. 26 Oct. 1864, Sophie Ellen, dau. of Lt. Col. II. W. Wood, Madras Army, and d. 19 Feb. 1928. She d. 7 Nov. 1933. They had issue,

Sir Claud Schuster, **Baron Schuster**, b. 22 Aug. 1869; educ. Winchester and New Coll. Oxford, B.A. 1892, M.A. 1909; Hon. Fell. St. Catharine's Coll. Camb.; Barrister-at-Law, Inner Temple, 1895; K.C. 1919; Bencher, 1924; Treasurer, 1947; Sec. London Gov. Act Commission, 1899-1902; Legal Asst. Board of Education, 1903-07; Legal Asst. and Asst., Sec. to same, 1907-11; Prin. Asst. Sec. (Legal Branch), 1911; Chief Registrar of Friendly Socs., 1909-12; Sec. Nat. Health Insurance Commission, 1912; mem. of and Legal Adviser to Nat. Health Insurance Jt. Cttee. 1913-15; Perm. Sec. to Lord Chancellor, and Clerk of the Crown in Chancery, 1915-44; Dir. Legal Div. Allied Commission for Australia (Brit. Element) 1944-46; J.P. co. London, J.P. and High Sheriff, 1941, co. Dorset; Officier de l'Ordre de la Couronne, Belgium, Hon. mem. Canadian Bar Asscn.; Pres. of the Alpine Club, of the Ski Club of Great Britain, and of the Eagle Ski Club; in addition to mountaineering his principal recreation was hunting; he was author of *Peaks and Pleasant Places*, 1911; *Men, Women and Mountains, : Days in the Alps and Pyrenees*, 1931; *Sweet Enemy*, 1933; and *Postscript to Adventure*. He was cr. Kt. Bach. 1913; C.V.O. 1918; K.C.B. 1919; G.C.B. 1927, and Baron Schuster, of Cerne, co. Dorset 28 June 1944. He m. 1 July 1896, Mabel Elizabeth, dau. of the Rev. W. W. Merry, D.D., Rector of Lincoln Coll. Oxford. She d. 6 Aug. 1936. He d. 28 June 1956. They had issue,

Christopher John Claud, b. 13 Jan. 1899; educ. Winchester; served in World War I, 2nd Lt. The Rifle Bde. and was k. in action at La Bohéme 10 Aug. 1918.

Elizabeth Alice, b. 10 Dec. 1902; educ. St. Paul's Sch. for Girls; J.P. Dorset; m. 11 Dec. 1925, (m. diss. by div.), T. F. Turner, K.C., and had issue.

ARMS—Ermine a lion passant or, on a chief gules, a portcullis chained between two hearts of the second.
CREST—On a wreath or and gules, a lion passant or, gorged with a collar flory counter flory gules and resting the dexter paw on an escutcheon argent, charged with a penner and inkhorn sable.
SUPPORTERS—Dexter, A lion ermine; Sinister, A pegasus or, each gorged with a collar flory counterflory gules.
MOTTO—Levavi oculos.
Lord Schuster's residence was 7 Campden Hill Court, London, W.8. His clubs were Alpine, Oxford and Cambridge, and Travellers.

SEAFORTH

PEERAGE—U.K. Baron Seaforth, of Brahan in Urray, in the county of Ross and Cromarty.
SURNAME—Stewart-Mackenzie.
CR.—19 Jan. 1921. **EXT.**—3 Mar. 1923.
HISTORY—Keith William Stewart-Mackenzie, of Seaforth, a cadet of the family of the Earls of Galloway, d. 18 June 1881, having had by his first wife Hannah Charlotte, (d. 5 June 1868) dau. of James Joseph Hope-Vere, of Craigie Hall, (Linlithgow M.), with other issue,

James Alexander Francis Humberston Stewart-Mackenzie, **Baron Seaforth** of Brahan in Urray, in the county of Ross and Cromarty, so cr. 19 Jan. 1921, b. 9 Oct. 1847; educ. Glenalmond, Harrow and R.M.C. Sandhurst; joined 9th Lancers, 1867; served in the Afghan War, 1878-80, (despatches twice, wounded); Brev. Major; Mil. Sec. to Gov. of Madras, 1886-88; Lt. Col. cmdg. 9th Lancers, 1891; ret. 1896. He was Convener of Ross-shire C.C., Chm. of many public welfare Cttees, and Hon. Col. 4th Bn. Seaforth Highlanders (Ross-shire Buffs). He m. 18 July 1899, Mary Margaret, C.B.E., D.G. St. J., only child of Edward Steinkopff, of Lydhurst, Haywards Heath, co. Sussex and d.s.p. 3 Mar. 1923.
ARMS—Quarterly 1 and 4, Azure a stag's head caboshed or, (Mackenzie of Seaforth and Kintail); 2 and 3, Or a fess chequy azure and argent, surmounted of a bend engrailed, within a double tressure flory counterflory gules (Stewart, Earl of Galloway).
CRESTS—1. A mountain in flames ppr. (Mackenzie); 2. A pelican in her piety ppr. (Stewart).
SUPPORTERS—Dexter, A savage wreathed about the head and middle with laurel, holding in his exterior hand a baton erect on his shoulder burning at the end, his hair inflamed also ppr; Sinister, A greyhound ppr.
MOTTOES—Luceo non uro. Virescit vulnere virtus.
Lord Seaforth's seat was Brahan Castle, Conon Bridge, co. Ross, and he was bur. in the private ground of the Dell of Brahan. His London residence was 47 Berkeley Square, W.

SEATON

PEERAGE—U.K. Baron Seaton of Seaton, co. Devon.
SURNAME—Colborne-Vivian, formerly Colborne.
CR.—14 Dec. 1839. **EXT.**—12 Mar. 1955.
HISTORY—John Colborne, of Lymington, co. Hants, described as a descendant of the Colborne family of Wythy Hill, Lydford, co. Somerset, was grandfather of Charles Colborne, of Lyndhurst, and Barnes, co. Surrey. The latter d. 1747 devising part of his property to his great-nephew,

Samuel Colborne, who m. Cordelia Anne, dau. of John Garstin, of Leragh Castle and Ballykerren, co. Westmeath, and had issue with a dau., Cordelia Anne who m. the Rev. Duke Yonge, Vicar of Antony Cornwall,, an only son,

Field Marshal Sir John Colborne, **1st Baron Seaton**, G.C.B., G.C.H., G.C.M.G., b. 16 Feb.

1778; educ. Christ's Hosp. and Winchester; entered the Army 1799, served in Egypt, 1801, and throughout the Peninsular War, cmd. 52nd Light Inf. at Waterloo, was Col. 2nd Life Guards, held appointments of Lt. Gov. of Guernsey, and of Upper Canada, was Gov. Gen. of Canada, Lord High Cmmr. of the Ionian Islands, and Cmdr. of the Forces in Ireland; was cr. 14 Dec. 1839, Baron Seaton of Seaton, co. Devon.; m. 21 June 1814, Elizabeth, dau. of the Rev. John Yonge, of Puslinch co. Devon, Rector of Newton Ferrers, Devon. She d. 28 Nov. 1872. He d. 17 April 1863. They had issue with two other daus. who d. unm.,

1. James, **2nd Baron Seaton** (see below).
2. Francis, Sir, K.C.B., Gen., Col. Royal Warwick Regt., cmd. in Hong Kong and the Straits Settlements, b. 23 April 1817; d. unm. 26 Nov. 1895.
3. Edmund, b. 1824; educ. Exeter Coll. Oxford, M.A.; m. 5 June 1873, Rhoda Ellen, dau. of George Blogg, of Bucklesbury, London. She d. 23 Nov. 1913. He d. 12 May 1878, having had issue a dau., Edith Cordelia, b. 3 Sept. 1876; m. 25 April, 1903, F. D. Mackrell, and had issue.
4. Graham, Rev., M.A. Oxford, Rector of Dittisham, co. Devon, 1853-1913, b. 10 Oct. 1825; m. 18 Sept. 1890, Florence Susanna, dau. of Major W. Porter, of Hembury Fort, co. Devon. She d. 1901, he d.s.p. 30 Oct. 1913.
5. John, Major, 60th Rifles, and Col. in the Egyptian Army, b. 1830; and d. unm. 13 Feb. 1890.
1. Jane, m. 30 Sept. 1857; Gen. Sir Alexander G. Montgomery-Moore, K.C.B., of Garvey House, co. Tyrone, who d. 17 Jan. 1919, and she d. 14 June 1919.

The eldest son,
James Colborne, **2nd Baron Seaton,** b. 1816; Mil. Sec. to the Cmdr. of Forces in Ireland; m. 12 Feb. 1851, Charlotte, dau. and coheiress of Sir Ulysses Burgh, 2nd and last Baron Downes, (1883 Ext. Peerage), and d. 11 Oct. 1888. She d. 26 April 1863. They had issue, with three other daus., who d. unm.,

1. John Reginald Upton, **3rd Baron Seaton** (see below).
2. Francis Lionel Lydstone, M.V.O., Lt. Col. and Col. cmdg. 8th Bn. City of London Regt., and Major Royal Irish Rifles; served in Sinde, 1878, in Afghanistan 1880, in Boer War, 1881, in Sudan, 1884-85, S. African War 1900, and in World War I, 1914-17; b. 29 July 1855; m. 30 April 1906, Alice Matilda Mary, dau. and heiress of Capt. W. R. G Farmer, of Nonsuch and Lagham, co. Surrey, and d.s.p. 8 Sept. 1924. She d. 13 May 1936.
3. James Ulysses Graham Raymond, **4th Baron Seaton** (see below).
1. Alice Constantia Helen, d. unm. 5 Sept. 1943.
2. Charlotte Annette Maria, twin with her brother James, d. 12 Feb. 1877.

The eldest son,
John Reginald Upton Eliott-Drake-Colborne, **3rd Baron Seaton,** who assumed by Royal Licence, 16 Aug. 1917, the additional surname and arms of Eliott and Drake, was b. 4 July 1854; was hon. Major in the Army, and Capt. Royal 1st Devon Yeo.; served in

S. African War, on Staff of G.O.C., Aldershot Div. and in World War I 1914-17, at Menos, Alexandria, and Salonica, (1914 star, two medals, and Medal of King Albert of Belgium); m. 22 June 1887, Elizabeth Beatrice, only child of Sir Francis Fuller-Eliott-Drake, 2nd Bt., of Nutwell Court, and Buckland Abbey, co. Devon. He d.s.p. 11 Aug. 1933. She d. 9 May 1937. He was s. in the Barony by his ygr. brother,

James Ulysses Graham Raymond Colborne-Vivian, **4th Baron Seaton,** b. 20 April 1863; Major S. Staffordshire Regt., served in the Nile Exped. 1884-85, (was severely wounded), in Sudan F.F. 1885-86, in S. African War 1899-1902, and in World War I, 1914-19; m. 21 June 1904, Caroline Mabel, eldest dau. of Sir Arthur Pendarves Vivian, K.C.B., (Swansea, B.). They assumed by Royal Licence, 20 July 1927, the additional surname of Vivian. She d. 3 June 1948. He d.s.p. 12 Mar. 1955.

ARMS—Argent on a chevron, between three bugle horns stringed sable, as many mullets of the first, on a chief embattled pendent from a riband gules, fimbriated azure, a representation of the gold cross and clasps presented to Sir John Colborne 1st Baron Seaton, in consideration of services at the battles of Corunna, Albuera, Ciudad Rodrigo, Nivelle, Nive, Orthes, and Toulouse, between two mural crowns or.
CREST—Out of a mural crown or, a reindeer's head argent attired gold. between a branch of laurel on the dexter, and a branch of palm on the sinister, both ppr.
SUPPORTERS—Dexter, A soldier of Her Majesty's 52nd (or Oxfordshire) Regt. of Foot habited and accoutered, in the exterior hand a musket, all ppr.; Sinister, A Canadian Red Indian, holding in his dexter hand a tomahawk, and in the exterior a spear, all ppr.
MOTTO—Sperate infestis.
The seat of Lord Seaton was Beechwood, Plympton, Devon.

SHAND

PEERAGE—U.K. Baron Shand, of Woodhouse, co. Dumfries.
SURNAME—Shand.
CR.—20 Aug. 1892. EXT.—6 Mar. 1904.
HISTORY—Alexander Shand, of Aberdeen had by his wife, Louisa, dau. of John Whyte, M.D., of Banff, had issue,

Alexander Burns Shand, **Baron Shand,** of Woodhouse, co. Dumfries, so cr. 20 Aug. 1892. He was b. 1828; educ. Edinburgh Univ. 1828-52, studying law; Advocate Scots Bar, 1853; Sheriff of Kincardine, 1862, and of Haddington and Berwick, 1869; Advocate Depute, 1860-62; a Judge of the Scottish Court of Session, 1872-90; settled in London, 1890; Hon. Bencher of Gray's Inn, 1892; made P.C. and mem. of Judicial Cttee of Privy Council, 1890; apptd. a lord of Appeal in House of Lords, 1892-1904. He m. 1857, Emily Merelina, dau. of John Clarke Meymott, of Leinster Square, W. He d.s.p. 6 Mar. 1904.
ARMS—Gules a boar's head couped, on a chief argent three mullets azure.
CREST—A dove holding a slip of olive ppr.
MOTTO—Virtute duce.

SHANDON

PEERAGE—U.K. Baron Shandon, of the City of Cork. (Also a baronetcy, cr. 15 Jan. 1916.)
SURNAME—O'Brien.
CR.—1 July 1918. **EXT.**—10 Sept. 1930.
HISTORY—Mark Joseph O'Brien, of Cork, and his wife, Jane, dau. of William Dunne, of Cork, had a ygst. son,
Sir Ignatius John O'Brien, Bt., and **Baron Shandon**, b. 31 July 1857; educ. the Vincentian Sch. and the Catholic Univ. of Ireland; joined reporting staff of the *Freeman's Journal*, 1876; Barrister-at-Law, King's Inns, 1881; Inner Bar, 1899, Q.C. 1899, Bencher, 1907; Serjeant-at-Law, 1910; Solicitor Gen. for Ireland, 1911-12; Attorney Gen. 1912-13; P.C. 1912; Lord Chancellor of Ireland, 1913-18 (the office being abolished a few years later, under the legislation setting up the Irish Free State). He was cr. a baronet 15 Jan. 1916, and Baron Shandon, of the City of Cork, 1 July 1918. He became a Barrister of the Middle Temple, 1923, having moved to England in 1918. He m. 11 Feb. 1886, Annie, dau. of John Talbot Scallan, of Dublin. She d. 1 Feb. 1929. He d.s.p. 10 Sept. 1930.
ARMS—Gules three lions passant guardant in pale per pale or and argent a chief ermine.
CREST—Issuant from a cloud an arm embowed charged for distinction with an ermine spot, the hand grasping a sword all ppr.
SUPPORTERS—Dexter, An Irish elk reguardant gules, attired unguled and charged on the shoulder with a pheon or; Sinister, A lion reguardant pean langued and armed gules charged on the shoulder with a trefoil slipped vert.
MOTTO—Lamh laidir an nachtar.
In Ireland his residence was Ardtona, Dundrum, co. Dublin; in England at his house in Kensington, where he died. His clubs were, University, Dublin, and National Liberal, London.

SHEFFIELD

PEERAGE—Ireland. Baron Sheffield, of Dunamore, co. Meath, 9 Jan. 1781.
Ireland. Baron Sheffield, of Roscommon, co. Roscommon 20 Sept. 1783.
U.K. Baron Sheffield, of Sheffield, co. York, 29 July 1802.
Ireland. Viscounty of Pevensey, and Earldom of Sheffield, 16 Jan. 1816.
SURNAME—Holroyd.
CR.—Dates as above. **EXT.**—21 April 1909, except for Barony cr. in 1783.
HISTORY—Isaac Holroyd, of Dunamore, co. Meath, 1708-1778, had with other issue an only surv. son,
John Baker Holroyd, **1st Earl of Sheffield**, and **1st Baron**, as above, who inherited the estates of his mother's family, the Bakers of Penn, co. Buckingham, and assumed the surname of Baker before that of Holroyd. He was cr. Baron Sheffield, of Dunamore, co. Meath, 9 Jan. 1781, with remainder to his male issue; he was cr. 20 Sept. 1783, Baron Sheffield, of Roscommon, co. Roscommon, 20 Sept. 1783, both peerages being in the peerage of Ireland. The second barony was limited to the male issue of his two daus. by his first marriage, in

default of heirs male of his body. He was further cr. Baron Sheffield, of Sheffield, co. York, 29 July 1802, in peerage of United Kingdom; and made Viscount of Pevensey, and Earl of Sheffield, in the peerage of Ireland 16 Jan. 1816. He was Pres. of the Board of Agriculture, a Lord of Trade, and a P.C. He was b. 1735; m. (1) 26 April 1767, Abigail, dau. of Lewis Way, of Richmond, co. Surrey, and by her (who d. 3 April 1793) had issue with a son who d. young,
1. Maria Josepha, m. 11 Oct. 1796, John Thomas Stanley, 1st Baron Stanley of Alderley, and d. 1 Nov. 1863, leaving issue, who eventually inherited the Irish Barony of Sheffield, cr. 1783, (see extant peerages, Sheffield, B.).
2. Louisa Dorothea, m. 14 Mar. 1797, Lt. Gen. Sir William Henry Clinton, G.C.B., and d. 14 May 1854, (Newcastle, D.) leaving issue.
Lord Sheffield m. (2) 26 Dec. 1794, Lady Lucy Pelham, dau. of 1st Earl of Chichester and she d.s.p. 18 Jan. 1797. Lord Sheffield m. (3) 20 Jan. 1798, Lady Anne North, (d. 18 Jan. 1832), dau. of 2nd Earl of Guilford, (as Lord North, P.M. to George III). By her Lord Sheffield had issue,
1. George Augustus Frederick Charles, **2nd Earl of Sheffield** (see below).
3. Anne Frederica, m. 14 June 1827, Hon. Arthur Legge, (Dartmouth, E.), and d. 31 Aug. 1829, leaving issue.
The Earl of Sheffield was a great friend of the celebrated Edward Gibbon, and the latter's *Miscellaneous Works* in 5 vols. were edited and produced with notes and narrative by Lord Sheffield in 1814 (second edition, the first edition having been published in 1795). Gibbon appointed Lord Sheffield as his chief executor, and in his will refers to him thus: "My obligations to the long and active friendship of Lord Sheffield I could never sufficiently repay." The *Miscellaneous Works* contain many letters to Lord Sheffield from Gibbon, whose body was buried in Lord Sheffield's family burial place, in Fletching, co. Sussex. The first Earl of Sheffield, d. 30 May 1821, and was s. by his only son,
George Augustus Frederick Charles Holroyd, **2nd Earl of Sheffield**, b. 16 Mar. 1802; m. 6 June 1825, Harriet (d. 1 Jan. 1889), dau. of 2nd Earl of Harewood, and d. 5 April 1876, having had issue,
1. Frederic Henry Stuart, b. 24 Oct. 1827; d. 21 Mar. 1829.
2. Henry North, **3rd Earl of Sheffield** (see below).
3. Douglas Edward, Barrister-at-Law, b. 20 June 1834; d. 9 Feb. 1882.
1. Susan Harriet, m. 26 June 1849, Edward William Vernon-Harcourt, and d. 5 April 1894, leaving issue, (Vernon, B.).
The elder surv. son,
Henry North Holroyd, **3rd Earl of Sheffield**, b. 18 Jan. 1832; Attaché to British Legation at Copenhagen 1852, and to the British Embassy at Constantinople, 1853-56, M.P. for E. Sussex, 1857-65; d. unm. 21 April 1909, when all his peerages became extinct except the Barony of Sheffield cr. 1783, which was inherited by his kinsman, the 4th Baron Stanley of Alderley.
ARMS—Quarterly 1 and 4, Azure on a fess dancettée argent between three griffins passant

wings endorsed or, as many escallops gules; 2 and 3, Azure five cinquefoils in saltire argent (Holroyd).
CREST—A demi griffin segreant wings endorsed sable holding between the claws a ducal coronet or.
SUPPORTERS—Dexter, A lion regardant ppr; Sinister, A horse bridled ppr.
MOTTO—Quem te Deus esse jussit.
The Earl's seat was Sheffield Park, near Uckfield, Sussex and his town house, 58 Portland Place, W.

SHERARD

PEERAGE—Ireland. Baron Sherard, of Leitrim.
SURNAME—Sherard.
CR.—10 July 1627. EXT.—14 June 1931.
HISTORY—Geoffrey Sherard, of Stapleford, co. Leicester, was High Sheriff of co. Rutland, 1468, 1480 and 1484. Of his two sons, the younger Robert was ancestor of the Sherards, of Lobethorpe, (Burke's Extinct Baronetcies), and the elder,
Thomas Sherard, of Stapleford, High Sheriff of Rutland, 10 and 21 Henry VII, m. Margaret, dau. of John Hellwell, and had a son and heir,
George Sherard, of Stapleford, High Sheriff co. Leicester, 9 Elizabeth I, by his wife, Rohesia, dau. of Sir Thomas Poultney, had a son,
Francis Sherard, of Stapleford, m. Anne, dau. of George Moore, of Bourne, co. Lincoln, and had issue three sons, of whom only the third left issue, namely,
William Sherard, **1st Baron Sherard,** of Stapleford, who was knighted by James I at Oatlands, 3 July 1622, and was cr. a peer in the peerage of Ireland as Baron Sherard, of Leitrim on 10 July 1627 (by Charles I). He m. 1621, Abigail dau. and coheir of Cecil Cave, by Anne his wife, who was dau. and sole heir of Anthony Bennet, of Greenwich. Lady Sherard was the widow of Henry Tresham. She d. 1659. Lord Sherard d. 16 April 1640. They had issue,
1. Bennet, **2nd Baron Sherard,** from whom descended the lines of the Barons Sherard, and the Earldom of Harborough, until 1732, when the succession to the peerage honours passed to the descendants of the second son of the 1st Lord Sherard.
2. Philip, of Whissendine, M.P. co. Rutland, 1660-81, whose grandson, Philip, became **4th Baron Sherard,** and 2nd Earl of Harborough. (The third Baron Sherard of the Irish creation was further cr. 19 Oct. 1714, as Baron Harborough, of Harborough, co. Leicester, in the peerage of Great Britain, with remainder in default of his own male issue, to Philip Sherard, of Whissendine mentioned above. Lord Sherard was further advanced to the Earldom of Harborough 8 May 1719, with a like reversionary clause in the letters patent as had already been granted in those of the G.B. barony. Full details of the line of descent of the Earls of Harborough is given in the 1883 Extinct Peerage, until the death of the 6th Earl, in 28 July 1859, when the Earldom and the G.B. barony of Harborough

became extinct, but the Irish Barony of Sherard was inherited by the descendants of),
3. George, b. 1624; m. 31 July 1651, Anne Croppenburgh, of London, and d. 1670, leaving by her (who d. 1669), with other issue, an elder son,
William, of Glatton, b. 1652; m. 1693, Catherine, dau. and coheir of Castle Sherard, of Glatton, and Folkesworth, co. Huntingdon and had issue,
Castel, of Glatton, b. 1695; m. 1729, Martha, dau. of Edward Ferrar, of Little Gidding, co. Huntingdon, and d. 1741, leaving with other issue who d.s.p., a son,
1a Philip Castel, Rev. of Glatton, b. 1767; m. 1796, Sarah Haughton, dau. of Montague James, of Jamaica and d. Nov. 1814, having had with other issue,
Castel, Rev., b. 1733; m. 1763, Jane, dau. of Rev. Richard Caryer, and d. 1803, having had with two other sons and four daus.
1b Philip Castel, **9th Baron Sherard** (see below).
2b Simon Haughton, Rev., b. 9 Feb. 1811; m. 19 Oct. 1843, Mary Halton, dau. of Sir Simon Haughton Clarke, 9th Bt., and d. 1882, leaving with other issue,
1c Castel, **10th Baron** (see below).
2c Philip Halton, **11th Baron** (see below).
2a Robert, Rev., rector of Burlingham St. Peter, Norfolk, b. 1777; m. 1804, Grace Martha, dau. of Rev. George Johnson, and d. 1835, leaving with other issue,
Charles Wale, b. 1820; m. 1856, Isabella, dau. of P. W. Welsh, of Melbourne, and d. 1889, having had with other issue,
Robert Castel, **12th Baron** (see below).
On the death of the 6th Earl of Harborough, who was also **8th Baron Sherard,** the Irish Barony passed to his kinsman,
Philip Castel Sherard, **9th Baron Sherard,** b. 7 Mar. 1804; m. 26 June 1834, Anne, dau. of Nathaniel Weekes, of Mangrove, Barbados, who d. at Dresden 13 April 1835. He had by her an only child,
Marianne Sarah, m. 6 July 1854, Sir Henry Bourchier Toke Wrey, Bt.
He d. 16 Feb. 1896. The 9th Baron Sherard d. 14 Mar. 1886, being s. by his nephew,
Castel Sherard, **10th Baron Sherard,** Cmdr. R.N., b. 17 Aug. 1849; m. 6 Oct. 1898, Mary Gertrude, dau. of Rev. Robert Mandeville Rodwell, Rector of High Laver, co. Essex, and d.s.p. 5 Oct. 1902, when he was s. by his brother,
Philip Halton Sherard, **11th Baron Sherard,** b. 2 May 1851, and d. unm. 1 May 1924, when he was s. by his cousin,
Robert Castel Sherard, **12th Baron Sherard,** b. 1858; d.s.p. 14 June 1931.
The family appears to have been entirely English and only the title connected with Ireland.

ARMS—Argent a chevron gules between three torteaux.
CREST—Out of a ducal coronet or, a peacock's tail erect ppr.
SUPPORTERS—Two rams argent, armed and unguled or.
MOTTO—Hostis honori invidia.

SHERBROOKE

PEERAGE—U.K. Viscount Sherbrooke, of Sherbrooke, co. Surrey.
SURNAME—Lowe.
CR.—25 May 1880. EXT.—27 July 1892.
HISTORY—Elizabeth, third dau. and coheir of Henry Sherbrooke, of Oxton, Newark, co. Nottingham (see B.L.G. 1952, Sherbrooke of Oxton), m. 1740, Samuel Lowe, of Southwell, co. Nottingham. He d. 1765. Their third son was,
Robert Lowe, of Southwell, co. Nottingham, High Sheriff, 1802, b. 1746; m. 1770, Anne, dau. of Richard Turner Beecher, and d. 28 July 1822, aged 76, having had,
The Rev. Robert Lowe, Rector of Bingham and Preb. of Southwell, b. 1789; m. July 1805, Ellen, (d. 15 Nov. 1852) dau. and coheir of the Rev. Reginald Pyndar, Rector of Madresfield, co. Worcester and d. 23 Jan. 1845, having had issue,
1. Henry Porter Sherbrooke, of Oxton Hall, co. Nottingham, b. 1810; m. 1840, Louisa Anne, dau. of William Fane, and d. 12 June 1887, leaving two sons and three daus. He had assumed in 1847 the surname of Sherbrooke in lieu of that of Lowe, on inheriting the estate of Oxton, co. Nottingham (for his descendants, see B.L.G. 1952, under Sherbrooke of Oxton).
2. Robert, Viscount Sherbrooke (see below).
3. Frederick Pyndar, Rev., b. 1813; m. Helen, dau. and coheir of J. M. Leake, of Thorpe Hall, co. Essex, and d. 12 Oct. 1872, leaving,
   (1) Reginald.
   (1) Helen.
1. Elizabeth Agnes Pyndar, b. 1809; d. unm. 3 Sept. 1860.
2. Ellen Pyndar.
3. Margaret Anne.
The second son,
Robert Lowe, Viscount Sherbrooke, of Sherbrooke, co. Surrey, (i.e. Sherbrooke being the name of his house at Warlingham, co. Surrey) so cr. 25 May 1880; was b. 4 Dec. 1811; educ. Winchester and Univ. Coll. Oxford, B.A. 1833; until 1840 a private tutor at Oxford; Fell. Magdalen Coll. 1835-36, M.A. 1836; Barrister-at-Law, Lincoln's Inn, 1842; practised as a lawyer in Sydney, Australia; nom. a member of the Legislative Council there 1843-44; elected for St. Vincent and Aucklands, 1845, and for Sydney, 1848; returned to England, 1850; Liberal M.P. Kidderminster, 1852-59; for Calne, 1859-68, and for Univ. of London, 1868-80; Joint Sec. Board of Control for India, 1852-55; Vice Pres. Board of Trade and Paymaster Gen. 1855-58; P.C. 1855; Chancellor of the Exchequer, and a Lord of the Treasury, 1868-73; Home Sec. 1873-74; F.R.S. 1871; cr. a peer, 25 May 1880

as Viscount Sherbrooke, of Sherbrooke, co. Surrey, and G.C.B. 1885. He m. (1) 29 Mar. 1836, Georgiana, (d. 3 Oct. 1884), dau. of George Orred, of Tranmore, co. Chester. He m. (2) 3 Feb. 1885, Caroline, Anne, (d. 7 Sept. 1914), dau. of Thomas Sneyd, of Ashcombe Park, co. Stafford, and d.s.p. 27 July 1892.
ARMS—Gules three mullets fesswise argent pierced of the field between two wolves passant of the second.
CREST—In front of a wolf's head erased ppr. gorged with a collar gemel, two mullets or pierced gules.
SUPPORTERS—Dexter, A wolf ppr; Sinister, A bay horse, each charged with a chain therefrom suspended a portcullis or.
The seat of Viscount Sherbrooke was Sherbrooke, Caterham, Surrey. His town house was 34 Lowndes Square, S.W. His clubs were Athenæum, and Brook's.

SHERWOOD

PEERAGE—U.K. Baron Sherwood, of Calverton, co. Nottingham.
SURNAME—Seely.
CR.—14 Aug. 1941. EXT.—1 April 1970.
HISTORY—Sir Charles Seely, 1st Bt., so cr. 19 Feb. 1896, had issue with other children, an eldest son,
Sir Charles Hilton Seely, 2nd Bt., b. 7 July 1859; educ. Harrow and Trin. Coll. Camb., M.A.; Major 9th Queen's Own Lancers, R.A.C., served in World War II, taken prisoner 1941-43 but escaped; Master of the Gunmakers' Co. 1957 and 1964; m. 9 Dec. 1891, Hilda Lucy, dau. of R.T.A. Grant, of West Cowes, I. of W. She d. 24 Aug. 1939. He d. 26 Feb. 1926. They had with other issue (for whom see extant peerages, Seely, Bt.), a second surv. son,
Sir Hugh Michael Seely, 3rd Bt., and Baron Sherwood, b. 2 Oct. 1898; educ. Eton; served as Lt. Gren. Guards and S. Notts. Hussars, and was S/Ldr. cmdg. No. 504 C. of Nottingham (F) Squadron, Aux.A.F., being Hon. A/Cdr. 1947; was M.P. E. Div. of Norfolk, 1923-24, and for Berwick-on-Tweed, 1935-41; Under Sec. of State for Air, 1941-45; was cr. Baron Sherwood, of Calverton, co. Nottingham, 14 Aug. 1941; m. (1) 23 Mar. 1942 (m. diss. by div. 1948), Hon. Molly Patricia, dau. of 1st Viscount Camrose, and widow of Capt. Roger C. G. Chetwode (Chetwode, B.). He m. (2) 16 Mar. 1970, Catherine Thornton, widow of J. O. Ranger, and d.s.p. 1 April, 1970. The barony of Sherwood then became extinct but the baronetcy was inherited by his brother, who became, Sir Victor Basil John Seely, 4th Bt., (for whom see Seely, Bt.).
ARMS—Azure three ears of wheat banded or, within a chaplet of roses argent.
CREST—Upon the trunk of a tree fesswise ppr. three ears of wheat banded or.
SUPPORTERS—On either side a pegasus argent winged or, charged on the breast with a hurt, thereon three ears of wheat banded gold.
MOTTO—I ripen and die, yet live.
Lord Sherwood's residences were 10 Berkeley Street, London, W.1. and Chichester House, Chichester Terrace, Brighton; also Brooke, I. of W.

SIMEY

PEERAGE—U.K. Life. Baron Simey of
Toxteth, co. Palatine of Lancaster.
SURNAME—Simey.
CR.—12 May 1965. **EXT.**—27 Dec. 1969.
HISTORY—Michael Simey, m. 24 June 1680
at Bishop Wearmouth, co. Durham. Ann
Henderson, and had with three daus., an only
son,
George Simey, of Hylton, co. Durham,
bapt. 14 June 1690 and had by his wife,
Catherine,
George Simey, Mariner of Bishop Wear-
mouth, bapt. 17 Oct. 1733; he had by his wife,
Catherine Boyes, a dau., and eight sons, of
whom, the seventh,
Ralph Simey, mariner, bapt. 2 Mar. 1769;
m. Mary Ross in America and had issue
(with three daus. and an elder son, George
Lowry, master mariner who left issue) a yr.
son,
Thomas Boyes Simey, shipbuilder, b. 20
Sept. 1798; d. 2 Feb. 1871 having had by his
wife, Isabella Harrison, with two other sons,
Henry and John, and four daus.,
1. Thomas who had issue, with four daus.
   (1) Erroll George Tyndall, Rev., Clerk
   in Holy Orders, M.A. Queen's Coll.
   Camb., Rector of Mordiford, co.
   Hereford.
   (2) Percy.
2. Ralph (see below).
3. Alfred, m. and had children.
The second son,
Ralph Simey, a solicitor, Clerk of the Peace
and C.C. Durham, b. 31 May 1841; m. 6 June
1861, Margaret dau. of Dr. John Iliff, LL.D.,
and d. 11 June 1911. She d. 1926. They had
with six daus., three sons,
1. Ralph Iliff, Barrister-at-Law, Inner
   Temple, B.A. Corpus Christi, Coll.
   Oxford, b. 28 Mar. 1862; m. 14 Aug.
   1901, Dora Emily Vernon, dau. of H. R.
   Reynolds, and d. 1944, having had issue,
   Gertrude Margaret Stewart, Barrister-at-
   Law, Inner Temple, 1929, B.A. St. Hugh's
   Coll. Oxford.
2. George Iliff (see below).
3. Athelstan Iliff, F.R.C.S., F.R.C.P.,
   B.A. King's Coll. Camb., m. 1912 Alma
   Margaret Alleyne and d.s.p. 1945.
The second son,
George Iliff Simey, Solicitor 1892, Clerk of
the Peace and C.C. Somerset 1905-27, b.
25 Feb. 1866; educ. Rugby and Balliol Coll.
Oxford; m. 21 May 1896. Alice Robson, dau.
of Rev. William Spensley and d. 17 April
1927 leaving issue,
1. William Spensley, Solicitor, B.A. Balliol
   Coll. Oxford, 1922, b. 21 Sept. 1897; m.
   21 Dec. 1929, Margaret Mary, dau. of
   R. J. Jenkins, and had issue,
   George Richard Spensley, Solicitor,
   1960, partner with his father in Ford,
   Simey and Ford, 1961; m. 29 Oct.
   1960, Penelope, dau. of Major H.
   Pares (B.L.G. 1952) and had issue,
   three daus.
2. George Spensley, b. 5 June 1899, d. unm.
   1926.
3. Thomas Spensley, **Baron Simey** (see
   below).
The third son,
Thomas Spensley Simey, **Baron Simey**, of

Toxteth, co. Palatine of Lancaster, so cr. as a
Life Peer, 12 May 1965, b. 25 Nov. 1906; B.A.
1928, M.A. 1931, Balliol Coll. Oxford;
Solicitor 1931, Lecturer in Public Adm.
1931-39, and Prof. of Social Science, Liverpool
Univ. 1939, mem. Treasury Cttee. of Inquiry
into Civil Service 1966, author of several studies
on welfare; m. 12 April 1935, Margaret Bayne,
dau. of J. A. Todd of Glasgow, and d. 27 Dec.
1969, having had issue,
Thomas Iliff, A.R.I., B.A., b. 12 June 1938;
m. 17 Aug. 1963, Fiona, dau. of A. G.
Porteous, of Menstrie, co. Clackmanan, and
had two sons.
Duncan Michael, b. 1964 and Rollo
Thomas, b. 1966.
Lord Simey's residence was Coed Nant, Gain,
Cilcain, Flintshire.

SIMONDS

PEERAGE—U.K. Life. Baron Simonds, of
Sparsholt, co. Southampton, 18 April 1944.
U.K. Baron (hereditary) Simonds, etc.
24 June 1952.
U.K. Viscount Simonds, of Sparsholt, co.
Southampton, 18 Oct. 1954.
SURNAME—Simonds.
CR.—Dates as above. **EXT.**—28 June 1971.
HISTORY—Louis de Luze Simonds, of
Audleys Wood, Basingstoke, of a family of
brewers well known in the south of England,
b. 1852; educ. in U.S.A.; m. 1880, Mary
Elizabeth, dau. of Surg. Gen. Gavin Ainslie
Turnbull, and d. 1916. She d. 1930. They had
issue,
1. Frederick Adolphus, b. 2 Jan. 1881;
   educ. Eton and Magdalen Coll. Oxford;
   served in S. African War, 1900-01 with
   service co. of 1st V.B. Royal Berks Regt.;
   was Chm. and Man. Director of H. & G.
   Simonds, Ltd. brewers, and Dir. of
   Saccone and Speed, Ltd.; was High
   Sheriff, co. Berks, and Pres. Warrant
   Holders' Asscn. 1937 and 1945; m. 1909,
   Amy FitzGerald, O.B.E., dau. of J. S.
   Hill, of St. Albans, co. Herts, and d. 17
   Aug. 1953. She d. 1969. They had issue,
   two sons.
2. Gavin Turnbull, **Viscount Simonds** (see
   below).
3. John de Luze, Major R.A., b. 7 May
   1884; k. in action 1917
4. Henry Duncan, Cmdr. R.N., b. 27 July
   1887; m. M.Z. and d. 1950 having had
   issue, an elder son,
   Thomas Audley de Luze, R.M.; m.
   7 May 1957, Mary Bernadette, dau. of
   A. R. Neelands, of Chelsea Square,
   London, S.W.3.
The second son,
Sir Gavin Turnbull Simonds, **Baron and
Viscount Simonds**, b. 28 Nov. 1881 educ.
Winchester, Scholar, and New Coll. Oxford,
Exhibitioner, B.A. 1904, M.A. 1943, Hon.
Fell. 1944; Fell. Winchester, 1933, Warden
1946; Barrister-at-Law, Lincoln's Inn, 1906;
K.C. 1924; Bencher, 1929; and Treasurer, 1951;
apptd. a Judge of the High Court of Justice,
Chancery Div. 1937-44; apptd. a Lord of
Appeal in Ordinary, 1944, and again, 1954;
Lord High Chancellor, 1951-54; High Steward
of Winchester 1951, and Freeman of the City

1963. He m. 28 Mar. 1912, Mary Hope, dau. of Judge F. H. Mellor, K.C., and had issue,
1. Gavin Alexander, b. 1 Aug. 1915; educ. Winchester and New Coll. Oxford; Barrister-at-Law, Lincoln's Inn, 1945; served in World War II, Capt. Royal Wilts Yeo.; d. unm. 19 Mar. 1951.
2. John Mellor, b. 1 Aug. 1915, twin with his brother; educ. Winchester and Magdalene Coll. Camb.; Barrister-at-Law, Inner Temple, 1939; m. 12 Aug. 1944, Barbara, dau. of T. Robinson, of Greenfield Mount, St. Helens, and widow of F/O A. J. Willock, R.A.F. He served in World War II, and was k. In action at Arnhem 23 Sept. 1944. His widow m. 3rdly Angus Macpherson, M.B., M.R.C.P.
He was cr. Kt. Bach. 1937; made P.C. 1944; cr. a life peer as Baron Simonds, of Sparsholt, co. Southampton, 18 April 1944; cr. an hereditary peer, same style, 24 June 1952, and cr. Viscount Simonds, of Sparsholt, co. Southampton, 18 Oct. 1954. Viscount Simonds d.s.p.m.s. 28 June 1971.
ARMS—Tierced in pale, azure, gules and vert, three trefoils slipped or.
CREST—An ermine ppr. resting the sinister paw upon the astronomical sign of Taurus sable, and holding in the mouth a trefoil slipped or.
SUPPORTERS—On either side an ermine ppr. each charged on the shoulder, the dexter with a hop leaf or, and the sinister with a bezant.
MOTTO—Simplex munditiis.

SNELL

PEERAGE—U.K. Baron Snell, of Plumstead, co. Kent.
SURNAME—Snell.
CR.—23 Mar. 1931. **EXT.**—21 April 1944.
HISTORY—Henry Snell, **Baron Snell,** b. 1 April 1865; educ. Nottingham Univ. Coll., London Sch. of Economics, and Heidelberg Univ.; was a politician and secularist, worked as a farm hand and in public houses, and joined the secularist movement and the I.L.P.; mem. L.C.C., 1919-25; Chm. 1934-35; M.P. for East Woolwich, as Labour man, 1922-31, having previously contested three times Huddersfield; cr. Baron Snell, of Plumstead, co. Kent, 23 Mar. 1931; had been sec. of Union of Ethical Societies, and Sec. Secular Education League, 1907-31; Chm. British Ethical Union, and Chm. L.C.C. 1934-38; was made P.C. 1937, and cr. C.H. 1943. Deputy Leader, House of Lords, 1940-44. He wrote several books and pamphlets, and d. 21 April 1944. Lord Snell's residence was 75 Semour Street, W.2. His club was Connaught.

SNOWDEN

PEERAGE—U.K. Viscount Snowden, of Ickornshaw, W.R. York.
SURNAME—Snowden.
CR.—24 Nov. 1931. **EXT.**—15 May 1937.
HISTORY—Joseph Snowden, of Cowling, co. York, who d. 1835 had a son,
John Snowden, of Cowling, b. 1829; m.

1851, Martha (d. 1922) dau. of Peter Nelson, of Cowling, and d. 1889, leaving with other issue,
Philip Snowden, **Viscount Snowden,** of Ickornshaw, b. 18 July 1864; educ. local board school and privately; entered the Civil Service as a clerk, and served in it 1886-93; while working in Inland Revenue had a severe bicycle accident, during convalescence from which he studied Socialism, and changed from Radicalism to support of Labour movement; worked as a journalist and author, and became Chm. of Independent Labour Party 1903-06, and 1917-20; contested Blackburn and Wakefield, and became Labour M.P. for Blackburn, 1906-18, a seat which he lost because he opposed the first World War; Labour M.P. for Colne Valley Div. of Yorkshire, 1922-31; made P.C. 1924; Chancellor of the Exchequer, 1924, and 1929-31; cr. Viscount Snowden, of Ickornshaw, W.R. York, 24 Nov. 1931; Lord Privy Seal 1932; m. 13 Mar. 1905, Ethel, J.P London, dau. of Alderman Richard Annakin, J.P., of Harrogate. She wrote several books, and was a mem. of the Labour Commission of Enquiry to Russia (1920). She d. 1951. He d.s.p. 15 May 1937. Viscount Snowden was one of the stalwarts of the Labour movement but when, in company with Ramsay Macdonald and Jimmy Thomas he changed over to sit in the National Government in 1931, his name was execrated among Socialists. His conduct of affairs at the Treasury was viewed by financial circles as being orthodox.
Viscount Snowden's home was Eden Lodge, Tilford, Surrey, and 72 Carlisle Mansions, Westminster, S.W.1.

**SOLWAY

PEERAGE—U.K. Baron Solway, of Kinmount, co. Dumfries.
SURNAME—Douglas.
CR.—7 June 1833. **EXT.**—3 Dec. 1837.
HISTORY—Sir Charles Douglas Douglas, 6th Marquess of Queensberry, b. 1777; m. 13 Aug. 1803, Lady Caroline Douglas-Scott, dau. of 3rd Duke of Buccleuch and Queensberry, and had issue eight daus. The Marquess who was a Representative Peer for Scotland, 1812-32, was cr. a peer of the U.K. as **Baron Solway** of Kinmount, co. Dumfries, on 7 June 1833 and d.s.p.m. 3 Dec. 1837 when the U.K barony became extinct and he was s. in the Marquessate and his other honours by his brother,
John Douglas, 7th Marquess of Queensberry, etc. (see extant peerages).

**SOMERS

PEERAGE—U.K. Viscount Eastnor and Earl Somers.
SURNAME—Somers-Cocks (formerly Cocks).
CR.—17 July 1821. **EXT.**—26 Sept. 1883.
HISTORY—Charles Cocks, 1st Baron Somers, (see extant peerages, Somers, B.) had an eldest son,
John Somers Cocks, 2nd Baron Somers, and **1st Earl Somers,** b. 6 May 1760; adm. Westminster Sch. 1774; St. Alban Hall, Oxford, 1778; M.P. West Looe, 1782-84, Grampound,

1784-1790; and Reigate, 1790-1806; s. as 2nd Baron 30 Jan. 1806; cr. Viscount Eastnor and Earl Somers, 17 July 1821; Lord Lt. of Herefordshire, 1817; m. (1) 19 Mar. 1785, Margaret, (d. 9 Feb. 1831) dau. of Rev. T. R. Nash, and had issue with a dau., d. unm.,

1. Edward Charles, Major in the Army, b. 1786; d. unm. k. in assault of Burgos 8 Oct. 1812.
2. John Somers, **2nd Earl Somers** (see below).
3. James Somers, Rev., Preb. of Hereford, and Canon of Worcester, b. 1790; d 1856.

The Earl m. (2) 3 June 1834, his cousin Jane, dau. of James Cocks, of London, a banker, and widow of Rev. George Waddington, and d. 5 Jan. 1841, being s. by his second son,
John Somers Somers-Cocks, **2nd Earl Somers,** b. 19 Mar. 1788; educ. Westminster Sch. 1797-1803; Cornet 16th Light Dragoons, 1803; Lt. 1805; Capt. 1806, 2nd Dragoon Guards, 1807, ret. 1812; M.P. Reigate, 1812-18 and 1832-41, and for Hereford, 1818-32; assumed surname of Somers before that of Cocks, 29 April 1841; Lord Lt. of Herefordshire 1845; m. 4 Mar. 1815, Lady Caroline Harriet Yorke, fourth dau. of 3rd Earl of Hardwicke and d. 5 Oct. 1852, having had with two daus. who d. young or unm.,

1. Charles Somers, **3rd Earl Somers** (see below).
1. Caroline Margaret, m. 1849, Rev. the Hon. C. L. Courtenay, Canon of Windsor, (Devon, E.), and d.s.p. 14 Nov. 1894.
2. Harriet Catherine, m. 1850, F. R. Wegg-Prosser, of Belmont, Hereford, and d. 1893, leaving issue.

The only son,
Charles Somers Somers-Cocks, **3rd Earl Somers,** b. 14 July 1819; m. 2 Oct. 1850, Virginia (d. 1910) dau. of James Pattle, B.C.S., and d. 26 Sept. 1883, having had issue three daus. The Earldom and Viscounty became extinct and the barony passed to his cousin,
Philip Reginald Cocks, 5th Baron Somers, (see extant peerages, Somers, B.).
ARMS—Quarterly 1 and 4, Sable a chevron between three stags' attires argent (Cocks). 2 and 3, Vert a fess dancettée ermine (Somers).
CRESTS—1. On a mount ppr. a stag lodged reguardant argent attired sable (Cocks). 2. A bay tree ppr., suspended therefrom by a strap gules a cuirass with epaulets and fasces argent charged with an ermine spot sable (Somers).
SUPPORTERS—On either side a lion ermine gorged with a collar indented vert.
MOTTO—Prodesse quam conspici.

SORENSON

PEERAGE—U.K. Life. Baron Sorenson, of Leyton, co. Essex.
SURNAME—Sorensen.
CR.—15 Dec. 1964. **EXT.**—8 Oct. 1971.
HISTORY—Jens (James) Sorenson, came to England from Denmark, being described as the son of one Soren of Silkeborg in that country, who was b. about 1815, and d. about 1875. Jens Sorensen who became a blacksmith in Islington, was b. 29 Dec. 1840, at Silkeborg;

m. Aug. 1866, Ann (d. 15 Sept. 1909), dau. of `J. Hilsdon, of Oxfordshire, and d. Oct. 1919, having had issue,

1. William James (see below).
2. Laurentz, a postmaster in S. Africa, b. 1869, had a wife named Elizabeth and d. 1915.
3. Frank, b. 1871; m. Lilian, dau. of M. Lock, and d.s.p. 1943.
4. Soren known as Sydney, b. 1873; m. Sylvia, dau. of L. Stetzel, of Hackney, and d. 1931. She d. 1931. They had issue, a dau. Sylvia who m. 1930, Frank Sloggett, and had issue, a son and a dau.
1. Ada, b. 1878; d. 1927.

The eldest son,
William James Sorensen, a silversmith, b. 3 May 1868; educ. St. Mary Abbot's Sch., Kensington, and in Denmark; m. 4 Aug. 1890, Alice Jemima, dau. of John Tester, of Worthing, a fisherman. She d. 18 April 1934. He d. 12 April 1925. They had issue,

1. Reginald William, **Baron Sorenson** (see below).
2. Edward John Laurentz, b. 29 Aug. 1899; m. 23 April 1927, Ethel May, dau. of W. J. Wallis, of Walthamstow, and had issue,
   Colin Edward, A.R.C.A., b. 1930; educ. Lower Sch. of John Lyon at Harrow and the Royal Coll. of Art; m. 1966, Mary Owen, M.A., dau. of Lt. Col. O. H. Burn, of Auckland N.Z., and had issue, Anna Mary Winifred, b. 1969.
   Janet Ethel, b. 1936; educ. Ickenham High Sch. and St. Katharine's Training Coll.
1. Elsie Alice, b. 10 Mar. 1894.
2. Irene Winifred, b. 26 Feb. 1896.

The elder son,
The Rev. the **Lord Sorenson,** Reginald William Sorenson, was b. 19 June 1891; educ. Elementary Sch. and in a Protestant Religious Community; he became an errand boy at age of 14, but studied for the ministry, and became for 21 years the Minister of the Free (Unitarian) Church at Walthamstow from 1916-37; he threw himself into political work, and became mem. of Walthamstow U.D.C., and Essex C.C. 1924-45, M.P. for Leyton West 1929-31, and 1935-50, also for Leyton 1950-64; A few weeks after being returned for Leyton, in 1964, Sorenson was offered a life peerage which he accepted, as he said, "after much reflection and some reluctance", the reason being to provide a seat for Mr. Patrick Gordon Walker, the Foreign Sec. who had been defeated at Smethwick. In the bye-election in Jan. 1965 a Conservative was elected in place of Walker, who did not eventually succeed until 1966. Lord Sorenson was much concerned with Indian affairs, and travelled all over the world to show his sympathy with the underdog. In 1965-68 he was Lord-in-Waiting to H.M. the Queen Elizabeth II. He wrote various books and pamphlets of a political nature. From the Federal Republic of Germany he received the Grand Cross of the Order of Merit. His creation as a life peer was that of Baron Sorenson, of Leyton, co. Essex, 15 Dec. 1964. He m. 22 Jan. 1916, Muriel, J.P. Essex, dau. of Rev. William Harvey Smith, Baptist Min. of Long Sutton, co. Lincoln, and d. 8 Oct. 1971, having had issue,

1. Michael Malcolm Reginald, b. 1919; educ. Sir George Monoux Gr. Sch., and Dalton Hall, Oxford; m. 1961, Jennifer, dau. of William Adams, of Stockbridge, Newcastle-upon-Tyne, and had issue, Richard, b. 1967, and Rachel Mary, b. 1969.
2. Brian John, b. 1923; educ. Sir George Monoux, Gr. Sch.; d. unm. 1947.
1. Moira Muriel, b. 1917; m. 1951, D. G. Clark, and had issue, two children, Bryony Sorensen, b. 1955, and Linden Sorensen, b. 1960.

Seat was 38 Woodside Park Avenue, Whipps Cross, Walthamstow, E.17. The Lord Sorenson's club was India.

SOUTHWARK

PEERAGE—U.K. Baron Southwark, of Southwark, co. London.
SURNAME—Causton.
CR.—13 July 1910. EXT.—23 Feb. 1929.
HISTORY—Alderman Sir Joseph Causton, printer, founder of Sir Joseph Causton and Sons Ltd., m. Mary Anne, (d. 1892), dau. of Edward Potter, and d. 27 May 1871, having, had with other issue, a second son,
Richard Knight Causton, **Baron Southwark,** b. 25 Sept. 1843; was Liberal M.P. for Colchester, 1880-85, and for West Southwark, 1888-1910; a lord of the Treasury, 1892-95; and Paymaster Gen. 1905-10; P.C. 1906; cr. Baron Southwark, of Southwark, co. London, 13 July 1910; Pres. of London Chamber of Commerce, 1913; twice Master of the Worshipful Co. of Skinners, a Lt. for the City of London; m. 10 Aug. 1871, Selina Mary, dau. of Sir Thomas Chambers, Q.C., M.P., Recorner of London. Lord Southwark d.s.p. 23 Feb. 1929. His widow d. 1 Jan. 1932. Lord Southwark's residence was 12 Devonshire Place, W. His clubs were Reform, National Liberal, Gresham and Devonshire.
Some of Messrs. Causton's records were destroyed in the war, and for this cause they were unable to supply details of Sir Joseph Causton's antecedents.

SOUTHWOOD

PEERAGE—U.K. Baron Southwood, of Fernhurst, co. Sussex. Viscount Southwood.
SURNAME—Elias.
CR.—Barony 11 June 1937. Viscounty 19 Feb. 1946. EXT.—10 April 1946.
HISTORY—Julius Salter Elias, **Baron and Viscount Southwood,** was b. 5 Jan. 1873 at Birmingham, the son of David Elias; he entered Odhams Press in 1894, and by 1898 had become a Director, and in 1920 Managing Dir., Chm. in 1934. His influence on the British Press was very great, for in the group of Odhams Publications, and through its associated cos. he became the publisher of *The People, The Daily Herald, News Review, Illustrated, Debrett's Peerage, Sporting Life, Woman* etc.; he printed the first issue of *John Bull* in 1906 for Horatio Bottomley, from whom he bought it in 1920. Viscount Southwood was instrumental in raising large sums for many charities,

and was Trustee for several charities in connection with the newspaper industry, also Pres. or Vice-Pres. of many other associations. He was cr. Baron Southwood, of Fernhurst, co. Sussex, 11 June 1937, and Viscount Southwood, 19 Feb. 1946. He m. 1906, Alice Louise, dau. of Charles Stone Collard, and d. 10 April 1946.
ARMS—Or on a bend azure, between four scrolls of paper two in chief and as many in base in saltire ppr. tied with a riband gules, three bees volant of the field.
CREST—In front of a terrestrial globe ppr. a staff in bend sinister gules, flying therefrom a pennon per pale sable and azure, thereon a flash of lightning or.
SUPPORTERS—On either side a lion or gorged with a collar pendent therefrom an escutcheon gules charged with a cap of Mercury gold.
BADGE—Two pens in saltire enfiled with a baron's coronet or.
MOTTO—Ars impressoria gentium concordia.
Viscount Southwood's residences were Tree Tops, Marley Heights, Fernhurst, nr. Haslemere, and Southwood Court, Highgate, N.6. The enormous expansion of Odhams under his direction, which caused Long Acre to be known coloquially as Odhams Street, was due to the skill with which he went on securing contracts for the printing side of the business.

STALBRIDGE

PEERAGE—U.K. Baron Stalbridge, of Stalbridge, co. Dorset.
SURNAME—Grosvenor.
CR.—22 Mar. 1886. EXT.—24 Dec. 1949.
HISTORY—Richard Grosvenor, 2nd Marquess of Westminster (see extant peerages Westminster, D.), had a fourth son,
Richard de Aquila Grosvenor, **1st Baron Stalbridge,** b. 28 Jan. 1837; M.A. Camb., F.R.G.S., M.P. for co. Flint, 1861-86; Vice Chamberlain to H.M. Household, 1872-74, and Patronage Sec. to the Treasury, 1880-85; made P.C., and cr. Baron Stalbridge, of Stalbridge, co. Dorset, 22 Mar. 1886; m. (1) 5 Nov. 1874, Hon. Beatrice Charlotte Elizabeth Vesey, (d. 15 Jan. 1876) dau. of 3rd Viscount de Vesci, and had issue,
1. Elizabeth Emma Beatrice, b. 7 Dec. 1875; m. 1 June 1899, Adm. Sir Aubrey Clare Hugh Smith and d. 31 Jan. 1931, leaving issue.

He m. (2) 3 April 1879, Eleanor Frances Beatrice, dau. of Robert Hamilton-Stubber, of Moyne, Queen's Co., and by her who d. 21 Mar. 1911, had further issue,
1. Hugh, **2nd Baron Stalbridge** (see below).
2. Gilbert, served in S. African War, 1900-02, and in World War I, Capt. 2nd Regt. King Edward's Horse, and Lt. The Rifle Brigade; b. 22 Aug. 1881; m. 4 July 1913, Effie, dau. of Rev. D. C. Cree, and d. 15 June 1939.
3. Richard Eustace, served in World War I, 1914-15 (despatches, M.C.), Capt. R.H.A.; b. 27 Jan. 1883; k. in action 13 Oct. 1915.
2. Blanche, twin with Hugh, m. 2 July 1901, Lt. Col. J. H. E. Holford, C.M.G., D.S.O., and had issue.

3. Eleanor Lilian, b. 18 Jan. 1885; m. 26 July 1906, Major Grant, and had issue.
The first Lord Stalbridge d. 18 May 1912, and was s. by his eldest son,
Hugh Grosvenor, **2nd Baron Stalbridge**, b. 5 May 1880; educ. Eton; served in S. African War, 1899-1902 (despatches twice) and in World War I (1914-18) (despatches twice, M.C.) Lt. 14th Hussars and Northamptonshire Yeo.; m. 10 Nov. 1903, Gladys Elizabeth, dau. of Brinsley de Courcy Nixon and d. 24 Dec. 1949. They had had issue,
Hugh Raufe, 2nd Lt. 7th Hussars, A.D.C. to Gov. of S. Australia, b. 17 Aug. 1904; B.A. Ch. Ch. Oxford; d. 6 Jan. 1930, as result of an aeroplane accident.
ARMS—Azure a garb or, a crescent of the last for difference.
CREST—A talbot statant or, charged with a crescent azure.
SUPPORTERS—On either side a talbot reguardant or, collared azure, charged on the shoulder with a crescent of the last.
MOTTO—Virtus non stemma.
Lord Stalbridge's residence was Pounds Farm, Eastbury, Newbury, Berks. His club was the Cavalry.

STAMFORDHAM

PEERAGE—U.K. Baron Stamfordham, of Stamfordham, co. Northumberland.
SURNAME—Bigge.
CR.—23 June 1911. EXT.—31 Mar. 1931.
HISTORY—William Bigge, of Newcastle-upon-Tyne, m. 1666, Isabel, dau. and heir of Thomas Dent, and d. 1690, having an only son,
Thomas Bigge, of Newcastle, m. about 1706, Elizabeth, dau. of Edward Hindmarsh, of the Six Clerks' Office, and had with other issue, an eldest son,
William Bigge, of Benton, co. Northumberland, High Sheriff, 1750, one of the Six Clerks in Chancery, b. 1707; m. 29 Jan. 1736, Mary, dau. and heir of Charles Clarke, of Ovingham, and d. 30 June 1785, having had with two others sons who d.s.p., an eldest son,
Thomas Charles Bigge, High Sheriff, co. Northumberland, 1772, b. 1739; m. 1772, Jemima, dau. of William Ord, of Fenham, and d. 10 Oct. 1794, having had with other issue,
1. Charles William (see below).
2. John Thomas, Chief Justice of Trinidad, b. 1780.
3. Thomas Hanway, of Newcastle, m. 1815, Charlotte, dau. of Rev. James Scott, Rector of St. Lawrence, Southampton, and d. 1824, having had issue.
1. Grace Julia, m. (1) 1817, her cousin Thomas C. Glyn, who d. 1827 (Glyn of Gaunts, Bt.), and (2) 1836, H. B. Sawbridge of East Haddon Hall, co. Northampton, and d. 1872.
The eldest son,
Charles William Bigge, of Linden and Ovingham, co. Northumberland, High Sheriff, 1802, b. 28 Oct. 1773; m. 27 Jan. 1802, Alicia, dau. of C. Wilkinson, of Newcastle, and d. 8 Dec. 1849, having had issue with seven other sons and four daus., a fifth son,

The Rev. John Frederick Bigge, Vicar of Stamfordham, co. Northumberland b. 12 July 1814; m. 14 Dec. 1843, Caroline Mary, dau. of Nathaniel Ellison, and d. 28 Feb. 1885. She d. 28 July 1901. They had issue,
1. Edward Ellison, of Ovingham, co. Northumberland and Watton House, co. Hertford, b. 15 Feb. 1846; m. 1887, Annie Elizabeth, dau. of John Straker, of Stagshaw, co. Northumberland and d. 1909 leaving issue.
2. Henry Charles, Rear Adm. R.N., b. 7 July 1847; m. Beatrice, dau. of Rev. Canon W. H. Wade, and d. 1908.
3. Arthur John, **Baron Stamfordham** (see below).
4. William Egelric, Sir, M.A. Oxford, Judge of the Chief Court, Lower Burma, b. 1850; d. unm. 1916.
5. Charles Wilkinson, of Humshaugh, co. Northumberland b. 1858; d. unm. 1916.
1. Alice Frances, m. 1880, 3rd Lord Teignmouth, who d.s.p. 1915.
2. Mary Augusta, m. 1874, J. H. Ridley, who d. 1904 leaving issue.
3. Julia Charlotte.
4. Caroline Amy.
The third son,
Sir Arthur John Bigge, **Baron Stamfordham,** b. 18 June 1849; Lt. R.A. 1869, Lt. Col. 1892, and ret. 1898; served in the Zulu War, 1879, (despatches), and was A.D.C. to Sir Evelyn Wood; he was a friend of the Prince Imperial who was k. in the Zulu War; Queen Victoria summoned Lt. Bigge to Balmoral so that he could give her particulars of the Prince's death; she was impressed with him and made him a Groom-in-Waiting, and Asst. Priv. Sec. 1880; he was a royal servant from that time until 1931, working for Queen Victoria, Edward VII and George V, mostly in capacity of Priv. Sec. He was cr. C.B. 1885; C.M.G. 1887; K.C.B. 1895; G.C.V.O. and K.C.M.G. 1901; I.S.O. 1903; K.C.S.I. 1906; G.C.I.E. 1911; G.C.B. 1916; and Baron Stamfordham, of Stamfordham, co. Northumberland, 23 June 1911. He m. 10 Feb. 1881, Constance, dau. of the Rev. William Frederick Neville, (Braybrooke, B.). and d 31 Mar. 1931. She d. 24 April 1922. They had issue,
1. John Neville, Lt. K.R.R.C., b. 14 Oct. 1887; educ. Eton and R.M.C. Sandhurst; k. in action in France, 15 May 1915.
1. Victoria Eugenie, b. 28 Nov. 1881; m. 25 Sept. 1909, Capt. H. R. A. Adeane, who was k. in action 2 Nov. 1914 having had issue.
2. Margaret, b. 5 July 1885.
ARMS—Ermine on a fess engrailed between three martlets sable beaked gules, as many ducal coronets or.
CREST—A cockatrice's head ermine, ducally crowned or, between two wings expanded azure, each charged with a ducal coronet of the second.
SUPPORTERS—Dexter, A scribe holding in the exterior hand a pen; Sinister, A man at arms supporting in the exterior hand a halbert all ppr.
MOTTO—Gladio stiloque ferax.

STANMORE

PEERAGE—U.K. Baron Stanmore, of Great Stanmore, co. Middlesex.
SURNAME—Hamilton-Gordon.
CR.—21 Aug. 1893. EXT.—13 April 1957.
HISTORY—The 4th Earl of Aberdeen had a ygst. son,
Sir Arthur Hamilton-Gordon, **1st Baron Stanmore**, b. 26 Nov. 1829; M.A. Camb.; M.P. Beverley, 1854-57; Lt. Gov. New Brunswick, 1861-66; Gov. and C. in C. of Trinidad, 1866-70; of Mauritius, 1871-74; of Fiji, 1875-80; and of New Zealand, 1880-82; High Cmr. and Consul Gen. for Western Pacific, 1877-83; Gov. of Ceylon, 1883-90; cr. C.M.G. 1859, K.C.M.G. 1871; G.C.M.G. 1878, and Baron Stanmore, of Great Stanmore, co. Middlesex, 21 Aug. 1893; m. 24 Sept. 1865, Rachel Emily, dau. of Sir George Shaw Lefevre, K.C.B. She d. 26 Jan. 1889. He d. 30 Jan. 1912, having had issue, with a dau. Rachel Nevil, b. 13 July 1869, and who d. unm. 22 Oct. 1947, a son and successor,
Sir George Arthur Maurice Hamilton-Gordon, **2nd Baron Stanmore**, b. 3 Jan. 1871; educ. Winchester and Trin. Coll. Camb., B.A. 1892; Capt. 3rd Bn. Hampshire Regt.; a Lord-in-Waiting to George V, 1914-22; a Dep. Speaker of the House of Lords, 1916; K.J. St. J., and Sec. Gen. of that Order, 1921-22; Treasurer of St. Bart's Hosp. 1921-37; Chief Liberal Whip in Lords, 1923-44; Lord Chm. of Cttees, and Dep. Speaker, House of Lords, 1944-46; cr. C.V.O. 1922, K.C.V.O. 1930, and made P.C. 1932; d. 13 April 1957.
ARMS—Quarterly 1 and 4, Azure three boars' heads couped within a double tressure, adorned with roses, thistles and fleurs-de-lis alternately, or (Gordon); 2 and 3, Quarterly (i) and (iv), Gules three cinquefoils pierced ermine, and (ii) and (iii), Argent a lymphad, the sails furled, the whole within a bordure sable (Hamilton).
CRESTS—1. Two arms from the shoulder naked, holding a bow or, to let fly an arrow argent. 2. Out of a ducal coronet or an oak tree, fructed and penetrated, transversely, in the main stem by a frame saw, inscribed with the word "Thorough" all ppr., the tree charged with an escutcheon argent thereon a heart gules.
SUPPORTERS—Dexter, A chief of the Fiji Islands habited and supporting with the exterior hand, a club, all ppr. Sinister, An adigar of the Island of Ceylon habited and holding in the exterior hand a staff of office, all ppr.
MOTTO—Haud immemor.

STERNDALE

PEERAGE—U.K. Baron Sterndale, of King Sterndale, co. Derby.
SURNAME—Pickford.
CR.—14 Nov. 1918. EXT.—17 Aug. 1923.
HISTORY—Thomas Edward Pickford, of Manchester, m. Georgiana Todd, dau. of Jeremiah Todd Naylor, of Manchester, and they had a second son,
Sir William Pickford, **Baron Sterndale**, b. 1 Oct. 1848; educ. Liverpool Coll. and Exeter Coll. Oxford, B.A. 1873; M.A. 1908; Barrister-at-Law, Inner Temple, 1874; Q.C. 1893;

Recorder of Oldham, 1901-04; Recorder of Liverpool, 1904-07; Bencher, Inner Temple, 1904; Commissioner of Assize North Eastern Circuit, 1906; Judge of the High Court of Justice, 1907-14; Lord Justice of Appeal, 1914-18; cr. Kt. Bach. 1907; P.C. 1914; mem. of Dardanelles Commission, 1916, Chm. 1917; Pres. of the Probate, Divorce and Admiralty Div. and Judge of the High Court of Justice, 1918-19; cr. Baron Sterndale, of King Sterndale, co. Derby, 14 Nov. 1918; Master of the Rolls, 1919-23; m. 18 Aug. 1880, Alice Mary, dau. of J. W. Brooks, of Sibton, co. Suffolk. She d. 5 Sept. 1884. He d. 17 Aug. 1923, leaving issue,
1. Dorothy Frances, O.B.E., J.P. Derby, mem. Post Office Advisory Council,
2. Mary Ada, C.B.E., M.A. Oxford, M.P. North Div. Hammersmith, d. unm. 6 Mar. 1934.

STEVENSON

PEERAGE—U.K. Baron Stevenson, of Holmbury, co. Surrey.
(Also a baronetcy cr. 21 Feb. 1917.)
SURNAME—Stevenson.
CR.—7 May 1924. EXT.—10 June 1926.
HISTORY—Archibald Stuart Stevenson, of Carriden, Kilmarnock, m. Elizabeth, dau. of James Morrison, and d. 1895. She d. 1894. They had an eldest son,
Sir James Stevenson, **Baron Stevenson**, b. 2 April 1873; educ. Kilmarnock Academy; entered firm of John Walker and Sons, the famous whisky makers, and became Man. Dir.; was Dir. of Area Organization, Ministry of Munitions, 1915-17; Vice Chm. of the Ministry of Munitions Advisory Cttee. 1917; held several other postwar appts. including that of a mem. of the Army Council, 1919; and mem. of the Air Council 1919-21; was cr. a baronet 21 Feb. 1917; G.C.M.G., 1922, and Baron Stevenson, of Holmbury, co. Surrey, 7 May 1924. He was Chm. of the Board of the British Empire Exhibition at Wembley, 1924 and 1925. He m. (1) 18 June 1897, Jessie Baird, dau. of James Hogarth, of Ardrossan; she d. 30 Sept. 1917. He m. (2) 1918, Stella, dau. of W. J. Fraser, of Hampstead, and widow of E. H. Johnstone. He d.s.p. 10 June 1926, and his widow d. 7 July 1935.
ARMS—Azure a chevron between in chief two fleurs-de-lis, and in base a sun in splendour issuant or.
CREST—A dexter hand couped at the wrist grasping a roll of parchment ppr. and a pipe or in saltire.
SUPPORTERS—On either side a squirrel charged on the shoulder with a thistle leaved and slipped ppr.
BADGE—A thistle leaved and slipped and a sprig of hazel fructed ppr. in saltire enfiled with a baron's coronet or.
MOTTO—Carry on.

STONHAM

PEERAGE—U.K. Life Baron Stonham, of Earl Stonham, co. Suffolk.
SURNAME—Collins.
CR.—2 Aug. 1958. EXT.—22 Dec. 1971.

HISTORY—Victor Collins, by his wife Eliza Sarah Williams, had issue,

Victor John Collins, who was b. 1 July 1903; educ. the Regent Street Polytechnic, and London Sch. of Economics, London Univ.; entered the family business of J. Collins and Sons, Shoreditch, in 1923. It was a furniture and basket making firm. "He was descended from Huguenot ancestors who had been weaving silk in Spitalfields, in the 17th century and his own family business dated from that period. He had also a 70 acre farm at Earl Stonham in Suffolk, where he specialized in growing willows for his own factory" (*The Times* obituary notice). He became Gov. Dir. of the family firm in 1931, and Dir. of several other private cos., was Pres. of Employers' Federation of Cane and Willow Worker Asscns. 1932; Chm. Nat. Basket and Willow Workers Asscns. 1941. He was Pres. of Nat. Willow Growers Asscn. 1946-53; Founder and first Chm. of Jt. Industrial Council for Basket-making Industry; M.P. Taunton Div. of Somerset 1945-50; for Shoreditch and Finsbury 1954-58; Jt. Parl. Under Sec. of State, Home Office, 1964-67; Min. of State Home Office, 1967-69 where he was given special responsibility for prisons, he having been before that Pres. of the Reform Council, and connected with other asscns. in connection with welfare of prisoners; served in Home Guard, 1941-45; awarded O.B.E. 1946; P.C. 1969, and cr. a life peer as **Baron Stonham,** of Earl Stonham, co. Suffolk, taking his title from his farm estate; m. 30 April 1929, Violet Mary, dau. of T. E. Savage, of Salop and Crouch End, N., and d. 23 Dec. 1971, having had issue,

Ian Greville, b. 24 Nov. 1941; educ. Queen's Coll. Taunton and Kingston Grm. Sch.

Lord Stonham lived at the Old Hall, Highgate, London, N.6.

STOPFORD OF FALLOWFIELD

PEERAGE—U.K. Life. Baron Stopford of Fallowfield, of Hindley Green in the co. Palatine of Lancashire.
SURNAME—Stopford.
CR.—5 Aug. 1958. **EXT.**—6 Mar. 1961.
HISTORY—John Stopford, of Upholland, Wigan, co. Lancaster, d. 25 Dec. 1889, leaving issue,

1. Thomas Rinck (see below).
2. John Bird, Rev. Canon, M.A. Camb.
3. Robert, M.D., of Southport, and afterwards of Sydney, Australia.
4. Keble, of Adelaide, Australia.

The eldest son,

Thomas Rinck Stopford, Mining Engineer, b. 12 Mar. 1856; educ. Upholland Grm. Sch. and Wigan Mining Coll.; m. 25 Aug. 1886, Mary Tyer (d. 14 Mar. 1927) dau. of James Johnson of Bolton, co. Lancs. and d. Mar. 1945 having had issue,

1. John Sebastian Bach, **Baron Stopford** of Fallowfield (see below).
2. Thomas Rinck, b. 18 Oct. 1892; educ. Manchester Grm. Sch. and Manchester Univ., B.Sc. 1912, M.Sc. 1913, became Industrial Research Chemist; m. 19 July

1928, Mercy Margaret (d. 11 Aug. 1956) dau. of Arthur Mellor, of Huddersfield, and had issue,
  (1) Arthur Robert, b. 11 Aug. 1932; served in World War II in R.A.F. 1950-52; m. 15 Mar. 1958, Janet, dau. of George W. Wood, of Huddersfield.
  (1) Joan Mercy Mary, b. 13 Feb. 1929; m. 23 Mar. 1957, Jeffrey Sykes of Huddersfield, and had issue.
  (2) Betsy Patricia, b. 30 Nov. 1935.
3. Eric, d. young.

The eldest son,

Sir John Sebastian Bach Stopford, **Baron Stopford** of Fallowfield, b. 25 June 1888; educ. Liverpool Coll., Manchester Grm. Sch. and Manchester Univ. M.B., Ch.B. 1911, M.D. 1915; F.R.S. 1927, Lecturer in Anatomy, afterwards Prof. of Anatomy, Manchester 1919-37; Prof. of Experimental Neurology, Manchester Univ. 1937-56; Dean of the Medical Sch. 1923-27, Vice Chancellor 1934-56, and Emeritus Prof. 1956; cr. M.B.E. 1919, Kt. Bach. 1941, K.B.E. 1955 and Baron Stopford of Fallowfield, of Hindley Green, in the co. Palatine of Lancaster, 5 Aug. 1958; m. 7 Sept. 1916, Lily, M.B., Ch.B., 1914, Hon. M.A., Manchester, 1957, dau. of John Allan, of Blackburn, co. Lancs, and d. 6 Mar. 1961 having had issue,

Thomas, b. 28 June 1921; educ. Manchester Grm. Sch.; served in World War II, 1939-45, as Capt. R.A.; m. 6 July 1943, Mary Howard, dau. of Alfred James Small, of Manchester and had issue,
  John Thomas, b. 10 Dec. 1944.

Lord Stopford's residence was at Knott Lea, Arnside, Westmorland. His club was the Athenaeum.

Lord Stopford was one of the 14 life peers created under the Life Peerages Act 1958, July. As such he was included with the remaining 13 in an appendix to the 1959 Burke's Peerage, with the explanation: "They were too late to be included in the main section of the volume for the present edition, but will be inserted in their proper alphabetical places in subsequent issues." This was fair enough but what was of amusing nature was that when the 1958 Act was passed the first sets of life peerages created under it were announced in lists apart from the twice yearly honours lists, as though for all the world, the newcomers were not quite in the same class as the hereditary peers. This strange practice soon ceased and became of course quite inoperative after 1964, the advent of the Labour Gov., since which date none but life peerages have been created.

STRATHCLYDE

PEERAGE—U.K. Baron Strathclyde, of Sandyford, co. Lanark.
SURNAME—Ure.
CR.—15 Jan. 1914. **EXT.**—2 Oct. 1928.
HISTORY—John Ure, of Cairndhu, Helensburgh, co. Dumbarton, D.L. cos. Lanark and Dumbarton, and for Glasgow, also Lord Provost of Glasgow, and LL.D., d. 1 Aug. 1901 having had by Isabella his wife, dau. of John Dibb, of Glasgow, a second son, .

Sir Alexander Ure, **Baron Strathclyde,** b. 24 Feb. 1853; educ. Glasgow and Edinburgh

Univs. M.A. Glasgow, 1872, LL.B. 1877; Advocate, Scots Bar, 1878; Lecturer on Consitutional Law and History, Glasgow, 1878-88; Q.C. 1897; Solicitor Gen. for Scotland 1905-09, Lord Advocate, 1909-13, and Lord Justice Gen. 1913-20. He was M.P. for Linlithgowshire, 1895-1913; made P.C. 1909; cr. Baron Strathclyde, of Sandyford, co. Lanark, 15 Jan. 1914, and G.B.E. 1917. He m. 1879, Margaret McDowell, dau. of Thomas Steven, of Ardlui House, Helensburgh, co. Dumbarton, and d. 2 Oct. 1928, having had issue,
Christobel Helen, b. 31 Mar. 1885; m. 17 Oct. 1911, Lt. Col. J. J. Readman, D.S.O., and d. 11 June 1918, leaving issue.

STRATHCONA AND MOUNT ROYAL

PEERAGE—U.K. Baron Strathcona and Mount Royal, of Glencoe, co. Argyll, and of Mount Royal, Quebec, Canada.
SURNAME—Smith.
CR.—23 Aug. 1897. **EXT.**—21 Jan. 1914.
HISTORY—Sir Donald Alexander Smith, **1st Baron Strathcona** and Mount Royal, was the second son of Alexander Smith, of Archieston, co. Moray, b. 1780, d. 1847. See extant peerages, Strathcona and Mount Royal, B., for present barony of that name.
Sir Donald Alexander Smith was b. 6 Aug. 1820 in Scotland, and went to Canada as a clerk in Hudson's Bay Co., becoming eventually Gov. of the Co.; a financier and politician who attained great distinction; was a conservative mem. of the Federal Parl.; and with a group of colleagues, who included his cousin, Baron Mount Stephen (see that title in present work), completed the greater part of the Great Northern Railway, 1879, and the Canadian Pacific Railway, 1885; he was cr. G.C.M.G., G.C.V.O. and Baron Strathcona and Mount Royal of Glencoe, co. Argyll, and of Mount Royal, Quebec, Canada, 23 Aug. 1897, with the usual remainder to the heirs male of his body and was later cr. Baron Strathcona and Mount Royal, of Mount Royal, Quebec, Canada, and of Glencoe, co. Argyll, 26 June 1900, with special remainder in default of male issue, to his daughter and her heirs male. He re-entered Parl. for Montreal constituency 1889; was High Commissioner for Canada in London, 1896-1914; mem. of the Royal Commission of the S. African War, 1902; raised Strathcona's Horse for that war; and lived the last years of his life in England, where he died. He m. Isabella Sophia, dau. of Richard Hardisty, Chief Factor of the Hudson Bay Co., and by her who d. 12 Nov. 1913, had issue,
Margaret Charlotte, Baroness Strathcona and Mount Royal.
At his death, on 21 Jan. 1914, Lord Strathcona's senior barony became extinct but he was s. in the junior barony by his dau., as above.
ARMS—Gules on a fess argent between in chief a demi-lion rampant or, and in base a canoe of the last, pointed to the sinister, manned with four men paddling ppr., in the bow thereof a flag of the second, flowing

towards the dexter, charged with the letters N.W., a hammer surmounted of a nail in saltire sable.
CREST—On a mount vert a beaver eating into a maple tree ppr.
SUPPORTERS—Dexter, A trooper of the regiment of Strathcona's Horse, supporting in his exterior hand, a rifle, all ppr.; Sinister, A navvy standing on a railway sleeper, chaired and railed all ppr. to illustrate the driving of the last spike of the Canadian Pacific Railway, on 7 Nov. 1885.
MOTTOES—Agmina Ducens; Perseverance (over the Crest).
Seats were—Glencoe, Argyllshire, Colonsay, Argyllshire; Silver Heights, Winnipeg; Norway House, Pictou, Nova Scotia; with town residences, 911 Dorchester Street, West, Montreal, and 28 Grosvenor Square, London, W.

STRATHNAIRN

PEERAGE—U.K. Baron Strathnairn, of Strathnairn and Jansi.
SURNAME—Rose.
CR.—31 July 1866. **EXT.**—16 Oct. 1885.
HISTORY—The Rt. Hon. George Rose, the great-grandson of David Rose, of Earlsfield and Termet (see B.L.G. 1952, Rose of Lewestonrose and Rose of Kilravock), was Keeper of the Records at Westminster and Sec. to the Treasury. He m. 7 July 1769, Theodora, dau. of Major John Duer, and d. 13 Jan. 1815. She d 6 Nov. 1834. They had issue, with a second son, William Stewart, a poet, d. 1843, and a dau. Frances Theodora, who d. unm. 1846, an elder son,
Sir George Henry Rose, P.C., M.A. St. John's Coll. Camb. b. 3 May 1770; m. 5 Feb. 1796, Frances, dau. of Thomas Duncombe, of Duncombe Park, and d. 18 June 1853, leaving with other issue,
Sir Hugh Henry Rose, **Baron Strathnairn**, b. 6 April 1801, at Berlin where he was educ.; entered the Army, Ensign, 1820; Major, 1826; Lt. Col. 1839; selected for special service in Syria against Mehemet Ali's Egyptian Army; 1840; deputy Adjt. Gen. to Omar Pasha; Col. and commander of British detachments in Syria; consul general Syria, 1841; Sec. of Embassy at Constantinople, and Brev. Col. 1851; Chargé d'Affaires, 1852; in Crimean War, apptd. Queen's Commissioner at H.Q. of French C. in C., and served at Alma and Inkerman; Major Gen. 1854; K.C.B. 1855; volunteered for service in India, 1857, and served with distinction there, retaking Gwalior, and winning victory of Morar; cmd. of Bombay Div.; G.C.B., Col. Lt. Gen. and C. in C. of Bombay Army, later C. in C. India, with rank of Gen. 1860; K.C.S.I. 1861; G.C.S.I. 1866; Cmdr. of forces in Ireland, 1865-70; cr. Baron Strathnairn of Strathnairn and Jansi, 31 July 1866; Gen. 1867; Col. Royal Horse Guards, 1869; Field Marshal, 1877; d. unm. at Paris, 16 Oct. 1885.

STRATHSPEY

PEERAGE—U.K. Baron Strathspey, of Strathspey.
SURNAME—Ogilvie Grant. (from 1811, previously Grant).
CR.—14 Aug. 1858. **EXT.**—31 Mar. 1884.
HISTORY—Sir John Charles Ogilvie Grant, 11th Baronet and 7th Earl of Seafield, (see extant peerages, Strathspey, B.), K.T., b. 4 Sept. 1815; served in R.N., was a Representative Peer for Scotland, 1853-58; was cr. **Baron Strathspey**, of Strathspey, co. Inverness, 14 Aug. 1858. He m. 12 Aug. 1850, Hon. Caroline Stuart (d. 16 Oct. 1911) dau. of 11th Baron Blantyre, and d. 18 Feb. 1881, being s. by his only child,
Sir Ian Charles Ogilvie Grant, 12th Bt., **2nd Baron Strathspey**, and 8th Earl of Seafield, b. 7 Oct. 1851; served in 1st Life Guards; d. unm. 31 Mar. 1884, when the barony of 1858 creation became extinct, and his other titles passed to his uncle,
Sir James Ogilvie Grant, 13th Bt., who was cr. Baron Strathspey, of Strathspey, 17 June 1884. He was also 9th Earl of Seafield.
On the death of Sir Ian Charles Ogilvie Grant, 12th Bt. and 2nd Baron Strathspey of the 1858 creation, his mother s. to the Grant and Seafield estates, and entailed them upon the 11th Earl of Seafield. (see Strathspey, B. and Seafield, E. in extant peerages).
ARMS—(as given in works of the period 1884). Quarterly 1 and 4, Grand Quarters, Quarterly I and IV, Argent a lion passant guardant gules, imperially crowned, ppr. (Ogilvie); II and III, Argent a cross engrailed sable, (Sinclair); 2 and 3 Grand Quarters, Gules three antique crowns or, (Grant).
CRESTS—1. A lion rampant gules holding between the paws a plumb rule erect ppr. (Ogilvie). 2. A mountain in flames ppr. (Grant).
SUPPORTERS—Dexter, A lion guardant or; Sinister, A naked man, ppr. wreathed about the head and middle with laurel, and in his exterior hand a club.
MOTTOES—(over 1st crest) Tout jour; (over 2nd crest) Craigellachie.

STRICKLAND

PEERAGE—U.K. Baron Strickland, of Sizergh Castle, co. Westmorland.
SURNAME—Strickland.
CR.—19 Jan. 1928. **EXT.**—22 Aug. 1940.
HISTORY—Cmdr. Walter Strickland, R.N. (1824-67) had with other issue (for antecedents see B.L.G. 1952, Hornyold Strickland of Sizergh), a son and heir,
Gerald Strickland, **Baron Strickland** of Sizergh Castle, co. Westmorland, b. 24 May 1861; educ. Oscott Coll. Birmingham, and Trin. Coll. Camb., B.A., LL.B.; Pres. of Cambridge Union 1887; Barrister-at-Law, Inner Temple, 1887; Asst. Sec. Malta 1888; Chief Sec. 1889-1902; Major Royal Malta Militia, Pres. of Maltese Cttee for Privileges; s. as 6th Count Della Catena, 1875, under decision of Privy Council 6 Feb. 1882; Gov. of the Leeward Islands, 1902-04; of Tasmania, 1904-09, of West Australia, 1909-13; and of New South Wales, 1913-17; Mem. of Malta Legislative Assembly 1921-32; M.P. for the Lancaster Div. of Lancashire, 1924-28; Min. of Justice and Min. of Police, Malta, 1927-32; mem. of the Senate and Leader of the Constitutional Party in opposition in Malta, 1933; cr. C.M.G. 1889; K.C.M.G. 1897; G.C.M.G. 1913; and Baron Strickland of Sizergh Castle, co. Westmorland, 19 Jan. 1928; m. (1) 26 Aug. 1890, Edeline, D.J. St. J., dau. of 7th Earl de la Warr. She d. 15 Dec. 1918. He m. (2) 31 Aug. 1926, Margaret, D.G. St. J., dau. of Edward Hulton, of Ashton-on-Mersey, co. Chester, and d.s.p.m.s. 22 Aug. 1940, having had issue,
1. Reginald, b. 1892, d. 1893.
2. Walter, b. Aug. 1901, d. July 1902.
1. Mary Christina, M.B.E. 1919, b. 4 June 1896; m. 7 July 1920, Henry Hornyold, J.P. (see B.L.G. article mentioned above) and had issue.
2. Cecilia Victoria, b. 26 July 1897; m. 18 Oct. 1927, Capt. Hubert de Trafford. (De Trafford, Bt.) and had issue.
3. Mabel Edeline, b. 8 Jan. 1899; O.B.E. 1944; attached Naval H.Q., Malta 1918-19; Man. Dir. Allied Malta Newspapers, and Editor of *Times of Malta* etc.
4. Margaret Angela, b. 1 Sept. 1900; d. infant.
5. Henrietta May, b. 6 Feb. 1903; m. 24 Sept. 1922, Cmdr. R. T. Bower, of 3 Oakhill Road, Putney, S.W.15, and had issue.
6. Constance Teresa, b. 16 Aug. 1912.
ARMS—Sable three escallops argent.
CREST—A bundle of holly vert fructed gules banded round the middle with a wreath argent and sable.
SUPPORTERS—Dexter, A figure habited as a knight in complete armour, supporting in the dexter hand a banner of St. George all ppr. representing the bearer of that banner at the battle of Agincourt; Sinister, A figure habited and in armour ppr. cloaked sable, charged on the left shoulder with a Maltese Cross argent; at the feet an anchor also ppr. representing the Admiral of the galleys of the Knights Hospitallers at the time they retreated from the island of Rhodes.
MOTTO—Sans mal.
Lord Strickland's seat was Sizergh Castle, Westmorland, and also Villa Bologna, Malta. Walter Charles Strickland of Sizergh who d. 1903, made an arrangement whereby the Sizergh estates came into the possession of his kinsman, Lord Strickland.
An account of Lord Strickland's family history is also given in Burke's Peerage, 1949, under the heading of Della Catena, a creation of 1745, in Malta, and now held by the head of the family of Hornyold-Strickland.

**STUART DE DECIES

PEERAGE—U.K. Baron Stuart De Decies, of Dromana, within the Decies, co. Waterford.
SURNAME—Villiers-Stuart.
CR.—10 May 1839. **EXT.**—23 Jan. 1874.
HISTORY—Lady Gertrude Amelia Mason-Villiers, dau. and sole heiress of the 2nd and last Earl of Grandison, m. 15 July 1802, Lord Henry Stuart, a ygr. son of the 1st Marquess of Bute. He d. 19 Aug. 1809. She d. 30 Aug. 1809. They had issue, with a ygr. son and a dau. (for

whom see under Bute, M. in extant peerages, and also in B.L.G. of Ireland, 1958 edition, William-Stuart of Dromana etc.), an elder son, Henry Villiers-Stuart, cr. **Baron Stuart De Decies,** of Dromana, within the Decies, co. Waterford, 10 May 1839. He was b. 8 June 1803; assumed along with his brother and sister, the additional surname of Villiers; he m. 12 Jan. 1826, both in the R.C. church and in accordance with Scottish law, Theresina Pauline Ott, of Vienna, and d. 23 Jan. 1874. They had issue, a son and dau., but the son, Henry Windsor Villiers-Stuart, of Dromana, was not able to satisfy the Cttee. of Privileges of the House of Lords as to the marriage of his parents, and this on account of his mother having been considered· as not free to marry in 1826. The peerage accordingly became extinct. Henry Villiers-Stuart had a very distinguished career. He became Vicar of Bulkington, co. Warwick, having been ordained in the C. of E. in 1850, and being M.A. of Durham Univ. 1852, but resigned his Orders in 1871 in accordance with the Clerical Disabilities Act of 1870, in order to stand for Parliament. He was M.P. co. Waterford, 1873-74, and 1880-85, and did much valuable work in Egypt, his report being published as a Gov. blue book. For his descendants see the article referred to above, in B.L.G. of Ireland, 1958, and also the D.N.B. ARMS—(of Baron Stuart De Decies). Quarterly 1 and 4, Or a fess chequy argent and azure within a double tressure flory counterflory gules (Stuart); 2 and 3, Argent on a cross gules five escallops or (Villiers). CRESTS—(1) A demi-lion rampant gules (Stuart). (2) A lion rampant argent ducally crowned or, (Villiers). SUPPORTERS—Dexter, A horse argent gorged with a wreath of shamrock vert; Sinister, A stag ppr. gorged as the dexter. MOTTO—Avito viret honore.

STUART OF WORTLEY

PEERAGE—U.K. Baron Stuart of Wortley, of the City of Sheffield.
SURNAME—Stuart-Wortley.
CR.—1 Jan. 1917. EXT.—24 April 1926.
HISTORY—The Rt. Hon. James Archibald Stuart-Wortley, third son of the 1st Baron Wharncliffe (see extant peerages, Wharncliffe, E.), m. 6 May 1846, Hon. Jane Lawley, only dau. of 1st Baron Wenlock (see present volume), and d. 1881, having had with other issue, a second son,
Charles Beilby Stuart-Wortley, **Baron Stuart** of Wortley, b. 5 Sept. 1851 educ. Rugby and Balliol Coll. Oxford, B.A. 1875, M.A. 1878; Barrister-at-Law, Inner Temple, 1876; Q.C. 1892; M.P. for undivided Borough of Sheffield, 1880-85 and for Hallam Div. of Sheffield, 1885-1916; Parl. Under Sec. of State for Home Dept., 1885-86, and 1886-92; made P.C. 1896; cr. Baron Stuart of Wortley, of the City of Sheffield, 1 Jan. 1917; m. (1) 16 Aug. 1880, Beatrice Catherine Harriet, dau. of Thomas Adolphus Trollope, the historian of Florence, (Trollope, Bt.), and had issue,
   1. Beatrice Susan Theodosia, b. 15 July 1881; m. 1 Dec. 1906, Capt. A. W. J. Cecil and had issue (Salisbury, M.).
He m. (2) 6 Jan. 1886, Alice Sophia Caroline,

dau. of Sir John Everett Millais, 1st Bt., and d.s.p.m. 24 April 1926, having by her had further issue,
   2. Clare Euphemia, b. 16 Oct. 1889; d. unm. 15 Jan. 1945.
ARMS—Quarterly 1 and 4, Argent, on a bend between six martlets gules, three bezants (Wortley), a canton charged with the arms of Stuart (as in 2nd quarter); 2 and 3, Or a fess chequy azure and argent within a double tressure flory counterflory gules (Stuart).
SUPPORTERS—Dexter, A horse argent bridled gules; Sinister, A stag ppr. attired or, each gorged with a collar flory counter flory of the second and charged on the shoulder with a mullet for difference.
CRESTS—1. An eaglet's leg erased or, issuant therefrom three ostrich feathers ppr. charged on the thigh with a fess chequy azure and argent. 2. A demi-lion rampant gules (on an escroll over, Nobilis ira).
MOTTO—Avito viret honore.

SUMNER

PEERAGE—U.K. Life. Baron Sumner, of Ibstone, co. Buckingham and (hereditary) U.K. Viscount Sumner.
SURNAME—Hamilton.
CR.—Barony 20 Oct. 1913. Viscounty 31 Jan. 1927. EXT.—24 May 1943.
HISTORY—Andrew Hamilton, of Withington, co. Lancaster, who d. 1906 had by Frances, his wife (d. 1869) dau. of Joseph Sumner, of Sharston, co. Chester, a second son,
Sir John Andrew Hamilton, **Baron Sumner** of Ibstone, co. Buckingham, b. 3 Feb. 1859; educ. Manchester Free Grammar Sch. and Balliol Coll. Oxford, B.A. 1882, M.A. 1884; Fell. of Magdalen Coll. 1882-89; Barrister-at-Law, Inner Temple, 1883; K.C. 1901; Bencher, 1909; Standing Counsel to the Univ. of Oxford, 1906-09; a Judge of the King's Bench Div. High Court of Justice, 1909-12; P.C. 1912; Lord Justice of Appeal, 1912-13; apptd. Lord of Appeal in Ordinary and cr. a Baron for life as Baron Sumner of Ibstone, co. Buckingham, 20 Oct. 1913; cr. Kt. Bach. 1909 and G.C.B. 1920. Chm. of House of Lords Cttee on Abeyances, 1926. He was cr. 31 Jan. 1927 a hereditary peer as **Viscount Sumner.** He was Treasurer, Inner Temple, 1930. He m. 20 Dec. 1892, Maude Margaret, dau. of the Rev. John Wood Todd, D.D., of Forest Hill, London, and d.s.p. 24 May 1934.
ARMS—Ermine, a chevron interlaced with another reversed between three cinquefoils gules.
CREST—A deer hound's head couped at the neck argent charged with two chevrons as in the arms.
MOTTO—Loi et loyaute.

SWANBOROUGH

PEERAGE—U.K. Life. Baroness Swanborough, of Swanborough, co. Sussex.
SURNAME—Isaacs.
CR.—22 Sept. 1958. EXT.—22 May 1971.
HISTORY—Stella Charnaud, was b. 6 Jan. 1894, dau. of Charles Charnaud; she was educ.

privately; m. as his 2nd wife, 6 Aug. 1931, Rufus Daniel Isaac, 1st Marquess of Reading (see extant peerages). He d. 30 Dec. 1935. The Dowager Marchioness of Reading had a very distinguished career. Chm. W. V. S. for Civil Defence 1938, Vice Chm. Imperial Relations Trust, mem. Council of Univ. of Sussex, Chm. Commonwealth Immigrants Advisory Council, 1962-65, mem. National Advisory Cttee. on Employment of Older Men and Women, and many other cttees; a Gov. of the B.B.C.; 1946-51; and Vice Chm. 1947-51; was cr. D.B.E. (Civil) 1941 and G.B.E. (Civil) 1944; a life peeress as **Baroness Swanborough** of Swanborough, co. Sussex, 22 Sept. 1958. She was Grand Officer of Order of Orange Nassau, of the Netherlands, 1952, D. St. J. 1957, and had the Nat. Achievement Award for Women, 1948, also American Red Cross, Civilian Service Bar and Silver Medal. She d. 22 May 1971.

ARMS—Argent a chevron vert between in chief two bees volant and in base three slips of rosemary two in saltire and one in pale leaved and flowered ppr.

SUPPORTERS—On either side a member of the W.V.S., the dexter in the uniform of an ordinary member, the sinister in the uniform worn by a member in the Welfare Section of the Civil Defence Corps, all ppr.

MOTTO—Not why we can't but how we can. The Dowager Marchioness of Reading, Baroness Swanborough, had by her seat at Swanborough Manor, Lewes, Sussex, and London house, 16 Lord North Street, Westminster, S.W.1.

SYDENHAM OF COMBE

PEERAGE—U.K. Baron Sydenham of Combe, of Dulverton, co. Somerset.
SURNAME—Clarke.
CR.—12 Feb. 1913. **EXT.**—7 Feb. 1933.
HISTORY—Henry Clarke, of Winchester, solicitor, b. 1675; m. Petronella or Martha, dau. of Paul Deverall, of Jamaica, merchant, by Anne, his wife, niece of Edward Hyde, Earl of Clarendon. She d. 1780. They had issue with three other sons and two daus., a third son,

The Rev. Richard Clarke, b. 1723; educ. Winchester and Univ. Coll. Oxford; m. (1) Eunice, dau. of John Rayner, attorney and clerk to the Skinners' Co., and (2) Mary, dau. of Henry Robarts, of Cornwall and niece and heir of Capt. William Charles Roberts, of Jamaica. He m. (3) Susannah, dau. of Thomas Tredway of London, and widow of John Crocket, of Carolina. He had issue by all three wives, but the line of descent is traced through his ygst. son of his third wife,

Gen. Tredway Clarke, Madras Artillery, H.E.I.C.S., who m. 1812, Sarah, dau. of Humphrey Sydenham, (Sydenham of Combe and Brimpton, Somerset, Burke's Extinct Baronetcies,), and d. 5 May 1858, having by her who d. 15 Jan. 1871, had a third son,

The Rev. Walter John Clarke, of Knoyle House, Folkestone, Vicar of Sinderby, co. Lincoln, 1843-47, b. 3 April 1813; B.A. 1835; M.A. 1838, Balliol Coll. Oxford; m. 17 Sept.

1847, Maria Frances, dau. of Rev. Joseph Mayor. She d. 15 April 1906. He d. 24 Aug 1903. They had issue,

1. George Sydenham, **Baron Sydenham** o Combe (see below).
2. Frederic Sydenham, b. 9 Dec. 1850; m 6 Sept. 1875, Annie, dau. of Alexande Christian, and had issue, three daus.
3. Walter Sydenham, b. 27 Nov. 1856; m 14 Nov. 1894, Augusta Janet, dau. o Rev. Henry Arkwright, and had issue, a son who d. young.
4. Percy Sydenham, b. 6 Feb. 1864; m 1 Nov. 1888, Agnes Herkok, and d 3 Sept. 1889, leaving issue, a son.
1. Frances Maria, b. 18 Jan. 1852; m 1 April 1884, Rev. Edward Pease Gregg and had issue.
2. Jesse Harriet, b. 7 Mar. 1853.
3. Catharine Charlotte, b. 21 Aug. 1855 m. 29 April 1886, Frank Charlton, an had issue.
4. Mary Adelaide, b. 31 Oct. 1858; m 13 Oct. 1887, H. T. Mackenzie and ha issue.
5. Ellen Georgina, b. 8 June 1862; m. 1884 R. F. Simpson, and d. 1893, leaving issue

The eldest son,

Sir George Sydenham Clarke, **Baron Syden ham** of Combe, b. 4 July 1848; educ. Repton Rossall, Haileybury, Wimbledon Sch. and the Royal Mil. Academy, Woolwich; joined Royal Engineers, 1868; on staff of Roya Indian Engineering Coll. Cooper's Hill 1871-80; served in Egyptian Exped. 1882; the Sudan Exped. 1885; and in Suakin in the Intell. Dept. and as Asst. Political Officer Sec. of the Colonial Defence Cttee. 1885-92 and several other cttees; Gov. of Victoria 1901-04; Sec. to the Cttee of Imperial Defence 1904-07; Gov. of Bombay, 1907-13; cr C.M.G. 1887; K.C.M.G. 1893; G.C.M.G 1905; G.C.I.E. 1907; and G.C.S.I. 1911; cr Baron Sydenham of Combe, of Dulverton, co Somerset, 12 Feb. 1913. He was Chm. of Brit Empire League, 1915-21; Pres. of Brit. Science Guild, 1917-20, F.R.S.; Vice-Pres. Roya Empire Soc.; K.J. St. J. He m. (1) Caroline Emily, D.G. St. J., dau. of Gen. Peregrine Henry Fellowes. She d. 9 Dec. 1908, having had issue, Constance Violet, b. 26 May 1879 d. unm. at Bombay, 21 Mar. 1909. Lord Sydenham m. (2) 4 Nov. 1910, Phyllis Angela Rosamond, D.G. St. J. dau. of George Morant of Farnborough Park, co. Hants, and widow of Capt. Arthur Reynolds.

Lord Sydenham who wrote several books, was a pessimist regarding the future of Britain and the Empire, foreseeing the decline o both.

ARMS—Azure on a chevron between three swans argent as many crosses couped gules.
CREST—In front of a saltire or issuing out o flames a demi dragon all ppr.
SUPPORTERS—Dexter, A kangaroo: Sinister, A Bengal tiger, both ppr. each gorged with a chain or, pendent therefrom an escutcheon, argent charged with a cross couped gules.
MOTTO—In medio tutissimus.

SYDNEY

PEERAGE—G.B. Baron Sydney, of Chisle-
hurst, co. Kent. 6 Mar. 1783.
  G.B. Viscount Sydney, of St. Leonards, co.
  Gloucester. 11 June 1789.
  U.K. Earl Sydney, 27 Feb. 1874.
SURNAME—Townshend.
CR.—Dates as above. **EXT.**—14 Feb. 1890.
HISTORY—Thomas Townshend, 2nd son of
the 2nd Viscount Townshend, (see extant
peerages, Townshend, M.) one of the Tellers of
the Exchequer, M.P. for Univ. of Cambridge,
b. 1701; m. 1780, Albinia (d. 1739) dau. of Col.
John Selwyn of Matson, co. Gloucester, and d.
1780, having had with other issue, an eldest
son,
  Thomas Townshend, **Baron and Viscount
Sydney**, b. 24 Feb. 1732; Sec. of State for Home
Dept.; cr. Baron Sydney, of Chiselhurst, co.
Kent, 6 Mar. 1783; and Viscount Sydney of
St. Leonards, co. Gloucester, 11 June 1789;
m. 19 May 1760, Elizabeth, (d. 1 May 1826),
eldest dau. and heiress of Richard Powys, of
Hintlesham, co. Suffolk, d. 30 June 1800,
having had issue, with two ygr. sons, who d.
unm. an eldest son,
  John Thomas Townshend, **2nd Viscount
Sydney**, b. 21 Feb. 1764; m. (1) 12 April 1790,
Hon. Sophia Southwell, dau. of 17th Baron de
Clifford. She d. 9 Nov. 1795. He had by her
two daus. (Townshend, M.) and m. (2) 27 May
1802, Lady Caroline Clements, dau. of 1st
Earl of Leitrim, and d. 20 Jan. 1831, having
by her (who d. 9 Aug. 1805) had further issue,
an only son and successor,
  John Robert Townshend, **3rd Viscount
Sydney**, and cr. **Earl Sydney**, 27 Feb. 1874. He
was b. 9 Aug. 1805; was P.C., G.C.B., M.A.
Camb. Capt. of Deal Castle, Lord Lt. of Kent,
was twice Lord Chamberlain, and twice Lord
Steward of the Household; m. 4 Aug. 1832,
Emily Caroline, (d. 1893) dau. of 1st Marquess
of Anglesey and d.s.p. 14 Feb. 1890.
ARMS—Quarterly 1 and 4, Azure a chevron
ermine between three escallops argent (Townshend); 2 and 3, Quarterly gules and or, in the
first quarter a mullet argent, and in the centre
fess point a crescent (Vere).
CREST—A stag trippant ppr.
SUPPORTERS—Dexter, A lion or, collared,
chained and charged on the shoulder with a
pheon azure; Sinister, A stag sable, armed
argent collared and chained or, charged on the
shoulder with an escallop of the second.
MOTTO—Droit et avant.

TAAFFE

PEERAGE—Ireland. Baron of Ballymote, and
Viscount Taaffe, of Corren, both in co.
Sligo.
SURNAME—Taaffe.
CR.—Barony and Viscounty 1 Aug. 1628.
SUSPENDED—28 Mar. 1919, on removal
of the title from the Roll of Peers. (see also
under Albany, D. and Cumberland, D.).
HISTORY—The Taaffes were a family seated in
the cos. of Louth and Sligo in Ireland. Sir
William Taaffe, of Harleston, distinguished
himself by his services to the Crown during the
rebellion of Tyrone in 1597, and also against
the Spanish invaders at Kinsale in 1601. His

brother Peter Taaffe, of Peppardstown, and
Dromin, co. Louth, was ancestor of the
Taaffes of Smarmore Castle, Ardee, co.
Louth (entered in Burke's Landed Gentry of
Ireland, 1958). Sir William had a second wife,
Ismay, the dau. of Sir Christopher Bellew, and
d. 1630, being s. by his only son,
  Sir John Taaffe, **1st Viscount Taaffe**, who
was cr. 1 Aug. 1628, Baron of Ballymote, and
Viscount Taaffe, of Corren, both in co. Sligo.
He m. Anne, dau. of 1st Viscount Dillon, and
d. 2 Jan. 1642, having had issue,
  1. Theobald, Sir, **2nd Viscount and 1st Earl
     of Carlingford** (see below).
  2. Lucas, Major Gen. in the Army, apptd.
     Gov. of Ross in 1649, to defend that
     place against Cromwell. He had to leave
     Ireland, and served in the armies of
     France and Spain as a Colonel. He d. in
     Ireland s.p.m.
  3. Francis, a Col. in the rebellion of 1641;
     m. an Italian lady and left a son, Charles
     who d.s.p.
  4. Edward, d. unm.
  5. William, m. Margaret, dau. of Connor
     O'Kennedy Roe, and had by her with
     three daus.,
       Francis, who m. Anne, dau. of John
       Crean, of Crean's Castle. Sligo, and
       had issue,
     (1) Nicholas, **6th Viscount** (see below).
     (1) Anne, m. John Brett, of Rathdoony,
         co. Sligo.
     (2) Mary m. Theodore Verdon, of
         Clunigashell, and d.s.p.
The eldest son of the 1st Viscount,
  Theobald Taaffe, **2nd Viscount Taaffe** and
1st Earl of Carlingford, so cr. 26 June 1661. He
took the royal side in the civil wars and his
estates were sequestered. He m. (1) Mary dau.
of Sir Nicholas White, of Leixlip and had by
her with other issue who d. young and unm.,
  1. Nicholas, 2nd Earl and **3rd Viscount** (see
     below).
  2. Francis, 3rd Earl and **4th Viscount** (see
     below).
  3. John, a Major in the Army, who was k.
     at Londonderry in 1689, in service of
     James II. He m. Lady Rose Lambert,
     dau. of 1st Earl of Cavan, and had
     Theobald, 4th Earl and **5th Viscount** (see
     below).
The 1st Earl m. (2) Anne, dau. of Sir William
Pershall, of Suggenhill and Canwell, co.
Stafford, and by her (who m. 2ndly the 11th
Lord Dunsany) had no issue. The 1st Earl d.
31 Dec. 1677, and was s. by his eldest son,
  Nicholas, Taaffe, 2nd Earl of Carlingford,
and **3rd Viscount Taaffe**, m. Mary, dau. and
heir of Humphret Weld, of Lulworth, (B.L.G.
1952) and d. at the battle of the Boyne, 1691,
cmdg. a regt. of foot for James II, and d.s.p.
He was s. by his brother,
  Francis Taaffe, 3rd Earl of Carlingford, and
4th Viscount Taaffe, who had a very distinguished career on the continent of Europe.
He obtained a commission from Charles, 5th
Duke of Lorraine as a Capt. in the Duke's
own regt. He later became Chamberlain to the
Emperor, a marshal of the Empire, and
counsellor of state. Owing to the high esteem
in which he was held in Europe, he was exempt-
ed from forfeiture of his peerages by an English
Act of Parliament, 1st William and Mary; in
the Acts passed in Ireland, 9th William and

Mary, it was provided that nothing should convict him of High Treason or involve his forfeiture. He thus s. as 3rd Earl, and d. Aug. 1704, when he was s. by his nephew,

Theobald Taaffe, 4th Earl of Carlingford, and **5th Viscount Taaffe,** who m. Amelia, dau. of the 3rd Earl of Fingall but d.s.p. when the Earldom of Carlingford, became extinct, but the Viscounty of Taaffe, and the barony of Ballymote, passed to the next male heir,

Nicholas Taaffe, (see above), **6th Viscount Taaffe,** and Count Taaffe of the Empire, Field Marshal in the Imperial Service, who as Chamberlain to the Emperor, Charles VI, received a golden key. He served with distinction against the Turks, in 1738, and won a great victory at Belgrade. He m. 30 Oct. 1729, Mary Anne, dau. and heiress of Count Spendler, of Linz, Upper Austria, and d. at his seat of Ellischau, in Bohemia, 30 Dec. 1769, having had issue,

1. John Philip, mem. of the Imperial Aulic Council of the Empire, b. in England, 1 Feb. 1733; m. 1 Feb. 1759, Maria Countess Chotek, Countess of the Empire, dau. of the High Chancellor, Count Chotek, in Austria, and d.v.p. Dec. 1765, leaving with a ygst. son, John, and a dau. Maria Anna,
   Rodolphus, **7th Viscount** (see below).
2. Francis, lord of the bedchamber, and Gen. in the Austrian army, Count of the Empire, m. 1772, Hon. Frances Maria, dau. of Lord Bellew, and d. 1803, s.p.

The 6th Viscount was s. by his grandson,

Rodolphus Taaffe, **7th Viscount Taaffe,** Lord of the Seignories of Freystadt, Deutschleuten and Roy, in the duchy of Silesia, Lt. Col. the Hadek Regt. of Hussars; b. in London, 6 Oct. 1762; m. 11 April 1787, Countess Josephine Haugwitz, dau. of Charles William, Count Haugwitz, and had issue,

1. Francis John Charles Joseph, **8th Viscount** (see below).
2. Louis Patrick John, **9th Viscount** (see below).
1. Clementina, m. 11 April 1811, Thaddeus, Count Amadéx de Várkony.

The 7th Viscount was a Count of the Empire. He d. in Vienna 7 June 1830. He was s. by his elder son,

Francis John Charles Joseph Taaffe, **8th Viscount Taaffe,** b. 23 May 1788; Count of the Empire, Chamberlain to the Emperor of Austria, and Major in the Austrian Army. He m. 11 April 1811, Countess Antonia Amadée de Várkony and d. 8 Feb. 1849, being s. by his brother,

Louis Patrick John Taaffe, **9th Viscount Taaffe,** b. 25 Dec. 1791; m. 10 June 1822, Princess Amelia, dau. of Charles Augustus, Prince of Berzenheim von Regécz and d. 21 Dec. 1855, having had issue,

1. Charles Rudolph Joseph Francis Clement, **10th Viscount** (see below).
2. Edward Francis Joseph, **11th Viscount** (see below).
1. Walburga Clementina Rudolphina Francesca, b. 23 Oct. 1825; d. 13 Sept. 1882.
2. Amelia Rudolphina Henrietta, b. 1829, d. 1830.
3. Amelia Walburga, b. 1830.

The elder son,

Charles Rudolph Joseph Francis Clement Taaffe, **10th Viscount Taaffe,** whose right was recognised by the Cttee. of Privileges of the House of Lords, 17 Aug. 1860, Count of the Holy Roman Empire, Chamberlain to the Emperor of Austria, a Gen. and Lt. Col. 12th Lancers in the Austrian Army, b. 26 April 1823, and d. unm. 19 Nov. 1873, being s. by his brother,

Edward Francis Joseph Taaffe, **11th Viscount Taaffe,** Knight of the Golden Fleece, Grand Cross of St. Maurice and St. Lazarus, Knight of St. John, etc., by. 24 Feb. 1833; m. 15 Feb. 1860, Maria Francisca, Countess Czaky von Keresztceg and Adorjan, and by her who d. 1912 had issue,

1. Henry, **12th Viscount** (see below).
1. Mary, b. 21 Sept. 1866; m. 21 Sept. 1889, Count Maximilian Condenhove, of Brunn, Austria, and had issue.
2. Louisa, Canoness of the Maria Schul at Brünn, b. 1868.
3. Helen, b. 1870; m. Sept. 1889, Baron Richard von Mattencloit, of Orlan, Silesia, and had issue.
4. Clementine, b. 1875, d. 1887.

The 11th Viscount held many appointments under the Austrian Crown, and was Min. of the Interior, in the Austrian Empire, 1867 and deputy pres. of the Austrian Ministry, 1868. He was also Prime Minister of Austria, 1879-93. He d. 29 Nov. 1895. He was s. by his only son,

Henry Taaffe, **12th Viscount Taaffe,** Count of the Holy Roman Empire, Lt. Kaiser Franz Joseph's Regt. of Dragoons of the Reserve, Austrian Army. He was b. 22 May 1872; m. 22 May 1897, Maria Magda Fuchs, and d. leaving issue,

Edward Charles Richard Taaffe, in whom was vested the right to petition for restoration to the Roll of Peers as 13th Viscount Taaffe and Baron of Ballymote.

ARMS—Gules a cross argent fretty azure.

CREST—A dexter arm in armour embowed brandishing a sword ppr. hilt and pommel or.

SUPPORTERS—Dexter, A horse argent, semée of estoiles sable; Sinister, A wyvern wings expanded ppr.

MOTTO—In hoc signo spes mea.

The seats (of the 12th Viscount, and Count Taaffe) were the Castles of Ellischau and Kilinetz, Bohemia.

TEMPLEWOOD

PEERAGE—U.K. Viscount Templewood, of Chelsea, co. Middlesex. (Also a Baronetcy 7 Aug. 1899.)

SURNAME—Hoare.

CR.—14 July 1944. **EXT.**—7 May 1959.

HISTORY—The earlier history of the Hoare family is given in Burke's Landed Gentry (1952) under Hoare of Ellisfield, and as regards the present branch, under Hoare of Annabella, Baronets, in extant peerage works. Edward Hoare was a Major in Cromwell's Army in Ireland, where he received large grants of land in Cork, and m. Mary dau. of John Woodcock, of Kilcragan, co. Kilkenny and d. 3 July 1690, having had issue, with another dau. who d. unm.,

1. Edward, the progenitor of the Hoares of Annabella, Bts.

2. Joseph (see below).
3. Enoch.
1. Esther, m. Samuel Terry, of Cork.
The second son,
Joseph Hoare, of Hoare's Lane and Wood-
hill, Cork, a mem. of the Soc. of Friends, and
a banker and merchant in Cork, m. (1) 3 Mar.
1692, Rachel, dau. of Francis Rogers, of Cork.
She d. 2 July 1700. By her he had issue, with
three other sons who d. in infancy, and two
daus.,
   1. Joseph, b. 17 Dec. 1695; m. (1) Sarah,
      dau. of Abraham Abell, of Cork, and
      had issue a dau. Rachel; m. (2) 1720.
      Margaret, dau. of Joseph Pike, and d.
      4 Oct. 1740 having had no further issue.
He m. (2) 19 Aug. 1708, Deborah Whelly, of
Clonmel, who d.s.p. 11 Jan. 1709-10.
He m. (3) 23 April 1713, Margaret (who d.
24 Jan. 1717/18), dau. of Edward Sattherwaite
of Townend, co. Lancaster, and by her had,
   2. Samuel (see below).
He m. (4) Mary, widow of Joseph Beale, of
Mount Mellick, and d. 14 Oct. 1729, having no
further issue by her.
The second son,
Samuel Hoare, went from Cork to London
where, in partnership with his father-in-law,
he made a large fortune. He was b. 20 Sept.
1716; m. 19 Feb. 1744, Grizell, dau. of Jonathan Gurnell, of Ealing. She d. 17 July 1756.
He d. at Stoke Newington, 30 Aug. 1796,
having had issue, with a dau. who d. unm.,
   1. Joseph, b. 1750; d. unm. 1775.
   2. Samuel (see below).
   3. Jonathan, b. 4 Nov. 1752; m. 19 June
      1783, Sarah, dau. of Thomas Beswick,
      and d. 15 Aug. 1819, having had issue, a
      dau. Sarah who d. unm.
   1. Margaret, b. 1748; m. 5 July 1769,
      Joseph Woods, of London, and had
      issue.
   2. Sarah, b. 1753; m. 26 Nov. 1777, Thomas
      Bradshaw, of Newtonards co. Down,
      and d. 21 Jan. 1819, having had issue.
   3. Grizell, b. 1758; m. (1) 16 Dec. 1801,
      William Birbeck, of Norwich, who d.
      2 June 1812, and (2) 14 Mar. 1828,
      William Allen, of London, and d.s.p. 1837.
The eldest surviving son,
Samuel Hoare, a partner in the banking firm
of Barnett, Hill, Barnett and Hoare, of London,
b. 29 May 1751; m. (1) 15 May 1776, Sarah,
the dau. and coheiress of Samuel Gurney, of
Norwich and London, and by her (who d.
31 Jan. 1783) had issue, with a dau. who d.
unm.,
   1. Samuel (see below).
   1. Hannah, m. 25 Nov. 1802, T. M. Pryor,
      of Baldock, co. Hertford, and d. 30 April
      1850, leaving issue.
   2. Grizell, m. David Powell, of Oughton, co.
      Essex, and d. 15 May 1832.
He m. (2) 17 June 1788, Hannah, who d. 21
Jan. 1856, the dau. of Henry Sterry, of Hatton
Garden, London, by whom he had no issue.
He d. 13 July 1825 being s. by his only son,
Samuel Hoare, banker, of Hamptead Heath
House, co. Middlesex, and of Cromer, co.
Norfolk, b. 16 Jan. 1783; m. 24 Dec. 1806, his
cousin, Louisa, (d. 6 Sept. 1836) dau. of John
Gurney, of Earlham, co. Norfolk (for full
account of the Gurney family of Walsingham
Abbey and Sprowston Hall, see B.L.G. 1952).
He d. 26 Dec. 1847, having had issue,

1. Samuel, banker, b. 1 Dec. 1807; m.
   8 Sept. 1831, Catherine Edwards, dau. of
   Rev. Robert Hankinson, and d.v.p.
   27 Oct. 1833, leaving by her who m.
   secondly Rear Adm. Sir William Parry,
   (1) Priscilla, m. Edward Hardcastle.
   (2) Louisa Gurney, m. 11 Jan. 1860, as
   his 2nd wife, Capt. Philip Hammond,
   and had issue.
2. John Gurney (see below).
3. Edward, Rev., Vicar of Holy Trinity,
   Tunbridge Wells, and Canon of Canterbury, b. 5 June 1812; m. 10 July 1839,
   Maria Eliza, who d. 27 July 1863, the
   only dau. of Sir Benjamin C. Brodie, 1st
   Bt., and d. 7 July 1894, leaving issue.
4. Joseph, of Childs Hill House, co. Middlesex, M.P. for Hull, a banker, inherited
   Hoare property in Cork, b. 21 Mar. 1814;
   m. (1) 13 July 1836, Anna Amelia, only
   dau. of Charles Buxton, of Weymouth,
   (Buxton, Bt.). She d. 19 July 1843. He m.
   (2) 20 April 1847, Rachel Juliana, dau. of
   Charles Barclay, of Bury Hill, co. Surrey,
   (B.L.G. 1952, Barclay of Bury Hill), and
   d.s.p. 1885.
5. Richard, of Marden Hill, co. Hertford,
   and North Lodge, Cromer, b. 13 June
   1824; m. 30 Oct. 1861, Susan, dau. of
   Col. William Tomkinson, of Willington
   Hall, co. Chester, and d. 18 Feb. 1901,
   leaving issue.
6. Francis, of Weylands, Cromer, and of
   London, b. 13 June 1828; m. 26 July
   1854, Eugenia (d. 1904), dau. of the Ven.
   the Archdeacon of Norwich, Robert
   Hankinson, and d. 26 Oct. 1903, leaving
   issue, with a dau. d. young,
   (1) Francis Robert, b. 26 Oct. 1855; d.
   unm. 2 May 1949.
   (2) Richard Gurney, twin with his
   brother, m. 13 Dec. 1888, Margaret
   Caroline, (d. 1943) dau. of S. Gurney
   Buxton, of Catton Hall, Norwich,
   (Buxton, Bt.), and d. 23 Feb. 1945
   having had issue
     Mabel, m. Oct. 1919, Capt. Geo-
     ffrey Wait, M.C., and had issue.
   (3) Alfred Ernest, O.B.E., of Chelsworth
   Hall, co. Suffolk, mem. C.C. West
   Suffolk, B.A. Camb., b. 29 Mar.
   1861; m. 27 Sept. 1894, Edith Gertrude, dau. of Richard Benyon, of
   Reading, and d. 7 Jan. 1930, leaving
   issue,
   1a Eustace Benyon, b. 28 May 1899;
     educ. Eton and Trin. Coll. Camb.,
     Major Gren. Guards; m. 11 Dec.
     1925, Lady Peggy Virginia Coven-
     try, dau. of Viscount Deerhurst,
     (Coventry, E.), and had issue,
     1b Samuel Julian, b. 21 Mar. 1930.
     2b Francis, b. 14 Mar. 1932.
     1b Virginia, b. 1 Mar. 1927; m.
      7 Dec. 1950, Oliver M. Watson
      (Manton, B.).
     2a Reginald Alfred, b. 27 Oct. 1900.
     1a Millicent Elizabeth, b. 31 Mar. 1897.
   (4) Harold Arthur, b. 20 Nov. 1862; d.
   20 Sept. 1927.
   (5) Gerald Eugene, b. 16 April 1868; m.
   5 June 1894, Rosabelle Mary, (d.
   1948), dau. of R. Hunter Muskett, of
   Hingham Hall, co. Norfolk, and d.
   20 Mar. 1922, leaving issue,

Robert Rawdon, D.S.O. 1940, M.C. 1918, b. 16 May 1897; educ. Beaumont Coll. Windsor; served in World War I, 1914-18 and in World War II, 1939-45, (despatches twice).

(1) Marion Louisa, m. 21 April 1881, Col. H. A. Barclay, of Hanworth Hall, co. Norfolk, and d. 4 July 1938, leaving issue.

1. Elizabeth, m. 23 June 1846, the Rev. Canon John Patteson, Rector of Thorpe, co. Norfolk, and d. 24 May 1902, having had issue.
2. Catherine Louisa, m. 27 Jan. 1842, Rev. E. F. E. Hankinson, Canon of Norwich, son of Rev. Robert Hankinson, and d.s.p. 1 Dec. 1844.

The eldest surviving son,
John Gurney Hoare, of Hampstead Heath House, co. Middlesex, and Cliff House, Cromer, co. Norfolk, b. 7 May 1810; m. 18 Mar. 1837, Caroline, dau. of Charles Barclay, of Bury Hill, co. Surrey, and d. 16 Feb. 1875. She d. 7 July 1878. They had issue,

1. Samuel, 1st Bt. (see below).
2. Robert Gurney, of Jesmond Park, co. Northumberland, b. 31 Aug. 1844; m. 20 Nov. 1867, his cousin Anne, the dau. of Rev. Edward Hoare, (see above). She d. 7 Aug. 1915. He d. 22 May 1899, leaving issue.
3. Charles Richard Gurney, of Lexden House, Colchester, b. 8 Oct. 1847; m. 18 Feb. 1873, Rachel Georgina dau. of G. I. Bevan, of Godmanchester. She d. 30 June 1911. He d. 9 Nov. 1915, leaving issue.
1. Anna Maria, m. 6 Dec. 1859, J. R. MacInnes.
2. Louisa Caroline, m. 3 Sept. 1861, Samuel Gurney Buxton, of Catton Hall, and d. 1 Mar. 1879 leaving issue, (Buxton Bt.).
3. Juliana Margaret, M.B.E., d. unm. 3 Mar. 1936.

The eldest son,
Sir Samuel Hoare, 1st Bt., so cr. 7 Aug. 1899, of Sidestrand Hall, co. Norfolk, and Hampstead, co. Middlesex, b. 7 Sept. 1841; educ. Trin. Coll. Camb., M.A.; M.P. Norwich, 1886-1906; a banker; m. 7 April 1866, Katharine Louisa Hart, dau. of R. V. Davis, of Frognal, Hampstead, and d. 29 Jan. 1915. She d. 14 Jan. 1931. They had issue,

1. Samuel John Gurney, 2nd Bt. and **Viscount Templewood** (see below).
2. Oliver Vaughan Gurney, b. 18 July 1882; educ. Harrow; and New Coll. Oxford, B.A. 1904; m. 24 April 1906, Phoebe Alice, dau. of Charles Van Neck, of Bracknell, co. Berks, and San Remo, Italy and d.s.p. 6 May 1957.
1. Muriel Annie Caroline, m. 2 June 1896, Edward Payne Press, of Avon Woods, Clifton, Bristol, and d. 4 Dec. 1937, leaving issue.
2. Annie Louisa, Mother-Gen. of the Community of St. Mary the Virgin at Wantage, d. 13 Mar. 1951.
3. Elma Katie, m. 27 Oct. 1892, Rt. Rev. Henry Luke Paget, D.D., Bishop of Chester, 1919-32, and had issue, (Paget of Harewood Place, Bt.).
4. Marjorie Gurney, d. unm. 13 Oct. 1931.
5. Christobel Mary, F.R. Hist. S., J.P. co.

Norfolk, mem. C.C. Norfolk, and C.A. 1949; mem. Erpingham R.D.C. 1919, and Chm. 1950; editor of *Norfolk Archaeology*, 1922-35, and author of *An East Anglian Soke*, m. 14 Oct. 1916, Rev. Charles Ivo Sinclair Hood, C.F., who d. 15 April 1918, of wounds received in action, leaving issue.

The eldest son,
Sir Samuel John Gurney Hoare, 2nd Bt., and **Viscount Templewood**, b. 24 Feb. 1880; educ. Harrow and New Coll. Oxford, B.A. 1903, M.A. 1910; a very prominent politician in the interwar period; M.P. for Chelsea, 1910-44; mem. of L.C.C. for Brixton, 1907; Sec. of State for Air, 1922-24; (Jan.) and Nov. 1924-June 1929, and April-May 1940; Sec. of State for India, 1931-35; and Sec. of State for Foreign Affairs, June 1935-Dec. 1935, having to resign over public agitation concerning the proposed Hoare-Laval Pact for Abyssinia; shortly afterwards injured his nose in a skating accident, a sport in which he was very skilled; First Lord of the Admiralty, June 1936-37, and Home Sec. May 1937-Sept. 1939; Lord Privy Seal, Sept. 1939-April 1940; from May 1940 to Dec. 1944, undertook the very difficult position of British Ambassador in Madrid; served in World War I as a G.S.O. (despatches twice) and had the following foreign orders and decorations: St. Anne and St. Stanislas, 2nd class of Russia, St. Maurice and St. Lazarus of Italy, and Gr. Cross of White Lion of Czechoslovakia, Gr. Cross of the Northern Star of Sweden, Gr. Cross of the Dannebrog of Denmark, and Gr. Cross of Order of Orange-Nassau, of the Netherlands; mem. of numerous commissions and Pres. of the Lawn Tennis Asscn. 1932; Freeman of Chelsea; Elder Bro. of Trinity House, 1936; Chan. of Reading Univ. 1937; Pres. .of the Howard League for Penal Reform, 1947, and Pres. of the Air League of the Brit. Empire, 1953; m. 17 Oct. 1909, Lady Maud Lygon, D.B.E. 1927, dau. of 6th Earl Beauchamp. She d. 27 Dec. 1962. Sir Samuel, was cr. C.M.G. 1917, made P.C. 1922, cr. G.B.E. 1927, G.C.S.I., 1934 and a peer as Viscount Templewood of Chelsea, Middlesex. He d.s.p. 7 May 1959.

ARMS—Sable, a double headed eagle displayed within a bordure indented argent.
CREST—A stag's head erased argent charged on the neck with a cross couped sable.
SUPPORTERS—On either side a stag or, charged on the neck with a cross couped sable.
MOTTO—Hora venit.
Viscount Templewood's seat was Templewood, Northrepps, Cromer, Norfolk.

TENTERDEN

PEERAGE—U.K. Baron Tenterden, of Hendon in the co. of Middlesex.
SURNAME—Abbott.
CR.—30 April 1927. **EXT.**—16 Sept. 1939.
HISTORY—John Abbott, of Canterbury, m. Alice, only dau. and heiress of Daniel Bunce, of Canterbury, and d. 14 Feb. 1795, having had with other issue, a second son,
Sir Charles Abbott, **1st Baron Tenterden,** b. 7 Oct. 1762; educ. Corpus Christi Coll.

Oxford; Barrister-at-Law, Inner Temple; one of the Puisne Judges of the Court of Common Pleas, 1815, and later the same year, a judge of the Court of King's Bench; cr. Kt. Bach. 1816, and 1818, apptd. Lord Chief Justice of England; cr. Baron Tenterden, of Hendon in the co. of Middlesex, 30 April 1827. He m. 13 July 1795, Mary, dau. of John Legier Lamotte, of the Grotto House, Basildon, co. Berks, and d. 4 Nov. 1832 having by her (who d. 20 Dec. 1832) had issue,

1. John Henry, **2nd Baron Tenterden** (see below).
2. Charles, b. 8 Aug. 1803; m. 9 Jan. 1834, Emily Frances, dau. of Lord George Stuart, Adm. R.N., 7th son of 1st Marquess of Bute and d. 17 Dec. 1838, having by her (who d. 16 June 1886) a son,
   Charles Stuart Aubrey, **3rd Baron Tenterden** (see below).
   1. Mary, d. 9 Aug. 1858.
   2. Catherine Alice, m. 11 May 1839, Lt. Gen. Sir John Rowland Smyth, brother of the Princess of Capua, and d. 31 Dec. 1865, having had issue,
      Penelope Mary Gertrude Smyth who m. her cousin, the 3rd Baron Tenterden, (see below).

The elder son,
John Henry Abbott, **2nd Baron Tenterden,** b. 6 Aug. 1796, and d. unm. 10 April 1870, being s. by his nephew,
Charles Stuart Aubrey Abbott, **3rd Baron Tenterden,** K.C.B., Per. Under Sec. of State for Foreign Affairs, b. 26 Dec. 1834; m. (1) 2 Aug. 1859, his cousin, Penelope Mary Gertrude Smyth (see above). She d. 30 Mar. 1879. He m. (2) 13 Jan. 1880, Emma Mary, dau. of Charles Bailey, of Lee Abbey, North Devon, and widow of Henry Rowcliffe, Q.C. She d. 21 May 1928. The 3rd Lord Tenterden d. 22 Sept. 1882, having had by his first wife,

1. Charles Stuart Henry, **4th Baron Tenterden** (see below).
   1. Audrey Mary Florence, m. (1) 30 Mar. 1882, Major R. G. Handcock, (Castlemaine, B.) who d.s.p. 1906. She m. (2) 1915, W. H. Nash and d. 24 Nov. 1945.
   2. Geraldine Alice Ellen, m. 1884, Lt. Col. C. Egan and d. 1919.
   3. Gwen Elea Villet, m. 1888, Hon. Edward Charles Macnaghten, later Sir Edward Macnaghten, Bt., (Machnaghten Bt.), and d. 5 Dec. 1891.

The only son,
Charles Stuart Henry Abbott, **4th Baron Tenterden,** Lt. 3rd Bn. the York and Lancaster Regt., b. 30 Oct. 1865; m. 10 Jan. 1906, Elfrida Charlotte only dau. of Major-Gen. Sir Alfred Turner, and d. 16 Sept. 1939, having had issue,
Charles Stuart Anthony Rowland, b. 25 July 1909; d. 14 Mar. 1928.
Gwen Elfrida Penelope, b. 22 July 1908; m. 1941, William Fisher, son of Alexander Fischer, of Budapest and had issue.

ARMS—Purpure a pile wavy, vairé argent and gules, between two water bougets in base or; on a canton of the third, a crosier erect azure.
CREST—A fox passant per pale, sable and argent, charged on the shoulder with a water bouget or.
SUPPORTERS—Dexter, A dragon, wings elevated vert gorged with the collar of Lord Chief Justice, and charged on the wing with a water bouget or; Sinister, A pelican wings elevated or, beaked, vulned and gorged, with a collar of roses gules.
MOTTO—Labore.

THANKERTON

PEERAGE—U.K. Life. Baron Thankerton, of Thankerton, co. Lanark.
SURNAME—Watson.
CR.—1 May 1929. **EXT.**—13 June 1948.
HISTORY—William Watson, Baron Watson, of Thankerton, co. Lanark, a life peer (see Watson in present work), had a third son.
William Watson, **Baron Thankerton,** b. 8 Dec. 1873; educ. Winchester and Jesus Coll. Camb., B.A., LL.B. 1895; Advocate of the Scots Bar, 1899; M.P. South Lanarkshire, 1913-18, and for Carlisle 1924-29; K.C. 1914; Hon. Bencher, Gray's Inn, 1928; Advocate Depute, 1919; Solicitor Gen. 1922; Lord Advocate for Scotland, 1922-24; and 1924-29; Procurator of the Church of Scotland, 1918-22; was made P.C. 1922, and cr. a Lord of Appeal in Ordinary and a life peer as Baron Thankerton, of Thankerton, co. Lanark, 1 May 1929. He m. 26 July 1903, Sophia Marjorie, dau. of John James Cowan, of Bavelaw Castle, Midlothian and d. 13 June 1948, having had issue,

1. William Douglas, b. 25 Jan. 1905; educ. Winchester, and Trin. Coll. Camb. B.A. 1926; W.S. Edinburgh; served in World War II, 1939-45 (despatches twice, Lt. Col. R.A., and T.D.), mem. Royal Co. of Archers, Queen's Bodyguard for Scotland; m. 16 June 1934, Enid Agnes, dau. of Colin Ballantyne.
2. David John, b. 29 July 1911; educ. Winchester, and Trin. Coll. Camb. B.A. 1933; Barrister-at-Law, Gray's Inn, 1934, Q.C., Advocate, Scotland, 1944; mem. of Royal Co. of Archers etc., d. unm. 27 Nov. 1959.
   1. Sophia Margaret, b. 2 July 1907; m. 20 June 1936, M. J. Callow.

ARMS—Or an oaktree growing out of a mount in base vert surmounted of a fess ermine charged with two mullets azure.
CREST—The stump of an oak tree with two branches sprouting from it, and grasped on either side by a hand issuing from a cloud all ppr.
MOTTO—A Deo Floruit.

THOMSON

PEERAGE—U.K. Baron Thomson, of Cardington, co. Bedford.
SURNAME—Thomson.
CR.—11 Feb. 1924. **EXT.**—5 Oct. 1930.
HISTORY—Gen. Harry Thomson, d. 1880 having had issue,
Major Gen. David Thomson, R.E., b. 1833; m. 26 Jan. 1867, Emily Lydia, dau. of Gen. Christopher Birdwood, (Birdwood, Bt.), and d. 23 Mar. 1911, having had issue,

1. Harry Verelst (1867-68).
2. Burns Travers, b. 15 Aug. 1870; d. 21 Feb. 1896.
3. Christopher Birdwood, **Baron Thomson** (see below).

4. Roger Gordon, C.M.G., 1918, D.S.O. 1916, Col. R.F.A., served in World War I (despatches five times and wounded), b. 4 April 1878; m. 7 April 1904, Florence Lucy, dau. of Major Gen. W. E. Delves Broughton, Bengal Army and had issue,
(1) Roger William David, Midshipman, R.N., b. 1906.
(1) Florence Margaret Gordon, m. 26 April 1925, R. Richardson-Bunbury, and had issue (Richardson-Bunbury Bt.).
(2) Betty Winifred.
5. Harry Tagert, b. 17 Aug. 1860.
1. Nellie de Winton, b. 2 June 1869; m. Elvin Harris and d. 1910.
2. Annie Gordon, (1872-72)
3. Winifred Marian, b. 29 May 1873; d. 15 Jan. 1901.
4. Mary Josephine, b. 3 May 1879; m. 16 May 1905, Rev. D. H. G. Sargent, and had issue.
5. Alice May Lydia, b. 3 May 1897.
The third son, Christopher Birdwood Thomson, **Baron Thomson**, b. 13 April 1875, in India, and educ. Cheltenham and the R.M.A. Woolwich; joined R.E. 1894; served in Mashonaland Campaign, 1896, and in the S. African War, 1900-02; Brev. Major, on reaching rank of Capt.; Instructor at Sch. of Mil. Engineering, Chatham, 1902-05; in West Africa, 1906-07; Staff Coll. Camberley, 1909-10; War Office, 1911-14, being present at the Balkan Wars, 1912-13, as representing the War Office; served in World War I, G.S.O. 1st grade, 1914-15; Mil. Attaché and Chief of Brit. Mil. Commission in Rumania, 1915-16; Cmdr. R.E. 60th Div. Palestine, 1917-18; Brig. Gen., Gen. Staff, Supreme War Council, Versailles, 1918; was cr. D.S.O. 1918, C.B.E. 1919, and ret. with rank of Brig. Gen. 1919; made P.C. 1924; Sec. of State for Air, 1924- and 1929-30. He was cr. 11 Feb. 1924, Baron Thomson, of Cardington, co. Bedford. (He had previously contested Bristol Central Div. 1922 and St. Albans, 1923.) He was mainly responsible for the Gov.'s decision on three years' scheme of air development, including the building of two airships, R.100 and R.101. He d. unm. in the diaster to the airship R.101 at Beauvais, France on 5 Oct. 1930. He was bur. at Cardington in a common grave with the rest of the victims after lying in state in Westminster Hall.

THRING

PEERAGE—U.K. Baron Thring, of Alderhurst, co. Surrey.
SURNAME—Thring.
CR.—17 Aug. 1886. EXT.—4 Feb. 1907.
HISTORY—Brouncker Thring, Gent., of Codford St. Peter, co. Wilts, d. 1708, leaving a son, John Thring, b. 1681; m. Katharine Wrench, and d. 16 May 1750, having had issue,
1. Brouncker, b. 1714, m. Anne Hewlett, and d. 1787. His son and grandson became in succession Rectors of Sutton Veny.
2. Wrench (see below).
The ygr. son,
Wrench Thring, Esq., of Codford St. Peter, b. 1718; m. 1752, Anne, dau. of John Ingram,

of Hindon, and d. 1781 leaving with a dau. Elizabeth who m. Rev. George Smith, a son,
John Thring, of Alford House, b. 1753; m. Elizabeth, dau. of William Everett, Esq., of Heytesbury, and d. 1830, leaving issue, with a dau., Alicia Anne, a son,
The Rev. John Gale Dalton Thring, of Alford House, co. Somerset, B.C.L., J.P. and D.L., b. Sept. 1784; m. 1811, Sarah, dau. of Rev. John Jenkyns, Preb. of Wells, and d. Dec. 1874, leaving by her (who d. 26 Sept. 1891, aged 102), with two daus.,
1. Theodore, of Alford House, B.A., Barrister-at-Law, Chm. of Quarter Sessions, b. 4 Aug. 1816; m. 1852 Julia Jane, dau. of William Mills, of Saxham Hall, co. Suffolk, and d. 28 Sept. 1891 leaving issue.
2. Henry, **Baron Thring** (see below).
3. Edward, Rev. M.A., Head master of Uppingham Grammar Sch.; b. 1823; m. 1853, Marie, dau. of Herr Koch, of Bonn, and d. 22 Oct. 1887, leaving issue.
4. Godfrey, Rev., Preb. of Wells, Rector of Alford with Hornblotton, Somerset, 1858-92, b. 1823; m. 18 Jan. 1870, Mary Jane, dau. of Charles Pinney, of Camp House, Clifton, Bristol, and had issue.
5. John Charles, Rev., B.A., of Chantry House, co. Wilts, b. 1824; m. 1858, Lydia Eliza Dyer, dau. of Capt. Samuel Meredith, R.N. and had issue.
The second son,
Sir Henry Thring, **Baron Thring**, b. 3 Nov. 1818; M.A. Camb., Barrister-at-Law, 1845; Counsel to Home Office, 1861-69; Parl. Counsel to Government, 1869-86, High Steward, Kingston-on-Thames; cr. K.C.B. and a peer as Baron Thring, of Alderhurst, Surrey, m. 14 Aug. 1856, Elizabeth, dau. of John Cardwell, of Liverpool and sister of 1st Viscount Cardwell, (see that title). He d. 4 Feb. 1907. She d. 27 Nov. 1897. They had issue,
Katharine Anne,
ARMS—Erminois on a fess plain azure, another wavy or, charged with three escallops sable, bordure invected gules.
CREST—A cock per pale, or and gules charged with two escallops counterchanged in the beak an ear of barley ppr.
Lord Thring's seat was Alderhurst, Englefield Green.

**THURLOW

PEERAGE—Great Britain. Baron Thurlow, of Ashfield, co. Suffolk.
SURNAME—Thurlow.
CR.—3 June 1778. EXT.—12 Sept. 1806.
HISTORY—Edward Thurlow, of a family very distinguished in the law, became Lord High Chancellor of Great Britain 1778-92. He was cr. 3 June 1778 **Baron Thurlow**, of Ashfield, co. Suffolk, with the usual remainder to the heirs male of his body. On 12 June 1792 he was further cr. Baron Thurlow (G.B.) of Thurlow, West Suffolk, with remainder, failing his male issue, to his nephews, Edward and Thomas Thurlow, and Edward South Thurlow. The Baron Thurlow d. unm. 12 Sept. 1806. The barony of 1778 became extinct but the barony cr. in 1792 was inherited by Lord Thurlow's nephew.
Edward Hovell-Thurlow, 2nd Baron

Thurlow of the 1792 creation. (see Thurlow in extant peerages).
ARMS—Argent on a chevron cottised sable, three portcullises with chains and rings argent.
CREST—A raven ppr. gorged with a chain and pendent therefrom a portcullis argent.
SUPPORTERS—On either side a greyhound or, collared and line reflexed over the back sable.

TOMLIN

PEERAGE—U.K. Life. Baron Tomlin of Ash, co. Kent.
SURNAME—Tomlin.
CR.—11 Feb. 1929. **EXT.**—12 Aug. 1935.
HISTORY—Francis Tomlin, of Ash, co. Kent, (see editions of B.L.G. previous to 1952), who d. 1751, was father of.
Thomas Minter Tomlin, of Twitham Hill, Ash, co. Kent, b. 1781; d. 29 Aug. 1857, being father of,
George Taddy Tomlin, of Comber House, Canterbury, Barrister-at-Law, Inner Temple, b. 9 July 1826; m. 23 Aug. 1865, Alice, dau. of Rev. Canon W. J. Chesshyre, of Barton Court, Canterbury, and d. 14 Feb. 1877, leaving issue, with three daus.,
1. Thomas James Chesshyre, **Baron Tomlin** (See below).
2. James William Sackett, Rev., M.A. New Coll. Oxford, Canon of Canterbury, and Warden of St. Augustine's Missionary Coll. Canterbury, b. 18 July 1871; m. 3 July 1906, Dorothy Edith, dau. of Rev. Canon Meyrick, and had issue.
The elder son,
Thomas James Chesshyre Tomlin, **Baron Tomlin**, b. 6 May 1867; educ. Harrow and New Coll. Oxford, M.A., B.C.L.; Barrister-at-Law, Middle Temple, 1891; Lincoln's Inn, 1891; K.C. 1913; Bencher 1918; Counsel to Royal Coll. of Physicians 1922; a Judge of the High Court of Justice, Chancery Div. 1923; apptd a Lord of Appeal in Ordinary, 11 Feb. 1929, and cr. a Baron for life as Baron Tomlin, of Ash, co. Kent; a mem. of the Univs. Cttee. of the Privy Council. He m. 18 July 1893, Marion Olivia, dau. of Col. W. G. Waterfield, and d. 13 Aug. 1935, having had issue,
1. Anthony Neville Chesshyre, b. 30 May 1895; d. in New Zealand, 6 Dec. 1917.
2. George Garrow, b. 7 Jan. 1898; Barrister-at-Law, Lincoln's Inn, B.A. Magdalene Coll. Camb. Lt. R.N. (ret.) served in World War I, and d. 13 Dec. 1931, at Nazeing, co. Essex, in a flying accident.
3. Stephen, sculptor, b. 2 Mar. 1901, m. 22 July 1927, Julia Frances, dau. of Oliver Strachey (Strachie, B.).
1. Joan Olivia, b. 24 Feb. 1906; m. 3 Nov. 1932, W. G. Trower, and had issue,
2. Helen Rosa, b. 24 Feb. 1906, m. 3 Nov. 1932, Dr. Frank Goldby and had issue.
ARMS—Argent on a fess between three battle-axes erect sable as many dexter hands couped at the wrist ppr.
CREST—In front of two battle-axes in saltire ppr. a dexter hand as in the arms.
SUPPORTERS—On either side a lion purpure, each charged on the shoulder with a fasces or.
MOTTO—Aidons nous mutuellement.

TOVEY

PEERAGE—U.K. Baron Tovey, of Langton Matravers, co. Dorset.
SURNAME—Tovey.
CR.—11 Feb. 1946. **EXT.**—12 Jan. 1971.
HISTORY—Lt. Col. Hamilton Tovey, R.E., had with other issue, two sons.
1. George Strangways, Lt. Col. R.A.; b. 1875; educ. St. Paul's; served in S. African War, 1899-1902, (despatches); and in World War I, 1914-18 (C.M.G. 1918, and D.S.O. 1916); m. 1910, Lilian Mary, dau. of the Rev. A. Conder, of Bognor, and d. 13 Jan. 1943. She d. 1939. They had one son and one dau.
2. John Cronyn, **Baron Tovey** (see below).
The second son,
Sir John Cronyn Tovey, **Baron Tovey**, of Langton Matravers, co. Dorset, so cr. 11 Feb. 1946, b. 7 Mar. 1885; served in World War I, (despatches D.S.O.); Capt. 1923; cmd. Destroyer Flotillas, 1925-26; Asst. Dir. of Tactical Sch. 1928-29; Naval Asst. to Second Sea Lord, 1930-32; cmd. H.M.S. *Rodney*, 1932-34; A.D.C. to King George V. 1935; Commodore R.N. Barracks, Chatham, 1935-37; Rear Adm. 1935; Rear Adm. Destroyers, Mediterranean, 1938-40; Vice Adm. 1939; Vice Adm. second in command, Mediterranean Fleet, 1940; C. in C. Home Fleet, 1940-43, Adm. 1942; Adm. of the Fleet, 1943; C. in C. the Nore, 1943-46; A.D.C. King George VI, 1945-46; cr. C.B. 1937; K.C.B. and K.B.E. 1941, G.C.B. 1943. He m. 28 Mar. 1916, Aida, dau. of John Rowe. He d.s.p. 12 Jan. 1971.
ARMS—Azure an eagle displayed and in chief three pierced mullets of six points or.
CREST—On a mural crown argent, an eagle displayed or, in the beak a spear bendwise the staff broken ppr.
SUPPORTERS—Dexter, An able seaman; Sinister, A stoker, both in square rig ppr.

**TRAQUAIR

PEERAGE—Scotland. Baron Stuart of Traquair, co. Peebles, cr. 19 April 1638. Scotland. Baron Linton and Cabarston and Earl of Traquair, 22 June 1683.
SURNAME—Stuart.
CR.—as above. **DORMANT**—2 Aug. 1861.
HISTORY—This peerage is entered in Burke's Extinct Peerage for 1883, but ends with the words, after the detail of the death of the 8th Earl, "since that time, the Earldom of Traquair has remained dormant."
In the Complete Peerage vol. (1959) covering this peerage, there is a reference in some detail to a claim being prepared by C. E. T. Stuart-Linton in 1949. Reference is also made to a work by the present writer, L. G. Pine (1940), *The Stuarts of Traquair*. The pedigree on which C. E. T. Stuart-Linton's claim was based was given in full in the 1952 edition of Burke's Landed Gentry. It also appeared in the 1939 edition of the same work, American Supplement. Very briefly the history is as follows:
The **8th Earl of Traquair**, when Lord Linton m. at Coldstream, Scotland, 28 April 1818, a Protestant lady, Elizabeth Mary Johnstone, and by her had issue,

Charles Alfred George Stuart, b. 7 Feb. 1819 in Dublin. He assumed the additional surname of Linton, ahd became a great friend of H.R.H. Adolphus Frederick, 1st Duke of Cambridge, and of his son, the 2nd Duke of Cambridge. About 1852 he was made the Gov. of a convict settlements in Australia. He m. Margaret MacMahon 1847 and d.v.p. ca. 1856, having had issue three sons, George, William and Adolphus, of whom the third son,

Adolphus Frederick Stuart-Linton, so named after the 1st Duke of Cambridge, of Cabarston House, Hove, co. Sussex, was b. 14 Aug. 1852, in Australia; m. 10 Dec. 1878, at the British Embassy in Paris, Rhoebe Rebecca Elizabeth Elwina, who d. 18 Feb. 1944, dau. of John Borland Finlay, of Finlayston House, Kittaning, Pa., and d. 18 Aug. 1914, having had issue,

    Charles Edward Traquair Stuart-Linton (see below).

    Fryda Amy Bertha, M.B.E., m. (1) 1917 (m. diss. by div. 1928), Ernest Gagné, and (2) 1938, Oliver Paul Jeffreys Corwin.

The only son,

Charles Edward Traquair Stuart-Linton, b. 7 Jan. 1884 at Nice, France; educ. Thompson's, Brighton, the Rev. Dr. West's, Ascham House, Bournemouth and Trinity Univ. Toronto; served in World War I, 1914-18, with the Canadian Expeditionary Force and was commissioned in the 109th Regt., and later served with the 1st Central Ontario Regt. and subsequently with the Brit. Mil. Mission to U.S.A., was attached to M.I.I.C. and later to M.I.5; and in World War II joined the Brit. Information Service in New York as a volunteer without pay, and also served on several committees in connection with the British War Effort. He m. 23 Nov. 1951, Inez Sargent, ygr. dau. of George Edward Hanks, of Portland, Oregon, U.S.A. and d.s.p. in his apartment at 2 Tudor City Place, New York, N.Y., 10021, in 1963 or 1964 (obituary appeared in *New York Times*).

The documents possessed by the late Mr. Stuart-Linton included the following: (a certificate of a marriage performed at Coldstream on 28 April 1818) "These are to certify all persons who it may concern that Charles Stuart, Lord Linton, of the County of Peebles, and Elizabeth Mary Johnston, of the County of Northumberland, who came before me declaring themselves to be both single persons were lawfully married by the way of the Church of England and agreeable to our Laws of the Kingdom and Kirk of Scotland. Given under my hand at Coldstream Bridge, Coldstream, Scotland, this 28 Day of April 1818.
Scribe and Witness   John Armstrong.
William Bigger.   Linton.
Witness—John Waugh. Elizabeth Mary Johnston."

The original of this document was in possession of the late C. E. T. Stuart-Linton. John Armstrong was the "priest" at Coldstream, and he is said to have performed a like ceremony for Lord Brougham and Vaux. There is no reason to doubt the validity of the matter, since, although irregular, the marriage is not invalid in Scots law. As a matter of fact when the printed book by L. G. Pine was sent in 1940 to the then Lord Lyon he urged the late Mr. C. E. T. Stuart-Linton to prepare his petition.

It may also be of interest to note that Lady Christina Stuart, the dau. of the 6th Earl of Traquair made a runaway marriage with Cyrus Griffin, of Virginia, at Coldstream in 1770, he becoming later the last President of the Continental Congress. A very great deal of information on the family in America has been compiled by John Insley Coddington, a distinguished American genealogist. This appeared in the National Genealogical Society Quarterly, vol. 52 no. 1 Mar. 1964, pages 25-36. This was under the heading: Ancestors and Descendants of Lady Christina Stuart (1741-1807), wife of the Hon. Cyrus Griffin of Virginia. Mr. Coddington has also obtained some more information about the earlier holders of the earldom, which differs from some details given in C.P.

In the view of the present writer it was most unfortunate that the suggestion of the Lord Lyon in 1940 was not acted upon by Mr. Stuart-Linton. It was not until after the second World War that he made strenuous efforts to trace any possible descendants of his father's two brothers, who might have been possible claimants to the earldom. Such descendants were not found despite efforts in both U.S.A. and Australia. I have been informed by Mr. Coddington that the two elder sons, George and William, had some connection with the neighbourhood of Bath, Ontario, Canada, on the northern shore of Lake Ontario. He adds that he once met an elderly doctor H. C. Burleigh, of Bath, Ontario who had some knowledge of the Stuart-Linton family and who stated that he had written to the writer on the matter. This letter was not received.

Two other notes may be of interest. Mr. C. Stewart Henderson, wrote an article on The Stewarts of Traquair, in *The Stewarts: An Historical and General Magazine*, Edinburgh; The Stewart Society, vol. 8 (1947) pp. 13-25.

It should also be mentioned that Mr. A. F. Stuart-Linton, father of the claimant, was an art connoisseur of note and possessed a large number of Old Masters which he bequeathed to his son, C. E. T. Stuart-Linton, and which included works by Rubens, Van Dyke, Hobbema, Claude, Vignon and Greuze, and the Altoviti Aprhodite a marble statue attributed by experts to Praxiteles, and later in possession of J. D. Rockfeller, Jr. Some of the paintings had formerly been in the collection of H.R.H. Adolphus Frederick, 1st Duke of Cambridge who gave them to A. F. Stuart-Linton.

TREDEGAR

PEERAGE—U.K. Baron Tredegar, 16 April 1859.
    Viscount Tredegar of Tredegar, co. Monmouth, 28 Dec. 1905. Ext. 11 Mar. 1913.
    Viscount Tredegar, of Tredegar, co. Monmouth 4 Aug. 1926. Ext. 27 April 1949. (Also a baronetcy cr. 15 Nov. 1792.)
SURNAME—Morgan.
CR.—As above. EXT.—(Barony of 1859 with baronetcy), 17 Nov. 1962.
HISTORY—Llewellyn ap Ivor, was lord of St. Clere and Gwinfar, co. Carmarthen, and descended from Cadifor Vawr, Lord of Kilsaint. He m. Angharad, dau. and heiress of Sir Morgan ap Meredyth, Lord of Tredegar,

and thus became, in right of his wife, owner of the Tredegar properties. He had issue,
1. Morgan (see below).
2. Ivor, of Werncleppa, whose last male heir, Roger Morgan, d. 1632, when his estate was inherited by the Tredegar line.
3. Philip, from whom descended the family of Lewis of St. Pierre, (B.L.G. 1894 edit.).

The eldest son,
Morgan ap Llewellyn, Lord of St. Clere, and of Tredegar, co. Monmouth, had issue by his wife Maud, dau. of Rhys ap Gronwy, lord of Kybor,
1. Llewellyn, his heir (see below).
2. Philip, of Langston, from whom descended the now extinct baronets, Morgan of Llanternam.

The elder son,
Llewellyn ap Morgan, lord of St. Clere and of Tredegar, m. Jonnet, dau. of David Vaughan ap David ap Llewellyn ap Philip of Rhuderin, co. Monmouth, and had issue,
Jevan ap Llewellyn ap Morgan of St. Clere and Tredegar, m. Elizabeth or Dennis, dau. of Thomas ap Llewellyn ap Howell ap Eynon Sais, and had issue,
Sir John Morgan, of St. Clere and Tredegar, m. Jonnet, dau. and heiress of John Mathew, of Llandaff, and had, with three other sons,
1. Morgan, of Tredegar, m. Margaret, dau. of Sir Thomas Morgan of Langston, and had a son, John, of Tredegar, (will dated 4 April 1513) whose son, William, d.s.p. in 1569.
2. Thomas (see below).

The ygr. son,
Thomas Morgan, of Machen, Esquire of the King's Body, Henry VII, m. Elizabeth, dau. of Roger Vaughan, of Talgarth, and had issue with six daus. and a ygr. son, John (from whom came the Morgans of Bassalegge), an elder son,
Rowland Morgan, of Machen, living 1570, m. (sett. dated 4 Nov. 1517) Blanch, dau. of John Thomas, of Treowen, co. Monmouth, and had issue with four daus. and a ygr. son, Harry, of Llanrumney, ancestor of the Morgans of Llanrumney, an elder son,
Thomas Morgan, of Machen and Tredegar, who by his wife Elizabeth, dau. of Roger Bodenham, of Rotherwas, co. Hereford, had issue,
Sir William Morgan, of Tredegar, (will proved 13 Sept. 1653), m. (1) 1598, Elizabeth, dau. of Sir William Wintour, of Lidney, co. Gloucester. He m. (2) Bridget (d. before 1627) dau. of Anthony Morgan, of Hayford, co. Northants, and d. circa 1653 having had issue by both his wives. By his first wife he had,
1. Thomas, his heir (see below).
2. Edward, of Kilfiggin, and Coyd Morgan, co. Monmouth, m. Elizabeth, and had issue a dau. and heiress who m. Henry Chambre and had issue.
3. William, of Tumney, m. Jane Morgan, of Hurst, co. Glamorgan, and d. 7 Sept. 1670. From him descended the family of Morgan-Clifford.
1. Elizabeth, m. 1633, William Morgan, of Dderrw, co. Brecon, and was bur. 28 June 1638, leaving issue (see below).

The eldest son,
Thomas Morgan, of Machen and Tredegar, m. (1) 1621, Rachel, dau. of Robert Hopton, and sister and coheir of Lord Hopton, of

Strattorn, and widow of Daid Kemeys, of Cefn Mably, and by her had issue, an only dau. Elizabeth, m. Sir Trevor Williams, 1st Bt. (title extinct 1758) and d. 1679 having had issue. He m. (2) 1 Oct. 1633, Elizabeth who d. 18 Oct. 1666, dau. and heiress of Francis Windham, of Sandhill, co. Somerset. By her he had seven sons and seven daus. He d. 13 May 1664, and was s. by his eldest son,
William Morgan, of Tredegar, m. (1) 4 Nov. 1661, Blanche, (d. 25 Mar. 1673), dau. of William Morgan, of Dderrw, co. Brecon, and by her had with other issue,
1. Thomas, of Tredegar, b. 7 Sept. 1664; m. 5 Sept. 1687, Martha, dau. of Sir Edward Mansel. She d. 20 Nov. 1695. He d.s.p. 1699.
2. John who s. to Tredegar (see below).
He m. (2), Elizabeth, dau. and co-heir of Edward Lewis, of Van Park, co. Glamorgan, and widow of Sir Francis Darell, of co. Bucks and d. 28 April 1680, being s. by his ygr. son,
John Morgan, of Tredegar and of Ruperra, Lord Lt. of the cos. of Monmouth and Brecon, b. 4 Jan. 1670; m. 9 Jan. 1699/1700, Martha (bur. 27 Oct. 1720) dau. of Gwyn Vaughan, of Trebarried, Brecon, and d. (will proved 1716) having had issue,
1. William, his heir (see below).
2. Thomas, heir to his nephew (see below).
1. Martha, m. 1725, Edward Harley 3rd Earl of Oxford, and d. 4 Jan. 1774.
2. Katherine, m. John Butler, of Warminghurst Park, Sussex, and d. 1748.

The elder son,
Sir William Morgan, K.B., of Tredegar, Lord Lt. cos. Monmouth and Brecon, b. 1700; m. Rachel, eldest dau. of 2nd Duke of Devonshire. She d. 18 June 1780. He d. 24 April 1731, aged 30 having had with other issue,
William (see below).
Elizabeth, b. 29 Mar. 1729; m. 6 July 1767, William Jones, of Clytha House, co. Monmouth, and d.s.p. 14 Jan. 1787.

The son and heir,
William Morgan, of Tredegar, b. 28 Mar. 1725; d. unm. 16 July 1763, being s. in the Tredegar estate by his uncle,
Thomas Morgan, of Tredegar and of Ruperra, Lord Lt. cos. Monmouth and Brecon, b. 20 May 1702; m. Jane, dau. and coheir of Maynard Colchester, of Westburyon-Severn, and d. 12 April 1769. She d. 5 Nov. 1767. They had issue,
1. Thomas, his heir (see below).
2. Charles, heir to his brother (see below).
3. John, heir to his brother Charles (see below).
1. Jane, who eventually s. to Tredegar.
2. Katherine, b. 11 Sept. 1735; m. Aug. 1754, Charles Vann, of Llanwern, co. Monmouth, and d. July 1784 leaving issue.

The eldest son,
Thomas Morgan, of Tredegar, Lord Lt. cos. Brecon and Monmouth, b. 8 June 1727; d. unm. 15 May 1771, and was s. by his next brother,
Charles Morgan, of Tredegar, Lord Lt. co. Brecon, b. 1 Dec. 1736; m. Mary, dau. and heiress of Thomas Parry, of Arkston, co. Hereford, and widow of Robert Minors Gouge, of Treagoe, co. Hereford, and d. 24 May 1787, being s. by his brother,
John Morgan, of Tredegar, M.P. co. Monmouth, b. 18 Feb. 1741/42; m. Louisa, dau. of

Charles Pym Burt and d.s.p. 27 June 1792, being s. at Tredegar by his elder sister,

Jane Morgan, of Tredegar, b. 10 June 1731; m. Feb. 1758 Sir Charles Gould, 1st Bt. P.C., Advocate Gen. and Judge Marshal of H.M.'s Forces, who was cr. a baronet 15 Nov. 1792. He assumed by Royal Licence 16 Nov. 1792, the name and arms of Morgan in lieu of those of Gould. He was son of King Gould, Dep. Judge Advocate. Lady Morgan d. 14 Feb. 1797. Sir Charles Morgan d. 6 Dec. 1806. They had issue,

1. Charles, 2nd Bt. (see below).
2. John, a Midshipman R.N., who was k. while serving under Lord Rodney 12 April 1782.
1. Jane, m. (1) Cpt. Henry Ball, R.N., who d.s.p. 14 Aug. 1792. She m. (2) 8 May 1793, Samuel Homfray, of Penydarron, co. Glamorgan, and d. 22 Dec. 1746 leaving issue.
2. Elizabeth, m. 10 Mar. 1795, Rowley Lascelles, of Catherel, co. Glamorgan, and d. 10 May 1836 leaving issue.

The elder son,

Sir Charles Morgan, 2nd Bt., Lt. Col., and Capt. Coldstream Guards, M.P. Brecon, 1787-96, and co. Monmouth, 1797-1831; b. 4 Feb. 1760; m. 1791 Mary Margaret, only child of Capt. George Stoney, R.N. She d. 24 Mar. 1808. By her he had issue,

1. Charles Morgan Robinson, **1st Baron Tredegar** (see below).
2. George Gould, M.P. Brecon, b. 12 July 1794; m. 7 July 1824, Eliza, dau. of Rev. William Beville, and d. 25 Aug. 1845, leaving by her (she m. 2ndly Capt. Claridge) with another dau. who d. unm.,
   (1) Eliza Angeline, m. 11 Dec. 1856, Major Gen. Sir G. H. S. Willis, G.C.B., and d. 1867.
   (2) Selina Rose Catherine, m. 10 April 1858, Rev. W. N. Tilson Marsh-Lucherton-Tilson, and d. 24 Mar. 1896.
3. Charles Augustus Samuel, Rev., Chancellor of Llandaff Cathedral, Rector of Machen, co. Monmouth, b. 2 Sept. 1800; m. 20 April 1837, Frances, dau. of Rowley Lascelles, and d. 5 Sept. 1875.
4. Charles Octavius Swinnerton, M.P. co. Monmouth, 1841-74; F.R.S., M.A., b. 15 Sept. 1803; d. unm. 5 Aug. 1888.
1. Maria Margaretta, m. 8 Mar. 1817, Lt. Gen. F. M. Milman, (Milman, Bt.), and d. 15 May 1875 leaving issue.
2. Charlotte Georgiana, m. 27 Feb. 1819, 3rd Baron Rodney, and d. 19 Feb. 1878.
3. Angelina Maria Cecilia, m. 12 April 1825, Sir Hugh Owen, 2nd Bt., and d. 4 Sept. 1844, leaving issue.

Sir Charles Morgan, 2nd Bt., d. 5 Dec. 1846, and was s. by his eldest son.

Sir Charles Morgan Robinson Morgan, 3rd Bt., and **1st Baron Tredegar**, M.P. and Lord Lt. co. Brecon, b. 10 April 1792; cr. a peer as Baron Tredegar, 16 April 1859; m. 6 Oct. 1827, Rosamund, (d. 3 Jan. 1883), only dau. of Gen. Godfrey Basil Mundy, by his wife, Sarah, dau. of 1st Baron Rodney, and had issue,

1. Charles Rodney, Coldstream Guards, M.P. Brecon, b. Dec. 1828; d.v.p. unm. 14 Jan. 1854.
2. Godfrey Charles, **2nd Baron** and **1st and last Viscount** (see below).

3. Frederick Courtenay, of Ruperra Castle, Newport, co. Monmouth, M.P. co. Monmouth, 1874-85, and S. Div. 1885-1906, Capt. Rifle Brig., b. 24 May 1834; m. 3 May 1858, Charlotte Ann, (d. 30 Mar. 1891) dau. of Charles A. Williamson, of Lawers, co. Perth, and d. 8 Jan. 1909, leaving issue,
   (1) Courtenay Charles Evan, **3rd Baron** (see below).
   (2) Frederic George, **5th Baron** (see below).
   (1) Blanche Frances, b. 10 Feb. 1859; m. 18 Sept. 1883, C. T. Hoare, and d. 31 Dec. 1948, leaving issue.
   (2) Violet Wilhelmina, b. 23 Sept. 1860; m. 28 Jan. 1894, Major B. St. Mundy, and d. 22 Dec. 1943 leaving issue,
4. Arthur John, b. 27 Aug. 1840; m. 31 Jan. 1894, Louisa Sarah (d. 9 Aug. 1925) dau. of W. C. Gammon and d.s.p.
5. George Gould, b. 15 Sept. 1845; d. unm. 3 Mar. 1907.
1. Rosamond Marian, m. 18 Dec. 1848, Sir William H. M. Style, 9th Bt., and d. 15 Jan. 1883 leaving issue.
2. Selina Maria, m. 5 Jan. 1853, D. R. Williamson, of Lawers co. Perth, and d. 31 Mar. 1922, leaving issue.
3. Fanny Henrietta, m. 9 Oct. 1854, Sir George F. Forestier-Walker, 2nd Bt., and d. 2 Sept. 1887, leaving issue.
4. Ellen Sarah, m. 14 May 1856, Lt. Col. H. G. Lindsay, of Glasnevin House, co. Dublin, and d. 19 May 1912, leaving issue, (Crawford, E.).
5. Georgiana Charlotte, m. (1) 28 Sept. 1857, Lord Francis Conyngham (Conyngham, M.) and (2) 27 April 1882, Lt. Col. A. G. Chichester, and d.s.p. 22 April 1886. (Templemore, B.).
6. Mary Anna, m. 16 July 1863, the 16th Viscount Hereford, and d. 14 Aug. 1924, leaving issue.

The 1st Lord Tredegar d. 16 April 1875, and was s. by his eldest surv. son,

Godfrey Charles Morgan, **2nd Baron Tredegar,** and **Viscount Tredegar,** b. 28 April 1831; Lord Lt. co. Monmouth, and Capt. 17th Lancers, (Crimean medal and four clasps) M.P. co. Brecon, 1858-75; Vice Chm. and Alderman, Monmouth C.C.; cr. Viscount Tredegar, of Tredegar, co. Monmouth, 28 Dec. 1905, and d. unm. 11 Mar. 1913, when the Viscounty became extinct, but he was s. in the barony and the baronetcy by his nephew,

Courtenay Charles Evan Morgan, **3rd Baron** and **1st Viscount Tredegar** (second creation), b. 10 April 1867; educ. Eton; joined Royal Monmouthshire Engineers 1884; Major and Hon. Lt. Col.; served in the S. African War, 1900-01, was Lt. R.N.V.R. 1914; served in World War I, 1914-18, cmd. H.M.Y. *Liberty* and was with Royal Naval Div.; cr. O.B.E., 1919; C.B.E. 1925; and on 4 Aug. 1926, Viscount Tredegar, of Tredegar, co. Monmouth; F.S.A., F.R.E.S., K.J. St. J., m. 5 Aug. 1890, Lady Katharine Agnes Blanche Carnegie, dau. of 9th Earl of Southesk. She d. 4 Oct. 1949. He d. 3 May 1934. They had issue with a dau. Gwyneth Erica b. 5 Jan. 1895, and d. Dec. 1924, an only son,

Evan Frederic Morgan, **4th Baron** and **2nd Viscount Tredegar,** F.R.S.A., F.R.S.L., F.R. Hort. S., F.Z.S., F.I.L., F.A.G.S., Privy

Chamberlain of Cape and Sword to Popes Benedict XV and Pius XI, Cmdr. with Star of Order of the Holy Sepulchre, Kt. of Devotion and Honour of the Sovereign and Mil. Order of Malta, Kt. of Justice of Constantinian Order of St. George, K.J. St. J., Almoner for Wales of O. St. J., b. 13 July 1893, educ. Eton and Ch. Ch. Oxford, served in World War I Lt. Welsh Guards, resigned commission in 1919 through ill health; m. (1) 21 April 1928, Hon. Lois Sturt, dau. of 2nd Baron Alington. She d. 18 Sept. 1937. He m. (2) 13 Mar. 1939 (m. annulled 1943), Princess Olga Sergievna Dolgorouky, dau. of Gen. Prince Serge Alexandrovltch Dolgorouky. He was known as a poet, writer and painter, had exhibited at the Paris Salon, and written novels and poems. He d.s.p. 27 April 1949, when the Viscounty became extinct and he was s. in the barony and the baronetcy by his uncle,

Frederick George Morgan, **5th Baron Tredegar,** b. 22 Nov. 1873; educ. Eton and Oxford Univ.; m. 14 April 1898, (m. diss. by div. 1921) Dorothy Syssyllt, dau. of Ralph Thurstan Bassett, of Bonvilston, co. Glamorgan. She d. 1 Oct. 1929. He d. 21 Aug. 1954 They had issue,

Frederic Charles John **6th Baron** (see below).
Syssyllt Avis, b. 24 Feb. 1903; m. 10 July 1926, (m. diss. by div., 1934), Peter H. Gurney.
The only son,

Frederic Charles John Morgan, **6th Baron Tredegar,** b. 26 Oct. 1908; educ. Eton; served in World War II 1939-45, with K.O.S.B., and on Staff; Asst. Almoner for Wales for Order of St. John; m. 4 Dec. 1954, Joanna, dau. of W. H. Law-Smith, of Adelaide, S. Australia, and formerly wife of Cmdr. A. B. Russell, R.N., and d.s.p. 17 Nov. 1962.

ARMS—Quarterly 1 and 4, Or a griffin segreant sable (Morgan); 2 and 3, Or on a chevron between three roses azure, as many thistles slipped of the field (Gould).
CREST—A reindeer's head couped or attired gules.
SUPPORTERS—Dexter, A lion sable; Sinister, A griffin sable, each charged on the shoulder with a thistle, slipped or.
MOTTO—Si Deus nobiscum, quis contra nos? The family seat was Tredegar Park, Newport, co. Monmouth. The residence of Lord Tredegar was Villa Belvedere, Beaulieu-sur-Mer, A.M., France.

TRENT

PEERAGE—U.K. Baron Trent, of Nottingham, co. Nottingham. (Also a baronetcy cr. 11 Jan. 1917.)
SURNAME—Boot.
CR.—18 Mar. 1929. **EXT.**—8 Mar. 1956.
HISTORY—This family is first traced at Diseworth, co. Leicester, where Richard Boot, d. 1577, leaving a son, Thomas Boot(e), who d. 1622 leaving by his wife, Margaret, a son, Thomas Boot, of Diseworth, who was father of,

Thomas Boot, of Diseworth, d. Aug. 1657, leaving by Elizabeth his wife, with three other sons and a dau., a second son,

Edward Boot, of Diseworth, d. 1688 leaving by Dorothy his wife, with two other sons and three daus.,

Jonathan Boot, of Ratcliffe-on-Scar, co. Nottingham, b. Feb. 1678; m. (1) 1706, Mary Endsor, (d. Nov. 1719) and (2) 20 May 1727, Sarah, dau. of William Plackit, of Ratcliffe and d. Mar. 1762, having had, by his first wife, three sons and a dau. of whom the eldest son,

Jonathan Boot, of Widmerpool, co. Nottingham, b. 1709; m. 15 Nov. 1730, Elizabeth Patchet (d. 7 Feb. 1752) and d. 1769, leaving an eldest surv. son,

John Boot, of Widmerpool, b. 1735; m. 7 June 1757, Ann Allen, and d. Feb. 1813, leaving an only son,

John Boot, of Willoughby, co. Nottingham, b. Feb. 1758; m. (1) 5 Feb. 1781, Ann Wartnaby (d.s.p. 9 Jan. 1782), and (2) 1 Dec. 1783, Sarah, Wilby, of Willoughby and d. April 1824, having by her had issue, with five other sons and two daus., a second son,

William Boot, of Holme Pierrepont, co. Nottingham, b. Mar. 1788; and d. 6 April 1861, having had by his wife, Sarah, an only son,

John Boot, of Nottingham, b. Oct. 1815; m. (1) 5 June 1838, Elizabeth, dau. of Thomas Mills, of Basingfield, co. Notts, She d. 14 Jan. 1848. He m. (2) 15 Feb. 1849, Mary, dau. of Benjamin Wills, of Nottingham, and by her (who d. 27 May 1885) had issue,

Sir Jesse Boot, 1st Bt. and **1st Baron Trent** of Nottingham, co. Nottingham, b. 2 June 1850, at Hockley Street, Nottingham; he was the founder of the world famous chemists' business, Boots Pure Drug Co. He was cr. Kt. Bach. 1909, a baronet, 11 Jan. 1917 and a peer, as Baron Trent, of Nottingham, co. Nottingham, 18 Mar. 1929. He m. 31 Aug. 1886, Florence Anne, dau. of William Rowe, of St. Heliers, Jersey, and d. 13 June 1931, having had issue,

1. John Campbell, 2nd Bt. and **2nd Baron Trent** (see below).
1. Dorothy Florence, m. 25 Nov. 1913, Capt. W. M. Bruce, C.B.E., R.N.R. and had issue, (Bruce of Downhill, Bt.).
2. Margery Amy, m. 18 Jan. 1921, A. M. Holman, and had issue.
The only son,

Sir John Campbell Boot, 2nd Bt. and **2nd Baron Trent,** b. 19 Jan. 1889; educ. the Leys Sch. Camb. and Jesus Coll. Camb.; Dir. of Boots Pure Drug Co.; served in World War I, Lt. 7th Terr. Bn. The Sherwood Foresters, 1914; Adj. 1915; Capt. 1916; Chm. and Man. Dir. of Boots Pure Drug Co., and assoc. cos.; m. 10 June 1914, Margaret Joyce, dau. of F. H. Pyman of Dunsley, co. York, and d. 8 Mar. 1956, leaving issue,

1. Barbara Jacqueline, b. 26 Sept. 1915; m. 26 June 1934, Major W. R. Norman (Norman Bt.), and had issue.
2. Jocelyne Mary, b. 6 Feb. 1917; m. 19 Nov. 1947, Major H. M. S. Gold, and had issue.
3. Margaret Anne, b. 31 July 1920; m. (1) 29 June 1940, (m. diss. by div. 1948), Major J. E. J. Davie, and had issue. She m. (2) 12 May 1949, A/V/M S. D. Macdonald.
4. Elizabeth Campbell, b. 26 Feb. 1927; m. 26 June 1947, Major Woodbine Parish (B.L.G. 1952), and had issue.
ARMS—Argent a chevron between in chief two galleys sable and in base a rose gules, barbed and seeded ppr.
CREST—A lion passant ppr. ducally gorged

and resting the dexter forepaw on a burning lamp or.

SUPPORTERS—Dexter, A stag reguardant; Sinister, A lion also reguardant, each charged on the shoulder with an acorn leaved and slipped, all ppr.

MOTTO—Droit et avant.

Lord Trent's seats were Ardnamurchan, Acharacle, Argyll; Lenton House, Lenton, Notts. Town house—32 Smith Square, Westminster. His club was Bath.

TREOWEN

PEERAGE—U.K. Baron Treowen, of Treowen and Llanarth, co. Monmouth. (Also a baronetcy cr. 19 July 1907).

SURNAME—Herbert.

CR.—20 June 1917. **EXT.**—18 Oct. 1933.

HISTORY—Sir Ivor John Caradoc Herbert, Bt., and **Baron Treowen,** was the eldest son of John Arthur Edward Jones, of Llanarth Court and Treowen, High Sheriff of co. Monmouth 1849. This Mr. Jones with his two brothers and one surv. sister changed their surname by Royal Licence, 20 Sept. 1848, to Herbert, as being representatives of an elder branch of the Herbert family which afterwards became Earls of Pembroke. The genealogy of this Herbert line is given in great detail in Burke's L.G. 1952 under Herbert of Upper Helmsley and Westow. There the descent is traced from Jenkin ap Adam of Llanvaplay and Wernddu, co. Monmouth who lived tempore Edward III and Richard II.

Sir Ivor John Caradoc Herbert, Bt. and **Baron Treowen,** was b. at Llanarth Court, 15 July 1851; educ. St. Mary's Coll. Oscot; joined Grenadier Guards, 1870, Capt. 1874, Brev. Major 1882, and Lt. Col. 1883; served in Egypt 1882, Nile Exped. 1884-85; and in the S. African War, 1899-1901; Mil. Attaché St. Petersburg, 1886-90; cmd. Canadian Land Forces with rank of Major Gen. 1890-95; Col. 1898; sat as Liberal for S. Division of Monmouthshire, 1906-17; was cr. C.B. 1890; C.M.G. 1895; a baronet 19 July 1907; and a peer as Baron Treowen, of Treowen and Llanarth, co. Monmouth, 20 June 1917. He m. 31 July 1873, Albertina Agnes Mary, dau. of Albert Denison, 1st Lord Londesborough (see that title in present work) and d.s.p.m. s. 18 Oct. 1933, having had by her (who d. 30 Oct. 1929),

Elidyr John Bernard, b. 13 Jan. 1917; B.A. King's Coll. Camb. Barrister-at-Law, Inner Temple, J.P. co. Monmouth, Capt. Royal Gloucestershire Hussars Yeo., k. in action in Palestine, 12 Nov. 1917.

Florence Mary Ursula, m. 20 April 1911, Walter Francis Roch.

ARMS—Per pale azure and gules three lions rampant argent.

CREST—A Moorish woman's head affrontée ppr. couped at the shoulders, with long hair sable, pendent from the ears double rings or, veil azure doubled argent, encircled by a wreath argent.

SUPPORTERS—Dexter, A dragon gules gorged with a collar argent; Sinister, An eagle argent armed and legged or, gorged with a collar gules.

MOTTO—Asgre lan Diogel ei Pherchen.

The seats of Lord Treowen were Llanarth Court, Raglan, and Llansantffraed and Llanover, Abergavenny; and Treowen, Monmouth.

TRURO

PEERAGE—U.K. Baron Truro, of Bowes, co. Middlesex.

SURNAME—Wilde.

CR.—15 July 1850. **EXT.**—8 Mar. 1899.

HISTORY—Thomas Wilde, Attorney, by his wife, Mary Anne Knight, had issue,

1. John, Sir, of Hopeville, Cape Town, Chief Justice of Cape of Good Hope, 1827-54, m. 1805, Jane Elizabeth Moore, and d. 1859, leaving issue, five sons.
2. Thomas, **Baron Truro** (see below).
3. Edward Archer, m. 1808, Marianne, dau. of W. Norris, M.D., and had,
   (1) Charles Norris, b. 10 June 1812; m. 19 Oct. 1837, his cousin, Emily Claudine Thomasine, only dau. of 1st Baron Truro, and d. 1885, leaving issue.
   (2) James Plaisted, Sir, Baron Penzance, (see that title in present work).
   (3) Alfred Thomas, Sir, K.C.B., C.S.I., Lt. Gen. Madras Army, m. Ellen Margaret, dau. of Col. Greene, C.B., and d. 1878, leaving issue.
   (4) Edward Archer, b. 1826; m. 1858, Mary Penelope, dau. of E. H. Donnithorne, of Colne Lodge, Twickenham, and d. 1889, leaving issue.

The second son,

Sir Thomas Wilde, **Baron Truro,** b. 7 July 1782; educ. St. Paul's; admitted an attorney, 1805; Barrister-at-Law, Inner Temple, 1817; distinguished himself in defence of Queen Caroline, 1820; serjeant-at-law, 1824; King's serjeant, 1827; Solicitor Gen. 1839; cr. Kt. Bach. 1840; M.P. (Whig) for Newark-on-Trent, 1831-32; and 1835-41; and for Worcester, 1841; Attorney Gen. 1841 and 1846; Lord Chief Justice of Common Pleas, 1846-50; P.C. 1846; Lord High Chancellor, 1850-52; cr. Baron Truro, of Bowes, co. Middlesex; 15 July 1850; m. (1) 13 April 1813, Mary, dau. of William Wileman, and widow of W. Devaynes, and by her (d. 13 June 1840) had surv. issue,

1. Charles Robert Claude, **2nd Baron Truro** (see below).
2. Thomas Montague Carrington, b. 17 Oct. 1818; m. 3 Feb. 1853, Emily, dau. of Charles Chapman, of Balham Hill, co. Surrey, and d. 10 Mar. 1878, leaving issue,
   Thomas Montague Morrison, **3rd Baron Truro** (see below).
1. Emily Thomasine Claudine, m. 19 Oct. 1837, her cousin, C. N. Wilde, (see above).

The 1st Baron Turo m. (2) 13 Aug. 1845, Augusta Emma, Mademoiselle D'Este, (d. 21 May, 1866) dau. of H.R.H. Augustus Frederick, Duke of Sussex, 6th son of George III, and d. 11 Nov. 1855, being s. by his elder son,

Charles Robert Claude Wilde, **2nd Baron Truro,** A.D.C. to Queen Victoria, Barrister-at-Law, Inner Temple, 1842; b. 1 Nov. 1816; m.

12 June, 1838, Lucy (d. 5 Oct. 1879) dau. of Robert Ray, and d.s.p. 27 Mar. 1891, being s. by his nephew,

Thomas Montague Morrison Wilde, **3rd Baron Truro**, Barrister-at-Law, Inner Temple, b. 11 Mar. 1856; m. 11 April 1883; Alice Hare, ygr. dau. of Capt. Eyre Maunsell, R.N. of Royal Crescent, Bath, and d.s.p. 8 Mar. 1899.
ARMS—Ermine on a cross sable a plate, on a chief of the second three martlets argent.
CREST—A hart lodged with a rose in its mouth, all ppr.
SUPPORTERS—Two ermines ppr.
MOTTO—Aequabiliter et diligenter.
The seats of the Barons Truro were Bowes, near Southgate, Middlesex, and Falconwood, Kent. Residence was Norton House, Norton, Malmesbury. Lord Truro's Club was Brooks's.

TURNOUR

PEERAGE—U.K. Baron Turnour, of Shillinglee, co. Sussex.
SURNAME—Turnour.
CR.—15 Feb. 1952. **EXT.**—26 Aug. 1962.
HISTORY—The family history of Turnour is given in extant peerages under the title of Earl Winterton. Baron Winterton was 6th Earl Winterton, Viscount Turnour and Baron Turnour of Gort, co. Galway, all in the peerage of Ireland. He was Edward Turnour and s. to these Irish peerages on the death of his father in 1907. He was b. 4 April 1883; educ. Eton and New Coll. Oxford; was M.P. for Horsham 1904-18, for Horsham and Worthing 1918-45 and for Horsham 1945-51, thus becoming the Father of the House of Commons. He served in World War I, 1914-18 in Gallipoli, Egypt and the Hedjaz, with the Sussex Yeo. and the Imperial Camel Corps, held many Gov. positions on cttees., etc., Chancellor of the Duchy of Lancaster 1937-39, Paymaster Gen. Jan-Nov. 1939; was made P.C., awarded T.D., and cr. **Baron Turnour** of Shillinglee, co. Sussex in the peerage of the United Kingdom on his retirement from the Commons. He m. 28 Feb. 1924, Hon. Cecilia Monica Wilson, dau. of the 2nd Baron Nunburnholme and d. 26 Aug. 1962, when the Barony of Turnour became extinct but the Irish peerages devolved upon the Earl's kinsman, Robert Chad Turnour who thus became 7th Earl Winterton.

Earl Winterton's case is a rare example of the confused position regarding Irish peerages. As an Irish peer who did not seek election to the House of Lords he was eligible to seek election to the House of Commons. When he retired from the Commons, the grant of a U.K. peerage enabled him to remain at Westminster in the House of Lords. There he would be out of courtesy addressed as an Earl, though his place on the Roll of the Lords was that of a Baron.
ARMS—Ermines on a cross quarter pierced argent four fers de moulin sable.
CREST—A lion passant guardant argent holding in the dexter paw a fer de moulin sable.
SUPPORTERS—Two lions argent semée of fers de moulin sable.
MOTTO—Esse quam videri.

TWEEDMOUTH

PEERAGE—U.K. Baron Tweedmouth of Edington, co. Berwick. Baron Marjoribanks (cr. 12 and ext. 19 June 1873). (Also a baronetcy cr. 25 April 1866.)
SURNAME — Marjoribanks. (Pronounced Marshbanks).
CR.—12 Oct. 1881. **EXT.**—23 April 1935.
HISTORY—Robert Marjoribanks of that ilk was father of Thomas Marjoribanks of that ilk, and of Ratho, to which he had a charter in 1540, and of Spotts, 1543, and of the lands of Marjoribanks in Annandale, 1560. This Thomas Marjoribanks, was an Advocate of the Scots Bar, Provost of Edinburgh 1541, M.P. for Edinburgh 1540-49, and became a Lord of Session, and Lord Clerk Register. He m. Janet Purves, and d. 1580 having with other issue, including a son, John, ancestor of Marjoribanks of Balbardie, another son,

James Marjoribanks, ancestor of the lines of Leuchie, Hallyards, Lees, and Preston, whose son,

Joseph Marjoribanks, a merchant in Edinburgh, m. Marion, dau. of Andrew Sympson, of Edinburgh, merchant and d. 1636 having had with other issue,

John Marjoribanks, of Leuchie, b. 1612; m. 1641, Elizabeth, dau. of John Trotter, of Morton Hall, co. Midlothian, and had with other issue,

1. Edward (see below).
2. James, of Lees, and of Bradheugh, estates which at the death of his grandson, James Pringle, descended to the great-grandson of his brother, Edward.

The elder brother,

Edward Marjoribanks, of Hallyards, which he acquired in 1699, was b. 1654; m. 1685, Agnes, dau. of Robert Murray, of Melgund, and had issue,

Edward Marjoribanks, of Hallyards, b. 1688; m. 1710, Janet, dau. of James Loch, of Drylaw, and had issue,

John Marjoribanks, of Hallyards, b. 1712; m. Katherine dau. and coheir of Ronald Campbell, of Kames and Balerno, and was s. by his son,

Edward Marjoribanks, of Hallyards and Lees, b. 1735. He s. to Lees and Bradheugh in 1754 at the death of his kinsman, James Pringle, and also became male representative of the family on the death of Major Gen. Alexander Marjoribanks, of Carlowrie, in 1774. As such he recorded his arms in Lyon Register, in 1787. He m. Grizel, dau. of Archibald Stewart and d. 1815, she d. 1817. They had with other issue,

1. John, Sir, cr. a baronet 6 May 1815, of Lees, co. Berwick, a baronetcy which became extinct with the 4th Bt., the great-grandson of Sir John. Sir John's fourth son,

David, M.P. for co. Berwick, and Lord Lt. of that county, was b. 2 April 1797, and assumed the surname and arms of Robertson, in lieu of those of Marjoribanks. He was cr. **Baron Marjoribanks**, of Ladykirk, 12 June 1873; m. 10 Sept. 1834, Mariana Sarah, dau. of Sir Thomas Haggerston, Bt., and by her (d. 19 Aug. 1889), had issue, three sons who all d. young, and two daus. Lord Marjoribanks d.

19 June 1873, seven days after the creation of the barony.

2. Edward (see below).

The ygr. (i.e. fourth) son,

Edward Marjoribanks, of Greenlands, and Ewden, co. Buckingham was b. 31 May 1776; was a partner in Coutts Bank from 1796-1868; m. Georgiana, dau. of Joseph Francis Louis Latour, of Hexton Park, and d. 17 Sept. 1868 having by her (who d. April 1849), with other issue, a third son,

Sir Dudley Coutts Marjoribanks, 1st Bt., and **1st Baron Tweedsmouth**, M.P. Berwick, 1853-81; cr. a baronet 25 July 1866, and a peer as Baron Tweedmouth of Edington, co. Berwick, 12 Oct. 1881. He was b. 29 Dec. 1820; m. 19 Oct. 1848, Isabella, sister of 1st Lord Magheramorne, and d. 4 Mar. 1894, having by her had issue. She d. 20 Mar. 1908. They had issue,

1. Edward, **2nd Baron Tweedmouth** (see below).
2. Stewart, b. 23 July 1852; d. 22 Jan. 1864.
3. Coutts, Lt. Queen's Own Cameron Highlanders, b. 6 Dec. 1860; m. 3 July 1895, Agnes Margaret, dau. of Col. Kinloch, and widow of Cmdr. J. E. T. Nicolls, R.N., and d. 1 Nov. 1924, having had issue,
   (1) John Coutts, b. 22 June, and d. 21 Aug. 1902.
   (1) Ishbel Agnes, b. 9 Nov. 1897; m. 17 Aug. 1921, Capt. Allen Villiers Surtees, and had issue.
4. Archibald John, b. 25 Nov. 1861; mem. of H.M.'s Bodyguard for Scotland, the Royal Co. of Archers; m. 17 Feb. 1897, Elizabeth dau. of Judge James Trimble Brown, of Nashville, Tennessee, U.S.A., and d. 4 Sept. 1900. She m. 2ndly 14 Aug. 1905, Rt. Hon. Sir Douglas McGarel Hogg, later 1st Viscount Hailsham (see extant peerages), and d. 10 May 1925. By the first marriage there was issue,
   Edward, Barrister-at-Law, Lincoln's Inn, Middle Temple and S.E. Circuit; M.P. for Eastbourne Div. Sussex, 1929; b. 14 Feb. 1900; educ. Eton (Capt. of School), and Ch. Ch. Oxford, 1st Class in Honour Mods, 1920, and 1st Class in Lit. Hum. 1922, also Pres. of Oxford Union, 1922; 2nd Lt. Scots Guards; author of *Life of Sir Edward Marshall Hall*. He d. unm. 2 April 1932.
   Isobel Marianne Frances, b. 7 Oct. 1898; m. (1) 30 Oct. 1920, Bertram Ellerbeck, (m. diss. by div. 1929), and m. (2) 1929, Capt. Beilby.
1. Mary Georgiana, m. 10 Dec. 1873, Sir Matthew White Ridley, Bt., later 1st Viscount Ridley and d. 14 Mar. 1899, leaving issue.
2. Annie Grizel, d. an infant, 20 Aug. 1856.
3. Ishbel Maria, G.B.E., LL.D., J.P., m. 7 Nov. 1877, John Campbell, Marquess of Aberdeen, K.T., and had issue.

The eldest son,

Edward Marjoribanks, **2nd Baron Tweedmouth**, K.T. and P.C., M.P. Berwickshire 1880-94; Alderman London C.C.; Barrister-at-Law, comptroller of H.M. Household 1886,; Lord Privy Seal and Chancellor of the Duchy of Lancaster, 1894-95; 1st Lord of the Admiralty, 1905-00; Lord Pres. of the Council,

1908; b. 8 July 1849; m. 9 June 1873, Lady Fanny Octavia Louisa Spencer-Churchill, dau. of 7th Duke of Marlborough, and d. 15 Sept. 1909, having by her (who d. 5 Aug. 1904) had issue,

Dudley Churchill Marjoribanks, **3rd Baron Tweedmouth**, C.M.G., D.S.O., M.V.O., Lt. Col. Royal Horse Guards, served in the S. African War, 1899-1901 and in the World War I, 1914; b. 2 Mar. 1874; m. 30 Nov. 1901, Lady Muriel Brodrick, dau. of 1st Earl of Midleton, and d.s.p.m. 23 April 1935, having had issue,

1. Moyra, m. 12 June 1923, Major R. F. Heyworth, and had issue.
2. Joan Millicent, m. 5 Mar. 1935 Sir Charles Michael Robert Vivian Duff-Assheton-Smith, 3rd Bt.

ARMS—Argent on a chief gules a cushion between two spur rowels of the field.

CREST—A lion's gamb, erect and erased, grasping a lance in bend both ppr.

SUPPORTERS—On either side a bear ppr., muzzled and collared or and charged on the shoulder with a spur rowel argent.

MOTTO—Advance with courage.

The seat of Lord Tweedmouth was Hutton Castle, Berwick-on-Tweed.

TWINING

PEERAGE—U.K. Life. Baron Twining of Tanganyika, in East Africa, and of Godalming, co. Surrey.

SURNAME—Twining.

CR.—18 Aug. 1958. **EXT.**—21 July 1967.

HISTORY—The Twining family has been traced in great detail in the counties of Gloucester and Worcester for 500 years, beginning with Henry Twining who held a mill in Painswick, co. Gloucester in 1486. He was b. ca. 1440 and m. Joan who was holder of a mill called Twynnyng. He d. ca. 1496 having had a son,

Thomas Twynnyng a landowner in Edge Tythyg, co. Glos. in 1518, who had issue,

John Twynning of The Mill, Painswick, and other properties held by him 1548. He m. Julian who was executrix of his will which was proved at Gloucester, 2 May 1550. She also was a mill owner in Edge Tything. Her will was proved 4 Sept. 1585 at Gloucester. They had issue, an eldest son,

John Twynning, of The Mill in Painswick, b. ca. 1530, mentioned in both father's and mother's wills, a considerable property owner, m. 5 Dec. 1559, Edith, dau. of Richard Foord, of Coaley, co. Glos. His will dated 28 Jan. 1596/7, proved at Gloucester 20 April 1597. Her will was dated 10 Feb. 1599. They were buried at Painswick, having had issue, with an elder son, Thomas, a second son,

John Twinninge, of The Mill, heir to his brother Thomas m. (1) 13 June 1580 Julian a Meyre (who d. Oct. 1598) and (2) Katherine, dau. of James Newarke, of Cranham, co. Glos. and was dead by 16 June 1612, having had issue, with a son William and other children,

John Twyning, of Evesham and of Wyre Piddle, co. Worcester, described as Gentleman, bapt. at Painswick, 9 Nov. 1599; m. twice and had two daus. by first wife (names not known). He m. (2) Joane dau. of Thomas Sanders of Moore in Fladbury, co. Worcester. His will

PLATE 18

BARON STRATHCONA AND MOUNT ROYAL.

VISCOUNT TAAFFE.

BARON TENTERDEN.

VISCOUNT TREDEGAR.

BARON WALLSCOURT.

BARON TWEEDMOUTH.

PLATE 19

BARON WANDSWORTH.

BARON WELBY.

EARL WAVELL

BARON WENLOCK.

VISCOUNT WOLSELEY.

was proved in P.C.C. 29 Nov. 1664. His second wife was bur. 28 July 1670 at Wyre Piddle. He had issue a son and heir,
Thomas Twyning, of Wyre Piddle in Fladbury, co. Worcester, Gentleman, aged 26 in 1606, m. 27 Oct. 1666, Hester, dau. of William Dingley of Naunton Beauchamp, co. Worcester and was bur. 16 Sept. 1669, having had issue,
John Twyning of Throckmorton, co. Worcester, bapt. 12 June 1668, and d. 23 April 1708, leaving by his wife Joane (whose will was proved 6 April 1723) a yst. son,
Richard Twining, of Pershore, co. Worcs. b. posthumously, 13 May 1708, and was bur. 20 Sept. 1741 at Fladbury leaving by his wife, Mary, a yst. son,
James Twining, of Pershore, bapt. 12 June 1739; m. 17 Mar. 1765, Elizabeth Brown and had with other children an eldest son,
Edward Twining of Pershore, b. 3 Mar. 1766; m. 11 June 1787, Frances Monday and had, with other children, a third son,
William Twining of Worcester, bapt. 14 Aug. 1796; m. 5 Sept. 1819, Mary Ann Kelsey of Worcester and was bur. 13 Sept. 1829, having with other issue a second son,
Edwin Twining of Dudley, co. Worcester and London, b. 25 Nov. 1822; m. 9 Oct. 1849, Lucy, dau. of James Greaves of Droitwich, co. Worcs. and d. 3 July 1879 leaving issue,
The Rev. William Henry Greaves Twining, Associate King's Coll., Univ. of London 1882, Clerk in Holy Orders. Author of *Some Facts in the History of the Twining Family* 1892-96, b. 24 Mar. 1853; m. 30 Oct. 1894, Agatha Georgina (d. 12 June 1962) dau. of Lt. Col. Robert Bourne (B.L.G. 1952, Bourne of Symondsbury House) and d. 27 Sept. 1932. They had issue with a dau. d. unm. 1921, two sons
1. Stephen Herbert, M.B.E., Director R. Twining & Co. Ltd., on Council of Royal Warrant Holders' Asscn., Author of *Some Early Twinings* (1927), 225 *Years in the Strand* (1931) and *The House of Twining* (250 years of Tea and Coffee) 1956. He was b. 28 July 1895; m. 23 Nov. 1929, Georgiana Elizabeth, dau. of Francis Gaskell, and d. 5 Mar. 1961 having had issue a son and two daus.
2. Edward Francis, Sir, **Baron Twining** (see below).
The second son,
Sir Edward Francis Twining, **Baron Twining,** b. 29 June 1899; educ. Lancing and R.M.C. Sandhurst, gazetted Worcs. Regt. 1918, served in 4th King's African Rifles 1923-28, entered Colonial Service in Uganda, 1929, held several colonial apptds.; was Gov. North Borneo, 1946-49 and Gov. Tanganyika 1949-58. He was cr. M.B.E. 1923, C.M.G. 1943, K.C.M.G. 1949, G.C.M.G. 1953 and a Life Peer as Baron Twining of Tanganyika in East Africa and of Godalming in the co. of Surrey, 18 Aug. 1958. He m. 21 July 1928, Helen Mary, O.B.E., M.R.C.S., D.P.H., dau. of Arthur E. De Buisson and d. 21 July 1967 having had issue,
1. John Peter, b. 8 June 1929; m. 1954, Mary Avis Jane, dau. of Brig. J. H. D. Bennett, and had issue.
2. William Lawrence, b. 22 Sept. 1934; m. 1957 Penelope Elizabeth, dau. of R. W. Morris and had issue.
ARMS—Sable a fesse embattled between in chief two mullets and in base a millrind or.

CREST—A dexter cubit arm grasping in the hand two snakes entwined round the arm ppr. and charged on the forearm with a millrind or.
SUPPORTERS—Dexter, A crested crane; Sinister, A giraffe, both ppr.
MOTTO—Fortiter ac firmiter.
*The above pedigree is registered in the Coll. of Arms, connection between this line and that of the famous tea firm is not established.

TYRRELL OF AVON

PEERAGE U.K. Baron Tyrrell of Avon, co. Southampton.
SURNAME—Tyrrell.
CR.—24 July 1929. **EXT.**—14 Mar. 1947.
HISTORY—The Rev. Henry Tyrrell, Rector of Kinnitty, King's Co., Ireland, b. 1 Nov. 1800, d. Oct. 1858, having had issue,
William Henry Tyrrell, Judge of the High Court, N.W. Provinces, India, who d. 18 June 1895 having by his wife Julia (d. 22 Mar. 1892) dau. of Col. Wakefield, had issue,
Sir William George Tyrrell,, **Baron Tyrrell** of Avon, b. 17 Aug. 1866; educ. privately and Balliol Coll. Oxford; entered the Foreign Office, 1889; Senior Clerk, 1907-18; Asst. Under Sec. of State for Foreign Affairs, 1918-25; Permanent Under Sec. 1925-28, Ambassador Extraordinary and Minister Plenipotentiary at Paris, 1928-34; Priv. Sec. to Sec. of State for Foreign Affairs, 1907-15; Pres. of the British Board of Film Censors, 1935. He was made P.C. 1928; cr. C.B. 1909; K.C.M.G. 1913; K.C.V.O. 1919; G.C.M.G. 1925; K.C.B. 1927; G.C.E. 1934, and Baron Tyrrell of Avon, co. Southampton, 24 July 1929. He m. 22 April 1891, Margaret Ann, dau. of David Urquhart, M.P. and d. 14 Mar. 1947, having had issue,
1. Hugo William Louis, Lt. R.N., b. 1891; k. in action Feb. 1918.
2. Francis Chichester Victor, 2nd Lt. Coldstream Guards, d. of wounds 15 Feb. 1915.
1. Margaret Julia, m. 1923, Ronald Kenneth Duncan Renton, and d. 11 Feb. 1925.
2. Harriet Anne Mary Tyrrell, assumed by deed poll 1930 the additional Christian names of Mary Tyrrell; m. (1) 30 April 1930 (marr. annulled 1932) Sir Adrian Holman; m. (2) 25 April 1934, Capt. Jack William Leslie Crawshay, M.C.
ARMS—Or two chevronels gules, on a chief azure, a fleur-de-lis of the first between two plates each charged with a cross all within a bordure engrailed of the second.
CREST—A leopard's face or, jessant de lis azure, between two plates each charged with a cross as in the arms.
SUPPORTERS—On either side a leopard or, gorged with a chain azure pendent therefrom a hurt charged with a fleur-de-lis gold.
MOTTO—Sans crainte.

UPJOHN

PEERAGE—U.K. Life. Baron Upjohn of Little Tey, co. Essex.
SURNAME—Upjohn.
CR.—26 Nov. 1963. **EXT.**—27 Jan. 1971.

HISTORY—William Bellingham Drew Upjohn (son of William Henry Rouse Upjohn) was a clerk in the Chambers of Mr. Justice Chitty. He was b. 1824; m. 29 Sept. 1852, Eliza Josephine, dau. of Thomas Ritchie, and d. 30 Dec. 1881, having had issue,

1. William Henry (see below).
2. Arthur Ritchie, b. 25 Jan. 1862; educ. City of London Sch. and London Univ.; admitted a Solicitor, 1880, and Barrister-at-Law, 1920; m. 5 Oct. 1880, Alice Augusta, dau. of W. Moon, of Lincoln's Inn Fields, and d. Sept. 1948, having by her (who d. 1945) had issue,
    (1) Beryl, b. 17 Feb. 1893; m. 9 Nov. 1918, H. T. Johnstone, and had issue, a son and a dau.
    (2) Marjorie, b. 24 June 1896; educ. Roedean and Lady Margaret Hall, Oxford, M.A.; m. 24 July 1920 (m. diss. by div. 1945), Sir Claude Grundy and had issue three sons and a dau.
    (3) Ursula, b. 23 Mar. 1899.

The elder son,

William Henry Upjohn, of Annesley Bank, Lyndhurst, co. Hants, b. 31 Aug. 1853; educ. King's Coll. Sch. and London Univ., LL.B.; Barrister-at-Law, 1881, and Q.C. 1897; m. 27 Dec. 1881, Lucy Martha, dau. of Rees Williams, of Cefn Pennar, Aberdare, and d. 16 July 1941, having by her (who d. 3 June 1943) had issue,

1. William Moon, b. 22 Oct. 1884; educ. Eton and Trin. Coll. Camb.; served in World War I with Welsh Guards; m. 3 July 1913, Dora Sybil Mary dau. of Sir George Anderson Critchett, 1st Bt., and was k. in action, 24 Aug. 1918, having had issue,
    Clive Henry Critchett, b. 21 Sept. 1914; educ. Eton and Trin. Coll. Camb., B.A. 1936, M.B. and B. Chir. 1940, M.A. and M.D. 1951; M.R.C.S., L.R.C.P.; served in World War II as Surg. Lt. R.N.V.R.; m. 22 Sept. 1962, Anna, M.B. B.S., dau. of J. L. Warrander, of Edinburgh and had issue, a dau.
    Melissa Mary, b. 18 May 1964.
2. Gerald Ritchie, **Baron Upjohn** (see below).
1. Lucy Margaret, b. 4 Mar. 1883; m. 1903, F. H. Swann, of Steeple, Corfe Castle, co. Dorset, and d. 26 July 1961, leaving issue.
2. Winifred, b. 1886.
3. Gwendoline, b. 28 May 1888; d. unm. 1946.

The ygr. son,

Sir Gerald Ritchie Upjohn, **Baron Upjohn** of Little Tey, co. Essex, was b. 25 Feb. 1903; educ. Eton and Trin. Coll. Camb., B.A. 1925, M.A. 1928; Barrister-at-Law, Lincoln's Inn, 1929; served in World War II, 1939-45, with Welsh Guards, Capt. and Technical Adjt. 2nd Welsh Guards, Col. 1943, Brig. 1944; was Vice Pres. Allied Control Comm. 1944; (despatches); K.C. 1943; Attorney Gen. Duchy of Lancaster, 1947-51; apptd. Judge of High Court, Chancery Div., 1951; a Lord Justice of Appeal 1960; Bencher, of Lincoln's Inn, 1948, and Treasurer, 1965; a Lord Justice of Appeal in Ordinary, 1963; was cr. C.B.E. 1945; Kt. Bach. 1951; P.C. 1960; cr. a life peer as Baron Upjohn, of Little Tey, co. Essex, 26 Nov. 1963; m. 22 May 1947, Marjorie Dorothy Bertha, dau. of Major Ernest Murray Lucas, of Lyndhurst, co. Hants (Lucas, Bt.). He d. 27

Jan. 1971. He was Fell. of Eton, Gov. of Felsted Sch., Chm. of St. George's Hospita Medical Sch. 1954-64.

ARMS—Sable a fess between in chief two lions' heads erased and in base as many leeks in saltire or.
CREST—A stork ppr. holding in the beak a balance or.
MOTTO—Quid quid agis age toto.
Lord Upjohn's residences were The Old Rectory, Little Tey, Colchester, Essex, and 309 Hawkins House, Dolphin Square, S.W.1. His clubs were Athenaeum, United University and Pratt's.

UTHWATT

PEERAGE—U.K. Life Baron Uthwatt, of Lathbury, co. Buckingham.
SURNAME—Uthwatt (formerly Andrewes, see below).
CR.—9 Jan. 1946. **EXT.**—24 April 1949.
HISTORY—For the full ancestry of this family, see B.L.G. 1952, under Andrewes, formerly of Maids Moreton Manor. The surname of Uthwatt originated from the action of the Rev. Henry Uthwatt Andrewes, (b. 1755) who assumed the surname of Uthwatt in lieu of that of Andrewes by Royal Licence, dated 18 Mar. 1803, for himself and his issue, when they should succeed and come into possession of the Great Linford Estates, this being in accordance with the will of his godfather, Henry Uthwatt, of Great Lindford, who d. 1735. From the Rev. Henry Uthwatt Uthwatt, descended (see B.L.G. as above) Thomas Andrewes Uthwatt, of Maids Moreton Manor, Bucks, to which he s. in 1916, also to Thorpenstie, on death of his cousin, Miss Andrewes; lord of the manor of Maids Moreton, and patron of the living, also of that of Great Linford; b. 15 Aug. 1846; m. 18 Jan. 1875, Anne, dau. of W. O'Donnell Hazlitt, of Dunmow, co. Donegal, and d. 14 June 1927, having had with other issue,

Sir Augustus Andrewes Uthwatt, **Baron Uthwatt**, b. 25 April 1879; educ. Ballarat Coll. Victoria, and Trin. Coll. Melbourne, M.A., LL.B., and Balliol Coll. Oxford, B.C.L. 1904; Barrister-at-Law, Gray's Inn, 1904, Bencher, 1929, Treasurer, 1939-40; a Justice of High Court, Chancery Div. 1941-46; a Lord of Appeal in Ordinary, 1946-49; cr. Kt. Bach. 1941, and a life peer as Baron Uthwatt, of Lathbury, co. Buckingham, 9 Jan. 1946, made P.C. 1946; m. 6 Aug. 1927, Mrs. Mary Baxter Bonhote, dau. of Rev. Charles Edwin Meeres, Vicar of Eastry, co. Kent, and d. 24 April 1949. Lord and Lady Uthwatt adopted, Mary Elizabeth Anne Duncan, who m. Rev. H. S. Deighton.

ARMS—Argent on a bend cotised sable three pierced mullets of the field.
CREST—A stag's head erased argent.
MOTTO—Lux in tenebris.

VANSITTART

PEERAGE—U.K. Baron Vansittart, of Denham, co. Buckingham.
SURNAME—Vansittart.
CR.—3 July 1941. **EXT.**—14 Feb. 1957.

HISTORY—William Van Sittart, of Juliers, was b. 1517, and d. 1573 having had a son, John Van Sittart, or Von Sittart, of Juliers, who was b. 1552, and who fled to Danzig to avoid persecution in 1598. He was placed under the ban of the Empire in 22nd Rudolph II. He d. at Danzig in 1612, leaving a son,

John William Von Sittart, b. 1582; m. 1616, Anne, dau. of John Roboan, of Danzig, and d. Jan. 1630/31, leaving by her (she m. 2ndly 1634, Stephen Kayser and d. May 1635), with others an eldest son,

William Von Sittart, of Danzig, b. 13 Dec. 1622; m. 18 Sept. 1646, Eve, (d. July 1676) dau. of Winholt Junckcr of Danzig, and d. Гсb. 1675, having had with others a second son,

Peter Van Sittart, described as a merchant venturer, who came to England in 1670, and became a Dir. of the East India Co., b. 13 Jan. 1650/51; m. 3 Oct. 1678, Susanna, dau. of Robert Sanderson, and had numerous issue, some of whom d. young. She d. 25 Mar. 1725. He d. 8 Mar. 1705. The eldest son,

Robert Van Sittart, Dir. H.E.I.C., purchased Shottesbrook, Berks. b. 26 June 1679; m. 15 April 1707 Elizabeth, sister of Sir Peter Vandeout, 1st Bt., (Burke's Extinct Baronetcies) and d.s.p. 28 Dec. 1719. His widow m. George Baker. Robert Van Sittart was s. by his brother,

Arthur Van Sittart, of Clewer, and of Moat Park, Windsor, and of Shottesbrooke, High Sheriff, Berks, b. 26 Dec. 1691; m. 23 May 1723, Maria, dau. and coheiress of Rt. Hon. Sir John Stonhouse, 3rd Bt., P.C., and d. 16 Sept. 1760. She d. 13 June 1782. They had issue,

1. Arthur (see below).
2. Robert, b. 28 Dec. 1728; Senior Fell. of All Souls, Oxford, D.C.L., Regius Prof. of Civil Law at Oxford, Recorder of Windsor, 1770; d. unm. 31 Jan. 1789.
3. Henry, of Foxley, co. Berks, H.E.I.C.S., Dir. 1769, Gov. of Bengal, 1760-64; M.P., b. 3 June 1732; m. 1 June 1754 Emelia, dau. of Nicholas Morse, Gov. of Madras, and d. Dec. 1769, leaving by her (who d. 2 Aug. 1819) with other issue,
   (1) Henry, of Foxley, H.E.I.C.S., mem. of Bengal Council; bapt. 30 April 1755; m. 3 Feb. 1723, Catherine Maria, dau. of Thomas Powney, H.E.I.C.S., and d. 7 Oct. 1786, having had issue by her who m. 2ndly G. N. Thompson,
      Henry Vansittart of Foxley, and of Kirkleatham, co. York, High Sheriff, 1820, b. 10 July 1784; m. 21 July 1812, Teresa, dau. of Charlotte, Viscountess Newcomen, (1883, Extinct Peerage) widow of Sir Charles Turner, Bt., and d. 22 April 1848, leaving an only dau., Teresa, of Foxley and Kirkleatham who m. 11 July 1841, Arthur Newcomen, and d. 29 April 1887, leaving issue.
   (2) Nicholas, Rt. Hon., of Foots Cray and North Cray, co. Kent, Chancellor of the Exchequer, 1812-23, b. 29 April 1766; cr. Baron Bexley, 1 Mar. 1823, (Extinct Peerage, 1883); m. 22 July 1806, Catherine Isabella, (d. 10 Aug. 1810), dau. of 1st Baron Auckland, and d.s.p. 8 Feb. 1851.

(1) Emelia, m. Edward Parry, of Little Dunham, co. Norfolk, and d. 25 Oct, 1791.
4. John, Lt. R.N., b. 11 Nov. 1733; k. in action, on board H.M.S. *Kent* in battle off Ortegal, 20 June 1747.
5. George, of Bisham Abbey (1952 B.L.G., Vansittart-Neale).
1. Anne, b. 1737; m. 11 Feb. 1761, Sir Robert Palk, Bt., (Haldon, in present work) and had issue.

The eldest son,

Arthur Vansittart, of Shottesbrook, and of Clewer, Col. in the Army, Vice Lt. for Berks, M.P. Bcrks, 1757-74; b. 26 Гсb. 1726; m. 7 Aug. 1773, Hon. Anne Hanger, (d. 9 June 1782), dau. of 1st Baron Coleraine, (1883 Extinct Peerage), and d. 12 Nov. 1806, having had with a dau. who d. unm.,

1. Arthur (see below).
2. Robert, H.E.I.C.S., inherited lordship of the manor of Driffield from 3rd Baron Coleraine, b. 12 Sept. 1778; d. unm. 26 Dec. 1832.
3. William, Rev., D.D., of Driffield, Preb. of Carlisle, Rector of Shottesbrooke, and of White Waltham, co. Berks, b. 30 Nov. 1779; m. 11 Feb. 1817, Charlotte Teresa, (d. 2 Aug. 1858), dau. of Gen. George Warde, of Woodland Castle, co. Glamorgan and of Squerryes, co. Kent, and d. 22 Nov. 1847, having had with other issue,
   (1) Spencer, of Coolbawn, Castleconnell, co. Limerick, Capt. Royal Regt. of Foot, b. 12 June 1824; m. 2 Sept. 1857, his cousin, Emily Theresa, dau. of Adm. Charles Warde, of Squerryes, (B.L.G. 1952), and widow of Robert Osborne, and d. May 1902, having by her who d. 18 Oct. 1891, with two other sons who d. in infancy,
      1a Spencer Charles Patrick, of Coolbawn, co. Limerick, b. 9 Mar. 1860; educ. Bradfield Coll.; m. 13 Nov. 1889, Hon. Matilda Massey, 2nd dau. of 6th Baron Massy and d. 9 Aug. 1928, leaving,
         1b Everina Lucy.
         2b Slaney Theresa, m. (1) Major E. C. Robertson, k. in action in France, 1915; and m. (2) 1926, Lt. Col. C. F. W. Hughes and had issue.
         3b Marjorie.
      1a Aileen Emily, m. 7 Aug. 1889, Capt. R. R. K. Stuart.
   (2) Frederick, Lt. 14th Light Dragoons, b. 1825; m. July 1855, Henrietta, dau. of James Lowe, and d.s.p. May 1902.
   (1) Katherine Mary, b. 23 Aug. 1827; m. 4 Aug. 1849, J. C. Conybeare, and d. 13 Jan. 1895, leaving issue.

The eldest son of Col. Arthur Vansittart,

Arthur Vansittart, of Shottesbrook and of Clewer, M.P. Windsor, 1804, bapt. 28 Dec. 1775; m. 17 June 1806, Hon. Caroline Eden, (d. 2 Mar. 1851) dau. of 1st Baron Auckland, and had issue,

1. Arthur, of Shottesbrook, and of Foots Cray, co. Kent, served as Cornet with 2nd Life Guards, b. 2 May 1807; m. 26 Mar. 1831, Diana Sara (d. Sept. 1881) dau. of Gen. Sir John Gustavus-Crosbie,

and d. 22 April 1859, having had with
another son, who d.v.p.,
  Coleraine Robert, b. 31 Aug. 1833;
  served in the Crimea, Capt. 11th
  Hussars; s. to Shottesbrook, but d.
  unm. 14 April 1886, when Shottesbrook was inherited by his sister, and
  Foots Cray by his cousin Robert
  Arnold Vansittart (see below).
  Rose Sophia, m. 27 Nov. 1856 Oswald
  Augustus Smith, of Shottesbrook Park,
  and d. 8 Jan. 1892, leaving issue.
2. Robert, of Driffield, and of Chuffs, co.
Berks, Lt. Col. Coldstream Guards, b.
24 Jan. 1811; m. 4 Nov. 1845, Elizabeth
Harriet, (d. 3 April 1906) dau. of J. W.
Fleming, of Stoneham Park, co. Hants
and d. 2 May 1872, having had with
other issue,
  (1) Robert Arnold Vansittart, M.B.E.,
  F.R.C.S., of Foots Cray Place, co.
  Kent, Capt. 7th Dragoon Guards,
  b. 21 Oct. 1851; m. 30 July 1878,
  Susan Alice, dau. of G. J. Blane, of
  Follejon Park, co. Berks, (B.L.G.
  1952), and d. 8 Jan. 1928 having by
  her who d. 13 Feb. 1919, had issue,
    1a Robert Gilbert, Sir, cr. **Baron
    Vansittart** (see below).
    2a Arnold Bexley, b. 24 Sept. 1889;
    educ. Oxford Univ. B.A., served
    in World War I, Lt. 11th Hussars,
    and d. unm. 1 May 1915, of
    wounds received in action.
    3a Guy Nicholas, b. 8 Sept. 1893; m.
    28 Mar. 1922, Margaret Helen,
    dau. of Sir Henry Proctor, of
    Ware Hill, co. Herts, and had
    issue,
      1b Sibell Alice.
      2b Honoria Edith.
      3b Marjorie Marie.
  (1) Catherine Caroline, m. 14 Jan. 1869,
  Thomas Campbell, and had issue,
  (B.L.G. Campbell of Colgrain).
  (2) Fanny, m. 26 April 1866, Walter Long,
  of Preshaw, and d. 1932, having had
  issue, (B.L.G. Wyndham of Dun-
  oon).
  (3) Edith, m. 25 Aug. 1870, R. P.
  Wethered, and d. 22 June 1924.
  (4) Mary Emily, m. 19 Jan. 1876, H. C.
  FitzHerbert, of Millbrook, Queen's
  Co., and d. having had issue.
  (5) Constance Mary, m. 1889, Col. C. W.
  Long, and had issue, (B.L.G. Long of
  Hurts Hall).
  (6) Evelyn Jane, m. 4 Nov. 1882, E. S.
  Neave, and d. 23 Aug. 1934, leaving
  issue.
3. William, H.E.I.C.S., M.P. Windsor, b.
2 May 1813; m. (1) 1 July 1839, Emily
(d. 25 May 1844) dau. of Lt. Col. R. L.
Anstruther, (Anstruther Bt.) and had
issue, with a son, William Henry, d. unm.,
  (1) Emily Eden, m. 1 Oct. 1861, George
  Palmer and d. 27 May 1905, leaving
  issue (Selborne, E.).
He m. (2) 2 Dec. 1847, Henrietta, dau. of
John Humphreys, and by her who d.
19 May 1852, had further issue,
  (2) Caroline Bertha, m. (1) 21 Nov. 1869,
  Reginald Wyniatt, and (2) 13 Sept.
  1882, H. D. Deane-Drummond, and
  d. 13 July 1919.

He m. (3) 6 Feb. 1866, Melanie, dau. of
Sir Richard Jenkins G.C.B., and d.
15 Jan. 1876, having had by her (who m.
2ndly Henry Pepys, and d. 1891) further
issue,
  (1) Charles Edward Bexley, b. Dec. 1867;
  m. (1) 28 July 1888 (m. diss. by div.
  1904) Constance Frances dau. of Sir
  Thomas Miller, 4th Bt., and had issue
  by her,
    1a Constance Hilda Maude Bexley,
    m. 5 Aug. 1915, J. C. Reid.
    2a Melanie Bexley, d. 5 June 1924.
  C. E. B. Vansittart m. (2) and had
  further issue.
4. George Nicholas, b. June 1814; m. 1
June 1852, Elizabeth Ann (d. 19 Nov.
1875) dau. of J. Mansfield of Midmar
Castle, co. Aberdeen, and d. 12 May
1889, having had issue,
  (1) Arthur George, H.M. Diplomatic
  Service, b. 22 Nov. 1854; d. unm.
  15 Nov. 1911.
  (2) Francis Robert, b. 8 Jan. 1858; d.v.p.
  (3) Coleraine Nicholas, b. 3 Dec. 1860;
  m. Marie (m. diss. by div. 1896), dau.
  of Gustave Vincent and had issue,
    1a Coleraine, b. 13 July 1889; d.
    young.
    2a Francis de Mansfield, b. 10 Feb.
    1891.
    1a Violet, b. 15 Aug. 1887.
  (1) Emily Christina,
5. Henry, H.E.I.C.S., Judge, b. 3 Nov. 1816;
m. May 1848, Mary Amelia, dau. of
Capt. H. Dobbie, R.N., and formerly
wife of Lt. William Jervis, I.A., and d.
13 Jan. 1896, having by her (who d. 18
June, 1886) had issue,
  (1) Henry, Lt. R.M.A., 1868-72, Barrister-
  at-Law, Middle Temple, 1872, b. 4
  Aug. 1849; m. (1) 19 Oct. 1878, Mary
  Virginia, dau. of F. J. Jessop, of
  Derby, and m. (2) Ellen Diamond-
  opolis, and d. 1930, having had a dau.
  Enid, b. 1890.
  (2) Charles, Finance Dept., Gov. of
  India, b. 1 Jan. 1853; m. 24 Feb. 1881,
  Katherine Frances, dau. of Lt. Gen.
  Charles Pollard, and had issue with a
  son, Herbert Charles d.v.p., two daus.,
  Violet Katherine, and Dorothy Mary.
  (3) Herbert, b. 13 April 1854; m. 12 Dec.
  1893, Mary Agatha, dau. of Adm.
  W. H. Dobbie, R.N., and had issue,
  two daus.
  (4) Eden, D.S.O., Col. 5th Royal
  Gurkhas, raised 10th Gurkha Rifles
  in Burma, and raised and cmd. 8th
  Service Bn. of Royal West Kent Regt.,
  1914, and served in World War I,
  1914-18, (wounded and despatches),
  b. 19 April 1857; m. 1889, Ethel Deey,
  dau. of Robert Spedding, I.C.S., and
  d. 17 Sept. 1936, leaving by her (who
  d. 6 Sept. 1935), a dau. Vera Mary
  Eden, b. 5 April 1891, and m. 27 Oct.
  1927, Major T. J. Carroll-Leahy,
  D.S.O., M.C.
  (1) Edith Catherine, m. 26 Dec. 1868,
  Major Gen. Nugent Barton and d.
  18 Oct. 1923.
  (2) Florence, m. 24 Oct. 1871, Major
  Gen. J. M. Stewart and d. 1 Sept.
  1920. (B.L.G. Stewart of Cairnsmore).

6. Nicholas, C.B., Post Capt. R.N., b. 7 Mar. 1819; served in the China War, 1842, at destruction of Brunee, 1846, in the Austro-Italian War, 1849, and in Russian War, 1855, also at Pei-Ho Forts action, when he d. unm. 17 July 1859, from wounds received at the storming.

7. Charles, Rev., M.A., Rector of Shottesbrooke, b. 8 Mar. 1820; m. 27 May 1845, (m. diss. by div. 1856) Frances Rosalie, dau. of Hans Busk, and d. 14 July 1878, having had issue, with another son and a dau., who d. unm.

  (1) Clement Arthur, served in the Pontifical Zouaves, 1866-70, (medal and Mentana Cross), b. 3 Nov. 1849; m. Marguerite, dau. of John M. Hopkins, of Carmarthen, and d. 22 Feb. 1930, leaving issue,

    Clement Percival, m. 26 April 1928, Doreen K. Miller, and had issue, David Arthur Nicholas, Oxf. and Bucks L.I., b. 29 Nov. 1931, m. 4 June 1955, Clare B. Conyers.

  (2) Cyril Bexley, Secret Chamberlain of the Cape and Sword of the Popes Pius IX and Leo XIII, b. 28 Aug. 1851; d. unm. at Rome 22 Aug. 1887.

1. Caroline, m. 9 July 1828, 6th Baron Vaux of Harrowden and d. 30 Sept. 1883 leaving issue.

2. Charlotte, Eleanor, m. 4 Aug. 1842, Rev. E. S. Pearce-Serocold, and d. 1891, leaving issue (B.L.G.).

3. Martha Louisa, m. 4 Aug. 1841, William Chapman, brother of Sir Montague Lowther Chapman, 3rd Bt. (extinct), of Killua Castle, Westmeath, and had issue.

4. Sophia, m. 7 Jan. 1841, T. A. Anstruther, H.E.I.C.S. and had issue (Anstruther, Bt.).

Mr. Arthur Vansittart (b. 1775), d. 31 May 1829. His great-grandson,

Sir Robert Gilbert Vansittart, **Baron Vansittart**, b. 25 June 1881; educ. Eton; Diplomatic Service, 1902, served as 1st Sec. Foreign Office, 1919, and at Paris, 1902, Teheran, 1907, Cairo, 1909, Stockholm, 1915, and Paris 1919, Sec. to Marquess Curzon, Sec. of State for Foreign Affairs, 1920-24, Asst. Under Sec. of State for Foreign Affairs, and Principal Priv. Sec. to Prime Minister, 1928-30, Perm. Under Sec. of State for Foreign Affairs, 1930-38, Chief Diplomatic Adviser to Foreign Sec. 1938-41; was author of over 20 books, including the highly controversial *Black Record*, describing the German record in politics and war. He m. (1) 7 Sept. 1921, Mrs. Gladys Robinson Duff (d. 3 July 1928) only dau. of Gen. W. C. Heppenheimer, of New Jersey U.S.A., and had issue,

  Cynthia, b. 31 Dec. 1922; m. 9 Jan. 1942 (m. diss. by div. 1954) Frederick Crocker Whitman, and had issue.

He m. (2) 29 July 1931, Sarita Enriqueta, dau. of Herbert Ward, of Paris, and widow of Sir Colville Adrian de Rune Barclay (Barclay Bt.). He was cr. M.V.O. 1906, C.M.G. 1920, C.B. 1927, K.C.B. 1929, G.C.M.G. 1931, G.C.B. 1938; made P.C. 1940, and cr. Baron Vansittart, of Denham, co. Buckingham. 3 July 1941. He d. 14 Feb. 1957.

ARMS—Ermine an eagle displayed sable, on a chief gules, a ducal coronet or, between two crosses pattée argent.

CREST—An eagle's head, couped at the breast, between two wings, elevated and displayed, sable, the whole resting on two crosses pattée argent.

SUPPORTERS—On either side a greyhound argent, gorged with a collar flory counter flory azure.

MOTTO—Fata viam invenient.

Lord Vansittart's residence was at Denham Place, Denham, Bucks. His clubs were the Athenaeum and St. James's.

WAKEFIELD

PEERAGE—U.K. Baron Wakefield of Hythe, co. Kent. Viscount Wakefield. (Also a baronetcy cr. 16 Feb. 1917.)

SURNAME—Wakefield.

CR.—Barony, 20 Jan. 1930. Viscounty, 28 June 1934. EXT.—15 Jan. 1941.

HISTORY—Thomas Wakefield of Upper Northgate Street, Chester, and formerly of Normanton Road, Derby, b. Aug. 1800; m. 1824, Juliana Carwithen, and d. 17 April 1860 having by her (d. 9 Feb. 1886 aged 89) an eldest son,

John Wakefield, of Wavertree Vale, co. Lancs., in H.M.'s Customs, b. 7 June 1825; m. 25 Dec. 1847, Mary, dau. of William Cheers, of Manchester, who d. 10 July 1892. He d. 6 Aug. 1890, leaving a fourth and ygst. son,

Sir Charles Cheers Wakefield, Bt., **Baron and Viscount Wakefield**, b. 12 Dec. 1859; educ. Liverpool Inst.; founded in City of London the firm of C. C. Wakefield, & Co., dealing in lubricating oils and appliances, 1899; used the trade name "Castrol"; Sheriff of City of London, 1907-08; Lt. for City, and Lord Mayor, 1915-16; was cr. Kt. Bach. 1908, a baronet 16 Feb. 1917; Baron Wakefield, of Hythe, co. Kent, 20 Jan. 1930 and Viscount Wakefield, 28 June 1934; Gov. Dir. of C. C. Wakefield & Co., and Chm. N. British and Mercantile Insurance Co.; m. 17 Feb. 1888, Sarah Frances, D.G. St. J., Vice Pres. League of Mercy, B.R.C. Medal in gold, dau. of John Graham, of Lancashire. Lord Wakefield who possessed many foreign orders, was a most generous donor to many charities, and a great supporter of flights by Sir Alan Cobham and Amy Johnson, and also of Sir Henry Seagrave's motor speed trials; he owned Miss England speed boats, and was Chm. of the R.A.F. Benevolent Fund. He was further cr. G.C.V.O. 1936. He d.s.p. 15 Jan. 1941.

ARMS—Or a chevron vert between in chief two roses gules barbed and seeded ppr. and in base a cross couped gules, on a chief of the second a two bladed air screw fesswise of the first.

CREST—Between two elephants tusks erect argent, a wyvern sans legs gules.

SUPPORTERS—Dexter, A lion or, charged on the shoulder with a wreath of laurel ppr. tied with a riband gules; Sinister, An eagle wings endorsed and inverted or, charged with a like wreath.

BADGE—A lymphad azure the sail gules charged with a four bladed air screw saltirewise, flags flying to the dexter also or.

MOTTO—Vigilans et audax.

Lord Wakefield's seat was at Hythe, co. Kent.

WALERAN

PEERAGE—U.K. Baron Waleran, of Uffculme, co. Devon. (Also a Baronetcy, cr. 24 Feb. 1876.)

SURNAME—Walrond.

CR.—23 Dec. 1905. **EXT.**—4 April 1966.

HISTORY—This family lived in the 12th century at Bradfelle, in the parish of Uffculme, co. Devon, where, in 1154, Richard de Bradfelle, grandson of Robert de Bradfelle, had a son, Richard de Bradfelle, ca. 1189, who had issue,

Richard Walrond, of Exeter, and of Bradfield, the first to use the present surname, who lived ca. 1216. His son,

William Walrond, of Bradfield, had with other issue, an eldest son,

John Walrond, of Bradfield, living ca. 1270 and was s. by his son,

John Walrond, of Bradfield and later of Stofford, co. Devon, which he acquired by marriage with Joan, dau. and heiress of John Stofford, and was s. by his son,

William Walrond, of Bradfield, living ca. 1327, m. the dau. of John Sambuel and had, with other issue, an eldest son,

William Walrond, of Bradfield, living 1399, had with other issue an elder son,

William Walrond of Bradfield, living 1401, m. Alice, dau. of Walter Hake, and had with other issue, a son and heir,

John Walrond, of Bradfield, living 1445, m. Alice, dau. of John Ufflett, and sister and heiress of Edmund Ufflett, and had with other issue, a son and heir,

John Walrond, of Bradfield, living 1465, m. Gennett, dau. of William Gilbert and had issue [(with a yr. son, William, ancestor of the Walronds of Bovey, co. Devon, whose heiress, Judith Walrond m. 1778, Lord Rolle and d.s.p. 1820, (see Burke's Extinct Peerage 1883) an elder son and heir,

John Walrond of Bradfield, living 1491 had by his wife, Margaret, dau. of John Moore, of Moore Hayes, co. Devon, (with a yr. son Osmond, ancestor of the Walronds of Dulford, co. Devon) an elder son,

Humphrey Walrond, of Bradfield, m. Eleanor, dau. of Henry Ogan, of Saltwinch, co. Somerset, and had with other issue, an elder son,

Henry Walrond, of Bradfield, m. Agnes, dau. and co-heiress of John Whitinge, of Woode, co. Devon, and had a son and heir,

Humphrey Walrond, of Bradfield, m. twice, (1) Mary dau. of Sir Thomas Willoughby, by whom he had six sons. She was bur. at Uffculme, 30 Nov. 1556, (2), Florence, dau. of Thomas Moore, of Taunton, by whom he had further issue, a dau. Elizabeth m. Sir William Guise. Florence was bur. 25 April 1582 and Humphrey Walrond 7 April 1586, being s. by his eldest son,

William Walrond of Bradfield, m. Mary, dau. of Nicholas Sandford, of Cerne, co. Dorset, and was bur. 19 July 1627, having had with three daus. a son,

Henry Walrond, of Bradfield, admitted Inner Temple, 11 May 1603, bapt. 18 July 1584; m. twice, (1) Penelope, dau. of Humphrey Sydenham, of Dulverton, co. Somerset, and had issue, and (2) Elizabeth—by whom he had more issue. He d. 1649 being s. by his eldest son,

William Walrond, of Bradfield, admitted Middle Temple, 31 Oct. 1631, b. 1610; m. Ursula Speccott, and d. 1669 being s. by his eldest son,

Sir William Walrond, of Bradfield, knighted at Bideford, 25 May 1671, bapt. 30 July 1639; m. Dinah, dau. and co-heiress of Sir Thomas Mompesson, Kt., and d.s.p. 1689, being s. by his brother,

Henry Walrond, of Bradfield, m. three times, (1) Margaret, dau. of Edward Foxwell and had with other issue, two sons, (2) Elizabeth, dau. of Sir William Strode Kt., but had no issue, (3) 1719, Elizabeth, (d. 1749) widow of James Holway, of Uffculme, by whom he had no issue. He d. 1724 being s. by his son,

William Walrond, of Bradfield, m. Ann, dau. of Francis Courtenay, and d. (will proved 31 Jan. 1745/46) having had with other issue, an eldest son, Courtenay and a third son, Henry. He was s. by,

Courtenay Walrond, of Bradfield, m. . . . Saunders of Bradninch, co. Devon, and d.s.p. 1761, being s. by his brother,

The Rev. Henry Walrond of Bradfield, Rector of Woolfardisworthy, near Crediton, co. Devon, m. 22 Jan. 1759, Dorothy Millford and was bur. 8 June 1787, having issue with two daus., a son,

William Henry Walrond, of Bradfield, b. 28 Jan. 1762; m. 9 June 1795, Mary Alford (d. 1843) and d. 20 Feb. 1845, having had issue two daus., twins and coheiresses, Frances and Margaret (d. unm.), of whom the elder,

Frances Walrond, of Bradfield, m. 6 July 1915, Benjamin Bowes Dickinson, son of John Dickinson, High Sheriff, Devon, 1824. By Royal Licence he assumed the name and arms of Walrond in lieu of those of Dickinson, 22 April 1845. He d. 15 July 1851. She d. 11 Nov 1866. They had with other children a second son,

Sir John Walrond Walrond, 1st Bt., so cr. 24 Feb. 1876, High Sheriff, Devon 1874, M.P. for Tiverton 1865-68, b. 1 Mar. 1818; m. 20 May 1845, the Hon. Frances Caroline Hood, dau. of 2nd Baron Bridport, and d. 23 April 1889, having had issue with a yr. son whose male issue died out, and six daus., an elder son,

Sir William Hood Walrond, 2nd Bt., and **1st Baron Waleran**, P.C., Capt. Grenadier Guards, M.P. for E. Devon, 1880-85, and for N.E. Div. 1885-1905, Patronage Sec. 1895-1902, Chancellor of the Duchy of Lancaster 1902-05, b. 26 Feb. 1849; was cr. Baron Waleran, of Uffculme, co. Devon; m. (1) 11 April 1871, Elizabeth Katharine, only dau. and heiress of J. S. Pitman of Dunchideock House, co. Devon, and by her who d. 11 Oct. 1911, had with an elder son, John d. unm. and two daus. a yr. son,

William Lionel Charles, of Bradfield, b. 22 May 1876, M.P. for N.E. Div. of Devon, 1906-15; m. 18 June 1904 Hon. Charlotte Margaret Lothian Coats, dau. of 1st Baron Glentanar; served in World War I in the Rly. Supply Detach. A.S.C., and d. 2 Nov. 1915 of illness contracted on service in France, having had issue with a yr. son, John Humphrey, d. 1942, an elder son,

William George Hood, 3rd Bt. and **2nd Baron Waleran** (see below).

The 1st Lord Waleran m. (2) 28 Oct. 1913, Helena Margaret, dau. of F. Morrison of Shanghai and d. 17 Mar. 1925 when he was s. by his grandson,

Sir William George Hood Walrond, 3rd Bt. and **2nd Baron Waleran**, b. 30 Mar. 1905; educ. Eton and Trin. Coll. Oxford; served in World War II 1939-45, (despatches), W/Cmdr. R.A.F.V.R., Asst. Priv. Sec. to Gov. of New Zealand 1927-30; m. (1) 6 June 1932 (m. diss. by div. 1934) Margaret Patricia, dau. of Capt. G. Blackader, of Montreal, (2) 16 Sept. 1936, (m. diss. by div. 1952) Betty, dau. of Sir Emsley Carr, and (3) 17 Dec. 1954, Valantine, dau. of E. O. Anderson and formerly wife of S/Ldr. G. M. Rothwell. Lord Waleran d. 4 April 1966.

ARMS—Argent three bulls' heads cabossed sable, armed or.
CREST—An heraldic tiger sejant sable semée of plates, waved and tufted or.
SUPPORTERS—Dexter, An heraldic tiger sable demée of plates crined and tufted or; Sinister, A double headed eagle, close, gules.
MOTTO—Sic vos non vobis.

WALLSCOURT

PEERAGE—Ireland. Baron Wallscourt, of Ardfry, co. Galway.
SURNAME—Blake.
CR.—31 July 1800. **EXT.**—27 May 1920.
HISTORY—In Burke's Landed Gentry of Ireland, (edition of 1958) the earliest known history of this family is given from the reign of Edward I (circa 1277). Geoffrey Blake, had a grant of land in Athenry from Robert Steven dated 20 Aug. 1391. His elder son, William Blake, burgess of Galway, was devisee under the will of his uncle, Henry Blake, in 1421. He helped to endow the parish church of St. Nicholas in Galway, 1435, and d. 1453 leaving by his wife (a dau. of Athy, of Galway) an eldest son,
John Blake, Mayor of Galway, 1487 who m. Anabel de Burgh and had with other issue, a third son,
Andrew Blake, living tempore Henry VII, whose ygst, son,
Walter Blake, had with an elder son, Marcus, who d. 1629, having been elected Mayor of Galway, a second son,
Robert Blake, of Ardfry, co. Galway, who had a grant by patent, dated 12 May 1612, of Ballinacourt (now Wallscourt) and of Ardfry, both in co. Galway, and also of lands in Mayo. He had with other issue,
1. Richard, Sir (see below).
2. John, ancestor of Blake de Burgh, of Coolcon.
3. Andrew, of Partgar, or Castlegrove, co. Galway, from whom descended the Blakes of Castlegrove, the Netterville Blakes, and the Blakes of Canada.
Robert Blake d. 15 Dec. 1615 (will dated 3 July 1612, proved at Tuam, 2 May 1616). His eldest son,
Sir Richard Blake, of Ardfry, M.P. co. Galway, 1639, Mayor of Galway, 1627, knighted by the Lord Deputy, Viscount Falkland, 8 Aug. 1624; Speaker of the Supreme Council of Kilkenny, 1648; m. Gyles, dau. of Alderman Andrew Kirwan, and d. 1663 (will dated 13 June 1663, and proved 20 July 1663) having with other issue, an eldest son,
Robert Blake, of Ardfry and Wallscourt, of which he had a regrant by patent 24 Feb. 1681;

m. Elizabeth dau. of Martin Lynch, of Levally, and d. 20 Mar. 1697, having had issue,
1. Richard (see below).
2. Andrew.
3. Joseph, of Grange, co. Galway, m. Mary, dau. of Ignatius Browne, (Oranmore, B.), and had issue with two other sons, an eldest son,
Richard (see below).
The eldest son,
Richard Blake, of Ardfry, m. (1) 1 Mar. 1681, Mary Magdalen, only dau. of Oliver Martyn sen. of Tullyra, and had issue, an eldest son, Robert. He m. (2) Dec. 1700, Ellzabeth, dau. of Robert Dillon, of Clonbrock, and d. 12 May 1735 having had further issue. He was s. by his eldest son,
Robert Blake, of Newgrove and Ardfry, m. Anstace, dau. of Rt. Hon. Denis Daly, (Dunsandle, B.) and d. 12 May 1741 (will proved 24 Dec. 1744) having by her (who d. 1 May 1739), had issue, with a dau. Mary who m. Sir Ulick Blake, 8th Bt., an only son,
Richard Blake, of Ardfry and of Newgrove, co. Galway, m. 1739, Marcia Maria, only child and heiress of Marcus ffrench, of Rahassane, co. Galway, and d. 3 July 1744, having by her (who d. 16 Oct. 1743) an only dau. and heiress, Anstace, who d. unm. 1753. At his death s.p.m. the representation of the family and the estates of Ardfry and Wallscourt passed to his kinsman,
Richard Blake, of Ardfry, son of Joseph Blake of Grange (see above) who m. Maria Young, and d. 1754 leaving an eldest son,
Joseph Blake of Ardfry, b. 2 Oct. 1739; m. Oct. 1764, Honoria, dau. of Dermot Daly, and d. 19 Jan. 1806, having by her (who d. 14 July 1784) had issue,
1. Joseph Henry, **1st Baron Wallscourt** (see below).
2. Ignatius Charles, Capt. of Dragoons, b. 21 Aug. 1773; m. June 1794, Helen, dau. of William Cashel, of Berwick-on-Tweed, and d. 6 Aug. 1797, having had issue, with a dau., Louisa Helena, m. Capt. R. Bourne R.N., a son,
Joseph Henry, **2nd Baron Wallscourt** (see below).
3. Henry James, Col. Galway Militia, b. 5 Oct. 1774; m. 14 Feb. 1796, Anne, dau. of John French, of Galway and d. 11 Nov. 1811, having had with other issue d.s.p. an eldest son,
Joseph Henry, **3rd Baron Wallscourt** (see below).
1. Joanna Harriet, m. (1) 1 Feb. 1783, Richard Burke, of Glinsk, (Burke Bt.), and (2) 1792, Dominick Daly and had issue.
2. Elizabeth Jemima, m. (1) 25 Jan. 1790, 16th Earl of Erroll who d.s.p. 1798. She m. (2) 12 Sept. 1816, Rt. Hon. John Hookham Frere, (see B.L.G. 1952, Frere of Maryfield), and d. 17 Jan. 1831.
3. Agnes Maria, m. 1807, Charles Aldrich and d. 1808.
4. Margaret, d. at Paris, aged 96, in Jan. 1862.
5. Honoria Louisa, m. 4 April 1810, 3rd Earl Cadogan, and d. 12 Sept. 1845.
The eldest son,
Joseph Henry Blake, **1st Baron Wallscourt,** b. 5 Oct. 1765; m. 18 Aug. 1784 Lady Louisa Catherine Mary Bermingham, dau. and

coheiress of 1st Earl of Louth, by whom (who m. 2ndly James Daly and d. 1827), he had issue an only dau., Anastasia, m. 1803, 2nd Lord Clonbrock. Mr. Blake, was M.P. co. Galway, and on 31 July 1800 was cr. a peer as Baron Wallscourt, of Ardfry, co. Galway, with remainder in default of the issue male of his body, to the heirs male of the body of his father; he d. 28 Mar. 1803, vita patris, and was s. in accordance with the special limitation by his nephew,

Joseph Blake, **2nd Baron Wallscourt,** b. 23 July 1795; d.s.p. 11 Oct. 1816, being s. in the barony by his first cousin,

Joseph Henry Blake, **3rd Baron Wallscourt,** b. 2 June 1797; m. 23 Sept. 1822, Elizabeth, dau. of William Lock, of Norbury, co. Surrey and d. 28 May 1849, having had by her (who d. 2 Jan. 1877) with two other sons, who d. young,

1. Erroll Augustus, **4th Baron Wallscourt** (see below).
1. Elizabeth Fredrica, m. 17 July 1866, Gen. the Hon. Arthur Upton (Templetown, V.), and d. 8 July 1902.
2. Elizabeth Nina, m. 26 Sept. 1859, Lt. Gen. the Hon. James William Bosville Macdonald and d. 21 July 1890. (Macdonald, B.).

The only surv. son,

Erroll Augustus Joseph Henry Blake, **4th Baron Wallscourt,** b. 22 Aug. 1841; Capt. Coldstream Guards, and Gentleman Usher to Lord Lt. of Ireland; m. (1) 7 Feb. 1874, Lady Jane Harriet Charlotte Stanhope, dau. of 7th Earl of Harrington, and by her (d. 8 Sept. 1889) had issue,

1. Charles William Joseph Henry, **5th Baron Wallscourt** (see below).
2. Erroll Wyndham Lincoln, b. 21 Dec. 1875; d. unm. 28 April 1910.
1. Elizabeth Honoria, b. 23 Aug. 1877; d. 10 Sept. 1880.
2. Elizabeth Lucy Eily, twin with her sister Elizabeth Honoria, m. 30 April 1907, Major Leycester Penrhyn Storr, D.S.O., who was reported missing in World War I, and had issue five daus.
3. Margaret Phyllis, b. 19 June 1883; m. 24 June 1908, W. E. Ffarington, of Worden Hall, co. Lancs. and d. 26 July 1910.

The 4th Baron m. (2) 25 Jan. 1896, Ethel Mary, dau. of Sir William Palliser, and d. 22 July 1918. The elder son,

Charles William Joseph Henry Blake, **5th Baron Wallscourt,** b. 12 Jan. 1875, m. 11 Dec. 1897, Ellen (d. 7 Feb. 1921) dau. of Joseph Mayo, and widow of P. Boisset, and d. 27 May 1920.

ARMS—Argent a fret gules.
CREST—A cat-a-mountain passant guardant ppr.
SUPPORTERS—Dexter, A cat-a-mountain guardant ppr. ducally gorged and chained or; Sinister, An antelope argent armed and unguled or collared and lined gules.
MOTTO—Virtus sola nobilitat.
The seat of the peers was Ardfry, Oranmore, co. Galway.

WANDSWORTH

PEERAGE—U.K. Baron Wandsworth, of Wandsworth, London.
SURNAME—Stern.
CR.—19 July 1895. **EXT.**—10 Feb. 1912.
HISTORY—Sydney James Stern, **Baron Wandsworth,** was b. in London, 1845, the eldest son of Viscount de Stern, by Sophia, his wife, (who d. 8 Dec. 1900), the dau. of Aaron Asher Goldsmid, of Cavendish Square, London, and the niece of Sir Isaac Lyon Goldsmid, 1st Bt., (see editions of Burke's Peerage between 1841 and 1896 when the Goldsmid baronetcy became extinct). He s. his father as Viscount de Stern and was cr. a peer as Baron Wandsworth, of Wandsworth, London, 19 July 1895. He was educ. Magdalene Coll. Camb.; J.P. cos. Surrey and London; Hon. Col. 4th Vol. Bn. East Surrey Regt.; M.P. for Stowmarket Div. of Suffolk, 1891-95; having unsuccessfully contested Mid. Div. of Surrey, 1880 and 1884, the borough of Ipswich, 1886, and the Tiverton Div. of Devonshire, 1885. He d. 10 Feb. 1912.
ARMS—Or on a pile sable, a lion rampant of the field, on a chief gules two horses' heads erased argent.
CREST—A lion passant ppr. gorged with a collar flory counterflory gules, resting the dexter forepaw on an escutcheon of the last charged with a horse's head argent.
SUPPORTERS—On either side, a horse argent gorged with a collar flory counter-flory and charged on the shoulder with an estoile within an annulet, all gules.
MOTTO—Vincit perseverantia.
Lord Wandsworth's residence was 10 Great Stanhope Street, Mayfair, W. and his clubs were Marlborough; Bachelors'; St. James's and New University.

WANTAGE

PEERAGE—U.K. Baron Wantage, of Lockinge, co. Berks.
SURNAME—Loyd-Lindsay.
CR.—23 July 1885. **EXT.**—10 June 1901.
HISTORY—The Hon. Robert Lindsay, 2nd son of James Lindsay, 5th Earl of Balcarres, and brother of Alexander Lindsay, 23rd Earl of Crawford, (see that title in extant peerages) was b. 25 Jan. 1754; m. 25 Nov. 1788, Elizabeth, dau. of Sir Alexander Dick, Bt., and d. 10 May 1836, leaving with other issue, a son and heir,

Lt. Gen. James Lindsay, of Balcarres, co. Fife, b. 17 April 1793; m. twice and by his second wife, Anne, dau. of Sir Coutts Trotter, Bt., had with other issue, a second son,

Sir Robert James Loyd-Lindsay, **Baron Wantage,** b. 16 April 1832; soldier and politician, joined Scots Guards, 1850, and served in the Crimea with great distinction, being awarded the V.C., 1857; m. 17 Nov. 1858, the Hon. Harriet Sarah Loyd (she d. 9 Aug. 1920), only surv. dau. and heir of Lord Overstone (see that title in present work), and assumed by Royal Licence, the additional surname and arms of Loyd (23 Oct. 1858); ret. as Lt. Col. 1859; was a pioneer in the Volunteer movement; M.P. for Berkshire, 1865-85; Fin. Sec. to the War Office, 1877-80; cr. K.C.B. 1881,

and Baron Wantage, of Lockinge, co. Berks, 23 July 1885; was prominent in freemasonry, and a keen agriculturist in Berkshire; helped to found Reading Univ. Coll.; d.s.p. 10 June 1901.
ARMS—Quarterly 1 and 4, Counter quartered, I and IV, Gules a fess chequy argent and azure (Lindsay); II and III, Or a lion rampant gules debruised of a ribband in bend sable (Abernethy) all within a bordure azure semée of stars or; 2 and 3, Per bend sinister ermine and argent an eagle displayed with two heads sable a border of the last bezantée, a canton or; for distinction (Loyd).
CRESTS—(1) A tent azure fringed and semée of stars or, ensigned with a pennon gules (Lindsay); (2) A buck's head ppr. erased sable attired or charged on the neck with a fess engrailed also sable, thereon three bezants (Loyd).
SUPPORTERS—Dexter, A stag ppr., ducally gorged and chained, chain reflexed over the back, and charged on the shoulder with a cross masculy pomettée or; Sinister, An eagle wings elevated sable, beaked, ducally gorged, chained, chain reflexed over the back and charged on the breast with a cross masculy pomettée or.
MOTTO—Astra, castra, numen, lumen.
Lord Wantage's seats were Lockinge Park, near Wantage; Overstone Park, Northampton; town residence, 2 Carlton House Garden, S.W. His clubs were Carlton; Athenaeum; Guards'; Travellers; Marlborough; Bachelors'; and United Service.

WARGRAVE

PEERAGE—U.K. Baron Wargrave of Wargrave, co. Berks. (Also a baronetcy cr. 25 June 1915.)
SURNAME—Goulding.
CR.—22 Nov. 1922. EXT.—17 July 1936.
HISTORY—William Goulding of Summerhill House, and Ballyrusheen, co. Cork, had by his second wife, with other issue, two sons, namely,
1. William Joshua, Sir, cr. a baronet 1904, (see extant peerages, Goulding of Millicent, Bt.).
2. Edward Alfred, Bt. and Baron Wargrave (see below).
The ygr. son,
Sir Edward Alfred Goulding, Bt. and Baron Wargrave, b. 5 Nov. 1862; educ. St. John's Coll. Camb., M.A., and Pres. of Cambridge Union, 1885; Barrister-at-Law, Inner Temple, 1887; M.P. East Wilts, 1895-1906, and for Worcester, 1908-22; mem. L.C.C. Hammersmith, 1895-1901; was cr. a baronet 25 June 1915, and Baron Wargrave of Wargrave, co. Berks, 22 Nov. 1922. He d.s.p. 17 July 1936.
ARMS—Argent a griffin segreant within an orle of martlets sable.
CREST—A dexter hand appaumée and couped at the wrist, encircled with a chaplet of oak leaves bendwise and transfixed with an arrow in bend sinister, all ppr.
SUPPORTERS—Two swans ppr. each charged with a cross flory or.
MOTTO—Virtute et valore.
Lord Wargrave's seat was Shiplake Court, Henley-on-Thames, Oxon.

WARING

PEERAGE—U.K. Baron Waring, of Foots Cray Place, Foots Cray, co. Kent. (Also a baronetcy, cr. 31 May 1919.)
SURNAME—Waring.
CR.—18 July 1922. EXT.—9 Jan. 1940.
HISTORY—John Waring, of Derringhy, co. Antrim, by Mary his wife, the dau. of the Rev. Peers, of Derringhy, had with other issue, an eldest son,
William Waring, of Waringstown, co. Down, High Sheriff, 1669; m. (1) 21 May 1656, Elizabeth, dau. of William Gardiner, and had issue. He m. (2) Jane, dau. of John Close, and by her had issue four sons. She d. 6 May 1724 He d. 27 July 1703. His fourth son,
John Waring, of Fidany, co. Down, and St. Clement Danes, London, d. 1727, leaving with other issue by his wife, Rebecca, an eldest son,
John Waring, of Bellmount, and Fidany, co. Down, b. Nov. 1696; m. twice (the second wife being Elizabeth Stothard whom he m. 25 April 1765) and d. 1772, having by his first marriage had issue,
John Waring, of Bellmount and later of Downpatrick, co. Down, who d. 1785 having had issue by his wife, Margaret, six sons and five daus., of whom the sixth son,
Samuel Waring, of Downpatrick and Lisburn, b. July 1785, had a son,
John Moore Johnson Waring, b. Dec. 1805; m. Elizabeth, dau. of James Shaw, of Dillsborough, co. Down, and d. 16 Sept. 1866, having had with other issue,
Samuel James Waring, of Liverpool, b. 1838; m. 4 July 1858, Sarah Ann, dau. of Thomas Wells, of Everton, and d. 23 June 1907, leaving with other issue, a second son,
Sir Samuel James Waring, Bt., and Baron Waring, b. 19 April 1860; educ. privately; in 1893 established the business of Waring & Sons, later Waring and Gillows 1932 Ltd., being Pres. thereof; High Sheriff of Denbighshire, 1907; Commissioner for Boy Scouts, co. Kent, patron of three livings, had Order of Medjidie, 2nd class; during World War I organized factories for production of aeroplanes, engines, and general war equipment; mem. of many committees and organizations; cr. a baronet 31 May 1919, and Baron Waring, of Foots Cray Place, Foots Cray, co. Kent, 18 July 1922; m. 15 Oct. 1890, Eleanor Caroline, dau. of Charles Bamford, of Brookhurst, co. Chester, and Llanrhaiadr Hall, Llanrhaiadr, co. Denbigh, and d.s.p.m.s. 9 Jan. 1940, leaving issue,
Arthur Samuel Bamford, b. 9 Mar. 1892; d.v.p. and unm. 23 April 1911.
Eleanor Gladys, b. 1894; m. 3 Oct. 1923, Capt. Arthur Cunliffe Bernard Critchley-Waring, D.S.O., (formerly Critchley) Argyll and Sutherland Highlanders, son of Godfrey Critchley-Salmonson, of Torquay, co. Devon, and had issue. They assumed the additional surname and arms of Waring by Royal Licence, 14 Aug. 1929.
ARMS—Argent on a bend between two trefoils slipped sable three mascles of the field.
CREST—In front of a stork's head ppr. a mascle fessways or.
SUPPORTERS—On either side a stork ppr. holding in the beak a trefoil slipped sable.

MOTTO—Nec vi nec astutia.

Lord Waring's seat was Foots Cray Place, Kent. His town house was 23 Portland Place, W.

WARRINGTON OF CLYFFE

PEERAGE—U.K. Baron Warrington of Clyffe, of Market Lavington, co. Wilts.

SURNAME—Warrington.

CR.—25 Oct. 1926. EXT.—26 Oct. 1937.

HISTORY—Thomas Warrington, of London, by his wife, Mary Jane, dau. of Henry George Radclyffe, was father of,

Sir Thomas Rolls Warrington, **Baron Warrington of Clyffe**, b. 29 May 1851, at Old Brompton, London; educ. Rugby and Trin. Col. Camb., M.A.; Barrister-at-Law, Lincoln's Inn, 1875; Q.C. 1895; Bencher, 1897; apptd. a Judge of the High Court, Chancery Div., 1904-15; Kt. Bach. 1904; a Lord Justice of Appeal, 1915; P.C. 1915; mem. of the Judicial Cttee. of the Privy Council and of the Gen. Council of the Bar, and retired 1926. He was cr. 25 Oct. 1926, Baron Warrington of Clyffe, of Market Lavington, co. Wilts. He m. 31 July 1883, Emma Maud, dau. of Decimus Sturges, Barrister-at-Law. He d.s.p. 26 Oct. 1937.

ARMS—Argent on a bend invected gules between two bulls' heads erased sable three eagles displayed of the field.

CREST—In front of a demi-eagle displayed erased sable holding in the beak a cross patee fitchée gules, an escutcheon argent charged with a bull's head as in the arms.

SUPPORTERS—On either side a bull sable armed, unguled and charged on the shoulder with a fasces erect or.

MOTTO—Constantia et labore.

Lord Warrington's seat was Clyffe Hall, Market Lavington, Devizes, Wilts.

WATSON

PEERAGE—U.K. Life. Baron Watson, of Thankerton, co. Lanark.

SURNAME—Watson.

CR.—28 April 1880. EXT.—14 Sept. 1899.

HISTORY—The Rev. Thomas Watson, of Covington, co. Lanark, by Eleanora, his wife the dau. of David McHaffie, had issue,

William Watson, **Baron Watson**, of Thankerton, co. Lanark, b. 1828; m. 1868, Margaret (d. 3 Mar. 1898), dau. of Dugald J. Bannatyne; Advocate Scots Bar, 1851; Dean of Faculty at Edinburgh; filled successively the offices of Solicitor Gen. and Lord Advocate for Scotland; M.P. for the Univs. of Aberdeen and Glasgow, 1876-1880; apptd. a Lord of Appeal in Ordinary, he was cr. a peer for life as Baron Watson, of Thankerton, co. Lanark, 28 April 1880. He d. 14 Sept. 1899 having had issue, a third son, William, Baron Thankerton (see that title in present work).

ARMS—Or an oak tree ppr. growing out of a mount in base vert surmounted of a fess ermine charged with two mullets azure.

CREST—The stump of an oak tree with two branches sprouting from it and grasped on either side by a hand issuing from a cloud all ppr.

SUPPORTERS—Dexter, A Highland deerhound ppr.; Sinister, A lion argent, each charged on the shoulder with a thistle leaved and slipped ppr.

MOTTO—A Deo Floruit.

WAVELL

PEERAGE—U.K. Viscount Wavell, of Cyrenaica, and of Winchester, co. Southampton. Earl Wavell and Viscount Keren of Eritrea, and of Winchester co. Southampton.

SURNAME—Wavell.

CR.—Viscount Wavell, 22 July 1943. Earl Wavell and Viscount Keren, 1 May 1947.

EXT.—24 Dec. 1953.

HISTORY—For a full account of the family of Wavell, in its various branches, see *The House of Wavell*, by L. G. Pine, which was based on the 25 years of research by Mr. G. Edward Wavell, a member of the Newchurch and London branch of the family, who are descended from the Rev. Richard Wavell, born 1633, (see below). An immense amount of material was collected by G. E. Wavell, and it is unlikely that it will be easy to add more details to the account. It was, however, the intention of the 2nd Earl Wavell to have work undertaken on the medieval background of the Wavells, in view of their five centuries connection with Winchester College.

Like all other English surnames, Wavell has undergone various changes before settling into its present form. The variants of the name can all be traced to an origin in the village of Vauville which stands on the bay of the same name in the western portion of the Cherbourg peninsula. The Seigneurs of Vauville were a younger branch of the Barons of Briquebec who, like many other of the ruling caste in Normandy, were descended from the old Norse stock. A William de Vauville or Wavilla is mentioned in charters both in Normandy and England in the 11th century, and in the reign of King John Sir Richard de Vauville (Wauvill) settled in Sussex, and during the period 1200-1400 the Wavells are to be found in Sussex, Bedfordshire and Somerset, for the most part as the holders of knights' fees. At the close of the Middle Ages the family was settled in the Isle of Wight.

The first of the line in the Isle of Wight was John Wavell who bought the manor of Atherfield from Sir Thomas Trenchard, married Jane Holbrooke and d. before 1592. He had two sons, Thomas and David. David Wavell, a freeholder in the Isle of Wight in 1606, had a ygr. son, Thomas Wavell, described as a Royalist Major, of Limerston and a strong cavalier. He was a trustee of his brother David's will in 1641. He had issue five sons and two daus., of whom the second son,

The Rev. Richard Wavell, b. 3 April 1633, at Limerston, Isle of Wight, was B.A. Oxford, 1657-8, and was in 1658 ministering at Egham, co. Surrey. He m. Anna Bale of Egham. He was later Pastor of Pinners' Hall, Old Broad Street, London, and was one of the ministers who were deprived of their livelihood by the act of Uniformity in 1662. In the period of persecution under Charles II, Richard Wavell was on one occasion obliged to give bail for his appearance at the Sessions, and had to appear at the bar before the magistrates. The then Lord Mayor of London, Sir Henry Tulse was his kinsman and it was owing to this fact that Wavell escaped the full rigour of the law against nonconformity. He d. 19 Dec. 1705 and was bur. in Bunhill Fields, leaving several children. One of his sons lived at Clapham and had estates at Richmond, co. Surrey, and he was the first of the family, at least in modern times, to use arms, which are engraved on his tomb at Holy Trinity Church, Clapham. From another son of the Rev. Richard Wavell, whose Christian name is unknown, came, John Wavell, who m. Ann Cowlam, 6 Jan. 1745 at Newchurch, Isle of Wight, and had four sons and three daus., of whom, the fourth son,

William Wavell, M.D., F.R.S., of Barnstaple, co. Devon, was surgeon, geologist and botanist. He was surgeon of Gracechurch Street London, 1779-80, at Barnstaple, 1793, and elected F.R.S. 1824. Sir Humphrey Davy in 1805 read a paper before the Royal Society on Wavell's discovery of Wavellite, described in the *Encyclopedia Britannica*, as a mineral consisting of hydrated aluminium phosphate, crystallizing in the orthorombic system etc. Dr. Wavell was bapt. 20 Dec. 1750; m. Mary Garrett, (d. 26 July 1788) dau. of William Smith, of Guildford. He d. 15 May 1829, having had issue,

1. William, Rev., b. circa 1781; educ. Winchester and Caius Coll. Camb., M.B. 1805, Tancred Student; deacon 21 Aug. 1808 and priest 2 Oct. 1808; m. 8 May 1809, Ann Poult on (d. 3 Dec. 1847) and d. 6 April 1811, having had issue, two daus.
2. Arthur Goodall (see below).
1. Maria Barston, b. 20 Oct. 1783; m. 30 Mar. 1807, Rev. John Dene, Rector of Horwood, and d. 6 Dec. 1839.

The second son,
Arthur Goodall Wavell, K.F., K.C.S., F.R.S., of Little Somborne House, near Stockbridge, co. Hants, was a Major Gen., b. 29 Mar. 1785; educ. Winchester; served in the Peninsular War receiving the Cross of Distinction, Mil. Cross of San Fernando and Order of Charles III; he then served in the Independence armies of Chile and Mexico and wrote numerous military works. He m. 1825, Anne (d. 7 Feb. 1882) yst. dau. of Sir William Paxton, of Middleton Hall, co. Carmarthen, and d. 10 July 1860, leaving issue,

1. Arthur Henry, Col. 1880, served in Crimean War 1855-56, in W. Indies 1857-59, E. Indies, 1865-75, and S. Africa, 1879-85; b. 12 June 1836; m. 14 Jan. 1880, Matilda Clara Beatrice (d. 19 June 1918) dau. of Rev. John Byng, and d. 16 Jan. 1891 leaving issue with, two daus. who d. unm.,
   (1) Arthur John Byng, M.C., F.R.G.S.,

   Major the Welsh Regt., served in the S. African War 1900-02, and in World War I, 1914-16, b. 27 May 1882, and k. in action 8 Jan. 1916 at Mwele, Brit. East Africa. He was unm. He was a fluent speaker of French, Italian, Arabic and Swahili and had travelled (in disguise, of course) to Mecca. An account of his exploits is given in Lord Tweedsmuir's book,

The Last Secrets. He described his journey to Mecca, in a book, *A Modern Pilgrim in Mecca*.
   (2) Raymond George who assumed the additional surname and arms of Paxton, b. 2 Feb. 1884; educ. Winchester and Magdalen Coll. Oxford, B.A. 1904; served in Coldstream Guards, 1914-21; m. 14 April 1921, Olive Louise, (d. 23 Oct. 1951) only dau. of Sir Arthur Lawson, 1st Bt., and d. 31 Mar. 1948, leaving issue, Phoebe Louisa, b. 12 May 1925.
   (3) George Augustus, b. 1886, d. 1887.
   (1) Veronica Beatrice, m. 1909, Rear Adm. Roger M. Bellairs, C.B., C.M.G., R.N., of Wyvenhoe, Farnham Royal, Bucks, and had issue,
2. William, of 30 Cambridge Square, Hyde Park, London, bapt. 16 Nov. 1838, educ. Haileybury and St. John's Coll. Camb., and entered the I.C.S., but retired on 31 Dec. 1877, in consequence of damage to his health from a murderous attack by a native. He m. 1881, Florence Darwin Huish, who d. 11 Jan. 1922. She was the granddau. of Erasmus Darwin (see that family in B.L.G. 1952). He d. 21 Nov. 1915, having had issue,
   Frances Gwendoline, b. 1882; m. 1905, Capt. Raymond England, R.A., of Bournemouth and had issue.
3. Llewellyn, of Somborne, Farnborough, co. Hants, b. 15 Nov. 1839, entered the Army 1856, gazetted Ensign in Indian Army and posted to 456th Native Infantry. He served right through the Indian Mutiny in the first European Bengal Fusiliers, and at the siege of Delhi was one of the first officers through the gate when it was blown in. He was described as that "brave boy, Wavell". He served in the battles of Narnone, Gungaree, Outtialee, Mynpoorie and the capture of Lucknow; also in the Chinese War 1860-62, the Afghan War 1879, and was promoted to Col. 1883; m. 24 June 1869, Emily Ann Martha, dau. of John Cooper Cobb, Solicitor, of Congleton, co. Chester. She d. 14 Aug. 1931. He d. 27 Nov. 1910. There is a brass memorial tablet to him in Winchester Cathedral. They had issue, two sons both of whom died as infants.
4. Archibald Graham (see below).
1. Anne Maria, b. 11 April 1829; d. unm. 2 Dec. 1909.
2. Sophia Matilda, b. circa 1831, m. 19 July 1853, Joseph Rusbridger, and d. 13 Oct. 1905 leaving issue.
3. Emily Caroline, b. 10 May 1833; m. 22 June 1859, William Macfarlane, of Notting Hill, and d. 13 Nov. 1903.
4. Laura Anne, b. 13 Nov. 1834; d. unm. 11 September 1882.
5. Mary Frederica, b. circa 1841, m. 3 July 1869, Capt. Frederick Boone, Madras Staff Corps, and d. 1872 in India.
6. Elizabeth Florence Paxton, b. 29 Dec. 1845; m. Feb. 1871, Col. Norton Knatchbull, (Brabourne, B.) and d. 17 May 1923, leaving issue.

The ygst son,
Archibald Graham Wavell, of Little Somborne, Ringwood, co. Hants, Major Gen. in

the Army, C.B., b. 18 Nov. 1843, entered the Army 1863; served in Zulu War 1879, in Tambookie and Basuto Campaigns, 1880-81, promoted Major, Norfolk Regt., (late 9th Foot) and transferred to Royal Highland Regt. (the Black Watch). Lt. Col. 1890, Col. 1895, was A.A.G. for recruiting at the War Office, in 1898, served in S. African War 1899-1900, mentioned in despatches, and awarded C.B. He was Chief of Staff, 3rd Army Corps, at Dublin, 1901-02, ret. 1902 with rank of Major Gen. He m. 7 Nov. 1880 Lillie, dau. of R. N. Percival, of Springfields, Bradwell, co. Chester. She d. 24 June 1926. He d. 2 Mar. 1935. Their children were,

1. Archibald Percival, **Earl Wavell** (see below).
1. Florence Anne Paxton (Nancy) A.R.R.C., b. 10 Mar. 1882.
2. Lillian Mary (Molly), b. 30 June 1884.

The only son,
Sir Archibald Percival Wavell, **1st Earl Wavell**, b. 5 May 1883; educ. Winchester and R.M.C., entered the Army as commissioned in the Black Watch, 8 May 1901; served in S. Africa, 1901-02, (medal with 4 clasps), on Indian Frontier, (medal with clasp), in World War I, 1914-18, (wounded, despatches, M.C.), Palestine, 1937-38, (medal with clasp), and in World War II, 1939-43, Cmdr. 6th Inf. Brig. Aldershot, 1930-34, Cmdr. 2nd Div. Aldershot 1935-37; cmd. troops in Palestine and Trans-jordan, 1937-38; G.O.C.S. Command, 1938-39; C. in C. Middle East 1939-41, in which position he completely defeated the Italians in Libya under Marshal Garziani and took over 133,000 Italian prisoners. Only German intervention, and the necessity of sending part of his forces to Greece, saved the Italian empire in Africa from complete dissolution. In Ethiopia the Italian army was compelled to surrender, and the Emperor of Ethiopia restored to his throne. Wavell was appointed C. in C. India 1941-43, and Supreme Cmdr. S.W. Pacific Area, 1942; [(for a full account of Wavell's life and career the reader is referred to the two vols. by John Connell named, *Wavell, Scholar and Soldier*, (1964) followed by *Wavell, Supreme Commander 1941-43*, which was not completed by Connell, owing to the latter's death (1969) but was edited and completed by Brig. Michael Roberts, D.S.O. In his final despatch on 20 June 1943, Wavell wrote: "This despatch marks the end of my active military career. During the present war, in just under four years, from Sept. 1939 to June 1943, I have directed some 14 campaigns in the Western Desert of North Africa, in British Somaliland, Eritrea, in Italian Somaliland, in Abyssinia, in Greece, in Crete, In Iraq, in Syria, in Iran, in Malaya, in the Dutch East Indies, in Burma, in Arakan. Some have been successful, others have failed." "In this my last despatch I should like to pay a tribute to the British soldier. He has shown himself in this war, as in all others, the finest all-round fighting man in the world. He has won so many victories that he never doubts of victory, he has suffered so many disasters and defeats on his way to victory that defeat seldom depresses him. He has adapted himself to desert and to jungle, to open plains and to mountains, to new foes, new conditions, new weapons with the same courage and humorous endurance of difficulties and dangers which he has always

shown. His staying power is a sure guarantee of final success.")]. Wavell was appointed Viceroy and Gov. Gen. of India 1943-47, and dismissed from that post because of the Labour Gov.'s desire to make a quick hand over in India. He was Constable of the Tower of London, 1948-50. He was cr. C.M.G. 1919, C.B. 1935; K.C.V.O. 1939; G.C.B. 1941; G.C.S.I.; G.C.I.E., was made P.C. and cr. Viscount Wavell of Cyrenaica, and of Winchester, co. Southampton, 20 July 1943, and Earl Wavell, and Viscount Keren, of Eritrea, of Winchester, co. Southampton, 1 May 1947. He held many foreign decorations. He m. 22 April 1915, Eugenie Marie, C.I. 1943. only dau. of Col. J. O. Quirk, C.B., D.S.O., and d. 24 May 1950, having had issue,

1. Archibald John Arthur, **2nd Earl** (see below).
1. Eugenie Pamela, b. 2 Dec. 1918; served in World War II, with B.R.C. and St. J. Amb., Cmdt. V.A.D. 5th Scottish Hosp. Cairo, 1942; m. 14 Mar. 1942, Lt. Col. A. F. W. Humphrys, M.B.E., Central India Horse, and had issue.
2. Felicity Ann, b. 21 July 1921; m. 20 Feb. 1947, Capt. P. M. Longmore, M.C., R.A., son of A/C./M. Sir Arthur Longmore, and had issue.
3. Joan Patricia Quirk, b. 23 April 1923; m. (1) 27 Jan. 1943, Major the Hon. Simon N. Astley, (see Baron Hastings), by whom she had issue. He d. 16 Mar. 1946 at Quetta, as a result of a motor accident. She m. (2) H. A. Gordon, M.C. and had further issue.

The only son,
Archibald John Arthur Wavell, **2nd Earl Wavell**, b. 11 May 1916; educ. Winchester; served in Palestine, 1936-39, (wounded, medal with clasp), and in World War II, 1939-45, (wounded, M.C. 1947), Major the Black Watch; was k. in a Mau Mau skirmish in Africa, 24 Dec. 1953.

ARMS—Azure a chevron between three fleurs-de-lis or, a bordure argent charged with six martlets gules.

CREST—A demi-lion holding between its paws a human heart vulned ppr.

SUPPORTERS—Dexter, A soldier of the Black Watch in field service uniform, supporting with his exterior hand a rifle; Sinister, A scholar of Winchester College in his gown, holding in his exterior hand a closed book, all ppr.

MOTTO—Pro patria.

WAVENEY

PEERAGE—U.K. Baron Waveney, of South Elmham, co. Suffolk.
SURNAME—Adair.
CR.—10 April 1873. **EXT.**—5 Feb. 1886.
HISTORY—Sir Robert Shafto Adair, 1st Bt., so cr. 2 Aug. 1838. (see extant peerages, under Adair, Bt.) had with other issue, an elder son,
Sir Robert Alexander Shafto Adair, 2nd Bt., and **Baron Waveney**, of South Elmham, co. Suffolk, so cr. 10 April 1873. He was b. 25 Aug. 1811; was Lord Lt. of Antrim, Hon. Col. Suffolk Artillery, M.P. for Cambridge, 1847-52, and 1854-57; m. 11 June 1836, Theodosia, dau.

of Gen. Hon. Robert Meade, (Clanwilliam, E.), She d. 10 May 1871. He d. 5 Feb. 1886. The Barony became extinct but he was s. in the baronetcy by his brother, Sir Hugh Edward Adair, 3rd Bt., from whom descend the present baronets (see extant works).

ARMS—Quarterly 1 and 4, Per bend or and argent three dexter hands couped and erect gules (Adair); 2 and 3, Gules on a bend argent three mullets azure (Shafto).

CREST—A man's head affrontée couped at the neck ppr.

SUPPORTERS—Dexter, A knight banneret armed, all ppr., holding banneret of family arms displayed; Sinister, An Irish chief armed, all ppr.

MOTTO—Loyal au mort.

WAVERTREE

PEERAGE—U.K. Baron Wavertree, of Delamere, co. Chester.

SURNAME—Walker.

CR.—27 Oct. 1919. EXT.—2 Feb. 1933.

HISTORY—Sir Andrew Barclay Walker, 1st Bt., of Walker of Gateacre, now Walker-Okeover (see extant peerages and baronetcies, where the representation of the ancient family of Okeover, extinct in the male line after nine centuries of continuous tenure of Okeover, is now vested in the Walker-Okeover Baronets), had issue a third son,

William Hall Walker, **Baron Wavertree**, b. 25 Dec. 1856; Educ. Elstree and Harrow; M.P. for Widnes Div. of S.W. Lancashire, 1900-19; Managing Dir. of Peter Walker & Co., Brewers, served in World War I, Hon. Col. 9th Bn. King's Liverpool Regt.; cr. Baron Wavertree, of Delamere, co. Chester, 27 Oct. 1919; T.D., O. St. J.; m. 29 Sept. 1896, Sophie Florence Lothrop, C.B.E., D. St. G., dau. of Algernon Thomas Brinsley Sheridan, of Frampton Court, Dorset, by Mary Lothrop, dau. of the Hon. John Lothrop Motley, U.S.A. Minister to the Netherlands, and famous historian of the Dutch Republic. Lord Wavertree d.s.p. 2 Feb. 1933. Lady Wavertree m. 2ndly 1947, F. M. B. Fisher, and d. 27 Nov. 1952.

ARMS—Or a saltire ermine charged with a stag's head erased ppr., on a chief azure a garb between two mullets of six points of the field.

CREST—A cornucopia ppr.

SUPPORTERS—Dexter, A horse; Sinister, A stag ppr., each charged on the shoulder with a garb or. both ppr.

MOTTO—Curia et industria.

Lord Wavertree's seats were Sandy Brow, Tarporley, Cheshire, and Horsley Hall, Gresford, co. Denbigh. His town house was Sussex Lodge, Regent's Park, N.W.

WEARDALE

PEERAGE—U.K. Baron Weardale, of Stanhope, co. Durham.

SURNAME—Stanhope.

CR.—10 Jan. 1906. EXT.—1 Mar. 1923.

HISTORY—Philip James Stanhope, fourth son of 5th Earl Stanhope (see Chesterfield

and Stanhope, in present work), b. 8 Dec. 1847; joined R.N. as naval cadet, 1861; retired as Midshipman, 1866; sat as Liberal M.P. for Wednesbury, 1886-92, for Burnley, 1893-1900, and for Harborough Div. of Leicestershire, 1904-05; Pres. of Inter-Parl. Union, 1906; m. 11 May 1877, at St. Petersburgh (Leningrad), Alexandra, widow of Count Tolstoy, and dau. of Count Kankrin, of the Baltic Provinces, by a dau. of Baron Von Stael Holstein, of the Baltic Provinces. He was a great supporter of the Save the Children Fund; was cr. 10 Jan. 1906, **Baron Weardale** of Stanhope, co. Durham. He d.s.p. 1 Mar. 1923. His widow who continued until her death as Vice Pres. of the Save the Children Fund, d. 14 Oct. 1934. His life was written in a short memoir by Edward Fuller (1923).

ARMS—Quarterly ermine and gules a crescent azure for difference.

CREST—Issuant from a tower azure a demi-lion rampant or, holding between the paws a grenade fired ppr.

SUPPORTERS—Dexter, A talbot ermine; Sinister, A lion or, ducally crowned gules, each charged on the shoulder with a mullet issuant from a crescent both azure.

MOTTO—A Deo et rege.

Lord Weardale's seat was Weardale Manor, Brasted Chart, Kent. His town house was 3, Carlton Gardens, Pall Mall, S.W.

WEBB-JOHNSON

PEERAGE—U.K. Baron Webb-Johnson, of Stoke-on-Trent, co. Stafford. (Also a baronetcy cr. 15 Mar. 1945.)

SURNAME—Webb-Johnson.

CR.—22 June 1948. EXT.—28 May 1958.

HISTORY—Robert Johnson of Armagh, b. circa 1756, had issue,

1. Robert. 2. Morgan. 3. James.
4. William. 5. Samuel (see below) and
1. Ann.

The fifth son,

Samuel Johnson, of Armagh, merchant b. 1800; m. 11 Mar. 1841, Rose Anne Canavan, of Armagh, and d. 1878, leaving issue,

1. Samuel (see below).
1. A dau., m. William Slater, of Burslem, Stoke-on-Trent, Art. Director to Doultons, the potters.
2. A dau. m. Alfred Thomas Townley, of Oswaldtwistle, co. Lancs.

The only son,

Samuel Johnson, M.D. 1870, Medical Offr. of Health, Stoke-on-Trent, b. 17 May 1846; educ. Royal Univ. of Ireland; m. 14 Sept. 1876, Julia Anne, dau. of James Webb, Army Agent, of Burslem, Stoke-on-Trent, and of Southwark, London, by his wife Clara Maria Kent, of Wantage, co. Berks, and d. 15 Nov. 1899. She d. 23 Jan. 1931. Their issue were:

1. Cecil, M.B., CH.B. Manchester, b. 9 May 1879; educ. High Sch. Newcastle-under-Lyme, Manchester and London Univs. and London Hosp.; m. 19 June 1929, Babette Tobin and d. leaving issue,
   (1) Rosemary, b. 5 Sept. 1921.
   (2) Myrtle Mary, b. 27 Feb. 1924.
2. Alfred Edward, Sir, Bt. and **Baron Webb-Johnson** (see below).

3. Stanley, b. 1 Mar. 1888; educ. Rossall and Manchester Univ. LL.B.; served in World War I and in World War II with 6th Bn. East Surrey Regt. and on Staff, Col. Delhi Contingent and Simla Rifles; Sen. Prof. Officer Bd. of Trade (Custodian of Enemy Property), Partner in Hasties, Lincoln's Inn, 1912-14; Legal Adviser to Gov. of India, 1920-45; Hon. A.D.C. to Viceroy, 1944-46; Chm. Pensions Appeal Tribunal 1946-49; m. 29 Feb. 1932, Beryl Buchanan, dau. of Steuart Binny of Dale House, Hassocks, co. Sussex, and had issue,
    (1) Steuart Alfred, b. 10 Mar. 1933; educ. Charterhouse and Magdalene Coll. Camb.
    (2) David Cecil, b. 13 April 1939; educ. Charterhouse.
1. Rosa, b. 27 July 1877; d. unm. 18 Aug. 1951.
2. Ethel, b. 8 Sept. 1881.
3. Mabel, b. 26 July 1883.
4. Kathleen, b. 8 Oct. 1884.
5. Norah Millicent, b. 1 Mar. 1888; m. 24 Jan. 1922 Lt. Col. Walter Thyne, I.A. and had issue.
The second son,
Sir Alfred Webb-Johnson, Bt., and **Baron Webb-Johnson,** b. 4 Sept. 1880; assumed by deed poll 20 July 1915, the surname of Webb-Johnson; educ. High Sch. Newcastle-under-Lyme, and Manchester Univ. M.B., Ch. B., 1903; F.R.C.S. Eng. 1906; Surgeon to Queen Mary from 1936; Vice Pres. and Cons. Surgeon Middlesex Hosp., Pres. Epsom Coll. and Royal Medical Benevolent Fund; Pres. Royal Coll. of Surgeons, (Eng.), 1941-49; and of Royal Soc. of Medicine, 1950-52; Chm. Army Medical Advisory Board, Col. R.A.M.C. (T.A.), served in World War I, 1914-19, (D.S.O., and despatches three times), Hunterian Prof. at Royal Coll. of Surgeons 1917; mem. Court of Examiners and Council of R.C.S.; Examiner in Surgery, Camb. Univ.; mem. Advisory Council of B.B.C.; m. 23 Nov. 1911, Cecilia Flora, C. St. J., and H. St. J., dau. of D. G. MacRae, of Norbiton, Surrey, founder of the *Financial Times.* He was K.J. St. J., cr. C.B.E. 1919, Kt. Bach. 1936; K.C.V.O. 1942, a baronet 15 Mar. 1945, and a peer as Baron Webb-Johnson, of Stoke-on-Trent, co. Stafford, 22 June 1948. He d. 28 May 1958.
ARMS—(Heralds' Coll. 1917) Argent on a fess between in chief a stag's head cabossed gules and in base an anchor azure a winged spur or between a lion couchant guardant and a serpent nowed ppr.
SUPPORTERS—Dexter, A figure habited in the robes of a Fellow of the Royal College of Surgeons; Sinister, A figure habited in the robes of a Knight of Justice of the Order of St. John of Jerusalem, both ppr.
MOTTO—Nunquam non paratus.

WEEKS

PEERAGE—U.K. Baron Weeks of Ryton, co. Palatine of Durham.
SURNAME—Weeks.
CR.—31 May 1956. EXT.—19 Aug. 1960.

HISTORY—Richard Morce Weeks, of Ryton, co. Durham, b. 7 Feb. 1811; m. Fanny Elizabeth. (d. 1898) dau. of John Nicholson, and d. 14 Feb. 1896, leaving issue three sons and four daus. (For one of these—John George Weeks there is a short account in 1952 B.L.G. Weeks of Thirston House). The third son,
Richard Llewellyn Weeks, of Riding Mill, co. Northumberland, b. 22 Nov. 1856; m. Susan Helen Walker, dau. of John McIntyre, and d. 1 April 1937, leaving issue, two sons and three daus. The second son,
Sir Ronald Morce Weeks, K.C.B., **Baron Weeks,** of Ryton, co. Pal. of Durham, b. 13 Nov. 1890; educ. Charterhouse and Gonville and Caius Coll. Camb. B.A. 1912, Hon. Fell. 1946; served in World War I 1914-18, with S. Lancs. Regt., and Rifle Brigade, (despatches three times, D.S.O. 1918, M.C. with Bar, and Croix de Guerre), and in World War II, 1939-45, Cmdr. Legion of Merit, U.S.A., Lt. Gen., Dir. Gen. of Army Equipment 1941-42, Dep. Chief of Imperial Gen. Staff, 1942-45, Dep. Mil. Gov. of Germany and Chief of Staff, British Zone, Control Commission for Germany 1945; Chm. Vickers Nuclear Engineering Ltd., and Finance Corp. for Industry Ltd., Dir. of many other companies; m. (1) (m. diss. by div. 1930) 21 April 1922, Evelyn Elsie, dau. of Henry Haynes, of Clifton, co. Nottingham; m. (2) 3 Feb. 1931, Cynthia Mary, dau. of J. W. Irvine, of Liverpool, and d. 19 Aug. 1960, having had issue,
1. Pamela Rose, b. 9 Nov. 1931; m. 6 April 1957, Lt. Cmdr. H. W. Plunkett-Ernle-Erle-Drax, R.N., (Dunsany, B.) and had issue.
2. Venetia Daphne, b. 29 Aug. 1933; m. 10 April 1954, Lt. Cmdr. Peter Troubridge, R.N., (Troubridge, Bt.) and had issue.
Lord Weeks, was cr. C.B.E. (mil) 1939, K.C.B. (mil) 1943, and Baron Weeks of, Ryton, co. Palatine of Durham, 31 May 1956.
ARMS—Sable in front of a miner's pick ppr. two battle-axes in saltire argent, on a chief or three annulets gules.
CREST—In front of a cubit arm grasping a scimitar ppr., pomel and hilt or, three annulets interlaced gold.
SUPPORTERS—Dexter, An eagle wings inverted and addorsed azure, the neck gorged with a mural crown and chained argent and standing with the dexter foot upon a drum and crossed drumsticks ppr.; Sinister, A lion or, the mane and tail azure, the neck gorged with a collar of steel ppr.
MOTTO—Praesto et persto.

WELBY

PEERAGE—U.K. Baron Welby, of Allington, co. Lincoln.
SURNAME—Welby.
CR.—16 April 1894. EXT.—29 Oct. 1915.
HISTORY—The Rev. John Earle Welby, 2nd son of Sir William Earle Welby, 1st Bt. (see extant peerages and baronetcies, Welby, Bt.), had with other issue, a fifth son,
Reginald Earle Welby, **Baron Welby,** of Allington, co. Lincoln, b. 3 Aug. 1832; educ. Eton and Trin. Coll. Camb., B.A. 1855; apptd. to Treasury, 1856, Priv. Sec. to Financial Sec.

1859-71; Princ. Clerk, Finance Dept., 1871-80; Asst. Fin. Sec. 1880-85, Perm. Sec. 1885-94, Chm. of L.C.C. 1899-1900; cr. C.B., 1874; K.C.B. 1882, G.C.B. 1892; P.C. 1913; cr. Baron Welby, of Allington, co. Lincoln 16 April 1894; d. unm. 29 Oct. 1915.

ARMS—Sable a fess between three fleurs-de-lis argent.

CREST—A cubit arm in armour issuing from clouds holding a sword over flames of fire all ppr.

SUPPORTERS—On either side a wolf regardant sable semée of fleurs-de-lis argent.

MOTTO—Per ignem per gladium.

WENLOCK

PEERAGE—U.K. Baron Wenlock, of Wenlock, co. Salop, cr. 10 Sept. 1831. Ext. 10 April 1834.
U.K. Baron Wenlock, of Wenlock, co. Salop, cr. 13 May 1839. Ext. 14 June 1932.
(Also a baronetcy cr. 16 Aug. 1641.)

SURNAME—Lawley.

CR.—As above. **EXT.**—As above.

HISTORY—Thomas Lawley, of Wenlock, co. Salop, s. to that estate on the death of his cousin, John Wenlock, Baron Wenlock, at the battle of Tewkesbury, 4 May 1471. The latter had been made Baron Wenlock, of Wenlock, co. Salop in 1461, but the barony became extinct at his death (see 1883 Extinct Peerage). Thomas Lawley is therein described as heir general to Baron Wenlock. The son and heir of the last named Thomas Lawley was, Edward Lawley, of Wenlock, whose son and heir was,

John Lawley, of Wenlock, who by his wife, Mary, dau. of Thomas Cressett, of Upton, had issue two sons, Thomas, of Wenlock, whose issue d. out in male line, and a ygr. son,

Richard Lawley, of Spoonhill, co. Salop, m. 1546 Barbara, dau. and heir of Edmund Rudgeley, and had issue, with three daus., an only son,

Francis Lawley, of Spoonhill, who m. Elizabeth, dau. and heir of Sir Richard Newport, of High Ercall, and by her (who m. 2ndly Sir Thomas Lawley, son of Thomas of Wenlock mentioned above), had with other issue, a second son,

Sir Thomas Lawley, **1st Bt.**, of Spoonhill, Salop, M.P. for Wenlock, 1625-26, and 1628-29, who was cr. a baronet 16 Aug. 1641; m. Anne, dau. and coheir of John Manning, and d. 19 Oct. 1646, having by her (who m. 2ndly Sir John Glynne) with other issue, an elder son,

Sir Francis Lawley, **2nd Bt.**, M.P. Wenlock, m. 1650, Anne, dau. of Sir Thomas Whitmore, 1st Bt., and d. Oct. 1696, leaving issue,
1. Thomas, **3rd Bt.** (see below).
2. Francis, d. unm.
3. Richard, of Ealing, d.s.p.
1. Mary, m. John Verney, 1st Viscount Fermanagh (1883 Extinct Peerages).
2. Esther, m. Robert Palmer, 2nd son of Sir Lewis Palmer, Bt.
3. Margaret m. (1) Leonard Powell, son of Sir Nathaniel Powell, Bt., and (2) Sir Nathan Wright, Bt.
The eldest son,
Sir Thomas Lawley, **3rd Bt.**, M.P. Wenlock,

m. (1) Rebecca, dau. of Sir Humphrey Winch, Bt. and by her had surv. issue,
1. Robert, **4th Bt.** (see below).
1. Anne, m. Sir John Cheshire.
2. Elizabeth m. (1) Thomas Coton, of Coton, co. Warwick, and (2) Sir Nicholas Laws.
He m. (2) 3 Mar. 1711-12, Elizabeth Perkins, widow, and d. 30 Sept. 1729, having by her had issue with a dau.,
2. George Bateman, m. 1738, Mary Tomlinson.
The eldest son,
Sir Robert Lawley, **4th Bt.**, m. 1726, Elizabeth, dau. of Sir Lambert Blackwell, 1st Bt., and d. 28 Nov. 1779, having by her (d. 21 Mar. 1774) had issue with two daus., an only son,
Sir Robert Lawley, **5th Bt.**, M.P. Warwickshire, m. Jane, only dau. and eventual heir of Beilby Thompson, of Escrick, co. York, (who d. Nov. 1816), and by her had issue, with four daus.,
1. Robert, **6th Bt.** and **Baron Wenlock** of the 1831 creation (see below).
2. Francis, **7th Bt.** (see below).
3. Paul Beilby, **8th Bt.**, and **1st Baron Wenlock** of the 1839 creation (see below).
Sir Robert, 5th Bt., d. 11 Mar. 1793, being s. by his eldest son,
Sir Robert Lawley, **6th Bt.**, and only **Baron Wenlock**, so cr. 10 Sept. 1831, m. 16 Sept. 1793, Anna Maria, dau. of Joseph Denison, of Denbies, co. Surrey, who d. 20 Aug. 1850. Lord Wenlock d.s.p. 10 April 1834, when his barony became extinct and he was s. as baronet by his ygr. brother,
Sir Francis Lawley, **7th Bt.**, M.P. co. Warwick, m. 18 May 1815, Mary Anne, eldest dau. and coheir of George Talbot, of Temple Guiting, co. Gloucester, who d. 21 Dec. 1878. He d.s.p. 30 Jan. 1851, when he was s. by his brother as baronet,
Sir Paul Beilby Lawley-Thompson, **8th Bt.**, who had been cr. **Baron Wenlock**, of Wenlock, co. Salop 13 May 1839. He obtained by Royal Licence permission to take the name and arms of Thompson 27 Sept. 1820, and again to take the name of Lawley before that of Thompson, 1 June 1839, and the arms of Thompson and Lawley quarterly and his issue to take the name and arms of Lawley only. He m. 10 May 1817, Hon. Caroline Neville, (d. 2 May 1868) dau. of 2nd Lord Braybrooke, and d. 9 May 1852, having had issue,
1. Beilby Richard, **2nd Baron Wenlock** (see below).
2. Robert Neville, b. 30 Aug. 1819; m. 10 Nov. 1852, Georgiana Emily, dau. of Gen. Lord Edward Somerset, (Beaufort, D.), and d.s.p. 1 Nov. 1891.
3. Stephen Willoughby, Rev., M.A. Oxford, b. 4 April 1823; d. unm. 23 Oct. 1905.
4. Francis Charles, Fell. of All Souls, Oxford, M.P. Beverley, 1852-53; b. 24 May 1825; m. 18 Dec. 1869, Henrietta Louisa Amelia, dau. of Rev. F. A. Zaiser, chaplain to King of Saxony, and d.s.p. 18 Sept. 1901.
1. Jane, m. 6 May 1846 Rt. Hon. James Stuart Wortley (Wharncliffe, E.), and d. 4 Feb. 1900.
The eldest son,
Sir Beilby Richard Lawley, **9th Bt.**, and **2nd Baron Wenlock**, b. 21 April 1818; m. m. 28 Nov. 1846, Lady Elizabeth Grosvenor,

dau. of 2nd Marquess of Westminster. She d. 16 Dec. 1899. He d. 6 Nov. 1880, having had issue,

1. Beilby, **3rd Baron Wenlock** (see below).
2. Richard Thompson, **4th Baron** (see below).
3. Algernon George, **5th Baron** (see below).
4. Arthur, **6th Baron** (see below).
5. Robert, b. 5 July 1863; m. 2 July 1924, Agnes, dau. of Rev. David Balsillie, and d. 18 Sept. 1924.

1. Caroline Elizabeth, M.B.E., m. 21 April 1870, Lt. Col. the Hon. Caryl Craven Molyneux, and d. 13 July 1934 (Sefton, E.).
2. Alethea Jane, m. 12 April 1890, Cavaliere Professore Taddeo Wiel, of Venice, and d. 13 April 1929.
3. Constance Mary, m. (1) 19 June 1877, Capt. the Hon. Eustace Vesey who d. 18 Nov. 1886 (De Vesci, V.). She m. (2) 7 July 1892, Hon. E. B. Portman, (Portman, V.).
4. Katharine, m. 28 April 1885, W. F. Forbes.

The eldest son,
Sir Beilby Lawley, **10th Bt.**, and **3rd Baron Wenlock**, P.C., G.C.S.I., G.C.I.E., K.C.B., Major Yorkshire Hussars, V.D., Gov. of Madras, 1891-95; a lord of the bedchamber to King George V when Prince of Wales, 1901-10, b. 12 May 1849; educ. Camb. Univ. B.A.; m. 14 May 1872, Lady Constance Mary Lascelles, C.I. dau. of 4th Earl of Harewood. She d. 23 Aug. 1932. He d. 15 Jan. 1912. They had issue, Irene Constance, D.G. St. J. b. 7 May 1889; m. 3 Dec. 1920, C. G. F. Adam, (Adam, Bt.), and had issue. The 3rd Baron Wenlock was s. by his brother,
Sir Richard Thompson, **11th Bt.**, and **4th Baron Wenlock**, C.B., Brev. Lt. Col. 7th Hussars, mil. sec. to Gov. of Madras, 1891-96, b. 21 Aug. 1856; m. 31 July 1909, Rhoda Edith, dau. of Rev. Canon W. J. Knox-Little, and d. 25 July 1918, being s. by his brother,
The Rev. Sir Algernon George Lawley, **12th Bt.**, and **5th Baron Wenlock**, M.A. Trin. Coll. Camb., Preb. of St. Paul's 1907-23, and Vicar of St. Peter's, Eaton Square, 1913-16, b. 25 Dec. 1857; m. 16 July 1896, May Ethel, (d. 12 Sept. 1934), dau. of Sir Stuart Alexander Donaldson, and d.s.p. 14 June 1921, being s. by his brother,
Sir Arthur Lawley, **13th Bt.**, and **6th Baron Wenlock**, G.C.S.I., G.C.I.E., K.C.M.G., administrator of Matabeleland, 1898-1901, Gov. of Western Australia, 1901-02, Lt. Gov. of the Transvaal 1902-05, and Gov. of Madras, 1905-11, K.J. St. J., b. 12 Nov. 1860; m. 15 Oct. 1885, Annie Ellen, G.B.E., D.G. St. J., dau. of Sir Edward Cunard 2nd Bt., and d.s.p.m.s. 14 June 1932, had issue,

1. Richard Edwin, b. 9 May 1887; d. unm. 4 Sept. 1909.

1. Ursula Mary, b. 8 June 1888; m. 21 July 1927, 1st Baron Wraxall and had issue.
2. Margaret Cecilia, b. 15 June 1889; m. 14 June 1919, Geoffrey Dawson, of Langcliffe Hall, Settle, and 23 Sussex Place, Regent's Park, editor of *The Times*, son of George Robinson, of Skipton-in-Craven, co. York, (Geoffrey Robinson changed his surname by Royal Licence, 3 July 1917 to that of Dawson; see B.L.G. 1952, Dawson of Langcliffe Hall).

ARMS—Argent a cross formée throughout, chequy sable and or.
CREST—A wolf statant sable.
SUPPORTERS—On either side a wolf sable gorged with a plain collar or, pendent therefrôm an escutcheon argent, charged with a chevron of the first, between three Moors' heads affrontée ppr.
MOTTO—Je veux de bonne guerre.
Lord Wenlock's seat was Monkhopton House, Bridgnorth, Salop.

WESTER WEMYSS

PEERAGE—U.K. Baron Wester Wemyss of Wemyss, co. Fife.
SURNAME—Wemyss.
CR.—18 Nov. 1919. **EXT.**—24 May 1933.
HISTORY—James Hay Erskine Wemyss, of Wemyss Castle, co. Fife, (see extant peerages, Wemyss and March, E.) had issue, a third son,
Rosslyn Erskine Wemyss, **Baron Wester Wemyss**, b. 12 April 1864; educ. Farnborough Sch; R.N. 1877; Lt. 1897; Cmdr. 1898; Capt. 1901; cmd. R.N.C. Osborne, 1903, and Dartmouth, 1905; Commodore of the R.N. Barracks, Devonport, 1909-11; Rear Adm. Second Battle Squadron, 1912-13, and 3rd Fleet, 1914; served in World War I, in the Gallipoli landings, 1915, and in charge of naval withdrawal from Suvla Bay and Anzac; Vice Adm. 1916; C. in C. Egypt and East Indies, 1916-17; Sea Lord of the Admiralty, 1917; first Sea Lord, and Chief of Naval Staff, 1917-19; Adm. and Adm. of the Fleet, 1919; he was cr. C.M.G. 1911; K.C.B. 1916; G.C.B. 1918; Baron Wester Wemyss, of Wemyss, co. Fife, 18 Nov. 1919, and had numerous foreign orders. He m. 21 Dec. 1903, Victoria, dau. of Rt. Hon. Sir Robert Burnett David Morier, P.C., G.C.B. and d.s.p.m. 24 May 1933. She d. 22 April 1945. They had issue,
Alice Elizabeth Millicent, Docteur ès Lettres of Toulouse who m. 11 Feb. 1953, Major F. H. Cunack,
ARMS—1 and 4, Or a lion rampant gules (Wemyss); 2 and 3, Argent a lion rampant sable (Giles); in the centre of the quarter a mullet of the second for difference.
CREST—A swan ppr.
SUPPORTERS—Dexter, A swan; Sinister, A sea lion, both ppr.
Lord Wester Wemyss wrote in 1924 *The Navy in the Dardanelles Campaign*, and his *Life* was written by his wife, pub. in 1935.

**WESTMEATH

PEERAGE—U.K. Marquess of Westmeath.
SURNAME—Nugent.
CR.—12 Jan. 1822. **EXT.**—5 May 1871.
HISTORY—George Thomas John Nugent, 8th Earl of Westmeath, b. 17 July 1785; a Representative Peer for Ireland, who was cr. 12 Jan. 1822, as **Marquess of Westmeath** with remainder to the heirs male of his body. He was m. three times, the second marriage being terminated by divorce, but he had no male issue, his only surv. child being, Lady Rosa Emily Mary Anne, who in 1840 m. the 1st

Baron Greville of Clonyn and had issue, (see extant peerages). The Marquess d.s.p.m. 5 May 1871, when the Marquessate became extinct but he was s. in the Earldom of Westmeath by his kinsman, Anthony Francis Nugent, Lord Riverston of Pallas, co. Galway, who then became 9th Earl of Westmeath. (see extant peerages, Westmeath, E.).

WHITBURGH

PEERAGE—U.K. Baron Whitburgh of Whitburgh, co. Midlothian.
SURNAME—Borthwick.
CR.—10 Dec. 1912. EXT.—29 Sept. 1967.
HISTORY—Sir Thomas Borthwick, 1st Bt., so created 21 July 1908 was to have been made a peer, this having been announced on 14 June 1912, but he d. 31 July 1912. King George V ordained 8 Feb. 1913 that Dame Letitia Mary Borthwick should enjoy the same style and title as if her husband had lived to hold the title and dignity of Baron Whitburgh. She was therefore termed, Lady Whitburgh (d. 1935), but the same royal ordinance did not thereby confer upon her any of the rights or privileges, or the precedence belonging by statute or common law to the widow of a peer. In the *London Gazette*, 28 Mar. 1913 it was stated that the yr. children of Sir Thomas Borthwick should have hold and enjoy the same title, place and precedence, as if their father had survived to be made a baron. The name of Sir Thomas's third son, William which was accidentally omitted from the declaration in the *Gazette*, was later added. In the meantime on 10 Dec. 1912 a barony was conferred on Sir Thomas Borthwick's eldest son, who had s. to his baronetcy and thus became,
Sir Thomas Banks Borthwick, 2nd Bt. and **Baron Whitburgh** of Whitburgh, co. Midlothian, b. 21 Aug. 1874; d. Sept. 29 1967 when the peerage became extinct but the baronetcy was inherited by his nephew, Sir John Thomas Borthwick, M.B.E., 3rd Bt. (see extant Peerage and Baronetage).
ARMS—Argent a cinquefoil sable on a chief invected sable two cinquefoils argent.
CREST—A staff raguly fesswise sable thereon a blackamoor's head in profile couped ppr.
SUPPORTERS—On either side an angel ppr. wings elevated argent vested gules supporting with the exterior hand a shepherd's crook or.
MOTTO—Qui conducit.

WILLIAMS

PEERAGE—U.K. Baron Williams of Ynyshir, co. Glamorgan.
SURNAME—Williams.
CR.—24 June 1948. EXT.—18 Feb. 1966.
HISTORY—William Williams, of Ynyshir, co. Glamorgan was father of,
Thomas Edward Williams, **Baron Williams,** b. 26 July 1892; educ. Secondary Schs. and Ruskin Coll. mem. Woolwich Borough Council, of L.C.C. and of the Nat. Executive of Labour Party; Chm. Co-op, Wholesale Soc. Ltd., and Pres. Co-op Congress, 1952-53; Commissioner Crown Estate; was made Cmdr. of the Order of Dannebrog of Denmark and

created Baron Williams of Ynyshir, co. Glamorgan, 24 June 1948. He m. 14 May 1921, Lavinia Mary, dau. of Charles Northam of Plumstead, S.E.18, and d. 18 Feb. 1966, having had issue, a dau., Gweneth Mary, b. 22 June 1927, m. (1) Hugh Sharp Eadie (m. diss. by div.) and (2) Dr. Donald Walter Alexander Brown of Windygates, Fife. Lord Williams lived at 35 Foxes Dale, Blackheath, S.E.3.

WILLIAMS OF BARNBURGH

PEERAGE—U.K. Life. Baron Williams of Barnburgh, of Barnburgh, W. Riding, co. York.
SURNAME—Williams.
CR.—2 Feb. 1961. EXT.—29 Mar. 1967.
HISTORY—James Williams of Wath, co. Yorks, m. Mary Ann Parton. She d. 1924. He d. 1913. Their son was,
Thomas Williams, **Baron Williams** of Barnburgh, b. 18 Mar. 1888; educ. Elementary sch., Swinton; a coal miner; M.P. Don. Div. Yorks, 1922-59; Min. of Agric. & Fisheries 1945-51; mem. Political Honours Scrutiny Cttee. 1961; made P.C. 1941 and cr. a life peer as Baron Williams of Barnburgh of Barnburgh, W. Riding co. Yorks 2 Feb. 1961. He m. 7 Sept. 1910, Elizabeth Ann, dau. of Thomas Andrews of Mexborough, co. Yorks, and d. 29 Mar. 1967, having had issue,
Horace, b. 3 Dec. 1914; m. (1) 5 April 1941 (m. diss. by div. 1947). Mary Joyce only child of Herbert Stanley Morrison, Baron Morrison of Lambeth (see that title) and (2) 1952, Margaret Dick Chisholm, dau. of William Green and had issue.
Doris, b. 20 April 1916; m. 1939 R. J. Lee and had issue.

WILMOT OF SELMESTON

PEERAGE—U.K. Baron Wilmot of Selmeston, co. Sussex.
SURNAME—Wilmot.
CR.—30 Jan. 1950. EXT.—22 July 1964.
HISTORY—Charles Wilmot, an engraver, was father of,
John Wilmot, **Baron Wilmot** of Selmeston, b. 2 April 1895, served in World War I in R.N.A.S.; mem. Inst of Bankers, Gilbert Prizeman in Banking, a writer on banking and finance, Chm. Illingworth Morris & Co. Ltd., and other cos., M.P. for East Fulham, 1933-35, winning the seat at a by-election, this being the famous and spectacular Labour gain of a seat considered safely Conservative, a result said to have adversely influenced the Cons. Gov.'s attitude towards re-armament. He was later M.P. for Kennington Div. of Lambeth, 1939-45, and for Deptford, 1945-50; held several ministerial appts., being Min. of Supply, 1945-47 and served on various committees, Chm. of Govs, of Old Vic., and mem. Nat. Theatre Council. He was made P.C. 1945 and Baron Wilmot of Selmeston, of Selmeston, co. Sussex, 30 Jan. 1950. His residence was Cobb Court, Selmeston. He d. 22 July 1964.
ARMS—Argent on a fesse gules between three eagles' heads erased sable, a unicorn couchant between two roses or.

CREST—A demi lion guardant sable semée of plates holding in the paws a battle axe argent. SUPPORTERS—Dexter, A unicorn gules armed crined and unguled or; Sinister, A panther sable semée of plates and incensed ppr., both gorged with a collar composed of alternate roses and escallops gold.

WINMARLEIGH

PEERAGE—U.K. Baron Winmarleigh, of Winmarleigh, co. Lancaster.
SURNAME—Patten, sometimes Wilson Patten (no hyphen—see below).
CR.—16 Mar. 1874. EXT.—11 July 1892.
HISTORY—This family of Patten was living in Lancashire for several centuries. In the *Victoria History of Lancashire* Vol. iii. p. 321, it is mentioned that the surname of Patten occurs as far back as a survey of 1465. Thomas and John Patten are entered in an assessment of 1649. A pedigree recorded by Thomas Patten in 1665 at the age of 28 is headed by Richard Patten of Wainfleet. Mary, the dau. of Thomas Patten in 1698 m. Thomas Wilson (1663-1755) who was apptd. Bishop of Sodor and Man in 1697. Of him it has been written: "He administered his hitherto neglected diocese with great devotion for nearly 60 years and contributed much to its material and spiritual well being by founding public libraries, providing a Manx translation of the Bible, and writing himself a Manx Catechism (1707)." (*Chambers Encyclopedia*, 1964, Thomas Wilson). His works, with a life written by John Keble, form 7 vols. in the *Library of Anglo-Catholic Theology*, 1847-63. A Theological Coll. in Man named after him was closed in 1943. Dr. Wilson left his estates (ultimately) to the Pattens, on condition that they should bear the surname of Wilson. Mary Wilson's brother,
Thomas Patten was a prosperous merchant, who deepened the channel of the Mersey. His son,
Thomas Patten, of Bank Hall, Warrington, which he built in 1705 with slag from his copper works cast into the shape of bricks, and which was bought in 1872 by Warrington Town Council and is now the Warrington Town Hall, also acquired the lordship of Winmarleigh. He d. 1772, being s. by his son,
Thomas Patten, High Sheriff, 1773, Lancashire, who m. a dau. of Peter Bold, of Bold. One of their sons, Peter Patten Bold (formerly Patten) left four daus. as coheirs and the Patten estates went on the death of Thomas Patten in 1806 to the third son,
Thomas Wilson Patten, of Bank Hall, who changed his surname to Wilson in accordance with the will of his cousin, Dr. Thomas Wilson D.D., (1703-84, son of Bishop Wilson, see above, and a chaplain to George II), from whom he inherited Woodchurch and other properties in the Wirral, Cheshire in 1800. When his son came of age in 1823 he was able to resume his surname of Patten, calling himself Wilson Patten without loss of these estates. (On the changes of name circa 1800 and 1823, Robert Pierpoint in *Notes and Queries*, 11th Ser., Vol. i, pp. 23-24 wrote that there was no hyphen between Wilson and Patten in M.I. in the old parish church at

Warrington). He m. Elizabeth, dau. of Nathan Hyde, of Ardwick, co. Lancs., and d. 7 Dec. 1827, having had issue,
1. Thomas Patten Wilson, who d. unm. 28 Oct. 1819, at Naples, aged 18.
2. John Wilson Patten, (after 1823 Wilson), **Baron Winmarleigh** (see below).
The second and surv. son,
John Wilson Patten (after 1823 Wilson), **Baron Winmarleigh**, b. 26 April 1802; educ. Eton and Magdalen, Coll. Oxford; M.P. for Lancs 1830-31 and for North Lancs 1832-74; Chm. of Cttees in House of Commons 1852-53; served in 3rd R. Lancs Mil., Col. 1842, cmd. Regt. at Gibralter 1854; Militia A.D.C. to Queen Victoria, 1857-1892; Chan. Duchy of Lancaster, 1867-68; P.C. 1867; Chief Sec. for Ireland, Sept.-Dec. 1868. P.C. Ireland 1868. He was cr. 16 Mar. 1874 Baron Winmarleigh, of Winmarleigh, co. Lancaster (this estate in Garstang had been bought by his great-grandfather, Thomas Patten in 1744, see above). Lord Winmarleigh built Winmarleigh House in 1871, and sold Bank House in 1872. He was Constable of Lancaster Castle, 1879-92. He m. 15 April 1828, Anna Maria, fourth and ygst. dau. and coheir of his paternal uncle Peter Patten Bold, formerly Patten of Bank Hall, and of Bold, co. Lancaster, by Mary, dau. of the Rev. John Parker, of Astle, co. Chester. She d. 4 Aug. 1846, and was bur. in the Patten chapel at Warrington. Lord Winmarleigh d.s.p.m.s. 11 July 1892. There is a marble bust of him in Warrington Museum and a life sized recumbent marble figure in the Patten chapel. His children were:
1. Eustace John Wilson Patten, b. 8 Feb. 1836; educ. Eton; served in 1st Life Guards, Cornet and Sub. Lt. 1855; Lt. 1857; Capt. 1863-69. He m. 12 Aug. 1863, Emily Constantia, 1st dau. of the Rev. Lord John Thynne, (Bath, M.) and d.v.p. 17 Dec. 1873. (She m. 2ndly, as his second wife, 29 Nov. 1875, Thomas Taylour, 3rd Marquess of Headfort. She had issue, by first marriage,
John Alfred Wilson Patten, b. 24 Oct. 1867; Lt. 1st Life Guards; d. unm. of typhoid fever, 20 Nov. 1889.
2. Arthur Wilson Patten, b. 4 Jan. 1840; educ. Eton; 2nd Lt. the Rifle Brigade, 1858; Lt. 1861; d. unm. 2 Jan. 1866 in Quebec, Canada.
ARMS—(The shields of both Wilson and Patten are illustrated in the *Victoria County History of Lancashire*, vol. vii, p.30 with two differences in the description, from the following, namely under Patten lozengy instead of fusilly, and under Wilson, salient instead of rampant). The following is taken from the *General Armory:*
Quarterly 1 and 4, Fusilly ermine and sable a canton gules (Patten); 2 and 3, Sable a wolf rampant or, in chief three estoiles of the second (Wilson).
CRESTS—(1) A griffin's head erased vert beaked or (Patten); (2) A demi-wolf rampant or (Wilson).
SUPPORTERS—Dexter, A griffin vert, beaked or, charged on the shoulder with a lozenge ermine; Sinister, A wolf or, charged on the shoulder with an estoile sable.
MOTTOES—Nulla pallescere culpa (Patten). Virtus ad sidera tollit (Wilson).

WINSTER

PEERAGE—U.K. Baron Winster, of Wither-slack, co. Westmorland.
SURNAME—Fletcher.
CR.—4 Feb. 1942. EXT.—7 June 1961.
HISTORY—William Fletcher, of Beckside, Cartmel, co. Lancaster, m. 10 Feb. 1715 Mary Dawson, of Hardcragg, Cartmel. She d. Mar. 1761. He d. 3 Aug. 1732. Their issue was (with a ygr. son William, b. 4 June 1721, and two daus., Isabel, b. 23 April 1718, and Mary, b. 16 July 1727) an elder son,
The Rev. John Fletcher, Curate of Lindale-in-Cartmel (a living endowed by Benjamin Fletcher in 1706 with a parsonage which stood on the Winster Moss), b. 6 Jan. 1716; m. 31 Mar. 1755, Dorothy (d. 6 May 1787), dau. of Richard Goad, of Grange-in-Cartmel, and of his wife, Alice Barrow of Kent's Bank, Cartmel, and d. 5 Sept. 1786, leaving issue the following, of whom two sons d. abroad of yellow fever,
1. William, bapt. 2 June 1756.
2. John (see below).
3. James, of Blackburn, bapt. 24 Jan. 1770; m. 11 Aug. 1800, Jane Boothman, and had issue,
   (1) John, of Hull, Rev., b. 11 Mar. 1801; m. 20 May 1822, Margaret Pilling.
   (2) James, b. 8 Dec. 1802; d. 12 Sept. 1805.
   (3) James, b. 28 July 1806; m. Miss Ripon.
   (1) Dorothy Goad, b. 10 June 1804; d. 21 Sept. 1805.
   (2) Dorothy Goad, b. 12 May 1810; m. E. Wilson, of Turn Side, Crosth-waite, co. Westmorland, and d. 13 Nov. 1890, leaving issue.
4. Richard Goad, bapt. 19 May 1744.
5. Thomas, bapt. 7 June 1766.
1. Elizabeth, bapt. 2 Aug. 1758.
2. Mary, bapt. 8 Feb. 1765; d. unm. 6 July 1791.
3. Dorothy, bapt. 17 Jan. 1722; d. unm. 29 Nov. 1792.
The second son,
The Rev. John Fletcher, Incumbent of Kirkby Kendal, bapt. 2 Oct. 1776; m. Miss Turner, and d. 20 Feb. 1797, leaving by her (who m. 2ndly an Army officer and d. in Egypt) an only child,
Mary Fletcher, m. Nicholas Hollywell, of Kay Moss, Witherslack, co. Westmorland, and had issue,
Joseph Fletcher, of Kay Moss, Witherslack, b. 30 Nov. 1811, assumed the surname of Fletcher in lieu of Hollywell; m. 26 Jan. 1835, Jane (d. 10 Mar. 1902) dau. of John Barker, and of Ellen, his 2nd wife, dau. of John Barnish, and d. 17 Aug. 1883, having had issue,
1. John, of Broughton House, Cartmel, b. 26 Dec. 1836; m. July 1872, Elizabeth Margaret Clarke, and d. 30 Sept. 1903, leaving issue, Annie, d. unm. 23 Nov. 1941.
2. Joseph, b. 19 Feb. 1839; d. 12 Sept. 1844.
3. Nicholas (see below)
1. Mary Jane, b. 25 Aug. 1841; d. 14 May 1842.
2. Mary Jane, b. 7 Mar. 1843; d. 13 Nov. 1844.
3. Ellen, b. 20 Sept. 1845; d. unm. 30 Dec. 1878.

4. Mary, b. 10 Feb. 1852; d. unm. 25 May 1902.
The third son,
Nicholas Fletcher, of Rampholme, Winder-mere, B.A. Peterhouse, Camb. (24th Wrangler, 1873) for many years Prof. of Mathematics at R.N.C. Greenwich, b. 20 Feb. 1848; m. 30 Jan. 1879, Dinah, dau. of James Wright, of Warwick, and d. 18 July 1905. She d. 1912. They had issue,
1. Robert d. an infant.
2. Reginald Thomas Herbert, **Baron Winster** (see below).
1. Lucy Mary Margaret, m. A. J. Magoris, and d. in Colombo, 1910.
2. Ella Mary Josephine, m. Haden Watkins, who d. in Korea, 1937.
The second son
Sir Reginald Thomas Herbert Fletcher, **Baron Winster**, b. 27 Mar. 1885; educ. privately and Shirley House, Blackheath; served in World War I, 1914-18; Lt. Cmdr. R.N., and in World War II; M.P. Basingstoke Div. of Hampshire, 1923-24, and Nuneaton Div. co. Warwick, 1935-41; Parl. Priv. Sec. to First Lord of the Admiralty, 1940-41; Min. of Civil Aviation, 1945-46; Gov. of Cyprus 1946-49; author of *The War on Our Doorstep*, and jt. author of *The Air Defences of Great Britain;* cr. Baron Winster, of Witherslack, co. Westmor-land, 4 Feb. 1942; made P.C. 1945; cr. K.C.M.G. 1948, and was K.G. St. J.; m. 13 Oct. 1909, Elspeth, S.S. St. J., dau. of the Rev. H. J. Lomax, of Abbotswood, and d. 7 June 1961.
ARMS—Argent a cross engrailed sable be-tween four pellets each charged with a pheon of the field; on a chief ermine an anchor between two escallops gules.
CREST—A horse's head couped argent charged on the neck with a trefoil slipped gules and in the mouth an arrow point upwards in bend or.
SUPPORTERS—On either side a seahorse ppr. gorged with a collar engrailed sable pendent therefrom by a riband azure a plate charged with two lions passant guardant in pale gules.
MOTTO—Martis non cupidinis.
Lord Winster's residence was Fivevents Way, Crowborough, Sussex. His club was the Athenaeum.

WINTERSTOKE

PEERAGE—U.K. Baron Winterstoke, of Blagdon, co. Somerset. (Also a baronetcy cr. 12 Aug. 1893).
SURNAME—Wills.
CR.—1 Feb. 1906. EXT.—29 Jan. 1911.
HISTORY—Sir William Henry Wills, Bt., **Baron Winterstoke**, was the second son of William Day Wills, and grandson of Henry Overton Wills, (see extant peerages, Wills of Blagdon, Bt.). He was b. 1 Sept. 1830 in Bristol and baptized there. He was educ. at Mill Hill Sch. and London Univ.; entered the firm of W. D. and H. O. Wills 1858, and be-came 1st Chm. of the Imperial Tobacco Co., 1901; he was Sheriff of Bristol, 1877-78; sat as Liberal M.P. for Coventry, 1880-85, and for East Bristol, 1895-1900; was a Dir. of the Great Western Railway and Pres. of the Bristol Fine Arts Academy; Chm. of the

Bristol Chamber of Commerce and Pro. Chancellor of the Univ. of Bristol, to the formation fund of which he contributed £35,000; he was also a donor of many gifts to Bristol including the Art Gallery. He was cr. a baronet, 12 Aug. 1893; and Baron Winterstoke, of Blagdon, co. Somerset, 1 Feb. 1906. He m. 11 Jan. 1853, Elizabeth, ygst. dau. of John Stancomb, of The Prospect, Trowbridge, by Mary, second dau. of William Perkins, of Trowbridge, and d.s.p. 29 Jan. 1911. She d. 10 Feb. 1896.

ARMS—Gules three suns in splendour in fess between two griffins passant or.

CREST—Issuant from an annulet or a demi griffin gules charged with a sun in splendour, and holding in the dexter claw a battle axe or.

SUPPORTERS—On either side a horse sable, maned, tailed and girthed or.

MOTTO—As God wills.

Lord Winterstoke's, seats were Coombe Lodge, Blagdon, Somerset; East Court, St. Laurence on Sea, Thanet. His town house was 25 Hyde Park Gardens, W. His clubs were Reform; National Liberal, and Royal Thames Yacht.

WITTENHAM

PEERAGE—U.K. Baron Wittenham, of Wallingford, co. Berks.

SURNAME—Faber.

CR.—29 June 1918. **EXT.**—1 Feb. 1931.

HISTORY—George Denison Faber, was the third son of Charles Wilson Faber, of Northaw House, co. Hertford, and ygr. brother of Baron Faber (see that title in present work, and for ancestry, B.L.G. 1952, Faber of Worsall Grange). He was b. 14 Dec. 1851; educ. Marlborough and Univ. Coll. Oxford, B.A. 1875; Barrister-at-Law, Lincoln's Inn, 1879; Registrar of the Privy Council, 1887-96; M.P. for York City, 1900-10, and for Clapham, 1910-18; he was a partner in the firm of Beckett and Co., Bankers, of Leeds; cr. 29 June 1918, **Baron Wittenham**, of Wallingford, co. Berks; m. 7 Oct. 1895, Hilda Georgiana, dau. of Sir Frederic Ulric Graham, 3rd Bt., of Netherby and d.s.p. 1 Feb. 1931.

ARMS—Or on a pale ermine a rose gules barbed and seeded ppr., a chief azure, thereon two mullets argent.

CREST—On the battlements of a tower or, in front of a cubit arm in scale armour, holding in the hand ppr. a rose gules slipped and leaved also ppr, two mascles interlaced fessways vert.

SUPPORTERS—On either side a wild boar ppr. collared and semée of roses argent.

MOTTO—Quisque faber fortunae suae.

Lord Wittenham's seat was Howbery Park, Wallingford, Berks.

WOODBRIDGE

PEERAGE—U.K. Baron Woodbridge, of Ipswich, co. Suffolk. (Also a baronetcy cr. 3 July 1917.)

SURNAME—Churchman.

CR.—17 June 1932. **EXT.**—3 Feb. 1949.

HISTORY—John Churchman, of Nacton, co.

Suffolk, bapt. 4 July 1732; son of Richard Churchman, of Nacton, co. Suffolk, (who was bur. 8 Oct. 1748) and Margaret his wife; m. 11 April 1747, Sarah Gelders, (bur. 3 Aug. 1772) and had issue,

William Churchman, of Ipswich, bapt. 2 July 1758; m. before 1794, Susannah Pawsey, and was bur. 15 July 1834, leaving issue,

William Churchman, of Ipswich, b. 18 Mar. 1794; m. (1) 30 Nov. 1820, Hannah Layton, (d. 18 April 1830), dau. of Arthur Watling, of Sotterley, co. Suffolk; m. (2) Dorcas (d.s.p. 29 Oct. 1874, aged 85) and d. 27 Mar. 1876, having issue by his first marriage,

Henry Charles Churchman, of Paget House, Ipswich, co. Suffolk, b. 12 Dec. 1827; m. 23 April 1857, Mary Anna, dau. and heiress of Charles Eade, of Hill House, Ipswich, and d. 8 July 1888, leaving by her who d. 8 Dec. 1896,

1. Henry Eade, Solicitor, b. 23 Aug. 1863; m. 24 Dec. 1902, Minnie Barker, dau. of John Thomas Jones, of Bridgetown, Barbados, W.I. She d. 7 Aug. 1930.
2. William Alfred, Sir, Bt., of W. Melton, co. Suffolk, D.L. and J.P. Suffolk, Mayor of Ipswich, 1899-1900, Lt. Col. and hon. Col. 4th. Bn. Suffolk Regt. 1906-12, and T/Lt. Col. cmdg. 2/5th Bn. Suffolk Regt., 1914-16, employed in Min. of Munitions, 1917-18, b. 23 Aug. 1863, twin with his brother, cr. Kt. Bach. 1920, and a Baronet, 29 June 1938; m. 21 Jan. 1891, Lois Adelaide, (d. 19 Feb. 1934) dau. of Alfred Wrinch, of Hill Crest, Ipswich, and d.s.p.m. 25 Nov. 1947, leaving issue, three daus., Dorothy, Nancy and Violet.
3. Arthur Charles, Sir, Bt. and **Baron Woodbridge** (see below).
1. Ellen Elizabeth, m. 22 April 1882, Frank Turner, of Lynwood, Felixstowe, co. Suffolk, and d. 5 Nov. 1935, leaving issue.

The third son,

Sir Arthur Charles Churchman, Bt. and **Baron Woodbridge**, b. 7 Sept. 1867; educ. privately and Ipswich Sch.; hon. Col. R.A., and Hon. Col. 429 Coast Regt. (Suffolk), R.A. (T.A.); Lt. Col. cmdg. Essex and Suffolk R.G.A. 1905-09, and Lt. Col. cmdg. 2/6th Bn. Suffolk Regt. 1914; M.P. Woodbridge Div. of Suffolk, 1920-29; Vice Chm. of British American Tobacco Co. Ltd., and partner in firm of W. A. & A. C. Churchman 1888-1902 (Churchman's Number One); D.L. and J.P., High Sheriff of Suffolk, 1931; High Steward of Ipswich from 1935; Mayor of Ipswich, 1901 and 1902; cr. a Baronet 3 July 1917, and a peer as Baron Woodbridge, of Ipswich, co. Suffolk, 17 June 1932. He m. 23 July 1891, Edith, only dau. of J. A. Harvey, M.I.M.E., of London and Ipswich, and d. 3 Feb. 1949, having had issue,

1. Henry Arthur, b. 3 April 1893; d. 28 Aug. 1908.
2. Charles Harvey, b. 19 Feb. 1895; educ. Pembroke Coll. Camb.; served in World War I, Lt. 6th Bn. Suffolk Regt., and was k. in action 3 May 1917.
3. Walter Eric, b. 30 Jan. 1896; d. 29 Dec. 1897.
1. Mary Helen, b. 7 Mar. 1897; m. (1) 30 Dec. 1916, Capt. C. E. Stuart, Suffolk Regt., who d. of wounds received in action, 15 Mar. 1917, and she m. (2)

27 Oct. 1921, John Woodman-Smith and
d. Mar. 1924, leaving issue.
  2. Vera Kate, b. 22 Feb. 1913; m. 26 Oct.
  1936, Peter William Barnett, and had
  issue.
ARMS—Barry of four argent and sable, on a
chief of the last two leopards' faces over all a
sword erect or.
CREST—Upon a roll of parchment a cock ppr.
SUPPORTERS—Dexter, A lion or; Sinister,
A leopard or, each charged on the shoulder
with a tripel-towered castle argent within a
chaplet of oak vert.
MOTTO—Post tenebras aurora.
Lord Woodbridge's residences were Abbey
Oaks, Sproughton, near Ipswich and 20
Kingston House, Princes Gate, S.W.7. His
clubs were Carlton, Junior Carlton, and Royal
Automobile.

WOLSELEY

PEERAGE—U.K. Baron Wolseley of Cairo
and Wolseley co. Stafford.
  U.K. Viscount Wolseley, of Wolseley, co.
Stafford.
SURNAME—Wolseley.
CR.—Barony, 25 Nov. 1882. Viscounty,
28 Sept. 1885. EXT.—Barony 25 Mar. 1913.
Viscounty 24 Dec. 1936.
HISTORY—Major Garnet Joseph Wolseley,
(see extant peerages, Wolseley of Mount
Wolseley, Bt.), had an eldest son,
  Garnet Joseph Wolseley, **Baron Wolseley**
and **1st Viscount Wolseley**, the famous Victorian general whose name became a synonym
for success, and whose brilliant administration of his commands gave rise to the common
expression, "all Sir Garnet". He was b. 4 June
1833, in county Dublin. He entered the Army
in 1852; he served in the following campaigns;
second Burma War, 1852-53; the Crimean
War, 1854-56; Indian Mutiny, 1857-59; China
War, 1860; was assistant quartermaster gen. in
Canada, 1861, and Col. 1865; cmd. the exped.
which put down the Red River rebellion of
Louis Riel, 1870; cmd. exped. against King
Koffee of Ashanti, 1873, and defeated him,
occupying Kumasi, 1874; was first administrator of Cyprus, 1878; sent out to end the
Zulu War, and captured King Cetewayo, 1879;
crushed rebellion of Arabi Pasha, at Tel-el-
Kebir and occupied Cairo, 1882; conducted
Nile campaign for relief of Gen. Gordon,
1883-85; and was C. in C. Ireland, 1890-95,
and C. in C. of British Army, 1895-99. He was
Field Marshal in the Army. He supported the
Army reforms of Viscount Cardwell, and
succeeded in getting most of the desired changes
brought about. He was made P.C., cr. K.P.,
G.C.B., G.C.M.G., and Baron Wolseley of
Cairo and Wolseley, 25 Nov. 1882; further cr.
Viscount Wolseley, of Wolseley, co. Stafford,
28 Sept. 1885, the latter creation being with remainder in default of male issue to his dau. and
her male issue. He m. 4 June 1867, Louisa, (d.
10 April 1920) dau. of Alexander Erskine, and
d. 25 Mar. 1913, leaving issue,
  Frances Garnet Wolseley, **Viscountess Wolseley,** and 2nd holder of title, b. 15 Sept. 1872;
founded the College of Gardening at Glynde,
and for this was given the Freedom of the City
of London, 1913; was author of several works,
Gardening for Women, Some of the Smaller

*Manor Houses of Sussex, Byegone Sussex in
and Around Steyning, Some Sussex Byways,* etc.
She d. unm. 24 Dec. 1936.
ARMS—(of Viscount Wolseley). Argent a
talbot passant gules, a mullet for difference.
CREST—Out of a ducal coronet or a wolf's
head ppr.
SUPPORTERS—Two wolves ppr. each charged on the shoulder with a laurel and palm
branch, in saltire gorged with a mural crown or,
and holding in the paw a sword erect ppr.
pommelled and hilted gold.
MOTTO—Homo homini lupus.
Viscountess Wolseley lived at Culpepers,
Ardingley, Sussex.

WOLVERHAMPTON

PEERAGE—U.K. Viscount Wolverhampton,
of Wolverhampton, co. Stafford.
SURNAME—Fowler.
CR.—4 May 1908. EXT.—9 Mar. 1943.
HISTORY—The Rev. Joseph Fowler, of
Arnley, near Leeds where he was b. July 1791,
said to have come of a family originally of
Cullompton, co. Devon and there engaged in
the cloth industry. He was educ. Bradford
Grammar Sch. and became a Wesleyan Minister in 1811. He m. (1) 1815, Mary, dau. of
John Moate, of Braithwaite, nr. Doncaster,
and had issue,
  1. Robert, d. in Canada.
  2. Mary.
She d. 1824. He m. (2) Jane, dau. of Timothy
Bentley, J.P., of Lockwood, Huddersfield, and
she d.s.p. 1828. He m. (3), 1829, Eliza, dau. of
Alexander Laing, of Glasgow, and d. 25 Mar.
1851, having by her had further issue,
  2. Henry Hartley, **1st Viscount Wolverhampton** (see below).
  2. Louisa, m. the Rev. William Tyack and
  d.s.p. 1893.
The only son of the third marriage,
  Henry Hartley Fowler, **1st Viscount Wolverhampton,** b. 16 May 1830 in Sunderland; educ.
Woodhouse Grove Sch. and St. Saviour's
Grammar Sch. Southwark; admitted a solicitor,
1852; Mayor of Wolverhampton, 1863; Liberal
M.P. for Wolverhampton, 1880-1908; Under
Sec. of State for the Home Dept. 1884-85; Fin.
Sec. to the Treasury, 1886; P.C. 1886; Pres.
of Local Gov. Board, 1892-94; Sec. of State
for India, 1894-95; Chancellor of the Duchy of
Lancaster, 1905-00, and Lord Pres. of the
Council, 1908-10. He was cr. G.C.S.I. 1895
and Viscount Wolverhampton, of Wolver-
hampton, co. Stafford, 4 May 1908; m. 6 Oct.
1857, Ellen, C.I. dau. of George Benjamin
Thorneycroft, of Chapel House, Wolver-
hampton, an iron master. She d. 6 Jan. 1911.
He d. 25 Feb. 1911. They had issue,
  1. Henry Ernest, **2nd Viscount Wolverhampton** (see below).
  1. Ellen Thorneycroft, m. 16 April 1902,
  A. L. Felkin, M.A.
  2. Edith Henrietta, m. 23 June 1903, Rev.
  W. R. Hamilton, and had issue.
The only son,
  Henry Ernest Fowler, **2nd Viscount Wolverhampton,** b. 4 April 1870; educ. Charterhouse
and Ch. Ch. Oxford; m. 8 June 1910, Evelyn
Henrietta, dau. of Arthur Wrottesley, 3rd
Baron Wrottesley, and d. 9 Mar. 1943.

ARMS—Per pale gules and sable on a chevron between in chief two lions passant and in base a portcullis all argent a rose gules barbed and seeded ppr.
CREST—Upon a rock ppr. a stork argent holding in the beak a cross moline sable.
SUPPORTERS—Dexter, A wolf or charged on the shoulder with an escutcheon gules thereon two keys in saltire wards upwards argent; Sinister, A royal tiger or striped sable charged on the shoulder with an escutcheon azure, thereon an estoile argent.
Viscount Wolverhampton's residence was Carrwood House, Overstrand, Norfolk, and his club the Reform.

WOOLAVINGTON

PEERAGE—Baron Woolavington, of Lavington, co. Sussex. (Also a baronetcy cr. 6 Feb. 1920.)
SURNAME—Buchanan.
CR.—24 Jan. 1922. EXT.—9 Aug. 1935.
HISTORY—Alexander Buchanan, of Glasgow, and Bankell, co. Stirling, had a ygst. son,
Sir James Buchanan, Bt., and **Baron Woolavington**, b. 16 Aug. 1849, at Brockville, Canada West, and baptized there; educ. privately; was the founder of James Buchanan, and Co. Whisky Distillers, 1880, and was its Chm. He was High Sheriff of Sussex, 1910; cr. a baronet 6 Feb. 1920, and a peer as Baron Woolavington, of Lavington, co. Sussex, 24 Jan. 1922, and a G.C.V.O. 1931. He m. 1892, Anne, dau. of Thomas Pounder. She d. 5 Oct. 1918, and was bur. in the parish church at Lavington Park. He d.s.p.m. at Lavington Park, 9 Aug., and was bur. 13 Aug. 1935, at Graffham Church, near Petworth, co. Sussex. He left issue,
Catherine, m. 18 Jan. 1922, Reginald Narcissus Macdonald-Buchanan, M.C., Capt. Scots Guards, son of John Macdonald, of Buenos Aires and had issue. They assumed by deed poll, 17 Jan. 1922, the additional surname of Buchanan.
Lord Woolavington's seat at Lavington Park is now occupied by Seaford College. The parish church at Lavington Park is rich in memorials, including those to Cardinal Manning who in his Anglican days was rector there and Archdeacon of Chichester.
ARMS—Or a lion rampant sable, armed and langued gules, holding in its sinister forepaw three ears of barley conjoined in stalk vert, a bordure invected of the second.

CREST—A dexter arm couped at the elbow holding in the hand a ducal coronet between two branches of laurel orleways ppr.
SUPPORTERS—Dexter, A ram ppr.; Sinister, A horse argent, each charged on the shoulder with three ears of barley ppr. banded azure.
MOTTO—Clarior hinc honos.

YSTWYTH

PEERAGE—U.K. Baron Ystwyth of Tan-y-Bwlch, co. Cardigan.
SURNAME—Davies.
CR.—18 Jan. 1921. EXT.—21 Aug. 1935.
HISTORY—John Davies of Nantoes and later of Crygie, co. Cardigan, b. 1716, m. Jane, dau. of Richard Morris and widow of Lewis Williams Llanbadarn Faw. She d. 26 Feb. 1806. He d. 27 April 1784. They had issue,
1. John Maurice, Capt. 31st Regt., b. 1752, m. and had issue.
2. Richard, b. 1769 d. an infant.
3. David of Crygie b. 1772.
4. Lewis (see below).
1. Mary, m. Pierce Evans of Piercefield.
2. Jane, m. William Tunstall of Stoke Castle, co. Salop.
3. Sarah, m. Lewis Morris of Tynant.
4. Elizabeth.
The fourth son,
Major Gen. Lewis Davies, C.B. of Tan-y-Bwlch, co. Cardigan, b. 1776, m. 1800, Jane, dau. and coheiress of Mathew Davies of Cwmcyfelin, co. Cardigan, and d. 10 May 1828 having had with other issue,
Matthew Davies, of Tan-y-Bwlch, co. Cardigan, b. 1802; m. 14 Nov. 1832, Emma, dau. and coheiress of John Davies of Surrey Sq., London and of Strawberry Hill. She d. 21 Aug. 1872. He d. 14 Nov. 1853 leaving issue an eldest son,
Matthew Lewis Vaughan Davies, **Baron Ystwyth,** b. 17 Dec. 1840; educ. Harrow, High Sheriff, co. Cardigan 1875, Liberal M.P. co. Cardigan 1895-1920, Pres. Agric. Dept. Univ. of Wales, cr. Baron Ystwyth, of Tan-y-Bwlch, co. Cardigan, 18 Jan. 1921. He m. Dec. 1889, Mary, dau. of Thomas Powell of The Gaer, Monmouth and widow of Alexander Jenkins of Hyde Park Gardens, London W. She d. 1 Mar. 1926. He d.s.p. 21 Aug. 1935.
Lord Ystwyth's seat was Tan-y-Bwlch, Aberystwyth.

Index

Index

303

ROLLAND'S SUPPLEMENT TO RIETSTAP'S ARMORIAL GÉNÉRAL

An illustrated series of European family Arms not already appearing in Rolland's Illustrations.

Vol. I	204pp	£3.15
Vols. II A-G	624pp ⎫	£12.60
III H-Z	936pp ⎭	
Vol. IV	420pp	£6.30
Vol. V	456pp	£6.30
Vol. VI	356pp	£6.30
Vol. VII	340pp	£6.30
Vol. VIII	320pp	£6.30

Vol. IX Index to Series 224pp £5.25

BURKE'S COLONIAL GENTRY

Pedigrees and Arms of Families in Australia Canada, New Zealand and the West Indies. 1891/5.
2 vols. bound in 1, 916pp & 120 illustrations of Arms.
Bound red buckram, gilt letters. £8.40

List of new and second-hand books on Heraldry and Genealogy, sent free on request.